# Blackburn Rovers

## The Official Encyclopaedia

# Blackburn Rovers

# The Official Encyclopaedia

**Mike Jackman**

Breedon Books
Publishing Company
Derby

First published in Great Britain by
The Breedon Books Publishing Company Limited
44 Friar Gate, Derby, DE1 1DA.
1994

ISBN 1 873626 70 3

Printed and bound by Hillman Printers, Frome, Somerset.
Covers printed by BDC Printing Services Limited of Derby

## *Dedication*

This book is dedicated to my late grandfather, James Robinson, whose love of Blackburn Rovers I have been fortunate to inherit. Writing this book brought back many happy memories of shared visits to Ewood Park.

**Note on abbreviations**

The following abbreviations have been used for wartime competitions throughout the book:

LSPT - Lancashire Section Principal Tournament
LSST - Lancashire Section Subsidiary Tournament
NWRL - North West Regional League
NRL - North Regional League
FLNS-FC - Football League Northern Section - First Competition
FLNS-SC - Football League Northern Section - Second Competition
FLN - Football League North
LWC - League War Cup

# *Acknowledgements*

I must place on record my sincere thanks to a number of individuals to whom I owe an enormous debt of gratitude. Without the input of Jim Creasy, Mike Davage and Garth Dykes, this book would have been impossible to undertake. These three football historians provided a constant supply of information and leads on the careers and birthdates of former players. I was also fortunate in being able to call on the services of fellow Blackburn statistician Derek Jones to check a number of appearance and goalscoring figures.

Thanks must also go to Michael Braham, Alan Harding, Bill Hume, Mark Chapman, Brian Tabner, Peter White and Peter Windle, who all provided varying degrees of invaluable assistance. Thanks, too, to Mrs Linda Churchward, daughter of the late Albert Clarke who scored 21 goals in the Second Division championship side of 1938-39. I am also grateful to Don Mackay for providing such an illuminating guide to his career as both player and manager.

As local newspapers provided such a rich source of information it goes without saying that I am particularly grateful to those librarians at Accrington, Blackburn, Bolton, Burnley, Nelson and Preston who constantly showed kindness and co-operation at many continued requests for 'old' newspapers. However, a special mention must be given to Ian Sutton and his staff at the Blackburn Reference Library for their unfailing help and efficiency over a number of years. I am especially grateful to Ian for helping with photographs from the Library's collection which appear in this book.

Once again a number of visits to the Football League offices at Lytham St Annes have been made and I would like to thank the officials of the League for allowing me access to their records. As always, particular thanks at the League must go to Mrs Lorna Parnell.

I must express my gratitude to the officials of Blackburn Rovers who once again allowed me to use the club's appearance books and kindly agreed for the book to be termed 'The Official Encyclopaedia of Blackburn Rovers'.

Thanks must also go to Roger Edworthy at the *Lancashire Evening Telegraph* and in particular to Mrs Lillian Duffy for her help in guiding me through the picture library at the *Telegraph*. Thanks must also go to John Napier and his staff at the newspaper who reproduced so many of the photographs to be found in this volume. I am also grateful for the work of Wally & Howard Talbot Photography who produced so many excellent photographs at very short notice. I am similarly grateful to John Barry Photography who performed a similar task.

I must also record my thanks to Anton Rippon and his staff at Breedon Books for the support and encouragement they have given throughout this project. Finally, I would be remiss not to thank my parents, Harry and Amelia Jackman, for the hundred and one different jobs they have undertaken and the support they have given to ensure the completion of this work.

# Introduction

During the autumn of 1992 I began work on updating my Complete Record of Blackburn Rovers which had been published in 1990. However, as the project progressed I found myself becoming increasingly drawn to the idea of producing a different concept than that of the 'Complete Record' series. Fortunately, Anton Rippon of Breedon Books was happy to support my ideas and hence the Encyclopaedia of Blackburn Rovers was born.

Although the format is different from my previous publication, the methods of research have remained the same. The pages of several local newspapers have been examined as well as many from further afield. In particular the *Blackburn Times, Northern Daily Telegraph* (later the *Lancashire Evening Telegraph*), *Lancashire Daily Post* (later the *Lancashire Evening Post*) and *The Cricket & Football Field* have proved invaluable sources of information. *The Scottish Referee* provided many leads on the movement of players in the days before World War One whilst the *Athletic News* provided so many invaluable references.

Once again official records have been perused at the Football League and documents from the Football Association have also been consulted.

In researching this new work I have taken the opportunity to have another look at the line-ups and goalscorers in every League and Cup game played by the club. As a result a few amendments have been made to certain players' details from those shown in my original work.

The book contains a potted biography of every player to appear in a senior League or Cup match rather than just a selection of players. Clearly such an undertaking is fraught with problems for a club whose first appearance in the FA Cup was in 1879. Victorian and Edwardian newspapers did not pay the same meticulous attention to goalscorers and line-ups as today's journalists. Furthermore, the pre and post-Blackburn careers of some of the early figures in the club's history remain shrouded in the mists of time. However, the contents of this book will hopefully shed some light on the majority of men who have worn those famous shirts of Blackburn Rovers.

With regard to the potted biographies I have tried to concentrate on the impact which a player made at Blackburn rather than appraise their career in general. However, it has been necessary to look at certain careers in a wider context in order to assess an individual contribution to Blackburn Rovers.

Mike Jackman
Blackburn
June 1994.

## ACCRINGTON FC

'Th 'Owd Reds' were founded in 1878 and provided frequent opposition for the Rovers in the years before the creation of the Football League. The two clubs met in an early experiment with artificial lighting in 1878 (See Floodlights). On 15 September 1888, Accrington visited the Leamington Ground to provide the opposition in Blackburn's opening fixture in the Football League. Perhaps the greatest service that Accrington did for Blackburn Rovers was to allow them to 'borrow' George Haworth, their England international half-back, for the 1885 FA Cup Final. The Rovers had already allowed Accrington to use Joe Beverley and Joe Sowerbutts for a friendly in April 1884 and in September 1886, Herbie Arthur appeared for 'Th 'Owd Reds' in their opening two friendly matches. Accrington visited Blackburn for the last time on 4 September 1895 when they were beaten 3-0 by a Rovers Reserve team. Within months of this match 'Th 'Owd Reds' had folded.

### Football League

|         |         |         | Home |     | Away |     |
|---------|---------|---------|------|-----|------|-----|
| 1888-89 |         | (FL)    | D    | 5-5 | W    | 2-0 |
| 1889-90 |         | (FL)    | W    | 3-2 | D    | 2-2 |
| 1890-91 |         | (FL)    | D    | 0-0 | W    | 4-0 |
| 1891-92 |         | (FL)    | D    | 2-2 | L    | 0-1 |
| 1892-93 |         | (Div 1) | D    | 3-3 | D    | 1-1 |

|       | P  | W | D | L | F  | A  |
|-------|----|---|---|---|----|----|
| Home  | 5  | 1 | 4 | 0 | 13 | 12 |
| Away  | 5  | 2 | 2 | 1 | 9  | 4  |
| Total | 10 | 3 | 6 | 1 | 22 | 16 |

### FA Cup

| 1887-88 | (3) | Away | W | 3-1 |
|---------|-----|------|---|-----|
| 1888-89 | (1) | Away | D | 1-1 |
|         | (R) | Home | W | 5-0 |

## ACCRINGTON STANLEY FC

Believed to have come into being around 1892 as Stanley Villa before changing their name to Accrington Stanley in 1893. Meetings between Blackburn Rovers and Accrington Stanley were far rarer than those between the Rovers and 'Th 'Owd Reds'. The most famous was undoubtedly the third round FA Cup-tie in January 1936, when Accrington of the Third Division North eliminated Second Division Rovers at Peel Park following an exciting draw at Ewood Park. Another memorable occasion saw Blackburn Rovers visit Peel Park for a floodlight friendly on 15 November 1954. At a time when the Rovers had not yet invested in floodlights, their Third Division North neighbours were rewarded with a record attendance of 17,634. The result was a hard fought 2-2 draw. When Accrington Stanley folded in March 1962, one of the two joint caretaker managers was Bill Smith, the former Blackburn Rovers utility player of the 1950s. Immediately after Accrington resigned from the League the Rovers signed Mike Ferguson who was, without doubt, the Accrington club's outstanding young player.

### FA Cup

| 1909-10 | (1) | Home* | W | 7-1 |
|---------|-----|-------|---|-----|
| 1936-37 | (3) | Home  | D | 2-2 |
|         | (R) | Away  | L | 1-3 |

* Match originally drawn to be played at Accrington.

### Wartime

|         |           | Home |     | Away |      |
|---------|-----------|------|-----|------|------|
| 1939-40 | (NWRL)    | L    | 0-2 | D    | 2-2  |
| 1944-45 | (FLNS-FC) | L    | 1-2 | W    | 4-1  |
|         | (FLNS-SC) | W    | 3-0 | L    | 2-3± |
|         |           | D    | 4-4 | W    | 4-3* |
|         |           | W    | 2-0*|      |      |

*Note: These matches were the Final of the Lancashire Cup competition.
±Note: Blackburn Rovers and Accrington Stanley met each other on five occasions in this competition.

## AGE

The youngest player to appear in the Football League for Blackburn Rovers was Harry Dennison who made his debut against Bristol City at Ewood Park on the 8 April 1911. At the time of his debut Dennison was aged 16 years and 155 days.

The oldest player to represent the Rovers in the Football League was Bob Crompton. The long-serving full-back made his final appearance at Bradford on 23 February 1920 at the age of 40 years and 151 days.

The 1993-94 season saw Kevin Moran have the honour of being the oldest outfield player in the Carling Premiership. Moran had celebrated his thirty-seventh birthday in April 1993 and was not only a regular in the Rovers line-up but was still playing for the Republic of Ireland in the World Cup Qualifying campaign.

The oldest player to represent England whilst still with the Rovers was Harry Healless who made his second, and final, international appearance against Scotland on 31 March 1928. Healless had celebrated his 35th birthday a few weeks earlier on 10 February. The youngest player to appear in an England jersey whilst with the Rovers was Jimmy Brown. The free-scoring centre-forward made his England debut, against Wales in February 1881, at the age of 18 years 210 days.

## AGNEW, Stephen Mark

Midfield. 1991-1993.
*5ft 9in; 10st 6lb.*
*Born: Shipley, 9 November 1965.*
*Debut: v Portsmouth (h) 17 August 1991.*
*Career: Barnsley associated schoolboy April 1982, becoming an apprentice in July 1982, before signing professional in November 1983; Blackburn Rovers June 1991 (£750,000); Portsmouth on loan November to December 1992; Leicester City February 1993 (£250,000).*

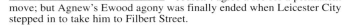

**Appearances:** Football League 2; Football League Cup 2; Total 4.

Don Mackay paid a record fee to bring this creative midfield player to Ewood Park during the summer of 1991. Unfortunately, the Blackburn public never had the opportunity to enjoy the vision and passing ability which had won Agnew so many admirers at Oakwell. After only four games for the Rovers he suffered a serious ankle injury which was to keep him side-lined until the final weeks of the season. Although restored to full fitness for the start of the 1992-93 campaign, Agnew found himself behind Tim Sherwood, Gordon Cowans and Mark Atkins in the queue for the midfield places. A loan move to Portsmouth ended when Pompey couldn't agree a fee for a permanent move; but Agnew's Ewood agony was finally ended when Leicester City stepped in to take him to Filbert Street.

## AINSCOW, Alan

Midfield. 1985-1989.
*5ft 8in; 11st 5lb.*
*Born: Bolton, 15 July 1953.*
*Debut: v Hull City (h) 1 February 1986.*
*Career: Blackpool apprentice July 1970, turning professional in July 1971; Birmingham City July 1978; Everton August 1981; Barnsley on loan November 1982 to December 1982; Eastern FC (Hong Kong) 1983; Wolverhampton Wanderers August 1984; Blackburn Rovers December 1985 on a non-contract basis before signing a full contract in June 1987; Rochdale June 1989; Horwich RMI August 1990; Flint Town United cs 1991.*
*Domestic honours with Blackburn Rovers: Full Members' Cup winner: 1987.*
**Appearances:** Football League 42 + 23; Play-offs 1 + 2; Football League Cup 2 + 1; Full Members' Cup 4 + 2; Total 49 + 28.
**Goals:** Football League 5; Football League Cup 1; Full Members' Cup 1; Total 7.

A bustling type of midfielder who was signed by Bobby Saxton on a non-contract basis to add a little depth to his threadbare squad. Saxton seemed strangely reluctant to use Ainscow in the first team and it wasn't until Don Mackay arrived that he was given a prolonged run at senior level. A player who was at his best foraging for the ball in midfield before feeding it to his front men, Ainscow enjoyed something of an 'Indian Summer' to his career whilst at Ewood Park.

## AIREY, John

Winger. 1959-1963.
*5ft 10in; 11st.*
*Born: Blackburn, 28 November 1937.*
*Debut: v Burnley (h) 7 March 1959.*
*Career: Blackburn Rovers January 1959 to cs 1963.*

**Appearances:** Football League 3.
**Goals:** Football League 1.
Airey had the unenviable task of understudying the likes of Douglas and MacLeod during his time at Blackburn. Although he made a goalscoring debut against old rivals Burnley in March 1959, Airey was given very few first-team opportunities during his stay at the club.

**AITKEN, Fergus McKenna**
Forward. 1921-1922.
*5ft 8in; 10st 8lb.*
*Born: Glasgow, 5 June 1896; Died: Kilmarnock, 13 July 1989.*
*Debut: v Chelsea (h) 27 August 1921.*
*Career: Petershill 1915-16; Benburb 1916-17; Third Lanark; Bury June 1919; Blackburn Rovers May 1921 (£2,000); Cardiff City November 1922; Birmingham March 1923; Southport March 1924; Bradford June 1926 until cs 1927.*
**Appearances:** Football League 8.
**Goals:** Football League 1.
A speedy right winger who came to Blackburn from Bury but failed to live up to the reputation he had gained at Gigg Lane. Although he began the 1921-1922 campaign as first choice on the left wing he was replaced by Joe Hodkinson after only six games. Brief spells at Cardiff City and Birmingham were equally unsuccessful, although Aitken enjoyed better fortune at Southport where he appeared in 78 League matches and scored three goals. After ending his career with a season at Bradford he returned to his native Glasgow to become a tram driver, rising to the rank of inspector before his retirement.

**AITKENHEAD, Walter Campbell Allison**
Inside-left/Half-back. 1906-1918.
*5ft 9in; 11st 8lb.*
*Born: Maryhill Glasgow, 21 May 1887; Died: Pleasington, nr. Blackburn, 19 July 1966.*
*Debut: v Derby County (h) 27 October 1906.*
*Career: Maryhill Harp; Partick Thistle May 1906; Blackburn Rovers October 1906; Preston North End 1915-16 (wartime guest); Retired 1918.*
*International honours with Blackburn Rovers: Scotland: 1 cap (1912).*
*Domestic honours with Blackburn Rovers: First Division championship: 1911-12 (29 apps, 15 gls); 1913-14 (35 apps, 9 gls).*
**Appearances:** Football League 210; FA Cup 28; Charity Shield 1; Total 239.
**Goals:** Football League 75; FA Cup 18; Charity Shield 2; Total 95.
A versatile performer who proved equally at home at wing-half or inside-forward and occasionally at the centre of defence. 'Wattie', as he was popularly known in Blackburn, was more than just a typically hard-working half-back. He was a

creative player who not only made opportunities for others but who had an eye for goal himself. In his later years he proved equally adept in a deeper role and was an automatic selection for the first team during the years when the Rovers enjoyed their greatest success in the Football League. World War One effectively ended his career, although he did appear as a guest for Preston North End. Although thoughts of a comeback with the Rovers were ended on medical grounds, Aitkenhead remained in Blackburn after his retirement in 1918. He was managing director of a local cotton firm from 1920 until the late 1950s and then became chairman of another textile company until about a year before his death.

**ALCOCK, Terence**
Centre-half. 1976-1977.
*6ft; 11st 8lb.*
*Born: Hanley, 9 December 1946.*
*Debut: v Burnley (h) 27 December 1976.*
*Career: Port Vale apprentice May 1962, turning professional in September 1964; Blackpool August 1967; Bury on loan February 1972; Blackburn Rovers on loan December 1976 to January 1977; Port Vale February 1977 to March 1977; Portland Timbers (USA) March 1977; Port Vale August 1977; Halifax Town September 1977.*
**Appearances:** Football League 3; FA Cup 2, Total 5.
**Goals:** Football League 1.

An experienced defender who had almost 300 League appearances behind him when he joined Blackburn on a month's loan in December 1976. He arrived at Blackburn following two away defeats in early December 1976 and helped the team to gain two draws over the Christmas period. As Alcock had not featured in Blackpool's first team since April 1976, the Seasiders allowed the Rovers to play him in their FA Cup-tie against Charlton Athletic, after which he returned to Bloomfield Road.

**ALDERSHOT FC**
Although members of the Football League between 1932 and 1991, Aldershot never climbed beyond the Third Division. As a result meetings between Aldershot and Blackburn Rovers were extremely rare whilst their paths never crossed in the cup competitions.

**Football League**

| | | | Home | | Away | |
|---|---|---|---|---|---|---|
| 1973-74 | | (Div 3) | L | 1-2 | L | 0-4 |
| 1974-75 | | (Div 3) | W | 2-0 | D | 1-1 |

| | P | W | D | L | F | A |
|---|---|---|---|---|---|---|
| Home | 2 | 1 | 0 | 1 | 3 | 2 |
| Away | 2 | 0 | 1 | 1 | 1 | 5 |
| Total | 4 | 1 | 1 | 2 | 4 | 7 |

**ALEXANDRA MEADOWS**
Alexandra Meadows, the home of the East Lancashire Cricket Club, became the home base of Blackburn Rovers in 1877. Whilst there were obvious drawbacks in renting Alexandra Meadows from the East Lancs Cricket Club, at least Blackburn Rovers finally had a home which was more in keeping with their ambitions. The ground had the advantage of being enclosed and also had its own pavilion. In such improved surroundings the club was able to broaden its horizons with regard to opponents. Thus club officials were able to turn their attentions to Scotland to find more taxing opponents for the Rovers.

The opening game at Alexandra Meadows on 2 January 1878 saw the club entertain Partick Thistle who had met and defeated Darwen FC the previous season. However, two goals from Dick Birtwistle enabled the Rovers to pull off a famous 2-1 victory over their illustrious Scottish opponents. The game saw A.N.Hornby make his debut for the Rovers and the full line up was as follows:

T.Greenwood; D.H.Greenwood, J.Baldwin, A.N.Hornby, J.Baguley, F.Hargreaves, W.Duckworth, J.Lewis, R.Birtwistle, A.L.Birch, T.Dean.

It proved to be the first of numerous encounters between Blackburn Rovers and the cream of Scottish Football.

Although Blackburn Rovers stayed at Alexandra Meadows for less than two seasons, it was the scene of some memorable moments in the history of the club. In 1878 the Rovers experimented with artificial light when they played Accrington on the evening of Monday, 4 November, 1878 *(see Floodlights).* Although the attendance was between five and six thousand, a number of people watched events from the neighbouring park and adjoining hillside. It was this free view which went some way to convincing the club that Alexandra Meadows was not an ideal venue.

It was whilst at Alexandra Meadows that the club undertook its first tentative steps into competitive football. In 1879 the club entered the inaugural Lancashire Cup competition and also entered the FA Cup for the first time.

**ALMOND, William**
Centre-half. 1888-1892.
*5ft 9in; 11st 10lb.*
*Born: Blackburn, Lancashire, 5 April 1868.*
*Debut: v Accrington (h) 15 September 1888.*
*Career: Witton (Blackburn); Blackburn Rovers May 1888; Accrington November 1892; Middlesbrough cs 1893; Nelson; Millwall Athletic cs 1894; Tottenham Hotspur August 1895; Millwall Athletic cs 1897; Clapton; Wandsworth.*
**Appearances:** Football League 58; FA Cup 9; Total 67.
**Goals:** Football League 3; FA Cup 1, Total 4.
Willie Almond missed only one game for Blackburn Rovers during the inaugural season of the Football League. However, although he had the ideal physique for the centre-half position, the following two seasons found him understudying George Dewar. He returned to the first team during the 1891-92 campaign but was allowed to join Accrington in November 1892. After leaving 'Th 'Owd Reds' he was never seen in the Football League again but eventually settled into Southern League football with Millwall and Tottenham Hotspur.

**ALTRINCHAM FC**
Non-League side, famed for their FA Cup exploits, who faced Rovers in the second round of the competition in 1973-74. At that time the Rovers

were in the Third Division whilst Altrincham played their football in the Northern Premier League. However, Altrincham had already claimed the scalp of Hartlepool in the first round and when they held the Rovers to a draw at Ewood Park another upset seemed likely. Blackburn's cause was not helped by the dismissal of Neil Wilkinson, but in the replay the Rovers had a fairly comfortable passage.

**FA Cup**

| 1973-74 | | | | |
|---|---|---|---|---|
| | (2) | Home | D | 0-0 |
| | (R) | Away | W | 2-0 |

## AMERICAN SOCCER LEAGUE

Blackburn Rovers were invited to the United States of America to compete in an international football tournament during the summer of 1964. The format of the tournament, which had been established for several years, involved a miniature league system together with a final for the leading teams. The Rovers had to face Heart of Midlothian from Scotland, Bahia from Brazil, Lanerossi from Italy and Werder Bremen of Germany.

Sadly, from a playing point of view, the team returned with a dismal record, winning only one of their six matches. A poor end to the English season meant confidence was already at a low ebb when the team reached the shores of America. Once in America injuries were to take their toll and the solitary victory was marred when Mike England was sent off for allegedly butting an opponent. None the less, the Rovers earned praise for their conduct throughout the tour despite their lack of fortune on the field.

| June | 3 | (n1) | Bahia | D | 1-1 |
|---|---|---|---|---|---|
| | 7 | (n1) | Werder Bremen | L | 2-3 |
| | 14 | (n2) | Lanerossi | L | 1-3 |
| | 21 | (n2) | Bahia | W | 3-1 |
| | 24 | (n2) | Heart of Midlothian | L | 0-2 |
| | 31 | (n2) | Heart of Midlothian | L | 0-1 |

n1 – played in Los Angeles
n2 – played in New York

**Appearances:**
R.Blore 1; A.Bradshaw 1; J.Bray 5; J.Byrom 1; R.Clayton 5; B.Douglas 5; F.Else 6; H.M.England 6; M.K.Ferguson 6; M.J.Harrison 5; G.A.Jones 6; W.Joyce 4; M.A.McEvoy 5; M.McGrath 3; K.R.Newton 5; H.C.Sims 2.

**Goalscorers:**
A.Bradshaw 1; B.Douglas 1; H.M.England 1; M.J.Harrison 1; G.A.Jones 1; M.A.McEvoy 1; K.R.Newton 1.

## ANDERSON, Benjamin Cummings
Half-back/Centre-forward. 1964-1968.
*6ft; 12st 3lb.*
*Born: Aberdeen, 18 February 1946.*
*Debut: v Leicester City (a) 6 February 1965.*
*Career: Peterlee Juniors; Blackburn Rovers March 1964; Bury July 1968 to March 1970; Cape Town City (South Africa); Crystal Palace November 1973 until June 1974.*
**Appearances:** Football League 21 + 7.
**Goals:** Football League 7.
A recruit from Scottish junior circles whose build meant he could be utilised either in defence or attack. His big break came towards the end of the 1966-67 campaign when he was asked to lead the attack after promotion had slipped away due to a lack of goals. He began the following season as first-choice centre-forward and scored in each of the opening three Second Division fixtures. Yet, although a strong and willing worker, Anderson never really looked like a natural leader of the attack and eventually lost his place. Whilst at Ewood Park, Anderson helped the second team to two Central League championships in 1964-65 and 1966-67. He appeared in 53 League games for Bury and 11 for Crystal Palace after leaving Blackburn.

## ANDERSON, Christopher Shelly
Outside-right. 1950-1953.
*5ft 6in; 9st 12lb.*

*Born: Wemyss, Fife, 28 January 1928.*
*Debut: v Manchester City (h) 18 November 1950.*
*Career: Lochore Welfare; Blackburn Rovers August 1950; Kidderminster Harriers July 1952; Nelson 1953; Stockport County June 1953; Southport July 1954 to cs 1955; Lion Brewery, Blackburn November 1955; Blackburn West October 1956; Highfield Athletic 1959-60 (possibly earlier).*
**Appearances:** Football League 13.
**Goals:** Football League 1.
Although he cost a mere £150 when he moved from junior football, Anderson proved to be a typically tricky Scottish player. He enjoyed an impressive debut against Manchester City at Ewood Park in November 1950 and seemed destined to mount a serious challenge for the right-wing spot. Unfortunately, his career never really took off and after 34 League games with Stockport County and a further 28 with Southport, he was to be found playing in the Blackburn Combination.

## ANDERSON, George E.
Centre-half. 1892-1897.
*5ft 8in; 12st.*
*Debut: v Preston North End (h) 29 October 1892.*
*Career: Leith Athletic; Blackburn Rovers October 1892; New Brighton Tower August 1897; Blackburn Rovers on loan April 1898; Blackburn Rovers cs 1898; New Brighton Tower; Blackpool February 1901; Cliftonville as coach in August 1905.*
**Appearances:** Football League 178; Test Matches 4; FA Cup 18; Total 200.
**Goals:** Football League 19; Test Matches 1; Total 20.
Geordie Anderson was one of a group of young men who were brought down from Scotland to provide the backbone of the Blackburn first team in the early 1890s. Anderson proved to be better than many of his contemporaries and became a regular fixture in the first team for five seasons. A magnificent half-back and inspirational captain, Anderson was a spirited individual both on and off the field. Unfortunately, a number of clashes with the committee with regard to his fitness led to his suspension by the club during the 1896-97 campaign and the following close season saw him leave for New Brighton Tower. However, with the club facing relegation in April 1898 the committee were forced to invite him back to play in two of the final League games and for the four Test matches. He did sufficiently well to be installed in his old position for the start of the 1898-99 season. A second spell with New Brighton Tower was followed by a move to Blackpool where he was played at centre-forward and topped the goalscorers in 1901-02 with 12 goals. When he retired from playing he was given a temporary position as team coach before moving to Cliftonville in a coaching capacity.

## ANDERSSON, Patrik Jonas
Central defender/Midfield. 1993.
*6ft 0¾in; 13st 11lb.*
*Born: Borgeby, Sweden, 18 August 1971.*
*Debut: v Wimbledon (h) 9 January 1993 (sub).*
*Career: Bairred; Malmö FF; Blackburn Rovers January 1993 (£800,000); Borussia Mönchengladbach (Germany) November 1993 (£425,000).*
*International honours with Blackburn Rovers: Sweden: 7 caps (1993)*
**Appearances:** Premier League 7 + 5; FA Cup 1; Football League Cup 2; Total 10 + 5.

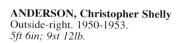

**Goals:** Football League Cup 1.
A member of the Swedish team that eliminated England from the 1992 European championships, Patrik Andersson attracted the attention of Norwich City and Leeds United before Kenny Dalglish brought him to Ewood Park. Highly rated in Sweden as a classy defender who likes to play constructive football. His debut in English football proved something of a culture shock when he came on as a substitute against Wimbledon following a facial injury to Kevin Moran. He found the pace and power of the Premier League difficult to come to terms with and was used as much in midfield as in his preferred central-defensive role during his first season at Blackburn. The 1992-93 season saw him unable to break into the first team, despite being a regular in the Swedish national team, and in November 1993 he was allowed to move to Germany.

## ANGLO-FRENCH FRIENDSHIP CUP

The Anglo-French Friendship Cup was inaugurated at the start of the 1960-61 season. Blackburn were invited to represent the Football League in this competition, along with Cardiff City, Derby County and Southampton, for the 1961-62 season. The Rovers were drawn to play FC Nancy on a home and away basis. The French team had a truly international flavour and included three Argentinians, a Pole and a Sudanese. Nancy visited Blackburn in December 1961, but proved to be a major disappointment. The French club failed to adapt to English conditions and their intricate passing movements were ill-suited to the clinging mud they found at Ewood Park. In a far from friendly encounter the Rovers were largely untroubled by their opponents and enjoyed a 3-1 victory in front of a crowd of 4,850. The men from Blackburn went close to winning the return in France in May 1962, but were eventually defeated by a single goal.

**1st Leg**
4  Dec  1961  (h)  W  3-1
**2nd Leg**
1  May  1962  (a)  L  0-1

**Appearances:** J.Byrom 2; R.Clayton 2; B.Douglas 2; M.McGrath 2; K.R.Newton 2; F.Pickering 2; K.G.Taylor 2; R.Craig 1; F.Else 1; H.M.England 1; J.Haverty 1; R.W.Jones 1; W.I.Lawther 1; J.B.Ratcliffe 1; M.Woods 1.
**Goals:** R.Clayton 1; W.I.Lawther 1; F.Pickering 1.

## ANGLO-SCOTTISH CUP

The Anglo-Scottish Cup came into being following the withdrawal of the sponsorship of Texaco from the Texaco Cup. The competition had originally been intended to be a mini British Cup but the withdrawal of Texaco saw the competition restricted to English and Scottish clubs. The initial stages of the competition were played during the pre-season period on a mini-league basis. Afterwards, four English and four Scottish clubs were paired in a two-legged quarter-final. The Rovers reached the quarter-final stages on two occasions but were unable to make further progress in a tournament which was to become dominated by English Second Division clubs. Building upon the interest generated during the Third Division championship campaign the Rovers were able to attract respectable crowds during the inaugural competition. However, although the pre-season games involved a series of local derby matches, interest in the competition began to wane in later years. During the six campaigns that the Rovers entered this competition they only attracted a five figure gate on three occasions. Two of these games, against Manchester City (10,612) and Motherwell (18,647), were played at Ewood in the 1975-76 campaign whilst the game against Burnley at Ewood in 1976-77 attracted a crowd of 11,012.

**1975-76**
| Aug | 2 | (a) | Sheffield U | L | 1-3 |
| | 6 | (h) | Manchester C | W | 1-0 |
| | 9 | (h) | Blackpool | W | 3-2 |
| Sep | 17 | (h) | Motherwell (QF) | D | 0-0 |
| | 29 | (a) | Motherwell | L | 1-2 |

**1976-77**
| Aug | 7 | (h) | Burnley | D | 1-1 |
| | 9 | (h) | Blackpool | W | 1-0 |
| | 10 | (a) | Bolton W | L | 0-2 |

**1977-78**
| Aug | 2 | (a) | Burnley | L | 1-2 |
| | 6 | (h) | Blackpool | W | 3-1 |
| | 10 | (h) | Bolton W | W | 2-0 |
| Sep | 14 | (a) | Hibernian (QF) | L | 1-2 |
| | 28 | (h) | Hibernian | L | 0-1 |

**1978-79**
| Aug | 5 | (a) | Blackpool | W | 1-0 |
| | 9 | (h) | Preston NE | W | 1-0 |
| | 12 | (h) | Burnley | D | 1-1 |

**1979-80**
| Aug | 1 | (a) | Blackpool | D | 2-2 |
| | 4 | (h) | Burnley | D | 2-2 |
| | 7 | (h) | Preston NE | D | 1-1 |

**1980-81**
| Jul | 30 | (a) | Blackpool | L | 0-2 |
| Aug | 2 | (a) | Preston NE | W | 1-0 |
| | 5 | (a) | Carlisle U | W | 4-1 |

**Appearances:** A.Parkes 17; S.M.Metcalfe 16 + 1; D.W.Fazackerley 15; N.Brotherston 14; G.M.Keeley 12; K.Hird 10 + 2; J.A.Bailey 10; G.N.Hawkins 10; P.W.Bradshaw 7; J.Waddington 7; D.Wagstaffe 7; K.G.Beamish 6; J.M.Butcher 6; P.G.Round 5 + 1; R.Jones 5; G.Oates 5;

R.Mitchell 4 + 2; J.Aston 4 + 1; J.A.Arnold 4; J.Curtis 4; J.M.Heaton 4; M.F.T.Hickman 4; H.Kendall 4; D.McKenzie 4; M.J.Rathbone 4; M.J.Wood 4; S.Garner 3 + 2; J.Craig 3 + 1; M.Fowler 3 + 1; R.L.Svarc 3 + 1; A.Burgin 3; A.Crawford 3; D.Martin 3; B.Morley 3; G.Taylor 3; N.Wilkinson 3; M.Speight 2 + 1; R.J.Coughlin 2; R.S.DeVries 2; G.Hutt 2; F.J.Lewis 2; A.P.Needham 2; S.J.Parker 2; R.Hoy 1 + 1; J.F.Kenyon 1 + 1; J.P.S.Branagan 1; J.Hall 1; J.Radford 1; K.Stonehouse 1; A.Morley 0 +1.
**Goalscorers:** N.Brotherston 7; K.G.Beamish 3; S.Garner 2; G.Oates 2; S.J.Parker 2; D.Wagstaffe 2; M.J.Wood 2; J.Craig 1; S.M.Metcalfe 1; R.Mitchell 1; A.Parkes 1; P.G.Round 1; M.Speight 1; K.Stonehouse 1; R.L.Svarc 1.

## ANTHONY, Walter
Outside-left. 1908-1914.
*5ft 6in; 11st.*
*Born: Nottingham, 21 November 1879; Died: 26 January 1950.*
*Career: Heanor Town; Osmaston February 1899; Nottingham Forest February 1904; Brighton & Hove Albion cs 1905; Blackburn Rovers February 1908; Stalybridge Celtic cs 1914.*
*Domestic honours with Blackburn Rovers: First Division championship: 1911-12 (27 apps, 1 gl); 1913-14 (1 app).*
**Appearances:** Football League 149; FA Cup 14; Charity Shield 1; Total 164.
**Goals:** Football League 11; FA Cup 3; Total 14.
Walter Anthony came to Blackburn in February 1908 from Brighton & Hove Albion along with Joe Lumley and Richard Wombwell. Anthony, who had appeared in 80 Southern League matches for the 'Seagulls', quickly established himself on the left wing for the Rovers. A fast and tricky type of winger, Anthony also possessed a powerful shot and was regarded as one of the quickest forwards in the game at that time. Contemporary reports suggest that if he had been able to be a little more robust in his play he may well have gone on to win greater honours. None the less, he remained a regular on the left wing at Ewood Park until the arrival of Joe Hodkinson in 1913.

## APPEARANCES

**Leading Appearance Makers**

| | | Football League | Test/Play-off Matches | FA Cup | FL Cup | FMC Cup | Charity Shield | Total |
|---|---|---|---|---|---|---|---|---|
| 1. | D.W.Fazackerley | 593+3 | 0 | 40 | 38 | 0 | 0 | 674 (671+3) |
| 2. | R.Clayton | 579+2 | 0 | 56 | 28 | 0 | 0 | 665 (663+2) |
| 3. | R.Crompton | 529 | 0 | 46 | 0 | 0 | 1 | 576 |
| 4. | S.Garner | 455+29 | 7+1 | 24+5 | 32+2 | 9 | 0 | 564 (527+37) |
| 5. | B.Douglas | 438 | 0 | 39+1 | 25 | 0 | 0 | 503 (502+1) |
| 6. | S.M.Metcalfe | 376+11 | 0 | 23 | 22+2 | 0 | 0 | 434 (421+13) |
| 7. | W.Eckersley | 406 | 0 | 26 | 0 | 0 | 0 | 432 |
| 8. | W.Bradshaw | 386 | 0 | 39 | 0 | 0 | 1 | 426 |
| 9. | G.M.Keeley | 365+5 | 0 | 19+1 | 23 | 5 | 0 | 418 (412+6) |
| 10. | H.Healless | 360 | 0 | 36 | 0 | 0 | 1 | 397 |
| 11. | A.Parkes | 345+5 | 0 | 21 | 21 | 0 | 0 | 392 (387+5) |
| 12. | N.Brotherston | 307+10 | 0 | 24+1 | 22 | 2+1 | 0 | 367 (355+12) |
| 13. | K.R.Newton | 306 | 0 | 21 | 30 | 0 | 0 | 357 |
| 14. | R.I.Pryde | 320 | 0 | 25 | 0 | 0 | 0 | 345 |
| 15. | J.Bruton | 324 | 0 | 20 | 0 | 0 | 0 | 344 |
| 16. | J.P.S.Branagan | 290+4 | 0 | 20 | 18 | 5 | 0 | 337 (333+4) |
| 17. | T.W.Gennoe | 289 | 8 | 18 | 15 | 4 | 0 | 334 |
| 18. | J.E.Bell | 323 | 0 | 10 | 0 | 0 | 0 | 333 |
| 19. | M.J.Rathbone | 270+3 | 0 | 15 | 14 | 4 | 0 | 306 (303+3) |
| 20. | A.Cowell | 278 | 0 | 26 | 0 | 0 | 1 | 305 |
| 21. | E.Crossan | 287 | 0 | 15 | 0 | 0 | 0 | 302 |
| 22. | A.Walmsley | 272 | 0 | 28 | 0 | 0 | 1 | 301 |

**Players with 250 or More Appearances in Football League**
| Fazackerley D.W. | 596 (593+3) |
| Clayton R. | 581 (579+2) |
| Crompton R. | 529 |
| Garner S. | 484 (455+29) |
| Douglas B. | 438 |
| Eckersley W. | 406 |
| Metcalfe S.M. | 387 (376+11) |
| Keeley G.M. | 370 (365+5) |
| Healless H. | 360 |
| Parkes A. | 350 (345+5) |
| Bruton J. | 324 |
| Bell J.E. | 323 |
| Pryde R.I. | 320 |

| | |
|---|---|
| Brotherston N. | 317 (307+10) |
| Newton K.R. | 306 |
| Branagan J.P.S. | 294 (290+4) |
| Gennoe T.W. | 289 |
| Crossan E. | 287 |
| Cowell A. | 278 |
| Rathbone M.J. | 273 (270+3) |
| Walmsley A. | 272 |
| McGrath M. | 268 |
| Miller I. | 268 (252+16) |
| Woods M. | 260 |
| Latheron E.G. | 256 |
| Puddefoot S.C. | 250 |
| Whittaker A. | 250 |

**Players with 25 or More Appearances in the FA Cup**

| | |
|---|---|
| Clayton R. | 56 |
| Forrest J.H. | 47 |
| Crompton R. | 46 |
| Douglas J. | 42 |
| Fazackerley D.W. | 40 |
| Douglas B. | 40 (39+1) |
| Bradshaw W. | 39 |
| Suter F. | 38 |
| Healless H. | 36 |
| Arthur J.W.H. | 35 |
| McIntyre H. | 34 |
| Brown J. | 32 |
| Lofthouse J.M. | 32 |
| Woods M. | 30 |
| McGrath M. | 29 |
| Walton N. | 29 |
| Garner S. | 29 (24+5) |
| Aitkenhead W.A.C. | 28 |
| Walmsley A. | 28 |
| McLean T. | 27 |
| Brandon T. | 26 |
| Cowell A. | 26 |
| Eckersley W. | 26 |
| Puddefoot S.C. | 26 |
| Roscamp J. | 26 |
| Townley W.J. | 26 |
| Brotherston N. | 25 (24+1) |
| Pryde R.I. | 25 |

**Players with 15 or more appearances in the Football League Cup**

| | |
|---|---|
| D.W.Fazackerley | 38 |
| S.Garner | 34 (32+2) |
| K.R.Newton | 30 |
| R.Clayton | 28 |
| B.Douglas | 25 |
| S.M.Metcalfe | 24 (22+2) |
| G.M.Keeley | 23 |
| N.Brotherston | 22 |
| A.Parkes | 21 |
| M.N.Atkins | 21 (17+4) |
| J.P.S.Branagan | 18 |
| D.Martin | 17 (16+1) |
| M.Woods | 17 |
| F.Else | 16 |
| E.C.J.Hendry | 16 |
| W.Wilson | 16 |
| T.W.Gennoe | 15 |
| R.Jones | 15 |
| M.McGrath | 15 |

**Consecutive Appearances**

The record for consecutive appearances is held by full-back Walter Crook. Between 22 December 1934 and 7 December 1946 Crook appeared in 208 Football League matches. In addition Crook appeared in the three matches of the ill-fated 1939-40 League season. Because of World War Two and the suspension of the Football League it meant that Crook's record spanned almost ten years.

**APPLEBY, James Patrick**
Centre-half. 1958-1961.
*6ft 1½in; 12st 7lb.*
*Born: Shotton Colliery, 15 June 1934.*
*Debut: v Aston Villa (a) 27 September 1958.*
*Career: Wingate Welfare; Burnley January 1953; Blackburn Rovers February 1958; Southport October 1961; Chester City June 1962 to cs*

1963; *Horden Colliery Welfare 1963 to 1967; Ryhope Colliery Welfare 1967-68; Horden Colliery Welfare manager.*
**Appearances:** Football League 2.
A rugged centre-half who was a regular in the Burnley Central League team for three seasons before moving to Blackburn. At Ewood Park he was destined to understudy Matt Woods and his cause was not helped by a disappointing debut performance in a 3-2 home defeat by Aston Villa in September 1958. He made his second appearance in August 1962 and was unfortunate enough to figure in a 6-1 defeat at Old Trafford. By this time Mike England had become the main challenger to Matt Woods and Appleby was allowed to join Southport shortly after the Old Trafford débâcle.

**ARCHIBALD, Steven**
Centre-forward. 1987-1988.
*5ft 10in; 11st 2lb.*
*Born: Glasgow, 27 September 1956.*
*Debut: v Birmingham City (h) 19 December 1987.*
*Career: Crofoot United; Fernhill Athletic; East Stirling; Clyde 1974; Aberdeen January 1978 (£25,000); Tottenham Hotspur May 1980 (£800,000); Barcelona (Spain) July 1984 (£900,000); Blackburn Rovers on loan December 1987 until end of season; Hibernian August 1988; Espanõl (Spain) January 1990; St Mirren November 1990; Reading on trial January 1992; Ayr United February 1992; Fulham non-contract player September 1992.*
**Appearances:** Football League 20; Play-offs 1; FA Cup 1; Total 22.
**Goals:** Football League 6.
Don Mackay rocked the football world when he persuaded Steve Archibald to forsake the splendour of the Nou Camp stadium in Barcelona for the more homely surroundings of Ewood Park in December 1987. One of most unlikely deals in the history of Blackburn Rovers came about after the signings of Mark Hughes and Gary Lineker had made Archibald surplus to requirements in Spain. His arrival at Ewood Park caused a surge of interest in the club and his on the field performances helped lift Rovers into the thick of the promotion race. Although Archibald only found the net on six occasions he produced a number of memorable displays, including an impressive two-goal performance in a vital top of the table clash with Aston Villa. Archibald, a Scottish international, was a skilful and strong running forward, who won championship medals with Aberdeen and Barcelona and a Cup winners' medal with Tottenham Hotspur. He also picked up runners-up medals for the League Cup competitions in Scotland and England as well as a European Cup runners-up medal with Barcelona.

**ARDILES, Osvaldo Cesar**
Midfield. 1988.
*5ft 6in; 9st 10lb.*
*Born: Argentina, 3 March 1952.*
*Debut: v Plymouth Argyle (a) 26 March 1988.*
*Career: Red Star Cordoba (Argentina); Instituto de Cordoba (Argentina); Huraçan (Argentina) 1975; Tottenham Hotspur July 1978 (£325,000); Paris St-Germain (France) on loan July 1982; Blackburn Rovers on loan March 1988 until end of season; Queen's Park Rangers August 1988; Fort Lauderdale Strikers (USA) June 1989; Swindon Town manager July 1989; Newcastle United manager April 1991 to February 1992; West Bromwich Albion manager May 1992; Tottenham Hotspur manager July 1993.*
**Appearances:** Football League 5; Play-offs 1+1; Total 6+1.
A hefty challenge from Plymouth Argyle's Nicky Marker, later to join Blackburn Rovers himself, severely dented Don Mackay's bold bid to install Ossie Ardiles into the engine room of his promotion chasing team. The injury he received kept him out of the vital Easter fixtures and although he returned to display his subtle midfield skills in four of the remaining games, Mackay's brave gamble came to nothing. However, although Ardiles only appeared in five League games for the club he was a big favourite with the fans. For over a decade the silky skills of the tiny Argentinian had illuminated English football and the Blackburn public were appreciative of the brief glimpse they were given of his enormous talent. A member of Argentina's 1978 World Cup winning team, Ardiles was brought to Tottenham by Keith Burkinshaw after the World Cup Final and went on to create a special niche in the hearts of the White Hart Lane fans. He helped Tottenham to win the FA Cup and the UEFA Cup in a ten year spell that was interrupted briefly when Ardiles went to France because of the Falklands War. After ending his playing career with Queen's Park Rangers he entered management with Swindon Town. After transforming their style of play he led them to the First Division after victory in the play-offs in 1989-90. However, an illegal payments scandal saw them denied their place in the top flight. In March 1991, Ardiles was appointed manager of Newcastle United and tried to introduce his own brand of total football to the Magpies. Sadly, his gamble of using young players failed and with Newcastle facing relegation to the Third Division

the decision was taken to terminate his employment. He enjoyed a successful 12 months at West Bromwich Albion, taking the club to promotion via the play-offs, before controversially leaving The Hawthorns to return to his beloved Tottenham Hotspur.

### ARENTOFT, Preben
Midfield/Left-back/Centre-back. 1971-1974.
*5ft 6½in; 10st 5lb.*
*Born: Copenhagen, Denmark, 1 November 1942.*
*Debut: v Shrewsbury Town (a) 2 October 1971.*
*Career: Brønshøj (Denmark); Morton September 1965; Newcastle United March 1969 (£18,000); Blackburn Rovers September 1971 (£15,000) to cs 1974.*
**Appearances:** Football League 94; FA Cup 10, Football League Cup 4; Total 108.
**Goals:** Football League 3.
Small and stocky in build, Ben Arentoft was a hard-working midfield player whose perceptive reading of the game had brought him four international caps for Denmark in his pre-Blackburn days. The high point of his career in England was helping Newcastle United to win the UEFA Cup in 1969 and he appeared in 50 League matches (including four as sub) for the Tyneside club before moving to Ewood Park in September 1971. Unfortunately, his cultured touch never looked suitable for the rough and tumble of Third Division midfield play and he quickly lost his place in the first team. An end of season trip to his native Denmark saw him moved to full-back with great success and as a result he became an automatic choice for the left-back position during the next two seasons. His masterful reading of the game and his intelligent use of the ball made him a great favourite at Ewood. The arrival of Gordon Lee as manager brought Arentoft's career to an end as the new manager preferred his defenders to be a little more rugged and vociferous. After being released in May 1974, the Dane returned to his native homeland to take up a business career.

### ARNOLD, James Alexander
Goalkeeper. 1979-1981
*6ft 2in; 12st 3lb.*
*Born: Stafford, 6 August 1950.*
*Debut: v Millwall (h) 18 August 1979.*
*Career: Stafford Rangers; Blackburn Rovers June 1979 (£25,000); Everton August 1981 (£200,000); Preston North End on loan October 1982; Port Vale August 1985; Kidderminster Harriers.*
**Appearances:** Football League 58; FA Cup 7; Football League Cup 3; Total 68.
Jim Arnold had just celebrated his 29th birthday when he made his Football League debut for Blackburn Rovers. Prior to this Arnold had played his football in non-League circles with Stafford Rangers and appeared for the England semi-professional team on two occasions in 1979. Arnold was brought to Ewood Park by Howard Kendall to challenge John Butcher for the goalkeeping position and very quickly made the green jersey his own. In contrast to the hesitancy of Butcher, Jim Arnold was always calm and cool under pressure. His handling was a delight and his intelligent positional play was a major asset as the club rose from likely relegation candidates to promotion challengers. During a remarkable spell of 15 League matches between January and April 1980, which saw 14 wins and one draw for the Rovers, Arnold conceded only four goals. He

missed the final three matches of the season with a finger injury and the 1980-81 campaign saw him forced on the side-lines for three months due to a persistent groin strain. Such was Howard Kendall's respect for his goalkeeper that when he moved to Everton in the summer of 1981 he quickly returned to Ewood Park to sign Jim Arnold for £200,000. At Everton he made 48 League appearances while Neville Southall was groomed to replace him. He returned to the Potteries in 1985 and ended his League career with 53 appearances for Port Vale before returning to non-League football with Kidderminster Harriers. He reappeared briefly at Ewood Park in the late 1980s when Don Mackay signed him to provide cover for his goalkeepers during an end of season promotion push.

### ARNOTT, Kevin W.
Midfield. 1981-1982 & 1982-1983
*5ft 10in; 11st 12lb.*
*Born: Gateshead, 28 September 1958.*
*Debut: v Shrewsbury Town (h) 25 November 1981.*
*Career: Sunderland September 1976; Blackburn Rovers on loan November 1981; Sheffield United June 1982; Blackburn Rovers on loan November 1982; Rotherham United on loan March 1983; Vasalund (Sweden); Chesterfield non-contract player November 1987.*
**Appearances:** Football League 28+1; FA Cup 2; Total 30+1.
**Goals:** Football League 3.
A creative midfield player who would probably have become a permanent member of the Ewood playing staff but for the club's precarious financial position during the early 1980s. Although he created a favourable impression at Blackburn during two separate loan spells his career never really fulfilled the early promise he had shown at Sunderland.

### ARSENAL FC
Founded in 1886 as Royal Arsenal, Woolwich. The Rovers first met the 'Gunners' in a friendly match on 1 April 1895 when the clubs shared a 2-2 draw in London. The clubs didn't meet in a League fixture until Arsenal won promotion to Division One in 1904. Since that time the 'Gunners' have provided opposition in almost every First Division & Premiership campaign that the Rovers have played. In 1897, Thomas Mitchell, the former Rovers secretary, became Arsenal's first professional manager, whilst Eddie Hapgood, who made 393 League appearances for Arsenal, became the Rovers manager in 1946. A number of Arsenal players have moved to Blackburn in the past including goalkeepers Jimmy Ashcroft and George Marks. The most famous name to make the trip in the opposite direction was Joe Hulme who went on to appear in 333 League games for the 'Gunners'.

### Football League

| | | | Home | | Away | |
|---|---|---|---|---|---|---|
| 1904-05 | (Div 1) | D | 1-1 | L | 0-2 |
| 1905-06 | (Div 1) | W | 2-0 | L | 2-3 |
| 1906-07 | (Div 1) | L | 2-3 | L | 0-2 |
| 1907-08 | (Div 1) | D | 1-1 | L | 0-2 |
| 1908-09 | (Div 1) | L | 1-3 | W | 1-0 |
| 1909-10 | (Div 1) | W | 7-0 | W | 1-0 |
| 1910-11 | (Div 1) | W | 1-0 | L | 1-4 |
| 1911-12 | (Div 1) | W | 4-0 | L | 1-5 |
| 1912-13 | (Div 1) | D | 1-1 | W | 1-0 |
| 1919-20 | (Div 1) | D | 2-2 | W | 1-0 |
| 1920-21 | (Div 1) | D | 2-2 | L | 0-2 |
| 1921-22 | (Div 1) | L | 0-1 | D | 1-1 |
| 1922-23 | (Div 1) | L | 0-5 | D | 1-1 |
| 1923-24 | (Div 1) | W | 2-0 | D | 2-2 |
| 1924-25 | (Div 1) | W | 1-0 | L | 0-1 |
| 1925-26 | (Div 1) | L | 2-3 | L | 2-4 |
| 1926-27 | (Div 1) | L | 1-2 | D | 2-2 |
| 1927-28 | (Div 1) | W | 4-1 | L | 2-3 |
| 1928-29 | (Div 1) | W | 5-2 | L | 0-1 |
| 1929-30 | (Div 1) | D | 1-1 | L | 0-4 |
| 1930-31 | (Div 1) | D | 2-2 | L | 2-3 |
| 1931-32 | (Div 1) | D | 1-1 | L | 0-4 |
| 1932-33 | (Div 1) | L | 2-3 | L | 0-8 |
| 1933-34 | (Div 1) | D | 2-2 | L | 1-2 |
| 1934-35 | (Div 1) | W | 2-0 | L | 0-4 |
| 1935-36 | (Div 1) | L | 0-1 | L | 1-5 |
| 1946-47 | (Div 1) | L | 1-2 | W | 3-1 |
| 1947-48 | (Div 1) | L | 0-1 | L | 0-2 |
| 1958-59 | (Div 1) | W | 4-2 | D | 1-1 |
| 1959-60 | (Div 1) | D | 1-1 | L | 2-5 |
| 1960-61 | (Div 1) | L | 2-4 | D | 0-0 |
| 1961-62 | (Div 1) | D | 0-0 | D | 0-0 |
| 1962-63 | (Div 1) | D | 5-5 | L | 1-3 |
| 1963-64 | (Div 1) | W | 4-1 | D | 0-0 |

## Football League continued

|         |         | Home |     | Away |     |
| ------- | ------- | ---- | --- | ---- | --- |
| 1964-65 | (Div 1) | L    | 1-2 | D    | 1-1 |
| 1965-66 | (Div 1) | W    | 2-1 | D    | 2-2 |

|       | P  | W  | D  | L  | F   | A   |
| ----- | -- | -- | -- | -- | --- | --- |
| Home  | 36 | 12 | 12 | 12 | 69  | 56  |
| Away  | 36 | 5  | 10 | 21 | 32  | 80  |
| Total | 72 | 17 | 22 | 33 | 101 | 136 |

## FA Premiership

|         |         | Home |     | Away |     |
| ------- | ------- | ---- | --- | ---- | --- |
| 1992-93 |         | W    | 1-0 | W    | 1-0 |
| 1993-94 |         | D    | 1-1 | L    | 0-1 |

|       | P | W | D | L | F | A |
| ----- | - | - | - | - | - | - |
| Home  | 2 | 1 | 1 | 0 | 2 | 1 |
| Away  | 2 | 1 | 0 | 1 | 1 | 1 |
| Total | 4 | 2 | 1 | 1 | 3 | 2 |

## FA Cup

|         |      |                         |     |       |
| ------- | ---- | ----------------------- | --- | ----- |
| 1900-01 | (1)  | Away                    | L   | 0-2   |
| 1925-26 | (4)  | Away                    | L   | 1-3   |
| 1927-28 | (SF) | Filbert Street Leicester | W  | 1-0   |
| 1965-66 | (3)  | Home                    | W   | 3-0   |

## Football League Cup

|         |     |      |   |     |
| ------- | --- | ---- | - | --- |
| 1967-68 | (4) | Away | L | 1-2 |

### ARTHUR, William John Herbert
Goalkeeper. 1880-1889 & 1891-1892.
*5ft 10½in.*
*Born: Blackburn, 14 February 1863; Died: Blackpool, 27 November 1930.*
*Debut: v Southport (h) 20 November 1883 (FAC).*
*Career: Lower Bank Academy; King's Own; Blackburn Rovers 1880; Southport Central 1890; Blackburn Rovers November 1890.*
*International honours with Blackburn Rovers: England: 7 caps (1885-87).*
*Domestic honours with Blackburn Rovers: FA Cup winner: 1884; 1885; 1886.*
**Appearances:** Football League 40; FA Cup 35; Total 75.
Although Herbie Arthur joined the club as a wing-half, it was as a goalkeeper that he made his senior debut in the friendly match with Aston Villa in March 1882. With Woolfall and Howorth ahead of him in the pecking order it wasn't until the 1883-84 season that Arthur finally became the first-choice goalkeeper. A member of a local well-to-do family, employment in the family business kept Arthur out of the professionalism debate which was raging at that time. There was little flamboyance about his style; he preferred to use positional play rather than spectacular leaps to keep his goal intact. He gained wide acclaim for his goalkeeping skills and won all the honours the game had to offer at that time. Unfortunately, Arthur was no longer in his prime when the Football League was founded in 1888. He began the first League season in goal, but a serious knee injury at the turn of the year kept him out of action for some time. From then on his career went into decline and in 1891 he began playing with Southport Central. However, he was brought back to Blackburn for the 1891-92 season and had the distinction of playing Burnley on his own. During a severe snowstorm all of the Blackburn side, apart from Arthur, left the field. As the Burnley side charged towards his goal the rather forlorn figure of Arthur successfully appealed for offside. He then proceeded to take so long over the free-kick that the referee was forced to abandon the match.

### ASHCROFT, James
Goalkeeper. 1908-1913.
*5ft 10in; 12st 6lb.*
*Born: Liverpool 12 September 1878; Died: North Liverpool, 9 April 1943.*
*Debut: v Bristol City (h) 1 September 1908.*
*Career: Wilby's United; Anfield Recreation Club; Garston Copperworks; Everton amateur September 1897; Gravesend United 1899; Woolwich Arsenal June 1900; Blackburn Rovers May 1908 (£350); Tranmere Rovers June 1913.*
*Domestic honours with Blackburn Rovers: First Division championship: 1911-12 (8 apps).*
**Appearances:** Football League 114; FA Cup 15; Total 129.
Jimmy Ashcroft, a former England international goalkeeper, joined Blackburn Rovers to solve the goalkeeping crisis created by the departures of Evans and McIver during the 1908 close season. Ashcroft had proved an exceptionally talented custodian during his time in London

and had been the first Arsenal player to win an England cap. Ashcroft was a goalkeeper whose strength was his consistency rather than brilliance and his debut season at Ewood Park saw him become the first goalkeeper to maintain an ever-present record in the League since Adam Ogilvie in 1895-96. Sound with shots both high and low; Ashcroft continued to hold onto the goalkeeping position despite suffering from muscular rheumatism. Injury and ill health finally forced the Rovers into bringing Alf Robinson to the club and Ashcroft's appearances grew increasingly infrequent. In June 1913 he returned to his native Merseyside to join Tranmere Rovers.

### ASTILL, Leonard Victor
Forward. 1936-1937.
*5ft 10in; 11st.*
*Born: Wolverhampton, 30 December 1916; Died: January 1988.*
*Debut: v Birmingham (a) 1 February 1936.*
*Career: Heath Town; Wolverhampton Wanderers amateur May 1934; Blackburn Rovers January 1936 (£1,000); Ipswich Town June 1937; Colchester United March 1938.*
**Appearances:** Football League 3; FA Cup 1; Total 4.
**Goals:** Football League 1.
Astill attracted the attention of representatives of the Ewood Club when they had travelled to watch a player whom the Wanderers would not release. However, Astill created such a favourable impression that when Wolves announced they were ready to part with him the Rovers moved swiftly to bring him to Ewood Park. Although he enjoyed an outstanding debut for the Rovers he quickly faded from the scene at a time when the club were fighting a losing battle against relegation. Astill never featured in a winning team on his four senior outings and during the 1937 close season he moved to Ipswich Town where he scored 13 goals in 31 League games.

### ASTON, John
Outside-left. 1978-1980
*5ft 10in; 11st 12lb.*
*Born: Manchester 28 June 1947.*
*Debut: v Crystal Palace (h) 19 August 1978.*
*Career: Manchester United apprentice June 1963, turning professional in July 1964; Luton Town July 1972; Mansfield Town September 1977; Blackburn Rovers July 1978 to cs 1980.*
**Appearances:** Football League 12+3; Football League Cup 1; Total 13+3.
**Goals:** Football League 2.
John Aston had over 300 League appearances behind him when he became Jim Iley's second close season signing of 1978. Sadly, for both player and manager, the move was not a success as Aston struggled to find the form that had made him an automatic selection at both Old Trafford and Kenilworth Road. An orthodox left-winger who relied on pace to beat his opponent, Aston's fortunes dipped as age curtailed his speed. Unlike Dave Wagstaffe, whom he replaced, Aston never won over the fans at Ewood and his signing became another issue which distanced the supporters from the manager. Aston remained at Ewood during Howard Kendall's first year of office but was only called upon on two occasions. Aston's ill-fated Ewood venture was in marked contrast to a career which had seen him help Manchester United to win the FA Youth Cup, Football League championship and the European Cup. At Luton, he had helped the Hatters to win promotion to the First Division in 1974. His father, also called John, was left-back in the Manchester United team which won the FA Cup in 1948.

### ASTON VILLA FC
Founded in 1874 by members of the Villa Cross Wesleyan Chapel, Aston. Blackburn Rovers and Aston Villa have a long history of opposition stretching back to the years before the creation of the Football League. The two former founding members of the Football League remained in the First Division together until 1935-36, when both clubs suffered the ignominy of relegation for the first time. The Rovers have met Villa in the Premiership, First, Second and Third Divisions of the Football League.

## Football League

|         |         | Home |     | Away |     |
| ------- | ------- | ---- | --- | ---- | --- |
| 1888-89 | (FL)    | W    | 5-1 | L    | 1-6 |
| 1889-90 | (FL)    | W    | 7-0 | L    | 0-3 |
| 1890-91 | (FL)    | W    | 5-1 | D    | 2-2 |
| 1891-92 | (FL)    | W    | 4-3 | L    | 1-5 |
| 1892-93 | (Div 1) | D    | 2-2 | L    | 1-4 |
| 1893-94 | (Div 1) | W    | 2-0 | L    | 1-2 |
| 1894-95 | (Div 1) | L    | 1-3 | L    | 0-3 |
| 1895-96 | (Div 1) | D    | 1-1 | L    | 1-3 |
| 1896-97 | (Div 1) | L    | 1-5 | L    | 0-3 |
| 1897-98 | (Div 1) | W    | 4-3 | L    | 1-5 |

| 1898-99 | (Div 1) | D | 0-0 | L | 1-3 |
|---------|---------|---|-----|---|-----|
| 1899-00 | (Div 1) | L | 0-4 | L | 1-3 |
| 1900-01 | (Div 1) | D | 2-2 | D | 3-3 |
| 1901-02 | (Div 1) | W | 4-0 | D | 1-1 |
| 1902-03 | (Div 1) | L | 0-2 | L | 0-5 |
| 1903-04 | (Div 1) | L | 0-3 | W | 3-2 |
| 1904-05 | (Div 1) | W | 4-0 | L | 0-3 |
| 1905-06 | (Div 1) | D | 1-1 | W | 1-0 |
| 1906-07 | (Div 1) | W | 2-1 | L | 2-4 |
| 1907-08 | (Div 1) | W | 2-0 | D | 1-1 |
| 1908-09 | (Div 1) | W | 3-1 | D | 1-1 |
| 1909-10 | (Div 1) | W | 3-2 | L | 3-4 |
| 1910-11 | (Div 1) | D | 0-0 | D | 2-2 |
| 1911-12 | (Div 1) | W | 3-1 | W | 3-0 |
| 1912-13 | (Div 1) | D | 2-2 | D | 1-1 |
| 1913-14 | (Div 1) | D | 0-0 | W | 3-1 |
| 1914-15 | (Div 1) | L | 1-2 | L | 1-2 |
| 1919-20 | (Div 1) | W | 5-1 | W | 2-1 |
| 1920-21 | (Div 1) | L | 0-1 | L | 0-3 |
| 1921-22 | (Div 1) | L | 1-2 | D | 1-1 |
| 1922-23 | (Div 1) | W | 4-2 | L | 0-2 |
| 1923-24 | (Div 1) | W | 3-1 | L | 0-1 |
| 1924-25 | (Div 1) | D | 1-1 | L | 3-4 |
| 1925-26 | (Div 1) | W | 3-1 | W | 2-1 |
| 1926-27 | (Div 1) | L | 0-2 | L | 3-4 |
| 1927-28 | (Div 1) | L | 0-1 | L | 0-2 |
| 1928-29 | (Div 1) | L | 2-5 | L | 1-2 |
| 1929-30 | (Div 1) | W | 2-0 | L | 0-3 |
| 1930-31 | (Div 1) | L | 0-2 | L | 2-5 |
| 1931-32 | (Div 1) | W | 2-0 | W | 5-1 |
| 1932-33 | (Div 1) | L | 0-5 | L | 0-4 |
| 1933-34 | (Div 1) | W | 2-1 | D | 1-1 |
| 1934-35 | (Div 1) | W | 5-0 | D | 1-1 |
| 1935-36 | (Div 1) | W | 5-1 | W | 4-2 |
| 1936-37 | (Div 2) | L | 3-4 | D | 2-2 |
| 1937-38 | (Div 2) | W | 1-0 | L | 1-2 |
| 1946-47 | (Div 1) | L | 0-1 | L | 1-2 |
| 1947-48 | (Div 1) | D | 0-0 | L | 2-3 |
| 1958-59 | (Div 1) | L | 2-3 | L | 0-1 |
| 1960-61 | (Div 1) | W | 4-1 | D | 2-2 |
| 1961-62 | (Div 1) | W | 4-2 | L | 0-1 |
| 1962-63 | (Div 1) | W | 4-1 | D | 0-0 |
| 1963-64 | (Div 1) | W | 2-0 | W | 2-1 |
| 1964-65 | (Div 1) | W | 5-1 | W | 4-0 |
| 1965-66 | (Div 1) | L | 0-2 | L | 1-3 |
| 1967-68 | (Div 2) | W | 2-1 | W | 2-1 |
| 1968-69 | (Div 2) | W | 2-0 | D | 1-1 |
| 1969-70 | (Div 2) | W | 2-0 | D | 1-1 |
| 1971-72 | (Div 3) | D | 1-1 | L | 1-4 |
| 1987-88 | (Div 2) | W | 3-2 | D | 1-1 |

|      | P   | W  | D  | L  | F   | A   |
|------|-----|----|----|----|-----|-----|
| Home | 60  | 32 | 11 | 17 | 129 | 85  |
| Away | 60  | 11 | 16 | 33 | 81  | 135 |
| Total| 120 | 43 | 27 | 50 | 210 | 220 |

**FA Premiership**

|         |   | Home |   | Away |
|---------|---|------|---|------|
| 1992-93 | W | 3-0  | D | 0-0  |
| 1993-94 | W | 1-0  | W | 1-0  |

|       | P | W | D | L | F | A |
|-------|---|---|---|---|---|---|
| Home  | 2 | 2 | 0 | 0 | 4 | 0 |
| Away  | 2 | 1 | 1 | 0 | 1 | 0 |
| Total | 4 | 3 | 1 | 0 | 5 | 0 |

**FA Cup**

| 1888-89 | (3) | Home | W | 8-1 |
|---------|-----|------|---|-----|
| 1922-23 | (1) | Away | W | 1-0 |
| 1929-30 | (5) | Away | L | 1-4 |
| 1979-80 | (5) | Home | D | 1-1 |
|         | (R) | Away | L | 0-1 |
| 1989-90 | (3) | Home | D | 2-2 |
|         | (R) | Away | L | 1-3 |

**ATHERTON, Dewi Lewis**
Midfield. 1967-1971.
*6ft; 11st 2lb.*
*Born: Bangor, 6 July 1951.*
*Career: Blackburn Rovers associated schoolboy July 1967, turning professional in July 1968, contract cancelled in October 1971; Bangor City 1971.*

**Appearances:** Football League 9+1; Football League Cup 1; Total 10+1.
Lightweight midfield player who never really graduated beyond the role of understudy during his time at Ewood Park. His only opportunities came towards the end of the ill-fated 1970-71 season when he was plunged into a team fighting a losing battle against relegation. He was to become an early casualty of Ken Furphy's rapid rebuilding programme and returned to his native Wales on leaving Blackburn.

**ATHERTON, Moses John**
Trainer. 1913-1933.
*Born: Ince, nr Wigan, c.1884; Died: Blackburn, 9 March 1956 (aged 72).*
*Career: Ince Park-road; Ince Imperial; Bryn Central; Wigan Town; Blackburn Rovers 1907; Eccles Borough; Great Harwood; Darwen; Blackburn Rovers 1912 groundsman & assistant trainer, becoming trainer in November 1913; Grimsby Town trainer January 1933; Blackburn Rovers masseur.*
Mo Atherton served Blackburn Rovers in various capacities during his long association with the club but is best known as trainer to the teams that won the First Division championship in 1913-14 and the FA Cup in 1928. Atherton first came to Ewood Park as a young centre-half but his only senior appearance was in a friendly match against his former club, Wigan Town, in September 1907. He had a season with the Reserves as centre-half and helped the club to lift the Lancashire Combination Second Division title. Mo then moved into non-League circles and captained both Eccles Borough and Great Harwood before ending his playing career with a few games at Darwen. In 1912 he returned to Ewood Park as groundsman and assistant trainer to Bob Holmes. He succeeded Holmes as first-team trainer in November 1913 and had the appointment confirmed in February 1914. That season saw the club lift the First Division title for the second time in three seasons and such was the esteem in which Atherton was held that the club gained permission to give him a championship medal similar to that of the players. Between that auspicious start and the training of the 1928 Cup Final team, Atherton was honoured by the Football Association on several occasions. He was appointed trainer of the England international team on five occasions including the game against Wales which was held at Ewood Park in 1923-24. His greatest personal honour came in 1925 when, on the recommendation of John Lewis, he was appointed trainer of the FA touring party destined for Australia. On 17 January 1933, Atherton sensationally quit Ewood Park and twenty-four hours later was installed as trainer at Grimsby Town. He served Grimsby until the outbreak of war and during that time the Mariners won the Second Division championship, in his first full season, and also reached the semi-final of the FA Cup. As late as 1950-51 he was acting as masseur to the Rovers while carrying on a long established private practice in the town.

**ATKINS, Mark Nigel**
Right-back/Midfield. 1988-
*6ft; 12st 5lb.*
*Born: Doncaster, 14 August 1968.*
*Career: Scunthorpe United July 1986; Blackburn Rovers June 1988 (£45,000).*
*Domestic honours for Blackburn Rovers: Second Division Play-off winner; 1992.*
**Appearances:** Premier League 32+14; Football League 162+11; Play-offs 9; FA Cup 9+3; Football League Cup 17+4; Full Members' Cup 5; Total 234+32.

**Goals:** Premier League 6; Football League 22; Football League Cup 4; Full Members' Cup 1; Total 33.
Mark Atkins came to Blackburn in June 1988 from Scunthorpe United as a replacement for the departed Chris Price. At Scunthorpe, Atkins had made his debut whilst still a schoolboy and had appeared in over 60 senior matches for the club. Atkins, like his predecessor Price, developed an eye for goal whilst playing at right-back for the Rovers. He remained the first-choice right-back under Mackay as the Rovers challenged to reach the top flight. However, as the club's fortunes slumped in 1990-91, Atkins found himself out of the side. The 1991-92 season brought the departure of Mackay and Tony Parkes, acting as caretaker manager, switched Atkins into a midfield role. It was in this position that Kenny Dalglish

preferred to use Atkins and the 1991-92 campaign saw him develop into a competitive midfield man who helped lift the club into the Premier League via the Play-offs. If he lacked the skill of some of his more illustrious colleagues there was no denying his commitment to the cause. His versatility made him a valuable member of the squad and whilst he didn't always find his way into the starting eleven during the Rovers first season in the Premier League, he was a more than useful substitute. However, as Dalglish continued to build his squad during the 1993-94 campaign Atkins found first team openings few and far between.

## ATTENDANCES

The record home attendance was set on 2 March 1929 when a crowd of 62,522 watched the sixth round FA Cup-tie with Bolton Wanderers. According to the *Blackburn Times* of 9 March 1929, the receipts for this match were £4,722 13s 6d.

The highest attendance for a home match in the Football League occurred on 26 December 1921 when 52,656 watched the First Division match against Preston North End.

The lowest home attendance since the Football League began to record attendances in 1925 was recorded on 7 May 1984 when the Second Division match against Cardiff City only attracted a crowd of 3,107. However, two Football League Cup-ties have seen crowds of lower than 2,000 recorded. On 8 October 1985 a crowd of 2,161 gathered at Ewood Park to watch Blackburn try to retrieve a five-goal deficit from the first leg of a second-round tie against Wimbledon. On 2 September 1986, a crowd of 2,831 watched the second-leg tie with Wigan Athletic after the Rovers had won the first leg of this first-round tie 3-1.

### Football & Premier League Attendance Figures

Until the 1925-26 season, records of attendances for Football League matches were not recorded by the Football League. For the seasons prior to this the figures below have been calculated from newspaper records and are, as such, in most cases based on approximations. Figures from 1925-26 onwards are taken from those recorded at the Football League in Lytham St Annes and from 1950 onwards from records which exist at Blackburn Rovers. In the odd case where there is a discrepancy the figures recorded at the club have taken precedence.

| Season | Aggregate | Average | Highest | Lowest |
|---|---|---|---|---|
| 1888-89 | 66,000 | 6,000 | 12,000 | 2,000 |
| 1889-90 | 83,600 | 7,600 | 15,000 | 4,000 |
| 1890-91 | 89,500 | 8,136 | 18,000 | 3,000 |
| 1891-92 | 65,000 | 5,000 | 10,000 | 2,000 |
| 1892-93 | 83,300 | 5,553 | 12,000 | 3,000 |
| 1893-94 | 94,000 | 6,267 | 12,000 | 2,000 |
| 1894-95 | 116,200 | 7,747 | 15,000 | 1,200 |
| 1895-96 | 110,000 | 7,333 | 20,000 | 3,000 |
| 1896-97 | 101,517 | 6,768 | 14,000 | 2,000 |
| 1897-98 | 120,628 | 8,042 | 17,000 | 4,000 |
| 1898-99 | 133,500 | 7,853 | 20,000 | 4,000 |
| 1899-00 | 113,326 | 6,666 | 14,000 | 300 |
| 1900-01 | 99,000 | 5,824 | 12,000 | 3,000 |
| 1901-02 | 129,000 | 7,588 | 20,000 | 2,000 |
| 1902-03 | 135,354 | 7,962 | 20,000 | 2,000 |
| 1903-04 | 153,557 | 9,033 | 25,000 | 2,000 |
| 1904-05 | 194,000 | 11,412 | 25,000 | 4,000 |
| 1905-06 | 239,500 | 12,605 | 29,000 | 3,000 |
| 1906-07 | 239,000 | 12,579 | 35,000 | 5,000 |
| 1907-08 | 255,000 | 13,421 | 30,000 | 8,000 |
| 1908-09 | 280,000 | 14,737 | 30,000 | 5,000 |
| 1909-10 | 269,000 | 14,158 | 30,000 | 3,000 |
| 1910-11* | 232,000 | 14,500 | 20,000 | 7,000 |
| 1911-12 | 351,309 | 18,490 | 36,195 | 7,159 |
| 1912-13 | 354,023 | 18,633 | 41,115 | 2,000 |
| 1913-14 | 405,126 | 21,322 | 48,000 | 10,000 |
| 1914-15 | 262,700 | 13,826 | 25,000 | 3,000 |
| 1919-20 | 361,388 | 17,209 | 40,000 | 6,000 |
| 1920-21 | 567,800 | 27,038 | 43,000 | 8,000 |
| 1921-22 | 491,656 | 23,412 | 52,656 | 15,000 |
| 1922-23 | 401,000 | 19,095 | 30,000 | 7,000 |
| 1923-24 | 377,000 | 17,952 | 35,000 | 5,000 |
| 1924-25* | 299,000 | 14,950 | 30,000 | 3,000 |
| 1925-26 | 376,298 | 17,919 | 29,991 | 9,190 |
| 1926-27 | 396,704 | 18,891 | 42,000 | 10,176 |
| 1927-28 | 401,521 | 19,120 | 39,300 | 9,656 |
| 1928-29 | 353,659 | 16,841 | 33,966 | 5,461 |
| 1929-30 | 393,002 | 18,714 | 25,591 | 8,544 |
| 1930-31 | 329,654 | 15,698 | 29,734 | 6,699 |
| 1931-32 | 276,691 | 13,176 | 40,059 | 7,885 |
| 1932-33 | 271,832 | 12,944 | 35,987 | 3,624 |
| 1933-34 | 294,105 | 14,005 | 31,636 | 5,949 |
| 1934-35 | 276,491 | 13,166 | 25,472 | 5,921 |
| 1935-36 | 325,465 | 15,498 | 33,016 | 5,664 |
| 1936-37 | 311,189 | 14,819 | 26,927 | 7,928 |
| 1937-38 | 310,345 | 14,778 | 19,855 | 7,088 |
| 1938-39 | 383,501 | 18,262 | 32,704 | 7,547 |
| 1946-47 | 553,699 | 26,367 | 35,646 | 18,129 |
| 1947-48 | 585,535 | 27,883 | 46,874 | 14,087 |
| 1948-49 | 473,076 | 22,527 | 31,526 | 13,418 |
| 1949-50 | 456,766 | 21,751 | 42,891 | 10,948 |
| 1950-51 | 521,428 | 24,830 | 44,612 | 9,770 |
| 1951-52 | 487,781 | 23,228 | 34,077 | 13,617 |
| 1952-53 | 486,314 | 23,158 | 29,920 | 12,794 |
| 1953-54 | 548,582 | 26,123 | 45,521 | 11,793 |
| 1954-55 | 565,482 | 26,928 | 36,273 | 17,469 |
| 1955-56 | 484,023 | 23,049 | 33,582 | 12,635 |
| 1956-57 | 484,913 | 23,091 | 32,380 | 15,003 |
| 1957-58 | 476,765 | 22,703 | 41,789 | 8,825 |
| 1958-59 | 640,430 | 30,497 | 43,192 | 17,613 |
| 1959-60 | 573,285 | 27,299 | 41,694 | 15,832 |
| 1960-61 | 406,218 | 19,344 | 29,236 | 12,746 |
| 1961-62 | 334,027 | 15,906 | 33,914 | 8,876 |
| 1962-63 | 336,013 | 16,001 | 30,243 | 8,564 |
| 1963-64 | 452,403 | 21,543 | 37,526 | 10,341 |
| 1964-65 | 338,301 | 16,110 | 29,363 | 8,990 |
| 1965-66 | 283,770 | 13,513 | 30,414 | 7,256 |
| 1966-67 | 309,136 | 14,721 | 26,380 | 8,567 |
| 1967-68 | 284,111 | 13,529 | 20,225 | 7,195 |
| 1968-69 | 222,951 | 10,617 | 21,224 | 4,777 |
| 1969-70 | 262,979 | 12,523 | 17,393 | 7,339 |
| 1970-71 | 168,706 | 8,034 | 11,210 | 3,971 |
| 1971-72 | 189,891 | 8,256 | 15,562 | 5,643 |
| 1972-73 | 211,927 | 9,214 | 16,346 | 5,710 |
| 1973-74 | 170,929 | 7,432 | 10,989 | 3,520 |
| 1974-75 | 290,957 | 12,650 | 24,007 | 5,858 |
| 1975-76 | 220,311 | 10,491 | 24,430 | 6,765 |
| 1976-77 | 212,727 | 10,130 | 22,189 | 5,923 |
| 1977-78 | 255,765 | 12,179 | 27,835 | 6,316 |
| 1978-79 | 181,519 | 8,644 | 17,790 | 4,684 |
| 1979-80 | 237,155 | 10,311 | 26,130 | 5,757 |
| 1980-81 | 245,357 | 11,684 | 19,222 | 8,465 |
| 1981-82 | 175,419 | 8,353 | 15,182 | 5,207 |
| 1982-83 | 148,445 | 7,069 | 14,021 | 3,797 |
| 1983-84 | 159,879 | 7,613 | 19,199 | 3,107 |
| 1984-85 | 202,585 | 9,647 | 22,137 | 5,121 |
| 1985-86 | 122,352 | 5,826 | 9,666 | 3,587 |
| 1986-87 | 145,452 | 6,926 | 13,019 | 4,149 |
| 1987-88 | 209,084 | 9,504 | 17,356 | 5,619 |
| 1988-89 | 204,499 | 8,891 | 16,927 | 5,724 |
| 1989-90 | 221,052 | 9,611 | 15,633 | 7,456 |
| 1990-91 | 187,143 | 8,137 | 13,437 | 5,969 |
| 1991-92 | 305,634 | 13,288 | 19,511 | 8,898 |
| 1992-93 | 341,197 | 16,247 | 20,305 | 13,556 |
| 1993-94 | 372,865 | 17,755 | 22,061 | 14,260 |

*Note:
The estimated attendances for three games in the 1910-11 season remain unknown. The aggregate and average given are based on 16 matches. The estimated attendance for one game in the 1924-25 season remains unknown. The aggregate and average given are based on 20 matches.

### Top Twenty Home Attendances

| | | | | | | |
|---|---|---|---|---|---|---|
| 1. | 62,522 v | Bolton W | FA Cup | 6 | Round | 2.3.29 |
| 2. | 60,011 v | Blackpool | FA Cup | 4 | Round | 7.3.25 |
| 3. | 54,400 v | Huddersfield T | FA Cup | 6 | Round R | 9.3.39 |
| 4. | 53,839 v | Burnley | FA Cup | 6 | Round R | 16.3.60 |
| 5. | 53,000 v | Everton | FA Cup | 4 | Round | 25.1.30 |
| 6. | 52,920 v | Burnley | FA Cup | 6 | Round | 8.3.52 |
| 7. | 52,656 v | Preston NE | Division One | | | 26.12.21 |
| 8. | 52,468 v | Liverpool | FA Cup | 3 | Round | 7.1.50 |
| 9. | 51,223 v | Blackpool | FA Cup | 4 | Round | 30.1.60 |
| 10. | 51,177 v | West Brom A | FA Cup | 5 | Round | 23.2.52 |
| 11. | 51,000 v | Liverpool | FA Cup | 6 | Round | 1.3.58 |
| 12. | 49,546 v | Liverpool | FA Cup | 4 | Round | 26.1.35 |
| 13. | 48,170 v | Tottenham H | FA Cup | 3 | Round R | 26.2.25 |
| 14. | 47,248 v | Sunderland | FA Cup | 5 | Round R | 16.2.39 |
| 15. | 46,874 v | Preston NE | Division One | | | 4.10.47 |
| 16. | 45,711 v | Wolverhampton W | FA Cup | 3 | Round | 24.2.12 |
| 17. | 45,521 v | Leicester C | Division One | | | 16.4.54 |
| 18. | 45,410 v | Derby County | FA Cup | 4 | Round | 26.1.29 |
| 19. | 45,320 v | Hull City | FA Cup | 4 | Round | 2.2.52 |
| 20. | 45,068 v | Huddersfield T | FA Cup | 3 | Round | 18.2.22 |

**AVERY, George**
Forward. 1879-1884.
*Born: High Wycombe, January 1860; Died: Blackburn, 8 March 1915 (aged 55).*
*Career: Queen's Own, Blackburn; Blackburn Rovers.*
*Domestic honours with Blackburn Rovers: FA Cup runners-up: 1882.*
**Appearances:** FA Cup 20. **Goals:** FA Cup 10.
A small and stocky forward who was a regular goalscorer during the early 1880s. Avery was a member of the first Blackburn team to reach an FA Cup Final in 1882. On that occasion the team were beaten by the Old Etonians by a single goal and although Avery featured in the semi-final side of 1883-84 he did not appear in the Cup Final. He had more luck in the Lancashire Cup, featuring in the cup-winning sides of 1882, 1883 and 1884. In later life he became the landlord of the Leamington Hotel in Blackburn, after having spent some time working in a rubber factory in New Jersey in the USA.

## AWAY FORM
### Away Defeats
The record for the most away defeats in each division is as follows:

| | | | |
|---|---|---|---|
| Premiership | 7 | defeats | 1992-93 |
| Division 1 | 16 | defeats | 1935-36 & 1965-66 |
| Division 2 | 16 | defeats | 1937-38 |
| Division 3 | 13 | defeats | 1971-72 |

The record for the fewest away defeats in each division is as follows:

| | | | |
|---|---|---|---|
| Premiership | 6 | defeats | 1993-94 |
| Division 1 | 4 | defeats | 1908-09 |
| Division 2 | 6 | defeats | 1989-90 |
| Division 3 | 7 | defeats | 1974-75 & 1979-80 |

### Away Draws
The record for the most away draws in each division is as follows:

| | | | |
|---|---|---|---|
| Premiership | 7 | draws | 1992-93 |
| Division 1 | 10 | draws | 1960-61 |
| Division 2 | 10 | draws | 1980-81 |
| Division 3 | 9 | draws | 1974-75 |

The record for the fewest away draws in each division is as follows:

| | | | |
|---|---|---|---|
| Premiership | 5 | draws | 1993-94 |
| Division 1 | 1 | draw | 1890-91 & 1903-04 |
| Division 2 | 2 | draws | 1954-55, 1955-56 & 1978-79 |
| Division 3 | 4 | draws | 1979-80 |

### Away Points
The record for the most away points in each division is as follows:

| | | | W | D | L | |
|---|---|---|---|---|---|---|
| Premiership | (3) | 37 points | 11 | 4 | 6 | 1993-94 |
| Division 1 | (2) | 23 points | 8 | 7 | 4 | 1908-09 |
| Division 2 | (2) | 23 points | 9 | 5 | 7 | 1957-58 |
| Division 2 | (3) | 35 points | 9 | 8 | 6 | 1989-90 |
| Division 3 | (2) | 28 points | 12 | 4 | 7 | 1979-80 |

The record for the fewest away points in each division is as follows:

| | | | W | D | L | |
|---|---|---|---|---|---|---|
| Premiership | (3) | 28 points | 7 | 7 | 7 | 1992-93 |
| Division 1 | (2) | 4 points | 1 | 2 | 14 | 1899-00 |
| Division 2 | (2) | 6 points | 1 | 4 | 16 | 1937-38 |
| Division 2 | (3) | 17 points | 4 | 5 | 12 | 1982-83 |
| | | 17 points | 2 | 9 | 10 | 1985-86 |
| Division 3 | (2) | 15 points | 5 | 5 | 13 | 1971-72 |

*Note: The number of points per win is shown in brackets.

### Away Wins
The record for the most away wins in each division is as follows:

| | | |
|---|---|---|
| Premiership | 11 wins | 1993-94 |
| Division 1 | 8 wins | 1908-09 & 1963-64 |
| Division 2 | 9 wins | 1956-57, 1957-58, 1987-88 & 1989-90 |
| Division 3 | 12 wins | 1979-80 |

The record for the fewest away wins in each division is as follows:

| | | |
|---|---|---|
| Premiership | 7 wins | 1992-93 |
| Division 1 | 1 win | 1899-00 & 1910-11 |
| Division 2 | 1 win | 1937-38 & 1970-71 |
| Division 3 | 5 wins | 1971-72 & 1973-74 |

**BAAH, Peter H.**
Outside-left. 1989-1992.
*5ft 9in; 10st 4lb.*
*Born: Littleborough, 1 May 1973.*
*Debut: v Millwall (a) 5 October 1991.*
*Career: Blackburn Rovers trainee July 1989, turning professional in June 1991; Rotherham United on loan April 1992; Fulham July 1992 until May 1994.*
**Appearances:** Football League 1.
A young player developed by the club whose sole first-team appearance came during the caretaker reign of Tony Parkes. The arrival of Kenny Dalglish coupled with the progress of Jason Wilcox and the arrival of a number of expensive new players closed the first-team door to Baah. He had a short spell on loan to Rotherham United in April 1992 but was not called upon for the first team. In the 1992 close season he joined Don Mackay at Fulham and was given a further opportunity to prove himself in the Football League.

**BAILEY, John Anthony**
Left-back. 1975-1978.
*5ft 8in; 10st 9lb.*
*Born: Liverpool 1 April 1957.*
*Debut: v Preston North End (a) 19 August 1975 (FLC) .*
*Career: Blackburn Rovers April 1975; Everton July 1979 (£300,000); Newcastle United October 1985 (£80,000); Bristol City December 1988 (free transfer). Retired February 1992 and joined the backroom staff at Everton. Left Goodison Park in April 1993.*
**Appearances:** Football League 115+5; FA Cup 7; Football League Cup 7; Total 129+5.
**Goals:** Football League 1.
After being rejected by Everton, John Bailey served his apprenticeship at Ewood Park and developed through the Youth and Central League team to become first-choice left-back under Jim Smith. An attacking player by nature Bailey was, none the less, an excellent defender. Strong in the tackle and extremely quick on the ground, Bailey developed a formidable partnership with Dave Wagstaffe on the left wing. His extrovert personality made him a great favourite with the Blackburn public and his talent was sufficient for Everton to pay £300,000 for his services. Back on his native Merseyside he represented the England 'B' team and won an FA Cup winners' medal in 1984 before the arrival of Pat van den Hauwe led to his departure in October 1985. His move to Newcastle was not a happy one and after only 40 League appearances he was freed at the end of the 1987-88 season. He enjoyed better times at Bristol City and helped them to reach the semi-final of the Littlewoods Cup in 1988-89. Bailey retired from playing in February 1992 and returned to Goodison Park for 12 months as a member of the backroom staff.

**BALDWIN, James J.**
Half-back. 1945-1950.
*5ft 6½in; 10st 2lb.*
*Born: Blackburn 12 January 1922; Died: Blackburn, 13 February 1985.*
*Debut: v Bolton Wanderers (a) 15 January 1946 (FAC).*
*Career: Mill Hill St Peters; Blackburn Rovers amateur August 1943, turning professional on December 1945; Leicester City February 1950 (£10,000); Great Yarmouth player-manager April 1956.*
**Appearances:** Football League 88; FA Cup 8; Total 96.
**Goals:** FA Cup 1.
Jimmy Baldwin was a perfect example of the 'local boy who made good'. A wartime recruit from the Sunday School League, he cost nothing but was sold for a sizeable sum at a time when the Rovers needed to boost their finances. A workmanlike half-back who was a great trier and especially strong in defence. After almost 100 senior outings for the club he lost his place to Jackie Campbell, a more constructive type of half-back, in November 1949. In February 1950 he moved to Leicester City and became their regular right-half during the early 1950s, helping them to the Second Division title in 1953-54. Following 180 League games for the Filbert Street club he tried his hand at management with Great Yarmouth.

**BALL, William Henry**
Right-half. 1897-1898 & 1901-1902
*5ft 8in; 11st 8lb.*
*Born: West Derby, Liverpool, 1876 (April quarter).*
*Career: Liverpool South End; Rock Ferry; Blackburn Rovers May 1897; Everton May 1898; Notts County May 1899; Blackburn Rovers May 1901; Newton Heath October 1902 to cs 1903.*
**Appearances:** Football League 20.
Ball first joined Blackburn from Rock Ferry with Ben Hulse in 1897 and both players quickly forced their way into the team. Ball appeared in 17 First Division matches during his first season with the club before he was allowed to move, somewhat surprisingly, to Everton only a year after joining the Rovers. The Goodison club had a wealth of talent in the half-back division and Ball spent only 12 months on Merseyside before moving to Notts County. After two years with County he indicated a desire to return to Blackburn and the departure of Jimmy Moir meant the directors were only too pleased to welcome him back into the fold.

Although he was always a hard-working player, Ball failed to establish himself second time around and after a season spent largely in the second team, he was allowed to join Newton Heath.

### BANCROFT, William H.
Chairman. 1971-1979.

When William Bancroft, a director of a Blackburn shuttle firm, was appointed to the Rovers' board in 1966 he became the club's youngest director. On the 12 January 1971, when aged 39, he became the youngest chairman in the history of Blackburn Rovers. His reign ended in March 1979 when he was forced to resign on medical grounds. His fellow directors had no hesitation in appointing him to the position of club president following his resignation.

Bancroft's introduction to the position of chairman proved something of a 'baptism of fire'. When he was elected chairman the club was deep in debt and within months of his appointment was relegated to the Third Division for the first time in its history. Yet Bancroft's reign was seen as the start of a new era in the club's history.

Bancroft appeared to represent a more 'open' style of management than had previously been seen at Ewood Park. Together with Ken Furphy he worked hard to improve the public relations system at the club. Although his revelations to fans were sometimes unpalatable, the Blackburn public responded to the improvement in communications between the club and those who stood on the terraces.

He crowned the club's centenary year by leading them to the Third Division title and played a leading role in the appointment of four managers, three of whom went on to higher things. In leading the club through a financial minefield he laid the foundations for others to build upon.

### BARKER, Simon
Midfield. 1982-1988.
*5ft 9in; 11st.*
*Born: Farnworth, 4 November 1964.*
*Debut: v Swansea City (a) 29 October 1983.*
*Career: Blackburn Rovers associated schoolboy July 1980, becoming an apprentice in July 1981 before turning professional in November 1982; Queen's Park Rangers July 1988 (£400,000).*
*International honours with Blackburn Rovers: England Under-21: 4 caps (1985-86).*
*Domestic honours with Blackburn Rovers: Full Members' Cup winner: 1987.*
**Appearances:** Football League 180+2; FA Cup 11; Football League Cup 9; Full Members' Cup 6; Total 206 + 2.
**Goals:** Football League 35; Football League Cup 4; Full Members' Cup 2; Total 41.

An attacking midfield player whose intelligent passing was capable of opening up the tightest of defences. Barker, a product of the club's youth development scheme, made his debut in October 1983 and quickly established himself as one of the most polished midfield players in the Second Division. A creative right-sided player who, despite his youth, was an excellent reader of the game, Barker developed the ability to 'thrust' into the penalty area and became a regular goalscorer. Twice he helped to take the club to the brink of the First Division and in so doing won England Under-21 honours. He was also named 'Man of the Match' for his part in the Full Members' Cup Final in March 1987. Although injuries plagued his final season at Ewood Park it was not surprising that Barker became the target of First Division clubs.

In July 1988, Rovers received a record £400,000 from Queen's Park Rangers for Barker, yet the midfielder found it difficult to break into the first team at Loftus Road. However, once he settled down, he developed a formidable partnership with Ray Wilkins in midfield.

### BARNSLEY FC
Founded in 1887 as Barnsley St Peter's. The Yorkshire side didn't meet the Rovers in a competitive match until January 1912 when Blackburn visited Barnsley, then in the Second Division, for an FA Cup-tie. Goals from Shea, Bradshaw and Aitkenhead ensured a narrow victory in front of a crowd of 30,800. The clubs didn't meet in the Football League until the Rovers dropped out of the First Division in 1936.

**Football League**

|         |         | Home |     | Away |     |
|---------|---------|------|-----|------|-----|
| 1936-37 | (Div 2) | D    | 1-1 | L    | 2-3 |
| 1937-38 | (Div 2) | W    | 5-3 | D    | 0-0 |
| 1948-49 | (Div 2) | W    | 5-3 | D    | 1-1 |
| 1949-50 | (Div 2) | W    | 4-0 | D    | 1-1 |
| 1950-51 | (Div 2) | L    | 3-4 | L    | 0-3 |
| 1951-52 | (Div 2) | W    | 2-1 | W    | 2-1 |
| 1952-53 | (Div 2) | W    | 2-0 | W    | 4-1 |
| 1955-56 | (Div 2) | W    | 5-1 | L    | 1-2 |
| 1956-57 | (Div 2) | W    | 2-0 | D    | 3-3 |
| 1957-58 | (Div 2) | W    | 3-1 | W    | 2-0 |
| 1971-72 | (Div 3) | W    | 4-0 | D    | 0-0 |
| 1979-80 | (Div 3) | L    | 0-1 | D    | 1-1 |
| 1981-82 | (Div 2) | W    | 2-1 | W    | 1-0 |
| 1982-83 | (Div 2) | D    | 1-1 | D    | 2-2 |
| 1983-84 | (Div 2) | D    | 1-1 | D    | 0-0 |
| 1984-85 | (Div 2) | D    | 0-0 | D    | 1-1 |
| 1985-86 | (Div 2) | L    | 0-3 | D    | 1-1 |
| 1986-87 | (Div 2) | W    | 4-2 | D    | 1-1 |
| 1987-88 | (Div 2) | L    | 0-1 | W    | 1-0 |
| 1988-89 | (Div 2) | W    | 2-1 | W    | 1-0 |
| 1989-90 | (Div 2) | W    | 5-0 | D    | 0-0 |
| 1990-91 | (Div 2) | L    | 1-2 | W    | 1-0 |
| 1991-92 | (Div 2) | W    | 3-0 | L    | 1-2 |

|       | P  | W  | D  | L | F  | A  |
|-------|----|----|----|---|----|----|
| Home  | 23 | 14 | 4  | 5 | 55 | 27 |
| Away  | 23 | 7  | 12 | 4 | 27 | 23 |
| Total | 46 | 21 | 16 | 9 | 82 | 50 |

**FA Cup**

| 1912-13 | (2) | Away | W | 3-2 |
|---------|-----|------|---|-----|
| 1928-29 | (3) | Home | W | 1-0 |
| 1955-56 | (4) | Away | W | 1-0 |

**Wartime**

|         |       | Home |     | Away |     |
|---------|-------|------|-----|------|-----|
| 1945-46 | (FLN) | W    | 3-1 | L    | 0-4 |

### BARRITT, Arthur
Secretary-manager. 1931-1936.
*Born: Burnley.*
*Career: North-East Lancashire League secretary; Burnley office staff 1919; Blackburn Rovers assistant secretary October 1925, becoming secretary in January 1927 and finally secretary-manager in March 1931 until his resignation in March 1936.*

Arthur Barritt enjoyed an association with Blackburn Rovers that lasted for ten and a half years. During that time he became regarded as one of the most dedicated officials that the club had ever employed. Yet, but for a single vote, he might well have spent his career in football administration at neighbouring Burnley. He had joined the Turf Moor office staff in 1919 and in January 1925 he had missed out on the post of secretary at Burnley by one vote; nine months later he was installed as assistant secretary at Blackburn.

Barritt was elevated to the position of secretary on 19 January 1927 following the resignation of Jack Carr from the position of secretary-manager. Barritt looked after administrative matters whilst the playing affairs were controlled by Bob Crompton. However, the removal of Crompton in 1931 thrust Barritt into the manager's chair.

Although he had an impressive background in football administration, Barritt had had no previous experience in handling the playing side of a football club. He inherited an ageing team that was beginning to show signs of slipping and it was to his credit that he managed to keep the club away from the relegation zone.

The serious economic situation that existed at the club forced Barritt to part with players of the calibre of Cunliffe and Dix in May 1933. The loss of the talented Dix was a particularly severe blow as Barritt had only signed him 12 months earlier. Although the club finished eighth in 1933-34, Rovers continued to struggle throughout Barritt's leadership.

The 1935-36 season found the team anchored at the basement of the First Division following a series of injuries to key players. As the team struggled on the field rumours were rife that relations between the manager and directors were beginning to sour. Differences over club policy and team selection led to a widening gulf between Barritt and the board of directors. As a result of this conflict Barritt tendered his resignation in March 1936.

Duncan Shearer celebrates his first goal for Rovers against Barnsley at Oakwell in March 1992.

## BARRON, James

Goalkeeper. 1935-1946.
*5ft 10in; 11st.*
*Born: Burnhope, 19 July 1913; Died: Newcastle, 15 September 1969.*
*Debut: v Sheffield Wednesday (a) 11 April 1936.*
*Career: Durham City; Blyth Spartans cs 1933; Blackburn Rovers March 1935; Bradford City wartime guest 1941-42; Gateshead wartime guest 1941-42 & 1943-44; Darlington wartime guest 1943-44; York City wartime guest 1944-45; Newcastle United wartime guest 1944-45; Darlington June 1946.*
*Domestic honours with Blackburn Rovers: Second Division championship: 1938-39 (41 apps); FA War Cup runners-up: 1940.*
**Appearances:** Football League 76; FA Cup 7; Total 83.
After two seasons of jostling for the role of first-team goalkeeper, Jim Barron was finally rewarded with 41 appearances during the Second Division championship campaign of 1938-39. Unfortunately, World War Two virtually ended his Ewood career although he featured in the 1940 War Cup Final team at Wembley. Barron spent the war years working in a steel works in his native North-East and as a result his appearances for Blackburn were fairly restricted. After 'guesting' for several teams Barron finally joined Darlington in June 1946 and made 23 League appearances for the Quakers. His son, also called Jim, kept goal for Nottingham Forest and Wolverhampton Wanderers during the 1960s.

## BARROW FC

Founded in 1901, Barrow were members of the Football League between 1921 and 1972. Although their paths didn't cross in the Football League the Rovers met Barrow in the Football League Cup in 1967 and also encountered the Holker Street club in the Lancashire Senior Cup. The most embarrassing encounter in the latter competition came on 15 October 1923 when the Rovers sent their first team to play Barrow, then in the Third Division North, and suffered a 3-2 defeat.

**Football League Cup**

| | | | | |
|---|---|---|---|---|
| 1965-66 | (2) | Home | W | 4-1 |

**Wartime**

| | | | |
|---|---|---|---|
| 1939-40 | (NWRL)* | L | 0-2 |
| | | L | 2-4 |

*Note: Both games in this competition were played at Barrow.

## BARTON, Alfred

Forward. 1882-1885.
*Born: Blackburn, c.1865; Died: Blackburn, 31 July 1938 (aged 73).*
*Debut: v Blackpool (h) 23 October 1882 (FAC).*
*Career: Blackburn Rovers 1882.*
**Appearances:** FA Cup 3.
**Goals:** FA Cup 6.
A player who appeared spasmodically during friendly matches in the early 1880s. He made a major impact in the FA Cup with hat-tricks against South Shore in 1882-83 and Rossendale in 1884-85. Sadly, injury kept him from appearing in the 1885 FA Cup Final when the Rovers lifted the trophy for a second time.

The son of a former cotton manufacturer, Barton was employed for many years at Roe Lee Mill in Blackburn. His sporting interests also included cricket and bowls.

## BARTON, David

Centre-half. 1982.
*6ft; 11st 7lb.*
*Born: Bishop Auckland, 9 May 1959.*
*Debut: v Wolverhampton Wanderers (a) 28 August 1982.*
*Career: Newcastle United May 1977; Blackburn Rovers on loan August 1982 to October 1982; Darlington on loan February 1983 before signing permanently.*
**Appearances:** Football League 8.
**Goals:** Football League 1.
Athletic Newcastle United defender who was brought to Ewood Park on loan on the eve of the 1982-83 season. Barton was thrust straight into the first team as Glenn Keeley was involved in a pay dispute with the club. Barton experienced mixed fortunes at Ewood for although he proved an ideal substitute for Keeley, he was sent off at Grimsby and missed two matches through suspension. Believed to be available for £50,000 from Newcastle, Barton suffered a serious injury in the match with Chelsea on 16 October 1982 when he caught his studs in the turf and badly twisted his knee. The injury ended any hopes of a permanent move to Blackburn and in February of the following year he was playing with Darlington.

## BARTON, John

Right-half. 1887-1891.
*5ft 7in; 9st 12lb.*

*Born; Blackburn, 5 October 1866; Died: Blackburn, 22 April 1910.*
*Debut: v Blackburn Olympic (h) 5 November 1887 (FAC).*
*Career: Witton FC (Blackburn); Blackburn West End; Blackburn Rovers 1887; Retired late 1891 due to injury. Later had a spell as trainer at Preston North End.*
*International honours with Blackburn Rovers: England: 1 cap (1890).*
*Domestic honours with Blackburn Rovers: FA Cup winner: 1890; 1891*
**Appearances:** Football League 40; FA Cup 12; Total 52.
**Goals:** Football League 2; FA Cup 2; Total 4.
Jack Barton, a coachbuilder by trade, joined Blackburn Rovers in 1887 and was a regular member of the second team for the next two years. Although his first-team opportunities were limited during this period he made a favourable impression on all who saw him. The 1889-90 season saw him force his way into the first team in the right-half position. His style of play was similar to that of Jimmy Forrest, being fluent and accurate in distribution. His outstanding form with the Rovers earned him international recognition and he was a member of the FA Cup winning sides of 1890 and 1891. Sadly a severe knee injury in the early part of the 1891-92 season brought his playing career to a premature end. After leaving the Rovers he became landlord of the Park Inn on Montague Street in Blackburn for nine years before taking over as the licensee of the Cambridge Hotel in the town. It was here that Barton died after a long illness, following an attack of pneumonia, at the age of 44.

**BARTON, John Birchall**
Goalkeeper. 1966-1972 & 1973.
*5ft 10in; 13st 4lb.*
*Born: Orrell, 27 April 1942.*
*Debut: v Derby County (a) 20 August 1966.*
*Career: Preston North End May 1957 groundstaff, turning professional in April 1959; Blackburn Rovers June 1966 (£6,000) to cs 1972, re-signed March 1973 until April 1973.*
**Appearances:** Football League 68; FA Cup 1; Football League Cup 3; Total 72.
Small and stocky goalkeeper who inherited the first-team spot from Fred Else. Ironically, Barton had understudied Else at Deepdale in his youth; making his debut for North End as a 16-year-old against Arsenal at Highbury. During seven seasons with Preston he made 48 appearances as first Else and then Alan Kelly restricted his senior outings. In contrast to his experiences at Deepdale he was an ever-present during his first season at Ewood Park. However, Barton never looked totally convincing as the Rovers tried to return to the First Division at the first attempt. His lack of height, combined with a touch of hesitancy, undermined his judgment of crosses. Barton also had an unfortunate tendency to make critical errors in important games and this was to cost the club a number of vital points. The signing of Adam Blacklaw in the 1967 close season ended Barton's reign as first-team goalkeeper and the remainder of his Ewood career was spent in the shadow of Blacklaw and Roger Jones. Following his release by the club he was re-signed in the spring of 1973 to understudy Paul Bradshaw when Jones was ruled out by injury.

**BARTON, John William**
Right-back. 1919-1920.
*5ft 9in; 11st 11lb.*
*Born: Southport, 1895 (July quarter).*
*Debut: v West Bromwich Albion (h) 3 January 1920.*
*Career: Holy Trinity School, Southport; Southport Working Lad's Club; National Telephone Co FC; Southport Park Villa; Burnley 1912; Rochdale 1913; Fulham wartime guest; Portsmouth wartime guest; Southport wartime guest 1917-18; Blackburn Rovers March 1919; Merthyr Town cs 1920; Pontypridd 1920-21; Rochdale 7 October 1921; Colwyn Bay United cs 1922; Manchester North End; Ashton National May 1928; Lytham St Anne's.*
**Appearances:** Football League 1; FA Cup 1; Total 2.
Barton was secured by the Rovers as Bob Crompton's successor and he certainly appeared to have the right credentials. Sturdily built, but reputedly quick over the ground, Barton had a reputation as a fearless tackler. Prior to coming to Ewood Park he had filled spells with various clubs and had filled a variety of positions including centre-forward, inside-right and right-back. He settled into the right-back position after being 'discovered' by Rochdale and seemed the ideal replacement for Crompton. However, Barton failed to make any impact at Ewood and the signing of David Rollo helped hasten his departure from the club.

**BATESON, Edward**
Outside-right. 1924-1925.
*5ft 7in; 10st.*
*Born: Settle.*
*Debut: v West Ham United (h) 19 January 1924.*
*Career: Giggleswick School; Blackburn Rovers amateur January 1924, turning professional in February 1924.*

**Appearances:** Football League 2.
Edward Bateson made his debut for Blackburn Rovers whilst still an amateur in January 1924. He made a favourable impression on the right wing, due largely to his speed, and turned professional the following month. His second opportunity came in February when he replaced Jack Crisp at outside-right for the home game with Sheffield United. Unfortunately, a leg muscle strain which had troubled him for some time was aggravated during a sprint for the ball early in the second half. Bateson had to leave the field for treatment and although he returned he was little more than a passenger. Although Bateson was retained at the end of the season he didn't appear in the first team again.

**BATTY, David**
Midfield. 1993-
*5ft 5in; 10st.*
*Born: Leeds, 2 December 1968.*
*Debut: v Tottenham Hotspur (h) 30 October 1993.*
*Career: Leeds United associated schoolboy November 1983, apprentice August 1985, turning professional in July 1987; Blackburn Rovers October 1993 (£2,750,000).*
*International honours with Blackburn Rovers: England: 1 cap (1994).*
**Appearances:** Premier League 26; FA Cup 4; Football League Cup 2; Total 32.

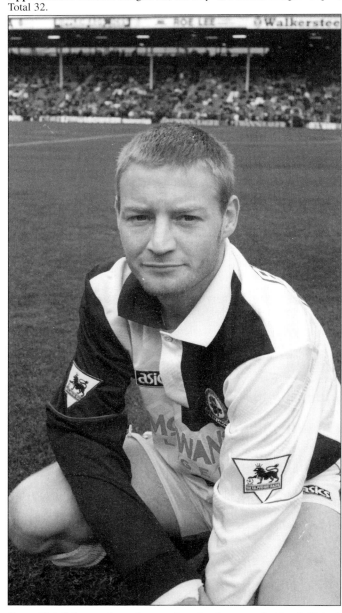

Kenny Dalglish caused a major surprise when he persuaded Leeds United to part with their talented England international midfielder. The need to raise funds following ground development meant that Leeds were unable to turn down the offer made by Dalglish, despite the displeasure of Leeds manager Howard Wilkinson.

An England international at Youth, Under-21, 'B' and senior level, David Batty was noted at Elland Road for his hard tackling performances at the heart of midfield. His tenacious midfield play was a major factor in lifting Leeds from the Second Division in 1989-90 and he became the driving force of the team which lifted the 1991-92 League title.

Whilst retaining his work-rate and ball winning tenacity, Batty freely admitted that he was allowed to express himself more creatively under Dalglish. Batty quickly became a cult figure with the Ewood faithful and seemed destined to add to the 14 international caps he collected whilst with Leeds United.

A foot injury robbed the club of the services of Batty for the final few League games of 1993-94 and this kept him out of the England squad at the end of the season. His popularity at Ewood was reflected by the fact that he was selected as the Player of the Year by the supporters.

**BAXENDALE, Frank**
Winger. 1935-1937.
*Born: Leyland 1914 (January quarter).*
*Debut: v Middlesbrough (h) 21 March 1936.*
*Career: Preston North End amateur September 1932; Dick Kerr's XI 1932-33; Leyland Motors; Blackburn Rovers amateur July 1933, turning professional in May 1935; Falkirk December 1937 (£960); Carlisle United August 1939.*
**Appearances:** Football League 12; FA Cup 1; Total 13.
**Goals:** Football League 3.
A nippy, lightly built winger from nearby Leyland, Frank Baxendale enjoyed a run of seven Second Division games during the 1936-37 season before losing his place to Billy Guest. Although primarily an outside-right, his appearances for the first team were, with the exception of one game, all on the left wing. With Guest firmly entrenched in the outside-left position the Rovers allowed Baxendale to join Falkirk in December 1937. Baxendale played in 82 Central League games for the Rovers and scored three goals. He returned to English football in August 1939, but the outbreak of war ended his first-class career.

**BAXTER, Thomas Thornton**
Right-back. 1927-1932.
*5ft 10½in; 11st 12lb.*
*Born: Blackburn, 18 April 1907; Died: Blackburn, 23 December 1981.*
*Debut: v West Ham United (a) 9 March 1929.*
*Career: Blackburn CE Central School; Blackburn Corinthians; Blackburn Schoolboys; Blackburn Works XI; Blackburn Rovers January 1927 to March 1932; Blackburn Borough Police Force.*
**Appearances:** Football League 36; FA Cup 3; Total 39.
A player who graduated through local junior circles to establish himself in the right-back position during the 1929-30 season. Baxter joined the Rovers as a full-time professional when the foundry at which he had been apprenticed closed down and thus disrupted his planned career in engineering. A tremendously hard working defender, Baxter was an astute distributor of the ball from defence. Unfortunately his career at Ewood was dogged by injuries. A serious injury at West Ham United in October 1930 kept him out of action for the rest of that season and after only four matches of the 1931-32 campaign he suffered yet another injury. Problems with a knee injury led to him asking to be released from his contract so that he could join the Blackburn Police Force. The club agreed and Baxter served for more than 25 years with the force.

**BAZAAR FUND**
The Blackburn Rovers 'Bazaar' was held in the Exchange Hall in Blackburn in early 1895. The aim of the week-long function was to raise a total of £1,500 to help liquidate the deficit caused by the club transferring its headquarters to Ewood Park.
The cost of that change was reported to be in the region of £2,700 and it was a great relief when the bazaar proved a huge success. A commemorative booklet on the history of the club was issued and the players, led by captain Harry Campbell, each donated a week's wage to the fund. As a result some £1,480 was raised, the net profit being £1,200.

**BEAMISH, Kenneth G.**
Forward. 1974-1976.
*6ft; 12st 6lb.*
*Born: Bebington, 25 August 1947.*
*Debut: v Grimsby Town (a) 17 August 1974.*
*Career: Tranmere Rovers July 1966; Brighton & Hove Albion March 1972; Blackburn Rovers May 1974 (£25,000); Port Vale September 1976 (£10,000); Bury September 1978 (£30,000); Tranmere Rovers November 1979; Swindon Town August 1981, later coach then manager March 1983 to June 1984; Blackburn Rovers commercial manager October 1986.*
*Domestic honours with Blackburn Rovers: Third Division championship: 1974-75 (43 apps, 11 gls).*

**Appearances:** Football League 86; FA Cup 3; Football League Cup 9; Total 98.
**Goals:** Football League 18; FA Cup 2; Football League Cup 5; Total 25.
A much-travelled striker who spent almost all of his career in the lower divisions but always scored goals wherever he went. During a playing career of 554 League appearances and 160 goals, Beamish played in three promotion sides: Tranmere Rovers in 1967, Brighton & Hove Albion in 1972 and Blackburn Rovers in 1975. He was Gordon Lee's second signing of the 1974 close season and, at that point, the fee of £25,000 was the most that Lee had paid for any player in his managerial career.

The money proved well spent as Beamish struck up an immediate understanding with the rejuvenated Don Martin. Between them they scored 26 goals as the Rovers claimed the Third Division title with Beamish contributing 11 goals. A wholehearted player, Beamish was a great favourite with the fans who made the terraces ring with the chant of 'Beamo, Beamo', a nickname by which he was always known at Blackburn. The cry, rather unkindly, could still be heard long after Beamish had left the club whenever an opponent missed a scoring opportunity – a comment of the player's failings in front of goal during his later years with the club.

Beamish found goals more difficult to come by in the Second Division and in September 1976 he was allowed to move to Port Vale. His travels continued until he finally settled at Swindon and joined the coaching staff before becoming manager in March 1983. He stayed in the hot seat at Swindon for one season before becoming the victim of boardroom politics and being replaced by Lou Macari. He declined the offer to remain with Swindon in a coaching capacity and spent some time out of the game before returning to Blackburn as commercial manager. As popular as ever, it was typical of the humour of the man to have 'Beamo' flash on the scoreboard whenever scoring opportunities were fluffed.

**BEAN, Alan**
Centre-half. 1952-1955.
*5ft 8½in; 10st 13lb.*
*Born: Doncaster, 17 January 1935.*
*Debut: v Luton Town (a) 15 November 1952.*
*Career: Blackburn Rovers April 1952 to cs 1955.*
**Appearances:** Football League 2.
Alan Bean was a product of Blackburn's youth development system and appeared in the club's first FA Youth Cup-tie against Blackpool in 1952-53. He was given an early first-team opportunity at Luton in November 1952, when Willie Kelly was tried at centre-forward. The team crashed to a six-goal defeat and although Bean was not the sole cause of the reversal he didn't appear in the first team again until September 1954.

**BEARDALL, James Thomas**
Centre-forward. 1968-1969.
*5ft 11in; 12st 3lb.*
*Born: Whitefield, 18 October 1946.*
*Debut: v Portsmouth (a) 20 April 1968.*
*Career: Bury youth team; Blackburn Rovers amateur May 1967, turning professional in March 1968; Oldham Athletic May 1969; Great Harwood March 1970 to May 1976.*
**Appearances:** Football League 4+2.
**Goals:** Football League 1.
Jim Beardall was seen towards the end of the 1968-69 season as an alternative to Jimmy Fryatt as leader of the attack. However, his reign was short-lived and after only three games he returned to the Central League team. Beardall had made his debut towards the end of the 1967-68 campaign but had been substituted after 57 minutes. His record in the Central League was a respectable one with 33 goals coming from 64 appearances, three of which were at centre-half.

Beardall was released by the Rovers at the end of the 1968-69 season and made the short move to Oldham Athletic. He made an immediate impact at Boundary Park with 10 goals in 22 League appearances (including one as sub). However, once his goals dried up he lost his place and after less than a season at Boundary Park he was released and joined Great Harwood.

**BEARDSMORE, Russell Peter**
Outside-left. 1991-1992.
*5ft 6in; 9st.*
*Born: Wigan, 28 September 1968.*
*Debut: v Wolverhampton Wanderers (a) 26 December 1991.*
*Career: Manchester United associated schoolboy April 1984, becoming an apprentice in June 1985 before turning professional in October 1986; Blackburn Rovers on loan December 1991; AFC Bournemouth June 1993 (Free).*
**Appearances:** Football League 1+1.
A midfield player who was versatile enough to play on either wing. He

made his Football League debut with Manchester United in September 1988 and a bright future was predicted for a player whose strength was his accuracy of passing. However, an influx of big money signings and a dip in his own form saw him become something of a 'forgotten man' at Old Trafford.

In December 1991, Kenny Dalglish gave him a chance to revive his career when he brought him to Ewood on a month's loan. Unfortunately, Beardsmore made little impact and returned to Old Trafford. In June 1993 he was freed by United and joined AFC Bournemouth in a bid to rebuild his career.

### BEATTIE, John Murdoch

Inside-forward. 1934-1937.
*5ft 10in; 12st.*
*Born: Newhills, 28 May 1912; Died: 10 January 1992.*
*Debut: v Aston Villa (a) 22 December 1934.*
*Career: Hall Russell FC (Aberdeen); Aberdeen professional August 1931; Wolverhampton Wanderers September 1933 (£1,500); Blackburn Rovers December 1934 (£5,000); Birmingham January 1937 (player exchange plus £2,000); Huddersfield Town 7 January 1938 (£2,500); Grimsby Town February 1938 (£2,500); Walsall; Retired during World War Two.*
**Appearances:** Football League 76; FA Cup 5; Total 81.
**Goals:** Football League 17; FA Cup 1; Total 18.
During the 1930s a number of First Division Clubs, Blackburn Rovers included, were prepared to pay large fees for this nomadic inside-forward. Beattie was of the forceful rather than traditional Scottish crafty school and packed a fierce shot in his right foot. In truth, although he was a regular fixture in the first team, Beattie proved something of a disappointment during his time at Blackburn. In Scotland he scored 12 goals in 60 League games for Aberdeen, whilst his career in England saw him score 52 goals in 217 League matches. He moved from Blackburn to Birmingham in the deal which brought Billy Guest to Ewood Park.

### BECKFORD, Jason Neil

Forward. 1991.
*5ft 9in; 12st 4lb.*
*Born: Manchester, 14 February 1970.*
*Debut: v Brighton & Hove Albion (a) 16 March 1991.*
*Career: Manchester City August 1987; Blackburn Rovers on loan March 1991; Port Vale on loan September 1991; Birmingham City January 1992 (£50,000)*
**Appearances:** Football League 3+1.
Don Mackay brought Beckford to Ewood Park when his injury hit side were struggling in the wrong half of the Second Division. Having failed to force his way into the first team at Maine Road, Beckford was on the transfer list, at his own request, when he moved to Blackburn. During his stay at Ewood Park, Beckford made three appearances on the right wing and was substitute on another occasion. However, he made little impression on a struggling side and returned to Manchester. He eventually moved to Birmingham City in January 1992, but was kept out of the game for some time through injury. Beckford's brother, Darren, played for Port Vale and Norwich City before joining Oldham Athletic in March 1993.

### BEE, Frank E.

Inside-left. 1949-1950.
*5ft 11½in; 10st 8lb.*
*Born: Nottingham, 23 January 1927.*
*Debut: v West Ham United (a) 5 March 1949.*
*Career: Nottingham Forest amateur; Sunderland June 1947; Blackburn Rovers March 1949 (£6,000) to cs 1950.*
**Appearances:** Football League 4.
Frank Bee failed to justify the £6,000 fee which Blackburn Rovers paid Sunderland to bring him to Ewood Park in June 1947. Although there was no doubting his scheming talents, his lack of pace proved too big a handicap to overcome. He made his four appearances in March 1949 but was not called upon during the 1949-50 season and was not retained at the end of that campaign.

### BEGLIN, James Martin

Left-back. 1990.
*5ft 11in; 11st.*
*Born: Waterford, 29 July 1963.*
*Debut: v Watford (h) 13 October 1990*
*Career: Shamrock Rovers; Liverpool May 1983; Leeds United July 1989; Plymouth Argyle on loan November 1989 to January 1990; Blackburn Rovers on loan October 1990.*
**Appearances:** Football League 6.
One of six loan players to appear in the senior team during the troubled 1990-91 season. Jim Beglin was a cultured left-back who won a

championship medal, FA Cup winners' medal and European Cup runners-up medal with Liverpool in the 1980s. His intelligent passing style was entirely suited to the Liverpool way of playing football. Sadly, a badly broken leg kept him out of the first team for 18 months and having failed to regain his place he was freed in the summer of 1989. He was a member of the Leeds team which won the Second Division title in 1989-90 despite spending part of the season on loan to Plymouth. Beglin produced several sound performances for the Rovers before returning to Elland Road. He retired from the game at the end of the 1990-91 season and later became a football commentator with Granada Television.

### BELL, Alexander

Half-back. 1913-1915.
*Born: Cape Town, South Africa 1882; Died: Chorlton-cum-Hardy, 30 November 1934.*

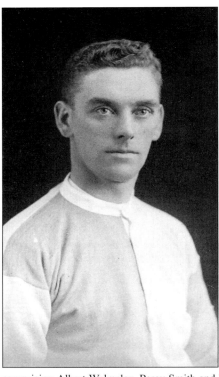

*Debut: v Derby County (h) 4 October 1913.*
*Career: Ayr Park-house; Newton Heath 1903 (£700); Black-burn Rovers July 1913 (£1,000); Coventry City trainer; Man-chester City trainer 1925-1934.*
*Domestic honours with Blackburn Rovers: First Division champ-ionship: 1913-14 (8 apps).*
**Appearances:** Football League 11; FA Cup 1; Total 12.
The signing of Manchester United's veteran left-half, Alex Bell, came as something of a surprise to many Blackburn supporters. Although Bell had 278 League appearances behind him with United few could believe that, in the twilight of his career, he would be able to force his way into a half-back line comprising Albert Walmsley, Percy Smith and Billy Bradshaw. This trio had been outstanding during the latter part of the 1912-13 season and Bell had to accept a supporting role on his arrival at Ewood Park. However, when called into the team to replace the injured Bradshaw, Bell gave an immaculate performance. He demonstrated that he had lost none of his attacking techniques and his ability to open up a game with long cross field passes proved invaluable. Although he only appeared in eight games during the 1913-14 season his defensive play was as sound as ever and as a result the half-back line was not weakened whenever one of the first-choice men was incapacitated.

### BELL, John Eric

Left-half. 1945-1957.
*5ft 8in; 9st 13lb.*
*Born: Bedlington, 13 February 1922.*
*Debut: v Portsmouth (a) 31 August 1946.*
*Career: Blyth Shipyard; Blackburn Rovers May 1945 to cs 1957. Joined the Blackburn coaching staff on retirement and was appointed second-team trainer in April 1964 before being released in May 1969.*
*International honours with Blackburn Rovers: Football League: 2 appearances (1950).*
**Appearances:** Football League 323; FA Cup 10; Total 333.
**Goals:** Football League 9.
Eric Bell arrived at Ewood Park as the war came to an end and was rarely out of the first team during

the next decade. Although primarily a foraging left-half, Bell was versatile enough to occupy full-back, inside-forward and left-wing positions with equal distinction. A solid, reliable performer who rarely captured the headlines, Bell was the model professional. By 1949-50 he had progressed to the fringe of a full cap and had represented the Football League. A sub-postmaster in Darwen during his playing days, Bell joined the coaching staff after hanging up his boots. During the 1960s he led the second team to the Central League championship on two occasions before being controversially released by the club in May 1969.

## BELL, Norman
Centre-forward. 1981-1984.
*6ft 1in; 13st 2lb.*
*Born: Sunderland, 16 November 1955.*
*Debut: v Shrewsbury Town (h) 25 November 1981.*
*Career: Wolverhampton Wanderers apprentice July 1971, turning professional in November 1973; New England Teamen (USA) on loan May 1980; Blackburn Rovers November 1981 to cs 1984; Darwen.*
**Appearances:** Football League 57+4; FA Cup 2; Football League Cup 2; Total 61+4.
**Goals:** Football League 10.
During his ten years at Molineux, Norman Bell made 100 senior appearances for the club (including 28 as sub) and scored 24 goals. Bell could play as an old-fashioned 'target' man or could be moved into midfield when the need arose. Because of his versatility, Bell was a popular choice for the substitute role and earned the reputation of 'super-sub' at Molineux. The role of substitute followed him across the Atlantic during the summer of 1980, when eight of his 20 appearances for New England were made from the bench.

Bell was signed by Bobby Saxton to give some height and power to the Blackburn forward line. Although not the most prolific of goalscorers, Bell came to Ewood with a reputation and as a result found himself closely marked by Second Division defences. Whilst this meant his own goalscoring remained moderate he was, none the less, able to create space and goalscoring opportunities for Simon Garner.

Bell suffered a serious knee injury in the opening fixture of the 1983-84 season and as a result had to retire from first-class football.

## BELL, Robert Charles
Central defender. 1971.
*6ft; 11st 11lb.*
*Born: Cambridge, 26 October 1950.*
*Debut: v Bolton Wanderers (h) 11 September 1971.*
*Career: Tottenham Hotspur apprentice May 1966 to August 1967; Ipswich Town apprentice September 1967, turning professional in November 1968; Blackburn Rovers September 1971; Crystal Palace September 1971; Norwich City on loan February 1972; playing in South Africa from 1973; York City February 1977 until March 1977; Fort Lauderdale Strikers (USA) April 1977 until June 1977.*
**Appearances:** Football League 2.
Bobby Bell's stay at Ewood Park proved only a fleeting one. He arrived at Blackburn on 9 September 1971 as part of the deal which took Allan Hunter to Ipswich Town. The Rovers received a cheque for £65,000 plus Bell, who was valued around £25,000, in exchange for their Northern Ireland defender. Bell was made captain and installed into the vacancy left by Hunter. However, 14 days later and after only 180 minutes of first-team action, Bell was sold to Crystal Palace for £50,000. Ken Furphy justified the deal by claiming that it made economic sense for the club and certainly the Rovers were able to use the money to fund Furphy's rebuilding programme. Bell's own career failed to live up to the promise he had shown as youngster at Ipswich and during his spell with Crystal Palace he only appeared in 31 League games. After a period in South Africa he failed to rebuild his career with York City and tried his luck in the North American Soccer League.

## BENNETT, John W.
Right-back. 1905-1906.
*5ft 9in; 11st 4lb.*
*Born: Liverpool, 1880.*
*Debut: v Wolverhampton Wanderers (a) 22 April 1905.*
*Career: Wavertree; Lincoln City May 1900; Wellingborough; Northampton Town cs 1901; Luton Town cs 1903; Leicester Fosse June 1904; Blackburn Rovers April 1905.*
**Appearances:** Football League 1.
Although John Bennett broke into the Football League with Lincoln City, it was in the Southern League that he established a reputation as a fine full-back. He came to Blackburn as understudy to Bob Crompton and, like so many others who had that unenviable task, found that first-team opportunities were severely restricted.

## BENSON, James R.
Forward. 1933-1936.
*5ft 10in; 11st 4lb.*
*Born: Markinch, c.1914.*
*Debut: v Chelsea (h) 17 November 1934.*
*Career: Markinch; St Johnstone; Brechin City on loan February 1933; Blackburn Rovers May 1933; Falkirk May 1936; Durham City; Hartlepools United.*
**Appearances:** Football League 2.
**Goals:** Football League 1.
A tenacious forward who came to Blackburn with Bob Pryde in May 1933. A strong centre-forward who was not easily shaken off the ball, Benson proved a prolific goalscorer for the Central League team during his spell at Ewood Park. He made his debut at inside-left and scored Rovers' only goal in a 2-1 defeat at the hands of Chelsea. Benson had to wait 13 months before his next first-team outing and this proved to be his last. He returned to Scotland in the spring of 1936 to join Falkirk.

## BERESFORD, James
Outside-right. 1887-1888.
*Debut: v Blackburn Olympic (h) 5 November 1887 (FAC).*
*Career: Staveley; Church 1883; Accrington September 1883; Church 1883; Blackburn Rovers 1887; Hyde.*
**Appearances:** Football League 12; FA Cup 2; Total 14.
**Goals:** Football League 4.
Beresford joined Blackburn Rovers at the start of the 1887-88 season and held one of the forward positions during the club's last season of friendly football. He appeared on the score-sheet fairly frequently and notched a hat-trick in the 9-2 win over Boston in September 1887. He figured in 12 Football League games for the club during the inaugural season of the competition.

In 1883-84, Beresford had unwittingly been the cause of Accrington being ejected from the FA Cup competition. At the beginning of that season he had appeared for Accrington against Rossendale in September 1883 and had scored twice in a 5-1 victory. However, competition for places was keen and Beresford returned to Church. Although no longer with the Accrington club, a gentleman, who was not connected with Accrington, paid him a sum of money to keep his name on the Accrington books.

A subsequent FA investigation found the Accrington club to be in breach of Rule 15, regarding the employment professional players and as a result Accrington were ejected from the FA Cup for that season.

## BERG, Henning
Right-back. 1993-
*6ft; 11st 9lb.*
*Born: Eidseoll, Norway, 1 September 1969.*
*Debut: v Crystal Palace (h) 2 February 1993 (sub).*
*Career: SK Lillestrøm (Norway); Blackburn Rovers January 1993 (£400,000).*
*International honours with Blackburn Rovers: Norway: 13 caps (1993-94).*
**Appearances:** Premier League 40+5; FA Cup 4; Football League Cup 5; Total 49+5.
**Goals:** Premier League 1.
Henning Berg agreed to join Blackburn Rovers shortly after coming on as

substitute in Norway's drawn World Cup tie with England at Wembley in October 1992. However, it wasn't until January 1993 that Berg was actually able to link up with the Rovers and the consistency of David May, coupled with injury to Berg himself, meant he was restricted to six first-team appearances (including 2 as sub).

Although Berg had never played at full-back prior to his arrival at Ewood Park, he emerged as one of the best attacking right-backs in the Premiership during 1993-94. A player who possesses both pace and power, Berg passes the ball with great accuracy and is good in the air. He became a regular member of the Norwegian team that won through to the 1994 World Cup Finals in America.

## BESTALL, John Gilbert
Manager. 1949-1953.
*Born: Beighton, 24 June 1900; Died: Doncaster, 11 April 1985.*
*Career: Sheffield Schoolboys; Beighton Miners Welfare; Rotherham United 1925; Grimsby Town November 1926 (£700) to May 1938; Birmingham coach-chief scout June 1938; Doncaster Rovers manager March 1946 to April 1949; Blackburn Rovers manager June 1949 to May 1953; Nelson manager cs 1953 to November 1954; Doncaster Rovers chief scout August 1958 to March 1959, then manager from March 1959 to August 1960.*

In accepting the position of manager of Blackburn Rovers in June 1949, Jackie Bestall became the fourth occupant of that office in three years. Bestall's first flirtation with management had been at Doncaster Rovers where his first season in charge saw the club capture the Third Division North title. This early success in management followed an outstanding career with Grimsby Town as a constructive inside-forward. He appeared in 427 games for the Blundell Park club and was capped by England before he turned to coaching with Birmingham.

Sadly, his success at Doncaster did not last and the club were relegated after only one season in the Second Division. However, when Blackburn Rovers parted company with Jack Bruton it was Jackie Bestall who they turned to in an attempt to revive their fortunes.

Like Hapgood before him, Bestall was keen to encourage the development of young players. During his reign at Ewood the club produced a whole crop of young talent, including Ronnie Clayton and Bryan Douglas, who were both to become regular first-team players and England internationals.

However, Bestall didn't put all his energies in planning the long-term future of the club. Throughout his time at Blackburn he was always prepared to bring experienced men to Ewood Park and the likes of Elvy, Kelly, Quigley, Briggs and Smith were all signed by Bestall.

Unfortunately, despite his best efforts, success continued to elude the club. Although the Rovers reached the 1951 FA Cup semi-final it was little compensation to a club whose supporters believed their rightful place was in the First Division.

As Bestall's problems began to mount during the 1952-53 campaign rumours, not for the first time in the club's history, began to circulate regarding disputes between the manager and his players. In May 1953 it was announced that Bestall had decided it would be in everyone's interest if he left Ewood Park. Although he had no future plans the parting was an amicable one.

Like his three immediate predecessors, Bestall had failed to lift the club's fortunes on the field. However, he had brought stability to a club that appeared to be drifting and, more importantly, had built a solid foundation on which Johnny Carey was to build so successfully.

After a short spell with Nelson, Bestall eventually returned to serve Doncaster Rovers as chief scout and then had a further period in charge of the Belle Vue club.

## BEVERLEY, Joseph
Right-back. 1882-1884 & 1886-1889.
*Born: Blackburn, 12 November 1856; Died: Blackburn, 21 May 1897.*
*Debut: v Nottingham Forest (a) 31 January 1880 (FAC).*
*Career: Blackburn Schoolboy football; James Street; Blackburn Olympic 1876; Blackburn Rovers October 1882; Blackburn Olympic cs 1884; Blackburn Rovers cs 1886 until cs 1889.*
*International honours with Blackburn Rovers: England: 3 caps (1884).*
*Domestic honours with Blackburn Rovers: FA Cup winner: 1884.*
**Appearances:** Football League 8; FA Cup 14; Total 22.

Joe Beverley was one of the founder members of Blackburn Olympic when that club was formed by the amalgamation of the James Street club with Black Star FC. This probably goes some way to explaining why he remained an Olympian at heart and turned his back on winning honours with Blackburn Rovers. At Olympic, Beverley had spent much of his time on the right wing or at centre-forward before he made the switch to right-back. Unable to force his way into the Blackburn Olympic side which won the FA Cup in 1883, he accepted an offer to play with Blackburn Rovers. Beverley was no stranger to the Rovers having made guest appearances for the club in the past.

His first season with the Rovers saw him win a Cup winners' medal and three England caps as well as becoming regarded as one of the finest backs in the country. However, the Olympic club was still close to his heart and he accepted an invitation to return to his former club in the summer of 1884. The move meant that this small but accomplished player not only lost out on two further Cup Final appearances but also brought his international career to an end.

In the summer of 1886 he returned to the Rovers and stayed with them until his retirement at the end of the 1888-89 season. Tragically, Beverley was fatally injured in May 1897 when a cylinder fell on his head whilst he was inspecting machinery at the Blackburn mill where he worked.

## BIBBY, Joseph
Full-back. 1920-1921.
*5ft 7in; 11st.*
*Born: Rishton, 1896 (January quarter); Died: Haslingden 1968 (July quarter).*
*Debut: v Sunderland (h) 11 September 1920.*
*Career: Blackburn Trinity; Blackburn Rovers amateur 5 March 1920, turning professional in March 1920; Wigan Borough June 1921; Dundee Hibernians cs 1922.*
**Appearances:** Football League 8.

Bibby, a strong and robust defender, joined the Rovers after leaving the Royal Navy. Although Bibby had never really played football before enlisting for the Navy he turned professional only a few weeks after to coming to Ewood as an amateur. He understudied David Rollo and Fred Duckworth for a season before the signing of Tom Wylie made him surplus to requirements. A short stay with Wigan was followed by a spell in Scotland.

## BIMPSON, James Louis
Outside-right/Centre-forward. 1959-1961.
*6ft 1in; 12st 5lb.*
*Born: Rainford, Lancashire, 14 May 1929.*
*Debut: v Newcastle United (a) 21 November 1959.*
*Career: Burscough; Liverpool January 1953; Blackburn Rovers November 1959; Bournemouth & Boscombe Athletic February 1961; Rochdale August 1961; Wigan Athletic July 1963.*
*Domestic honours with Blackburn Rovers: FA Cup runners-up: 1960.*
**Appearances:** Football League 22; FA Cup 7; Total 29.
**Goals:** Football League 5; FA Cup 3; Total 8.

Though not recognised as a regular first-teamer, Louis Bimpson appeared in each round of Blackburn's journey to the FA Cup Final in 1960. During that season he scored only twice in 16 League appearances, but in the FA Cup he missed only two of the nine games and scored three goals.

Fighting for a first-team place was nothing new to Louis Bimpson when he came to Blackburn in November 1959. During his eight seasons at Anfield, Bimpson made only 94 League appearances for the club. He was regarded as a centre-forward on Merseyside and despite his 39 League goals he found himself in the shadow of Billy Liddell at Anfield. His best season with Liverpool saw him notch 11 goals in 15 games in 1958-59.

At Ewood Park he was used in the outside-right position and made a major contribution to the club's success in the FA Cup. The 1960-61 season saw him once again on the fringe of the first team, making only 6 League appearances. In August 1961, Bimpson was transferred to Rochdale where he helped the Spotland Club to beat the Rovers in the semi-final of the 1961-62 Football League Cup.

## BINNS, Clifford Herman
Goalkeeper. 1930-1936.
*6ft; 11st 9lb.*
*Born: Cowling, 9 March 1907; Died: Rochdale, 1977 (January quarter).*
*Debut: v Burnley (a) 15 March 1930.*
*Career: Todmorden School; Knott United; Portsmouth Rovers; Burnley trial; Preston North End trial; Halifax Town amateur 20 April 1928, turning professional in June 1928; Blackburn Rovers January 1930 (£1,500); Workington cs 1933; Blackburn Rovers October 1933; Barnsley December 1936 until 1945-46 (£500); Halifax Town 1940-41 wartime guest; Leeds United 1942-43 wartime guest; Lincoln City 1943-44 wartime guest; Carlisle United 1945-46 wartime guest.*
**Appearances:** Football League 183; FA Cup 13; Total 196.

Cliff Binns made his debut in the derby clash with Burnley in March 1930 when illness and loss of form led to the exclusion of Jock Crawford. Although Binns had been at the club for barely two months when called into the first team he lived up to the high reputation he had gained at Halifax Town. A capable goalkeeper who put his height to good use when dealing with crosses; it was said of Binns that he "caught the ball like an alert cricketer". The 1930-31 season saw him become the first goalkeeper to maintain an ever-present record since Jimmy Ashcroft in 1908-09.

The following two seasons saw Binns under increasing pressure as the defensive frailties of the team began to show. His form became more erratic and a series of injuries did little to restore his confidence. In May 1933 he was placed on the transfer list and his Ewood career appeared to be at an end. Relations between the club and player appeared further strained when Binns successfully appealed to the Football League to reduce the size of the fee demanded by the Rovers.

Unable to secure an engagement with a League club he joined Workington in the North Eastern League. It was here that Binns rebuilt his confidence and rediscovered his best form. Back at Ewood Park, injury to Bill Gormlie had thrown the club into something of a crisis and as a result Binns was brought back to Blackburn in October 1933 to provide cover for Jack Hughes. Within a couple of months Binns had forced his way into the first team and remained the first-choice goalkeeper until loss of form brought about his demotion and subsequent transfer to Barnsley in December 1936. At Oakwell he regained his form and helped the Yorkshire club to win the 1938-39 Third Division North championship.

## BINNS, Eric
Centre-half. 1955-1957.
*6ft; 12st 8lb.*
*Born: Halifax, 13 August 1924.*
*Debut: v Leicester City (a) 27 August 1955.*
*Career: Huddersfield Town; Halifax Town May 1946; Goole Town; Burnley March 1949; Blackburn Rovers May 1955; Runcorn cs 1957.*
**Appearances:** Football League 23.
Binns was signed from Burnley to provide cover for the ageing Willie Kelly. However, after two games of the 1955-56 season, Kelly was axed and Binns was promoted to the first team. Following defeats in their opening two fixtures, Binns helped the team to keep a clean sheet on his debut and was given an extended run in the side. However, his lack of pace and mobility was gradually exposed and when four consecutive matches were lost in December 1955, Binns was replaced by Kelly. Although he made four appearances early in 1956-57, the arrival of Matt Woods in November 1956 ended his first-team career.

## BIRCHALL, John
Left-half/Centre-half. 1903-1907.
*5ft 10in; 12st.*
*Born: Prescott.*
*Debut: v Derby County (a) 14 February 1903.*
*Career: Prescott Ramblers; Whiston Ramblers; St Helens Recreation; Liverpool; Blackpool August 1900; Blackburn Rovers February 1903 (£200); Leyton on trial October 1907 but not retained.*
**Appearances:** Football League 39; FA Cup 1; Total 40.
**Goals:** Football League 3.
Blackburn Rovers were able to snap up John Birchall when financial difficulties forced Blackpool to part with their talented half-back. At Bloomfield Road he had earned a reputation as a sound tackler who could pass accurately and support his forwards. Consistency rather than brilliance was his strength and at Ewood Park he settled into the left-half position for the final nine games of the 1902-03 campaign. The signing of Billy Bradshaw from Accrington Stanley relegated Birchall to the second team for a time before his conversion to the centre-half position saw him restored to the first team. He began the 1905-06 season out of the senior team and had the misfortune to break a leg at Sheffield Wednesday in November 1905 at a time when he had just forced his way back into the team. Sadly, Birchall made only one more League appearance for the club after this injury and left Blackburn in the summer of 1907 without having fulfilled the promise he had shown during his time at Blackpool.

## BIRCHENALL, Alan John
Midfield. 1978-1979.
*6ft; 12st 8lb.*
*Born: East Ham, 28 August 1945.*
*Debut: v Charlton Athletic (h) 30 September 1978.*
*Career: Thorneywood Thistle; Sheffield United June 1963; Chelsea November 1967 (£100,000); Crystal Palace June 1970 (£100,000); Leicester City September 1971; Notts County on loan March 1976; San Jose Earthquakes (USA) on loan April 1977; Notts County September 1977; Memphis Rogues (USA) April 1978; Blackburn Rovers September 1978; Luton Town March 1979; Hereford United October 1979; Trowbridge player-manager cs 1980.*
**Appearances:** Football League 17+1; FA Cup 2; Total 19+1.
Alan Birchenall was signed by Jim Iley, together with Joe Craig, only four days before the manager was sacked by the club. At the age of 33, Birchenall was viewed as a short-term solution to the problems the club had in midfield. In his prime, Birchenall had been a successful striker for whom a number of clubs were prepared to pay six-figure fees to sign. However, the blond-haired veteran was unable to lift the spectre of relegation at Ewood and in March 1979 he moved to Luton Town before the last rites were given on Blackburn's ill-fated season.

## BIRMINGHAM CITY FC
Founded in 1875 by members of Trinity Church, Bordesley, as Small Heath Alliance. In 1888 they changed their name to Small Heath FC and in 1905 adopted the name Birmingham. In 1945 they became known as Birmingham City. The first meeting between the clubs produced a 9-1 scoreline in favour of the Rovers and featured hat-tricks by Chippendale and Killean. The home match with Birmingham on 28 September 1929 produced a 7-5 win for the Rovers with Syd Puddefoot scoring four goals.

## Football League

| | | | Home | | Away | |
|---|---|---|---|---|---|---|
| 1894-95 | (Div 1) | W | 9-1 | D | 1-1 |
| 1895-96 | (Div 1) | W | 2-1 | L | 1-2 |
| 1901-02 | (Div 1) | W | 3-1 | L | 0-2 |
| 1903-04 | (Div 1) | D | 1-1 | L | 1-2 |
| 1904-05 | (Div 1) | L | 1-4 | L | 0-2 |
| 1905-06 | (Div 1) | W | 5-1 | L | 0-3 |
| 1906-07 | (Div 1) | W | 1-0 | L | 0-2 |
| 1907-08 | (Div 1) | W | 1-0 | D | 1-1 |
| 1921-22 | (Div 1) | D | 1-1 | L | 0-1 |
| 1922-23 | (Div 1) | D | 1-1 | D | 1-1 |
| 1923-24 | (Div 1) | W | 4-1 | D | 1-1 |
| 1924-25 | (Div 1) | W | 7-1 | D | 1-1 |
| 1925-26 | (Div 1) | D | 4-4 | L | 0-2 |
| 1926-27 | (Div 1) | W | 3-2 | L | 1-3 |
| 1927-28 | (Div 1) | D | 4-4 | L | 1-2 |
| 1928-29 | (Div 1) | W | 4-1 | L | 0-4 |
| 1929-30 | (Div 1) | W | 7-5 | W | 2-1 |
| 1930-31 | (Div 1) | W | 2-1 | L | 1-4 |
| 1931-32 | (Div 1) | L | 1-2 | L | 1-2 |
| 1932-33 | (Div 1) | W | 2-0 | L | 1-3 |
| 1933-34 | (Div 1) | W | 3-1 | L | 0-2 |
| 1934-35 | (Div 1) | W | 3-1 | L | 0-1 |
| 1935-36 | (Div 1) | L | 1-2 | L | 2-4 |
| 1950-51 | (Div 2) | L | 2-3 | L | 2-3 |
| 1951-52 | (Div 2) | L | 1-4 | W | 1-0 |
| 1952-53 | (Div 2) | L | 1-2 | W | 2-1 |
| 1953-54 | (Div 2) | W | 3-0 | D | 0-0 |
| 1954-55 | (Div 2) | D | 3-3 | L | 1-3 |
| 1958-59 | (Div 1) | W | 3-2 | L | 0-3 |
| 1959-60 | (Div 1) | W | 2-1 | L | 0-1 |
| 1960-61 | (Div 1) | W | 2-0 | D | 1-1 |
| 1961-62 | (Div 1) | W | 2-0 | L | 1-2 |
| 1962-63 | (Div 1) | W | 6-1 | D | 3-3 |
| 1963-64 | (Div 1) | W | 3-0 | D | 2-2 |
| 1964-65 | (Div 1) | W | 3-1 | D | 5-5 |
| 1966-67 | (Div 2) | W | 1-0 | D | 1-1 |
| 1967-68 | (Div 2) | L | 1-2 | D | 1-1 |
| 1968-69 | (Div 2) | W | 3-2 | L | 1-3 |
| 1969-70 | (Div 2) | D | 1-1 | L | 0-3 |
| 1970-71 | (Div 2) | D | 2-2 | L | 0-1 |
| 1984-85 | (Div 2) | W | 2-1 | W | 2-0 |
| 1986-87 | (Div 2) | W | 1-0 | D | 1-1 |
| 1987-88 | (Div 2) | W | 2-0 | L | 0-1 |
| 1988-89 | (Div 2) | W | 3-0 | L | 0-2 |

| | P | W | D | L | F | A |
|---|---|---|---|---|---|---|
| Home | 44 | 29 | 8 | 7 | 117 | 61 |
| Away | 44 | 4 | 13 | 27 | 40 | 84 |
| Total | 88 | 33 | 21 | 34 | 157 | 145 |

## FA Cup
| | | | | | |
|---|---|---|---|---|---|
| 1932-33 | (4) | Away | L | 0-3 |
| 1934-35 | (5) | Home | L | 1-2 |

## Football League Cup
| | | | | | |
|---|---|---|---|---|---|
| 1980-81 | (3) | Away | L | 0-1 |

## BIRTWISTLE, Alfred
Full-back. 1875-1880.
*Born: Blackburn.*
*Debut: v Tyne Association (h) 1 November 1879 (FAC).*
*Career: Blackburn Rovers 1875.*
**Appearances:** FA Cup 3.
One of the founder playing members of Blackburn Rovers, Alfred Birtwistle featured in all three of the club's FA Cup fixtures in 1879-80. The following season saw him replaced with Fergie Suter as D.H.Greenwood's partner at full-back.

## BIRTWISTLE, Fred
Full-back/Forward. 1875-1885.
*Born: Great Harwood.*
*Debut: v Sheffield Providence (h) 6-2.*
*Career: Blackburn Rovers 1875.*
**Appearances:** FA Cup 2.
**Goals:** FA Cup 1.
In his *History of Blackburn Rovers* published in 1925, Charles Francis stated that Fred Birtwistle was a full-back who hailed from Great

Harwood. Newspaper reports from the club's early seasons also show Alfred Birtwistle occupying a full-back berth in several matches. Fred Birtwistle was also credited with two forward appearances in the FA Cup.

## BIRTWISTLE, Richard
Forward. 1875-1880.
Chairman. 1901-1905.
*Born: Great Harwood c.1853; Died: Lytham St Annes, 16 December 1929.*
*Debut: v Tyne Association (h) 1 November 1879.*
*Career: Cob Wall FC; Turton FC; Blackburn Rovers 1875.*
**Appearances:** FA Cup 4.
**Goals:** FA Cup 1.
Richard Birtwistle was one of 17 men who formed the Blackburn Rovers Football Club at a meeting at the St Leger Hotel in Blackburn in November 1875. Birtwistle was a member of a local family who had various interests in the cotton industry. Whilst his father and grandfather were well-known cotton manufacturers, Richard became a yarn agent and one of the most influential figures in Lancashire football.

He scored Blackburn's only goal in their inaugural match and was a regular member of sides fielded by the club in its formative years. He was later to become a committee man, director and finally club chairman of Blackburn Rovers.

Dick Birtwistle attended the inaugural meeting of the Lancashire Football Association and served on that body during the 1879-80 season. He resumed his connection with the Lancashire Football Association in 1901 and remained a member of that body until resigning through ill health in June 1927. He was elected vice-chairman in 1919 and also received a long-service medal. Such was the respect that he had earned that he was made a Life Member of the Association and presented with a silver casket in recognition of his service to the Lancashire Association. No man had a greater knowledge or understanding of the history of football in Lancashire than Dick Birtwistle.

## BLACKBURN, Arthur
Full-back. 1895-1898, 1899 & 1901-1902.
*5ft 11in; 12st 7lb.*
*Born : Blackburn, 1877.*
*Debut: v Sheffield United (a) 9 September 1899.*
*Career: Mellor FC; Blackburn Rovers March 1895; Wellingborough cs 1898; Blackburn Rovers 1899; Southampton May 1900; Blackburn Rovers 1901.*
**Appearances:** Football League 4.
Arthur Blackburn was playing in the second team at Blackburn Rovers when he was persuaded to try his luck in the Southern League with Southampton. Although the Rovers didn't want to lose Blackburn they couldn't offer him first-team football as Bob Crompton and Alan Hardy were established in the full-back positions.

Plagued by injury problems, he appeared in only nine Southern League matches for the Saints before returning to Ewood Park.

Whilst his brother Fred was a leading light in the Rovers team, Arthur failed to make much impression and his second stint at Ewood ended after only two appearances in the First Division. He turned to coaching in later life and worked in Rotterdam, Holland.

## BLACKBURN ASSOCIATION XI
A friendly fixture was played on 20 December 1879, between Blackburn Rovers and a representative XI from the town on "the ground near the cattle market". According to the correspondent of *The Blackburn Standard* the match attracted a "considerable number of spectators" and he went on to comment that "The fact that the Rovers, whose successes of late have made them so popular, were competing with a team composed of the best players of the clubs in the Blackburn Association, added extra interest to the match, and speculation was rife as to its probable result." On a frosty ground the Rovers enjoyed a convincing 5-2 victory. The teams that day were as follows:
Blackburn Rovers: Howorth; F.Birtwistle, D.H.Greenwood, F.W.Hargreaves, Leyland, J.Hargreaves, Lewis, Avery, Brown, Astley, Pickup.
Blackburn Association XI: H.Walsh; T.McQuirk, T.Holden, J.Battersby, J.McQuirk, J.Leaver, G.Hacking, Frost, T.Hacking, R.Foy, R.Cooper.

## BLACKBURN & DISTRICT XI
An exhibition match was played on the 16 September 1882, on the ground of the Bradford (Park Avenue) Football Club between Blackburn Rovers and a Blackburn & District XI. The result was a 5-1 victory for the Rovers and after the match the teams were entertained by the Bradford Club at the Alexandra Hotel. The teams that day were as follows:
Blackburn Rovers: Arthur; Suter, Shorrock, McIntyre, Harvey, Douglas, Duckworth, Brown, Strachan, Avery, J.Hargreaves.
Blackburn & District XI: Woolfall (Blackburn Rovers); Wood

(Blackburn Rovers). Chippendale (Church), Latham (Blackburn Rovers)., Ramsdale (Witton), Snape (Witton), Lofthouse (Blackburn Rovers), McGill (Everton), Thornber (Blackburn Rovers), Blenkhorn (Blackburn Rovers), Barton (Blackburn Rovers).

## BLACKBURN, Frederick
Outside-left. 1897-1905.
*5ft 6½in; 10st 12lb.*
*Born: Mellor, nr Blackburn, September 1877.*
*Debut: v Notts County (a) 5 March 1898.*
*Career: Mellor FC; Blackburn Rovers May 1897; West Ham United May 1905; Retired cs 1913; Barking (coach) 1931.*
*International honours with Blackburn Rovers: England: 3 caps (1901-04)*
*Football League: 1 appearance (1901).*
**Appearances:** Football League 192; FA Cup 12; Test Matches 2; Total 206.
**Goals:** Football League 25; FA Cup 5; Test Matches 1; Total 31.
Fred Blackburn arrived at Ewood Park from his local village team as an inside-forward. However, once he was converted into a ball-playing outside-left, Blackburn went on to become one of the most exciting players of his era. His ability to cross the ball with great accuracy created numerous opportunities for his colleagues, whilst Blackburn's own shooting powers brought him a number of goals. He gained international recognition with the Rovers before moving to West Ham United in May 1905.

He quickly established himself in the 'Hammers' side and remained a first-team regular for several seasons. During his later years with the London Club he was converted to a wing-half and played his last game for West Ham in 1913. He spent some time in the Merchant Navy before returning to football in the 1930s as a coach at non-League Barking. Fred Blackburn's young brother, Arthur, also played with the Rovers before moving to Southampton.

## BLACKBURN OLYMPIC FC
Formed by the fusion of Black Star FC and James Street FC; two local clubs who were determined to offer a challenge to the emerging Blackburn Rovers. The decision to amalgamate resulted in the new club taking to the field in 1878 under the name of Blackburn Olympic. The name 'Olympic' was chosen by James Edmondson, the club's captain and treasurer. Initially based in the Pleckgate area of town the club eventually moved to the Hole 'ith wall ground of the defunct King's Own club.

Blackburn Olympic was largely made up of working men who regarded the Rovers as something of a 'gentleman's club'. However, the Olympic club had its own patron in Sidney Yates of the local iron foundry, W.&J.Yates.

In the first meeting between Olympic and Rovers the 'gentleman's club' made the mistake of underestimating their working class opponents and slumped to a 3-1 defeat. However, there was no disgrace in this as Blackburn Olympic quickly became one of the strongest teams in the area and won the inaugural East Lancashire Charity Cup in 1881-82.

The greatest achievement of the club was in winning the FA Cup in 1882-83. A 2-1 victory over Old Etonians resulted in the trophy leaving the capital for the first time in its history. The Blackburn Olympic team was as follows: G.Gibson (professional), T.Dewhurst (weaver), T.Hacking (dentist's assistant), J.T.Ward (cotton machine operator), J.Costley (spinner), J.Hunter (professional), J.Yates (weaver), W.Astley (weaver), T.Gibson (Iron-moulder's dresser), S.A.Warburton (master plumber), A.Matthews (picture framer).

As professionalism grew the fortunes of Blackburn Olympic began to wane. Although they continued to meet Blackburn Rovers in friendly matches until 1889, the people of Blackburn turned more and more to the successful Rovers. The final blow for the Olympic came when they were not elected to the newly formed Football League in 1888. Players left, defeats became increasingly embarrassing and the club passed quietly into the pages of history.

### FA Cup
| | | | | |
|---|---|---|---|---|
| 1884-85 | (2) | Home | W | 3-2 |
| 1887-88 | (2) | Home | W | 5-1 |

## BLACKBURN PARK ROAD FC
Formed in 1875, Blackburn Park Road played in the Audley area of the town but never achieved the success of Blackburn Rovers or Blackburn Olympic. The club failed to achieve much success in the FA Cup competition during the 1880s and on 29 October 1881 the Rovers beat them 9-1 in the first round of the competition. A month earlier Jimmy Brown had scored 5 goals for the Rovers in a 14-0 victory in a friendly fixture in front of 2,000 spectators. The Park Road club did cause some minor embarrassment to the Rovers towards the end of the 1887-88 season when they invited Derby Junction, conquerors of the Rovers in the FA Cup, to Blackburn and beat them 3-0.

**FA Cup**

| | | | | | |
|---|---|---|---|---|---|
| 1881-82 | | (a) | Home | W | 9-1 |

## BLACKLAW, Adam Smith

Goalkeeper. 1967-1970.
*5ft 11½in; 14st 13lb.*
*Born: Aberdeen, 2 September 1937.*
*Debut: v Millwall (a) 19 August 1967.*
*Career: Aberdeen Schools; Burnley groundstaff 1954, turning professional in October 1954; Blackburn Rovers July 1967 (£15,000); Blackpool June 1970; Great Harwood cs 1971.*
**Appearances:** Football League 96; FA Cup 5; Football League Cup 9; Total 110.

Eddie Quigley brought Adam Blacklaw to Ewood Park to replace the inconsistent John Barton in the summer of 1967. The former Burnley player had proved a formidable barrier to Blackburn in numerous derby matches and the Rovers supporters immediately took to the big and brave Scotsman.

Blacklaw, who had made his debut as a 19-year-old at Turf Moor, had been with the Clarets for some 13 years. When Colin McDonald's career was tragically cut short by injury in 1959, Blacklaw became the club's first-choice goalkeeper. He won a championship medal in 1960 and an FA Cup runners-up medal with the Clarets in 1962. Whilst at Turf Moor, Blacklaw appeared in 318 First Division games.

The vastly experienced Blacklaw seemed an ideal choice to fill the goalkeeping position as Quigley tried to build a promotion winning side. For two and a half seasons he was first choice until injury and a loss of form caused Quigley to look elsewhere for a younger man.

The signing of Roger Jones brought Blacklaw's Ewood career to an end and, with Barton preferred as understudy, the veteran 'keeper was allowed to join Blackpool on a free transfer. Blacklaw made one appearance for Blackpool during the 1970-71 campaign and then joined Great Harwood. On returning to the Burnley area he became a publican and was later the steward at a local golf course.

## BLACKPOOL FC

Founded in 1887. Blackpool amalgamated with South Shore FC on 12 December 1899. The first meeting between the clubs in senior competition was an FA Cup-tie in 1925 when a crowd of 60,011 at Ewood Park saw Blackburn win by a goal from Syd Puddefoot. The gate was the highest in the club's history up to that point and has only been bettered by the 62,522 that watched the Cup-tie against Bolton Wanderers in 1929.

**Football League**

| | | | Home | | Away | |
|---|---|---|---|---|---|---|
| 1930-31 | | (Div 1) | W | 5-0 | D | 1-1 |
| 1931-32 | | (Div 1) | W | 5-1 | L | 1-2 |
| 1932-33 | | (Div 1) | W | 6-5 | L | 0-3 |
| 1936-37 | | (Div 2) | W | 2-0 | L | 0-2 |
| 1946-47 | | (Div 1) | D | 1-1 | L | 0-1 |
| 1947-48 | | (Div 1) | D | 1-1 | L | 0-1 |
| 1958-59 | | (Div 1) | D | 0-0 | D | 1-1 |
| 1959-60 | | (Div 1) | W | 1-0 | L | 0-1 |
| 1960-61 | | (Div 1) | W | 2-0 | L | 0-2 |
| 1961-62 | | (Div 1) | D | 1-1 | L | 1-2 |
| 1962-63 | | (Div 1) | D | 3-3 | L | 1-4 |
| 1963-64 | | (Div 1) | L | 1-2 | L | 2-3 |
| 1964-65 | | (Div 1) | W | 4-1 | L | 2-4 |
| 1965-66 | | (Div 1) | L | 1-3 | L | 2-4 |
| 1967-68 | | (Div 2) | W | 2-1 | L | 1-2 |
| 1968-69 | | (Div 2) | D | 1-1 | W | 1-0 |
| 1969-70 | | (Div 2) | W | 2-1 | D | 0-0 |
| 1975-76 | | (Div 2) | L | 0-2 | D | 1-1 |
| 1976-77 | | (Div 2) | L | 0-1 | D | 1-1 |
| 1977-78 | | (Div 2) | L | 1-2 | L | 2-5 |
| 1979-80 | | (Div 3) | W | 2-0 | L | 1-2 |

| | P | W | D | L | F | A |
|---|---|---|---|---|---|---|
| Home | 21 | 10 | 6 | 5 | 41 | 26 |
| Away | 21 | 1 | 5 | 15 | 18 | 42 |
| Total | 42 | 11 | 11 | 20 | 59 | 68 |

**FA Cup**

| | | | | | |
|---|---|---|---|---|---|
| 1924-25 | (4) | Home | W | 1-0 |
| 1959-60 | (4) | Home | D | 1-1 |
| | (R) | Away | W | 3-0 |

**Wartime**

| | | | Home | | Away | |
|---|---|---|---|---|---|---|
| 1916-17 | | (LSPT) | W | 4-0 | L | 1-2 |
| | | (LSST) | L | 2-3 | L | 1-4 |
| 1917-18 | | (LSPT) | D | 2-2 | L | 1-4 |
| | | (LSST) | L | 1-4 | L | 0-2 |
| 1918-19 | | (LSPT) | L | 0-3 | L | 0-2 |
| | | (LSST) | D | 1-1 | L | 1-6 |
| 1939-40 | | (NWRL) | D | 1-1 | L | 2-3 |
| 1941-42 | | (FLNS-FC) | W | 2-1 | L | 1-4 |
| 1942-43 | | (FLNS-FC) | L | 2-4 | L | 2-7 |
| | | (FLNS-SC) | D | 3-3 | L | 2-4 |
| 1943-44 | | (FLNS-FC) | D | 1-1 | L | 0-8 |
| | | (FLNS-SC) | W | 3-1 | D | 2-2 |
| 1944-45 | | (FLNS-FC) | D | 2-2 | L | 1-2 |
| | | (FLNS-SC) | W | 7-4 | L | 1-3 |
| 1945-46 | | (FLN) | D | 1-1 | L | 2-5 |

## BLACKPOOL ST JOHN'S FC

Formed around 1877 and a forerunner of Blackpool Football Club. This club met Blackburn Rovers in the first round of the FA Cup in 1882 when the Rovers recorded an impressive 11-1 victory. A crowd of 1,000 saw Jimmy Brown notch four goals for the Rovers whilst Alfred Barton scored a hat-trick. In terms of records the score remains second only to the 11-0 thrashing of Rossendale in the same competition in 1884.

**FA Cup**

| | | | | | |
|---|---|---|---|---|---|
| 1882-83 | | (a) | Home | W | 11-1 |

## BLACKSHAW, John

Centre-forward. 1900-1901.
*Born: Blackburn.*
*Debut: v Notts County (h) 6 April 1901.*
*Career: Park Road; Blackburn Rovers August 1900; Darwen; Trawden Forest October 1902; Oswaldtwistle Rovers cs 1903.*
**Appearances:** Football League 2.

A player who played two games for Blackburn Rovers in a matter of three days against both Nottingham clubs. Whilst the Rovers lost to County by two goals to nil they managed to beat Forest by a single goal. However, Blackshaw was not called upon again and after a couple of seasons of second-team football he was allowed to move to Darwen. Although he was given several first-team opportunities with Darwen he failed to make much impression and was soon playing in more junior circles.

## BLENKHORN, Robert

Half-back. 1881-1887.
*Debut: v Blackpool South Shore (a) 1 December 1883 (FAC)*
*Career: Blackburn Rovers 1881 to 1887.*
**Appearances:** FA Cup 3.

Although Bob Blenkhorn had a long association with the club during the 1880s, he found it difficult to establish himself in one of the half-back positions. With Jimmy Douglas and Jim Forrest installed in the first team, Blenkhorn had to settle for the role of understudy. However, he was an adaptable type of player and from time to time filled in at full-back and in the forward line.

## BLORE, Reginald

Forward. 1963-1965.
*5ft 9in; 12st.*
*Born: Sesswick, nr Wrexham, 18 March 1942.*
*Debut: v Arsenal (h) 30 November 1963.*
*Career: Liverpool Schoolboys; Liverpool amateur May 1958, turning professional in May 1959; Southport July 1960; Blackburn Rovers November 1963 (£6,000); Oldham Athletic December 1965 (£8,000); Bangor City 1970-71; Ellesmere Port 1971-72.*
*International honours with Blackburn Rovers: Wales Under-23: 3 caps (1964-65).*
**Appearances:** Football League 11.

Reg Blore was the first incoming transfer at Ewood Park for 14 months when he joined the club in November 1963. A versatile player who could fill most of the forward positions he was snapped up for £6,000 to provide cover for Fred Pickering. The stockily built Blore was a Welsh Under-23 international and had just turned down a move to Oxford United when the Rovers stepped in to bring him to Ewood Park. Although he had joined

Southport on a free transfer he had caused quite a stir at Haig Avenue by scoring 55 goals in 139 League games. At Blackburn, Blore was never more than an understudy and in two years made only 11 first-team appearances. He enjoyed better fortunes at Boundary Park where he appeared in 181 League games before moving into non-League football.

## BODELL, Norman
Coach. 1975-1978.
*Born: Manchester, 29 January 1938.*
*Career: Rochdale September 1956; Crewe Alexandra May 1963; Halifax Town October 1966; Barrow coach 1968, then manager from February 1969 until February 1970; Preston North End coach 1974; Blackburn Rovers coach July 1975 until April 1978; Birmingham City coach April 1979 until 1981, then chief scout until 1983; West Bromwich Albion chief scout in 1990.*

Norman Bodell was brought to Ewood Park by Jim Smith, a former playing colleague of Bodell at Halifax Town, in July 1975. A qualified FA coach, Bodell had previously been working with Bobby Charlton at Preston North End before making the short move to Ewood Park. Bodell was highly rated by Smith and when the latter moved to Birmingham City in March 1978, there was immediate speculation that Bodell would join him at St Andrew's. Following the departure of Smith, Bodell was put in charge of team affairs at Ewood Park until a new manager could be appointed. Under his caretaker managership, the team won only two of eight League fixtures. As the team travelled to meet Mansfield Town on 15 April 1978, Jim Iley was installed as manager and Norman Bodell left Ewood Park to join Jim Smith at Birmingham City.

## BOGAN, Thomas
Outside-right. 1953-1954.
*5ft 9in.*
*Born: Glasgow, 18 May 1920; Died: 23 September 1993.*
*Debut: v Oldham Athletic (a) 26 September 1953.*
*Career: Strathclyde 1937; Blantyre Celtic 1939; Renfrew Juniors 1943; Hibernian September 1944; Glasgow Celtic January 1946; Preston North End September 1948; Manchester United August 1949; Aberdeen March 1951; Southampton December 1951; Blackburn Rovers August 1953 to June 1954; Macclesfield Town June 1954.*
**Appearances:** Football League 1.

Tommy Bogan made his reputation in the years immediately after World War Two as a winger with Celtic. He represented the Scottish League and appeared set for a successful career in English football. Sadly, Bogan failed to make much impression at any of his English clubs. His most successful spell was at Old Trafford where he scored 7 goals in 29 League outings. At Ewood Park he was one of four players tried in the outside-right spot in 1953-54 before the arrival of Frank Mooney in February 1954.

## BOLTON WANDERERS FC
Founded in 1874 as Christ Church FC, the club changed its name to Bolton Wanderers in 1877. One of the original members of the Football League, Bolton have met Blackburn Rovers in the First, Second and Third Divisions of the Football League. It was for a sixth-round FA Cup-tie against Bolton Wanderers on 2 March 1929 that a record crowd of 62,522 was seen at Ewood Park. The game ended in a 1-1 draw and 65,295 watched Bolton win 2-1 in the replay at Burnden Park.

### Football League

|         |        | Home |     | Away |     |
|---------|--------|------|-----|------|-----|
| 1888-89 | (FL)   | D    | 4-4 | L    | 2-3 |
| 1889-90 | (FL)   | W    | 7-1 | L    | 2-3 |
| 1890-91 | (FL)   | L    | 0-2 | L    | 0-2 |
| 1891-92 | (FL)   | W    | 4-0 | L    | 2-4 |
| 1892-93 | (Div 1)| W    | 3-0 | L    | 1-2 |
| 1893-94 | (Div 1)| L    | 0-1 | L    | 1-2 |
| 1894-95 | (Div 1)| W    | 2-1 | W    | 3-1 |
| 1895-96 | (Div 1)| W    | 3-2 | D    | 1-1 |
| 1896-97 | (Div 1)| W    | 1-0 | D    | 0-0 |
| 1897-98 | (Div 1)| L    | 1-3 | W    | 2-1 |
| 1898-99 | (Div 1)| W    | 4-1 | W    | 2-0 |
| 1900-01 | (Div 1)| W    | 2-0 | L    | 0-1 |
| 1901-02 | (Div 1)| W    | 2-0 | L    | 0-4 |
| 1902-03 | (Div 1)| W    | 4-2 | W    | 2-1 |
| 1905-06 | (Div 1)| W    | 4-1 | L    | 0-1 |
| 1906-07 | (Div 1)| L    | 2-3 | L    | 2-5 |
| 1907-08 | (Div 1)| W    | 3-2 | L    | 1-3 |
| 1909-10 | (Div 1)| W    | 4-2 | W    | 2-1 |
| 1911-12 | (Div 1)| W    | 2-0 | L    | 0-2 |
| 1912-13 | (Div 1)| W    | 6-0 | D    | 1-1 |
| 1913-14 | (Div 1)| W    | 3-2 | L    | 0-1 |
| 1914-15 | (Div 1)| D    | 2-2 | L    | 2-3 |
| 1919-20 | (Div 1)| D    | 2-2 | L    | 1-2 |
| 1920-21 | (Div 1)| D    | 2-2 | L    | 1-2 |
| 1921-22 | (Div 1)| L    | 1-2 | D    | 1-1 |
| 1922-23 | (Div 1)| W    | 1-0 | L    | 0-3 |
| 1923-24 | (Div 1)| W    | 3-1 | L    | 0-3 |
| 1924-25 | (Div 1)| L    | 0-2 | L    | 0-6 |
| 1925-26 | (Div 1)| W    | 3-0 | D    | 2-2 |
| 1926-27 | (Div 1)| L    | 0-3 | L    | 1-5 |
| 1927-28 | (Div 1)| L    | 1-6 | L    | 1-3 |
| 1928-29 | (Div 1)| L    | 1-3 | W    | 3-0 |
| 1929-30 | (Div 1)| W    | 3-1 | L    | 1-2 |
| 1930-31 | (Div 1)| D    | 2-2 | D    | 1-1 |
| 1931-32 | (Div 1)| W    | 3-1 | L    | 1-3 |
| 1932-33 | (Div 1)| W    | 3-2 | L    | 2-4 |
| 1935-36 | (Div 1)| L    | 0-3 | L    | 1-3 |
| 1946-47 | (Div 1)| W    | 2-1 | D    | 0-0 |
| 1947-48 | (Div 1)| W    | 4-0 | L    | 0-1 |
| 1958-59 | (Div 1)| D    | 1-1 | L    | 1-3 |
| 1959-60 | (Div 1)| W    | 1-0 | W    | 3-0 |
| 1960-61 | (Div 1)| W    | 3-1 | D    | 0-0 |
| 1961-62 | (Div 1)| L    | 2-3 | D    | 1-1 |
| 1962-63 | (Div 1)| W    | 5-0 | D    | 0-0 |
| 1963-64 | (Div 1)| W    | 3-0 | W    | 5-0 |
| 1966-67 | (Div 2)| D    | 0-0 | W    | 1-0 |
| 1967-68 | (Div 2)| W    | 2-1 | L    | 1-2 |
| 1968-69 | (Div 2)| L    | 2-3 | D    | 1-1 |
| 1969-70 | (Div 2)| W    | 3-1 | L    | 0-1 |
| 1970-71 | (Div 2)| L    | 0-2 | D    | 1-1 |
| 1971-72 | (Div 3)| L    | 0-3 | L    | 0-1 |
| 1972-73 | (Div 3)| L    | 0-3 | W    | 1-0 |
| 1975-76 | (Div 2)| D    | 1-1 | W    | 1-0 |
| 1976-77 | (Div 2)| W    | 3-1 | L    | 1-3 |
| 1977-78 | (Div 2)| L    | 0-1 | L    | 2-4 |
| 1980-81 | (Div 2)| D    | 0-0 | W    | 2-1 |
| 1981-82 | (Div 2)| L    | 0-2 | D    | 2-2 |
| 1982-83 | (Div 2)| D    | 1-1 | L    | 0-1 |

|       | P   | W  | D  | L  | F   | A   |
|-------|-----|----|----|----|-----|-----|
| Home  | 58  | 31 | 10 | 17 | 121 | 84  |
| Away  | 58  | 12 | 13 | 33 | 65  | 104 |
| Total | 116 | 43 | 23 | 50 | 186 | 188 |

### FA Cup

| 1881-82 | (2)  | Home   | W | 6-2 |
|---------|------|--------|---|-----|
| 1928-29 | (6)  | Home   | D | 1-1 |
|         | (R)  | Away   | L | 1-2 |
| 1935-36 | (3)  | Home   | D | 1-1 |
|         | (R)  | Away   | W | 1-0 (aet) |
| 1945-46 | (3)  | Away   | L | 0-1 |
|         |      | Home   | L | 1-3 |
| 1957-58 | (SF) | Maine Road, Manchester L 1-2 |
| 1960-61 | (4)  | Away   | D | 3-3 |
|         | (R)  | Home   | W | 4-0 |

### Football League Cup

| 1964-65 | (2) | Away | W | 5-1 |
|---------|-----|------|---|-----|
| 1970-71 | (2) | Away | L | 0-1 |

### Wartime

|         |          | Home |     | Away |      |
|---------|----------|------|-----|------|------|
| 1916-17 | (LSPT)   | W    | 5-1 | D    | 0-0  |
| 1917-18 | (LSPT)   | L    | 1-2 | L    | 2-5  |
| 1918-19 | (LSPT)   | L    | 2-3 | L    | 0-3  |
| 1939-40 | (NWRL)   | W    | 3-1 | L    | 0-2  |
|         | (LWC)    | W    | 5-1 | W    | 3-1  |
| 1940-41 | (NRL)    |      |     | L    | 0-2* |
| 1941-42 | (FLNS-FC)| D    | 3-3 | D    | 2-2  |
| 1942-43 | (FLNS-FC)| W    | 4-2 | D    | 3-3  |
|         | (FLNS-SC)| W    | 7-1 | L    | 1-3+ |
|         |          | L    | 1-3 | W    | 1-0  |
| 1943-44 | (FLNS-FC)| W    | 3-1 | W    | 4-1  |
|         | (FLNS-SC)| W    | 2-0 | L    | 1-4  |
| 1944-45 | (FLNS-FC)| W    | 2-1 | D    | 0-0  |
| 1945-46 | (FLN)    | L    | 0-1 | W    | 2-1  |

*Note: Blackburn Rovers did not play a home match with Bolton Wanderers in this competition.
+Note: Blackburn Rovers and Bolton Wanderers played each other at home and away on two occasions in this competition.

**BOND, Richard**
Outside-right. 1922-1923.
5ft 6½in; 10st 12lb.
*Born: Garstang, Lancashire, 14 December 1883; Died: Preston, 25 April 1955.*
*Debut: v Aston Villa (a) 26 August 1922.*
*Career: Army football (Royal Field Artillery); Preston North End August 1902; Bradford City July 1909 (£950); Blackburn Rovers May 1922 (£450); Lancaster Town August 1923. Retired 1924. Garstang FC 1926-27.*
**Appearances:** Football League 24; FA Cup 2; Total 26.
**Goals:** Football League 2; FA Cup 1; Total 3.
In the first three seasons after the end of World War One no fewer than 15 players were tried in the outside right position by Blackburn Rovers. It was in a bid to solve this problem position that the club turned to Dickie Bond, the veteran Bradford City winger, in May 1922.

When Bond had joined Bradford in the summer of 1909 he was acknowledged as the finest outside-right in the country. He had won a Second Division championship medal with Preston North End and had helped take the Deepdale club to a runners' up position in the top flight. At Valley Parade he appeared in 301 first Division matches, scoring 60 goals, and added a further three England caps to the five he had won at Deepdale.

However, although Bond began the 1922-23 season on the right wing for the Rovers, it was clear that his best days were behind him. In March 1923 the Rovers paid £3,125 to sign Jack Crisp from West Bromwich Albion and this signalled the end of Bond's career. In August 1923 he joined Lancaster Town after a League career which had seen him score 96 goals in 473 appearances.

**BOOTH, Thomas Edward**
Right-half. 1896-1900.
*Born: Ardwick, 25 April 1874; Died: Blackpool, 7 September 1939.*
*Debut: v Liverpool (h) 5 September 1896.*
*Career: Hooley Hill FC; Ashton North End; Blackburn Rovers May 1896; Everton May 1900; Preston North End 1908; Carlisle United coach November 1908; Retired 1909.*
*International honours with Blackburn Rovers: England: 1 cap (1898); Football League: 2 appearances (1897-98).*
**Appearances:** Football League 111; FA Cup 9; Test Matches 3; Total 123.
**Goals:** Football League 10; FA Cup 1; Total 11.
As a young man Tom Booth learned the trade of a felt hatter in the village of Hooley Hill. However, his prowess on the football field was quickly noticed and he became a professional with Ashton North End. As Ashton progressed into the Lancashire League a number of big clubs became attracted to the ever-improving Booth. In May 1896 he joined Blackburn Rovers and was to remain at Ewood for four seasons.

He forced his way into the first team on a regular basis at the end of October 1896 and retained his place until his departure to Everton in May 1900. Although Booth began as a right-half the departure of Geordie Anderson to New Brighton Tower saw him move to centre-half in October 1897. He was again at right-half when Anderson returned to Ewood for the 1898-99 season, but the following campaign, Booth's last at Blackburn, found him once more in the central position.

Booth was coolness personified on the football field. No matter how rugged the opponent he never flinched from a challenge and remained a calming influence on his colleagues.

At the end of the 1899-1900 season he was enticed to Merseyside by an attractive offer from Everton. At Goodison Park he captained the side and went on to win a second England cap in 1903, his first having been won with Blackburn in 1898. Sadly, injury prevented Booth from appearing in the 1906 FA Cup Final and when Everton reached the final again 12 months later, Booth was no longer a first-team regular.

He left Everton for Preston North End in 1908 and in November of that year he moved to Carlisle United as coach. At that time Carlisle were struggling in the North Eastern League and had not even won a game when Booth arrived. However, by the end of the season they had 24 points and were to finish fourth from bottom. Booth retired from football in 1909.

**BOOTHMAN, James**
Left-back. 1917-1919.
*5ft 7in; 11st 12lb.*
*Born: Blackburn, 1890 (April quarter).*
*Debut: v Sheffield Wednesday (h) 18 October 1919.*
*Career: St John's (Blackburn); Victoria Cross (Blackburn); Fleetwood; Blackburn Trinity; Blackburn Rovers 1917; Lancaster Town; Fleetwood cs 1920; Lancaster Town.*
**Appearances:** Football League 2.
An experienced player in local junior circles, James Boothman joined the

club during World War One. He scored twice in 50 wartime appearances for the club but when peace returned the found himself understudying Fred Duckworth. His two senior appearances in the Football League came in October 1919, after which he returned to non-League football.

**BOOTLE FC**
Originally founded as Bootle St John's in 1878, Bootle challenged Everton for football supremacy on Merseyside in the 1880s. The club eventually became members of the Football League in 1892. However, they remained in the Second Division for only a season before resigning and being replaced by Liverpool FC. Bootle met Blackburn in the third round of the FA Cup in 1890 when a Nat Walton hat-trick and two goals from Jack Southworth helped the Rovers to a convincing 7-0 victory.

**FA Cup**

| | | | | |
|---|---|---|---|---|
| 1889-90 | (3) | Away | W | 7-0 |

**AFC BOURNEMOUTH**
Founded in 1899 as Boscombe Football Club, the club changed its name to Bournemouth & Boscombe Athletic in 1932. In 1935, Bob Crompton became manager of the club but left after only eight months. The club's present title was adopted in 1972. Although they had previously met in a friendly, Blackburn and Bournemouth did not meet in competitive football until the Rovers were relegated to the Third Division in 1971.

**Football League**

| | | Home | | Away | |
|---|---|---|---|---|---|
| 1971-72 | (Div 3) | W | 2-1 | L | 0-1 |
| 1972-73 | (Div 3) | W | 2-1 | L | 0-3 |
| 1973-74 | (Div 3) | W | 4-3 | W | 2-1 |
| 1974-75 | (Div 3) | W | 1-0 | D | 0-0 |
| 1987-88 | (Div 2) | W | 3-1 | D | 1-1 |
| 1988-89 | (Div 2) | W | 2-0 | L | 1-2 |
| 1989-90 | (Div 2) | D | 1-1 | W | 4-2 |

| | P | W | D | L | F | A |
|---|---|---|---|---|---|---|
| Home | 7 | 6 | 1 | 0 | 15 | 7 |
| Away | 7 | 2 | 2 | 3 | 8 | 10 |
| Total | 14 | 8 | 3 | 3 | 23 | 17 |

**FA Cup**

| | | | | |
|---|---|---|---|---|
| 1992-93 | (3) | Home | W | 3-1 |

**Football League Cup**

| | | | | |
|---|---|---|---|---|
| 1993-94 | (2) | Home | W | 1-0 |
| | | Away | D | 0-0 |

**BOURTON, Clarence Frederick Tom**
Centre-forward. 1928-1931.
*5ft 9½in; 12st.*
*Born: Bristol, 30 September 1908; Died: Bath, 20 April 1981.*
*Debut: v Bury (h) 10 November 1928.*
*Career: Poulton United (Bristol District League) 1926; Bristol City January 1927; Blackburn Rovers May 1928 (£4,000 joint fee for Bourton and Albert Keating); Coventry City July 1931 (£750); Plymouth Argyle October 1937; Bristol City January 1938, including a spell as caretaker manager from October 1938 until May 1939. Retired 1944.*
**Appearances:** Football League 63; FA Cup 9; Total 72.
**Goals:** Football League 37; FA Cup 5; Total 42.
Clarrie Bourton was an old-style centre-forward who scored goals wherever he played. Although his approach was more suited to the rough and tumble of Third Division football, Bourton nevertheless maintained a highly respectable goals-per-game ratio whilst at Blackburn.

Bourton joined Blackburn as the makeweight in a £4,000 deal which also brought Albert Keating to Ewood Park. However, after scoring 11 goals in 12 Central League games he was promoted to the first team in place of Jack Roscamp. He scored on his debut and on his fourth appearance in the senior team he notched all four goals against Manchester United in a 4-1 victory at Old Trafford. The following season saw him score 21 goals in only 23 League appearances, including another haul of 4 in an away match, this time at Sheffield United.

Unfortunately, Bourton was unable to maintain this strike rate and the 1930-31 season saw him lose his centre-forward spot to Les Bruton. In July 1931 he moved to Coventry City and rewrote the record books at Highfield Road when he finished with 49 goals at the end of his first season with the club. In January 1938 he returned to his native Bristol to link up with Bristol City, the club from whom Blackburn Rovers had signed him in 1928.

**BOW, William**
Inside-right, 1902-1904

*5ft 9in; 11st.*
*Born: Edinburgh,1884.*
*Debut: v Middlesbrough (h) 1 September 1902.*
*Career: Edinburgh St Bernard's September 1901; Blackburn Rovers August 1902 (£250); Darwen; Nelson cs 1905; Great Harwood.*
**Appearances:** Football League 20; FA Cup 3; Total 23.
**Goals:** Football League 2.
Billy Bow joined the Rovers as a replacement for Peter Somers on the eve of the 1902-03 campaign. Although a little on the light side and primarily an inside-left it was none the less felt that he would be an adequate replacement for Somers. Fast and tricky, Bow possessed a strong shot and had attracted the attention of a number of top clubs both north and south of the border before moving to Blackburn. Although he featured in 18 League games during his first season at Ewood the following campaign saw him virtually overlooked when it came to first-team opportunities. After leaving Blackburn he appeared in local non-League circles.

### BOWDLER, John Charles Henry
Outside-left. 1892-1893.
*Born: Shrewsbury, December 1868; Died: Shrewsbury, 18 July 1927.*
*Debut: v Newton Heath (h) 3 September 1892.*
*Career: Shrewsbury School; Shrewsbury Town 1885-1890; Wolverhampton Wanderers May 1890; Blackburn Rovers July 1892; Shrewsbury Town April 1893-97.*
**Appearances:** Football League 22; FA Cup 4; Total 26.
**Goals:** Football League 5; FA Cup 2; Total 7.
As a former pupil of Shrewsbury School, Jack Bowdler enjoyed the same type of public school background as Jack Lewis and Arthur Constantine. In the same way that Lewis and Constantine had helped form Blackburn Rovers, Bowdler was involved in the formation of Shrewsbury Town. As the club's best player he became the first Shrewsbury Town player to join a Football League club when he signed for Wolves in May 1890. He coupled speed and good ball control with a fierce shot and the ability to play on either wing or at inside-forward.

Although he was an automatic choice for the outside-left position, Bowdler remained with the Rovers for only one season. He returned to Shrewsbury in April 1893 and two years later became a qualified solicitor. It was in 1895 that the Rovers made an unsuccessful attempt to get him to return to Ewood Park.

Bowdler was later to serve Shrewsbury Town as secretary and then chairman as well as becoming a member of the Shropshire Football Association. Bowdler was also active in local politics and served on the Shrewsbury council from 1901 and was also agent to the local MP for a number of years.

### BOWMAN, Adam
Forward. 1903-1907.
*5ft 10½in; 12st.*
*Born: Forfar, Angus.*
*Debut: v West Bromwich Albion (h) 21 March 1903.*
*Career: St Johnstone; East Stirling; Everton December 1901; Blackburn Rovers March 1903; Brentford May 1907; Leeds City May 1908; Brentford cs 1909; Portsmouth November 1909; Leith Athletic; Accrington Stanley March 1912.*
**Appearances:** Football League 99; FA Cup 5; Total 104.
**Goals:** Football League 42; FA Cup 1; Total 43.
Adam Bowman had only appeared in 9 League games for Everton when Blackburn Rovers signed him and put him straight into the first team. He responded with 5 goals in the remaining 7 games of the 1902-03 season. Although he began as a bustling centre-forward with the Rovers, it was as an inside-left that he enjoyed his greatest success with the club. A tricky player with a keen eye for an opening near goal, Bowman was the club's leading goalscorer in seasons 1904-05 and 1905-06. He left Blackburn for Brentford in May 1907 and scored 21 goals in 30 League appearances for the 'Bees' during the 1907-08 season.

### BRACEGIRDLE, Ernest
Winger. 1906-1911.
*5ft 5½in; 10st 4lb.*
*Born: Knutsford, 1886; Died: Knutsford, 1954.*
*Debut: v Woolwich Arsenal (h) 24 November 1906.*
*Career: Knutsford; Northwich Victoria; Blackburn Rovers May 1906; Crewe Alexandra cs 1911; Northwich Victoria cs 1913; Manchester United wartime guest 1915-16; Oldham Athletic wartime guest 1918-19; Altrincham October 1919*

**Appearances:** Football League 60; FA Cup 5; Total 65.
**Goals:** Football League 6; FA Cup 1; Total 7.
Two goals on his debut suggested Ernest Bracegirdle might well fulfil the high expectations that everyone had of him at Ewood Park. Although small in build, he possessed plenty of pace and enjoyed running at defenders with the ball. The fact that he once notched six goals in a game for Knutsford, together with the power of his shooting, suggested that he had an eye for goal. Sadly, Bracegirdle merely flattered to deceive. The arrival of Walter Anthony from Brighton & Hove Albion in February 1908 limited his first-team opportunities and in the summer of 1911 he moved to Crewe Alexandra.

### BRADBURY, John Joe Longstaff
Outside-right. 1897.
*5ft 7½in; 11st.*
*Born: South Bank 1878.*
*Debut: v Derby County (a) 4 September 1897.*
*Career: Stockport County; Lincoln City January 1896; Ashton North End September 1896; Blackburn Rovers May 1897; Ashton North End November 1897; Derby County May 1899; Barnsley June 1900; Bristol City June 1901; New Brompton May 1902; Millwall Athletic May 1904; Carlisle United cs 1906.*
**Appearances:** Football League 2.
Having failed to make an impression at Stockport or Lincoln, Bradbury came to prominence with Aston North End in the Lancashire League. He joined the Rovers in May 1897 and began the 1897-98 season in the first team. Defeats in the opening two fixtures resulted in Bradbury being replaced by Thomas Briercliffe and in November 1897 he was allowed to return to Ashton North End. Although Bradbury was to return to the Football League with short spells at Derby County, Barnsley and Bristol City, he enjoyed his greatest success with New Brompton and Millwall in the Southern League.

### BRADFORD (PARK AVENUE) FC
Formed in 1907 and members of the Football League between 1908 and 1970, the Bradford club was voted out of the League in 1970 and was disbanded in 1974.

**Football League**

|  |  | Home |  | Away |  |
|---|---|---|---|---|---|
| 1914-15 | (Div 1) | D | 2-2 | W | 2-1 |
| 1919-20 | (Div 1) | D | 3-3 | L | 2-5 |
| 1920-21 | (Div 1) | W | 1-0 | D | 1-1 |
| 1936-37 | (Div 2) | D | 1-1 | W | 2-1 |
| 1937-38 | (Div 2) | D | 0-0 | L | 1-7 |
| 1938-39 | (Div 2) | W | 6-4 | W | 4-0 |
| 1948-49 | (Div 2) | L | 2-3 | L | 0-2 |
| 1949-50 | (Div 2) | L | 0-1 | D | 2-2 |

|  | P | W | D | L | F | A |
|---|---|---|---|---|---|---|
| Home | 8 | 2 | 4 | 2 | 15 | 14 |
| Away | 8 | 3 | 2 | 3 | 14 | 19 |
| Total | 16 | 5 | 6 | 5 | 29 | 33 |

### BRADFORD CITY FC
Founded in 1903 and elected to the Second Division of the Football League in the same year. Bradford City and Blackburn Rovers have met in the First, Second and Third Divisions of the Football League since their first League meeting in 1908-09. Blackburn's home record against City has been particularly impressive over the years with the Yorkshiremen only recording one win at Ewood Park in 17 attempts.

**Football League**

|  |  | Home |  | Away |  |
|---|---|---|---|---|---|
| 1908-09 | (Div 1) | D | 1-1 | W | 2-0 |
| 1909-10 | (Div 1) | W | 2-0 | L | 0-2 |
| 1910-11 | (Div 1) | W | 3-0 | L | 0-1 |
| 1911-12 | (Div 1) | W | 3-1 | L | 0-1 |
| 1912-13 | (Div 1) | W | 5-0 | W | 2-0 |
| 1913-14 | (Div 1) | D | 0-0 | W | 2-0 |
| 1914-15 | (Div 1) | W | 2-1 | L | 0-3 |
| 1919-20 | (Div 1) | W | 4-1 | L | 1-3 |
| 1920-21 | (Div 1) | L | 2-3 | W | 4-3 |
| 1921-22 | (Div 1) | W | 3-1 | D | 1-1 |
| 1936-37 | (Div 2) | W | 3-0 | D | 2-2 |
| 1971-72 | (Div 3) | W | 1-0 | W | 2-1 |
| 1985-86 | (Div 2) | W | 3-0 | L | 2-3 |
| 1986-87 | (Div 2) | W | 2-1 | L | 0-2 |
| 1987-88 | (Div 2) | D | 1-1 | L | 1-2 |
| 1988-89 | (Div 2) | W | 2-1 | D | 1-1 |
| 1989-90 | (Div 2) | D | 2-2 | W | 1-0 |

|        | P  | W  | D | L | F  | A  |
|--------|----|----|---|---|----|----|
| Home   | 17 | 12 | 4 | 1 | 39 | 13 |
| Away   | 17 | 6  | 3 | 8 | 21 | 25 |
| Total  | 34 | 18 | 7 | 9 | 60 | 38 |

**FA Cup**

| 1909-10 | (2)  | Away                      | W | 2-1 |
|---------|------|---------------------------|---|-----|
| 1910-11 | (SF) | Bramall Lane, Sheffield L | 0-3 |   |
| 1935-36 | (4)  | Away                      | L | 1-3 |

**Wartime**

|         |           | Home    | Away    |
|---------|-----------|---------|---------|
| 1941-42 | (FLNS-SC) | W   2-0 | L   0-5 |

### BRADFORD, David William
Midfield. 1969-1974.
*5ft 5in; 9st 8lb.*
*Born: Manchester, 22 February 1953.*
*Debut: v Rotherham United (h) 14 August 1971.*
*Career: Blackburn Rovers apprentice November 1969, turning professional in August 1971; Sheffield United July 1974; Peterborough United on loan October 1976 until November 1976; West Bromwich Albion on loan December 1976 until January 1977 before a permanent transfer in February 1977; Detroit Express (USA) March 1978; Washington Diplomats (USA) 1981; Coventry City October 1981; Tulsa Roughnecks (USA) April 1982; Seattle Sounders (USA) May 1983; Tulsa Roughnecks (USA) May 1984; Rossendale United September 1985.*
**Appearances:** Football League 58+6; FA Cup 5; Football League Cup 4; Total 67+6.
**Goals:** Football League 3.

David Bradford was only 18 years old when Ken Furphy selected him and another 18-year-old, Gerry McDonald, to form a midfield partnership at the start of the 1971-72 season. After losing his place after four games he was later brought back to favour to partner the experienced Terry Garbett in midfield. Once he linked up with Garbett he began to produce the quick incisive passing movements which led Furphy to describe him as 'the first million pound footballer'.

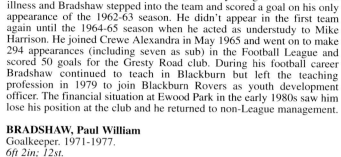

He couldn't quite recapture his earlier form during the next 18 months and following the arrival of Gordon Lee in January 1974, Bradford found himself out of favour with the new management. He was placed on the transfer list at his own request after Lee had made it clear that Bradford would not be part of his future plans.

In July 1974, Bradford followed Terry Garbett and Tony Field to Bramall Lane to link up again with Ken Furphy. The manager who regarded him so highly was able to sign him for a bargain £10,000 fee. Bradford appeared in 60 League matches for the 'Blades' and had a loan spell with Peterborough before signing for West Bromwich Albion, following a loan period at the club, in February 1977. Unable to break into the first team at The Hawthorns he accepted an invitation to link up with Ken Furphy at Detroit Express.

His style of play was well suited to the North American Soccer League and, apart from an abortive attempt to resurrect his League career with Coventry City, Bradford remained in America to finish his playing career. After retiring from football he returned to Blackburn to take over a post office in the Brownhill area of the town.

### BRADSHAW, Alan
Forward. 1960-1965.
*5ft 8in; 10st 8lb.*
*Born: Blackburn, 14 September 1941.*
*Debut: v Wolverhampton Wanderers (a) 1 September 1962.*
*Career: Blackburn Rovers non-contract player January 1960, becoming an amateur in May 1962, before turning professional in March 1964; Crewe Alexandra May 1965; Great Harwood manager April 1976; Blackburn Rovers youth development officer; Padiham manager cs 1982 until September 1982; coaching in Sarawak, Malaysia September 1982; Clitheroe manager.*
**Appearances:** Football League 11.
**Goals:** Football League 2.

Alan Bradshaw was a PE student at Loughborough College when he made his first-team debut with the Rovers. Bobby Craig was stricken with illness and Bradshaw stepped into the team and scored a goal on his only appearance of the 1962-63 season. He didn't appear in the first team again until the 1964-65 season when he acted as understudy to Mike Harrison. He joined Crewe Alexandra in May 1965 and went on to make 294 appearances (including seven as sub) in the Football League and scored 50 goals for the Gresty Road club. During his football career Bradshaw continued to teach in Blackburn but left the teaching profession in 1979 to join Blackburn Rovers as youth development officer. The financial situation at Ewood Park in the early 1980s saw him lose his position at the club and he returned to non-League management.

### BRADSHAW, Paul William
Goalkeeper. 1971-1977.
*6ft 2in; 12st.*
*Born: Altrincham, 28 April 1956.*
*Debut: v Tranmere Rovers (h) 17 February 1974.*
*Career: Altrincham & District schools; Altrincham & Cheshire Boys; Blackburn Rovers associated schoolboy May 1971, becoming an apprentice in August 1971, before turning professional July 1973; Wolverhampton Wanderers September 1977; Vancouver Whitecaps (Canada) August 1984; West Bromwich Albion April 1985; Walsall coach June 1986; Bristol Rovers non-contract player March 1987; Newport County July 1987; West Bromwich Albion September 1988; Peterborough United July 1990; Kettering Town cs 1991.*
*International honours with Blackburn Rovers: England Youth International.*
**Appearances:** Football League 78; FA Cup 4; Football League Cup 5; Total 87

A blond giant of a goalkeeper who got his chance as a 17-year-old at Ewood Park when Roger Jones suffered a serious knee injury in February 1974. Although he had to take a back seat during the Third Division championship season, Bradshaw was promoted to the number-one position following the sale of Jones to Newcastle United in March 1976.

Although tall, Bradshaw was deceptively agile and had a safe pair of hands. He was such an outstanding prospect that he had only played 78 League games when Wolves paid £140,000 to take him to Molineux.

Shortly after arriving at Wolves he earned the first of four England Under-21 caps and went on to appear in 200 League matches for the club. On leaving Wolves he played in the North American Soccer League with Vancouver Whitecaps before returning to England to continue his League career.

### BRADSHAW, William
Left-half. 1903-1920.
*5ft 8in; 10st 10lb.*
*Born: Padiham, Lancashire, 1884 (April quarter).*
*Debut: v Wolverhampton Wanderers (a) 12 September 1903.*
*Career: Padiham; Accrington Stanley; Blackburn Rovers April 1903; Rochdale player-manager April 1920.*
*International honours with Blackburn Rovers: England: 4 caps (1910-19). Football League: 4 appearances (1904-11). Domestic honours with Blackburn Rovers: First Division championship: 1911-12 (36 apps, 3 gls); 1913-14 (27 apps, 3 gls).*
**Appearances:** Football League 386; FA Cup 39; Charity Shield 1; Total 426.
**Goals:** Football League 36; FA Cup 3; Total 39.

Billy Bradshaw began his footballing career in his native Padiham before

joining Accrington Stanley of the Lancashire Combination. Along with his elder brother Jack, he helped Stanley win the Lancashire Combination championship in 1902-03 before joining Blackburn Rovers in April 1903.

Although not the most robust of players, Bradshaw's positional play enabled him to intercept the ball without having to resort to tackling. However, when called upon to win the ball, Bradshaw rarely came out of a tackle second best. His natural athleticism meant that Bradshaw was able to play as a forward or half-back; although it was in the latter position in which he excelled. Apart from his intelligent reading of the game his greatest asset was his ability to pass the ball. His distribution was second to none and he helped to create numerous opportunities for his playing colleagues. A member of the team which won the First Division title twice in the years immediately preceding World War One, Bradshaw was also capped four times for England.

Bradshaw returned to Ewood Park after the war but the intervening years had taken their toll and injuries effectively ended his career at Blackburn. In April 1920 he joined Rochdale as player-manager but, unable to attend training sessions, he was given a free transfer shortly into the 1920-21 season.

## BRANAGAN, James Patrick S.
Right-back. 1979-1987.
*5ft 10in; 11st 7lb.*
*Born: Barton, 3 July 1955.*
*Debut: v Colchester United (h) 27 October 1979.*
*Career: Oldham Athletic associated schoolboy November 1971, turning professional in July 1973; Cape Town City (South Africa) May 1977; Huddersfield Town November 1977; Blackburn Rovers October 1979 (£20,000); Preston North End June 1987; York City September 1987; Chorley 1989-90.*
*Domestic honours with Blackburn Rovers: Full Members' Cup winner: 1987 (sub – didn't play)*
**Appearances:** Football League 290+4; FA Cup 20; Football League Cup 18; Full Members' Cup 5; Total 333+4.
**Goals:** Football League 5.
Perhaps it was no surprise that Jim Branagan should carve out a career as a rugged no-nonsense defender. His father, Ken, had enjoyed a long and successful career with Manchester City and Oldham Athletic as a reliable full-back. Indeed, it was at one of his father's old club's that Jim began his career. However, after failing to make much impression at Boundary Park he tried his luck in South Africa with Cape Town City. On returning to England he joined Huddersfield Town but once again found himself languishing in the second team. In October 1979, Howard Kendall plucked him from obscurity and gave him the right-back berth in what was to become a promotion winning team.

An honest and hard-working defender whose uncompromising approach to the game made him a great favourite at Ewood Park. His height meant he was capable of moving to the centre of defence on occasions whilst his rugged tackling style was utilised in midfield in a number of games. However, it was his full-back partnership with Mick Rathbone for which he is best remembered. Sadly, both were to miss appearing at Wembley in the Full Members' Cup final before leaving the club in the summer of 1987.

## BRANDON, Thomas
Right-back. 1889-1891 & 1893-1900.
*5ft 9½in; 12st 10lb.*
*Born: Kilbirnie, Ayrshire, 26 February 1869.*
*Debut: v Everton (a) 7 September 1889.*
*Career: Clippsons; Johnstone FC cs 1885; Port Glasgow Athletic cs 1886; Renfrew Athletic; St Mirren cs 1887; Blackburn Rovers August 1889; Sheffield Wednesday 1891; Nelson August 1893; Blackburn Rovers December 1893; St Mirren 1900*
*International honours with Blackburn Rovers: Scotland: 1 cap (1896); Football League: 1 appearance (1891).*
*Domestic honours with Blackburn Rovers: FA Cup winner: 1891*
**Appearances:** Football League 216; FA Cup 26; Test Matches 3; Total 245.
**Goals:** Football League 2.
Tom Brandon was a hard-tackling full-back who arrived at Blackburn in August 1889 after an impressive early career in his native Scotland. After winning an FA Cup medal with the Rovers in 1891 he was enticed across the Pennines to join his cousin Harry at Sheffield Wednesday. The Rovers objected at the way in which Brandon was lured to Yorkshire, being promised a public house in the town, and complained to the League. As a result Wednesday were placed on the League's 'black list' for a time.

Brandon captained the Sheffield Wednesday team which gained admission to the Football League in 1892 before becoming unsettled in Yorkshire. He left the League for a short time to play with Nelson before his move back to Blackburn could be completed.

Big and burly, Brandon was not a cultured full-back, but one who used his physical assets to the full. Brandon was the first Blackburn Rovers player to appear in 200 Football League matches for the club. During his later years with the Rovers he was also a popular landlord in the town. In 1900 he returned to Scotland to end his playing career with St Mirren and in 1904 he was reported to be living in Rhode Island, USA.

His son, Thomas, joined the Rovers before World War One and played for the club during the war years. However, he never featured in peacetime football for Blackburn but enjoyed various degrees of success with West Ham United, Hull City, Bradford and Wigan Borough.

## BRAY, John
Right-back. 1953-1965.
*5ft 9in; 11st 8lb.*
*Born: Rishton, 16 March 1937; Died: Rainford, nr Liverpool, 29 September 1992.*
*Debut: v Everton (h) 21 September 1959.*
*Career: Clayton Schoolboys; Bangor Street Youth Club; Blackburn Rovers groundstaff May 1953, turning professional in March 1954; Bury April 1965; Drumcondra; Great Harwood, later becoming their player-manager.*
*Domestic honours with Blackburn Rovers: FA Cup runners-up: 1960.*
**Appearances:** Football League 153; FA Cup 19; Football League Cup 12; Total 184.
**Goals:** Football League 2.

John Bray was a strong, barrel-chested full-back who could play on either flank. His attacking style and no-nonsense approach to the game led to him affectionately being known as 'The Tank'. Bray joined the Blackburn groundstaff as a youngster and signed professional forms in March 1954. During his early days with the club Bray fluctuated between the full-back and half-back position before finally settling down in a full-back berth. Bray's enthusiastic and robust style of play quickly earned him a first-team place following a successful debut in September 1959. Bray appeared in the ill-fated 1960 FA Cup Final and during the early 1960s formed a solid full-back partnership with Keith Newton.

Injuries forced Bray to step down in 1964-65 and enabled younger and quicker men to establish themselves in the first team. In April 1965, Bray joined Bury and made 32 League appearances for the Gigg Lane club before moving to Drumcondra in Ireland. He returned to Blackburn to play non-League football with Great Harwood and later became their player-manager. In 1970-71 he led the club to the first round of the FA Cup for the first and only time in the club's history.

After leaving football Bray became a works foreman in Blackburn and later moved to the Isle of Whithorn in Scotland. Tragically he died in September 1992 whilst visiting Louis Bimpson, a fellow member of the 1960 FA Cup team.

## BRAYSHAW, Walter
Inside-right. 1925-1926.
*5ft 8in; 11st.*
*Debut: v Sunderland (h) 18 April 1925.*
*Career: Mexborough Rovers; Sheffield United May 1919; Exeter City May 1920; Denaby United cs 1921; Blackburn Rovers April 1925; Southend United May 1926; Denaby United January 1928.*
**Appearances:** Football League 9.
**Goals:** Football League 1.
Walter Brayshaw was hailed as an exciting young prospect when he arrived at Ewood Park in April 1925. He made an immediate impact on his debut, scoring the Rovers goal in a 1-1 home draw with Sunderland. The following season saw him begin as the first-choice inside-right but, following defeat in the opening three fixtures, he was axed to make way for Ted Harper. This was the season that Harper created a club record of 43 goals in only 37 League matches and needless to say Brayshaw found his first-team opportunities extremely limited. At the end of the season he left the club to join Southend United.

## BRENNAN, Thomas James
Inside-left. 1933-1935.
*5ft 9in; 10st 9lb.*
*Born: Calderbank, Lanark, 7 February 1911.*
*Debut: v Liverpool (h) 10 March 1934.*
*Career: Longriggend Rob Roy; Brentford March 1928; Gillingham May 1929; Crystal Palace December 1930; Tunbridge Wells Rangers June 1932; Blackburn Rovers November 1933 (£500); Stockport County June 1935.*
**Appearances:** Football League 13.
**Goals:** Football League 1.
Brennan was a talented schemer and dribbler in the traditional Scottish mould. He had won international honours as a schoolboy and earned a

favourable reputation with Longriggend Rob Roy in junior circles in Scotland. He crossed the border as a 17-year-old to join Brentford but moved to Gillingham before being called upon for the senior team. It was with Crystal Palace that Brennan made his Football League debut but after two appearances he drifted out of the League with Tunbridge Wells. He arrived at Ewood Park in November 1933 and played in eight of the last ten games of the season. He began the following campaign as first-choice inside-left but was dropped after three games and made only two further appearances for the club before joining Stockport County in the summer of 1935.

## BRENTFORD FC
Formed in 1889 and founder members of the Third Division South in 1920. Brentford first met Blackburn Rovers in competitive football in 1935-36 during what was to be Blackburn's first relegation season. The clubs last met in the League in the old Third Division, although their paths crossed several times in the 1980s in Cup competitions.

### Football League

|         |         | Home |     | Away |     |
|---------|---------|------|-----|------|-----|
| 1935-36 | (Div 1) | W    | 1-0 | L    | 1-3 |
| 1946-47 | (Div 1) | L    | 0-3 | W    | 3-0 |
| 1948-49 | (Div 2) | W    | 2-1 | W    | 1-0 |
| 1949-50 | (Div 2) | W    | 4-1 | L    | 0-2 |
| 1950-51 | (Div 2) | W    | 3-2 | L    | 2-3 |
| 1951-52 | (Div 2) | W    | 3-0 | D    | 1-1 |
| 1952-53 | (Div 2) | W    | 3-0 | L    | 2-3 |
| 1953-54 | (Div 2) | D    | 2-2 | W    | 4-1 |
| 1972-73 | (Div 3) | W    | 2-1 | L    | 0-4 |
| 1979-80 | (Div 3) | W    | 3-0 | L    | 0-2 |

|       | P  | W  | D | L | F  | A  |
|-------|----|----|---|---|----|----|
| Home  | 10 | 8  | 1 | 1 | 23 | 10 |
| Away  | 10 | 3  | 1 | 6 | 14 | 19 |
| Total | 20 | 11 | 2 | 7 | 37 | 29 |

### FA Cup

| 1988-89 | (5) | Home | L | 0-2 |
|---------|-----|------|---|-----|

### Football League Cup

| 1982-83 | (2) | Away | L | 2-3 |
|---------|-----|------|---|-----|
|         |     | Home | D | 0-0 |
| 1988-89 | (2) | Home | W | 3-1 |
|         |     | Away | L | 3-4 |

## BRENTWOOD FC
An amateur club from Essex who played host to Blackburn Rovers in the sixth round of the 1885-86 FA Cup competition. Two goals from Nat Walton and one from Herbert Fecitt, in front of a crowd of 3,000, sent Rovers into a semi-final clash with the Swifts.

### FA Cup

| 1885-86 | (6) | Away | W | 3-1 |
|---------|-----|------|---|-----|

## BRIBERY
It was in 1903 that the directors of Blackburn Rovers found themselves at the centre of a footballing scandal.

The 1902-03 season saw the Rovers locked in a relegation battle with Bolton Wanderers and Grimsby Town. Fortunately, the appalling start which Bolton made to the season, their first win delayed until 23 games into the campaign, meant that even with a late revival they were unable to escape the bottom spot. Thus as the final weeks of the season dawned it was a straight fight between the Rovers and Grimsby Town as to who would accompany the 'Trotters' into the Second Division. Following a 4-2 win over the depressed Wanderers the Rovers claimed five points from their remaining four games. It proved sufficient to lift them into 16th position and condemn Grimsby Town to an early return to a Second Division they had only left in 1901.

Three of the points which the Rovers gained came from the most unlikely of sources. On 10 April they visited a Bury team who had just beaten Sheffield Wednesday, the champions-to-be, and who were destined to go on and capture the FA Cup with a 6-0 win over Derby County. Three days later, with just a point separating the Rovers from Grimsby, Blackburn visited Goodison Park and gained an unexpected 3-0 win. Rovers safety was ensured with a 3-1 win over Newcastle the following Saturday.

The fact that three points had come from neighbouring clubs merely fuelled speculation that Grimsby Town had been the victim of a conspiracy between the Lancashire clubs. It was claimed that the Lancashire clubs had got together to keep Blackburn in the First Division at the expense of a club on the other side of the country. Feelings were so

strong that Grimsby protested to the Football League over the results against Bury and Everton.

An official inquiry was held and the following statement was issued:
'We are of the opinion that Mr J Walmsley, the secretary of Blackburn Rovers FC, endeavoured to arrange that Rovers should be allowed to win the match (against Everton). We are satisfied that, so far as Everton officials were concerned, such efforts were not successful. There was no evidence to suggest that their players had been approached, so no action will be taken against Everton.'

Nothing was said about the Bury game and as a result of the finding of the inquiry Walmsley was suspended *sine die* from future football management. Everton were also censured for not reporting the matter but there was no evidence to be found against any other official at Ewood Park. Thus, although Grimsby might have felt the verdict to be a moral victory, it was the Rovers who remained in the top flight and Grimsby Town who descended into the Second Division.

## BRIERCLIFFE, Thomas
Outside-right. 1897-1900.
*Debut: v Stoke (a) 18 September 1897.*
*Career: St Luke's Juniors; Wheelton; Bacup; Clitheroe; Blackburn Rovers May 1897; Stalybridge Rovers cs 1900, Woolwich Arsenal September 1901; Plymouth Argyle 1905; Brentford cs 1907; Darwen 1907.*
**Appearances:** Football League 56; Test Matches 1; FA Cup 4; Total 61.
**Goals:** Football League 10.
Known as 'Chip', Briercliffe was a strong and pacey winger who was one of the most effective wide players of his day. The Rovers were so keen to sign him that they brought him to the club whilst he was still suffering from a broken collar-bone. Briercliffe filled the gap on the right wing left by Jamie Haydock but on occasions also played as an inside-right. During his spell in London he was a member of the Arsenal team that won promotion to the First Division – contributing 18 goals from the outside-right position.

## BRIGGS, Thomas Henry
Centre-forward. 1952-1958.
*6ft; 12st 7lb.*
*Born: Chesterfield, 27 November 1923; Died: Grimsby, 10 February 1984.*
*Debut: v Bury (a) 29 November 1952.*
*Career: Doncaster junior football; Royal Navy football; Plymouth Argyle amateur November 1945, turning professional in March 1946; Grimsby Town June 1947; Coventry City January 1951 (£19,550); Birmingham City September 1951; Blackburn Rovers November 1952 (£15,000); Grimsby Town March 1958 (£2,000); Glentoran player-manager March 1959 until June 1961.*
**Appearances:** Football League 194; FA Cup 10; Total 204.
**Goals:** Football League 140; FA Cup 3; Total 143.

In terms of goals per game, Tommy Briggs remains the most prolific goalscorer in the club's modern history. A centre-forward in the traditional mould, Briggs relied on others to create the chances which he converted with great consistency. He had first shown his proficiency in front of goal at Grimsby Town where 78 goals in 116 League games had earned him an England 'B' cap in 1950. In 1949-50, he not only topped the goalscorers at Grimsby, but his 36 goals made him the leading marksman in the Football League. At Coventry City he scored 7 goals in 11 games but never really settled and moved to Birmingham City in a deal which involved a fee and a player exchange. At St Andrew's, Briggs scored 22 goals in 50 League appearances before

Rovers goalkeeper John Butcher foils Brighton's Gerry Ryan at the Goldstone Ground in April 1979.

moving to Ewood Park with Bill Smith in November 1952. Surrounded by players who could create the type of chances which were his lifeblood, Briggs became a hugely popular figure with the supporters.

He topped 30 goals in four successive seasons whilst missing only three League games during that time. On 5 February 1955 he created a new club record when he scored seven goals in succession in the 8-3 win over Bristol Rovers at Ewood Park. His goals took the club to the brink of the First Division on four occasions, but when promotion was finally achieved Briggs had already left the club. Although he began the 1957-58 season in the first team his form was not what it had been. Doubts about his fitness and a return of three goals from 12 games suggested that his Ewood career was drawing to a close. In March 1958 he was allowed to return to Grimsby Town for a small fee and a year later he moved to Ireland to become player-manager of Glentoran. Briggs remained in Ireland for almost two seasons before returning to live and work in Grimsby.

## Full Career Record in England.

|  | League | | FA Cup | | Total | |
|---|---|---|---|---|---|---|
|  | App | Gls | Apps | Gls | Apps | Gls |
| Plymouth Argyle | | | | | | |
| 1946-47 | 0 | 0 | 0 | 0 | 0 | 0 |
| Grimsby Town | | | | | | |
| 1947-48 | 24 | 5 | 1 | 0 | 25 | 5 |
| 1948-49 | 34 | 26 | 2 | 1 | 36 | 27 |
| 1949-50 | 41 | 36 | 2 | 4 | 43 | 40 |
| 1950-51 | 17 | 11 | 0 | 0 | 17 | 11 |
| Coventry City | | | | | | |
| 1950-51 | 7 | 3 | 0 | 0 | 7 | 3 |
| 1951-52 | 4 | 4 | 0 | 0 | 4 | 4 |
| Birmingham City | | | | | | |
| 1951-52 | 33 | 18 | 2 | 1 | 35 | 19 |
| 1952-53 | 17 | 4 | 0 | 0 | 17 | 4 |
| Blackburn Rovers | | | | | | |
| 1952-53 | 17 | 9 | 1 | 0 | 18 | 9 |
| 1953-54 | 41 | 32 | 3 | 1 | 44 | 33 |
| 1954-55 | 41 | 33 | 1 | 0 | 42 | 33 |
| 1955-56 | 41 | 31 | 4 | 2 | 45 | 33 |
| 1956-57 | 42 | 32 | 1 | 0 | 43 | 32 |
| 1957-58 | 12 | 3 | 0 | 0 | 12 | 3 |
| Grimsby Town | | | | | | |
| 1957-58 | 9 | 5 | 0 | 0 | 9 | 5 |
| 1958-59 | 10 | 4 | 0 | 0 | 10 | 4 |
| Total | 390 | 256 | 17 | 9 | 407 | 265 |

## BRIGHTON & HOVE ALBION FC

Founded in 1900 as Brighton & Hove Rangers, the club changed its name to Brighton & Hove Albion in 1901. Members of the Southern League from 1902 to 1920, Brighton & Hove Albion were founder members of the Third Division South in 1920-21. Although the clubs had crossed paths in the two national Cup competitions it was another 51 years before Brighton and Blackburn met in the Football League. Curiously, Blackburn have been involved in three multi-transfer deals with Brighton over the years. In February 1908 the Rovers signed Walter Anthony, Richard Wombwell and Joseph Lumley from Brighton whilst in August 1972 Dave Turner and Kit Napier arrived together from the Goldstone Ground. In May 1974, Gordon Lee brought Pat Hilton and Ken Beamish to Ewood Park from Brighton.

## Football League

|  |  | Home | | Away | |
|---|---|---|---|---|---|
| 1971-72 | (Div 3) | D | 2-2 | L | 0-3 |
| 1973-74 | (Div 3) | W | 3-1 | L | 0-3 |
| 1974-75 | (Div 3) | W | 1-0 | W | 1-0 |
| 1977-78 | (Div 2) | L | 0-1 | D | 2-2 |
| 1978-79 | (Div 2) | D | 1-1 | L | 1-2 |
| 1983-84 | (Div 2) | D | 2-2 | D | 1-1 |
| 1984-85 | (Div 2) | W | 2-0 | L | 1-3 |
| 1985-86 | (Div 2) | L | 1-4 | L | 1-3 |
| 1986-87 | (Div 2) | D | 1-1 | W | 2-0 |

| | | | | |
|---|---|---|---|---|
| 1988-89 | (Div 2) | W | 2-1 | L | 0-3 |
| 1989-90 | (Div 2) | D | 1-1 | W | 2-1 |
| 1990-91 | (Div 2) | L | 1-2 | L | 0-1 |
| 1991-92 | (Div 2) | W | 1-0 | W | 3-0 |

| | P | W | D | L | F | A |
|---|---|---|---|---|---|---|
| Home | 13 | 5 | 5 | 3 | 18 | 16 |
| Away | 13 | 4 | 2 | 7 | 14 | 22 |
| Total | 26 | 9 | 7 | 10 | 32 | 38 |

**FA Cup**

| | | | | |
|---|---|---|---|---|
| 1961-62 | (3) | Away | W | 3-0 |

**Football League Cup**

| | | | | |
|---|---|---|---|---|
| 1967-68 | (2) | Home | W | 3-1 |

## BRISTOL CITY FC

Founded in 1894 as Bristol South End, the club changed its title to Bristol City in 1897 and joined the Second Division of the Football League in 1901. Blackburn and Bristol City met in the First Division in the years before World War One and on 13 April 1908, Billy Davies scored all four goals for Blackburn in a 4-1 win at Ashton Gate. Bristol City were relegated from the First Division at the end of the 1910-11 season and since that time all the League meetings between the clubs have taken place in the Second Division.

**Football League**

| | | | Home | | Away | |
|---|---|---|---|---|---|---|
| 1906-07 | (Div 1) | L | 0-1 | L | 0-3 |
| 1907-08 | (Div 1) | W | 4-1 | D | 2-2 |
| 1908-09 | (Div 1) | D | 1-1 | W | 4-1 |
| 1909-10 | (Div 1) | W | 5-2 | D | 2-2 |
| 1910-11 | (Div 1) | W | 2-0 | L | 0-1 |
| 1955-56 | (Div 2) | L | 4-6 | L | 0-2 |
| 1956-57 | (Div 2) | W | 3-1 | L | 0-3 |
| 1957-58 | (Div 2) | W | 5-0 | D | 0-0 |
| 1966-67 | (Div 2) | W | 1-0 | D | 2-2 |
| 1967-68 | (Div 2) | W | 2-0 | D | 0-0 |
| 1968-69 | (Div 2) | L | 1-3 | L | 0-1 |
| 1969-70 | (Div 2) | D | 3-3 | L | 0-4 |
| 1970-71 | (Div 2) | D | 2-2 | D | 1-1 |
| 1975-76 | (Div 2) | L | 1-2 | L | 0-1 |
| 1980-81 | (Div 2) | W | 1-0 | L | 0-2 |
| 1990-91 | (Div 2) | L | 0-1 | L | 2-4 |
| 1991-92 | (Div 2) | W | 4-0 | L | 0-1 |

| | P | W | D | L | F | A |
|---|---|---|---|---|---|---|
| Home | 17 | 9 | 3 | 5 | 39 | 23 |
| Away | 17 | 1 | 6 | 10 | 13 | 30 |
| Total | 34 | 10 | 9 | 15 | 52 | 53 |

**FA Cup**

| | | | | |
|---|---|---|---|---|
| 1950-51 | (3) | Away | L | 1-2 |

## BRISTOL ROVERS FC

Founded in 1883 as Black Arabs FC, the club changed its name to Eastville Rovers in 1884. In 1897 the club became known as Bristol Eastville Rovers and in 1898 the 'Eastville' was dropped from the club's name. The club was among the original members of the Third Division of the Football League in 1920 but didn't meet Blackburn Rovers in the League until the 1953-54 season. It was against Bristol Rovers on 5 February 1955 that Tommy Briggs created a new goalscoring record by netting seven goals in an 8-3 win at Ewood Park.

**Football League**

| | | | Home | | Away | |
|---|---|---|---|---|---|---|
| 1953-54 | (Div 2) | D | 1-1 | W | 2-1 |
| 1954-55 | (Div 2) | W | 8-3 | L | 1-2 |
| 1955-56 | (Div 2) | W | 2-0 | L | 0-1 |
| 1956-57 | (Div 2) | W | 2-0 | W | 1-0 |
| 1957-58 | (Div 2) | W | 2-0 | L | 0-4 |
| 1971-72 | (Div 3) | L | 1-2 | L | 0-3 |
| 1972-73 | (Div 3) | D | 0-0 | L | 0-3 |
| 1973-74 | (Div 3) | L | 0-2 | L | 0-3 |
| 1975-76 | (Div 2) | L | 1-2 | D | 1-1 |
| 1976-77 | (Div 2) | D | 0-0 | D | 0-0 |
| 1977-78 | (Div 2) | L | 0-1 | L | 1-4 |
| 1978-79 | (Div 2) | L | 0-2 | L | 1-4 |
| 1989-81 | (Div 2) | W | 2-0 | W | 1-0 |
| 1990-91 | (Div 2) | D | 2-2 | W | 2-1 |
| 1991-92 | (Div 2) | W | 3-0 | L | 0-3 |

| | P | W | D | L | F | A |
|---|---|---|---|---|---|---|
| Home | 15 | 6 | 4 | 5 | 24 | 15 |
| Away | 15 | 4 | 2 | 9 | 10 | 30 |
| Total | 30 | 10 | 6 | 14 | 34 | 45 |

**FA Cup**

| | | | | |
|---|---|---|---|---|
| 1930-31 | (4) | Home | W | 5-1 |
| 1953-54 | (3) | Away | W | 1-0 |
| 1974-75 | (3) | Home | L | 1-2 |

**Football League Cup**

| | | | | |
|---|---|---|---|---|
| 1961-62 | (2) | Away | D | 1-1 |
| | (R) | Home | W | 4-0 |

## BRITT, Martin Charles

Centre-forward. 1966-67.
*5ft 10in; 12st 4lb.*
*Born: Leigh-on-Sea, 17 January 1946.*
*Debut: v Leeds United (h) 19 March 1966.*
*Career: West Ham United apprentice July 1961, turning professional in January 1963; Blackburn Rovers March 1966 (£16,000) to June 1967.*

**Appearances:** Football League 8; Football League Cup 1; Total 9.
It came as something of a surprise when Blackburn Rovers signed this little-known but promising reserve centre-forward from West Ham United. Tall and strong, Britt had played for London Schoolboys and had also had international trials at that level. He had progressed through the junior ranks at West Ham and had actually made his first-team debut for the 'Hammers' against the Rovers in May 1963. It was during that season that Britt was capped three times for the England Youth team.

At Ewood Park he was thrust straight into a side that was struggling at the foot of the table but made little impact on his debut when he was up against Jack Charlton, the England centre-half. Britt was dropped after three games and although he was quickly recalled he ended the season out of the first team.

He began the 1966-67 campaign in the Central League side and scored 12 goals in 12 games; but his solitary senior appearance was not a success. In December 1966, Britt underwent tests on a knee injury that had caused him problems since the opening Central League fixture. Tragically the injury proved a serious one and just before Christmas he was told the heartbreaking news that he would not play again.

## BRITTON, Francis

Left-half. 1930-1934.
*5ft 8in; 10st 3lb.*
*Born: Bristol, 1910 (April quarter).*
*Debut: v Manchester City (a) 3 April 1931.*
*Career: Bristol St George; Bristol Rovers amateur September 1927; Blackburn Rovers June 1930; Oldham Athletic June 1934; Accrington Stanley February 1935; Reading one month's trial 23 August 1935; Aldershot October 1935; Worcester City March 1936; Hereford United August 1936; Cradley Heath; Stourbridge; Evesham Town.*
**Appearances:** Football League 45; FA Cup 3; Total 48.
**Goals:** Football League 8; FA Cup 1; Total 9.
Frank Britton had to live in the shadow of a more famous brother throughout his footballing life. Cliff Britton, like his younger brother Frank, began his professional career with Bristol Rovers. However, the brothers went their separate ways; Cliff to Everton and nine England caps, Frank to Ewood Park and a battle for first-team football. Frank Britton was a stocky player whose strengths were his determination to succeed and a willingness to play anywhere. His favoured position was left-half, but he also turned out at inside-left and centre-forward. He had a short but unsuccessful spell with Oldham before returning to East Lancashire to finish the 1934-35 campaign with Accrington Stanley. Despite scoring nine goals in 11 games for Stanley he returned south in the summer of 1935.

## BROOKS, Ernest William

Outside-right. 1920-1921.
*5ft 6in; 10st 7lb.*

*Born: Brierley Hill, 1894 (April quarter).*
*Debut: v Bradford (h) 24 January 1920.*
*Career: Birmingham League Football; Blackburn Rovers January 1920; Wolverhampton Wanderers May 1921; Brierley Hill Alliance to July 1925.*
**Appearances:** Football League 3.
The brother of Sammy Brooks, the Wolverhampton Wanderers winger, Ernest Brooks was signed from Birmingham League football midway through the 1919-20 campaign. He was one of nine players who were used in the outside-right position during that season but, although a hard worker, lost his place through injury after only three matches. He didn't appear in the first team again and in May 1921 he joined his brother at Wolves, but failed to make the first team at Molineux.

**BROTHERSTON, Noel**
Winger/Midfield. 1977-1987.
*5ft 7in; 11st 4lb.*
*Born: Belfast, 18 November 1956.*
*Debut: v Notts county (a) 20 August 1977.*
*Career: North Down Schools; Tottenham Hotspur apprentice 1972, turning professional in April 1974; Blackburn Rovers July 1977; Bury June 1987; Scarborough on loan October 1988; Motola (Sweden) on loan 1989; Chorley cs 1990.*
*International honours with Blackburn Rovers: Northern Ireland: 27 caps (1980-85); Northern Ireland Under-21: 1 cap (1978).*
**Appearances:** Football League 307+10; FA Cup 24+1; Football League Cup 22; Full Members' Cup 2+1; Total 355+12.
**Goals:** Football League 40; FA Cup 4; Football League Cup 2; Full Members' Cup 1; Total 47.
This talented Irishman was snapped up by Jim Smith on a free transfer in July, 1977. Brotherston had progressed through the junior ranks at White Hart Lane before making his debut for Tottenham in 1976.

Although the prematurely balding Brotherston made only one appearance for Spurs, he proved a revelation in his first season at Ewood Park. Despite playing as a winger he finished his first campaign with Blackburn as top scorer with 11 goals and established a reputation as one of the trickiest wingers outside of the top flight.

Brotherston was a player who relied on skill and trickery rather than outright pace to beat an opponent. He was also capable of scoring spectacular goals from long range as well as being a goal poacher in the six-yard box.

Capped 27 times for Northern Ireland, he appeared in the successful Irish team that won through to the 1982 World Cup finals in Spain. Unfortunately, the emergence of Norman Whiteside in the Northern Ireland team meant that Brotherston's appearances in Spain were restricted to that of substitute.

The latter part of his time at Ewood Park was plagued by injuries and a loss of form. As a result, Brotherston was no longer a regular member of the side when the club reached the Full Members' Cup Final in 1987.

Don Mackay released Brotherston at the end of the 1986-87 season and the winger joined Third Division Bury. He lost his first-team place towards the end of his first season at Gigg Lane and the following campaign saw him loaned to Scarborough. He moved to Sweden in the spring of 1989 to play for Motola, a First Division Club, on loan. Brotherston joined Chorley at the start of the 1990-91 season but only appeared in one game for the club.

**BROWN, Charles**
Right-back. 1898-1899.
*Debut: v Bury (a) 14 February 1899.*
*Career: Mossend Swifts; Leith Athletic April 1895; Blackburn Rovers June 1898; Mossend Swifts May 1899; Leith Athletic September 1901.*
**Appearances:** Football League 1.
A right-back from Scottish junior football who had the misfortune to arrive at Ewood Park as Tom Brandon and Bob Crompton were about to form a new full-back partnership. Although he deputised for Brandon on one occasion it was clear his opportunities were going to be limited and in the summer of 1899 he returned to Scottish junior circles.

**BROWN, James**

Centre-forward. 1879-1889.
*5ft 5in.*
*Born: Blackburn, 31 July 1862; Died: Oldham, 4 July 1922.*
*Debut: v Tyne Association (h) 1 November 1879 (FAC)*
*Career: Mintholme College; Blackburn Rovers 1879*
*International honours with Blackburn Rovers: England: 5 caps (1881-85).*
*Domestic honours with Blackburn Rovers: FA Cup winner: 1884; 1885; 1886; FA Cup runners-up: 1882.*
**Appearances:** Football League 4; FA Cup 32; Total 36.
**Goals:** FA Cup 29.
At 5ft 5in and weighing less than 10st, Jimmy Brown was hardly the build of a traditional centre-forward. However, in ten years with the club he proved to be one of the greatest goalscorers to wear the famous 'Blue & White'.

Brown joined the club after leaving Mintholme College and was quickly promoted to the first team. In an era when physical strength often dominated, Brown's delicate touch and devastating place were capable of destroying the best of defences.

A solicitor's clerk by profession, Brown became a firm favourite with the Blackburn public and his shrewd tactical brain made him an obvious candidate for the captaincy.

Brown led the side to three FA Cup triumphs in the 1880s and was capped on five occasions by England. However, following the third FA Cup victory in 1886, Brown bowed out of the Blackburn team.

He returned to the first team during the inaugural season of the Football League in 1888-89. Sadly, Brown was a mere shadow of the player he had been and, although only in his late 20s, Brown retired from the game at the end of the season.

**BROWN, Richard Anthony**
Right-back. 1990-
*5ft 10½in; 12st 12lb.*
*Born: Nottingham, 13 January 1967.*
*Debut: v Port Vale (h) 11 September 1991.*
*Career: Nottingham Forest associated schoolboy June 1981; Derby County; Ilkeston Town; Sheffield Wednesday December 1984; Ilkeston Town July 1986; Grantham Town January 1987; Boston United July 1987; Kettering Town July 1988 (£500); Blackburn Rovers September 1990 (£15,000); Maidstone United on loan February 1991 until March 1991.*
**Appearances:** Premier League 2; Football League 24+2; FA Cup 2; Football League Cup 1+1; Full Members' Cup 1; Total 30+3.
Richard Brown turned professional with Sheffield Wednesday in December 1984 but failed to make the grade at Hillsborough. He was given the chance to revive his League career at Ewood Park following a period in non-League football. Although Don Mackay paid a fee in the region of £15,000 to bring Brown to Blackburn, the versatile defender had to wait 12 months before getting his chance in the first team.

Brown made his first-team debut under the caretaker managership of Tony Parkes in September 1991. He was recalled by Kenny Dalglish and remained in the team for four months, as the Rovers headed the Second Division table, before again losing his place. Although he was brought back for the four vital end of season matches which took the Rovers into the Play-offs, Brown was left out of the Play-off matches themselves.

Captain of the Central League team during 1992-93, Brown found his first-team opportunities limited as Kenny Dalglish assembled a squad packed with big money signings.

**BRUTON, John**
Outside-right. 1929-1939.
Manager. 1947-1948.
*5ft 8in; 10st.*
*Born: Westhoughton, nr Bolton, 21 November 1903; Died: Bournemouth, 13 March 1986.*
*Debut: v Leeds United (h) 7 December 1929.*
*Career: Westhoughton Sunday School; Hindley Green; Wigan Borough amateur June 1922; Bolton Wanderers amateur December 1923; Horwich RMI 1924-25; Burnley March 1925 (£125); Blackburn Rovers December 1929 (£6,500). Retired during World War Two and became assistant secretary. Blackburn Rovers assistant manager September 1947, becoming manager in December 1947 until May 1948; Bournemouth & Boscombe manager*

*March 1950 to March 1956; later part-time scout and coach for Portsmouth and Bournemouth. Blackburn Rovers scout in August 1961. International honours with Blackburn Rovers: Football League: 1 appearance (1934).*
*Domestic honours with Blackburn Rovers: Second Division championship: 1938-39 (1 app)*
**Appearances:** Football League 324; FA Cup 20; Total 344.
**Goals:** Football League 108; FA Cup 7; Total 115.
Blackburn Rovers paid a club record £6,500 to bring Jack Bruton to Ewood Park from neighbouring Burnley in December 1929. Bruton, a former miner, was a supreme athlete who not only possessed electrifying pace, but who was also a skilful schemer and consistent goalscorer. During his time at Burnley he was capped on three occasions for England and scored 42 goals in 167 League appearances for the Turf Moor club.

At Blackburn he proved remarkably consistent, missing only one League game in four seasons between 1931 and 1935. He was awarded a benefit at Blackburn in 1935 and remained a regular in the first team until the 1937-38 season. He made one appearance during the Second Division championship winning season of 1938-39 before becoming a member of the backroom team at Ewood Park.

After spells as assistant trainer and assistant secretary he was unexpectedly thrust into the manager's chair when Will Scott succumbed to illness early in September 1947. When Scott returned at the end of the month Bruton was appointed his assistant and within weeks of this appointment he was short-listed for the vacant manager's job at Manchester City. However, with a question mark over Scott's health, Burton decided to remain loyal to the club and withdrew his name from the Maine Road short-list.

When Scott tendered his resignation in December 1947, Bruton stepped up and was given the task of avoiding relegation to the Second Division. Unfortunately, one win in the last ten games sealed Rovers' fate. However, the directors remained loyal to Bruton and he quickly took steps to try to revive the club's flagging fortunes. In a bid to put more punch into the attack, Bruton signed Dennis Westcott from Wolves and brought Jackie Wharton from Preston to supply the crosses for his new centre-forward. In defence he had unearthed an exciting prospect in the shape of Bill Eckersley.

Success, however, proved as elusive as ever and Rovers only managed 14th place in the Second Division. In May 1949 he was summoned to a meeting with the directors and was informed that they wanted a change of direction. As a result both Bruton and his first-team trainer, Horace Cope, were released by the club.

The parting of the ways was a somewhat bitter one with Bruton claiming that he had to submit his team selection to the board who then had the power to alter it if they so desired. He also claimed that he did not have full control over the buying and selling of players. On ending his 20-year association with the club he said, "My earnest wish is that the next manager will receive more co-operation".

Bruton returned to management in 1950 with Bournemouth & Boscombe Athletic and after leaving the club in 1956 he had spells as a scout with Portsmouth, Bournemouth and Blackburn Rovers.

**BRUTON, Leslie Hector Ronald**
Centre-forward. 1929-1932.
*5ft 10in; 11st 7lb.*
*Born: Coventry, 1 April 1903; Died: Coventry, 2 April 1989.*
*Career: Foleshill; Peterborough & Fletton United ; Southampton November 1922 (£15); Peterborough & Fletton United cs 1926; Raith Rovers November 1928; Blackburn Rovers May 1929 (£295); Liverpool February 1932; Leamington Town July 1933. Later on Coventry City's training staff.*
**Appearances:** Football League 38; FA Cup 4; Total 42.
**Goals:** Football League 23; FA Cup 5; Total 28.
A breathtaking 31 goals in 27 appearances for Raith Rovers was enough to persuade Blackburn Rovers to bring Leslie Bruton back to England after his brief adventure in Scottish football. Bruton could play in any of the forward positions and his robust approach earned him the nickname of the 'human tank'. Although he maintained a highly respectable goalscoring record whilst at Blackburn he failed to make the sort of impact that had been expected. Although capable of cultured play and, given the right service, a dangerous marksman, his lack of pace proved a major handicap in the top flight.

**BRYANT, Clifford Samuel A.**
Half-back. 1932-1936.
*5ft 9in; 11st.*
*Born: Bristol, 1913 (July quarter).*
*Debut: v Newcastle United (a) 22 April 1933.*
*Career: Bristol Rovers amateur October 1930, turning professional in May 1931; Blackburn Rovers August 1932; Wrexham May 1936 to cs 1937.*

**Appearances:** Football League 4; FA Cup 1; Total 5.
A former England Schoolboy international who was described by contemporaries as being cultured in his play without being showy. Although he never let anyone down on his rare first-team outings he was denied the opportunity of further appearances because of the wealth of half-back talent that was available at the time. He moved to Wrexham in May 1936 but was restricted to eight League appearances during his one season at the Racecourse Ground.

**BRYANT, William**
Outside-right. 1900-1902.
*5ft 7in; 12st.*
*Born: Rotherham, 1874.*
*Debut: v Liverpool (a) 1 September 1900.*
*Career: Rotherham Town August 1894; Newton Heath April 1896; Blackburn Rovers cs 1900.*
**Appearances:** Football League 25.
**Goals:** Football League 8.
Bryant was a fast and tricky winger who was unfortunate in having Arnold Whittaker and Fred Blackburn as rivals for the wide positions. Unable to dislodge either man from the first team Bryant was given the opportunity to play in the inside positions and was even tried in the half-back line. Although he scored 6 goals in 15 appearances during the 1900-01 season, Bryant failed to establish himself away from his favoured outside-right position.

**BURGIN, Andrew**
Full-back/Midfield. 1974-1977.
*5ft 8½in; 9st 8lb.*
*Born: Sheffield, 6 March 1947.*
*Debut: Brighton & Hove Albion (h) 7 September 1974.*
*Career: Sheffield Wednesday apprentice August 1962, turning professional in March 1964; Rotherham United August 1967; Detroit Cougars (USA) April 1968; Halifax Town on loan December 1968 until March 1969 before signing permanently in March 1969; Blackburn Rovers September 1974 until January 1977.*
*Domestic honours with Blackburn Rovers: Third Division championship: 1974-75 (40 apps, 1 gl).*
**Appearances:** Football League 45; FA Cup 3; Football League Cup 2; Total 50.
**Goals:** Football League 1.
Problems with the left-back position prompted Gordon Lee to turn to Halifax Town's long-serving Andy Burgin in September 1974. Although Burgin had started his career at Hillsborough, he had made only one League appearance for Sheffield Wednesday before moving to Rotherham United. At Millmoor his career again appeared to stall and after only nine League appearances he moved to the Shay. At Halifax he quickly established himself at right-back and went on to make 243 League appearances for the Yorkshire club. At first Burgin played at right-back at Ewood while Mick Heaton switched to the left. However, as Heaton seemed ill at ease on the left, Burgin was switched before being moved into midfield for a short time. During the latter part of the 1974-75 Third Division title campaign, Burgin performed with great consistency in the left-back spot and seemed destined to make the position his own for some time. Unfortunately, a freak accident in September 1975 ended his playing career. In the game at Southampton, Burgin collided with Mike Hickman and received a leg injury that was to force his premature retirement from professional football.

**BURKE, Marshall**
Midfield. 1980-1982.
*5ft 7in; 9st 11lb.*
*Born: Glasgow, 26 March 1959.*
*Debut: v West Ham United (h) 13 December 1980 (sub).*
*Career: Burnley March 1977; Leeds United May 1980; Blackburn Rovers December 1980; Lincoln City October 1982; Cardiff City on loan December 1983; Scarborough; Tranmere Rovers September 1984; Scarborough; Northwich Victoria; Colne Dynamos August 1986; Blackburn Rovers; Morecambe; Colne Dynamos.*
**Appearances:** Football League 34+5; FA Cup 1; Football League Cup 3; Total 38+5.
**Goals:** Football League 7; FA Cup 1; Total 8.
A hard-working midfield player who is one of a select band of players to have appeared with both Blackburn Rovers and Burnley. Burke, a former Scottish Schoolboy and Youth international, was a product of the youth policy at Turf Moor and made 24 League appearances (including two as sub) for the Clarets before moving across the Pennines to Elland Road. Burke had yet to make his first-team debut at Leeds when Howard Kendall added him to his promotion chasing squad in December 1980. Considering the threadbare nature of the Ewood squad it proved to be a useful acquisition and the former Turf Moor man retained a first-team

A great header by Mike Harrison puts Rovers two goals in front against Burnley at Turf Moor in October 1965 and there is nothing that Burnley defender John Angus can do about it.

place for almost 12 months. Burke went on to appear in 50 League games for Lincoln City before dropping out for the Football League. He tried unsuccessfully to resurrect his career with Tranmere Rovers before returning to Scarborough. After a short spell with Northwich Victoria he returned to Lancashire to sign for the ambitious Colne Dynamos in August 1986. He experienced mixed fortunes during his first season at Colne and spent his time playing for the Dynamos Reserve side and Blackburn Rovers Reserves. He played with Morecambe for a time before returning to Colne to appear in the 1987 FA Vase Final, coming off the bench to help defeat Emley at Wembley in extra-time.

## BURNLEY FC

Founded in 1881 as Burnley Rovers, the club dropped the title 'Rovers' in 1882 and became one of the original members of the Football League in 1888. In the early years of Blackburn Rovers it was Darwen who generated the most hostility amongst Blackburn supporters but since the formation of the Football League Burnley have become accepted as the traditional 'enemy'. This rivalry remains as intense today as it ever did despite the fact that the teams have only met on eight occasions in the Football League since the mid-1960s.

There have of course been a number of memorable clashes between the old foes and Burnley remain the only club in the Football League whom the Rovers have defeated 7-1 both home and away. Another convincing victory for the Rovers occurred on 9 January 1929 when the Clarets crashed 8-3 at Ewood Park. The meeting in the sixth round of the FA Cup in March 1960 produced two titanic battles. The first clash at Turf Moor saw the Rovers coming from 3-1 down to snatch a dramatic late equaliser in front of 51,501 spectators. A crowd of 53,839 watched the Rovers win the replay 2-0 to earn a place in the semi-finals.

However, not all the meetings between the clubs have gone in favour of the men from Ewood Park. Burnley proved triumphant in both of the Test Matches played in April 1898 and the Rovers would have been consigned to the Second Division for the first time in their history but for the intervention of their neighbours from Turf Moor. It was Burnley who successfully proposed that the First Division should be enlarged and that relegated Rovers and Newcastle United should retain their places with the elite.

The meetings between the two clubs have also produced their lighter moments. On 22 February 1890 the Rovers won 2-1 at Burnley when the

home side felt aggrieved that the referee had disallowed a goal which might have earned them a point. The Clarets were none too pleased to discover that the referee was in fact the brother of the Rovers goalkeeper. However, the snowstorm incident involving Herbie Arthur probably remains the most amusing moment between the two clubs.

## Football League

| | | Home | | Away | |
|---|---|---|---|---|---|
| 1888-89 | (FL) | W | 4-2 | W | 7-1 |
| 1889-90 | (FL) | W | 7-1 | W | 2-1 |
| 1890-91 | (FL) | W | 5-2 | W | 6-1 |
| 1891-92 | (FL) | D | 3-3 | L | 0-3 |
| 1892-93 | (Div 1) | W | 2-0 | D | 0-0 |
| 1893-94 | (Div 1) | W | 3-2 | L | 0-1 |
| 1894-95 | (Div 1) | W | 1-0 | L | 1-2 |
| 1895-96 | (Div 1) | W | 1-0 | L | 0-6 |
| 1896-97 | (Div 1) | W | 3-2 | W | 1-0 |
| 1898-99 | (Div 1) | L | 0-2 | L | 0-2 |
| 1899-1900 | (Div 1) | W | 2-0 | L | 0-1 |
| 1913-14 | (Div 1) | D | 0-0 | W | 2-1 |
| 1914-15 | (Div 1) | W | 6-0 | L | 2-3 |
| 1919-20 | (Div 1) | L | 2-3 | L | 1-3 |
| 1920-21 | (Div 1) | L | 1-3 | L | 1-4 |
| 1921-22 | (Div 1) | W | 3-2 | W | 2-1 |
| 1922-23 | (Div 1) | W | 2-1 | L | 1-3 |
| 1923-24 | (Div 1) | D | 1-1 | W | 2-1 |
| 1924-25 | (Div 1) | L | 0-3 | W | 5-3 |
| 1925-26 | (Div 1) | W | 6-3 | W | 3-1 |
| 1926-27 | (Div 1) | L | 1-5 | L | 1-3 |
| 1927-28 | (Div 1) | W | 2-1 | L | 1-3 |
| 1928-29 | (Div 1) | D | 1-1 | D | 2-2 |
| 1929-30 | (Div 1) | W | 8-3 | L | 2-3 |
| 1936-37 | (Div 2) | W | 3-1 | D | 0-0 |
| 1937-38 | (Div 2) | D | 3-3 | L | 1-3 |
| 1938-39 | (Div 2) | W | 1-0 | L | 2-3 |
| 1947-48 | (Div 2) | L | 1-2 | D | 0-0 |
| 1958-59 | (Div 1) | W | 4-1 | D | 0-0 |
| 1959-60 | (Div 1) | W | 3-2 | L | 0-1 |
| 1960-61 | (Div 1) | L | 1-4 | D | 1-1 |

| | | | | | | |
|---|---|---|---|---|---|---|
| 1961-62 | (Div 1) | W | 2-1 | W | 1-0 |
| 1962-63 | (Div 1) | L | 2-3 | L | 0-1 |
| 1963-64 | (Div 1) | L | 1-2 | L | 0-3 |
| 1964-65 | (Div 1) | L | 1-4 | D | 1-1 |
| 1965-66 | (Div 1) | L | 0-2 | W | 4-1 |
| 1976-77 | (Div 2) | D | 2-2 | L | 1-3 |
| 1977-78 | (Div 2) | L | 0-1 | W | 3-2 |
| 1978-79 | (Div 2) | L | 1-2 | L | 1-2 |
| 1982-83 | (Div 2) | W | 2-1 | W | 1-0 |

| | P | W | D | L | F | A |
|---|---|---|---|---|---|---|
| Home | 40 | 21 | 6 | 13 | 91 | 71 |
| Away | 40 | 13 | 7 | 20 | 58 | 70 |
| Total | 80 | 34 | 13 | 33 | 149 | 141 |

### Test Matches

| | | Home | | Away | |
|---|---|---|---|---|---|
| 1897-98 | | L | 1-3 | L | 0-2 |

### FA Cup

| | | | | | |
|---|---|---|---|---|---|
| 1912-13 | (4) | Home | L | 0-1 |
| 1951-52 | (6) | Home | W | 3-1 |
| 1958-59 | (4) | Home | L | 1-2 |
| 1959-60 | (6) | Away | D | 3-3 |
| | (R) | Home | W | 2-0 aet |

### Wartime

| | | Home | | Away | |
|---|---|---|---|---|---|
| 1916-17 | (LSPT) | L | 1-4 | L | 0-2 |
| | (LSST) | W | 4-0 | L | 1-4 |
| 1917-18 | (LSPT) | W | 3-1 | L | 1-6 |
| | (LSST) | W | 2-1 | L | 0-3 |
| 1918-19 | (LSPT) | L | 3-4 | W | 1-0 |
| | (LSST) | L | 2-4 | L | 1-5 |
| 1939-40 | (NWRL) | W | 1-0 | D | 0-0 |
| 1940-41 | (NRL) | D | 1-1 | L | 1-2 |
| | | W | 3-2 | L | 1-2* |
| 1941-42 | (FLNS-FC) | W | 3-2 | D | 0-0 |
| | (FLNS-SC) | W | 6-2 | L | 0-2 |
| 1942-43 | (FLNS-FC) | D | 3-3 | L | 0-1 |
| | (FLNS-SC) | W | 3-1 | D | 0-0 |
| 1943-44 | (FLNS-SC) | W | 2-0 | L | 1-5 |
| 1944-45 | (FLNS-FC) | L | 0-2 | D | 1-1 |
| | (FLNS-SC) | L | 2-4 | L | 1-4 |
| 1945-46 | (FLN) | W | 4-2 | W | 4-1 |

*Note: Blackburn Rovers and Burnley played each other twice at home and away in this competition.

### BURTON, John Henry

Forward. 1906-1908.
*Debut: v Everton (h) 17 March 1906.*
*Career: Grangetown FC; Blackburn Rovers March 1906 initially on trial; West Ham United July 1908; Birmingham September 1909; Nelson October 1910; Cardiff City cs 1911; Southend United May 1914.*
**Appearances:** Football League 4.

Burton came to Blackburn on trial during the 1905-06 season as a creative ball-playing forward with an eye for goal. He was joined at Ewood Park by Eddie Latheron, a playing colleague at Grangetown, and both players were given a run in the second team.

Although Burton made his senior debut several months before Latheron, it was the latter who went on to become a first-team regular. Having made his debut within days of his arrival, Burton had to wait until January 1908 before his next opportunity. After three appearances during January and February 1908, Burton was allowed to move to West Ham United in the close season.

A season in London was followed by 12 months with Birmingham before he returned to Lancashire with Nelson in October 1910. However, the most productive period of Burton's career came with a move to Cardiff City during the summer of 1911. In 1912-13, he scored 11 goals for Cardiff as they came top of the Second Division of the Southern League.

### BURTON TOWN FC

Burton Town was born around the turn of the century and became the main team in Burton following the demise of Burton United. They were drawn against Blackburn Rovers in the third round of the 1931-32 FA Cup competition when they were members of the Birmingham & District League and the Rovers were in the First Division. Burton reached the third round by defeating Gateshead who were in the Third Division North of the Football League. However, two goals apiece by Jack Bruton and Arthur Cunliffe ensured that the Rovers did not fall victim to the giant

killers from Burton. The club was disbanded in 1939.

### FA Cup

| | | | | |
|---|---|---|---|---|
| 1931-32 | (3) | Away | W | 4-0 |

### BURTON WANDERERS

Formed in 1871, the club became founder members of the Midland League in 1889. Burton Wanderers played in the Second Division between 1894 and 1897 before returning to the Midland League. In 1901 they merged with Burton Swifts to become Burton United and played in the Second Division of the Football League until the club was disbanded in 1910. Having won through four qualifying rounds of the FA Cup in 1894-95, Wanderers played hosts to Blackburn Rovers in the first-round proper of the competition. Two goals from Jamie Haydock were sufficient to send the Rovers into the next round.

### FA Cup

| | | | | |
|---|---|---|---|---|
| 1894-95 | (1) | Away | W | 2-1 |

### BURY FC

Founded in 1885, Bury joined the Second Division of the Football League in 1894 and won the title in their first season of League membership. Blackburn and Bury have met in three divisions of the Football League as well as in both major Cup competitions. In 1887-88 the clubs met in the first round of the FA Cup and the Rovers clocked up a 10-0 victory. However, just prior to the match Bury, who were fielding a number of ineligible players, scratched from the competition. Although this fact was kept from the players until the game was over the official result was a 'walkover' for Blackburn.

### Football League

| | | Home | | Away | |
|---|---|---|---|---|---|
| 1895-96 | (Div 1) | L | 0-2 | L | 0-2 |
| 1896-97 | (Div 1) | L | 1-2 | L | 0-3 |
| 1897-98 | (Div 1) | D | 1-1 | L | 0-1 |
| 1898-99 | (Div 1) | D | 0-0 | L | 2-3 |
| 1899-1900 | (Div 1) | W | 3-2 | L | 0-2 |
| 1900-01 | (Div 1) | L | 0-2 | W | 1-0 |
| 1901-02 | (Div 1) | L | 0-3 | L | 0-2 |
| 1902-03 | (Div 1) | L | 0-3 | D | 1-1 |
| 1903-04 | (Div 1) | D | 2-2 | L | 0-3 |
| 1904-05 | (Div 1) | L | 0-2 | W | 2-0 |
| 1905-06 | (Div 1) | W | 3-0 | L | 0-5 |
| 1906-07 | (Div 1) | W | 4-1 | D | 0-0 |
| 1907-08 | (Div 1) | W | 1-0 | D | 1-1 |
| 1908-09 | (Div 1) | L | 0-1 | D | 1-1 |
| 1909-10 | (Div 1) | W | 5-1 | L | 1-2 |
| 1910-11 | (Div 1) | W | 6-2 | D | 2-2 |
| 1911-12 | (Div 1) | W | 2-0 | W | 2-1 |
| 1924-25 | (Div 1) | L | 0-1 | D | 1-1 |
| 1925-26 | (Div 1) | L | 1-2 | L | 1-3 |
| 1926-27 | (Div 1) | D | 2-2 | W | 2-0 |
| 1927-28 | (Div 1) | L | 0-1 | W | 3-2 |
| 1928-29 | (Div 1) | D | 1-1 | L | 0-1 |
| 1936-37 | (Div 2) | L | 2-3 | D | 1-1 |
| 1937-38 | (Div 2) | W | 2-1 | L | 1-2 |
| 1938-39 | (Div 2) | W | 1-0 | W | 4-2 |
| 1948-49 | (Div 2) | L | 1-2 | L | 1-3 |
| 1949-50 | (Div 2) | W | 2-1 | L | 0-3 |
| 1950-51 | (Div 2) | L | 2-4 | W | 3-1 |
| 1951-52 | (Div 2) | L | 1-2 | W | 2-0 |
| 1952-53 | (Div 2) | W | 4-0 | L | 0-1 |
| 1953-54 | (Div 2) | W | 4-2 | D | 0-0 |
| 1954-55 | (Div 2) | D | 1-1 | L | 1-2 |
| 1955-56 | (Div 2) | W | 3-1 | W | 4-0 |
| 1956-57 | (Div 2) | W | 6-2 | D | 2-2 |
| 1966-67 | (Div 2) | W | 2-1 | W | 2-1 |
| 1968-69 | (Div 2) | W | 3-0 | W | 3-1 |
| 1974-75 | (Div 3) | W | 1-0 | W | 2-1 |
| 1979-80 | (Div 3) | L | 1-2 | W | 2-1 |

| | P | W | D | L | F | A |
|---|---|---|---|---|---|---|
| Home | 38 | 17 | 6 | 15 | 68 | 53 |
| Away | 38 | 13 | 9 | 16 | 48 | 57 |
| Total | 76 | 30 | 15 | 31 | 116 | 110 |

### FA Cup

| | | | | |
|---|---|---|---|---|
| 1913-14 | (2) | Home | W | 2-0 |
| 1928-29 | (5) | Home | W | 1-0 |

## Football League Cup

| 1979-80 | (1) | Away | W | 3-0 |
| | | Home | W | 3-2 |

## Wartime

| | | Home | | Away | |
|---|---|---|---|---|---|
| 1916-17 | (LSPC) | D | 2-2 | L | 0-1 |
| 1917-18 | (LSPC) | L | 1-4 | L | 1-5 |
| 1918-19 | (LSPC) | L | 0-1 | W | 4-3 |
| 1939-40 | (NWRL) | L | 1-2 | L | 1-2 |
| 1940-41 | (NRL) | W | 3-2 | L | 1-3* |
| | | W | 3-1 | L | 1-3 |
| | | W | 4-0 | | |
| 1941-42 | (FLNS-FC) | W | 2-0 | W | 3-0 |
| 1942-43 | (FLNS-FC) | W | 6-2 | L | 0-6 |
| | (FLNS-SC) | W | 7-4 | D | 2-2 |
| 1943-44 | (FLNS-FC) | W | 5-1 | L | 0-1 |
| | (FLNS-SC) | D | 2-2* | | |
| 1944-45 | (FLNS-SC) | W | 4-2 | W | 3-2 |
| 1945-46 | (FLN) | L | 2-3 | L | 2-3 |

*Note: Blackburn Rovers and Bury played each other three times at Ewood Park and twice at Gigg Lane in this competition.

*Note: Blackburn Rovers and Bury only played each other at Ewood Park in this competition.

## BUSBY, Vivian Dennis
Centre-forward. 1981-1982.
*6ft; 11st 12lb.*
*Born: Slough, 19 June 1949.*
*Debut: v Derby County (h) 14 February 1981.*
*Career: Hatters Lane School; Buckinghamshire trial; Terries (High Wycombe); Wycombe Wanderers 1966; Queen's Park Rangers trial; Chelsea trial; Fulham trial 1969; Luton Town January 1970; Newcastle United on loan December 1971 until February 1972; Fulham August 1973 (£25,000); Norwich City September 1976 (£50,000); Stoke City November 1977 (£50,000); Sheffield United on loan January 1980 to March 1980; Tulsa Roughnecks (USA) March 1980; Blackburn Rovers February 1981 (exchange deal for Duncan McKenzie); York City non-contract player August 1982, becoming assistant manager in 1984; Sunderland assistant manager May 1987 until November 1991; Hartlepool United manager February 1993 to November 1993.*
**Appearances:** Football League 8.
**Goals:** Football League 1.
Viv Busby was entering the veteran stage of his career when he moved to Ewood Park in 1981. Howard Kendall, who had worked with Busby at Stoke City, hoped that the striker would be able to score the goals that would take his goal shy team into the First Division. Unfortunately Busby, who had been playing in America prior to coming to Ewood, rarely looked like recapturing the form he had shown earlier in his career and lost his place after only eight matches.

## BUTCHER, John Melvin
Goalkeeper. 1976-1982.
*6ft 2in; 12st 3lb.*
*Born: Newcastle, 27 May 1956.*
*Debut: v Bristol Rovers (a) 8 March 1977.*
*Career: Blackburn Rovers amateur 1974, turning professional in March 1976; Oxford United July 1982; Halifax Town on loan September until October 1983; Bury on loan December 1983; Chester City August 1984; Bury on loan October 1985 until November 1985; Altrincham cs 1987; Macclesfield Town 1989.*
**Appearances:** Football League 104; FA Cup 5; Football League Cup 7; Total 116.

When financial problems caused the sale of Paul Bradshaw to Wolverhampton Wanderers in September 1977, Jim Smith was forced to thrust his promising young understudy into the first team. John Butcher had the perfect build for a goalkeeper, tall and slim, and seemed destined to follow in the footsteps of his two immediate predecessors. Sadly, Butcher failed to live up to those expectations. Brilliant one match and truly awful the next, Butcher lacked the consistency required of a top-class goalkeeper. His indecision when dealing with crosses and basic handling errors cost the club vital

points during the promotion push of 1977-78. Yet, for all his faults, Butcher appeared to have the makings of a good goalkeeper. His confidence was not helped when he became the target of the 'terrace critics' and during the 1978-79 relegation season he lost his place to Neil Ramsbottom.

The remainder of his time at Ewood Park was spent understudying Jim Arnold and Terry Gennoe and only a serious injury to Arnold in the 1980-81 season gave him an extended run in the team. In the summer of 1982, Jim Smith returned to Ewood Park to offer Butcher the opportunity to rebuild his career with Oxford United. During his time at the Manor Ground he made only 16 League appearances and had two loan spells in the lower divisions. He enjoyed better fortunes with Chester City, making 84 League appearances whilst with the club.

## BUTT, Leonard
Inside-forward. 1937-1947.
*5ft 5in; 10st 12lb.*
*Born: Wilmslow, 26 August 1910; Died: Macclesfield, June 1994.*
*Debut: v Norwich City (a) 23 January 1937.*
*Career: Wilmslow Albion; Ashton National Gas; Stockport County amateur June 1928, turning professional in August 1928; Macclesfield May 1932; Huddersfield Town May 1935; Blackburn Rovers 23 January 1937; Manchester United wartime guest 1939-40 & 1940-41; Huddersfield Town wartime guest 1940-41 & 1941-42; Wrexham wartime guest 1940-41; Manchester City wartime guest 1941-42; York City wartime guest 1941-42; Chelsea wartime guest 1942-43; Stockport County wartime guest 1943-44; Aldershot wartime guest 1943-44; York City January 1947; Mansfield Town October 1947; Mossley player-coach June 1948.*
*Domestic honours with Blackburn Rovers: Second Division championship: 1938-39 (41 apps, 16 gls); War League Cup runners-up: 1940.*
**Appearances:** Football League 110; FA Cup 7; Total 117.
**Goals:** Football League 44; FA Cup 4; Total 48.
A player who could both create and score goals with equal aplomb, Len Butt was the perfect inside-forward. Ranked as one of the cleverest craftsmen of his day, Butt was a regular member of the team which brought the Second Division title to Ewood Park in 1938-39.

The success he enjoyed at Blackburn was in marked contrast to his early days in the game when a move from Wilmslow Albion to Stockport County was so unsuccessful that he drifted back into non-League football. Fortunately, Butt rediscovered the form which had first alerted Stockport to his ability and in 1936 Huddersfield Town threw him a life-line to resurrect his career in the Football League.

He came to Ewood Park with Jock Wightman in January 1937 and his speed and guile quickly endeared him to the supporters. After helping to win the Second Division title he also appeared in the 1940 War Cup Final during the first season of wartime football.

Sadly, the war years and a knee operation took the edge off his game and when League football returned in 1946-47 he left Ewood Park for York City.

## BYERS, John Edwin
Outside-left. 1923-1924.
*5ft 8in; 11st.*
*Born: Selby, 1897 (July quarter); Died: Worcester, November 1931.*
*Debut: v Chelsea (h) 28 April 1923.*
*Career: Selby Town; Knaresborough; Huddersfield Town November 1921; Blackburn Rovers April 1923; West Bromwich Albion January 1924 to July 1928; Worcester City July 1928; Torquay United May 1929; Kidderminster Harriers August 1931, retired cs 1932.*
**Appearances:** Football League 27; FA Cup 1; Total 28.
**Goals:** Football League 2.
Jack Byers was an outstandingly quick outside-left who enjoyed a brief career at Ewood Park. He had been signed from Huddersfield Town where he had scored 4 goals in 12 League matches but had found outings with the senior team limited. He was an ever-present at Ewood Park until a fracas with Tom Wylie resulted in his departure from the club. The players had just returned to Blackburn after a humiliating defeat by Corinthians when the players started a brawl at the station. Wylie was exonerated of all blame for the incident but Byers was suspended and transferred to West Bromwich Albion within the week. At The Hawthorns he scored 11 goals in 104 League appearances.

## BYRNE, David Stuart
Outside-right. 1989.
*5ft 8in; 11st.*
*Born: Hammersmith, 5 March 1961.*
*Debut: v Barnsley (a) February 1989.*
*Career: Brentford schoolboy forms; Southall; Hounslow; Harrow Borough; Hounslow; Kingstonian October 1983; Gillingham July 1985;*

*Millwall August 1986 (£5,000); Cambridge United on loan September 1988; Blackburn Rovers on loan February 1989; Plymouth Argyle March 1989; Bristol City on loan February 1990; Watford November 1990; Reading on loan August 1991; Fulham on loan January 1992; St Johnstone January 1993.*
**Appearances:** Football League 4.
David Byrne arrived at Ewood Park on loan in February 1989 to bolster the club's promotion drive. Byrne was a winger who could operate in midfield and created a favourable impression during his four games with the club. His sudden departure, to sign for Plymouth Argyle, came as something of a shock to the club. The most successful period in Byrne's nomadic career came at Millwall when he was a member of the squad which won the Second Division championship in 1987-88 season.

**BYROM, John**
Forward. 1959-1966 & 1976-1977.
*5ft 10in; 11st 8lb.*
*Born: Blackburn, 28 July 1944.*
*Debut: v Birmingham City (h) 11 November 1961.*
*Career: Blackburn Schoolboys; Blackburn Rovers schoolboy forms August 1959, joining the groundstaff in June 1960, before becoming a professional in August 1961; Bolton Wanderers June 1966 (£25,000); Blackburn Rovers September 1976, retired cs 1977.*
*International honours with Blackburn Rovers: England Youth International.*
**Appearances:** Football League 121+3; FA Cup 16; Football League Cup 9; Total 146+3.
**Goals:** Football League 50; FA Cup 12; Football League Cup 2; Total 64.
John Byrom was a classic case of the local boy who made good. A

product of local schoolboy football, Byrom was capped by England Youth and after only a handful of Central League appearances he was thrust into the First Division side in November 1961. He jostled for a regular place in the forward line for two seasons but, despite a reasonable goals-per-game ratio, the emergence of Andy McEvoy and Fred Pickering restricted him to only three appearances in 1963-64 season.

When Pickering left for Everton, Byrom forced his way ahead of George Jones, who had been bought as Pickering's replacement, to partner McEvoy in the first team. In 1964-65 he scored 25 goals in 40 League games and looked set to form a prolific partnership with the Irish striker.

The 1965-66 campaign saw the Rovers tumble towards the Second Division as both Byrom and McEvoy struggled to score goals in League matches. Whilst Byrom scored seven goals in only five FA Cup-ties, his return in League matches was a meagre three goals in 28 appearances (including two as sub).

The summer of 1966 saw the club begin to rebuild for life in the Second Division and following the arrival of Allan Gilliver from Huddersfield Town, Byrom was allowed to move to Bolton Wanderers. In retrospect the £25,000 fee received for Byrom looked akin to daylight robbery. He notched 113 League goals for the 'Trotters' over the next decade and seemed to take great delight in netting a number of goals against his old club.

In 1976, Jim Smith gambled on Byrom, now in the veteran stage of his career, solving his goalscoring problems. Sadly, age was against him and a series of injuries meant his return to Ewood Park was not a great success. At the end of the season Byrom brought the curtain down on a career which, although successful, did not quite fulfil its early promise.

**BYROM, Thomas**
Inside-forward. 1911-1920.
*5ft 7in; 10st 10lb.*
*Born: Blackburn, 1889 (January quarter).*
*Debut: v Chelsea (a) 20 March 1915.*
*Career: Blackburn St Phillip's; Blackburn Victoria Cross; Blackburn Rovers June 1911; Burnley wartime guest; Rochdale June 1920; Oldham Athletic December 1920 (£1,150) to May 1921; Chorley September 1922.*
**Appearances:** Football League 13.
**Goals:** Football League 3.

One of a number of local-born players whose career was severely disrupted by World War One. Byrom made a sensational debut by scoring twice in a 3-1 win over Chelsea in March 1915; but during wartime football he was restricted to just six appearances for the club. After nine appearance during the first post-war season he made the short move to Rochdale in June 1920. At Spotland he proved an immediate success and nine goals in 18 Central League games was sufficient to persuade Oldham Athletic to take him to Boundary Park. The move was not a success and after only five senior outings he was released.

**CAIRNS, Ronald**
Forward. 1953-1959.
*5ft 7in; 10st 4lb.*
*Born: Chopwell, 4 April 1934.*
*Debut: v Sheffield Wednesday (h) 26 December 1955.*
*Career: Chopwell Juniors; Consett; Blackburn Rovers September 1953; Rochdale June 1959; Southport July 1964; Wigan Athletic 1965-66; Darwen 1967, becoming manager cs 1970.*
**Appearances:** Football League 26.
**Goals:** Football League 7.
A utility forward who broke into the team during the 1957-58 promotion season when he scored seven goals in 15 League appearances. However, with Dobing and Vernon in possession of the inside-forward positions, Cairns was allowed to move to Rochdale in June 1959. He scored 66 goals in 195 League games for the Spotland club before ending his League career with 13 goals in 34 games for Southport.

**CALLADINE, Charles Frederick**
Half-back/Inside-forward. 1936-1938.
*5ft 9¼in; 11st.*
*Born: Wessington, Derbyshire, 24 January 1911; Died: Matlock, 29 October 1983.*
*Debut: v Arsenal (h) 8 February 1936.*
*Career: Wessington FC 1927; Ivanhoe FC; Scunthorpe United 1928; Birmingham May 1930; Blackburn Rovers February 1936; Guildford City August 1938. Retired during World War Two.*
**Appearances:** Football League 48; FA Cup 1; Total 49.
**Goals:** Football League 6; FA Cup 1; Total 7.
Charlie Calladine was a powerful defender whose vigorous play was also utilised at inside-forward by the Rovers. Calladine had featured in 115 League games for Birmingham before joining Blackburn in February 1936. He vied with Wally Halsall for a half-back position during his first few months at the club but began the 1936-37 season as first-choice left-half. Although he lost his place to Norman Christie towards the end of October 1936, he returned at inside-left the following January. Calladine spent most of the 1937-38 season out of the team before moving to non-League Guildford City.

**CALLOWAY, Laurence John**
Left-back. 1968-1970.
*5ft 11in; 12st 2lb.*
*Born: Birmingham, 17 June 1945.*
*Debut: v Plymouth Argyle (h) 24 April 1968.*
*Career: Wolverhampton Wanderers apprentice July 1961, turning professional in October 1962; Rochdale July 1964; Blackburn Rovers March 1968; Southport August 1970; York City June 1971; Shrewsbury Town December 1972; San Jose Earthquakes (USA) May 1974 to 1979; California Surf (USA) coach 1981; Seattle Sounders (USA) coach 1983; Salt Lake Sting (USA) coach; San Francisco Bay Blackhawks (USA) coach.*
**Appearances:** Football League 17 + 8; FA Cup 2; Football League Cup 1 + 1; Total 20 + 9.
**Goals:** Football League 1.
The arrival of Laurie Calloway from Rochdale was thought to herald the departure of Keith Newton from Blackburn. However, the club were able to hold on to Newton for another 18 months and Calloway had to settle for a role on the bench. Calloway, a hard-tackling and athletic full-back, was a popular figure at Ewood Park despite spending most of his time as either substitute or in the Central League team. In 1970 he moved to Southport in the deal which brought Alex Russell to Ewood Park from Haig Avenue. After 368 appearances in the Football League with his various clubs Calloway joined the exodus to the North American Soccer League. He became a coach in America after his playing days were over and in 1991 he led the San Francisco Bay Blackhawks to the American Professional Soccer League title.

**CALVEY, Mitchell**
Centre-forward. 1893-1894.
*Born: Blackburn.*
*Debut: v West Bromwich Albion (h) 13 January 1894.*
*Career: Belfast Distillery 1892-93; Blackburn Rovers August 1893;*

*Manchester City May 1894; Bacup cs 1894; Baltimore (USA) October 1894.*
**Appearances:** Football League 6; FA Cup 5; Total 11.
**Goals:** Football League 3; FA Cup 2; Total 5.
Although a native of Blackburn, Calvey came to the Rovers after playing a season with Belfast Distillery. Calvey made only six League appearances during the 1893-94 campaign but figured in most of the important Cup engagements. Sadly, Calvey was not a success. Contemporary reporters believed that, despite his willingness to run, he lacked sufficient class for a team like the Rovers. "Calvey gets too excited to play a safe game. He exhibits a spectators enthusiasm at times and loses some good openings", said the *Lancashire Daily Post*.

## CAMBRIDGE UNITED FC
Formed in 1919 and known as Abbey United until 1951. Cambridge were elected to the Football League in 1970. Cambridge first met Blackburn in 1973-74, having won promotion from the Fourth Division the previous season. Cambridge have remained welcome visitors to Ewood Park as they have failed to take a point and only scored two goals at Ewood Park in seven meetings. Indeed, Cambridge didn't score a goal, at home or away, against Blackburn until the seventh League meeting between the clubs.

**Football League**

|         |         | Home |     | Away |     |
|---------|---------|------|-----|------|-----|
| 1973-74 | (Div 3) | W    | 2-0 | W    | 2-0 |
| 1978-79 | (Div 2) | W    | 1-0 | W    | 1-0 |
| 1980-81 | (Div 2) | W    | 2-0 | D    | 0-0 |
| 1981-82 | (Div 2) | W    | 1-0 | L    | 0-1 |
| 1982-83 | (Div 2) | W    | 3-1 | L    | 0-2 |
| 1983-84 | (Div 2) | W    | 1-0 | L    | 0-2 |
| 1991-92 | (Div 2) | W    | 2-1 | L    | 1-2 |

|       | P  | W | D | L | F  | A |
|-------|----|---|---|---|----|---|
| Home  | 7  | 7 | 0 | 0 | 12 | 2 |
| Away  | 7  | 2 | 1 | 4 | 4  | 7 |
| Total | 14 | 9 | 1 | 4 | 16 | 9 |

**Football League Cup**

| 1992-93 | (6) | Home | W | 3-2 |
|---------|-----|------|---|-----|

## CAMERON, John
Left-back. 1904-1907.
*5ft 9in; 12st 9lb.*
*Born: Kirkwoodin, Lanarkshire.*
*Debut: v Middlesbrough (a) 16 April 1904.*
*Career: Kirkwood Thistle; St Mirren 1899; Blackburn Rovers April 1904; Chelsea October 1907 (£900); Burslem Port Vale July 1913.*
**Appearances:** Football League 64; FA Cup 3; Total 67.
Jock Cameron came to Ewood Park in April 1903 to partner Bob Crompton at full-back. Although he was an ever-present during the 1904-05 season, the emerging Arthur Cowell deposed him at left-back the following year. Cameron's remaining appearances for Blackburn were as understudy to both Crompton and Cowell. A quick, hard-tackling full-back, Cameron was clearly too good to linger in the second team and in October 1907 he moved south to join Chelsea. He was an automatic choice at Stamford Bridge for six seasons and was also appointed captain.

## CAMERON, William Smith
Half-back/Centre-forward/Winger. 1908-1913.
*5ft 8in; 12st.*
*Born: Mossend, Lanarkshire, 1884; Died: Bolton, 15 October 1958.*
*Debut: v Bury (a) 17 April 1908.*
*Career: Burnbank Athletic 1902-03; Albion Rovers 1903-04; Renton 1903-04; Glossop 1904; Bolton Wanderers May 1906; Blackburn Rovers April 1908; Bury January 1914; Hamilton Academical wartime guest; Bury player-manager, May 1919 to May 1923; Rochdale manager August 1930 to December 1931.*
*Domestic honours with Blackburn Rovers: First Division championship: 1911-12 (13 apps, 1 gl).*
**Appearances:** Football League 70; FA Cup 12; Total 82.
**Goals:** Football League 18; FA Cup 1; Total 19.
Cameron was a genuine utility player who could play in a number of

positions with equal aplomb. Like so many players of his kind, Cameron never really established himself for long spells in the first team but tended to be moved about to cover gaps. His best season at Ewood was 1909-10 when he scored ten goals in 17 League appearances. After World War One he turned his hand to management and in 1923 was involved in a bribery scandal which resulted in him receiving a life suspension from the game. In 1929 the suspension was revoked and he returned to football for a short time as manager of Rochdale.

## CAMPBELL, Austen Fenwick
Left-half. 1923-1929.
*5ft 9in; 11st 10lb.*
*Born: Hamsterley, County Durham, 5 May 1901; Died: Blackburn, 8 September 1981.*
*Debut: v Sheffield United (a) 23 February 1923.*
*Career: Spen Black & White; Leadgate Park; Coventry City 1919-20; Leadgate Park June 1921; Blackburn Rovers February 1923; Huddersfield Town September 1929; Hull City November 1935; Darwen cs 1936 to 1938.*

*International honours with Blackburn Rovers: England: 2 caps (1928); Football League: 2 appearances (1928).*
*Domestic honours with Blackburn Rovers: FA Cup winner: 1928.*
**Appearances:** Football League 161; FA Cup 23; Total 184.
**Goals:** Football League 7; FA Cup 2; Total 9.
'Aussie' Campbell will forever be remembered at Ewood Park for his 'Man of the Match' performance in the 1928 FA Cup Final. Campbell, a neat and tidy footballer, had joined Blackburn Rovers in February 1923 from Leadgate Park. A natural left-footer, Campbell had a superb physique and his hard-tackling was a feature of the half-back line at Blackburn during the 1920s. Yet Campbell was more than just a destructive half-back. He was also a forceful forager who liked to get forward in support of the front men and was not averse at trying his luck in front of goal. His abilities were finally recognised by England in 1928, just a few months after his memorable Cup Final display. In September 1929, Campbell joined the club which he had helped to destroy at Wembley. He returned to Wembley with Huddersfield in 1930, but on that occasion he was on the losing side. He remained at Huddersfield until joining Hull City in November 1935. Campbell returned to East Lancashire to play non-League football with Darwen in the summer of 1936. He continued to live in Blackburn and worked for many years in a local brewery. It was with some affection that Aussie Campbell kept one special souvenir of the 1928 FA Cup Final for the rest of his days, namely the match ball.

## CAMPBELL, Henry
Inside-right. 1889-1894.
*5ft 6in; 10st 10lb.*
*Born: Renton, Dunbartonshire, 1867; Died: Blackburn, November 1915.*
*Debut: v Everton (a) 7 September 1889.*
*Career: Renton Athletic; Renton FC; Blackburn Rovers August 1889 to cs 1894.*
*Domestic honours with Blackburn Rovers: FA Cup winner: 1890.*
**Appearances:** Football League 98; FA Cup 15; Total 113.
**Goals:** Football League 22; FA Cup 4; Total 26.
A dyer by trade, Henry Campbell's first experience with an organised team was with Renton Athletic, with whom he played for one season. He was then invited to appear on the left wing in the second team of the famous Renton club. During the 1887-88 season he was promoted to the first team at Renton and occupied the inside-right position. After two seasons of first-team football in Scotland he came south to Blackburn in August 1889. He readily adapted to the short and accurate passing style of the Rovers and became a great favourite with the supporters. His perceptive understanding of the game enabled him to dictate tactics and initiate many of the team's attacking moves. In 1890 he added an FA Cup winners' medal to the Scottish Cup winners' medal he had won with Renton. He was capped for Scotland in 1889 before moving south to England.

## CAMPBELL, John
Outside-left. 1896-1898.
*Born: Govan, Glasgow, 1877.*
*Debut: v West Bromwich Albion (h) 1 September 1896.*

*Career: Ferntower FC; Renton Union; Linthouse; Partick Thistle July 1895; Blackburn Rovers May 1896; Glasgow Rangers May 1898; West Ham United 1902; Hibernian 1903 to cs 1906.*

**Appearances:** Football League 55; Test Matches 2; FA Cup 1; Total 58.

**Goals:** Football League 10.

A skilful little winger who was brought to Ewood Park to link up with John Wilkie, his former left-wing partner at Partick Thistle. The pair were a permanent fixture on the left for two seasons before both were lured back to Scotland to join Rangers. Campbell enjoyed tremendous success at Ibrox and shared in the winning of four League titles as well as being a member of the Rangers team which lost the 1899 Cup Final. Campbell was capped on four occasions for Scotland and appeared once for the Scottish League during his time with Rangers. After 28 goals in 53 League appearances with the Ibrox club, Campbell returned to England to try his luck with West Ham United in the Southern League. However, after only one goal in 18 League games he returned to Scotland to end his career with Hibernian.

## CAMPBELL, John J.
Half-back/Forward. 1945-1956.

*5ft 7in; 10st 7lb.*

*Born: Liverpool, 17 March 1922.*

*Debut: v Bolton Wanderers (a) 5 January 1946 (FAC).*

*Career: Liverpool April 1943; Blackburn Rovers December 1945; Oldham Athletic July 1956 to March 1957. Later youth coach at Blackburn.*

**Appearances:** Football League 224; FA Cup 21; Total 245.

**Goals:** Football League 19; FA Cup 1; Total 20.

Jackie Campbell joined Blackburn Rovers when the club was still playing in the temporary Wartime League North. Although his career at Ewood fluctuated more than most he proved to be a larger than life character who became a loyal club servant. As a winger, Campbell was a little too apt to over elaborate whilst as an inside man he proved durable rather than outstanding. However, an emergency conversion to right-half during the 1949-50 season completely changed his career at Ewood Park. 'Nudger', as he was known to colleagues, remained in the right-half spot until December 1952, when he once more reverted to the right-wing position. Although no longer a first-team regular during his last two seasons with the club, Campbell remained a valuable utility player. However, in July 1956 he finally left Ewood in search of first-team football at Boundary Park. He left Oldham in March 1957 after scoring five goals in 26 League games and was to return to Ewood Park as a coach to the youth team. Campbell was one of the men responsible for the successful FA Youth Cup winning team of 1959.

## CAMPBELL, William Cecil
Inside-forward. 1893.

*Debut: v Preston North End (h) 7 October 1893.*

*Career: Royal Arsenal 1889 to 1891; Preston North End 1891; Middlesbrough; Darwen May 1892; Blackburn Rovers August 1893; Newton Heath November 1893; Notts County March 1894; Newark cs 1894.*

**Appearances:** Football League 1.

Campbell was one of football's more colourful characters in the 1890s; a player of undoubted skill, but whose personality led him to clash with authority on more than one occasion. Campbell came to Blackburn in August 1893, after a successful season with Darwen. It came as something of a surprise when the Darwen committee decided to dispense with his services as he was a popular member of the Barley Bank side. A suspension by the Football Association meant that Campbell's debut for the Rovers had to be delayed until the beginning of October. He made his debut against Preston North End, one of his former clubs, but was a huge disappointment. He didn't appear fully fit and one commentator stated that "W.C.Campbell came out after suspension but he appeared to be suspended even during play." Whatever the reasons for his abject showing, the player didn't remain with the club for long. He announced he was leaving to take an appointment in South Africa, but in November 1893 had joined Newton Heath and four months later he moved to Notts County. He was released at the end of the season and became a traveller for a firm of cigar and tobacco manufacturers. At the same time it was reported that he had signed for Newark and had been appointed captain. In May 1894, Campbell had been hauled before the Football League Management Committee following complaints that he had made an illegal approach for John Murray of Blackburn Rovers, on behalf of Notts County. Notts County denied all knowledge of Campbell's actions and the player agreed that he had acted on his own after hearing that County wanted a good back. As a result Campbell received a two year suspension by the management committee.

## CARDIFF CITY FC
Formed in 1899 as Riverside FC, the club amalgamated with Riverside Albion in 1902 and in 1908 changed its name to Cardiff City FC. Originally members of the Southern League, Cardiff were elected to the Second Division of the Football League in 1920. In 1925 they beat Rovers in the semi-final of the FA Cup and went on to become the only club to take the trophy out of England. The clubs had first crossed paths in a friendly in November 1913 when Blackburn travelled to Wales and suffered a narrow defeat.

**Football League**

| | | | Home | | Away | |
|---|---|---|---|---|---|---|
| 1921-22 | (Div 1) | L | 1-3 | W | 3-1 |
| 1922-23 | (Div 1) | W | 3-1 | L | 0-5 |
| 1923-24 | (Div 1) | W | 2-1 | L | 0-2 |
| 1924-25 | (Div 1) | W | 3-1 | L | 0-3 |
| 1925-26 | (Div 1) | W | 6-3 | L | 1-4 |
| 1926-27 | (Div 1) | W | 1-0 | W | 1-0 |
| 1927-28 | (Div 1) | D | 0-0 | D | 1-1 |
| 1928-29 | (Div 1) | W | 2-0 | D | 1-1 |
| 1948-49 | (Div 2) | W | 2-1 | L | 0-1 |
| 1949-50 | (Div 2) | W | 1-0 | L | 1-2 |
| 1950-51 | (Div 2) | W | 2-0 | L | 0-1 |
| 1951-52 | (Div 2) | L | 0-1 | L | 1-3 |
| 1957-58 | (Div 2) | W | 4-0 | L | 3-4 |
| 1960-61 | (Div 2) | D | 2-2 | D | 1-1 |
| 1961-62 | (Div 2) | D | 0-0 | D | 1-1 |
| 1966-67 | (Div 2) | W | 4-1 | D | 1-1 |
| 1967-68 | (Div 2) | D | 1-1 | L | 2-3 |
| 1968-69 | (Div 2) | W | 1-0 | L | 1-2 |
| 1969-70 | (Div 2) | W | 1-0 | D | 0-0 |
| 1970-71 | (Div 2) | D | 1-1 | L | 1-4 |
| 1976-77 | (Div 2) | W | 2-1 | L | 1-2 |
| 1977-78 | (Div 2) | W | 3-0 | D | 1-1 |
| 1978-79 | (Div 2) | L | 1-4 | L | 0-2 |
| 1980-81 | (Div 2) | L | 2-3 | W | 2-1 |
| 1981-82 | (Div 2) | W | 1-0 | W | 3-1 |
| 1982-83 | (Div 2) | D | 1-1 | W | 1-0 |
| 1984-85 | (Div 2) | W | 2-1 | W | 2-1 |

| | P | W | D | L | F | A |
|---|---|---|---|---|---|---|
| Home | 27 | 17 | 6 | 4 | 49 | 26 |
| Away | 27 | 6 | 7 | 14 | 29 | 48 |
| Total | 54 | 23 | 13 | 18 | 78 | 74 |

**FA Cup**

| | | | | |
|---|---|---|---|---|
| 1924-25 | (SF) | Meadow Lane, Nottingham L | 1-3 |
| 1957-58 | (5) | Away | D | 0-0 |
| | (R) | Home | W | 2-1 |

## CAREY, John James
Manager. 1953-1958 & 1970-71.

*Born: Dublin, 23 February 1919.*

*Career: St James' Gate (Ireland); Manchester United November 1936 to 1953; Blackburn Rovers manager June 1953 to October 1958; Everton manager October 1958 to April 1961; Leyton Orient manager August 1961 to July 1963; Nottingham Forest manager July 1963 to December 1968; Blackburn Rovers administrative manager January 1969, then manager October 1970 to June 1971.*

After a highly successful playing career with Manchester United, football management seemed the natural metamorphosis for Johnny Carey. Carey, who came to England to join Manchester United in November 1936, started his football career as an inside-forward, but was later converted to wing-half before finally settling in the full-back position. A versatile and gifted player, Carey was capped by both the Republic of Ireland and Northern Ireland as well as becoming the 1949 Footballer of the Year.

In 1948 he led United to FA Cup success, defeating Blackpool at Wembley, while in 1951-52 he was a member of the side that won the First Division championship. He retired from playing in 1953, after appearing in 306 League games for United and was appointed manager at Ewood Park. Although keen to pursue and improve the existing youth policy, Carey was shrewd enough to realise that young talent needed to be carefully nursed through the formative years. In the meantime, Carey looked to bring more experienced players to the club in order to fulfil his immediate tactical plans.

Carey was keen to encourage attacking football and it was to encourage this philosophy that two new wingers were brought to the club. He introduced Frank Mooney, a youngster from Old Trafford, and Bobby Langton, the old Rovers star, to his team. With Eddie Crossan, Tommy Briggs and Eddie Quigley, filling the inside positions, the Blackburn public enjoyed a feast of attacking football. In 1953-54 the team notched 86 goals and the following four seasons saw totals of 114, 84, 83 and 93 goals.

Whilst keeping Rovers in the forefront of the promotion race, Carey began to introduce the youngster's who would form the team known as 'the Carey Chick's'. The introduction of Bryan Douglas and Ronnie Clayton on a regular basis was followed by the promotion of Roy Vernon and Peter Dobing from the second team. Carey went to Ireland to sign Mick McGrath, whilst Harry Leyland and Matt Woods were former Everton players who were signed to boost the defence. The transformation was complete when Ally MacLeod arrived from St Mirren to replace the departed Langton. After four, heart-breaking, near misses, promotion was finally achieved in 1957-58.

As the club took their place in the First Division, another batch of young talent was already being developed in the youth team. However, Carey was not to remain at Ewood Park long enough to see this new batch develop. His achievements at Blackburn had not gone unnoticed elsewhere and in September 1958 he announced his intention to leave Blackburn in order to become manager of Everton. He remained at Ewood until a successor was found and finally took over at Goodison Park on 20 October 1958.

He returned to Ewood Park to add Roy Vernon to a host of new signings that he assembled on Merseyside. After two disappointing seasons he led Everton to fifth place in the First Division; the club's highest post-war position. It was not enough. In April 1961, in one of football's more bizarre incidents, Carey was sacked by the Everton chairman whilst the two shared a London taxi.

Carey moved to Leyton Orient and his first season in charge saw the club promoted to the First Division. Without the resources to strengthen the side, Carey could do little as the club slipped back into the Second Division after only one season in the top flight. In July 1963 he left London to join Nottingham Forest.

At Forest he had the resources to build an impressive looking team and in 1966-67 he took the club to second place in the First Division and an FA Cup semi-final. However, the 1968-69 season saw Forest drop into the relegation zone and in December 1968 the club committee terminated his employment at the City Ground. In January 1969 the directors at Ewood Park invited Carey to return to the club and take over the position of administrative manager. Thus the directors reunited Carey with Eddie Quigley, one of his former players at Ewood, who was to remain as team manager.

The 1970-71 season began badly for the club and by October it was clear that relegation to the Third Division was a distinct possibility. In October 1970 the directors decided that the two managers should swop positions in a bid to prevent the club from dropping into the Third Division for the first time in its history. Carey and Quigley had totally different philosophies to the game and when Carey took over he was quoted as saying: "Football is not a tactical battle that can be worked out entirely on a blackboard. When they're on the field the players must stand or fall by their own decisions."

The New Year brought a brief revival and hopes were raised that Carey could, indeed, save the club. However, the sale of Ken Knighton to Hull City was a severe blow to the club's hopes, even though it released funds for Carey to bring Fred Pickering back to the club. Sadly, Pickering, clearly past his best, made little impact on the side and the club were duly relegated to the Third Division. In June 1971, both Carey and Quigley paid the price which relegation usually demands. Alas, the jovial Irishman had been unable to work his magic for a second time.

## CARLISLE UNITED FC

Formed in 1903 following a merger between Carlisle Red Rose and Shaddongate United. Carlisle entered the Football League in 1928, when they became members of the Third Division North. The clubs first met in a friendly in February 1953, when Tommy Briggs scored four goals in a 6-3 victory for the Rovers. The clubs had to wait until the 1966-67 season before they met in competitive football and then, in a matter of weeks, they met in the Football League, Football League Cup and the FA Cup.

### Football League

|  |  | Home |  | Away |  |
|---|---|---|---|---|---|
| 1966-67 | (Div 2) | W | 2-0 | W | 2-1 |
| 1967-68 | (Div 2) | W | 1-0 | L | 0-1 |
| 1968-69 | (Div 2) | L | 0-2 | L | 1-4 |
| 1969-70 | (Div 2) | W | 1-0 | W | 1-0 |
| 1970-71 | (Div 2) | L | 0-2 | L | 0-1 |
| 1975-76 | (Div 2) | W | 1-0 | W | 1-0 |
| 1976-77 | (Div 2) | L | 1-3 | D | 1-1 |
| 1979-80 | (Div 3) | L | 1-2 | D | 1-1 |
| 1982-83 | (Div 2) | W | 3-2 | L | 1-3 |
| 1983-84 | (Div 2) | W | 4-1 | W | 1-0 |
| 1984-85 | (Div 2) | W | 4-0 | W | 1-0 |
| 1985-86 | (Div 2) | W | 2-0 | L | 1-2 |

|  | P | W | D | L | F | A |
|---|---|---|---|---|---|---|
| Home | 12 | 8 | 0 | 4 | 20 | 12 |
| Away | 12 | 5 | 2 | 5 | 11 | 14 |
| Total | 24 | 13 | 2 | 9 | 31 | 26 |

### FA Cup

| 1966-67 | (3) | Home | L | 1-2 |
|---|---|---|---|---|

### Football League Cup

| 1966-67 | (4) | Away | L | 0-4 |
|---|---|---|---|---|
| 1969-70 | (3) | Away | L | 1-2 |

### Wartime

|  |  | Home |  | Away |  |
|---|---|---|---|---|---|
| 1939-40 | (NWRL) | D | 1-1 | W | 2-1 |

## CARR, John

Manager. 1922-1926.
*Born: Seaton Burn, Newcastle, 1876; Died: 17 March 1948.*
*Career: Seaton Burn; Newcastle United December 1899, retired cs 1912, then assistant trainer 1912-1922; Blackburn Rovers manager February 1922, becoming secretary-manager October 1925, resigned December 1926.*

As a player, with Newcastle United, Jack Carr had won all the honours that the early twentieth-century game had to offer. During his long career with Newcastle United, his only club, Carr had won two England caps, three championship medals, an FA Cup winners' medal and two runners-up medals. Having retired from the game in 1912, Carr had been employed as assistant trainer to Newcastle United and appeared ideally suited to step into management.

He became the first manager in the history of the club when Blackburn appointed him to that position in February 1922. In the aftermath of war, Carr faced a monumental task at Blackburn. Prior to the outbreak of World War One, the club had enjoyed its most successful period since the formation of the Football League. Sadly the team that had captured the League crown in 1912 and 1914 was now in need of rebuilding and this was the task that fell to Jack Carr. Luckily, the club had the resources to enable Carr to become active in the transfer market in a bid to revive former glories.

However, despite a succession of new faces, success continued to elude the new manager. During his reign at Ewood Park, Blackburn finished in the top ten on only one occasion and the FA Cup brought some embarrassing exits. Although he led the club to a semi-final appearance against Cardiff City in 1925, defeats at the hands of Corinthians and South Shields were hardly in keeping with the glorious past of Blackburn Rovers in the knock-out competition. However, despite his difficulties on the field, the club were pleased with his administrative capabilities and, following the death of R.B.Middleton, appointed him secretary-manager on 1 October 1925. It therefore came as something of a shock to everyone at Ewood Park when Carr handed in his resignation on 22 December 1926.

## CARTER, Donald Frederick

Outside-left. 1948.
*Born: Midsomer Norton, 11 September 1921.*
*Debut: v Southampton (a) 21 August 1948.*
*Career: Welton School; Somerset County Schoolboys; Norton St John's; Stourbridge April 1938; Bury January 1939 (£250); Blackburn Rovers June 1948 (£5,000); New Brighton November 1948; Northwich Victoria cs 1951.*
**Appearances:** Football League 2.

Carter began the 1948-49 campaign as the first-choice outside-left in succession to Bobby Langton. Carter, who had scored 27 goals in 56 League games with Bury, had cost a sizeable fee and the club had high expectations of him. However, after two games he was axed and replaced with Jackie Wharton, another close season signing. The consistency of Wharton meant there was no way back for Carter and in November 1948 he moved to New Brighton where he scored 19 goals in 105 League games.

## CARTER, James
Goalkeeper. 1897-1899.
Born: Preston.
*5ft 11in; 11st 7lb.*
*Debut: v Liverpool (a) 18 December 1897.*
*Career: Preston North End; Sheppey United; Millwall Athletic 1896-97; Blackburn Rovers May 1897; New Brompton September 1899.*
**Appearances:** Football League 43; FA Cup 2; Total 45.
James Carter made only 17 Southern League appearances for Millwall Athletic before Blackburn Rovers brought him back to his native county. Carter had started his footballing career as back-up to the legendary Jim Trainer at Preston North End and had moved south in search of first-team football. Although he had been expected to start the 1897-98 campaign in the first team, a broken finger before the season started meant he had to wait until Christmas before he could oust Albert Knowles from the team. Carter immediately caught the eye in a struggling team and held his place until the end of the season. The following campaign saw Carter's form wane and although he missed only seven matches there were doubts as to whether the Rovers would want to re-sign him. In fact the Rovers couldn't afford to replace him and offered him terms for the new campaign. However, Carter decided to try his luck elsewhere and much to the surprise of everyone at Ewood Park he opted to return south and join New Brompton.

## CARVER, Jesse
Centre-half. 1927-1936.
*5ft 9in; 12st.*
*Born: Liverpool, 7 July 1911.*
*Debut: v Sunderland (h) 20 September 1930.*
*Career: Aigburth Church of England School; Blackburn Rovers amateur December 1927, signing professional in October 1928; Newcastle United June 1936 (£2,000); Workington; Leicester City; Bury April 1939; Leicester City (wartime guest). Retired during the War. Huddersfield Town (assistant trainer) 1946-47; Dutch FA coach 1947; then coach to Lazio, Juventus, Valdagho and Torino in Italy; West Bromwich Albion (coach) 1952; returned to Italy to become coach at Torino and then AC Roma manager in 1953; Coventry City (manager) June to December 1955; Lazio January 1956; Tottenham Hotspur (coach) October 1958 to March 1959; later in Portugal and USA coaching before returning to England during the 1960s to retire.*

**Appearances:** Football League 143; FA Cup 3; Total 146.
**Goals:** Football League 2.
Jessie Carver proved that a combination of strong tacking and intelligent positional play would more than compensate for a lack of inches in a defender. Carver arrived at Ewood Park as a youngster in 1929, but it was not until the 1932-33 campaign that he established himself as the regular first-team centre-half. For two and a half seasons he dominated the centre-half position and was unfortunate to lose his place due to a cartilage operation. The emergence of Bob Pryde during the relegation campaign of 1935-36, coupled with a dispute over a benefit, led to a souring of relations between Carver and the Rovers. In June 1936 he agreed to join Newcastle United for a fee of £2,000 and remained on Tyneside for three seasons.

He returned to Lancashire to sign for Bury in 1939 but before the hostilities had ended he had retired from playing and taken up the position of assistant trainer at Huddersfield Town. In 1947 Carver began a globe-trotting coaching career when he joined the Dutch Football Association as coach to the national team. He became one of Europe's top coaches and worked in Italy with Lazio, Juventus, Torino and AC Milan. In England he had spells with Coventry City as manager and Tottenham Hotspur as coach. Carver also spent some time in Portugal and the United States of America before finally retiring to England in the 1960s.

## CENTRAL LEAGUE
Blackburn Rovers were founder members of the Central League in 1911.

Below is their complete record in the competition. Appearances and goalscorers are given for those seasons when the club won either the Central League championship or the Central League Second Division championship.

| | P | W | D | L | F | A | Pts | Pos |
|---|---|---|---|---|---|---|---|---|
| 1911-12 | 32 | 12 | 6 | 14 | 60 | 54 | 30 | 12 |
| 1912-13 | 38 | 15 | 10 | 13 | 70 | 61 | 40 | 11 |
| 1913-14 | 38 | 18 | 7 | 13 | 93 | 72 | 43 | 5 |
| 1914-15 | 38 | 14 | 4 | 20 | 71 | 87 | 32 | 17 |
| **League Suspended 1915-1919** | | | | | | | | |
| 1919-20 | 42 | 18 | 6 | 18 | 79 | 82 | 42 | 9 |
| 1920-21 | 42 | 14 | 14 | 14 | 74 | 71 | 42 | 12 |
| 1921-22 | 42 | 17 | 9 | 16 | 68 | 72 | 43 | 12 |
| 1922-23 | 42 | 15 | 9 | 18 | 54 | 76 | 39 | 13 |
| 1923-24 | 42 | 8 | 5 | 29 | 40 | 96 | 21 | 22 |
| 1924-25 | 42 | 19 | 9 | 14 | 71 | 48 | 47 | 7 |
| 1925-26 | 42 | 23 | 8 | 11 | 98 | 64 | 54 | 2 |
| 1926-27 | 42 | 20 | 2 | 20 | 102 | 97 | 42 | 10 |
| 1927-28 | 42 | 14 | 5 | 23 | 93 | 119 | 33 | 20 |
| 1928-29 | 42 | 12 | 8 | 22 | 85 | 111 | 32 | 22 |
| 1929-30 | 42 | 20 | 8 | 14 | 91 | 82 | 48 | 6 |
| 1930-31 | 42 | 18 | 12 | 12 | 104 | 87 | 48 | 8 |
| 1931-32 | 42 | 22 | 10 | 10 | 101 | 67 | 54 | 3 |
| 1932-33 | 42 | 23 | 5 | 14 | 95 | 66 | 51 | 3 |
| 1933-34 | 42 | 13 | 13 | 16 | 73 | 78 | 39 | 14 |
| 1934-35 | 42 | 14 | 11 | 17 | 69 | 69 | 39 | 14 |
| 1935-36 | 42 | 15 | 8 | 19 | 76 | 88 | 38 | 14 |
| 1936-37 | 42 | 13 | 4 | 25 | 78 | 107 | 30 | 19 |
| 1937-38 | 42 | 17 | 6 | 20 | 85 | 90 | 39 | 16 |
| 1938-39 | 42 | 15 | 4 | 23 | 74 | 94 | 34 | 20 |
| **League Suspended 1939-1945** | | | | | | | | |
| 1945-46 | 40 | 12 | 9 | 19 | 65 | 83 | 33 | 16 |
| 1946-47 | 42 | 16 | 4 | 22 | 79 | 95 | 36 | 16 |
| 1947-48 | 42 | 12 | 10 | 20 | 61 | 79 | 34 | 16 |
| 1948-49 | 42 | 12 | 11 | 19 | 59 | 71 | 35 | 17 |
| 1949-50 | 42 | 15 | 7 | 20 | 47 | 72 | 37 | 16 |
| 1950-51 | 42 | 14 | 11 | 17 | 56 | 72 | 39 | 16 |
| 1951-52 | 42 | 14 | 10 | 18 | 68 | 73 | 38 | 17 |
| 1952-53 | 42 | 17 | 7 | 18 | 63 | 67 | 41 | 13 |
| 1953-54 | 42 | 16 | 6 | 20 | 62 | 83 | 38 | 15 |
| 1954-55 | 42 | 15 | 9 | 18 | 78 | 82 | 39 | 15 |
| 1955-56 | 42 | 15 | 9 | 18 | 63 | 78 | 39 | 14 |
| 1956-57 | 42 | 12 | 11 | 19 | 55 | 72 | 35 | 16 |
| 1957-58 | 42 | 13 | 5 | 24 | 61 | 98 | 31 | 22 |
| 1958-59 | 42 | 19 | 6 | 17 | 86 | 83 | 44 | 10 |
| 1959-60 | 42 | 21 | 9 | 12 | 85 | 65 | 51 | 6 |
| 1960-61 | 42 | 24 | 5 | 13 | 90 | 66 | 53 | 5 |
| 1961-62 | 42 | 19 | 10 | 13 | 82 | 63 | 48 | 5 |
| 1962-63 | 42 | 16 | 5 | 21 | 77 | 80 | 37 | 15 |
| 1963-64 | 42 | 12 | 10 | 20 | 64 | 91 | 34 | 18 |
| 1964-65 | 42 | 26 | 8 | 8 | 90 | 41 | 60 | 1 |
| 1965-66 | 42 | 25 | 5 | 12 | 107 | 62 | 55 | 3 |
| 1966-67 | 42 | 27 | 8 | 7 | 93 | 43 | 62 | 1 |
| 1967-68 | 42 | 19 | 10 | 13 | 82 | 51 | 48 | 7 |
| 1968-69 | 42 | 11 | 11 | 20 | 56 | 69 | 33 | 19 |
| 1969-70 | 42 | 10 | 10 | 22 | 41 | 63 | 30 | 20 |
| 1970-71 | 42 | 11 | 6 | 25 | 47 | 84 | 28 | 21 |
| 1971-72 | 42 | 9 | 9 | 24 | 39 | 93 | 27 | 22 |
| 1972-73 | 42 | 7 | 7 | 28 | 34 | 80 | 21 | 22 |
| 1973-74 | 42 | 12 | 9 | 21 | 41 | 63 | 33 | 18 |
| 1974-75 | 42 | 4 | 15 | 23 | 35 | 77 | 23 | 22 |
| 1975-76 | 42 | 12 | 8 | 22 | 58 | 85 | 32 | 18 |
| 1976-77 | 42 | 13 | 9 | 20 | 51 | 83 | 35 | 18 |
| 1977-78 | 42 | 18 | 5 | 19 | 53 | 70 | 41 | 10 |
| 1978-79 | 42 | 11 | 13 | 18 | 53 | 69 | 35 | 16 |
| 1979-80 | 42 | 14 | 7 | 21 | 60 | 85 | 35 | 17 |
| 1980-81 | 42 | 7 | 9 | 26 | 33 | 78 | 23 | 22 |
| 1981-82 | 42 | 10 | 14 | 18 | 58 | 81 | 34 | 17 |
| **Central League Division One** | | | | | | | | |
| 1982-83 | 30 | 12 | 6 | 12 | 49 | 53 | 30 | 9 |
| 1983-84 | 30 | 10 | 6 | 14 | 38 | 46 | 36 | 11 |
| 1984-85 | 34 | 17 | 7 | 10 | 57 | 43 | 58 | 7 |
| 1985-86 | 34 | 14 | 4 | 16 | 57 | 49 | 46 | 10 |
| 1986-87 | 34 | 5 | 8 | 21 | 27 | 72 | 23 | 17 |
| **Central League Division Two** | | | | | | | | |
| 1987-88 | 34 | 21 | 7 | 6 | 69 | 24 | 70 | 1 |
| **Central League Division One** | | | | | | | | |
| 1988-89 | 34 | 13 | 2 | 19 | 55 | 62 | 41 | 12 |
| 1989-90 | 34 | 14 | 8 | 12 | 69 | 59 | 50 | 10 |
| 1990-91 | 34 | 12 | 8 | 14 | 56 | 51 | 44 | 10 |

Blackburn Rovers Reserves, Central League champions 1966-67. Back row (left to right): Blore, Mulvaney, George Jones, Anderson, Holt, Horrey, Eric Bell (assistant trainer). Front row: McGrath, Hall, Mr A.Duckett (director), Bob Jones, Wilson, Rogers.

| 1991-92 | 34 | 17 | 8 | 9 | 58 | 43 | 59 | 4 |
| 1992-93 | 34 | 18 | 10 | 6 | 60 | 37 | 64 | 3 |
| 1993-94 | 34 | 14 | 7 | 13 | 40 | 47 | 49 | 8 |

**1964-65 Central League championship appearances**
R.Blore 39; A.Holden 38; B.C.Anderson 33; E.Rogers 31; R.Mulvaney 31; D.E.Holt 30; R.G.Horrey 30; M.Hall 27; R.W.Jones 27; W.Wilson 26; G.A.Jones 25; A.Bradshaw 24; H.C.Sims 24; J.Bray 18; M.Whittle 12; M.McGrath 9; K.S.Cooper 7; E.G.Coxon 4; M.Darling 4; F.Else 4; G.F.V.Sharples 4; M.Warren 4; J.Byrom 2; R.Clayton 2; W.J.Howie 2; M.A.McEvoy 2; M.J.Harrison 1; A.R.Howard 1; I.Kendall 1.

**1964-65 Central League championship goalscorers**
R.Blore 25; G.A.Jones 12; R.G.Horrey 9; B.C.Anderson 6; A.Bradshaw 6; E.Rogers 5; R.Mulvaney 4; A.Holden 3; M.A.McEvoy 3; J.Byrom 2; W.J.Howie 2; H.C.Sims 2; M.J.Harrison 1; D.E.Holt 1; G.F.V.Sharples 1; M.Whittle 1; W.Wilson 1; own-goals 6.

**1966-67 Central League championship appearances**
J.Roberts 40; D.Helliwell 39; M.Whittle 39; E.G.Coxon 37; D.Halstead 34; E.Rogers 33; B.C.Anderson 27; S.M.Metcalfe 24 + 2; R.Mulvaney 23; I.Kendall 22 + 3; M.A.McEvoy 19; M.Darling 16; I.Ledgard 14; M.C.Britt 12; P.E.Jones 12; G.F.V.Sharples 11; D.E.Holt 10; W.Wilson 10; M.J.Harrison 9; G.A.Jones 7; F.Lord 5; R.Charter 4 + 1; J.Williams 4; T.M.J.Aspinall 2 + 1; A.H.Gilliver 2; R.W.Jones 2; J.T.Beardall 1; M.K.Ferguson 1; B.Mulligan 1; A.Smith 1; J.L.Tomlinson 1.

**1966-67 Central League championship goalscorers**
M.A.McEvoy 17; M.C.Britt 12; M.Darling 12; E.Rogers 12; I.Kendall 7; B.C.Anderson 6; M.J.Harrison 6; G.A.Jones 6; D.Helliwell 3; R.Mulvaney 2; G.F.V.Sharples 2, M.Whittle 2; A.H.Gilliver 1; D.E.Holt 1; F.Lord 1; S.M.Metcalfe 1; own-goals 2.

**1987-88 Central League Division Two championship appearances**
L.Johnrose 33; A.J.Diamond 31 + 1; K.J.Hill 31; D.May 30 + 1; P.Bolton 28 + 2; D.Collier 23; J.Millar 23; J.M.Wilcox 22 + 8; M.A.Patterson 20; C.R.Skinner 16 + 16; S.P.Curry 15 +1; A.Ainscow 15; I.Miller 14; H.A.Gayle 13; R.Driver 10 + 13; D.Fanthom 10; S.Holmes 7 + 9; A.J.Dawson 7; M.Lee 6 + 13; S.Barker 6; D.Mail 3; D.Gornall 2 + 3; S.Sellars 2; N.Tilly 2; M.Mylott 1 + 1; S.Garner 1; T.W.Gennoe 1; A.Jackson 1; C.S.Sulley 1.
(Note: Substitute appearances include all occasions when named as substitute and not just appearances on the pitch).

**1987-88 Central League Division Two championship goalscorers**
A.J.Diamond 26; S.P.Curry 9; L.Johnrose 8; J.M.Wilcox 4; I.Miller 3;

M.A.Patterson 3; R.Driver 2; S.Garner 2; H.A.Gayle 2; K.J.Hill 2; D.May 2; A.Ainscow 1; A.J.Dawson 1; S.Sellars 1; C.R.Skinner 1; own-goals 2.

**CHADWICK, Edgar Wallace**
Forward. 1887-1888.
*5ft 6in; 10st 7lb.*
*Born: Blackburn, Lancashire, 14 June 1869; Died: Blackburn, 14 February 1942.*
*Debut: v Blackburn Olympic (h) 5 November 1887 (FAC).*
*Career: Little Dots FC 1884; Blackburn Olympic 1886; Blackburn Rovers cs 1887; Everton July 1888; Burnley May 1899; Southampton August 1900; Liverpool May 1902; Blackpool May 1904; Glossop May 1905; Darwen 1906; Retired 1908. The Hague and Haarlem FC (Holland) 1908; England amateur team coach November 1908; Blackburn Rovers wartime guest 1916-17.*
**Appearances:** FA Cup 4.
**Goals:** FA Cup 3.
Edgar Chadwick first appeared in the Blackburn Rovers team at the start of the 1887-88 season. A regular goalscorer throughout his season with Rovers, Chadwick scored one of the goals which helped to eliminate Blackburn Olympic, his old club, from the FA Cup. As the Rovers prepared for the inaugural season of the Football League, Chadwick's father began to scout around for better opportunities for his gifted son. The result was that Chadwick left the Rovers and began the 1888-89 season at Goodison Park. On Merseyside, Chadwick became one of the major figures of his era. A quick and constructive player who could shoot with either foot, Chadwick was capped seven times by England and won a championship medal with Everton. He also won a Southern championship medal with Southampton and represented the Football League. During his career he netted 127 goals in 413 appearances in the Football League and scored 18 goals for Southampton in 52 Southern League matches. On retirement he moved abroad and became involved in coaching in Germany and Holland, before returning to Blackburn to work as a baker. He made a final appearance for Blackburn Rovers during wartime football when he lined up at outside-left against Manchester United on 11 November 1916 at the age of 47.

**CHADWICK, Francis Robert**
Right-half. 1946-1955.
*5ft 10in; 10st 3lb.*
*Born: Blackburn, 9 November 1927.*
*Debut: v West Bromwich Albion (a) 19 March 1949.*
*Career: Blackburn Rovers amateur May 1946, turning professional in June 1946; York City July 1955 to June 1956.*
**Appearances:** Football League 11.
**Goals:** Football League 1.
Although he made only a handful of first-team appearances, Frank Chadwick remained a loyal servant to Blackburn Rovers for nine years. He began as understudy to Jimmy Baldwin and Jackie Campbell for the right-half spot and by the start of the 1952-53 season had only two first-team appearances to his credit. The second half of the 1952-53 campaign saw Campbell move to outside-right and Chadwick enjoyed his best spell with the club and featured in nine League games. These proved to be his last for the Rovers and a further two seasons of Central League football were followed by a move to York City. At York he was not called upon for first-team duty and left the club after only one season.

**CHADWICK, Miles**
Outside-left. 1905-1908.
*Debut: v Aston Villa (h) 2 September 1905.*
*Career: Spring Bank Rovers (Blackburn); Blackburn St Phillip's; Darwen; Blackburn Rovers cs 1905; Darwen cs 1908.*
**Appearances:** Football League 51; FA Cup 1; Total 52.
**Goals:** Football League 7.
Miles Chadwick was a pacey outside-left whose main strength was his

ability to race past opposing defenders and deliver accurate centres. Small and slight in build, Chadwick earned a regular first-team spot for much of the 1905-06 season and a bright future was predicted for this teetotaller and non-smoker. Unfortunately, although Chadwick rarely shirked a challenge, he failed to find the consistency that the club desired and the 1906-07 season saw him involved in a battle with Arthur Dawson for the left-wing position. As neither man appeared totally convincing the Rovers signed Ernest Bracegirdle for the start of the 1907-08 campaign and then added Walter Anthony later in the season. Chadwick became surplus to requirements and in the summer of 1908 he returned to Darwen.

## CHAIRMEN
The following have held the position of chairman at Blackburn Rovers Football Club:

| | |
|---|---|
| J.Lewis | 1875-1888 |
| E.S.Morley | 1888-1901 |
| R.Birtwistle | 1901-1905 |
| L.Cotton | 1905-1919 |
| C.Cotton | 1919-1921 |
| J.W.Walsh | 1921-1933 |
| W.Tempest | 1933-1938 |
| J.Cotton | 1938-1943 |
| J.Caton | 1944-1948 |
| F.Wood | 1948-1952 |
| T.Blackshaw | 1952-1956 |
| G.N.Forbes | 1956-1960 |
| J.Wilkinson | 1960-1964 |
| D.Hull | 1964-1968 |
| C.R.Davies | 1968-1970 |
| A.L.Fryars | 1970-1971 |
| W.H.Bancroft | 1971-1979 |
| D.T.Keighley | 1979 |
| D.Brown | 1979-1982 |
| W.Fox | 1982-1991 |
| R.D.Coar | 1991- |

## CHAMBERS, Peter
Left-half. 1897-1899.
*5ft 9in; 11st 10lb.*
*Born: Workington, 1878.*
*Debut: v Sheffield Wednesday (a) 13 November 1897.*
*Career: Black Diamonds; Blackburn Rovers October 1897; Bedminster 1899; Bristol City 1900 to 1906; Swindon Town 1907 to 1912.. Retired.*
**Appearances:** Football League 33.
Peter Chambers came to Blackburn Rovers after helping the Black Diamonds club of Workington to League and Cup honours in Cumberland. Chambers made only sporadic first-team appearances during the 1897-98 campaign, but had become first-choice left-half at the start of the following season. However, with 'Kelly' Houlker pressing him for the left-half spot, Chambers moved south to join Southern League Bedminster in 1899. In 1900, Bedminster merged with Bristol City and Chambers was one of the players who helped to the club make the transition to the Football League in 1901-02. Chambers won a Second Division championship medal with Bristol City in 1905-06 before moving to Swindon Town in 1907.

## CHAMPIONSHIPS
Blackburn Rovers have won a divisional championship on four occasions. These have been as follows:

### 1911-12 First Division
This was the first time that the First Division title came to Ewood Park. A mid-season run which brought ten wins, six draws and only one defeat from 17 matches went some way to ensuring that Blackburn lifted the title. The top three positions were as follows:

| | P | W | D | L | F | A | Pts |
|---|---|---|---|---|---|---|---|
| Blackburn Rovers | 38 | 20 | 9 | 9 | 60 | 43 | 49 |
| Everton | 38 | 20 | 6 | 12 | 46 | 42 | 46 |
| Newcastle United | 38 | 18 | 8 | 12 | 64 | 50 | 44 |

A total of 21 players appeared during the season in League matches. Appearances and goalscorers are listed below:

**Appearances:** A.Walmsley 37; W.Bradshaw 36; J.Simpson 35; R.Compton 33; A.Cowell 31; P.J.Smith 31; A.Robinson 30; W.C.A.Aitkenhead 29; W.Anthony 27; G.R.Chapman 23; E.G.Latheron 22; J.Orr 19; J.Clennell 18; W.S.Cameron 13; W.Davies 11; J.Ashcroft 8; T.Suttie 7; J.Johnston 5; H.Dennison 1; W.Garbutt 1; B.Proctor 1.

Billy Bradshaw (left) and Albert Walmsley training at Ewood in 1913-14, when Rovers won their second Football League championship title in three seasons.

**Goalscorers:** W.C.A.Aitkenhead 15; G.R.Chapman 9; J.Clennell 9; J.Orr 9; E.G.Latheron 7; W.Bradshaw 3; W.Davies 2; J.Simpson 2; W.Anthony 1; W.S.Cameron 1; P.J.Smith 1; own-goals 1.

### 1913-14 First Division
The Rovers won their opening five matches and remained unbeaten in their opening ten fixtures. Record signing Danny Shea began to blend with Simpson, Latheron and Hodkinson in a forward line that constantly created openings. Problems with the centre-forward position were solved when a large fee brought Percy Dawson from Hearts for the final games of the season. The team created a new club record in losing only seven matches. The top three positions were as follows:

| | P | W | D | L | F | A | Pts |
|---|---|---|---|---|---|---|---|
| Blackburn Rovers | 38 | 20 | 11 | 7 | 78 | 42 | 51 |
| Aston Villa | 38 | 19 | 6 | 13 | 65 | 50 | 44 |
| Middlesbrough | 38 | 17 | 9 | 12 | 77 | 60 | 43 |

A total of 21 players appeared during the season in League matches. Appearances and goalscorers are listed below:

**Appearances:** A.Cowell 38; A.Walmsley 37; D.Sea 36; E.G.Latheron 35; J.Simpson 34; R.Crompton 33; J.Hodkinson 33; P.J.Smith 33; A.Robinson 28; W.Bradshaw 27; G.R.Chapman 19; W.C.A.Aitkenhead 17; J.J.Crabtree 10; A.McGhie 9; A.Bell 8; P.H.Dawson 8; J.Orr 5; J.Clennell 4; J.Johnston 2; W.Anthony 1; G.Porteous 1.
**Goalscorers:** D.Shea 28; E.G.Latheron 13; G.R.Chapman 9; W.C.A.Aitkenhead 7; W.Bradshaw 3; P.H.Dawson 3; A.McGhie 3; P.J.Smith 3; J.Hodkinson 2; J.Orr 2; J.Simpson 1; J.Clennell 1; J.Simpson 1; A.Walmsley 1; own-goals 2.

Rovers' Second Division championship team of 1938-39. Back row (left to right): Bob Crompton (manager), Walter Crook, Bob Pryde, Arnold Whiteside, Jimmy Baron, Frank Chivers, Ernest Lanceley. Front row: Billy Rogers, Len Butt, Jock Weddle, Albert Clarke, Bobby Langton.

## 1938-39 Second Division

Bob Crompton had returned in triumph towards the end of the previous campaign and, after saving the club from relegation, took them to the title in his first season in charge. Never out of the top six all season, they went to the top just before Christmas and, apart from one Saturday, remained in the top spot. The top three positions were as follows:

| | P | W | D | L | F | A | Pts |
|---|---|---|---|---|---|---|---|
| Blackburn Rovers | 42 | 25 | 5 | 12 | 94 | 60 | 55 |
| Sheffield United | 42 | 20 | 14 | 8 | 69 | 41 | 54 |
| Sheffield Wednesday | 42 | 21 | 11 | 10 | 88 | 59 | 53 |

A total of 19 players appeared during the season in League matches. Appearances and goalscorers are listed below:

**Appearances:** W.Crook 42; J.R.Weddle 42; J.Barron 41; L.Butt 41; R.I.Pryde 41; W.Rogers 41; F.C.Chivers 38; A.Clarke 38; R.Langton 37; A.Whiteside 33; W.A.Hough 31; E.Lanceley 11; W.Guest 8; G.G.Hardy 7; F.W.Hall 6; P.Dickie 2; J.Bruton 1; W.R.Lee 1; G.Matier 1.
**Goalscorers:** A.Clarke 21; W.Rogers 18; L.Butt 16; J.R.Weddle 16; R.Langton 14; W.Crook 2; W.Guest 1; R.I.Pryde 1; A.Whiteside 1; own-goals 4.

## 1974-75 Third Division

The race for the Third Division title developed into a battle between Blackburn Rovers and Plymouth Argyle. The turning point proved to be the meeting of the two teams at Ewood Park in February 1975. Two weeks earlier the Rovers had visited Home Park and surrendered their leadership of the table after going down by two goals to one. In the return at Ewood, Plymouth raced to a two-goal lead and looked like cementing their position at the top of the table. However, Ken Beamish pulled a goal back just before half-time and a spirited second-half display saw Plymouth routed by five goals to two. The title was virtually sealed with a 4-1 victory at Port Vale, Gordon Lee's old club, on the last Saturday of the season. Two days later the Rovers clinched the title with a 0-0 draw against Wrexham in front of a crowd of 21,290.

| | P | W | D | L | F | A | Pts |
|---|---|---|---|---|---|---|---|
| Blackburn Rovers | 46 | 22 | 16 | 8 | 68 | 45 | 60 |
| Plymouth Argyle | 46 | 24 | 11 | 11 | 79 | 58 | 59 |
| Charlton Athletic | 46 | 22 | 11 | 13 | 76 | 61 | 55 |

A total of 20 players appeared in League matches during the season. Appearances and goalscorers are listed below:

**Appearances:** R.Jones 46; A.Parkes 46; G.Oates 45; K.Beamish 43; D.Martin 42 + 1; S.M.Metcalfe 42 + 1; G.N.Hawkins 42; J.M.Heaton 40 + 2; A.Burgin 40; D.W.Fazackerley 22 + 1; J.Waddington 21; M.F.T.Hickman 18 + 1; M.J.Wood 18; P.J.Hilton 16; J.F.Kenyon 9 + 3; J.Mullen 5 + 4; R.Hoy 6 + 1; B.Endean 2 + 5; N.Wilkinson 2; K.Hird 1 + 1.
**Goalscorers:** D.Martin 15; K.G.Beamish 11; M.F.T.Hickman 7; S.M.Metcalfe 7; G.Oates 6; A.Parkes 5; D.W.Fazackerley 4; J.Waddington 4; P.J.Hilton 2; A.Burgin 1; G.N.Hawkins 1; J.M.Heaton 1; J.F.Kenyon 1; own-goals 3.

## CHAPMAN, George R.

Centre-half/Centre-forward. 1908-1910 & 1911-1919.
*5ft 10in; 12st.*
*Born: Broxburn, 23 October 1886.*
*Debut: v Bristol City (h) 1 September 1908.*
*Career: Heart of Midlothian; Raith Rovers cs 1907; Blackburn Rovers August 1908; Glasgow Rangers May 1910; Blackburn Rovers October 1911; Accrington Stanley 1919.*
*Domestic honours with Blackburn Rovers: First Division championship: 1911-12 (23 apps, 9 gls); 1913-14 (19 apps, 9 gls).*
**Appearances:** Football League 138; FA Cup 14; Total 152.
**Goals:** Football League 34; FA Cup 8; Total 42.

Although George Chapman did not quite fulfil his original promise as a centre-half, he rendered excellent service to the club in a variety of positions. Chapman arrived at Ewood Park during the summer of 1907 and apart from a season with Glasgow Rangers, he remained with the club until 1919. Chapman began his career at Blackburn as a centre-half and his prowess as a sprinter proved a great help to the back division. On returning from Glasgow Rangers, Chapman was given the centre-forward

Malcolm Darling, Blackburn's inside-left, tries a shot at goal against Charlton Athletic at The Valley in October 1969, as Peter Reeves, Charlton's left-half, races to intercept.

berth during the first of the club's two title-winning seasons. His pace, fearlessness and powerful shooting quickly earned him the respect of First Division defenders. However, a lack of control over the ball in tight situations prevented Chapman from developing into a top-class centre-forward. Although Chapman had lost his first-team place by the outbreak of World War One, he went on to score ten goals in 30 wartime appearances for the club. On 30 September 1916, he scored all the Blackburn goals in the 6-1 victory over Rochdale at Ewood Park.

### CHAPPELL, Leslie Alan
Midfield. 1968-1969.
*5ft 8in; 10st 5lb.*
*Born: Nottingham, 6 February 1947.*
*Debut: v Sheffield United (h) 21 September 1968.*
*Career: Rotherham United non-contract player May 1962, before becoming an apprentice in April 1963 and signing professional in February 1965; Blackburn Rovers May 1968 (in exchange for Allan Gilliver); Reading July 1969; Doncaster Rovers December 1974; Swansea City July 1976 to July 1981, then club coach.*
**Appearances:** Football League 7.
When Eddie Quigley signed Les Chappell, in a deal which saw Allan Gilliver move to Rotherham United, he described him as a quick moving, lively goal-poacher in the Jimmy Greaves mould. Sadly, Chappell was dogged by ill fortune throughout his 12 months at Blackburn and became Ewood's forgotten man. After waiting six weeks in the Central League team to prove himself, Chappell was injured after only half an hour of his senior debut. When he had finally recovered from the injury, his child was taken seriously ill and he returned to Rotherham to be closer to his family. He returned to first-team action towards the end of the season but, although he was signed ostensibly as a goal-getter, most of his appearances were in midfield. He was freed at the end of the 1968-69 season.

### CHARLTON ATHLETIC FC
Founded in 1905, Charlton Athletic became members of the Third Division South in 1921. Although Blackburn and Charlton didn't meet in the Football League until after World War Two, the clubs have since played each other in the First, Second and Third Divisions. The most memorable meeting in the Football League took place at the Valley on 26 April 1958. In the last match of the season the Rovers needed to win to accompany West Ham United into the First Division whilst Charlton needed only a point to clinch promotion. A crowd of 45,435 watched a pulsating battle which saw the Rovers race to a 4-1 lead before having to hang on to a 4-3 win. The 1974-75 season gave both clubs something to celebrate with the Rovers clinching the Third Division title and Charlton accompanying them into the Second Division by finishing in third place. On 28 March 1987, the clubs met at Wembley in the Final of the Full Members' Cup. Although Charlton were then a First Division side, it was Second Division Rovers who won the trophy thanks to a single Colin Hendry strike.

### Football League

|         |         | Home |     | Away |     |
|---------|---------|------|-----|------|-----|
| 1946-47 | (Div 1) | W    | 1-0 | W    | 2-0 |
| 1947-48 | (Div 1) | D    | 0-0 | W    | 1-0 |
| 1957-58 | (Div 1) | D    | 1-1 | W    | 4-3 |
| 1966-67 | (Div 2) | W    | 2-1 | D    | 0-0 |
| 1967-68 | (Div 2) | W    | 3-2 | L    | 0-3 |
| 1968-69 | (Div 2) | L    | 0-1 | L    | 0-4 |
| 1969-70 | (Div 2) | W    | 3-0 | D    | 0-0 |
| 1970-71 | (Div 2) | W    | 1-0 | W    | 4-2 |
| 1972-73 | (Div 3) | W    | 3-1 | W    | 2-1 |
| 1973-74 | (Div 3) | D    | 1-1 | L    | 3-4 |
| 1974-75 | (Div 3) | W    | 3-1 | L    | 1-2 |
| 1975-76 | (Div 2) | W    | 2-0 | L    | 1-2 |
| 1976-77 | (Div 2) | D    | 0-0 | L    | 0-4 |
| 1977-78 | (Div 2) | W    | 2-1 | D    | 2-2 |

| 1978-79 | (Div 2) | L | 1-2 | L | 0-2 |
|---|---|---|---|---|---|
| 1981-82 | (Div 2) | L | 0-2 | L | 0-2 |
| 1982-83 | (Div 2) | W | 2-0 | L | 0-3 |
| 1983-84 | (Div 2) | D | 1-1 | L | 0-2 |
| 1984-85 | (Div 2) | W | 3-0 | L | 0-1 |
| 1985-86 | (Div 2) | D | 0-0 | L | 0-3 |
| 1990-91 | (Div 2) | D | 2-2 | D | 0-0 |
| 1991-92 | (Div 2) | L | 0-2 | W | 2-0 |

|  | P | W | D | L | F | A |
|---|---|---|---|---|---|---|
| Home | 22 | 11 | 7 | 4 | 31 | 18 |
| Away | 22 | 6 | 4 | 12 | 22 | 40 |
| Total | 44 | 17 | 11 | 16 | 53 | 58 |

**FA Cup**

| 1946-47 | (5) | Away | L | 0-1 |
|---|---|---|---|---|
| 1976-77 | (3) | Away | D | 1-1 |
|  | (R) | Home | W | 2-0 |

**Full Members' Cup**

| 1986-87 | (F) | Wembley | W | 1-0 |
|---|---|---|---|---|

## CHARTER, Raymond
Right-back. 1966-1971.
*5ft 8½in; 10st 6lb.*
*Born: Ashton, 10 January 1950.*
*Debut: v Oxford United (h) 14 March 1970.*
*Career: Blackburn Rovers apprentice July 1966, turning professional in January 1968; Stockport County July 1971.*
**Appearances:** Football League 13+5; FA Cup 0+1; Total 13+6.
A quick moving full-back who began as a front player at Ewood Park. Charter never failed to give 100 per cent and appeared to have established himself in the first team when he figured in the last nine games of the 1969-70 season. However, the following campaign saw Freddie Goodwin moved to right-back and Charter returned to Central League football. He had better luck at Stockport where he appeared in 91 (including four as sub) League games (including four as sub) and scored two goals.

## CHELSEA FC
Chelsea were formed in 1905 and elected to the Second Division of the Football League in the same year. They won promotion to the First Division in 1907 and so began a long association with Blackburn Rovers. In May 1988, Blackburn met Chelsea in the first stages of the First Division Play-offs. Chelsea participated as a First Division club and succeeded in clinching a 6-1 victory over the two legs. However, in the Play-off Final they lost their First Division status to Middlesbrough.

**Football League**

|  |  | Home | | Away | |
|---|---|---|---|---|---|
| 1907-08 | (Div 1) | W | 2-0 | L | 0-1 |
| 1908-09 | (Div 1) | W | 2-0 | D | 1-1 |
| 1909-10 | (Div 1) | W | 1-0 | L | 1-3 |
| 1912-13 | (Div 1) | D | 1-1 | W | 6-1 |
| 1913-14 | (Div 1) | W | 3-1 | L | 0-2 |
| 1914-15 | (Div 1) | W | 3-2 | W | 3-1 |
| 1919-20 | (Div 1) | W | 3-1 | L | 1-2 |
| 1920-21 | (Div 1) | D | 0-0 | W | 2-1 |
| 1921-22 | (Div 1) | D | 1-1 | L | 0-1 |
| 1922-23 | (Div 1) | D | 0-0 | D | 1-1 |
| 1923-24 | (Div 1) | W | 3-0 | L | 0-2 |
| 1930-31 | (Div 1) | W | 2-0 | L | 2-3 |
| 1931-32 | (Div 1) | D | 2-2 | W | 2-1 |
| 1932-33 | (Div 1) | L | 1-3 | D | 2-2 |
| 1933-34 | (Div 1) | W | 4-2 | L | 0-3 |
| 1934-35 | (Div 1) | L | 1-2 | L | 2-4 |
| 1935-36 | (Div 1) | W | 1-0 | L | 1-5 |
| 1946-47 | (Div 1) | L | 1-2 | W | 2-0 |
| 1947-48 | (Div 1) | D | 1-1 | L | 0-1 |
| 1958-59 | (Div 1) | L | 0-3 | W | 2-0 |
| 1959-60 | (Div 1) | W | 1-0 | L | 1-3 |
| 1960-61 | (Div 1) | W | 3-1 | L | 2-5 |
| 1961-62 | (Div 1) | W | 3-0 | D | 1-1 |
| 1963-64 | (Div 1) | D | 2-2 | L | 0-1 |
| 1964-65 | (Div 1) | L | 0-3 | L | 1-5 |
| 1965-66 | (Div 1) | L | 0-1 | L | 0-1 |
| 1975-76 | (Div 2) | D | 1-1 | L | 1-3 |
| 1976-77 | (Div 2) | L | 0-2 | L | 1-3 |
| 1980-81 | (Div 2) | D | 1-1 | D | 0-0 |
| 1981-82 | (Div 2) | D | 1-1 | D | 1-1 |
| 1982-83 | (Div 2) | W | 3-0 | L | 0-2 |
| 1983-84 | (Div 2) | D | 0-0 | L | 1-2 |

| 1988-89 | (Div 2) | D | 1-1 | W | 2-1 |
|---|---|---|---|---|---|

|  | P | W | D | L | F | A |
|---|---|---|---|---|---|---|
| Home | 33 | 14 | 12 | 7 | 48 | 34 |
| Away | 33 | 7 | 6 | 20 | 39 | 63 |
| Total | 66 | 21 | 18 | 27 | 87 | 97 |

**Football League Play-offs**

|  |  | Home | | Away | |
|---|---|---|---|---|---|
| 1987-88 |  | L | 0-2 | L | 1-4 |

**FA Premiership**

|  |  | Home | | Away | |
|---|---|---|---|---|---|
| 1992-93 |  | W | 2-0 | D | 0-0 |
| 1993-94 |  | W | 2-0 | W | 2-1 |

|  | P | W | D | L | F | A |
|---|---|---|---|---|---|---|
| Home | 2 | 2 | 0 | 0 | 4 | 0 |
| Away | 2 | 1 | 1 | 0 | 2 | 1 |
| Total | 4 | 3 | 1 | 0 | 6 | 1 |

**FA Cup**

| 1908-09 | (2) | Home | W | 2-1 |
|---|---|---|---|---|
| 1930-31 | (5) | Away | L | 0-3 |
| 1983-84 | (3) | Home | W | 1-0 |

**Full Members' Cup**

| 1986-87 | (4) | Home | W | 3-0 |
|---|---|---|---|---|

## CHESTER CITY FC
Founded in 1884 with the amalgamation of Chester Rovers and Kings School Old Boys. Chester were elected into the Third Division North of the Football League in 1931. In 1983 they added 'City' to their name. Although Blackburn first met Chester in a friendly fixture in 1891, their paths only crossed in 1979-80 in League football.

**Football League**

|  |  | Home | | Away | |
|---|---|---|---|---|---|
| 1979-80 | (Div 3) | W | 2-0 | D | 0-0 |

|  | P | W | D | L | F | A |
|---|---|---|---|---|---|---|
| Home | 1 | 1 | 0 | 0 | 2 | 0 |
| Away | 1 | 0 | 1 | 0 | 0 | 0 |
| Total | 2 | 1 | 1 | 0 | 2 | 0 |

## CHESTERFIELD FC
Originally founded in 1866 and reformed in 1871, Chesterfield were elected to the Football League in 1899. The club underwent another change in structure in 1904 and became known as Chesterfield Town. The club left the Football League in 1909 and Chesterfield Corporation took control of the club's affairs. Chesterfield continued in the Midland League until returning to the newly formed Third Division North of the Football League in 1921.

**Football League**

|  |  | Home | | Away | |
|---|---|---|---|---|---|
| 1936-37 | (Div 2) | W | 5-2 | W | 4-0 |
| 1937-38 | (Div 2) | D | 3-3 | L | 0-3 |
| 1938-39 | (Div 2) | W | 3-0 | W | 2-0 |
| 1948-49 | (Div 2) | L | 0-2 | D | 0-0 |
| 1949-50 | (Div 2) | D | 1-1 | L | 1-2 |
| 1950-51 | (Div 2) | D | 1-1 | L | 1-4 |
| 1971-72 | (Div 3) | W | 1-0 | L | 0-2 |
| 1972-73 | (Div 3) | L | 0-1 | L | 1-3 |
| 1973-74 | (Div 3) | W | 2-1 | L | 0-3 |
| 1974-75 | (Div 3) | W | 2-0 | W | 2-1 |
| 1979-80 | (Div 3) | W | 1-0 | W | 1-0 |

|  | P | W | D | L | F | A |
|---|---|---|---|---|---|---|
| Home | 11 | 6 | 3 | 2 | 19 | 11 |
| Away | 11 | 4 | 1 | 6 | 12 | 18 |
| Total | 22 | 10 | 4 | 8 | 31 | 29 |

**FA Cup**

| 1960-61 | (3) | Away | D | 0-0 |
|---|---|---|---|---|
|  | (R) | Home | W | 3-0 |

**Wartime**

|  |  | Home | | Away | |
|---|---|---|---|---|---|
| 1945-46 | (FLN) | L | 0-7 | L | 0-4 |

**CHIPPENDALE, Henry**
Winger. 1891-1897.
5ft 8½in; 11st 3lb.
Born: Blackburn, 2 October 1870; Died: Blackburn, 29 September 1952.
Debut: v Burnley (h) 26 September 1891.
Career: Nelson; Blackburn Rovers September 1891, retired cs 1897.
Later served as a Football League linesman to November 1908.
International honours with Blackburn Rovers: England: 1 cap (1894).
**Appearances:** Football League 134; FA Cup 13; Total 147.
**Goals:** Football League 50; FA Cup 2; Total 52.
Harry Chippendale had a surprisingly good turn of speed considering his bulky appearance. His build was also a useful asset in dealing with defenders and Chippendale was a difficult player to contain when in full flight. Coupled with an ability to send in pin-point crosses, Chippendale also possessed a fierce shot and notched a half century of goals in the Football League. Chippendale and Jimmy Whitehead formed a formidable left-wing partnership and it was fitting that Whitehead should be in the England team when Chippendale won his sole international cap. Unfortunately, his England debut coincided with Ireland managing to avoid defeat at English hands for the first time. Sadly, Chippendale and Whitehead were two of six players who didn't appear for England again following this upset. Outside of the game Harry was employed at Hornby's Brookhouse Mill in Blackburn and was later to become a manager with the firm.

**CHIVERS, Francis Cornelius**
Left-half. 1938-1942.
5ft 8in; 10st 8lb.
Born: Drybrook, Gloucester, 1909 (October quarter); Died: Don Valley, 4 April 1942.
Debut: v Luton Town (h) 19 March 1938.
Career: Goldthorpe United; Barnsley amateur May 1930, turning professional in October 1930; Huddersfield Town January 1936; Blackburn Rovers March 1938; Huddersfield Town wartime guest 1940-41.
Domestic honours with Blackburn Rovers: Second Division championship: 1938-39 (38 apps); League War Cup runners-up: 1940.
**Appearances:** Football League 48; FA Cup 7; Total 55.
**Goals:** Football League 2; FA Cup 1; Total 3.
Frank Chivers was the driving force of the successful 1938-39 Second Division championship team. Along with Arnold Whiteside and Bob Pryde, Chivers formed a half-back line that was widely recognised as one of the best in the country. Chivers had actually come to Ewood Park as a centre-forward from Huddersfield Town in March 1938. Ironically, Chivers' second goal in his Huddersfield career came against Blackburn Rovers at Leeds Road in February 1936. He scored a total of 16 goals in 50 League games for Huddersfield before making the move to Ewood Park. Chivers played in the final ten games of the 1937-38 season at Blackburn as either a centre-forward or an inside-left. However, after missing the opening five matches of the 1938-39 campaign he was introduced into the team in the left-half position. It was in this position that he enjoyed his greatest success at Blackburn. A dogged defender, Chivers was not only tenacious in his search for the ball but was also tireless in his support of the forwards. Following the outbreak of war he returned to work in the coal-mines but still made regular appearances for the Rovers. He figured in 88 wartime matches and scored three goals before tragically being killed in a mining accident in April 1942.

**CHRISTIE, Norman T.**
Centre-half. 1934-1937.
5ft 10in; 11st 7lb.
Born: Jarrow, 24 November 1913.
Debut: v Aston Villa (a) 22 September 1934.
Career: Newcastle United trial; Bishop Auckland; Huddersfield Town July 1931; Blackburn Rovers December 1934 to 1937.
**Appearances:** Football League 43; FA Cup 7; Total 50.
Norman Christie was secured from Huddersfield Town to fill the gap left by the injured Jesse Carver in December 1934. Christie, a Physical Education teacher in Huddersfield, proved so successful that he was quickly elevated to the captaincy. A skilful and enthusiastic player, Christie was a constructive type of centre-half whose long sweeping passes were a source of many attacking moves. Unfortunately, he was dogged by injury and eventually lost his place to Bob Pryde midway through the 1936-37 campaign.

**CLARK, Samuel James Hugh**
Left-back. 1933-1937.
5ft 9in; 10st 9lb.
Born: Whitletts, Cotsbridge, 15 November.
Debut: v Birmingham (a) 1 February 1936.
Career: Petershill; Blackburn Rovers August 1933; Halifax Town May 1937.

**Appearances:** Football League 1.
After 15 appearances for the Central League team at outside-left, Sam Clarke was tried in the back division. He made a favourable impression and was unfortunate not to receive more than one opportunity in a team that was ultimately to be relegated. Having been a winger, Clark liked nothing more than to get forward and join in the attack. Unfortunately, this left gaps at the back and it was this weakness that probably cost him more first-team opportunities.

**CLARKE, Albert**
Forward. 1938-1944.
5ft 7in; 10st 3lb.
Born: Sheffield, 25 December 1916; Died: 1944 (killed in action during World War Two whilst serving with the Devon Regiment).
Debut: v Tranmere Rovers (h) 27 August 1938.
Career: Mosborough Trinity; Frickley Colliery; Mexborough Town; Torquay United June 1934; Birmingham January 1936; Blackburn Rovers July 1938; Torquay United wartime guest 1939-40; Newport County wartime guest; Cardiff City wartime guest 1941-42.
Domestic honours with Blackburn Rovers: Second Division championship: 1938-39 (38 apps, 21 gls); League War Cup runners-up: 1940.
**Appearances:** Football League 38; FA Cup 4; Total 42.
**Goals:** Football League 21; FA Cup 2; Total 23.
Although he only figured in one season of peace-time football, Albert 'Nobby' Clarke carved his own niche in the club's history. He scored two goals on his debut and went on to finish as the leading goalscorer during the club's Second Division championship season. Although not the biggest of forwards, his stamina and enthusiasm made him a formidable opponent. At Birmingham he had proved his versatility by appearing in a number of positions, but at Ewood Park he was a permanent fixture at inside-left. Clarke was a tricky dribbler whose blistering pace made him a difficult man to mark. He immediately struck up a good understanding with Jock Weddle and when the latter wandered from his centre-forward position to the wing, Clarke was always ready to nip into the space which was left. Clarke appeared in all eight of the League War Cup games of 1939-40 and made two further appearances in that competition in 1940-41. However, although he remained on the registered playing staff, Clarke made no further appearances for Blackburn in wartime football. Sadly, Clarke became a casualty of war in 1944 when he was killed in action whilst serving with his regiment.

**CLAYTON, Kenneth**
Half-back. 1950-1961.
5ft 8¼in; 10st 6lb.
Born: Preston, 6 April 1933.
Debut: v Birmingham City (h) 22 November 1952.
Career: Blackburn Rovers amateur July 1949, signing professional in May 1950 to cs 1961; Ashton United 1961.
**Appearances:** Football League 72; FA Cup 5; Total 77.
The older brother of Ronnie Clayton, Ken came to Ewood Park as an amateur at the same time as his brother but was able to sign professional forms ahead of Ronnie. However, whilst Ronnie became an established first-team player, Ken had to settle for Central League football and by the end of the 1954-55 season had only three first-team appearances to his credit. After losing the opening two games of the 1955-56 season Johnny Carey decided to pair the Clayton brothers in the two wing-half positions. Ken Clayton made the most of his opportunity and quickly established himself as the perfect partner for his brother in the half-back line. The partnership remained intact until Ken suffered a broken leg towards the end of the 1956-57 season. The injury gave Mick McGrath a chance to establish himself at left-half and Ken was only to make three more senior appearances before being released at the end of the 1960-61 season.

**CLAYTON, Ronald**
Right-half. 1950-1969.
5ft 10½in; 11st 7lb.
Born: Preston, 5 August 1934.
Debut: v Queen's Park Rangers (h) 25 April 1951.
Career: Blackburn Rovers amateur July 1949, signing professional in August 1951; Morecambe player-manager July 1969; Great Harwood 1970.
International honours with Blackburn Rovers: England: 35 caps (1955-60); England Under-23: 6 caps (1955-57); England 'B': 1 cap (1955); Football League: 10 appearances (1955-60).
Domestic honours with Blackburn Rovers: FA Cup runners-up: 1960.
**Appearances:** Football League 579+2; FA Cup 56; Football League Cup 28; Total 663+2.
**Goals:** Football League 15; FA Cup 1; Total 16.
Second only to Bob Crompton in the Ewood Park 'Hall of Fame', Ronnie Clayton was the epitome of the perfect club professional. An old-

fashioned wing-half, Clayton remained faithful to Blackburn Rovers for 20 years and as result missed out on some of the more tangible rewards that the game began to offer with the lifting of the maximum wage. He arrived at Ewood with younger brother Ken in the summer of 1949 but didn't sign professional forms until August 1951. Even at that early stage his promise was such that the Rovers manager at the time, Jackie Bestall, predicted an international future for the talented youngster. Clayton was an athletic half-back who was strong in the tackle and powerful in the air. A feature of his play was his ability to surge forward in support of his forwards and to instigate attacking moves from deep positions.

Like Crompton before him, Clayton coupled his footballing ability with natural leadership qualities. In September 1955 he won his first England Under-23 cap and a month later he appeared for the England 'B' team. The sequence was completed in November 1955 when he made his debut for the full England team. At international level he appeared in the final stages of the 1958 World Cup in Sweden and captained his country in the last five of his 35 England appearances. On the domestic level he was the driving force behind the club's successful promotion campaign of 1957-58.

Clayton readily adapted to life in the First Division and in 1960 he led the team to Wembley in the FA Cup. However, in remaining loyal to what was regarded as an unfashionable club, Clayton missed out on the domestic honours in the game. During his time at Blackburn the club experienced mixed fortunes both on and off the field and yet Clayton always maintained the same level of enthusiasm and endeavour. As age blunted his attacking runs, Clayton moved to the centre of defence. Whilst age had slowed the legs, his touch and timing remained undiminished and, coupled with his intelligent reading of the game, enabled him to become an accomplished centre-back.

Clayton finally bowed out of Ewood at the end of the 1968-69 season and became player-manager of non-League Morecambe. However, his flirtation with management was a brief one and he quickly returned to East Lancashire to play for Great Harwood. At the Showground he linked

up with a host of former Blackburn colleagues including Bryan Douglas, Roy Vernon and Bob Jones. On 24 November 1970 he figured in the Great Harwood team which played host to Rotherham United in the first round of the FA Cup. Sadly, there was to be no glory for Harwood as Third Division Rotherham ran out 6-2 winners. One of the greatest ambassadors that Blackburn Rovers have ever had, Ronnie Clayton can still be found at Ewood Park today supporting the club he served so loyally for so many years.

**Career Record with Blackburn Rovers:**

|  | League | | FA Cup | | FL Cup | | Total | |
|---|---|---|---|---|---|---|---|---|
|  | Apps | Gls | Apps | Gls | Apps | Gls | Apps | Gls |
| 1950-51 | 1 | 0 | 0 | 0 | 0 | 0 | 1 | 0 |
| 1951-52 | 22 | 0 | 7 | 0 | 0 | 0 | 29 | 0 |
| 1952-53 | 12 | 0 | 1 | 0 | 0 | 0 | 13 | 0 |
| 1953-54 | 4 | 0 | 2 | 0 | 0 | 0 | 6 | 0 |
| 1954-55 | 42 | 2 | 1 | 0 | 0 | 0 | 43 | 2 |
| 1955-56 | 42 | 1 | 4 | 0 | 0 | 0 | 46 | 1 |
| 1956-57 | 34 | 4 | 1 | 0 | 0 | 0 | 35 | 4 |
| 1957-58 | 36 | 1 | 6 | 1 | 0 | 0 | 42 | 2 |
| 1958-59 | 40 | 1 | 2 | 0 | 0 | 0 | 42 | 1 |
| 1959-60 | 38 | 1 | 9 | 0 | 0 | 0 | 47 | 1 |
| 1960-61 | 41 | 0 | 5 | 0 | 5 | 0 | 51 | 0 |
| 1961-62 | 38 | 4 | 5 | 0 | 7 | 0 | 50 | 4 |
| 1962-63 | 35 | 1 | 1 | 0 | 5 | 0 | 41 | 1 |
| 1963-64 | 41 | 0 | 3 | 0 | 1 | 0 | 45 | 0 |
| 1964-65 | 39 | 0 | 2 | 0 | 3 | 0 | 44 | 0 |
| 1965-66 | 39 | 0 | 5 | 0 | 1 | 0 | 45 | 0 |
| 1966-67 | 41 | 0 | 1 | 0 | 3 | 0 | 45 | 0 |
| 1967-68 | 23 | 0 | 0 | 0 | 3 | 0 | 26 | 0 |
| 1968-69 | 11 +2 | 0 | 1 | 0 | 0 | 0 | 12+2 | 0 |
|  | 579 +2 | 15 | 56 | 1 | 28 | 0 | 663+2 | 16 |

**CLEGHORN, Thomas**
Left-half. 1894-1896.
*5ft 5in; 11st.*
*Born: Leith, Edinburgh, 1871.*
*Debut: v Stoke (h) 15 September 1894.*
*Career: Leith Athletic; Blackburn Rovers August 1894; Liverpool March 1896; Portsmouth August 1899 to 1902.*
**Appearances:** Football League 45; FA Cup 3; Total 48.
**Goals:** Football League 3.
A busy, hard-working half-back who was hugely popular with the Blackburn public during his two seasons with the club. Not only was Cleghorn a demon tackler, but his intelligent use of the ball created numerous opportunities for his forwards. A player who never knew when he was beaten, Cleghorn had the personality to rouse the crowds simply by his own enthusiastic efforts. After leaving Ewood he enjoyed successful spells with Liverpool and Portsmouth and helped Pompey to lift the Southern League championship in 1901.

**CLENNELL, Joseph**
Inside-left. 1911-1914.
*5ft 8in; 11st.*
*Born: New Silksworth, Co. Durham, 19 February 1889; Died: Blackpool, 28 February 1965.*
*Debut: v Tottenham Hotspur (h) 22 April 1911.*
*Career: Silksworth United; Seaham Harbour; Blackpool May 1910; Blackburn Rovers April 1911 (£900); Everton January 1914 (£1,500); Cardiff City October 1921 (£3,500); Stoke City February 1925; Bristol Rovers July 1926; Rochdale October 1927 to March 1928; Ebbw Vale player-manager 1928; Barry Town cs 1928; Bangor player-coach July 1929; Belfast Distillery manager; Great Harwood April 1931; Accrington Stanley coach 1934.*
*Domestic honours with Blackburn Rovers: First Division championship: 1911-12 (18 apps ,9 gls); 1913-14 (4 apps, 1 gl).*
**Appearances:** Football League 26; FA Cup 1; Total 27.
**Goals:** Football League 12.
Joe Clennell enjoyed one good season with Blackburn Rovers and helped the club to capture the League title for the first time in its history. A hard running and skilful

striker, Clennell was still a raw youngster when he came to Blackburn in April 1911. He became a first-team regular towards the end of the title-winning season but the two following campaigns saw him out of favour and in January 1914 he moved to Everton. At Goodison Park, Clennell developed into a brilliant schemer who also possessed a fine shot. He won another championship medal whilst on Merseyside, in 1914-15, and appeared for the Football League in 1920. Clennell scored 30 goals in 60 League matches for Everton before moving to Cardiff City in 1921. He enjoyed something of a nomadic existence during the latter part of his career, but Clennell returned to East Lancashire in 1931 to play for Great Harwood and later had a spell as coach to Accrington Stanley. Tragically, Joe Clennell died in a car accident in 1965.

### CLINTON, Thomas Joseph
Right-back. 1955-1956.
*5ft 9in; 11st 2lb.*
*Born: Dublin, 13 April 1926.*
*Debut: v Sheffield Wednesday (h) 26 December 1955.*
*Career: Dundalk; Everton March 1948; Blackburn Rovers April 1955; Tranmere Rovers June 1956 to June 1957.*
**Appearances:** Football League 6; FA Cup 2; Total 8.
Clinton, a former Republic of Ireland international, was signed by Blackburn to provide experienced cover for the full-back positions. He was brought to England by Everton, but he found it difficult to retain a regular first-team spot during his seven seasons at Goodison Park despite winning three international caps. The emergence of Ken Taylor towards the end of the 1955-56 campaign brought his Ewood career to an end and he returned to Merseyside to finish his career with Tranmere Rovers.

### CLITHEROE FC
Founded in 1879, Clitheroe met Blackburn Rovers in the first round of the FA Cup on 24 October 1885. The match was played at Clitheroe in front of 1,500 spectators and resulted in a 2-0 victory for the Rovers. This was the start of what was to be the third successful campaign for Blackburn in the FA Cup in successive years.

### CLOUGH, Albert Eric
Left-back. 1919-1921.
*5ft 8in; 11st 3lb.*
*Debut: v Bradford (h) 24 January 1920.*
*Career: St Matthew's; Audley Central; Great Harwood; Blackburn Rovers amateur early 1919, turning professional in November 1919; Blackpool May 1921; Great Harwood; Lancaster 1922.*
**Appearances:** Football League 1.
Albert Clough was described as having 'the makings of an excellent defender' by the correspondent of a local football annual at the start of the 1920-21 season. Clough had made his debut in the 3-3 draw with Bradford in January 1920, but this proved to be his only senior appearance. He made a major impact in the Central League when he scored a hat-trick on the day he was tried at outside-left. Clough was allowed to join Blackpool in May 1921.

### COCKSHUTT, James William
Centre-forward. 1890-1892.
*Born: Darwen, Lancs, 1873; Died: 13 April 1938.*
*Debut: v Sunderland (a) 16 April 1892.*
*Career: Blackburn Rovers August 1890; Brierfield; Burnley December 1893; Nelson cs 1894; Reading cs 1897; Grimsby Town May 1898; Nelson October 1900.*
**Appearances:** Football League 1.
Although considered to be rather short for the centre-forward position, James Cockshutt proved a spirited competitor at a number of clubs during the 1890s. As a youngster he was understudy to Jack Southworth at Blackburn and was a member of the team that won the Lancashire Combination title in 1892-93. He won further honours with Nelson in 1895-96 when he helped them to win the Lancashire League.

### CODDINGTON, John William
Centre-half. 1967-1970.
*6ft 1in; 12st 4lb.*
*Born: Worksop, 16 December 1937.*
*Debut: v Millwall (a) 19 August 1967.*
*Career: Worksop Boys' Club; Huddersfield Town groundstaff September 1953, becoming a part-time professional in January 1955, and a full-time professional in June 1958; Blackburn Rovers June 1967 (£20,000); Stockport County on loan January 1970 before signing permanently in March 1970; Great Harwood July 1971; Bradford City chief coach; Drogheda February 1973; Middlesbrough coach; Horden Colliery Welfare manager.*
**Appearances:** Football League 72+1; FA Cup 5; Football League Cup 6; Total 83+1.

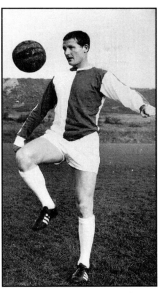

**Goals:** Football League 3.
Convinced that a pairing of Ronnie Clayton and George Sharples lacked sufficient height to compete for the ball in the air, Eddie Quigley persuaded John Coddington, Huddersfield's long serving captain, to move to Ewood Park. Coddington, who Quigley installed as captain, was in the traditional mould of centre-halves. Strong in the air, what skill he lacked on the ball he made up for with his strong tackling and sheer physical presence. He was a commanding figure during the 1967-68 season but the following campaign saw him exposed to pace. It was a cruel twist of fate that Coddington should best be remembered at Ewood Park for a twice missed penalty against Crystal Palace in March 1968. His two attempts to score from the spot on a heavy pitch saw him embark on a run-up which many a fast bowler would have been proud. Sadly, on both occasions the contact with the ball was so poor that the goalkeeper had to wait for the ball to reach him. Having lost his place to Dick Mulvaney, Coddington ended his League career with Stockport County. He returned to East Lancashire to play for Great Harwood before moving into coaching.

### COLCHESTER UNITED FC
Formed in 1937, Colchester United were elected to the Football League in 1950. Although relegated to the GM Vauxhall Conference in 1992, Colchester bounced back to the Football League after only one season in exile. Colchester first met Blackburn Rovers during the 1974-75 Third Division championship campaign when they were managed by Jim Smith. When Gordon Lee left Blackburn for Newcastle at the end of that season, the Rovers chose Smith to become his replacement. Whilst the Rovers have an excellent record in League matches against Colchester, 'The U's' inflicted an embarrassing League Cup defeat on the men from Ewood in 1977.

**Football League**

|         |         | Home |     | Away |     |
|---------|---------|------|-----|------|-----|
| 1974-75 | (Div 3) | W    | 3-2 | L    | 0-2 |
| 1979-80 | (Div 3) | W    | 3-0 | W    | 1-0 |

|       | P | W | D | L | F | A |
|-------|---|---|---|---|---|---|
| Home  | 2 | 2 | 0 | 0 | 6 | 2 |
| Away  | 2 | 1 | 0 | 1 | 1 | 2 |
| Total | 4 | 3 | 0 | 1 | 7 | 4 |

**Football League Cup**

|         |     |      |   |     |
|---------|-----|------|---|-----|
| 1977-78 | (2) | Home | D | 1-1 |
|         | (R) | Away | L | 0-4 |

### COLLIER, Darren James
Goalkeeper. 1987-1993.
*6ft; 12st 6lb.*
*Born: Stockton, 1 December 1967.*
*Debut: v Ipswich Town (a) 13 May 1989.*
*Career: Middlesbrough non-contract player; Blackburn Rovers non-contract player December 1987, signing as a professional in June 1988; Darlington July 1993 (free).*
**Appearances:** Football League 27; Football League Cup 3; Full Members' Cup 1; Total 31.
Darren Collier turned professional with Blackburn Rovers after having had a spell on Middlesbrough's book as a non-contract player. At Ewood he became the club's number-two goalkeeper following the departure of Vince O'Keefe and made 14 appearances during the 1989-90 season. When Terry Gennoe was injured in the first match of the following campaign, Collier found himself thrust into the first team. Not the biggest of goalkeepers, Collier always looked better in dealing with ground shots than challenging for crosses. With the team struggling for results, Don Mackay brought Mark Grew on loan from Port Vale and Collier returned to his understudy role. His number-two position was confirmed when the club spent £250,000 to bring Bobby Mimms from Tottenham Hotspur in December 1990. He was not selected at all during the 1991-92 season and following the signings of Matt Dickins and Frank Talia, his Ewood career appeared to be rather bleak. He was named as substitute goalkeeper on a

number of occasions during 1992-93 whilst both Dickins and Talia were gaining valuable experience on loan to other clubs. At the end of the season he was give a free transfer and returned to the North-East to join Darlington.

**COMSTIVE, Paul Thomas**
Midfield. 1978-1983.
*6ft 1in; 12st 7lb.*
*Born: Southport, 25 November 1961.*
*Debut: v Sheffield Wednesday (a) 7 October 1980.*
*Career: Blackburn Rovers non-contract player December 1978, signing as a professional in October 1979; Rochdale on loan September 1982; Wigan Athletic August 1983 (free); Wrexham November 1984 (free); Burnley August 1987 (£8,000); Bolton Wanderers September 1989 (£37,000); Chester City November 1991 (£10,000); Southport cs 1993.*
**Appearances:** Football League 3+3.
Although Paul Comstive joined Blackburn Rovers as a midfield player, it was as a utility man that he enjoyed his greatest success during a rather nomadic career. Although tall and well built, Comstive found it difficult to establish himself in a midfield berth at Ewood Park. In August 1983, after a loan spell with Rochdale, he moved to Wigan Athletic on a free transfer. Comstive found no shortage of employers in the lower divisions and by the time he moved to Southport in the summer of 1993 he had amassed over 300 appearances in the Football League.

**CONLON, Bryan**
Centre-forward. 1970-1972.
*6ft 1in; 12st 7lb.*
*Born: Shildon, 14 January 1943.*
*Debut: v Watford (a) 15 August 1970.*
*Career: Shildon Morden Council School; Sheffield Wednesday trail; Newcastle United May 1961; South Shields May 1962; Darlington August 1964; Millwall November 1967; Norwich City December 1968; Blackburn Rovers May 1970; Crewe Alexandra on loan January 1972 to February 1972; Cambridge United March 1972; Hartlepool United September 1972 to June 1974; Shildon Athletic July 1974 to December 1975.*
**Appearances:** Football League 43+2; FA Cup 2; Football League Cup 3+1; Total 48+3.
**Goals:** Football League 7.
Bryan Conlon was a craggy centre-forward who enjoyed his best days with Darlington, scoring 27 goals in 74 appearances (including three as sub) in the Football League. Although he found no shortage of employers, Conlon was never the most prolific of goalscorers. During his subsequent career his goals tally only reached double figures at the Den where he scored 13 goals in 41 League appearances (including one as sub). Conlon came to Blackburn in a part-exchange deal which took Malcolm Darling to Norwich City in May 1970. In a struggling team he never looked capable of providing the fire-power that would keep the club in the Second Division. Asked to battle alone in the middle, Conlon finished the season with a meagre haul of six goals from 30 appearances; although this was enough to make him the joint top goalscorer for the season. Conlon was involved in a curious incident when he was controversially sent off for dissent in the relegation battle with Orient in December 1970. The Orient players were so incensed with the decision that they offered to support him at the subsequent hearing. The result of the hearing was that Conlon escaped a ban and received a suspended sentence and a small fine. In 1971-72, Conlon, a tall and powerfully built individual, was used as a central defender by Ken Furphy – a case of poacher turned gamekeeper. The experiment ended when the Rovers signed John McNamee and Conlon was allowed to continue his travels.

**CONNELLY, John Michael**
Winger. 1966-1970.
*5ft 8½in; 11st 2lb.*
*Born: St Helens, 18 July 1938.*
*Debut: v Ipswich Town (h) 24 September 1966.*
*Career: St Helens Town; Burnley November 1956; Manchester United April 1964 (£56,000); Blackburn Rovers September 1966 (£40,000); Bury June 1970 (free). Retired cs 1972.*
**Appearances:** Football League 148+1; FA Cup 6; Football League Cup 9; Total 163+1.
**Goals:** Football League 36; FA Cup 2; Football League Cup 1; Total 39.
Jack Marshall pulled off a major coup when he persuaded John

Connelly to come to Ewood Park only two months after appearing in England's opening World Cup fixture. Although this proved to be the last of Connelly's 20 England caps, there was no doubt that he was still a winger of real quality. Connelly was already well known to Blackburn supporters due to his lengthy service with neighbouring Burnley. He had joined the Turf Moor Club in November 1956 and went on to appear in 215 League games for the Clarets. A winger of terrific pace, Connelly could play on either wing and was an opportunist marksman in front of goal. During his time with Burnley he scored 86 League goals and was top scorer with 20 goals during the championship winning season of 1959-60. He joined Manchester United in April 1964 and added a second championship medal to his collection in 1964-65. Connelly scored 22 goals in 80 League appearances (including one as sub) at Old Trafford before moving to Blackburn. Connelly gave excellent service to the Rovers for four seasons. He was the top League goalscorer for the club in 1966-67 and was equal top in 1968-69. Released at the end of the 1969-70 season he made the short move to Bury where he scored 37 goals in 128 League games before retiring in 1973. On leaving football he concentrated on his fish and chip shop in Brierfield, near Burnley.

**COOK, Leslie**
Right-back. 1939-1949.
*5ft 9in; 10st 1lb.*
*Born: Blackburn, 11 November 1924.*
*Debut: v Huddersfield Town (a) 14 September 1946.*
*Career: Blackburn Rovers amateur June 1939, turning professional in February 1943; Coventry City 20 July 1949; Rugby Town 1955.*
**Appearances:** Football League 76; FA Cup 8; Total 84.
A rugged, wholehearted player who was used in a variety of positions during his ten years at Ewood Park. Apart from 84 appearances in first-class matches, Cook also appeared in 65 wartime games. Noted for his hard tackling, Cook had been capped at schoolboy level for England in 1939 when playing at left-half. However, it was as right-back that he finally settled into the Blackburn team, appearing in 39 League matches in 1946-47. He eventually lost his place to David Gray before having a run of 14 games at right-half in 1948-49. At the end of the season a disagreement over a benefit led to him joining Coventry City, where he was to appear in a further 88 League games.

**COOMBS, Ernest Horace**
Centre-forward. 1933-1934.
*Born: Frome, 1 May 1908; Died: Frome, 16 May 1971.*
*Debut: v Stoke City (a) 9 December 1933.*
*Career: Colefield; Writhlington; Bristol Rovers amateur September 1931, turning professional in September 1931; Bristol City May 1932; Bath City 1932-33; Blackburn Rovers November 1933; Bath City September 1934; Cheltenham Town August 1935; Somerset Constabulary January 1936.*
**Appearances:** Football League 6.
A prolific goalscoring record in junior football led to Bristol Rovers offering Coombs the opportunity to step up into the Football League in September 1931. However, after only one season he switched his allegiance to Bristol City and the following season was back in non-League circles with Bath City. A double hat-trick in a friendly against Cardiff City was one of the feats that attracted him to Blackburn Rovers in November 1933. After a run of six games without a goal Coombs was replaced by the veteran Harper and was never again selected for the first team. In September 1934 he returned to non-League football.

**COPE, Harold**
Goalkeeper. 1926-1930.
*5ft 8in; 11st.*
*Born: Rawmarsh, 9 February 1902; Died: 7 July 1980.*
*Debut: v Burnley (h) 16 October 1926.*
*Career: Parkgate Works FC; Rawmarsh Athletic; Mexborough Town cs 1921; Birmingham trial April 1922; Barnsley amateur May 1922, turning professional in August 1922; Mexborough Town 1925; Blackburn Rovers October 1926; Swindon Town May 1930; Stalybridge Celtic August 1932; Harrow Sheet Metal Works December 1934.*
**Appearances:** Football League 25.
Harold Cope was signed by Blackburn Rovers following injuries to Ronnie Sewell and Jock Crawford. With both senior goalkeepers out of action the Rovers turned to Cope, a former Barnsley goalkeeper, who was playing with Mexborough Town. Although stockily built, Cope was deceptively quick off his line and fearless when challenging for the ball. Sadly, after establishing himself in the first team, injury cost him his place and gave Jock Crawford the chance to regain the number-one position. When the club signed Cliff Binns in January 1930, Cope opted to join Swindon Town rather than play Central League football.

Rovers clear their lines against Corinthians in 1924, when the amateurs inflicted an embarrassing FA Cup defeat on the Rovers.

**COPE, Horace Walter**
Trainer. 1946-1949.
*Born: Treeton, nr Sheffield, 24 May 1899; Died: Nottingham, December 1961.*
*Career: Treeton United; Notts County 1920; Arsenal December 1926 (£3,125); Bristol Rovers July 1933 (£1,500); Norwich City reserve trainer July 1934; Southampton trainer March 1937; Blackburn Rovers trainer early 1946 to May 1949.*
Horace Cope came to Ewood Park after World War Two to join Eddie Hapgood, a former playing colleague at Highbury. Indeed, Cope had understudied Hapgood for the left-back position at Arsenal and for this reason made only 65 League appearances for the Gunners. Cope remained at Ewood following Hapgood's early departure and went on to serve Will Scott and Jack Bruton as the club's senior trainer. Cope was axed by the Rovers along with Jack Bruton in May 1949. Only a week before his departure he had acted as trainer for the Football League side in an inter-League match in Dublin. Following his dismissal at Blackburn, Cope left the game to take charge of a social club in Yorkshire before becoming a publican in Nottingham.

**CORINTHIANS FC**
Founded in 1882, the Corinthians were, at one time, the top amateur side in the country. During the 1880s they travelled to Blackburn for a number of friendly encounters and invariably came out on top. The first meeting between the clubs, at Blackburn on the 15 December 1884, resulted in an 8-1 win for the Corinthians. Their rules forbade them from entering the FA Cup and it was not until 1922 that they finally participated in the competition. In their second season of FA Cup football they were drawn to meet Blackburn Rovers at home in the first round. The match was played at Crystal Palace on 12 January 1924 and resulted in an embarrassing 1-0 defeat for the Rovers.

**COTTON, Lawrence**
Chairman. 1905-1919.
As a young man Lawrence Cotton had been a playing member and secretary of Christ Church Cricket and Football Club. However, it was with Blackburn Rovers that Cotton carved his own niche in the sporting history of his home town. A director of the club from 1891 to 1901, Cotton returned to the boardroom in 1903 and became chairman on 28 March 1905 and retained that position until 19 February 1919. During his chairmanship he raised the Rovers from a position where relegation to the Second Division seemed likely, to one in which two League championships were captured in the space of three seasons. To achieve this feat he sanctioned the expenditure of some £12,000 between 1906 and 1914 to bring the very best players to Ewood Park. In particular the arrival of Jock Simpson, Danny Shea, Joe Hodkinson and Percy Dawson turned the team into one of true championship material.

As well as a massive outlay on players, Cotton was also responsible for turning Ewood Park into one of the finest grounds in the country. This was done at a cost of around £33,000. In 1893, Lawrence Cotton went into business as a cotton manufacturer in partnership with his brother Clement. It was Clement who followed Lawrence into the position of chairman at Ewood Park in 1919. In December 1892, Lawrence Cotton was elected to the Council but retired from office after only four years. However, in 1917 he became Mayor of Blackburn, a post he held until his death, and in 1919 he was made an Alderman of the town in recognition for his services to Blackburn. It was the pressure of his civic duties that forced him to step down from the chairmanship of Blackburn Rovers in February 1919. However, the following June, with his brother installed as chairman, Lawrence Cotton became the club's first-ever president. It was a position he retained until his death at his residence at Clayton Green on 7 May 1921.

**COUGHLIN, Russell**
Midfield. 1979-1980.
*5ft 8in; 11st 6lb.*
*Born: Swansea, 15 February 1960.*
*Debut: v Cambridge United (h) 28 March 1979.*
*Career: Manchester City amateur July 1976, turning professional in March 1978, Blackburn Rovers March 1979 (£40,000); Carlisle United*

*October 1980 (£20,000); Plymouth Argyle July 1984 (£20,000); Blackpool December 1987 (£75,000); Shrewsbury Town on loan September 1990; Swansea City October 1990; Exeter City August 1993.*
**Appearances:** Football League 22+2; Football League Cup 1+1; Total 23+3.
Stocky midfielder who came to Ewood Park after failing to break into the first team at Maine Road. He joined the Rovers as the club was fighting for Second Division survival but, despite some promising performances, was unable to make sufficient difference to a struggling side. He featured in several of Howard Kendall's early team selections but lost his place as Kendall settled on a winning formula. After leaving the Rovers he enjoyed great success with several clubs in the lower divisions.

### COUPE, Thomas
Goalkeeper. 1899-1900.
*Born: Rishton.*
*Debut: v Liverpool (a) 3 February 1900.*
*Career: Great Harwood; Blackburn Rovers March 1899; Accrington Stanley June 1900; Blackburn Rovers December 1901; Chorley May 1902; Great Harwood; Accrington Stanley; Padiham cs 1904.*
**Appearances:** Football League 1.
An unhappy debut resulted in a 3-1 defeat at Liverpool and effectively ended Coupe's claims for a first-team place. He moved to Accrington Stanley in the summer of 1900, but returned to Ewood Park in December 1901 to appear with the Reserves in the Lancashire Combination. He continued to find plenty of employment in non-League circles after ending his second stint with Blackburn.

### COVENTRY CITY FC
Although formed in 1883, Coventry City did not meet Blackburn Rovers in a competitive match until the 1936-37 season. Coventry became members of the Second Division in 1919 and it was in that division that all the Football League meetings between the clubs were played. In 1992-93 the clubs met for the first time in top-flight football during the inaugural season of the Premier League. It was Coventry who pipped Blackburn to promotion to the First Division in 1966-67 and whilst the fortunes of the Rovers fluctuated during the next 25 years, Coventry enjoyed uninterrupted membership of the old First Division.

**Football League**

|  |  | Home |  | Away |  |
|---|---|---|---|---|---|
| 1936-37 | (Div 2) | L | 2-5 | W | 1-0 |
| 1937-38 | (Div 2) | L | 1-3 | L | 2-3 |
| 1938-39 | (Div 2) | L | 0-2 | W | 1-0 |
| 1948-49 | (Div 2) | W | 2-0 | W | 1-0 |
| 1949-50 | (Div 2) | L | 0-1 | D | 1-1 |
| 1950-51 | (Div 2) | W | 1-0 | L | 1-6 |
| 1951-52 | (Div 2) | L | 0-1 | W | 2-1 |
| 1966-67 | (Div 2) | L | 0-1 | L | 0-2 |

|  | P | W | D | L | F | A |
|---|---|---|---|---|---|---|
| Home | 8 | 2 | 0 | 6 | 6 | 13 |
| Away | 8 | 4 | 1 | 3 | 9 | 13 |
| Total | 16 | 6 | 1 | 9 | 15 | 26 |

**FA Premiership**

|  | Home |  | Away |  |
|---|---|---|---|---|
| 1992-93 | L | 2-5 | W | 2-0 |
| 1993-94 | W | 2-1 | L | 1-2 |

|  | P | W | D | L | F | A |
|---|---|---|---|---|---|---|
| Home | 2 | 1 | 0 | 1 | 4 | 6 |
| Away | 2 | 1 | 0 | 1 | 3 | 2 |
| Total | 4 | 2 | 0 | 2 | 7 | 8 |

**FA Cup**

| 1979-80 | (4) | Home | W | 1-0 |
|---|---|---|---|---|

### COWANS, Gordon Sidney
Midfield. 1991-1993.
*5ft 9in; 10st 7lb.*
Born: Cornforth, 27 October 1958.
*Debut: v Middlesbrough (h) 30 November 1991.*
*Career: County Durham & District Schools; Aston Villa apprentice July 1974, turning professional in September 1976; Bari (Italy) July 1985 (£500,000); Aston Villa July 1988 (£250,000); Blackburn Rovers November 1991 (200,000); Aston Villa June 1993 (free); Derby County February 1994 (£75,000).*
*Domestic honours with Blackburn Rovers: Second Division Play-off winners: 1992.*
**Appearances:** Premier League 23+1; Football League 26; Play-offs 3;

FA Cup 5; Football League Cup 4; Total 61+1.
**Goals:** Premier League 1; Football League 1; FA Cup 1; Total 3.
Kenny Dalglish brought the vastly experienced Cowans to Ewood Park to be his midfield general in the chase for a Premier League place. A former England international, Cowans had spent his entire career with Aston Villa apart from a three year spell in Italy with Bari. His vision and ability to pass the ball with great accuracy played a major part in the ultimate success of the quest for Premier League football at Ewood Park. It came as something of a surprise when Cowans began the 1992-93 season out of the first team. However, he overcame the challenges of Mark Atkins and Patrik Andersson and won a regular place during the latter part of the campaign. Ironically, his best performance of the season came against Aston Villa at Ewood Park when the Rovers ended Villa's hopes of winning the title. Cowans was allowed to return to Aston Villa on a free transfer in the summer of 1993 when it was thought that Roy Keane would opt to come to Ewood Park.

### COWELL, Arthur
Left-back. 1905-1922.
*5ft 7½in; 10st 10lb.*
*Born: Blackburn, 20 May 1886; Died: Lower Darwen, 12 February 1959.*
*Debut: v Notts County (a) 23 September 1905.*
*Career: Blackburn St Peter's; Nelson 1904; Blackburn Rovers May 1905. Retired cs 1920 to become a member of the training staff at Ewood Park, becoming first-team trainer in 1933 until 1937; Wrexham trainer May 1937 then manager from June 1938 to August 1938.*

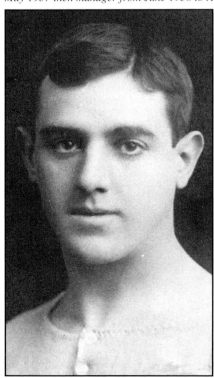

*International honours with Blackburn Rovers: England: 1 cap (1910); Football League: 1 appearance (1909).*
*Domestic honours with Blackburn Rovers: Football League championship: 1911-12 (31 apps); 1913-14 (38 apps).*
**Appearances:** Football League 278; FA Cup 26; FA Charity Shield 1; Total 305.
Arthur Cowell and Bob Crompton formed one of the finest full-back partnerships in the long history of Blackburn Rovers. They came together on 23 September 1905 and appeared for the last time in tandem, in peacetime football, on 24 April 1915. During that time Blackburn Rovers claimed the First Division title twice and reached two FA Cup semi-finals. Locally, they were seen as the perfect com-

bination. Although Cowell was smaller in build than Crompton, he possessed the speed which enabled him to cover any gaps which occurred in the Rovers' defence. Furthermore, despite his size, Cowell was a relentless tackler whose accurate distribution often set up many threatening counter-attacks. However, unlike Crompton, who became a fixture in the England team for over a decade, Cowell received only one international cap. World War One effectively ended the playing careers of both men. Although younger than Crompton, Cowell was unable to revive his career following the return of League football due to a serious injury. He was restricted to a solitary appearance during the 1919-20 season and although he spent the next two years trying to regain full fitness he finally had to accept his playing days were over. On hanging up his boots he joined the training staff at Ewood Park and following Mo Atherton's departure in January 1933 he was appointed first-team trainer. He left Ewood Park in May 1937 to become trainer at Wrexham and enjoyed a short spell as manager with the Welsh club in 1938. During his later years he became a newsagent in Kirkham and then Darwen.

## COXON, Eric Gary
Right-back. 1963-1969.
*5ft 7in; 10st 8lb.*
*Born: Liverpool, 31 May 1946.*
*Debut: v Rotherham United (h) 6 May 1967.*
*Career: Everton apprentice July 1961; Blackburn Rovers December 1963; Northwich Victoria cs 1969.*

**Appearances:** Football League 10.
Gary Coxon joined Blackburn Rovers after serving his apprenticeship with Everton. However, if the energetic young full-back thought he would receive more first-team opportunities at Ewood Park he was to be sadly disappointed. The pairing of Keith Newton and Billy Wilson restricted Coxon to a handful of League appearances and during the summer of 1969 he entered non-League football with Northwich Victoria.

## CRABTREE, James Joseph MC
Goalkeeper. 1913-1920.
*6ft 2in; 10st 11lb.*
*Born: Clitheroe, February 1895; Died: Clitheroe, 1 December 1965.*
*Debut: v Bradford City (a) 25 February 1914.*
*Career: Stonyhurst College; Clitheroe Amateurs; Blackburn Rovers amateur April 1913, turning professional in March 1914; Rochdale August 1920 to May 1923; Accrington Stanley February 1924 to May 1925.*
*International honours with Blackburn Rovers: England: 1 Amateur cap.*
*Domestic honours with Blackburn Rovers: First Division championship: 1913-14 (10 apps).*

**Appearances:** Football League 12.
James Crabtree was an unknown quantity when he appeared in ten of the final 11 games that clinched the First Division title in 1913-14. Although he made his debut just short of his 19th birthday, his exceptional reach and natural ability enabled him to keep five clean sheets in those vital ten games. Crabtree served with distinction during World War One, winning the Military Cross for bravery and rising from the ranks to a commission. He returned to Ewood after the war but made only two appearances before moving to join Rochdale. Whilst at Spotland he appeared at inside-left in one game and scored two goals. Crabtree returned to East Lancashire in February 1924 to join Accrington Stanley but retired shortly afterwards to become a referee.

## CRAIG, Joseph
Centre-forward. 1978-1981.
*5ft 9in; 11st 2lb.*
*Born: Bridge of Allan, Stirlingshire, 14 May 1954.*
*Debut: v Charlton Athletic (h) 30 September 1978.*
*Career: Sauchie Juniors; Partick Thistle August 1972; Glasgow Celtic September 1976 (£60,000); Blackburn Rovers September 1978 (£40,000); Hamilton Academical March 1981 to 1983; Cowdenbeath coach 1985, becoming acting manager in December 1985 then manager in April 1986 until June 1987; Armadale Thistle November 1987; Airdrieonians coach 1988 to May 1991.*
**Appearances:** Football League 44+4; FA Cup 3; Football League Cup 3+1; Total 50+5.
**Goals:** Football League 8; FA Cup 1; Football League Cup 1; Total 10.
Joe Craig was signed by Jim Iley just four days before the club terminated his contract as manager. Craig, who was capped for Scotland in 1977, was highly regarded north of the border as a hard-working striker. He had formed a twin spearhead at Parkhead with Kenny Dalglish and in 1976-77 had actually out-scored the man who was to become such a legendary figure in the game. When Jim Iley brought Craig to Ewood Park he became the first player signed from a Scottish club since Ally MacLeod in the late 1950s. Although he came with a reputation as a prolific goalscorer, Craig found goals in short supply at Blackburn. He failed to make much impression in a struggling team and couldn't supply the goals required to keep the club in the Second Division. Howard Kendall began the 1979-80 season with Craig at centre-forward but was later to favour the emerging promise of young Simon Garner. Unable to break into the first team Craig chose to return to Scotland in March 1981.

## CRAIG, Robert M.
Inside-forward. 1962.
*5ft 4in; 10st 12½lb.*
*Born: Airdrie, 8 April 1935.*
*Debut: v Sheffield Wednesday (h) 26 April 1962.*
*Career: Blantyre Celtic; Third Lanark; Sheffield Wednesday November 1959; Blackburn Rovers April 1962 (£20,000); Glasgow Celtic October 1962 (£15,000); St Johnstone 1963-64; Oldham Athletic March 1964 (£5,000); Toronto City (Canada) Johannesburg Wanderers (South Africa); Third Lanark.*
**Appearances:** Football League 8; Football League Cup 2; Total 10.
**Goals:** Football League 3.
Bobby Craig was a diminutive inside-forward in the typically tricky Scottish mould. Craig had learned his trade in Scotland with Third Lanark before moving south to England in November 1959 to join Sheffield Wednesday. Jack Marshall brought this ball playing schemer to Blackburn towards the end of the 1961-62 season. Having made his debut in the penultimate match of that campaign, Craig began the 1962-63 season with an opening day hat-trick at Ipswich Town. Unfortunately, Craig's wife failed to settle in Blackburn and as a result his form began to suffer. In October 1962 he was placed on the transfer list and was snapped up by Celtic. He returned to England briefly in 1964 to score four goals in 18 appearances for Oldham Athletic.

## CRAWFORD, Andrew
Inside-forward. 1979-1981.
*5ft 7in; 10st 4lb.*
*Born: Filey, 30 January 1959.*
*Debut: v Gillingham (a) 6 October 1979.*
*Career: Filey Town; Derby County apprentice September 1975, turning professional in March 1978; Manawata (New Zealand) on loan 1979; Blackburn Rovers October 1979 (£50,000); AFC Bournemouth November 1981 (£40,000); Cardiff City October 1983; Middlesbrough October 1983; Stockport County December 1984; Torquay United non-contract player March 1985; Poole Town 1988.*
**Appearances:** Football League 56; A Cup 8; Football League Cup 4; Total 68.
**Goals:** Football League 21; FA Cup 5; Total 26.
Andy Crawford was but a fleeting meteor on the Blackburn skyline. He came to Blackburn as a relatively unknown striker who had been

lingering in the Central League team at Derby County. However, under Howard Kendall, he scored 18 goals in 36 Third Division matches for Blackburn and helped the club to promotion at the first attempt. Yet at a time when his career ought to have flourished, Crawford demanded a transfer and found himself returned to football's backwaters. However, despite his sudden demise from the first team at Ewood Park, Crawford had carved a niche in the club's history with his goalscoring exploits as the club climbed the Third Division table. The diminutive striker's return of 18 League goals was the best individual scoring feat since the days of Andy McEvoy in the 1960s. Crawford left Blackburn for Bournemouth in November 1981 and his career briefly flourished on

the south coast. Ten goals helped the club to promotion from the Fourth Division, but two years later he was given a free transfer. After a trial with Cardiff failed to produce a contract he spent ten months at Middlesbrough but made only nine appearances (including one as sub). Brief spells with Stockport County and Torquay United failed to revive his career and at the end of the 1984-85 campaign he drifted out of League football. Sadly, Crawford's career failed to fulfil the potential he had shown in that first explosive season at Ewood Park.

**CRAWFORD, John Chalmers**
Goalkeeper. 1925-1932.
*5ft 11in; 12st 8lb.*
*Born: Stirling, 11 October 1902; Died: Stirling, May 1973.*
*Debut: v Bolton Wanderers (a) 22 April 1925.*
*Career: Alloa Athletic; Blackburn Rovers March 1925; East Stirling on loan September 1932.*
*Domestic honours with Blackburn Rovers: FA Cup winners: 1928.*
**Appearances:** Football League 155; FA Cup 17; FA Charity Shield 1; Total 173.
'Jock' Crawford arrived at Ewood Park in March 1925 and gradually established himself as the number-one custodian at the club. However, the former Alloa Athletic goalkeeper was forced to fight his way into the team. In 1925-26 he vied with Ronnie Sewell for the goalkeeper's jersey and in 1926-27, as Sewell bowed out, he found Harold Cope challenging for the place between the posts. In his early days at the club Crawford appeared to lack a little in confidence, particularly when dealing with high balls in the area. However, by the start of the 1927-28 campaign he had rectified his faults and become firmly established as the number-one goalkeeper at Ewood Park. The 1927-28 season saw him win an FA Cup winners' medal and he was invited to attend a Scottish trial. After appearing in 40 League games during the 1928-29 campaign, Crawford's form suddenly and unexpectedly began to wane. A loss of confidence, together with illness, affected his performances and gave opportunities to others to force their way ahead of Crawford. Sadly, he found it impossible to re-establish himself and he was released at the end of the 1931-32 season.

**CRAWFORD, Robert**
Right-half. 1934-1936.
*5ft 7½in; 11st 2lb.*
*Born: Glespin, Scotland, 4 February 1901; Died: Fulwood, Preston, 23 October 1965.*
*Debut: v Birmingham (h) 2 February 1935.*
*Career: Glenbuck Cherrypickers; Raith Rovers; Preston North End November 1921; Blackpool September 1932; Blackburn Rovers August 1934; Southport May 1936 to February 1938; Lancaster Town cs 1938.*
**Appearances:** Football League 5.
At the age of 33, Bobby Crawford was well into the veteran stage of his career when Blackburn Rovers swooped to bring him to Ewood Park in August 1934. Crawford, a talented left-half, had given 13 years of outstanding service to Preston North End and Blackpool before moving to Blackburn. Dour and uncompromising in defence, Crawford was also capable of constructive attacking play from the half-back position. He was signed by Blackburn to lead the Central League team and guide the younger players in that side. His five appearances for the senior team were all at right-half.

**CRAWLEY, Felix Patrick**
Left-back. 1921-1923.

*5ft 10in; 12st 10lb.*
*Born: Paisley, 22 May 1894; Died: Detroit, USA, April 1945.*
*Debut: v Preston North End (h) 26 December 1921.*
*Career: Croy Celtic; Kirkintilloch Rob Roy; Blackburn Rovers October 1921; Lincoln City September 1923; Accrington Stanley August 1924 to January 1926; Toronto Bell Telephone (Canada) 1926; Toronto Dunlops (Canada); Detroit All Stars (USA) coach.*
**Appearances:** Football League 24; FA Cup 2; Total 26.
**Goals:** Football League 1.
Frank Crawley enjoyed an outstanding debut in the Christmas fixture with Preston North End in 1921, until he clashed with Tommy Roberts of North End and promptly received his marching orders. Crawley suffered another set back in August 1922 when he broke a bone in his leg in a public trial match. However, by the end of September he was back in action and for a time he was tried at centre-forward in the Central League team. In January 1923 he actually appeared at centre-forward for the first team at Cardiff, but a 5-0 reverse meant the experiment was not continued. The consistency of Tom Wylie meant Crawley had to settle for second-team football at Ewood Park and in September 1923 he tried his luck with Lincoln City. Eleven months later he was back in East Lancashire with Accrington Stanley and made 11 appearances for the Peel Park club before emigrating to Canada. Whilst playing in Canada, Crawley won three international caps during a Canadian tour of New Zealand in 1927.

**CREWE ALEXANDRA FC**
Founded in 1876 and one of the original members of the Second Division in 1892, Crewe Alexandra lost their League status in 1896 but returned to the fold in 1921 as founder members of the Third Division North. They have never met Blackburn in a League game but there have been two meetings in the FA Cup. Crewe also played at Ewood Park in December 1993, when they met Accrington Stanley in the second round of the FA Cup. In March 1889, Blackburn played an FA Cup semi-final and the replay at the Alexandra Ground, Crewe.

**FA Cup**

| 1972-73 | (2) | Home | L | 0-1 |
|---------|-----|------|---|-----|
| 1992-93 | (4) | Away | W | 3-0 |

**CRICKETERS**
Many players have taken up the willow during the summer months and represented local cricket teams. However, a number of men who represented Blackburn Rovers proved sufficiently talented to appear at county level. Those who have appeared in first-class cricket include:

Albert Neilson Hornby, popularly known as 'Monkey' was the most famous cricketer to don the colours of Blackburn Rovers. He made his first-class debut for Lancashire in Blackburn, against Yorkshire, in 1867. He went on to appear in 292 matches for Lancashire and was captain between 1880 and 1891 and also captained the side during part of the 1892-93 season and in 1897-98. During his career in first-class cricket he scored 16,109 runs (including 16 centuries) at an average of 24.07. He also took 11 wickets, 313 catches and made three stumpings. He made his England Test debut in the side which lost to Australia at the Melbourne Cricket Ground in January 1878.

Hornby figured in two other Test matches for England and on both occasions he was captain. In August 1882 he led the England side which lost to Australia by seven runs at the Kennington Oval and in July 1884 he captained England to a draw against Australia at Old Trafford.

Fred Hargaves made his first-class debut for Lancashire against Derbyshire at Derby in 1881. Although he didn't score he did take two catches. Hugh McIntyre was another Rovers player who made his sole appearance for Lancashire against Derbyshire. McIntyre kept wicket for the county in the match at Derby in 1884 and took one catch and made two stumpings. With the bat he was not out for one run.

Arthur Paul kept goal for Blackburn Rovers in one match but appeared in 95 games for Lancashire between 1889 and 1900 as a right-handed batsman who occasionally kept wicket. He made his debut against Oxford University at Old Trafford in 1889 and went on to score 2,958 runs at an average of 21.91. He partnered Archie Maclaren in a second wicket stand of 363 against Somerset at Taunton in 1895. At the time this was a Lancashire record and Paul reached 177, his highest first-class innings.

Joe Hulme left Ewood Park for Arsenal in February 1926 and between 1929 and 1939 represented Middlesex. He appeared in 223 matches and scored 8,015 runs at an average of 26.63. Hulme also took 89 wickets. Another player who appeared with the Rovers in the 1920s and who played county cricket was Syd Puddefoot. Puddefoot couldn't match the record of Hulme but did appear in a handful of first-class matches for Essex.

Jim Melville had played as a professional in League cricket whilst playing football for Barrow, Blackburn Rovers, Hull City and

Northampton Town in the 1920s and 1930s. In 1946 he made his debut at county level when he was selected to play for Warwickshire. He appeared in two games for Warwickshire and returned a highest score of 13 against Kent at Edgbaston and took 3-34 against Hampshire at Coventry. Henry Horton was another player who successfully managed to enjoy a career in both football and cricket. He joined Blackburn in January 1947 and went on to play for Southampton (1951-54) and Bradford (1954-55) whilst continuing a successful career in first-class cricket. Horton made 11 appearances for Worcestershire between 1946 and 1949, and appeared in 405 matches for Hampshire between 1953 and 1967. He was an umpire between 1973 and 1975.

### CRISP, John
Outside-right. 1923-1927.
*5ft 5in; 11st.*
*Born: Hamstead, Birmingham, 27 November 1894; Died: February 1939.*
*Debut: v Newcastle United (h) 10 March 1923.*
*Career: Albert Road School; Aston Boys; Walsall trial; Aston Villa trial 1910; Leicester Fosse amateur September 1913; Ordnance FC; West Bromwich Albion amateur May 1914; Ward End Works guest player during World War One; Blackburn Rovers March 1923 (£3,125); Coventry City February 1927; Stourbridge September 1928; Bromsgrove Rovers September 1929; Cheltenham Town November 1933. Retired 1935.*
**Appearances:** Football League 98; FA Cup 10; Total 108.
**Goals:** Football League 18; FA Cup 1; Total 19.
Jack Crisp was a member of the West Bromwich Albion side which won the League championship in 1919-20 and only a substantial sum brought him to Ewood Park in March 1923. He made an immediate impact at Ewood Park, scoring on each of his first three appearances for the club. His ability to play on either wing saw him switched to outside-left in March 1924 to accommodate the arrival of Joe Hulme. Although nippy, his main assets were his bravery, ability to cross the ball accurately and, for a winger, his surprising power in the air.

### CROMPTON, Alan
Midfield. 1976-1978.
*5ft 9in; 10st 8lb.*
*Born: Manchester, 6 March 1958.*
*Debut: v Orient (h) 12 March 1977 (sub).*
*Career: Sunderland apprentice February 1975, turning professional in March 1975; Blackburn Rovers July 1976; Wigan Athletic 1978 to 1980; Runcorn; Telford; Northwich Victoria.*
**Appearances:** Football League 2+2.
A young midfield player who came to Ewood Park after failing to make the grade at Roker Park. Crompton was given limited opportunities in the first team towards the end of the 1976-77 campaign. However he failed to make much impression and in the summer of 1978 he moved to Wigan Athletic following their election to the Football League. His two seasons at Springfield Park saw him appear in only 14 League games (including seven as substitute). After leaving Wigan he served several non-League clubs.

### CROMPTON, George Ellis
Forward. 1905-1910.
*5ft 8in; 11st 7lb.*
*Born: Ramsbottom, nr Bury, 17 July 1886; Died: Barnstaple, 17 May 1953.*
*Debut: v Birmingham (h) 10 November 1906.*
*Career: Padiham; Blackburn Rovers May 1905; Tottenham Hotspur December 1910; Exeter City July 1912; Bristol Rovers May 1913 (£400); Exeter City June 1921; Barnstaple Town player-coach June 1926; Llanelli 1929; Barry Town player-coach 1930.*
**Appearances:** Football League 35; FA Cup 1; Total 36.
**Goals:** Football League 20.
Although a regular goalscorer, Ellis Crompton found it impossible to gain a regular place in the Ewood Park forward line between 1905 and 1910. However, his record was sufficient to persuade Tottenham Hotspur to part with a large fee to take him to London. Crompton was unable to settle in the capital and after one goal in nine games he moved to Southern League Exeter City. He moved to Bristol Rovers in 1913 and proved a versatile performer during his time at Eastville. In 1921 he returned to Exeter City as an inside-forward but soon switched to a half-back position and became captain of the team.

### CROMPTON, Robert
Right-back. 1896-1920.
*5ft 10½in; 13st.*
*Born: Blackburn, 26 September 1879; Died: Blackburn, 15 March 1941.*
*Career: Moss Street School, Blackburn; Rose & Thistle, Blackburn; Blackburn Trinity; Blackburn Rovers 30 September 1896 to May 1920,*

*when he retired, then director June 1921 to March 1931 and also honorary manager December 1926 to February 1931; Bournemouth & Boscombe Athletic manager June 1935 to February 1936; Blackburn Rovers coaching capacity April 1938 then manager May 1938 to March 1941.*
*International honours with Blackburn Rovers: England: 41 caps (1902-14); Football League: 17 appearances (1902-14).*
*Domestic honours with Blackburn Rovers: First Division championship: 1911-12 (33 apps); 1913-14 (33 apps).*
**Appearances:** Football League 529; FA Cup 46; FA Charity Shield 1; Total 576.
**Goals:** Football League 14.
Bob Crompton played an active part in the life of Blackburn Rovers for almost half a century. He made his debut on 10 April 1897 and appeared for the final time with the senior team at Bradford on 23 February 1920. He then became a director of the club and took the position of honorary manager following the departure of Jack Carr in December 1926. Forced out of the club in controversial circumstances during the 1930-31 season, he was recalled in April 1938 and the following month was appointed manager.

Rovers won two First Division titles under his leadership as a player and he remained a regular in the England team for over a decade. As manager he won the FA Cup in 1928 and in 1938-39 he lifted the Second Division title, only 12 months after saving the club from being relegated to the Third Division North. Quite simply he was the greatest 'Rover' of them all.

Although the young Crompton had won many admirers whilst playing for Moss Street School, Rose & Thistle and Blackburn Trinity he was none the less reluctant to sign professional forms. Crompton was keen to complete his apprenticeship as a plumber and as a talented swimmer and polo player he was reluctant to jeopardise his amateur status.

Fortunately, Crompton chose to become a professional with the Rovers but, at the same time, he also became a partner in a local plumbing firm and was said to be responsible for several important inventions in this area. Indeed, rumours persisted throughout his life that these inventions had made him a wealthy man. Although Crompton always maintained that these stories were greatly exaggerated, his lifestyle suggested otherwise. The fact that he owned his own car – when few in society did – and that he was later invited to join the board of directors suggests that he was a man of some substance. As a player, Crompton was a first-class tactician and had natural leadership qualities despite never being 'one of the boys'.

A private man who appeared a rather solitary figure and one who remained aloof from his playing colleagues, Crompton nevertheless commanded the respect of everyone at the club. Although his playing style was based on strength, he always played the game in the true 'Corinthian' spirit and insisted that colleagues did likewise. Strong in the air, Crompton could pass the ball with great accuracy and was resolute in the tackle.

When he finally retired from playing he had made a record 529 League appearances for the club; a record which has only been bettered by Ronnie Clayton and Derek Fazackerley. In 1921, Crompton was invited to join the board of directors and following the surprise departure of Jack Carr in December 1926 he was nominated to become 'honorary manager' by his fellow directors. At the time the club was not enjoying the best of fortunes but Crompton gradually turned things around. Victory in 1928 FA Cup Final was a welcome, if unexpected, boost and provided Crompton with the trophy that had eluded him as a player. The League position also improved with Rovers finishing 12th, seventh and sixth during the first three years of his reign.

Already a legend with the people of the town, Crompton's success as a manager merely underlined his 'Midas' touch. In management, as in playing, Crompton remained very much his own man. Unfortunately, his autocratic style was not appreciated by everyone at the club. Crompton believed that the game was about passing and that future success would require the ability to pass the ball accurately and at greater speed than ever before. It was not the philosophy that an ageing team would readily accept and, whilst Crompton was always prepared to listen to others, he was not a man to compromise. Matters came to a head in February 1931 when the chairman announced that he had received a letter from the players listing a number of grievances against the manager. Being a man of principle, Crompton immediately withdrew from all managerial duties until the matter was settled. The immediate result was that the Rovers crashed out of the FA Cup at the hands of Chelsea at Stamford Bridge.

In March 1931, the club held its annual meeting amidst a background of newspaper reports which suggested that more than one player had come to regret the way in which events had developed. At this meeting Crompton had to offer himself for re-election as a director and, although no mention was made of the dispute, the votes went against him. Asked for his thoughts on the severing of a 34-year association with the club, Crompton commented, "I must thank all the people who voted for me. My 34 years experience with the Rovers has been a nice time and I have enjoyed every year I have been connected with the club. One is naturally a little disappointed at the result. It is all in the game however. One has to take it as it is given, I thank you all."

In June 1935 he surprised many people in Blackburn by accepting the managership of Bournemouth & Boscombe Athletic.

However, Crompton returned to Blackburn after only eight months on the south coast as the call for his return to Ewood Park began to grow. During his absence from the club the Rovers had slipped into the Second Division for the first time in their history. Whilst the local Press, who had been bitterly critical of the decision to allow Crompton to leave Ewood, actively campaigned for his return, Bob Crompton maintained a dignified silence. In truth he had become an almost Arthurian figure; a man waiting in the wings to rescue his beloved Blackburn Rovers in their time of need. The time of need came in March 1938 when the club appeared to be destined to taste football in the Third Division North.

The directors bowed to the growing clamour for Crompton's return and announced that he had accepted an invitation to offer what help he could to Reg Taylor, the club's beleaguered secretary-manager. Crompton returned to Ewood Park on 2 April 1938 and steered the team to safety. Hailed as a saviour, Crompton accepted the invitation to become the club's full-time manager in May 1938. He quickly assessed the playing strength of the club and set about building a team which would win the Second Division championship within 12 months.

The outbreak of war prevented Crompton from re-establishing the club in the First Division, although he did have the consolation of returning to Wembley with the Rovers in the 1940 League War Cup

Final. Sadly, this proved to be the last major occasion that Crompton shared with the club. On 15 March 1941 he watched the Rovers defeat Burnley 3-2 at Ewood Park and later that evening he collapsed and died. An association between club and man which had begun in 1896 was finally at an end.

**Bob Crompton's playing record with Blackburn Rovers:**

| | League | | FA Cup | | Charity Shield | | Total | |
|---|---|---|---|---|---|---|---|---|
| | Apps | Gls | Apps | Gls | Apps | Gls | Apps | Gls |
| 1896-97 | 2 | 0 | 0 | 0 | 0 | 0 | 2 | 0 |
| 1897-98 | 1 | 0 | 0 | 0 | 0 | 0 | 1 | 0 |
| 1898-99 | 33 | 1 | 1 | 0 | 0 | 0 | 34 | 1 |
| 1899-00 | 34 | 1 | 4 | 0 | 0 | 0 | 38 | 1 |
| 1900-01 | 24 | 0 | 1 | 0 | 0 | 0 | 25 | 0 |
| 1901-02 | 31 | 0 | 1 | 0 | 0 | 0 | 32 | 0 |
| 1902-03 | 28 | 0 | 3 | 0 | 0 | 0 | 31 | 0 |
| 1903-04 | 32 | 1 | 3 | 0 | 0 | 0 | 35 | 1 |
| 1904-05 | 27 | 3 | 0 | 0 | 0 | 0 | 27 | 3 |
| 1905-06 | 36 | 0 | 1 | 0 | 0 | 0 | 37 | 0 |
| 1906-07 | 28 | 1 | 5 | 0 | 0 | 0 | 33 | 1 |
| 1907-08 | 33 | 1 | 1 | 0 | 0 | 0 | 34 | 1 |
| 1908-09 | 31 | 1 | 3 | 0 | 0 | 0 | 34 | 1 |
| 1909-10 | 25 | 0 | 2 | 0 | 0 | 0 | 27 | 0 |
| 1910-11 | 31 | 1 | 6 | 0 | 0 | 0 | 37 | 1 |
| 1911-12 | 33 | 0 | 7 | 0 | 1 | 0 | 41 | 0 |
| 1912-13 | 31 | 0 | 4 | 0 | 0 | 0 | 35 | 0 |
| 1913-14 | 33 | 0 | 3 | 0 | 0 | 0 | 36 | 0 |
| 1914-15 | 34 | 4 | 1 | 0 | 0 | 0 | 35 | 4 |
| 1919-20 | 2 | 0 | 0 | 0 | 0 | 0 | 2 | 0 |
| Total | 529 | 14 | 46 | 0 | 1 | 0 | 576 | 14 |

**Wartime Record**

| | App | Gls |
|---|---|---|
| 1916-17 | 20 | 0 |
| 1917-18 | 2 | 0 |
| 1918-19 | 8 | 0 |
| Total | 30 | 0 |

### CROMPTON, Wilfred
Outside-right. 1927-1932.
*5ft 6½in; 10st 4lb.*
*Born: Blackburn, 1 April 1908; Died: Lytham, 22 June 1971.*
*Debut: v Grimsby Town (h) 14 September 1929.*
*Career: Blackburn Parish Higher Grade School; Blackburn Rovers amateur May 1927, turning professional in November 1927; Burnley May 1932; Gillingham June 1934; Luton Town November 1934 until February 1937 when he retired through injury.*
**Appearances:** Football League 20.
**Goals:** Football League 5.
The youngest son of Bob Crompton, Wilfred came into the team when his father was not only a director but also honorary team manager of the club. Despite the difficulties of living in the shadow of a famous father, Wilfred won, and retained, a first-team place on merit. He developed into a two-footed winger whose accurate centring was a constant danger to opposing teams. Although the stockily built Crompton had an eye for goalscoring opportunities, his run as a first-team regular ended with the arrival of Jack Bruton from Burnley. After two seasons of limited opportunities with the senior team he moved to Burnley.

### CROOK, James Albert
Inside-right. 1899-1900.
*Debut: v Manchester City (h) 2 September 1899.*
*Career: Stalybridge Rovers; Blackburn Rovers May 1899; Stalybridge Rovers cs 1900.*
**Appearances:** Football League 9.
**Goals:** Football League 2.
Crook made an impressive debut for the club, scoring the second goal in the 4-3 win over Manchester City, at Ewood Park, on the opening day of the 1899-1900 season. He figured at inside-right in the opening six games of the season but was axed following four defeats and only two victories. He appeared in the final three games of the season before returning to Stalybridge Rovers in the summer of 1900.

### CROOK, Walter
Left-back. 1931-1947.
*5ft 10in; 10st 4lb.*
*Born: Whittle-le-Woods, 28 April 1912; Died: Mellor, 27 December 1988.*
*Debut: v Liverpool (h) 19 March 1932.*
*Career: Blackburn Nomads; Blackburn Rovers January 1931; Aldershot*

*wartime guest 1939-40 and 1940-41; Chelsea wartime guest 1939-40; Blackpool wartime guest 1944-45; Bolton Wanderers May 1947; Ajax (Holland) coach; Accrington Stanley manager June 1951 until February 1953; Ajax manager; Wigan Athletic manager October 1954; Preston North End head trainer-coach for 18 years.*
*International honours with Blackburn Rovers: England: 1 wartime appearance (1939).*
*Domestic honours with Blackburn Rovers: Second Division championship: 1938-39 (42 apps, 2 gls); War Cup winners: 1940.*
**Appearances:** Football League 218; FA Cup 19; Total 237.
**Goals:** Football League 2.
Walter Crook graduated through the junior teams at Ewood Park before making his first-team debut just a few weeks before his 20th birthday. Crook had to spend a further two seasons learning his trade in the Central League team before earning an extended run in the first team midway through the 1934-35 season. Given his opportunity on 22 December 1934, Crook remained an ever-present in the senior team until the outbreak of war and the suspension

of the League programme in September 1939. Crook figured in the first 17 matches of the 1946-47 campaign to establish his own niche in the record books with 208 consecutive Football League appearances for the club. A natural left-footer, despite playing a few games on the right, Crook made the left-back position his own. Crook was a rugged character whose aggressive approach inspired his playing colleagues and delighted supporters. He became the club captain and led the team to the Second Division championship in 1939-40. Although he played in the 1940 War Cup Final, military service was to keep him away from Ewood Park for most of the war years. When he returned, Crompton was dead and Crook found himself unable to come to terms with the management of Eddie Hapgood. As a result he was placed on the transfer list at his own request and in May 1947 made the short move to Burnden Park. Injury was to force him into premature retirement and into a new career in coaching. He took the struggling Ajax club of Amsterdam to the championship within two years of his arrival in Holland. Crook returned to East Lancashire to take over the reigns at Accrington Stanley in June 1951. However, his time at Peel Park was not a happy one and he tendered his resignation in February 1953. After leaving Accrington, Crook returned to Holland for a spell and was then out of football until being appointed manager of Wigan Athletic in October 1954. He later spent 18 years on the coaching staff of Preston North End before becoming disillusioned with the game.

**CROSSAN, Edward**
Inside-forward. 1947-1957.
*5ft 6in; 10st.*
*Born: Londonderry, 17 November 1925.*
*Debut: v Sunderland (h) 31 January 1948.*
*Career: Glentoran; Derry City; Blackburn Rovers November 1947 (£3,000); Tranmere Rovers July 1957; Cork Hibernians September 1958.*
*International honours with Blackburn Rovers: Northern Ireland: 3 caps (1949-1955).*
**Appearances:** Football League 287; FA Cup 15; Total 302.
**Goals:** Football League 73; FA Cup 1; Total 74.
Eddie Crossan was a gifted Irishman who graced Ewood Park in the 1950s and who, with greater dedication, would surely have won more than three international caps. The mercurial Crossan possessed incredible natural ability and quickly became a favourite with the Blackburn public. His brilliant close control enabled him to mesmerise opponents with his silky skills. Yet, sadly, Crossan was a flawed diamond. As with so many other brilliant individualists, lack of consistency proved to be his Achilles' heel. Although he scored 73 League goals for the club, many of them outstanding efforts, Crossan is still remembered as the man who missed most frequently from short range. Whatever his flaws, Crossan revelled in the most successful forward line that the club has ever produced. He left the club in August 1957, when age was beginning to blunt his skills, and played for Tranmere Rovers for a season before

returning to his native Ireland. Johnny Crossan, his younger brother, a less gifted but more consistent inside-forward, won 23 caps for Ireland during a career that included spells within Standard Liege, Sunderland, Manchester City and Middlesbrough.

**CROWE, Christopher**
Inside-forward. 1960-1962.
*5ft 6in; 10st 5lb.*
*Born: Newcastle upon Tyne, 11 June 1939.*
*Debut: v West Ham United (a) 19 March 1960.*
*Career: Edinburgh schools; Edinburgh junior football; Leeds United amateur October 1954, turning professional in June 1956; Blackburn Rovers March 1960 (£25,000); Wolverhampton Wanderers February 1962 (£30,000); Nottingham Forest August 1964 (£30,000); Bristol City January 1967 (£15,000); Auburn FC (Sydney, Australia) May 1969; Walsall September 1969 (£1,000); Bath City February 1971.*
*International honours with Blackburn Rovers: England Under-23: 2 caps (1961).*
**Appearances:** Football League 51; FA Cup 5; Football League Cup 6; Total 62.
**Goals:** Football League 6; FA Cup 1; Football League Cup 4; Total 11.
A former schoolboy international for Scotland and a youth international for England, Chris Crowe was signed by Dally Duncan following the departure of Roy Vernon to Everton. Crowe had scored 27 goals in 95 League games with Leeds United and began the 1960-61 season as the first-choice number-ten. However, despite winning two England Under-23 caps with the Rovers, Crowe failed to produce the type of form which had been expected from him. At the time of his transfer to Wolves in February 1963 he had been axed in favour of Ian Lawther. The blond-haired Crowe enjoyed better fortunes at Molineux and was capped by England in October 1963. Crowe appeared in 384 League games (including four appearances as sub) during his career and scored 83 goals.

**CRYSTAL PALACE FC**
Founded in 1905, Crystal Palace immediately became members of the Southern League. Palace were founder members of the Third Division in 1920 and didn't meet Blackburn Rovers until the 1966-67 season. Since that time, apart from one season in the Third Division, the clubs have met only in the Second Division of the Football League. In 1988-89 the clubs met in the Final of the Second Division Play-offs. The Rovers took what appeared to be a commanding 3-1 lead to Selhurst Park for the second leg of the tie. Sadly, the London side, aided by a controversial penalty, overwhelmed the Rovers and ran out 3-0 winners. The Rovers visited Selhurst Park for their inaugural match in the Premier League and on a memorable day Alan Shearer, Blackburn's record signing, scored two goals of outstanding quality in a 3-3 draw.

**Football League**

|  |  | Home | Away |
|---|---|---|---|
| 1966-67 | (Div 2) | W 2-1 | L 1-2 |
| 1967-68 | (Div 2) | W 2-1 | L 0-1 |
| 1968-69 | (Div 2) | L 1-2 | L 0-1 |
| 1974-75 | (Div 3) | D 1-1 | L 0-1 |
| 1977-78 | (Div 2) | W 3-0 | L 0-5 |
| 1978-79 | (Div 2) | D 1-1 | L 0-3 |
| 1981-82 | (Div 2) | W 1-0 | W 2-1 |
| 1982-83 | (Div 2) | W 3-0 | L 0-2 |
| 1983-84 | (Div 2) | W 2-1 | W 2-0 |
| 1984-85 | (Div 2) | L 0-1 | D 1-1 |
| 1985-86 | (Div 2) | L 1-2 | L 0-2 |
| 1986-87 | (Div 2) | L 0-2 | L 0-2 |
| 1987-88 | (Div 2) | W 2-0 | L 0-2 |
| 1988-89 | (Div 2) | W 5-4 | D 2-2 |

|  | P | W | D | L | F | A |
|---|---|---|---|---|---|---|
| Home | 14 | 8 | 2 | 4 | 24 | 16 |
| Away | 14 | 2 | 2 | 10 | 8 | 25 |
| Total | 28 | 10 | 4 | 14 | 32 | 41 |

**Football League Play-offs**

|       | Home |     | Away |     |
| ----- | ---- | --- | ---- | --- |
| 1988-89 | W | 3-1 | L | 0-3 |

**FA Premiership**

|       | Home |     | Away |     |
| ----- | ---- | --- | ---- | --- |
| 1992-93 | L | 1-2 | D | 3-3 |

|       | P | W | D | L | F | A |
| ----- | - | - | - | - | - | - |
| Home  | 1 | 0 | 0 | 1 | 1 | 2 |
| Away  | 1 | 0 | 1 | 0 | 3 | 3 |
| Total | 2 | 0 | 1 | 1 | 4 | 5 |

**CUNLIFFE, Arthur**
Outside-left. 1928-1933.
*5ft 6½in; 10st.*
*Born: Blackrod, Lancashire, 5 February 1909; Died: Bournemouth, 28 August 1986.*
*Debut: v Manchester United (h) 4 January 1930.*
*Career: Adlington 1923; Chorley August 1927; Blackburn Rovers January 1928; Aston Villa May 1933 (£8,000 – joint transfer with R.W.Dix); Middlesbrough December 1935; Burnley April 1937; Hull City June 1938; Brighton & Hove Albion wartime guest 1941-42; Reading wartime guest 1942-43; Aldershot wartime guest 1943-44; Rochdale wartime guest 1944-45; Stoke City wartime guest 1944-45; Rochdale August 1945, becoming trainer in July 1947; Bournemouth & Boscombe Athletic trainer July 1950, becoming physiotherapist between 1971 and 1974.*
*International honours with Blackburn Rovers: England: 2 caps (1932).*
**Appearances:** Football League 129; FA Cup 11; Total 140.
**Goals:** Football League 47; FA Cup 8; Total 55.
Although Arthur Cunliffe began his career on the right wing, it was not until he switched to the opposite flank that he began to make his mark on the professional game. He proved to be the archetypal left-winger – fast, direct and with excellent ball control. Yet, Cunliffe could also score goals as well as supply the crosses for others and it was his goal-scoring flair that brought him two international caps whilst at Ewood Park. It was during the 1932-33 season that Cunliffe formed a formidable left-wing partnership with Ronnie Dix. Their exploits did not go unnoticed and a combined fee of £8,000 proved too good for the cash starved Rovers to refuse. After leaving Ewood, Cunliffe embarked on a somewhat nomadic career before finally settling in Bournemouth where he became trainer and later physiotherapist to Bournemouth & Boscombe Athletic.

**CUNLIFFE, Thomas**
Outside-left. 1906-1908.
*Debut: v Preston North End (h) 13 April 1906.*
*Career: Holey Hill; Earlestown; Blackburn Rovers March 1906; Chorley cs 1908.*
**Appearances:** Football League 1.
Thomas Cunliffe joined Blackburn Rovers with Herbert France from Earlestown, a Lancashire Combination club, in March 1906. Injuries to established players enabled both men to make a premature debut against Preston North End on Good Friday, 1906. It was not a happy experience for Cunliffe, who appeared completely overwhelmed by the situation. In the event it proved to be the only first-team call he received during his time at Ewood Park.

**CURRY, Sean Patrick**
Centre-forward. 1987-1989.
*5ft 8in; 10st 11lb.*
*Born: Liverpool, 13 November 1966.*
*Debut: v Millwall (h) 21 February 1987.*
*Career: Liverpool June 1983; Blackburn Rovers January 1987; Hartlepool United August 1989; Preston North End October 1989 to March 1990.*
**Appearances:** Football League 25+13; Play-offs 0+2; FA Cup 0+1; Football League Cup 3+2; Total 28+18.
**Goals:** Football League 6.
Small and stocky striker who was signed from Liverpool during the caretaker managership of Tony Parkes in January 1987. Curry was a neat and tidy footballer who lacked the height and pace to be truly successful in the traditional centre-forward role. Despite his skill, Curry failed to make a lasting impression at Ewood and was released in the summer of 1989.

**CURTIS, John**
Right-back. 1977-1979.
*5ft 8in; 10st.*
*Born: Poulton-le-Fylde, 2 September 1954.*
*Debut: v Notts County (a) 20 August 1977.*

*Career: Blackpool apprentice July 1970, turning professional in September 1972; Blackburn Rovers July 1977; Wigan Athletic on loan March 1979 to April 1979; Wigan Athletic August 1979; Morecambe.*
**Appearances:** Football League 9+1; Football League Cup 2; Total 11+1.
John Curtis had a wealth of Second Division experience behind him when Jim Smith signed him on a free transfer during the summer of 1977. He had appeared in 102 League matches (including six as sub) for Blackpool and Smith had no hesitation in giving him the number-two shirt at the start of the 1977-78 season. However, Curtis was not a success and, within weeks of his debut, Smith had replaced him with Kevin Hird. The successful conversion of Hird from midfielder to full-back meant the two seasons that Curtis had at Ewood Park were largely spent in the Central League team.

**DALGLISH, Kenneth Mathieson** MBE
Manager. 1991-
*Born: Dalmarnock, Glasgow, 4 March 1951.*
*Career: Glasgow Schools; Drumchapel Amateurs; Glasgow United; Celtic August 1967; Cumbernauld United for a spell; Liverpool August 1977 (£400,000), becoming player-manager in June 1985 until February 1991; Blackburn Rovers manager October 1991.*
*Playing honours:*
*Scotland: Schoolboy & Youth levels; Scotland Under-23: 4 caps; Scotland: 102 caps.*
*Celtic: Scottish League championship: 1972; 1973; 1974; 1977; Scottish Cup winners: 1972; 1974; 1975; 1977; Scottish Cup runners-up: 1973; Scottish League Cup winners 1975; Scottish League Cup runners-up: 1972; 1973; 1974; 1977.*
*Liverpool: Football League championship: 1979; 1980; 1982; 1983; 1984; Football League Cup winners: 1981; 1982; 1983; 1984; Football*

*League Cup runners-up: 1978; European Cup winners: 1978; 1981; 1984; European Cup runners-up: 1985; European Super Cup winners: 1977; European Super Cup runners-up: 1978; 1985.*
*Managerial honours:*
*Liverpool: Football League championship: 1986; 1988; 1990; FA Cup winners: 1986; 1989; FA Cup runners-up: 1988; Football League Cup runners-up: 1987.*
*Blackburn Rovers: Second Division Play-off winners: 1992.*
One glance at the list of honours above indicates just what a remarkable career Kenny Dalglish has enjoyed on both sides of the border. Not only does he hold the record for Scottish international appearances, but he is also joint holder of the Scottish international goalscoring record and is still the only man to score 100 goals in both Scottish and English League football.

When Don Mackay was relieved of managerial duties at Ewood Park in August 1991, Kenny Dalglish was the only man that Jack Walker, the club's wealthy benefactor, wanted as manager of Blackburn Rovers. To many it appeared a flight of fantasy that a club like the Rovers would be able to entice Dalglish out of his self-imposed retirement. However, Mr Walker was undeterred and on 12 October 1991, a press conference was called, prior to the home game with Plymouth Argyle, to announce that Dalglish had accepted the challenge to restore the fortunes of Blackburn Rovers. At the same press conference Dalglish introduced Ray Harford as his assistant and announced his intention of retaining the existing coaching staff of Tony Parkes, Asa Hartford and Jim Furnell.

Dalglish quickly set about the task of using the funds that were available to him and a succession of big money signings moved to Ewood Park. The team soared to the top of the Second Division before a run of six successive defeats in March and April threatened even a Play-off place. Fortunately, eight points from the final six games clinched the last Play-off spot. After overcoming Derby County at the semi-final stage, Dalglish saw the Rovers snatch the final Premier League place with a 1-0 victory over Leicester City at Wembley.

Whilst the cynics claimed that the Rovers had bought their success, the fact remains that Dalglish showed remarkable judgment in rebuilding his team during the season whilst maintaining a promotion challenge. The summer of 1992 saw the arrival of Alan Shearer for £3.4 million, a new British record fee, and Stuart Ripley for £1.1 million. Dalglish immediately integrated his new signings into the team and on 3 October, just a year after taking control at Ewood Park, he saw his Blackburn team demolish Norwich City, leaders of the Premier League, 7-1 at Ewood Park to take the top spot themselves.

A memorable first season in the Premier League saw the Rovers finish fourth in the League, reach the semi-final of the League Cup and the sixth round in the FA Cup. Dalglish continued to build his team during the 1993-94 season and in the space of three months he rocked the football world with the signings of Paul Warhurst (£2.75 million), David Batty (£2.75 million) and Tim Flowers (£2.4 million – a world record fee for a goalkeeper). However, Dalglish quickly bedded the new players into his team and the public of Blackburn were treated to a standard of football that had not been seen at Ewood Park for 30 years.

The 1993-94 season exceeded all expectations in that the club made a strong challenge for the Premiership title despite being 16 points adrift of Manchester United at one stage. However, under the astute leadership of Dalglish the club went into the final stages of the season neck and neck with United before finally having to settle for second place. In finishing as runners-up, Dalglish ensured that Blackburn Rovers would participate in European football for the first time in their history. Ironically, due to the ban on English clubs which followed the tragedy at Heysel in 1985, Dalglish will also enter European competition in 1994-95 for the first time in his career as a manager.

### DALY, Patrick John
Forward. 1957-1962.
*5ft 7in; 9st 8lb.*
*Born: Manchester, 3 January 1941.*
*Debut: v Sheffield Wednesday (a) 16 January 1960.*
*Career: Manchester Boys; Lancashire Boys; Blackburn Rovers non-contract player May 1957, signing professional in January 1958; Southport February 1962; Hyde United August to September 1962; Runcorn October 1962; Witton Albion 1964 to 1966; Rhyl December 1966 to 1967; Witton Albion 1967 to possibly 1969.*
**Appearances:** Football League 3; Football League Cup 1; Total 4.
An ability to create openings for

others was one of the main assets in Paddy Daly's armoury. Unfortunately, in an era when the club possessed a number of such players Daly was destined to spend his time at Ewood as a regular in the Central League team. He fared little better at Southport and after only ten League appearances for the Haigh Avenue club he joined the non-League circuit.

### DARLING, Malcolm
Forward. 1964-1970.
*5ft 7½in; 10st.*
*Born: Arbroath, 4 July 1947.*
*Debut: v Newcastle United (h) 13 November 1965.*
*Career: Lucarty Juniors; Blackburn Rovers October 1964; Norwich City May 1970; Rochdale October 1971; Bolton Wanderers September 1973; Chesterfield August 1974; Stockport County on loan March 1977 to June 1977; Sheffield Wednesday August 1977; Hartlepool United September 1977; Morecambe 1977; Bury March 1978; Great Harwood Town manager cs 1985.*
**Appearances:** Football League 114+14; FA Cup 8; Football League Cup 4+1; Total 126+15.
**Goals:** Football League 30; FA Cup 4; Total 34.
A lively utility forward who joined the Rovers from Scottish junior football and graduated through the Central League team at Ewood Park. He got his first-team chance during the disastrous 1965-66 campaign and scored a goal on his debut against Newcastle United at Ewood Park. The 4-2 victory was only the third Blackburn Rovers win in 16 League matches but Darling did enough to earn a run in the senior team. During the next four seasons, Darling enjoyed long spells in the first team but never quite seemed to realise his full potential. As a goalscorer his best moment came in January 1969 when he scored a hat-trick in the 4-0 win over Portsmouth in the FA Cup. He left Ewood Park for Norwich City in an exchange deal which brought Bryan Conlon to Blackburn. During a somewhat nomadic career, Darling scored 86 League goals in 360 appearances (including 28 as sub).

### DARLINGTON FC
Although Darlington Football Club was a founder member of the Third Division North in 1921, the Quakers have met Blackburn Rovers only once in competitive football. The clubs met at Ewood Park on 14 December 1974 in the second round of the FA Cup. A Graham Oates goal was sufficient to give the Rovers a 1-0 win and earn a third-round tie against Bristol Rovers.

### DARROCH, John
Left-back. 1901-1902.
*5ft 7½in; 11st.*
*Born: Alexandria, Dumbarton, 1872.*
*Debut: v Manchester City (a) 14 December 1901.*
*Career: Renton; Sheffield Wednesday; Dundee April 1895; Bury May 1896; Blackburn Rovers December 1901; Dundee August 1902 to cs 1907.*
**Appearances:** Football League 17; FA Cup 1; Total 18.
The signing of Jack Darroch was something of a calculated gamble on the part of the directors of Blackburn Rovers. Having tried Hardy, Blackburn and Eastham at left-back without success the club turned to Darroch, Bury's veteran defender, in December 1901. At 29 years of age and having spent his entire career at right-back, the signing of Darroch raised more than a few eyebrows in Blackburn. The veteran provided adequate support for Crompton during the remainder of the 1901-02 campaign but eight months after arriving at Ewood Park, he was allowed to return to his native Scotland.

### DARWEN FC
Formed in 1870, the Barley Bank club provided the fledgling Blackburn Rovers with some of the most hostile moments in their history. Relationships between the club were soured in 1880 when Fergie Suter defected from Barley Bank to join the Rovers. Suter, a stonemason by trade, had joined Darwen for the 1879-80 season from Glasgow Rangers. Whilst Darwen refuted claims that Suter was paid for playing for the few ever witnessed him carrying out his trade in the town. His move Blackburn was made for what were termed as 'personal reasons. However, angered Darwen officials interpreted this as meaning being offered better terms by the Rovers. Certainly there is good to suggest that Suter was the first professional player with B Rovers.

On 27 November 1880, Darwen travelled to Blackburn play the Rovers in a friendly fixture. A crowd of 10,000 watched rugged, bruising encounter which ended with Suter becoming e iled in a brawl with Marshall of Darwen. Feelings between th two sets of supporters were such that a large number of them decide to join Suter and Marshall in battle. With little chance of restoring c er there was no alternative but to abandon the match. The hostile atmosphere between the clubs was such that it didn't always need an incident on the field to cause uproar. A few months after the fracas between Suter and Marshall the clubs were drawn to meet each other in the fourth round of the Lancashire Cup but neither club could find an agreeable date and an exasperated Lancashire Football Association finally ejected both clubs from the competition. Darwen were so incensed that they withdrew from the following season's competition to avoid any possible clash with the Rovers. Blackburn Rovers faced Darwen in the second round of the FA Cup in 1879-80. This was only the second game that the Rovers had played in this competition and thanks to two goals from Jimmy Brown and another from John Hargreaves, they recorded a 3-1 victory. The teams were paired in the fourth round of the 1881-82 FA Cup competition when goals from John Hargreaves (2), Jimmy Brown and John Duckworth (2) gave the Rovers a convincing 5-1 victory. However, Darwen had their revenge during the following season when they eliminated Rovers from the FA Cup with a single-goal victory. The last FA Cup meeting took place in 1887-88 when the Rovers enjoyed a comfortable 3-0 victory in front of an attendance of 10,000 spectators.

### Football League

| | | | Home | | Away | |
|---|---|---|---|---|---|---|
| 1891-92 | | (FL) | W | 4-0 | W | 5-3 |
| 1893-94 | | (Div 1) | W | 4-1 | W | 3-2 |

| | P | W | D | L | F | A |
|---|---|---|---|---|---|---|
| Home | 2 | 2 | 0 | 0 | 8 | 1 |
| Away | 2 | 2 | 0 | 0 | 8 | 5 |
| Total | 4 | 4 | 0 | 0 | 16 | 6 |

### FA Cup

| | | | | | |
|---|---|---|---|---|---|
| 1879-80 | | (2) | Home | W | 3-1 |
| 1881-82 | | (4) | Home | W | 5-1 |
| 1882-83 | | (2) | Away | L | 0-1 |
| 1887-88 | | (5) | Away | W | 3-0 |

### DARWEN OLD WANDERERS FC

Formed in 1879, Darwen Old Wanderers visited Blackburn Rovers on two occasions to play Cup-ties. On 5 December 1885, goals from Joe Sowerbutts (2), Jimmy Brown (2), Herbert Fecitt and Joe Lofthouse gave the Rovers a comfortable 6-1 victory in the third round of the FA Cup. Two seasons earlier the Rovers had eliminated the Wanderers from the Lancashire Cup competition.

### DAVIES, William

Centre-forward. 1905-1913.
*5ft 9½in; 11st.*
*Born: Wrexham, 13 April 1882; Died: Preston, 21 January 1966.*
*Debut: v Aston Villa (h) 2 September 1905.*
*Career: Wrexham National School; Wrexham St Giles; Wrexham Victoria; Wrexham 1902; Blackburn Rovers April 1905, retired 1913.*
*International honours with Blackburn Rovers: Wales: 9 caps (1908-12).*
*Domestic honours with Blackburn Rovers: First Division championship: 1911-12 (11 apps, 2 gls).*
**Appearances:** Football League 132; FA Cup 11; Total 143.
**Goals:** Football League 67; FA Cup 3; Total 70.
'Tinker' (a nickname he picked up from his employment as a master tinsmith) Davies joined the Rovers in April 1905 and scored a hat-trick on his debut with the Reserves. Davies was a natural goalscorer who was not averse to taking the shortest route to goal. However, as well as his pace and power, he had the natural instincts of a goalscorer that lurked around the penalty area waiting to snap up any opportunity that came his way. Capped nine times for Wales, Davies was at Ewood by injuries during his time top scorer at the Park but still finished as that his in four of the seasons married his the club. Davies Blackburn the daughter of a motor engineer and went into a Bob Cromping partnership with football in. He retired from concentrate April 1913 to interests. his business

### DAVIS, Edwin

Goalkeeper. 1922-1925.
*6ft ½in; 13st 5lb.*
*Born: Bristol, 1891 (January quarter); Died: Bristol, 6 March 1954.*
*Debut: v Everton (h) 16 September 1922.*
*Career: Bristol City April 1911; Brentford trial 1912; Clapton Orient December 1912; Huddersfield Town October 1913; Blackburn Rovers July 1922; Bristol City May 1925; Bath City player-manager in 1930.*
**Appearances:** Football League 24; FA Cup 1; Total 25.
Ted Davis was signed from Huddersfield Town at a time when Blackburn Rovers already had an outstanding goalkeeper in Ronnie Sewell. Davis, himself a first-class custodian, got his opportunity when Sewell injured a wrist in the fourth game of the 1922-23 season. He grabbed the chance with both hands and Sewell found himself relegated to the Central League team. Davis was the model of consistency and thoroughly deserved his position as the club's number-one custodian. However, his reign proved to be short lived as Sewell soared to a new peak in performance that even the reliable Davis could not equal. Finding himself in the Central League team for the next two seasons, Davis jumped at the opportunity of joining Bristol City in May 1925.

### DAWSON, Arthur

Outside-left. 1903-1907.
*Born: Rishton, 1882.*
*Debut: v Aston Villa (h) 9 April 1904.*
*Career: Blackburn Crosshill; Blackburn Rovers January 1903; Nelson August 1907; Burnley cs 1908.*
**Appearances:** Football League 18.
**Goals:** Football League 4.
In many ways a classic winger in that he had the ability to cross the ball accurately on the run. His speed and shooting ability ought to have paved the way for a successful career but somehow Dawson could never quite make the outside-left position his own.

### DAWSON, Alistair J.

Defender. 1987-1989.
*5ft 10in; 11st 10lb.*
*Born: Johnstone, Renfrewshire, 25 February 1958.*
*Debut: v Hull City (a) 15 August 1987.*
*Career: Johnstone High School; Glasgow Rangers 1975; Blackburn Rovers August 1987 to cs 1989 (£50,000); Airdrieonians 1989; St Andrew's (Malta) manager.*
**Appearances:** Football League 32+8; FA Cup 1; Football League Cup 3; Total 36+8.
Ally Dawson was a former Scottish international whose signing seemed something of a major coup for Don Mackay. A cultured player who could play at full-back or in the centre of defence, Dawson had enjoyed a highly successful career with the Ibrox club. Unfortunately, he was plagued by injuries during his time at Ewood and rarely had the opportunity to display the form which had brought him so much success north of the border.

### DAWSON, Percival Hall

Centre-forward. 1914-1923.
*5ft 11in; 12st.*
*Born: Cullercoats, 1890 (October quarter).*
*Debut: Tottenham Hotspur (h) 28 February 1914.*
*Career: Whitley Athletic; North Shields; Heart of Midlothian (£2,400) January 1911; Blackburn Rovers February 1914 (£2,500); Preston Colliery cs 1923; Barrow 1923-24.*
**Appearances:** Football League 140; FA Cup 11; Total 151.
**Goals:** Football League 71; FA Cup 2; Total 73.
Percy Dawson's arrival at Ewood Park clinched the club's second League title in three years; but Dawson himself did not collect any silverware. His eight games and three goals were not enough to allow him to qualify for a medal. But for World War One, Percy Dawson might well have developed into one of football's great centre-forwards. During his first full season at Blackburn he notched 20 goals in 28 appearances as the Rovers failed to retain their title. Sadly, his career was badly affected by the war and, when he returned to Ewood in 1919, he found himself in a completely different team to the one he joined. Dawson himself was no

longer the player he had been. The classy touches were still there, but the ageing legs now found it difficult to respond to the footballer's instincts. However, as one of the few experienced men at the club, Dawson strove manfully to hold the front line together for four seasons. During this time he managed to score over 40 goals in the League despite his diminishing power in front of goal. Dawson hung up his boots in 1923-24 to go into the licensed trade in his native North-East and he remained their until his retirement in the late 1950s.

## DEFEATS
The record for the most defeats in a season in each division is as follows:

| | | | |
|---|---|---|---|
| Premiership | 11 | defeats | 1992-93 |
| Division 1 | 30 | defeats | 1965-66 |
| Division 2 | 22 | defeats | 1978-79 & 1990-91 |
| Division 3 | 18 | defeats | 1971-72 & 1973-74 |

The record for the fewest defeats in a season in each division is as follows:

| | | | |
|---|---|---|---|
| Premiership | 8 | defeats | 1993-94 |
| Division 1 | 6 | defeats | 1888-89 |
| Division 2 | 8 | defeats | 1957-58 & 1980-81 |
| Division 2 | 8 | defeats | 1974-75 |

The record for worst home and away defeats is as follows:
Home 1-7 Notts County 14 March 1891 & Middlesbrough 29 November 1947.
Away 0-8 Arsenal 25 February 1933 & Lincoln City 29 August 1953.

## DEFENSIVE RECORD
Blackburn Rovers established their best defensive record in the Football League during the 1980-81 season. Under the leadership of Howard Kendall the Rovers conceded just 29 goals as they narrowly failed to win promotion for the second successive season. This was the second time in two seasons that the Rovers had created a new defensive record. Twelve months earlier the team had conceded 36 goals in 46 games in winning promotion from the Third Division.

## DENNIS, William
Right-back. 1919-1921.
*5ft 9in; 12st.*
*Born: Mossley, 21 September 1896.*
*Debut: v Middlesbrough (h) 15 September 1919.*
*Career: Army football; Ashton PSA; Birkenhead Comets; Stalybridge Celtic 1918; Blackburn Rovers May 1919; Stalybridge Celtic July 1921; Manchester United May 1923; Chesterfield February 1924; Wigan Borough May 1928 to April 1930; Macclesfield Town May 1930; Hurst July 1931; Mossley trainer October 1934.*
**Appearances:** Football League 5.
William Dennis came to Blackburn Rovers as one of the most highly-rated players in the Lancashire Combination. A hard tackler who could also feed his forwards, Dennis spent much of his time at Ewood in the Central League side before returning to Stalybridge in the summer of 1921.

## DENNISON, Harry
Outside-left. 1911-1920.
*5ft 8in; 10st 10lb.*
*Born: Bradford, 4 November 1894.*
*Debut: v Bristol City (h) 8 April 1911.*
*Career: Blackburn Grammar School; Blackburn Trinity; Blackburn Rovers amateur January 1911, turning professional in February 1911; Rochdale cs 1920; Wigan Borough June 1922; Stalybridge Celtic July 1923; Stockport County May 1924; Stalybridge Celtic; Hurst August 1928.*
*Domestic honours with Blackburn Rovers: First Division championship: 1911-12 (1 app).*
**Appearances:** Football League 3.
Harry Dennison created his niche in the history of Blackburn Rovers when he became the youngest player to appear in the Football League for the club. However, Dennison had to leave his home-town club to carve out a first-team career. After World War One, Dennison enjoyed two successful seasons with Rochdale, in which he was top scorer on each

occasion, before going on to become the leading goalscorer at Wigan in 1922-23. A schoolmaster by profession, Dennison was a fine dribbler who possessed wonderful ball control and on his day could be a match winning forward.

## DERBY COUNTY FC
Derby County was founded in 1884 as the football section of Derbyshire County Cricket Club. Derby County and Blackburn Rovers have a long record of rivalry in competitive football. As well as 94 Football League matches the clubs have met on no fewer than ten occasions in the FA Cup. However, perhaps the most crucial meetings between the clubs took place in the Second Division Play-off semi-final in 1991-92 season. The first leg at Ewood Park produced a titanic battle which saw Derby race into an early 2-0 lead. However, the Rovers fought back to level the score by half-time, thanks to goals by Scott Sellars and Mike Newell. In a rousing second-half, David Speedie scored two goals as the Rovers took a grip of the tie with a 4-2 win. The second leg at Derby produced another pulsating tie which again saw Derby take a lead. However, a brave Kevin Moran header put the Rovers back in the driving seat and, despite a second Derby goal, the Rovers managed to hang on for a 5-4 aggregate win.

### Football League

| | | Home | | Away | |
|---|---|---|---|---|---|
| 1888-89 | (FL) | W | 3-0 | W | 2-0 |
| 1889-90 | (FL) | W | 4-2 | L | 0-4 |
| 1890-91 | (FL) | W | 8-0 | L | 5-8 |
| 1891-92 | (FL) | L | 0-2 | D | 1-1 |
| 1892-93 | (Div 1) | D | 2-2 | L | 0-3 |
| 1893-94 | (Div 1) | L | 0-2 | L | 2-5 |
| 1894-95 | (Div 1) | D | 0-0 | D | 0-0 |
| 1895-96 | (Div 1) | L | 0-2 | D | 0-0 |
| 1896-97 | (Div 1) | W | 5-2 | L | 0-6 |
| 1897-98 | (Div 1) | D | 1-1 | L | 1-3 |
| 1898-99 | (Div 1) | W | 3-0 | D | 0-0 |
| 1899-00 | (Div 1) | W | 2-0 | W | 2-0 |
| 1900-01 | (Div 1) | W | 1-0 | L | 0-4 |
| 1901-02 | (Div 1) | W | 3-1 | D | 1-1 |
| 1902-03 | (Div 1) | L | 2-4 | L | 0-1 |
| 1903-04 | (Div 1) | W | 2-1 | L | 0-3 |
| 1904-05 | (Div 1) | W | 3-1 | D | 1-1 |
| 1905-06 | (Div 1) | W | 3-0 | W | 2-1 |
| 1906-07 | (Div 1) | W | 5-1 | W | 3-2 |
| 1912-13 | (Div 1) | L | 0-1 | D | 1-1 |
| 1913-14 | (Div 1) | W | 3-1 | W | 3-2 |
| 1919-20 | (Div 1) | W | 2-0 | D | 0-0 |
| 1920-21 | (Div 1) | W | 2-0 | W | 1-0 |
| 1926-27 | (Div 1) | D | 4-4 | W | 5-4 |
| 1927-28 | (Div 1) | W | 3-2 | L | 0-6 |
| 1928-29 | (Div 1) | W | 3-1 | L | 1-5 |
| 1929-30 | (Div 1) | L | 0-3 | L | 3-4 |
| 1930-31 | (Div 1) | W | 1-0 | D | 1-1 |
| 1931-32 | (Div 1) | W | 3-2 | D | 1-1 |
| 1932-33 | (Div 1) | D | 3-3 | L | 1-2 |
| 1933-34 | (Div 1) | W | 2-1 | D | 1-1 |
| 1934-35 | (Div 1) | L | 2-5 | D | 1-1 |
| 1935-36 | (Div 1) | D | 0-0 | L | 0-1 |
| 1946-47 | (Div 1) | D | 1-1 | L | 1-2 |
| 1947-48 | (Div 1) | L | 3-4 | L | 0-5 |
| 1953-54 | (Div 2) | L | 0-3 | D | 2-2 |
| 1954-55 | (Div 2) | W | 5-2 | W | 3-0 |
| 1957-58 | (Div 2) | W | 3-1 | W | 3-0 |
| 1966-67 | (Div 2) | D | 0-0 | W | 3-2 |
| 1967-68 | (Div 2) | W | 3-0 | D | 2-2 |
| 1968-69 | (Div 2) | D | 1-1 | L | 2-4 |
| 1980-81 | (Div 2) | W | 1-0 | D | 2-2 |
| 1981-82 | (Div 2) | W | 4-1 | D | 1-1 |
| 1982-83 | (Div 2) | W | 2-0 | W | 2-1 |
| 1983-84 | (Div 2) | W | 5-1 | D | 1-1 |
| 1986-87 | (Div 2) | W | 3-1 | L | 2-3 |
| 1991-92 | (Div 2) | W | 2-0 | W | 2-0 |

| | P | W | D | L | F | A |
|---|---|---|---|---|---|---|
| Home | 47 | 29 | 9 | 9 | 108 | 59 |
| Away | 47 | 12 | 17 | 18 | 65 | 97 |
| Total | 94 | 41 | 26 | 27 | 173 | 156 |

### Play-offs

| | Home | | Away | |
|---|---|---|---|---|
| 1991-92 | W | 4-2 | L | 1-2 |

Kevin Moran scores with a brave header against Derby County at the Baseball Ground in May 1992 to clinch a place in the Play-off Final.

**FA Cup**

| | | | | |
|---|---|---|---|---|
| 1891-92 | (1) | Home | W | 4-1 |
| 1893-94 | (3) | Away | W | 4-1 |
| 1901-02 | (1) | Home | L | 0-2 |
| 1902-03 | (2) | Away | L | 0-2 |
| 1903-04 | (3) | Away | L | 1-2 |
| 1911-12 | (2) | Away | W | 2-1 |
| 1928-29 | (4) | Home | D | 1-1 |
| | (R) | Away | W | 3-0 |
| 1931-32 | (4) | Away | L | 2-3 |
| 1976-77 | (5) | Away | L | 1-3 |

**Football League Cup**

| | | | | |
|---|---|---|---|---|
| 1962-63 | (2) | Away | D | 1-1 |
| | (R) | Home | W | 3-1 |

**DERBY JUNCTION FC**

Derby Junction caused a major upset in the 1887-88 FA Cup competition when they won through to the semi-final stage. Although Derby had enjoyed a fairly easy passage up to the sixth round stage, all of their victories had been by a one-goal margin. Thus when they were drawn at home to Blackburn Rovers in the sixth round, it was expected that the Rovers would go through. However, despite a Jack Southworth goal, the Rovers were to suffer an embarrassing defeat by two goals to one at the quaintly named Arboretum Field. It was probably the biggest upset that the club had suffered in the competition up to that time. To add insult to injury, Blackburn Park Road invited Derby Junction to Blackburn for an end-of-season friendly and defeated them 3-0. The site of this major upset is still a grassed recreation area, not far from Derby County's Baseball Ground.

**DERBYSHIRE, James Edward**

Left-back. 1902-1903.
*Born: Hawks Lane, nr Bury.*
*Debut: v Aston Villa (h) 27 September 1902.*
*Career: Hawks Lane St Mary's; Turton; Blackburn Rovers January 1902; Nelson 1903; Darwen; Turton September 1904.*
**Appearances:** Football League 11
A full-back whose pace and tough tackling made him a formidable opponent. He got his chance to partner Bob Crompton in the 1902-03 season but dropped out of contention following an injury at Stoke in December 1902. After battling back to full fitness, his claims to a first-team place were, surprisingly, overlooked by the committee and in 1903 he joined Nelson.

**DEVINE, Peter**

Centre-forward. 1982-1984.
*5ft 8in; 11st 6lb.*
*Born: Blackburn, 25 May 1960.*
*Debut: v Derby County (h) 2 May 1983.*

*Career: Brooklands, Blackburn; Mill Hill Old Boys, Blackburn; Mill Hill Working Men's club, Blackburn; Bury trial; Chorley; Vancouver Whitecaps (Canada); Bristol City July 1981; Blackburn Rovers non-contract player September 1982; Chorley; Burnley June 1984; Chorley; Clitheroe; Lancaster City; Haslingden.*
**Appearances:** Football League 8.
**Goals:** Football League 2.
Peter Devine enjoyed a varied career in football before joining Blackburn Rovers as a non-contract player in September 1982. Having made his debut towards the end of the 1982-83 season he figured briefly in the first team during the following campaign. He scored two goals in seven appearances during November and December 1983 before Chris Thompson returned to the first team and closed the door on Devine. In the summer of 1984 he tried his luck with Burnley and made 56 League appearances (including ten as sub) before a motor accident on holiday ended his League career. Devine later returned to Ewood Park to take charge of the club's Community Development Scheme. Whilst working at Ewood he continued playing in local non-League circles.

**DEVLIN, Hugh**

Left-back. 1896.
*Born: Glasgow, 1875.*
*Debut: v West Bromwich Albion (h) 1 September 1896.*
*Career: Cambuslang; Blackburn Rovers May 1896.*
**Appearances:** Football League 1.
Devlin was yet another player who came from north of the border with an excellent reputation. Quick thinking and possessing the ability to clear the ball powerfully, only his slender build appeared to be against him as he arrived in English football. Sadly, his promise was never fulfilled as injury was to restrict him to one appearance in the Football League.

**DE VRIES, Roger Stuart**

Left-back . 1980-1981.
*5ft 8½in; 11st 5lb.*
*Born: Willerby, Hull, 25 October 1950.*
*Debut: v Cardiff City (a) 16 August 1980.*
*Career: Hull schools football; Hull City amateur August 1967, turning professional in September 1967; Blackburn Rovers July 1980; Scunthorpe United October 1981.*
**Appearances:** Football League 13; FA Cup 1; Football League Cup 3; Total 17.
A natural left-back who came to Ewood Park in the twilight of his career. For almost a decade he had been a regular in the Hull City side and had proved himself to be a consistent and reliable defender in 318 League appearances (including four as sub). Concerned that Jim Branagan and Mick Rathbone both favoured the right, Howard Kendall installed De Vries in the number-three shirt for the start of the 1980-81 campaign. Although a neat and tidy footballer, De Vries was soon ousted by Rathbone and left the club to end his career with Scunthorpe United.

**DEWAR, George**
Centre-half/Half-back. 1889-1897.
*5ft 8½in; 11st 7lb.*
*Born: Dumbarton, 20 July 1867; Died: 2 September 1915.*
*Debut: v Everton (a) 7 September 1889.*
*Career: Dumbarton Athletic 1884; Dumbarton September 1887; Blackburn Rovers August 1889; New Brighton Tower June 1897; Southampton May 1898.*
*International honours with Blackburn Rovers: Football League: 1 appearance (1891).*
*Domestic honours with Blackburn Rovers: FA Cup winners: 1890; 1891.*
**Appearances:** Football League 174; FA Cup 22; Total 196.
**Goals:** Football League 7; FA Cup 3; Total 10.
An upholsterer by trade, George Dewar was not the most stylish of half-backs, but was certainly one of the most effective. Dewar had won two Scottish caps before joining Blackburn's band of Scottish professionals in August 1889. During his first three seasons with the club he was asked to fill the centre-half position but eventually settled into the right-half berth. Strong and quick, his hard tackling and good ball control made him a popular favourite with the crowd. During the 1897 close season he chose to join two Blackburn colleagues, Geordie Anderson and Josh Hargreaves, at New Brighton Tower. The move was not a success and in May 1898 he travelled south to play for Southampton in the Southern League. However, Dewar was now well into the veteran stage of his career and he made only four appearances in the Southern League during his year with Southampton before returning to his native Scotland.

**DEWHURST, John**
Centre-forward. 1899-1905.
*5ft 9in; 12st 2lb.*
*Born: Padiham, Lancashire, 1877.*
*Debut: v Preston North End (h) 14 October 1899.*
*Career: Padiham 1898; Darwen 1899; Blackburn Rovers April 1899; Brentford cs 1905; Bury October 1905; Accrington Stanley cs 1912.*
**Appearances:** Football League 169; FA Cup 13; Total 182.
**Goals:** Football League 43; FA Cup 4; Total 47.
Jack Dewhurst came to Blackburn from neighbouring Darwen and established himself as the regular centre-forward for the club in the early 1900s. Never the most prolific of goalscorers, Dewhurst enjoyed his best season in 1901-02 when he scored 16 goals in 34 League games. Dewhurst was versatile enough to be moved to the centre-half position on occasions and gave the Rovers excellent service for six seasons. The parting of the ways came when Dewhurst expressed the desire for a benefit as well as the maximum wage. As a result the Rovers allowed him to move to Brentford but within a matter of weeks, at the beginning of 1905-06 season, Dewhurst was back in Lancashire with Bury.

**DEWHURST, Robert Matthew**
Central defender. 1989-1993.
*6ft 3in; 13st 1lb.*
*Born: Keighley, 10 September 1971.*
*Debut: v Hull City (h) 28 August 1990.*
*Career: Blackburn Rovers trainee February 1989, before signing professional in October 1990; Darlington on loan December 1991 to February 1992; Huddersfield Town on loan October 1992; Wycombe Wanderers on loan January 1993; Released by Blackburn Rovers in November 1993; Hull City November 1993.*
**Appearances:** Football League 13; Football League Cup 2; Full Members; Cup 1; Total 16.
Bob Dewhurst graduated through the youth development scheme at Ewood and made his first-team debut, against Hull City in August 1990, a month before turning professional. Good in the air, Dewhurst enjoyed a short run in the first team before returning to Central League football in January 1991. The 1991-92 season saw him out of the reckoning at Ewood and he spent three months on loan to Darlington. The following season found him in a similar position and he enjoyed brief spells on loan in the lower divisions with Huddersfield Town and Wycombe Wanderers. In November 1993 he was given a free transfer in a bid to help him get first-team football.

**DIAMOND, Anthony John**
Centre-forward. 1982-1989.
*5ft 10in; 10st 4lb.*
*Born: Rochdale, 23 August 1968.*
*Debut: v Sunderland (h) 6 September 1986.*
*Career: Blackburn Rovers associated schoolboy September 1982, becoming a non-contract player in July 1984; Wigan Athletic on loan October 1988 to November 1988; Blackpool August 1989; Chorley on loan September 1990 to October 1990; Atherton LR.*
*International honours with Blackburn Rovers: Northern Ireland Under-23: 1 cap (1989); Northern Ireland Youth International.*

**Appearances:** Football League 9+17.
**Goals:** Football League 3.
A rather lightweight centre-forward who graduated through the junior ranks at Ewood Park. Although quick, he lacked the physique for the centre-forward position and, although a regular goalscorer in the Central League side, was more frequently used as a substitute with the senior team. He scored two goals in six League games whilst on loan to Wigan Athletic before moving to Blackpool at the start of the 1989-90 season. He struggled to make any impression at Bloomfield Road and was loaned to Chorley before bowing out of League football and signing for Atherton LR.

**DICKIE, Percy**
Half-back/Inside-forward. 1937-1942.
*5ft 5in; 9st 12lb.*
*Born: Aberdeen.*
*Debut: v Fulham (h) 20 September 1937.*
*Career: Mugiemoss; Aberdeen 1929; St Johnstone late 1932; Blackburn Rovers 17 September 1937; Manchester City wartime guest 1940-41; Bradford wartime guest 1942-43; Walsall wartime guest 1942-43; Leicester City wartime guest 1943-44 & 1944-45.*
*Domestic honours with Blackburn Rovers: Second Division championship: 1938-39 (2 apps).*
**Appearances:** Football League 19; FA Cup 2; Total 21.
**Goals:** Football League 1.
Percy Dickie was a utility player who came to Ewood Park after spending eight years in the Scottish First Division. A rift between St Johnstone and Dickie developed when the Scottish club refused to agree to Dickie's demand for a benefit after five years' service. As a result he was not in contention for a first-team place at the Perth club when Blackburn stepped in to bring him to Ewood Park. The stockily built Dickie quickly settled into the right-half position but was unable to retain his place in the face of competition from Halsall and Whiteside. Dickie also appeared in 28 wartime matches for the club.

**DICKENS, Matthew James**
Goalkeeper. 1992-.
*6ft 4in; 14st.*
*Born: Sheffield, 3 September 1970.*
*Debut: v Wolverhampton Wanderers (h) 14 April 1992.*
*Career: Sheffield United associated schoolboy October 1986, becoming a trainee in July 1987 and signing as a professional in July 1989; Lincoln City February 1991; Blackburn Rovers march 1992 (£250,000); Blackpool on loan January to April 1993; Lincoln City on loan November to December 1993.*
**Appearances:** Football League 1.
Matt Dickens was signed by Kenny Dalglish to provide cover for Bobby Mimms during the final promotion push of the 1991-92 season. He suffered a nightmare experience on his debut when he misjudged a long range shot and presented Wolves with a late winning goal. Unable to reclaim a first team place he has been on loan to both Blackpool and Lincoln City. At the end of the 1993-94 season he found himself battling with Frank Talia for the position of number-three goalkeeper at Ewood.

**DINNIS, Richard R.**
Coach. 1971-1975.
*Born: Clitheroe.*
*Career: Burnley amateur; Blackburn Rovers 1969 on the coaching staff, becoming caretaker manager 7 December 1974 until 16 January 1975, before reverting to coaching duties; Newcastle United coach cs 1975, then manager February to November 1977; Philadelphia Furies (USA) coach January to June 1978; Blackburn Rovers coaching staff March to October 1979; Bristol City scout; Middlesbrough coach 1985-87; Barrow manager December 1992 to October 1993.*
Richard Dinnis was a physical education teacher in Darwen before accepting the invitation to take over as the trainer-coach to the Central League team at Ewood Park. A fully qualified FA coach, Dinnis was put in charge of the first team following the departure of Ken Furphy to Sheffield United in December 1973. His six League games in charge ended with three wins and three defeats whilst he overcame Altrincham in the FA Cup after a replay before going out to Everton at Goodison Park. When Gordon Lee was appointed to the manager's position in January 1975, Dinnis returned to the Central League team. Dinnis followed Gordon Lee to Newcastle United in the summer of 1975 and was upgraded to manager when Lee left for Everton in January 1977. He helped Newcastle to finish in fifth position in the First Division and qualify for a place in the UEFA Cup. Unfortunately, a poor run during the early part of 1977-78 and a quick exit from Europe resulted in his dismissal in November 1977. Following a spell in America Dinnis rejoined the coaching staff at Ewood Park as John Pickering fought to keep the club in the Second Division. Dinnis left Ewood for a second time early in the reign of Howard Kendall and then coached at Middlesbrough

and in Saudi Arabia before becoming manager of Barrow in the Northern Premier League.

### DIX, Ronald William
Inside-forward. 1932-1933.
*5ft 8½in; 11st.*
*Born: Bristol, 5 September 1912.*
*Debut: v Chelsea (a) 27 August 1932.*
*Career: Bristol Schools; South Central School; Bristol Rovers amateur May 1927, turning professional in September 1929; Blackburn Rovers May 1932 (£3,000); Aston Villa May 1933; Derby County February 1937 (£4,875); Tottenham Hotspur June 1939; Bristol City wartime guest 1939-40 & 1940-41; Chester wartime guest 1940-41; Blackpool wartime guest 1941-42, 1942-43, 1943-44 & 1944-45; Bradford wartime guest 1944-45; Liverpool wartime guest 1944-45; Wrexham wartime guest 1944-45 & 1945-46; York City wartime guest; Reading November 1947, retired June 1949.*
**Appearances:** Football League 38; FA Cup 2; Total 40.
**Goals:** Football League 14; FA Cup 1; Total 15.
Ronnie Dix was the outstanding schoolboy footballer of his generation and at the tender age of 15 was a regular with the reserve team at Bristol Rovers. A former England Schoolboy international, Dix, at 15 years 180 days, became the youngest ever Football League goalscorer on 3 March 1928, when he scored in a 3-0 win over Norwich City. It was not surprising that a number of big clubs became interested in this outstanding young prospect. Both Everton and Aston Villa were keen on his services but negotiations between Everton and Dix failed to produce a contract. A Football League enquiry prevented Villa from stepping in to sign Dix and when Everton lost interest it was Blackburn Rovers who stepped in to sign him. Dix revelled in the Ewood team and struck up an immediate understanding with Jack Bruton on the right wing. He scored 14 League goals in his only season at Ewood Park, the same as Arthur Cunliffe and only three less than top scorer Ernie Thompson. On 2 May 1933 the Blackburn public were shocked to learn that financial difficulties had forced the club to sell Dix and Cunliffe to Aston Villa for the bargain fee of £8,500. Dix appeared in over 400 Football League matches during his career and scored 130 goals. He won his only England cap in 1939.

### DIXON, Edward Stanley
Inside-forward/Centre-half. 1923-1926.
*5ft 11in; 12st 8lb.*
*Born: Choppington, Northumberland, 26 May 1894; Died: Bedlington, Northumberland, 13 August 1979.*
*Debut: v Newcastle United (h) 10 March 1923.*
*Career: Barrington Albion; Newcastle United amateur December 1913, turning professional in February 1915; Blackburn Rovers March 1923 (£1,100); Hull City May 1926 to 1930; East Riding Amateurs 1930.*
**Appearances:** Football League 29; FA Cup 2; Total 31.
**Goals:** Football League 1; FA Cup 2; Total 3.
Stan Dixon was a dour performer whose fearless tackling was utilised both in defence and attack by Blackburn Rovers. Dixon had been at Newcastle for ten years, scoring nine goals in 53 League games. Dixon was given his chance at centre-half at Blackburn following injuries to Reilly, Pool and Williamson. However, although he appeared in the final 11 games of the 1922-23 season, Dixon was unable to establish himself as a regular at Ewood. He had better fortune at Hull City where he finished his professional career with a further three goals in 99 League games for the 'Tigers'.

### DOBING, Peter A.
Forward. 1955-1961.
*5ft 9in; 11st.*
*Born: Manchester, 1 December 1938.*
*Debut: v Bristol City (a) 2 September 1956.*
*Career: Blackburn Rovers 2 December 1955; Manchester City 20 July 1961 (£37,500); Stoke City 16 August 1963.*
*International honours with Blackburn Rovers: England Under-23: 7 caps (1959-61); Football League: 3 appearances (1959-60).*
*Domestic honours with Blackburn Rovers: FA Cup winners: 1960.*
**Appearances:** Football League 179; FA Cup 22; Football League Cup 4; Total 205.
**Goals:** Football League 88; F A Cup 16; Total 104.
The son of a former Salford Rugby League player, Peter Dobing first attracted the attention of Blackburn Rovers as a schoolboy in Crewe. In the face of stiff competition from other clubs, Johnny Carey brought him to Ewood Park as a 16-year-old and put him in the 'A' team. On his 17th birthday he signed as a professional and was promoted to the Central League side. Dobing made his senior debut as a 17-year-old and made rapid progress as a goalscoring inside-right and centre-forward. He was already a first-team regular when he helped the youth side to reach the last eight of the FA Youth Cup in 1956-57. A well-built and energetic

youngster, Dobing's main assets were his strong running and powerful shooting. In four seasons from 1957-58 to 1960-61 he finished as the top goalscorer at the club. His 20 League goals in 1957-58 helped the club to gain promotion to the First Division and he notched five goals in the run to the 1960 FA Cup Final. Although he won honours at Under-23 and Football League levels, Dobing was unable to break into the senior England team despite a move to Manchester City in July 1961. Although he scored 31 goals in 82 League games at Maine Road, the move was not a happy one for Dobing and in August 1963 he joined Stoke City. During his ten years at the Victoria Ground, Dobing performed with great consistency, scoring 80 goals in 303 League games. In 1971-72 he returned to Wembley to help Stoke win the Football League Cup.

### DOBSON, Anthony John
Central defender. 1991-1993.
*6ft 1in; 12st 2lb.*
*Born: Coventry, 5 February 1969.*
*Debut: v Ipswich Town (h) 19 January 1991.*
*Career: Coventry City associated schoolboy March 1983, becoming an apprentice in May 1985 before turning professional in July 1986; Blackburn Rovers January 1990 (£250,000); Portsmouth on loan October 1993, signing permanently in December 1993 (£150,000).*

**Appearances:** Premier League 15+4; Football League 21+1; FA Cup 2; Football League Cup 5; Full Members' Cup 1; Total 44+5.

A former England Under-21 international, Tony Dobson, along with Steve Livingstone, was signed by Don Mackay from Coventry City in January 1990. Although the club was struggling at the foot of the Second Division, the input of funds by Jack Walker enabled Mackay to bring the pair from Coventry for a substantial fee. Dobson immediately caught the eye in the centre of defence and he played a major part in the club's climb up the table. Dobson struggled to find his form during the early games of the 1991-92 season and was dropped after only four matches. Overlooked by Kenny Dalglish, Dobson appeared to have little future at the club and it was a major surprise when the manager selected him at left-back for the opening matches of the 1992-93 season. Dobson was unfortunate to be sent off at Wimbledon in September 1992, and his subsequent suspension saw Alan Wright moved to left-back and Gordon Cowans return to the first team. Dobson was unable to force his way back into the team on a regular basis and the signing of Graeme Le Saux finally sealed his fate. Unable to break into the team during the 1993-94 season campaign, this rugged, left-sided defender was allowed to join Portsmouth on an extended loan before finally completing a transfer to the Fratton Park club.

**DOIG, John Edward**
Goalkeeper. 1889.
*5ft 9¾in; 12st 2lb.*
*Born: Letham, Forfarshire, 29 October 1866; Died: St Helens, 7 November 1919.*
*Debut: v Notts County (h) 16 November 1889.*
*Career: St Helens FC (Arbroath); Arbroath; Blackburn Rovers October 1889 (£35); Arbroath; Sunderland September 1890; Liverpool August 1904 to 1908; St Helen's Recreation.*
**Appearances:** Football League 1.
According to the correspondent of the *Blackburn Times*, Ned Doig 'made a favourable impression on the spectators' on his debut for the club. The correspondent remarked of Doig that 'his duties were very light but they were smartly performed'. It was hoped that Doig would sign for the Rovers but unfortunately he chose to return to his native Scotland. He was finally brought to English football by Sunderland in September 1890 and went on to make 421 League appearances for the Roker Park club as well as appearing in 35 FA Cup-ties. He won four League championship medals with Sunderland and became recognised as one of the great goalkeepers of his era, appearing on five occasions for Scotland. He moved to Liverpool in 1904 and won a Second Division championship medal during his stay on Merseyside. He retired from League football after 51 appearances with Liverpool.

**DONCASTER ROVERS FC**
Formed in 1879 and elected to the Second Division of the Football League in 1901, Doncaster Rovers failed to gain re-election in 1903, but returned 12 months later. However, the club found itself out of the League again in 1905 and didn't return until being elected to the Third Division North in 1923. All the League meetings between Blackburn and Doncaster have taken place in the Second Division.

**Football League**

|  |  | Home |  | Away |  |
|---|---|---|---|---|---|
| 1936-37 | (Div 1) | W | 2-0 | W | 1-0 |
| 1950-51 | (Div 2) | W | 4-2 | W | 1-0 |
| 1951-52 | (Div 2) | D | 3-3 | L | 0-1 |
| 1952-53 | (Div 2) | W | 2-1 | D | 3-3 |
| 1953-54 | (Div 2) | W | 2-0 | W | 2-0 |
| 1954-55 | (Div 2) | W | 7-2 | W | 3-1 |
| 1955-56 | (Div 2) | D | 1-1 | D | 2-2 |
| 1956-57 | (Div 2) | D | 2-2 | D | 1-1 |
| 1957-58 | (Div 2) | W | 3-2 | W | 5-1 |

|  | P | W | D | L | F | A |
|---|---|---|---|---|---|---|
| Home | 9 | 6 | 3 | 0 | 26 | 13 |
| Away | 9 | 5 | 3 | 1 | 18 | 9 |
| Total | 18 | 11 | 6 | 1 | 44 | 22 |

**Football League Cup**

| 1969-70 | (2) | Home | W | 4-2 |
|---|---|---|---|---|

**DONNELLY, Darren Charles**
Forward. 1988-1993.
*5ft 10in; 11st 6lb.*
*Born: Liverpool, 28 December 1971.*
*Debut: v Charlton Athletic (h) 13 April 1991 (sub).*
*Career: Blackburn Rovers associated schoolboy April 1986, becoming a trainee in July 1988 and turning professional in June 1990; Chester City August 1993.*
**Appearances:** Football League 1+1.
Darren Donnelly graduated through the junior ranks at Ewood Park before breaking into the first team towards the end of the 1990-91 season. He made his first full appearance in the senior team at Millwall on the last day of the season and appeared to have a bright future ahead of him. Although not the biggest of front men, Donnelly was a regular goalscorer for the Central League team and three or four years earlier would probably have been given the opportunity of an extended first-team run. However, the arrival of a number of expensive forwards meant Donnelly was not selected for the first team again and in the summer of 1993 he was freed by the club. In August 1993 he signed for Chester City in a bid to rebuild his career.

**DONNELLY, James**
Full-back. 1919-1922.
*5ft 11in; 12st 6lb.*
*Born: Mayo, 18 December 1899.*
*Debut: v Bolton Wanderers (h) 20 November 1920.*
*Career: Army football (Royal Artillery); Blackburn Rovers November 1919; Accrington Stanley May 1922; Southend United May 1924; Brentford August 1925; Thames Association July 1928, then player-manager cs 1931 to cs 1932; Grajanski coach (Yugoslavia); Gunes coach (Turkey).*
**Appearances:** Football League 8; FA Cup 2; Total 10.
Donnelly came to Blackburn Rovers on the recommendation of Alexander McGhie, with whom he served in the Royal Artillery in France during World War One. He had to wait 12 months before making his debut and deputised for David Rollo and Fred Duckworth on ten occasions during the 1920-21 season. Although he remained with the Rovers until May 1922 he was not called upon again for the first team. He enjoyed greater success at neighbouring Peel Park where he made 54 appearances for Accrington Stanley.

**DOUGAN, Alexander Derek**
Centre-forward. 1959-1961.
*6ft 2in; 12st.*
*Born: Belfast, 20 January 1938.*
*Debut: v Arsenal (a) 14 March 1959.*
*Career: Belfast schoolboy football; Distillery 1955; Portsmouth August 1957; Blackburn Rovers March 1959; Aston Villa August 1961 (£15,000); Peterborough United June 1963 (£21,000); Leicester City May 1965 (£25,000); Wolverhampton Wanderers March 1967 (£50,000) until retiring in May 1975; Kettering Town manager 1975 to 1977. After*

*a spell as a sports presenter with Yorkshire Television he became chairman and chief executive with Wolverhampton Wanderers from 1982 to 1983.*
*International honours with Blackburn Rovers: Northern Ireland: 5 caps (1959-61); Northern Ireland 'B': 1 cap (1959).*
*Domestic honours with Blackburn Rovers: FA Cup runners-up: 1960.*
**Appearances:** Football League 59; FA Cup 14; Football League Cup 3; Total 76.
**Goals:** Football League 26; FA Cup 4; Football League Cup 4; Total 34.
Derek Dougan had won caps for Northern Ireland at schoolboy, youth and amateur levels whilst playing as a centre-half or wing-half. It was as a central defender that Dougan signed for Distillery, but on crossing the water to join Portsmouth he found himself converted into a centre-forward. Although he only scored nine goals

in his 33 League outings with 'Pompey', his promise was sufficient to persuade Dally Duncan to bring him to Ewood Park.

He scored on his debut at Highbury and quickly developed a rapport with the Blackburn supporters. Nicknamed 'Cheyenne' after the central character of a popular western series on television, Dougan revelled in the adulation of the younger element of the Ewood crowd. On the field he was a gangling talent whose ability was matched only by his unpredictability. Dougan's high point with the club came in the FA Cup semi-final of 1959-60 when he scored both goals which defeated Sheffield Wednesday.

As unpredictable as ever, his low point came just a few weeks later when he handed in a transfer request on the way to Wembley. Dougan then turned out for the Rovers at Wembley when there were serious doubts about his fitness and made little impact on a disappointing game. During the 1960-61 season his form continued to fluctuate and in August 1961 he was sold to Aston Villa. His career seemed to be in a terminal decline when Villa sold him to Peterborough United after only two seasons. However, at Peterborough he transformed his career and 38 goals in 77 League games had the First Division clubs again clamouring for his services. He joined Leicester City in May 1965, but it was his move to Wolves in March 1967 which finally gave him the stage he had sought throughout his career.

At Molineux he developed into one of the best centre-forwards in the country; displaying subtle ground skills to match his aerial power. He won a League Cup winners' medal and a UEFA Cup runners-up medal with Wolves and became a most articulate chairman of the Professional Footballers Association. He was capped 43 times for Northern Ireland and on retirement from League football accepted the position of manager with Kettering Town. In August 1982 he returned to Wolves as chairman and chief executive but left the club in January 1985 as the boardroom politics intensified at Molineux.

## DOUGLAS, Bryan
Outside-right/Inside-forward. 1952-1969.
*5ft 6in; 10st.*
*Born: Blackburn, 27 May 1934.*
*Debut: v Notts County (a) 4 September 1954.*
*Career: Blackburn Schoolboys; Lower Darwen YC; Blackburn Rovers 15 April 1952; Great Harwood June 1969.*
*International honours with Blackburn Rovers: England: 36 caps (1957-63); England 'B': 1 cap (1956); England Under-23: 5 caps (1956-57); Football League: 4 appearances (1958-1962).*
*Domestic honours with Blackburn Rovers: FA Cup runners-up: 1960.*
**Appearances:** Football League 438; FA Cup 39+1; Football League Cup 25; Total 502+1.
**Goals:** Football League 101; FA Cup 9; Football League Cup 5; Total 115.
For a youngster who was practically born on the Ewood Park doorstep it was not surprising that Bryan Douglas' sole ambition was to play for his local club. Douglas realised that ambition when he signed professional forms in April 1952, just a few days after the club had lost an FA Cup semi-final. Little did Douglas realise that he would appear in three semi-finals for the club and, along with Ronnie Clayton, become the most famous 'Rover' in the modern history of Blackburn Rovers. Success did not come quickly for Douglas as National Service disrupted his early career and delayed his first-team debut until September 1954.
Although small and deceptively frail looking, Douglas proved a revelation once he was moved from inside-forward to the right wing. His perfect balance and control over the ball meant he was a wizard at dribbling past opponents. Early in his career there were those who felt he had a tendency to over-elaborate and be a little selfish on the ball. However, the Douglas philosophy was not to give the ball away too

cheaply and his ability to send pinpoint passes into the penalty area quickly silenced the critics. In 1957-58 he helped the Rovers gain promotion to the First Division, scoring an all important penalty in the crucial 4-3 victory over Charlton Athletic in the final match of the season. It was in this season that his talents were rewarded with the first of his 36 England caps. Although he inherited the mantle of Matthews and Finney in the England team as an out and out winger, he came to be used more and more as an inside-forward with the Rovers. As a scheming inside-left, Douglas had the ability to spray the ball around and create openings for others. It was Douglas who supplied the ammunition for Pickering and McEvoy in 1963-64 when their prolific goalscoring took the club to the top of the First Division.

Douglas also enjoyed running at opponents from the centre of midfield and his shuffling gait bemused some of the best defenders in the game. A major factor in the relegation of the club from the First Division in 1965-66 was the absence of Douglas through injury. A cartilage operation and succession of other injuries restricted him to only 16 appearances during that ill-fated season. However, he returned the following season to try to inspire the team to a quick return to the top flight. Sadly, he was unsuccessful in what was to prove to be his last season as a truly effective member of the first team. Dogged by injuries during his final two seasons at Ewood Park, Douglas decided to retire from the first-class game at the end of the 1968-69 season. He signed for non-League Great Harwood and was later reunited at the Northern Premier League club with Ronnie Clayton, Roy Vernon and a host of other former Ewood colleagues.

## DOUGLAS, James

Right-half. 1880-1892.
*Born: Renfrew, 3 September 1859; Died: Renfrew, September 1919.*
*Debut: v Sheffield Wednesday (a) 18 December 1880 (FAC).*
*Career: Renfrew Grammar School; Paisley Institution; Renfrew FC; Barrow Rangers 1880; Blackburn Rovers 1880. Retired c.1892.*
*Domestic honours with Blackburn Rovers: FA Cup winners: 1884; 1885; 1886; FA Cup runners-up: 1882.*
**Appearances:** Football League 34; FA Cup 42; Total 76.
**Goals:** FA Cup 8.

One of a triumvirate of Scottish professionals who were the mainstay of the FA Cup winning sides of the 1880s. Douglas had won international recognition with Renfrew in 1880 before turning his back on further international caps in order to join the exodus of Scottish professionals to England. In 1880 he joined Barrow Rangers, but before the year was out had opted to play with Blackburn Rovers. Originally a terrier-like inside-forward, it was as a skilful wing-half that Douglas made his mark with Blackburn Rovers. Although he weighed little more than eight stones, he was, none the less, a remarkably tough little character who even performed admirably as a centre-half for Blackburn. Like McIntyre and Suter, his fellow Scotsmen, Douglas was hugely popular with the Blackburn public. For a time he became a licensee in Blackburn before returning to his original trade of pattern maker. Along with the other Scottish imports, Jimmy Douglas helped raise the standard of the early Rovers' teams and so establish them as one of the country's leading clubs. Unlike McIntyre and Suter, Douglas remained at Blackburn long enough to make 34 League appearances.

## DOWNES, Steven F.

Forward. 1976.
*5ft 10in; 11st 7lb.*
*Born: Leeds, 2 February 1949.*
*Debut: v West Bromwich Albion (a) 13 March 1976.*
*Career: Leeds MDBC; Rotherham United April 1967; Sheffield Wednesday December 1969; Chesterfield August 1972; Halifax Town July 1974; Blackburn Rovers on loan March 1976 to April 1976.*
**Appearances:** Football League 6.

Steve Downes was signed on loan in March 1976 as the Rovers fought to retain their newly won Second Division status. Injury had brought a premature end to the season for Bobby Svarc and with little or no money available for a replacement, Jim Smith was forced into the loan market. Downes, apart from a two year spell with Chesterfield, had played all of his football in his native Yorkshire. However, he had never quite recaptured the form which had brought 128 goals in 62 League appearances (including eight as sub) with Rotherham United. His six matches at Ewood brought seven important points but Downes was unable to find the target himself.

## DRAWS

The record for the greatest number of drawn games in each division is as follows:

| | | | |
|---|---|---|---|
| Premiership | 11 | draws | 1992-93 |
| Division 1 | 15 | draws | 1920-21 |
| Division 2 | 18 | draws | 1980-81 |
| Division 3 | 16 | draws | 1984-75 |

The record for the least number of drawn games in each division is as follows:

| | | | |
|---|---|---|---|
| Premiership | 9 | draws | 1993-94 |
| Division 1 | 2 | draws | 1890-91 & 1893-94 |
| Division 2 | 5 | draws | 1938-39 |
| Division 3 | 9 | draws | 1971-72 & 1979-80 |

The club's highest scoring draw is 5-5 and this scoreline has featured in three League matches. Accrington and Blackburn drew 5-5 in Blackburn's opening League game at the Leamington Ground on 15 September 1888. The same scoreline was recorded against Arsenal at Ewood Park in 1962-63 and against Birmingham City at St Andrew's in 1964-65. The greatest number of drawn games in an FA Cup-tie is two. This has happened on four occasions: Portsmouth (first round 1899-1900), Tottenham Hotspur (second round 1906-07), Portsmouth (second round 1924-25) and Sunderland (fifth round 1938-39).

## DUCKWORTH, Frederick

Left-back. 1910-1922.
*5ft 6½in; 10st 7lb.*
*Born: Blackburn.*
*Debut: v Preston North End (h) 30 August 1919.*
*Career: Bastwell Etrurians (Blackburn); St Stephen's (Blackburn); Furthergate; Blackburn Trinity; Blackburn YMCA; Blackburn Rovers 18 January 1910 to 1921-22.*
*International honours with Blackburn Rovers: England: 2 Victory International appearances (1919).*
**Appearances:** Football League 60; FA Cup 3; Total 63.

A smallish man who was much more powerful than he looked and one who timed tackles to perfection. Fred Duckworth had first joined the club in January 1910 but had to wait until August 1919 before making his debut in a Football League match. However, he had featured prominently during the club's wartime activities and was rewarded with two appearances in the Victory Internationals of 1919. Always cool under pressure, Duckworth had a knack of getting out of awkward situations with the minimum of fuss. His strong clearances and accurate passing made him a great favourite with the Blackburn public.

## DUCKWORTH, John

Forward. 1878-1883.
*Born: Blackburn, 1858.*
*Debut: v Tyne Association (h) 1 November 1879 (FAC).*
*Career: Blackburn Rovers 1878.*
*Domestic honours with Blackburn Rovers: FA Cup runners-up: 1882.*
**Appearances:** FA Cup 13.
**Goals:** FA Cup 7.

The brother of Walter Duckworth, who was a member of the original team and also the club's first secretary. John Duckworth came into the team just when his brother was coming to the end of his playing career. A goalscoring winger, Duckworth scored two goals in the first match that Blackburn Rovers played in the FA Cup competition. Duckworth went on to appear in the 1882 Cup Final for Blackburn Rovers but had retired by the time of the club's great exploits in the competition.

## DUCKWORTH, Joseph Cullen

Goalkeeper. 1919-1920.
*5ft 10in; 12st.*
*Born: Blackburn, 29 April 1898.*
*Debut: v Bolton Wanderers (a) 27 December 1919.*
*Career: Moss Street School, Blackburn; Accrington Stanley 1914; Blackburn Rovers amateur April 1915, signing professional in August 1919; Aberdare July 1921; Reading June 1924; Brighton & Hove Albion June 1930; York City July 1932.*
**Appearances:** Football League 5; FA Cup 2; Total 7.

Duckworth signed for the club as an amateur just before the League programme was abandoned for the duration of World War One. He returned to Ewood in 1919 to become a professional and found himself understudying Alf Robinson. Sadly, Duckworth failed to make the most of his opportunities and when ten goals went past him in three games in the opening weeks of 1920, his Ewood fate was sealed. The club signed Ronnie Sewell and although Duckworth remained at Ewood for another season he didn't reappear in the first team. The player enjoyed better fortunes with his subsequent clubs and in 1926 he won a Third Division South championship medal with Reading. Duckworth went on to make over 300 appearances in the Football League for his various clubs.

## DUCKWORTH, Thomas Crook

Outside-right. 1903-1905.
*Born: Blackpool, 1882.*
*Debut: v Derby County (a) 5 March 1904 (FAC).*
*Career: Blackpool April 1901; West Ham United; Blackburn Rovers*

*November 1903; Blackpool June 1905.*
**Appearances:** Football League 1; FA Cup 1; Total 2.
A speedy type of winger who found it difficult to establish himself at three different clubs. He scored three goals in ten League appearances with Blackpool in 1901-02 before trying his luck with West Ham United. Duckworth failed to make the first team in London and returned to Lancashire to join Blackburn Rovers in November 1903. With Arnold Whittaker in possession of the right-wing position, Duckworth was limited to just one FA Cup appearance during the 1903-04 season. He made one League appearance the following campaign and then returned to Blackburn for the 1905-06 season. During his second stint at Bloomfield Road he scored two goals in four League outings.

**DUERDEN, James**
Forward. 1888-1889.
*Debut: v Accrington (a) 19 January 1889.*
*Career: Livesey; Blackburn Rovers 1888; Burnley July 1890; Rossendale cs 1891.*
**Appearances:** Football League 2.
James Duerden appeared in two League games during the inaugural season of the Football League. He featured on the left wing on his debut and on his second appearance was at centre-half. Duerden was not retained for a second season of League football at Ewood but re-emerged at Turf Moor in 1890.

**DUNCAN, Douglas 'Dally'**
Manager. 1958-1960.
*Born: Aberdeen 14 October 1909; Died: Brighton, 2 January 1990.*
*Career: Aberdeen Richmond 1927; Hull City August 1928; Derby County March 1932 (£2,000); guest for Notts County (1939-40 & 1940-41), Reading (1939-40) and Nottingham Forest (1941-42) during World War Two; Luton Town player-coach October 1946, then player-manager June 1947 to October 1958; Blackburn Rovers manager October 1958 to July 1960; coached Brighton schoolboys for a year and ran a guest house in Brighton; Luton Town scout.*
'Dally' Duncan had enjoyed a successful playing career, winning 14 caps for Scotland, before turning to management. The former outside-left had taken Luton Town into the First Division whilst the Hatters and so came to Ewood Park as a man of proven ability. Taking over in October 1958, Duncan successfully led the club to tenth position on their return to the First Division. However, the real success of the 1958-59 campaign was the winning for the FA Youth Cup, a fact which suggested that Duncan would have a new crop of youngsters around which to build the future of the club.

Unfortunately, the first team began to break up before the youngsters were ready to step up. Injury began to take its toll of Bill Eckersley, whilst the uneasy relationship between Duncan and Roy Vernon ended in the Welshman joining Johnny Carey at Everton. Although the team made a good start to the 1960-61 campaign, results fell away as internal problems began to mount. Between Boxing Day and the end of the season the Rovers collected a meagre haul of six points from 17 games. Fortunately, their good start to the campaign enabled them to finish in 17th position. Ironically, as their League form slumped, the team embarked upon a run in the FA Cup which was to take them all the way to Wembley. Sadly, the Wembley date offered little consolation for the troubled Duncan. Uproar over the distribution of Cup Final tickets and a transfer request from Derek Dougan, on the way to Wembley, did little to boost morale. A crushing defeat in the Final, albeit with only ten men after Whelan broke his leg, simply added to the pressure on the manager.

Although Duncan had a fine record in management with Luton Town, he was never able to win over the supporters in the same way as Johnny Carey. The Blackburn public wanted the type of football that Carey had provided and as a disappointing season ended rumour of a rift between the manager and directors began to grow. Clearly unhappy with the way events had gone the board asked Duncan for his resignation. However, having the security of a long contract, the Rovers' manager declined the request, but in July 1960 he was unceremoniously removed by the directors. Duncan lived in retirement in Brighton until his death in 1990.

**DUNCAN, William McKiddie**
Inside-left. 1933-1935.
*5ft 6in; 11st.*
*Born: Dundee, 20 July 1913.*
*Debut: v Tottenham Hotspur (h) 1 January 1934.*
*Career: Dundee Stobswell; Blackburn Rovers January 1933; Carlisle United February 1935; Gillingham July 1935.*
**Appearances:** Football League 2; FA Cup 1; Total 3.
He joined Blackburn as a 19 year old after being selected as reserve for a junior international between Scotland and Wales. At the time of his signing for Rovers he was sought after by a number of Scottish and English clubs. Although there was no doubting the quality that he

possessed, Duncan failed to do himself justice at Ewood Park. Duncan, a very talented dribbler, made a rapid leap from third team to first team but after three successive appearances he faded from the scene.

**DUNKLEY, Albert E.**
Outside-left. 1903-1904.
*Born: Northampton, 1877.*
*Debut: v Small Heath (a) 17 October 1903.*
*Career: Northampton Town 1897; Leicester Fosse May 1900; Northampton Town February 1901; New Brompton cs 1901; Queens Park Rangers; Blackburn Rovers August 1903; Bristol Rovers cs 1904; Blackpool August 1906.*
**Appearances:** Football League 4.
**Goals:** Football League 1.
Albert Dunkley was one of football's nomads during the early 1900s. He had the distinction of being the outside-left in the first side ever fielded by Northampton Town and also topped their goalscorers during their first season of competitive football in the Northants League. Dunkley came to Blackburn for the start of the 1903-04 season to understudy Fred Blackburn. Although his first-team opportunities were limited, Dunkley managed to make a goal-scoring debut against Small Heath when he scored a consolation goal in a 2-1 defeat. At the end of the season, Dunkley continued on his travels and moved to Bristol Rovers where he won a Southern League championship medal in 1905.

**DUNNING, William**
Forward. 1968-1972.
*5ft 9in; 10st.*
*Born: Bury, 15 November 1952.*
*Debut: v Cardiff City (a) 14 November 1970.*
*Career: Blackburn Rovers apprentice July 1968, turning professional in November 1970, released cs 1972.*
**Appearances:** Football League 10+3.
**Goals:** Football League 2.
A lively but rather lightweight striker whose professional career was ended by a serious back injury. Bill Dunning enjoyed a brief run of eight games during the middle of the 1970-71 season when the club was at the foot of the Second Division. Although he brought a refreshing enthusiasm into the team he did little to suggest he could lift the club's ailing fortunes.

**DUXBURY, Michael**
Full-back. 1990-1992.
*5ft 9in; 11st 2lb.*
*Born: Accrington, 1 September 1959.*
*Debut: v Barnsley (h) 15 September 1990.*
*Career: Manchester United associated schoolboy May 1975, becoming and apprentice in July 1976 before turning professional in October 1976; Blackburn Rovers August 1990 (free); Bradford City on loan from January 1992 until signing permanently on a free transfer in March 1992, freed May 1994.*
**Appearances:** Football League 25+2; FA Cup 2; Football League Cup 1; Full Members' Cup 0+1; Total 28+3.
Don MacKay managed to bring this former England international to Ewood Park in the face of stiff competition from other clubs. A tough tackling defender and hard-working midfield player Duxbury, a former England international, had been given a free transfer by Manchester United after appearing in 299 League games (including 25 as substitute) for the club. Versatility had enabled Duxbury to retain a first-team place at Old Trafford for a decade and Mackay hoped that he would prove as successful as his former United colleagues Frank Stapleton and Kevin Moran. Sadly, Duxbury was plagued by injury during his time at Blackburn and was never able to establish himself in the first team. In January 1992, Kenny Dalglish allowed Duxbury to link up with Frank Stapleton at Bradford City on loan and two months later the move became permanent.

**EAST LANCASHIRE CHARITY CUP**
The origins of this competition date back to May 1882, when representatives of Blackburn Rovers, Blackburn Olympic, Darwen and Accrington were invited to a meeting at the White Bull Hotel in Blackburn. This gathering decided to form a new competition which would enable the clubs to raise money for charitable purposes. Thus the East Lancashire Charity Cup came into being. The first draw saw the Rovers visit Blackburn Olympic and Accrington met in the other tie. The game at Darwen was played on 26 May 1882 and resulted in a convincing 4-1 victory for the Rovers.

The Final was held over until the start of the following season and on 7 August 1882 the Rovers crashed 5-2 at home to Blackburn Olympic. Financially the competition proved quite successful with the two Blackburn clubs raising £90 between them, in subscriptions, whilst

Darwen raised £23 and Accrington almost £9. Subscriptions and gate money together amounted to a final total of £240. The East Lancashire Charity Cup itself cost £146 12s 0d and contained a football scene on one side and on the reverse a representation of the Infirmary. It was the Blackburn and East Lancashire Infirmary that benefited to the tune for £40 from the first competition.

The competition was a regular event in East Lancashire during the 1880s and early 1890s. However, once the Football League was established it was not uncommon for reserve teams to be fielded in the competition. As a result of this, interest in the competition began to wane and on occasions the event was postponed altogether. Blackburn Rovers opted to use mainly weakened teams in this competition following the formation of the Football League. However, during the early 1900s they again reverted to a first-team formation in a number of these matches and as a result enjoyed some overwhelming victories. The largest margin of victory was recorded on 28 September 1910 when Blackburn travelled to Accrington Stanley and romped to a 9-1 win thanks to five goals from Wattie Aitkenhead. After World War One the competition became the preserve of reserve teams and interest gradually faded away.

## EASTHAM, John Bilborough
Full-back. 1901-1905.
*Born: Blackburn, 1883 (January quarter); Died: Stalybridge, 3 May 1932.*
*Debut: v Sunderland (a) 2 November 1901.*
*Career: St Peter's School, Blackburn; Blackburn Rovers March 1901; Glossop September 1905; Southampton May 1906.*
**Appearances:** Football League 48; FA Cup 4; Total 52.
The disappointing form of John Darroch, the veteran full-back signed from Bury, gave Jack Eastham the opportunity to establish himself as Bob Crompton's partner. A local lad, Eastham found the going tough at first but was to develop into a rugged defender. Sadly, Eastham was plagued by injury and the arrival of Tom Riley and Jock Cameron restricted his first-team opportunities. In September 1905 he moved to Glossop and on Boxing Day 1905, he kept goal during Glossop's 4-2 home defeat at the hands of Chelsea. He appeared in 26 League games for Glossop before moving to Southampton. Although he took time to settle at the Dell he eventually went on to appear in 161 Southern League matches. He retired at the end of the 1911-12 season and returned to live in the Blackburn area.

## ECCLES, Terence S.
Central defender/Centre-forward. 1968-1973.
*6ft 0½in; 13st.*
*Born: Leeds, 2 March 1952.*
*Debut: v Norwich City (a) 31 January 1970.*
*Career: Blackburn Rovers apprentice August 1968, turning professional in August 1969; Mansfield Town July 1973; Huddersfield Town January 1977; Ethnikos (Greece) June 1978; York City September 1979.*
**Appearances:** Football League 33+13; FA Cup 1; Football League Cup 2; Total 36+13.
**Goals:** Football League 6; Football League Cup 1; Total 7.
Although a natural centre-half, it was at right-back that 'Tex' Eccles first broke into the senior team at Ewood Park. After a run of four games in 1969-70 he returned to the Central League team before being recalled to the centre of defence during the following campaign. As the club hurtled towards relegation to the Third Division, Johnny Carey switched Eccles to the centre-forward position. Initially, he did quite well and three goals in four games suggested that he might be good enough to help the club avoid relegation. However, his goals dried up and he eventually lost his place in attack when Fred Pickering returned to Ewood In March 1971. Eccles began the 1971-72 season as leader of the attack but was replaced when Ken Furphy undertook his rapid rebuilding of the team. In July 1973 he was transferred to Mansfield Town and was their leading goalscorer with 20 goals in 1973-74. The following season his 17 goals helped Mansfield win the Fourth Division title and he remained at Field Mill until moving to Huddersfield Town in January 1977. After leaving Yorkshire he enjoyed a year in Greece before ending his Football League career with York City, where he scored 18 goals in 64 League matches.

## ECKERSLEY, William
Left-back. 1948-1961.
*5ft 6in; 10st 1lb.*
*Born: Southport, 16 July 1925; Died: 25 October Blackburn 1982.*
*Debut: v Manchester United (a) 1 May 1948.*
*Career: High Park, Southport; Blackburn Rovers March 1948 until cs 1961.*
*International honours with Blackburn Rovers: England: 17 caps (1950-53); England 'B': 3 caps (1950); Football League: 6 appearances (1950-53).*
**Appearances:** Football League 406; FA Cup 26; Total 432.

**Goals:** Football League 20; FA Cup 1; Total 21.
The talented Bill Eckersley graduated from lorry driver and junior footballer in Southport to England's first-choice left-back in a matter of three years. He came to Blackburn in March 1948 and, with the club already doomed to relegation, was given his first-team chance in the final match of the campaign. An ever-present the following season, Eckersley established himself as the club's outstanding player. Calm and cool under pressure, Eckersley was not only a tenacious tackler, but also a most constructive attacking full-back. Although lacking in height and weight, Eckersley had a tremendous heart and a determined will to win.

One of the finest players to wear the blue and white colours, Eckersley was selected as Alf Ramsey's regular full-back partner in the England team. In total he won 17 caps for England between 1950 and 1953, before the 6-3 Wembley defeat by Hungary ended the international careers of both Eckersley and Ramsey. Eckersley, as club captain, led by example on the field, whilst his sharp sense of humour kept dressing-room morale high. Unfortunately, despite his success at international level, honours at club level eluded Eckersley.

A succession of promotion near misses and two FA Cup semi-finals were all he had to show for his long association with Blackburn Rovers until promotion to the First Division was finally achieved in 1957-58. Plagued by injury, Eckersley only appeared in six League games during his final two seasons at Ewood and was forced to miss out on the 1960 FA Cup Final. He retired in 1961 and a crowd of 21,000 turned out to pay him an emotional farewell at his testimonial match. Sadly, life outside of the game was not quite so kind to Eckersley. A confectionery business in the Ewood area didn't quite work out as he had hoped and he returned to driving before his untimely death in October 1982. Fittingly, his ashes were scattered on the Ewood turf, by his sons Billy and Stephen, in an emotional ceremony prior to a first-team match.

## EDDLESTON, Joseph
Centre-forward. 1919-1921.
*5ft 6½in; 10st 6lb.*
*Born: Oswaldtwistle, Lancashire, 29 December 1896; Died: Blackburn, 24 March 1959.*
*Debut: v Burnley (a) 20 September 1919.*
*Career: St Mary's RC Oswaldtwistle; Blackburn Rovers May 1919; Nelson April 1921; Swindon Town August 1926; Accrington Stanley July 1932; Fleetwood August 1933.*
**Appearances:** Football League 7.
**Goals:** Football League 3.
In the years immediately after World War One, Joe Eddleston was one of a number of young players trying to establish themselves at Ewood Park. Despite scoring three goals in seven outings during the 1919-20 season, Eddleston was not called upon again and dropped out of the Football

League to join Nelson in April 1921. However, within weeks of joining the Seedhill club, Eddleston found himself once more in the ranks of Football League players when Nelson were elected to the newly formed Third Division North. Although not the biggest of men, Eddleston proved a reliable marksman and notched 95 goals in 183 League games. He spent six years at Swindon Town (203 appearances, 64 goals) before returning to Lancashire to join Accrington Stanley. He scored 12 goals in 40 appearances at Peel Park and it was whilst with Stanley that he recorded his 400th Football League appearance.

**EDDS, Ernest Frederick**
Outside-left. 1949-1951.
*5ft 7½in; 11st 2lb.*
*Born: Plymouth, 19 March 1926.*
*Debut: v Tottenham Hotspur (h) 24 December 1949.*
*Career: Portsmouth April 1944 amateur; Plymouth Argyle October 1946; Blackburn Rovers December 1949; Torquay United June 1951; Plymouth Argyle October 1953; Swindon Town July 1955.*
**Appearances:** Football League 18; FA Cup 1; Total 19.
**Goals:** Football League 3; FA Cup 1; Total 4.
Ernie Edds became the eighth player to be used by Blackburn Rovers in the outside-left position following the sale of Bobby Langton to Preston North End in August 1948. Although he had figured prominently at centre-forward for Plymouth, the small and lightly built Edds enjoyed a run of 14 League games following his arrival from Plymouth. However the following season found him in the Central League team and, unable to regain his place in the first team he opted to join Torquay United in June 1951.

**EDGE, Arthur Stanley**
Goalkeeper. 1914-1915.
*Born: Freshfields, 24 September 1892.*
*Debut: v Liverpool (h) 21 September 1914.*
*Career: Blackburn Grammar School; Rossall School; Cambridge University; Blackburn Rovers amateur March 1914.*
**Appearances:** Football League 9.
The war clouds gathering over Europe gave Arthur Edge his chance of senior football at Ewood Park. At the start of the 1914-15 campaign, Edge was the club's third-choice custodian and there appeared little likelihood that he would be involved with the senior team. However, James Crabtree enlisted in the Army almost as soon as the season started and an injury to Alf Robinson meant Edge was thrown into the first team before the end of September. Edge, a student at Jesus College, Cambridge, had first come to the notice of the Rovers after being given his blue in his second year at university. He understudied Robinson throughout the 1914-15 season before receiving his degree and becoming a captain in the Army. When hostilities ended he took up a career in commerce.

**ELLIS, Robert**
Forward. 1908-1910.
*5ft 7½in; 10st 10lb.*
*Born: Park Head, Glasgow.*
*Debut: v Bristol City (h) 1 September 1908.*
*Career: Vale of Leven; Workington; Blackburn Rovers June 1908 until cs 1910; Workington.*
**Appearances:** Football League 1.
**Goals:** Football League 1.
Ellis was signed by Blackburn Rovers in June 1908, along with Jack Lawrie, from Workington. Ellis was a tricky inside-forward who was said

to be a splendid header of the ball. The hard-working Ellis made his debut in the opening match of the 1908-09 season and scored the goal which enabled Blackburn to share the points with Bristol City in a 1-1 draw. However, this proved to be the only senior appearance that Ellis made for the club.

**ELSE, Frederick**
Goalkeeper. 1961-1966.
*5ft 10in; 11st 4lb.*
*Born: Golborne, 31 March 1933.*
*Debut: v Cardiff City (h) 19 August 1961.*
*Career: Standish St Wilfreds; Wigan; Standish St Wilfreds; Axwell Park; Preston North End August 1953; Blackburn Rovers August 1961 (£20,000); Barrow July 1966.*

**Appearances:** Football League 187; FA Cup 18; Football League Cup 16; Total 221.
Fred Else joined Blackburn Rovers as a result of the lifting of the maximum wage restriction on professional footballers. Else was in dispute with Preston North End when Jack Marshall stepped in to bring the former England 'B' international to Ewood Park. The signing of Else was a major coup for Blackburn as the player was regarded by many as the finest uncapped goalkeeper of his generation. Else had built his reputation at Deepdale on being able to read the game and his excellent judgement and anticipation meant that he rarely had to rely on the spectacular to keep his goal intact. An athletic and agile custodian, Else appeared to be the perfect man for Marshall to have behind his attacking team. His safe and confident handling quickly established him as a great favourite at Ewood Park, but the consistency of Ron Springett and the emergence of Gordon Banks kept him out of the England set-up. Following a broken collar-bone in 1964-65 his form began to wane. Confidence was further dented during the ill-fated 1965-66 relegation season when Else was one of a number of senior players who struggled to find their form. At the end of the season he was given a free transfer and joined Barrow. He played 148 League games for Barrow and eventually became their manager for a short spell before their demise from the Football League.

**ELVY, Reginald**
Goalkeeper. 1951-1956.
*6ft 2½in; 11st 8lb.*
*Born: Churwell, 25 November 1920; Died: Kingsthorpe, 13 July 1991.*
*Debut: v Cardiff City (h) 10 November 1951.*
*Career: Halifax Town amateur March 1944; turning professional in March 1944; Bolton Wanderers March 1947; Blackburn Rovers November 1951; Northampton Town July 1956 to 1959.*

**Appearances:** Football League 192; FA Cup 16; Total 208.
An injury to Jack Patterson in November 1951 created a goalkeeping crisis at Ewood Park and led to the arrival of Reg Elvy. Elvy, who was quietly playing out his career in the Central League team at Burnden Park, was not the club's first choice to replace Patterson. The Rovers had hoped to sign Ken Greaves, a Lancashire county cricketer, from Bury, but illness to Greaves forced the Ewood club to turn to Elvy. Elvy had joined Bolton Wanderers after making 22 League appearances for Halifax Town. However, the consistency of Stan Hanson at Burnden Park meant that Elvy had only added another 31 League appearances to his total before moving to Ewood Park.

At the age of 31, Elvy was finally given the opportunity to

carve out a first-team career in professional football. He literally seized it with both hands and made 152 consecutive appearances from November 1951 to April 1955. Tall and rangy, with long arms and large hands, Elvy proved to be a more than capable goalkeeper. His height allowed him to dominate his area when dealing with crosses and yet for a tall man he was surprisingly quick at getting down to ground shots. At a time when the buccaneering style of play at Ewood Park often left him exposed, Elvy maintained a high level of consistency in his performances. The parting of the ways came at the end of the 1955-56 season when, despite making 40 League appearances, concern was expressed about his slowing reflexes and failing eyesight. Elvy, who had worn contact lenses during matches, was released on a free transfer and found employment at Northampton Town. He went on to appear in a further 67 League matches for the Cobblers before hanging up his gloves.

## ENDEAN, Barry
Centre-forward. 1971-1975.
*5ft 10in; 11st 10lb.*
*Born: Chester-le-Street, Co.Durham, 22 March 1946.*
*Debut: v Aston Villa (a) 30 October 1971.*
*Career: Watford September 1968; Charlton Athletic February 1971 (£11,111); Blackburn Rovers October 1971 (p/e for Eamon Rogers); Huddersfield Town March 1975; Workington on loan October 1975 to November 1975 and December 1975 until January 1976; Hartlepool United March 1976 to June 1977.*
**Appearances:** Football League 65+14; FA Cup 5; Football League Cup 3+1; Total 73+15.
**Goals:** Football League 18; Football League Cup 1; Total 19.
Blackburn Rovers received Barry Endean and £7,777 pounds from Charlton Athletic in exchange for Eamon Rogers on 27 October 1971. In signing for Blackburn Rovers, Endean found himself reunited with Ken Furphy, his former manager at Watford. It was at Watford that Endean had made a sensational start to his Football League career with seven goals in his first three League games. He left Watford after scoring 28 goals in 77 League games to try his luck in London with Charlton Athletic.

However, Endean found goals hard to come by at the Valley and scored only one goal in his 27 League games for the club. Endean was brought to Ewood Park during the major rebuilding programme that Furphy launched during the opening months of the 1971-72 campaign. Unfortunately, Endean was unable to reproduce his Watford form for Furphy and failed to score in his 14 League games (including two appearances as sub). It wasn't until the close season tour of Czechoslovakia that Endean found his form and convinced Furphy not to enter the transfer market to find a replacement. It was during the latter part of the 1972-73 season that Endean finally won a regular place in the team. This followed an operation to remove his tonsils that necessitated a blood transfusion which left him under par for some considerable time. Once he found his niche in the team Endean became a popular figure with the supporters because of his willingness to fight for every ball. His never-say-die attitude allowed Furphy to use him in midfield as well as at centre-forward and he finished the 1972-73 season with nine League goals.

He scored another nine goals in the Third Division during the following campaign but lost his place towards the end of the season as Gordon Lee experimented with the playing staff that he had inherited. The arrival of Ken Beamish and Graham Oates, coupled with Lee's decision to restore Don Martin to the team, resulted in Endean finding himself relegated to the bench for much of the 1974-75 season. As the season reached its climax he was allowed to join Huddersfield Town in a deal which brought Bobby Hoy to Ewood Park.

## ENGLAND, Harold Michael
Centre-half. 1957-1966.
*6ft 2in; 13st 2lb.*
*Born: Greenfield, North Wales, 2 December 1941.*
*Debut: v Preston North End (h) 3 October 1959.*
*Career: Blackburn Rovers non-contract player May 1957, turning professional in April 1959; Tottenham Hotspur 19 August 1966; Seattle Sounders (USA) May 1975; Cardiff City 19 August 1975; Seattle Sounders (USA) May 1976 to August 1979.*
*International honours with Blackburn Rovers: Wales: 20 caps (1962-66); Wales Under-23: 11 caps (1959-65).*
*Domestic honours with Blackburn Rovers: FA Youth Cup winners: 1959.*
**Appearances:** Football League 165; FA Cup 12; Football League Cup 7; Total 184.
**Goals:** Football League 21.
A member of the FA Youth Cup winning side of 1959, Mike England went on to become possibly the finest centre-half of his generation. Tall and lean, England was a natural athlete who could fill a variety of positions. He made his debut at right-half and played at right-back in the

opening 12 games of the 1960-61 season.

The consistency of Matt Woods meant England had to settle for Central League football before finally establishing himself at left-half towards the end of 1962-63. The departure of Woods at the end of that season enabled England to finally capture the number-five shirt at Ewood Park. England quickly matured into an outstanding defender. His height made him dominant in the air, whilst on the ground his strength and speed made him a daunting prospect for even the quickest of forwards. Yet his game was not just based on power. For a big man, England had the deftest of touches and his instant control and accurate distribution put him on a level above most First Division defenders.

His vision and ability to read the game meant the could be used as an attacking wing-half and he also had a successful spell at centre-forward during the 1965-66 relegation campaign. When the club were relegated at the end of 1965-66 season it was clear that England would not settle for Second Division football. When he joined Tottenham Hotspur for £95,000 in August 1966, England had no equal in Britain and few in Europe. At Tottenham he won FA Cup, League Cup and UEFA Cup winners' medals and appeared in 300 League games for the White Hart Lane club.

Already a regular on the international scene before he left Ewood Park, England went on to win 44 caps for Wales and, following spells with Seattle Sounders and Cardiff City, became the Welsh international team manager. He took Wales to the brink of appearing in the final stages of both the World Cup and European Championships. Unfortunately, luck always appeared to desert the Welsh at crucial times and in February, 1988, England was controversially dismissed.

## EVANS, Lorenzo
Winger. 1898-1899.
*Born: Preston, 1878.*
*Debut: v Newcastle United (h) 10 December 1898.*
*Career: Blackburn Rovers September 1898; Glossop North End amateur July 1899 to cs 1900; Blackpool cs 1900 to cs 1903.*
**Appearances:** Football League 2.
Lorenzo Evans joined the club in September 1898 and acted as understudy for William Williams and Daniel Hurst in the wide positions. His debut against Newcastle was a disappointing affair as he squandered several goalscoring opportunities during a convincing 4-2 win. He received a second call up two weeks later when Hurst was injured for the meeting with Liverpool at Ewood Park on Christmas Eve 1898. Although he improved on his initial appearance in the team it was clear that he was not quite up to the standard of the men he was understudying. The summer of 1899 saw him try his luck with Glossop. An architect by profession, Evans played as an amateur with Glossop.

## EVANS, Robert Owen
Goalkeeper. 1903-1908.
*5ft 10½in; 12st.*
*Born: Wrexham, August 1881; Died: Coventry, 8 March 1962.*
*Debut: v Everton (a) 1 September 1903.*
*Career: Olympic Juniors 1895; Stansby Villa; Wrexham August 1898; Blackburn Rovers April 1903 (£150); Croydon Common May 1908; Coventry City May 1909; Birmingham June 1913; Nuneaton May 1914.*
*International honours with Blackburn Rovers: Wales: 1 cap.*

**Appearances:** Football League 104; FA Cup 9; Total 113.

Bob Evans came to Ewood Park from Wrexham in April 1903 and was installed as the first-choice goalkeeper for the start of the following season. The promotion of Evans ahead of Billy McIver caused a certain amount of controversy amongst the supporters at the time. However, the confident manner with which Evans dealt with all types of shots quickly endeared him to the Blackburn faithful. Evans was an agile custodian who dominated his area and rarely misjudged the flight of crosses. Evans had won four caps with Wrexham and was capped on one occasion whilst at Ewood Park. His career with Blackburn Rovers came to a close when a serious knee injury appeared to rob him of some of his mobility. He moved to Croydon Common in May 1908 but a year later he joined Coventry City. During four seasons with Coventry he appeared in 126 Southern League games and 13 FA Cup-ties for the club. He retired from soccer after suffering from shell shock during World War One and later became an administrator in junior football.

## EVER-PRESENTS

Since the formation of the Football League in 1888 an ever-present record has been maintained in League matches on 90 occasions. A total of 67 different players have managed this feat in either the Football League or the Premier League. The record for the most ever-present seasons is held jointly by Walter Crook and Derek Fazackerley who both went through a League campaign without missing a game on five occasions. The record for the most ever-present players in one season was set as early as 1889-90 when four players completed all 22 Football League fixtures. Although this record has never been broken it was equalled in 1954-55 when four players appeared in each of the 42 League games. The full list of ever-present players is shown below together with the number of matches they appeared in.

| Player | Season | Apps |
|---|---|---|
| W.C.A.Aitkenhead | 1909-10 | (38) |
| J.Ashcroft | 1908-09 | (38) |
| M.N.Atkins | 1988-89 | (46) |
| S.Barker | 1986-87 | (42) |
| J.B.Barton | 1966-67 | (42) |
| J.E.Bell | 1949-50 | (42) |
|  | 1954-55 | (42) |
| C.H.Binns | 1930-31 | (42) |
| J.P.S.Branagan | 1980-81 | (42) |
| T.Brandon | 1889-90 | (22) |
| T.H.Briggs | 1956-57 | (42) |
| J.Bruton | 1931-32 | (42) |
|  | 1932-33 | (42) |
|  | 1934-35 | (42) |
| L.Butt | 1937-38 | (42) |
| J.Cameron | 1904-05 | (34) |
| H.Campbell | 1889-90 | (22) |
| J.J.Campbell | 1952-53 | (42) |
| J.Carver | 1933-34 | (42) |
| H.Chippendale | 1894-95 | (30) |
| R.Clayton | 1954-55 | (42) |
|  | 1955-56 | (42) |
| A.Cowell | 1913-14 | (38) |
| R.Crompton | 1899-00 | (34) |
| W.Crook | 1935-36 | (42) |
|  | 1936-37 | (42) |
|  | 1937-38 | (42) |
|  | 1938-39 | (42) |
| B.Douglas | 1956-57 | (42) |
|  | 1964-65 | (42) |
| G.Dewar | 1890-91 | (22) |
|  | 1892-93 | (30) |
| J.Dewhurst | 1901-02 | (34) |
| W.Eckersley | 1948-49 | (42) |
| F.Else | 1963-64 | (42) |
| R.Elvey | 1952-53 | (42) |
|  | 1953-54 | (42) |
| D.W.Fazackerley | 1972-73 | (46) |
|  | 1973-74 | (46) |
|  | 1975-76 | (42) |
|  | 1979-80 | (46) |
| M.K.Ferguson | 1965-66 | (42) |
| J.Forbes | 1889-90 | (22) |
|  | 1890-91 | (22) |
| S.Garner | 1983-84 | (42) |
| W.Guest | 1937-38 | (42) |
| E.C.Harper | 1923-24 | (42) |
| R.Haworth | 1901-02 | (34) |
| E.C.J.Hendry | 1987-88 | (44) |
| K.Hird | 1977-78 | (42) |
| J.Hodkinson | 1914-15 | (38) |
| J.H.A.Hulme | 1924-25 | (42) |
| B.Hulse | 1898-99 | (34) |
| A.Hunter | 1970-71 | (42) |
| R.Jones | 1970-71 | (42) |
|  | 1972-73 | (46) |
|  | 1974-75 | (46) |
| W.Joyce | 1964-65 | (42) |
| G.M.Keeley | 1980-81 | (42) |
| W.M.Kelly | 1953-54 | (42) |
| R.Langton | 1954-55 | (42) |
| H.K.Leyland | 1957-58 | (42) |
| J.A.Lowey | 1983-84 | (42) |
| M.McGrath | 1957-58 | (42) |
| D.Martin | 1969-70 | (42) |
| I.Miller | 1981-82 | (42) |
| R.A.Mimms | 1992-93 | (42) |
| F.Mooney | 1954-55 | (42) |
| J.W.Murray | 1892-93 | (30) |
| A.Ogilvie | 1894-95 | (30) |
|  | 1895-96 | (30) |
| A.Parkes | 1974-75 | (46) |
|  | 1976-77 | (42) |
| J.G.Patterson | 1950-51 | (42) |
| M.J.Rathbone | 1982-83 | (42) |
|  | 1984-85 | (42) |
|  | 1985-86 | (42) |
| N.S.Reid | 1987-88 | (44) |
| A.Rigby | 1925-26 | (42) |
| S.Sellars | 1988-89 | (46) |
| John Southworth | 1889-90 | (22) |
| R.Suart | 1952-53 | (42) |
|  | 1953-54 | (42) |
| L.Thorpe | 1920-21 | (42) |
| J.R.Weddle | 1938-39 | (42) |
| W.Wilson | 1967-68 | (42) |
|  | 1969-70 | (42) |
| M.Woods | 1957-58 | (42) |
|  | 1960-61 | (42) |
| T.Wylie | 1923-24 | (42) |

## EVERTON FC

Founded in 1878 as St Domingo Church Sunday School Club, the club changed its name to Everton in 1879 and became one of the founder members of the Football League in 1888. Only Sheffield United, Aston Villa and Bolton Wanderers have faced Blackburn Rovers in more Football League games than Everton. It was against Everton at Ewood Park on 16 September 1922 that Johnny McIntyre scored four goals in five minutes to earn a 5-1 victory for the Rovers. The Goodison Park club have something of a record for 'poaching' some of the most promising forward talent at Ewood Park. In the 1888 close season Edgar Chadwick made the move to Merseyside and in 1893 Jack Southworth made a similar journey. During the late 1950s and early 1960s it was Everton who poached Roy Vernon and Fred Pickering from the playing staff at Ewood Park and Johnny Carey from the manager's chair.

**Football League**

| Season |  | Home |  | Away |  |
|---|---|---|---|---|---|
| 1888-89 | (FL) | W | 3-0 | L | 1-3 |
| 1889-90 | (FL) | L | 2-4 | L | 2-3 |
| 1890-91 | (FL) | W | 2-1 | L | 1-3 |
| 1891-92 | (FL) | D | 2-2 | L | 1-3 |
| 1892-93 | (Div 1) | D | 2-2 | L | 0-4 |
| 1893-94 | (Div 1) | W | 4-3 | D | 2-2 |
| 1894-95 | (Div 1) | W | 4-3 | L | 1-2 |
| 1895-96 | (Div 1) | L | 2-3 | W | 2-0 |
| 1896-97 | (Div 1) | W | 4-2 | W | 3-0 |
| 1897-98 | (Div 1) | D | 1-1 | D | 1-1 |
| 1898-99 | (Div 1) | L | 1-3 | L | 1-2 |
| 1899-00 | (Div 1) | W | 3-1 | D | 0-0 |
| 1900-01 | (Div 1) | W | 2-1 | D | 0-0 |
| 1901-02 | (Div 1) | W | 3-1 | W | 2-0 |
| 1902-03 | (Div 1) | W | 3-2 | W | 3-0 |
| 1903-04 | (Div 1) | L | 0-2 | L | 1-3 |
| 1904-05 | (Div 1) | W | 1-0 | L | 0-1 |
| 1905-06 | (Div 1) | L | 1-2 | L | 2-3 |
| 1906-07 | (Div 1) | W | 2-1 | L | 0-2 |
| 1907-08 | (Div 1) | W | 2-0 | L | 1-4 |
| 1908-09 | (Div 1) | D | 0-0 | D | 4-4 |
| 1909-10 | (Div 1) | W | 2-1 | W | 2-0 |
| 1910-11 | (Div 1) | L | 0-1 | L | 1-6 |

| 1911-12 | (Div 1) | W | 2-1 | W | 3-1 |
| 1912-13 | (Div 1) | L | 1-2 | L | 1-2 |
| 1913-14 | (Div 1) | W | 6-0 | D | 0-0 |
| 1914-15 | (Div 1) | W | 2-1 | W | 3-1 |
| 1919-20 | (Div 1) | W | 3-2 | L | 0-3 |
| 1920-21 | (Div 1) | D | 0-0 | L | 1-2 |
| 1921-22 | (Div 1) | D | 2-2 | L | 0-2 |
| 1922-23 | (Div 1) | W | 5-1 | L | 0-2 |
| 1923-24 | (Div 1) | W | 2-0 | D | 0-0 |
| 1924-25 | (Div 1) | W | 3-0 | L | 0-1 |
| 1925-26 | (Div 1) | D | 2-2 | L | 0-3 |
| 1926-27 | (Div 1) | D | 3-3 | L | 0-1 |
| 1927-28 | (Div 1) | W | 4-2 | L | 1-4 |
| 1928-29 | (Div 1) | W | 2-1 | L | 2-5 |
| 1929-30 | (Div 1) | W | 3-1 | D | 2-2 |
| 1931-32 | (Div 1) | W | 5-3 | L | 0-5 |
| 1932-33 | (Div 1) | W | 3-1 | L | 1-6 |
| 1933-34 | (Div 1) | D | 1-1 | L | 1-7 |
| 1934-35 | (Div 1) | W | 6-2 | L | 2-5 |
| 1935-36 | (Div 1) | D | 1-1 | L | 0-4 |
| 1946-47 | (Div 1) | W | 4-1 | L | 0-1 |
| 1947-48 | (Div 1) | L | 2-3 | L | 1-4 |
| 1951-52 | (Div 2) | W | 1-0 | W | 2-0 |
| 1952-53 | (Div 2) | W | 3-1 | W | 3-0 |
| 1953-54 | (Div 2) | D | 0-0 | D | 1-1 |
| 1958-59 | (Div 1) | W | 2-1 | D | 2-2 |
| 1959-60 | (Div 1) | W | 3-1 | L | 0-2 |
| 1960-61 | (Div 1) | L | 1-3 | D | 2-2 |
| 1961-62 | (Div 1) | D | 1-1 | L | 0-1 |
| 1962-63 | (Div 1) | W | 3-2 | D | 0-0 |
| 1963-64 | (Div 1) | L | 1-2 | W | 4-2 |
| 1964-65 | (Div 1) | L | 0-2 | W | 3-2 |
| 1965-66 | (Div 1) | L | 1-2 | D | 2-2 |

|  | P | W | D | L | F | A |
|---|---|---|---|---|---|---|
| Home | 56 | 32 | 12 | 12 | 124 | 81 |
| Away | 56 | 11 | 13 | 32 | 68 | 121 |
| Total | 112 | 43 | 25 | 44 | 192 | 202 |

## FA Premiership

|  | Home | | Away | |
|---|---|---|---|---|
| 1992-93 | L | 2-3 | L | 1-2 |
| 1993-94 | W | 2-0 | W | 3-0 |

|  | P | W | D | L | F | A |
|---|---|---|---|---|---|---|
| Home | 2 | 1 | 0 | 1 | 4 | 3 |
| Away | 2 | 1 | 0 | 1 | 4 | 2 |
| Total | 4 | 2 | 0 | 2 | 8 | 5 |

## FA Cup

| 1894-95 | (2) | Away | D | 1-1 |
|---|---|---|---|---|
|  | (R) | Home | L | 2-3 |
| 1896-97 | (3) | Away | L | 0-2 |
| 1897-98 | (1) | Away | L | 0-1 |
| 1929-30 | (4) | Home | W | 4-1 |
| 1956-57 | (3) | Away | L | 0-1 |
| 1957-58 | (4) | Away | W | 2-1 |
| 1970-71 | (3) | Away | L | 0-2 |
| 1973-74 | (3) | Away | L | 0-3 |
| 1985-86 | (4) | Away | L | 1-3 |

## Wartime

|  |  | Home | | Away | |
|---|---|---|---|---|---|
| 1916-17 | (LS-PT) | L | 1-5 | W | 5-2 |
| 1917-18 | (LS-PT) | L | 0-6 | L | 1-2 |
| 1918-19 | (LS-PT) | L | 1-4 | L | 0-9 |
| 1941-42 | (FLNS-SC) | D | 0-0 | D | 0-0 |
| 1943-44 | (FLNS-FC) | L | 1-3 | D | 0-0 |
| 1945-46 | (FLN) | W | 2-1 | L | 1-4 |

## EWOOD PARK

In 1882, four local tradesmen were responsible for the construction of a general sports ground in the Ewood area of Blackburn. The ground, which opened in April 1882, had cost £10,000 to build and during the 1880s it was the venue for a range of activities including football, athletics, and dog racing. It is believed that this is the ground that Blackburn Rovers played four matches on during April 1882. The matches against Sheffield Wednesday, Edinburgh Hibernians, Aston Villa and Dumbarton were played at a ground called 'Ewood Bridge' between 9-23 April 1882.

The new ground was certainly a lucky omen for the club as all four

The Nuttall Street Stand following redevelopment in 1907

The Nuttall Street Stand on fire in July 1984.

matches were won in convincing fashion. When the rent at their Leamington Ground reached an unacceptable level it was to the sports ground at Ewood that the committee of Blackburn Rovers turned. In 1890 the club took a ten-year lease on the Ewood Park ground at an annual rent of £60 for the first five years and £70 for the remainder. A total of £1,000 was spent on bringing the ground up to standard and on 13 September 1890, Blackburn Rovers staged their opening game at Ewood Park against Accrington. Although the opening fixture ended in a disappointing 0-0 draw, the club's new home was an immediate success. In April 1891, the Rovers were invited to stage an international fixture with Scotland at Ewood Park. The following year the club experimented with artificial light at Ewood during the benefit match for Jack Southworth. The potential of the new ground was clear for all to see and in 1893 the committee sanctioned the purchase of the ground for the princely sum of £2,500. Despite the obvious optimism there were still initial problems to overcome. Having experienced crowd problems in 1890, during a friendly with Darwen, the ground witnessed a further disturbance in January 1896 when part of a stand collapsed.

During the late 1890s the club failed to recapture the glories of its pre-League days and as a result there was little finance available for ground development. It was not until 1905, under the leadership of Lawrence Cotton, that the directors determined to improve facilities at Ewood Park. It was in that year that the Darwen End, with a capacity of 12,000, was covered at a cost of £1,680. However, the major project which the club undertook was the construction of the Nuttall Street grandstand in 1906. Designed by Archibald Leitch, a well-known architect of football stadiums, this stand was opened on New Year's Day 1907, when Preston North End visited Ewood Park.

The summer of 1907 brought further work on all parts of the ground. The Nuttall Street side of the ground now contained seated accommodation for 4,500 and standing capacity for 6,000 in the enclosure in front of the seated area. Underneath the seating the building contained directors' room, secretary's office, boardroom, 'gate' office, tea rooms, refreshment bars and splendid changing rooms. As well as work to the Nuttall Street side, the Darwen End had fifty rows of terracing put down during the summer of 1907. At the Blackburn and Darwen ends of the ground the old tumble-down hoarding, which had done duty since the ground was built, was replaced with brick walls surrounded by terra cotta work.

The ground, which now had a 40,000 capacity, was painted in a blue and white colour scheme. The winning of the First Division championship in 1912 and 1914 brought further ground development in

The famous cobbled street and tram-line at the back of old Blackburn End. Today the scene has been replaced by an impressive double-decker stand.

The old Blackburn End showing the famous 'Rovers' sign.

the shape of the Riverside Stand. By 1915 the ground capacity was reported to be 70,866. Little was spent on ground improvements in the aftermath of World War One as money had to be diverted to the rebuilding of the playing staff. It was during the 1920s that Ewood Park witnessed its largest crowds. In March 1925, some 60,011 watched the local derby with Blackpool in the fourth round of the FA Cup.

On 6 March 1929 a reported 62,522 were crammed into the ground for a sixth round FA Cup-tie with Bolton Wanderers. In the years between these two games the financial position had improved sufficiently to allow the club to replace the wooden perimeter railing with a concrete wall and to re-roof the Riverside Stand. Improvements continued to be made to the terracing on all sides of the ground and in 1958 the club followed the growing trend of erecting floodlights. Two years later the successful FA Cup run enabled the club to cover the Blackburn End and thus complete the covering of all four sides of the ground. The net major development occurred in 1976 when the club spent £20,000 on upgrading the floodlighting system.

This proved to be the start of a major programme of ground improvements which were necessitated by the 1975 Safety of Sports Grounds Act. The summer of 1984 brought a potentially damaging fire in the Nuttall Street Stand but, fortunately, damage was confined to the Blackburn End wing of the structure. At this point the directors took the bold decision to redevelop this section of the stand into executive boxes and a restaurant. Named the John Lewis Complex in honour of one of the club's founder members, the development cost in the region of a quarter of a million pounds but generated much needed finance over the next decade. The club suffered a further setback in the late 1980s when the roof of the stand on the Riverside side of the ground was deemed to be unstable in high winds.

Further investigations revealed that the whole structure was unsound due to crumbling foundations. The club had no alternative but to close one side of the ground and make preparations to demolish the existing stand. Thanks to the generosity of local firm Walkersteel, materials were supplied to provide a new stand with 700 seats. The Walkersteel stand, as

it was now called, was further developed to take in the whole of the Riverside part of the ground and thus provide seating for 5,017 spectators. It was in this area that the club also operated a family enclosure. Whilst facilities for the supporters were being developed the club also turned its attentions to the state of the playing surface.

This had been steadily deteriorating over the years and in the summer of 1989 the pitch was dug up and a revolutionary new surface, with under-soil heating, was laid. The new 'Techturf' surface was developed and marketed by ICI, the club sponsor at the time and based on technology which had been patented by the Blackburn firm of Netlon. The new surface was based on natural grass growing through Netlon meshing and was said to be capable of withstanding two of three times the wear of ordinary pitches.

The arrival of Jack Walker to the seat of power at Ewood Park was the signal for major redevelopment work to begin. Plans were announced to turn the whole ground into a 30,000 all-seater stadium and mid-way through the 1992-93 season the Darwen End was closed and demolished to allow rebuilding work to begin. At the close of the season the Blackburn End was demolished and another two-tier stand was constructed. The lower tier of the Darwen End opened at the start of the 1993-94 season with the upper tier opening in November. In December the lower tier of the Blackburn End was opened and a month later the FA Cup-tie with Portsmouth saw the historic Nuttall Street Stand used for the last time before its demolition.

Keen to retain links with their glorious past the club arranged for the famous boardroom in the Nuttall Street stand to be carefully dismantled and rebuilt in the new Blackburn End stand during the summer of 1994. Although the old boardroom, which fittingly was to be situated next to a club museum, would still be used for board meetings it was no longer be used to entertain guests on match day. A new suite for directors and guests was to be constructed in the new Nuttall Street stand. In January 1994, the directors announced that the new stand on the Nuttall Street side of the ground would be named the Jack Walker Stand in honour of the man who was responsible for the transformation of Blackburn Rovers. As Blackburn Rovers approached the middle of the last decade

The Blackburn End Stand under construction.

Ewood Park before the Walker 'revolution'.

The Nuttall Street Stand during demolition in January 1994.

of the 20th century, they could once again claim to have one of the finest stadiums in the country.

## EXETER CITY FC

Founded in 1904, Exeter City were members of the Southern League before joining the Football League Division Three in 1920. Exeter caused something of a shock in the 1927-28 FA Cup competition. They held the Rovers to a 2-2 draw in a fourth-round tie at St James' Park and were only overcome after extra-time in the Ewood Park replay. They had more success in 1978-79 when they knocked the Rovers out of the Football League Cup, despite being in a lower division. In 1979-80 they were the only team to take a point from the Rovers during a run which resulted in 14 wins from 15 games. Ironically, it was Exeter City who brought the run to an end with a 2-0 victory over Blackburn at St James' Park.

### Football League

|  |  | Home |  | Away |  |
| --- | --- | --- | --- | --- | --- |
| 1979-80 | (Div 3) | D | 1-1 | L | 0-2 |

|  | P | W | D | L | F | A |
| --- | --- | --- | --- | --- | --- | --- |
| Home | 1 | 0 | 1 | 0 | 1 | 1 |
| Away | 1 | 0 | 0 | 1 | 0 | 2 |
| Total | 2 | 0 | 1 | 1 | 1 | 3 |

### FA Cup

| 1927-28 | (4) | Away | D | 2-2 |
| --- | --- | --- | --- | --- |
|  | (R) | Home | W | 3-1 aet |

### Football League Cup

| 1978-79 | (2) | Away | L | 1-2 |
| --- | --- | --- | --- | --- |

## FAIRBROTHER, Ronald Wilson

Centre-half. 1922-1929.
*6ft 1½in; 11st.*
*Born: Poulton-le-Fylde, 28 April 1902; Died: Alderley Edge, 18 April 1969.*
*Debut: v Liverpool (a) 15 March 1924.*
*Career: Manchester University; Manchester City amateur; Manchester United amateur; Northern Nomads; Blackburn Rovers amateur April 1922 until cs 1929.*
**Appearances:** Football League 1.

Fairbrother, a doctor in obstetrics, joined the club as an amateur in 1922 and remained on the books until the summer of 1929. During this period Fairbrother played most of his football with Northern Nomads and made only fleeting appearances for the Central League team at Ewood Park. He won an Amateur Cup winners' medal in 1926 and was also capped for the England Amateur international team whilst with Nomads. On 15 March 1924, Fairbrother was called into the senior team at Blackburn for the trip to Anfield. His height proved a valuable asset in defence and although his passing lacked a little in accuracy, most commentators agreed that he had made an excellent debut. After the Liverpool match Fairbrother returned to the amateur game and was not called upon to appear in the Blackburn senior team again.

## FAMILIES

The history of Blackburn Rovers has seen several instances of family involvement both on and off the field. In the formative years of the club the Greenwood family played an important part in the affairs of Blackburn Rovers. Thomas Greenwood was the club's first goalkeeper and also held the position of captain whilst his brother Harry was a useful full-back who could also play in the forward line. Another Greenwood brother who became a leading light with the Rovers was Doctor Haydock Greenwood who, like Harry, was a full-back but one who was good enough to win England honours. Thomas Greenwood also lined up in a side which contained Arthur Thomas, his brother-in-law.

Two brothers who both figured with England during the 1880s were Fred and John Hargreaves. When Fred Hargreaves was capped by England in 1880 he became the first Blackburn Rovers player to receive full international honours. The brothers also appeared together for the club in the 1882 FA Cup Final when the Rovers lost to the Old Etonians by a single goal. On 15 September 1888, Jack and James Southworth became the first brothers to appear in the Football League for the Rovers. The inaugural match in the Football League saw James at left-back whilst Jack appeared at centre-forward and scored the club's first League goal in the 5-5 draw with Accrington.

The most recent case of brothers holding down a first-team place at Ewood Park was that of Ronnie and Ken Clayton in the mid-1950s. Although they came to Ewood together as youngsters in 1949, it was not until 1955-56 that they became the regular half-back pairing. The partnership ended in April 1957 when Ken broke his leg. In the boardroom there has only been one case of two brothers who have held

the position of chairman. Between 1905-1919, Lawrence Cotton held the position at the club and when the pressure of civic duties forced him to step down and accept the position of president, his brother Clement was elected chairman. The death of Lawrence Cotton in 1921 saw Clement give up the chairmanship to follow in his brother's footsteps and become president of the club. The most famous father and son relationship at the club involved Bob and Wilfred Crompton. Wilfred was the youngest son of the legendary England international and at time of his debut in September 1929, his father was acting as the honorary team manager. Another famous father who saw his son follow in his footsteps at Ewood Park was Jim Forrest. Jimmy Forrest had won five FA Cup winners' medals with the club and 11 England caps during his 12 years as a player with the club. In 1906 he had become a director of Blackburn Rovers and saw his son, also called James, make his debut for the club in February 1922.

## FARRELL, Gerard W.

Left-back. 1971-1973.
*5ft 7in; 10st 6lb.*
*Born: Liverpool, 19 March 1952.*
*Debut: v Rochdale (h) 9 October 1971.*
*Career: Wolverhampton Wanderers apprentice July 1968, turning professional in May 1970; Blackburn Rovers on loan from October 1971 until signing permanently in January 1972 until February 1973; Johannesburg Rovers (South Africa); Morecambe.*
**Appearances:** Football League 21+1; FA Cup 2; Total 23+1.
**Goals:** Football League 1.

Gerry Farrell came to Blackburn during the autumn of 1971 as part of Ken Furphy's dramatic rebuilding programme. Initially brought to the club on loan, Farrell did enough to win a full contract and was given the number-three shirt in the first team. Whilst Farrell brought enthusiasm to the position, he lacked consistency and eventually lost his place to Mick Wood. However, when Wood was injured, towards the end of the 1971-72 season, Farrell was restored for the last four matches. Although three of those four games were won, Furphy was clearly not happy with Farrell at left-back. An end of season tour of Czechoslovakia saw Furphy successfully experiment with Benny Arentoft at left-back. After that Farrell was only called upon when Arentoft was injured or deputising in the centre of defence. The former Wolves full-back was released in February 1973 and tried his luck in South Africa.

## FATALITIES

The only fatality to be suffered by the club as a result of an incident on the field occurred with the death of Robert Marshall on 3 January 1928. Bob Marshall, a part-timer who had been signed from Altrincham at the start of the 1926-27 season, was the regular left-back with the Central League side but had yet to make his debut in the Football League. On Boxing Day 1927, Marshall collided with an opponent in the Central League fixture with Blackpool at Bloomfield Road. Although he left the field it was not thought that the injury was a serious one and after the game he left with his fiancée for a nearby house in which they were staying. However, that evening he was taken ill with chronic abdominal pains and as a result was operated on in Blackpool Victoria Hospital. After a slight improvement his condition worsened and on 3 January 1928 he died.

## FAULKNER, Robert

Outside-right. 1919-1920.
*5ft 9in; 11st.*
*Born: Glasgow.*
*Debut: v Chelsea (a) 28 February 1920.*
*Career: Maryhill, Glasgow; Blackburn Rovers August 1919; Queen's Park Rangers cs 1920; South Shields June 1922; Toronto Irish July 1924.*
**Appearances:** Football League 9.

Although Faulkner came to Blackburn with a good reputation, he failed to establish himself in the problem outside-right position. Faulkner was one of ten players who were tried on the right wing during the 1919-20 campaign. In many respects he was as successful as any with the Rovers taking ten out of a possible 18 points during his run of nine senior outings. Faulkner moved to London in the summer of 1920 and appeared in 50 League games with Queen's Park Rangers before joining South Shields during the 1922 close season.

## FAWCETT, William F.

Outside-right. 1919-1920.
*5ft 8in; 11st.*
*Debut: v Manchester City (h) 15 November 1919.*
*Career: Blackburn Rovers amateur November 1919.*
**Appearances:** Football League 5.
**Goals:** Football League 1.

Although the Rovers crashed 4-1 to Manchester City on his debut,

William Fawcett had the consolation of scoring Blackburn's only goal after only four minutes. One commentator remarked: "He possesses skill and speed, and was generally smarter than his opponents." However, despite this promising beginning, Fawcett failed to establish himself at Ewood Park, being one of nine players to fill the outside-right position in 1919-20.

## FAZACKERLEY, Derek William

Central defender. 1969-1987.
*5ft 11in; 12st 3lb.*
*Born: Preston, 5 November 1951.*
*Debut: v Hull City (a) 23 February 1971.*
*Career: Blackburn Rovers apprentice July 1969, turning professional in January 1970; Chester City player-assistant manager January 1987; York City July 1988; Bury December 1988; Darwen; Kumu (Finland) player-coach May 1990; Newcastle United 1990 as reserve-team coach, becoming first-team coach in 1992.*
*Domestic honours with Blackburn Rovers: Third Division championship: 1974-75 (22+1 apps, 4 gls).*
**Appearances:** Football League 593+3; FA Cup 40; Football League Cup 38; Total 671+3.
**Goals:** Football League 24; FA Cup 1; Football League Cup 1; Total 26.

Although Derek Fazackerley was an unfamiliar name outside of Blackburn, to the Ewood faithful he became known as 'Mr Consistency'. He was never honoured at international level or the subject of major transfer speculation, yet Fazackerley went on to write a new page in the history of Blackburn Rovers when he broke the club's appearance record, previously held by Ronnie Clayton. Like Clayton before him, Fazackerley was the perfect club professional. That he should have gone on to rewrite the appearance record is all the more remarkable when it is remembered that he broke into the team during the bleakest period in the club's history.

Fazackerley made his debut as the club hurtled towards the Third Division and it was in the sparse surroundings of Third Division football that he mastered his trade. As a youngster he was fortunate in being tutored in the arts of defensive play by the likes of John McNamee and Graham Hawkins. Indeed, throughout his career he was at his best when playing alongside a traditional centre-half, almost as a sweeper. In Glenn Keeley, Fazackerley found the perfect partner and the pair would not have been disgraced on the First Division stage. 'Faz', as he was popularly known at Blackburn, was a tough-tackling defender who was a commanding figure in the air.

However, his major strengths as a defender were his pace and timing. Such was his judgement that tackles were rarely mistimed, even when under severe pressure, and on those occasions when he was caught out, his pace enabled him to recover lost ground with apparent ease. In 1979, Blackburn almost lost his services to Oldham Athletic but fortunately Fazackerley declined a move to Boundary Park after a fee of £60,000 had been agreed. Shortly afterwards Howard Kendall arrived at Ewood Park and the Keeley-Fazackerley partnership was given the encouragement it required. In January 1987, seemingly at the end of his playing career, Fazackerley was allowed to join Chester City as player-assistant manager.

He made 66 League appearances for Chester before rejoining his old Blackburn boss, Bobby Saxton, at York City in the summer of 1988. The move was not a success and following Saxton's departure, Fazackerley elected to join is old friend, Martin Dobson, at Bury. He retired from

League football in the summer of 1989 having made 692 League appearances (including ten as sub). After a short spell playing for Darwen he accepted a coaching appointment with Kumu in Finland in May 1990. During 1990-91 he was appointed reserve-team coach at Newcastle United and was promoted to first-team coach in 1992. Under the managership of Kevin Keegan he played an important part in helping to lift the first Division title in 1993 and take United into the Premiership.

Career Record with Blackburn Rovers:

| | League | | FA Cup | | FL Cup | | Total | |
|---|---|---|---|---|---|---|---|---|
| | App | Gls | App | Gls | App | Gls | App | Gls |
| 1970-71 | 14 | 0 | 0 | 0 | 0 | 0 | 14 | 0 |
| 1971-72 | 39 | 0 | 2 | 1 | 2 | 0 | 43 | 1 |
| 1972-73 | 46 | 2 | 3 | 0 | 1 | 0 | 50 | 2 |
| 1973-74 | 46 | 2 | 5 | 0 | 3 | 0 | 54 | 2 |
| 1974-75 | 22 +1 | 4 | 1 | 0 | 2 | 0 | 25 +1 | 4 |
| 1975-76 | 42 | 1 | 1 | 0 | 2 | 0 | 45 | 1 |
| 1976-77 | 37 +1 | 0 | 4 | 0 | 3 | 0 | 44 +1 | 0 |
| 1977-78 | 28 | 0 | 2 | 0 | 2 | 0 | 32 | 0 |
| 1978-79 | 37 | 3 | 2 | 0 | 1 | 0 | 40 | 3 |
| 1979-80 | 46 | 1 | 7 | 0 | 4 | 0 | 57 | 1 |
| 1980-81 | 38 | 0 | 1 | 0 | 5 | 0 | 44 | 0 |
| 1981-82 | 39 | 1 | 1 | 0 | 3 | 0 | 43 | 1 |
| 1982-83 | 38 | 0 | 1 | 0 | 2 | 1 | 41 | 1 |
| 1983-84 | 39 | 4 | 3 | 0 | 2 | 0 | 44 | 4 |
| 1984-85 | 39 | 4 | 4 | 0 | 2 | 0 | 45 | 4 |
| 1985-86 | 36 +1 | 1 | 3 | 0 | 2 | 0 | 41 +1 | 1 |
| 1986-87 | 7 | 1 | 0 | 0 | 2 | 0 | 9 | 1 |
| | 593 +3 | 24 | 40 | 1 | 38 | 1 | 671 +3 | 26 |

## FEAR, Keith W.

Forward. 1977-1978.
*5ft 7in; 10st 8lb.*
*Born: Bristol, 8 August 1952.*
*Debut: v Burnley (a) 26 December 1977.*
*Career: Bristol City associated schoolboy May 1966, turning professional in June 1969; St Louis Stars (USA) April 1976 to August 1976; Hereford United on loan September 1977 until October 1977; Blackburn Rovers on loan December 1977 until January 1978; Plymouth Argyle February 1978; Brentford November 1979; Chester City January 1980.*
**Appearances:** Football League 5; FA Cup 1; Total 6.
**Goals:** Football League 2.

Keith Fear was a talented inside-forward who enjoyed a brief loan spell at Ewood Park as a replacement for the injured Jack Lewis. He became an instant hero to the Ewood faithful when he scored the second goal in a memorable 3-2 victory over Burnley at Turf Moor on Boxing Day 1977. The most successful period of his playing career was with Bristol City where he scored 32 goals in 151 League appearances (including 25 as sub).

## FECITT, Herbert Lincoln

Inside-left. 1882-1891.
*Born: Blackburn 1865 (January quarter).*
*Debut: v Blackpool South Shore (a) 1 December 1883 (FAC).*

*Career: King's Own; Blackburn Rovers 1882; Accrington 1887; Blackburn Rovers cs 1888; Northwich Victoria October 1892.*
*Domestic honours with Blackburn Rovers: FA Cup winners: 1885; 1886.*
**Appearances:** Football League 21; FA Cup 23; Total 44.
**Goals:** Football League 13; FA Cup 13; Total 26.

The career of Herbert Fecitt spanned the years when Blackburn Rovers dominated the FA Cup competition. Fecitt himself was a member of two of the successful Cup winning sides and earned a reputation as a dashing inside-forward. He was not only a player who could create chances for others, but one who was also a notable marksman in his own right. Fecitt's career with Blackburn Rovers appeared to be over when he was allowed to move to Accrington in 1887. However, following the departure of Edgar Chadwick to

Everton, the Blackburn committee turned to Fecitt to fill one of the inside-forward positions as the club began the inaugural season of the Football League. In 1899-1900 he was in charge of the second team at Ewood Park.

### FENTON, William Hartas
Outside-left. 1948-1951.
*5ft 7½in; 10st 11lb.*
*Born: West Hartlepool, 23 June 1926; Died: York, 14 April 1973.*
*Debut: v Grimsby Town (h) 15 January 1949.*
*Career: Barnsley November 1944; Horden Colliery Welfare; Blackburn Rovers December 1948; York City May 1951; Scarborough cs 1957.*
**Appearances:** Football League 33; FA Cup 1; Total 34.
**Goals:** Football League 7.
Apart from a run of 17 games between December 1950 and April 1951, Fenton failed to establish himself at Ewood Park during his two and a half year stay. A fast and direct left-winger, with an eye for goal, Fenton enjoyed great success following his transfer to York City in May 1951. In his first season at York he scored 31 goals in 45 League games to establish a new goalscoring record and went on to become the third highest scorer in York's history.

### FERGUSON, James
Right-half. 1907-1911.
*5ft 9in; 12st.*
*Born: Glasgow, 1885.*
*Debut: v Bury (h) 2 September 1907.*
*Career: Strathclyde; Airdrieonians; Blackburn Rovers May 1907; St Johnstone October 1912.*
**Appearances:** Football League 32.
**Goals:** Football League 1.
Ferguson spent much of his time at Ewood Park understudying Albert Walmsley for the right-half position. He enjoyed his greatest success with the club in 1908-09 when he appeared at right-half in 17 League games. However, the following season saw him restricted to only four appearances – two at centre-half and two at left-half. Unable to win a regular first-team place he returned to play in Scotland.

### FERGUSON, Michael Kevin
Outside-right/Midfield. 1962-1968.
*5ft 10in; 11st 4lb.*
*Born: Burnley, 9 March 1943.*
*Debut: v Ipswich Town (a) 18 August 1962.*
*Career: Burnley Schools; Plymouth Argyle amateur March 1959; Accrington Stanley July 1960; Blackburn Rovers March 1962 (£2,500); Aston Villa May 1968 (£50,000); Queen's Park Rangers November 1969 (£15,000); Cambridge United July 1973; Rochdale July 1974; Los Angeles (on loan) summer 1975; IA Akranes (Iceland) April 1976; Rossendale coach; Halifax Town December 1976; Rochdale (manager) October 1977 to December 1978.*
*Then managed a side in Sweden and later Apoel Nicosia before working in the Arab Emirates with Don Revie c.1985. Became a scout with Tottenham Hotspur in November 1989.*

**Appearances:** Football League 220; FA Cup 15; Football League Cup 14; Total 249.
**Goals:** Football League 29; FA Cup 1; Football League Cup 6; Total 36.
A mercurial talent who entertained, enraged and enthralled the fans during his time at Ewood Park. 'Fergie', as he was popularly known, became a cult figure with supporters following his move to Blackburn in March 1962. Following the demise of Accrington Stanley from the Football League in March 1962, Ferguson became a target of both Blackburn Rovers and Preston North End. On Wednesday 14 March, the two managers travelled to Accrington determined to sign Ferguson. Fortunately, Jack Marshall learned of the player's whereabouts before Jimmy Milne, his counterpart at Preston, and was able to sign Ferguson for a modest fee. At Accrington Ferguson had impressed as an immensely talented inside-forward. However, under the guidance of Marshall he blossomed into a tricky outside-right. At Ewood Park he became a member of one of the most exciting team's that the club had produced.

Ferguson revelled in the style of football which Marshall encouraged and turned in a number of dazzling performances. A natural crowd pleaser, Ferguson would beat an opponent, wait for him to recover, and then beat him again. Sadly, Ferguson proved to be a flawed diamond. The flaw, which frustrated both fans and management alike, was a suspect temperament. It was seen at its worst in a vital promotion match with Coventry City at Ewood Park on Easter Saturday 1967. A tense battle was still goalless when Ferguson received his marching orders for lashing out at an opponent following a stiff challenge. Coventry went on to win the game and earn promotion to the First Division. Capable of playing full-back, midfield or orthodox winger, Ferguson remained with the club for one more season before moving to Aston Villa in May 1968.

### FIELD, Anthony
Forward. 1971-1974.
*5ft 7in; 11st.*
*Born: Halifax, 6 June 1946.*
*Debut: v Mansfield Town (h) 23 October 1971.*
*Career: Illingworth United; Halifax Town July 1963; Barrow August 1966; Southport March 1968; Blackburn Rovers October 1971; Sheffield United March 1974; New York Cosmos (USA) April 1976; Memphis Rogues (USA) 1978 to 1980.*
**Appearances:** Football League 104+2; FA Cup 10; Football League Cup 4; Total 118+2.
**Goals:** Football League 45; FA Cup 7; Football League Cup 2; Total 54.
Tony Field began his career in football's bargain basement at Halifax Town and ended up with the millionaires of New York, where he rubbed shoulders with Pelé and Franz Beckenbauer. During his trek from Halifax to New York he stopped off in Blackburn to briefly lift the gloom that had

descended on the club following relegation to the Third Division. Field was beginning to make a name for himself at Southport when Ken Furphy parted with £17,500 and Freddie Goodwin to bring him to Ewood Park.

He quickly established himself as a firm favourite with the fans and became the club's most consistent goalscorer since the days of Andy McEvoy. When Field arrived at Ewood the club were rapidly sliding towards the Fourth Division. However his 17 goals in 33 League appearances lifted Rovers to mid-table respectability. A yard quicker than most Third Division defenders, Field delighted the fans with his dazzling runs and deadly finishing. Yet Field was not just a goalscorer, he was a player who was capable of creating chances for others. When Furphy left for Sheffield United he quickly returned to Ewood to pay £75,000 to take Field across the Pennines.

He found goalscoring a little tougher in the First Division and was reunited with Furphy once more when he joined New York Cosmos in 1976. Field spent two successful seasons with the Cosmos in the company of Pelé, Beckenbauer and Carlos Alberto before joining Memphis Rogues in 1978. He enjoyed three more seasons in the NASL before the Memphis club folded as the football boom began to wane.

### FINNIGAN, Anthony
Midfield. 1988-1990.
*6ft; 12st.*
*Born: Wimbledon, 17 October 1962.*
*Debut: v Chelsea (a) 27 August 1988.*
*Career: Fulham November 1980; Corinthian Casuals; Crystal Palace February 1985; Blackburn Rovers July 1988; Hull City August 1990; Swindon Town March 1991; Brentford non-contract player January 1992 to March 1992; Earnest Borel (Hong Kong); Barnet September 1993; Hendon; Dulwich Hamlet.*
**Appearances:** Football League 21+15; FA Cup 5; Football League Cup 3; Full Members' Cup 3+1; Total 32+16.
**Goals:** FA Cup 1; Full Members' Cup 1; Total 2.
Tony Finnigan endured a rather turbulent two seasons at Ewood Park after signing for Don Mackay in July 1988. He had appeared in 105 League games (including 11 as sub) with Crystal Palace after having failed to make the grade with Fulham. Finnigan featured in midfield for the Rovers but his rather 'laid-back' style did little to endear him to the Blackburn public. Although capable of scoring spectacular goals,

Finnigan had a tendency to pass the ball sideways and backwards and as a result became a target for the displeasure of the supporters. After leaving Blackburn in August 1990, his career continued to slide and in 1992 he ended up playing in Hong Kong. He tried to revive his League career with Barnet at the start of the 1993-94 season.

## FIRST MATCH

The first match to be played by Blackburn Rovers took place at Church on 11 December 1875. A brief report of the game was carried in the columns of *The Blackburn Times* on 18 December 1875. The result was

A newspaper report of Blackburn Rovers' first-ever match, against Church in December 1875.

a 1-1 draw and although the team was not named it is generally thought to have consisted of the following players: Thomas Greenwood; Jack Baldwin, Fred Birtwistle, Arthur Thomas, J.T.Syckelmore, Walter Duckworth, John Lewis, Tom Dean, Arthur Constantine, Harry Greenwood and Richard Birtwistle.

## FLOODLIGHTS

Blackburn Rovers experimented with artificial lighting as early as 1878. On Monday, 4 November 1878 the Rovers played hosts to Accrington at Alexandra Meadows for a match which was to be played under electric light. The ground was illuminated by the Gramme light, one light being fixed at the east end and one at the west. Each lamp was on a scaffold some 30 or 40 feet high and was supposed to have 6,000 candle power. The man responsible for this feat was William Edward Staite who had invented the machine and lamps which could provide illumination for large areas.

The lights were turned on at 7pm and burned steadily until 9.20pm. As one would expect the match created much interest within the town and an attendance numbered close to 6,000 paid to enter Alexandra Meadows. However, in addition to those in the ground a large number of people chose to watch the match from the hillside in the neighbouring park. The leather ball was painted white so that the players could see it more clearly. The result was a convincing 3-0 win for the Rovers. A second experiment with artificial light took place at Ewood Park when the Rovers beat Darwen 3-0 under Wells' Light in a benefit match for Jack Southworth.

In the 1950s a growing number of clubs were erecting floodlights and on 5 November 1954 the Rovers attracted a record attendance of 17,634 to Peel Park, Accrington when they went to play a floodlit friendly. In 1958 the Rovers finally erected floodlights at Ewood Park and on 10 November they entertained Werder Bremen at Ewood Park. A crowd of 20,806 watched Peter Dobing (2) and Ally MacLeod score the goals which gave the Rovers a 3-1 win over the German club. In 1976 the Rovers upgraded the floodlighting system at Ewood Park at a cost of £20,000. A prestige friendly was arranged with Aberdeen who were under the managership of Ally MacLeod, one of the goalscorers in the Werder Bremen match. Unfortunately, a dismal night and a crowd of less than 4,000 meant that the club recouped little of the initial outlay.

## FLOWERS, Timothy David

Goalkeeper. 1993-
*6ft 2in; 14st.*
*Born: Kenilworth, 3 February 1967.*
*Debut: v Queen's Park Rangers (a) 6 November 1993.*
*Career: Wolverhampton Wanderers associated schoolboy March 1981; then apprentice August 1983, turning professional in August 1984;*

*Southampton on loan in April 1986; Southampton June 1986 (£70,000); Swindon Town on loan March 1987; Swindon Town on loan November 1987; Blackburn Rovers November 1993 (£2,400,000).*
*International honours with Blackburn Rovers: England: 1 cap (1994).*
**Appearances:** Premier League 29; FA Cup 4; Total 33.

The signing of Tim Flowers for a world-record fee for a goalkeeper was a further indication of the determination of Jack Walker to develop Blackburn Rovers into a major footballing power. Acknowledged as one of the outstanding goalkeepers in the country, Flowers had won his first England cap against Brazil in the summer of 1993. He had been linked with the Rovers for several months but Southampton were naturally reluctant to lose his services. Once the decision was taken to allow Flowers to leave a deal with Liverpool was agreed for the player.

However, Flowers was adamant that he wanted to play for Blackburn Rovers and when he refused to speak to Liverpool, Kenny Dalglish stepped in to bring him to Ewood Park. Flowers quickly settled down at the club and developed a good rapport with the supporters. An excellent shot stopper, Flowers handles crosses with confidence and sweeps up well behind his defence. Ironically his first clean sheet for Blackburn came in his second appearance, his home debut for the club, when Southampton visited Ewood Park.

## FOOTBALL ASSOCIATION CHALLENGE CUP

The Football Association Challenge Cup came about as a result of a meeting held in the offices of the Sportsman, London 20 July, 1871. It was here that C.W.Alcock, the Honorary Secretary of the Football Association and of the Wanderers FC, proposed that a Challenge Cup should be established and that all clubs belonging to the Association should be invited to participate. The first Final in 1872 saw the Wanderers defeat Royal Engineers 1-0 in front of 2,000 spectators. Blackburn Rovers entered the competition for the first time in 1879 and in 1882 appeared in their first final. It was during the 1880s that the club dominated the competition and in 1886, after their third successive victory in a final, the Football Association presented the club with a silver shield in honour of their achievement. Results of all FA Cup matches are listed in the following pages:

| | | | | | |
|---|---|---|---|---|---|
| 1879-80 | (1) | Tyne Association | Home | W | 5-1 |
| | (2) | Darwen | Home | W | 3-1 |
| | (3) | Nottingham Forest | Away | L | 0-6 |
| 1880-81 | (1) | Sheffield Providence | Home | W | 6-2 |
| | (2) | Sheffield Wednesday | Away | L | 0-4 |
| 1881-82 | (1) | Blackburn Park Road | Home | W | 9-1 |
| | (2) | Bolton Wanderers | Home | W | 6-2 |
| | (3) | Bye | | | |
| | (4) | Darwen | Home | W | 5-1 |
| | (5) | Wednesbury Old Athletic | Home | W | 3-1 |
| | (SF) | Sheffield Wednesday | St Johns, Huddersfield | D | 0-0 |
| | (R) | Sheffield Wednesday | Whalley Range Manchester | W | 5-1 |
| | (F) | Old Etonians | Kennington Oval | L | 0-1 |
| 1882-83 | (1) | Blackpool St Johns | Home | W | 11-1 |
| | (2) | Darwen | Away | L | 0-1 |
| 1883-84 | (1) | Southport | Home | W | 7-0 |
| | (2) | South Shore | Away | W | 7-0 |
| | (3) | Padiham | Home | W | 3-0 |
| | (4) | Staveley | Home | W | 5-1 |
| | (5) | Upton Park | Away | W | 3-0 |
| | (SF) | Notts County | Lower Grounds, Aston, Birmingham | W | 1-0 |
| | (F) | Queen's Park | Kennington Oval | W | 2-1 |
| 1884-85 | (1) | Rossendale | Home | W | 11-0 |
| | (2) | Blackburn Olympic | Home | W | 3-2 |
| | (3) | Witton | Home | W | 5-1 |
| | (4) | Romford | Home | W | 8-0 |
| | (5) | Bye | | | |
| | (6) | West Bromwich Albion | Away | W | 2-0 |
| | (SF) | Old Carthusians | Trent Bridge, Nottingham | W | 5-1 |
| | (F) | Queen's Park | Kennington Oval | W | 2-0 |
| 1885-86 | (1) | Clitheroe | Away | W | 2-0 |
| | (2) | Oswaldtwistle Rovers | Home | W | 1-0 |
| | (3) | Darwen Old Wanderers | Home | W | 6-1 |
| | (4) | Staveley | Home | W | 7-1 |
| | (5) | Bye | | | |
| | (6) | Brentwood | Away | W | 3-1 |
| | (SF) | Swifts | Derby Cricket Ground | W | 2-1 |
| | (F) | West Bromwich Albion | Kennington Oval | D | 0-0 |
| | (R) | West Bromwich Albion | Racecourse Ground Derby | W | 2-0 |
| 1886-87 | (1) | Halliwell – walkover | | | |
| | (2) | Renton | Away | D | 2-2 aet |
| | (R) | Renton | Home | L | 0-2 |
| 1887-88 | (1) | Bury – walkover | | | |
| | (2) | Blackburn Olympic | Home | W | 5-1 |
| | (3) | Accrington | Away | W | 3-1 |
| | (4) | Bye | | | |
| | (5) | Darwen | Away | W | 3-0 |
| | (6) | Derby Junction | Away | L | 1-2 |
| 1888-89 | (1) | Accrington | Away | D | 1-1 |
| | (R) | Accrington | Home | W | 5-0 |
| | (2) | Swifts – walkover | | | |
| | (3) | Aston Villa | Home | W | 8-1 |
| | (SF) | Wolves | Alexandra Ground, Crewe | D | 1-1 |
| | (R) | Wolves | Alexandra Ground, Crewe | L | 1-3 |
| 1889-90 | (1) | Sunderland | Home | W | 4-2 aet |
| | (2) | Grimsby Town | Home | W | 3-0 |
| | (3) | Bootle | Away | W | 7-0 |
| | (SF) | Wolves | Racecourse Ground, Derby | W | 1-0 |
| | (F) | Sheffield Wednesday | Kennington Oval | W | 6-1 |
| 1890-91 | (1) | Middlesbrough Ironopolis* | Away | W | 3-0 |
| | (2) | Chester | Home | W | 7-0 |
| | (3) | Wolves | Home | W | 2-0 |
| | (SF) | West Bromwich Albion | Victoria Ground, Stoke | W | 3-2 |
| | (F) | Notts County | Kennington Oval | W | 3-1 |

* Blackburn Rovers first played Middlesbrough Ironopolis at Middlesbrough on the 17 January 1891 and won 2-1 after extra-time. However, a replay was ordered after a protest by the home club.

Rovers in about 1879, when they made their FA Cup debut. Back row (left to right): T.Greenwood, D.Greenwood; Second row: F.Birtwistle, J.Baldwin, J.Haworth, A.Thomas. Front row: H.Ibbotson (umpire), Johnny Duckworth (squatting), T.Dean, Dick Birtwistle, John Lewis, F.Hargreaves, W.Duckworth

| 1891-92 | (1) | Derby County | Home | W | 4-1 |
|---|---|---|---|---|---|
| | (2) | West Bromwich Albion | Away | L | 1-3 |
| 1892-93 | (1) | Newton Heath | Home | W | 4-0 |
| | (2) | Northwich Victoria | Home | W | 4-1 |
| | (3) | Sunderland | Home | W | 3-0 |
| | (SF) | Wolves | Town Ground, Nottingham | L | 1-2 |
| 1893-94 | (1) | West Bromwich Albion | Away | W | 3-2 |
| | (2) | Newton Heath | Away | D | 0-0 aet |
| | (R) | Newton Heath | Home | W | 5-1 |
| | (3) | Derby County | Away | W | 4-1 |
| | (SF) | Notts County | Bramall Lane, Sheffield | L | 0-1 |
| 1894-95 | (1) | Burton Wanderers | Away | W | 2-1 |
| | (2) | Everton | Away | D | 1-1 |
| | (R) | Everton | Home | L | 2-3 |
| 1895-96 | (1) | West Bromwich Albion | Home | L | 1-2 |
| 1896-97 | (1) | Sheffield United | Home | W | 2-1 |
| | (2) | Wolves | Home | W | 2-1 |
| | (3) | Everton | Away | L | 0-2 |
| 1897-98 | (1) | Everton | Away | L | 0-1 |
| 1898-99 | (1) | Liverpool | Away | L | 0-2 |
| 1899-00 | (1) | Portsmouth | Away | D | 0-0 |
| | (R) | Portsmouth | Home | D | 1-1 aet |
| | (2R) | Portsmouth | Villa Park, Birmingham | W | 5-0 |
| | (2) | Preston North End | Away | L | 0-1 |
| 1900-01 | (1) | Woolwich Arsenal | Away | L | 0-2 |

| 1901-02 | (1) | Derby County | Home | L | 0-2 |
| 1902-03 | (1) | Sheffield Wednesday | Away | D | 0-0 |
| | (R) | Sheffield Wednesday | Home | W | 1-0 |
| | (2) | Derby County | Away | L | 0-2 |
| | | | | | |
| 1903-04 | (1) | Liverpool | Home | W | 3-1 |
| | (2) | Nottingham Forest | Home | W | 3-1 |
| | (3) | Derby County | Away | L | 1-2 |
| | | | | | |
| 1904-05 | (1) | Sheffield Wednesday | Home | L | 1-2 |
| | | | | | |
| 1905-06 | (1) | Stoke | Away | L | 0-1 |
| | | | | | |
| 1906-07 | (1) | Manchester City | Home | D | 2-2 |
| | (R) | Manchester City | Away | W | 1-0 |
| | (2) | Tottenham Hotspur | Home | D | 1-1 |
| | (R) | Tottenham Hotspur | Away | D | 1-1 aet |
| | (2R) | Tottenham Hotspur | Villa Park, Birmingham | L | 1-2 |
| | | | | | |
| 1907-08 | (1) | Leicester Fosse | Away | L | 0-2 |
| | | | | | |
| 1908-09 | (1) | Notts County | Away | W | 1-0 |
| | (2) | Chelsea | Home | W | 2-1 |
| | (3) | Manchester United | Away | L | 1-6 |
| | | | | | |
| 1909-10 | (1) | Accrington Stanley | Home | W | 7-1 |
| | (2) | Bradford City | Away | W | 2-1 |
| | (3) | Newcastle United | Away | L | 1-3 |
| | | | | | |
| 1910-11 | (1) | Southend United | Home | W | 5-1 |
| | (2) | Tottenham Hotspur | Home | D | 0-0 |
| | (R) | Tottenham Hotspur | Away | W | 2-0 |
| | (3) | Middlesbrough | Away | W | 3-0 |
| | (4) | West Ham United | Away | W | 3-2 |
| | (SF) | Bradford City | Bramall Lane, Sheffield | L | 0-3 |
| | | | | | |
| 1911-12 | (1) | Norwich City | Home | W | 4-1 |
| | (2) | Derby County | Away | W | 2-1 |
| | (3) | Wolves | Home | W | 3-2 |
| | (4) | Manchester United | Away | D | 1-1 |
| | (R) | Manchester United | Home | W | 4-2 aet |
| | (SF) | West Bromwich Albion | Anfield, Liverpool | D | 0-0 |
| | (R) | West Bromwich Albion | Hillsborough, Sheffield | L | 0-1 aet |
| | | | | | |
| 1912-13 | (1) | Northampton Town | Home | W | 7-2 |
| | (2) | Barnsley | Away | W | 3-2 |
| | (3) | Reading | Away | W | 2-1 |
| | (4) | Burnley | Home | L | 0-1 |
| | | | | | |
| 1913-14 | (1) | Middlesbrough | Home | W | 3-0 |
| | (2) | Bury | Home | W | 2-0 |
| | (3) | Manchester City | Home | L | 1-2 |
| | | | | | |
| 1914-15 | (1) | Swansea Town | Away | L | 0-1 |
| | | | | | |
| 1919-20 | (1) | Wolves | Home | D | 2-2 |
| | (R) | Wolves | Away | L | 0-1 |
| | | | | | |
| 1920-21 | (1) | Fulham | Home | D | 1-1 |
| | (R) | Fulham | Away | L | 0-1 |
| | | | | | |
| 1921-22 | (1) | Southport | Home | D | 1-1 |
| | (R) | Southport | Away | W | 2-0 |
| | (2) | Swindon Town | Away | W | 1-0 |
| | (3) | Huddersfield Town | Home | D | 1-1 |
| | (R) | Huddersfield Town | Away | L | 0-5 |
| | | | | | |
| 1922-23 | (1) | Aston Villa | Away | W | 1-0 |
| | (2) | South Shields | Away | D | 0-0 |
| | (R) | South Shields | Home | L | 0-1 |
| | | | | | |
| 1923-24 | (1) | Corinthians | Away | L | 0-1 |
| | | | | | |
| 1924-25 | (1) | Oldham Athletic | Home | W | 1-0 |
| | (2) | Portsmouth | Home | D | 0-0 |
| | (R) | Portsmouth | Away | D | 0-0 |
| | (2R) | Portsmouth | Arsenal Stadium, Highbury | W | 1-0 |
| | (3) | Tottenham Hotspur | Away | D | 2-2 |
| | (R) | Tottenham Hotspur | Home | W | 3-1 |

| | | | | | | |
|---|---|---|---|---|---|---|
| | (4) | Blackpool | Home | W | 1-0 | |
| | (SF) | Cardiff City | Meadow Lane, Nottingham | L | 1-3 | |
| 1925-26 | (3) | Preston North End | Home | D | 1-1 | |
| | (R) | Preston North End | Away | W | 4-1 | |
| | (4) | Arsenal | Away | L | 1-3 | |
| | | | | | | |
| 1926-27 | (3) | Southport | Away | L | 0-2 | |
| | | | | | | |
| 1927-28 | (3) | Newcastle United | Home | W | 4-1 | |
| | (4) | Exeter City | Away | D | 2-2 | |
| | (R) | Exeter City | Home | W | 3-1 | aet |
| | (5) | Port Vale | Home | W | 2-1 | |
| | (6) | Manchester United | Home | W | 2-0 | |
| | (SF) | Arsenal | Filbert Street, Leicester | W | 1-0 | |
| | (F) | Huddersfield Town | Wembley | W | 3-1 | |
| | | | | | | |
| 1928-29 | (3) | Barnsley | Home | W | 1-0 | |
| | (4) | Derby County | Home | D | 1-1 | |
| | (R) | Derby County | Away | W | 3-0 | |
| | (5) | Bury | Home | W | 1-0 | |
| | (6) | Bolton Wanderers | Home | D | 1-1 | |
| | (R) | Bolton Wanderers | Away | L | 1-2 | |
| | | | | | | |
| 1929-30 | (3) | Northampton Town | Home | W | 4-1 | |
| | (4) | Everton | Home | W | 4-1 | |
| | (5) | Aston Villa | Away | L | 1-4 | |
| | | | | | | |
| 1930-31 | (3) | Walsall | Home | D | 1-1 | |
| | (R) | Walsall | Away | W | 3-0 | |
| | (4) | Bristol Rovers | Home | W | 5-1 | |
| | (5) | Chelsea | Away | L | 0-3 | |
| | | | | | | |
| 1931-32 | (3) | Burton Town | Away | W | 4-0 | |
| | (4) | Derby County | Away | L | 2-3 | |
| | | | | | | |
| 1932-33 | (3) | Lincoln City | Away | W | 5-1 | |
| | (4) | Birmingham | Away | L | 0-3 | |
| | | | | | | |
| 1933-34 | (3) | Manchester City | Away | L | 1-3 | |
| | | | | | | |
| 1934-35 | (3) | Middlesbrough | Away | D | 1-1 | |
| | (R) | Middlesbrough | Home | W | 1-0 | |
| | (4) | Liverpool | Home | W | 1-0 | |
| | (5) | Birmingham | Home | L | 1-2 | |
| | | | | | | |
| 1935-36 | (3) | Bolton Wanderers | Home | D | 1-1 | |
| | (R) | Bolton Wanderers | Away | W | 1-0 | aet |
| | (4) | Bradford City | Away | L | 1-3 | |
| | | | | | | |
| 1936-37 | (3) | Accrington Stanley | Home | D | 2-2 | |
| | (R) | Accrington Stanley | Away | L | 1-3 | aet |
| | | | | | | |
| 1937-38 | (3) | Tottenham Hotspur | Away | L | 2-3 | |
| | | | | | | |
| 1938-39 | (3) | Swansea Town | Home | W | 2-0 | |
| | (4) | Southend United | Home | W | 4-2 | |
| | (5) | Sunderland | Away | D | 1-1 | |
| | (R) | Sunderland | Home | D | 0-0 | aet |
| | (2R) | Sunderland | Hillsborough, Sheffield | W | 1-0 | aet |
| | (6) | Huddersfield Town | Away | D | 1-1 | |
| | (R) | Huddersfield Town | Home | L | 1-2 | |
| | | | | | | |
| 1945-46 | (3) | Bolton Wanderers | Away | L | 0-1 | |
| | | Bolton Wanderers | Home | L | 1-3 | |
| | | | | | | |
| 1946-47 | (3) | Hull City | Home | D | 1-1 | |
| | (R) | Hull City | Away | W | 3-0 | |
| | (4) | Port Vale | Home | W | 2-0 | |
| | (5) | Charlton Athletic | Away | L | 0-1 | |
| | | | | | | |
| 1947-48 | (3) | West Ham United | Home | D | 0-0 | |
| | (R) | West Ham United | Away | W | 4-2 | |
| | (4) | Southampton | Away | L | 2-3 | |
| | | | | | | |
| 1948-49 | (3) | Hull City | Away | L | 1-2 | aet |
| | | | | | | |
| 1949-50 | (3) | Liverpool | Home | D | 0-0 | |
| | (R) | Liverpool | Away | L | 1-2 | |

| Season | Round | Opposition | Venue | Result | Score |
|---|---|---|---|---|---|
| 1950-51 | (3) | Bristol City | Away | L | 1-2 |
| 1951-52 | (3) | Nottingham Forest | Away | D | 2-2 |
| | (R) | Nottingham Forest | Home | W | 2-0 |
| | (4) | Hull City | Home | W | 2-0 |
| | (5) | West Bromwich Albion | Home | W | 1-0 |
| | (6) | Burnley | Home | W | 3-1 |
| | (SF) | Newcastle United | Hillsborough, Sheffield | D | 0-0 aet |
| | (R) | Newcastle United | Elland Road, Leeds | L | 1-2 |
| 1952-53 | (3) | Luton Town | Away | L | 1-6 |
| 1953-54 | (3) | Bristol Rovers | Away | W | 1-0 |
| | (4) | Hull City | Home | D | 2-2 |
| | (R) | Hull City | Away | L | 1-2 |
| 1954-55 | (3) | Swansea Town | Home | L | 0-2 |
| 1955-56 | (3) | Northampton Town | Away | W | 2-1 |
| | (4) | Barnsley | Away | W | 1-0 |
| | (5) | West Ham United | Away | D | 0-0 |
| | (R) | West Ham United | Home | L | 2-3 |
| 1956-57 | (3) | Everton | Away | L | 0-1 |
| 1957-58 | (3) | Rotherham United | Away | W | 4-1 |
| | (4) | Everton | Away | W | 2-1 |
| | (5) | Cardiff City | Away | D | 0-0 |
| | (R) | Cardiff City | Home | W | 2-1 |
| | (6) | Liverpool | Home | W | 2-1 |
| | (SF) | Bolton Wanderers | Maine Road, Manchester | L | 1-2 |
| 1958-59 | (3) | Leyton Orient | Home | W | 4-2 |
| | (4) | Burnley | Home | L | 1-2 |
| 1959-60 | (3) | Sunderland | Away | D | 1-1 |
| | (R) | Sunderland | Home | W | 4-1 |
| | (4) | Blackpool | Home | D | 1-1 |
| | (R) | Blackpool | Away | W | 3-0 |
| | (5) | Tottenham Hotspur | Away | W | 3-1 |
| | (6) | Burnley | Away | D | 3-3 |
| | (R) | Burnley | Home | W | 2-0 |
| | (SF) | Sheffield Wednesday | Maine Road, Manchester | W | 2-1 |
| | (F) | Wolves | Wembley | L | 0-3 |
| 1960-61 | (3) | Chesterfield | Away | D | 0-0 |
| | (R) | Chesterfield | Home | W | 3-0 |
| | (4) | Bolton Wanderers | Away | D | 3-3 |
| | (R) | Bolton Wanderers | Home | W | 4-0 |
| | (5) | Sheffield United | Away | L | 1-2 |
| 1961-62 | (3) | Brighton & Hove Albion | Away | W | 3-0 |
| | (4) | Stoke City | Away | W | 1-0 |
| | (5) | Middlesbrough | Home | W | 2-1 |
| | (6) | Fulham | Away | D | 2-2 |
| | (R) | Fulham | Home | L | 0-1 |
| 1962-63 | (3) | Middlesbrough | Home | D | 1-1 |
| | (R) | Middlesbrough | Away | L | 1-3 |
| 1963-64 | (3) | Grimsby Town | Home | W | 4-0 |
| | (4) | Fulham | Home | W | 2-0 |
| | (5) | Oxford United | Away | L | 1-3 |
| 1964-65 | (3) | Leicester City | Away | D | 2-2 |
| | (R) | Leicester City | Home | L | 1-2 |
| 1965-66 | (3) | Arsenal | Home | W | 3-0 |
| | (4) | West Ham United | Away | D | 3-3 |
| | (R) | West Ham United | Home | W | 4-1 |
| | (5) | Norwich City | Away | D | 2-2 |
| | (R) | Norwich City | Home | W | 3-2 |
| | (6) | Sheffield Wednesday | Home | L | 1-2 |
| 1966-67 | (3) | Carlisle United | Home | L | 1-2 |
| 1967-68 | (3) | Swindon Town | Away | L | 0-1 |
| 1968-69 | (3) | Stockport County | Home | W | 2-0 |

|  |  |  |  |  |
|---|---|---|---|---|
|  | (4) Portsmouth | Home | W | 4-0 |
|  | (5) Manchester City | Home | W | 1-4 |
| 1969-70 | (3) Swindon Town | Home | L | 0-4 |
| 1970-71 | (3) Everton | Away | L | 0-2 |
| 1971-72 | (1) Port Vale | Home | D | 1-1 |
|  | (R) Port Vale | Away | L | 1-3 |
| 1972-73 | (1) Lincoln City | Away | D | 2-2 |
|  | (R) Lincoln City | Home | W | 4-1 |
|  | (2) Crewe Alexandra | Home | L | 0-1 |
| 1973-74 | (1) Willington Town | Away | D | 0-0 |
|  | (R) Willington Town | Home | W | 6-1 |
|  | (2) Altrincham | Home | D | 0-0 |
|  | (R) Altrincham | Away | W | 2-0 |
|  | (3) Everton | Away | L | 0-3 |
| 1974-75 | (1) Matlock Town | Away | W | 4-1 |
|  | (2) Darlington | Home | W | 1-0 |
|  | (3) Bristol Rovers | Home | L | 1-2 |
| 1975-76 | (3) Luton Town | Away | L | 0-2 |
| 1976-77 | (3) Charlton Athletic | Away | D | 1-1 |
|  | (R) Charlton Athletic | Home | W | 2-0 |
|  | (4) Orient | Home | W | 3-0 |
|  | (5) Derby County | Away | L | 1-3 |
| 1977-78 | (3) Shrewsbury Town | Home | W | 2-1 |
|  | (4) Orient | Away | L | 1-3 |
| 1978-79 | (3) Millwall | Away | W | 2-1 |
|  | (4) Liverpool | Away | L | 0-1 |
| 1979-80 | (1) Kidderminster Harriers | Away | W | 2-0 |
|  | (2) Stafford Rangers | Home | W | 2-0 |
|  | (3) Fulham | Home | D | 1-1 |
|  | (R) Fulham | Away | W | 1-0 |
|  | (4) Coventry City | Home | W | 1-0 |
|  | (5) Aston Villa | Home | D | 1-1 |
|  | (R) Aston Villa | Away | L | 0-1 |
| 1980-81 | (3) Notts County | Away | L | 1-2 |
| 1981-82 | (3) West Bromwich Albion | Away | L | 2-3 |
| 1982-83 | (3) Liverpool | Home | L | 1-2 |
| 1983-84 | (3) Chelsea | Home | W | 1-0 |
|  | (4) Swindon Town | Away | W | 2-1 |
|  | (5) Southampton | Home | L | 0-1 |
| 1984-85 | (3) Portsmouth | Away | D | 0-0 |
|  | (R) Portsmouth | Home | W | 2-1 |
|  | (4) Oxford United | Away | W | 1-0 |
|  | (5) Manchester United | Home | L | 0-2 |
| 1985-86 | (3) Nottingham Forest | Away | D | 1-1 |
|  | (R) Nottingham Forest | Home | W | 3-2 |
|  | (4) Everton | Away | L | 1-3 |
| 1986-87 | (3) Portsmouth | Away | L | 0-2 |
| 1987-88 | (3) Portsmouth | Home | L | 1-2 |
| 1988-89 | (3) Welling United | Away | W | 1-0 |
|  | (4) Sheffield Wednesday | Home | W | 2-1 |
|  | (5) Brentford | Home | L | 0-2 |
| 1989-90 | (3) Aston Villa | Home | D | 2-2 |
|  | (R) Aston Villa | Away | L | 1-3 |
| 1990-91 | (3) Liverpool | Home | D | 1-1 |
|  | (R) Liverpool | Away | L | 0-3 |
| 1991-92 | (3) Kettering Town | Home | W | 4-1 |
|  | (4) Notts County | Away | L | 1-2 |

| 1992-93 | (3) | AFC Bournemouth | Home | W | 3-1 |
|---|---|---|---|---|---|
| | (4) | Crewe Alexandra | Away | W | 3-0 |
| | (5) | Newcastle United | Home | W | 1-0 |
| | (6) | Sheffield United | Home | D | 0-0 |
| | (R) | Sheffield United | Away | D | 2-2 aet |
| | | (Sheffield United won 5-3 on penalties) | | | |
| 1993-94 | (3) | Portsmouth | Home | D | 3-3 |
| | (R) | Portsmouth | Away | W | 3-1 |
| | (4) | Charlton Athletic | Away | D | 0-0 |
| | (R) | Charlton Athletic | Home | L | 0-1 |

Blackburn Rovers had played 107 clubs in the FA Cup up to the end of the 1993-94 season.
Below is their record against each club.

| | P | W | D | L | F | A |
|---|---|---|---|---|---|---|
| Accrington | 3 | 2 | 1 | 0 | 9 | 2 |
| Accrington Stanley | 3 | 1 | 1 | 1 | 10 | 6 |
| AFC Bournemouth | 1 | 1 | 0 | 0 | 3 | 1 |
| Altrincham | 2 | 1 | 1 | 0 | 2 | 0 |
| Arsenal | 4 | 2 | 0 | 2 | 5 | 5 |
| Aston Villa | 7 | 2 | 2 | 3 | 14 | 12 |
| Barnsley | 3 | 3 | 0 | 0 | 5 | 2 |
| Birmingham City | 2 | 0 | 0 | 2 | 1 | 5 |
| Blackburn Olympic | 2 | 2 | 0 | 0 | 8 | 3 |
| Blackburn Park Road | 1 | 1 | 0 | 0 | 9 | 1 |
| Blackpool | 3 | 2 | 1 | 0 | 5 | 1 |
| Blackpool St John's | 1 | 1 | 0 | 0 | 11 | 1 |
| Bolton Wanderers | 10 | 3 | 3 | 4 | 19 | 15 |
| Bootle | 1 | 1 | 0 | 0 | 7 | 0 |
| Bradford City | 3 | 1 | 0 | 2 | 3 | 7 |
| Brentford | 1 | 0 | 0 | 1 | 0 | 2 |
| Brentwood | 1 | 1 | 0 | 0 | 3 | 1 |
| Brighton & Hove Albion | 1 | 1 | 0 | 0 | 3 | 0 |
| Bristol City | 1 | 0 | 0 | 1 | 1 | 2 |
| Bristol Rovers | 3 | 2 | 0 | 1 | 7 | 3 |
| Burnley | 5 | 2 | 1 | 2 | 9 | 7 |
| Burton Town | 1 | 1 | 0 | 0 | 4 | 0 |
| Burton Wanderers | 1 | 1 | 0 | 0 | 2 | 1 |
| Bury | 2 | 2 | 0 | 0 | 3 | 0 |
| Cardiff City | 3 | 1 | 1 | 1 | 3 | 4 |
| Carlisle United | 1 | 0 | 0 | 1 | 1 | 2 |
| Charlton Athletic | 5 | 1 | 2 | 2 | 3 | 3 |
| Chelsea | 3 | 2 | 0 | 1 | 3 | 4 |
| Chester City | 1 | 1 | 0 | 0 | 7 | 0 |
| Chesterfield | 2 | 1 | 1 | 0 | 3 | 0 |
| Clitheroe | 1 | 1 | 0 | 0 | 2 | 0 |
| Corinthians | 1 | 0 | 0 | 1 | 0 | 1 |
| Coventry City | 1 | 1 | 0 | 0 | 1 | 0 |
| Crewe Alexandra | 2 | 1 | 0 | 1 | 3 | 1 |
| Darlington | 1 | 1 | 0 | 0 | 1 | 0 |
| Darwen | 4 | 3 | 0 | 1 | 11 | 3 |
| Darwen Old Wanderers | 1 | 1 | 0 | 0 | 6 | 1 |
| Derby County | 10 | 4 | 1 | 5 | 18 | 16 |
| Derby Junction | 1 | 0 | 0 | 1 | 1 | 2 |
| Everton | 10 | 2 | 1 | 7 | 10 | 18 |
| Exeter City | 2 | 1 | 1 | 0 | 5 | 3 |
| Fulham | 7 | 2 | 3 | 2 | 7 | 6 |
| Gateshead (South Shields) | 2 | 0 | 1 | 1 | 0 | 1 |
| Grimsby Town | 2 | 2 | 0 | 0 | 7 | 0 |
| Huddersfield Town | 5 | 1 | 2 | 2 | 6 | 10 |
| Hull City | 6 | 2 | 2 | 2 | 10 | 7 |
| Kettering Town | 1 | 1 | 0 | 0 | 4 | 1 |
| Kidderminster Harriers | 1 | 1 | 0 | 0 | 2 | 0 |
| Leicester City | 3 | 0 | 1 | 2 | 3 | 6 |
| Leyton Orient | 3 | 2 | 0 | 1 | 8 | 5 |
| Lincoln City | 3 | 2 | 1 | 0 | 11 | 4 |
| Liverpool | 10 | 3 | 2 | 5 | 9 | 13 |
| Luton Town | 2 | 0 | 0 | 2 | 1 | 8 |
| Manchester City | 5 | 1 | 1 | 3 | 6 | 11 |
| Manchester United | 8 | 4 | 2 | 2 | 17 | 12 |
| Matlock Town | 1 | 1 | 0 | 0 | 4 | 1 |
| Middlesbrough | 7 | 4 | 2 | 1 | 12 | 6 |
| Middlesbrough Ironopolis | 1 | 1 | 0 | 0 | 3 | 0 |
| Millwall | 1 | 1 | 0 | 0 | 2 | 1 |
| Newcastle United | 5 | 2 | 1 | 2 | 7 | 6 |
| Northampton Town | 3 | 3 | 0 | 0 | 13 | 4 |
| Northwich Victoria | 1 | 1 | 0 | 0 | 4 | 1 |

| | P | W | D | L | F | A |
|---|---|---|---|---|---|---|
| Norwich City | 3 | 2 | 1 | 0 | 9 | 5 |
| Nottingham Forest | 6 | 3 | 2 | 1 | 11 | 12 |
| Notts County | 6 | 3 | 0 | 3 | 7 | 6 |
| Old Carthusians | 1 | 1 | 0 | 0 | 5 | 1 |
| Old Etonians | 1 | 0 | 0 | 1 | 0 | 1 |
| Oldham Athletic | 1 | 1 | 0 | 0 | 1 | 0 |
| Oswaldtwistle Wanderers | 1 | 1 | 0 | 0 | 1 | 0 |
| Oxford United | 2 | 1 | 0 | 1 | 2 | 3 |
| Padiham | 1 | 1 | 0 | 0 | 3 | 0 |
| Portsmouth | 13 | 5 | 6 | 2 | 20 | 10 |
| Port Vale | 4 | 2 | 1 | 1 | 6 | 5 |
| Preston North End | 3 | 1 | 1 | 1 | 5 | 3 |
| Queen's Park | 2 | 2 | 0 | 0 | 4 | 1 |
| Reading | 1 | 1 | 0 | 0 | 2 | 1 |
| Renton | 2 | 0 | 1 | 1 | 2 | 4 |
| Romford | 1 | 1 | 0 | 0 | 8 | 0 |
| Rossendale United | 1 | 1 | 0 | 0 | 11 | 0 |
| Rotherham United | 1 | 1 | 0 | 0 | 4 | 1 |
| Sheffield Providence | 1 | 1 | 0 | 0 | 6 | 2 |
| Sheffield United | 4 | 1 | 2 | 1 | 5 | 5 |
| Sheffield Wednesday | 10 | 5 | 2 | 3 | 18 | 12 |
| Shrewsbury Town | 1 | 1 | 0 | 0 | 2 | 1 |
| South Shore | 1 | 1 | 0 | 0 | 7 | 0 |
| Southampton | 2 | 0 | 0 | 2 | 2 | 4 |
| Southend United | 2 | 2 | 0 | 0 | 9 | 3 |
| Southport | 4 | 2 | 1 | 1 | 10 | 4 |
| Stafford Rangers | 1 | 1 | 0 | 0 | 2 | 0 |
| Staveley | 2 | 2 | 0 | 0 | 12 | 2 |
| Stockport County | 1 | 1 | 0 | 0 | 2 | 0 |
| Stoke City | 2 | 1 | 0 | 1 | 1 | 1 |
| Sunderland | 7 | 4 | 3 | 0 | 14 | 5 |
| Swansea City | 3 | 1 | 0 | 2 | 2 | 3 |
| Swifts | 1 | 1 | 0 | 0 | 2 | 1 |
| Swindon Town | 4 | 2 | 0 | 2 | 3 | 6 |
| Tottenham Hotspur | 9 | 3 | 4 | 2 | 15 | 11 |
| Tyne Association | 1 | 1 | 0 | 0 | 5 | 1 |
| Upton Park | 1 | 1 | 0 | 0 | 3 | 0 |
| Walsall | 2 | 1 | 1 | 0 | 4 | 1 |
| Wednesbury Old Athletic | 1 | 1 | 0 | 0 | 3 | 1 |
| Welling United | 1 | 1 | 0 | 0 | 1 | 0 |
| West Bromwich Albion | 11 | 5 | 2 | 4 | 15 | 15 |
| West Ham United | 7 | 3 | 3 | 1 | 16 | 11 |
| Willington | 2 | 1 | 1 | 0 | 6 | 1 |
| Witton | 1 | 1 | 0 | 0 | 5 | 0 |
| Wolverhampton Wanderers | 10 | 4 | 2 | 4 | 13 | 15 |

## FOOTBALL ASSOCIATION CHALLENGE CUP FINALS
Blackburn Rovers have appeared in eight FA Cup Finals during their history. Below is a record of their appearances in those Finals.

**1881-82 v Old Etonians (at Kennington Oval) L 0-1, 6,000.**
Hopes of lifting the trophy were dashed after 20 minutes when Anderson placed a long shot beyond the reach of Howorth. Although the Rovers attacked with the wind at their backs in the second half, the Old Etonians were able to keep them at bay and thus prevent the Rovers from returning to Lancashire with the trophy.
**Old Etonians**: J.F.P.Rawlinson; T.H.French, P.J.de Paravivini, Hon A.F.Kinnaird, C.W.Foley, P.C.Novelli, A.T.B.Dunn, R.H.McCauley, H.C.Goodhart, J.B.T.Chevalier, W.J.Anderson.
*Scorer: Anderson.*
**Blackburn Rovers**: Howorth; McIntyre, Suter, Sharples, F.W.Hargreaves, Duckworth, Douglas, Strachan, Brown, J.Hargreaves, Avery.

**1883-84 v Queen's Park (at Kennington Oval) W 2-1, 12,000.**
The match was something of an international event with one of England's top clubs facing Scotland's premier team. The Rovers had the referee to

The Blackburn Rovers team which faced Sheffield Wednesday in the 1890 FA Cup Final. Back row (left to right): James Southworth, John Southworth, Mr R.Birtwistle, Horne, Dewar. Middle row: Lofthouse, Campbell, Forbes, Walton, Townley. Front: Barton, Forrest.

thank for keeping them in the game when two early Queen's Park goals were disallowed for offside. The decisions appeared to upset the Scots and after 30 minutes Joe Sowerbutts began a move which ended with Jimmy Brown scoring the opening goal. The Rovers increased their lead when Jimmy Forrest broke up a promising Queen's Park attack and raced down the wing. His cross was misjudged by the goalkeeper and floated over Gillespie before it finally dropped into the goal. Although Christie pulled a goal back, the result never looked in doubt.

**Blackburn Rovers**: Arthur: Beverley, Suter, McIntyre, J.Hargreaves, Forrest, Lofthouse, Douglas, Sowerbutts, Inglis, J.Brown.
*Scorers: Brown, Forrest.*
**Queen's Park**: Gillespie; McDonald, Arnott, Gow, Campbell, Allan, Harrower, Dr.J.Smith, W.Anderson, Watt, Christie.
*Scorer: Christie.*

### 1884-1885 v Queen's Park (at Kennington Oval) W 2-0, 15,000.

This was a repeat of the previous season's Final and ended in a similar result. The game was noteworthy for the fact that the Rovers fielded three half-backs instead of the normal two. The Rovers had George Haworth, the Accrington half-back, in the side and excluded Nat Walton from the forward line. The Rovers held the upper hand throughout and went ahead when Jimmy Brown hit a fierce shot against the crossbar and saw Jimmy Forrest knock the rebound into the goal. Brown scored the second goal when Herbert Fecitt sent a shot across goal and Brown touched the ball past Arnott.

**Blackburn Rovers**: Arthur; Turner, Suter, Haworth, McIntyre, Forrest, Lofthouse, Douglas, Brown, Fecitt, Sowerbutts.
*Scorers: Forrest, Brown.*
**Queen's Park**: Gillespie; Arnott, MacLeod, McDonald, Campbell, Sellars, Anderson, McWhannel, Hamilton, Allan, Gray.

### 1885-86 v West Bromwich Albion (at Kennington Oval) D 0-0, 15,156.

A third consecutive appearance in the FA Cup Final proved a disappointing affair. Albion had the better of the first half and the Rovers had to work hard to keep the score level. A major factor in the first-half performance was the impressive display given by Herbie Arthur. Hopes of a brighter second period failed to materialise and matters were not helped when Turner twisted an ankle. At the end of the day the Rovers were glad of the opportunity to have another bite of the cherry.

**Blackburn Rovers**: Arthur; Turner, Suter, Heyes, McIntyre, Forrest, Strachan, Douglas, Brown, Fecitt, Sowerbutts.
**West Bromwich Albion**: Roberts; H.Green, H.Bell, Horton, C.Perry, Timmins, Woodhall, T.Green, Bayliss, Loach, G.Bell.

### Replay v West Bromwich Albion (at Derby) W 2-0, 16,144.

The replay saw the Cup Final moved from London for the first time in its history. The venue was the County Cricket Ground at Derby and whilst West Bromwich remained unchanged, the Rovers brought in Walton for Heyes. The Rovers took the initiative from the beginning and after 26 minutes found themselves ahead. Roberts chose to fist Forrest's looping cross but only found Walton. In a flash Walton had controlled the ball and sent Fecitt running towards the Albion goal. Fecitt quickly released the ball to Sowerbutts and his superb shot found the corner of the goal. The game swung from end to end but after 62 minutes the Rovers finally took control of matters with their second goal. A long ball from McIntyre was instantly controlled by Brown in the middle of the field. He set off towards the Albion goal and as a defender lunged to tackle, Brown hit a glorious drive past Roberts to seal the result for Blackburn. For the third consecutive season the country's premier football trophy was captured by Blackburn Rovers. To commemorate the feat the Football Association

Triumphant Rovers in the Wembley tent after beating Huddersfield Town in the 1928 FA Cup Final. Front (from left to right): Jock Hutton, Harry Healless (captain with Cup), George Thornewell, Arthur Rigby and Peter Holland. Behind: Bill Rankin, Tommy Mitchell, Herbert Jones, Jock Crawford, Tommy McLean.

presented the club with a silver shield in honour of their achievement.

**Blackburn Rovers**: Arthur; Turner, Suter, Douglas, McIntyre, Forrest, Walton, Strachan, Brown, Fecitt, Sowerbutts.
*Scorers: Sowerbutts, Brown.*
**West Bromwich Albion**: Roberts, H.Green, H.Bell, Horton, C.Perry, Timmins, Woodhall, T.Green, Bayliss, Loach, G.Bell.

**1889-90 v Sheffield Wednesday (at Kennington Oval) W 6-1, 20,000.**
The 1890 FA Cup competition saw the first 'Roses' Cup Final. With a side packed with internationals, the Rovers were hot favourites to bring the trophy back to Blackburn. The experience of the Blackburn men certainly gave them the edge over a Wednesday team that looked completely overawed by the occasion. The Rovers wore an all-white strip and took the lead as early as the sixth minute when Townley beat the Wednesday 'keeper. A second goal was scored by Walton and after 35 minutes the game was as good as over when Townley notched his second goal. The second half followed a similar pattern to the first with Jack Southworth adding his name to the list of scorers. Although Mumford pulled a goal back it was not enough to turn the tide. Further goals from Townley and Lofthouse enabled the Rovers to win the Cup for a fourth time and by the most decisive of margins. In helping the Rovers to win the trophy, Billy Townley became the first man to hit a hat-trick in an FA Cup Final.

**Blackburn Rovers**: Horne; James Southworth, Forbes, Barton, Dewar, Forrest, Lofthouse, Campbell, Jack Southworth, Walton, Townley.
*Scorers: Townley 3, Walton, Jack Southworth, Lofthouse.*
**Sheffield Wednesday**: Smith; Brayshaw, Morley, Dungworth, Betts, Waller, Ingram, Woodhouse, Bennett, M.Mumford, Cawley.
*Scorer: M.Mumford.*

**1890-91 v Notts County (at Kennington Oval) W 3-1, 23,000.**
A week before they were due to face Notts County at the Kennington Oval, the Rovers crashed 7-1 at home to County in the Football League.

For the Cup Final the Rovers restored Pennington in goal and welcomed back Jimmy Forrest and Jack Southworth. However, the loss of Harry Campbell, through illness, was a major blow to the club's prospects. Whether County had been lulled into a false sense of security is unclear. However, they were certainly bemused by the flowing football of the Rovers and conceded three first-half goals. The goals from Dewar, Southworth and Townley put the Rovers in a commanding position and although Oswald pulled a goal back it was never enough to inspire a County revival.

**Blackburn Rovers**: Pennington; Brandon, Forbes, Barton, Dewar, Forrest, Lofthouse, Walton, Jack Southworth, Hall, Townley.
*Scorers: Dewar, Southworth, Townley.*
**Notts County**: Thraves; Ferguson, Hendry, H.Osborne, Calderhead, Shelton, McGregor, McInnes, Oswald, Locker, H.B.Daft.
*Scorer: Oswald.*

**1927-28 v Huddersfield Town (at Wembley) W 3-1, 92,041.**
Huddersfield Town went into the 1928 Cup Final as firm favourites to win the trophy. The Yorkshire team, which boasted a number of internationals, were chasing the championship whilst the Rovers were languishing at the wrong end of the table. Blackburn, though, had clearly not read the script because Roscamp gave the Rovers a first-minute lead. The build-up to the goal saw Roscamp display uncharacteristic finesse when he chipped the ball over a Huddersfield defender. Unfortunately the ball was slightly overhit and Mercer, in the Town goal, appeared to have the ball covered. As Mercer stood on his line to collect the ball, Roscamp dipped his shoulder and moved in for the kill. As he charged into Mercer the ball squirmed from the 'keeper's grip and floated over the line whilst Mercer made a desperate lunge to keep it out. With Aussie Campbell tackling fearlessly in midfield the Rovers capitalised on their success with a second goal after 22 minutes. A cross from Rigby found McLean some 18 yards from goal. McLean, primarily the schemer of the forward line, cracked in a glorious shot which hit the back of the net before

The Rovers squad inspect the Wembley pitch before the 1960 FA Cup Final against Wolves. From left to right: Ally MacLeod, Derek Dougan, Eddie Thomas, Bryan Douglas, Dave Whelan, Roy Isherwood, Mike England (behind Isherwood), Ronnie Clayton, Harry Leyland, Matt Woods, Peter Dobing, John Bray and Mick McGrath.

Mercer had a chance to move. Huddersfield fought back in the second half thanks to a tactical switch which saw Jackson moved from the wing to play inside. The move soon paid dividends when Jackson hit a terrific shot which Crawford could only turn on to a post before the ball rebounded into the net. As Huddersfield poured forward, Healless and Campbell worked tirelessly to try to stem the tide. Their work was rewarded five minutes from time when Roscamp scored a second goal with a low shot.

**Blackburn Rovers**: Crawford; Hutton, Jones, Healless, Rankin, Campbell, Thornewell, Puddefoot, Roscamp, McLean, Rigby.
*Scorers: Roscamp 2, McLean.*
**Huddersfield Town**: Mercer; Goodall, Barkas, Redfern, Wilson, Steele, Jackson, Kelly, Brown, Stephenson, Smith.
*Scorer: Jackson.*

### 1959-60 v Wolverhampton Wanderers (at Wembley) L 0-3, 98,776.
The 1960 FA Cup Final was to prove a disastrous event in the history of Blackburn Rovers. Problems with ticket distribution had left many supporters feeling totally disillusioned with the club before the team even got to Wembley. On the eve of the final Derek Dougan handed in a transfer request and then appeared in the Final when less than fully fit. With Dougan struggling, the Rovers were further handicapped when Dave Whelan broke his leg. In the circumstances it was hardly surprising that Wolves should stroll to a 3-0 victory in what was a boring affair. An own-goal by Mick McGrath sent Wolves on their way and a minute later Whelan broke his leg and the game was all but over. Two second-half goals from Deeley gave a rather robust Wolves side a convincing victory in a disappointing game.
**Wolverhampton Wanderers**: Finlayson; Showell, Harris, Clamp, Slater, Flowers, Deeley, Stobart, Murray, Broadbent, Horne.
*Scorers: McGrath own-goal, Deeley 2.*
**Blackburn Rovers**: Leyland; Bray, Whelan, Clayton, Woods, McGrath, Bimpson, Dobing, Dougan, Douglas, MacLeod.

### FOOTBALL ASSOCIATION CHALLENGE CUP MEDALS
Jimmy Forrest holds a unique record in having appeared for Blackburn Rovers in five FA Cup winning teams. He won his five medals in 1884, 1885, 1886, 1890 and 1891 and in so doing equalled the five medals won by A.F.Kinnaird (Wanderers 1873, 1877, 1878 & with Old Etonians 1879 & 1882) and C.H.R.Wollaston (Wanderers 1872, 1873, 1876, 1877 & 1878). Joe Lofthouse won four medals by appearing in the 1884, 1885, 1886, 1890 & 1891 sides. Aussie Campbell had the unusual experience of gaining a winners' medal with the Rovers in 1928 against Huddersfield Town and then picked up a runners-up medal with Huddersfield Town when they lost to Arsenal in the 1930 Cup Final.

### FOOTBALL ASSOCIATION CHARITY SHIELD
The FA Charity Shield match was inaugurated in 1908. During the first five years of the competition the champions of the Football League met the champions of the Southern League. Subsequently the game involved the Football League champions and the holders of the FA Cup. Blackburn Rovers have been involved in the match on two occasions. In May 1912, as Football League champions, they faced Queen's Park Rangers, the Southern League champions, at White Hart Lane. The match was originally planned to be played at the start of the 1912-13 season. However, due to the Titanic disaster the match was brought forward so that the proceeds could be donated to the Titanic Relief Fund. In October 1928, as FA Cup holders, Blackburn Rovers made their second appearance in the Charity Shield when they played Everton, the reigning champions, at Old Trafford. The end of the 1993-94 season saw Blackburn Rovers receive an invitation to play in the Charity Shield at the start of the 1994-95 season. The opportunity came about because Manchester United completed the double and Blackburn, as the team who finished second in the Premiership, appeared as obvious candidates to provide the opposition at Wembley in August 1994.

### 4 May 1912 v Queen's Park Rangers (at White Hart Lane) W 2-1.
*Aitkenhead 2.*
Robinson; Crompton, Cowell, Walmsley, Smith, Bradshaw, Simpson, Latheron, Aitkenhead, Clennell, Anthony.
*Att: 7,111.*

### 24 October 1928 v Everton (at Old Trafford) L 1-2.
*Thornewell.*
Crawford; Roxburgh, Jones, Healless, Baxter, O'Dowd, Thornewell, Puddefoot, Roscamp, T.McLean, Rigby.
*Att: 4,000.*

## FOOTBALL ASSOCIATION YOUTH CUP

Blackburn Rovers won the FA Youth Cup for the only time in their history in 1959 when they faced West Ham United in a two-leg tie. The first-leg was played at Upton Park on 27 April in front of a crowd of 10,750. A goal by Alan Bradshaw earned the Rovers a 1-1 draw against a West Ham side that included future England captain, Bobby Moore. In a crowd of 28,500 flocked to Ewood Park on 4 May for the second-leg. In a pulsating tie, Barry Griffith saved a penalty which enabled the Rovers to take the game into extra-time. During the period, Paddy Daly scored the goal which gave the Rovers a 2-1 aggregate win. The trophy was presented to Fred Pickering, the Blackburn captain, by Sir Stanley Rous, the secretary of the Football Association. The Rovers team for both games was as follows: Griffith; Wells, Pickering, England, Newton, Leech, Ratcliffe, Bradshaw, Jervis, Daly, Mulvey.

## FOOTBALL LEAGUE

The Football League was formed in 1888 to meet the needs of the professional clubs in the North of England and in the Midlands. Prior to 1888, although clubs participated in the FA Cup and various local county competitions, the bulk of the fixtures were made up with friendly games.

It was not unusual for such matches to be subject to last-minute cancellations or delayed kick-offs. Furthermore, there was no guarantee that clubs would field their strongest team in these games. With clubs paying an increasing number of professional players it was felt in some quarters that the game needed to be run in a more business like manner. On 2 March 1888, William McGregor, an Aston Villa committee member, wrote to five clubs – Blackburn Rovers, Bolton Wanderers, Preston North End, West Bromwich Albion and Aston Villa – outlining a plan for regular home and away fixtures between 12 leading clubs. The result of this letter was a meeting at the Anderton Hotel in London on 22 March. Blackburn Rovers were one of several clubs represented at this meeting and further meetings which resolved to invite six clubs from the North (Accrington, Blackburn Rovers, Bolton Wanderers, Burnley, Everton and Preston North End), and six from the Midlands (Aston Villa, Derby County, Notts County, Stoke, West Bromwich Albion and Wolves) to form the Football League for the start of the 1888-89 season.

Blackburn Rovers record in the Football League between 1888-89 and 1991-92 is as follows:

| | P | Home W | Home D | Home L | Home F | Home A | Away W | Away D | Away L | Away F | Away A | Overall W | Overall D | Overall L | Overall F | A | Pts | Pos |
|---|---|---|---|---|---|---|---|---|---|---|---|---|---|---|---|---|---|---|
| **The Football League** | | | | | | | | | | | | | | | | | | |
| 1888-89 | 22 | 7 | 4 | 0 | 44 | 22 | 3 | 2 | 6 | 22 | 23 | 10 | 6 | 6 | 66 | 45 | 26 | 4th |
| 1889-90 | 22 | 9 | 0 | 2 | 59 | 18 | 3 | 3 | 5 | 19 | 23 | 12 | 3 | 7 | 78 | 41 | 27 | 3rd |
| 1890-91 | 22 | 7 | 1 | 3 | 29 | 19 | 4 | 1 | 6 | 23 | 24 | 11 | 2 | 9 | 52 | 43 | 24 | 6th |
| 1891-92 | 26 | 8 | 3 | 2 | 39 | 26 | 2 | 3 | 8 | 19 | 39 | 10 | 6 | 10 | 58 | 65 | 26 | 9th |
| **Division One** | | | | | | | | | | | | | | | | | | |
| 1892-93 | 30 | 5 | 8 | 2 | 29 | 24 | 3 | 5 | 7 | 18 | 32 | 8 | 13 | 9 | 47 | 56 | 29 | 9th |
| 1893-94 | 30 | 13 | 0 | 2 | 48 | 15 | 3 | 2 | 10 | 21 | 38 | 16 | 2 | 12 | 69 | 53 | 34 | 4th |
| 1894-95 | 30 | 9 | 5 | 1 | 40 | 15 | 2 | 5 | 8 | 19 | 34 | 11 | 10 | 9 | 59 | 49 | 32 | 5th |
| 1895-96 | 30 | 10 | 1 | 4 | 26 | 18 | 2 | 4 | 9 | 14 | 32 | 12 | 5 | 13 | 40 | 50 | 29 | 8th |
| 1896-97 | 30 | 8 | 1 | 6 | 27 | 25 | 3 | 2 | 10 | 8 | 37 | 11 | 3 | 16 | 35 | 62 | 25 | 14th |
| 1897-98 | 30 | 4 | 7 | 4 | 20 | 22 | 3 | 3 | 9 | 19 | 32 | 7 | 10 | 13 | 39 | 54 | 24 | 15th |
| 1898-99 | 34 | 9 | 5 | 3 | 41 | 23 | 5 | 3 | 9 | 19 | 29 | 14 | 8 | 12 | 60 | 52 | 36 | 6th |
| 1899-00 | 34 | 12 | 2 | 3 | 38 | 22 | 1 | 2 | 14 | 11 | 39 | 13 | 4 | 17 | 49 | 61 | 30 | 14th |
| 1900-01 | 34 | 9 | 4 | 4 | 24 | 18 | 3 | 5 | 9 | 15 | 29 | 12 | 9 | 13 | 39 | 47 | 33 | 9th |
| 1901-02 | 34 | 12 | 2 | 3 | 36 | 16 | 3 | 4 | 10 | 16 | 32 | 15 | 6 | 13 | 52 | 48 | 36 | 4th |
| 1902-03 | 34 | 9 | 2 | 6 | 27 | 24 | 3 | 3 | 11 | 17 | 39 | 12 | 5 | 17 | 44 | 63 | 29 | 16th |
| 1903-04 | 34 | 7 | 5 | 5 | 29 | 23 | 4 | 1 | 12 | 19 | 37 | 11 | 6 | 17 | 48 | 60 | 28 | 15th |
| 1904-05 | 34 | 9 | 3 | 5 | 28 | 18 | 2 | 2 | 13 | 12 | 33 | 11 | 5 | 18 | 40 | 51 | 27 | 13th |
| 1905-06 | 38 | 10 | 5 | 4 | 34 | 18 | 6 | 3 | 10 | 20 | 34 | 16 | 8 | 14 | 54 | 52 | 40 | 9th |
| 1906-07 | 38 | 10 | 3 | 6 | 40 | 25 | 4 | 4 | 11 | 16 | 34 | 14 | 7 | 17 | 56 | 59 | 35 | 12th |
| 1907-08 | 38 | 10 | 7 | 2 | 35 | 23 | 2 | 5 | 12 | 16 | 40 | 12 | 12 | 14 | 51 | 63 | 36 | 14th* |
| 1908-09 | 38 | 6 | 6 | 7 | 29 | 26 | 8 | 7 | 4 | 32 | 24 | 14 | 13 | 11 | 61 | 50 | 41 | 4th |
| 1909-10 | 38 | 13 | 6 | 0 | 47 | 17 | 5 | 3 | 11 | 26 | 38 | 18 | 9 | 11 | 73 | 55 | 45 | 3rd |
| 1910-11 | 38 | 12 | 2 | 5 | 40 | 14 | 1 | 9 | 9 | 22 | 40 | 13 | 11 | 14 | 62 | 54 | 37 | 12th |
| 1911-12 | 38 | 13 | 6 | 0 | 35 | 10 | 7 | 3 | 9 | 25 | 33 | 20 | 9 | 9 | 60 | 43 | 49 | 1st |
| 1912-13 | 38 | 10 | 5 | 4 | 54 | 21 | 6 | 8 | 5 | 25 | 22 | 16 | 13 | 9 | 79 | 43 | 45 | 5th |
| 1913-14 | 38 | 14 | 4 | 1 | 51 | 15 | 6 | 7 | 6 | 27 | 27 | 20 | 11 | 7 | 78 | 42 | 51 | 1st |
| 1914-15 | 38 | 11 | 4 | 4 | 51 | 27 | 7 | 3 | 9 | 32 | 34 | 18 | 7 | 13 | 83 | 61 | 43 | 3rd |
| 1919-20 | 42 | 11 | 4 | 6 | 48 | 30 | 2 | 7 | 12 | 16 | 47 | 13 | 11 | 18 | 64 | 77 | 37 | 20th |
| 1920-21 | 42 | 7 | 9 | 5 | 36 | 27 | 6 | 6 | 9 | 21 | 32 | 13 | 15 | 14 | 57 | 59 | 41 | 11th |
| 1921-22 | 42 | 7 | 6 | 8 | 35 | 31 | 6 | 6 | 9 | 19 | 26 | 13 | 12 | 17 | 54 | 57 | 38 | 15th |
| 1922-23 | 42 | 12 | 7 | 2 | 32 | 19 | 2 | 5 | 14 | 15 | 43 | 14 | 12 | 16 | 47 | 62 | 40 | 14th |
| 1923-24 | 42 | 14 | 5 | 2 | 40 | 13 | 3 | 6 | 12 | 14 | 37 | 17 | 11 | 14 | 54 | 50 | 45 | 8th |
| 1924-25 | 42 | 7 | 6 | 8 | 31 | 26 | 4 | 7 | 10 | 22 | 40 | 11 | 13 | 18 | 53 | 66 | 35 | 16th |
| 1925-26 | 42 | 11 | 6 | 4 | 59 | 33 | 4 | 5 | 12 | 32 | 47 | 15 | 11 | 16 | 91 | 80 | 41 | 12th |
| 1926-27 | 42 | 9 | 5 | 7 | 40 | 40 | 6 | 3 | 12 | 37 | 56 | 15 | 8 | 19 | 77 | 96 | 38 | 18th |
| 1927-28 | 42 | 13 | 5 | 3 | 41 | 22 | 3 | 4 | 14 | 25 | 56 | 16 | 9 | 17 | 66 | 78 | 41 | 12th |
| 1928-29 | 42 | 11 | 6 | 4 | 42 | 26 | 6 | 5 | 10 | 30 | 37 | 17 | 11 | 14 | 72 | 63 | 45 | 7th |
| 1929-30 | 42 | 15 | 2 | 4 | 65 | 36 | 4 | 5 | 12 | 34 | 57 | 19 | 7 | 16 | 99 | 93 | 45 | 6th |
| 1930-31 | 42 | 14 | 3 | 4 | 54 | 28 | 3 | 5 | 13 | 29 | 56 | 17 | 8 | 17 | 83 | 84 | 42 | 10th |
| 1931-32 | 42 | 12 | 3 | 6 | 57 | 41 | 4 | 3 | 14 | 32 | 54 | 16 | 6 | 20 | 89 | 95 | 38 | 16th |
| 1932-33 | 42 | 11 | 6 | 4 | 48 | 41 | 3 | 4 | 14 | 28 | 61 | 14 | 10 | 18 | 76 | 102 | 38 | 15th |
| 1933-34 | 42 | 16 | 5 | 0 | 57 | 21 | 2 | 2 | 17 | 17 | 60 | 18 | 7 | 17 | 74 | 81 | 43 | 8th |
| 1934-35 | 42 | 12 | 5 | 4 | 42 | 23 | 2 | 6 | 13 | 24 | 55 | 14 | 11 | 17 | 66 | 78 | 39 | 15th |
| 1935-36 | 42 | 10 | 6 | 5 | 32 | 24 | 2 | 3 | 16 | 23 | 72 | 12 | 9 | 21 | 55 | 96 | 33 | 22nd |
| **Division Two** | | | | | | | | | | | | | | | | | | |
| 1936-37 | 42 | 11 | 3 | 7 | 49 | 32 | 5 | 7 | 9 | 21 | 30 | 16 | 10 | 16 | 70 | 62 | 42 | 12th |
| 1937-38 | 42 | 13 | 6 | 2 | 51 | 30 | 1 | 4 | 16 | 20 | 50 | 14 | 10 | 18 | 71 | 80 | 38 | 16th |
| 1938-39 | 42 | 17 | 1 | 3 | 59 | 23 | 8 | 4 | 9 | 35 | 37 | 25 | 5 | 12 | 94 | 60 | 55 | 1st |
| **Division One** | | | | | | | | | | | | | | | | | | |
| 1946-47 | 42 | 6 | 5 | 10 | 23 | 27 | 8 | 3 | 10 | 22 | 26 | 14 | 8 | 20 | 45 | 53 | 36 | 17th |
| 1947-48 | 42 | 8 | 5 | 8 | 35 | 30 | 3 | 5 | 13 | 19 | 42 | 11 | 10 | 21 | 54 | 72 | 32 | 21st |
| **Division Two** | | | | | | | | | | | | | | | | | | |
| 1948-49 | 42 | 12 | 5 | 4 | 41 | 23 | 3 | 3 | 15 | 12 | 40 | 15 | 8 | 19 | 53 | 63 | 38 | 14th |

| Season | P | W | D | L | F | A | W | D | L | F | A | W | D | L | F | A | Pts | Pos |
|---|---|---|---|---|---|---|---|---|---|---|---|---|---|---|---|---|---|---|
| 1949-50 | 42 | 10 | 5 | 6 | 30 | 15 | 4 | 5 | 12 | 25 | 45 | 14 | 10 | 18 | 55 | 60 | 38 | 16th |
| 1950-51 | 42 | 13 | 3 | 5 | 39 | 27 | 6 | 5 | 10 | 26 | 39 | 19 | 8 | 15 | 65 | 66 | 46 | 6th |
| 1951-52 | 42 | 11 | 3 | 7 | 35 | 30 | 6 | 3 | 12 | 19 | 33 | 17 | 6 | 19 | 54 | 63 | 40 | 14th |
| 1952-53 | 42 | 12 | 4 | 5 | 40 | 20 | 6 | 4 | 11 | 28 | 45 | 18 | 8 | 16 | 68 | 65 | 44 | 9th |
| 1953-54 | 42 | 15 | 4 | 2 | 54 | 16 | 8 | 5 | 8 | 32 | 34 | 23 | 9 | 10 | 86 | 50 | 55 | 3rd |
| 1954-55 | 42 | 14 | 4 | 3 | 73 | 31 | 8 | 2 | 11 | 41 | 48 | 22 | 6 | 14 | 114 | 79 | 50 | 6th |
| 1955-56 | 42 | 13 | 4 | 4 | 55 | 29 | 8 | 2 | 11 | 29 | 36 | 21 | 6 | 15 | 84 | 65 | 48 | 4th |
| 1956-57 | 42 | 12 | 6 | 3 | 49 | 32 | 9 | 4 | 8 | 34 | 43 | 21 | 10 | 11 | 83 | 75 | 52 | 4th |
| 1957-58 | 42 | 13 | 7 | 1 | 50 | 18 | 9 | 5 | 7 | 43 | 39 | 22 | 12 | 8 | 93 | 57 | 56 | 2nd |
| **Division One** | | | | | | | | | | | | | | | | | | |
| 1958-59 | 42 | 12 | 3 | 6 | 48 | 28 | 5 | 7 | 9 | 28 | 42 | 17 | 10 | 15 | 76 | 70 | 44 | 10th |
| 1959-60 | 42 | 12 | 3 | 6 | 38 | 29 | 4 | 2 | 15 | 22 | 41 | 16 | 5 | 21 | 60 | 70 | 37 | 17th |
| 1960-61 | 42 | 12 | 3 | 6 | 48 | 34 | 3 | 10 | 8 | 29 | 42 | 15 | 13 | 14 | 77 | 76 | 43 | 8th |
| 1961-62 | 42 | 10 | 6 | 5 | 33 | 22 | 4 | 5 | 12 | 17 | 36 | 14 | 11 | 17 | 50 | 58 | 39 | 16th |
| 1962-63 | 42 | 11 | 4 | 6 | 55 | 34 | 4 | 8 | 9 | 24 | 37 | 15 | 12 | 15 | 79 | 71 | 42 | 11th |
| 1963-64 | 42 | 10 | 4 | 7 | 44 | 28 | 8 | 6 | 7 | 45 | 37 | 18 | 10 | 14 | 89 | 65 | 46 | 7th |
| 1964-65 | 42 | 12 | 2 | 7 | 46 | 33 | 4 | 8 | 9 | 37 | 46 | 16 | 10 | 16 | 83 | 79 | 42 | 10th |
| 1965-66 | 42 | 6 | 1 | 14 | 30 | 36 | 2 | 3 | 16 | 27 | 52 | 8 | 4 | 30 | 57 | 88 | 20 | 22nd |
| **Division Two** | | | | | | | | | | | | | | | | | | |
| 1966-7 | 42 | 13 | 6 | 2 | 33 | 11 | 6 | 7 | 8 | 23 | 35 | 19 | 13 | 10 | 56 | 46 | 51 | 4th |
| 1967-68 | 42 | 13 | 5 | 3 | 34 | 16 | 3 | 6 | 12 | 22 | 33 | 16 | 11 | 15 | 56 | 49 | 43 | 8th |
| 1968-69 | 42 | 9 | 6 | 6 | 30 | 24 | 4 | 5 | 12 | 22 | 39 | 13 | 11 | 18 | 52 | 63 | 37 | 19th |
| 1969-70 | 42 | 15 | 2 | 4 | 42 | 19 | 5 | 5 | 11 | 12 | 31 | 20 | 7 | 15 | 54 | 50 | 47 | 8th |
| 1970-71 | 42 | 5 | 8 | 8 | 20 | 28 | 1 | 7 | 13 | 17 | 41 | 6 | 15 | 21 | 37 | 69 | 27 | 21st |
| **Division Three** | | | | | | | | | | | | | | | | | | |
| 1971-72 | 46 | 14 | 4 | 5 | 39 | 22 | 5 | 5 | 13 | 15 | 35 | 19 | 9 | 18 | 54 | 57 | 47 | 10th |
| 1972-73 | 46 | 12 | 8 | 3 | 34 | 16 | 8 | 7 | 8 | 23 | 31 | 20 | 15 | 11 | 57 | 47 | 55 | 3rd |
| 1973-74 | 46 | 13 | 4 | 6 | 38 | 21 | 5 | 6 | 12 | 24 | 43 | 18 | 10 | 18 | 62 | 64 | 46 | 13th |
| 1974-75 | 46 | 15 | 7 | 1 | 40 | 16 | 7 | 9 | 7 | 28 | 29 | 22 | 16 | 8 | 68 | 45 | 60 | 1st |
| **Division Two** | | | | | | | | | | | | | | | | | | |
| 1975-76 | 42 | 8 | 6 | 7 | 27 | 22 | 4 | 8 | 9 | 18 | 28 | 12 | 14 | 16 | 45 | 50 | 38 | 15th |
| 1976-77 | 42 | 12 | 4 | 5 | 31 | 18 | 3 | 5 | 13 | 11 | 36 | 15 | 9 | 18 | 42 | 54 | 39 | 12th |
| 1977-78 | 42 | 12 | 4 | 5 | 33 | 16 | 4 | 9 | 8 | 23 | 44 | 16 | 13 | 13 | 56 | 60 | 45 | 5th |
| 1978-79 | 42 | 5 | 8 | 8 | 24 | 29 | 5 | 2 | 14 | 17 | 43 | 10 | 10 | 22 | 41 | 72 | 30 | 22nd |
| **Division Three** | | | | | | | | | | | | | | | | | | |
| 1979-80 | 46 | 13 | 5 | 5 | 34 | 17 | 12 | 4 | 7 | 24 | 19 | 25 | 9 | 12 | 58 | 36 | 59 | 2nd |
| **Division Two** | | | | | | | | | | | | | | | | | | |
| 1980-81 | 42 | 12 | 8 | 1 | 28 | 7 | 4 | 10 | 7 | 14 | 22 | 16 | 18 | 8 | 42 | 29 | 50 | 4th |
| 1981-82 | 42 | 11 | 4 | 6 | 26 | 15 | 5 | 7 | 9 | 21 | 28 | 16 | 11 | 15 | 47 | 43 | 59 | 10th |
| 1982-83 | 42 | 11 | 7 | 3 | 38 | 21 | 4 | 5 | 12 | 20 | 37 | 15 | 12 | 15 | 58 | 58 | 57 | 11th |
| 1983-84 | 42 | 9 | 11 | 1 | 35 | 19 | 8 | 5 | 8 | 22 | 27 | 17 | 16 | 9 | 57 | 46 | 67 | 6th |
| 1984-85 | 42 | 14 | 3 | 4 | 38 | 15 | 7 | 7 | 7 | 28 | 26 | 21 | 10 | 11 | 66 | 41 | 73 | 5th |
| 1985-86 | 42 | 10 | 4 | 7 | 30 | 20 | 2 | 9 | 10 | 23 | 42 | 12 | 13 | 17 | 53 | 62 | 49 | 19th |
| 1986-87 | 42 | 11 | 4 | 6 | 30 | 22 | 4 | 6 | 11 | 15 | 33 | 15 | 10 | 17 | 45 | 55 | 55 | 12th |
| 1987-88 | 44 | 12 | 8 | 2 | 38 | 22 | 9 | 6 | 7 | 30 | 30 | 21 | 14 | 9 | 68 | 52 | 77 | 5th |
| 1988-89 | 46 | 16 | 4 | 3 | 50 | 22 | 6 | 7 | 10 | 24 | 37 | 22 | 11 | 13 | 74 | 59 | 77 | 5th |
| 1989-90 | 46 | 10 | 9 | 4 | 43 | 30 | 9 | 8 | 6 | 31 | 29 | 19 | 17 | 10 | 74 | 59 | 74 | 5th |
| 1990-91 | 46 | 8 | 6 | 9 | 26 | 27 | 6 | 4 | 13 | 25 | 39 | 14 | 10 | 22 | 51 | 66 | 52 | 19th |
| 1991-92 | 46 | 14 | 5 | 4 | 41 | 21 | 7 | 6 | 10 | 29 | 32 | 21 | 11 | 14 | 70 | 53 | 74 | 6th |

* Equal with Woolwich Arsenal

Blackburn Rovers in 1947-48, when they were relegated from the First Division. Back row (left to right): J.Baldwin, D.Gray, K.Holliday, S.Hayhurst, D.Westcott, W.Eckersley. Front row: J.Campbell, L.Graham, E.Bell, E.Murphy, D.Carter.

## FOOTBALL LEAGUE CUP

Although the Football League Cup did not come into being until 1960, the idea of a Cup competition for League clubs was nothing new. Suggestions for such a competition had been mooted within a few years of the formation of the Football League. Between 1933 and 1946 the Football League ran a Third Division Cup competition in which teams from the Northern and Southern sections met teams of the same division in a knockout competition. However the winners of the two sections did not meet in an overall Final.

During World War Two the League operated its own Cup competition and in June 1940, Blackburn Rovers met West Ham United in the Final at Wembley. Sadly the Rovers lost this first wartime Final and in 1945 the FA Cup returned and thus ended the life of the League Cup competition.

The idea for a League Cup competition was revived by Alan Hardaker, the Secretary of the Football League, and in 1960-61 the inaugural competition was held. Initially, a number of top First Division clubs boycotted the competition and it was not until Wembley became the venue of the Final, with a UEFA Cup place as reward for the winner, that the competition gained respectability. The Football League Cup has never been a particularly successful competition for the Rovers. The club has never appeared in a Final and has only made the last four on two occasions.

In 1961-62 the Rovers were surprisingly defeated in a two-legged semi-final by Rochdale. At the time the Rovers were a respected First Division outfit whilst the men from Spotland were plying their trade in 1960-61 in the Fourth Division. The Rovers didn't reach the semi-final stage again until 1992-93 when Sheffield Wednesday denied the Rovers a trip to Wembley.

Whilst the competition has brought little in the way of glory it has certainly witnessed a number of embarrassing exits. Perhaps the worst of these was the 5-1 defeat by Workington at Ewood Park in 1964-65.

The full record of Blackburn Rovers in the Football League Cup is as follows:

| | | | | | |
|---|---|---|---|---|---|
| 1960-61 | (1) | York City | Away | W | 3-1 |
| | (2) | Swansea Town | Away | W | 2-1 |
| | (3) | Rochdale | Home | W | 2-1 |
| | (4) | Wrexham | Home | D | 1-1 |
| | (R) | Wrexham | Away | L | 1-3 aet |
| 1961-62 | (1) | Peterborough United | Away | W | 3-1 |
| | (2) | Bristol Rovers | Away | D | 1-1 |
| | (R) | Bristol Rovers | Home | W | 4-0 |
| | (3) | Nottingham Forest | Away | W | 2-1 |
| | (4) | Ipswich Town | Home | W | 4-1 |
| | (5) | Rotherham United | Away | W | 1-0 |
| | (SF) | Rochdale | Away | L | 1-3 |
| | | Rochdale | Home | W | 2-1 |
| 1962-63 | (2) | Derby County | Away | D | 1-1 |
| | (R) | Derby County | Home | W | 3-1 |
| | (3) | Leeds United | Home | W | 4-0 |
| | (4) | Rotherham United | Home | W | 4-1 |
| | (5) | Sunderland | Away | L | 2-3 |
| 1963-64 | (2) | Notts County | Away | L | 1-2 |
| 1964-65 | (2) | Bolton Wanderers | Away | W | 5-1 |
| | (3) | Workington | Away | D | 0-0 |
| | (R) | Workington | Home | L | 1-5 |
| 1965-66 | (2) | Northampton Town | Home | L | 0-1 |
| 1966-67 | (2) | Barrow | Home | W | 4-1 |
| | (3) | York City | Away | W | 2-0 |
| | (4) | Carlisle United | Away | L | 0-4 |
| 1967-68 | (2) | Brighton & Hove Albion | Home | W | 3-1 |
| | (3) | Middlesbrough | Home | W | 3-2 |
| | (4) | Arsenal | Away | L | 1-2 |
| 1968-69 | (2) | Stoke City | Home | D | 1-1 |
| | (R) | Stoke City | Away | W | 1-0 |
| | (3) | Swindon Town | Away | L | 0-1 |
| 1969-70 | (1) | Stockport County | Away | W | 2-0 |
| | (2) | Doncaster Rovers | Home | W | 4-2 |
| | (3) | Carlisle United | Away | L | 1-2 |
| 1970-71 | (2) | Bolton Wanderers | Away | L | 0-1 |
| 1971-72 | (1) | Workington | Home | W | 2-0 |
| | (2) | Lincoln City | Home | D | 0-0 |
| | (R) | Lincoln City | Away | L | 1-4 |
| 1972-73 | (1) | Rochdale | Home | L | 0-1 |
| 1973-74 | (1) | Southport | Away | D | 1-1 |
| | (R) | Southport | Home | W | 3-1 aet |
| | (2) | Orient | Away | L | 0-2 |
| 1974-75 | (1) | Stockport County | Away | W | 2-0 |
| | (2) | Northampton Town | Away | D | 2-2 |
| | (R) | Northampton Town | Home | W | 1-0 |
| | (3) | Hartlepool | Away | D | 1-1 |
| | (R) | Hartlepool | Home | L | 1-2 |
| 1975-76 | (1) | Preston North End | Away | L | 0-2 |
| | | Preston North End | Home | D | 0-0 |

| | | | | | |
|---|---|---|---|---|---|
| 1976-77 | (1) | Rochdale | Away | W | 1-0 |
| | | Rochdale | Home | W | 4-1 |
| | (2) | Stockport County | Home | L | 1-3 |
| 1977-78 | (2) | Colchester United | Home | D | 1-1 |
| | | Colchester United | Away | L | 0-4 |
| 1978-79 | (2) | Exeter City | Away | L | 1-2 |
| 1979-80 | (1) | Bury | Away | W | 3-0 |
| | | Bury | Home | W | 3-2 |
| | (2) | Nottingham Forest | Home | D | 1-1 |
| | (R) | Nottingham Forest | Away | L | 1-6 |
| 1980-81 | (1) | Huddersfield Town | Home | D | 0-0 |
| | | Huddersfield Town | Away | D | 1-1 aet* |
| | (2) | Gillingham | Home | D | 0-0 |
| | | Gillingham | Away | W | 2-1 |
| | (3) | Birmingham City | Away | L | 0-1 |

*Blackburn won on away-goals rule.

| | | | | | |
|---|---|---|---|---|---|
| 1981-82 | (2) | Sheffield Wednesday | Home | D | 1-1 |
| | | Sheffield Wednesday | Away | W | 2-1 |
| | (3) | Nottingham Forest | Home | L | 0-1 |
| 1982-83 | (2) | Brentford | Away | L | 2-3 |
| | | Brentford | Home | D | 0-0 |
| 1983-84 | (2) | Ipswich Town | Away | L | 3-4 |
| | | Ipswich Town | Home | L | 1-2 |
| 1984-85 | (2) | Oxford United | Home | D | 1-1 |
| | | Oxford United | Away | L | 1-3 aet |
| 1985-86 | (2) | Wimbledon | Away | L | 0-5 |
| | | Wimbledon | Home | W | 2-1 |
| 1986-87 | (1) | Wigan Athletic | Away | W | 3-1 |
| | | Wigan Athletic | Home | W | 2-0 |
| | (2) | Queen's Park Rangers | Away | L | 1-2 |
| | | Queen's Park Rangers | Home | D | 2-2 |
| 1987-88 | (2) | Liverpool | Home | D | 1-1 |
| | | Liverpool | Away | L | 0-1 |
| 1988-89 | (2) | Brentford | Home | W | 3-1 |
| | | Brentford | Away | L | 3-4 |
| | (3) | Tottenham Hotspur | Away | D | 0-0 |
| | (R) | Tottenham Hotspur | Home | L | 1-2 aet |
| 1989-90 | (2) | Exeter City | Away | L | 0-3 |
| | | Exeter City | Home | W | 2-1 |
| 1990-91 | (2) | Rotherham United | Away | D | 1-1 |
| | | Rotherham United | Home | W | 1-0 |
| | (3) | Queen's Park Rangers | Away | L | 1-2 |
| 1991-92 | (2) | Hull City | Home | D | 1-1 |
| | | Hull City | Away | L | 0-1 |
| 1992-93 | (2) | Huddersfield Town | Away | D | 1-1 |
| | | Huddersfield Town | Home | W | 4-3 aet |
| | (3) | Norwich City | Home | W | 2-0 |
| | (4) | Watford | Home | W | 6-1 |
| | (5) | Cambridge United | Home | W | 3-1 |
| | (SF) | Sheffield Wednesday | Home | L | 2-4 |
| | | Sheffield Wednesday | Away | L | 1-2 |
| 1993-94 | (2) | AFC Bournemouth | Home | W | 1-0 |
| | | AFC Bournemouth | Away | D | 0-0 |
| | (3) | Shrewsbury Town | Home | D | 0-0 |
| | (R) | Shrewsbury Town | Away | W | 4-3 aet |
| | (4) | Tottenham Hotspur | Away | L | 0-1 |

Blackburn Rovers had played 50 clubs in the Football League Cup up to the end of the 1993-94 season. Below is their record against each club.

| | P | W | D | L | F | A |
|---|---|---|---|---|---|---|
| Arsenal | 1 | 0 | 0 | 1 | 1 | 2 |
| Barrow | 1 | 1 | 0 | 0 | 4 | 1 |
| Birmingham City | 1 | 0 | 0 | 1 | 0 | 1 |
| Bolton Wanderers | 2 | 1 | 0 | 1 | 5 | 2 |
| AFC Bournemouth | 2 | 1 | 1 | 0 | 1 | 0 |
| Brentford | 4 | 1 | 1 | 2 | 8 | 8 |
| Brighton & Hove Albion | 1 | 1 | 0 | 0 | 3 | 1 |
| Bristol Rovers | 2 | 1 | 1 | 0 | 5 | 1 |
| Bury | 2 | 2 | 0 | 0 | 6 | 2 |
| Cambridge United | 1 | 1 | 0 | 0 | 3 | 2 |
| Carlisle United | 2 | 0 | 0 | 2 | 1 | 6 |
| Colchester United | 2 | 0 | 1 | 1 | 1 | 5 |
| Derby County | 2 | 1 | 1 | 0 | 4 | 2 |
| Doncaster Rovers | 1 | 1 | 0 | 0 | 4 | 2 |
| Exeter City | 3 | 1 | 0 | 2 | 3 | 6 |
| Gillingham | 2 | 1 | 1 | 0 | 2 | 1 |
| Hartlepool | 2 | 0 | 1 | 1 | 2 | 3 |
| Huddersfield Town | 4 | 1 | 3 | 0 | 6 | 5 |
| Hull City | 2 | 0 | 1 | 1 | 1 | 2 |
| Ipswich Town | 3 | 1 | 0 | 2 | 8 | 7 |
| Leeds United | 1 | 1 | 0 | 0 | 4 | 0 |
| Lincoln City | 2 | 0 | 1 | 1 | 1 | 4 |
| Liverpool | 2 | 0 | 1 | 1 | 1 | 2 |
| Middlesbrough | 1 | 1 | 0 | 0 | 3 | 2 |
| Northampton Town | 3 | 1 | 1 | 1 | 3 | 3 |
| Norwich City | 1 | 1 | 0 | 0 | 2 | 0 |
| Nottingham Forest | 4 | 1 | 1 | 2 | 4 | 9 |
| Notts County | 1 | 0 | 0 | 1 | 1 | 2 |
| Orient | 1 | 0 | 0 | 1 | 0 | 2 |
| Oxford United | 2 | 0 | 1 | 1 | 2 | 4 |
| Peterborough United | 1 | 1 | 0 | 0 | 3 | 1 |
| Preston North End | 2 | 0 | 1 | 1 | 0 | 2 |
| Queen's Park Rangers | 3 | 0 | 1 | 2 | 4 | 6 |
| Rochdale | 6 | 4 | 0 | 2 | 10 | 7 |
| Rotherham United | 4 | 3 | 1 | 0 | 7 | 2 |
| Sheffield Wednesday | 4 | 1 | 1 | 2 | 6 | 8 |
| Shrewsbury Town | 2 | 1 | 1 | 0 | 4 | 3 |
| Southport | 2 | 1 | 1 | 0 | 4 | 2 |
| Stockport County | 3 | 2 | 0 | 1 | 5 | 3 |
| Stoke City | 2 | 1 | 1 | 0 | 2 | 1 |
| Sunderland | 1 | 0 | 0 | 1 | 2 | 3 |
| Swansea Town | 1 | 1 | 0 | 0 | 2 | 1 |
| Swindon Town | 1 | 0 | 0 | 1 | 0 | 1 |
| Tottenham Hotspur | 3 | 0 | 1 | 2 | 1 | 3 |
| Watford | 1 | 1 | 0 | 0 | 6 | 1 |
| Wigan Athletic | 2 | 2 | 0 | 0 | 5 | 1 |
| Wimbledon | 2 | 1 | 0 | 1 | 2 | 6 |
| Workington | 3 | 1 | 1 | 1 | 3 | 5 |
| Wrexham | 2 | 0 | 1 | 1 | 2 | 4 |
| York City | 2 | 2 | 0 | 0 | 5 | 1 |

## FORBES, George P.
Centre-forward. 1937-1946.
*5ft 11½in; 11st 13lb.*
Born: Cheadle, 21 July 1914.
Debut: v Newcastle United (h) 30 January 1937.
Career: Hyde United; Blackburn Rovers January 1937; Barrow June 1946. Retired 1951.
**Appearances:** Football League 2; FA Cup 1; Total 3.
**Goals:** Football League 1.
George Forbes made his debut on a snow covered and frozen Ewood Park surface after very little experience with the Central League team. Although he headed the fourth Blackburn goal in a 6-1 victory, his inexperience enabled the visiting defenders to generally keep a tight reign on him. A lack of speed was his major flaw and after making a second appearance, in March 1937, he returned to the Central League team. During the Second World War he was converted into a full-back and made 155 appearances for the club in wartime football. During the summer of 1946 he was transferred to Barrow and went on to appear in 177 games for the club.

## FORBES, John
Left-back. 1888-1894.
*5ft 8in; 10st 10lb.*
Born: Bonhill, Dunbartonshire, 13 January 1862; Died: Blackburn, 31 January 1928.
Debut: v Aston Villa (a) 13 October 1888.

Career: Star of Leven FC; Vale of Leven 1879; Blackburn Rovers August 1889, retired 1894.
Domestic honours with Blackburn Rovers: FA Cup winners: 1890; 1891.
**Appearances:** Football League 106; FA Cup 20; Total 126.
**Goals:** Football League 1; FA Cup 1; Total 2.
John Forbes was a cultured full-back who relied on speed rather than power to overcome opponents. He came to Blackburn from his native Scotland in August 1889 and had a major influence on Blackburn Rovers as both player and director. This dual role was nothing new to Forbes as he had been both player and shareholder whilst with Vale of Leven. Forbes had enjoyed great success in Scotland and had appeared in the 1883 and 1885 Scottish Cup Finals. Shortly after his move to Blackburn he was invited to join the committee which guided the club's affairs.

On the field he led the Rovers to two successive Cup Final victories, in 1892 and 1893, before ill health forced him into premature retirement. Fortunately, Forbes was well prepared for life away from the football field. Shortly after his arrival in the town he had set up a gentlemen's outfitters which continued to prosper until its closure in 1973. Forbes retained his association with Blackburn Rovers after retirement by accepting a seat on the board of directors. He remained on the board until his death and was later followed into the boardroom by both his brother and nephew.

## FOREIGN PLAYERS
Blackburn Rovers introduced a foreign-born player to their team in March 1949 with the signing of Bob Priday from Liverpool. South African born Priday had played in South African football before joining Liverpool in December 1945. The relegation campaign of 1965-66 saw the Rovers field John Roberts, an Australian international goalkeeper, in three end of season matches. Although Roberts remained to play Central League football at Ewood Park, these were his only first-team appearances. The first Scandinavian player to appear in the first team at Ewood Park was Preben Arentoft, a Danish international signed from Newcastle United in September 1971.

Don Mackay was the first manager to really explore foreign fields as a possible source of players. However, although a number were brought to Ewood Park on a trial basis, Mackay failed to find anyone who he felt would readily adapt to English conditions. In March 1988 he brought Ossie Ardíles, the Argentinian international, to Ewood Park on loan to aid what was to prove an unsuccessful push for promotion. The 1990-91 season saw Mackay play Claus Reitmaier, a triallist German 'keeper from Wiener SC of Austria, in the first-round tie of the Zenith Data Systems Cup. Everton won 4-1 at Ewood Park and Mackay allowed Reitmaier to return to Austria as the £200,000 transfer fee was outside his price range.

South-African born Roy Wegerle joined the Rovers from Queen's Park Rangers in March 1992. Wegerle, who was qualified through marriage to play for the United States of America, made his international debut whilst with the Rovers. Two more Scandinavians arrived at Ewood Park during the 1992-93 season.

Patrik Andersson was a Swedish international who joined the club from Malmö whilst Norwegian international Henning Berg came from Lillestrøm. Although Berg became the regular right-back during 1993-94, Andersson was unable to settle in English football and was transferred to Borussia Mönchengladbach in November 1993.

## FORREST, James Henry
Left-half. 1883-1895.
*5ft 7in; 10st 4lb.*
*Born: Blackburn, 24 June 1864; Died: Blackburn, 30 December 1925.*
*Debut: v Southport (h) 20 November 1883 (FAC).*
*Career: Imperial United; King's Own 1879; Witton 1880; Blackburn Rovers January 1883; Darwen 12 October 1895.*
*International honours with Blackburn Rovers: England: 11 caps (1884-90).*
*Domestic honours with Blackburn Rovers: FA Cup winners: 1884; 1885; 1886; 1890; 1891.*
**Appearances:** Football League 148; FA Cup 47; Total 195.
**Goals:** Football League 2; FA Cup 5; Total 7.
Jimmy Forrest holds a unique position in the history of Blackburn Rovers in that he remains the only man to have won five FA Cup winners' medals with the club. Forrest was a man of rare and remarkable talents. He made his first-team debut in a friendly encounter with Wednesbury Old Athletic in January 1883 and such was his progress that in 1884 he was capped by England. A tape sizer in the cotton trade, Forrest was a tireless left-half who combined rugged defending with excellent distribution. His passing ability was such that he became the key playmaker in the Rovers team.

Although primarily a wing-half, Forrest was versatile enough to turn out at full-back and centre-half and be equally effective. His defensive role was aided by his intelligent reading of the game. In an age when brawn often overcame brain, Forrest was able to use his positional sense

to enable him to intercept the ball rather than having to rely on tackling.

A contemporary writer said of him: 'Though rather light, had no superior; kicks with great precision, very quick in dodging and turning; a clever player.' Forrest became one of the early professional players and recalled in later life how professionals had been treated when playing with amateurs.

In 1886, Forrest had to play against Scotland in a much tighter shirt than his amateur colleagues to distinguish him as a professional player. Whilst with the Rovers he was reported to have been paid £1 a match and in 1890 a benefit raised a further £100 for the player. In October 1895, Forrest left the Rovers after a bitter dispute over his pay. Forrest claimed that the committee wanted him to ask to be reinstated as an amateur so that they could retain his services without a fixed wage.

The committee denied this and claimed that Forrest was unhappy about being asked to play for the second team. The result of the dispute was that Forrest left for Darwen and stated that his new club were prepared to pay him more than he had ever earned at Blackburn. In 1906 the rift between Forrest and Blackburn Rovers was healed when he was invited to join the board of directors. He remained a valuable member of the board until his death in December 1925.

### FORREST, James Henry
Half-back/Full-back. 1920-1927.
*5ft 7in; 11st 2lb.*
*Born: Blackburn, 28 October 1895.*
*Debut: v Burnley (h) 4 February 1922.*
*Career: Tramways; Blackburn Rovers May 1920 to 1927.*
**Appearances:** Football League 16; FA Cup 2; Total 18.
Forrest was versatile enough to play a fair game in any position, yet failed to win a regular spot in the team. The son of the former Rovers and England international, Forrest came to Ewood whilst his father was still a member of the board. He began as a hard-working half-back but his game improved once he was moved to the full-back position. However, throughout his time at Ewood he was destined to fill the role of understudy.

### FOUNDING
Blackburn Rovers was born in the heart of industrial Lancashire in 1875. The club, whose image is inextricably rooted in the smoking chimneys of the town's cotton mills and the rows of cobbled terraced streets, was the brainchild of two former public schoolboys. John Lewis and Arthur Constantine called a meeting at the St Leger Hotel in King William Street, Blackburn with a view to forming a football club. The 17 men who attended the meeting were, in the main, from the commercial strata of Blackburn society. Lewis accepted the position of treasurer whilst Walter Duckworth, a former pupil at Clitheroe Grammar School, became secretary.

The position of captain went to Thomas Greenwood, one of five brothers who played an important part in the success of the game in the Blackburn district. Thomas remained captain until the end of the 1878-79 season whilst two other brothers, Harry and Doctor Haydock, also

appeared with the Rovers. The early teams fielded by Blackburn Rovers included other men who, like the Greenwoods, came from the town's leading commercial families.

Other early players who were equally 'well connected' included Arthur Thomas, brother-in-law of Thomas Greenwood, who had a brother who was an alderman of Blackburn whilst A.L.Birch was the son of the Vicar of Blackburn. J.T.Sycelmore was a regular with the first team and a master at the Grammar School. In January 1878, A.N.Hornby, a member of one of the town's foremost mill-owning families, made his debut for the club against Partick Thistle.

The background of its early players goes some way to explaining why Blackburn Rovers would emerge from the myriad of small clubs to become a major power in the game. The involvement of so many of Blackburn's prominent families meant that the Rovers gained the support of many of the town's leading commercial figures. However, the fact that so many of the players came from a 'middle' class background meant that they were often physically stronger than local opponents, who were often made up of millworkers, who played their football after work.

The first season produced an income of £2 8s 0d, which was made up entirely from subscriptions. At this stage the club did not have a ground of their own and as a result there were no ground receipts. None the less, John Lewis was able to balance the books as the only outlay was 15 shillings which was spent on the only football the club possessed.

### FOWLER, Martin
Midfield. 1978-1980.
*5ft 11in; 12st 10lb.*
*Born: York, 17 January 1957.*
*Debut: v Crystal Palace (h) 19 August 1978.*
*Career: Huddersfield Town apprentice April 1972, turning professional on January 1974; Blackburn Rovers June 1978; Hartlepools United March 1980 to May 1980; Stockport County August 1980; Scunthorpe United September 1980 March 1983.*
**Appearances:** Football League 36+2; FA Cup 1; Football League Cup 3; Total 40+2.
A hard working midfield player who could also fill in at right back. Fowler was signed by Jim Iley and given a berth in midfield ahead of Stuart Metcalfe at the start of the 1979-80 season. Although Fowler retained a place in the team for most of the season he did little to suggest that he could prevent the club from sliding into the Third Division. The arrival of Howard Kendall in the role of player-manager closed the first-team door on Fowler and in March 1980 he joined Hartlepools United.

### FOX, William
Chairman. 1982-1991.
Bill Fox had been a supporter of Blackburn Rovers since 1938. On leaving grammar school in 1943 he joined the family business of fruit and vegetable wholesalers. He was elected to the board of directors at Ewood Park in June 1976 and three years later he was made vice-chairman. In April 1982 he was appointed chairman of the club he had supported since boyhood. Fox inherited the chairmanship at a time when financial pressures threatened to send the Rovers into the same downward spiral that had been experienced at neighbouring clubs.

However, with prudent management, which did not always make him popular with supporters, Fox was able to steer the club through troubled financial waters. In 1986 Fox followed in the footsteps of two former Blackburn directors, John Lewis and Walter Tempest, in being elected to the League Management Committee. In August 1989 he became president of the Football League.

However, Fox was to be thwarted in his attempts to install Gordon Taylor as chief executive of the Football League. Having played a major part in preventing the break-up of the Football League in the late 1980s, it fell to Fox to oversee the restructuring of the Football League following the establishment of the FA Premier League.

Whilst his style of running the club did not meet with universal approval, Fox built the platform which enabled Jack Walker to take the club into a different dimension. Sadly, Fox did not live long enough to see the ultimate goal of promotion achieved. The man who had witnessed so many promotion near misses, died after a short illness on 8 December 1991.

### FRANCE, Herbert
Centre-forward. 1906-1907.
*Debut: v Preston North End (h) 13 April 1906.*
*Career: Hooley Hill; Earlestown; Blackburn Rovers March 1906; St Helens Recreation; Earlestown cs 1908; Hurst 1910.*
**Appearances:** Football League 4.
Herbert France came to Blackburn with Thomas Cunliffe, a playing colleague at Earlestown. Both men had impressed Blackburn officials whilst playing for the Lancashire Combination club and both were given their first-team debuts in the Good Friday derby with Preston North End

in April 19(•5. Although on the small side, France was a hard-working player and of the two he made the most favourable impression. Yet in truth neither man was of First Division standard and France quickly returned to Lancashire Combination football.

## FRASER, Nathan James
Inside-right. 1935-1937.
*6ft 0½in; 11st 9lb.*
*Born: Glasgow.*
*Debut: v Accrington Stanley (h) 16 January 1937 (FAC).*
*Career: Glasgow Ashfield; Dumbarton; Blackburn Rovers October 1935; Wrexham June 1937; Tranmere Rovers October 1938 to December 1938.*
**Appearances:** FA Cup 1.
**Goals:** FA Cup 1.
Fraser had the misfortune to make his debut for the club on the day that Accrington Stanley came to Ewood Park and almost pulled off a major shock in the FA Cup. In fact it was the tall Fraser who grabbed the goal, with a near post header, that kept the Rovers in the competition for a few days more. However despite helping the Rovers snatch a 2-2 draw, Fraser lacked the pace to trouble the Stanley defence and he didn't appear in the replay. Whilst he may have considered it a blessing in disguise to miss the humiliating 3-1 defeat at Peel Park, Fraser was in fact destined never to reappear in the senior team at Ewood Park.

## FRYATT, James Edward
Centre-forward. 1968-1970.
*6ft; 12st.*
*Born: Swaythling, nr Southampton, 2 September 1940.*
*Debut: v Bury (a) 19 October 1968.*
*Career: Moor End Youth Club, Southampton; Charlton Athletic part-time October 1957, turning professional in September 1958; Southend United June 1960 (£600); Bradford June 1963 (£2,500); Southport March 1966 (£4,000); Torquay United March 1967 (£5,000); Stockport County October 1967 (£7,000); Blackburn Rovers October 1968 (£24,000); Oldham Athletic February 1970 (£8,000); Southport November 1971; Philadelphia Atoms (USA) cs 1973 to August 1973 and cs 1974 until August 1974; Stockport County September 1974; Torquay United December 1974 monthly contract; Chorley January to March 1975; Hartford Bi-Centennials (USA) April to June 1975; Philadelphia Atoms (USA) July to August 1975; Las Vegas Quicksilver 1977 assistant manager and then manager.*
**Appearances:** Football League 29+8; FA Cup 4; Total 33+8.
**Goals:** Football League 5; FA Cup 3; Total 8.
At first glance the moustachioed, mutton chop whiskered Fryatt could well have been mistaken for a character from a Dickensian novel. In reality Jimmy Fryatt was a much sought after goalscorer who retired from English football with a record of 189 League goals in 598 appearances (including ten as sub). Although he possessed a fierce shot with either foot, it was in the air that the heavily built Fryatt was at his most dangerous. Despite his build, Fryatt had the ability to hang in the air and yet still head the ball with tremendous power. His reputation as a regular marksman, albeit in the lower spheres, persuaded Eddie Quigley that he was the man to score the goals that would take the Rovers out of the Second Division. Sadly, although he created a number of chances with his heading ability, Fryatt found goals in short supply at a higher level. After leaving Ewood Park, Fryatt enjoyed great success at Oldham and Southport before trying his luck in the North American Soccer League. He scored 17 goals in 50 matches in America and later settled there to become a croupier in Las Vegas.

## FULHAM FC
Founded in 1879 as St Andrew's Sunday School, West Kensington. The club became known as Fulham St Andrew's because of the location of the ground. Fulham entered the Second Division of the Football League in 1907 but first met Blackburn Rovers in competitive football in the 1920-21 FA Cup. Relegation to the Second Division in 1936 brought the Rovers in direct competition with Fulham in the Football League.

### Football League

| | | | Home | | Away |
|---|---|---|---|---|---|
| 1936-37 | (Div 2) | L | 0-2 | D | 1-1 |
| 1937-38 | (Div 2) | D | 2-2 | L | 1-3 |
| 1938-39 | (Div 2) | W | 2-1 | W | 3-2 |
| 1948-49 | (Div 2) | W | 1-0 | D | 1-1 |
| 1952-53 | (Div 2) | D | 2-2 | L | 1-2 |
| 1953-54 | (Div 2) | W | 5-1 | W | 3-2 |
| 1954-55 | (Div 2) | W | 3-1 | L | 1-5 |
| 1955-56 | (Div 2) | W | 1-0 | L | 0-3 |
| 1956-57 | (Div 2) | W | 2-0 | L | 2-7 |
| 1957-58 | (Div 2) | D | 1-1 | D | 1-1 |
| 1959-60 | (Div 1) | W | 4-0 | W | 1-0 |
| 1960-61 | (Div 1) | W | 5-1 | D | 1-1 |
| 1961-62 | (Div 1) | L | 0-2 | L | 0-2 |
| 1962-63 | (Div 1) | L | 0-1 | D | 0-0 |
| 1963-64 | (Div 1) | W | 2-0 | D | 1-1 |
| 1964-65 | (Div 1) | W | 2-0 | L | 2-3 |
| 1965-66 | (Div 1) | W | 3-2 | L | 2-5 |
| 1968-69 | (Div 2) | D | 2-2 | D | 1-1 |
| 1975-76 | (Div 2) | L | 0-1 | D | 1-1 |
| 1976-77 | (Div 2) | W | 1-0 | L | 0-2 |
| 1977-78 | (Div 2) | W | 4-0 | D | 0-0 |
| 1978-79 | (Div 2) | W | 2-1 | W | 2-1 |
| 1982-83 | (Div 2) | D | 0-0 | L | 1-3 |
| 1983-84 | (Div 2) | L | 0-1 | W | 1-0 |
| 1984-85 | (Div 2) | W | 2-1 | L | 2-3 |
| 1985-86 | (Div 2) | W | 1-0 | D | 3-3 |

| | P | W | D | L | F | A |
|---|---|---|---|---|---|---|
| Home | 26 | 16 | 5 | 5 | 47 | 22 |
| Away | 26 | 5 | 10 | 11 | 32 | 53 |
| Total | 52 | 21 | 15 | 16 | 79 | 75 |

### FA Cup

| | | | | |
|---|---|---|---|---|
| 1920-21 | (1) | Home | D | 1-1 |
| | (R) | Away | L | 0-1 |
| 1961-62 | (6) | Away | D | 2-2 |
| | (R) | Home | L | 0-1 |
| 1963-64 | (4) | Home | W | 2-0 |
| 1979-80 | (3) | Home | D | 1-1 |
| | (R) | Away | W | 1-0 |

## FULL MEMBERS' CUP
This was a knock-out competition involving First and Second Division clubs which was introduced in the wake of the ban on English clubs from European competitions. Although a trip to Wembley was the reward for the two Finalists the first year of the competition,1985-86, saw only 21 of the 44 Full Members of the Football League enter the competition. Blackburn Rovers did not participate in the inaugural competition but took part the following season when every Second Division club entered the event.
It proved to be a wise decision as they went on to lift the trophy at Wembley on Sunday 28 March 1987 following a narrow 1-0 victory over Charlton Athletic. The 1986-87 season saw the competition attract sponsorship from Simod and from 1989-90 the competition became known as the Zenith Data Systems Cup. The 1991-92 competition proved to be the last as the break up of the Football League and formation of the Premier League brought about its demise. After their initial success the Rovers made very little progress in the competition. Although they reached the Third Round in 1988-89, their other four attempt at reclaiming the trophy ended at the first hurdle. Although Wembley caught the imagination of the Blackburn public the early rounds of the competition attracted very little support.

### Full Members' Cup

| | | | | | |
|---|---|---|---|---|---|
| 1986-87 | (1) | Huddersfield Town | Away | W | 2-1* |
| | (2) | Sheffield United | Home | W | 1-0 |
| | (3) | Oxford United | Home | W | 4-3 |
| | (4) | Chelsea | Home | W | 3-0 |
| | (SF) | Ipswich Town | Home | W | 3-0 |
| | (F) | Charlton Athletic | Wembley | W | 1-0 |

*After Extra-time

### Simod Cup

| | | | | | |
|---|---|---|---|---|---|
| 1987-88 | (1) | Swindon Town | Home | L | 1-2 |
| 1988-89 | (1) | Manchester City | Home | W | 3-2* |
| | (2) | Sunderland | Home | W | 2-1 |
| | (3) | Ipswich Town | Away | L | 0-1 |

*After extra-time

### Zenith Data Systems Cup

| | | | | | |
|---|---|---|---|---|---|
| 1989-90 | (1) | Leeds United | Away | L | 0-1 |
| 1990-91 | (1) | Everton | Home | L | 1-4 |
| 1991-92 | (1) | Port Vale | Away | L | 0-1 |

## FULL MEMBERS' CUP FINAL 1987
If the early rounds of the Full Members' Cup competition had been greeted with indifference by the public of Blackburn, the same could not be said of the Final. The match itself was largely forgettable but it would be impossible to over-estimate the importance of the occasion to Blackburn Rovers. On Sunday, 28 March 1987, almost 30,000 Lancastrians travelled south on a journey that would finally lay to rest the

The jubilant team set off on their lap of honour after winning the Full Members' Cup against Charlton Athletic in 1987. From left to right are Ian Miller, Chris Price, Simon Garner, Simon Barker, Glenn Keeley, Vince O'Keefe and Alan Ainscow.

spectre of the 1960 FA Cup Final. Whilst Charlton Athletic were battling against relegation from the First Division, the Rovers themselves had suffered a hugely disappointing season. Having been anchored to the foot of the Second Division the club had dispensed with Bobby Saxton in December and appointed Don Mackay as his replacement.

The new manager had lifted the club out of the relegation zone and seen his new team reach Wembley for the first time since 1960. As a spectacle the game was largely a non-event. In truth, Charlton had the better chances but failed to capitalise on the opportunities they created. The Blackburn fans had Vince O'Keefe to thank for keeping the Charlton forwards at bay. O'Keefe, the Rovers' number-two 'keeper, had never enjoyed the same popularity as Terry Gennoe but on this occasion a string of fine saves made him an instant hero.

The game remained deadlock for 85 minutes and appeared to be drifting towards extra-time. The whole scenario changed when Alan Ainscow worked the ball out to Ian Miller on the right wing. The veteran winger finally found himself in a one-on-one situation with his opponent and made full use of the situation. With one touch he had caught the Charlton defender flat footed and was flying towards the Charlton penalty area. His perfect cross to the far side of the area tempted Bolder off his line in an attempt to intercept it. Although Bolder stretched he found he could only get his fingertips to the ball with the result that it fell invitingly at the feet of Colin Hendry. The blond striker wasted no time in sending a superb angled shot off the inside of the near post and into the net. It was a moment which sent 30,000 Blackburn supporters into ecstasy.

The final whistle brought incredible scenes of joy for Rovers' long-suffering fans. The trophy was presented to Glenn Keeley who made his only mistake of the day and promptly dropped it. However, nothing could disguise the joy of the 30,000 fans who stood and cheered as the players danced around Wembley. On the Monday evening the team returned in triumph to the town and were given an ecstatic welcome by the thousands who had gathered in the town centre. The team were given a civic reception and for a brief moment the burden of past glories was finally lifted. The Full Members' Cup may have been considered a second-rate competition to some, but 30,000 Blackburn Rovers fans know differently.

**Blackburn Rovers**: O'Keefe; Price, Sulley, Barker, Keeley, Mail, Miller, Ainscow, Hendry, Garner, Sellars. Subs: Patterson (for Sellars), Branagan (not used).

**Charlton Athletic**: Bolder; Humphrey, Reid, Peake, Thompson, Miller, Milne, Lee, Melrose, Walsh, Shipley. Subs: Gritt, Shirtcliff (not used).

Referee: Mr B.T.Stevens (Stonehouse, Glos).

*Attendance: 43,789*

### FURNELL, James

Reserve-team manager 1981-1991.

Youth-team manager 1981-

*Born: Clitheroe, 23 November 1937.*

*Career: Burnley November 1954; Liverpool February 1962 (£18,000); Arsenal November 1963 (£15,000); Rotherham United September 1968 (£9,000); Plymouth Argyle December 1970, retired May 1976 and joined the staff. Exeter City chief scout; Plymouth Argyle reserve-team manager 1979; Blackburn Rovers reserve & youth-team manager cs 1981, concentrating solely on youth development from June 1991.*

Jim Furnell came to Ewood Park during the summer of 1981 to continue his long association with Bobby Saxton. The two had been members of the Plymouth Argyle side which had accompanied Rovers out of the Third Division in 1975.

Furnell, a goalkeeper, appeared in 430 League games with his various clubs before hanging up his gloves and becoming a member of the staff at Home Park. When Saxton began his managerial career at Exeter City he appointed Furnell as his chief scout. In January 1979, Saxton returned to Home Park as manager and Furnell followed to take charge of the reserve team.

At Ewood Park, Furnell took charge of the Central League and was also responsible for overseeing youth development. With the club in serious financial difficulties, youth development was of vital importance to the club. The early 1980s saw Simon Barker and Mark Patterson graduate from the junior ranks to become regular first-team players. Under the guidance of Furnell, a series of home grown products like Keith Hill, Tony Diamond, Lenny Johnrose and Craig Skinner found their way into the first team. Whilst these were all sold on to other clubs, Jason Wilcox and David May remained to establish themselves in

Premier League football to underline the importance a sound youth development policy.

## FURPHY, Kenneth
Manager. 1971-1973.
*Born: Stockton, 28 May 1931.*
*Career: Everton November 1951; Runcorn December 1951; Darlington August 1953 becoming player-youth-team coach in the late 1950s; Workington player-manager July 1962; Watford player-manager November 1964; Blackburn Rovers manager July 1971; Sheffield United manager December 1973 until October 1975; New Year Cosmos coach January 1976; Detroit Express coach 1978 to 1980; Washington Diplomats coach 1981.*

The arrival of Ken Furphy in July 1971 proved a major watershed in the history of Blackburn Rovers. It was a signal for a change of direction for a club which had, perhaps, for too long dwelt on memories of a more glorious past. If Furphy was to fail in his ultimate goal of lifting the club from the Third Division, there can be no doubting that it was he who laid the foundations for future success. An FA Staff coach, Furphy was a young track suit manager who had proved himself capable of managing on a shoestring budget. A playing career in the lower divisions had

equipped him with the necessary experience for coping with limited resources and Furphy had shown himself capable of achieving success with very little at his disposal. As player-manager at Workington he had guided the club into the Third Division and in 1964 had caused one of the most embarrassing moments in the history of Blackburn Rovers.

It was Furphy who led Workington, of the Fourth Division, to Ewood Park for a third round League Cup replay against First Division Rovers. In a competition which has brought a number of embarrassments to the club, the 5-1 home defeat by Workington remains the biggest. Shortly afterwards he moved to Watford and steered them into the Second Division and a

semi-final appearance in the 1970 FA Cup competition. With little money available, Furphy had to wheel and deal at Ewood to rebuild a side that looked like dropping straight through the Third Division. The months of September and October 1971 brought a procession of comings and goings from Ewood Park the like of which the club had never seen before. The result was that the club was able to consolidate its position in the Third Division and the following season enjoyed a record breaking run of 19 League games without defeat.

Although Furphy had not been able to deliver a promotion place, his work had not gone unnoticed elsewhere. In November 1973 he was offered the vacant managership of Sheffield United. The Rovers offered to match any salary that Sheffield could offer but the lure of the First Division proved too strong.

Furphy was not long in returning to Ewood Park to take Terry Garbett, Tony Field and David Bradford to Bramall Lane. Ironically, at a time when the Rovers were about to embark on their most successful period for many years, Furphy's own career was on the wane. A string of poor results at Bramall Lane brought the sack in October 1975 and the following year he joined the growing exodus to the North American Soccer League. As coach to New York Cosmos he was able to field a team which included Garbett and Field as well as the legendary Pelé and Chinaglia. He returned to England in the early 1980s and became involved in radio work in the south-west of England, often commentating on Blackburn matches played in that area.

## GALLACHER, Bernard
Left-back. 1990.
*5ft 9in; 11st.*
*Born: Johnstone, 22 March 1967.*
*Debut: v West Bromwich Albion (a) 17 November 1990.*
*Career: Aston Villa apprentice August 1983, turning professional on April 1985; Blackburn Rovers on loan 1990; Doncaster Rovers non-contract player September 1991 to October 1991; Brighton & Hove Albion non-contract player October 1991 before signing a contract in December 1991.*
**Appearances:** Football League 4.
Don Mackay had tracked Bernard Gallacher for some time before bringing him to Ewood Park on loan. Originally an outside-left, Gallacher

was unfortunate to suffer a number of injuries. As his form began to dip, Gallacher lost his place in the Villa line-up. Unfortunately, a move to Ewood Park did little to boost his confidence and a proposed deal between the clubs collapsed. After leaving Blackburn his career went into decline until Brighton came to his rescue.

## GALLACHER, Kevin William
Forward. 1993-
*5ft 7in; 9st 11lb.*
*Born: Clydebank, 23 November 1966.*
*Debut: v Liverpool (h) 3 April 1993.*
*Career: Duntocher Boys Club; Dundee United November 1983; Coventry City January 1990 (£900,000); Blackburn Rovers March 1993 (£1,500,000).*
*International honours with Blackburn Rovers: Scotland: 5 caps (1993).*

**Appearances:** Football League 36+3; FA Cup 4; Football League Cup 4; Total 44+3.
**Goals:** Football League 12; FA Cup 1; Total 13.

A winger cum striker of great pace, Kevin Gallacher came to Ewood Park in a deal which saw Coventry City receive Roy Wegerle and one million pounds. With Alan Shearer side-lined through injury, Gallacher struck up an immediate under-standing with Mike Newell and used his space to threaten opposing defenders. His debut brought a goal in the 4-1 win over Liverpool and established him as a favourite with the crowd.

A member of a footballing family, Gallacher is the grandson of the leg-endary Patsy Gal-lacher who played for Celtic between 1911 and 1925. Kevin Gallacher began his profes-sional career with Dundee United and appeared in two Scottish Cup Finals and the 1987 UEFA

Cup Final before moving to England in 1990. Although hampered by injuries at Coventry, Gallacher was able to resurrect his international career. Kenny Dalglish made a surprise move to bring Gallacher to Ewood Park just before the transfer deadline in March 1993.

His five goals in nine appearances helped the Rovers to claim 21 points and finish in fourth place. The return of Alan Shearer in 1993-94 saw Gallacher moved to play in the left-wing position that he had occupied at Coventry. However, an injury to Mike Newell allowed Gallacher to form a strike partnership with Shearer and underline his value to the team as a versatile front runner. Tragically, Gallacher's season came to a premature end when he suffered a triple fracture of the right leg in a freak accident at Highbury in February 1994.

## GALLACHER, Patrick
Inside-forward. 1936-1938.
*Born: Glasgow, 9 January 1913; Died; Hastings, June 1983.*
*Debut: v Fulham (h) 17 October 1936.*
*Career: Dunoon Athletic; Millwall November 1933; Third Lanark 1934; Blackburn Rovers October 1936 (£1,250); Bournemouth & Boscombe Athletic June 1938; Weymouth player-manager June 1948.*

**Appearances:** Football League 11.

Patrick Gallacher came to Ewood Park with a reputation for being something of an entertainer. Gallacher was in the typically Scottish mould of tricky individualist. When he joined the Rovers in October 1936, it was stated that he had a tendency to be over individualistic and than this was his major weakness. Sadly, Gallacher could not master the need for the discerning pass, and despite his undoubted skill, he failed to make much impact at Blackburn.

## GARBETT, Terence Graham
Midfield. 1971-1974.
*5ft 9in; 11st 12lb.*
*Born: Lanchester, Durham, 9 September 1945.*
*Debut: v Bolton Wanderers (h) 11 September 1971.*
*Career: Pelton Fell; Middlesbrough August 1963; Watford August 1966; Blackburn Rovers September 1971 (£16,000); Sheffield United February 1974 (£30,000); New York Cosmos (USA) April 1976 to 1979.*
**Appearances:** Football League 90; FA Cup 9; Football League Cup 4; Total 103.
**Goals:** Football League 6; FA Cup 1; Total 7.

Having assessed the playing staff at Blackburn, new manager Ken Furphy wasted no time in returning to his former club to sign Terry Garbett. Garbett was an attacking midfield player who had scored 46 goals in 200 (including four as sub) League appearances with the Vicarage Road club. Garbett provided Furphy with the experience he required to enable him to use untried youngsters like Gerry McDonald and David Bradford in midfield. Garbett overcame a cartilage operation in 1972-73 to become a commanding figure at the heart of the Rovers team. In December 1973, Furphy moved to Sheffield United and such was his regard for Garbett that he returned to Blackburn to take his former skipper to the First Division club. Garbett, didn't enjoy the best of fortunes at Bramall Lane and after 31 (including five as sub) appearances followed Furphy to the North American Soccer League.

## GARBUTT, William
Outside-right. 1908-1912.
*Born: Stockport.*
*Debut: v Bristol City (h) 1 September 1908.*
*Career: Royal Artillery; Reading; Woolwich Arsenal December 1905; Blackburn Rovers May 1908; Genoa trainer-coach May 1912 until 1927; then coaching spells with AS Roma 1927; Napoli 1929; Athletic Bilbao 1935; Genoa 1946.*
*International honours with Blackburn Rovers: Football League: 1 appearance (1910).*
*Domestic honours with Blackburn Rovers: Football League championship: 1911-12 (1 app).*
**Appearances:** Football League 81; FA Cup 4; Total 85.
**Goals:** Football League 10.

Billy Garbutt was a typically tricky winger whose adept dribbling and accurate centres created numerous goals for Blackburn Rovers. He made his debut at the start of the 1908-09 season and for the next two and a half seasons was regarded as the first-choice outside-right. He eventually lost his place following the signing of Jock Simpson and made only one appearance during the successful championship campaign of 1911-12. In May 1912 he moved to Italy to become trainer-coach with Genoa and under his influence the club won the Italian championship in 1914-15. He stayed in Italy until the mid-1930s when he moved to Spain. He returned to Italy during World War Two and was interned for a time. On his release he evaded the Fascists by living under an assumed Italian name in the mountains where sadly, he lost his wife during a British air raid. He returned to coach in Genoa but lost a leg in a motor accident and eventually returned to England.

## GARNER, Simon
Striker. 1976-1992.
*5ft 9in; 11st 12lb.*
*Born: Boston, 23 November 1959.*
*Debut: v Exeter City (a) 29 August 1978 (FLC).*
*Career: Boston United; Blackburn Rovers apprentice August 1976, turning professional in July 1978; West Bromwich Albion August 1992 (£30,000); Wycombe Wanderers February 1994 (free).*
*Domestic honours with Blackburn Rovers: Full Members' Cup winners: 1987.*

The second goal of Simon Garner's hat-trick against Manchester City on 15 April 1989, ensured his own niche in the history of Blackburn Rovers. As he walked off Ewood Park that day, he did so in the knowledge that he had scored more goals in the Football League than any other player in the long and illustrious history of the club. Garner broke into the first

team at a time when the club were struggling for Second Division survival. Initially used in midfield, Garner was given the centre-forward position by Howard Kendall during the successful promotion campaign of 1979-80.

Ironically, it had been during the reign of Howard Kendall that the Rovers had almost sold Garner to Halifax Town for £40,000. Fortunately, a move to the Shay held little appeal to Garner and he opted to fight for a place at Ewood Park. It was under the managership of Bobby Saxton that Garner began to flourish as a prolific goalscorer. His pace and power made him a real handful for most Second Division defenders. Quick to pounce on defensive errors, Garner was a master at snapping up any half chance that came his way. Throughout the 1980s he was recognised as one of the deadliest marksmen in the game and yet, strangely, no First Division club offered him a platform at the highest level.

He remained a loyal servant to Blackburn Rovers during the period when the club was continually pipped for promotion to the top flight. He was awarded a well-deserved testimonial year in 1988 and remained a constant favourite with the Ewood faithful.

Sadly, Garner was no longer a member of the first team when promotion to the Premier League was won via the Play-offs. The summer of 1992 saw him join Ossie Ardiles at West Bromwich Albion but, unfortunately, injuries restricted his appearances at the Hawthorns and in February 1994, Garner joined Wycombe Wanderers on a free transfer.

Simon Garner's Playing record with Blackburn Rovers:

|  | League | | Play-Offs | | FA Cup | | FL Cup | | FM Cup | | Total | |
|---|---|---|---|---|---|---|---|---|---|---|---|---|
|  | App | Gls | App | Gls | App | Gls | App | Gls | App | Gls | App | Gls |
| 1978-79 | 20 +5 | 8 | 0 | 0 | 2 | 0 | 1 | 0 | 0 | 0 | 23 +5 | 8 |
| 1979-80 | 25 +3 | 6 | 0 | 0 | 5 | 0 | 1 +2 | 0 | 0 | 0 | 31 +5 | 6 |
| 1980-81 | 31 +2 | 7 | 0 | 0 | 0 +1 | 0 | 5 | 1 | 0 | 0 | 36 +3 | 8 |
| 1981-82 | 35 +1 | 14 | 0 | 0 | 1 | 2 | 3 | 2 | 0 | 0 | 39 +1 | 18 |
| 1982-83 | 40 +1 | 22 | 0 | 0 | 1 | 1 | 2 | 0 | 0 | 0 | 43 +1 | 23 |
| 1983-84 | 42 | 19 | 0 | 0 | 3 | 1 | 2 | 3 | 0 | 0 | 47 | 23 |
| 1984-85 | 37 | 12 | 0 | 0 | 0 +2 | 0 | 2 | 2 | 0 | 0 | 39 +2 | 14 |
| 1985-86 | 36 +2 | 12 | 0 | 0 | 3 | 0 | 2 | 0 | 0 | 0 | 41 +2 | 12 |
| 1986-87 | 39 +1 | 10 | 0 | 0 | 1 | 0 | 4 | 1 | 6 | 4 | 50 +1 | 15 |
| 1987-88 | 40 | 14 | 2 | 0 | 1 | 1 | 2 | 0 | 0 | 0 | 45 | 15 |
| 1988-89 | 43 +1 | 20 | 4 | 2 | 3 | 1 | 4 | 2 | 2 | 0 | 56 +1 | 25 |
| 1989-90 | 42 +1 | 18 | 1 +1 | 0 | 2 | 0 | 1 | 0 | 1 | 0 | 47 +2 | 18 |
| 1990-91 | 11 +1 | 1 | 0 | 0 | 2 | 1 | 1 | 0 | 0 | 0 | 14 +1 | 2 |
| 1991-92 | 14 +11 | 5 | 0 | 0 | 0 +2 | 0 | 2 | 0 | 1 | 0 | 17 +13 | 5 |
|  | 455 +29 | 168 | 7 +1 | 2 | 24 +5 | 7 | 32 +2 | 11 | 10 | 4 | 528 +37 | 192 |

**Appearances:** Football League 3.

Although an adequate reserve, Garstang was regarded by contemporaries as rather too slow for first-team football. He figured in three successive League games in November 1890 as understudy to Tom Brandon. However, there was never any likelihood of him seriously challenging Brandon for his first-team place and he was not retained for the 1891-92 season.

Simon Garner's Goal Chart with Blackburn Rovers

| Opponents | Football League | Play-Offs | FA Cup | FL Cup | FM Cup | Total |
|---|---|---|---|---|---|---|
| Derby County | 11 | 0 | 0 | 0 | 0 | 11 |
| Barnsley | 9 | 0 | 0 | 0 | 0 | 9 |
| Crystal Palace | 7 | 1 | 0 | 0 | 0 | 8 |
| Grimsby Town | 8 | 0 | 0 | 0 | 0 | 8 |
| Oldham Athletic | 8 | 0 | 0 | 0 | 0 | 8 |
| Oxford United | 4 | 0 | 0 | 2 | 1 | 7 |
| Portsmouth | 6 | 0 | 1 | 0 | 0 | 7 |
| Carlisle United | 6 | 0 | 0 | 0 | 0 | 6 |
| Sunderland | 6 | 0 | 0 | 0 | 0 | 6 |
| Chelsea | 4 | 0 | 0 | 0 | 1 | 5 |
| Huddersfield Town | 4 | 0 | 0 | 1 | 0 | 5 |
| Sheffield United | 4 | 0 | 0 | 0 | 1 | 5 |
| Shrewsbury Town | 5 | 0 | 0 | 0 | 0 | 5 |
| Brighton & HA | 4 | 0 | 0 | 0 | 0 | 4 |
| Burnley | 4 | 0 | 0 | 0 | 0 | 4 |
| Hull City | 4 | 0 | 0 | 0 | 0 | 4 |
| Ipswich Town | 0 | 0 | 0 | 3 | 1 | 4 |
| Leicester City | 4 | 0 | 0 | 0 | 0 | 4 |
| Manchester City | 4 | 0 | 0 | 0 | 0 | 4 |
| Middlesbrough | 4 | 0 | 0 | 0 | 0 | 4 |
| Millwall | 4 | 0 | 0 | 0 | 0 | 4 |
| Plymouth Argyle | 4 | 0 | 0 | 0 | 0 | 4 |
| Sheffield Wednesday | 1 | 0 | 1 | 2 | 0 | 4 |
| Swindon Town | 3 | 0 | 1 | 0 | 0 | 4 |
| West Bromwich Albion | 2 | 0 | 2 | 0 | 0 | 4 |
| Birmingham City | 3 | 0 | 0 | 0 | 0 | 3 |
| Cambridge United | 3 | 0 | 0 | 0 | 0 | 3 |
| Cardiff City | 3 | 0 | 0 | 0 | 0 | 3 |
| Fulham | 3 | 0 | 0 | 0 | 0 | 3 |
| Leeds United | 3 | 0 | 0 | 0 | 0 | 3 |
| Luton Town | 3 | 0 | 0 | 0 | 0 | 3 |
| Norwich City | 3 | 0 | 0 | 0 | 0 | 3 |
| Rotherham United | 3 | 0 | 0 | 0 | 0 | 3 |
| Stoke City | 3 | 0 | 0 | 0 | 0 | 3 |
| Wolverhampton W. | 3 | 0 | 0 | 0 | 0 | 3 |
| AFC Bournemouth | 2 | 0 | 0 | 0 | 0 | 2 |
| Brentford | 0 | 0 | 0 | 2 | 0 | 2 |
| Liverpool | 0 | 0 | 2 | 0 | 0 | 2 |
| Notts County | 2 | 0 | 0 | 0 | 0 | 2 |
| Queen's Park Rangers | 1 | 0 | 0 | 1 | 0 | 2 |
| Watford | 1 | 1 | 0 | 0 | 0 | 2 |
| Aston Villa | 1 | 0 | 0 | 0 | 0 | 1 |
| Bradford City | 1 | 0 | 0 | 0 | 0 | 1 |
| Bury | 1 | 0 | 0 | 0 | 0 | 1 |
| Charlton Athletic | 1 | 0 | 0 | 0 | 0 | 1 |
| Chesterfield | 1 | 0 | 0 | 0 | 0 | 1 |
| Newcastle United | 1 | 0 | 0 | 0 | 0 | 1 |
| Port Vale | 1 | 0 | 0 | 0 | 0 | 1 |
| Swansea City | 1 | 0 | 0 | 0 | 0 | 1 |
| Walsall | 1 | 0 | 0 | 0 | 0 | 1 |
| West Ham United | 1 | 0 | 0 | 0 | 0 | 1 |
| Wimbledon | 1 | 0 | 0 | 0 | 0 | 1 |
| Wrexham | 1 | 0 | 0 | 0 | 0 | 1 |

**GARSTANG, Harry**

Right-back. 1890-1891.
*Debut: v Everton (h) 8 November 1890.*
*Career: Blackburn Rovers 30 August 1890.*

**GARSTANG, John**

Forward. 1897-1899.
*Born: Blackburn.*
*Debut: v Bolton Wanderers (h) 11 September 1897.*
*Career: Blackburn Etrurians; Blackburn Rovers December 1897; Chorley; Witton; Blackburn Crosshill.*
**Appearances:** Football League 4.

Garstang signed for Blackburn Rovers after helping Blackburn Etrurians to win the Lancashire Amateur Cup. He was a lively centre-forward who made his debut in the second game of the 1897-98 season. The Rovers crashed by three goals to one at home to Bolton Wanderers with the result that Garstang didn't receive another first-team call until the following season. Garstang made three appearances during the 1898-99 season before moving into local junior football. In 1904 he became a director at Ewood Park and, apart from a break of 12 months, served the club in that capacity until 1924.

**GATE, William Henry**

Outside-left. 1901-1902.
*5ft 5in; 10st.*
*Debut: v Grimsby Town (a) 12 October 1901.*
*Career: Newton Heath October 1899; Darwen cs 1900; Blackburn Rovers 14 August 1901; Southport Central 1905 to 1910; Chorley 1910-11.*
**Appearances:** Football League 4.
**Goals:** Football League 1.

An outside-left who was signed from Darwen at the start of the 1901-02 season. Gate received an early opportunity to understudy Fred Blackburn, appearing in four League games in October and November 1901. However, once Blackburn was restored to the left-wing position, Gate had to be content with second-team football.

**GAYLE, Howard A.**

Outside-right/Centre-forward. 1987-1992.
*5ft 10in; 10st 9lb.*
*Born: Liverpool, 18 May 1958.*
*Debut: v Hull City (a) 15 August 1987.*
*Career: Liverpool apprentice June 1974, turning professional in November 1977; Fulham on loan January 1980; Newcastle United on loan November 1982; Birmingham City on loan January 1983; Birmingham City June 1983; Sunderland August 1984 (£75,000); Dallas Sidekicks (USA) summer 1986; Stoke City March 1987; Blackburn Rovers August 1987 (£5,000) to May 1992; Halifax Town September 1992; Carlisle United trial October 1992; Accrington Stanley September 1993.*
**Appearances:** Football League 97+19; Play-offs 8; FA Cup 5+2; Football League Cup 6+3; Full Members' Cup 3+1; Total 119+25.
**Goals:** Football League 29; Play-offs 3; Football League Cup 1; Full Members' Cup 1; Total 34.

Howard Gayle acquired almost cult status amongst a section of the Blackburn crowd during his time at Ewood Park. The first coloured player to win a regular first-team place at Ewood, the nomadic Gayle enjoyed the best spell of his career with Blackburn Rovers. Gayle had begun his career on his native Merseyside with Liverpool but was unable to break into the first team. His subsequent career took him to a number of clubs and he gained a reputation for being difficult to handle.

He faced an uncertain future when Don Mackay threw him a lifeline to resurrect his career with the Rovers. His prospects looked even bleaker when injuries severely restricted his appearances during the 1987-88 season. However, Mackay persevered with him and the following season saw Gayle form a prolific goalscoring partnership with Simon Garner. Gayle scored 19 goals in 45 League outings and helped take the Rovers to the brink of the First Division with two goals in the home leg of the Play-off final with Crystal Palace. Gayle continued to give good service to the club until a series of injuries again began to restrict his appearances. The arrival of Kenny Dalglish and a number of big signings brought an end of his Ewood career and he was given a free transfer as the 1991-92 season drew to a close.

### GENNOE, Terence William
Goalkeeper. 1981-1992.
*6ft 2in; 13st 3lb.*
*Born: Shrewsbury, 16 March 1953.*
*Debut: v Sheffield Wednesday (h) 29 August 1981.*
*Career: Meole Brace Junior School; The Wakeman School; Bricklayers Sports, Shrewsbury; Bury May 1973; Blackburn Rovers on loan March 1974; Leeds United on loan March 1975 to April 1975; Halifax Town May 1975 (£3,000); Southampton February 1978 (£35,000); Everton on loan September 1980 to October 1980; Crystal Palace on loan January 1981 to February 1981; Blackburn Rovers August 1981 (£60,000), retired in May 1992 to become the club's Education Officer and goalkeeping coach.*

Bobby Saxton turned to Terry Gennoe to fill the vacancy left by the departed Jim Arnold during the summer of 1981. The newly appointed Saxton paid £60,000 to bring Gennoe from Southampton where he had created a club record with six successive clean sheets. It proved to be money well spent as the Shropshire born 'keeper went on to create two more goalkeeping records at Ewood Park.

He beat the record for goalkeeping appearances, held by Roger Jones, and then went on to become the oldest man to occupy the goalkeeping position at Ewood Park. Gennoe

had actually been a member of the playing staff at Ewood in the early 1970s when Gordon Lee signed him to provide cover for Paul Bradshaw when Roger Jones was side-lined through injury. However, the excellence of Jones and the potential of Bradshaw meant that Gennoe was allowed to return to Bury. A former England Youth international, Gennoe had signed schoolboy forms with Shrewsbury Town before taking a place at Madeley Teacher Training College. Whilst at Madeley he played Sunday football with the Bricklayers Arms and was spotted by a Bury scout. On completing his college course he opted to join Bury instead of staying on at college to gain extra qualifications.

Although he broke a leg in a pre-season game, Gennoe was determined to make his way in professional football. Whilst at Gigg Lane he was loaned out to Blackburn and Leeds United without making any senior appearances. Having been restricted to just three outings with the senior team at Bury he signed for Halifax Town in May 1975. It was at the Shay that Gennoe established himself in the Football League and began to attract the attention of larger clubs. In February 1978, after making 78 League appearances for Halifax, Gennoe signed for Southampton. Although his Southampton days brought a Football League Cup runners-up medal in 1979, Gennoe found his first-team opportunities rather limited. It was for this reason that he chose to leave the Dell after 36 League games to join Blackburn Rovers.

A tall, commanding figure in the six-yard box, Gennoe dominated on crosses and yet for a big man was exceptionally agile when dealing with ground shots. Gennoe read the game perfectly from his goalkeeping position and was always a calming influence on his defence in pressure situations. His reputation in the game was reflected when he was named in the 1984-85 PFA Second Division team. In creating a new appearance record, Gennoe had to overcome a spate of injuries and a serious viral illness during the 1986-87 season. Although Gennoe missed the 1987 Full Members' Cup Final, he got a chance to rebuild his first-team career when Vince O'Keefe broke his leg in the fifth match of the 1987-88 season.

Gennoe made the most of his chance and like good wine, appeared to improve with age. However, injuries eventually began to take their toll and Gennoe made his final first-team appearance in the opening fixture of the 1990-91 season. The arrival of Bobby Mimms in December 1991, coupled with continual problems with a knee injury finally led to Gennoe announcing his retirement at the end of the 1991-92 season. However, his services were not lost to the club as he was appointed to the coaching staff and also became the club's Education Officer. It was in the latter capacity

that Gennoe was able to utilise his teaching qualifications to work with schoolchildren whilst running the club's Learning Through Football programme.

Appearances with Blackburn Rovers:

|  | League | Play-Offs | FA Cup | FL Cup | FM Cup | Total |
|---|---|---|---|---|---|---|
| 1981-82 | 35 | 0 | 1 | 3 | 0 | 39 |
| 1982-83 | 33 | 0 | 1 | 2 | 0 | 36 |
| 1983-84 | 30 | 0 | 3 | 2 | 0 | 35 |
| 1984-85 | 37 | 0 | 4 | 1 | 0 | 42 |
| 1985-86 | 32 | 0 | 3 | 1 | 0 | 36 |
| 1986-87 | 11 | 0 | 0 | 0 | 1 | 12 |
| 1987-88 | 39 | 2 | 1 | 2 | 1 | 45 |
| 1988-89 | 43 | 4 | 3 | 3 | 2 | 55 |
| 1989-90 | 28 | 2 | 2 | 1 | 0 | 33 |
| 1990-91 | 1 | 0 | 0 | 0 | 0 | 1 |
|  | 289 | 8 | 18 | 15 | 4 | 334 |

### GIBRALTAR TOURNAMENT 1976
The Rovers stepped in at the last minute to replace Southampton, who had just won the FA Cup, in an end of season tournament that also included Lincoln City, Sheffield United and Wolverhampton Wanderers. Jim Smith used the tournament to give outings to Andy Needham and Bobby Mitchell before deciding whether to offer them terms for the following season. In their opening fixture the Rovers lost by the odd goal in five to Wolverhampton Wanderers. The Blackburn goals were scored by Ken Beamish and Kevin Hird. The second game saw the Rovers draw 3-3 with Lincoln City thanks to goals from Andy Needham, Tony Parkes and John Waddington. The Rovers gained third place in the competition by winning the penalty shoot-out with Lincoln 11-10.

### GIBSON, Thomas Kenyon
Left-back. 1880.
*Born: Blackburn.*
*Debut: v Nottingham Forest (a) 31 January 1880.*
*Career: James Street; Blackburn Olympic 1878; Blackburn Rovers guest 1880.*
**Appearances:** FA Cup 1.

Thomas Gibson was unquestionably the greatest Olympian of them all. A member of the team which brought the FA Cup to Blackburn in 1883, Gibson remained loyal to the cause of Olympic despite the growing importance of Blackburn Rovers. Although he chose to stay with Olympic, Gibson made occasional appearances for Blackburn Rovers, including one FA Cup-tie in January 1880.

### GILLESPIE, Matthew
Forward. 1892-1893.
*Born: Strathclyde.*
*Debut: v Accrington (h) 1 October 1892.*
*Career: Glasgow Thistle; Blackburn Rovers June 1892; Leith Athletic cs 1893.*
**Appearances:** Football League 6.
**Goals:** Football League 1.

Matthew Gillespie was one of a number of Scottish players brought to the club by Thomas Mitchell. Sadly, players like Mann, Murray, Sawers and Gillespie were not of the calibre of earlier Scottish imports and Gillespie returned to Scotland after only one season at Blackburn.

### GILHESPY, Thomas William Cyril
Outside-right. 1929-1930.
*5ft 8in; 11st 2lb.*
*Born: Fence Houses, Co.Durham 18 February 1898.*
*Debut: v West Ham United (h) 31 August 1929.*
*Career: Fencehouses FC; Chester-le-Street; Sunderland October 1920; Liverpool August 1921; Bristol City May 1925; Blackburn Rovers June 1929; Reading June 1930; Mansfield Town July 1931; Crewe Alexandra August 1932 to 1933.*
**Appearances:** Football League 5.
**Goals:** Football League 1.

Cyril Gilhespy arrived at Blackburn with a reputation as a speedy winger who had been a vital part of Bristol City's 1926-27 promotion winning team. Although he made an impressive debut, scoring in a 3-3 draw with West Ham United, Gilhespy struggled to retain a place in the first team. His fate at Ewood Park was sealed with the arrival of Jack Bruton from Burnley in December 1929. With Bruton firmly entrenched in the first team, Gilhespy was allowed to join Reading during the summer of 1930.

### GILLINGHAM FC
Formerly known as New Brompton, Gillingham Football Club became one of the original members of the Football League Division Three in

1920. Blackburn Rovers have only met Gillingham on four occasions in the Football League and have maintained an impressive record in those Third Division clashes. The clubs met in the second round of the Football League Cup in 1980-81 when Gillingham held Rovers to a goalless draw at Ewood Park. However, goals from Duncan McKenzie and Kevin Stonehouse gave the Rovers a 2-1 victory at the Priestfield Stadium.

**Football League**

|  |  | Home |  | Away |  |
|---|---|---|---|---|---|
| 1974-75 | (Div 3) | W | 4-1 | D | 1-1 |
| 1979-80 | (Div 3) | W | 3-1 | W | 2-1 |

|  | P | W | D | L | F | A |
|---|---|---|---|---|---|---|
| Home | 2 | 2 | 0 | 0 | 7 | 2 |
| Away | 2 | 1 | 1 | 0 | 3 | 2 |
| Total | 4 | 3 | 1 | 0 | 10 | 4 |

**Football League Cup**

| 1980-81 | (2) | Home | D | 0-0 |
|---|---|---|---|---|
|  |  | Away | W | 2-1 |

## GILLIVER, Allan H.
Centre-forward. 1966-1968.
*6ft 1½in; 13st.*
*Born: Swallownest, 3 August 1944.*
*Debut: v Derby County (a) 20 August 1966.*
*Career: Huddersfield Town June 1961; Blackburn Rovers June 1966; Rotherham United May 1968; Brighton & Hove Albion July 1969; Lincoln City February 1971; Bradford City June 1972; Stockport County June 1974; Boston United; Bradford City non-contract player August 1978.*
**Appearances:** Football League 32+2; FA Cup 1; Football League Cup 4; Total 37+2.
**Goals:** Football League 9.
Few could have realised the repercussions that the signing of Allan Gilliver would have on professional football following his arrival at Ewood Park in June 1966. The Rovers had tried to sign Gilliver a few months earlier in a last ditch attempt to prevent relegation from the First Division. However, as Huddersfield were chasing promotion they were reluctant to allow Gilliver to leave.

The move was eventually completed in the summer and Gilliver arrived at Blackburn with a record of 22 goals in 45 League appearances for Huddersfield. A strongly built centre-forward, Gilliver began in fine style with a goal in each of his first two appearances. However, after five games he was kept out of action with back trouble and although he returned for a further four games it was clear that the problem with his back was a serious one. Gilliver was forced to take a prolonged break from football after a slipped disc was diagnosed which necessitated an operation.

Unhappy with the circumstances involving the injury, the Rovers took the matter to the Football League. A commission was held which examined all the relevant facts and then ordered Huddersfield Town to repay £18,000 of the transfer fee. In the wake of this decision it was decided to introduce formal medical examinations as part of transfer transactions. Gilliver returned to first-team action at Ewood Park the following season but failed to fulfil the promise he had shown in his days at Huddersfield. Gilliver became unhappy with life at Ewood Park and clashed with Eddie Quigley. As a result he was traded to Rotherham United in exchange for Les Chappell.

## GLAISTER, George
Outside-left. 1937-1947.
*5ft 8in; 11st.*
*Born: Bywell, Northumberland, 18 May 1918.*
*Debut: v Bolton Wanderers (a) 5 January 1946 (FAC).*
*Career: North Shields 1936-37; Blackburn Rovers May 1937; Stockport County May 1947; Halifax Town August 1950; Accrington Stanley September 1951; Bangor City cs 1952.*
**Appearances:** Football League 8; FA Cup 2; Total 10.
**Goals:** Football League 1.
George Glaister joined the Rovers as a young professional from North Shields in May 1937. Sadly his career at Blackburn was seriously disrupted by World War Two. Although he scored 14 goals in 69 wartime appearances, Glaister was unable to win a regular first-team place following the restoration of the Football League. A transfer to Stockport County saw him record 21 goals in 92 League appearances; his best period in League football. He returned to East Lancashire in September 1951 when Walter Crook, a former Ewood Park teammate, signed him for Accrington Stanley from Halifax Town. At the Shay he had scored seven goals in 34 League outings but Glaister failed to solve the outside-

left problem at Peel Park and after one goal in 24 League games he dropped out the Football League during the summer of 1952.

## GLENN, David Anthony
Right-back. 1983-1985.
*5ft 8in; 11st 4lb.*
*Born: Wigan, 30 November 1962.*
*Debut: v Portsmouth (h) 19 November 1983 (sub).*
*Career: Wigan Athletic apprentice July 1979, turning professional on November 1980; Blackburn Rovers November 1983; Chester City July 1985 until 1988; Fleetwood; Chorley 1992.*
**Appearances:** Football League 23+1; FA Cup 3; Total 26+1.
David Glenn came to Blackburn on a free transfer from Wigan Athletic and was almost immediately thrust into the first team. With Mick Rathbone missing for much of the campaign, due to a broken leg, Glenn was given an extended run in the Second Division. Although not the most graceful of athletes, Glenn did remarkably well and appeared to be quite at home in higher company. His inclusion in the team meant that Jim Branagan had to cross over to left-back and the following season, with Rathbone fit again, Glenn was rather unfortunate to lose his place as Bobby Saxton reunited Branagan and Rathbone. Glenn moved to Chester City in the summer of 1985 and appeared in 73 League games (including three as substitute) for the Cheshire club.

## GLOSSOP FC
Formed as Glossop North End in 1886, the club were members of the Football League between 1898 and 1915. They won promotion to the First Division after only one season in the Football League and at that point chose to drop the 'North End' from their name. They were relegated after only one season in the top flight with a record of only four wins, ten draws and 20 defeats. Despite their dismal record, Blackburn Rovers were the only team not to defeat Glossop in a First Division fixture during that season. The three points that Glossop took from Blackburn was their best return from any of their First Division opponents.

**Football League**

|  |  | Home |  | Away |  |
|---|---|---|---|---|---|
| 1899-01 | (Div 1) | D | 2-2 | L | 2-4 |

|  | P | W | D | L | F | A |
|---|---|---|---|---|---|---|
| Home | 1 | 0 | 1 | 0 | 2 | 2 |
| Away | 1 | 0 | 0 | 1 | 2 | 4 |
| Total | 2 | 0 | 1 | 1 | 4 | 6 |

## GLOVER, Alexander
Winger. 1951-1954.
*Born: Glasgow, 28 February 1922.*
*Debut: v Queen's Park Rangers (a) 3 September 1951.*
*Career: 257 Boys' Brigade, Glasgow; Linthouse Victoria; Partick Thistle May 1943; Bradford March 1948; Luton Town 1949; Blackburn Rovers September 1951; Barrow August 1954.*
**Appearances:** Football League 64; FA Cup 7; Total 71.
**Goals:** Football League 4; FA Cup 1; Total 5.
Alec Glover joined the Rovers after the club began the 1951-52 season with only one point from their opening five games. Glover had scored five goals in 48 League appearances with Bradford and a further six goals in 56 games with Luton Town following his move to English football in March 1948. A winger who could operate on either flank, Glover was immediately introduced to an outside-right position which had been filled by Chris Anderson and Harry Parker in the opening games. However, it wasn't until December that the club's fortunes began to improve and by this time Glover had been switched to the left wing. Glover was unable to retain a regular place in the side throughout his stay at Ewood Park and the return of Bobby Langton in September 1953 further restricted his first-team opportunities. He ended his career with seven goals in 86 League outings with Barrow.

## GLOVER, John William
Left-back. 1897-1899.
*Born: West Bromwich, 28 October 1876; Died: Dudley, 20 April 1955.*
*Debut: v Derby County (a) 4 September 1897.*
*Career: Christ Church School; West Bromwich Unity; Great Bridge Unity; Halesowen; Rudge-Whitworth FC; West Bromwich Albion; Blackburn Rovers May 1897; New Brompton 1899 (£100); Liverpool June 1900 (£350); Birmingham October 1903 (£250); Brierley Hill Alliance August 1908; Retired 1910.*
**Appearances:** Football League 25; FA Cup 1; Total 26.
Although born in West Bromwich, John Glover had to come to Ewood Park to break into League football. Although he didn't progress beyond the reserves at the Hawthorns, Glover found himself installed as first-choice left-back at Blackburn. He made 23 League appearances during

his first campaign at Ewood without ever really looking convincing in his partnership with Tom Brandon. He played in the first game of the 1898-99 season but was then replaced by Bob Crompton and made only one further senior appearance for the club. His best spell in football came when he partnered Frank Stokes at Birmingham. He joined the club when they were still known as Small Heath and went on to make 124 League appearances for them.

## GOALKEEPING RECORDS

Bill Hughes holds the record for the longest period from a goalkeeper's debut to conceding his first goal. Hughes was within a minute of keeping a clean sheet in each of his first three games for the club in 1948-49. However, the record for the longest unbeaten spell between one goal and the next is held by Adam Blacklaw. The former Turf Moor favourite was unbeaten for 582 minutes, a period which covered the end of the 1968-69 season and the start of the following campaign. During the 1978-79 Third Division promotion campaign, Jim Arnold managed to create a record by keeping 19 clean sheets.

This was equalled by Bobby Mimms in the Premier League during the 1992-93 season. In keeping those 19 clean sheets, Mimms created a new record for the number of clean sheets in top flight football. The record for the most Football League appearances by a goalkeeper is held by Terry Gennoe with 289 appearances between 1981 and 1990. However, Reg Elvy with 152 holds the record for the longest run of consecutive League games. In November 1993 the Rovers established a new world record transfer fee for a goalkeeper when they paid Southampton £2,400,000 for Tim Flowers.

## GOALSCORING RECORDS

Listed below are individual goalscoring records concerning Blackburn Rovers:

**Most Goals in a career**: 192, Simon Garner 1978-92.

**Most Goals in a season**: 44, Ted Harper (League 43; FA Cup 1) 1925-26.

**Ted Harper's Record Breaking Season**:
### 9 September 1925 v Newcastle United (away) W 7-1.
*Scorers: Harper 5, Hulme, Rigby.*
This was Harper's first game of the season after being restored to the first team following three defeats in the opening three matches. His first goal came when Joe Hulme delivered a perfect centre and Harper drove the ball over the advancing goalkeeper. His second goal, which was the third for Blackburn, came when Chandler failed to close Jock McKay down and the resultant pass left Harper with the goal at his mercy. The fourth Blackburn goal provided Harper with his hat-trick. Wilson, in the Newcastle goal, badly misjudged the flight of an Arthur Rigby centre and Harper reacted more quickly than the United defenders to pounce on the loose ball. With the Newcastle defence in total disarray, Harper struck once more with a sixth goal for the Rovers. His fifth came shortly afterwards when he drew Wilson out of the goal before scoring from close range.

### 12 September 1925 v West Bromwich Albion (h) L 1-2.
*Scorer: Harper (pen).*
Harper's goal came 30 seconds from the end of the game when he was knocked over as he tried to dribble his way through a packed defence. He took the ensuing penalty and beat Ashmore in the Albion goal with a low drive.

### 19 September 1925 v Sheffield United (a) D 1-1.
*Scorer: Harper.*
Harper struck his seventh goal of the season after 39 minutes play at Bramall Lane. Arthur Rigby deflected the ball inside for Harper to squeeze between Pantling and Cook of United and drive the ball past Anderson in the Sheffield goal.

### 21 September 1925 v Sunderland (h) W 3-0.
*Scorer: Rigby, Harper 2.*
A long clearance from Jock Crawford in the Blackburn goal found Joe Hulme on the right wing. The winger immediately touched it inside for Harper to run at goal. Although he had defenders in close attention, Harper ended his run with a slanting drive which went in near the far post to give the Rovers a 2-0 lead. Harper's second goal came after 55 minutes when Syd Puddefoot placed the ball through the middle of the Sunderland defence. Harper wasted no time in controlling the ball and his first-time shot sped past McInroy's left hand to give the Rovers a 3-0 victory.

### 26 September 1925 v Cardiff City (h) W 6-3.
*Scorer: Harper 3, Rigby, Hulme, McKay.*

Harper struck the first of his three goals after only eight minutes when Farquharson failed to hold a 30-yard drive from Syd Puddefoot. Harper was on the loose ball in a flash to open the scoring for the Rovers. Harper's second goal, a somewhat scrambled affair, came when the Rovers held a commanding 4-1 lead. Once again it was his natural predatory instincts which enabled him to be in the right position to latch on to the ball as it bobbed about in the area. Harper completed his hat-trick with a picture-book goal. He moved through the middle of the Cardiff defence with ease before leaving Farquharson helpless with a shot into the corner of the net.

### 3 October 1925 v Tottenham Hotspur (a) L 2-4.
*Scorers: Harper, Rigby.*
Harper scored his goal only five minutes after Tottenham had taken the lead. A Tottenham defender missed his tackle and Harper wasted no time in beating the goalkeeper with a shot that curled in towards the far post.

### 10 October 1925 v Manchester City (h) D 3-3.
*Scorers: Puddefoot 2, Harper.*
Once again it was the predatory instincts of Harper which brought him his 14th goal in seven games. A cross from Arthur Rigby was forced against the post before Harper rushed in to smash the ball into the net to give the Rovers a 3-2 lead.

### 24 October 1925 v Notts County (a) W 4-1.
*Scorers: Rigby, Roscamp, Harper 2 (1 pen).*
After 67 minutes play the Rovers were awarded a penalty when Rigby was brought down in the area. Harper blasted his shot into the net off the bar. Seven minutes from the end Harper scored his second goal thanks to a dreadful goalkeeping error. Iremonger completely missed the ball as he rushed from his goal to clear and was left completely stranded on the edge of the penalty area. Although Harper was to the left of goal he wasted no time in driving the ball into the net to put the Rovers 4-1 up.

### 31 October 1925 v Burnley (a) W 3-1.
*Scorer: Harper 3.*
The local derby with Burnley brought Harper his third hat-trick of the season. It was after 62 minutes that Harper finally broke the deadlock in what was proving to be an extremely tight affair. Once again Arthur Rigby provided Harper with the perfect centre and the centre-forward took advantage of a slight hesitation by the Burnley 'keeper to put the Rovers ahead. Twenty minutes later, Harper brilliantly headed home a perfect cross from Joe Hulme. Within two minutes the same two players had combined again to produce a third goal for the Rovers. Once again Hulme beat his man before sending in a cross which Harper headed into the back of the net.

### 7 November 1925 v Leeds United (h) D 2-2.
*Scorers: Harper (pen), McIntyre.*
For the second game in succession Ted Harper chose the 62nd minute to make his mark on the match. Trailing by two goals to nil, the Rovers got back in the game when Joe Hulme sent over a cross which struck a Leeds player. There was a half-hearted appeal from the Blackburn players for a penalty and to the surprise of many the referee stopped the game to speak to a linesman. The result was that a spot-kick was given and Harper wasted no time in putting the penalty away to put the Rovers back in the game.

### 21 November 1925 v Arsenal (h) L 2-3.
*Scorer: Harper 2 (1 pen).*
A rash tackle by Mackie of Arsenal on Arthur Rigby gave Ted Harper another chance to score from the spot. The referee was a Mr Harper and the Arsenal 'keeper was also called Harper. Once the penalty was given, Harper beat his namesake with a rising ball into one corner. With the Rovers trailing by three goals to one, Harper gave his team a lifeline when he scored a fine solo goal in the 84th minute. He went through on the right wing and though harassed by opponents he screwed a ground shot inside the far post.

### 5 December 1925 v Liverpool (h) D 1-1.
*Scorer: Harper.*
On an icy pitch, Harper put the Rovers ahead after only eight minutes. A long range effort from Jack Roscamp appeared to be well covered by the Liverpool 'keeper when Harper touched the ball with his head and deflected it into the net.

### 25 December 1925 v Everton (h) D 2-2.
*Scorer: Harper 2.*
The Rovers went behind to Everton on a snow covered Ewood Park on Christmas Day 1925. However, within three minutes of the Everton goal, Harper had equalised matters with a low shot. Once again, Everton took

the lead but Harper bundled the ball over the line in a goalmouth scramble after 50 minutes to clinch a point for the Rovers.

**2 January 1926 v Bury (a) L 1-3.**
*Scorer: Harper.*
There was a certain amount of luck about Harper's goal against Bury at Gigg lane. Jock McKay completely botched his attempt at a shot but was fortunate enough to recover possession. He slipped the ball to Harper who made no mistake with a shot which easily beat Harrison in the Bury goal.

**16 January 1926 v Birmingham (h) D 4-4**
*Scorers: McIntyre, Crisp 2, Harper.*
With 68 minutes played and Blackburn leading 3-1, Arthur Rigby swung a fast low ball into the middle towards Harper. Although only half-facing the goal, Harper side-footed it into the net with great aplomb.

**23 January 1926 v West Bromwich Albion (a) D 1-1.**
*Scorer: Harper.*
Ted Harper created a fine shooting chance for Johnny McIntyre after only 12 minutes of the game at the Hawthorns. McIntyre drove the ball towards the Albion goal only to see it blocked. However, the ball found its way back to McIntyre and the Scot quickly turned it inside for Harper to score from close range.

**30 January 1926 v Arsenal (a) L 1-3 (FA Cup fourth round).**
*Scorer: Harper.*
Ted Harper opened the scoring in the cup-tie after half-an-hour. A neat build up involving Roxburgh, McIntyre, Crisp and Harper resulted in Harper converting a centre from Jack Crisp.

**13 February 1926 v Tottenham Hotspur (h) W 4-2.**
*Scorers: Harper 2, Rigby, Crisp.*
The first of a brace of goals from Harper came after 30 minutes play when Syd Puddefoot lifted a pin-point pass straight through the heart of the Tottenham defence. From 20 yards out, Harper chipped the ball over the advancing goalkeeper to put the Rovers one goal ahead. Harper's second goal put the Rovers 2-1 up and once again he profited from a good cross. A corner kick by Jack Crisp wasn't cleared by the Tottenham defence and Harper hooked the loose ball into the roof of the net.

**1 March 1926 v Sheffield United (h) W 3-1.**
*Scorers: Harper, Webster (own-goal), Rigby.*
Harper opened the scoring after 25 minutes when a close passing move ended with Harper converting Holland's cross.

**13 March 1926 v Burnley (h) W 6-3.**
*Scorers: Puddefoot 2, Rigby 3, Harper.*
Harper had to wait until three minutes from the end of this local derby before getting his name on the score-sheet. Harper controlled a difficult ball and managed to hook it past the Burnley 'keeper.

**17 March 1926 v Manchester City (a) W 1-0.**
*Scorer: Harper.*
The only goal of the game came after 56 minutes when Harper met a centre by Rigby and saw his half-hit shot creep into the City goal.

**20 March 1926 v Leeds United (a) L 1-2.**
*Scorer: Harper.*
Harper opened the scoring for Blackburn when he latched on to a long pass by Johnny McIntyre. He took it in his stride, slipped a tackle, swerved and as the 'keeper dashed out, Harper lifted the ball over the goalkeeper and into the net.

**3 April 1926 v Arsenal (a) L 2-4.**
*Scorer: Harper 2.*
A long pass by Aussie Campbell and a neat piece of inter-play by Mitchell and Puddefoot resulted in a score which Harper converted with little difficulty. After giving the Rovers a 1-0 lead, Harper was called upon to level matters after Arsenal had gone into a 2-1 lead. A corner from Mitchell was followed by a goalmouth mêlée which ended with Harper converting yet another close-range opportunity.

**6 April 1926 v Huddersfield Town (a) L 1-3.**
*Scorer: Harper (pen).*
With the Rovers 3-0 down, Harper's 89th minute penalty was of little consequence. The penalty was given after Mitchell had been sent sprawling in the area and Harper sent the Huddersfield 'keeper the wrong way.

**10 April 1926 v Manchester United (h) W 7-0.**
*Scorers: Campbell, Harper 4, Mitchell, Puddefoot.*

Harper struck the first of his four goals after Aussie Campbell had given the Rovers an early lead. On 5 minutes the ball was swung in from the left and with Steward, the United goalkeeper, unable to collect the ball, Harper was able to knock the ball back across the face of the goal into the far corner of the net. With his second goal, after 28 minutes, Harper equalled the League record of 39 goals in a season. Harper collected the ball just inside of his own half, tipped it over an opponent's head and set off on a 40-yard run. With a defender at his heels, Harper pushed the ball past Steward as he advanced from his goal. The second half was only nine minutes old when Harper created a new League record. He picked the ball up on the edge of the centre circle and set off goalwards. He shook off a tackle and placed the ball past Steward as the United 'keeper made another fruitless dash from his line. The whole of the Blackburn team raced to congratulate Harper on establishing a new record. After 73 minutes Mitchell beat Moore and dropped over a delightful centre which Harper nodded past Steward.

**24 April 1926 v Aston Villa (h) W 3-1.**
*Scorers: Harper 2 (1 pen), Mitchell .*
Harper opened the scoring after 16 minutes following a foul on himself in the penalty area. The decision looked a harsh one but Harper calmly put the spot-kick away. Harper's final goal of the season came after 17 minutes when he scrambled home a cross from Walter.

**Most Goals in a Game**
Seven – Tommy Briggs v Bristol Rovers (h) Second Division, 5 February 1953.

**First Goal**: Briggs scored his first goal in match after 33 minutes when Bristol held a 2-1 lead. Good work by Eddie Crossan and Eddie Quigley created the opportunity for Briggs to beat Radford, the Bristol 'keeper, with a low drive.
**Second Goal**: Briggs again got the Rovers on level terms when he scored his second goal after 48 minutes. Frank Mooney was pulled down on the junction of the by-line and the penalty area and Eddie Crossan stepped up to take the free-kick. He floated the ball over the goalkeeper and Briggs met it on the far post to bring the scores level at 3-3.
**Third Goal**: A fourth Blackburn goal arrived on 62 minutes when Bobby Langton raced on to a perfect pass from Eddie Quigley. The winger pulled the ball back for Briggs who, with outstretched foot, managed to turn it into the net.
**Fourth Goal**: Briggs was put through again after 78 minutes. An inch perfect pass from Bill Smith saw Briggs bear down on goal. Although not noted for his fancy footwork, Briggs left four defenders floundering in his wake before he smashed a glorious low drive past Radford.
**Fifth Goal**: Briggs scored his fifth goal after only 84 minutes when Quigley again picked out Briggs and the Bristol 'keeper once again found the ball flying past him.
**Sixth Goal**: A sixth goal came for Briggs shortly after he had had the misfortune to hit a Bristol post. A cross from Frank Mooney was met on the volley by Briggs and the ball soared into the roof of the net like a rocket.
**Seventh Goal**: As the game drew to a close Langton, the club's penalty-taker, was hauled down in the area. Langton and the rest of the team urged a reluctant Briggs to take the kick. Although the tension amongst the crowd was electric, Briggs remained as unconcerned as ever as he put the ball on the spot. Within a flash he had calmly driven the ball past Radford and scored his seventh goal.

**Leading Goalscorers in League games are given below in a season by season listing:**

| | | |
|---|---|---|
| 1888-89 | 17 | J.Southworth |
| 1889-90 | 22 | J.Southworth |
| 1890-91 | 26 | J.Southworth |
| 1891-92 | 22 | J.Southworth |
| 1892-93 | 11 | W.Sawers |
| 1893-94 | 14 | H.Chippendale |
| 1894-95 | 12 | H.Chippendale |
| 1895-96 | 7 | H.Chippendale, J.Haydock, P.Turnbull |
| 1896-97 | 7 | J.Wilkie |
| 1897-98 | 9 | J.Proudfoot |
| 1898-99 | 14 | D.J.Hurst |
| 1899-00 | 11 | A.Whittaker |
| 1900-01 | 8 | A.Whittaker |
| 1901-02 | 16 | J.Dewhurst |
| 1902-03 | 10 | A.Whittaker |
| 1903-04 | 14 | L.P.Watson |
| 1904-05 | 12 | A.Bowman |
| 1905-06 | 15 | A.Bowman |
| 1906-07 | 17 | J.Martin |
| 1907-08 | 11 | W.Davies |

| | | |
|---|---|---|
| 1908-09 | 19 | W.Davies |
| 1909-10 | 12 | W.C.A.Aitkenhead |
| 1910-11 | 17 | W.Davies |
| 1911-12 | 15 | W.C.A.Aitkenhead |
| 1912-13 | 14 | E.G.Latheron |
| 1913-14 | 28 | D.Shea |
| 1914-15 | 20 | P.H.Dawson |
| 1919-20 | 17 | E.Hawksworth |
| 1920-21 | 17 | P.H.Dawson |
| 1921-22 | 12 | P.H.Dawson |
| 1922-23 | 12 | J.McKay |
| 1923-24 | 18 | E.C.Harper |
| 1924-25 | 12 | J.M.McIntyre, J.McKay |
| 1925-26 | 43 | E.C.Harper |
| 1926-27 | 35 | E.C.Harper |
| 1927-28 | 15 | T.Mitchell |
| 1928-29 | 16 | J.Roscamp |
| 1929-30 | 21 | C.F.T.Bourton |
| 1930-31 | 19 | J.Bruton |
| 1931-32 | 21 | J.E.Thompson |
| 1932-33 | 17 | J.E.Thompson |
| 1933-34 | 15 | J.Bruton, E.C.Harper |
| 1934-35 | 18 | J.Bruton, J.E.Thompson |
| 1935-36 | 15 | J.E.Thompson |
| 1936-37 | 16 | J.Bruton |
| 1937-38 | 20 | L.Butt |
| 1938-39 | 21 | A.Clarke |
| 1946-47 | 12 | J.Smith |
| 1947-48 | 15 | L.Graham |
| 1948-49 | 21 | D.Westcott |
| 1949-50 | 16 | D.Westcott |
| 1950-51 | 13 | L.Graham |
| 1951-52 | 11 | E.Quigley |
| 1952-53 | 18 | E.Quigley |
| 1953-54 | 32 | T.H.Briggs |
| 1954-55 | 33 | T.H.Briggs |
| 1955-56 | 31 | T.H.Briggs |
| 1956-57 | 32 | T.H.Briggs |
| 1957-58 | 20 | P.A.Dobing |
| 1958-59 | 24 | P.A.Dobing |
| 1959-60 | 18 | P.A.Dobing |
| 1960-61 | 18 | P.A.Dobing |
| 1961-62 | 14 | W.I.Lawther |
| 1962-63 | 23 | F.Pickering |
| 1963-64 | 32 | M.A.McEvoy |
| 1964-65 | 29 | M.A.McEvoy |
| 1965-66 | 10 | G.A.Jones, M.A.McEvoy |
| 1966-67 | 11 | J.M.Connelly |
| 1967-68 | 8 | M.K.Ferguson |
| 1968-69 | 10 | J.M.Connelly, M.Darling, D.Martin |
| 1969-70 | 13 | D.Martin |
| 1970-71 | 6 | B.Conlon, E.Rogers |
| 1971-72 | 17 | A.Field |
| 1972-73 | 17 | A.Field |
| 1973-74 | 11 | A.Field |
| 1974-75 | 15 | D.Martin |
| 1975-76 | 7 | K.G.Beamish, A.Parkes |
| 1976-77 | 10 | R.L.Svarc |
| 1977-78 | 11 | N.Brotherston |
| 1978-79 | 8 | S.Garner |
| 1979-80 | 18 | A.Crawford |
| 1980-81 | 10 | K.Stonehouse |
| 1981-82 | 14 | S.Garner |
| 1982-83 | 22 | S.Garner |
| 1983-84 | 19 | S.Garner |
| 1984-85 | 15 | C.D.Thompson |
| 1985-86 | 12 | S.Garner |
| 1986-87 | 11 | S.Barker |
| 1987-88 | 14 | S.Garner |
| 1988-89 | 20 | S.Garner |
| 1989-90 | 18 | S.Garner |
| 1990-91 | 10 | F.A.Stapleton |
| 1991-92 | 23 | D.R.Speedie |
| 1992-93 | 16 | A.Shearer |
| 1993-94 | 31 | A.Shearer |

**Players with 50 or more goals in League football**

| | |
|---|---|
| S.Garner | 168 |
| T.H.Briggs | 140 |
| E.C.Harper | 121 |
| J.Bruton | 108 |
| B.Douglas | 101 |
| J.Southworth | 97 |
| E.G.Latheron | 94 |
| E.Quigley | 92 |
| M.A.McEvoy | 89 |
| P.A.Dobing | 88 |
| J.E.Thompson | 82 |
| S.C.Puddefoot | 79 |
| W.C.A.Aitkenhead | 75 |
| E.Crossan | 73 |
| P.H.Dawson | 71 |
| W.Davies | 67 |
| D.Shea | 62 |
| F.Pickering | 61 |
| R.Langton | 57 |
| D.Martin | 57 |
| A.Whittaker | 57 |
| J.Byron | 50 |
| H.Chippendale | 50 |

**Players with ten or more goals in the FA Cup**

| | |
|---|---|
| J.Brown | 29 |
| J.Southworth | 24 |
| W.C.A.Aitkenhead | 18 |
| P.A.Dobing | 16 |
| J.E.Sowerbutts | 16 |
| W.J.Townley | 14 |
| H.L.Fecitt | 13 |
| J.Byrom | 12 |
| J.M.Lofthouse | 12 |
| N.Walton | 12 |
| G.Avery | 10 |
| E.G.Latheron | 10 |
| M.A.McEvoy | 10 |

**Players with five or more goals in the Football League Cup**

| | |
|---|---|
| S.Garner | 11 |
| W.I.Lawther | 10 |
| E.Rogers | 9 |
| F.Pickering | 8 |
| M.C.Newell | 7 |
| A.Shearer | 7 |
| M.K.Ferguson | 6 |
| K.G.Beamish | 5 |
| B.Douglas | 5 |

**GODWIN, Verdi**
Outside-right/Centre-forward. 1945-1948.
*5ft 7in; 10st 10lb.*
*Born: Blackburn, 11 February 1926.*
*Debut: v Huddersfield Town (a) 14 September 1946.*
*Career: Moss Street School, Blackburn; Local junior football; Blackburn Rovers amateur May 1945, turning professional in March 1946; Manchester City June 1948; Stoke City June 1949; Mansfield Town January 1950; Middlesbrough on trial November 1951 to December 1951; Grimsby Town on trial January 1952 to February 1952; Brentford March 1952; Southport July 1954; Barrow August 1955; Tranmere Rovers August 1956; King's Lynn July 1957; Netherfield late 1957-58; New Brighton 1958-59; Macclesfield Town 1959-60; Colwyn Bay 1960-61.*
**Appearances:** Football League 27.
**Goals:** Football League 6.
Verdi Godwin became one of football's nomads during the late 1940s and 1950s. Blackburn Rovers was his home-town club and Godwin, equally adept at centre-forward or outside-right, appeared on 17 occasions during the final season of wartime football. He challenged for a first-team place for two seasons after the war but failed to establish himself and moved to Manchester City in June 1948.

**GOODWIN, Frederick James**
Full-back/Midfield. 1970-1971.
*5ft 10in; 11st 1lb.*
*Born: Stockport, 4 January 1944.*
*Debut: v Birmingham City (h) 4 March 1970.*
*Career: Wolverhampton Wanderers groundstaff April 1959, turning professional in January 1961; Stockport County January 1966; Blackburn Rovers March 1970; Southport October 1971; Port Vale August 1972; Macclesfield Town; Stockport County August 1974; New Mills 1976-77; Stalybridge Celtic; Ashton United (coach).*
**Appearances:** Football League 63+1; FA Cup 1; Football League Cup 4; Total 68+1.

**Goals:** Football League 4.

Freddie Goodwin proved a useful signing for Eddie Quigley because of his ability to play as an attacking full-back or in midfield. Goodwin had arrived at Ewood Park as a hard-working midfielder who had spent the majority of his career labouring in the lower divisions. A regular member of the first team throughout his time at Ewood Park, Goodwin was allowed to leave Blackburn in the exchange deal which brought Tony Field to the club.

### GORDON, Patrick
*Outside-right. 1894-1895.*
*Born: Scotland.*
*Debut: v Burnley (h) 17 November 1894.*
*Career: Renton; Everton August 1890; Liverpool June 1893; Blackburn Rovers October 1894; Liverpool South End cs 1895.*
**Appearances:** Football League 12; FA Cup 3; Total 15.
**Goals:** Football League 2; FA Cup 1; Total 3.
The signing of Patrick Gordon caused a number of eyebrows to be raised amongst Blackburn supporters. Gordon, a speedy right winger who was equally effective at inside-forward, came to Blackburn with excellent credentials. In Scotland he had understudied several Scottish internationals at Renton, whilst in England he had won an FA Cup runners-up medal in 1893 with Everton and a Second Division championship medal with Liverpool in 1894.

However, the outside-right position, for which he had been signed, was not thought to be a weakness. James Haydock had made a good impression after getting into the Blackburn team and Gordon found himself making his debut in an inside-forward position. Contemporary critics were hardly impressed with his form and one wrote that 'Gordon is scarcely worth his place in the team after all. The wiseacres on the Rovers' committee think him a dashing outside-right. But he is not. Haydock is the best they have had for a long time.' The committee obviously agreed for after a season of sporadic appearances, Gordon was allowed to return to the Liverpool area.

### GORMAN, James
*Right-back. 1930-1937.*
*5ft 10in; 11st 8lb.*
*Born: Liverpool, 3 March 1910.*
*Debut: v Blackpool (a) 3 January 1931.*
*Career: Burscough Rangers; Skelmersdale United; Blackburn Rovers March 1930; Sunderland January 1937; Hartlepools United October 1945.*
**Appearances:** Football League 213; FA Cup 12; Total 225.
Originally a centre-forward, Gorman was converted into a full-back whilst playing with Skelmersdale United. Although he had been closely watched by Everton it was Blackburn Rovers who gave him the chance to establish himself in the Football League. Signed as a likely successor to Jock Hutton, Gorman made his debut in January 1931 and quickly established himself in the first team. A stalwart defender, Gorman was endowed with a fine physique and electrifying pace. Due to the deficiencies of his forwards, Gorman developed into a fine attacking full-back. However, a number of contemporary commentators felt that he was inclined to take too many risks. The 1935-36 campaign brought relegation to the Second Division and ultimately led to a transfer request from Gorman. In January 1937 he joined Sunderland and within months of his arrival he was helping his new club to win the FA Cup. Like so many other players of his era, his career was virtually ended by World War Two. He played wartime football with Sunderland and Hartlepools United but didn't reappear when the Football League began again in 1946.

### GORMLIE, William Joseph
*Goalkeeper. 1930-1935.*
*5ft 11in; 12st.*
*Born: Liverpool, 1911 (April quarter); Died: Brussels, Belgium, July 1976.*
*Debut: v Sunderland (h) 13 February 1932.*
*Career: Hotel Imperial XI; Fleetwood Windsor Villa; Blackburn Rovers amateur July 1930, turning professional in May 1931; Northampton Town June 1935; Lincoln City July 1939; Later manager of Anderlecht, Osled and Racing Club Jetta; also coached the Belgium national team between 1947 and 1953.*
**Appearances:** Football League 44.
A former page boy at the Blackpool Tower Ballroom, Bill Gormlie faced competition from Jock Crawford and Cliff Binns for the goalkeeping position at Blackburn Rovers. However, by the start of the 1932-33 season, Crawford had been released and Gormlie had edged himself ahead of Binns in terms of selection. A player of real ability, Gormlie had the necessary reflexes for making brilliant saves. However, on occasions, the team in

front of him appeared incapable of keeping a clean sheet. Gormlie was further handicapped by a succession of injuries and illnesses which virtually ended his career at Ewood. The progress of Jack Hughes allowed the club to let Gormlie move to Northampton Town in June 1935.

### GOW, John
*Goalkeeper. 1890-1891.*
*Debut: v Sunderland (h) 11 October 1890.*
*Career: Vale of Leven; Renton; Blackburn Rovers October 1890; Northwich Victoria June 1891; West Manchester.*
**Appearances:** Football League 15; FA Cup 3; Total 18.
John Gow made a memorable debut at Blackburn when a bit of sharp practice on his part prevented Sunderland scoring. Gow got out of difficulty at one point by bending the crossbar so that the ball sailed over rather than under the bar. Gow had learned his trade in Scotland as understudy to James Wilson, a Scottish international. He served Rovers well during the 1890-91 season before his Blackburn career ended in controversy. Having missed the 1890 FA Cup semi-final, Gow was immediately restored to the team and looked a certainty for the Cup Final team. However, a shattering 7-1 home defeat at the hands of Notts County, the team who were due to play Blackburn in the Final seven days later, led to the axe falling on Gow. Although recalled for the final League match, Gow let it be known that he didn't want to continue with the club. In September 1891, he informed the committee that he was going to return to Scotland and join Renton, but actually moved to Northwich Victoria.

### GRAHAM, Leslie
*Forward. 1946-1953.*
*5ft 7¾in; 10st 6lb.*
*Born: Manchester, 14 May 1924.*
*Debut: v Grimsby Town (h) 20 September 1947.*
*Career: Blackburn Rovers amateur May 1945, turning professional April 1947; Newport County February 1953 (£2,500); Watford July 1955 (free); Newport County September 1957 (£1,250); Cambridge City July 1959; Merthyr Town player-manager 1959-60; Cwmbran manager; Tottenham Hotspur scout.*
**Appearances:** Football League 150; FA Cup 7; Total 157.
**Goals:** Football League 42; FA Cup 2; Total 44.
Les Graham got the chance to play League football after being recommended to Blackburn Rovers by an army major who had seen him play in India. A skilful ball player with an eye for goal, Graham got his chance in September 1947 and made an immediate impact with a goal on his debut. He finished his first season with the senior team as top scorer with 15 goals in 32 League games. Although his form fluctuated from time to time, Graham remained a regular in the first team until the 1952-53 season. Unable to retain his place, Graham opted for a move to Newport County in February 1953. Apart from two seasons at Watford, Graham spent the remainder of his League career in South Wales with Newport.

### GRAY, David
*Right-back. 1948-1953.*
*5ft 7in; 10st 6lb.*
*Born: Dundee, 8 February 1922.*
*Debut: v Southampton (a) 21 August 1948.*
*Career: Lochee Harp; Dundee Violets; Glasgow Rangers; Preston North End 19 May 1947; Blackburn Rovers 21 August 1948; Dundee cs 1954.*
**Appearances:** Football League 107; FA Cup 4; Total 111.
**Goals:** Football League 5.
David Gray came to Ewood Park as part of the deal which took Bobby Langton to Deepdale. Gray had failed to make much impression at Preston following his move from Scotland and was something of an unknown quantity when he arrived in Blackburn. In the event it proved to be an inspired signing. Both Gray and Bill Eckersley, his partner at full-back, were players who possessed speed and flair. During the next two seasons they formed an impressive partnership until Gray began to be hampered by injuries. Having failed to make a senior appearance for two seasons, Gray returned to his native Scotland in the summer of 1954.

### GREEN, Alan
*Left-back. 1945-1947.*
*5ft 8in; 10st 12lb.*
*Debut: v Bolton Wanderers (a) 5 January 1945 (FAC).*
*Career: Blackburn Rovers January 1945.*
**Appearances:** FA Cup 2.
A full-back who got his senior chance during World War Two. Green first appeared at left-back against Rochdale in January 1945. During wartime football he made 36 appearances for the senior team as well as appearing in two FA Cup-ties. However, with the restoration of the Football League he found it impossible to break into the first team.

## GREENWOOD, Doctor Haydock
Full-back. 1875-1883.
*Born: Blackburn, 31 October 1860; Died: Buxton, 3 November 1951.*
*Debut: v Tyne Association (h) 1 November 1879 (FAC).*
*Career: Blackburn Rovers 1875 until 1883. Represented Malvern College XI 1878-79.*
*International honours with Blackburn Rovers: England: 2 caps (1882).*
**Appearances:** FA Cup 10.
Doctor Haydock Greenwood was the youngest of seven brothers who were members of a local wealthy family. Two of his brothers Thomas and Harry, preceded him into the Blackburn Rovers team and Thomas was also the first captain of the club. However, it was the youngest Greenwood who went on to earn the greatest recognition, winning two England caps in 1882. Although not the fleetest of players, Greenwood was a powerful defender who went on to form an outstanding full-back partnership with Fergie Suter. Whilst Suter can lay claim to being the club's first professional player, Greenwood was an amateur in the true sense of the word. A former public schoolboy, he was invited to become involved with the famous Corinthians in 1883. Injury robbed him of a place in the 1882 FA Cup Final and the following season his appearances became increasingly spasmodic.

## GREGORY, David Harry
Forward. 1978.
*5ft 9in; 11st 6lb.*
*Born: Peterborough, 6 October 1951.*
*Debut: v Crystal Palace (h) 19 August 1978.*
*Career: Chatteris Town; Peterborough United August 1973; Stoke City June 1977; Blackburn Rovers on loan August 1978 to September 1978; Bury September 1978; Portsmouth December 1979; Wrexham August 1982; Peterborough United August 1986.*
**Appearances:** Football League 5; Football League Cup 1; Total 6.
**Goals:** Football League 3; Football League Cup 1; Total 4.
The failure to bring Dave Gregory to Ewood Park proved a fatal blow to the managership of Jim Iley. Within months of accepting the position at Blackburn, Iley found himself under mounting pressure as the team made a stumbling start to the 1978-79 season. The only ray of light in the rapidly deepening gloom was the form of Dave Gregory who had been brought to Ewood on a month's loan. Gregory, a lively inside-forward with an eye for goal, was offered terms by Iley but chose to sign for Third Division Bury. Whilst his decision hastened Iley's departure from Ewood Park, Gregory went on to enjoy a successful career with a number of clubs. When he retired from League football he had scored 108 goals in 480 League appearances (including 53 as sub).

## GREW, Mark Stuart
Goalkeeper. 1991.
*5ft 11in; 12st 8lb.*
*Born: Bilston, 15 February 1958.*
*Debut: v Watford (h) 13 October 1991.*
*Career: West Bromwich Albion June 1976; Wigan Athletic on loan December 1978; Notts County on loan March 1979; Leicester City July 1983 (£25,000); Oldham Athletic on loan 28 October 1983; Ipswich Town March 1984 (£60,000); Fulham on loan September 1985; West Bromwich Albion on loan January 1986; Derby County March 1986; Port Vale June 1986 (free); Blackburn Rovers on loan October to December 1991; Cardiff City August 1992 (free).*
**Appearances:** Football League 13; Football League Cup 1; Total 14.
A more than competent goalkeeper who figured in a number of loan deals during his career. It was such a deal which brought him to Ewood Park in October 1991. At the time Grew was out of favour at Port Vale whilst the Rovers were struggling at the wrong end of the Second Division. With Terry Gennoe ruled out with injury and the form of Darren Collier giving cause for concern, Don Mackay opted to bring the experienced Grew to Ewood. The move proved successful for both parties. Grew regained his best form and as a result the Rovers gained some much needed points. The loan period came to an end in December 1991 when Jack Walker provided the finance to bring Bobby Mimms from Tottenham Hotspur for £250,000. Grew returned to the Potteries and regained his first-team place with Port Vale before moving to Cardiff City during the summer of 1992.

## GRIFFITHS, Barry
Goalkeeper. 1960-1964.
*5ft 11in; 11st 6lb.*
*Born: Manchester, 21 November 1940.*
*Debut: v Newcastle United (h) 9 April 1960.*
*Career: Sheffield Wednesday; Blackburn Rovers non-contract player June 1960 signing professional in May 1961, released April 1964; Altrincham; Witton; Stalybridge Celtic.*
**Appearances:** Football League 2.
A member of the successful FA Youth Cup winning side of 1959, Barry

Griffiths vied with Bob Jones and Brian Reeves for the reserve goalkeeping spot. Griffiths made 46 appearances with the Central League team but was only called into the first team on two occasions. He understudied Harry Leyland in April 1960 and gave a confident enough performance. However his second game, against Blackpool in April 1963, proved something of a nightmare with the Rovers losing by four goals to one. He was released by the club 12 months later and went into non-League football.

## GRIMSBY TOWN FC
Founded as Grimsby Pelham in 1878. The club dropped the name 'Pelham' the following year and became one of the original members of the Second Division of the Football League in 1892. Grimsby have been welcome visitors to Ewood Park over the years, having failed to register a single win in Lancashire in 26 visits in the League and two in FA Cup-ties. In 1979-80 both clubs won promotion to the Second Division when Grimsby Town lifted the Third Division title and the Rovers finished in second place.

| Football League | | Home | | Away | |
|---|---|---|---|---|---|
| 1901-02 | (Div 1) | W | 2-0 | L | 1-2 |
| 1902-03 | (Div 1) | W | 2-0 | L | 1-4 |
| 1929-30 | (Div 1) | W | 4-1 | L | 3-5 |
| 1930-31 | (Div 1) | W | 5-2 | L | 0-2 |
| 1931-32 | (Div 1) | W | 3-2 | L | 3-4 |
| 1934-25 | (Div 1) | D | 2-2 | W | 2-1 |
| 1935-36 | (Div 1) | W | 1-0 | D | 1-1 |
| 1946-47 | (Div 1) | D | 1-1 | L | 1-2 |
| 1947-48 | (Div 1) | W | 4-0 | D | 2-2 |
| 1948-49 | (Div 2) | D | 3-3 | W | 2-1 |
| 1949-50 | (Div 2) | W | 3-0 | W | 2-1 |
| 1950-51 | (Div 2) | W | 2-0 | D | 1-1 |
| 1956-57 | (Div 2) | W | 2-0 | W | 3-1 |
| 1957-58 | (Div 2) | W | 3-0 | W | 4-3 |
| 1972-73 | (Div 3) | D | 0-0 | L | 0-2 |
| 1973-74 | (Div 3) | W | 1-0 | L | 2-4 |
| 1974-75 | (Div 3) | D | 1-1 | W | 2-1 |
| 1979-80 | (Div 3) | D | 0-0 | W | 2-1 |
| 1980-81 | (Div 2) | W | 2-0 | D | 0-0 |
| 1981-82 | (Div 2) | W | 2-0 | D | 1-1 |
| 1982-83 | (Div 2) | W | 2-1 | L | 0-5 |
| 1983-84 | (Div 2) | D | 1-1 | L | 2-3 |
| 1984-85 | (Div 2) | W | 3-1 | D | 1-1 |
| 1985-86 | (Div 2) | W | 3-1 | L | 2-5 |
| 1986-87 | (Div 2) | D | 2-2 | L | 0-1 |
| 1991-92 | (Div 2) | W | 2-1 | W | 3-2 |

| | P | W | D | L | F | A |
|---|---|---|---|---|---|---|
| Home | 26 | 18 | 8 | 0 | 56 | 19 |
| Away | 26 | 8 | 6 | 12 | 41 | 56 |
| Total | 52 | 26 | 14 | 12 | 97 | 75 |

| FA Cup | | | | | |
|---|---|---|---|---|---|
| 1889-90 | | (2) | Home | W | 3-0 |
| 1963-64 | | (3) | Home | W | 4-0 |

## GROVES, Arthur
Inside-left. 1929-1933.
*5ft 10in; 11st.*
*Born: Killamarsh, Yorkshire, 27 September 1907; Died: 27 September 1979.*
*Debut: v Manchester United (h) 13 April 1929.*
*Career: Langwith Colliery; Halifax Town May 1927; Blackburn Rovers December 1928; Derby County July 1933 (£550); Portsmouth January 1936; Stockport County June 1939; Atherstone Town 1945; Heanor Athletic player-coach.*
**Appearances:** Football League 65; FA Cup 3; Total 68.
**Goals:** Football League 26.
A scheming type of inside forward who had a fine turn of speed and an elusive body shot. Although regarded as a play maker, Groves also had an eye for goal and in 1929-30 he notched ten goals in only 16 League games. Groves was never able to match that record and the 1930-31 season found him out of the first team. The following two seasons found him in and out of the team and in July 1933 he opted to join Derby County. At Derby he scored 17 goals in 64 League games, although his main function was to create opportunities for Jack Bowers.

## GUEST, William Francis
Outside-left. 1937-1947.
*5ft 8in; 10st 11lb.*
*Born: Brierley Hill, 8 February 1914; Died: November 1973.*

*Debut: v Norwich City (a) 23 January 1937.*
*Career: Brierley Hill Juniors; Bromley Juniors; Kingswinford; Birmingham amateur August 1928, turning professional in February 1932; Blackburn Rovers January 1937 (in part-exchange for Jack Beattie); Walsall August 1947; Peterborough United 1949; Kidderminster Harriers; Lovell's Athletic; Hinckley United; Bilston United; Brandwood Rovers coach.*
*Domestic honours with Blackburn Rovers: Second Division championship: 1938-39 (8 apps, 1 gl); League War Cup runners-up: 1940.*
**Appearances:** Football League 88; FA Cup 6; Total 94.
**Goals:** Football League 30; FA Cup 2; total 32.
Billy Guest was an industrious outside-left who possessed a powerful shot. He joined Blackburn Rovers in a part-exchange deal which took Jack Beattie to Birmingham in January 1937. The lively Guest appeared to have solved the club's long standing problem with the outside-left position. Sixteen games in the 1936-37 season brought nine goals, including four in the 9-1 win over Nottingham Forest at Ewood Park in April 1937. Guest was an ever-present the following season but after four games of the 1938-39 season he was axed in favour of Bobby Langton. Guest scored nine goals in 35 appearances during wartime football and in 1946-47 he was used as an inside-forward in a number of games. However, with Langton in possession of the left-wing spot, Guest moved to Walsall in August 1947.

### HALIFAX TOWN FC
Founded in 1911, Halifax Town joined the Football League in 1921 with the formation of the Third Division North. It was another 50 years before Blackburn Rovers and Halifax Town met in the Football League for the first time. The meetings were restricted to the four seasons that Blackburn spent in the Third Division in early 1970s. At the end of the 1992-93 season, as Blackburn celebrated fourth place in the Premier League, Halifax Town were relegated from the Football League into the GM Vauxhall Conference.

**Football League**

| | | | Home | | Away |
|---|---|---|---|---|---|
| 1971-72 | (Div 3) | W | 2-0 | W | 1-0 |
| 1972-73 | (Div 3) | W | 3-0 | D | 2-2 |
| 1973-74 | (Div 3) | D | 1-1 | D | 1-1 |
| 1974-75 | (Div 3) | W | 1-0 | D | 1-1 |

| | P | W | D | L | F | A |
|---|---|---|---|---|---|---|
| Home | 4 | 3 | 1 | 0 | 7 | 1 |
| Away | 4 | 1 | 3 | 0 | 5 | 4 |
| Total | 8 | 4 | 4 | 0 | 12 | 5 |

**Wartime**

| | | | Home | | Away |
|---|---|---|---|---|---|
| 1940-41 | (NRL) | L | 0-1 | D | 1-1 |
| | | | | D | *3-3 |
| 1941-42 | (FLNS-FC) | W | 2-0 | D | 0-0 |
| 1944-45 | (FLNS-FC) | W | 4-0 | L | 1-2 |

*Note: Blackburn played at Halifax twice in this competition.

### HALL, Coombe
Inside-left. 1890-1895.
*5ft 4½in; 11st 10lb.*
*Born: Scotland: 1872; Died: Port Elizabeth, South Africa, March 1932.*
*Debut : v Burnley (a) 18 October 1890.*
*Career: Edinburgh St Bernard's; Blackburn Rovers October 1890; Edinburgh St Bernard's March 1895; Wanderers (South Africa); Port Elizabeth (South Africa).*
*Domestic honours with Blackburn Rovers: FA Cup winners: 1891.*
**Appearances:** Football League 79; FA Cup 9; Total 88.
**Goals:** Football League 26; FA Cup 4; Total 30.
Coombe Hall was known as the 'Pocket Hercules' during his footballing days on account of his small stature and great strength. Hall joined the Rovers in October 1890 and during his first season with the club he helped to retain the FA Cup with five goals in six FA Cup-ties. Although primarily an inside-left, Hall proved a versatile player and appeared at full-back and centre-half as well as in variety of forward positions. He returned to Scotland and was a member of the St Bernard's team which won the 1895 Scottish Cup Final. Subsequently he went to live in South Africa.

### HALL, Frederick William
Centre-half. 1935-1946.
*5ft 11½in; 13st.*
*Born: Chester-le-Street, 18 November 1917.*
*Debut: v Leicester City (a) 2 January 1937.*
*Career: Ouston Juniors; Blackburn Rovers November 1935; Arsenal wartime guest 1944-45 & 1945-46; Tottenham Hotspur wartime guest 1944-45 & 1945-46; Sunderland August 1946; Barrow September 1955;*

*Ransome & Marles August 1956.*
**Appearances:** Football League 29; FA Cup 1; Total 30.
A utility defender who appeared in all three of the half-back positions and at right-back during his time at Ewood Park. A rugged defender, Hall lacked the necessary passing ability to make a constructive half-back, but his intuitive reading of the game and his tough tackling made him a natural centre-half. Hall had skirted around the fringe of the first team in the late 1930s, but it was during wartime football that his reputation began to grow. He had made a favourable impression whilst guesting with Tottenham Hotspur and as a result was selected as reserve for the Victory International against France in 1945. However, he was unable to agree terms with Eddie Hapgood at Ewood and in August 1946 he joined Sunderland. He became captain of the Roker Park club and went on to make 215 League appearances for them before ending his League career with Barrow.

### HALL, George
Inside-forward. 1897-1898.
*Born: Northern Ireland.*
*Debut: v Derby County (a) 4 September 1897.*
*Career: Belfast Distillery; Blackburn Rovers May 1897.*
**Appearances:** Football League 1.
**Goals:** Football League 1.
George Hall made his debut for Ireland against England at Nottingham on 20 February 1897, whilst still with Belfast Distillery. Unfortunately, Ireland lost by six goals and Hall was not selected for the Irish side again. However, three months after making his international debut, Hall was signed by Blackburn Rovers to fill the inside-right position at Ewood Park. Hall made a good start with a goal on his debut in the opening fixture of the 1897-98 season. Unfortunately, this was not sufficient to prevent the Rovers from suffering a 3-1 defeat. The following week saw Hall relegated to the second team and the sturdily-built Irishman was never called upon again for first-team action.

### HALSALL, Walter George
Left-half. 1932-1938.
*6ft; 11st.*
*Born: Liverpool, 29 March 1912.*
*Debut: v Leeds United (h) 26 August 1933.*
*Career: Bootle Celtic; Liverpool amateur; Marine FC; Burscough Rangers; Bolton Wanderers amateur December 1931; Blackburn Rovers amateur November 1932, signing professional in February 1933; Birmingham July 1938; Chesterfield May 1939. Retired during World War Two.*
**Appearances:** Football League 63; FA Cup 6; Total 69.
**Goals:** Football League 4; FA Cup 1; Total 5.
Wally Halsall was a constructive left-half who graduated through the ranks at Ewood to become a first-team regular at the start of the 1933-34 season. Sadly, injury plagued his career at the club and his position was not helped when the Rovers signed Charlie Calladine from Birmingham in February 1936. Frustrated at the lack of first-team opportunities, Halsall himself moved to Birmingham in July 1938. He remained at St Andrew's for only a season before being released following Birmingham's relegation to the Second Division.

### HAMILL, Alexander
Forward. 1935-1936.
*5ft 9in; 12st 3lb.*
*Born: Dumbarton, 1912.*
*Debut: v Grimsby Town (h) 31 August 1935.*
*Career: Hamilton Academy; Hamilton Welfare; Renton Thistle; Cowdenbeath 1930; Blackburn Rovers August 1935 (£250); Barnsley November 1936; Carlisle United June 1938. Retired during World War Two.*
**Appearances:** Football League 21; FA Cup 3; Total 24.
**Goals:** Football League 4.
A Scot who joined Cowdenbeath when 18 and served the Scottish Club for five years before moving to Blackburn in August 1935. He had the good fortune to make his debut, as deputy for Jack Bruton, on the day he crossed the border. Subsequently he occupied every position in the forward line and gave a very good account of himself at centre-forward. A bustling type of player, he was signed by Barnsley for a fee approaching three times that which the Rovers paid for him.

### HAMILL, Kevin Joseph
Goalkeeper. 1936.
*Born: Liverpool, 6 March 1914; Died: Liverpool, 1975 (October quarter).*
*Debut: v Portsmouth (h) 18 April 1936.*
*Career: Seaforth Social Club; Liverpool amateur; Blackburn Rovers amateur April 1936; Seaforth Social Club April 1936.*
**Appearances:** Football League 1.

An amateur goalkeeper who enjoyed a brief moment in the spotlight at Ewood Park. In a season which was to bring relegation to the Second Division, no fewer than five goalkeepers appeared in the first team. With the club's three professional goalkeepers, Binns, Hughes and Barron, all on the injured list the Rovers received special permission from the Football League to use Hamill in the home match with Portsmouth. Although to blame for the only goal that Portsmouth scored Hamill performed well enough, considering his background, and helped the team to their first win in seven games. However, for the final two games of the season the club turned to John Pratt, an amateur from Preston.

**HAMILTON, David**
Midfield. 1981-1985.
*5ft 7½in; 9st 12lb.*
*Born: South Shields, 7 November 1960.*
*Debut: v Watford (h) 10 January 1981 (sub).*
*Career: Sunderland September 1978; Blackburn Rovers January 1981; Cardiff City on loan March to May 1985; Wigan Athletic August 1986; Chester City August 1989; Burnley August 1990; Chorley cs 1992; Barrow December 1993.*
**Appearances:** Football League 104+10; FA Cup 1+1; Football League Cup 7; Total 112+11.
**Goals:** Football League 7.
David Hamilton was signed by Howard Kendall as a possible successor to his own midfield role. Hamilton proved an adaptable utility man and performed equally well in defence as in midfield. After spending some time in the role of understudy, Hamilton finally won a midfield spot during the 1982-83 season. The following season saw Mick Rathbone suffer a broken leg and Hamilton was switched to defence. His form wavered during the season and in 1984-85 his Ewood career seemed to be at an end when he was loaned to Cardiff City. However, he returned for one more season of first-team football with Blackburn before joining Wigan Athletic in August 1986. Hamilton also enjoyed spells with Chester City and Burnley before moving into non-League football in the summer of 1992.

**HAND, John**
Centre-half. 1906-1907.
*Born: Middlesbrough.*
*Debut: v Aston Villa (h) 29 December 1906.*
*Career: Blackburn Rovers September 1906; Hartlepools United.*
**Appearances:** Football League: 2.
Hand got his first-team opportunity in place of Joe Wilson in the last match of 1906. He made a creditable start to his career in League football and was retained for the game at home to Preston North End on New Year's Day 1907. Although the Rovers managed to snatch a 1-1 draw, the absence of Wilson was keenly felt and this was the last appearance Hand made for the first team. He went on to become a founder member of the Hartlepools United team and was in their line-up on 12 September 1908 when they played their first competitive game in the North Eastern League.

**HANNAH, Gardner**
Right-half. 1895-1896.
*5ft 6in; 11st 9lb.*
*Born: Dunfermline, 1874.*
*Debut: v Sheffield Wednesday (a) 11 January 1896.*
*Career: Airdrieonians; Blackburn Rovers March 1895.*
**Appearances:** Football League 3.
A clever little half-back who came across the border with a good reputation. Hannah was a fearless tackler who liked to get forward and have a crack at goal. A hard-working player who possessed plenty of pace, Hannah had the misfortune to be in competition with Dewar, Anderson, Cleghorn and Killean for the half-back positions.

**HAPGOOD, Edris Albert**
Manager. 1946-1947.
*Born: Bristol, 24 September 1908; Died: Leamington Spa, 20 April 1973.*
*Career: Bristol Rovers trial May 1927; Kettering Town cs 1927; Arsenal October 1927 (£750); Chelsea wartime guest 1942-43 & 1943-44 & 1944-45; Luton Town wartime guest 1943-44 & 1944-45; Blackburn Rovers manager January 1946 until February 1947; Shrewsbury Town player-coach August 1947; Watford manager February 1948 until March 1950; Bath City manager March 1950 until February 1956.*
As a player with the great Arsenal side of the 1930s, Eddie Hapgood had won four League championship medals, an FA Cup winners' medal and 30 England caps. However, his first tentative steps into football management were to prove less memorable or successful. Hapgood had been approached to take over the managership of Blackburn Rovers whilst he was still serving with the RAF in 1944. His RAF posting delayed his arrival at Ewood and problems with housing meant that

Hapgood did not take over the managerial reigns until New Year's Day 1946.
The former Arsenal and England left-back made two appearances for the first team in the Football League North, but his main task was to build a side to be ready for the restoration of the Football League. Without the financial resources to bring in new blood, Hapgood decided to put his faith in a crop of youngsters. A few ageing stars from the Second Division championship side remained to provide experience, whilst Hapgood appointed Horace Cope, an old Arsenal colleague, as trainer. The manager returned to Highbury to sign George Marks, a young goalkeeper who had begun to establish himself in wartime football. Although Hapgood fashioned a workmanlike side, it failed to achieve any degree of consistency.
The result was that the Rovers made a disappointing start to their delayed return to the First Division. Hapgood laid himself open to criticism when he continued with the policy of ignoring more experienced campaigners in favour of untried youth. As a result a number of the club's more seasoned professionals became unsettled. Early in 1947, the first signs for a rift between manager and directors began to appear. With the club entrenched at the wrong end of the table the directors embarked on a dramatic rebuilding programme. In a short space of time the club had acquired Jock Weir, Jack Oakes and Frank McGorrighan for a sizeable outlay. However, Hapgood had not instigated the signings and their arrival at Ewood Park merely highlighted the gulf that had developed between the manager and his employers.
On 19 February 1947, it was announced that Eddie Hapgood had tendered his resignation as manager of Blackburn Rovers. On leaving Ewood he resumed his playing career with Shrewsbury Town in the Midland League. However, in February 1948 he returned to football management when he accepted the managership of Watford. He later had a spell in charge of Bath City before becoming the warden of a youth hostel.

**HARDY, Allan**
Left-back. 1900-1902.
*5ft 9½in; 12st 8lb.*
*Born: Ilkeston, 1873.*
*Debut: v Nottingham Forest (h) 5 March 1900.*
*Career: Ilkeston 1898; Wigan County December 1899; Blackburn Rovers January 1900 to cs 1902.*
**Appearances:** Football League 42.
A cricket professional with Wigan Cricket Club, Allan Hardy also turned out for Wigan County during the winter months. He gained a reputation as one of the best left-backs in the Lancashire Combination and was snapped up by the Rovers in January 1900. He played in nine of the final 12 matches of the season and began the following campaign as Bob Crompton's partner. Tragically, the 1902-03 season brought a leg injury from which Hardy was unable to recover and which forced him into retirement.

**HARDY, George G.**
Half-back. 1938-1939.
*5ft 11½in; 12st 7lb.*
*Born: Newbold Verdun, Leicestershire, 1912 (January quarter).*
*Debut: v Tranmere Rovers (h) 27 August 1938.*
*Career: Leicestershire schoolboy football; Nuneaton Town 1932; Aston Villa February 1934; Blackburn Rovers August 1938.*
**Appearances:** Football League 7.
An Aston Villa reserve half-back who made only six League appearances during his time at Villa Park. He was immediately installed in the centre-half position at Blackburn but failed to provide the leadership which Bob Crompton hoped he would bring. Injury forced him out of the team and Bob Pryde was switched to centre-half as Frank Chivers stepped into the left-half spot. The moves were such a success that there was no way back for Hardy.

**HARDY, Jacob Henry**
Outside-right. 1922-1923.
*Born: Bishop Auckland, 1898 (July quarter).*
*Debut: v Liverpool (a) 17 February 1923.*
*Career: Shildon Athletic July 1922; Blackburn Rovers September 1922.*
**Appearances:** Football League 1.
Jacob Hardy was the fifth outside-right to be used in the space of six games during January and February 1923. The disappointing form of the veteran Dickie Bond, who had been signed from Bradford City in the close season, gave Hardy an unexpected opportunity of first-team football. Hardy was given a baptism of fire at Liverpool and had little opportunity to make an impression. Although he put some nice centres over, it was his pin-point corner kicks which caught the eye. Within weeks of his debut the club had signed Jack Crisp and Hardy never appeared for the first team again.

**HARESNAPE, Robert**
Outside-right. 1888-1889.
*Born: Blackburn, 1866.*
*Debut: v West Bromwich Albion (h) 22 September 1888.*
*Career: Witton (Blackburn); Blackburn Rovers May 1888; Burnley August 1889; Irwell Springs November 1891.*
**Appearances:** Football League 9; FA Cup 4; Total 13.
**Goals:** Football League 2; FA Cup 6; Total 8.
Bob Haresnape acted as understudy for James Beresford during the club's first season of League football. However, it was in the FA Cup that he came into his own with six goals in only four appearances. Unable to win a regular place in the Blackburn team, Haresnape joined Burnley in August 1889.

**HARFORD, Raymond**
Assistant manager. 1991-
*Born: Halifax, 1 June 1945.*
*Career: Charlton Athletic amateur May 1961, turning professional in May 1964; Exeter City January 1966; Lincoln City July 1967; Mansfield Town June 1971; Port Vale December 1971; Colchester United January 1973; Romford July 1975; Colchester United coach September 1975; Fulham youth-team manager cs 1981, becoming assistant manager cs 1982 and manager in April 1984; Luton Town assistant manager July 1986, then manager June 1987 until January 1990; Wimbledon assistant manager February 1990, then manager June 1990; Blackburn Rovers assistant manager October 1991.*
Ray Harford is generally acknowledged as one of the finest coaches in the modern game. Although his own playing career was rather modest in terms of top flight football, he has been in constant demand as a manager and coach since retiring from playing. Harford enjoyed his greatest success as manager at Luton Town following his appointment to the position in June 1987. During his first season in charge he saw the Hatters finish ninth in the First Division and defeat Arsenal in the Football League Cup Final.

In the same season he also visited Wembley in the Simod Cup, where Luton were surprisingly defeated by Reading, and reached the semi-final of the FA Cup. Harford was sacked by Luton in January 1990, but a month later he had joined Bobby Gould at Wimbledon as assistant manager. When Gould left the club, Harford was appointed caretaker manager before taking over permanently in December 1990. However, in August 1991, he announced his intention to resign as manager and gave the club six months' notice. When Kenny Dalglish walked into Ewood Park in October 1991, he had Ray Harford by his side as his number two. The pair were to prove an excellent combination with Dalglish always quick to point out the importance of Harford's contribution to success of the club.

**HARGREAVES, A.**
Forward. 1892-1895.
*Debut: v Derby County (a) 22 October 1892.*
*Career: Blackburn Rovers June 1892.*
**Appearances:** Football League 2.
Little is known about this player apart from the fact that he joined the club from the Accrington district. Although registered with the Football League in June 1892, his Christian name was never recorded. At the time the Rovers also had Joshua Hargreaves registered with them and some sources have credited that player with two appearances during 1892-93. However, as Joshua was transferred to Northwich Victoria in early October 1892, it is likely that it was A.Hargreaves who appeared in the forward line on 22 October 1892 and 2 January 1893.

**HARGREAVES, David G.**
Forward. 1977-1979.
*5ft 8½in; 11st 4lb.*
*Born: Accrington, 27 August 1954.*
*Debut: v Blackpool (a) 4 February 1978.*
*Career: Accrington Stanley; Blackburn Rovers December 1977; Accrington Stanley; Padiham.*
**Appearances:** Football League 2.
David Hargreaves made a belated entry into the Football League when he signed for Blackburn Rovers at the age of 23. Hargreaves had an impressive goalscoring record with Accrington Stanley but did not enjoy the best of fortune at Ewood Park. He made his debut in the disastrous 5-2 defeat at Blackpool – a result which proved a severe blow to the club's promotion hopes. Within a fortnight of his debut the club had signed John Radford from West Ham United and Hargreaves returned to the Central League team. Sadly, injuries prevented Hargreaves from doing himself justice at Ewood and he returned to non-League football with Accrington Stanley.

**HARGREAVES, Frederick William**
Half-back. 1877-1882.
*Born: Blackburn, 16 August 1858; Died: Wiltshire, nr Blackburn, 5 April 1897.*
*Debut: v Tyne Association (h) 1 November 1879 (FAC).*
*Career: Malvern College; Blackburn Rovers 1877.*
*International honours with Blackburn Rovers: England: 3 caps (1880-82).*
*Domestic Honours with Blackburn Rovers: FA Cup runners-up 1882.*
**Appearances:** FA Cup 12.
**Goals:** FA Cup 1.
Fred Hargreaves had the distinction of becoming the first Blackburn Rovers player to win an international cap. The son of the Blackburn coroner, Hargreaves was one of three former Malvern College pupils to represent Blackburn Rovers during the club's formative years. With his younger brother John, Fred appeared in the Blackburn team which was beaten by a single goal in the 1882 FA Cup Final. Whilst John went on to pick up a winners' medal in 1884, Fred had already retired from the game by the time the Rovers reached their second Final. An outstanding half-back, Fred was a rugged tackler and a player whose willingness to drive forward in support of his front men made him a popular character at the club. Like his brother John, Fred Hargreaves died at a tragically early age.

**HARGREAVES, John**
Forward. 1878-1884.
*Born: Blackburn, 13 December 1860; Died: Blackburn, 13 January 1903.*
*Debut: v Tyne Association (h) 1 November 1879 (FAC).*
*Career: Malvern College 1878; Blackburn Rovers 1878-1884.*
*International honours with Blackburn Rovers: England: 2 caps (1881).*
*Domestic honours with Blackburn Rovers: FA Cup winner: 1884; FA Cup runners-up: 1882.*
**Appearances:** FA Cup 11.
**Goals:** FA Cup 5.
Jack Hargreaves received his initiation to the game at Malvern College. He made his first appearance for the Rovers against Turton during a school vacation. Although he complained about the rough tactics employed by the opposition, Hargreaves became a regular member of the Blackburn Rovers team between 1878 and 1884. Jack, like his brother Fred, won international honours for England and appeared in two Cup Finals for the Rovers. A solicitor by profession, Jack was something of an all round athlete and whilst at college he headed the cricket averages at both batting and bowling.

**HARGREAVES, Joshua**
Forward. 1891-1892 & 1893-1897 & 1898.
*5ft 5in; 10st 6lb.*
*Debut: v Darwen (a) 2 September 1893.*
*Career: Blackburn Rovers August 1991; Northwich Victoria October 1992; Blackburn Rovers cs 1893; New Brighton Tower cs 1897; Blackburn Rovers on loan April 1898.*
**Appearances:** Football League 54; Test Matches 2; FA Cup 5; Total 61.
**Goals:** Football League 19.
Josh Hargreaves was continually discarded during the 1890s as the Blackburn committee tried a succession of men in the centre-forward position. However, the committee always returned to Hargreaves and Josh was always willing to take up the challenge. Although not the biggest of men, Hargreaves was a willing worker and was held in such esteem that the committee invited him back to Blackburn when the club was faced with the possibility of relegation in April 1898. At this time Hargreaves was plying his trade with New Brighton but agreed to play in the final two League matches and the first two test matches for his old club.

**HARGREAVES, Thomas**
Centre-forward. 1935-1946.
*5ft 9½in; 12st.*
*Born: Blackburn, 29 October 1917.*
*Debut: v Manchester United (a) 26 February 1938.*
*Career: Feniscowles Council School; Crosshill (Blackburn); Blackburn Rovers amateur October 1935, turning professional in October 1936; Accrington Stanley wartime guest 1939-40; Rochdale May 1946.*
**Appearances:** Football League: 4.
**Goals:** 2.
Although Tom Hargreaves joined the professional ranks at Ewood in October 1936, he still preferred to follow his original calling as a joiner and trained in the evenings. After graduating through the 'A' team, Hargreaves moved from inside-right to centre-forward during the 1937-38 season. A dozen goals in as many Central League games earned Hargreaves a first-team debut in February 1938. Although the team were beaten by Manchester United, Hargreaves had the satisfaction of scoring

the only Blackburn goal. Sturdily built, Hargreaves was blessed with good ball control and a strong shot but his lack of pace prevented him from winning a regular place in the first team. After World War Two he appeared briefly with Rochdale, making seven League appearances for the Spotland club.

### HARPER, Edward Cashfield
Centre-forward. 1923-1927 & 1933-1935.
*5ft 10in; 11st.*
*Born: Sheerness, Kent, 22 August 1901; Died: Blackburn, 22 July 1959.*
*Debut: v Chelsea (a) 25 August 1923.*
*Career: Whitstable Town; Sheppey United; Blackburn Rovers May 1923; Sheffield Wednesday November 1927; Tottenham Hotspur March 1929 (£5,500); Preston North End December 1931 (£5,000); Blackburn Rovers November 1933, joining the coaching staff in May 1935 until May 1948.*
*International honours with Blackburn Rovers: England: 1 cap (1926).*
**Appearances:** Football League 171; FA Cup 6; Total 177.
**Goals:** Football League 121; FA Cup 1; Total 122.
Ted Harper was brought to Ewood Park purely on the strength of his goalscoring record with Sheppey United. In truth there were few other facets to his game. A rather clumsy looking individual whose ball control was negligible, Ted Harper was, none the less, one of the most prolific goalscorers to appear in the colours of Blackburn Rovers.

Harper scored 18 goals, the highest individual tally since before World War One, during his first season with the club. Unable to reproduce this form during his second term with the club, Harper was eventually replaced by Syd Puddefoot, the former West Ham United man who had been playing with Falkirk. However, the 1925-26 season saw Harper and Puddefoot form a prolific goalscoring partnership. It was in this season that a change in the offside rule was exploited to the full by Puddefoot and Harper, with the result that Harper created a new Football League record of 43 League goals.

Although he gained an international cap in 1926, his game had too many weaknesses for him to win a regular place in the England side. However, few could fault his courage or his natural instinct to be in the right place at the right time. This instinctive positional sense, coupled with the ability to use either foot and head with telling accuracy, made him one of the most feared marksmen of his era.

He left Ewood during the 1927-28 season to join Sheffield Wednesday and scored 13 goals in 18 games for the Yorkshire club. In March 1929, Tottenham Hotspur paid a sizeable fee to take Harper to White Hart Lane and were rewarded with 62 goals in 63 League games.

Harper returned to Lancashire in December 1931 to join Preston North End and in November 1933 he signed for a second spell at Ewood Park. On hanging up his boots he joined the coaching staff at Ewood Park before retiring from the game in 1948. Whilst he may not have been the most skilful of players, Harper broke individual goalscoring records at Blackburn Rovers, Tottenham Hotspur and Preston North End.

### HARRIS, Joseph
Centre-forward. 1951-1953.
*5ft 9in; 11st 1lb.*
*Born: Belfast, 8 April 1929.*
*Debut: v West Ham United (a) 13 January 1951.*
*Career: Belfast Distillery; Larne; Blackburn Rovers January 1951; Oldham Athletic March 1953; Belfast Crusaders July 1954.*
**Appearances:** Football League 35; FA Cup 1; Total 36.
**Goals:** Football League 14.
Joe Harris had the misfortune to break the same leg twice in two years at a time when he was trying to establish himself at Ewood Park. It was a tragic blow for the youngster who had cost the Rovers two transfer fees to bring him to Blackburn in January 1951. The Rovers had to pay £300 to Larne, for whom he was playing, and £3,000 to Distillery, the club who still held his registration. Harris, a free scoring centre-forward, had joined Distillery as a 15-year-old but failed to agree terms with the club at the start of the 1950-51 season. As a result he went outside of the Irish League to join Larne before coming to England. It was hoped that Harris would finally solve the troublesome centre-forward position for the Rovers, a problem which had existed since the departure of Dennis Westcott almost 12 months earlier. Harris began with a goal on his debut and went on to score ten goals in the remaining 17 League fixtures. Sadly, after such a bright beginning, injuries took their toll and the arrival of Tommy Briggs in November 1952 put an end to any hopes of a return to the senior team. He joined Oldham to take part in the final stages of their successful promotion campaign but struggled to find his form the following season. In the summer of 1954, Harris returned to Ireland to play his football.

### HARRISON, Michael John
Outside-left. 1962-1967.
*5ft 10in; 11st 8lb.*
*Born: Ilford, 18 April 1940.*
*Debut: v West Ham United (h) 22 September 1962.*
*Career: Chelsea April 1957; Blackburn Rovers September 1962 (£18,000); Plymouth Argyle September 1967; Luton Town June 1968; Dover Town July 1970.*
**Appearances:** Football League 160; FA Cup 14; Football League Cup 7; Total 181.
**Goals:** Football League 40; FA Cup 2; Football League Cup 1; Total 43.
A former England Schoolboy and Under-23 international, Mike Harrison joined Blackburn Rovers in September 1962 to replace the inconsistent Joe Haverty. Although he had been capped three times at Under-23 level, Harrison had been unable to dislodge Frank Blunstone from the outside-left position at Stamford Bridge and so jumped at the opportunity of regular First Division football at Ewood Park. Tall and well built, Harrison was exceptionally quick and packed a powerful shot. An expert penalty taker, Harrison relied on pure power to blast the ball past startled goalkeepers. That he did not win more honours in the game was probably due to his reluctance to physically impose himself on defenders. None the less, Harrison gave the club excellent service during his time at Ewood Park and will always be remembered as a member of one of the most thrilling forward lines that the club has ever produced. When he finally lost his first-team place he moved to Plymouth Argyle in 1967 but after 15 League appearances he joined Luton Town. He retired from the game after a further 32 League appearances for the 'Hatters'.

### HARTFORD, Richard Asa
Reserve-team manager 1991-1993.
*Born: Clydebank, 24 October 1950.*
*Career: Drumchapel Amateurs; West Bromwich Albion apprentice April 1966, becoming a professional in November 1967; Manchester City August 1974 (£225,000); Nottingham Forest June 1979 (£500,000); Everton August 1979 (£400,000); Manchester City October 1981 (£350,000); Fort Lauderdale Strikers (United States of America) May 1984; Bolton Wanderers player-coach July 1985; Stockport County player-manager June 1987 until April 1989; Shrewsbury Town coach July 1989, then manager January 1990 until January 1991; Boston United player February 1991; Blackburn Rovers reserve-team manager cs 1991; Stoke City assistant manager November 1993.*
Asa Hartford was appointed manager of the Central League team at Ewood Park during the summer of 1991. As a player he had won 50 caps for Scotland and was acknowledged as one of the finest midfield players of his era. It was this wealth of experience that Don Mackay hoped Hartford would pass on to the younger players at the club. Within weeks of his arrival at Blackburn, Mackay was axed and Hartford found himself acting as the number two to caretaker manager Tony Parkes. Parkes and Hartford managed to lift the club into a mid-table position before the arrival of Kenny Dalglish and Ray Harford in October 1992. Dalglish, a former Scottish international colleague of Hartford, not only retained Hartford in the position of manager to the second team but also involved him with the first team. Under Hartford the reserve team enjoyed one of its most successful spells in the First Division of the Central League. In November 1993, Joe Jordan, newly appointed manager of Stoke City, persuaded Hartford to accept the number two position with the Potteries club.

### HARTLEPOOL UNITED FC
Hartlepool United FC was formed in 1908 as Hartlepools United. John Hand, a former Blackburn Rovers centre-half, was a member of the Hartlepools United side that first entered competitive League football in September 1908. At that time Hartlepools United were members of the North Eastern League but in 1921 they became founder members of the Third Division North of the Football League. Hartlepool United and Blackburn Rovers have never met in a Football League fixture but in 1974-75, Hartlepool pulled off a surprise victory in the Football League Cup against the Rovers.

Football League Cup
| 1974-75 | (3) | Away | D | 1-1 |
|---------|-----|------|---|-----|
|         | (R) | Home | L | 1-2 |

### HARTLEY, Dilworth
Half-back. 1890-1894.
*Debut: v West Bromwich Albion (a) 3 October 1890.*
*Career: Blackburn Rovers August 1890; Darwen June 1894.*
**Appearances:** Football League 6.
Dilworth Hartley was one of eight players who were tried in the right-half position during the 1891-92 season. The following season saw George Dewar moved into that position and Hartley was restricted to just two appearances. In June 1894 he moved to neighbouring Darwen.

## HARVEY, Arthur

Left-back. 1906-1907.
*Debut: v Manchester United (a) 16 February 1907.*
*Career: Shildon Athletic; Blackburn Rovers amateur October 1906.*
**Appearances:** Football League 1.

Arthur Harvey had the misfortune to face Billy Meredith, the Welsh wizard, on his debut in February 1907. Without the steadying influence of Bob Crompton and Arthur Cowell the Blackburn defence was led a merry dance by Meredith and none more so than the young Harvey. Although the youngster made some good clearances the Rovers could do nothing to prevent Manchester United cruising to a 4-2 victory and Harvey was never selected for the first team again.

## HAT-TRICK HEROES

Most hat-tricks in a season: 8 in 1963-64.
Most individual hat-tricks in a season: 5 John Southworth 1890-91; Andy McEvoy 1963-64.
Most hat-tricks in a career whilst at Blackburn: 12 John Southworth.

A full breakdown of players who have scored a hat-trick in a

Andy McAvoy scores one of his three goals in the third-round FA Cup game against Grimsby Town in January 1964.

The second goal of David Speedie's hat-trick over Newcastle at Ewood Park in February 1992.

League, FA Cup or Football League Cup game is given below.

**1880-81**

| | | | | | | | | | | |
|---|---|---|---|---|---|---|---|---|---|---|
| James Brown | (3) | 30 | Oct | 1880 | v | Sheffield Providence | Home | W | 7-2 | FA Cup |

**1882-83**

| | | | | | | | | | | |
|---|---|---|---|---|---|---|---|---|---|---|
| Alfred Barton | (3) | 23 | Oct | 1882 | v | Blackpool St Johns | Home | W | 11-1 | FA Cup |
| James Brown | (4) | 23 | Oct | 1882 | v | Blackpool St Johns | Home | W | 11-1 | FA Cup |

**1883-84**

| | | | | | | | | | | |
|---|---|---|---|---|---|---|---|---|---|---|
| James Brown | (4) | 19 | Jan | 1884 | v | Staveley | Home | W | 5-1 | FA Cup |

**1884-85**

| | | | | | | | | | | |
|---|---|---|---|---|---|---|---|---|---|---|
| Alfred Barton | (3) | 13 | Oct | 1884 | v | Rossendale | Home | W | 11-0 | FA Cup |
| Herbert Fecitt | (4) | 13 | Oct | 1884 | v | Rossendale | Home | W | 11-0 | FA Cup |

**1888-89**

| | | | | | | | | | | |
|---|---|---|---|---|---|---|---|---|---|---|
| John Southworth | (3) | 3 | Nov | 1888 | v | Burnley | Away | W | 7-1 | Football League |
| John Southworth | (3) | 17 | Nov | 1888 | v | Aston Villa | Home | W | 5-1 | Football League |
| Robert Haresnape | (4) | 3 | Mar | 1889 | v | Aston Villa | Home | W | 8-1 | FA Cup |
| John Southworth | (3) | 3 | Mar | 1889 | v | Aston Villa | Home | W | 8-1 | FA Cup |

**1889-90**

| | | | | | | | | | | |
|---|---|---|---|---|---|---|---|---|---|---|
| Nathaniel Walton | (4) | 16 | Nov | 1889 | v | Notts County | Home | W | 9-1 | Football League |
| John Southworth | (3) | 16 | Nov | 1889 | v | Notts County | Home | W | 9-1 | Football League |
| John Southworth | (4) | 30 | Nov | 1889 | v | West Bromwich Albion | Home | W | 5-0 | Football League |
| John Southworth | (4) | 4 | Jan | 1890 | v | Stoke | Home | W | 8-0 | Football League |
| Nathaniel Walton | (3) | 15 | Feb | 1890 | v | Bootle | Away | W | 7-0 | FA Cup |
| William Townley | (3) | 29 | Mar | 1890 | v | Sheffield Wednesday | at the Oval | W | 6-1 | FA Cup |

**1890-91**

| | | | | | | | | | | |
|---|---|---|---|---|---|---|---|---|---|---|
| John Southworth | (3) | 6 | Sep | 1890 | v | Derby County | Away | L | 5-8 | Football League |
| John Southworth | (3) | 6 | Dec | 1890 | v | Aston Villa | Home | W | 5-1 | Football League |
| Coombe Hall | (4) | 3 | Jan | 1891 | v | Derby County | Home | W | 8-0 | Football League |
| John Southworth | (3) | 3 | Jan | 1891 | v | Derby County | Home | W | 8-0 | Football League |
| John Southworth | (3) | 31 | Jan | 1891 | v | Chester | Home | W | 7-0 | FA Cup |
| John Southworth | (3) | 4 | Mar | 1891 | v | Accrington | Away | W | 4-0 | Football League |

**1891-92**

| | | | | | | | | | | |
|---|---|---|---|---|---|---|---|---|---|---|
| John Southworth | (3) | 21 | Nov | 1891 | v | Bolton Wanderers | Home | W | 4-0 | Football League |
| John Southworth | (4) | 16 | Jan | 1892 | v | Derby County | Home | W | 4-1 | FA Cup |

**1893-94**

| | | | | | | | | | | |
|---|---|---|---|---|---|---|---|---|---|---|
| Harry Chippendale | (3) | 3 | Feb | 1893 | v | Nottingham Forest | Home | W | 6-1 | Division One |
| James Haydock | (3) | 24 | Feb | 1893 | v | Derby County | Away | W | 4-1 | FA Cup |

**1894-95**

| | | | | | | | | | | |
|---|---|---|---|---|---|---|---|---|---|---|
| Coombe Hall | (3) | 15 | Sep | 1894 | v | Stoke | Home | W | 6-0 | Division One |
| Harry Chippendale | (3) | 5 | Jan | 1895 | v | Small Heath | Home | W | 9-1 | Division One |
| Edward Killean | (3) | 5 | Jan | 1895 | v | Small Heath | Home | W | 9-1 | Division One |

**1899-1900**

| | | | | | | | | | | |
|---|---|---|---|---|---|---|---|---|---|---|
| Arnold Whittaker | (3) | 14 | Oct | 1899 | v | Preston North End | Home | W | 3-0 | Division One |
| Frederick Blackburn | (3) | 5 | Feb | 1900 | v | Portsmouth | at Villa Park | W | 5-0 | FA Cup |

**1900-01**

| | | | | | | | | | | |
|---|---|---|---|---|---|---|---|---|---|---|
| William Bryant | (3) | 29 | Oct | 1900 | v | Aston Villa | Away | D | 3-3 | Division One |

**1901-02**

| | | | | | | | | | | |
|---|---|---|---|---|---|---|---|---|---|---|
| Hugh Morgan | (3) | 15 | Feb | 1902 | v | Stoke | Home | W | 6-1 | Division One |

**1903-04**

| | | | | | | | | | | |
|---|---|---|---|---|---|---|---|---|---|---|
| Frederick Pentland | (3) | 5 | Dec | 1903 | v | Newcastle United | Home | W | 4-0 | Division One |

**1905-06**

| | | | | | | | | | | |
|---|---|---|---|---|---|---|---|---|---|---|
| Adam Bowman | (3) | 24 | Feb | 1906 | v | Wolverhampton W | Home | W | 3-1 | Division One |

**1906-07**

| | | | | | | | | | | |
|---|---|---|---|---|---|---|---|---|---|---|
| James Robertson | (3) | 20 | Apr | 1907 | v | Manchester City | Home | W | 4-0 | Division One |

**1908-09**

| | | | | | | | | | | |
|---|---|---|---|---|---|---|---|---|---|---|
| William Davies | (4) | 21 | Nov | 1908 | v | Everton | Away | D | 4-4 | Division One |
| Ellis Crompton | (3) | 22 | Mar | 1909 | v | Sunderland | Home | W | 8-1 | Division One |
| William Davies | (4) | 13 | Apr | 1909 | v | Bristol City | Away | W | 4-1 | Division One |

**1910-11**

| | | | | | | | | | | |
|---|---|---|---|---|---|---|---|---|---|---|
| Edwin Latheron | (3) | 26 | Nov | 1910 | v | Sheffield Wednesday | Home | W | 6-1 | Division One |

**1912-13**

| | | | | | | | | | | |
|---|---|---|---|---|---|---|---|---|---|---|
| William Cameron | (4) | 26 | Oct | 1912 | v | Bolton Wanderers | Home | W | 6-0 | Division One |
| Wattie Aitkenhead | (3) | 18 | Jan | 1913 | v | Northampton Town | Home | W | 7-2 | FA Cup |
| Wattie Aitkenhead | (3) | 10 | Feb | 1913 | v | Middlesbrough | Home | W | 5-2 | Division One |
| John Orr | (3) | 10 | Mar | 1913 | v | Liverpool | Home | W | 5-1 | Division One |
| Daniel Shea | (3) | 29 | Mar | 1913 | v | Chelsea | Away | W | 6-1 | Division One |

**1913-14**

| | | | | | | | | | | |
|---|---|---|---|---|---|---|---|---|---|---|
| Daniel Shea | (4) | 6 | Sep | 1913 | v | Liverpool | Home | W | 6-2 | Division One |
| George Chapman | (3) | 20 | Sep | 1913 | v | Middlesbrough | Home | W | 6-0 | Division One |
| Daniel Shea | (3) | 20 | Sep | 1913 | v | Middlesbrough | Home | W | 6-0 | Division One |
| Edwin Latheron | (3) | 8 | Nov | 1913 | v | Everton | Home | W | 6-0 | Division One |
| Wattie Aitkenhead | (3) | 25 | Dec | 1913 | v | Preston North End | Home | W | 5-0 | Division One |
| Daniel Shea | (3) | 26 | Dec | 1913 | v | Preston North End | Away | W | 5-1 | Division One |
| Wattie Aitkenhead | (3) | 10 | Jan | 1913 | v | Middlesbrough | Home | W | 3-0 | FA Cup |

**1914-15**

| | | | | | | | | | | |
|---|---|---|---|---|---|---|---|---|---|---|
| Percy Dawson | (4) | 28 | Nov | 1914 | v | Burnley | Home | W | 6-0 | Division One |

**1919-20**

| | | | | | | | | | | |
|---|---|---|---|---|---|---|---|---|---|---|
| Percy Dawson | (3) | 11 | Dec | 1919 | v | Bradford City | Home | W | 4-1 | Division One |
| Norman Rodgers | (3) | 24 | Apr | 1920 | v | Manchester United | Home | W | 5-0 | Division One |
| Norman Rodgers | (3) | 1 | May | 1920 | v | Sheffield United | Home | W | 4-0 | Division One |

**1922-23**

| John McIntyre | (4) | 16 | Sep | 1922 | v | Everton | Home | W | 5-1 | Division One |
|---|---|---|---|---|---|---|---|---|---|---|

**1924-25**

| John McIntyre | (3) | 13 | Sep | 1924 | v | Burnley | Away | W | 5-3 | Division One |
|---|---|---|---|---|---|---|---|---|---|---|

**1925-26**

| Ted Harper | (5) | 9 | Sep | 1925 | v | Newcastle United | Away | W | 7-1 | Division One |
|---|---|---|---|---|---|---|---|---|---|---|
| Ted Harper | (3) | 26 | Sep | 1925 | v | Cardiff City | Home | W | 6-3 | Division One |
| Ted Harper | (3) | 31 | Oct | 1925 | v | Burnley | Away | W | 3-1 | Division One |
| Arthur Rigby | (3) | 13 | Mar | 1926 | v | Burnley | Home | W | 6-3 | Division One |
| Ted Harper | (4) | 10 | Apr | 1926 | v | Manchester United | Home | W | 7-0 | Division One |

**1926-27**

| Syd Puddefoot | (3) | 11 | Sep | 1926 | v | West Ham United | Away | W | 5-1 | Division One |
|---|---|---|---|---|---|---|---|---|---|---|
| Ted Harper | (3) | 25 | Dec | 1926 | v | Huddersfield Town | Home | W | 4-2 | Division One |
| Ted Harper | (4) | 14 | Feb | 1927 | v | West Ham United | Away | W | 4-1 | Division One |

**1927-28**

| Ted Harper | (3) | 24 | Sep | 1927 | v | Birmingham | Home | D | 4-4 | Division One |
|---|---|---|---|---|---|---|---|---|---|---|
| Tom Mitchell | (3) | 5 | Nov | 1927 | v | Arsenal | Home | W | 4-1 | Division One |

**1928-29**

| Jack Roscamp | (3) | 8 | Sep | 1928 | v | Bolton Wanderers | Away | W | 3-0 | Division One |
|---|---|---|---|---|---|---|---|---|---|---|
| Clarrie Bourton | (4) | 1 | Dec | 1928 | v | Manchester United | Away | W | 4-1 | Division One |
| Albert Keating | (3) | 9 | Mar | 1929 | v | West Ham United | Away | D | 3-3 | Division One |

**1929-30**

| Syd Puddefoot | (4) | 28 | Sep | 1929 | v | Birmingham | Home | W | 7-5 | Division One |
|---|---|---|---|---|---|---|---|---|---|---|
| Arthur Groves | (3) | 9 | Nov | 1929 | v | Burnley | Home | W | 8-3 | Division One |
| Arthur Cunliffe | (3) | 8 | Feb | 1930 | v | Huddersfield Town | Home | W | 5-2 | Division One |
| Clarrie Bourton | (4) | 3 | Mar | 1930 | v | Sheffield United | Away | W | 7-5 | Division One |

**1930-31**

| Les Bruton | (3) | 22 | Nov | 1930 | v | Huddersfield Town | Home | W | 5-3 | Division One |
|---|---|---|---|---|---|---|---|---|---|---|
| Les Bruton | (3) | 24 | Jan | 1931 | v | Bristol Rovers | Home | W | 5-1 | FA Cup |

**1931-32**

| Ernie Thompson | (3) | 19 | Dec | 1931 | v | Aston Villa | Away | W | 5-1 | Division One |
|---|---|---|---|---|---|---|---|---|---|---|
| Arthur Cunliffe | (3) | 9 | Apr | 1932 | v | West Ham United | Away | W | 3-1 | Division One |

**1932-33**

| Frank Britton | (3) | 2 | Jan | 1933 | v | Blackpool | Home | W | 6-5 | Division One |
|---|---|---|---|---|---|---|---|---|---|---|

**1933-34**

| Ernie Thompson | (3) | 26 | Aug | 1933 | v | Leeds United | Home | W | 4-2 | Division One |
|---|---|---|---|---|---|---|---|---|---|---|
| Ernie Thompson | (3) | 4 | Nov | 1933 | v | Wolverhampton W | Home | W | 7-1 | Division One |
| Ted Harper | (3) | 24 | Mar | 1934 | v | Leicester City | Home | W | 3-0 | Division One |

**1934-35**

| Les Talbot | (3) | 1 | Dec | 1934 | v | Huddersfield Town | Home | W | 4-2 | Division One |
|---|---|---|---|---|---|---|---|---|---|---|
| Ernie Thompson | (3) | 6 | Apr | 1935 | v | Wolverhampton W | Home | W | 4-2 | Division One |

**1936-37**

| Billy Guest | (4) | 10 | Apr | 1937 | v | Nottingham Forest | Home | W | 9-1 | Division Two |
|---|---|---|---|---|---|---|---|---|---|---|

**1938-39**

| Albert Clarke | (3) | 19 | Nov | 1938 | v | Newcastle United | Home | W | 3-0 | Division Two |
|---|---|---|---|---|---|---|---|---|---|---|

**1946-47**

| Jack Smith | (3) | 7 | Sep | 1946 | v | Everton | Home | W | 4-1 | Division One |
|---|---|---|---|---|---|---|---|---|---|---|

**1947-48**

| Les Graham | (3) | 24 | Apr | 1948 | v | Sheffield United | Home | W | 4-0 | Division One |
|---|---|---|---|---|---|---|---|---|---|---|

**1949-50**

| Dennis Westcott | (3) | 19 | Sep | 1949 | v | Brentford | Home | W | 4-1 | Division Two |
|---|---|---|---|---|---|---|---|---|---|---|
| Dennis Westcott | (3) | 12 | Nov | 1949 | v | Barnsley | Home | W | 4-0 | Division Two |

**1952-53**

| Bill Holmes | (3) | 30 | Aug | 1952 | v | Everton | Home | W | 3-1 | Division Two |
|---|---|---|---|---|---|---|---|---|---|---|

**1953-54**

| Tommy Briggs | (3) | 27 | Aug | 1953 | v | Brentford | Away | W | 4-1 | Division Two |
|---|---|---|---|---|---|---|---|---|---|---|
| Tommy Briggs | (4) | 2 | Jan | 1954 | v | Lincoln City | Home | W | 6-0 | Division Two |
| Tommy Briggs | (3) | 16 | Jan | 1954 | v | Notts County | Away | W | 5-0 | Division Two |

**1954-55**

| Eddie Crossan | (3) | 23 | Oct | 1954 | v | Rotherham United | Home | W | 4-1 | Division Two |
|---|---|---|---|---|---|---|---|---|---|---|
| Eddie Quigley | (3) | 6 | Nov | 1954 | v | Middlesbrough | Home | W | 9-0 | Division Two |
| Frank Mooney | (3) | 6 | Nov | 1954 | v | Middlesbrough | Home | W | 9-0 | Division Two |
| Eddie Quigley | (3) | 15 | Jan | 1955 | v | Notts County | Home | L | 4-5 | Division Two |
| Tommy Briggs | (7) | 5 | Feb | 1955 | v | Bristol Rovers | Home | W | 8-3 | Division Two |

**1955-56**

| Eddie Crossan | (3) | 12 | Nov | 1955 | v | Port Vale | Home | W | 7-1 | Division Two |
|---|---|---|---|---|---|---|---|---|---|---|

**1956-57**

| Tommy Briggs | (3) | 22 | Sep | 1956 | v | Sheffield United | Home | W | 3-1 | Division Two |
|---|---|---|---|---|---|---|---|---|---|---|

**1957-58**

| Ally MacLeod | (3) | 28 | Dec | 1957 | v | Notts County | Home | W | 3-0 | Division Two |
|---|---|---|---|---|---|---|---|---|---|---|
| Peter Dobing | (3) | 4 | Jan | 1958 | v | Rotherham United | Away | W | 4-1 | FA Cup |
| Peter Dobing | (4) | 24 | Mar | 1958 | v | Bristol City | Home | W | 5-0 | Division Two |
| Bryan Douglas | (3) | 4 | Apr | 1958 | v | Doncaster Rovers | Away | W | 5-1 | Division Two |
| Roy Vernon | (3) | 19 | Apr | 1958 | v | Leyton Orient | Home | W | 4-1 | Division Two |

**1958-59**

| Peter Dobing | (3) | 25 | Oct | 1958 | v | Arsenal | Home | W | 4-2 | Division One |
|---|---|---|---|---|---|---|---|---|---|---|
| Tom Johnston | (3) | 20 | Dec | 1958 | v | Newcastle United | Home | W | 3-0 | Division One |

**1959-60**

| Derek Dougan | (4) | 12 | Dec | 1959 | v | West Ham United | Home | W | 6-2 | Division One |
|---|---|---|---|---|---|---|---|---|---|---|

**1960-61**

| | | | | | | | | | | |
|---|---|---|---|---|---|---|---|---|---|---|
| Derek Dougan | (3) | 20 | Aug | 1960 | v | Manchester United | Away | W | 3-1 | Division One |

**1961-62**

| | | | | | | | | | | |
|---|---|---|---|---|---|---|---|---|---|---|
| Eddie Thomas | (4) | 16 | Oct | 1961 | v | Bristol Rovers | Home | W | 4-0 | Football Lge Cup |
| John Byrom | (3) | 26 | Dec | 1961 | v | West Ham United | Away | W | 3-2 | Division One |

**1962-63**

| | | | | | | | | | | |
|---|---|---|---|---|---|---|---|---|---|---|
| Bobby Craig | (3) | 18 | Aug | 1962 | v | Ipswich Town | Away | D | 3-3 | Division One |
| Fred Pickering | (3) | 10 | Nov | 1962 | v | West Bromwich Albion | Away | W | 5-2 | Division One |
| Fred Pickering | (3) | 13 | May | 1963 | v | Wolverhampton W | Home | W | 5-1 | Division One |

**1963-64**

| | | | | | | | | | | |
|---|---|---|---|---|---|---|---|---|---|---|
| Andy McEvoy | (4) | 7 | Sep | 1963 | v | Tottenham Hotspur | Home | W | 7-2 | Division One |
| Fred Pickering | (3) | 9 | Nov | 1963 | v | Everton | Away | W | 4-2 | Division One |
| Andy McEvoy | (3) | 23 | Nov | 1963 | v | West Bromwich Albion | Away | W | 3-1 | Division One |
| Fred Pickering | (3) | 30 | Nov | 1963 | v | Arsenal | Home | W | 4-1 | Division One |
| Fred Pickering | (3) | 26 | Dec | 1963 | v | West Ham United | Away | W | 8-2 | Division One |
| Andy McEvoy | (3) | 26 | Dec | 1963 | v | West Ham United | Away | W | 8-2 | Division One |
| Andy McEvoy | (3) | 4 | Jan | 1964 | v | Grimsby Town | Home | W | 4-0 | FA Cup |
| Andy McEvoy | (4) | 7 | Mar | 1964 | v | Leicester City | Home | W | 5-2 | Division One |

**1964-65**

| | | | | | | | | | | |
|---|---|---|---|---|---|---|---|---|---|---|
| Andy McEvoy | (3) | 17 | Oct | 1964 | v | Sheffield United | Home | W | 4-0 | Division One |
| Andy McEvoy | (3) | 5 | Dec | 1964 | v | Nottingham Forest | Away | W | 5-2 | Division One |
| John Byrom | (3) | 2 | Jan | 1965 | v | Aston Villa | Home | W | 5-1 | Division One |
| John Byrom | (3) | 20 | Mar | 1965 | v | West Ham United | Home | W | 4-0 | Division One |

**1965-66**

| | | | | | | | | | | |
|---|---|---|---|---|---|---|---|---|---|---|
| George Jones | (3) | 11 | Dec | 1965 | v | Northampton Town | Home | W | 6-1 | Division One |
| John Byrom | (3) | 12 | Feb | 1966 | v | West Ham United | Away | D | 3-3 | FA Cup |
| Andy McEvoy | (3) | 16 | Feb | 1966 | v | West Ham United | Home | W | 4-1 | FA Cup |

**1968-69**

| | | | | | | | | | | |
|---|---|---|---|---|---|---|---|---|---|---|
| Malcolm Darling | (3) | 25 | Jan | 1969 | v | Portsmouth | Home | W | 4-0 | FA Cup |

**1969-70**

| | | | | | | | | | | |
|---|---|---|---|---|---|---|---|---|---|---|
| Don Martin | (3) | 20 | Sep | 1969 | v | Millwall | Home | W | 4-0 | Division Two |
| John Connelly | (3) | 13 | Dec | 1969 | v | Preston North End | Home | W | 4-2 | Division Two |

**1971-72**

| | | | | | | | | | | |
|---|---|---|---|---|---|---|---|---|---|---|
| Tony Field | (3) | 5 | Feb | 1972 | v | Barnsley | Home | W | 4-0 | Division Three |

**1972-73**

| | | | | | | | | | | |
|---|---|---|---|---|---|---|---|---|---|---|
| Tony Field | (3) | 27 | Nov | 1972 | v | Lincoln City | Home | W | 4-1 | FA Cup |

**1974-75**

| | | | | | | | | | | |
|---|---|---|---|---|---|---|---|---|---|---|
| Don Martin | (3) | 2 | Oct | 1974 | v | Gillingham | Home | W | 4-1 | Division Three |

**1979-80**

| | | | | | | | | | | |
|---|---|---|---|---|---|---|---|---|---|---|
| Andy Crawford | (3) | 19 | Apr | 1980 | v | Reading | Home | W | 4-2 | Division Three |

**1983-84**

| | | | | | | | | | | |
|---|---|---|---|---|---|---|---|---|---|---|
| Simon Garner | (5) | 10 | Sep | 1983 | v | Derby County | Home | W | 5-1 | Division Two |
| Simon Garner | (3) | 14 | Apr | 1984 | v | Portsmouth | Away | W | 4-2 | Division Two |

**1984-85**

| | | | | | | | | | | |
|---|---|---|---|---|---|---|---|---|---|---|
| Jimmy Quinn | (3) | 6 | May | 1985 | v | Sheffield United | Away | W | 3-1 | Division Two |

**1985-86**

| | | | | | | | | | | |
|---|---|---|---|---|---|---|---|---|---|---|
| Mark Patterson | (3) | 19 | Apr | 1986 | v | Sheffield United | Home | W | 6-1 | Division Two |

**1986-87**

| | | | | | | | | | | |
|---|---|---|---|---|---|---|---|---|---|---|
| Simon Garner | (4) | 6 | Sep | 1986 | v | Sunderland | Home | W | 6-1 | Division Two |

**1988-89**

| | | | | | | | | | | |
|---|---|---|---|---|---|---|---|---|---|---|
| Simon Garner | (3) | 3 | Sep | 1988 | v | Oldham Athletic | Home | W | 3-1 | Division Two |
| Simon Garner | (3) | 15 | Apr | 1989 | v | Manchester City | Home | W | 4-0 | Division Two |

**1989-90**

| | | | | | | | | | | |
|---|---|---|---|---|---|---|---|---|---|---|
| Simon Garner | (3) | 30 | Sep | 1989 | v | Barnsley | Home | W | 5-0 | Division Two |

**1990-91**

| | | | | | | | | | | |
|---|---|---|---|---|---|---|---|---|---|---|
| Frank Stapleton | (3) | 27 | Oct | 1990 | v | Wolverhampton W | Away | W | 3-2 | Division Two |

**1991-92**

| | | | | | | | | | | |
|---|---|---|---|---|---|---|---|---|---|---|
| David Speedie | (3) | 15 | Feb | 1992 | v | Newcastle United | Home | W | 3-1 | Division Two |
| David Speedie | (3) | 2 | May | 1992 | v | Plymouth Argyle | Away | W | 3-1 | Division Two |

**1993-94**

| | | | | | | | | | | |
|---|---|---|---|---|---|---|---|---|---|---|
| Alan Shearer | (3) | 23 | Oct | 1993 | v | Leeds United | Away | D | 3-3 | Premiership |

**HAVERTY, Joseph**
Outside-left. 1961-1962.
*5ft 3½in; 10st 1lb.*
*Born: Dublin, 17 February 1936.*
*Debut: v Cardiff City (h) 19 August 1961.*
*Career: Home Farm (Dublin); St Patrick's Athletic (Dublin); Arsenal July 1954; Blackburn Rovers July 1961 (£17,500); Millwall September 1962; Celtic September 1964; Bristol Rovers December 1964 to June 1965; Shelbourne; Chicago Spurs (USA) May 1967; Kansas City Spurs March 1968.*
*International honours with Blackburn Rovers: Republic of Ireland: 2 caps (1961).*
**Appearances:** Football League 27; Football League Cup 4; Total 31.
**Goals:** Football League 1.
Blackburn Rovers signed Joe Haverty in July 1961 in a bid to fill the void left by Ally MacLeod. Haverty was a diminutive outside-left whose tricky wing play had made him a great favourite with the Highbury

crowd. Sadly, Haverty failed to live up to his reputation and lost his place to Barrie Ratcliffe during the middle of the 1961-62 campaign. Although restored for the final games of the season, Haverty failed to find any great consistency. Like so many players of his type, a tendency to over elaborate undermined his work on occasions. Having tried both Haverty and Ratcliffe without success in the opening games of the 1962-63 campaign, the club signed Mike Harrison from Chelsea. A few days after Harrison's arrival, Haverty was allowed to return to London to join Millwall.

**HAWKINS, Graham Norman**
Central Defender. 1974-1978.
*6ft; 11st.*
*Born: Darlaston, 5 March 1946.*
*Debut: v Grimsby Town (a) 17 August 1974.*
*Career: Wednesbury High School; East Staffordshire Boys; Wolverhampton Wanderers apprentice August 1962, turning professional*

*in April 1963; Preston North End January 1968; Blackburn Rovers June 1974 (£18,000); Port Vale January 1978; Blackburn Rovers reserve-team coach; Stoke City reserve-team coach; Shrewsbury Town assistant manager cs 1980; Wolverhampton Wanderers manager August 1982 until April 1984; Middle East coaching; Blackburn Rovers chief scout March 1990 to summer 1990.*
*Domestic honours with Blackburn Rovers: Third Division championship: 1974-75 (42 apps 1gl).*
**Appearances:** Football League 108+1; FA Cup 4; Football League Cup 8; Total 120+1.
**Goals:** Football League 4.
Gordon Lee signed Graham Hawkins to be the defensive kingpin in what was to become a championship winning side. Tall and blond, Hawkins was a powerful header of the ball and a player who never shirked a physical challenge. He had served his apprenticeship with Wolverhampton Wanderers before making almost 250 League appearances with Preston North End. Lee turned to Hawkins to organise the defence during matches and it was for this reason that he was asked to play when not always fully fit. However, with younger players like Waddington and Fazackerley to partner him in defence, Hawkins was able to have a major influence on the side that won the Third Division title. A wealth of experience of Second Division football proved just as vital when the Rovers struggled for survival following their promotion. Once again his influence played a major part in enabling the club to retain its newly won Second Division status. On reaching the age of 30, Hawkins found that injuries began to restrict his senior appearances. As he approached the veteran stage of his career he had to give way to the challenge of youth in the shape of Glenn Keeley. In January 1978 he joined Port Vale and began to take an interest in coaching. He returned to Ewood for a brief spell as coach to the reserve team before joining Stoke City in a similar capacity. He returned Wolverhampton Wanderers as manager in August 1982 after serving Shrewsbury Town as assistant manager. Hawkins took Wolves into the First Division but found success to be fleeting and with relegation imminent he was sacked in April 1985. After leaving Wolves, Hawkins continued his coaching career in the Middle East. In March 1990 he returned to Ewood Park for a third time to accept the position of chief scout; Hawkins had resigned his position at Ewood and had accepted a coaching appointment in Kuwait when the Gulf region was thrown into turmoil by the Iraqi Invasion of Kuwait.

**HAWKSWORTH, Ernest**
Inside-forward. 1919-1925.
*5ft 7in; 11st 8lb.*
*Born: Rochdale, 6 December 1894; Died: Rochdale, 7 July 1961.*
*Debut: v Preston North End (h) 30 August 1919.*
*Career: Sudden Villa; Rochdale 1912-13; Hull City (wartime guest); Blackburn Rovers March 1919 (£500) to cs 1925; New Brighton October 1926; Bury coach September 1927.*
**Appearances:** Football League 96; FA Cup 4; Total 100.
**Goals:** Football League 34.
During the first two seasons after World War One, Hawksworth shared the goalscoring burden with Percy Dawson. Before the outbreak of war he had joined Rochdale as an amateur and had earned a quick promotion to the first team. He appeared for Hull City in wartime football whilst serving in the First Dragoon Guards. He served with the Royal Scots in France and was twice wounded before returning to Rochdale in January 1919 to resume his footballing career. Two months later he had signed for Blackburn Rovers. A neat and tidy footballer, Hawksworth finished his first season at Ewood as top scorer with 17 League goals. The 1920-21 season brought a further 14 League goals as he finished second only to Percy Dawson in the goalscoring department. As new players arrived at the club Hawksworth, despite his impressive record, found his appearances becoming increasingly infrequent. In October 1926 he finally moved to New Brighton.

**HAWORTH, George**
Half-back. 1884-1885.
*5ft 7in; 11st 10lb.*
*Born: Accrington, 17 October 1864.*
*Debut: v Witton (h) 22 December 1884 (FAC).*
*Career: Christ Church FC 1878; Accrington FC 1882 until 1892; Preston North End on loan 1883-84; Blackburn Rovers on loan 1884-85.*
*Domestic honours with Blackburn Rovers: FA Cup winners: 1885.*
**Appearances:** FA Cup 2.
George Haworth was the captain of Accrington FC and probably the most famous player that 'Th' Owd Reds' produced. Popularly known as 'Jud', Haworth was a hard-tackling half-back who had the pace of a forward. He played as a guest for Preston North End in 1883-84 and featured in the third round and Final of the 1894-95 FA Cup competition with Blackburn Rovers. Haworth gave an outstanding display in the 2-0 win over Queen's Park in the Final at the Kennington Oval in May 1885. Haworth, a regular

performer with Lancashire between 1882 and 1888, was capped five times for England during his career and remained loyal to 'Th' Owd Reds' for a decade.

**HAWORTH, Robert**
Half-back. 1897-1904.
*5ft 9in; 11st.*
*Born: Blackburn, 1879.*
*Debut: v Burnley (a) 26 November 1898.*
*Career: Christ Church 1897; Darwen; Blackburn Rovers May 1897; Fulham cs 1904; Brentford 1906.*
**Appearances:** Football League 122; FA Cup 7; Total 129.
**Goals:** Football League 5.
It fell to Bob Haworth to fill the centre-half position following the departure of Geordie Anderson to new Brighton Tower. Haworth had been spotted as a youngster whilst playing in local junior circles and was converted into a defender with the reserve team at Ewood Park. Haworth was a defender who liked to play his way out of trouble and his skilful feeding of the forward line meant he could operate at either half-back or centre-half. Haworth could also play in either full-back position and his versatility made him a valued member of the playing staff. Haworth left Blackburn in the summer of 1904 after losing his first-team place at Ewood Park.

**HAWORTH, Ronald**
Forward. 1922-1924.
*5ft 7in; 11st.*
*Born: Lower Darwen, nr Blackburn, 10 March 1901; Died: Blackburn, 1973 (October quarter).*
*Debut: v Middlesbrough (a) 15 April 1922.*
*Career: Blackburn Sunday school football; Blackburn Rovers amateur March 1922; Hull City June 1924; Manchester United May 1926; Darwen August 1927.*
**Appearances:** Football League 25.
**Goals:** Football League 7.
Ronald Haworth experienced a rapid rise from local Sunday School football to the First Division within a matter of weeks in 1922. He appeared to make a successful transition to life at a higher level and scored three goals in his five appearances at the end of the 1921-22 season. However, he found goals more difficult to come by during the next campaign and only scored four in 18 appearances. The 1923-24 season found him languishing in the Central League team apart from two senior outings on the left-wing and in June 1924 he moved to Hull City. He scored ten goals in 36 League outings for Hull, before moving to Manchester United where he appeared in a further two League games.

**HAYDOCK, James**
Outside-right. 1890-1897.
*5ft 6in; 10st 7lb.*
*Born: Blackburn, 1873; Died: Blackburn, 24 March 1900.*
*Debut: v Wolverhampton Wanderers (h) 27 September 1890.*
*Career: Borough Road College; Blackburn Rovers August 1890.*
**Appearances:** Football League 66; FA Cup 13; Total 79.
**Goals:** Football League 21; FA Cup 6; Total 27.
A schoolteacher at the Furthergate School in Blackburn, Haydock was one of the greatest outside-rights that the club has ever produced. He made his debut in September 1890 and although he scored a goal he had to wait until the final game of the season before his second League appearance. It wasn't until the latter part of the 1893-94 season that he finally won a regular first-team berth, but even then he had to settle for an inside-forward position. The summer of 1894 brought the departure of Billy Townley and with Harry Chippendale switched to the left-wing, Haydock was finally given his opportunity on the right. He formed an excellent partnership with Jimmy Whitehead on the right and in 1895 he was chosen for England but was not available to play on the day of the match. Despite being dogged by ill-health he rendered excellent service to the club before illness compelled him to retire from the game in 1897. His breakdown in health also prevented him from continuing his profession of schoolteacher and in March 1900 he died at the tragically early age of 27.

**HAYHURST, Stanley**
Goalkeeper. 1943-1948.
*5ft 10in; 10st 9lb.*
*Born: Leyland, Lancashire, 13 May 1925.*
*Debut: v Manchester United (h) 14 December 1946.*
*Career: Leyland Motors; Royal Navy football; Blackburn Rovers January 1943; Tottenham Hotspur October 1948; Barrow June 1950 (£1,500); Grimsby Town January 1951 (£3,500); Weymouth Town July 1953.*
**Appearances:** Football League 27.

Stan Hayhurst came to Blackburn Rovers during World War Two and appeared in nine wartime games with the club. When peace was restored, Hayhurst found himself understudying George Marks for the goalkeeping position. However, following the departure of Marks, Hayhurst was given the opportunity to begin the 1948-49 season as the first-choice custodian. Unfortunately, Hayhurst's form began to waver and in October 1948 he became part of the deal which brought Bill Hughes to Blackburn from Tottenham Hotspur. Hayhurst found himself as understudy to Ted Ditchburn at White Hart Lane and the consistency of the England 'keeper meant Hayhurst was restricted to second-team football whilst in London. He began to rebuild his career with Barrow and after 26 League appearances he moved to Grimsby Town. Hayhurst appeared in 62 League games for the Mariners before joining non-League Weymouth.

### HEALLESS, Harry
Half-back. 1915-1933.
*5ft 9in; 11st 6lb.*
*Born: Blackburn, 10 February 1893; Died: Whitefield, 11 January 1972.*
*Debut: v Sheffield United (a) 20 October 1919.*
*Career: Blackburn Athletic; Victoria Cross; Blackburn Trinity; Blackburn Rovers amateur April 1915, becoming a professional during World War One. Retired in 1933 to become a member of the coaching staff at Blackburn; Almelo (Holland) coach 1935; Haslingden Gane player October 1937; Blackburn Rovers coach 1951 until 1953.*
*International honours with Blackburn Rovers: England: 2 caps (1924-28); Football League: 1 appearance (1923).*
*Domestic honours with Blackburn Rovers: FA Cup winners: 1928.*
**Appearances:** Football League 360; FA Cup 36; FA Charity Shield 1; Total 397.
**Goals:** Football League 12; FA Cup 1; Total 13.
Harry Healless played for several junior clubs in Blackburn before making his first senior appearance for the Rovers on 30 December 1916 against Manchester City at Maine Road. This was one of only two

wartime appearances that Healless made for the club, but it was during the war years that he signed as a professional for the Rovers. Although rather lightweight in build, Healless was capable of filling any of the half-back positions. It was as a forward that he first broke into the senior team during the 1919-20 season.

Although not the most gifted of individuals, Healless more than made up for his shortcomings by his tremendous, appetite for work. His strong running, tough tackling and aerial ability made him a commanding figure in the Blackburn half-back line for over a decade. His natural organisational abilities made him an obvious choice for the captaincy and his proudest moment came in 1928 when he held the FA Cup aloft after leading his home town club to

victory. Capped twice by England he continued to give loyal service to the Rovers until just short of his 40th birthday. On retiring from the game he was put in charge of the 'A' team at Ewood Park but left in 1935 to accept a coaching position in Holland with Almelo. He returned to Lancashire in October 1937 to play as an amateur for Haslingden Gane and after World War Two he could still be found playing in the local leagues. In 1951 he returned to Ewood Park to become the senior coach but left that position when Johnny Carey was appointed to the managership.

### HEATON, James Michael
Right-back. 1971-1977.
*5ft 6in; 10st 10lb.*
*Born: Sheffield, 15 January 1947.*
*Debut: v Rochdale (h) 9 October 1971.*
*Career: Sheffield United apprentice April 1962, turning professional in November 1964; Blackburn Rovers October 1971 to January 1977 (£7,000); Great Harwood January 1978; Blackburn Rovers reserve-team coach 1978, later first-team coach; Everton assistant manager cs 1981; Blackburn Rovers Community development officer 1988; Workington manager 1989; Manchester City assistant manager January 1990 until May 1991; Clitheroe coach October 1991.*
*Domestic honours with Blackburn Rovers: Third Division championship: 1974-75 (40+2 apps 1gl).*

**Appearances:** Football League 169+2; FA Cup 9; Football League Cup 10; Total 188+2.
**Goals:** Football League 1.
Mick Heaton was an ebullient character who was brought to Ewood Park by Ken Furphy as part of his rapid rebuilding of the first team in October 1971. At the time Heaton had been languishing in the Central League team at Bramall Lane having made only 33 League appearances (including two as sub) for Sheffield United. Furphy immediately installed

Heaton into the right-back position and his never-say-die approach made him a natural candidate for the captaincy. Small and agile, Heaton was not a stylist but made up for his lack of polish with an enormous appetite for work. His tigerish approach on the field epitomised the managerial philosophy of Gordon Lee and it was fitting that Heaton should play a leading part in the side which lifted the Third Division title. Heaton was at the peak of his career when he suffered a serious knee injury during the 1975-76 season.

Despite a brave attempt at a comeback, Heaton was never to appear in the first team again and eventually left the game to open a sports shop in the Brownhill district of Blackburn. In 1978 he returned to Ewood Park to look after the Central League team and, following the appointment of Howard

Kendall to the manager's position, was promoted to first-team coach. After winning promotion to the Second Division with Blackburn, Kendall took Heaton with him to Goodison Park during the summer of 1980. Whilst on Merseyside, Heaton shared in the success which brought League, FA Cup and European glory to Goodison Park in the 1980s. Shortly after Kendall left to take charge of Athletic Bilbao, Heaton himself left Goodison Park by mutual consent.

Heaton's search for a managerial position proved unsuccessful and in 1988 he returned to Ewood Park to take charge of the Community Development Programme at the club. In 1989, he took charge of Workington in the Northern Premier League, but lost that position before the end of the year. In January 1990, Heaton was reunited with Kendall when the latter returned from Spain to take charge of Manchester City. However, when Kendall left to return to Everton, Heaton became a casualty of the managerial merry-go-round and lost his position at Maine Road in May 1991.

### HEATON, Thomas
Left-half. 1915-1923.
*5ft 9in; 11st.*
*Born: Blackburn, 2 June 1897.*
*Debut: v Aston Villa (h) 15 April 1920.*
*Career: Blackburn Rovers 19 April 1915 (amateur), turning professional during World War One; Oldham Athletic 27 June 1923 (£150); Manchester North End August 1927; Toronto district (Canada) player, then manager; Retired 1930 after breaking his leg.*
**Appearances:** Football League 57; FA Cup 2; Total 59.
**Goals:** Football League 1.
A sturdily built half-back who favoured a somewhat physical approach to defending. However, Heaton was also capable of thoughtful constructive play and had the ability to feed his forwards with great accuracy. His 'never-say-die' attitude was exactly what the club required in the immediate post-war years. As the club began to turn to the transfer market to strengthen the playing staff, Heaton was allowed to move to Boundary Park and appeared in 59 League games for the 'Latics'.

## HELLIWELL, David
Inside-left. 1963-1969.
*5ft 8½in; 9st 12lb.*
*Born: Blackburn, 28 March 1948.*
*Debut: v Huddersfield Town (a) 3 September 1966.*
*Career: Blackburn Rovers amateur August 1963, becoming an apprentice in June 1964, before turning professional in May 1966; Lincoln City May 1969; Workington July 1970; Rochdale July 1976.*
**Appearances:** Football League 15; Football League Cup 1; Total 16.
**Goals:** Football League 1.
Nicknamed 'Spider', the fraily built Helliwell appeared to be a leading contender to replace Bryan Douglas in midfield. He made his first-team debut following the club's relegation to the Second Division but failed to command a regular place. The emergence of Eamon Rogers and Stuart Metcalf curtailed hopes of a first-team career for Helliwell at Ewood Park. Helliwell moved to Lincoln City in May 1969, but again found it difficult to establish himself and he left Sincil Bank after only 13 League outings (including two as sub). However, he enjoyed great success during six years with Workington, scoring 20 goals in 197 League games (including 13 as sub). Helliwell ended his career with a spell at Spotland Road where 11 of his 31 League appearances were made as substitute.

## HENDRY, Edward Colin James
Central defender. 1987-1990 & 1991-
*6ft 1in; 12st 4lb.*
*Born: Keith, 7 December 1965.*
*Debut: v Ipswich Town (h) 11 March 1987 (Full Members' Cup).*
*Career: Dundee May 1984; Blackburn Rovers March 1987; Manchester City November 1989 (£700,000); Blackburn Rovers November 1991 (£700,000).*
*International honours with Blackburn Rovers: Scotland: 6 caps (1993-94).*

*Domestic honours with Blackburn Rovers: Full Members' Cup winners: 1987; Second Division Play-off winners: 1992.*
**Appearances:** Premier League 63+1; Football League 125+7; Play-offs 9; FA Cup 10+1; Football League Cup 16; Full Members' Cup 7; Total 230+9.
**Goals:** Premier League 1; Football League 26; Full Members' Cup 1; Total 28.

Colin Hendry originally came to Ewood Park from Dundee in March 1987. He made his debut at centre-half against Ipswich Town in the Full Members' Cup but three days later was moved to centre-forward and scored in the home win over Stoke City. Within weeks of his arrival from reserve-team football at Dundee, Hendry became a 'Roy of the Rovers' figure when he scored the only goal of the 1987 Full Members' Cup Final at Wembley. Henry spent much of his first few weeks at Blackburn in the centre-forward position but the start of the 1987-88 campaign saw him installed at centre-half.

Tall and blond, Hendry's buccaneering style of play made him a firm favourite with the Blackburn supporters. Hendry dominated in the air and was always prepared to fling himself at the ball no matter what danger surrounded him. A tough and resolute defender, his long legs enabled him to make last-ditch tackles with apparent ease. During his first spell at the club the rashness of youth led to errors and, despite his willingness to go forward, questions were raised about his lack of pace. However, his striker's eye for goal and ability to initiate attacking moves more than compensated for his lack of experience. A contract dispute at the start of the 1989-90 resulted in Don Mackay leaving him out of the team and in November 1989, a rather reluctant Hendry left Ewood Park for Maine Road. Hendry quickly became a favourite with the Manchester City fans and he retained a regular first-team place until the arrival of Keith Curle.

Only two years after leaving Ewood Park, Hendry returned to Blackburn when Kenny Dalglish made him one of his early signings for the club. Under the guidance of Dalglish, Hendry became a far more polished defender than he had been during his first spell at the club. Hendry appeared in all but one of the club's Premier League fixtures in 1992-93 and the consistency of his defending was recognised when he was rewarded with his first international cap for Scotland. Unfortunately, the 1993-94 campaign began with Hendry on the injured list and, although he regained his first-team place, further injuries disrupted his season.

## HEREFORD UNITED FC
Formed in 1924 and, after a proud record as one of the FA Cup's giant killers, became members of the Football League in 1972. Hereford and Blackburn first met in the Third Division in 1973-74 when Hereford completed the double over the Rovers. The Edgar Street ground has brought little luck for the Rovers who have returned pointless from their three visits.

**Football League**

|  |  | Home | | Away | |
|---|---|---|---|---|---|
| 1973-74 | (Div 3) | L | 1-2 | L | 0-1 |
| 1974-75 | (Div 3) | W | 1-0 | L | 3-6 |
| 1976-77 | (Div 2) | W | 1-0 | L | 0-1 |

|  | P | W | D | L | F | A |
|---|---|---|---|---|---|---|
| Home | 3 | 2 | 0 | 1 | 3 | 2 |
| Away | 3 | 0 | 0 | 3 | 3 | 8 |
| Total | 6 | 2 | 0 | 4 | 6 | 10 |

## HERRON, Alan
Centre-half. 1950-1959.
*5ft 10in; 11st 2lb.*
*Born: Ashington, 6 October 1932.*
*Debut: v Nottingham Forest (a) 28 April 1956.*
*Career: Newcastle United amateur; Blackburn Rovers August 1950; Wigan Athletic cs 1959.*
**Appearances:** Football League 4.
Alan Herron spent nine seasons with Blackburn Rovers without enjoying a prolonged run in the first team. He understudied Willie Kelly for the centre-half position during the early 1950s but was overlooked whenever Kelly was forced to miss a game. Herron made his delayed debut in April 1956, on the day that Mick McGrath earned his first senior call. However, whilst McGrath went on to become an established first-team player, Herron drifted back into the Central League team. Herron appeared in three consecutive matches the following season before the arrival of Matt Woods permanently closed the first-team door to him.

## HEYES, Joseph
Half-back. 1885-1888.
*Debut: v Clitheroe (a) 24 October 1885 (FAC).*
*Career: Blackburn Rovers 1885.*
*Domestic honours with Blackburn Rovers: FA Cup winners: 1885.*
**Appearances:** FA Cup 12.
**Goals:** FA Cup 1.
Joe Heyes enjoyed his best run with the Blackburn first team during the FA Cup campaign of 1885-86. Heyes was a regular member of the team which brought the trophy back to the club for a third successive season.

Heyes (pictured right) duly took his place in the side which appeared in the Final at the Kennington Oval against West Bromwich Albion on 3 April 1886. The game ended in a 0-0 draw and Heyes, who appeared somewhat overcome by the occasion, failed to produce the form which had earned him a first-team spot. The replay took place at Derby seven days later and the Rovers opted to bring Nat Walton back into the team in place of Heyes. Heyes overcame the disappointment of missing out on the replay and became a regular member of the half-back line until the end of the 1887-88 season.

## HEYWOOD, James
Full-back. 1907-1910.
*5ft 6½in.*
*Born: 1883.*
*Debut: v Everton (h) 8 April 1907.*
*Career: Stockport County August 1905; Blackburn Rovers April 1907; Glossop January 1910; Nelson 1912-13.*
**Appearances:** Football League 15; FA Cup 1; Total 16.
Jimmy Heywood was held in such esteem at Stockport County that his departure for Blackburn Rovers in April 1907 was greeted with utter dismay by the supporters. Heywood was a strong and competitive defender whose skill and energy would have guaranteed him a first-team place at most clubs. However, at Blackburn the full-back positions were dominated by Bob Crompton and Arthur Cowell with the result that Heywood was restricted to spasmodic appearances. In 1910 he moved to Glossop but returned to Lancashire during the 1912-13 season to join Nelson.

## HICKMAN, Michael Frederick Thomas
Centre-forward. 1975.
*5ft 10in; 11st 3lb.*
*Born: Elstead, Surrey, 2 October 1946.*
*Debut: v Plymouth Argyle (a) 4 February 1975 (sub).*
*Career: Brighton & Hove Albion amateur September 1963, turning professional in June 1965; Grimsby Town June 1968; Blackburn Rovers February 1975 (£10,000); Torquay United October 1975 (£2,500) becoming trainer in 1977.*
*Domestic honours with Blackburn Rovers: Division Three championship: 1974-75 (18+1 apps, 7gls).*
**Appearances:** Football League 23+3; Football League Cup 2; Total 25+3.
**Goals:** Football League 8.
A 'player's player' is a description that could truly be applied to Mike Hickman. A tireless worker, he had the ability play anywhere and never gave less than 100 per cent. At Grimsby Town he had been a member of the side which won the Fourth Division championship and had scored 48 goals in 254 League appearances (including seven as sub). He joined the Rovers at a time when the chase for promotion was just beginning to show signs of wavering. However, Hickman proved an inspirational signing and his added steel provided the boost the club needed. Perhaps his most memorable performance came in the 5-2 win over promotion rivals Plymouth Argyle at Ewood Park when he scored two goals in an exhilarating second-half display. He left the club in rather controversial circumstances in October 1975 amid rumours of a disagreement between himself and coach Norman Bodell.

## HIGGINS, George
Left-back. 1946-1951.
*5ft 6in; 10st 1lb.*
*Born: Dundee, 16 June 1925.*
*Debut: v Huddersfield Town (h) 18 January 1947.*
*Career: Lochee Harp; Blackburn Rovers October 1946; Bolton Wanderers July 1951; Grimsby Town May 1954; Scarborough July 1957.*
**Appearances:** Football League 53; FA Cup 3; Total 56.
George Higgins found himself promoted to the first team at Ewood Park following the departure of Walter Crook to Bolton Wanderers. In selecting Higgins to play alongside Les Cook, Eddie Hapgood placed his trust in a pair of 21-year-olds to fill the full-back positions. Higgins began the 1947-48 season pairing the equally inexperienced Bob Tomlinson and made 28 appearances as the Rovers dropped into the Second Division.

Higgins found himself overlooked during the next two seasons as David Gray and Bill Eckersley became automatic choices for the full-back positions. He made a further 13 appearances in 1950-51 before moving to Bolton Wanderers in July 1951. Higgins appeared in 69 League games at Bolton and made a further 47 League appearances at Grimsby Town before moving to Scarborough in the summer of 1957.

## HILDERSLEY, Ronald C.
Midfield. 1988-1990.
*5ft 4in; 9st 2lb.*
*Born: Kirkcaldy, 6 April 1965.*
*Debut: v Chelsea (a) 27 August 1988.*
*Career: Manchester City apprentice July 1981, turning professional in April 1983; Chester City on loan January 1984; Chester City August 1984; Rochdale non-contract player August 1985; Preston North End June 1986; Cambridge United on loan February 1988; Blackburn Rovers July 1988; Wigan Athletic August 1990; Halifax Town November 1991.*
**Appearances:** Football League 25+5; FA Cup 3; Football League Cup 0+1; Total 28+6.
**Goals:** Football League 4; FA Cup 1; Total 5.
A busy little midfield player who was snapped up by Don Mackay on a free transfer from Preston North End. Despite a rather nomadic career, Hildersley was rarely able to establish himself at his various clubs and it was only at Deepdale that he reached a half century of League games. He enjoyed a brief run in the first team at Ewood Park midway through the 1988-89 season. However, the following campaign saw him largely ignored and in the summer of 1990 he moved to Wigan Athletic.

## HILL, Brian
Outside-left. 1969-1971.
*5ft 10in; 10st 8lb.*
*Born: Mansfield, 15 December 1942.*
*Debut: v Swindon Town (h) 9 August 1969.*
*Career: Ollerton Colliery; Grimsby Town August 1960; Huddersfield Town November 1966 (£20,000); Blackburn Rovers June 1969 (£30,000); Torquay United July 1971; Boston United cs 1972; Market Rasen player-manager.*
**Appearances:** Football League 34+3; FA Cup 2; Football League Cup 4; Total 40+3.
**Goals:** Football League 4; Football League Cup 1; Total 5.
Brian Hill was one of three major signings made by Eddie Quigley during the summer of 1969. However, whilst Allan Hunter and Ken Knighton were both sold on at a large profit, Hill left Ewood on a free transfer at the end of the 1970-71 season. This was in stark contrast to the success that Hill had experienced earlier in his career with Grimsby Town. A record of 26 goals in 180 League games had been sufficient for Huddersfield Town to pay £20,000 for the services of this slim left-winger who relied on pace and cunning to beat an opponent. Hill never quite achieved the same level of success at Leeds Road with six goals in 88 League appearances (including three as sub). Eddie Quigley turned to Hill after failing to sign Geoff Salmons from Sheffield United. Sadly, the move was not a success as Hill appeared too frail to beat the more robust of defenders. He finished his League career at Torquay before drifting into non-League football.

## HILL, Keith John
Central defender. 1984-1992.
*6ft; 11st 3lb.*
*Born: Bolton, 17 May 1969.*
*Debut: v Liverpool (h) 23 September 1987 (FLC).*
*Career: Blackburn Rovers associated schoolboy 1984, non-contract player July 1986, given a contract in May 1987; Plymouth Argyle September 1992 (as part of a package deal for Nicky Marker).*
**Appearances:** Premier League 0+1; Football League 89+6; Play-offs 0+2; FA Cup 5+1; Football League Cup 6; Full Members' Cup 3; Total 103+10.
**Goals:** Football League 4; Football League Cup 1; Total 5.
Keith Hill graduated through the junior ranks at Ewood Park to make his first-team debut in September 1987. Good in the air, Hill could play at full-back as well as in the centre of defence. He deputised for both Colin Hendry and David Mail during the 1988-89 season but began the following campaign as the first-choice centre-half. Injury and the arrival of Kevin Moran kept him out of the team during the second half of the 1989-90 campaign.

Injuries and loss of form plagued Hill the following season and it wasn't until October 1991 that he retained a permanent place in the team. Once again a dip in form cost him his place in the starting line-up and Hill played no part in the successful Play-off campaign in May 1992. Hill made one appearance, as a substitute, in the Premier League before Kenny Dalglish traded him to Plymouth Argyle in the deal which brought Nicky Marker to Ewood Park.

**HILTON, Patrick John**
Outside-left. 1974-1975.
*5ft 8in; 10st.*
*Born: Aylesham, 1 May 1954.*
*Debut: v Grimsby Town (a) 17 August 1974.*
*Career: Canterbury City; Brighton & Hove Albion February 1973; Blackburn Rovers May 1974; Gillingham on loan September 1975 before signing during the same month for £3,000; Aldershot on loan March to April 1977; Southport July 1977; Dover; 1978-80; Folkestone 1980; Thanet United; Gillingham youth team manager.*
*Domestic honours with Blackburn Rovers: Third Division championship: 1974-75 (16 apps, 2gls).*
**Appearances:** Football League 16; Football League Cup 5; Total 21.
**Goals:** Football League 2.
It was, perhaps, rather apt that Gordon Lee should make his first move into the transfer market at Ewood Park a free transfer signing. At Port Vale, Lee had earned a reputation of being able to manage on a shoestring and the signing of Hilton proved he still had an eye for a bargain. Although not a first-team regular with Brighton, Hilton began the 1974-75 campaign in the number-11 shirt for the Rovers. On the hard early season grounds, Hilton proved an energetic winger who liked nothing better than to run at defenders. However, as the season wore on he found the heavier grounds more difficult to deal with and his lightweight build was hardly conducive to Third Division football. Hilton lost his place after 16 League matches and in September 1975 he joined Gillingham. He failed to establish himself at any of his subsequent clubs before moving into non-League football.

**HINDLE, Harry**
Centre-half. 1901-1903.
*5ft 8in; 12st.*
*Born: Wilpshire, nr Blackburn, c.1883.*
*Debut: v Bury (a) 28 March 1902.*
*Career: St James Road (Blackburn Sunday School League); Oswaldtwistle Rovers; Blackburn Rovers May 1901; Nelson cs 1903.*
**Appearances:** Football League 2.
Harry Hindle was an athletic defender despite his rather heavy build. One commentator wrote of the young Hindle: 'He plays coolly and with great confidence, feeding his forwards delightfully and at times sending in long distance dropping shots which are full of menace to an opposing side.' Hindle played at centre-half with the second team but made his debut at left-half. Unable to dislodge Sam McClure or Neil Logan from the first team, Hindle moved to Nelson in the summer of 1903.

**HINDSON, Gordon**
Winger. 1975.
*5ft 9in; 11st 4lb.*
*Born: Quaking Houses, County Durham, 8 January 1950.*
*Debut: v West Bromwich Albion (h) 11 October 1975.*
*Career: Newcastle United August 1968; Luton Town October 1971; Carlisle United on loan September 1975 to October 1975; Blackburn Rovers on loan October 1975 to December 1975; Hartford Connecticut (USA) 1976; Evenwood Town 1976; Consett 1976, appointed coach August 1979; Spennymoor United January 1981; Gateshead November 1981.*
**Appearances:** Football League 10.
A skilful left-winger who spent two months at Ewood Park as the Rovers tried to re-establish themselves in the Second Division. As an authentic 'old fashioned' winger, Hindson was extremely popular with the Blackburn supporters and many regretted the fact that financial problems prevented the Rovers from bringing him to Ewood on a permanent basis. Hindson had appeared in seven League games with Newcastle United before moving south to Luton Town. At Kenilworth Road he appeared in 68 League games (including six as sub) before a broken ankle finally ended his League career.

**HIRD, Kevin**
Midfield/Right-back. 1970-1979.
*5ft 6in; 9st.*
*Born: Colne, 11 February 1955.*
*Debut: v Watford (a) 13 April 1974.*
*Career: Blackburn Rovers apprentice October 1970, turning professional in February 1973; Leeds United March 1979 (£357,000); Burnley August 1984 until cs 1986; Colne Dynamoes cs 1986; Barnoldswick United September 1991.*
*Domestic honours with Blackburn Rovers: Third Division championship: 1974-75 (1+1 apps).*
**Appearances:** Football League 129+3; FA Cup 8; Football League Cup 7+1; Total 144+4.
**Goals:** Football League 20; Football League Cup 1; Total 21.
Kevin Hird was a highly talented young midfielder who was converted

into a right-back with great success. Hird developed through the junior ranks at Ewood Park before being given his first-team debut by Gordon Lee towards the end of the 1973-74 season. Hird was overlooked during the 1974-75 Third Division title-winning campaign, but re-emerged from the shadows the following season as Jim Smith tried to keep the club in the Second Division. Hird's speed and power were well suited to the wide right-sided midfield role that he initially occupied at Ewood Park. However, injuries and loss of form amongst his full-backs compelled Smith to try Hird in the right-back position during the 1976-77 campaign. Although Hird looked comfortable in this position he was allowed to revert to midfield once the immediate crisis at the club was over.

However, the disappointing form of the newly arrived John Curtis led Smith to switch Hird to right-back at the start of the following season. In tandem with John Bailey, Hird developed into one the finest attacking full-backs outside of the First Division. Although Hird had limited defensive qualities, particularly in the air, his speed and powerful shooting made him a constant threat to opposing defenders. In March 1979, Leeds paid the club what was then a record fee to take Hird to Elland Road. He stayed with Leeds until the summer of 1984 and then, rather surprisingly, opted to drop into the Third Division to join Burnley. Relegated to the Fourth Division in his first season at Turf Moor, Hird remained at Burnley for one more season before leaving the Football League to join Colne Dynamoes. Hird joined the coaching staff of the ambitious non-League outfit and also organised his own coaching schools for youngsters.

**HODKINSON, Joseph**
Outside-left. 1913-1923.
*5ft 8in; 10st 7lb.*
*Born: Lancaster, 1889 (April quarter); Died: Lancaster, 18 June 1954.*
*Debut: v Notts County (a) 25 January 1913.*
*Career: Lancaster St Mary's; Lancaster Town; Glossop North End September 1909; Blackburn Rovers January 1913 (£1,000); Lancaster Town April 1923. Retired January 1925.*
*International honours with Blackburn Rovers: England: 3 caps (1913-19); England Victory international: 1 appearance (1920); Football League: 3 appearances (1913-14).*
*Domestic honours with Blackburn Rovers: First Division championship: 1913-14 (33 apps, 2gls).*
**Appearances:** Football League 228; FA Cup 16; Total 244.
**Goals:** Football League 19; FA Cup 1; Total 20.
Joe Hodkinson was an orthodox left-winger who possessed plenty of pace and the ability to deliver the ball with pin-point accuracy. Hodkinson had begun his footballing career with Lancaster Town whilst working as a labourer at a linoleum works. Even at an early age his ability to beat an opponent and deliver accurate crosses did not go unnoticed by other clubs. In 1909 he was signed by Glossop and helped their reserve team to win the Lancashire Combination title. Hodkinson duly graduated to the

first team at Glossop and was regarded as the quickest winger in the Second Division. Having attracted the attention of a number of First Division clubs, Hodkinson signed for Blackburn in January 1913. A strict teetotaller and non-smoker, Hodkinson was almost blinkered in his approach to the game. Hodkinson saw his task quite simply as that of being the provider for his inside men. Whilst other wingers would cut inside to take a speculative dip at goal, Hodkinson would diligently look to beat his full-back and deliver the perfect cross. Hodkinson helped bring a second League championship to Ewood Park and won two England caps before his career was halted by

World War One. He won a further England cap in 1919 and played at Ewood for a further four seasons before returning to Lancaster Town in April 1923.

### HOLDEN, Alan
Left-half. 1959-1966.
*5ft 7in; 10st 8lb.*
*Born: Haslingden, 12 October 1941.*
*Debut: v Notts County (a) 25 September 1963 (FLC).*
*Career: Blackburn Rovers non-contract player October 1959, signing as a professional in January 1962; Stockport County July 1966.*
**Appearances:** Football League 1; Football League Cup 1; Total 2.
A painter by profession, Alan Holden was a regular in the Central League team at Ewood Park during the early 1960s and made 38 appearances for the Central League championship side of 1964-65. However, with international players vying for the half-back places in the senior team, Holden had little opportunity to graduate beyond reserve-team football. He moved to Stockport County in July 1966 but made only one League appearance for the club.

### HOLDEN, William
Goalkeeper. 1888.
*Born: Darwen, 1860.*
*Debut: v Preston North End (a) 29 December 1888.*
*Career: Darwen; Blackburn Rovers on loan December 1888; Darwen December 1888.*
**Appearances:** Football League 1.
Holden was borrowed from neighbouring Darwen when the club was faced with a goalkeeping crisis during the Christmas period of 1888. Holden came with a reputation of being able to look after himself and he was immediately thrown into the local derby against Preston North End at Deepdale. However, North End won the game by a single goal and Holden was allowed to return to Darwen.

### HOLE, Barrington Gerard
Midfield. 1966-1968.
*5ft 11in; 11st 4lb.*
*Born: Swansea, 16 September 1942.*
*Debut: v Derby County (a) 20 August 1966.*
*Career: Cardiff City September 1959; Blackburn Rovers July 1966 (£40,000); Aston Villa September 1968 (£60,000); Swansea City July 1970 (£20,000) until May 1972.*
*International honours with Blackburn Rovers: Wales: 7 caps (1966-68).*
**Appearances:** Football League 79; FA Cup 2; Football League Cup 7; Total 88.
**Goals:** Football League 13; Football League Cup 2; Total 15.

Barrie Hole was one of the most cultured attacking wing halves of his era. Tall and slim, Hole was not a powerful midfield dynamo but his intelligent reading of the game and his constructive use of the ball made him a joy to watch. An extra-ordinarily gifted ball player, Hole also possessed the ability to ghost into the opposing penalty area, completely free of markers, and score a number of vital goals.

The son of Billy Hole, a pre-war Welsh international with Swansea Town, Barrie's two older brothers, Colin and Alan, were also professional footballers with Swansea Town. Although born in Swansea, Barrie broke with family tradition to begin his footballing career at Ninian Park. A Welsh schoolboy international, Hole was also capped at Under-23

and full international level whilst with Cardiff. He became the first specialist midfield player to sign for Blackburn Rovers when Jack Marshall brought him to Ewood Park following relegation to the Second Division. Marshall combined Hole with Bryan Douglas in a 4-2-4 system and the successful pairing came close to taking the Rovers back to the First Division at the first attempt. Hole remained at Blackburn for two seasons before joining Aston Villa early in the 1968-69 season. His time at Villa Park was not the happiest of his career and in July 1970 he returned to Wales to join Swansea City. After a brief spell at the Vetch Field he left the game to become a shopkeeper in Swansea.

### HOLLAND, Peter Byrom
Forward. 1919-1928.
*5ft 6in; 11st.*
*Born: Hindley, 5 October 1898.*
*Debut: v Preston North End (a) 6 September 1919.*
*Career: Durham Schoolboys; New Herrington Swifts; Houghton Rovers; Hull City; Blackburn Rovers wartime guest 1917-18 then signing permanently in March 1919; Watford September 1928 (£1,250); West Ham United October 1930; Tunbridge Well Rangers cs 1931.*
**Appearances:** Football League 116; FA Cup 9; Total 125.
**Goals:** Football League 24; FA Cup 1; Total 25.
A lively little forward who gave many years loyal service to Blackburn Rovers without ever winning a regular first-team place. It was not until 1927-28 that he topped 20 League games in a season and the following year he joined Watford. An industrious type of forward who appeared in a variety of positions for the Rovers, Holland had made nine appearances during wartime football for the club, having made his first appearance in December 1918.

### HOLLIDAY, Kenneth Joseph
Centre-half/Full-back. 1946-1952.
*6ft ½in; 12st 9lb.*
*Born: Darwen, 19 August 1925.*
*Debut: v Middlesbrough (a) 17 April 1948.*
*Career: Darwen Juniors; Blackburn Rovers amateur June 1946, turning professional in October 1946; Accrington Stanley July 1952; Barrow May 1955; Nelson cs 1956; Darwen; Padiham.*
**Appearances:** Football League 29; FA Cup 1; Total 30.
This red-headed defender joined Blackburn Rovers after World War Two. Holliday, who could play at centre-half or full-back, made his debut at right-back in April 1948 but was thought to be more likely to settle at centre-half. However, when Bob Pryde left Ewood Park in the summer of 1949, Bill Holt got the nod ahead of Holliday for the centre-half position. Apart from a run of nine games in 1951-52, when Holliday covered for Ron Suart at right-back, much of his time at Ewood was spent in the Central League team. In July 1952 he moved to Peel Park and proved a reliable defender for Stanley during his three seasons with the club. Holliday appeared in 96 League games for Stanley, scoring five goals, before moving to Barrow in May 1955.

### HOLMES, William
Centre-forward. 1952-1953.
*5ft 10½in; 11st 9lb.*
*Born: Hunslet, 29 October 1926.*
*Debut: v Queen's Park Rangers (h) 1 January 1952.*
*Career: Morecambe 1947-48; Wolverhampton Wanderers 1948-49; Doncaster Rovers amateur October 1950; Morecambe; Burnley 1951; Morecambe; Blackburn Rovers amateur cs 1951; Morecambe; Bradford City 25 September 1953; Southport 2 July 1954.*
**Appearances:** Football League 21; FA Cup 4; Total 25.
**Goals:** Football League 16; FA Cup 3; Total 19.
A physical education teacher from Morecambe, Holmes failed to make much impression at any of his Football League clubs. An England amateur international with Wolves he appeared in the Central League team at Burnley but wasn't signed on League forms. He first appeared in the Football League with Doncaster Rovers but after two games returned to non-League circles. Holmes was signed by Jackie Bestall on amateur forms during the summer of 1951 and on New Year's Day 1952 he made a goalscoring debut against Queen's Park Rangers. Although he scored seven goals in eight games he failed to capture the centre-forward position on a regular basis. However, a hat-trick against Everton at Ewood Park on 30 August 1952 helped to take his tally to six goals in seven appearances at the start of the 1952-53 season. Once again he lost his place in the team and in September 1953 he tried to rebuild his career at Bradford City. The following season he joined Southport and enjoyed his best spell in League football with 21 goals in 56 League games.

### HOLT, David Ephraim
Centre-half. 1963-1967.
*6ft ½in; 11st 8lb.*

*Born: Whickham, Durham, 7 January 1945.*
*Debut: v Sheffield United (a) 29 March 1966.*
*Career: Blackburn Rovers April 1963 to cs 1967, but registration retained until June 1969.*
**Appearances:** Football League 10; Football League Cup 1; Total 11.
David Holt joined the Rovers as a youngster and won a Central League championship medal with the club in 1964-65. However, with Mike England in possession of the number-five shirt, Holt had little opportunity to break into the first team. Following the departure of England to Tottenham Hotspur, Jack Marshall selected Dick Mulvaney ahead of Holt for the centre-half position. However Mulvaney suffered a perforated ear drum in the League Cup-tie with Barrow in September 1966 and Holt finally got a run in the senior team. Unfortunately, three of the five games Holt appeared in were lost and Marshall turned to Keith Newton and Ben Anderson before finally settling on George Sharples to partner Ronnie Clayton in the heart of defence. Holt became disenchanted with the game and decided to retire from professional football to go into business.

## HOLT, William Kenneth
Centre-half. 1949-1953.
*5ft 11¼in; 12st 5lb.*
*Born: Boldon, 31 March 1926.*
*Debut: v Brentford (h) 7 May 1949.*
*Career: Boldon Colliery Welfare; Blackburn Rovers January 1949 to June 1953; Weymouth cs 1953; Barrow June 1954 to June 1957.*
**Appearances:** Football League 78; FA Cup 2; Total 80.
Bill Holt made his debut in the final game of the 1949-50 season and such was his impact that he began the following campaign as the first-choice centre-half. Holt, a hard-working defender, appeared the natural successor to Bob Pryde. However, by the end of the 1950-51 season it had become clear that his lack of pace was a serious weakness in the heart of defence. The arrival of Willie Kelly in September 1951 brought an end to Holt's tenure of the centre-half position at Ewood. His only appearance in 1952-53 was as a makeshift centre-forward and in the close season he moved to Weymouth. He returned to the Football League in June 1954 to sign for Barrow and went on to appear in 72 League games during three seasons with that club.

## HOME DEFEATS
The record for the most home defeats in each division is as follows:
| | | | |
|---|---|---|---|
| Premiership | 4 | defeats | 1992-93 |
| Division 1 | 14 | defeats | 1965-66 |
| Division 2 | 9 | defeats | 1990-91 |
| Division 3 | 6 | defeats | 1973-74 |

The record for the fewest home defeats in each division is as follows:
| | | | |
|---|---|---|---|
| Premiership | 2 | defeats | 1993-94 |
| Division 1 | 0 | defeats | 1988,89, 1909-10, 1911-12 & 1933-34 |
| Division 2 | 1 | defeat | 1957-58, 1980-81 & 1983-84 |
| Division 3 | 1 | defeat | 1974-75 |

## HOME DRAWS
The record for the most home draws in each division is as follows:
| | | | |
|---|---|---|---|
| Premiership | 5 | draws | 1993-94 |
| Division 1 | 9 | draws | 1920-21 |
| Division 2 | 11 | draws | 1983-84 |
| Division 3 | 8 | draws | 1972-73 |

The record for the fewest home draws in each division is as follows:
| | | | |
|---|---|---|---|
| Premiership | 4 | draws | 1992-93 |
| Division 1 | 0 | draws | 1889-90 & 1893-94 |
| Division 2 | 1 | draw | 1938-39 |
| Division 3 | 4 | draws | 1971-72 & 1973-74 |

## HOME POINTS
The record for the most home points in each division is as follows:
| | | | | | | |
|---|---|---|---|---|---|---|
| Premiership | (3) | 47 points | 14 | 5 | 2 | 1993-94 |
| Division 1 | (2) | 37 points | 16 | 5 | 0 | 1933-34 |
| Division 2 | (2) | 35 points | 17 | 1 | 3 | 1938-39 |
| Division 2 | (3) | 52 points | 16 | 4 | 3 | 1988-89 |
| Division 3 | (2) | 37 points | 15 | 7 | 1 | 1974-75 |

The record for the fewest home points in each division is as follows:
| | | | | | | |
|---|---|---|---|---|---|---|
| Premiership | (3) | 43 points | 13 | 4 | 4 | 1992-93 |
| Division 1 | (2) | 13 points | 6 | 1 | 14 | 1965-66 |
| Division 2 | (2) | 18 points | 5 | 8 | 8 | 1970-71 & 1978-79 |
| Division 2 | (3) | 30 points | 8 | 6 | 9 | 1990-91 |
| Division 3 | (2) | 30 points | 13 | 4 | 6 | 1973-74 |

*Note: The number of points per win is shown in brackets.

## HOME WINS
The record for the most home wins in each division is as follows:
| | | | |
|---|---|---|---|
| Premiership | 14 | wins | 1993-94 |
| Division 1 | 16 | wins | 1933-34 |
| Division 2 | 17 | wins | 1938-39 |
| Division 3 | 15 | wins | 1974-75 |

The record for the fewest home wins in each division is as follows:
| | | | |
|---|---|---|---|
| Premiership | 13 | wins | 1992-93 |
| Division 1 | 4 | wins | 1897-98 |
| Division 2 | 5 | wins | 1970-71 & 1978-79 |
| Division 3 | 12 | wins | 1972-73 |

## HOPE, Philip
Right-back. 1924-1926.
*6ft; 13st 7lb.*
*Born: Kimblesworth, 24 April 1897.*
*Died: Ouston, Durham, 3 January 1969.*
*Debut: v Manchester City (a) 14 February 1925.*
*Career: Northumberland Schools League; Washington Colliery; Croxdale Colliery; Sunderland trial; Durham City; Norwich City amateur January 1920, turning professional in August 1920; Blackburn Rovers May 1924; Southend United September 1926; Clapton Orient June 1927; Washington Colliery October 1928; Rochdale May 1929 to May 1930.*
**Appearances:** Football League 6; FA Cup 2; Total 8.
The 1925-26 *Lancashire Daily Post Football Annual* described Hope in the following terms: 'A big-framed youngster from Norwich, who is exceptionally powerful. Craft and experience are his big needs, while his tackling could be better.' Hope had been signed as a possible successor to the ageing David Rollo, but in truth he rarely looked comfortable against First Division opponents. Hope, who had appeared in 108 League games for Norwich, returned to the lower divisions in September 1926 when he signed for Southend United.

## HOPWOOD, W.
Right-back. 1884-1885.
*Debut: v Rossendale (h) 13 October 1884 (FAC).*
*Career: Blackburn Rovers 1884.*
**Appearances:** FA Cup 1.
Little is known about this full-back who appeared at right-back in the 11-0 win over Rossendale in the 1884-85 FA Cup. Hopwood had appeared earlier in the season in a friendly fixture with Burnley at Turf Moor on 27 September 1884 when the Rovers had enjoyed a 4-2 victory. However, the acquisition of Richard Turner from the Bolton Association solved the full-back problems caused by the departure of Joe Beverley. As a result there was little scope for Hopwood to progress in the first team.

## HORNBY, Albert Neilson
Forward. 1878-1880.
*Debut: v Sheffield Providence (h) 30 October 1880 (FAC).*
*Career: Brookhouse; Blackburn Rovers 1878.*
**Appearances:** FA Cup 1.
**Goals:** FA Cup 1.
Albert Neilson Hornby, popularly known as 'Monkey', was a member of one of the town's leading commercial families. Hornby was blessed with a fine physique and indomitable courage and he excelled at cricket, rugby, hurdling, running, boxing and soccer. An England rugby international on nine occasions, Hornby became interested in the Association code when he formed his own team, known as Hornby's Team, at the family's Brookhouse Mills. The game that was played by this team, which later became known as Brookhouse, was played under a mixture of Rugby and Association rules. Hornby, who was a natural leader, captained the side and his players were made up from the workers of the family cotton mill.

Hornby made his debut for Blackburn Rovers on 2 January 1878, when the famous Partick Thistle visited Blackburn for a friendly fixture. Two goals from Dick Birtwistle, the son of another mill owner, ensured that Hornby ended his first game with the Rovers on the winning side. On one occasion whilst playing for the Rovers, Hornby was reputed to have become slightly confused about the two codes of football.

He was said to have caught the ball, tucked it under his arm and sped towards the opposing goal completely unaware of the uproarious laughter of spectators and players. Hornby made only fleeting appearances with the Rovers but enjoyed great success on the cricket field with Lancashire. He played for Lancashire between 1867 and was captain from 1880 to 1891. He went on to have further spells as captain and also played for England on three occasions.

**HORNE, John Kay**
Goalkeeper. 1890.
*5ft 10½in; 11st 8lb.*
*Born: Huncoat, 1862; Died: Hesketh Bank, 30 October 1926.*
*Debut: v Bootle (a) 15 February 1890 (FAC).*
*Career: Accrington; Windsor; Grimsby Town; Bury; Accrington; Burslem Port Vale; Accrington; Blackburn Rovers January 1890; Accrington; Notts County February 1891; Darwen.*
*Domestic honours with Blackburn Rovers; FA Cup winners: 1890.*
**Appearances:** Football League 2; FA Cup 3; Total 5.
Jack Kay Horne followed his brother Dick into the Accrington team in the mid-1880s. Horne had started his footballing career in the second team at Accrington before playing with Windsor, Grimsby Town and Bury. On leaving Bury he returned to succeed his brother as goalkeeper for 'Th' Owd Reds'. A chemist by profession, Horne had retired from senior football when he was approached to help the Rovers overcome their goalkeeping problems during the final stages of the 1889-90 season. At one time he was regarded as one of the safest goalkeepers in the country and was on the verge of international honours. He assisted the Rovers over the latter stages of the 1889-90 FA Cup competition and enjoyed a relatively easy Final as the Rovers overwhelmed Sheffield Wednesday by 6-1.

**HORNE, William E.**
Goalkeeper. 1891-1892.
*Born: Huncoat.*
*Debut: v Notts County (h) 12 September 1891.*
*Career: Accrington; Blackburn Rovers September 1891; Nelson.*
**Appearances:** Football League 7.
Horne was one of three goalkeeping brothers from the Accrington area. Dick Horne had been a stalwart for Accrington in the years before the formation of the Football League and his brother John inherited the goalkeeping position at Accrington before travelling further afield to play his football. William Horne made his Football League debut with Accrington in November 1890, when he appeared at inside-right against Sunderland. This was his only senior appearance for Accrington and in September 1891 he followed his brother John into the ranks for Blackburn Rovers. He featured in seven League games in September and October 1891 before Herbie Arthur was recalled from Southport Central to become the number-one custodian at the club.

**HORREY, Rowland George**
Outside-right. 1963-1966.
*5ft 9½in; 11st.*
*Born: Bishop Auckland, 9 March 1943.*
*Debut: v Stoke City (a) 13 March 1965.*
*Career: Ferryhill Athletic; Blackburn Rovers December 1963; York City July 1966 to June 1968; Cambridge United cs 1968 to January 1972.*
**Appearances:** Football League 3; Football League Cup 1; Total 4.
Rowland Horrey was plucked from junior football to understudy Mike Ferguson in the outside-right position. However, with Reg Blore and Alan Bradshaw also capable of filling the right-wing position, Horrey found his first-team opportunities severely limited. In 1964-65 he made his debut in the Football League and also scored nine goals and made 30 appearances for the team which lifted the Central League title. Unable to break into the first team on a regular basis, he moved to York City in July 1966 and scored nine goals in 74 League appearances for the club before joining non-League Cambridge United. Horrey was a member of the Cambridge team which was elected to the Football League in 1970 and made 38 appearances (including one as sub) and scored four goals for United in the League.

**HORTON, Henry**
Half-back/Inside-forward. 1947-1951.
*5ft 10½in; 12st 2lb.*
*Born: Malvern, Worcester, 18 April 1923.*
*Debut: v Stoke City (h) 26 April 1947.*
*Career: Worcester City; Blackburn Rovers January 1947 (£2,000);*

Southampton June 1951; Bradford May 1954; Hereford United September 1955.
**Appearances:** Football League 92; FA Cup 6; Total 98.
**Goals:** Football League 5.
Henry Horton cost a sizeable fee to bring him to Ewood Park from non-League football. Although he had joined the club as a wing-half who could also operate in the forward line, it was at centre-half that Horton made his first-team debut. However, it was in the left-half or inside-left positions that Horton enjoyed his greatest success at Ewood. A hard-working type of player, Horton also played cricket for Worcestershire and on moving to Southampton joined Hampshire County Cricket Club. He ended his footballing career with Bradford in 1954-55 before returning to non-League football with Hereford. However, Horton continued to play County Cricket until 1967 and then joined the list of first-class umpires.

**HOSIE, James**
Half-back. 1900-1901.
*5ft 11in; 12st 4lb.*
*Born: Glasgow, 1876.*
*Debut: v Liverpool (a) 1 September 1900.*
*Career: Glasgow Juniors; Glasgow Perthshire 1897; Reading; Blackburn Rovers May 1900; Manchester City January 1901; Stockport County October 1902; Bristol City August 1903.*
**Appearances:** Football League 3.
Hosie was one of the three players who joined Blackburn Rovers from Reading at the turn of the century. Although much was expected of him he lost his place to Jimmy Moir after only one match. Moir proved to be a revelation in the right-half position and Hosie was allowed to move to Manchester City in January 1901. He enjoyed first-team football at each of his three subsequent clubs and was highly regarded wherever he went.

**HOUGH, William Arthur**
Right-back. 1936-1942.
*5ft 8in; 10st 3lb.*
*Born: Greenfield, Wales, 1908 (July quarter).*
*Debut: v Stockport County (a) 23 October 1937.*
*Career: Connah's Quay & Shotton; Holywell Arcadians; New Brighton amateur August 1930, turning professional in September 1930; Preston North End December 1930; Blackburn Rovers December 1936 to 1942.*
*Domestic honours with Blackburn Rovers: Second Division championship: 1938-39 (31 apps); League War Cup runners-up: 1940.*
**Appearances:** Football League 49; FA Cup 7; Total 56.
Hough had appeared as an inside-forward in only four League games for New Brighton when Preston North End snapped him up in December 1930. At Deepdale he was converted into a full-back and proved himself to be a steady rather than spectacular performer. Although the Rovers signed Billy Hough just prior to selling Jimmy Gorman to Sunderland, the former North End full-back had to wait until February 1938 before winning a regular first-team place. He began the 1938-39 season as first-choice left-back but injury forced him out of the team and when he was restored to fitness he was unable to dislodge Ernest Lanceley. Hough appeared in 40 wartime matches before leaving the club.

**HOULKER, Albert Edward**
Left-half. 1894-1902 & 1906-1907.
*5ft 6½in; 10st 5lb.*
*Born: Blackburn, 27 April 1872; Died: Blackburn, 27 May 1962.*
*Debut: v Bolton Wanderers (a) 12 September 1896.*
*Career: Blackburn Hornets; Oswaldtwistle Rovers; Cob Wall (Blackburn); Park Road (Blackburn); Blackburn Rovers August 1894; Portsmouth May 1902; Southampton May 1903; Blackburn Rovers May 1906; Retired 1907; Colne cs 1909; Blackburn Rovers January 1918.*
*International honours with Blackburn Rovers: England: 1 cap (1902); Football League: 1 appearance (1902).*
**Appearances:** Football League 151; Test Matches 3; FA Cup 9; Total 163.
**Goals:** Football League 2.
Houlker was a small, but athletic, half-back who arrived at Ewood Park in August 1894 after playing for local junior clubs. Known to everyone as 'Kelly', he proved a versatile performer who filled all three of the half-back positions during his time at the club. Houlker, who favoured the left-hand side of the field, was an astute reader of the game who was noted for his total commitment and non-stop running. In May 1902, he won the first of his five England caps and then, surprisingly, opted to leave Blackburn in favour of Portsmouth. The fact that Houlker, at a time when he had just won his first international cap, should choose to leave Blackburn in favour of a club in the Southern League was a bitter blow the followers of Blackburn Rovers. It was a fact which the local press were quick to pick up on. They suggested that the Ewood board would find Houlker difficult to replace and inferred that Blackburn appeared to be the only top club prepared to part with its best players. His stay with

Pompey was a brief one and in May 1903 he moved along the South coast to join Southampton. In 1904 he helped the Saints to win the Southern League Championship, but in 1906 announced his retirement. However, the Rovers persuaded him to change his mind and added him to their squad. He played fairly regularly until the end of the 1907-08 campaign when he again announced his retirement. In 1909 he was enticed out of retirement by Colne and was to make two final appearances for Blackburn Rovers, in wartime football, towards the end of the 1917-18 season. Houlker continued to live and work in Blackburn until his death in April 1962, at the age of 90.

## HOWORTH, Roger
Goalkeeper.
*Born: Blackburn, 1859.*
*Debut: v Tyne Association (h) 1 November 1879 (FAC).*
*Career: Blackburn Rovers; Accrington on loan 1881; Blackburn Olympic 1884-85.*
*Domestic honours with Blackburn Rovers: FA Cup runners-up: 1882.*
**Appearances:** FA Cup 12.
Roger Howorth was a well built, one might even say corpulent, figure who possessed a powerful kick. Despite his build, Howorth had an athletic flair and was a more than capable cricketer during the summer months. Howorth began to force his way into the team during the second half of the 1878-79 season as the club looked for a successor for Tom Greenwood. The only serious challenger to Howorth was Woolfall but it was not until the 1881-82 season that Howorth established himself as the first choice custodian. He appeared in the 1882 FA Cup Final but by the time the Rovers reached the Final again, in 1884, he had been replaced by Herbie Arthur.

Howorth created his own niche in the history of Blackburn Rovers when he scored a goal in the Lancashire Cup-tie with Clitheroe on 26 November 1881. In a game that the Rovers won by ten goals to one, Howorth, no doubt feeling rather unemployed, moved up field for a corner and found himself on the score-sheet. In 1880-81 season, Howorth appeared for Accrington in two Lancashire Cup matches. The second of these was the Final against Blackburn Park Road which resulted in a 6-4 victory for Accrington at the Barley Bank Ground, Darwen. He appeared for Blackburn in two Lancashire Cup Finals and also represented Lancashire on three occasions. The son of a Blackburn Alderman, his family were heald and reed manufacturers and Howorth worked in the family firm until he retired.

## HOY, Robert
Winger. 1974-1976
*5ft 7½in; 10st.*
*Born: Halifax, 10 January 1950.*
*Debut: v Tranmere Rovers (h) 15 March 1975 (sub).*
*Career: Huddersfield Town amateur January 1966, becoming an apprentice in November 1966 before signing professional in November 1967; Blackburn Rovers March 1975 (£5,000 + Barry Endean); Halifax Town June 1976; York City August 1977; Rochdale December 1977 until cs 1981; Bradford City trial September 1983.*
*Domestic honours with Blackburn Rovers: Third Division championship: 1974-75 (6+1 apps).*
**Appearances:** Football League 13+6; FA Cup 1; Football League Cup 0+2; Total 14+8.
Bobby Hoy became the final piece in Gordon Lee's title-winning squad when he moved to Ewood Park in March 1975. Hoy had spent almost nine years at Leeds Road and had appeared in three divisions of the Football League. The pinnacle of his success at Huddersfield had come with the lifting of the Second Division championship in 1969-70. However, as the club's fortunes began to wane, Hoy found it increasingly difficult to maintain a regular first-team place. As an orthodox winger Hoy gave Lee some fresh options during the final two months of the season. With Jimmy Mullen nursing a broken leg and Pat Hilton struggling to make an impact on Third Division defences, the arrival of Hoy was a welcome boost to the squad. However, as at Huddersfield, Hoy failed to establish himself in the starting eleven and often had to settle for a place on the bench. In the summer of 1976 he returned to Yorkshire to join Halifax Town.

## HOYNE, James
Inside-right. 1901-1903.
*5ft 7in; 10st 6lb.*
*Debut: v Notts County (h) 29 March 1902.*
*Career: Sale Holmfield; Blackburn Rovers November 1901; Hyde St Georges coach September 1903; Stalybridge Rovers; Heywood United cs 1907.*
**Appearances:** Football League 2.
A busy little inside-forward who lacked the physical strength to withstand the tough tackling defenders of the period. On his debut against Notts

County on Easter Saturday 1902 he earned the Rovers a penalty when a fierce shot was handled in the area. He played a lively game against Wolves two days later but his inability to withstand strong challenges effectively curtailed his Ewood career.

## HUDDERSFIELD TOWN FC
Founded in 1908, Huddersfield Town played one season in the North Eastern League before becoming members of the Midland League. In 1910 the club was elected to the Second Division of the Football League and won promotion to the First Division in 1919-20. Huddersfield were one of the country's leading teams during the 1920s, winning the First Division championship on three occasions and twice finishing in the runners-up spot. In 1928 they met Blackburn Rovers in the FA Cup Final at a time when the Rovers were struggling at the wrong end of the table and Huddersfield were chasing a League and Cup 'double'. It was a major surprise when the Rovers lifted the trophy by virtue of a 3-1 win. The Rovers have met Huddersfield in three different divisions of the Football League and in three major Cup competitions.

### Football League

| | | | Home | | Away | |
|---|---|---|---|---|---|---|
| 1920-21 | (Div 1) | L | 1-2 | D | 0-0 |
| 1921-22 | (Div 1) | W | 2-0 | L | 0-3 |
| 1922-23 | (Div 1) | D | 0-0 | W | 2-0 |
| 1923-24 | (Div 1) | W | 1-0 | L | 0-1 |
| 1924-25 | (Div 1) | L | 2-3 | D | 0-0 |
| 1925-26 | (Div 1) | W | 2-1 | L | 1-3 |
| 1926-27 | (Div 1) | W | 4-2 | L | 0-5 |
| 1927-28 | (Div 1) | D | 1-1 | L | 1-3 |
| 1928-29 | (Div 1) | D | 1-1 | W | 2-0 |
| 1929-30 | (Div 1) | W | 5-2 | D | 0-0 |
| 1930-31 | (Div 1) | W | 5-3 | D | 1-1 |
| 1931-32 | (Div 1) | W | 3-0 | D | 1-1 |
| 1932-33 | (Div 1) | W | 4-2 | W | 3-0 |
| 1933-34 | (Div 1) | D | 2-2 | L | 3-5 |
| 1934-35 | (Div 1) | W | 4-2 | L | 0-6 |
| 1935-36 | (Div 1) | W | 2-1 | D | 1-1 |
| 1946-47 | (Div 1) | D | 2-2 | W | 1-0 |
| 1947-48 | (Div 1) | L | 1-2 | D | 1-1 |
| 1952-53 | (Div 2) | D | 1-1 | W | 3-0 |
| 1956-57 | (Div 2) | W | 3-2 | W | 2-0 |
| 1957-58 | (Div 2) | D | 1-1 | L | 1-2 |
| 1966-67 | (Div 2) | W | 2-0 | L | 1-3 |
| 1967-68 | (Div 2) | D | 0-0 | L | 1-2 |
| 1968-69 | (Div 2) | D | 0-0 | L | 1-2 |
| 1969-70 | (Div 2) | L | 0-2 | W | 1-0 |
| 1973-74 | (Div 3) | W | 1-0 | L | 0-1 |
| 1974-75 | (Div 3) | D | 1-1 | W | 2-1 |
| 1983-84 | (Div 2) | D | 2-2 | W | 2-0 |
| 1984-85 | (Div 2) | L | 1-3 | D | 1-1 |
| 1985-86 | (Div 2) | L | 0-1 | D | 0-0 |
| 1986-87 | (Div 2) | L | 1-2 | W | 2-1 |
| 1987-88 | (Div 2) | D | 2-2 | W | 2-1 |

| | P | W | D | L | F | A |
|---|---|---|---|---|---|---|
| Home | 32 | 13 | 12 | 7 | 57 | 43 |
| Away | 32 | 11 | 9 | 12 | 36 | 44 |
| Total | 64 | 24 | 21 | 19 | 93 | 87 |

### FA Cup
| 1921-22 | (3) | Home | D | 1-1 |
|---|---|---|---|---|
| | (R) | Away | L | 0-5 |
| 1927-28 | (F) | Wembley | W | 3-1 |
| 1938-39 | (6) | Away | D | 1-1 |
| | (R) | Home | L | 1-2 |

### Football League Cup
| 1980-81 | (1) | Home | D | 0-0 |
|---|---|---|---|---|
| | | Away | D | 1-1 aet* |
| 1992-93 | (2) | Away | D | 1-1 |
| | | Home | W | 4-3 aet |

*Blackburn won on the away goals rule.

### Full Members' Cup
| 1986-87 | (1) | Away | W | 2-1 aet |
|---|---|---|---|---|

### Wartime
| | | Home | | Away | |
|---|---|---|---|---|---|
| 1945-46 | (FLN) | L | 1-6 | W | 2-0 |

**HUDSON, George Anthony**
Centre-forward. 1955-1960.
*5ft 11in; 12st 6lb.*
*Born: Manchester, 14 March 1937.*
*Debut: v Manchester City (h) 18 April 1959.*
*Career: Manchester junior football; Blackburn Rovers amateur May 1955, turning professional in January 1958; Accrington Stanley July 1960; Peterborough United October 1961 (£5,000); Coventry City April 1963 (£20,000); Northampton Town March 1966; Tranmere Rovers January 1967 to cs 1969 (£15,000).*
**Appearances:** Football League 4.
**Goals:** Football League 1.

George Hudson came to Ewood Park as a young amateur player and did sufficiently well to be offered professional terms in January 1958. Although he was later to gain a reputation as a robust, goalscoring centre-forward, his time at Ewood was spent largely in the Central League team. He appeared in the final four games of the 1958-59 season but was unable to dislodge Derek Dougan from the number-nine shirt during the following campaign. It was not until he moved to Accrington Stanley in July 1960 that Hudson made a major impact in the Football League. At Peel Park in 1960-61 he equalled the club record of 35 goals in a season. Struggling financially, Stanley reluctantly agreed to sell Hudson to Peterborough United for a bargain fee of only £5,000.

A record of 39 goals in 65 League appearances was enough for Coventry City to pay Peterborough £20,000 to take Hudson to Highfield Road in April 1963. In 1963-64, his 25 goals in 32 appearances helped Coventry to lift the Third Division title and it was his goalscoring ability that persuaded Northampton Town to sign him just before the transfer deadline in 1966. Faced with relegation from the First Division after only one season, Hudson was signed to try to keep the 'Cobblers' in the top flight. Sadly, six goals in only 11 First Division appearances was not enough to prevent Northampton descending into the Second Division with Blackburn Rovers. Hudson ended his League career with Tranmere Rovers and helped the Merseyside club to secure promotion from the Fourth Division in 1966-67. Hudson retired from League football with a record of 164 goals in 298 appearances (including one as sub).

**HUGHES, John Iorweth**
Goalkeeper. 1933-1937.
*5ft 9in; 11st 8lb.*
*Born: Rhosllanerchrugog, nr Wrexham, 29 January 1913.*
*Debut: v Birmingham (h) 4 February 1933.*
*Career: Rhos National School; Plas Bennion; Llanerch Celts; Aberystwyth Town; Afongoch; Druids; Llanerch Celts; Rhos FC; Blackburn Rovers amateur January 1933, turning professional in March 1933; Dick Kerr's XI on loan 1932-33; Mansfield Town June 1937; Nelson; Bacup Borough 1946-47; Rossendale United 1947-48; Darwen 1948-49; Third Lanark.*
*International honours with Blackburn Rovers: Wales: 1 cap (1935).*
**Appearances:** Football League 47; FA Cup 3; Total 50.

Jack Hughes came to Ewood Park as an amateur in January 1933 and on 4 February he was preferred to the club's three professional 'keepers and selected for the first team. Although not blessed with height, Hughes was a strong and agile custodian whose good positioning and quick thinking made him a formidable last line of defence. He signed professional terms in March and, as a result, Cliff Binns was placed on the transfer list and allowed to drift out of the League to sign for Workington. At this time Hughes was seen as the number two to Bill Gormlie at Ewood but received an unexpected promotion when Gormlie was injured after only 11 games of the 1933-34 campaign. Although the team won four of the next seven games, the Rovers chose to recall Binns from Workington and install him in the first team in place of Hughes. With Binns showing excellent form and Hughes suffering a serious spinal injury in 1935, it was not until the 1936-37 season that Hughes was able to regain the goalkeeping position at Ewood Park. However, the form of Hughes was no longer what it had been and, with the promising Jimmy Barron on the staff, Hughes was allowed to move to Mansfield Town.

**HUGHES, William Arthur**
Goalkeeper. 1948-1950.
*6ft 2in; 12st 6lb.*
*Born: Colwyn Bay, 2 February 1919; Died: 11 March 1992.*
*Debut: v West Bromwich Albion (h) 23 October 1948.*
*Career: Colwyn Bay United 1935 to 1937; Larne 1937; Newry Town; Huddersfield Town May 1939; Arsenal wartime guest 1943-44; Tottenham Hotspur wartime guest 1944-45 & 1945-46 before signing permanently in December 1945; Blackburn Rovers October 1948; Nelson cs 1950; Rochdale September 1950; Crystal Palace February 1951.*
*International honours with Blackburn Rovers: Wales: 5 caps (1948-49).*
**Appearances:** Football League 27; FA Cup 1; Total 28.

The outbreak of World War Two put paid to the hopes that Bill Hughes had of launching his League career with Huddersfield Town. Fortunately, impressive wartime performances with Tottenham Hotspur earned him a permanent contract at White Hart Lane in December 1945. However, the consistency of Ted Ditchburn meant Hughes had only two League appearances to his name when he left London to join Blackburn Rovers in October 1948. Although Hughes won international recognition whilst at Ewood, his indecision on crosses caused some alarm in the Blackburn ranks. Injury cost him his place after 19 League appearances and allowed Jack Patterson to stake a claim for the first-team position.

Apart from a brief spell in September and October 1949, when Patterson himself was injured, Hughes never regained the first-team position at Ewood. Alarmed that reserve-team football would end his international career Hughes asked for a transfer. Although retained for the 1950-51 season he failed to appear at Ewood but chose to play for Nelson in the Lancashire League. He returned to League action in September 1950 when Rochdale agreed to pay a reduced transfer fee for Hughes. Sadly, after a bright start Hughes was unable to retain his place at Spotland and in February 1951 he returned to London to join Crystal Palace.

**HULL CITY FC**
Hull City Football Club was founded in 1904 and elected to the Second Division of the Football League in 1905. Blackburn and Hull City did not meet in competitive football until after World War Two. Apart from the 1979-80 season, when both clubs were in the Third Division, all League meetings between the clubs have taken place in the Second Division.

**Football League**

| | | | Home | | Away | |
|---|---|---|---|---|---|---|
| 1949-50 | | (Div 2) | W | 4-2 | L | 1-3 |
| 1950-51 | | (Div 2) | D | 2-2 | D | 2-2 |
| 1951-52 | | (Div 2) | W | 1-0 | L | 0-3 |
| 1952-53 | | (Div 2) | W | 2-0 | L | 0-3 |
| 1953-54 | | (Div 2) | W | 3-1 | W | 2-1 |
| 1954-55 | | (Div 2) | W | 4-0 | W | 4-1 |
| 1955-56 | | (Div 2) | W | 2-0 | W | 3-0 |
| 1966-67 | | (Div 2) | W | 4-1 | W | 3-2 |
| 1967-68 | | (Div 2) | W | 2-0 | D | 1-1 |
| 1968-69 | | (Div 2) | D | 1-1 | W | 3-1 |
| 1969-70 | | (Div 2) | W | 2-1 | L | 0-3 |
| 1970-71 | | (Div 2) | L | 0-1 | D | 0-0 |
| 1975-76 | | (Div 2) | W | 1-0 | W | 1-0 |
| 1976-77 | | (Div 2) | W | 1-0 | L | 0-1 |
| 1977-78 | | (Div 2) | D | 1-1 | W | 1-0 |
| 1979-80 | | (Div 3) | W | 1-0 | W | 1-0 |
| 1985-86 | | (Div 2) | D | 2-2 | D | 2-2 |
| 1986-87 | | (Div 2) | L | 0-2 | D | 0-0 |
| 1987-88 | | (Div 2) | W | 2-1 | D | 2-2 |
| 1988-89 | | (Div 2) | W | 4-0 | W | 3-1 |
| 1989-90 | | (Div 2) | D | 0-0 | L | 0-2 |
| 1990-91 | | (Div 2) | W | 2-1 | L | 1-3 |

| | P | W | D | L | F | A |
|---|---|---|---|---|---|---|
| Home | 22 | 15 | 5 | 2 | 41 | 16 |
| Away | 22 | 9 | 6 | 7 | 30 | 30 |
| Total | 44 | 24 | 11 | 9 | 71 | 46 |

**FA Cup**

| | | | | | |
|---|---|---|---|---|---|
| 1946-47 | (3) | Home | D | 1-1 | |
| | (R) | Away | W | 3-0 | |
| 1948-49 | (3) | Away | L | 1-2 | aet |
| 1951-52 | (4) | Home | W | 2-0 | |
| 1953-54 | (4) | Home | D | 2-2 | |
| | (R) | Away | L | 1-2 | |

**Football League Cup**

| | | | | |
|---|---|---|---|---|
| 1991-92 | (1) | Home | D | 1-1 |
| | | Away | L | 0-1 |

**HULME, Joseph Harold Anthony**
Outside-right. 1924-1926.
*5ft 7½in; 10st 4lb.*
*Born: Stafford, 26 August 1904; Died: Winchmore Hill, 26 September 1991.*
*Debut: v Aston Villa (h) 1 March 1924.*
*Career: Stafford YMCA; York City 1923; Blackburn Rovers February 1924 (£250); Arsenal February 1926 (£3,500); Huddersfield Town January 1938. Retired cs 1938. Tottenham Hotspur assistant secretary February 1944, becoming manager in October 1945 until May 1949.*
**Appearances:** Football League 73; FA Cup 9; Total 82.
**Goals:** Football League 6; FA Cup 2; Total 8.

Joe Hulme was a bright young prospect when he joined Blackburn Rovers from York City in February 1924. Although Hulme had only been at York a short time he was immediately thrown into the first team at Ewood Park. A fast and tricky winger, Hulme made the outside-right position his own and was a model of consistency throughout his time at Blackburn. In February 1926, Herbert Chapman persuaded the Rovers to part with their exciting young prospect in exchange for a sizeable fee. Hulme went on to become an integral part of the Arsenal side which was to dominate football in the 1930s.

Although injury restricted him to only eight appearances in the 1933-34 title-winning season, Hulme shared in three other championship successes (1931, 1934 and 1935) as well as two FA Cup triumphs (1930 and 1936). He also appeared in the Arsenal team which lost the 1932 Cup Final. Hulme was capped on eight occasions by England and ended his playing career with a season at Huddersfield Town in 1937-38. When he retired, Hulme had appeared in 414 League matches and 50 FA Cup-ties and had scored a total of 132 goals for his various League clubs. During the summer months Hulme played cricket for Middlesex and between 1929 and 1939, he appeared in 223 matches, scoring 8,015 runs at an average of 26.63. He also took 89 wickets.

## HULSE, Benjamin Daniel
Inside-forward. 1897-1900.
*Born: Liverpool, 1875 (July quarter); Died: Liverpool, 30 May 1950.*
*Debut: v Stoke (a) 18 September 1897.*
*Career: Rock Ferry; Blackburn Rovers May 1897; New Brighton Tower August 1900; Millwall Athletic cs 1901 to 1904.*
**Appearances:** Football League 85; Test Matches 3; FA Cup 5; Total 93.
**Goals:** Football League 22; FA Cup 3; Total 25.
Ben Hulse was a workmanlike inside-forward whose lack of finesse prevented him from developing into an outstanding player. Whilst he possessed plenty of dash and ball control, Hulse was regarded as something of a 'plodder' at Ewood Park. Yet, despite this criticism, Hulse held a regular first-team place for three seasons and no one could deny that he was a grafter in the true sense of the word. He ended his career with Millwall, scoring 35 goals in 60 Southern League matches.

## HUNTER, Allan
Central defender. 1969-1971.
*6ft; 12st 7lb.*
*Born: Sion Mills, County Tyrone, Ireland, 30 June 1946.*
*Debut: v Swindon Town (h) 9 August 1969.*
*Career: Coleraine amateur 1962, becoming a professional in 1965; Oldham Athletic January 1967 (£5,000); Blackburn Rovers June 1969 (£30,000); Ipswich Town September 1971 (£60,000 + Robert Bell); Colchester United player-manager 5 May 1982 until 18 January 1983, later returned as assistant manager until November 1987.*
*International honours with Blackburn Rovers: Northern Ireland: 6 caps (1969-71).*
**Appearances:** Football League 84; FA Cup 2; Football League Cup 5; Total 91.
**Goals:** Football League 1.
Doubts about the capabilities of John Coddington led Eddie Quigley to bring Allan Hunter to Ewood Park to form a new central defensive partnership with Dick Mulvaney. Hunter, who had joined Oldham Athletic following an unsuccessful trial with Leeds United, was a tall, long-legged centre-back whose cool and cultured defending was in stark contrast to his predecessor at Ewood. The pairing of Mulvaney and Hunter was a great success as only 50 goals were conceded in the League during 1969-70. Capped by Northern Ireland, Hunter developed into one of the most outstanding defenders outside of the First Division.

Unable to prevent the club from being relegated to the Third Division in 1970-71, Hunter was clearly too good to linger in the lower divisions. With the Rovers desperate to generate the revenue to revamp their squad, Ken Furphy allowed Hunter to move to Ipswich Town in a cash plus player exchange deal. Hunter went on to enjoy great success under Bobby Robson at Ipswich. He won an FA Cup winners' medal in 1978 and appeared in 280 League games for the club before joining Colchester United as player-manager in May 1982. Hunter, who gained 58 caps for Northern Ireland, didn't enjoy the same success in management that he had as a player and resigned his position at Colchester in January 1983. He was later to return to Colchester for a spell as assistant manager before leaving the game in November 1987.

## HURST, Daniel James
Outside-left. 1897-1901.
*Born: Cockermouth, 1876 (October quarter).*
*Debut: v West Bromwich Albion (h) 2 February 1898.*
*Career: Black Diamonds, Workington; Blackburn Rovers October 1897; Workington March 1900; Manchester City May 1901; Newton Heath May 1902 until cs 1903.*

*International honours with Blackburn Rovers: Football League: 1 appearance (1899).*
**Appearances:** Football League 53; Test Matches 2; FA Cup 5; Total 60.
**Goals:** Football League 17; Test Matches 2; Total 19.
Daniel Hurst made a major impact on the Test Match series of 1897-98 for Blackburn Rovers. Hurst, who had previously only appeared in two League matches, was drafted into the outside-left position after the first two games in the series had been lost. He scored two goals in a 4-2 win over Newcastle United and when the Rovers retained their First Division place due to a restructure of the League format, Hurst found himself promoted to the first team.

The 1898-99 season brought Hurst 14 goals in 31 League games and took him to the brink of international honours. However, a seemingly bright future suddenly turned sour in March 1900 when he was relegated to the reserve team following a dip in form. Hurst refused to turn out for the second team and returned to Workington leaving the Blackburn directors with little option but to suspend him for the rest of the season. Hurst attempted to revive his League career in Manchester, making 15 League appearances with Manchester City before joining Newton Heath in May 1902. He scored four goals in 16 League games with the latter before leaving the game in the summer of 1903.

## HUTCHINS, Donald
Outside-left. 1972-1974.
*5ft 7in; 10st 2lb.*
*Born: Middlesbrough, 8 May 1948.*
*Debut: v Bristol Rovers (a) 12 August 1972.*
*Career: Stockton; Leicester City February 1966; Plymouth Argyle July 1969; Blackburn Rovers July 1972; Bradford City June 1974 until cs 1981.*
**Appearances:** Football League 37+3; FA Cup 1+1; Football League Cup 2+1; Total 40+5.
**Goals:** Football League 6.
Don Hutchins had proved himself to be a winger with a flair for goals whilst with Plymouth Argyle. The 1971-72 season had seen him score 12 goals for the Pilgrims whilst the season before he had been the club's leading goalscorer with 11 goals. Sadly, Hutchins rarely produced such form at Ewood Park. As the Rovers mounted a serious promotion challenge during the latter part of the 1972-73 campaign, Hutchins spent long spells out the team. When he was recalled for the vital promotion clash against Notts County he fluffed the only clear-cut chance that the team created. He enjoyed his most productive spell at Ewood when Gordon Lee became manager but in June 1974 he was allowed to join Bradford City as part of the deal which brought Graham Oates to Blackburn. Hutchins enjoyed great success at Valley Parade, appearing in 256 League games (including four as sub) and scoring 44 League goals during his time at the club.

## HUTT, Geoffrey
Left-back. 1975.
*5ft 8in; 12st.*
*Born: Hazlewood, 28 September 1949.*
*Debut: v Sunderland (h) 20 September 1975.*
*Career: Huddersfield Town apprentice June 1966, turning professional in September 1967; Blackburn Rovers on loan September 1975 to October 1975; Haarlem (Holland) June 1976; York City February 1977; Halifax Town April 1978 to cs 1980.*
**Appearances:** Football League 10.
**Goals:** Football League 1.
Jim Smith turned to the experienced Hutt when injury robbed him of the services of Andy Burgin after only five games of the 1975-76 season. At Huddersfield, Hutt had appeared in every game of the 1969-70 Second Division championship campaign before suffering three relegations in four years with the Leeds Road club. A steady rather than outstanding full-back, Hutt might well have been retained by Smith if the financial position at Ewood had been a little healthier.

## HUTTON, John
Right-back. 1926-1933.
*5ft 8in; 13st 7lb.*
*Born: Dalziel, Motherwell, 29 October 1898.*
*Debut: v Burnley (h) 16 October 1926.*
*Career: Motherwell Hearts; Larkhill Thistle; Bellshill Athletic 1918; Aberdeen April 1919; Blackburn Rovers October 1926 (£5,000). Retired March 1933.*
*International honours with Blackburn Rovers: Scotland: 3 caps (1927-28).*
*Domestic honours with Blackburn Rovers: FA Cup winners: 1928.*
**Appearances:** Football League 127; FA Cup 19; Total 146.
**Goals:** Football League 4; FA Cup 1; Total 5.
Weighing in at over 13st, Jock Hutton could hardly be described as one

of football's most natural athletes. None the less he remained a popular personality with crowds on both sides of the border during a distinguished playing career. A product of junior football in Scotland, Hutton had begun his career as an inside-forward before his instinctive defensive qualities led to him moving to full-back. He enjoyed a highly successful career with Aberdeen and won seven Scottish caps as well as captaining the Scottish League side. Hutton was a hard-tackling defender who refused to use his weight unfairly. The master of the well-timed tackle, Hutton proved surprisingly agile for such a big man. He possessed a tremendous shot and liked nothing better than to get forward and have a pop at goal. Following his move to Blackburn he won three more Scottish caps and an FA Cup winners medal before injuries began to restrict his first-team appearances. Hutton was placed on the transfer list in December 1932, but decided to retire from the game the following March after having failed to fully overcome his injury problems.

### ILEY, James
Manager. 1978.
*Born: South Kirkby, 15 December 1935.*
*Career: Pontefract; Sheffield United June 1953; Tottenham Hotspur August 1957 (£16,000); Nottingham Forest July 1959 (£16,000); Newcastle United September 1962 (£17,000); Peterborough United player-manager January 1969 until September 1972; Cambridge United scout 1972-73; Barnsley manager April 1973; Blackburn Rovers manager April 1978 until October 1978; Bury manager July 1980 until February 1984; Exeter City manager June 1984 until April 1985; Charlton Athletic scout.*
Jim Iley endured a short but turbulent managerial reign at Ewood Park between April and October 1978. His departure from the club, only 172 days after his arrival was the culmination of one the most bitter episodes in the history of Blackburn Rovers. Iley had been appointed to succeed Jim Smith on 14 April 1978 and joined up with the players for the fixture at Mansfield Town the following day. This was one of only four games left in a season which had ended with the disappointing departure of Smith following the club's slide from the promotion placings. The appointment of Iley had followed the tried and trusted policy of selecting a man who had proved himself capable of managing a club on a small budget.

However, whereas Furphy, Lee and Smith had all experienced promotion with their respective clubs, Iley had built a strong Barnsley outfit without gaining the ultimate prize. Iley's own playing career had been more in keeping with the aspirations of the Rovers rather than the Fourth Division in which he worked with Barnsley. A long playing career as a half-back in the First Division was followed by a stint as player-manager with Peterborough United before his move to Oakwell. In contrast to the stability he had achieved at Barnsley, his reign at Ewood Park seemed to stumble from one crisis to another. Ironically, it was during the close season that Iley's position at Ewood began to be undermined. His decision to allow the veteran Dave Wagstaffe to leave for Blackpool brought universal condemnation from Blackburn supporters.

When the circumstances surrounding Wagstaffe's reluctant departure came to light the criticisms of the new manager merely intensified. Iley's position was not helped when John Aston, the outside-left Iley had signed before Wagstaffe's departure, failed to find any sort of early season form. Whilst Wagstaffe had developed other facets of his game to compensate for his ageing legs, Aston still relied on pace as the main weapon of his armoury. Sadly age had blunted the effectiveness of this weapon and he

posed little threat to Second Division defenders. With the Wagstaffe affair still hanging over Ewood Park the club was rocked by an eve-of-season clash between Iley and Stuart Metcalfe, the club's star midfield man.

The manager and player disagreed over the latter's style of play and Iley caused a sensation by putting Metcalfe on the substitute's bench for the opening home fixture with Crystal Palace. However, Iley, staring defeat in the face, was forced to introduce Metcalfe in a last ditch attempt to salvage a point. When Metcalfe came on and scored the equalising goal it was a further blow to the manager's credibility as far as the supporters were concerned. Only one point was gained from the opening three League games and defeat in the League Cup at Third Division Exeter City merely added to the pressure on Iley.

The one bright spot in a disappointing start to the campaign had been the form of Dave Gregory, a forward who was on loan from Stoke City. However, the manager came under further fire when Gregory rejected a permanent move to Ewood and opted to join Third Division Bury. The flames of discontent were further fanned by the local Press which carried endless letters from supporters who questioned the manager's judgement. Indeed some of the back page comment was highly unfavourable to the beleaguered manager. In a bid to lift the mounting pressure, Iley entered the transfer market to sign Joe Craig from Celtic and Alan Birchenall from Memphis Rogues. Iley hoped that Craig, a Scottish international striker, and the veteran midfielder Birchenall would be able to halt the alarming slide. However, the moves came too late to save the luckless Iley.

Only four days after sanctioning the double signing, the Ewood directors decided to end Iley's 172-day reign at Ewood Park. Iley accepted his sacking in the philosophical way that managers do but was quick to point out that injuries and the media had much to do with his downfall. After leaving Blackburn he continued to work in football management and had spells in charge of Bury and Exeter City before joining the scouting staff of Charlton Athletic.

### IMRIE, William Noble
Right-half. 1929-1934.
*5ft 10½in; 12st 2lb.*
*Born: Methil, Fife, 4 March 1908; Died: c.December 1944 while in the RAF.*
*Debut: v Newcastle United (h) 16 September 1929.*
*Career: Kirkcaldy Juniors; East Fife Juniors; Dunnikier Juniors; St Johnstone; Blackburn Rovers September 1929 (£4,475); Newcastle United March 1934 (£6,500); Swansea Town July 1938 (£800); Swindon Town July 1939.*
**Appearances:** Football League 165; FA Cup 11; Total 176.
**Goals:** Football League 23; FA Cup 1; Total 24.
The *Lancashire Daily Post Football Annual* of 1930-31 described Bill Imrie as 'a young lion of physical endeavour' and added that he 'Can kick like a full-back or go through like a forward, and his throw-ins have great power.' In short, he was the supreme competitor. Imrie won two Scottish caps with St Johnstone before moving to Ewood Park in September 1929. At Blackburn he made the right-half position his own and even had a spell at centre-half during the 1931-32 season. The red-haired Imrie moved to relegation bound Newcastle United in March 1932 and became an inspirational captain of the Magpies.

### INGLIS, John
Forward. 1884.
*Debut: v Upton Park (a) 9 February 1884 (FAC).*
*Career: Patrick FC; Glasgow Rangers; Blackburn Rovers October 1883.*
*Domestic honours with Blackburn Rovers: FA Cup winners: 1883-84.*
**Appearances:** FA Cup 3.
**Goals:** FA Cup 1.
The arrival of John Inglis, a Scottish international, from Glasgow Rangers was not greeted with universal approval in Blackburn. The correspondent of the *Blackburn Times* was particularly critical of his signing and commented: 'There is one point about Blackburn Rovers which does not give entire satisfaction, and that is the introduction of Inglis of the Glasgow Rangers. It is 'hard lines' on Sowerbutts or whoever else is supplanted, that after the faithful services of the past he should be pushed out in this manner, and besides that there is a class of people in the town who would rather lose the Cup on their merits than win it with the aid of a specially introduced stranger.'

Inglis had first appeared for the club in the Lancashire Cup-tie with Blackpool South Shore in October 1883. However, he didn't reappear until the friendly fixture with Darwen on 8 February 1884, but gave a good account of himself and scored one of the goals in a convincing 8-0 victory. The club had already announced that Inglis would appear for the team in the FA Cup-ties but they refrained from using him in friendlies. However, a month after the Cup Final, Inglis made a further appearance for the club in a friendly fixture with Sheffield Wednesday. Any lingering doubts as to the ethics of using Inglis disappeared when he helped the Rovers to win the FA Cup for the first time in the club's history.

## IPSWICH TOWN FC
Founded in 1880, Ipswich Town were elected to the Third Division South of the Football League in 1938. Ipswich and Blackburn have met in Division One and Two of the Football League and were both founder members of the Premier League in 1992-93. Ipswich provided the opposition at the semi-final stage of the 1986-87 Full Members' Cup competition when the Rovers went on to win the trophy at Wembley.

**Football League**

|         |         | Home |     | Away |     |
|---------|---------|------|-----|------|-----|
| 1954-55 | (Div 2) | W    | 4-1 | D    | 1-1 |
| 1957-58 | (Div 2) | D    | 0-0 | L    | 1-2 |
| 1961-62 | (Div 1) | D    | 2-2 | L    | 1-2 |
| 1962-63 | (Div 1) | L    | 0-1 | D    | 3-3 |
| 1963-64 | (Div 1) | W    | 3-1 | D    | 0-0 |
| 1966-67 | (Div 2) | L    | 1-2 | D    | 1-1 |
| 1967-68 | (Div 2) | W    | 2-1 | D    | 1-1 |
| 1986-87 | (Div 2) | D    | 0-0 | L    | 1-3 |
| 1987-88 | (Div 2) | W    | 1-0 | W    | 2-0 |
| 1988-89 | (Div 2) | W    | 1-0 | L    | 0-2 |
| 1989-90 | (Div 2) | D    | 2-2 | L    | 1-3 |
| 1990-91 | (Div 2) | L    | 0-1 | L    | 1-2 |
| 1991-92 | (Div 2) | L    | 1-2 | L    | 1-2 |

|       | P  | W | D | L  | F  | A  |
|-------|----|---|---|----|----|----|
| Home  | 13 | 5 | 4 | 4  | 17 | 13 |
| Away  | 13 | 1 | 5 | 7  | 14 | 22 |
| Total | 26 | 6 | 9 | 11 | 31 | 35 |

**FA Premiership**

|         | Home |     | Away |     |
|---------|------|-----|------|-----|
| 1992-93 | W    | 2-1 | L    | 1-2 |
| 1993-94 | D    | 0-0 | L    | 0-1 |

|       | P | W | D | L | F | A |
|-------|---|---|---|---|---|---|
| Home  | 2 | 1 | 1 | 0 | 2 | 1 |
| Away  | 2 | 0 | 0 | 2 | 1 | 3 |
| Total | 4 | 1 | 1 | 2 | 3 | 4 |

**Football League Cup**

| 1961-62 | (4) | Home | W | 4-1 |
|---------|-----|------|---|-----|
| 1983-84 | (2) | Away | L | 3-4 |
|         |     | Home | L | 1-2 |

**Full Members' Cup**

| 1986-87 | (SF) | Home | W | 3-0 |
|---------|------|------|---|-----|
| 1988-89 | (3)  | Away | L | 0-1 |

## IRELAND, Simon
Outside-left. 1992.
*5ft 10in; 10st 7lb.*
*Born: Halifax, 23 November 1971.*
*Debut: v Manchester City (a) 30 January 1993 (sub).*
*Career: Huddersfield Town July 1990; Wrexham on loan March 1992; Blackburn Rovers November 1992 (£200,000); Mansfield Town on loan March 1994.*
**Appearances:** Premier League 0+1.
Kenny Dalglish invested £200,000 in Simon Ireland after watching the young winger give his defence a torrid time in a League Cup fixture at Ewood Park. On his arrival from Huddersfield, Ireland was put into the Central League team but came into the first-team squad in January 1993. Sadly, his season came to a premature end when he suffered a broken ankle in a Central League game.

## IRVINE, James Alan
Midfield/Outside-right. 1989-1991.
*5ft 9in; 11st 3lb.*
*Born: Glasgow, 12 July 1958.*
*Debut: v Plymouth Argyle (a) 28 October 1989.*
*Career: Queens Park; Everton May 1981; Crystal Palace August 1984 (£50,000); Dundee United June 1987; Blackburn Rovers on loan from October 1989 before signing permanently in November 1989. Retired May 1992 and was appointed assistant youth-team manager with Blackburn Rovers.*
**Appearances:** Football League 40+18; Football League Cup 3; Full Members' Cup 0+1; Total 43+19.
**Goals:** Football League 3.
Alan Irvine was an orthodox outside-right who joined Blackburn Rovers

towards the end of his playing career. Irvine had first tried his luck in England with Everton after helping Queen's Park win the Scottish Second Division title. Although he appeared in the Everton side that lost the 1984 League Cup Final to Liverpool, Irvine failed to win a regular first-team place during his stay on Merseyside. After 51 League appearances (including nine as sub), Irvine tried his luck in London with Crystal Palace. He featured in 108 League matches (including one as sub) at Selhurst Park before returning to Scotland to link up with Dundee United. Having turned to coaching at Dundee, Irvine jumped at the chance of continuing his playing career with Blackburn Rovers. His dribbling and crossing qualities made him a popular character during his short spell in the first team at Ewood Park. Although he retired from senior football in May 1992 to take up the post of assistant youth-team manager at the club, Irvine continued to turn out with the Central League team.

## ISHERWOOD, Roy Edward
Outside-right. 1956-1962.
*5ft 6in; 10st 12lb.*
*Born: Blackburn, 24 January 1934.*
*Debut: v Huddersfield Town (h) 19 October 1957.*
*Career: Blackburn Rovers non-contract player September 1956, becoming a professional in October 1957 until June 1962; Chelmsford City cs 1962.*
**Appearances:** Football League 49; FA Cup 2; Football League Cup 6; Total 57.
**Goals:** Football League 9.
Roy Isherwood had the unenviable task of understudying Bryan Douglas during his time at Ewood Park. He made his debut in October 1957 and scored the goal which enabled to Rovers to take a point from the home game with Huddersfield Town. However, Isherwood had to wait until November 1958 before his next senior outing. Until the 1961-62 season his first-team outings were restricted to those occasions when injury or international duty kept Douglas out of the Blackburn line-up. However, after three games of the 1961-62 campaign, Douglas was moved to inside-left and Isherwood was given the opportunity to establish himself on the right wing. Sadly, he proved unequal to the task and was dropped after six games. The summer of 1962 saw him move to Chelmsford City and return to the plumbing trade which he had left to sign professional forms at Ewood.

## ISLE OF MAN FOOTBALL FESTIVAL
The Isle of Man Football Festival was begun in the early 1980s and linked to the Lancashire Manx Cup competition. The Isle of Man tournament was a pre-season event for which the winners of the previous season's Lancashire Manx Cup automatically qualified. The Rovers appeared in this event on three occasions and reached the Final twice. In 1984, the Rovers lost 1-0 to Sunderland in the Final whilst 12 months later they won the competition thanks to a 1-0 victory over Stoke City.

## JACKSON, Harold
Inside-left. 1948-1949.
*Born: Blackburn, 30 December 1918.*
*Debut: v Barnsley (a) 1 January 1949.*
*Career: Meadowcroft's; Stanhill; Darwen 1936-37 Burnley January 1942; Manchester City June 1946; Preston North End December 1947; Blackburn Rovers December 1948; Chester July 1949.*
**Appearances:** Football League 1; FA Cup 1; Total 2.
As a youth Harry Jackson had had trials with several clubs including Everton, Blackpool and Blackburn Rovers before linking up with Burnley during World War Two. By the time the Football League was restored for the 1946-47 season, Jackson had moved to Maine Road. However, after only eight League appearances with Manchester City he moved to Preston North End in December 1947. Twelve months at Deepdale produced five goals in 18 games and on Christmas Eve 1948, Jackson got the move he wanted when he signed for his home-town club.

He was signed primarily by Jack Bruton to provide cover for Dennis Westcott in the centre-forward position. However, his ability to play on the left wing made him a valuable addition to the playing staff at Ewood. Jackson made his debut at Barnsley on New Year's Day 1949 in the inside-left position but was given little opportunity to shine. None the less, on a day when the Rovers were less than impressive nobody worked harder than Jackson to try to win the game for Blackburn. He retained his place the following week when the Rovers were disappointingly eliminated from the FA Cup by Hull City. This was to prove to be Jackson's last appearance for the Rovers and in July 1948 he continued his travels with a move to Chester.

## JACKSON, J.Thomas
Centre-forward. 1897-1899.
*Debut: v Nottingham Forest (h) 15 January 1898.*

*Career: Padiham; Blackburn Rovers November 1897.*
**Appearances:** Football League 26; Test Matches 2; FA Cup 1; Total 29.
**Goals:** Football League 10.
Jackson came from Padiham in November 1897 and made his debut the following January when he deputised for the injured Briercliffe on the right wing. Jackson made an immediate impact on the side, laying on the cross which enabled Proudfoot and Campbell to work an opening for Wilkie to snatch an equalising goal against Nottingham Forest. This was Jackson's only League appearance of the season although he was recalled to the team, in his more usual centre-forward position, for the final two Test Matches. Jackson was given the centre-forward position for the 1898-99 campaign and scored ten goals in 25 League appearances before Ben Hulse was moved from inside-forward to replace Jackson in the middle.

**JACQUES, Thomas Edmund**
Left-half. 1912-1915.
*5ft 10in; 11st 12lb.*
*Born: Blackburn, 13 November 1890.*
*Debut: v Everton (h) 26 December 1912.*
*Career: Victoria Cross (Blackburn); Blackburn Trinity; Mill Hill Woodfold (Blackburn); Accrington Stanley; Darwen; Blackburn Rovers March 1912; Nelson; Great Harwood 1923-24. Returned to Nelson as groundsman and assistant trainer during the 1924 close season. First-team trainer at Nelson from July 1926 until cs 1928.*
**Appearances:** Football League 2.
Jacques graduated through local junior circles before joining Blackburn Rovers in March 1912. During his time at Ewood Park, Jacques was never regarded as anything more than an understudy and following World War One he returned to non-League football with Nelson. He was with the Seedhill club when they joined the Football League and he appeared in 17 games in the Third Division North and scored one goal before joining Great Harwood. Jacques later returned to Nelson as groundsman and assistant trainer and later served as first-team trainer for two seasons.

**JEFFERSON, Thomas**
Forward. 1880-1882.
*Debut: v Sheffield Wednesday (a) 18 December 1880 (FAC).*
*Career: Blackburn Rovers 1880.*
**Appearances:** FA Cup 1.
Jefferson was a regular member of the Blackburn forward line during the latter part of the 1880-81 season. Selected for the friendly encounter with Turton on 13 November 1880, Jefferson retained his place for the rest of the campaign and was a steady, if unprolific, goalscorer. He lost his first-team place the following season to Tot Strachan.

**JOHNROSE, Leonard**
Forward. 1984-1992.
*5ft 10in; 11st 5lb.*
*Born: Preston, 29 November 1969.*
*Debut: v West Bromwich Albion (a) 12 December 1987.*
*Career: Blackburn Rovers associated schoolboy January 1984, becoming a trainee in July 1986, before signing as a professional in June 1988; Preston North End (on loan) January 1992 to February 1992; Hartlepool United February 1992; Bury December 1991.*
**Appearances:** Football League 20+22; FA Cup 0+3; Football League Cup 2+1; Full Members' Cup 2; Total 24+26.
**Goals:** Football League 11; Football League Cup 1; Total 12.
Lenny Johnrose graduated through the club's youth development scheme to become a member of the first-team squad under Don Mackay. A quick moving front runner, Johnrose was adaptable enough to fill a midfield role when required. However, much of his time at Ewood was spent in the Central League team or on the substitute's bench. Johnrose drifted out of contention once Kenny Dalglish and a number of expensive signings arrived at the club. Johnrose left Ewood Park in February 1992 to carve out a first-team career in the lower divisions.

**JOHNSON, Arthur**
Goalkeeper. 1950-1955.
*6ft; 13st 2lb.*
*Born: Liverpool, 23 January 1933.*
*Debut: v Doncaster Rovers (h) 27 August 1951.*
*Career: Southport junior football; Blackburn Rovers January 1950; Halifax Town March 1955; Wrexham June 1960; Chester August 1962 until October 1962.*
**Appearances:** Football League 1.
Arthur Johnson made his debut for Blackburn Rovers as an 18-year-old in August 1951 against Doncaster Rovers. Unfortunately, Johnson was held directly responsible for all three of Doncaster's goals in a 3-3 draw. Although he remained at Ewood Park for a little over five years, the Doncaster game proved to be his only senior appearance. He appeared in 79 Central League games for the club before moving to Halifax in March

1955. Although Johnson failed to make the grade at Blackburn, he went on to appear in 271 League games for his three subsequent clubs, including 216 for Halifax Town.

**JOHNSTON, James**
Right-back. 1910-1914.
*5ft 8in; 12st.*
*Born: Rothesay, 1886; Died: Rothesay, October 1953 (aged 67).*
*Debut: v Aston Villa (a) 1 October 1910.*
*Career: Rothesay Royal Victoria; Maryhill; Blackburn Rovers January 1910.*
**Appearances:** Football League 14.
A strong, sturdy defender who was secured from Maryhill FC with a view to being groomed as the ultimate successor to Bob Crompton. Although a keen tackler, Johnston failed to challenge the ageing Crompton and his time at Ewood Park was largely spent with the second team.

**JOHNSTON, Thomas Bourhill**
Centre-forward. 1958-1959.
*5ft 11in; 12st 6lb.*
*Born: Loanhead, nr Aberdeen, 18 August 1927.*
*Debut: v Grimsby Town (h) 8 March 1958.*
*Career: Loanhead Mayflower; Peeble Rovers May 1949; Falkirk on trial; Third Lanark on trial; Kilmarnock November 1949; Darlington April 1951; Oldham Athletic March 1952; Norwich City June 1952 (£500); Newport County October 1954 (£3,000); Leyton Orient February 1956 (£6,000); Blackburn Rovers March 1958 (£15,000); Leyton Orient February 1959 (£7,500); Gillingham September 1961 (£3,000); Folkestone Town player-coach July 1962; Lytham St Annes.*
**Appearances:** Football League 36; FA Cup 2; Total 38.
**Goals:** Football League 22; FA Cup 1; Total 23.
Johnny Carey brought Tom Johnston to Ewood Park to fill the void left by Tommy Briggs. Once it had become apparent that Briggs was no longer the force he had been, Carey switched young Peter Dobing to the centre-forward position. However, as the Second Division promotion race began to reach its climax, Carey was shrewd enough to realise that he needed a reincarnation of Tommy Briggs to lead his line and thus allow Dobing to operate in his preferred inside-right position. The man chosen by Carey was the much travelled Johnston. Johnston had spent his early life down the pit and a mining accident left him with a withered arm which had to be bandaged whenever he played football. Like Briggs before him, Johnston was a traditional leader of the attack.

A strong, bustling type of striker, Johnston had few equals in the air and was always ready to snap up an opening in front of goal. He rewrote the goalscoring records at Leyton Orient in 1956-57 with 27 League goals and then broke his own record the following season with 35 goals in 30 games. At Ewood he provided exactly the sort of leadership that Carey wanted from his centre-forward. Two goals on his debut helped the Rovers to a convincing 3-0 win over Grimsby and Johnston helped the Rovers to win nine of their final 11 League games. Johnston scored eight goals in those 11 games and it proved sufficient to win promotion to the First Division. Although approaching the veteran stage of his career, Johnston notched 14 goals in 25 First Division games before returning to Leyton Orient in February 1959. During his Football League career Johnston scored 243 goals in 413 appearances. Johnston later moved to Poulton-le-Fylde to open a betting shop and also played a few games for Lytham St Annes. In February 1972 he emigrated to Australia.

**JONES, George Alexander**
Forward. 1964-1966.
*5ft 11in; 11st 9lb.*
*Born: Radcliffe, Lancashire, 21 April 1945.*
*Debut: v Birmingham City (a) 13 March 1964.*
*Career: Bury apprentice September 1961, turning professional in June 1962; Blackburn Rovers March 1964 (£30,000); Bury November 1966 (£18,000); Oldham Athletic March 1973 (£10,000); Halifax Town February 1976 (£2,000); Southport January 1977; Lancaster City cs 1978; Radcliffe Borough player-coach November 1978, player-manager January 1979; Prestwich Heyes; Hyde United; Prestwich Heyes.*
**Appearances:** Football League 36+3; FA Cup 2; Football League Cup 1; Total 39+3.
**Goals:** Football League 14; FA Cup 1; Total 15.
The youngest player to appear with Bury in the Football League, George

Jones was signed by Blackburn Rovers in March 1964. Jones, who had been a member of the England team which had won the UEFA Youth Tournament in 1963, was signed following Fred Pickering's big money move to Everton. Although Jones scored two goals in the remaining eight games of the season, the 18-year-old, not surprisingly, found it difficult to adjust to First Division football. The following season saw him overlooked in favour of John Byrom and he made only three appearances during the whole of the 1964-65 campaign. As the club headed for the Second Division during the disastrous 1965-66 campaign, Jones received more first-team opportunities and finished the season as the club's joint top scorer in League matches with ten goals. Still only 21, Jones was allowed to return to Bury in November 1966. Jones enjoyed a highly successful career in the lower divisions winning a Third Division championship medal with Oldham Athletic in 1974, and by the time he retired he had appeared in 503 League matches (including 20 as sub) and scored 162 goals. His son Alex played with Oldham Athletic, Stockport County, Preston North End and Rochdale in the 1980s and 1990s.

### JONES, Herbert
Left-back. 1925-1934.
*5ft 8in; 11st.*
*Born: Blackpool, 3 September 1896; Died: Fleetwood, 11 September 1973.*
*Debut: v Bury (a) 2 January 1926.*
*Career: Victoria School; South Shore Strollers; Army Football; Fleetwood 1920; Blackpool May 1922; Blackburn Rovers December 1925 (£3,850); Brighton & Hove Albion June 1934; Fleetwood cs 1935. International honours with Blackburn Rovers: England: 6 caps (1927-28); Football League: 3 appearances (1927-29).*
*Domestic honours with Blackburn Rovers: FA Cup winners: 1928.*
**Appearances:** Football League 247; FA Cup 14; Total 261.
Herbert Jones, known to everyone at Ewood Park, as 'Taffy', was the very antithesis of his partner, Jock Hutton. Whilst Hutton was a somewhat rotund and physically imposing defender, Jones was a mild, almost frail looking individual. However, he was the perfect example of how brain can triumph over brawn. His game embodied all that is best about the art of defensive play and he relied entirely on speed and guile to overcome his opponents. His intelligent positional play and fearless, but perfectly timed, tackles earned him six England caps within the space of 12 months. Jones had arrived at Ewood Park in December 1925 after making 80 League appearances with Blackpool and he ended his career with 37 League games with Brighton & Hove Albion. On leaving Brighton he returned to the Fylde area to join Fleetwood and at the age of 40 led his new club to the Lancashire Junior Cup Final in 1937.

### JONES, Thomas Robert
Half-back. 1901-1903.
*Debut: v Nottingham Forest (a) 4 October 1902.*
*Career: Llandudno; Blackburn Rovers August 1901.*
**Appearances:** Football League 11; FA Cup 1; Total 12.
Although Blackpool hoped to secure the services of Jones, it was Blackburn Rovers who finally got his signature. The former Welsh trialist, who had been working in St Annes before coming to Ewood Park in August 1901, made all his appearances for the Rovers during the 1901-02 season. Sadly, Jones never looked to be of the quality that the Rovers required.

### JONES, Robert William
Goalkeeper. 1958-1966.
*6ft 1in; 11st 4lb.*
*Born: Liverpool, 28 March 1932.*
*Debut: v West Bromwich Albion (a) 15 November 1958.*
*Career: Southport July 1951; Chester August 1953; Blackburn Rovers March 1958; Great Harwood cs 1966, later becoming manager until July 1972.*
**Appearances:** Football League 49; Football League Cup 3; Total 52.

Bob Jones served Blackburn Rovers for eight years without ever being regarded as the number-one goalkeeper at the club. He moved to Ewood Park after making 167 League appearances for Chester and prior to that he had appeared in 22 League games with Southport. Jones came to Ewood Park to understudy Harry Leyland and it wasn't until the start of the 1960-61 season that he got the opportunity of a prolonged run in the first team.

However, as soon as Leyland had recovered from a cartilage operation, Jones found himself relegated to the Central League team. With Leyland beginning to show signs of inconsistency, Jones found himself battling with Brian Reeves for the goalkeeping position at Ewood. Jones made a total of 20 League appearances during the 1960-61 season and this was to prove his most successful stint with the first team. During the summer of 1961 Jack Marshall moved to bring Fred Else to the club from Preston North End and Jones was once more shunted to the reserve team. Jones continued to act as understudy to Else until both men were released following the club's relegation to the Second Division in 1966.

### JONES, Roger
Goalkeeper. 1970-1976.
*5ft 11in; 12st 4lb.*
*Born: Upton-on-Seven, 8 November 1946.*
*Debut: v Millwall (a) 20 January 1970.*
*Career: Portsmouth apprentice 26 August 1963, turning professional in November 1964; Bournemouth & Boscombe Athletic May 1965; Blackburn Rovers January 1970 (£30,000); Newcastle United March 1976 (£20,000 not paid); Stoke City December 1976; Derby County July 1980 (£25,000); Birmingham City (on loan) February 1982 to March 1982; York City August 1982 (£5,000). Retired May 1985 and became a coach at York City. Then became reserve-team coach at Sunderland.*
*Domestic honours with Blackburn Rovers: Third Division championship: 1974-75 (46 apps).*
**Appearances:** Football League 242; FA Cup 15; Football League Cup 15; Total 272.
Roger Jones might easily have slipped out of League football when Portsmouth decided to scrap their reserve team in the late 1960s. Fortunately for Blackburn Rovers, Jones found employment at Bournemouth and went on to establish himself as one of the country's best young goalkeepers. Jones had already won England Under-23 honours when Eddie Quigley decided that the Bournemouth 'keeper was the man to replace the ageing Blacklaw and the inconsistent Barton at Ewood Park. A fee of £30,000 had to be paid to entice Bournemouth to part with Jones and it was a severe blow when injury limited him to just five games during the latter part of the 1969-70 season. However, the fee for Jones proved a wise investment as he went on to establish a new appearance record at the club for a goalkeeper. Although not the tallest of men, his judgement of crosses was impeccable and he totally dominated the six-yard box.

His naturalism produced a string of world-class saves which would surely have brought international recognition had he been playing in a higher division. Unfortunately, Jones held the goalkeeping position at Ewood during one of the bleakest periods in the club's history. An ever-present during the successful Third Division championship campaign of 1974-75, Jones began to attract the attention of bigger clubs. In March 1976, Gordon Lee returned to his former club to take Jones to Newcastle United for the ridiculously low fee of £20,000. Because Jones had a history of knee trouble it was agreed that the fee would be paid in instalments depending on the number of games he played. Surprisingly, Jones was only selected for Newcastle on five occasions and as a result the club refused to pay a fee to the Rovers.

The performances of Jones at his subsequent clubs was to make a complete nonsense of the decision taken by Newcastle. Jones moved to Stoke City and made 101 League appearances for the Potteries club before joining Derby County in July 1980. Although he was now into the veteran stage of his career, Jones appeared in 59 League games for the 'Rams' and also played in four games on loan for Birmingham City. He ended his playing career with 122 appearances for York City and helped the club to win the Fourth Division championship. He joined the coaching staff at York and then followed the management team of Dennis Smith and Viv Busby from York to Sunderland. At Sunderland he was put in charge of the reserve team and acted as assistant manager for a time when Malcolm Crosby was appointed manager following the departure of Smith. It was whilst Jones was serving in the latter capacity that Sunderland reached the 1992 FA Cup Final.

### JOY, William Joseph
Goalkeeper. 1896-1897.
*Born: Preston, 1864; Died: Preston, 6 June 1947.*

*Debut: v Burnley (h) 3 October 1896.*
*Career: Preston North End; Blackburn Rovers July 1896; Darwen November 1897.*
**Appearances:** Football League 3.
Billy Joy signed for Blackburn Rovers after a long career with Preston North End. During much of his time at Deepdale, Joy had been second choice and at the time of his leaving he was acting as understudy to Jim Trainer. He came to Blackburn to act as cover for Adam Ogilvie but the consistency of the number-one 'keeper meant Joy was restricted to just three League appearances. He had the misfortune to concede a goal after only 20 seconds of his debut in the derby with Burnley. Unable to establish himself in the first team at Blackburn, Joy was allowed to move to Darwen in November 1897.

### JOYCE, John William
Goalkeeper. 1902-1903.
*6ft; 16st.*
*Born: Burton upon Trent, 26 June 1877; Died: Greenwich, June 1956.*
*Debut: v Middlesbrough (h) 1 September 1902.*
*Career: Burton Pioneers 1895; Woodville 1896; Overseal Town 1897; Southampton May 1898; Millwall Athletic May 1900; Burton United August 1901; Blackburn Rovers May 1902; Tottenham Hotspur 1903; Millwall Athletic cs 1903; Tottenham Hotspur mid 1909-10; Millwall 1915. Assistant trainer at Millwall from 1919 to May 1938.*
**Appearances:** Football League 14.
Considering his build it was with tongue in cheek that Joyce was known throughout his career as 'Tiny'. Joyce was 24 years old when he joined the Rovers and had been a professional footballer since the age of 16. He signed for Blackburn at a time when it was fashionable to have 'big' men between the posts and certainly Joyce was well qualified with regard to this criteria. Unfortunately, Joyce failed to live up to expectations during his time at Ewood Park. His goalkeeping became increasingly eccentric as did his excursions further up the field. Shots which should have been held were punched and his wanderings outside of his area became increasingly costly. He conceded five goals on two occasions and allowed four to pass him in two other games. His 14 games in goal produced three wins, two draws and nine defeats with a total of 34 goals being conceded. On his return to London he enjoyed great success with Millwall Athletic and later Tottenham Hotspur. On his retirement he became assistant trainer with Millwall.

### JOYCE, Walter
Left-half/Left-back/Midfield. 1964-1967.
*5ft 11in; 12st 10lb.*
*Born: Oldham, 10 September 1937.*
*Debut: v Nottingham Forest (h) 8 February 1964.*
*Career: Lancashire Schoolboys; Burnley amateur July 1953, signing professional in November 1954; Blackburn Rovers February 1964 (£10,000); Oldham Athletic September 1967. Joined the coaching staff at Oldham 1969-70; Rochdale manager 1973 to May 1976; Bolton Wanderers coach & assistant manager until December 1985; Preston North End coach cs 1986.*
**Appearances:** Football League 119+1; FA Cup 9; Football League Cup 6; Total 134+1.
**Goals:** Football League 4.

Walter Joyce was a rugged defender whose no-nonsense approach made him hugely popular with Blackburn supporters. Joyce, who made 70 League appearances whilst at Turf Moor, came to Ewood Park to provide cover for the half-back positions. Joyce was not the most subtle of footballers but his enthusiasm and versatility made him a valued member of the Blackburn squad. During the 1966-67 season Eddie Quigley, then first-team coach, switched Joyce to a midfield role so that he could man mark the play maker in the opposing side. Joyce revelled in this new role and completely nullified the threat which many talented ball players posed to the Rovers. Joyce left Ewood Park in September 1967 to join Oldham Athletic and made 71 League appearances (including three as sub) before joining the coaching staff at Boundary Park. Joyce went on to occupy several managerial and coaching positions during his career. His son, Warren has played professional football with Bolton Wanderers, Preston North End, Plymouth Argyle and Burnley.

### JUBILEE FUND MATCHES
The idea behind the Jubilee Fund matches of 1938 and 1939 was to build up a fund of £10,000 from the receipts of a series of 'derby' matches. These were to be played on the Saturday before the official opening of the season. The fund was the brainchild of Charles E.Sutcliffe, a solicitor from Rawtenstall and president of the Football League. The fund was to be a forerunner of the post-war Players Provident Fund and was to provide financial support for players, former players and club officials should the need arise. It was also hoped that the fund would support educational and vocational training for players. In 1938, the 44 matches attracted a total attendance of 459,000 with the fund benefiting to the tune of approximately £25,000. In 1939, with war clouds gathering, attendances at these matches fell to 352,000. As far as Blackburn Rovers was concerned the 1938 Jubilee match against Burnley was something of a flop with only 4,600 attending the game at Ewood Park on 20 August 1938. Receipts of £262 compared badly with those in other parts of the country as the Blackburn public viewed the match as little more than a glorified practice game. Two goals from Jock Weddle and a Nobby Clarke penalty enabled the Rovers to record a 3-2 win. The reserve-team match at Burnley, which the home side won 3-0, brought in only about £50.

### KEATING, Albert Edward
Inside-forward. 1928-1931.
*5ft 10in; 12st 4lb.*
*Born: Swillington Common, nr Leeds, 28 June 1902.*
*Debut: v Sheffield Wednesday (h) 1 September 1928.*
*Career: Prudhoe Castle; Newcastle United January 1923 (£130); Bristol City December 1925 (£650); Blackburn Rovers May 1928; Cardiff City February 1931; Bristol City November 1932; North Shields 1933; Throckley Welfare cs 1935. Later became a Tyneside referee.*
**Appearances:** Football League 17.
**Goals:** Football League 5.
Albert Keating came to Ewood Park with Clarrie Bourton in a deal which cost the club £4,000. At Blackburn, Keating had little luck with injuries and had to undergo a cartilage operation which kept him side-lined for some time. Tall and strong, Keating was a forceful inside-forward whose outstanding performance with the Rovers came at West Ham United in March 1928, when he notched a hat-trick in a 3-3 draw. He joined Cardiff City in February 1931 after failing to agree terms with Bristol Rovers. His brother, Reg, was another much travelled player of the 1920s.

### KEELEY, Glenn Matthew
Centre-half. 1976-1987.
*6ft; 12st.*
*Born: Barking, Essex, 1 September 1954.*
*Debut: v Cardiff City (a) 28 August 1976.*
*Career: Ipswich Town apprentice July 1970, turning professional in August 1972; Newcastle United July 1974 (£70,000); Blackburn Rovers August 1976 (£30,000); Birmingham City on loan August 1982; Everton on loan October 1982 to December 1982; Oldham Athletic August 1987 (£15,000); Colchester United on loan February 1988; Bolton Wanderers September 1988 to April 1989; Chorley 1989; Clitheroe 1991. Domestic honours with Blackburn Rovers: Full Members' Cup winners: 1987.*
**Appearances:** Football League 365+5; FA Cup 19+1; Football League Cup 23; Full Members' Cup 6; Total 413+6.

**Goals:** Football League 23; Full Members' Cup 1: Total 24.
Glenn Keeley, a former England youth international, came to Blackburn in August 1976 after having failed to establish himself on Tyneside with Newcastle United. Keeley had only appeared in five League games for Ipswich Town when Newcastle paid a substantial fee to take the promising young defender to Tyneside. Although he had appeared in the 1976 League Cup Final, Keeley was seen as surplus to requirements at Newcastle after only 44 League games (including one as sub). A number of embarrassing errors in his early appearances with Blackburn, coupled with the fact that the club already had three proven central defenders in Fazackerley, Hawkins and Waddington, led many Blackburn supporters to question his acquisition.

Yet Keeley had the character to prove the doubters wrong and during his 11 seasons with the club he went on to acquire almost cult status with the same supporters who had doubted the wisdom of his signing. His height enabled him to dominate opposing forwards in the air whilst his tackling was resolute, if not downright intimidating at times. His early days at Ewood were littered with rash tackles that not only incurred the wrath of referees but also earned him the affectionate nickname of 'Killer' Keeley. Yet, beneath the reckless tackles, short fuse and endless brushes with authority, there lurked a defender of no little skill. Howard Kendall was the first manager to be able to harness the aggressive nature of Keeley's play and mould it into a tight defensive unit.

He immediately put Keeley at the heart of his defence with Derek Fazackerley and reaped the benefits of one of the best central defensive partnerships outside of the First Division. It was Kendall who gave Keeley the opportunity to establish himself in the First Division when he took him to Everton on loan in November 1982. Keeley, who was in a contract dispute with the Rovers, had spent most of the season in the Central League team and jumped at the opportunity to prove his worth at Goodison. Kendall immediately pitched Keeley into the electric atmosphere of a Merseyside derby.

Sadly the gamble didn't work. His lack of pace was exploited by Liverpool and a professional foul resulted in his early departure from the game and ended his dreams of a First Division future within 30 minutes of his Goodison debut. Keeley returned to Ewood Park and once again established himself at the heart of the defence. He was such an inspirational figure that Bobby Saxton made him his club captain and in 1987 he led the team to victory in the Full Members' Cup Final at Wembley. It proved to be a glorious end to his Ewood career. A few weeks later he turned out in his testimonial match at Ewood and this was to prove to be his last appearance for the club. His contract expired in the summer of 1987 and with the promising Colin Hendry available, the Rovers were reluctant to agree to Keeley's request for a two-year deal.

Unable to get the security he desired at Ewood, Keeley opted to join Oldham Athletic in August 1987. However, the move was not a success as Keeley failed to settle on the plastic surface of Boundary Park. A brief period was spent on loan with Colchester United before a permanent move took Keeley to Bolton Wanderers in September 1988. Early in 1989 his contract was cancelled so that he could pursue a commercial pilot's licence in the United States. However, Keeley returned to England at the start of the 1989-90 season and entered the world of non-League football with Chorley in the GM Vauxhall Conference.

## KELLY, Michael
Outside-left. 1900-1901.
*5ft 7in; 11st.*
*Born: Blackburn, 1877.*
*Debut: v Liverpool (a) 1 September 1900.*
*Career: Clitheroe 1897; Ashton North End 1897; Bury January 1898; Reading 1900; Blackburn Rovers May 1900.*
**Appearances:** Football League 3.
Kelly joined the Rovers from Reading with James Hosie in May 1900. Although both players began the 1900-01 season in the first team they were both axed after only one match. Kelly found himself having to understudy the remarkably consistent Fred Blackburn and as a result his first-team opportunities were few and far between.

## KELLY, William Muir
Centre-half. 1951-1957.
*5ft 9½in; 10st 11lb.*
*Born: Hill O'Beath, Cowdenbeath, 14 August 1922.*
*Debut: v Bury (h) 15 September 1951.*
*Career: Airdrieonians; Blackburn Rovers September 1951; Mossley July 1957; Accrington Stanley September 1957 to July 1958; Darwen.*
**Appearances:** Football League 186; FA Cup 16; Total 202.
**Goals:** Football League 1.
Although not the tallest man to play at centre-half for Blackburn Rovers, Kelly was certainly one of the toughest and one who fully lived up to his 'Iron Man' image. A dour, rugged Scot, Willie Kelly built his career on sheer aggression. There were few frills to his style of play and yet many more skilful opponents found themselves totally dominated by him. At a time when Johnny Carey put the emphasis on attack, it was Willie Kelly who was asked to shoulder the responsibility for organising the defence. It was a duty from which he never flinched and often turned out when not fully fit. For four seasons Kelly was the cornerstone of the Blackburn defence. However, when Eric Binns replaced him after two games of the 1955-56 season, Kelly appeared to be on his way out of Ewood Park.

His ageing legs were beginning to flounder and the Rovers agreed to a transfer request following his axing from the first team. However, four successive defeats at the beginning of December 1955 saw Kelly restored to the team and such was his consistency that the penultimate game of the season was the only one he missed.

However, not even the 'Iron man' could defy the challenge of youth forever and the signing of Matt Woods in November 1956 ended Kelly's first-team reign. In September 1957 he moved to Accrington Stanley but was forced into retirement, after 24 League appearances, when the end of regionalised football required him to take more time from work than was possible. On leaving Peel Park he moved into non-League football with Darwen.

## KENDALL, Howard
Midfield. 1979-1981.
*5ft 7in; 10st 13lb.*
*Born: Ryton-on-Tyne, 22 May 1946.*
*Debut: v Millwall (h) 18 August 1979.*
*Career: Ryton & District Schools; Preston North End apprentice August 1961, turning professional in May 1963; Everton March 1967 (£80,000); Birmingham City February 1974 (deal involving Bob Latchford); Stoke City August 1977 (£40,000); Blackburn Rovers player-manager July 1979; Everton manger May 1981, signing as a non-contract player in August 1981; Athletic Bilbao (Spain) manager June 1987 to November 1989; Manchester City manager December 1989; Everton manager November 1990 until December 1993.*
**Appearances:** Football League 79; FA Cup 6; Football League Cup 7; Total 92.
**Goals:** Football League 6; Football League Cup 1; Total 7.
Howard Kendall had enjoyed a highly successful playing career after creating football history in May 1964 when, still 20 days short of his 18th birthday, he became the youngest player to appear in an FA Cup Final. At the time Kendall was with Preston North End, but it was whilst at Everton that he achieved his greatest success, forming one third of the legendary Kendall, Ball and Harvey midfield trio at Goodison Park.

Kendall had taken his first steps in coaching at Stoke City when the Potteries club won promotion to the First Division at the end of the 1978-79 season. At the same time the Rovers had dropped into the Third Division for the second time in the club's history and it was Kendall who the directors appointed as the first-ever player-manager at Ewood Park in July 1979.

When Kendall came to Blackburn he found a club that was still suffering the traumas of relegation. Morale was low and John Bailey, the club's most promising youngster, was on his way to Everton.

Despite a poor start to the 1979-80 campaign, Kendall gradually began to mould a team together. He spent a total of £90,000 on four players who were hardly household names. Jim Arnold was a goalkeeper from non-League Stafford Rangers, whilst Stuart Parker was a centre-forward who was returning to England after a short spell playing abroad. Both Jim Branagan and Andy Crawford were languishing in the reserves at Huddersfield Town and Derby County respectively when Kendall brought them to Blackburn.

Gradually, Kendall began to turn things around at Ewood and the team began to steadily climb the Third Division table. Success was built on a firm foundation as Kendall turned Branagan, Keeley, Fazackerley and Rathbone into one of the tightest defensive units outside of the First Division. Kendall himself commanded the midfield aided by the hardworking Tony Parkes. The final member of his midfield trio was Duncan McKenzie and it was he who wrought havoc with opposing defences as the Rovers embarked on a run which brought an incredible 29 points from a possible 30. A 2-1 win at Bury in the penultimate game of the season ensured that Kendall was successful in leading the club to promotion in only his first season of football management.

After strengthening the midfield with Mick Speight from Sheffield United, Kendall took the team to the top of the Second Division. Once again, mean defending was the route Kendall took to achieve success. If the entertainment value was low results and the Second Division table made pleasant reading. However, in the final analysis it was a failure to score goals that ultimately cost the Rovers a place in the First Division. Crawford was but a mere shadow of the player he had been and Kendall had little or no money available to bring in an expensive striker. He tried to remedy the problem by bringing John Lowey from Sheffield Wednesday and Viv Busby from the United States. However, neither looked liked ending the goal drought and in obtaining Busby, Kendall had to part with McKenzie. The attacking frailties within his side were brought home on the final day of the season when Swansea City pipped the Rovers for promotion on goal-difference.

It came as no surprise to anyone in Blackburn when Everton approached the club for permission to talk to Kendall about succeeding Gordon Lee at Goodison Park. Although Kendall had earlier rejected overtures by Crystal Palace the lure of his beloved Everton was too much to resist.

Surprisingly, Kendall did not achieve overnight success on his return to Merseyside and pressure began to grow on both manager and directors. However, the Everton directors stayed loyal to Kendall and in return he rewarded them with one of the most successful periods in the club's history. The FA Cup, European Cup-winners' Cup and, most important of all, the League title were all won under Kendall's leadership.

At the height of his success, Kendall surprisingly turned his back on English football in June 1987 to take charge of Athletic Bilbao. He remained in Spain, despite an offer to become the manager of Newcastle United, until he was sacked in November 1989 following a run of disappointing results. Within weeks of returning to England he was appointed manager of Manchester City and in January 1990 he appointed Mick Heaton, his former Blackburn and Everton coach, as his assistant. However, before the end of the year he had accepted the invitation to return to Goodison Park to try to recapture the success he had experienced in the 1980s. Sadly, with little money at his disposal, Kendall was unable to lift Everton to the same heights that he had enjoyed before and in December 1993, with a power struggle taking place in the boardroom, Kendall unexpectedly tendered his resignation.

### KENNEDY, Andrew John
Centre-forward. 1988-1990.
*6ft 1in; 12st.*
*Born: Stirling, 8 October 1964.*
*Debut: v Bradford City (a) 5 October 1988 (sub).*
*Career: Sauchie Athletic; Glasgow Rangers; Seiko FC (Hong Kong) on loan; Birmingham City March 1985 (£50,000); Sheffield United on loan March 1987; Blackburn Rovers June 1988; Watford August 1990; Bolton Wanderers on loan October 1991 to November 1991; Brighton & Hove Albion September 1992.*
**Appearances:** Football League 49+10; Play-offs 1+1; FA Cup 3; Football League Cup 4; Total 57+11.
**Goals:** Football League 23; FA Cup 1; Play-offs 1; Total 25.

Andy Kennedy was a popular character at Ewood Park during the two years he spent with the club. Tall and strong, Kennedy also possessed blistering pace which enabled him to wander into wide positions and exploit unsuspecting full-backs. His ability to play in a wide position enabled Don Mackay to play Kennedy in the same team as Howard Gayle and Simon Garner during the 1988-89 campaign and the following season he was able to link up with Frank Stapleton and Garner in a three-man attack. Unfortunately, Kennedy appeared to be rather injury prone and in August 1990 he moved to Watford as part of the deal which brought Lee Richardson to Ewood Park. In many respects Kennedy's career never quite fulfilled the promise he showed at Ewood. Indeed after his departure from Blackburn Kennedy struggled to establish himself at a number of clubs.

### KENNEDY, Fred
Inside-left. 1933-1934.
*5ft 6in; 11st 7lb.*
*Born: Bury, 1902 (October quarter); Died: Failsworth, November 1963.*
*Debut: v Leeds United (h) 26 August 1933.*
*Career: Rossendale United 1920; Manchester United May 1923; Everton March 1925 (£2,000); Middlesbrough May 1927 (£600); Reading May 1929 (£500); Oldham Athletic November 1930 (£200); Rossendale United September 1931; Northwich Victoria December 1931; Racing Club de Paris (France) September 1932; Blackburn Rovers August 1933; Racing Club de Paris (France) June 1934; Stockport County July 1937.*
**Appearances:** Football League 29.
**Goals:** Football League 8.
Although Fred Kennedy found no shortage of employers during his career, he failed to establish himself at any of his clubs. His greatest

success came in France with League and Cup honours with Racing Club de Paris. His spell at Ewood was no more successful than his time with other English clubs. He began the 1933-34 campaign in his favoured inside-left position at Ewood Park and formed an impressive striking partnership with Ernie Thompson. However, a broken leg brought a premature end to Thompson's campaign and Thomas Brennan was preferred to Kennedy at inside-left during the final two months of the season. During the summer of 1934 Kennedy opted to return to France.

### KENNEDY, Patrick Antony
Left-back. 1956-1959.
*5ft 11in; 12st.*
*Born: Dublin, 9 October 1934.*
*Debut: v Barnsley (a) 18 September 1957.*
*Career: Johnville (Dublin); Manchester United February 1953; Blackburn Rovers September 1956; Southampton July 1959; Oldham Athletic July 1960.*

**Appearances:** Football League 3.
Johnny Carey paid Manchester United a small fee to bring Paddy Kennedy to Ewood Park in September 1956. Kennedy who, like Carey, was an Irishman was signed as a possible successor to Bill Eckersley in the left-back position. He received an early opportunity to fill in for Eckersley but suffered a serious knee injury in only his third appearance. Whilst he was out of action Dave Whelan took the opportunity to impress Carey and Kennedy was consigned to the Central League for the rest of his time at Ewood. Kennedy was to have brief spells with Southampton and Oldham Athletic after leaving Ewood but when he retired from the game he only had a total of six League appearances to show for his time at four clubs.

### KENYON, John Francis
Forward. 1972-1976.
*5ft 8½in; 11st 1lb.*
*Born: Blackburn, 2 December 1953.*
*Debut: v Tranmere Rovers (h) 31 March 1973 (sub).*
*Career: Great Harwood; Blackburn Rovers December 1972; Wigan Athletic; Great Harwood.*
*Domestic honours with Blackburn Rovers: Third Division championship: 1975 (9+3 apps, 1 gl).*
**Appearances:** Football League 32+14.
**Goals:** Football League 7.
A Blackburn-born striker who joined the Rovers midway through the 1972-73 season. Although a regular marksman with the Central League side, Kenyon failed to establish himself with the senior team. His most productive season was 1973-74 when he scored five goals in 24 Third Division appearances (including four as sub).

### KERR, John
Forward/Half-back. 1919-1921.
*5ft 9in; 11st.*
*Born: Annfield, Annan, Dumfriesshire.*
*Debut: v Middlesbrough (h) 15 September 1919.*
*Career: Army football; Queen's Park; Blackburn Rovers amateur March 1919; Brentford amateur January 1921, turning professional in June 1922 and remaining until 1924.*
**Appearances:** Football League 16.
Kerr came to Ewood Park as an outside-left from the Scottish club Queen's Park in March 1919. Although he appeared on the left wing on six occasions, it was at half-back that he gave his best performances whilst at Blackburn. However, with Levi Thorpe and Tommy Heaton in possession of the half-back positions on a regular basis the Rovers allowed Kerr to join Brentford in January 1921.

### KERR, James Peter
Midfield. 1970-1971.
*5ft 9in; 11st.*
*Born: Glasgow, 2 September 1949.*
*Debut: v Middlesbrough (a) 12 September 1970.*
*Career: Bury September 1966; Blackburn Rovers May 1970 (£65,000); Coventry City youth coach November 1971; Highlands Park (South*

*Africa) on loan March 1972.*
**Appearances:** Football League 11.
Eddie Quigley paid a record fee to bring this talented young midfield player from Bury in May 1970. Kerr was recognised as one of the outstanding young talents in the country and was sought after by a number of clubs. An injury picked up in pre-season kept Kerr out of action for the opening five League games of the 1970-71 season. However, he returned to action in September and appeared in 11 matches before a knee injury brought his season to a premature close. Sadly, the injury proved a serious one and specialists told Kerr that his career as a professional footballer was over because of the condition of his knee. He was sent to Lilleshall on a coaching course and was appointed a junior coach at Ewood. In November 1971 he accepted an offer to join the coaching staff at Coventry City and attempted a playing comeback with the Central League team at Highfield Road and also went to South Africa to play. Sadly, Jimmy Kerr was unable to resurrect his promising playing career in the Football League.

### KETTERING TOWN FC
Kettering Town were members of the GM Vauxhall Conference when they visited Ewood Park for a third round FA Cup-tie in January 1992. Kettering came to Ewood with an excellent record of giant killing behind them and in the second round had eliminated Maidstone United of the Fourth Division. However, goals from Speedie, Newell (2) and Cowans ensured Rovers a passage to the next round.

**FA Cup**

| | | | | |
|---|---|---|---|---|
| 1991-92 | (3) | Home | W | 4-1 |

### KIDDERMINSTER HARRIERS FC
Blackburn Rovers met Kidderminster Harriers in the first round of the 1979-80 FA Cup competition. The game provided an early opportunity for Jim Arnold, the former England semi-professional international, to play against his former club. This was the last time that Blackburn appeared in the first round of the FA Cup. Goals from Andy Crawford and Joe Craig gave the Rovers a 2-0 victory in front of a crowd of 4,500.

**FA Cup**

| | | | | |
|---|---|---|---|---|
| 1979-80 | (1) | Away | W | 2-0 |

### KILLEAN, Edward
Forward/Left-half/Left-back. 1894-1898.
*5ft 9in; 11st 6lb.*
*Born: Blackburn, 1874.*
*Debut: v Liverpool (h) 1 September 1894.*
*Career: 3rd Coldstream Guards; Blackburn Rovers August 1894; Glossop North End November 1898 (£70); Southampton cs 1900; New Brompton cs 1901; Blackpool December 1903.*
**Appearances:** Football League 88; Test Matches: 3; FA Cup 6; Total 97.
**Goals:** Football League 6.
Ted Killean was a stylish half-back who had the ability to pass the ball around even when hampered by the opposition. He had originally been earmarked at Ewood to fill the gap left by the departure of Jack Southworth to Everton but he lacked the necessary attributes of a top class centre-forward. As a result he was moved to the inside-left position before being converted into an outstanding defender. Although noted for a mercurial temperament, Killean gave outstanding service to the Rovers during his four seasons at the club. After leaving Ewood he embarked on a rather nomadic career before returning to Lancashire in December 1903 to sign for Blackpool.

### KNIGHTON, Kenneth
Midfield. 1969-1971.
*5ft 9in; 11st 5lb.*
*Born: Mexborough, 20 February 1944.*
*Debut: v Swindon Town (h) 9 August 1969.*
*Career: Barnsley schoolboy football; Wath Wanderers; Wolverhampton Wanderers non-contract player August 1959, becoming an apprentice in August 1960 before turning professional in February 1961; Oldham Athletic November 1966 (£12,000); Preston North End December 1967*

*(£35,000); Blackburn Rovers July 1969 (£45,000); Hull City March 1971 (£60,000); Sheffield Wednesday August 1973, joining the coaching staff in January 1976; Sunderland coach, becoming manager in June 1979 until April 1981; Orient manager October 1981 until May 1983; Dagenham Town manager May 1984 until October 1985; Trowbridge Town manager until January 1988.*
**Appearances:** Football League 70; FA Cup 2; Football League Cup 4; Total 76.
**Goals:** Football League 11; Football League Cup 1; Total 12.
A buccaneering midfield player who excelled in both defence and attack. Knighton had begun his working life as a trainee miner before being given the opportunity to play professional football with Wolverhampton Wanderers. Although he joined Wolves as a half-back, a number of his early games for the club were in the right-back position. However, it was as a driving half-back that he carved out a successful career with a number of clubs. His abilities were recognised in 1969 when he was asked to tour New Zealand with an FA XI.

Knighton came to Blackburn in the summer of 1969 when Eddie Quigley gambled £100,000 on signing Knighton, Alan Hunter and Brian Hill in a bid to win promotion to the First Division. Although the bid didn't succeed, Knighton impressed everyone at Ewood with his all round ability. The following season found the Rovers rooted to the foot of the Second Division and in desperate need of new blood. Unfortunately, without the financial resources to strengthen the squad, Johnny Carey had to reluctantly sanction the sale of Knighton to Hull City to raise much needed funds. After retiring from playing Knighton became involved in coaching and enjoyed spells as manager of Sunderland and Leyton Orient before leaving League football in 1983.

### KNOWLES, Albert
Goalkeeper. 1897-1900.
*5ft 10in.*
*Debut: v Derby County (a) 4 September 1897.*
*Career: Whalley & District; Clitheroe Amateurs; Whalley & District October 1894; Blackburn Rovers May 1897.*
**Appearances:** Football League 31; FA Cup 4; Total 35.
Although the majority of his displays were sound, Albert Knowles was one of those goalkeepers who had a tendency to make crucial errors which cost points. In every other way he was thoroughly capable and efficient but this Achilles' heel prevented him from making a more lasting impact at Blackburn Rovers.

### KOPEL, Frank
Full-back. 1969-1972.
*5ft 8½in; 11st.*
*Born: Falkirk, 28 March 1949.*
*Debut: v Bristol City (h) 22 March 1969.*
*Career: Manchester United 4 April 1966; Blackburn Rovers 15 March 1969 to 1 February 1972; Dundee United February 1972 until cs 1982; Arbroath assistant manager until October 1983; Forfar Athletic assistant manager 1991-92.*
**Appearances:** Football League 23+2.
Eddie Quigley paid a small fee to Manchester United to bring Frank Kopel to Ewood Park as cover for the impending departure of Keith Newton. In December 1969 the long awaited transfer of Newton was finally completed when Everton took him to Goodison Park. The departure of Newton gave Kopel the chance to break into the first team after spending several months in the Central League team. However, the former Manchester United defender looked far from comfortable and it came as no surprise when he lost his place. The 1970-71 season saw Kopel make only fleeting appearances for the first team and in April 1971 he missed a crucial penalty in the home defeat by Millwall, a result which virtually condemned the club to the Third Division. The following season saw Kopel allowed to leave Ewood to return to his native Scotland to join Dundee United. Kopel was to enjoy great success at Dundee and appeared in European football with the Scottish club.

### KYLE, Archibald
Inside-left. 1908-1909.
*5ft 6in; 10st 7lb.*
*Debut: v Bury (a) 17 April 1908.*
*Parkhead; Glasgow Rangers cs 1904; Blackburn Rovers April 1908; Bo'ness August 1909; Clyde September 1910; St Mirren cs 1911; Hamilton Academical cs 1914.*
**Appearances:** Football League 36; FA Cup 2; Total 38.
**Goals:** Football League 8.
Archie Kyle appeared in the Rangers team that played a friendly at Ewood Park on Christmas Day 1905. Although just beginning his career as a Scottish First Division player, Kyle gave an excellent exhibition of forward play. He went on to become a regular in the Rangers team and earned a reputation as one of the smartest forwards in Scottish football. A

clever dribbler and a good shot, Kyle represented the Scottish League on two occasions before moving to Ewood Park in April 1908. During the 1908-09 season, Kyle struck up a good understanding with Billy Davies, the Welsh international centre-forward, which enabled the latter to score 19 goals in 27 appearances. At the end of the campaign, Kyle returned to Scotland and remained active in the Scottish League until World War One.

## LANCASHIRE FOOTBALL ASSOCIATION
In the late summer of 1878 John Lewis, co-founder of Blackburn Rovers, was one of three men who met at the Volunteer Inn, Bromley Cross to discuss the formation of a Lancashire Football Association. On 28 September 1878, a meeting was held at the Co-operative Hall, Darwen which brought about the creation of the Lancashire Association. Blackburn Rovers Football Club was represented at this meeting along with officials of 22 other clubs and the club duly became one of the founder members of the Association.

Relations between Blackburn Rovers and the Lancashire Association became strained on several occasions during the early years of the Association. Indeed, at one point John Lewis severed his connection with the Association and such was his displeasure with that body that he threatened to destroy it. In May 1881, the Rovers resigned their membership of the Lancashire Association and only returned when it became clear that other members would not be allowed to play friendly fixtures with the club.

The majority of clashes between the Rovers and the Association revolved around the long running dispute with Darwen Football Club. The Lancashire Football Association played a leading role in the debate over professionalism in the 1880s and although it has had more professional clubs in its membership than any other County Association, it still found time to nurture the amateur game. The Association, which has its offices in Wellington Street, St Johns, Blackburn, celebrated its centenary in 1978.

## LANCASHIRE FOOTBALL COMBINATION
The Lancashire Combination was formed in 1891 and continued in existence for 91 years before being laid to rest in 1981 with the formation of the North West Counties League. The initial Lancashire Combination gave Blackburn Rovers, Bolton Wanderers and Preston North End the opportunity to provide competitive football for their reserve teams.

The Rovers fielded their second team in the Lancashire Combination until the formation of the Central League in 1911. Blackburn Rovers Reserves won the championship in each of the first three years of the competition and finished as runners-up in 1895-96. The team did not compete in the Combination during season 1900-01 and season 1906-07 saw the Rovers relegated to the Second Division. However, the following season saw them lift the Second Division title. In 1954-55 the Rovers fielded their 'A' team in the Second Division of the Combination. The complete record of Blackburn Rovers in the Lancashire combination is as follows:

**Blackburn Rovers Reserves:**
Division One

| | P | W | D | L | F | A | Pts | Pos |
|---|---|---|---|---|---|---|---|---|
| 1891-92 | 14 | 10 | 3 | 1 | 44 | 17 | 23 | 1 |
| 1892-93 | 20 | 14 | 1 | 5 | 59 | 30 | 29 | 1 |
| 1893-94 | 16 | 13 | 2 | 1 | 62 | 13 | 28 | 1 |
| 1894-95 | 24 | 10 | 2 | 12 | 45 | 49 | 22 | 8 |
| 1895-96 | 26 | 15 | 6 | 5 | 61 | 34 | 36 | 2 |
| 1896-97 | 28 | 15 | 5 | 8 | 59 | 44 | 35 | 5 |
| 1897-98 | 30 | 14 | 7 | 9 | 67 | 51 | 35 | 5 |
| 1898-99 | 28 | 14 | 5 | 9 | 72 | 55 | 33 | 6 |
| 1899-00 | 30 | 14 | 4 | 12 | 78 | 48 | 32 | 6 |
| 1901-02 | 34 | 11 | 7 | 16 | 56 | 77 | 29 | 13 |
| 1902-03 | 34 | 13 | 9 | 12 | 66 | 53 | 35 | 8 |
| 1903-04 | 34 | 17 | 6 | 11 | 75 | 64 | 40 | 6 |
| 1904-05 | 34 | 11 | 6 | 17 | 53 | 75 | 28 | 15 |
| 1905-06 | 38 | 13 | 12 | 13 | 65 | 69 | 38 | 9 |
| 1906-07 | 38 | 11 | 5 | 22 | 67 | 85 | 27 | 17 |

Second Division

| | P | W | D | L | F | A | Pts | Pos |
|---|---|---|---|---|---|---|---|---|
| 1907-08 | 38 | 30 | 3 | 5 | 141 | 34 | 63 | 1 |

First Division

| | P | W | D | L | F | A | Pts | Pos |
|---|---|---|---|---|---|---|---|---|
| 1908-09 | 38 | 15 | 10 | 13 | 85 | 61 | 40 | 7 |
| 1909-10 | 38 | 14 | 8 | 16 | 59 | 77 | 36 | 11 |
| 1910-11 | 38 | 16 | 8 | 14 | 66 | 63 | 40 | 5 |

Blackburn Rovers 'A' team:
Second Division

| | P | W | D | L | F | A | Pts | Pos |
|---|---|---|---|---|---|---|---|---|
| 1954-55 | 38 | 15 | 5 | 18 | 84 | 93 | 35 | 10 |

## LANCASHIRE LEAGUE
Today the Lancashire League is the competition in which the Blackburn Rovers Football Club fields its 'A' and 'B' teams. However, the original Lancashire League, which was formed in 1889-90 and continued in existence until 1902-03, provided competition for a number of senior clubs in the area. The only club from Blackburn amongst the founder members of the Lancashire League was the Park Road Football Club.

In 1892-93, Accrington left the Football League to become members of the Lancashire League following the club's relegation to the Second Division. Accrington believed that membership of the Lancashire League would be more economical than the Second Division of the Football League. It proved not to be the case and Accrington folded early in the 1894-95 season.

In 1900 Blackburn Rovers decided to allow their reserve team to participate in the Lancashire League instead of the Lancashire Combination. However, after only one season the reserve team reverted back to the Combination. The record of the reserve team during that season in the Lancashire League is shown below.

| | P | W | D | L | F | A | Pts | Pos |
|---|---|---|---|---|---|---|---|---|
| 1900-01 | 20 | 6 | 8 | 6 | 34 | 31 | 20 | 5 |

## LANCASHIRE MANX CUP
The Lancashire Manx Cup saw the resurrection of the old Lancashire Senior Cup trophy for what was to become a regular pre-season tournament. Initially sponsored by the Isle of Man Tourist Board, the competition was played during the pre-season and involved eight teams who were split into two groups. The top two teams met in the Final and the winner of the competition was invited to appear in the Isle of Man Football Festival the following summer.

The competition was seen as a replacement for the old Anglo-Scottish Cup competition and the derby element enabled clubs to attract larger than usual gates for games that gave the players much needed match practice. The Rovers reached the Final six times in the 1980s and proved victorious on four occasions. The club ceased to enter the competition after gaining promotion to the Premier League.

**1982-83**
| (GM) | Blackpool | Home | D | 2-2 |
|---|---|---|---|---|
| (GM) | Bolton Wanderers | Away | W | 1-0 |
| (GM) | Preston North End | Home | W | 3-1 |
| (F) | Bury | Away | L | 1-2 |

**1983-84**
| (GM) | Blackpool | Home | W | 4-2 |
|---|---|---|---|---|
| (GM) | Burnley | Away | D | 1-1 |
| (GM) | Preston North End | Home | W | 4-1 |
| (F) | Bury | Home | D | 0-0* |

*Blackburn Rovers won on 3-1 on penalties.

**1984-85**
| (GM) | Bury | Home | W | 3-2 |
|---|---|---|---|---|
| (GM) | Bolton Wanderers | Away | D | 1-1 |
| (GM) | Preston North End | Home | W | 1-0 |
| (F) | Wigan Athletic | Away | L | 1-2 |

**1985-86**
| (GM) | Wigan Athletic | Home | D | 2-2 |
|---|---|---|---|---|
| (GM) | Blackpool | Home | W | 6-0 |
| (GM) | Preston North End | Home | D | 0-0 |
| (F) | Burnley | Home | W | 1-0 |

**1986-87**
| (GM) | Rochdale | Home | D | 1-1 |
|---|---|---|---|---|
| (GM) | Blackpool | Away | D | 0-0 |
| (GM) | Bury | Away | L | 1-3 |

**1987-88**
| (GM) | Bolton Wanderers | Away | W | 2-1 |
|---|---|---|---|---|
| (GM) | Burnley | Away | L | 1-2 |
| (GM) | Blackpool | Home | W | 3-2 |
| (F) | Wigan Athletic | Home | D | 2-2* |

*Blackburn Rovers won 4-3 on penalties.

**1988-89**
| (GM) | Blackpool | Away | D | 2-2 |
|---|---|---|---|---|
| (GM) | Burnley | Away | W | 3-1 |
| (GM) | Preston North End | Home | L | 2-3 |

**1989-90**
| (GM) | Wigan Athletic | Away | W | 3-0 |
|---|---|---|---|---|
| (GM) | Burnley | Away | W | 2-0 |
| (GM) | Bolton Wanderers | Away | L | 1-3 |
| (F) | Blackpool | Away | W | 1-0 |

**1990-91**
| (GM) | Bury | Away | D | 0-0 |
|---|---|---|---|---|
| (GM) | Preston North End | Away | L | 2-4 |
| (GM) | Rochdale | Away | W | 2-0 |

**1991-92**
| (GM) | Preston North End | Away | D | 1-1 |
|---|---|---|---|---|

Ally Dawson lifts the old Lancashire Manx Cup after Blackburn beat Blackpool in the 1989 Final at Bloomfield Road

| (GM) | Burnley | Away | D | 1-1 |
|------|---------|------|---|-----|
| (GM) | Bury | Away | L | 0-1 |

**Appearances:** S.Garner 27+1; T.W.Gennoe 20; I.Miller 18+1; J.P.S.Branagan 16; M.J.Rathbone 16; S.Barker 15; D.W.Fazackerley 15; G.M.Keeley 14+1; N.Brotherston 14; J.A.Lowey 13+1; M.N.Atkins 13; K.J.Hill 12; D.Mail 11+1; E.C.J.Henry 11; D.Hamilton 10; S.Sellars 10; H.A.Gayle 9+3; C.S.Sulley 9; J.V.O'Keefe 8; J.Millar 7+2; N.Bell 7; C.W.Randell 7; N.S.Reid 6+1; A.Finnigan 6; A.J.Kennedy 6; K.B.Moran 6; M.A.Patterson 6; J.M.Quinn 6; F.A.Stapleton 5+2; J.A.Irvine 5+1; A.Ainscow 5; C.J.Price 5; C.D.Thompson 5; A.J.Diamond 4+2; D.Collier 4; A.J.Dawson 4; R.C.Hildersley 4; L.J.Richardson 4; J.M.Wilcox 3+1; S.P.Curry 3; M.Duxbury 3; R.A.Mimms 3; S.Munro 3; P.T.A.Shepstone 3; K.Stonehouse 3; L.Johnrose 2+2; M.Burke 2; A.J.Dobson 2; S.Livingstone 2; S.M.Agnew 1; P.T.Comstive 1; M.B.Salmon 1; C.R.Skinner 1; D.May 0+2; D.P.Murphy 0+1.

**Goalscorers:** S.Garner 13; A.J.Kennedy 4; S.Barker 3; N.Brotherston 3; J.M.Quinn 3; C.D.Thompson 3; D.W.Fazackerley 2; A.J.Diamond 2; L.Johnrose 2; J.A.Lowey 2; J.Millar 2; I.Miller 2; M.A. Patterson 2; S.Sellars 2; P.T.A.Shepstone 2; F.A.Stapleton 2; S.P.Curry 1; H.A.Gayle 1; A.Finnigan 1; D.Hamilton 1; E.C.J.Hendry 1; G.M.Keeley 1; K.Stonehouse 1; Own-goals 5.

## LANCASHIRE CUP/LANCASHIRE SENIOR CUP

The Lancashire Cup was first competed for in the 1879-80 season. The draw for the first round was made on 16 August 1879 at the Coffee Tavern on Darwen Street in Blackburn. The Rovers faced an away tie at Enfield and it took a replay before they were able to progress to the second round.

The Rovers went on to win through to the Final which was held at the Barley Bank Ground in Darwen. An attendance of between 9,000 and 10,000 gathered to watch the meeting of Blackburn Rovers and Darwen

*Below* Blackburn Rovers in 1882, when they won the Lancashire Cup for the first time. Back row (left to right): D.H.Greenwood, R.Howarth, J.Hargreaves, F.Suter, W.Duckworth (umpire). Middle row: J.Duckworth, H.McIntyre, H.Sharples, F.W.Hargreaves, T.Strachan, G.Avery. Front row: J.Brown, J.Douglas.

and produced receipts of £167. The Rovers were beaten 3-0 in front of a grandstand which consisted of borrowed forms placed on lorries. The competition became so popular that in 1885 the Association had to establish a second competition.

This new competition became known as the Lancashire Junior Cup because it involved many of the junior clubs who had little chance of defeating the senior clubs in the county. As a result of the formation of the Junior Cup, the original Lancashire Cup competition became known as the Lancashire Senior Cup. Having won the Lancashire Cup in 1881-82 for the first time, Blackburn Rovers registered 11 victories in the competition before World War One.

For much of this time, particularly in the years before the formation of the Football League, the competition was treated as one of great importance by the Lancashire clubs. However, once the Football League was formed a number of clubs, the Rovers included, chose to field weakened teams in the Lancashire Senior Cup competition.

After World War One an attempt was made to revive the fortunes of the Lancashire Senior Cup by changing the format of the competition. Clubs were split into four groups and results of matches played in the Football League were used to determine the winner of each group. The four teams then met on a knock-out basis in semi-finals to produce the Finalists. By the mid-1920s the competition had again reverted to a traditional knock-out format. Once again it was largely the preserve of reserve teams although clubs in the Third Division North tended to field their senior men in the competition.

After World War Two the competition continued to decline in importance with only Third, and later Fourth Division clubs fielding their strongest teams. On 5 December 1967 the Rovers suffered an embarrassing exit from the competition at the hands of non-League Morecambe. Unhappy with his team's performance at Cardiff on the previous Saturday, Eddie Quigley selected his strongest team for the visit to Morecambe. Only Keith Newton was missing from the line-up which had lost in Wales as Quigley believed the Morecambe fixture would be the ideal opportunity to restore lost confidence. Sadly, the plan backfired and Morecambe pulled off a major shock with a 2-1 victory over the men from the Second Division. The Rovers team that evening was as follows: Blacklaw: Coxon, Wilson, Clayton (Sharples), Coddington, Hole, Ferguson, Rogers, Gilliver, Darling, Connelly.

The Lancashire Senior Cup competition was finally halted in the early 1970s. However, the attractive trophy was resurrected with the introduction of the Lancashire Manx Cup in 1982.

**LANCELEY, Ernest**
Right-back. 1932-1941.
*5ft 11½in; 12st.*
*Born: Mexborough, 1 September 1910; Died: Blackburn, 27 February 1992.*
*Debut: v Manchester City (a) 6 October 1934.*
*Career: Mexborough Athletic; Charlton Athletic May 1931; Dartford cs 1932; Blackburn Rovers July 1932. Retired during World War Two.*
*Domestic honours with Blackburn Rovers: Second Division championship: 1938-39 (11 apps).*
**Appearances:** Football League 52; FA Cup 2; Total 54.
Lanceley was transferred to Blackburn Rovers before he had the opportunity to make his debut for non-League Dartford. However, the former Charlton Athletic defender had to wait two years at Ewood before being called into the first team. Lanceley eventually won the right-back spot in January 1937 but had the misfortune to break his leg the following October. Whilst he was out of action Billy Hough took the right-back spot and Lanceley had to wait until March 1939, when Hough himself was injured, before returning to the first team on a regular basis. Lanceley went on to appear in 43 wartime games but was unable to resume his career after the war because of injury. He worked at ICI in Darwen until his retirement in 1973.

**LANGTON, Robert**
Outside-left. 1937-1949 & 1953-1956.
*5ft 6in; 10st 10lb.*
*Born: Burscough, 8 September 1918.*
*Debut: v Swansea Town (h) 10 September 1938.*
*Career: Burscough Victoria; Blackburn Rovers amateur September 1937, turning professional in November 1937; Glentoran wartime guest 1945; Preston North End August 1948 (£14,000); Bolton Wanderers (£20,000) November 1949; Blackburn Rovers September 1953; Ards June 1956; Wisbech Town July 1957; Kidderminster Harriers cs 1959; Wisbech Town September 1959; Colwyn Bay October 1960; King's Lynn trainer/coach July 1962; Wisbech Town coach cs 1963; Burscough Rangers manager 1968.*
*International honours with Blackburn Rovers: England: 7 caps (1946-47); Football League: 2 appearances (1947-48).*
*Domestic honours with Blackburn Rovers: Second Division championship: 1938-39 (37 apps, 14 gls)*
**Appearances:** Football League 212; FA Cup 18; Total 230.

A trip down memory lane for Ernie Lanceley and Bob Pryde.

**Goals:** Football League 57; FA Cup 1; Total 58.

Bobby Langton arrived at Ewood Park as a promising young winger in September 1937. He initially signed amateur forms but his potential was such that within two months the club had invited him to join the professional ranks. Within 12 months of his arrival at Ewood he had graduated to the senior team and scored 14 goals in 37 games during his first campaign in League football. A speedy winger who could put in crosses from all angles, Langton possessed a strong shot and enjoyed cutting inside and having a crack at goal.

The outbreak of war severely hindered his progress and Langton spent much of the war in India. Although he appeared in the opening three games of the 1939-40 aborted League programme he didn't reappear for Blackburn until December 1944. Langton scored seven goals in 32 wartime games for the club before returning to Ewood for the 1946-47 season. During the war he had also appeared in the Glentoran team which reached the Irish Cup Final and had represented the Irish League against the Combined Services in Belfast. Whilst the club's fortunes began to wane during the immediate post-war years, Langton's star was very much in the ascendancy.

Having been capped by England, Langton moved to Preston North End in August 1948 following Blackburn's relegation to the Second Division. After scoring 14 goals in 55 League appearances with Preston, Langton moved to Bolton Wanderers in November 1949 for a fee that was a club record at the time. A regular in the Bolton team until 1953, Langton scored 16 goals in 118 League appearances and appeared in the 1953 FA Cup Final. Langton returned to Ewood Park in September 1953 and although his speed had diminished, Langton had added guile and cunning to his armoury. He enjoyed three seasons at Ewood on the left-wing before leaving the Football League to play in Ireland with Ards. He was later to return to England to embark upon an extensive career in non-League football.

### LAPHAM, Edgar Harold
Centre-forward. 1934-1936.
*5ft 8½in; 10st 7lb.*
*Born: Liverpool, 1911 (October quarter).*
*Debut: v Sheffield Wednesday (h) 7 December 1935.*
*Career: Marine FC; Everton on trial March 1933; Blackburn Rovers amateur November 1934; Accrington Stanley February 1936; Wrexham July 1936 until May 1939.*
**Appearances:** Football League 2.

A hat-trick for the Central League team against Bolton Wanderers in November 1935 earned Harold Lapham a promotion to the senior team. He appeared in two consecutive matches for the Rovers but failed to get on the score-sheet and returned to the Central League team. A strong running, bustling type of centre-forward, Lapham made the short move to Peel Park in February 1936. He scored twice in his first three appearances for Accrington but then found goals hard to find. In the summer of 1936 he moved to Wrexham and enjoyed better fortune at the Racecourse Ground, scoring 40 goals in 69 League appearances.

### LAPHAM, William H.
Half-back. 1879-1881.
*Debut: v Tyne Association (h) 1 November 1879 (FAC).*
*Career: Blackburn Rovers 1879.*
**Appearances:** FA Cup 2.

Latham appeared at half-back on a regular basis during the 1879-80 season. He participated in the very first FA Cup game that the club undertook in November 1879. Although he missed the second round match with Darwen, Latham was a member of the side which crashed 6-0 to Nottingham Forest in the third round. The pairing of Fred Hargreaves and Hugh McIntyre in the back division early in the 1880-81 season virtually ended Latham's appearances in the first team.

### LATHERON, Edwin Gladstone
Inside-forward. 1906-1917.
*5ft 5in; 10st 8lb.*
*Born: Grangetown, nr Middlesbrough, 1887; Died: Killed in action in France, 14 October 1917.*
*Debut: v Middlesbrough (h) 22 December 1906.*
*Career: Grangetown FC; Blackburn Rovers March 1906.*
*International honours with Blackburn Rovers: England: 2 caps (1913-14); Football League: 5 appearances (1909-15).*
*Domestic honours with Blackburn Rovers: Football League championship: 1911-12 (22 apps, 7 gls); 1913-14 (35 apps, 13 gls).*
**Appearances:** Football League 256; FA Cup 24; FA Charity Shield 1; Total 281.
**Goals:** Football League 94; FA Cup 10; Total 104

An England international at the peak of his powers, Eddie Latheron played his final game for Blackburn Rovers on 17 March 1917. Five days later he marched off to war and seven months after that he became

another victim of the carnage in Europe. Latheron had arrived at Ewood Park almost by accident in March 1906. He had visited Blackburn with his Grangetown club to play an FA Amateur Cup-tie with Crosshill.

Representatives of the Ewood club had gone to the match to watch another of the Grangetown players but found it was Latheron who caught the eye. A fee of £25 was paid to bring Latheron to Blackburn and in December 1906 he made his debut against Middlesbrough at Ewood Park. A skilful inside-forward, who could play on either side of the field, Latheron quickly established himself in the senior team. Although not the tallest of men, Latheron was good in the air and more than compensated for his lack of inches with his touch and timing on the ball. Indeed, Latheron had all the qualities needed to make a great player and above all he possessed a totally unselfish attitude on the field.

Although a prolific goalscorer in his own right, Latheron was always prepared to do the fetching and carrying for others. Quite simply he was the perfect team player. His engaging personality endeared him to friend and opponent alike and his courageous play and unquenchable enthusiasm made him a popular figure with the public of Blackburn.

It was therefore a devastating blow when Alex McGhie, his close friend and playing colleague at Ewood, relayed the news back from France that a German shell had extinguished one of Blackburn Rovers' brightest flames. Latheron was 28 when he died and left a widow and child; he also left the memory of a rare and gifted talent which fate decreed would never have the opportunity to mature.

### LAW, James
Outside-right. 1899-1900.
*Debut: v Sunderland (h) 11 November 1899.*
*Career: Blackburn Rovers July 1899.*
**Appearances:** Football League 3.
**Goals:** Football League 1.

Law got his chance of first-team football when Daniel Hurst was called up to appear for the Football League. Although he scored on his debut, Law was unable to strike up an immediate understanding with Fred Blackburn on the left-wing. Ironically, it was over the New Year period that Law got his only other opportunity with the senior team when a cold kept Blackburn out of the side for two games.

### LAWRIE, John
Outside-right. 1908.
*5ft 6½in; 10st 7lb.*
*Born: Knightsbridge, Glasgow.*
*Debut: v Aston Villa (a) 3 October 1908.*
*Career: Partick Thistle February 1905; Workington; Blackburn Rovers August 1908; Bristol Rovers cs 1909.*

**Appearances:** Football League 2.

Lawrie was unfortunate that in both his appearances with the senior team he found himself playing with a colleague at inside-right who was out of position. In both games Archie Kyle, a natural left-sided player, partnered Lawrie on the right-wing with disappointing results. Laurie was introduced in place of Billy Garbutt but after two indifferent games which brought a draw and a defeat, Garbutt was reinstated and Lawrie never appeared in the senior team again.

## LAWTHER, William Ian

Centre-forward. 1961-1963.
*5ft 10in; 11st 4lb.*
*Born: Belfast, 20 October 1939.*
*Debut: v Cardiff City (h) 19 August 1961.*
*Career: Crusaders; Sunderland March 1958; Blackburn Rovers July 1961; Scunthorpe United July 1963 (£12,000); Brentford November 1964; Halifax Town August 1968; Stockport County July 1971 to June 1976.*
*International honours with Blackburn Rovers: Northern Ireland: 2 caps (1961-62).*
**Appearances:** Football League 59; FA Cup 5; Football League Cup 11; Total 75.
**Goals:** Football League 21; FA Cup 1; Football League Cup 10; Total 32.

Ian Lawther came to Blackburn with a glowing reputation in the summer of 1961 but found himself axed after only two senior games. Fortunately, the Northern Ireland international returned to establish himself at inside-right and finished the 1961-62 season as top scorer with 20 League and Cup goals. Although he began the 1962-63 season at centre-forward, he was moved to inside-right after only five games to make way for Fred Pickering. However, his form dipped and midway through the season he found himself out of the side. He refused terms at the end of the season and in July 1963, Scunthorpe United paid a record fee to sign him. Lawther finally retired in 1976 after 575 (+21 sub) appearances and 178 goals in the Football League. During his later years he also played in the centre of defence.

## LEAMINGTON STREET GROUND

By the early 1880s, Blackburn Rovers were rapidly establishing themselves as one of the leading clubs in the area. The club's officials felt that if they were to become one of the leading club's in the country, then it was necessary to find a ground of their own rather than continue sharing the town's leading cricket ground.

On 15 October 1881, Blackburn Rovers played Blackburn Olympic at a new venue on Leamington Street (now Leamington Road). Having taken the lease on the ground at Leamington Street, the club spent £500 to build a grandstand which contained seating for 700 people.

The ground also contained a pavilion and a large refreshment pavilion. The nine years spent at Leamington Street represented one of the most successful periods during the club's history. Three FA Cup Finals were won in successive years and the club entered the Football League whilst still at the Leamington Ground. The Ground itself received recognition when England played three international matches there in 1881 and 1885 against Wales, and in 1887 against Scotland. The club's reputation and the increasing popularity of the Leamington Ground enticed the landlord to attempt to increase the rent to an unacceptable level.

Unwilling to succumb to these demands, despite having the resources to meet them, the club officials gambled on finding a new home. As a result of this decision Blackburn Rovers opened the 1890-91 season at Ewood Park. The Leamington area was the site of rapid house building and the site of the Leamington Ground was quickly covered with terraced housing.

## LEAVER, Derek

Inside-forward. 1949-1955.
*5ft 7in; 10st 2lb.*
*Born: Blackburn 13 November 1930.*
*Debut: v Manchester City (a) 18 November 1950.*
*Career: Blackburn Rovers May 1949; Bournemouth & Boscombe Athletic July 1955; Crewe Alexandra March 1956.*
**Appearances:** Football League 14.
**Goals:** Football League 5.

Derek Leaver was a local lad who made a dream debut by scoring one of the goals in a 4-1 win at Maine Road. Leaver was just one of a number of locally-born players to be given their chance during Jackie Bestall's reign at Ewood. During his time at the club Leaver appeared in a variety of forward positions without ever establishing himself on a permanent basis. In search of first-team football he moved to Bournemouth during the summer of 1955 and scored five goals in 29 League appearances before joining Crewe Alexandra. His stint at Gresty Road brought six goals in a further 28 League games.

## LEAVER, William

Forward. 1897-1898.
*Born: Blackburn, 1877.*
*Debut: v Everton (a) 29 January 1898 (FAC).*
*Career: Blackburn Rovers May 1897 until cs 1898.*
**Appearances:** FA Cup 1.

Leaver made his sole appearance for Blackburn Rovers in the first round of the 1897-98 FA Cup competition. Leaver came into the side at inside-right in place of the injured Ben Hulse. Sadly, he was unable to strike up an understanding with Briercliffe on the right wing as the Rovers slumped to a single goal defeat.

## LEE, Gordon

Manager. 1974-1975.
*Born: Hednesford, 13 July 1934.*
*Career: Littleworth School; Girton Road Gasworks; Hednesford Town 1951; Aston Villa October 1955; Shrewsbury Town player-coach July 1966; Port Vale manager May 1968; Blackburn Rovers manager January 1974; Newcastle United manager June 1975; Everton manager February 1977 until May 1981; Preston North End manager December 1981 until December 1983; KR Reykjavik (Iceland) coach; coached in the Middle East; Leicester City coach January 1988, then assistant manager, then caretaker manager January to May 1991.*

Gordon Lee was appointed to succeed Ken Furphy on 14 January 1974 and took up his duties at Ewood Park two days later. Like Furphy, Lee had proven himself to be capable of being able to achieve success on a limited budget. Although he was to remain at Ewood for only 18 months, Lee became the first manager to lead a Blackburn side to a championship success, albeit in the Third Division, since Bob Crompton won the Second Division title in 1938-39.

Lee, who spent the majority of his playing career with Aston Villa, entered football management at Port Vale in May 1968. In 1971 he led the Potteries club to the Third Division and managed to keep them there despite having limited resources at his disposal. It was this success that attracted him to the directors of Blackburn Rovers after Ken Furphy had moved to Sheffield United. The Gordon Lee philosophy to football was basically a very simple one. It was Lee's belief that success in football could only be achieved by hard work and complete dedication to the team effort.

Yet there was more to Lee's philosophy than just sweat. As a manager he had the gift of being able to motivate average players into reaching standards that many thought them incapable of achieving. However, if his strength lay in getting the best out of the average player, many felt that his Achilles' heel was in trying to deal with so-called 'star' players. Within a short time of his arrival at Blackburn it became clear that a number of the existing staff did not share Lee's approach to the game. Using his first few months at Ewood to assess the relative merits of the squad, Lee began to accumulate the finance required to rebuild his first-team squad. To the consternation of the supporters Lee accepted offers from Furphy for both Tony Field and Terry Garbett.

The close of the season brought free transfers to Kit Napier, Ben Arentoft, John O'Mara and Dave Turner whilst David Bradford was allowed to join Field and Garbett at Sheffield United for a modest fee. Ironically, Lee's first move into the transfer market was to bring Pat Hilton from Brighton & Hove Albion on a free transfer. However, in paying £25,000 to Brighton for Ken Beamish, his second signing for the club, Lee parted with the biggest fee that he had ever spent in his managerial career.

The summer of 1974 saw Graham Hawkins, Graham Oates and Jimmy Mullen appear at Ewood Park whilst Andy Burgin, Mike Hickman and Bobby Hoy all arrived at strategic moments in the season. As well as bringing in new faces, Lee also inspired the likes of Tony Parkes and Stuart Metcalfe to show their true worth in midfield. However, his most astute move was to resurrect the career of the veteran Don Martin. The former Northampton Town player had spent much of Furphy's reign languishing in the Central League team but repaid Lee's faith in him with 15 League goals. When the Third Division championship was won, Lee became the centre of a controversial tug-of-war with Newcastle United.

Once again, the Ewood directors found that a contract was no protection against the lure of the First Division. After leaving Blackburn, Lee experienced an extraordinarily varied career. He left Newcastle in February 1977 to become manager of Everton but was sacked in May 1981. A brief spell abroad was followed by two years at Deepdale. After leaving Preston he again found employment abroad before linking up with David Pleat at Leicester City. His association with Leicester ended when Brian Little became manager at Filbert Street.

## LEE, John B.
Forward. 1937.
*Born: Blackburn.*
*Debut: v Accrington Stanley (a) 20 January 1937 (FAC).*
*Career: Blackburn Rovers January 1937; Corinthian Casuals.*
**Appearances:** FA Cup 1.
Jack Lee was a Blackburn lad who became an Oxford Blue and turned out for a time with the Central League team. He received an unexpected call up to the first team for the replayed FA Cup-tie against Accrington Stanley in January 1937. Although a centre-forward, Lee was chosen to play in the inside-right position. Unfortunately an ankle injury forced him to end the game on the right wing as the Rovers crashed to a 3-1 defeat. It proved to be Lee's only appearance with the senior team. He later lived and worked in London and turned out at centre-forward for the Corinthian Casuals.

## LEE, William R.
Centre-half. 1936-1946.
*6ft; 11st 1lb.*
*Born: Darwen, 24 October 1919.*
*Debut: v Sheffield Wednesday (a) 8 September 1938.*
*Career: Feniscowles; Pleasington; Blackburn Rovers amateur December 1936, turning professional in January 1938; Barrow May 1946.*
*Domestic honours with Blackburn Rovers: Second Division championship: 1938-39 (1 app).*
**Appearances:** Football League 1.
The debut of young Billy Lee coincided with Blackburn's first defeat of the season after an opening run of three successive victories. Sadly, the promotion of the inexperienced Lee proved somewhat premature. The correspondent of *The Blackburn Times* remarked that Lee was slow and hesitant in his tackling and far too easily drawn out of position. The game proved to be his only appearance for the senior team as Lee did not return to Ewood after the war. In May 1946 he joined Barrow and went on to appear in 158 League games for the club.

## LEEDS UNITED FC
Founded in 1919 after Leeds City had been wound up. Leeds City had been in existence since 1904 and had been members of the Second Division of the Football League since 1905. Leeds United entered the Second Division in 1920 and finished as champions of that division in 1923-24. The following season Leeds and Blackburn met for the first time in the Football League. The most successful period in the history of Leeds, the late 1960s and early 1970s, coincided with a wane in the fortunes of Blackburn Rovers. As a result the clubs did not meet in the League between 1964-65 and 1982-83. Whilst Leeds maintained superiority in the Football League, the Rovers have enjoyed better luck in the Premier League meetings.
### Football League

| | | Home | | Away | |
|---|---|---|---|---|---|
| 1924-25 | (Div 1) | L | 2-3 | D | 1-1 |
| 1925-26 | (Div 1) | D | 2-2 | L | 1-2 |
| 1926-27 | (Div 1) | W | 4-1 | L | 1-4 |
| 1928-29 | (Div 1) | L | 0-1 | W | 1-0 |
| 1929-30 | (Div 1) | W | 2-1 | L | 2-4 |
| 1930-31 | (Div 1) | W | 3-1 | L | 2-4 |
| 1932-33 | (Div 1) | D | 1-1 | L | 1-3 |
| 1933-34 | (Div 1) | W | 4-2 | L | 0-4 |
| 1934-35 | (Div 1) | D | 1-1 | L | 1-5 |
| 1935-36 | (Div 1) | L | 0-3 | W | 4-1 |
| 1946-47 | (Div 1) | W | 1-0 | W | 1-0 |
| 1948-49 | (Div 2) | D | 0-0 | L | 0-1 |
| 1949-50 | (Div 2) | L | 0-1 | L | 1-2 |
| 1950-51 | (Div 2) | W | 2-1 | W | 1-0 |
| 1951-52 | (Div 2) | L | 2-3 | L | 0-1 |
| 1952-53 | (Div 2) | D | 1-1 | W | 3-0 |
| 1953-54 | (Div 2) | D | 2-2 | L | 2-3 |
| 1954-55 | (Div 2) | L | 1-2 | L | 0-2 |
| 1955-56 | (Div 2) | L | 2-3 | W | 2-1 |
| 1958-59 | (Div 1) | L | 2-4 | L | 1-2 |
| 1959-60 | (Div 1) | W | 3-2 | W | 1-0 |
| 1964-65 | (Div 1) | L | 0-2 | D | 1-1 |
| 1965-66 | (Div 1) | L | 2-3 | L | 0-3 |

| | | Home | | Away | |
|---|---|---|---|---|---|
| 1982-83 | (Div 2) | D | 0-0 | L | 1-2 |
| 1983-84 | (Div 2) | D | 1-1 | L | 0-1 |
| 1984-85 | (Div 2) | W | 2-1 | D | 0-0 |
| 1985-86 | (Div 2) | W | 2-0 | D | 1-1 |
| 1986-87 | (Div 2) | W | 2-1 | D | 0-0 |
| 1987-88 | (Div 2) | D | 1-1 | D | 2-2 |
| 1988-89 | (Div 2) | W | 2-0 | L | 0-2 |
| 1989-90 | (Div 2) | L | 1-2 | D | 1-1 |

| | P | W | D | L | F | A |
|---|---|---|---|---|---|---|
| Home | 31 | 11 | 9 | 11 | 48 | 46 |
| Away | 31 | 7 | 7 | 17 | 32 | 53 |
| Total | 62 | 18 | 16 | 28 | 80 | 99 |

### FA Premiership

| | | Home | | Away | |
|---|---|---|---|---|---|
| 1992-93 | | W | 3-1 | L | 2-5 |
| 1993-94 | | W | 2-1 | D | 3-3 |

| | P | W | D | L | F | A |
|---|---|---|---|---|---|---|
| Home | 2 | 2 | 0 | 0 | 5 | 2 |
| Away | 2 | 0 | 1 | 1 | 5 | 8 |
| Total | 4 | 2 | 1 | 1 | 10 | 10 |

### Football League Cup

| | | | | | |
|---|---|---|---|---|---|
| 1962-63 | (3) | Home | | W | 4-0 |

### Wartime

| | | Home | | Away | |
|---|---|---|---|---|---|
| 1945-46 | (FLC) | D | 0-0 | W | 4-1 |

## LEICESTER CITY FC
Founded in 1884 by old boys of Wyggeston School, the club was originally known as Leicester Fosse. Elected to the Second Division of the Football League in 1894, the club changed its name to Leicester City in 1919. Although Leicester and Blackburn first met in League football in 1908-09, the most important meeting between the clubs took place at Wembley in May 1992. By defeating Leicester 1-0 in the Second Division Play-off Final, the Rovers clinched a place in the newly-formed Premier League. The Leicester club was unfortunate in losing a second successive Play-off Final at Wembley in 1993, when Swindon Town pulled off an unlikely 4-3 victory. However, Leicester proved triumphant at the third attempt when they defeated Derby County in the 1994 First Division Play-off Final. Included in the Leicester squad, although they didn't play on the day, were Steve Agnew and David Speedie.

### Football League

| | | Home | | Away | |
|---|---|---|---|---|---|
| 1908-09 | (Div 1) | W | 3-0 | W | 4-2 |
| 1925-26 | (Div 1) | D | 0-0 | L | 1-2 |
| 1926-27 | (Div 1) | W | 2-1 | L | 0-4 |
| 1927-28 | (Div 1) | D | 0-0 | L | 0-6 |
| 1928-29 | (Div 1) | D | 1-1 | L | 1-2 |
| 1929-30 | (Div 1) | W | 3-1 | D | 1-1 |
| 1930-31 | (Div 1) | W | 3-0 | L | 1-3 |
| 1931-32 | (Div 1) | W | 6-0 | L | 0-1 |
| 1932-33 | (Div 1) | D | 1-1 | D | 1-1 |
| 1933-34 | (Div 1) | W | 3-0 | W | 2-1 |
| 1934-35 | (Div 1) | D | 0-0 | W | 1-0 |
| 1936-37 | (Div 2) | D | 0-0 | L | 0-1 |
| 1948-49 | (Div 2) | W | 2-0 | L | 1-3 |
| 1949-50 | (Div 2) | W | 3-0 | D | 3-3 |
| 1950-51 | (Div 2) | W | 1-0 | L | 0-2 |
| 1951-52 | (Div 2) | W | 2-1 | L | 1-2 |
| 1952-53 | (Div 2) | W | 2-0 | L | 1-2 |
| 1953-54 | (Div 2) | W | 3-0 | L | 0-4 |
| 1955-56 | (Div 2) | L | 2-3 | W | 2-0 |
| 1956-57 | (Div 2) | D | 1-1 | L | 0-6 |
| 1958-59 | (Div 1) | W | 5-0 | D | 1-1 |
| 1959-60 | (Div 1) | L | 0-1 | W | 3-2 |
| 1960-61 | (Div 1) | D | 1-1 | W | 4-2 |
| 1961-62 | (Div 1) | W | 2-1 | L | 0-2 |
| 1962-63 | (Div 1) | W | 2-0 | L | 0-2 |
| 1963-64 | (Div 1) | W | 5-2 | L | 3-4 |
| 1964-65 | (Div 1) | W | 3-1 | W | 3-2 |
| 1965-66 | (Div 1) | L | 0-2 | L | 0-2 |
| 1969-70 | (Div 2) | W | 3-1 | L | 1-2 |
| 1970-71 | (Div 2) | D | 2-2 | D | 1-1 |
| 1978-79 | (Div 2) | D | 1-1 | D | 1-1 |
| 1981-82 | (Div 2) | L | 0-2 | L | 0-1 |
| 1982-83 | (Div 2) | W | 3-1 | W | 1-0 |

Howard Gayle beats Leicester goalkeeper Martin Hodge but shoots wide in April 1989.

| | | | | | | |
|---|---|---|---|---|---|---|
| 1987-88 | | (Div 2) | D | 3-3 | W | 2-1 |
| 1988-89 | | (Div 2) | D | 0-0 | L | 0-4 |
| 1989-90 | | (Div 2) | L | 2-4 | W | 1-0 |
| 1990-91 | | (Div 2) | W | 4-1 | W | 3-1 |
| 1991-92 | | (Div 2) | L | 0-1 | L | 0-3 |

| | P | W | D | L | F | A |
|---|---|---|---|---|---|---|
| Home | 38 | 20 | 12 | 6 | 74 | 33 |
| Away | 38 | 11 | 6 | 21 | 44 | 77 |
| Total | 76 | 31 | 18 | 27 | 118 | 110 |

**Play-offs**

| | | | | | |
|---|---|---|---|---|---|
| 1991-92 | (F) | Wembley | W | 1-0 | |

**FA Cup**

| | | | | | |
|---|---|---|---|---|---|
| 1907-08 | (1) | Away | L | 0-2 | |
| 1964-65 | (3) | Away | D | 2-2 | |
| | (R) | Home | L | 1-2 | |

**LE SAUX, Graeme Pierre**
Left-back/Midfield. 1993-
*5ft 10in; 11st 2lb.*
*Born: Jersey, 17 October 1968.*
*Debut: v Liverpool (h) 3 April 1993.*
*Career: St Paul's (Jersey); Chelsea December 1988; Blackburn Rovers March 1993 (£400,000 plus Steve Livingstone).*
*International honours with Blackburn Rovers: England: 3 caps (1994).*
**Appearances:** Premier League 49+1; FA Cup 4; Football League Cup 4; Total 57+1.
**Goals:** Premier League 2.
Graeme Le Saux was spotted by Chelsea whilst playing for a local Jersey side, St Paul's. During his time at Stamford Bridge, Le Saux enjoyed various spells in the senior team at either left-back or on the left-wing. At the time of his move to Ewood Park, on the eve of the 1993 transfer deadline, Le Saux was out of favour at Stamford Bridge. The former England Under-21 and 'B' international quickly settled into the left-back spot at Ewood in place of the injured Alan Wright. A quick and skilful defender, Le Saux is an excellent crosser of the ball and has developed into an outstanding attacking left-back. He proved a revelation during the 1993-94 season and his form was so good that Alan Wright, himself a talented England Under-21

international, was unable to regain the left-back spot. In March 1994 his form was rewarded with a place in the first England squad to be selected by Terry Venables and on 9 March 1994 he made his international debut against Denmark.

### LEWIS, Frederick John
Inside-right. 1977-1978.
*5ft 10in; 11st 4lb.*
*Born: Long Eaton, Derbyshire, 22 March 1948.*
*Debut: v Tottenham Hotspur (h) 24 August 1977.*
*Career: Long Eaton United; Lincoln City March 1967; Grimsby Town January 1970 (£3,000); Blackburn Rovers August 1977; Doncaster Rovers August 1978.*
**Appearances:** Football League 24+4; Football League Cup 2; Total 26+4.
**Goals:** Football League 6.
Jack Lewis came to Ewood Park with a record of 74 goals in 258 League appearances (including 27 as sub) with Grimsby Town. Lewis, who was a member of the Welsh international squad, was brought to Ewood Park to improve the firepower available to Jim Smith. Unfortunately, Lewis did not enjoy the best of fortune at Blackburn and missed the middle part of the season through injury. After only a year at Ewood Lewis, who had played in a variety of positions with Grimsby, was allowed to join Doncaster Rovers.

### LEWIS, John
Forward. 1875-1880.
*Club treasurer 1881 to 1884 & committee member 1875 to 1897.*
*Born: Market Drayton, 30 March 1855; Died: Blackburn, 13 January 1926.*
*Debut: v Tyne Association (h) 1 November 1879 (FAC).*
*Career: Blackburn Rovers 1875 until 1880 as a player. A member of the committee until 1897 and club treasurer between 1881 and 1894.*
**Appearances:** FA Cup 3.
**Goals:** FA Cup 1.
A founder member of Blackburn Rovers Football Club, John Lewis played for the club in its formative years before going on to become an outstanding referee and administrator. The son of a Methodist preacher, Lewis and Arthur Constantine called the meeting at the St Leger Hotel in Blackburn which was to witness the birth of Blackburn Rovers. An athletic forward, his enthusiasm for the game was such that Lewis would turn out for any club that would have him whenever the Rovers were without a game. Sadly, injury curtailed his playing career and Lewis turned his attention to refereeing and administration.

His success as a referee earned him the title 'The Prince of Referees' and he officiated at the 1895, 1897 and 1898 FA Cup Finals. He retired from refereeing in 1905, at the age of 50, but was constantly in demand to turn out for important matches. In 1920, at the age of 65, he took control of the Final of the Olympic Games. Lewis enjoyed equal success in the field of administration. Apart from his position with the Rovers, Lewis was also a founder and council member of the Lancashire Football Association. In 1894 he became a member of the Football League Management Committee for one season before being re-elected in 1900. In total he served for 25 years on that body and was vice-president of the Football League from 1901 to 1925. In 1911 he was appointed a Football Association councillor, and in 1923 he became vice-president of the Football Association; a position he held until his death in 1926.

His Methodist upbringing and work for the Temperance movement were mirrored in his attitude to the sport. All his match fees as a referee were donated to charity and his impartiality was beyond reproach. However, his insistence that everyone should follow his own high standards led to more than one brush with both authority and football crowds. His bluntness often enraged those who incurred his wrath and his autocratic nature meant that he was a respected, rather than loved, figure.

In 1928, Charles E.Sutcliffe, president of the Lancashire Football Association, wrote of Lewis that: '...with all his failings he was one of the greatest men that ever took part in the conduct, control, and government of the game.' It was entirely appropriate that the directors of the modern Blackburn Rovers should recognise his importance by naming the complex of executive boxes and restaurant, which was constructed in the 1980s, after him.

### LEYLAND, Harry Kenneth
Goalkeeper. 1956-1961.
*5ft 10½in; 12st 6lb.*
*Born: Liverpool, 12 May 1930.*
*Debut: v West Ham United (a) 20 August 1956.*
*Career: Everton August 1950 to June 1956; Tonbridge cs 1956; Blackburn Rovers August 1956; Tranmere Rovers March 1961; Wigan Athletic player-manager.*
*Domestic honours with Blackburn Rovers: FA Cup runners-up: 1960.*

**Appearances:** Football League 166; FA Cup 18; Football League Cup 4; Total 188.

Harry Leyland was on his way out of League Football when he joined Blackburn Rovers in August 1956. Released by Everton, Leyland had been unable to find a berth at another League club and had agreed to join Ron Saunders, also freed by Everton, in a move to non-League Tonbridge. On the eve of the new season Leyland was thrown a lifeline by Johnny Carey who saw the former Evertonian as the ideal man to replace Reg Elvy. Leyland, who had appeared in 36 League matches during his five year stint at Goodison, was a complete contrast to the departed Elvy. A smaller, stockier man, Leyland looked far from athletic but was to prove that looks can be deceptive.

At Ewood Park he was shown to be an agile and brave 'keeper whose infectious humour benefited the whole team. Initial weaknesses in handling improved, particularly after the signing of Matt Woods, a former playing colleague at Everton. With Woods proving a tower of strength to the defence, Leyland grew in confidence and consistency. An ever-present during the successful promotion campaign of 1957-58, Leyland also picked up an FA Cup runners-up medal in 1960. However, it was at this time that Leyland was beginning to show increasing signs of vulnerability.

Matters were not helped by a succession of injuries but during the 1960-61 season it became clear that Leyland would have to be replaced. Leyland left for Tranmere Rovers before the campaign ended and enjoyed a new lease of life on his return to Merseyside. He went on to appear in a further 180 League matches with Tranmere before bowing out of League football to become player-manager of Wigan Athletic.

### LEYTON ORIENT FC
Originally founded in 1881, the club was known as Clapton Orient until 1946 when it became known as Leyton Orient. It was under the management of Johnny Carey, a former Blackburn Rovers manager, that Leyton Orient enjoyed its only season as a First Division club. In 1966, the club dropped Leyton from its name and simply became known as The Orient Football Club. In 1987 the club again adopted the title of Leyton Orient. Meetings between the Orient club, in its different guises, and Blackburn Rovers have been tight but fairly infrequent affairs.

**Football League**

|  |  |  | Home |  | Away |  |
|---|---|---|---|---|---|---|
| 1956-57 | (Div 2) | D | 3-3 | D | 1-1 |
| 1957-58 | (Div 2) | W | 4-1 | L | 1-5 |
| 1962-63 | (Div 1) | D | 1-1 | D | 1-1 |
| 1970-71 | (Div 2) | D | 0-0 | D | 1-1 |
| 1975-76 | (Div 2) | D | 1-1 | D | 1-1 |
| 1976-77 | (Div 2) | D | 2-2 | W | 1-0 |
| 1977-78 | (Div 2) | W | 1-0 | D | 0-0 |
| 1978-79 | (Div 2) | W | 3-0 | L | 0-2 |
| 1980-81 | (Div 2) | W | 2-0 | D | 1-1 |
| 1981-82 | (Div 2) | W | 2-0 | D | 0-0 |

|  | P | W | D | L | F | A |
|---|---|---|---|---|---|---|
| Home | 10 | 5 | 5 | 0 | 19 | 8 |
| Away | 10 | 1 | 7 | 2 | 7 | 12 |
| Total | 20 | 6 | 12 | 2 | 26 | 20 |

**FA Cup**

| 1958-59 | (3) | Home | W | 4-2 |
|---|---|---|---|---|
| 1976-77 | (4) | Home | W | 3-0 |
| 1977-78 | (4) | Away | L | 1-3 |

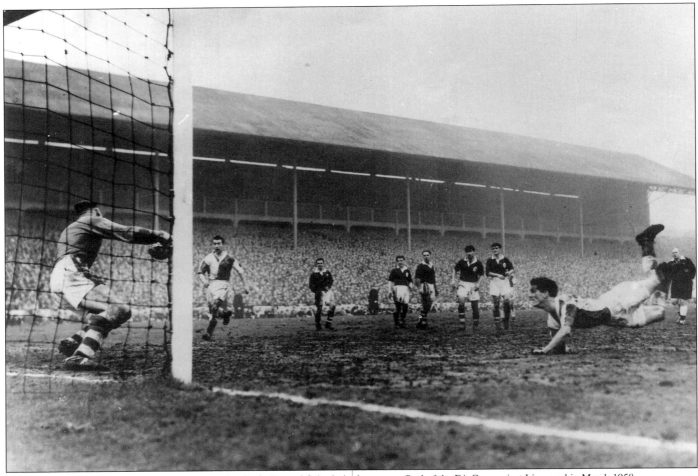

Ronnie Clayton scores with a diving header in Rovers' 2-1 win in the quarter-final of the FA Cup against Liverpool in March 1958.

**Football League Cup**

| | | | | |
|---|---|---|---|---|
| 1973-74 | (2) | Away | L | 0-2 |

## LINCOLN CITY FC

Founded in 1883 and one of the founder members of the Second Division of the Football League in 1892. Blackburn and Lincoln did not meet each other in competitive football until 1932-33 when they were drawn together in the third round of the FA Cup. All the League meetings between the clubs have been in the Second Division and apart from the first meeting in 1948-49, all these games were played during the 1950s.

**Football League**

| | | | Home | | Away |
|---|---|---|---|---|---|
| 1948-49 | (Div 2) | W | 7-1 | L | 0-3 |
| 1952-53 | (Div 2) | L | 0-2 | L | 1-4 |
| 1953-54 | (Div 2) | W | 6-0 | L | 0-8 |
| 1954-55 | (Div 2) | W | 1-0 | L | 1-2 |
| 1955-56 | (Div 2) | L | 0-2 | L | 0-3 |
| 1956-57 | (Div 2) | L | 3-4 | W | 2-1 |
| 1957-58 | (Div 2) | L | 0-1 | D | 1-1 |

| | P | W | D | L | F | A |
|---|---|---|---|---|---|---|
| Home | 7 | 3 | 0 | 4 | 17 | 10 |
| Away | 7 | 1 | 1 | 5 | 5 | 22 |
| Total | 14 | 4 | 1 | 9 | 22 | 32 |

**FA Cup**

| | | | | |
|---|---|---|---|---|
| 1932-33 | (3) | Away | W | 5-1 |
| 1972-73 | (1) | Away | D | 2-2 |
| | (R) | Home | W | 4-1 |

**Football League Cup**

| | | | | |
|---|---|---|---|---|
| 1971-72 | (2) | Home | D | 0-0 |
| | (R) | Away | L | 1-4 |

## LIVERPOOL FC

Liverpool Football Club was formed in 1892 as a result of a rent dispute involving the members of the Everton Football Club. The majority of the Everton members left the Anfield Ground to move to Goodison Park and those who remained formed a new club, Liverpool. A long history of meetings between Blackburn and Liverpool began in 1894 following the Anfield Club's first promotion to the top division. Liverpool went on to dominate English football for the best part of three decades following their promotion to the First Division in 1962. In October 1991, Blackburn Rovers rocked the football world when former Anfield favourite Kenny Dalglish was appointed manager at Ewood Park.

**Football League**

| | | Home | | Away | |
|---|---|---|---|---|---|
| 1894-95 | (Div 1) | D | 1-1 | D | 2-2 |
| 1896-97 | (Div 1) | W | 1-0 | L | 0-4 |
| 1897-98 | (Div 1) | W | 2-1 | W | 1-0 |
| 1898-99 | (Div 1) | L | 1-3 | L | 0-2 |
| 1899-00 | (Div 1) | W | 2-0 | L | 1-3 |
| 1900-01 | (Div 1) | W | 3-1 | L | 0-3 |
| 1901-02 | (Div 1) | D | 1-1 | L | 0-1 |
| 1902-03 | (Div 1) | W | 3-1 | L | 2-5 |
| 1903-04 | (Div 1) | L | 2-3 | W | 2-1 |
| 1905-06 | (Div 1) | D | 0-0 | W | 3-1 |
| 1906-07 | (Div 1) | D | 1-1 | W | 2-0 |
| 1907-08 | (Div 1) | L | 1-3 | L | 0-2 |
| 1908-09 | (Div 1) | W | 1-0 | D | 1-1 |
| 1909-10 | (Div 1) | D | 1-1 | L | 1-3 |
| 1910-11 | (Div 1) | L | 1-2 | D | 2-2 |
| 1911-12 | (Div 1) | W | 1-0 | W | 2-1 |
| 1912-13 | (Div 1) | W | 5-1 | L | 1-4 |
| 1913-14 | (Div 1) | W | 6-2 | D | 3-3 |
| 1914-15 | (Div 1) | W | 4-2 | L | 0-3 |
| 1919-20 | (Div 1) | L | 0-2 | L | 0-3 |
| 1920-21 | (Div 1) | D | 1-1 | L | 0-2 |
| 1921-22 | (Div 1) | D | 0-0 | L | 0-2 |
| 1922-23 | (Div 1) | W | 1-0 | L | 0-3 |
| 1923-24 | (Div 1) | D | 0-0 | D | 0-0 |
| 1924-25 | (Div 1) | W | 3-1 | D | 0-0 |
| 1925-26 | (Div 1) | D | 1-1 | D | 2-2 |
| 1926-27 | (Div 1) | W | 2-1 | D | 2-2 |

| 1927-28 | (Div 1) | W | 2-1 | L | 2-4 |
|---|---|---|---|---|---|
| 1928-29 | (Div 1) | W | 2-1 | D | 1-1 |
| 1929-30 | (Div 1) | W | 1-0 | D | 1-1 |
| 1930-31 | (Div 1) | D | 3-3 | L | 1-2 |
| 1931-32 | (Div 1) | L | 1-3 | L | 2-4 |
| 1932-33 | (Div 1) | D | 2-2 | D | 2-2 |
| 1933-34 | (Div 1) | W | 3-1 | L | 0-4 |
| 1934-35 | (Div 1) | L | 0-2 | L | 0-2 |
| 1935-36 | (Div 1) | D | 2-2 | L | 1-4 |
| 1946-47 | (Div 1) | D | 0-0 | L | 1-2 |
| 1947-48 | (Div 1) | L | 1-2 | L | 1-2 |
| 1954-55 | (Div 1) | W | 4-3 | L | 1-4 |
| 1955-56 | (Div 2) | D | 3-3 | W | 2-1 |
| 1956-57 | (Div 2) | D | 2-2 | W | 3-2 |
| 1957-58 | (Div 2) | D | 3-3 | L | 0-2 |
| 1962-63 | (Div 1) | W | 1-0 | L | 1-3 |
| 1963-64 | (Div 1) | L | 1-2 | W | 2-1 |
| 1964-65 | (Div 1) | W | 3-2 | L | 2-3 |
| 1965-66 | (Div 1) | L | 1-4 | L | 2-5 |

| | P | W | D | L | F | A |
|---|---|---|---|---|---|---|
| Home | 46 | 20 | 16 | 10 | 80 | 65 |
| Away | 46 | 8 | 11 | 27 | 52 | 104 |
| Total | 92 | 28 | 27 | 37 | 132 | 169 |

**FA Premiership**

| | | Home | | Away | |
|---|---|---|---|---|---|
| 1992-93 | | W | 4-1 | L | 1-2 |
| 1993-94 | | W | 2-0 | W | 1-0 |

| | P | W | D | L | F | A |
|---|---|---|---|---|---|---|
| Home | 2 | 2 | 0 | 0 | 6 | 1 |
| Away | 2 | 1 | 0 | 1 | 2 | 2 |
| Total | 4 | 3 | 0 | 1 | 8 | 3 |

**FA Cup**

| 1898-99 | (1) | Away | L | 0-2 |
|---|---|---|---|---|
| 1903-04 | (1) | Home | W | 3-1 |
| 1934-35 | (4) | Home | W | 1-0 |
| 1949-50 | (3) | Home | D | 0-0 |
| | (R) | Away | L | 1-2 |
| 1957-58 | (6) | Home | W | 2-1 |
| 1978-79 | (4) | Away | L | 0-1 |
| 1982-83 | (3) | Home | L | 1-2 |
| 1990-91 | (3) | Home | D | 1-1 |
| | (R) | Away | L | 0-3 |

**Football League Cup**

| 1987-88 | (2) | Home | D | 1-1 |
|---|---|---|---|---|
| | | Away | L | 0-1 |

**Wartime**

| | | Home | | Away | |
|---|---|---|---|---|---|
| 1916-17 | (LSPT) | L | 0-2 | L | 1-3 |
| 1917-18 | (LSPT) | L | 1-6 | L | 0-7 |
| 1918-19 | (LSPT) | L | 1-2 | L | 0-1 |
| 1940-41 | (NRL) | L | 0-3 | D | 1-1 |
| 1941-42 | (FLNS-SC) | | | D | 0-0 |
| | | | | W | 3-2 aet* |
| 1945-46 | (FLN) | L | 0-5 | L | 0-4 |

*Both games were played away from home with the second game also being in the Lancashire Senior Cup.

**LIVINGSTONE, Stephen**
Centre-forward. 1991-1993.
*6ft 1in; 12st 7lb.*
*Born: Middlesbrough, 8 September 1969.*
*Debut: v Ipswich Town (h) 19 January 1991.*
*Career: Coventry City YTS August 1985, turning professional in July 1986; Blackburn Rovers January 1991 (£450,000); Chelsea March 1993 (in exchange for Graeme Le Saux); Port Vale loan September 1993; Grimsby Town loan October 1993, signing permanently in December 1993.*
**Appearances:** Premier League 1+1; Football League 24+4; FA Cup 1; Football League Cup 2; Total 28+5.
**Goals:** Football League 10; FA Cup 1; Total 11.
The son of Joe Livingstone, a former professional with Middlesbrough, Carlisle United and Hartlepool United, Steve moved to Ewood Park with Tony Dobson in January 1991. At Coventry he had created a major impact when asked to stand in for Kevin Drinkell in January 1990. Four goals in a League Cup replay against Sunderland were followed by three

goals in the next two League games. However, although Livingstone appeared, and scored, in the League Cup semi-final against Nottingham Forest, he was unable to win a regular place at Highfield Road.

Don Mackay returned to his former club to sign Livingstone and Dobson in a bid to lift the Rovers from the lower reaches of the Second Division. Livingstone, although looking a trifle slow, made an excellent start to his Ewood career with seven goals in his first ten games. The 1991-92 season saw him passed over for selection as questions were raised about his fitness. The departure of Don Mackay and the arrival of Kenny Dalglish brought little change to his position with David Speedie and the newly-arrived Mike Newell being given the striking positions. Even when Newell was injured Livingstone was overlooked as the club moved to bring Roy Wegerle to Ewood. Livingstone remained out of favour until the closing stages of the 1992-93 Cup competitions.

However, once the Rovers had lost their League Cup semi-final and FA Cup quarter-final, Livingstone was transferred to Chelsea as part of the deal which brought Graeme Le Saux to Blackburn. Livingstone had little luck at Stamford Bridge, being injured on his senior debut and sent off in his reserve-team debut. The appointment of Glenn Hoddle to the manager's position at Chelsea saw Livingstone loaned to Port Vale and Grimsby Town before a permanent transfer to the latter club was finalised.

**LOAN TRANSFERS**
Blackburn Rovers have a long tradition of taking players on loan from other clubs. In the days before the formation of the Football League the club borrowed players on several occasions to play in important FA Cup games. On 31 January 1879, Thomas Gibson, the Blackburn Olympic full-back, appeared for the Rovers in an FA Cup match with Nottingham Forest. This was the first occasion that the club used a player from another club in an FA Cup-tie.

However, the most famous example of these early loan deals occurred when George Haworth was borrowed from Accrington to appear in the 1885 FA Cup Final. Haworth had earlier appeared for the Rovers in the third round of the competition having missed out on Accrington's own FA Cup match against Southport. Ironically, although Accrington won that match, they were later ejected from the competition for fielding ineligible players. The Rovers helped Accrington out in September 1886 when Herbie Arthur was allowed to travel with 'Th' Owd Reds' to appear in two friendly fixtures in Scotland.

The Rovers became involved in a number of loan deals during the closing weeks of the 1897-98 season. Faced with relegation to the Second Division, the Rovers arranged for five former players to return to Ewood to try to lift the club out of danger. Geordie Anderson, Thomas Tierney and Joshua Hargreaves all came from New Brighton Tower, whilst Harry Marshall and Peter Turnbull returned from their Scottish clubs. Anderson, Hargreaves and Marshall also stayed to appear in the 'Test Match' series.

In February 1900 the Rovers signed Peter Somers from Celtic for £200 in a curious 'loan' transfer. Blackburn officials wanted Somers to remain in Blackburn after two very successful seasons with the club and offered Celtic an increased fee for his services. However, the Celtic manager insisted on his return and Somers departed for Scotland at the end of the 1901-02 season.

It was in the early 1970s that the loan system became an integral part of the transfer system. Since that time the Rovers have used it extensively to cover senior players who have been side-lined by injury and also as a means of looking at players before signing them on a permanent basis.

Players who have spent time at Ewood Park on loan in recent times include:

| Alcock T. | CH | Blackpool | December 1976 to January 1977 |
|---|---|---|---|
| Archibald S. | CF | Barcelona | December 1987 to May 1988 |
| Ardíles O.C. | M | Tottenham Hotspur | March to May 1988 |
| Arnott K.W. | M | Sunderland | November 1981 |
| | | & Sheffield United | November 1982 |
| Askew W. | M | Middlesbrough | March to May 1982 |
| Barton D. | CH | Newcastle United | August to October 1982 |
| Beardsmore R.P. | W | Manchester United | December 1991 |
| Beckford J. | F | Manchester City | March 1991 |
| Beglin J. | LB | Leeds United | October 1990 |
| Boyd, L.M. | CH | Leeds United | March 1972 |
| Byrne D.S. | M | Millwall | February 1989 |
| Crossley I.W. | G | Coventry City | March 1972 |
| Downes S.F. | F | Halifax Town | March to April 1976 |
| Farrell G.W. | LB | Wolverhampton Wanderers | October 1970 to January 1971 |
| Fear K. | IF | Bristol City | December 1977 to January 1978 |
| Foyle M.J. | F | Southampton | March 1984 |
| Gallagher B. | FB | Aston Villa | November to December 1990 |
| Gennoe T.W. | G | Bury | March 1974 |
| Gillibrand I.V. | M | Arsenal | January to March 1968 |

| Gray N.R | CH | Orient | October to November 1982 |
| Gregory D.H. | F | Stoke City | August to September 1978 |
| Grew M.S. | G | Port Vale | October to December 1990 |
| Hindson G. | OL | Luton Town | October to December 1975 |
| Hutt G. | LB | Huddersfield Town | September to October 1975 |
| Irvine J.A. | M | Dundee United | October to November 1989 |
| Lambert C.J.P. | W | Reading | August to September 1993 |
| Marriott A. | G | Nottingham Forest | December 1989 to January 1990 |
| Mimms R.A. | G | Everton | January to March 1987 |
| Outterside M.J. | RB | Sunderland | December 1985 to January 1986 |
| Rathbone M.J | FB | Birmingham City | March to April 1979 |
| Shanahan T.C. | M | Ipswich Town | September to October 1971 |
| Sherwood T.C. | M | Norwich City | February 1992 |
| Silvester P.D. | CF | Southend United | October to November 1976 |
| Starbuck P.M. | CF | Nottingham Forest | September 1990 |
| Sulley C.D. | FB | Dundee United | March to April 1987 |
| Thorley D. | M | Stoke City | March to May 1980 |
| Wagstaffe D | OL | Wolverhampton W | January to February 1976 |

Blackburn players who have spent time on loan to other clubs on recent times include:

| Agnew S.M. | M | Portsmouth | November to December 1992 |
| Ashworth P.A. | CF | AFC Bournemouth | September to October 1975 |
| Baah P.H. | W | Rotherham United | April 1992 |
| Brown R.A. | FB | Maidstone United | February to March 1991 |
| Byrom D.J. | CH | Chester City | October 1982 to January 1983 |
| Coddington J.W. | CH | Stockport County | January to March 1970 |
| Comstive P.T. | M | Rochdale | September to October 1982 |
| | | | & February to March 1983 |
| Conlon B. | CF | Crewe Alexandra | January to February 1972 |
| Curtis J. | RB | Wigan Athletic | March to April 1979 |
| Dewhurst R. | CH | Darlington | December 1991 to February 1992 |
| Diamond A.J. | CF | Wigan Athletic | October to November 1988 |
| Dickins M.J | G | Blackpool | January to April 1993 |
| | | & Lincoln City | November to December 1993 |
| Dobson A.J. | D | Portsmouth | September to December 1993 |
| Duxbury M. | FB | Bradford City | January to March 1992 |
| Fowler M. | M | Hartlepool United | March to May 1980 |
| Hamilton D. | M | Cardiff City | March to May 1985 |
| Hilton P.J. | OL | Gillingham | September to October 1975 |
| Holt M. | FB | Aston Villa | April 1992 |
| Ireland S.P. | OL | Mansfield Town | March to April 1994 |
| Johnrose L. | F | Preston North End | January to February 1992 |
| Keeley G.M. | CH | Everton | October to December 1982 |
| Murphy D.P. | F | Drogheda | October 1982 to January 1983 |
| | | & Bohemians | February to May 1983 |
| Needham A.P. | CF | Aldershot | March to April 1977 |
| O'Keefe J.V. | G | Bury | October 1983 |
| | | & Blackpool | December 1986 to January 1987 |
| | | | & February to May 1989 |
| Pearce C.L. | G | Rochdale | August to September 1980 |
| | | & Barnsley | September to October 1981 |
| Randell C.W. | M | Newport County | March 1984 |
| Salmon M.B. | G | Leeds United | August to September 1982 |
| Svarc R.L. | F | Watford | September 1977 |
| Talia F. | G | Hartlepool United | December 1992 to March 1993 |
| Thorne P.L. | F | Wigan Athletic | March to April 1994 |

## LOFTHOUSE, Joseph Morris
Forward. 1882-1887 & 1889-1893.
*5ft 8in; 11st 12lb.*
*Born: Witton, Blackburn, 14 April 1865; Died: 10 June 1919.*
*Debut: v Darwen (a) 2 December 1882 (FAC).*
*Career: Blackburn Grammar School; King's Own FC (Blackburn); Blackburn Rovers 1882; Accrington cs 1887; Blackburn Rovers cs 1889; Darwen September 1893; Walsall December 1893; Magyar Athletic Club, Budapest (Hungary) coach February 1902; New Brompton trainer 1902-03; Everton assistant trainer August 1903.*
*International honours with Blackburn Rovers: England: 6 caps (1885-90).*
*Domestic honours with Blackburn Rovers: FA Cup winners: 1884; 1885; 1890; 1891.*
**Appearances:** Football League 51; FA Cup 32; Total 83.
**Goals:** Football League 18; FA Cup 12; Total 30.
Although Joe Lofthouse played for a time in the centre and on the left-wing, it was as an outside-right that he had most success with Blackburn Rovers. Gifted with a rare turn of speed, Lofthouse loved to dribble past opponents and once in possession of the ball he was very difficult to dispossess. Lofthouse was noted for his accurate crosses and was fond of long range shooting. Lofthouse had been captain of the Grammar School team at the age of 11 and was later to captain the King's Own side. He joined the reserve team of Blackburn Rovers but was playing occasional

first-team games at the age of 16. Lofthouse left the Rovers in 1887 to play for Accrington for a couple of seasons but returned to the Rovers in 1889. He won four FA Cup winners' medals with the club and was capped by England on six occasions whilst with the Rovers. Lofthouse *pictured left)* also won an England cap whilst with Accrington.

## LOGAN, Neil
Half-back. 1902-1903.
*Debut: v Middlesbrough (h) 1 September 1902.*
*Career: Blantyre; Sheffield United November 1897; Swindon Town cs 1898; Blackburn Rovers June 1902.*
**Appearances:** Football League 22.
**Goals:** Football League 2.
Neil Logan had joined Sheffield United at the age of 18 and had also had experience with Swindon Town before joining Blackburn Rovers in June 1902. Although he began the season at left-half, Logan also had a spell at centre-half before finally being discarded in January 1903. He was released at the end of the season as his rather lethargic style of play seemed ill suited to the requirements of the Rovers.

## LONG SERVICE
Bob Crompton holds the record for the longest serving player in the history of Blackburn Rovers. The former England full-back completed 23 years and 7 months on the playing staff at Ewood Park before entering the boardroom and later the manager's office at Blackburn. In 1961 the Football League initiated a players' long service award with a statuette being presented to honour 20 years' loyal service with one club. The only Blackburn Rovers player to receive such an award was Ronnie Clayton in 1969.

## LONGMUIR, Archibald MacDonald
Forward. 1921-1923.
*5ft 9in; 11st.*
*Born: Ardrossan, Ayrshire, 17 April 1897.*
*Debut: v Birmingham (a) 26 November 1921.*
*Career: Ardrossan Winton Rovers; Glasgow Celtic 1920; Blackburn Rovers November 1921 (£1,000); Oldham Athletic August 1923 (£500); Wrexham June 1924 (£400) to May 1930.*
**Appearances:** Football League 24; FA Cup 5; Total 29.
**Goals:** Football League 2.
Although Archie Longmuir had gained a reputation as something of a sharpshooter in the Celtic reserve team, the goals certainly dried up during his stay at Ewood Park. Two seasons in which he failed to live up to his reputation ended with his transfer to Oldham Athletic for only half of what he had originally cost the Rovers. His time at Boundary Park was no more successful and within 12 months he had moved on to Wrexham. It was at the Racecourse Ground that his career finally took off when he was given a wide berth as opposed to the inside-forward position he had occupied at Ewood. He appeared in 223 League games and scored 36 goals for the Welsh club in six seasons.

## LORD, Frank
Centre-forward. 1966-1967.
*6ft; 12st 11lb.*
*Born: Chadderton, 13 March 1936.*
*Debut: v Millwall (h) 3 December 1966.*
*Career: Chadderton Secondary Modern School; Royton Amateurs; Rochdale October 1958; Crewe Alexandra July 1961 (£3,000); Plymouth Argyle November 1963 (£12,000); Stockport County February 1966; Blackburn Rovers December 1966 (£8,000), appointed youth-team coach cs 1967; Chesterfield August 1967; Plymouth Argyle player-coach October 1967; Preston North End caretaker-manager February to March 1973; Crystal Palace coach 1973 to July 1975; Cape Town (South Africa) manager late 1970s; Hereford United manager December 1979 to September 1982; Penang State (Malaysia) manager January 1983.*
**Appearances:** Football League 10.
**Goals:** Football League 1.
The signing of Frank Lord from Stockport County in December 1966 was seen as something of a gamble by Blackburn Rovers. Although the much travelled and powerfully built Lord had never been with any of football's elite, he was, none the less, a proven goalscorer in the lower divisions.

Eddie Quigley, the newly installed coach at Ewood Park, had managed Lord at Stockport and was keen to bring him to Blackburn. Lord had few frills to his game, but plenty of power and was noted for his aerial ability. The gamble didn't work and in the summer of 1967 Lord was put in charge of the youth team at Ewood Park. He moved to Chesterfield in August 1967 and began a coaching career which was to take him to various parts of the world. He returned to Ewood briefly in the 1980s in the role of chief scout.

**LOW, David**
Left-half. 1924-1927.
*5ft 8½in; 10st 10lb.*
*Born: New Herrington, 1904.*
*Debut: v Birmingham (h) 2 April 1925.*
*Career: New Herrington Swifts; Blackburn Rovers February 1924; Swindon Town June 1927; Crook Town cs 1933.*
**Appearances:** Football League 13.
Although small in stature, David Low was thought to have the makings of a fine half-back when he arrived at Ewood Park from the North-East. Low was a constructive player who, though lacking in inches, lacked nothing in courage or endeavour. However, with Harry Healless and Aussie Campbell firmly entrenched in the half-back positions, Low had to leave Ewood Park to find regular first-team football.

**LOWE, John**
Goalkeeper. 1890-1891.
*Born: Denton cs 1866; Died: Blackpool, 23 May 1911.*
*Debut: v Derby County (a) 6 September 1890.*
*Career: Denton; Blackburn Rovers January 1890; Bury 1891.*
**Appearances:** Football League 2.
On his debut at Derby, John Lowe contrived to pull the crossbar down on top of him. However, despite this rather embarrassing start, Lowe was believed to have the makings of an excellent goalkeeper. Sadly, nerves got the better of him in his second game with the senior team and the club allowed him to move to Bury. Lowe went on to appear in 26 League games for the Gigg Lane Club. Lowe, a painter by trade, died at the tragically early age of 45 due to the effects of lead poisoning.

**LOWEY, John Anthony**
Centre-forward/Midfield. 1980-1986.
*5ft 11in; 12st 7lb.*
*Born: Manchester, 7 March 1958.*
*Debut: v Bristol Rovers (h) 29 November 1980.*
*Career: Manchester United associated schoolboy 1973-74, becoming an apprentice in July 1974 and turning professional in March 1975; Chicago Sting; Port Vale July to August 1977; Blackburn Rovers non-contract player September 1977; Port Vale October 1977; California Surf; Sheffield Wednesday October 1978; Blackburn Rovers November 1980; Wigan Athletic July 1986; Chesterfield on loan November 1986; York City on loan March 1987; Preston North End August 1987; Chester City March 1988.*
**Appearances:** Football League 136+5; FA Cup 6; Football League Cup 9; Total 151+5.
**Goals:** Football League 14; FA Cup 1; Football League Cup 1; Total 16.
John Lowey was brought to Ewood Park by Howard Kendall in a bid to end the goal drought which threatened to disrupt the club's bid for a second successive promotion. Lowey was no stranger to Ewood Park having appeared with the Central League team as a non-contract player in September 1977. Lowey was unable to provide the firepower Kendall required and ended the 1980-81 season with two goals from 19 appearances.

Although he began the following campaign in the number-nine shirt, Lowey lost his place in the team following the arrival of Norman Bell in November. It was not until the second half of the 1982-93 campaign that Lowey returned to the team on a regular basis. By this time he was no longer regarded as a striker but had been converted into an industrious midfield player. Although not the most prolific of marksmen, Lowey was an ever-present in midfield during the 1983-84 season.

The following campaign saw him lose his place to Colin Randell, but Lowey returned to senior action again during the middle part of the 1985-86 season. Lowey left Ewood Park during the summer of 1986 but failed to make much impact at any of his subsequent clubs. Indeed, apart from his 42 League appearances (including seven as sub) with Sheffield Wednesday and his time at Blackburn, Lowey's appearances failed to reach double figures at any of his other clubs.

**LUKE, Charles**
Outside-right. 1938.
*5ft 3in.*
*Born: Esh Winning, Durham. 16 March 1909: Died: Whitstable, 16 October 1983.*

*Debut: v West Ham United (h) 5 February 1938.*
*Career: Bishop Auckland; Huddersfield Town January 1931; Sheffield Wednesday February 1936; Blackburn Rovers February 1938; Chesterfield December 1938.*
**Appearances:** Football League 10.
**Goals:** Football League 2.
A diminutive outside-right who came to Blackburn Rovers as a goalscoring winger but who failed to do himself justice at Ewood Park. Luke possessed plenty of pace and had developed into a tricky winger whilst with Huddersfield Town. A total of 40 goals in 130 League appearances at Leeds Road persuaded Sheffield Wednesday to sign him in February 1936. At Hillsborough, Luke scored eight goals in 42 League games before his transfer to Blackburn Rovers in February 1938. At Ewood, Luke was asked to fill in for Jack Bruton on the right wing but lost his place after only ten appearances. The arrival of Billy Rogers from Preston North End in June 1938 meant that Luke spent the 1938-39 campaign in the Central League until his move to Chesterfield in December 1938.

**LUTON TOWN FC**
Founded in 1885 by the amalgamation of Wanderers and Excelsior. Luton Town were one of the pioneers of professional football in the South of England and were elected to the Football League in 1897. The club failed to gain re-election in 1900 and didn't return to the Football League until 1920. Meetings between Blackburn Rovers and Luton Town have almost exclusively been in the Second Division.

**Football League**

| | | | Home | | Away | |
|---|---|---|---|---|---|---|
| 1937-38 | (Div 2) | D | 2-2 | L | 1-4 | |
| 1938-39 | (Div 2) | W | 2-0 | D | 1-1 | |
| 1948-49 | (Div 2) | W | 4-1 | L | 0-2 | |
| 1949-50 | (Div 2) | D | 0-0 | L | 2-5 | |
| 1950-51 | (Div 2) | W | 1-0 | D | 1-1 | |
| 1951-52 | (Div 2) | W | 2-1 | D | 1-1 | |
| 1952-53 | (Div 2) | D | 1-1 | L | 0-6 | |
| 1953-54 | (Div 2) | W | 2-0 | L | 1-2 | |
| 1954-55 | (Div 2) | D | 0-0 | L | 3-7 | |
| 1958-59 | (Div 1) | W | 3-1 | D | 1-1 | |
| 1959-60 | (Div 1) | L | 0-2 | D | 1-1 | |
| 1970-71 | (Div 2) | W | 1-0 | L | 0-2 | |
| 1975-76 | (Div 2) | W | 3-0 | D | 1-1 | |
| 1976-77 | (Div 2) | W | 1-0 | L | 0-2 | |
| 1977-78 | (Div 2) | W | 2-0 | D | 0-0 | |
| 1978-79 | (Div 2) | D | 0-0 | L | 1-2 | |
| 1980-81 | (Div 2) | W | 3-0 | L | 1-3 | |
| 1981-82 | (Div 2) | L | 0-1 | L | 0-2 | |

| | P | W | D | L | F | A |
|---|---|---|---|---|---|---|
| Home | 18 | 11 | 5 | 2 | 27 | 9 |
| Away | 18 | 0 | 7 | 11 | 15 | 43 |
| Total | 36 | 11 | 12 | 13 | 42 | 52 |

**FA Cup**

| | | | | | |
|---|---|---|---|---|---|
| 1952-53 | (3) | Away | L | 1-6 | |
| 1975-76 | (3) | Away | L | 0-2 | |

**McALLISTER, Thomas**
Inside-left. 1904-1906.
*5ft 9in; 12st.*
*Debut: v Aston Villa (h) 2 September 1905.*
*Career: Castleford Town; Blackburn Rovers March 1904; Brentford cs 1906; Leeds City May 1908 to 1910; Halifax Town.*
**Appearances:** Football League 2.
Contemporary critics generally agreed that Tom McAllister had a great deal to offer in terms of ability. 'A brainy footballer' is how the correspondent of *The Blackburn Times* described McAllister. However, disciplinary problems, and the consistency of Adam Bowman, restricted him to two appearances at senior level before joining Brentford in the summer of 1906. At Brentford he enjoyed better fortune and scored nine goals in 28 Southern League games in 1906-07. The following season he was joined at Brentford by Bowman, and during this season McAllister was converted into a left-half. In May 1908 he joined Leeds City and made 53 League appearances, mainly at right-half, before leaving in 1910.

**McCAIG, Robert A.M.**
Winger. 1948-1951.
*5ft 6in; 9st 3lb.*
*Born: Lockerbie, Dumfries, 15 August 1923.*
*Debut: v Leeds United (a) 29 January 1949.*

*Career: Lockerbie Accies; Queen of the South 1944; Carlisle United August 1948; Blackburn Rovers December 1948; Stockport County August 1951; Halifax Town January 1952; Crewe Alexandra August 1952 until March 1954.*
**Appearances:** Football League 30; FA Cup 2; Total 32.
**Goals:** Football League 2.
A record of four goals in four Central League matches was sufficient to earn Bob McCaig a rapid promotion to the first team at Ewood Park. The former Carlisle United player had only been with the club a month when he made his League debut at Elland Road in January 1949. Although McCaig, who had only five League appearances to his credit at Carlisle, retained his place for the next match his lack of experience saw him returned to Central League football. The following campaign brought two goals in 20 appearances and his ability to play on either wing suggested he would become a valuable asset to the squad. However, the opening seven games of the 1950-51 season proved to be his last and although the club appeared to have no automatic choice for the outside-right position, McCaig was allowed to join Stockport County in August 1951.

**McCALL, William**
Winger. 1920-1922.
*5ft 9in; 11st 2lb.*
*Born: Maxwellstown, c.1898.*
*Debut: v Middlesbrough (h) 18 December 1920.*
*Career: Queen of the South Wanderers; Blackburn Rovers December 1920; Wolverhampton Wanderers June 1922; Southampton January 1923 until May 1923; Queen of the South September 1925.*
**Appearances:** Football League 11.
Bill McCall became the season's fourth occupant of the outside-right position when he made his senior debut in December 1920. He was said to be a quick orthodox winger but, following the signing of Bert Ralphs in January 1921, his first-team appearances were few and far between. Three of his four appearances during the 1921-22 season were at inside-left and in June 1922 he moved to Wolves in a bid to find first-team football. However, after failing to make the senior team at Molineux, McCall moved to Southampton in January 1923. Although he scored on his debut for the Saints, McCall made only eight League appearances for the club before leaving The Dell in May 1923.

**McCALLUM, Neil**
Outside-right. 1890.
*Born: Bonhill, Dumbartonshire; Died: 5 November 1920.*
*Debut: v Burnley (a) 22 February 1890.*
*Career: Renton; Glasgow Celtic May 1888; Blackburn Rovers February 1890; Glasgow Celtic 1890; Nottingham Forest August 1892; Notts County June 1895; Heanor Town cs 1896.*
**Appearances:** Football League 2.
A hugely popular Scottish winger who enjoyed great success north of the border with Renton and Celtic. A typically tricky winger, McCallum was capped by Scotland whilst with Renton and also appeared for the Scottish League team. He won two Scottish Cup winners' medals with Celtic before coming to Blackburn in February 1890. McCallum only appeared twice for the Rovers before returning to Scotland and Celtic. His second venture in English football, with Nottingham Forest, was rather more successful as McCallum enjoyed a record of 13 goals in 37 League games.

**McCLEERY, William**
Inside-forward. 1924-1927.
*5ft 8in; 10st 6lb.*
*Born: Belfast.*
*Debut: v Arsenal (a) 4 October 1924.*
*Career: Queen's Island, Belfast; Blackburn Rovers May 1924 to cs 1927; Shelbourne cs 1927; Linfield 1927-28.*
**Appearances:** Football League 23; FA Cup 2; Total 25.
**Goals:** Football League 5.
Willie McCleery came to Blackburn with Fred Morton from the Queen's Island club of Belfast in May 1924. The two players had formed the left-wing partnership for Queen's Island when the club lifted the 1923-24 Irish championship. A former amateur international, McCleery was a quick and clever individualist who could play in either of the inside-forward positions. In 1924-25 he scored five goals in 22 League games with the Rovers and appeared set for a bright future at Ewood. However, the following campaign saw him restricted to only one senior appearance and in the summer of 1927 he returned to Ireland to join Shelbourne. During the 1927-28 season he was transferred to Linfield and went on to win nine Irish caps whilst with that club.

**McCLELLAND, Charles**
Inside-left. 1948-1949.
*5ft 7½in; 9st 4lb.*

*Born: Manchester, 8 January 1924.*
*Debut: v Nottingham Forest (a) 22 January 1949.*
*Career: Bolton Wanderers wartime guest 1943-44 and 1944-45; Hyde United; Blackburn Rovers August 1946; Droylsden on loan November 1946; Hyde United on loan November 1946; Exeter City June 1949; Portland United cs 1955; Cheltenham Town.*
**Appearances:** Football League 13; FA Cup 5; Total 18.
**Goals:** Football League 2; FA Cup 5; Total 7.
Charlie McClelland was born on the day that his father scored five goals for Middlesbrough in an FA Cup-tie against Leeds United. Jimmy McClelland represented Raith Rovers, Southend United, Middlesbrough, Bolton Wanderers, Preston North End, Blackpool and Bradford between the wars, so it was not surprising that Charlie should follow in his father's footsteps. He began his career with Bolton Wanderers during the war but moved to Ewood Park from Hyde United in August 1946. He failed to win a regular place in the Blackburn side and appeared to save his best games for the FA Cup. Whilst at Ewood Park, McClelland had the unusual experience of appearing for three clubs – Droylsden, Hyde United and Blackburn Rovers – within a week in November 1946. He moved to Exeter in June 1949 and scored 60 goals for the Grecians in 183 League appearances.

**McCLURE, Samuel**
Centre-half. 1899-1906.
*5ft 10½in; 12st 9lb.*
*Born: Workington, 11 February 1878; Died: Workington, 17 July, 1906.*
*Debut: v Aston Villa (a) 23 September 1899.*
*Career: St Michael's School, Workington; Black Diamonds, Workington; Everton May 1898; Black Diamonds; Blackburn Rovers April 1899.*
**Appearances:** Football League 144; FA Cup 8; Total 152.
**Goals:** Football League 12.
Sam McClure was probably one of the finest natural athletes to wear the blue and white shirt of Blackburn Rovers. At school he had been an outstanding sportsman before beginning his footballing career in the Cumberland Senior League with Black Diamonds FC of Workington. At the time McClure was playing as a goalkeeper and Everton were quick to spot his potential and signed him in May 1898. Unable to break into the senior team on Merseyside, McClure returned to Black Diamonds and began to appear in outfield positions.

When Everton cancelled his registration officials of Blackburn Rovers were quick to snap him up as an outfield player. Although McClure was eventually to find his niche in the centre-half position, his ability to play at wing-half and in the forward line made him a valued utility player. Tall and quick, McClure had both agility and strength and although he was capable of delicate artistry on the field, his rugged approach meant that it was impossible for opponent's to physically intimidate him. As one would expect, McClure was not only a popular teammate, but was also a hugely popular figure with the supporters.

In 1904, a bout of illness affected McClure so badly that it threatened to bring his career to a premature end. However, his battling nature and great inner strength enabled him to recover sufficiently to become a regular with the reserves and make occasional first-team appearances. Sadly, although his mischievous sense of humour remained intact, McClure was no longer the player he had been. Tragedy struck in July 1906 when McClure was again struck down by ill health, but this time there was to be no recovery. An abscess in the ear spread inwards towards the brain and a life lived to the full with seemingly boundless energy was ended at the age of 28.

**McCULLOCH, Samuel S.**
Centre-half. 1926-1929.
*5ft 9in; 11st 6lb.*
*Born: Glasgow, 21 May 1906.*
*Debut: v West Bromwich Albion (h) 19 April 1927.*
*Career: Petershill FC; Blackburn Rovers September 1926; Thames Association September 1929; Accrington Stanley August 1931; Bury May 1936; Leyland Motors October 1938.*
**Appearances:** Football League 1.
During his three years with Blackburn Rovers Sam McCulloch was never regarded as anything more than second-team material. With Bill Rankin firmly entrenched in the first team, McCulloch moved south to Thames Association in September 1929. He was with the London club when they gained admission to the Football League in 1930, but returned to Lancashire in 1931 to join Accrington Stanley. He appeared in 188 League games for Stanley before moving to Bury in May 1936. Despite his consistency at Accrington, McCulloch was unable to break into the senior team at Gigg Lane.

**McDONALD, Gerard**
Midfield. 1969-1973.
*5ft 7½in; 9st 6lb.*

*Born: Milnthorpe, 3 December 1952.*
*Debut: v Rotherham United (h) 14 August 1971.*
*Career: Blackburn Rovers apprentice May 1969, turning professional in August 1971; Halifax Town July 1973 to June 1974.*
**Appearances:** Football League 19+2; FA Cup 0+2; Football League Cup 3; Total 22+4.
**Goals:** Football League 2.
Despite limited Central League experience, Gerry McDonald was thrown into the rigours of Third Division football at the start of the 1971-72 season. His youthful enthusiasm was utilised in midfield by Ken Furphy during the first four months of the campaign. However, as the demands of first-team football began to take their toll on the young McDonald, Furphy replaced him with David Bradford. McDonald didn't appear for the club during the 1972-73 season and was allowed to join Halifax Town at the end of that campaign. McDonald was to make 13 League appearances (including three as sub) whilst at the Shay.

### McDONALD, John
Right-back. 1903-1905.
*Born: Ayr, 1882.*
*Debut: v Stoke (a) 31 October 1903.*
*Career: Arden Villa; Ayr FC; Blackburn Rovers May 1903 (£90); Leeds City July 1905; Grimsby Town August 1906; Queen's Park Rangers cs 1907 to 1913.*
**Appearances:** Football League 1.
Although he had earned a good reputation for himself with Ayr FC in the Scottish Second Division, John McDonald was not a success at Ewood Park. Tall and strong, McDonald made his debut for Blackburn at centre-half when Stoke crushed the Rovers by six goals to two on the Victoria Ground. The following match saw Sam McClure restored to the first team and McDonald reverted to his former role of understudy to Bob Crompton. He left Ewood at the end of the 1904-05 season and enjoyed more successful spells with Leeds City and Grimsby Town. In 1908 he was a member of the Queen's Park Rangers side which won the Southern League championship.

### McDONALD, John
Inside-forward. 1920-1922.
*5ft 8in; 11st 4lb.*
*Born: Glasgow.*
*Debut: v Sunderland (a) 5 April 1920.*
*Career: Linfield; Blackburn Rovers March 1920 (£800); Dundee July 1922 to 1925.*
**Appearances:** Football League 33; FA Cup 2; Total 35.
**Goals:** Football League 7.
A club mate of David Rollo at Linfield before signing for Blackburn in March 1920. McDonald was an inside-forward who specialised in creating chances for others and won a regular place in the team during the 1920-21 season. Unfortunately, a serious knee injury restricted him to just 16 appearances and although seven other players were tried in the inside-right position it was McDonald who caught the eye. The following season he failed to regain his earlier form and was discarded as Jock McKay and Johnny McIntyre arrived at the club.

### McEVOY, Matthew Andrew
Inside-forward/Half-back. 1956-1967.
*5ft 8¾in; 11st 4lb.*
*Born: Dublin, 15 July 1938; Died: Bray, May 1994.*
*Debut: v Luton Town (h) 20 April 1959.*
*Career: Bray Wanderers; Blackburn Rovers October 1956; Limerick August 1967.*
*International honours with Blackburn Rovers: Republic of Ireland: 17 caps (1961-67).*
**Appearances:** Football League 183; FA Cup 17; Football League Cup 13; Total 213.
**Goals:** Football League 89; FA Cup 10; Football League Cup 4; Total 103.

Andy McEvoy was a perfect example of the team that became known as 'Marshall's Misfits'. Originally an indifferent inside-forward, McEvoy was later converted into a wing-half and held down a regular first-team place during the second half of the 1960-61 season. However, when Mick McGrath was restored to the senior team, McEvoy returned for a further spell in Central League football. It was Jack Marshall who finally transformed McEvoy's career when he converted him back into an inside-forward and saw him become one of the deadliest marksmen in the First Division. McEvoy had been moved to partner Fred Pickering in the forward line during the latter part of the 1962-63 season. Although the move was not an instant success, Marshall was prepared to give the partnership time to develop. The manager's patience was rewarded the following season when McEvoy scored 32 goals in 37 League games.

A regular in the Republic of Ireland side, McEvoy was the archetypal goal poacher. Always lurking in and around the penalty area, his blistering pace and deadly finishing were a lethal combination. Without doubt, McEvoy owed much of his success to the genius of Bryan Douglas in midfield. It was Douglas who carved out many of the opportunities which McEvoy and Pickering converted with unerring regularity. In 1963-64, the partnership seemed destined to take the club to the brink of championship success until the sale of Pickering to Everton shattered all title aspirations. Although he had to adjust to a new partner, in the shape of John Byrom, during the 1964-65 season, McEvoy still managed to score 29 goals in 40 League games to finish the First Division's joint leading goalscorer with Jimmy Greaves.

Like so many of his colleagues, McEvoy enjoyed little success during the relegation campaign of 1965-66, saving his best performances for the FA Cup. Relegation to the Second Division affected McEvoy more than most and he spent much of the 1966-67 campaign in the championship winning Central League team. Disillusioned with professional football, McEvoy returned to Ireland to become a tram driver and play football for Limerick on a part-time basis. McEvoy continued to appear for the Irish club until the early 1970s.

### MacFARLANE, Robert
Full-back. 1893.
*Debut: v Burnley (h) 18 November 1893.*
*Career: Paisley St Mirren; Blackburn Rovers November 1893; Nelson December 1893; Blackburn Rovers 1894; Everton November 1894; Liverpool December 1894.*
**Appearances:** Football League 2.
Robert MacFarlane had the misfortune to be used as a pawn in a game which would see Tom Brandon return to Blackburn Rovers. Brandon had announced his wish to leave Sheffield Wednesday, the club he had joined from Blackburn in 1891, and having failed to reach agreement with the Yorkshire club had joined Nelson at the start of the 1893-94 season. However, it was well known that Brandon was wanted by Blackburn and that the player was equally keen to return to the club. MacFarlane, a strapping young Scot from St Mirren, had been blooded in a friendly with Aston Villa on 13 November 1893. Five days later he made his League debut when influenza kept John Murray out of the team.

However, with Jimmy Forrest preferred as partner to Murray and the Rovers keen to obtain Tom Brandon's release from Sheffield Wednesday, MacFarlane attempted to return to Scotland. On 9 December, MacFarlane received a surprise recall to the senior team but within the week he had been registered with Nelson. The move to Nelson followed Wednesday's agreement to the transfer of Brandon to Blackburn and the Rovers allowed Nelson to have MacFarlane for the remainder of the season. Although registered with Blackburn for the 1894-95 season, MacFarlane did not reappear in the first team and was transferred to Everton in November 1894. He ended his playing career with Liverpool before quitting the game to join the police force on Merseyside.

### McGHIE, Alexander
Forward. 1910-1920.
*5ft 9in; 11st.*
*Born: Liverpool.*
*Debut: v Sunderland (h) 8 October 1910.*
*Career: Liscard Central; Kirkdale; Ashton Town; Blackburn Rovers April 1910 to cs 1920.*
*Domestic honours with Blackburn Rovers: First Division championship: 1913-14 (9 apps, 3 gls).*
**Appearances:** Football League 23; FA Cup 2; Total 25.
**Goals:** Football League 3.
Alex McGhie could play with equal success in any of the forward positions, although it was at outside-right that he enjoyed his greatest success. Although he remained on the playing staff for ten years, McGhie never really established himself as a first-team regular. The fact that outside-right was his best position and that the club had paid a record fee to give Jock Simpson that role probably explains his lack of success. However, as a utility forward, McGhie proved a great asset to the club. McGhie, who also scored one goal in 42 wartime appearances for the club, acted as assistant secretary for a time during his playing career at Blackburn.

## McGORRIGHAN, Francis Owen

Inside-left. 1947.
*5ft 11½in; 11st 8lb.*
*Born: Easington, Co Durham, 20 November 1921.*
*Debut: v Derby County (h) 15 February 1947.*
*Career: Durham Schools; Easington Colliery Welfare; Horden Colliery Welfare; Eppleton Colliery Welfare; Middlesbrough amateur March 1944, turning professional in April 1944; Carlisle United 1945-46; Hull City August 1946; Blackburn Rovers February 1947 (£6,000); Hull City September 1947; Southport July 1948 until January 1949; Scarborough August 1950; Wisbech Town 1952. Retired through injury c.1953.*
**Appearances:** Football League 5.
A play-making inside-forward, Frank McGorrighan was added to the Ewood staff immediately after the signings of Jock Weir and Jack Oakes from Scotland. He went straight into the first team but had to make way for the newly arrived Alec Venters after only four matches. Like Oakes and Weir, McGorrighan failed to make much impact at Ewood Park and in September 1947 he was allowed to return to Hull City.

## McGRATH, Michael

Left-half. 1954-1966
*5ft 8in; 11st 11lb.*
*Born: Dublin, 7 April 1936.*
*Debut: v Nottingham Forest (a) 28 April 1955.*
*Career: Home Farm; Blackburn Rovers August 1954; Bradford August 1966; Bangor City.*
*International honours with Blackburn Rovers: Republic of Ireland: 18 caps (1958-65); Republic of Ireland 'B': 1 cap (1957); Football League: 1 appearance (1960).*
*Domestic honours with Blackburn Rovers: FA Cup runners-up: 1960.*
**Appearances:** Football League 268; FA Cup 29; Football League Cup 15; Total 312.
**Goals:** Football League 8; FA Cup 3; Football League Cup 1; Total 12.

Mick McGrath was a quiet Irishman who, together with Ronnie Clayton and Matt Woods, formed one of the most formidable half-back lines in the club's history. McGrath was one of a number of young Irish players brought to the club by Johnny Carey during the mid-1950s. Although he arrived at Ewood in August 1954, McGrath had to wait until the start of the 1957-58 season before finally winning a regular place at left-half. He appeared in all 42 League games that season as the Rovers won promotion to the First Division on the final day of the campaign.

A hard-tackling, attacking half-back, McGrath quickly became a regular in the Republic of Ireland team and in 1960 he also appeared for the Football League against the League of Ireland at Ewood Park. A member of the ill-fated 1960 FA Cup Final team, McGrath had the misfortune to put through his own goal to open the scoring for Wolves. A perfect clubman, McGrath retained his place under Jack Marshall until March 1966 when he joined Bradford.

At Park Avenue he had the distinction of being the last Bradford player to win an international cap and, not surprisingly, he was also made club captain. After making 50 League appearances for Bradford he moved into non-League football to join Northern Premier League club Bangor City. In later years he helped out with the Rovers' youth teams and then became involved in local junior soccer. Today he still lives in the Brownhill district of Blackburn.

## McGROGAN, Felix

Outside-left. 1934-1936.
*5ft 8in; 10st 6lb.*
*Born: Dumbarton, 27 July 1914.*
*Debut: v Manchester City (h) 12 October 1935.*
*Career: Renfrew FC; Blackburn Rovers September 1934; Dunfermline Athletic June 1936; Falkirk May 1937; Kilmarnock January 1938; Dumbarton August 1940; Third Lanark August 1943.*
**Appearances:** Football League 4.
**Goals:** Football League 1.

A speedy type of winger who collected his fair share of goals in a career spent almost exclusively in Scottish football. Unfortunately, his one spell in England, with Blackburn Rovers, proved something of a disappointment. At the time of his signing he was thought to be a fine prospect whose play was in the mould of Jack Bruton. However, although he possessed the ability to cross accurately, McGrogan was unable to retain his place after a run of four games in the autumn of 1935 and returned to his native Scotland the following summer.

## McINTYRE, Hugh

Half-back. 1879-1886.
*Born: Glasgow, 27 June 1885.*
*Debut: v Darwen (h) 6 December 1879 (FAC).*
*Career: Glasgow Northern; Partick Thistle; Glasgow Rangers 1878-79; Blackburn Rovers guest appearances during 1879-80, signing permanently in 1880.*
*Domestic honours with Blackburn Rovers: FA Cup winners: 1884; 1885; 1886; FA Cup runners-up: 1882.*
**Appearances:** FA Cup 34.
**Goals:** FA Cup 4.
Perhaps the most versatile player ever to wear the blue and white colours of Blackburn Rovers. During his time with the club McIntyre occupied goalkeeping, full-back, half-back, centre-half and centre-forward positions with equal aplomb. The former Partick Thistle man was one of the triumphant of Scots – Suter and Douglas being the others – that formed the basis of the successful FA Cup winning sides of the 1880s. McIntyre had first come to the notice of Blackburn officials during friendly matches with Partick Thistle.

His reputation was further enhanced during a spell with Rangers and the 1879-80 season saw him making occasional guest appearances for the Rovers. The 1880-81 season saw McIntyre move to Blackburn on a permanent basis and so end his international career after only one Scottish cap. However, the loss of international honours was compensated with four FA Cup Final appearances and three winners' medals. McIntyre, although he possessed as much footballing finesse as any of his colleagues, was the man who brought a touch of 'steel' to the Blackburn side. His professional standing, like so many of the Scottish imports of the period, was somewhat vague. There is no doubt that Blackburn Rovers paid McIntyre for his services but it is also probable that club helped him to find employment within the town. Although an upholsterer by profession, McIntyre was eventually to become a very successful hotelier.

An all round athlete, McIntyre appeared as wicketkeeper for Lancashire and in the late 1880s he found employment in South America as a groundsman at a cricket club. By 1886-87, McIntyre was making only limited appearances for the Rovers, almost all of which were in goal, and it was believed that he eventually moved to London.

## McINTYRE, John McGregor

Inside-forward/Left-half. 1922-1928.
*5ft 9in; 11st.*
*Born: Glasgow, 4 January 1895; Died: Blackpool, February 1974.*
*Debut: v Oldham Athletic (h) 14 January 1922.*
*Career: Denny Athletic; Partick Thistle August 1912; Fulham February 1917; Sheffield Wednesday March 1920; Blackburn Rovers January 1922; Blackpool January 1928.*

**Appearances:** Football League 175; FA Cup 19; Total 194.
**Goals:** Football League 38.
John McIntyre began his professional career in Scotland with Partick Thistle in August 1912 and was reported to earn 30 shillings per week, plus an extra ten shillings whenever he made the League team. He made his debut on 7 September 1912 against Falkirk and went on to enjoy a successful career in England with Fulham and Sheffield Wednesday. It was whilst at Hillsborough that an unsuccessful attempt was made to convert McIntyre into a centre-forward. It was his reputation as a goal maker which attracted Blackburn Rovers and after arriving at Ewood Park he was quickly integrated into the team as a scheming inside-forward. However, four goals in five minutes against Everton at Ewood on 16 September 1922 showed he still had a flair for goals. During his time at Blackburn he had a spell on the left wing before ending his Ewood career at left-half. Despite his ageing legs, McIntyre readily adapted to his deeper role and proved just as successful

in the half-back line as he had as an inside-forward. In January 1928 he moved to Blackpool and ended his career at Bloomfield Road.

## McIVER, William

Goalkeeper. 1901-1908.
*5ft 9in; 11st 4lb.*
*Born: Whittle-le-Woods, 1877; Died: Darwen, 10 April 1934.*
*Debut: v Stoke (a) 19 October 1901.*
*Career: Whittle-le-Woods; Darwen; Blackburn Rovers July 1901; Brentford June 1908; West Hartlepools; Stockport County August 1911; Darwen; Nelson; Blackburn Trinity; Blackburn Rovers wartime guest 1916-17.*
**Appearances:** Football League 126; FA Cup 6; Total 132.
Although one of the smallest goalkeepers in the Football League, Billy McIver proved to be a fairly reliable custodian during his seven years at Ewood Park. Equally adept at dealing with high and low shots, McIver had to endure a number of false dawns to his Ewood career. 'Tiny' Joyce and Bob Evans both displaced McIver after the former Darwen 'keeper had appeared to have won the position as number one goalkeeper at the club. However, on each occasion that he was relegated to the second team McIver fought back to reclaim his first-team place. Unfortunately, despite his brilliant agility, a lack of inches was deemed as a major weakness in his armoury and in May 1908 the club signed Jimmy Ashcroft from Woolwich Arsenal.

McIver was given a free transfer and joined the colony of former Blackburn players who made the trek to Brentford. Whilst with Brentford, McIver appeared in 40 Southern League games for the club and on 3 April 1909 he scored two penalties against Millwall whilst playing in goal. The years before World War One found McIver playing in local non-League football but in 1916-17 he was again to be found between the posts at Ewood as a wartime guest. McIver also appeared in two games in 1918-19 and made a total of 22 wartime appearances for the club.

## McKAY, John

Inside-forward. 1921-1927.
*5ft 7½in; 10st.*
*Born: Glasgow, 1 November 1898.*
*Debut: v Huddersfield Town (h) 12 November 1921.*
*Career: Boys Bridge football; St Anthony's c.1916; Glasgow Celtic 1919; Blackburn Rovers November 1921; Middlesbrough March 1927 (£3,750); Hibernian cs 1936 to 1937.*
*International honours with Blackburn Rovers: Scotland: 1 cap (1924).*
**Appearances:** Football League 150; FA Cup 11; Total 161.
**Goals:** Football League 46; FA Cup 3; Total 49.

Jock McKay and Archie Longmuir were signed from Celtic in a double deal in November 1921. McKay, still very much a reserve at Parkhead, had scored six goals in ten League appearances during his two seasons with Celtic. The curly-haired McKay arrived at Ewood Park at a time when the club was trying to regain its position as one of the country's premier First Division sides. Although not the tallest of forwards, McKay was capable of the most intricate pieces of footwork and his mesmerising dribbling ability was matched with a powerful shot.

Sadly, McKay was unable to provide the consistency needed for success at either team or individual level. McKay was capped by Scotland in 1924 but a tendency towards showmanship probably cost him an extended run in the national side. At Ewood his most productive seasons were between 1922 and 1925 when he scored 12 goals in each campaign. A number of these goals came from the penalty-spot and the natural showman in McKay turned each spot kick into a game within a game. A succession of feints and jinks often left the opposing goalkeeper totally bemused before McKay actually kicked the ball.

Having failed to hold down a regular first-team place during the previous 12 months, McKay left Ewood Park for Middlesbrough in March 1927. He scored 19 goals in 104 matches for Middlesbrough and was their reserve-team coach for a time before returning to Scotland to join Hibernian in 1936.

## MACKAY, Donald Scrimgeour

Manager. 1987-1991.
*Born: Partick, 19 March 1940.*
*Career: Forfar Athletic October 1958 to June 1962; Dundee United July 1962 to June 1972; Southend United July 1972 to July 1974; Bristol City coach July 1974 until March 1978; Norresundby (Denmark) coach March 1978 until June 1980; Dundee manager June 1980 until December 1983; Coventry City assistant manager October 1984, then manager December 1984 until April 1986; Glasgow Rangers reserve & youth manager April 1986 until February 1987; Blackburn Rovers manager February 1987 until September 1991; Fulham manager January 1992 until March 1994.*

Don Mackay is a member of the small band of former goalkeepers who have gone on to make a successful career in management. Mackay spent most of his playing career in Scotland as a goalkeeper with Forfar Athletic and Dundee United before crossing the border to end his playing days with Southend United. After hanging up his gloves he turned to

coaching at Bristol City and also experienced football in Denmark as well as gaining managerial experience with Dundee. Mackay became assistant manager to Bobby Gould at Coventry City and in December 1984 he was promoted to the manager's position following Gould's departure from Highfield Road. He clashed with the directors over club policy and resigned as manager in April 1986.

He returned to Scotland and Glasgow Rangers and became youth and reserve-team manager at Ibrox under Graeme Souness. His appointment to the vacant managership of Blackburn Rovers in February 1987 came as something of a surprise to the majority of supporters.

The new manager was a complete contrast to his predecessor at Ewood Park. Whereas Bobby Saxton had seemed ill at ease with the media, Mackay, a more gregarious character, appeared to relish the challenge of promoting the name of Blackburn Rovers. His audacious raids into the transfer market to bring Steve Archibald, Ossie Ardíles, Kevin Moran and Frank Stapleton to Ewood Park captured wide media attention. Mackay appointed Tony Parkes as his assistant and kept faith with the rest of the backroom team following his arrival from Rangers. However, on the field he found he had inherited an ageing team that needed to be dismantled and rebuilt.

Mackay quickly set about the task and returned to Scotland to bring Colin Hendry and Chris Sulley to Blackburn from Dundee and Dundee United respectively. Indeed, throughout his reign as manager Blackburn supporters had to become accustomed to Scottish accents as Mackay brought a number of his fellow countrymen to Ewood Park. Mackay made a favourable impression on everyone at the club during his first few months in charge. During this period he led the club to Wembley for the first time since 1960 and returned victorious with the Full Members' Cup.

Whilst recognising the financial limitations of the club, Mackay was anything but timid in his approach to the transfer market. In December 1987 he rocked the football world when he took Steve Archibald on an extended loan deal from Barcelona. In March 1988 he followed this up by reuniting Archibald with Ossie Ardíles, the former Argentinian World Cup star who had played with Archibald at Tottenham Hotspur. Although the ultimate prize of promotion eluded him, Mackay justifiably felt that he had gone a long way in refuting the accusation that Blackburn lacked ambition.

Although he refrained from any major signings, Mackay's second season at Ewood proved even more successful than the first. Mackay was able to keep the team in the leading group in the Second Division without recourse to the type of transfer activity which a number of competing clubs had become involved in. Although his own signings were far more modest by comparison, he none the less moulded them into a competitive unit which was more than a match for some of the so called glamour sides of the division.

A 3-1 lead in the first leg of the 1988-89 Play-off Final against Crystal Palace appeared to signal the end of the club's long exile from the First Division. However, once again promotion proved elusive as Palace gained a 3-0 victory in the second leg to claim the final promotion place.

If Blackburn Rovers ended the 1988-89 season in a far healthier state than they started it the fact remained that the failure to gain promotion was a major blow to everyone at the club. The 1989-90 season brought further big name players to Ewood Park in the shape of Frank Stapleton from Le Havre and Kevin Moran from Sporting Gijon. However, this was the season when Mackay was to have his managerial abilities put to the test. A dispute with Colin Hendry ended in the popular young Scot leaving Ewood to join Manchester City.

Mackay put his faith in youngsters like Keith Hill and David May and, when they made the mistakes which go with youth, the manager found himself under fire from the terraces. Surprisingly, for a man who had been so active in the transfer market, it was his failure to strengthen the team in the wake of indifferent performances which saw the manager under the same sort of fire that Bob Saxton had faced in 1984-85.

Although the Rovers reached the Play-offs for the third successive season, an early exit at the hands of Swindon Town brought renewed criticism of Mackay's management. The 1990-91 season found the Rovers entrenched at the foot of the Second Division and facing the very real possibility of being relegated to the Third Division. Fortunately, an influx of capital from Jack Walker enabled Mackay to bring Bobby Mimms, Tony Dobson and Steve Livingstone to the club for the sort of fees that the club had never before been able to afford.

With Second Division survival achieved, Mackay spent the summer of 1991 trying to attract big name players to Ewood Park. However, attempts to sign Teddy Sherringham and Gary Lineker failed to materialise and Mackay had to be content with the signings of Stuart Munro and Steve Agnew. On the eve of the season David Speedie was added to the new arrivals and the 1991-92 campaign began with a genuine air of optimism. Unfortunately, the opening results were a major disappointment and after only two weeks of the new campaign Don Mackay became the first managerial casualty of the season.

In January 1992 he joined Fulham and lifted the club from the lower reaches of the Third Division to the brink of the play-off positions. Ironically, at a time when Blackburn Rovers could afford to pay record transfer fees, Mackay again found himself having to ply his trade at a club with limited financial resources. His reign at Craven Cottage came to a surprising end in March 1994 and following his dismissal Fulham slipped into the relegation zone and found themselves dropping into the Third Division at the end of the season.

## McKEE, William A.

Half-back. 1949-1953.
*5ft 8½in; 11st.*
*Born: Warrington, 6 June 1928.*
*Debut: v Chesterfield (a) 21 April 1951.*
*Career: Earlestown; Blackburn Rovers November 1949.*
**Appearances:** Football League 1.

McKee was brought to Ewood as a junior in November 1949 and made his Central League debut in the derby match with Burnley at Ewood Park on 29 April 1950. He gave an excellent performance at right-half and appeared in 24 Central League matches during the 1950-51 campaign. It was during this season that McKee found himself thrust into first-team action for an end of season encounter with Chesterfield. The experience was not a happy one for McKee who, according to one report, endured 'a chastening experience' during a 4-1 defeat. He returned to the Central League team for two more seasons before being given a free transfer at the end of the 1952-53 season.

## McKENZIE, Duncan

Forward. 1979-1981.
*5ft 9in; 11st.*
*Born: Grimsby, 10 June 1950.*
*Debut: v Preston North End (h) 24 March 1979.*
*Career: Nottingham Forest amateur July 1967, turning professional in July 1968; Mansfield Town on loan March 1970; Mansfield Town on loan February 1973 to March 1973; Leeds United August 1974; Anderlecht June 1976; Everton December 1976; Chelsea September 1978; Blackburn Rovers March 1979 (£80,000); Tulsa Roughnecks 1981; Chicago Sting; Hong Kong football.*
**Appearances:** Football League 74; FA Cup 8; Football League Cup 8; Total 90.
**Goals:** Football League 16; FA Cup 1; Football League Cup 4; Total 21.

A brilliant individualist who had the misfortune to parade his silky skills at a time when 'work-rate' was king. In an age when the 'entertainer' was often castigated rather than complimented, McKenzie became one of football's nomads. Although constantly in demand, McKenzie rarely stayed at a club for any length of time despite being hugely popular with the spectators.

McKenzie was not a midfielder in the modern sense of the word, nor was he an out-and-out striker. He was, quite simply, one of the finest dribblers to grace a football field and his ability to turn defences inside out was a throw back to a different era. McKenzie was brought to Ewood Park by John Pickering in a last ditch effort to keep the club in the Second Division. A club record fee of £80,000 was paid for McKenzie but he arrived too late to save the club from a second spell of Third Division

football. That promotion back to the Second Division was achieved in one season was as much down to McKenzie's attacking flair as Howard Kendall's defensive organisation. McKenzie delighted the public of Blackburn with his dazzling displays which left many Third Division defences in tatters.

Although he held his place for the first half of the 1980-81 season, it became clear that Kendall did not see McKenzie as a long term fixture in his Blackburn team. Early in 1981, Kendall agreed to allow McKenzie to move to Tulsa Roughnecks in a deal which brought Viv Busby to Ewood Park. After spells in America and Hong Kong, McKenzie returned to England to live on Merseyside and became a radio and newspaper correspondent and popular after-dinner speaker.

## McKEOWN, Thomas Michael

Left-back. 1891-1892.
*Born: Lugar, Ayrshire, 1869; Died: Glasgow, 26 October 1903.*
*Debut: v Aston Villa (a) 5 September 1891.*
*Career: Lugar Boswell; Hibernian 1887; Glasgow Celtic cs 1888; Blackburn Rovers August 1891; Morton cs 1892; Cowlairs May 1893; Hamilton Harp January 1896; Lugar Boswell September 1896; Hibernian June 1897; Carfin October 1897; Lugar Boswell October 1899.*
**Appearances:** Football League 19; FA Cup 2; Total 21.

The departure of Tom Brandon for Sheffield Wednesday resulted in the arrival for the experienced Mick McKeown from Scotland. The signing of the former Scottish international was seen as something of a stop-gap measure and it soon became clear that he was severely lacking in terms of pace. However, McKeown quickly learned to used his head to outsmart his opponents and, after an indifferent start to the season, he settled into the left-back position. His clever positional play and sound clearances suggested that he would be retained and it came as something of a surprise when he was released at the end of the 1891-92 season. McKeown returned to Scotland but was to die at a tragically early age when he was asphyxiated whilst cleaning out a vat at a bottle works in 1903.

## McKINNELL, James Templeton Broadfoot

Left-half. 1920-1926.
*5ft 9in; 11st 3lb.*
*Born: Dalbeattie, Dumfries, 27 March 1895.*
*Debut: v Middlesbrough (a) 1 January 1921.*
*Career: Queen of the South 1919; Blackburn Rovers December 1920; Darlington July 1926 (£300); Nelson July 1929 to cs 1930; Northampton Town assistant trainer August 1933.*
**Appearances:** Football League 111; FA Cup 13; Total 124.

Jimmy McKinnell experienced a disappointing start to his Blackburn career following his move from Scotland in December 1920. He made ten appearances in both inside-forward positions during the 1920-21 campaign without every really suggesting that he might offer a long term solution to either position. However, he finally found his true position when he appeared at left-half in the last five games of the 1921-22 season. The 1925-26 *Lancashire Daily Post Annual* said of McKinnell: 'A strong tackler, and, at his best, the cleverest constructive half on Rovers 'books.'

However, it was in this season that he lost his way at Ewood and in July 1926 he was allowed to move to Darlington. Although well into the veteran stage of his career, McKinnell returned to Lancashire to join struggling Nelson in the summer of 1929. Clearly coming towards the end of his playing career McKinnell only appeared in ten League games for the Seedhill club during the 1929-30 season. He was later to serve Northampton Town as assistant trainer for ten years before becoming a painter and decorator in that town.

## McKINNON, Paul
Centre-forward. 1986-1987.
*6ft 2in; 13st 7lb.*
*Born: Camberley, 1 August 1958.*
*Debut: v Sunderland (a) 21 December 1986.*
*Career: Chelsea; Camberley; Woking 1974 to 1977; Sutton United 1977 to 1980 (£15,000); Malmö FF (Sweden) 1980 to 1982; Sutton United 1982; Royden Sports (Hong Kong) 1983; Trellebor FF (Sweden) 1983; Sutton United 1983-1986; Teg SK (Sweden) 1986; Sutton United 1986; Blackburn Rovers December 1986 to May 1987 (£8,000); Orebro SK (Sweden) May 1987; Sutton United 1987-88; Orebro SK (Sweden) May 1987; Sutton United 1987-88; Orebro SK (Sweden) 1988; Sutton United 1988-1991; Slough Town 1991; Sutton United; Walton & Hersham.*
**Appearances:** Football League 5; FA Cup 1; Full Members' Cup 1; Total 7.
The signing of Paul McKinnon from non-League football proved a desperate gamble by Bobby Saxton to lift the Rovers from the foot of the Second Division. At a time when he allowed a proven goalscorer in Jimmy Quinn to leave Ewood Park, Saxton put his faith in a player who had yet to appear in the Football League. It seemed an unlikely move for the normally cautious Saxton despite the fact that McKinnon had appeared in the major European competitions with Malmö FF. Although there was no doubting his endeavour, McKinnon never got to grips with the pace of the game in the Football League. His prospects were not helped when Saxton was sacked within days of McKinnon making his debut for the club. It soon became clear that Don Mackay did not see McKinnon as part of his future plans and in May 1987 he returned to Sweden. On returning from Sweden, McKinnon returned to Sutton United and was a member of the team which eliminated Coventry City from the third round of the FA Cup in January 1989.

## McLEAN, John Calderwood
Half-back. 1931-1933.
*5ft 11in; 12st.*
*Born: Busby, Lanarks, 30 March 1908; Died: Bristol, April 1988.*
*Debut: v Sheffield United (a) 1 January 1932.*
*Career: Kirkintilloch Rob Roy c.1928; Blackburn Rovers July 1931; Bristol Rovers May 1933; Street FC player-manager May 1938.*
**Appearances:** Football League 8.
A powerfully-built defender, John McLean had spent three years in Scottish junior football intermediate football before joining Blackburn Rovers in the summer of 1931. He was said to be one of the best pivots in Scottish junior circles but at Ewood he was always used as a half-back. McLean made two appearances at right-half in 1931-32 and six appearances on the opposite flank the following season. However he was unable to win a regular place in the side and in May 1933 he moved to Bristol Rovers. McLean was allowed to revert to his natural centre-half position at Bristol and his rugged approach to defending brought him 134 first-team appearances. In May 1938 he was given a free transfer and became player-manager of Street FC.

## McLEAN, Thomas
Inside-forward. 1927-1935.
*5ft 5in; 10st.*
*Born: Lochgelly, 26 December 1903.*
*Debut: v Newcastle United (h) 12 March 1927.*
*Career: Lochgelly United; Arbroath; St Johnstone c.1925; Blackburn Rovers February 1927; Exeter City June 1935; Barlow February 1937.*
*Domestic honours with Blackburn Rovers: FA Cup winners: 1928.*
**Appearances:** Football League 247; FA Cup 27; FA Charity Shield 1; Total 275.
**Goals:** Football League 44; FA Cup 5; Total 49.
Tommy McLean was an unorthodox inside-forward whose incisive dribbling could open the tightest of defences. The pigeon-toed McLean, who was a former miner, was a wizard on the ball and possessed an often mystifying ability to ghost past defenders as if the ball was tied to his feet. Although he did not have a particularly strong shot, McLean scored the second Blackburn goal in the 1928 FA Cup Final with a blistering shot. Indeed, he regularly chipped in with a regular supply of goals throughout his time at Ewood. Like so many other ball-playing Scotsmen, McLean often perplexed and exasperated his own teammates. Like their opponents, many of the Blackburn players never quite knew what to expect next from McLean.

However, he won the hearts of the public and was one of the most popular players at the club during his stay in Blackburn. Although not the biggest of men, McLean had the strength and stamina befitting someone who had spent ten years in a coal mine in his native Scotland. As a result, McLean was more than capable of looking after himself on the pitch if opposing defenders tried to physically intimidate him. Equally at home in either inside-forward position, McLean also performed admirably at wing-half during the 1932-33 season. McLean left Ewood for Exeter in June 1935 and two years later joined Barrow on a free transfer.

## McLEAN, William
Outside-right. 1953-1955.
*5ft 7in; 10st 4lb.*
*Born: Liverpool, 14 August 1931.*
*Debut: v Derby County (a) 9 September 1953.*
*Career: Burscough; Blackburn Rovers February 1953 to June 1955.*
**Appearances:** Football League 12; FA Cup 2; Total 14.
Injuries gave Billy McLean an early opportunity to show his paces with the first team at Derby County in September 1953. Although he showed he had the makings of a serviceable winger, Johnny Carey elected to return McLean to the reserves for further grooming. The signing of Bobby Langton from Bolton Wanderers at the end of September enabled Carey to switch Alex Glover to the right-wing in order to give McLean the time to learn his trade in the Central League team. However, when Glover failed to impress Carey quickly promoted McLean to the senior team. With McLean unable to find the required consistency, Carey moved to bring Frank Mooney from Manchester United in February 1954. The following season found Mooney in outstanding form and having failed to reappear in the senior team, McLean was released in the summer of 1955.

## MacLEOD, Alistair Reid
Outside-left. 1956-1961.
*5ft 10in; 11st 7lb.*
*Born: Glasgow, 26 February 1931.*
*Debut: v Swansea Town (a) 18 August 1956.*
*Career: Third Lanark; St Mirren 1955; Blackburn Rovers June 1956; Hibernian 1961; Third Lanark 1963; Ayr United player-coach 1965, becoming manager April 1966; Aberdeen manager November 1975; Scotland manager May 1977 to September 1978; Ayr United manager September 1978; Motherwell manager February 1979 to August 1981; Airdrieonians manager; Ayr United manager November 1985.*
*Domestic honours with Blackburn Rovers: FA Cup runners-up: 1960*
**Appearances:** Football League 193; FA Cup 23; Football League Cup 2; Total 218.
**Goals:** Football League 47; FA Cup 6; Total 53.
Ally MacLeod was a hugely popular figure at Ewood Park during the late 1950s. A former Scottish schoolboy international, MacLeod played his early football with Third Lanark and St Mirren before moving to Ewood Park in June 1956. Tall, blond and rather ungainly, MacLeod was a speedy winger with an eye for goal.

Nicknamed 'Noddy' because of a peculiar nodding motion his head made when running, MacLeod scored 17 goals in 38 League games during the promotion season for 1957-58. Although he was unable to maintain that goalscoring record, MacLeod was a regular on the Blackburn left flank for five seasons.

He appeared in the 1960 FA Cup Final and was one of the few Blackburn players to do himself justice on the day. MacLeod returned to his native Scotland in 1961 to join Hibernian and in 1963 he rejoined Third Lanark. He became player-coach to Ayr United in 1965 and a few months later he accepted the position of manager. It was the start of a highly successful managerial career in Scotland which culminated in him being appointed the Scottish team manager. He took Scotland to the 1978 World Cup finals in Argentina but fate was to treat him cruelly. Fortunately, Ayr United offered him a retreat from the acrimonious atmosphere which prevailed after the World Cup failure.

Following the departure of Jim Iley, MacLeod had the opportunity to become manager of Blackburn Rovers but turned down the offer out of loyalty to Ayr United. MacLeod's managerial abilities remained in constant demand in Scotland until the early 1990s.

## McLUCKIE, George Robertson
Outside-left. 1952-1953.
*5ft 11in; 11st 12lb.*

*Born: Falkirk, 19 September 1931.*
*Debut: v Plymouth Argyle (a) 1 November 1952.*
*Career: Lochore Welfare; Blackburn Rovers August 1952; Ipswich Town May 1953; Reading June 1958 to March 1961.*
**Appearances:** Football League 20; FA Cup 1; Total 21.
**Goals:** Football League 2; FA Cup 1; Total 3.
Circumstances dictated that George McLuckie was blooded in the first team rather earlier than had been expected. Sadly, with few alternatives open to him, Jackie Bestall had to keep faith with the youngster rather longer than was beneficial for the player's own good. By the end of the season Alex Glover had regained the left-wing position and in May 1953, McLuckie joined Ipswich Town. He enjoyed regular first-team football at Portman Road and scored 24 goals in 141 League games before moving to Reading. He ended his career with a further eight goals in 85 League games for Reading.

### McNAMEE, John
Centre-half. 1971-1973.
*6ft; 13st 7lb.*
*Born: Coatbridge, 11 June 1941.*
*Debut: v Tranmere Rovers (a) 26 November 1971.*
*Career: Bellshill Athletic; Glasgow Celtic 1959; Hibernian June 1964; Newcastle United December 1966; Blackburn Rovers November 1971 to June 1972; Hartlepool November 1973 to December 1973; Lancaster City; Workington manager June 1975 to December 1975; registered as a player from August 1975 to May 1976.*
**Appearances:** Football League 56; FA Cup 1; Total 57.
**Goals:** Football League 9; FA Cup 1; Total 10.

A rough, tough centre-half in the traditional mould, John McNamee had few frills to his game. Quite simply he was a man born to play centre-half and he did it with relish. McNamee spent his early career in his native Scotland before joining Newcastle United in December 1966. He enjoyed great popularity on Tyneside and played alongside Benny Arentoft in the Newcastle team in the late 1960s. When he moved to Blackburn in November 1971, he found a club becalmed in the lower reaches of the Third Division and experiencing the worst period in its history.

McNamee made an immediate impact at Ewood and brought some much needed steel to the heart of the defence. Although his fitness was questionable, McNamee had the ability to organise the defence and instruct younger players, like Derek Fazackerley, in the finer arts of defensive play. Unfortunately, McNamee was plagued by injury during his second season at the club and was often patched up to play when clearly not fit. Towards the end of the 1972-73 season there were rumours of disciplinary problems and when the club failed to win promotion McNamee was given a free transfer. Although he only spent a short time at the club, John McNamee did more than most to lift the gloom which had descended on Ewood following relegation from the Second Division. He brought self-respect, as well as steel, back into the team and for that he will always have a special niche in the history of the club.

### McOWEN, William Arthur
Goalkeeper. 1887-1890.
*5ft 6½in; 9st 8lb.*
*Born: Darwen, 1871 (April quarter); Died: Darwen, 27 December 1950.*
*Debut: v Preston North End (h) 12 January 1889.*
*Career: Cherry Tree (Blackburn); Blackburn Olympic; Blackburn Rovers cs 1887; Darwen July 1890; Liverpool cs 1892 to 1894; Blackpool; Nelson.*
**Appearances:** Football League 14; FA Cup 1; Total 15.
Billy McOwen joined Blackburn Rovers as a promising young understudy to Herbie Arthur during the summer of 1887. He played in the opening friendly fixture at Park Road on 27 August 1887 when the Rovers went down to a surprising 4-2 defeat. Whilst not the biggest of men there could be no doubting his bravery or athleticism. However, despite his promise the Rovers' committee seemed reluctant to give him an extended trial in the team even when Arthur's own form gave cause

for concern. The breaking point between player and club was reached when Jack Horne was brought to Blackburn to play in the successful FA Cup run of 1889-90 at the expense of McOwen. The player vowed never to wear a Blackburn shirt again and returned to his native Darwen to play against the Rovers in the East Lancashire Charity Cup Final in June 1890. After two seasons at Darwen he joined Liverpool and helped them win the Second Division championship in 1894 when they conceded only 16 goals and didn't lose a game. After leaving Liverpool he resumed his career as a dentist and played as an amateur for Blackpool and later Nelson.

### McSHANE, Henry
Outside-left. 1937-1946.
*5ft 5in; 11st.*
*Born: Holytown, Lanarkshire, 8 April 1920.*
*Debut: v Chesterfield (h) 25 December 1937.*
*Career: Bellshill Athletic; Blackburn Rovers amateur January 1937, turning professional in February 1937; Manchester City wartime guest 1940-41; Huddersfield Town September 1946; Bolton Wanderers July 1947; Manchester United September 1950; Oldham Athletic February 1954 (£750); Chorley player-coach 1955-56; Wellington Town 1956-57; Droylsden September 1958.*
**Appearances:** Football League 2.
Harry McShane had to join Blackburn Rovers as an amateur because, at 15 years of age, he was too young to sign professional forms. He made his debut, as a 17-year-old, on Christmas Day 1937 in the home match with Chesterfield. However, the arrival of Billy Rogers in June 1938 meant McShane had to be content with reserve-team football during the Second Division championship campaign of 1938-39. World War Two severely disrupted his career and when peace returned he moved to Huddersfield Town after failing to win a first-team place at Ewood Park. A winger who relied on pace and simplicity, McShane spent a season at Leeds Road before joining Bolton Wanderers in July 1947. He scored six goals in 93 League games at Burnden Park before making the short journey to Manchester United in September 1950.

Sadly, a cartilage problem restricted him to 12 League appearances in 1951-52 and prevented him from collecting a League championship medal. McShane ended his League career with 41 games for Oldham Athletic before becoming the player-coach of Chorley. Harry is the father of film actor Ian McShane who appeared in the popular television series *Lovejoy*. Harry worked in the personnel department of Massey Ferguson for 16 years following his retirement from football and became a scout for Manchester United. McShane was also instrumental in the formation of the Manchester United Old Boys Association.

### MAIL, David
Central defender. 1982-1990.
*5ft 11in; 11st 12lb.*
*Born: Bristol, 12 September 1962.*
*Debut: v Derby County (a) 25 September 1982.*
*Career: Aston Villa, associated schoolboy January 1979, becoming an apprentice in July 1979 and turning professional in July 1980; Blackburn Rovers January 1982; Hull City July 1990.*
*Domestic honours with Blackburn Rovers: Full Members' Cup winners: 1987.*
**Appearances:** Football League 200+6; Play-offs 8; FA Cup 12; Football League Cup 12+1; Full Members' Cup 9; Total 241+7.
**Goals:** Football League 4.

A free-transfer signing from Aston Villa, David Mail went on to establish a reputation as an exceptionally quick and reliable central defender at Ewood Park. Although he had been a member of Aston Villa's successful FA Youth Cup winning squad in 1980, he had failed to progress into the first team at Villa Park. In January 1982, Bobby Saxton brought Mail to Ewood Park to provide cover for Glenn Keeley and Derek Fazackerley. The beginning of the 1982-83 season found Keeley in dispute with the club and Mail received an earlier than expected opportunity to make his mark in the first team.

The opportunity arose when David Barton, who had been signed on loan from Newcastle with a view to replacing Keeley, received a serious injury. Mail did sufficiently well that he found himself retained in the team at right-back once Keeley had made his peace with the club. Although not the tallest of central defenders, Mail was sound in the air, whilst his speed and tough tackling made him a formidable opponent on the ground. With Derek Fazackerley coming to the end of his illustrious career at Ewood Park, Mail found himself partnering Keeley at the heart of the Blackburn defence.

At his best when partnering a traditional type of centre-half, Mail struck up an impressive partnership with Colin Hendry following Keeley's departure from Ewood Park in the summer of 1987. Mail was a member of the successful Full Members' Cup winning side of 1987 and also appeared in three disappointing Play-off campaigns for the club. The 1989-90 season saw Mail surprisingly overlooked in favour of Keith Hill and David May. However, by the turn of the year the reliable Mail had regained his first-team place. Sadly, this was to be his last season at Ewood Park. Following the tragic death of his wife Mail moved to Hull City in July 1990.

### MAKEL, Lee R.
Midfield. 1992-
*5ft 10in; 9st 10lb.*
*Born: Sunderland, 11 January 1973.*
*Debut: v Norwich City (h) 28 October 1992 (sub) (FLC).*
*Career: Newcastle United associated schoolboy February 1987, becoming a trainee in June 1989, before signing professional in February 1991; Blackburn Rovers July 1992 (£160,000).*
**Appearances:** Premier League 1+2; Football League Cup 0+3; Total 1+5.

Lee Makel had only appeared in 12 League games (including six as sub) for Newcastle United when Kenny Dalglish swooped to bring the youngster to Ewood Park. Although slight in build, Makel is, none the less, an effective attacking midfield player whose excellent distribution is capable of splitting the best of defences. Since his arrival from Newcastle he has been groomed in the Central League team and has been restricted to occasional appearances on the bench in the Football League Cup. His first Premier League appearance was in the home game with Middlesbrough on 20 March 1993 when his neat intricate skills earned him the 'Man of the Match' award.

### MALCOLM, William
Inside-forward. 1923-1924.
*5ft 6in; 10st.*
*Born: Alloa.*
*Debut: v Chelsea (h) 28 April 1923.*
*Career: Blackburn Rovers April 1923; Bo'ness March 1924.*
**Appearances:** Football League 2.

Malcolm, a Scottish junior international, formed a new left-wing partnership with Jack Byers against Chelsea at Ewood Park in April 1923. Of the two débutants, Malcolm made the least impression and contemporary critics suggested that the young Scot was out of his depth. His second appearance for the club was also against Chelsea but this time at Stamford Bridge in the third game of the 1923-24 season. Malcolm, who was deputising for Jock McKay, was unfortunate to sustain a knee injury during the game which severely restricted his mobility. This proved to be his last appearance for the senior team as he returned to Scotland in March 1924 to join Bo'ness.

### MANAGERS
It is perhaps ironic that the most successful period in the club's history, when the FA Cup was won five times and the League championship twice, occurred in the period before World War One. During that period the club operated without a manager but relied on a system of secretaries, trainers and a committee to formulate team policy. The first man to occupy the position of manager at Ewood Park was Jack Carr who was appointed in February 1922. The six and half years that Jack Marshall spent in charge at Ewood Park is the longest peacetime reign of any manager at the club. Bob Crompton actually spent seven years as manager but they were spread over two terms (the first as 'honorary' manager) and also included two seasons of wartime football.

The Ewood hot-seat has not been a happy experience for many of the occupants with only Marshall, Crompton, Johnny Carey, Bobby Saxton and Arthur Barritt remaining for more than five years. Three men, Jim Iley, John Pickering and Will Scott, have failed to survive until the first anniversary of their appointment. Of the 23 men who have held the position only Crompton, Jack Bruton and Eddie Quigley were former players at the club although Howard Kendall also appeared for the club as player-manager. To date, Kendall remains the only player-manager that the club have employed although Eddie Hapgood appeared in a couple of wartime matches following his appointment as manager.

Two men, Arthur Barritt and Reg Taylor held the position of secretary-manager, whilst Bruton had also served as assistant secretary before becoming manager. Bruton, Quigley and Pickering remain the only three men to be promoted to the managership from the position of assistant manager. Four men, Richard Dinnis, Norman Bodell, John Pickering and Tony Parkes, have held the position of caretaker manager whilst a permanent appointment has been made. However, only Pickering went on to become full time manager at the club. Below is a complete list of the managers that have been employed by the club.

| Manager | From | To |
|---|---|---|
| Jack Carr | February 1922 | December 1926 |
| Bob Crompton | December 1926 | February 1931 |
| Arthur Barritt | February 1931 | April 1936 |
| Reg Taylor | October 1936 | May 1938 |
| Bob Crompton | May 1938 | March 1941 |
| Eddie Hapgood | January 1946 | February 1947 |
| Will Scott | April 1947 | December 1947 |
| Jack Bruton | December 1947 | May 1949 |
| Jackie Bestall | June 1949 | May 1953 |
| Johnny Carey | June 1953 | October 1958 |
| Dally Duncan | October 1958 | June 1960 |
| Jack Marshall | September 1960 | February 1967 |
| Eddie Quigley | February 1967 | October 1970 |
| Johnny Carey | October 1970 | June 1971 |
| Ken Furphy | August 1971 | December 1973 |
| Gordon Lee | January 1974 | June 1975 |
| Jim Smith | June 1975 | March 1978 |
| Jim Iley | April 1978 | October 1978 |
| John Pickering | December 1978 | May 1979 |
| Howard Kendall | June 1979 | May 1981 |
| Bobby Saxton | May 1981 | December 1986 |
| Don Mackay | February 1987 | September 1991 |
| Kenny Dalglish | October 1991 | |

### MANCHESTER CITY FC
Manchester City began life in 1880 as St Mark's of West Gorton. The club underwent various amalgamations and several name changes – to West Gorton (St Marks) in 1881; to Gorton in 1884 and to Ardwick in 1887 – before emerging as Manchester City in 1894. Ardwick joined the Alliance in 1891 and became members of the Second Division of the Football League in 1892. Manchester City and Blackburn Rovers have a long history of meetings in the top two divisions of the Football League and more recently in the Premiership. Whilst Blackburn have had slightly the better of League meetings, Manchester City have enjoyed better luck in FA Cup meetings. The fifth-round Cup-tie at Ewood Park on 24 February 1969 was the last occasion that an attendance of over 40,000 – official figure 42,315 – was registered at Ewood.

### Football League

| | | | Home | | Away | |
|---|---|---|---|---|---|---|
| 1899-00 | (Div 1) | W | 4-3 | D | | 1-1 |
| 1900-01 | (Div 1) | W | 1-0 | W | | 3-1 |
| 1901-02 | (Div 1) | L | 1-4 | D | | 1-1 |
| 1903-04 | (Div 1) | L | 2-5 | L | | 0-1 |
| 1904-05 | (Div 1) | W | 3-1 | L | | 1-2 |
| 1905-06 | (Div 1) | D | 1-1 | D | | 1-1 |
| 1906-07 | (Div 1) | W | 4-0 | D | | 0-0 |
| 1907-08 | (Div 1) | D | 0-0 | L | | 0-2 |
| 1908-09 | (Div 1) | W | 3-2 | D | | 3-3 |
| 1910-11 | (Div 1) | W | 2-0 | D | | 0-0 |
| 1911-12 | (Div 1) | W | 2-0 | L | | 0-3 |
| 1912-13 | (Div 1) | D | 2-2 | L | | 1-3 |
| 1913-14 | (Div 1) | W | 2-1 | W | | 2-1 |
| 1914-15 | (Div 1) | L | 0-1 | W | | 3-1 |
| 1919-20 | (Div 1) | L | 1-4 | L | | 2-8 |
| 1920-21 | (Div 1) | L | 0-2 | D | | 0-0 |
| 1921-22 | (Div 1) | W | 3-1 | D | | 1-1 |
| 1922-23 | (Div 1) | D | 0-0 | L | | 1-2 |
| 1923-24 | (Div 1) | L | 0-1 | L | | 1-3 |
| 1924-25 | (Div 1) | W | 3-1 | W | | 3-1 |
| 1925-26 | (Div 1) | D | 3-3 | W | | 1-0 |

Mike Newell celebrates his first goal in the Premier League, against Manchester City in August 1992.

| | | | | | | | |
|---|---|---|---|---|---|---|---|
| 1928-29 | (Div 1) | D | 2-2 | | W | 2-1 |
| 1929-30 | (Div 1) | L | 1-3 | | D | 1-1 |
| 1930-31 | (Div 1) | L | 0-1 | | L | 0-3 |
| 1931-32 | (Div 1) | D | 2-2 | | L | 1-3 |
| 1932-33 | (Div 1) | W | 1-0 | | W | 3-2 |
| 1933-34 | (Div 1) | W | 3-0 | | L | 1-3 |
| 1934-35 | (Div 1) | W | 1-0 | | D | 3-3 |
| 1935-36 | (Div 1) | W | 4-1 | | L | 0-2 |
| 1938-39 | (Div 2) | D | 3-3 | | L | 2-3 |
| 1947-48 | (Div 1) | W | 1-0 | | W | 3-1 |
| 1950-51 | (Div 1) | W | 4-1 | | L | 0-1 |
| 1958-59 | (Div 1) | W | 2-1 | | W | 1-0 |
| 1959-60 | (Div 1) | W | 2-1 | | L | 1-2 |
| 1960-61 | (Div 1) | W | 4-1 | | L | 0-4 |
| 1961-62 | (Div 1) | W | 4-1 | | L | 1-3 |
| 1962-63 | (Div 1) | W | 4-1 | | W | 1-0 |
| 1983-84 | (Div 2) | W | 2-1 | | L | 0-6 |
| 1984-85 | (Div 2) | L | 0-1 | | L | 1-2 |
| 1987-88 | (Div 2) | W | 2-1 | | W | 2-1 |
| 1988-89 | (Div 2) | W | 4-0 | | L | 0-1 |

| | P | W | D | L | F | A |
|---|---|---|---|---|---|---|
| Home | 41 | 24 | 8 | 9 | 83 | 53 |
| Away | 41 | 11 | 10 | 20 | 48 | 77 |
| Total | 82 | 35 | 18 | 29 | 131 | 130 |

**FA Premiership**

| | Home | | Away | |
|---|---|---|---|---|
| 1992-93 | W | 1-0 | L | 2-3 |
| 1993-94 | W | 2-0 | W | 2-0 |

| | P | W | D | L | F | A |
|---|---|---|---|---|---|---|
| Home | 2 | 2 | 0 | 0 | 3 | 0 |

| | | | | | | |
|---|---|---|---|---|---|---|
| Away | 2 | 1 | 0 | 1 | 4 | 3 |
| Total | 4 | 3 | 0 | 1 | 7 | 3 |

**FA Cup**

| | | | | | |
|---|---|---|---|---|---|
| 1906-07 | (1) | Home | D | 2-2 |
| | (R) | Away | W | 1-0 |
| 1913-14 | (3) | Home | L | 1-2 |
| 1933-34 | (3) | Away | L | 1-3 |
| 1968-69 | (5) | Home | L | 1-4 |

**Full Members' Cup**

| | | | | |
|---|---|---|---|---|
| 1988-89 | (1) | Home | W | 3-2 aet |

**Wartime**

| | | Home | | Away | |
|---|---|---|---|---|---|
| 1916-17 | (LSPT) | W | 2-1 | L | 0-8 |
| 1917-18 | (LSPT) | L | 0-4 | L | 0-1 |
| 1918-19 | (LSPT) | W | 2-1 | L | 1-5 |
| 1940-41 | (NRL) | D | 2-2 | D | 1-1 |
| | (LWC) | L | 2-4 | L | 2-5 |
| 1941-42 | (FLNS-SC) | W | 3-0 | W | 2-1 |
| 1942-43 | (FLNS-SC) | W | 2-0 | L | 0-4 |
| 1943-44 | (FLNS-SC) | W | 4-2* | L | 0-3 |
| 1945-46 | (FLN) | D | 0-0 | L | 2-4 |

*Note: This match was also in the Football League War Cup competition and extra time was played.

## MANCHESTER UNITED FC

The first club to bring the European Cup to England is thought to have begun in 1878. A group of railway workers at the carriage and wagon department of the Lancashire & Yorkshire Railway Company's engine shed at Newton Heath formed a club called Newton Heath (LYR). In 1889, the club joined the Football Alliance and in 1892 they became members of the Football League. At the turn of the century the club was struggling financially and in April 1902 it was reformed and adopted the name of Manchester United. The club went on to become one of the world's most famous clubs and under the leadership of Sir Matt Busby they pioneered European football in England. In Johnny Carey, Manchester United provided Blackburn Rovers with one of their most popular and successful managers.

## Football League

| | | | Home | | Away | |
|---|---|---|---|---|---|---|
| 1892-93 | (Div 1) | W | 4-3 | | D | 4-4 |
| 1893-94 | (Div 1) | W | 4-0 | | L | 1-5 |
| 1906-07 | (Div 1) | L | 2-4 | | D | 1-1 |
| 1907-08 | (Div 1) | L | 1-5 | | W | 2-1 |
| 1908-09 | (Div 1) | L | 1-3 | | W | 3-0 |
| 1909-10 | (Div 1) | W | 3-2 | | L | 0-2 |
| 1910-11 | (Div 1) | W | 1-0 | | L | 2-3 |
| 1911-12 | (Div 1) | D | 2-2 | | L | 1-3 |
| 1912-13 | (Div 1) | D | 0-0 | | D | 1-1 |
| 1913-14 | (Div 1) | L | 0-1 | | D | 0-0 |
| 1914-15 | (Div 1) | D | 3-3 | | L | 0-2 |
| 1919-20 | (Div 1) | W | 5-0 | | D | 1-1 |
| 1920-21 | (Div 1) | W | 2-0 | | W | 1-0 |
| 1921-22 | (Div 1) | W | 3-0 | | W | 1-0 |
| 1925-26 | (Div 1) | W | 7-0 | | L | 0-2 |
| 1926-27 | (Div 1) | W | 2-1 | | L | 0-2 |
| 1927-28 | (Div 1) | W | 3-0 | | D | 1-1 |
| 1928-29 | (Div 1) | L | 0-3 | | W | 4-1 |
| 1929-30 | (Div 1) | W | 5-4 | | L | 0-1 |
| 1930-31 | (Div 1) | W | 4-1 | | W | 1-0 |
| 1937-38 | (Div 2) | D | 1-1 | | L | 1-2 |
| 1946-47 | (Div 1) | W | 2-1 | | L | 0-4 |
| 1947-48 | (Div 1) | D | 1-1 | | L | 1-4 |
| 1958-59 | (Div 1) | L | 1-3 | | L | 1-6 |
| 1959-60 | (Div 1) | D | 1-1 | | L | 0-1 |
| 1960-61 | (Div 1) | L | 1-2 | | W | 3-1 |
| 1961-62 | (Div 1) | W | 3-0 | | L | 1-6 |
| 1962-63 | (Div 1) | D | 2-2 | | W | 3-0 |
| 1963-64 | (Div 1) | L | 1-3 | | D | 2-2 |
| 1964-65 | (Div 1) | L | 0-5 | | L | 0-3 |
| 1965-66 | (Div 1) | L | 1-4 | | D | 2-2 |

| | P | W | D | L | F | A |
|---|---|---|---|---|---|---|
| Home | 31 | 14 | 7 | 10 | 66 | 55 |
| Away | 31 | 8 | 8 | 15 | 38 | 61 |
| Total | 62 | 22 | 15 | 25 | 104 | 116 |

## FA Premiership

| | | Home | | Away | |
|---|---|---|---|---|---|
| 1992-93 | | D | 0-0 | L | 1-3 |
| 1993-94 | | W | 2-0 | D | 1-1 |

| | P | W | D | L | F | A |
|---|---|---|---|---|---|---|
| Home | 2 | 1 | 1 | 0 | 2 | 0 |
| Away | 2 | 0 | 1 | 1 | 2 | 4 |
| Total | 4 | 1 | 2 | 1 | 4 | 4 |

## FA Cup

| | | | | |
|---|---|---|---|---|
| 1892-93 | (1) | Home | W | 4-0 |
| 1893-94 | (2) | Away | D | 0-0 aet |
| | (R) | Home | W | 5-1 |
| 1908-09 | (3) | Away | L | 1-6 |
| 1911-12 | (4) | Away | D | 1-1 |
| | (R) | Home | W | 4-1 aet |
| 1927-28 | (6) | Home | W | 2-0 |
| 1984-85 | (5) | Home | L | 0-2 |

## Wartime

| | | Home | | Away | |
|---|---|---|---|---|---|
| 1916-17 | (LSPT) | L | 1-2 | L | 0-1 |
| 1917-18 | (LSPT) | L | 0-5 | L | 1-6 |
| 1918-19 | (LSPT) | D | 1-1 | L | 0-1 |
| 1939-40 | (LWC) | L | 1-2 | W | 3-1 |
| 1940-41 | (NRL) | D | 5-5 | L | 0-9 |
| | | L | 0-2 | D | 0-0 |
| 1941-42 | (FLNS-SC) | L | 1-2 | L | 1-3 |
| | | D | 1-1 | W | 1-0 |
| 1942-43 | (FLNS-SC) | W | 4-2 | L | 2-5 |
| 1943-44 | (FLNS-SC) | W | 2-1 | L | 1-2 |
| 1945-46 | (FLN) | L | 1-3 | L | 2-6 |

## MANN, George W.
Outside-right. 1892-1894.
*Born: 1873.*
*Debut: v Preston North End (h) 29 October 1892.*
*Career: East Stirlingshire; Blackburn Rovers October 1892; Manchester City July 1894; Bristol City August 1897.*
**Appearances:** Football League 2.
**Goals:** Football League 1.
Although George Mann came to Blackburn with an impressive reputation, his time at Ewood Park was not particularly successful. He made his first-team debut against Preston North End, replacing Harry Chippendale on the right wing, and scored a goal the following week in a 4-4 draw with Newton Heath. However, these were to prove his only senior outings and in July 1894 he moved to Manchester City. He enjoyed greater success in Manchester, where he operated as a right-half, and scored five goals in 59 League appearances. A player who could kick with either foot, Mann was also a formidable opponent in the air and developed into a fine attacking half-back. Although he was highly regarded in Manchester, Mann moved to Bristol City at a time when that club was beginning to embrace professionalism. He scored 13 goals in 41 non-League games during his time in Bristol.

## MANNING, John
Centre-half. 1907-1908.
*5ft 9in; 11st 6lb.*
*Debut: v Middlesbrough (h) 21 September 1907.*
*Career: Kirkcaldy United; Raith Rovers 1904; Blackburn Rovers May 1907; Northampton Town cs 1908.*
**Appearances:** Football League 4.
John Manning became the second Scottish signing in as many days when he followed James Ferguson to Ewood Park in May 1907. Although he didn't begin the 1907-08 season in possession of the centre-half position, he was quickly drafted in to replace Sam Wolstenholme. He made his debut in the 2-0 win over Middlesbrough on 21 September 1907, but just a month later the resounding 5-1 home defeat by Manchester United proved to be his last outing with the senior team.

## MANSFIELD TOWN FC
The present day Mansfield Town Football Club was founded in June 1910. However, this was not the first club to bear the title Mansfield Town. A club which bore this title played in the Midlands Counties League and Notts, Derby & District League in the 1890s. The present club came into being when Mansfield Wesley changed its name to Mansfield Town in 1910. Former members of the Central Alliance and Midland League, Mansfield Town joined the Third Division South of the Football League in 1931. Blackburn Rovers and Mansfield Town didn't meet in the League until the 1971-72 season.

## Football League

| | | Home | | Away | |
|---|---|---|---|---|---|
| 1971-72 | (Div 3) | D | 1-1 | L | 0-1 |
| 1977-78 | (Div 2) | W | 3-1 | D | 2-2 |
| 1979-80 | (Div 3) | D | 0-0 | W | 1-0 |

| | P | W | D | L | F | A |
|---|---|---|---|---|---|---|
| Home | 3 | 1 | 2 | 0 | 4 | 2 |
| Away | 3 | 1 | 1 | 1 | 3 | 3 |
| Total | 6 | 2 | 3 | 1 | 7 | 5 |

## MANSON, Robert
Inside-forward. 1906-1908.
*Debut: v Sheffield United (a) 20 January 1906.*
*Career: Brynn Central; Stockport County cs 1905; Blackburn Rovers January 1906.*
**Appearances:** Football League 16.
**Goals:** Football League 3.
A plucky inside-forward who was plagued by injuries during his time with Blackburn Rovers. Manson came to Ewood Park to challenge James Robertson and Adam Bowman for an inside-forward berth with the first team. However, for a time, all three turned out together and Manson occupied the centre-forward position in three games. He scored two goals in ten League games during 1905-06 but injuries restricted him to only a further six appearances (and one goal) during the remainder of his time at the club.

## MARKER, Nicholas Robert Thomas
Central defender/Midfield. 1992-
*6ft; 12st 11lb.*
*Born: Budleigh Salterton, 3 May 1965.*
*Debut: v Oldham Athletic (h) 26 September 1992 (sub).*
*Career: Exeter City associated schoolboy September 1979, becoming an*

*apprentice in July 1981, before turning professional in May 1985; Plymouth Argyle October 1987; Blackburn Rovers October 1992 (in exchange for £250,000 plus Keith Hill and Craig Skinner).*

**Appearances:** Premier League 28+10; FA Cup 4; Football League Cup 3; Total 35+10.

A central defender who is capable of playing in midfield, Nicky Marker's versatility has been put to good use by Kenny Dalglish. Good in the air and strong in the tackle, Marker has been used as a 'stopper' in the heart of defence and has also been used as the anchor man in midfield. Marker made his debut in the Football League with Exeter City when he was only 16 years of age. He appeared in 202 League games (including six as sub) for the Grecians before moving to Plymouth Argyle in October 1987. At Plymouth he was best remembered by Blackburn fans as the man whose tackle brought an early end to the debut of Ossie Ardíles with the Rovers. He remained at the heart of the Plymouth defence for five seasons and had appeared in 202 League games (including one as sub) for Argyle before his move to Ewood Park.

The outstanding form of Kevin Moran and Colin Hendry meant that Marker had few opportunities to enjoy an extended run in the first team at Blackburn during the 1992-93 season. However, Maker figured more prominently in team selection during the 1993-94 season and impressed everyone with his ability and total commitment to Blackburn Rovers.

## MARKS, William George

Goalkeeper. 1946-1948.
*5ft 11in; 11st 8lb.*
*Born: Amesbury, 9 April 1915.*
*Debut: v Portsmouth (a) 31 August 1946.*
*Career: Salisbury Corinthians; Arsenal amateur March 1936, turning professional in May 1936; Margate; Arsenal May 1938; Blackburn Rovers August 1946 (£5,000); Bristol City August 1948; Reading October 1948, becoming trainer-coach in 1954-55; Bulford United player 1955-56.*

**Appearances:** Football League 67; FA Cup 7; Total 74.

George Marks was capped on eight occasions by England between 1941 and 1943 and his arrival at Ewood Park in August 1946 was seen as something of a major coup for Eddie Hapgood. The manager was well acquainted with the potential of Marks as they had been together at Highbury immediately before the war. Although Marks had appeared in only two League games for Arsenal he had become the first choice at Highbury during the war and his potential was quickly apparent to everyone at Ewood. Marks displayed outstanding form in the Blackburn goal until he received a serious jaw injury at Deepdale in December 1946.

The injury kept him out of action for a month but when he returned he was unable to recapture his earlier form. Matters were not helped by the fact that he had been given permission by Hapgood to continue to live and train in the West Country and travel to Blackburn for matches. The departure of Hapgood and his replacement with Will Scott and then Jack Burton appeared to have little affect on Marks' position in the first team. However, Bruton was never happy with his goalkeeper's domestic arrangements and when his increasingly erratic form began to cost points he axed Marks in favour of Stan Hayhurst. Marks responded by asking for a transfer and although recalled for the final two games of the 1947-48 season, Bruton allowed him to join Bristol City in the close season.

## MARRIOTT, Andrew

Goalkeeper. 1989-1990.
*6ft; 12st 7lb.*
*Born: Sutton-in-Ashfield, 11 October 1970.*
*Debut: v Sheffield United (a) 30 December 1989.*
*Career: Arsenal associated schoolboy October 1985, becoming a trainee in July 1987 and turning professional in October 1988; Nottingham Forest June 1989; West Bromwich Albion on loan September 1989; Blackburn Rovers on loan December 1989 to January 1990; Colchester United on loan March 1990; Burnley on loan August 1991; Wrexham on loan October 1993, before signing permanently in December 1993.*

**Appearances:** Football League 2.

Andy Marriott came to Ewood Park on loan as an unknown teenager in December 1989. He was borrowed from Nottingham Forest to help the club overcome something of a goalkeeping crisis. When Marriott arrived at Ewood, Terry Gennoe was almost ready to return to senior action following a serious injury and Darren Collier had been promoted to first-team goalkeeper. However, Collier's confidence was at a low ebb after conceding 18 goals in only five games. Thus Marriott was thrust into the first team for the two games over the New Year holiday period. The youngster made a good impression, playing in an away win at Sheffield United and helping the team to claim a point from the home match with Bradford City. Marriott, a former England schoolboy and youth international, went on to appear for England Under-21 whilst at Forest and appeared in ZDS and League Cup Finals for the Nottingham club.

However, he was never really able to establish himself at the City Ground and in December 1993 he moved to Wrexham following a loan spell at the Racecourse Ground.

## MARSHALL, Henry

Left-half. 1892-1894.
*5ft 6½in; 12st 10lb.*
*Born: Portobello, 1872.*
*Debut: v Derby County (a) 22 October 1892.*
*Career: Portobello Thistle; Edinburgh St Bernard's; Heart of Midlothian 1892; Blackburn Rovers October 1892; Heart of Midlothian June 1896; Blackburn Rovers on loan April 1898; Celtic February 1899; Clyde 1903.*

**Appearances:** Football League 53; Test Matches 4; FA Cup 9; Total 66.
**Goals:** Football League 2.

Popularly known as 'The Portobello Boatman' because he owned a vessel that operated there, Harry Marshall was a resolute, yet cultured half-back who enjoyed a tremendously successful career north of the border. Marshall first came to prominence with Heart of Midlothian and it was from that club that he joined the Rovers in October 1892. He proved to be an outstanding half-back and became a permanent fixture in the Blackburn team. However, a serious leg injury in the second game of the 1894-95 season threatened to end his career in football. It was thought that he would not play again and he returned to his native Scotland to continue his normal occupation of boatman.

On his return to Scotland Marshall confounded those who had written him off and fought his way back to fitness. He again began to play with Heart of Midlothian and in April 1898 he returned to Blackburn to try to save the Rovers from relegation to the Second Division. He appeared at centre-half in the final two League games and remained to figure in all four test matches before returning to Scotland. Marshall went on to enjoy great personal success with Celtic and was capped by Scotland on two occasions during this period.

## MARSHALL, John Gilmore

Manager. 1960-1967.
*Born: Bolton, 29 May 1917.*
*Career: Burnley November 1936, retired through injury 1946; Bury coach 1949; Stoke City coach; Sheffield Wednesday trainer-coach 1954; Rochdale manager October 1958 to September 1960; Blackburn Rovers manager September 1960 to February 1967; Sheffield Wednesday assistant manager, then manager February 1968 to June 1969; Bury manager May to September 1969; Blackburn Rovers physiotherapist July 1970 to 1979.*

Jack Marshall was the man chosen to pick up the pieces at Ewood following the departure of Dally Duncan during the summer of 1960. His employers at Rochdale were reluctant to let him go and insisted on a successor being installed before they would release him. As a result the 1960-61 season was already six games old before Marshall was allowed to move to Ewood Park. Marshall was a vastly experienced coach and had been trainer to the England 'B' team during his spell at Hillsborough in the mid-1950s. Like Carey before him, Marshall had an attacking philosophy to the game which was well received at Ewood Park. Marshall's first two seasons at Blackburn were a time for rebuilding.

As well as bringing in a number of new faces, Marshall was also prepared to experiment with the players he inherited from Duncan. These positional changes saw Fred Pickering move from full-back to centre-forward whilst Keith Newton switched from half-back to full-back. Another key move saw Andy McEvoy revert to his original inside-forward position after having been tried as a half-back. In the transfer market the signings of Fred Else, Mike Harrison and Mike Ferguson proved astute business and the team known as 'Marshall's Misfits' began to make a real impression on the First Division.

Marshall provided the Blackburn public with side that produced exhilarating displays of attacking football. Orchestrated by Bryan Douglas in midfield, McEvoy and Pickering became a prolific goalscoring partnership which threatened to bring the First Division title to Ewood Park for the first time since before World War One. Sadly, consistency proved an elusive quality and hopes for a championship finally died when Pickering was sold to Everton in March 1964. A mid-table place in 1964-65 was followed by a disastrous 1965-66 season which saw the club hurtle towards the Second Division. As the club lost their First Division status Marshall's own contract with the club ran out. Without the security of a new contract, Marshall set about rebuilding the team during the summer of 1966.

The impending sale of Mike England allowed him to bring in Barrie Hole, John Barton and Allan Gilliver during the close season and in September he added John Connelly from Manchester United. However, although the team started promisingly, consistency continued to elude them and in November the directors appointed Eddie Quigley as Marshall's assistant and gave him responsibility for all coaching at the club. Amidst a spate of transfer requests and continued erratic form, Marshall found himself bearing the brunt of the criticism which followed the club's exit from the FA Cup. In February 1967, an unhappy Marshall finally tendered his resignation as manager of Blackburn Rovers.

Marshall returned to football as assistant manager to Alan Brown at Sheffield Wednesday and inherited the managerial position following Brown's departure in February 1968. He also had a spell in charge of Bury before returning to Ewood Park in July 1970 as physiotherapist. Marshall retired to his native Bolton in 1979.

## MARTIN, Donnah
Centre-forward. 1968-1975.
*5ft 10in; 10st 7lb.*
*Born: Corby, 15 February 1944.*
*Debut: v Norwich City (h) 24 February 1968.*
*Career: Northampton Town July 1962; Blackburn Rovers February 1968 (£30,000); Northampton Town November 1975; Dunstable; Corby player-manager.*
*Domestic honours with Blackburn Rovers: Third Division championship: 1975 (42+1 apps, 15gls)*
**Appearances:** Football League 218+6; FA Cup 10+1; Football League Cup 16+1; Total 244+8.
**Goals:** Football League 57; FA Cup 2; Football League Cup 4; Total 63.

A former England youth international, Don Martin was a member of the Northampton Town side which won promotion to the First Division in 1965. Eddie Quigley paid a fee of £30,000 to bring Martin to Ewood in the hope that he could supply the firepower that his shot-shy attack lacked. Tall, but not particularly well built, Martin proved to be deceptively strong and quick. He was a very skilful player whose perceptive reading of the game could be utilised in midfield as well as attack. A broken ankle in the third game of the 1970-71 season kept him out of first-team football for most of the campaign.

The loss of Martin was keenly felt and was a major factor in the club's relegation from the Second Division. Under the managership of Ken Furphy, Martin found himself being played in the centre of defence before being shunted into the Central League team. At a time when it appeared that Martin's career at Ewood was at an end the club were rocked by the departure of Furphy to Sheffield United. When Gordon Lee joined the club he offered Martin the opportunity to revive his career as a centre-forward. Martin was to enjoy a glorious 'Indian summer' to his Ewood career when he finished as top goalscorer during the 1974-75 Third Division championship campaign. He played in the opening games of the following season before returning to Northampton Town in November 1975 to finish his League career.

During his two stints with Northampton, Martin scored 69 League goals in 227 games (including 15 as sub). Martin earned his own particular niche in Ewood history on a rain sodden afternoon in September 1968 when playing against Sheffield United. He chased a floated free-kick into the United area only to find that Alan Hodgkinson, United's former England goalkeeper, had comfortably collected the ball whilst standing on his line. Undeterred, Martin continued his run, dipped his shoulder and gently nudged Hodgkinson and the ball over the line. Despite the appeals of the incredulous defenders the referee allowed the goal to stand. It was a throwback to another era and was certainly among the last, if not the last, of its type in the Football League.

## MARTIN, John
Centre-forward. 1906-1908.
*5ft 11½in; 12st 7lb.*
*Born: South Shields, 1885.*
*Debut: v Bristol City (a) 15 September 1906.*
*Career: Kingston Villa; South Shields, Lincoln City May 1904; Blackburn Rovers May 1906; Brighton & Hove Albion May 1908; Millwall May 1909.*
**Appearances:** Football League 57; FA Cup 5; Total 62.
**Goals:** Football League 25; FA Cup 2; Total 27.

Jack Martin was brought to Blackburn to score goals and he finished his first season at the club as the top goalscorer with 17 goals from 36 League games. He had a little more height and weight than a number of his colleagues in the forward line and he used it to good effect. The 1907-08 season was not quite so successful for Martin and on more than one occasion he had to give way to both Billy Davies and Ellis Crompton for the centre-forward position. In May 1908 he moved to Brighton & Hove Albion and ended the 1908-09 season as their top marksman with 18 goals in 37 Southern League games. However after only one season at Brighton he moved to Millwall and 12 goals in 39 Southern League games ensured he finished 1909-10 as the club's leading goalscorer He finished his second season at Millwall as the top marksman with 12 goals from 31 Southern League games.

## MATIER, Gerald
Goalkeeper. 1937-1939.
*5ft 10¼in; 11st 7lb.*
*Born: Lisburn, 1 December 1912; Died: Lisburn, September 1984.*
*Debut: v Swansea Town (h) 1 January 1938.*
*Career: Coleraine; Blackburn Rovers July 1937; Bradford City August 1939; Dundalk; Brideville; Glentoran; Plymouth Argyle September 1946; Torquay United November 1946.*
*Domestic honours with Blackburn Rovers: Second Division championship: 1938-39 (1 app).*
**Appearances:** Football League 20; FA Cup 1; Total 21.

Gerry Matier briefly challenged Jim Barron for the number-one goalkeeping position at Ewood Park during the 1937-38 season. During the latter part of that campaign the brilliant, but inconsistent, Matier appeared in 19 of the final 20 League games. A goalkeeper who was never afraid to venture from his line, Matier was always prepared to dive bravely at the feet of any oncoming forward. Injury and inconsistent form restricted him to only one appearance during the 1938-39 Second Division championship campaign and in August 1939 Matier signed for Huddersfield Town. Matier spent the war years playing in his native Ireland but joined Plymouth Argyle in 1946. He failed to appear in the Football League with either Huddersfield Town or Plymouth but ended his career with 17 League appearances for Torquay United.

## MATLOCK TOWN FC
Formed in 1885, Matlock Town were members of the Northern Premier League when Blackburn Rovers visited them in the first round of the 1974-75 FA Cup competition. Goals from Don Martin, Ken Beamish (2) and Tony Parkes ensured a comfortable 4-1 win for a Blackburn team which was heavily involved in the Third Division title race.

## MAY, David
Central defender/Right-back. 1984-1994
*6ft; 11st 4lb.*
*Born: Oldham, 24 June 1970.*

*Debut: v Swindon Town (a) 1 April 1989.*
*Career: Blackburn Rovers associated schoolboy October 1984, becoming a trainee in July 1986 before signing professional in June 1988; Manchester United May 1994.*
*Domestic honours with Blackburn Rovers: Second Division Play-off winners: 1992.*
**Appearances:** Premier League 74; Football League 49; Play-offs 3; FA Cup 10; Football League Cup 12+1; Full Members' Cup2; Total 150+1.
**Goals:** Premier League 2; FA Cup 1; Football League Cup 2; Total 5.

An exceptionally quick central defender, who can also play at right-back, David May has developed into one of the country's outstanding defenders under the tutelage of Messrs Dalglish and Harford. May, a product of the Ewood youth system, was given an early opportunity to establish himself in the senior team by Don Mackay at the beginning of the 1989-90 season. Injury kept him out until November 1990 when he returned to the first team at the expense of Keith Hill. Although May enjoyed a run in the team during the early part of the 1991-92 season he lost his place when Dalglish and Harford arrived and spent the majority of that season playing Central League football.

Having figured in only two League games for the new management team, May received a surprise call up to play at right-back in the Play-offs. The move was a great success and May began the 1992-93 campaign as the first-choice right-back. The emergence of Henning Berg at right-back allowed May revert to the centre of defence. Excellent in the air and with a sound positional sense, the 1993-94 season saw May mature into one of the Premiership's most impressive defenders. Out of contract at the end of the season, May opted to join Manchester United when Blackburn's terms failed to meet his expectations. The fee of £1.25 million made him the most expensive player to leave Ewood Park.

### MELVILLE, James
Centre-half/Left-half. 1928-1933.
*6ft 1in; 12st 4lb.*
*Born: Barrow-in-Furness, 15 March 1909; Died: Coventry, 2 August 1961.*
*Debut: v Grimsby Town (a) 18 January 1930.*
*Career: Vickerstown FC (Barrow); Barrow amateur July 1926; Blackburn Rovers June 1928; Hull City December 1933; Northampton Town June 1934.*
**Appearances:** Football League 25.
Originally an inside-left, Melville was converted into a half-back to make more use of his physique. However, he still retained the subtle touches of an inside-forward and his intelligent use of the ball allowed him to be become one of the more constructive type of half-backs. At Blackburn he was unable to force his way into the first-team on a regular basis – his five League appearances in 1931-32 being his best seasonal tally. In December 1933 he moved to Hull City before ending his career with Northampton Town. Jim was also a more than capable cricketer and in 1932 became professional with Millom CC. In 1946 he made two appearances with Warwickshire in County Cricket.

### METCALFE, Stuart Michael
Midfield. 1964-1980 & 1982-1983.
*5ft 7in; 9st.*
*Born: Blackburn, October 1950.*
*Debut: v Cardiff City (h) 27 April 1968.*
*Career: Blackburn Rovers schoolboy March 1964, becoming an apprentice in June 1966, before turning professional in January 1968; Carlisle United July 1980; Carolina Lightning 1981; Blackburn Rovers non-contract player October 1982; Crewe Alexandra January to February 1983; Blackburn Rovers non-contract player February 1983; Feniscowles (Blackburn).*
*Domestic honours with Blackburn Rovers: Third Division championship: 1974-75 (42+1 apps, 7 gls)*
**Appearances:** Football League 376+11; FA Cup 23; Football League Cup 22+2; Total 421+13.
**Goals:** Football League 21; FA Cup 1; Football League Cup 3; Total 25.
A former Blackburn schoolboy player who went on to represent England at youth level. Stuart Metcalfe joined his home-town club on schoolboy forms in March 1964 and came to prominence in the Central League championship team of 1966-67. By his 18th birthday, the slightly frail figure of Metcalfe was a familiar sight on the right wing of the senior team at Ewood. Although he began his career as a tricky outside-right, Eddie Quigley quickly realised that Metcalfe could make a bigger contribution to the team from a more central position.

Thus Metcalfe, despite his build, was moved into midfield and it was from there that he developed into a creative playmaker. Relegation to the Third Division meant a difficult transitional phase in his career as he tried to get to grips with the more physical approach of football in a lower division. After only eight League appearances (including two as sub) in 1971-72 season, Metcalfe finally re-established himself under Ken Furphy during the following campaign. However, it was under the managership of Gordon Lee that Metcalfe's midfield partnership with Tony Parkes began to blossom. His probing passes and powerful running combined well with the hard-working Parkes. Although never the most prolific of goalscorers, Metcalfe managed seven goals (two of them penalties) during the 1974-75 Third Division championship campaign.

Metcalfe was awarded a testimonial match in 1978 and, although no longer a regular member of the first team, appeared in 18 League games (including two as sub) when the Rovers again won promotion from the Third Division in 1979-80. In July 1980 he finally severed his connection with the club and moved to Carlisle United.

After 25 League appearances (including two as sub) with the Cumbrian club he tried his luck in America with Carolina Lightning. In October 1982 he returned to Ewood Park as a non-contract player and made one further appearance for the Rovers before ending his League career with three League games for Crewe Alexandra.

### MIDDLESBROUGH FC
Formed in 1876, Middlesbrough became a professional club in 1889 but elected to revert back to amateur status in 1892. The club accepted professionalism again in 1899 and in that year they were elected to the Second Division of the Football League. Blackburn Rovers and Middlesbrough have a long history of meetings in the Football League and have produced some high-scoring encounters. Perhaps the most memorable for Blackburn supporters was the 9-0 win at Ewood Park on 6 November 1954. Both Eddie Quigley and Frank Mooney completed their hat-tricks whilst Eddie Crossan scored twice and Bobby Langton got the ninth goal. Ironically, on an afternoon when Blackburn Rovers recorded their biggest-ever win in the Football League, Tommy Briggs, one of the most potent strikers in the history of the club, failed to find the back of the net.

### Football League

| | | Home | | Away | |
|---|---|---|---|---|---|
| 1902-03 | (Div 1) | L | 0-1 | L | 0-4 |
| 1903-04 | (Div 1) | D | 1-1 | W | 2-0 |
| 1904-05 | (Div 1) | L | 0-2 | L | 1-2 |
| 1905-06 | (Div 1) | D | 1-1 | D | 1-1 |
| 1906-07 | (Div 1) | W | 4-1 | W | 1-0 |
| 1907-08 | (Div 1) | W | 2-0 | L | 0-3 |
| 1908-09 | (Div 1) | D | 0-0 | L | 0-1 |
| 1909-10 | (Div 1) | D | 1-1 | W | 3-1 |
| 1910-11 | (Div 1) | W | 5-1 | W | 3-2 |
| 1911-12 | (Div 1) | W | 2-1 | L | 1-2 |
| 1912-13 | (Div 1) | W | 5-2 | D | 0-0 |
| 1913-14 | (Div 1) | W | 6-0 | L | 0-3 |
| 1914-15 | (Div 1) | W | 4-0 | W | 4-1 |
| 1919-20 | (Div 1) | L | 0-2 | D | 2-2 |
| 1920-21 | (Div 1) | W | 3-2 | D | 1-1 |
| 1921-22 | (Div 1) | D | 2-2 | W | 1-0 |
| 1922-23 | (Div 1) | W | 2-0 | W | 2-1 |
| 1923-24 | (Div 1) | W | 2-0 | L | 0-2 |
| 1927-28 | (Div 1) | W | 3-0 | L | 0-2 |
| 1929-30 | (Div 1) | W | 7-0 | W | 4-2 |
| 1930-31 | (Div 1) | L | 4-5 | L | 1-4 |
| 1931-32 | (Div 1) | W | 4-2 | W | 2-0 |
| 1932-33 | (Div 1) | W | 4-2 | L | 0-4 |
| 1933-34 | (Div 1) | D | 0-0 | L | 1-3 |
| 1934-35 | (Div 1) | W | 3-2 | D | 3-3 |
| 1935-36 | (Div 1) | D | 2-2 | L | 1-6 |
| 1946-47 | (Div 1) | L | 1-2 | W | 1-0 |
| 1947-48 | (Div 1) | L | 1-7 | D | 1-1 |
| 1954-55 | (Div 2) | W | 9-0 | L | 3-4 |
| 1955-56 | (Div 2) | W | 2-1 | L | 0-1 |
| 1956-57 | (Div 2) | W | 1-0 | L | 1-2 |
| 1957-58 | (Div 2) | D | 3-3 | W | 3-2 |
| 1967-68 | (Div 2) | W | 3-0 | D | 0-0 |
| 1968-69 | (Div 2) | D | 1-1 | L | 0-2 |
| 1969-70 | (Div 2) | W | 4-0 | L | 1-4 |
| 1970-71 | (Div 2) | D | 1-1 | D | 1-1 |
| 1982-83 | (Div 2) | D | 1-1 | W | 5-1 |
| 1983-84 | (Div 2) | W | 1-0 | W | 2-1 |
| 1984-85 | (Div 2) | W | 3-0 | W | 2-1 |
| 1985-86 | (Div 2) | L | 0-1 | D | 0-0 |
| 1987-88 | (Div 2) | L | 0-2 | D | 1-1 |
| 1989-90 | (Div 2) | L | 2-4 | W | 3-0 |
| 1990-91 | (Div 2) | W | 1-0 | W | 1-0 |
| 1991-92 | (Div 2) | W | 2-1 | D | 0-0 |

| | P | W | D | L | F | A |
|---|---|---|---|---|---|---|
| Home | 44 | 24 | 11 | 9 | 103 | 54 |
| Away | 44 | 16 | 11 | 17 | 59 | 71 |
| Total | 88 | 40 | 22 | 26 | 162 | 125 |

### FA Premiership

| | | Home | | Away | |
|---|---|---|---|---|---|
| 1992-93 | | D | 1-1 | L | 2-3 |

| | P | W | D | L | F | A |
|---|---|---|---|---|---|---|
| Home | 1 | 0 | 1 | 0 | 1 | 1 |
| Away | 1 | 0 | 0 | 1 | 2 | 3 |
| Total | 2 | 0 | 1 | 1 | 3 | 4 |

**FA Cup**

| | | | | |
|---|---|---|---|---|
| 1910-11 | (3) | Away | W | 3-0 |
| 1913-14 | (1) | Home | W | 3-0 |
| 1934-35 | (3) | Away | D | 1-1 |
| | (R) | Home | W | 1-0 |
| 1961-62 | (5) | Home | W | 2-1 |
| 1962-63 | (3) | Home | D | 1-1 |
| | (R) | Away | L | 1-3 |

**Football League Cup**

| | | | | |
|---|---|---|---|---|
| 1967-68 | (3) | Home | W | 3-2 |

**Wartime**

| | | Home | | Away | |
|---|---|---|---|---|---|
| 1945-46 | (FLN) | D | 3-3 | L | 1-5 |

## MIDDLESBROUGH IRONOPOLIS FC

Founded in 1889, Middlesbrough Ironopolis became members of the Second Division of the Football League in 1893-94. The club folded after one season of Football League membership. Blackburn Rovers and Middlesbrough Ironopolis met in the first round of the FA Cup in 1890-91 when Ironopolis were members of the Northern League. The game was originally played on 17 January 1891 in front of a crowd of approximately 10,000. Goals from Jack Southworth and Coombe Hall gave the Rovers a 2-1 win and passage into the next round.

However, the Ironopolis club lodged a protest and the Football Association ordered that the first game was null and void and should be replayed. Seven days after the original fixture, on 24 January 1891, Blackburn took the same eleven to Middlesbrough for the second game. Two goals from Coombe Hall and an own-goal by Stevenson of Ironopolis gave the Rovers a convincing 3-0 victory in front of 7,000 spectators.

## MIDDLETON, Robert Bradley
Secretary. 1903-1925.
A native of Yorkshire, Middleton was originally a schoolmaster in Rotherham and played football as an amateur for Wiston. He represented his club on the Sheffield Association and was also known to be a more than capable referee. He eventually left the scholastic profession to become the secretary of Rotherham Town Football Club and after two years he accepted a similar position with Darwen Football Club. His next move saw him chosen from a list of 50 applicants for the vacant secretaryship of Blackpool Football Club. He proved a considerable asset to the seaside club and his work at Bloomfield Road did not go unnoticed by the directors of Blackburn Rovers.

He was one of four men who were short-listed for the position of secretary at Ewood Park during the summer of 1903 and in July he was finally appointed to the position. Although genial and courteous, Middleton was a shrewd operator who was held in the highest esteem at Ewood Park. His ability to pull off major coups in the transfer market, despite fierce competition from other clubs, earned him national recognition. During his term of office the club twice won the League championship and Ewood Park was transformed into one of the finest grounds in the country. The League Management Committee recognised his services to football when they presented him with a commemorative gold medal to celebrate his 21 years as a football secretary. Middleton died on 1 September 1925 whilst still in office at Ewood Park.

## MILLAR, John
Left-back/Midfield. 1987-1991.
*5ft 7in; 10st.*
*Born: Coatbridge, 8 December 1966.*
*Debut: v Manchester City (a) 5 September 1987.*
*Career: Clyde Amateurs; Chelsea August 1984; Hamilton Academical on loan; Northampton Town on loan January 1987; Blackburn Rovers July 1987 (£25,000); Heart of Midlothian cs 1991 (free).*
**Appearances:** Football League 122+4; Play-offs 9; FA Cup 4; Football League Cup 9+1; Full Members' Cup 2; Total 146+5.
**Goals:** Football League 1.
A former Scottish youth international, John Millar was snapped up by Don Mackay during the 1987 close season. Although predominantly a left-back when he came to Ewood, Mackay used him a great deal in midfield. Millar, a combative little player, added some much needed aggression to the midfield but ultimately lacked the craft needed in that position. Millar, who had also played cricket for Scotland, returned to his native land during the summer of 1992 after being rather surprisingly released by the Rovers. He enjoyed a highly successful first season back in Scotland, scoring seven goals in 41 League appearances with Hearts.

## MILLER, Archibald B.
Left-half. 1947-1948.
5ft 11in; 11st 4lb.
Born: Larkhall, 5 September 1913.
Debut: v Liverpool (a) 22 November 1947.
Career: Royal Albert June 1932, Heart of Midlothian October 1932; Falkirk January 1940; Heart of Midlothian April 1941; Blackburn Rovers November 1947; Kilmarnock June 1948 (£1,000); Carlisle United September 1950; Heart of Midlothian 1951; Workington February 1952.
**Appearances:** Football League 6.
A player who was at the peak of his career when World War Two broke out. Miller enjoyed a long association with Heart of Midlothian and gradually made the left-half position his own. He came to Blackburn towards the end of his career and failed to establish himself in a struggling side. His first-team appearances all occurred within the first month of his stay in Lancashire and it was no surprise when he returned to Scotland in the June 1948.

## MILLER, Ian
Outside-right. 1981-1989.
*5ft 9in; 11st 7lb.*
*Born: Perth, 13 May 1955.*
*Debut: v Sheffield Wednesday (h) 29 August 1981.*
*Career: Bury August 1973; Nottingham Forest March 1975; Doncaster Rovers August 1975; Swindon Town July 1978; Blackburn Rovers August 1981 (£60,000); Port Vale July 1989; Scunthorpe United August 1990; Port Vale August 1991; Stafford Rangers January 1992; Port Vale youth-team coach 1993.*
*Domestic honours with Blackburn Rovers: Full Members' Cup winners: 1987.*

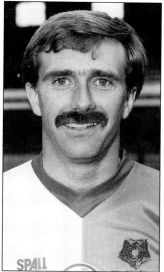

**Appearances:** Football League 252+16; Play-offs 4; FA Cup 12+1; Football League Cup 10+2; Full Members' Cup 5+3; Total 283+22.
**Goals:** Football League 16; Football League Cup 1; Full Members Cup 1; Total 18.
Bob Saxton paid a fee of £60,000 to Swindon Town to bring Miller to Ewood Park shortly after the manager's own arrival at the club. Miller was an orthodox outside-right whose strength was his ability to push the ball past the full-back and then beat him for speed. He favoured attacking the dead-ball line and a succession of telling crosses often led to great excitement in the opposing goalmouth. Although his crosses were not always as accurate as he might have liked, his ability to generate such excitement made him a great favourite with the fans.

Miller had begun his professional career with Bury before joining Nottingham Forest after only 15 appearances (including six as sub) with the Gigg Lane club. He failed to make the first team at the County Ground but scored 14 goals in 124 League appearances following a move to Doncaster Rovers. Miller had scored nine goals in 127 League appearances (including four as sub) for Swindon Town before his transfer to Ewood Park.

As well as his attacking role on the wing, Miller worked hard on the right-hand side of midfield and provided valuable defensive cover for the full-back. The highlight of his eight years at Ewood Park was undoubtedly a Wembley appearance in the Full Members' Cup in 1987; the only goal of the game came from a typical run and cross by Miller. As age began to slow him down his first-team appearances became increasingly restricted but, none the less, he remained a useful man to have on the bench.

During his last two seasons at Ewood he acted as club captain and in recognition of his services the club allowed him to move on a free transfer. Port Vale offered him the chance of a new career and after retiring from playing he became involved in coaching at the Potteries club after a spell as the Community Scheme organiser.

## MILLS, Andrew
Full-back. 1897-1898.
*5ft 9in; 11st 5lb.*
*Born: Knighton, 15 December 1877.*
*Debut: v Preston North End (h) 9 October 1897.*
*Career: Knighton; Blackburn Rovers May 1897; Swindon Town cs 1898;*

*Brighton United cs 1899; Leicester Fosse May 1900.*
**Appearances:** Football League 2.
Although Mills was to become a highly regarded defender during his time with both Swindon and Leicester, the consistency of Brandon and Glover meant that his season at Blackburn was spent in the second team. He was a Welsh trialist at both Swindon and Leicester and appeared in 64 Football League games for the Fosse.

### MILLWALL FC
Founded in 1885 as Millwall Rovers by employees of the Morton & Co jam and marmalade factory. The club became known as Millwall Athletic in 1889. League meetings between Blackburn Rovers and Millwall, apart from the 1979-80 season, have all taken place in the Second Division.

**Football League**

|  |  | | Home | | Away | |
|---|---|---|---|---|---|---|
| 1938-39 | (Div 2) | W | 3-1 | L | 1-4 |
| 1966-67 | (Div 2) | W | 1-0 | D | 1-1 |
| 1967-68 | (Div 2) | W | 2-0 | W | 2-1 |
| 1968-69 | (Div 2) | L | 2-4 | D | 2-2 |
| 1969-70 | (Div 2) | W | 4-0 | L | 1-3 |
| 1970-71 | (Div 2) | L | 0-2 | L | 0-2 |
| 1976-77 | (Div 2) | W | 2-0 | W | 1-0 |
| 1977-78 | (Div 2) | W | 2-1 | D | 1-1 |
| 1978-79 | (Div 2) | D | 1-1 | D | 1-1 |
| 1979-80 | (Div 3) | D | 1-1 | L | 0-1 |
| 1985-86 | (Div 2) | L | 1-2 | W | 1-0 |
| 1986-87 | (Div 2) | W | 1-0 | D | 2-2 |
| 1987-88 | (Div 2) | W | 2-1 | W | 4-1 |
| 1990-91 | (Div 2) | W | 1-0 | L | 1-2 |
| 1991-92 | (Div 2) | W | 2-1 | W | 3-1 |

|  | P | W | D | L | F | A |
|---|---|---|---|---|---|---|
| Home | 15 | 10 | 2 | 3 | 25 | 14 |
| Away | 15 | 5 | 5 | 5 | 21 | 22 |
| Total | 30 | 15 | 7 | 8 | 46 | 36 |

**FA Cup**

| 1978-79 | (3) | Home* | W | 2-1 |
|---|---|---|---|---|

*Drawn to play away but, owing to an FA ban, played at Ewood Park.

### MILNE, John Vance
Outside-left. 1932-1935.
*5ft 7½in 10st 2lb.*
*Born: Stirling, 25 March 1911.*
*Debut: v West Bromwich Albion (a) 20 January 1934.*
*Career: Glasgow Ashfield 1931; Blackburn Rovers March 1932; Arsenal June 1935 (£5,000); Middlesbrough December 1937; Dumbarton during World War Two. In Mexico from mid to late 1940s.*
**Appearances:** Football League 45; FA Cup 4; Total 49.
**Goals:** Football League 13; FA Cup 2; Total 15.
Blackburn Rovers faced stiff competition to bring Milne to Ewood Park from Scottish junior circles. The 20-year-old forward had learned his football with the Boys' Brigade in Stirling before moving to Glasgow. He joined the Rovers in March 1932 and was groomed in the Central League team before making his senior debut in January 1934. In the last five minutes of his debut he broke the base of a thumb and had to play for a time with his hand in plaster. His fourth appearance saw him switched to the right flank to understudy Jack Burton and he responded with two goals in the first eight minutes. However, it was on the left wing that he established himself at Ewood as a winger who possessed both tricks and pace. It came as something of a bombshell when he was transferred to Arsenal in June 1935, after only a season and a half of first-team football. Whilst at Highbury he won a championship medal in 1938 and was also capped by Scotland.

### MIMMS, Robert Andrew
Goalkeeper. 1987 & 1990-
*6ft 2in; 12st 13lb.*
*Born: York, 12 October 1963.*
*Debut: v Leeds United (a) 24 January 1987.*
*Career: Halifax Town associated schoolboy October 1979, becoming an apprentice in April 1980, before signing as a professional in August 1981; Rotherham United November 1981 (£15,000); Everton June 1985 (£150,000); Notts County on loan March 1986; Sunderland on loan December 1986; Blackburn Rovers on loan January to March 1987; Manchester City on loan September to October 1987; Tottenham Hotspur February 1988 (£325,000); Aberdeen on loan February to April 1990; Blackburn Rovers December 1990 (£250,000).*
*Domestic honours with Blackburn Rovers: Second Division Play-off winners: 1992.*

**Appearances:** Premier League 55; Football League 73; Play-offs 3; FA Cup 9; Football League Cup 14; Full Members' Cup 1; Total 155.
Bobby Mimms was transferred to Rotherham United after only three months as a professional at The Shay and without any League experience

behind him. He made his Football League debut with Rotherham United against Blackburn Rovers on 8 May 1982 but had to wait until March 1984 before becoming the first-choice goalkeeper at Millmoor. He won two England Under-21 caps whilst with Rotherham and made 83 League appearances for the club before he was transferred to Everton in June 1985 to act as understudy to Neville Southall.

Mimms had several loan spells with other clubs, including one at Ewood Park, whilst with Everton. He appeared in the 1986 FA Cup Final for the Goodison club, but finished on the losing side when Liverpool completed a League and Cup 'double'. He moved to Tottenham Hotspur in February 1988 after making only 29 League appearances during his time at Goodison Park. Unfortunately, Mimms didn't enjoy the best of fortune at White Hart Lane and after only one season he found himself understudying Erik Thorstvedt. In December 1990, Don Mackay created a new transfer record at Ewood Park when he paid £250,000 to bring Mimms back to Blackburn. Mimms had been extremely popular during his earlier loan spell at the club and this popularity continued following his move from London.

The 'keeper regained his confidence at Ewood and played a major part in helping the Rovers win a place in the Premier League. Although a tall and well-built 'keeper, Mimms is extremely agile and an excellent shot stopper. Although thought to be at his weakest in dealing with crosses the fact remains that he kept 20 clean sheets during the 1992-93 season. He continued to perform with consistency during the early part of the 1993-94 campaign despite increasing speculation that the club were about to sign Tim Flowers. However, following the arrival of Flowers, for a world-record fee for a goalkeeper, Mimms has had to settle for a place on the substitute's bench.

### MITCHELL, Albert James
Outside-left. 1948-1949.
*Born: Cobridge, 22 January 1922.*
*Debut: Portsmouth (h) 13 March 1948.*
*Career: Burslem Albion; Stoke City April 1939 amateur; Blackburn Rovers February 1948 (£4,000); Kettering Town; Northampton Town May 1949; Luton Town July 1951; Middlesbrough September 1954; Southport August 1956 to June 1957; Wellington July 1957; Kidderminster Harriers 1958-59; Stafford Rangers player-manager.*
**Appearances:** Football League 3.
Blackburn Rovers brought Bert Mitchell from Stoke City in February 1948 as the club was sliding towards the Second Division. Although Mitchell was a natural outside-left, his three appearances for Blackburn were all on the opposite flank. At the end of the season he was put on the retained list but refused to accept the terms he was offered and drifted out of League football. He had a season with Kettering Town before being picked up by Northampton Town in the 1949 close season. He went on to appear in over 250 League matches with his various clubs between 1949 and 1957.

### MITCHELL, Robert
Forward. 1976-1978.
*5ft 9in; 11st 4lb.*
*Born: South Shields, 4 January 1955.*
*Debut: v Plymouth Argyle (a) 24 August 1976 (sub).*
*Career: Sunderland January 1972. Blackburn Rovers July 1976; Grimsby Town June 1978; Carlisle United August 1982; Rotherham United March 1983; Hamrun FC (Malta) 1985; Lincoln City January 1986.*
**Appearances:** Football League 17+12; FA Cup 2; Total 19+12.
**Goals:** Football League 6; FA Cup 1; Total 7.
Bobby Mitchell was taken on an end-of-season trip to Gibraltar in May 1976 after having been released by Sunderland. He impressed Jim Smith sufficiently to be offered a contract and began the 1976-77 season on the fringe of the first team. Mitchell remained at Ewood for two seasons and,

although never really able to establish himself in the first team, he proved a more than useful substitute. During the summer of 1978 he left Ewood in search of first-team football and developed into a very sound midfield player with Grimsby Town. He scored six goals in 142 League appearances with the Mariners and won a Third Division championship medal in 1979-80.

## MITCHELL, T.
Outside-right. 1889.
*Debut: v Derby County (h) 15 April 1889.*
*Career: Blackburn Rovers 1889.*
**Appearances:** Football League 1.
**Goals:** Football League 2.
Very little is known about this player and even the initial of his Christian name must be treated with some caution as in some sources it has been given as 'W'. His one appearance with the senior team was in the final League match of the 1888-89 season. Although an E.H.Mitchell was registered with the club at the Football League for the 1889-90 season it not believed to be the same player who appeared in the match with Derby.

## MITCHELL, Thomas B.
Secretary. 1884-1896.
*Born: Kirkmahoe, Dumfries c.1843; Died: August 1921 (aged 78).*
Thomas Mitchell was thought to have come to Blackburn some time around 1867. From the moment Blackburn Rovers was conceived, Mitchell became passionately interested in the affairs of the club. At first he was simply a dedicated supporter who travelled the length and breadth of the country with his favourite team. Mitchell became the club secretary at a time when the Rovers were establishing themselves as a major force in the game. He proved to be a popular choice and had an excellent knowledge of the game, having refereed in England, Scotland, Ireland and Wales. In the year of his appointment the club won the FA Cup and during the 12 years that he was secretary the trophy returned to Ewood on a further four occasions.

A keen supporter of the Football League, Mitchell was responsible for steering the club through the formative years of that competition. During his time as secretary, Mitchell was a frequent visitor to Scotland in search of new talent and he was responsible for bringing players like Forbes, Brandon, Dewar, Campbell, Gow, Anderson and Marshall to Blackburn. He resigned as secretary in October 1896, but at the request of the committee did not immediately vacate his office. Mitchell was appointed as the first professional manager of Woolwich Arsenal for the 1897-98 season but resigned in March 1898.

## MITCHELL, Thomas
Outside-left. 1926-1929.
*5ft 8½in; 11st 4lb.*
*Born: Trimdon Grange; Died: Blackpool, July 1970*
*Debut: v Huddersfield Town (h) 11 February 1926.*
*Career: Trimdon Grange; Hartlepools United June 1922; Stockport County July 1924; Blackburn Rovers February 1926 (£2,100).*
**Appearances:** Football League 73; FA Cup 9; Total 82.
**Goals:** Football League 27; FA Cup 4; Total 31.
Tom Mitchell was tried with varying degrees of success in the centre-forward position even though his real position was on the left-wing. It was in the 1927-28 season that he made the move to centre-forward after having failed to win a regular place at outside-left. He was unfortunate to miss out on a place in the 1928 FA Cup Final team having scored four goals in four games earlier in the competition. Although big and strong, it was said that Mitchell lacked the aggression to be a truly effective leader of the attack. As the club continued to progress towards Wembley, Bob Crompton opted for the more physical approach of Jack Roscamp in the centre-forward position. The success of Roscamp meant that Mitchell returned to Central League football and was restricted to just eight League appearances during the 1928-29 season.

## MOIR, James
Right-half. 1900-1901 & 1903-1906.
*5ft 9in; 10st 8lb.*
*Born: Bonhill, Dumbartonshire, 1880.*
*Debut: v Newcastle United (h) 8 September 1900.*
*Career: Glasgow Celtic October 1898; Vale of Leven December 1899; Glasgow Celtic April 1900; Blackburn Rovers June 1900; Glasgow Celtic May 1901; Blackburn Rovers November 1903.*
**Appearances:** Football League 77; FA Cup 3; Total 80.
Jimmy Moir was virtually an unknown youngster when he moved to Blackburn Rovers in June 1900. When he arrived at Ewood it was assumed that he would be an understudy to James Hosie who had just arrived from Reading. However, Moir quickly established himself as the outstanding half-back at the club and deposed Hosie after only one League game. He appeared in 32 League games during the 1900-01

season and the Rovers were keen to keep him at Ewood Park. However, the Celtic manager wanted him back at Parkhead and in May 1901, Moir appeared in all four of Celtic's Glasgow Charity Cup matches. Although not a regular during the 1901-02 season, Moir established himself as the first-choice right-half at Celtic during the following campaign. In November 1903 he was again brought to Ewood Park but didn't really achieve the same level of success during his second spell with the club.

## MONKS, Albert
Inside-right. 1902-1904.
*5ft 6in; 11st 3lb.*
*Born: 1879.*
*Debut: v Notts County (h) 29 November 1902.*
*Career: Ashton North End; Glossop May 1899; Stalybridge Rovers; Bury May 1901; Everton May 1902; Blackburn Rovers November 1902; Nelson; Swindon Town May 1905 to cs 1906.*
**Appearances:** Football League 24; FA Cup 3; Total 27.
**Goals:** Football League 4; FA Cup 1; Total 5.
Albert Monks was said to be a skilful manipulator of the ball who possessed a powerful shot. Although he failed to make the first team at Goodison Park, Monks was immediately drafted into the Blackburn team following his move from Everton. Whilst not the most prolific of goalscorers, Monks provided valuable support for Jack Dewhurst and then Adam Bowman in the centre-forward position. Restricted to only five League games during the 1903-04 season, Monks played for a short time with Nelson before moving south to join Swindon Town.

## MOONEY, Francis
Outside-right. 1954-1956.
*5ft 7½in; 11st 4lb.*
*Born: Fauldhouse, 1 January 1932.*
*Debut: v Oldham Athletic (h) 13 February 1954.*
*Career: Bathgate St M; Manchester United May 1949; Blackburn Rovers February 1954; Carlisle United May 1956.*
**Appearances:** Football League 58; FA Cup 1; Total 59.
**Goals:** Football League 19.
Blackburn manager Johnny Carey had been impressed by the lively Mooney when they were playing colleagues at Old Trafford. During his first season in charge at Ewood Park, Carey was unable to fill the outside-right position with any degree of consistency and so returned to Old Trafford to sign Mooney. The stockily built Scot cost next to nothing but made an immediate impression at Ewood Park. He had pace and the ability to deliver the type of crosses on which Tommy Briggs would thrive. However, in 1954-55 he was to prove that he also had an eye for goal with a return of 16 goals in 42 League matches. The following season saw his form inexplicably waver and the emergence of Bryan Douglas on the right wing ended his first-team opportunities at Ewood Park. He moved to Carlisle in May 1956 and went on to score 23 goals in 124 League games for the Cumbrian club.

## MOORE, Norman Woodliffe
Centre-forward. 1950-1951.
*5ft 10in; 11st 7lb.*
*Born: Grimsby, 15 October 1919.*
*Debut: v Coventry City (a) 18 March 1950.*
*Career: Grimsby Schools; Grimsby Town March 1939; Wrexham wartime guest 1941-42 & 1942-43; Chester wartime guest 1943-44; Charlton Athletic wartime guest 1943-44; Norwich City wartime guest 1945-46; Hull City April 1947; Blackburn Rovers March 1950; Bury August 1951; Goole Town July 1952; Wisbech Town 1953.*
**Appearances:** Football League 7.
**Goals:** Football League 1.
The peak of Moore's career occurred before he joined Blackburn Rovers in March 1950. It was as a hard-working centre-forward at Hull City in the immediate post-war years that Moore achieved his greatest success. He had scored one goal in seven League games for Grimsby Town before the outbreak of war and had guested at various clubs during the war years. However, a return of 46 goals from 81 League appearances with Hull was the most productive period of his career and in 1948-49 he won a Third Division North championship medal with the club. He was signed by Jackie Bestall to replace the free-scoring Dennis Westcott who had been sold to Manchester City a few weeks earlier. Sadly, a return of one goal

from six games suggested that he would not provide the leadership that Bestall required. He made just one appearance during the 1950-51 season before moving to Bury in August 1951. He made only two League appearances for the Gigg Lane club before drifting into non-League football.

### MORAN, Kevin Bernard
Central defender. 1990-
*5ft 11in; 12st 9lb.*
*Born: Dublin, 29 April 1956.*
*Debut: v Stoke City (h) 27 January 1990.*
*Career: Manchester United February 1978; Sporting Gijon (Spain) August 1988; Blackburn Rovers January 1990.*
*International honours with Blackburn Rovers: Republic of Ireland: 24 caps (1990-94).*
*Domestic honours with Blackburn Rovers: Second Division Play-off winners: 1992.*
**Appearances:** Premier League 55; Football League 88+4; Play-offs 5; FA Cup 10+1; Football League Cup 8+1; Full Members' Cup 1; Total 167+6.
**Goals:** Premier League 5; Football League 5; Play-offs 1; FA Cup 1; Total 12.
After ten years at Old Trafford, Kevin Moran appeared to be approaching the end of his career when he opted to move to Spain to join Sporting Gijon in August 1988. In January 1990, Don Mackay pulled off something of a coup when he persuaded Moran to return to England to join the Rovers. In signing for Blackburn Moran turned down the chance to be reunited with Ron Atkinson, his former Old Trafford boss, who wanted him to join Sheffield Wednesday. Moran has played a crucial role in lifting Blackburn Rovers from a club anchored in the lower reaches of the Second Division to one that has become one of the most powerful clubs in the country.

Indeed, his bravely headed goal at Derby in the semi-final of the Second Division Play-offs proved vital in taking the Rovers to a Wembley Final with Leicester City. Shortly after joining the Rovers, Moran figured in all five of the Republic of Ireland's World Cup campaign during the summer of 1990. Although well into the veteran stage of his career, Moran appeared in 41 League games (including four as sub) and captained the team to Play-off success at Wembley in 1991-92. Those who believed that the tough-tackling central defender would find life in the Premier League too quick for his ageing legs were soon proved wrong.

The 1992-93 season found him in imperious form and his ability to read the game and to organise the team on the field proved invaluable. A defender who is never afraid to challenge for the ball, Moran has suffered some terrible facial injuries during his career but continues to give total commitment. Although injuries finally began to take their toll during the 1993-94 season, Moran remains an outstanding defender and captain. Away from football the quiet Irishman holds a Bachelor of Commerce degree and has an interest in a greetings card business back in his native Dublin.

### MORELAND, John
Inside-forward. 1898-1899.
*Debut: v Stoke (h) 8 April 1898.*
*Career: Blackburn Rovers March 1898.*
**Appearances:** Football League 20; Test Matches 1; Total 21.
**Goals:** Football League 6.
Moreland made his debut for the Rovers as the club were desperately trying to retain their First Division standing. Although he only figured in one of the test matches, Moreland became a regular in the inside-left position after the first match of the 1898-99 season. He scored six goals in 18 League games during that campaign before failing to turn up for the home game with Notts County on 2 January 1899. With no explanation

forthcoming for his non-appearance he was suspended *sine die* by the club and never appeared again for Blackburn Rovers.

### MORGAN, Hugh
Inside-left. 1900-1903.
*5ft 5½in; 11st.*
Born: Longriggend, Lanarks, 20 September 1869.
Debut: v Liverpool (a) 1 September 1900.
Career: Longriggend Wanderers; St Mirren June 1896; Liverpool March 1898; Blackburn Rovers June 1900 until cs 1903.
**Appearances:** Football League 77; FA Cup 2; Total 79.
**Goals:** Football League 18.
Hugh Morgan's best days were supposedly behind him when he joined Blackburn Rovers in June 1900. The dapper little Scotsman had scored 15 goals in 59 League outings whilst on Merseyside and as luck would have it his Blackburn debut was at Anfield against Liverpool. An artist on the ball, Morgan was a typically tricky Scot whose footwork was always neat and tidy. However, as well as skill, Morgan also had an appetite for hard work and an eye for goal. He enjoyed three successful seasons at Ewood and was particularly effective during his first two campaigns at the club when Peter Somers, a fellow Scot, occupied the inside-right position.

### MORLEY, Brian J.
Left-back. 1976-1981.
*5ft 7in; 11st 3lb.*
*Born: Fleetwood, 4 October 1960.*
*Debut: v Wrexham (a) 10 March 1979.*
*Career: Blackburn Rovers associated schoolboy February 1976, becoming an apprentice in July 1977, signing professional in October 1978; Tranmere Rovers August 1981.*
**Appearances:** Football League 20; Football League Cup 4; Total 24.
Brian Morley got the chance of first-team football following the departure of John Bailey to Everton in the summer of 1979. Morley, who had appeared in just three League games prior to the start of the 1979-80 season, was given the left-back position after the opening game of that campaign. However, he failed to grasp the opportunity to impress the newly appointed Howard Kendall and the manager eventually settled on a pairing of Branagan and Rathbone in the full-back positions. The success of these two players meant that Morley was not called upon again for first-team action before moving to Tranmere in August 1981. At Prenton Park, Morley, scored two goals in 16 League appearances (including six as sub).

### MORLEY, Dr E.S.
Chairman. 1888-1901.
A man noted for his cigars and velvet coats, Dr E.S.Morley was also a man of strong conviction and one who was not afraid to speak his mind. Morley became connected with Blackburn Rovers in 1880 and was quickly appointed a vice-president of the club. He became chairman of the club in 1888 and remained in that office until 1901. Failing health forced him to give up his position as chairman but he retained his seat on the board of directors right up to his death.

Dr Morley was not one of those who welcomed the legalisation of professionalism in 1885. He regarded football as a recreation and deplored the introduction of the business element that arrived with professionalism.

He was later to moderate his views on professionalism and in an interview he gave to the *Blackburn Times* in September 1887 he said: "I have changed my opposition to favour for the professional, because I prefer an out-and-out pro to a lying, deceitful, and scheming semi-amateur."

However, Dr Morley still had grave reservations about paying men to play football. He said: "The big wages they secure enable them to loaf away their time when they have no football to play, and in encouraging them to days of idleness and loafing in public houses we are doing an injury to the men themselves. This will be seen in time, and the heavily paid pro will be put to rout."

Dr Morley would no doubt have been astounded at the way in which the professional game was to develop during the following century. However, one issue on which he was clearly ahead of his time was that regarding the length of the football season. Even in 1887, Morley felt that the public would soon lose interest in the game if the clubs did not agree to cut down on the number of matches they played. In attacking the ever expanding football season Morley said: "It wearies the public of the game, makes players stale in their proper season, and games in winter lose their attractions."

### MORRIS, Peter A.
Outside-left. 1978-1980.
*5ft 7in; 9st 8lb.*

*Born: Farnworth, 23 November 1958.*
*Debut: v West Ham United (a) 30 December 1978 (sub).*
*Career: Preston North End October 1976; Blackburn Rovers July 1978 to April 1980.*
**Appearances:** Football League 2+2; FA Cup 1+1; Total 3+3.
Peter Morris was a fleet-footed outside-left who arrived at Ewood Park in the summer of 1978. When Jim Iley signed Morris he already had Dave Wagstaffe and the newly signed John Aston available for the left-wing position. However, the early departure of Wagstaffe and the failure of Aston gave Morris an unexpected opportunity to stake a claim for a first-team place. Unfortunately, with the team struggling at the foot of the table Morris found it difficult to make much impression against Second Division defences.

**MORRISON, Andrew C.**
Central defender 1993-
*5ft 11in; 12st.*
*Born: Inverness, 30 July 1970.*
*Debut: v Wimbledon (h) 5 February 1994 (sub).*
*Career: Plymouth Argyle trainee November 1986, turning professional in July 1987; Blackburn Rovers August 1993 (£250,000 including Wayne Burnett in part-exchange).*
**Appearances:** Premier League 1+4; FA Cup 1; Total 2+4.

Andy Morrison is a robust central defender who bears more than a passing resemblance to the late John Bray. Although Morrison first appeared for the club during a pre-season tour of Ireland, injuries meant that he had to wait until February 1994 before making his Premiership debut with the club. He got his opportunity when Tim Sherwood suffered a serious shoulder injury early in the match with Wimbledon at Ewood Park. However, Morrison quickly adapted to the pace of Premiership football and like Nicky Marker, a former teammate at Plymouth, has become a valuable member of the first-team squad.

**MORTIMER, Robert**
Centre-forward. 1937-1938.
*5ft 8½in; 11st 4lb.*
*Born: Bolton 1908 (April quarter).*
*Debut: v Southampton (h) 2 October 1937.*
*Career: Connah's Quay & Shotton; Barrow amateur February 1927, turning professional in July 1927; Bolton Wanderers August 1928; Northampton Town June 1931; Brentford May 1933; Bournemouth & Boscombe Athletic May 1934; Accrington Stanley June 1935; Portsmouth February 1936; Accrington Stanley September 1936; Blackburn Rovers October 1937 (with W.G.Tyson for a combined fee of £1,200); York City June 1938 (£300) until September 1939; Horwich RMI September 1946.*
**Appearances:** Football League 16.
**Goals:** Football League 4.
A stocky centre-forward whose lack of height was more than compensated for by his natural predatory instincts in front of goal. His goalscoring ability first came to light when he became Accrington Stanley's leading goalscorer for the 1935-36 campaign with 19 goals in 25 League games. In February 1936 he moved to Portsmouth but was unable to break into the first team and returned to Peel Park on a free transfer in September 1936. It was during the 1936-37 season that Mortimer left an indelible mark on the minds of officials at Ewood Park.

He scored both goals in a pulsating 2-2 draw in the third round of the FA Cup at Ewood Park and a further two goals in the replay which enabled Accrington to pull off a shock 3-1 win. In October 1937 he moved to Ewood Park and replaced Tommy Sale at centre-forward. However, although he scored two goals on his debut, Mortimer found scoring a more difficult art in the Second Division and, as a result, his appearances became more sporadic.

Mortimer ended his League career with a move to York City and finished the 1938-39 season as that club's leading goalscorer with 22 goals from 35 League games. After leaving football he had a grocery and mixed business in his native Bolton.

**MOST MATCHES**
The record for the most matches to have been played in the shortest space of time was created in April 1894. Within the space of one month the club played 18 matches of which 16 were friendlies and two were in the East Lancashire Charity Cup. Details of the 18 matches are given below:

| April 7 | Linfield Athletic | Home | W | 4-0 |
|---|---|---|---|---|
| 9 | Darwen | Away | W | 2-1 |
| 11 | Celtic | Away | D | 0-0* |
| 12 | Liverpool | Away | W | 5-0 |
| 13 | Burnley | Home | L | 1-2 |
| 14 | Stoke City | Home | W | 5-0 |
| 15 | Heart of Midlothian | Away | L | 1-2 |
| 17 | East Stirling | Away | W | 3-1 |
| 18 | Wishaw Thistle | Away | W | 10-2 |
| 19 | Preston North End | Home | L | 0-2 |
| 20 | Burnley | Away | L | 1-2 |
| 20 | Accrington (ELCC) | Away | D | 1-1 |
| 21 | Preston North End | Away | L | 0-6 |
| 23 | Darwen | Home | W | 4-0 |
| 24 | Liverpool | Away | W | 3-1 |
| 25 | Southport Central | Away | W | 2-1 |
| 26 | Accrington (ELCC) | Home | W | 4-0 |
| 28 | Bolton Wanderers | Away | W | 4-0 |

*Note: This match was played in Manchester.

**MULLEN, James**
Outside-left. 1974-1976.
*5ft 8½in; 10st 10lb.*
*Born: Oxford, 16 March 1947.*
*Debut: v Crystal Palace (a) 22 October 1974 (sub).*
*Career: Oxford City; Reading November 1966; Charlton Athletic November 1967; Rotherham United February 1969; Blackburn Rovers August 1974; Bury June 1976; Rochdale on loan March 1977 to May 1977.*
*Domestic honours with Blackburn Rovers: Third Division championship: 1974-75 (5+4 apps).*
**Appearances:** Football League 6+4; FA Cup 2; Total 8+4.
An experienced winger who was desperately unlucky with injuries during his short stay at Ewood Park. Injuries kept him out of the side almost as soon as he joined the club but his worst moment came against Peterborough United in February 1975 when he broke his leg just when he seemed to be settling into the side. After this he only featured in two more senior matches for the club before joining Bury.

**MULVANEY, Richard**
Central defender. 1964-1971.
*5ft 11in; 12st 5lb.*
*Born: Sunderland, 5 August 1942.*
*Debut: v Leicester City (h) 26 September 1964.*
*Career: Silksworth Colliery; Billingham Synthonia; Merton Colliery; Blackburn Rovers February 1964; Oldham Athletic August 1971; Rochdale October 1974 to October 1976; Gateshead; Chester-le-Street.*
**Appearances:** Football League 135+6; FA Cup 2; Football League Cup 8; Total 145+6.
**Goals:** Football League 4.
Dick Mulvaney waited until he had completed his apprenticeship, as an acetylene welder, in a Sunderland shipyard before accepting the opportunity to play professional football. He joined the Rovers in February 1964 and found himself understudying Mike England for the centre-half position at Ewood Park. Mulvaney had to bide his time in the second team but picked up two Central League championship medals whilst with the club. He made his first breakthrough in 1965-66 when Mike England was moved to the centre-forward position. However, with the Rovers anchored at the foot of the First Division, England reverted to centre-half and Mulvaney returned to the Central League.

When England was transferred to Tottenham Hotspur on the eve of the 1966-67 season Mulvaney, as expected, was given the number-five shirt. Sadly, he perforated an ear drum in a League Cup match with Barrow in September and was out of action for some time. In his absence George Sharples took the opportunity to form a reliable defensive partnership with Ronnie Clayton and Mulvaney was unable to force his way back into the team. A question mark appeared over his Ewood career when Eddie Quigley signed John Coddington, the experienced Huddersfield Town centre-half, in the summer of 1967.

Although Mulvaney only started six League games during the 1967-68 season, the following campaign saw him partnering Coddington on a number of occasions. By the start of the 1969-70 season, Eddie Quigley had settled on Mulvaney and Allan Hunter as his new defensive partnership. However, this pairing was broken up when Mulvaney became involved in a row with the club over where he lived. He was reported to have claimed that he wanted to return to his native North-East and insisted on living on the other side of the Pennines so that he had easier access to his native area. Whilst the club relaxed their rules on where a player lives, Mulvaney eventually took his case to the Football Association Appeal Tribunal. A transfer fee of £50,000 was placed on his head but further appeals resulted in a tribunal stating that he could become a free agent.

Relations between the club and Mulvaney were not improved when he accepted an offer to join Oldham Athletic rather than return to the North-East. Mulvaney enjoyed three very successful years at Boundary Park, appearing in 92 League games (including four a sub) and scoring two goals. He ended his professional career with 73 League appearances (including one as sub) and four goals for Rochdale. After leaving football he returned to the shipyards of his native North-East and non-League football. Tragically, osteoarthritis in his spine, a legacy of his footballing injuries, meant Mulvaney had to give up work at the age of 44. His brother Jimmy, who died in 1982, was a former professional footballer with Hartlepool United, Barrow and Stockport County.

## MUNRO, Stuart
Left-back. 1991-1993.
*5ft 11in; 11st.*
*Born: Falkirk, 15 September 1962.*
*Debut: v Ipswich Town (h) 31 August 1991.*
*Career: Bo'ness United; St Mirren 1980; Alloa Athletic cs 1982; Glasgow Rangers February 1984; Blackburn Rovers July 1991 (£350,000); Bristol City February 1993 (free).*
**Appearances:** Football League 1.
Stuart Munro was a big money signing from Rangers who was dogged by injury during the early part of his stay at Ewood Park. Munro, who had won four Scottish League championship medals and three Skol Cup medals with Rangers, was unable to regain his place once he had been restored to full fitness. Munro, a skilful attacking full-back, had been signed by Don Mackay and appeared in the opening match of the 1991-92 season. However, by the time he had overcome his injury problems the Rovers had replaced Mackay with Kenny Dalglish and the new manager had paid £400,000 to Blackpool to install Alan Wright in the left-back position.

The consistency of Wright meant Munro was confined to the Central League team for the remainder of the season. Following their promotion to the Premier League, Dalglish preferred Tony Dobson as Wright's understudy and in February 1993 he allowed Munro to join Bristol City on a free transfer. Munro became a regular in the first team at Ashton Gate and was a member of the team that enjoyed a memorable FA Cup victory over Liverpool at Anfield in February 1994.

## MURPHY, Donal Patrick
Forward. 1982-1983.
*5ft 11in; 11st.*
*Born: Dublin, 23 February 1955.*
*Debut: v Norwich City (a) 24 April 1982 (sub).*
*Career: Coventry City August 1972; Shamrock Rangers late 1973; Coventry City early 1975; Millwall on loan October to November 1977; Torquay United May 1978; Plymouth Argyle June 1980; Torquay United on loan December 1981; Blackburn Rovers February 1982; Drogheda on loan October 1982 to January 1983; Bohemians on loan February to May 1983; Drogheda Untied cs 1983; University College Dublin cs 1984.*
**Appearances:** Football League 1+2.
Donal Murphy joined Blackburn Rovers at a time when money was tight and the playing squad was somewhat threadbare. However, although Murphy had appeared in 182 League games (including 19 as sub) at his various clubs prior to coming to Ewood, he was unable to force his way into the Blackburn team. His only senior outings were towards the end of the 1981-82 campaign and the following season he was allowed to return to Ireland on loan.

## MURPHY, Thomas Edward
Inside-left. 1947-1949.
*Born: Middlesbrough, 25 March 1921.*
*Debut: v Everton (a) 25 December 1947.*
*Career: South Bank; Middlesbrough May 1939; Blackburn Rovers December 1947; Halifax Town March 1949 to June 1954; Redcar Albion September 1955.*
**Appearances:** Football League 31; FA Cup 3; Total 34.
**Goals:** Football League 6; FA Cup 1; Total 7.
Eddie Murphy was one of a number of new players who were brought to

Ewood Park in the immediate post-war years. Murphy made the inside-left position his own during the second half of the 1947-48 season, scoring three goals in 20 League appearances. Unfortunately, the campaign ended with Blackburn being relegated to the Second Division and Murphy lost his place after only two games of the new season. Although he enjoyed a brief return during the middle part of the campaign he was allowed to join Halifax Town in March 1949. At The Shay Murphy enjoyed great success and scored 30 goals in 217 League appearances.

## MURRAY, John Winning
Full-back. 1892-1896.
*Born: Strathblane, Stirlingshire, 24 April 1865; Died: 16 September 1922.*
*Debut: v Newton Heath (h) 3 September 1892.*
*Career: Wanderers FC; Vale of Leven; Sunderland September 1890; Blackburn Rovers May 1892. Retired April 1896.*
**Appearances:** Football League 109; FA Cup 13; Total 122.
Employed in the calico printing industry throughout his working life, John Murray solved the right-back problems which had been created by the departure of Tom Brandon to Sheffield Wednesday. However, when Brandon returned from Yorkshire, Murray moved to the left-back spot and the two proved a formidable combination. Murray, a somewhat burly figure for an athlete, used his build and enthusiasm to intimidate many an opposing winger. His approach to the game made him a natural for the captaincy and such was his loyalty to the cause that he answered the call to assist the reserve team following his retirement. His son Bobby was later to appear for the club as a goalkeeper.

## MURRAY, Robert William
Goalkeeper. 1908-1912.
*5ft 10in; 11st 2lb.*
*Born: Alexandria*
*Debut: v Bristol City (h) 13 September 1909.*
*Career: Brinscall; Crosshills; Darwen September 1908; Blackburn Rovers February 1909; Nelson 1912; Darwen.*
**Appearances:** Football League 10.
The son of John Winning Murray, a former Rovers full-back, Bobby Murray progressed through local junior circles before signing for Darwen in September 1908. By December of that year he was featuring with the Reserves at Ewood Park and in February 1909 he joined the playing staff at Blackburn on a full-time basis. Although he was generally reliable, Murray never established himself ahead of Jimmy Ashcroft and in 1911-12 he was third choice behind Alf Robinson and Ashcroft.

## NAPIER, Christopher Robin Anthony
Forward. 1972-1974.
*5ft 11½in; 11st 6lb.*
*Born: Dunblane, Perth, 26 September 1943.*
*Debut: v Bolton Wanderers (h) 2 September 1972.*
*Career: Blackpool non-contract player May 1960, signing professional in November 1960; Preston North End June 1963; Workington July 1964; Newcastle United November 1965; Brighton & Hove Albion September 1966; Blackburn Rovers August 1972 until cs 1974.*
**Appearances:** Football League 53+1; FA Cup 7; Football League Cup 3; Total 63+1.
**Goals:** Football League 10; FA Cup 3; Total 13.
Napier, who was nicknamed Kit, scored over 100 goals in the lower divisions of the Football League but failed to make much impression when given his First Division opportunity with Newcastle United. In many ways it was surprising that this tall and lean striker should enjoy his greatest success outside of the top flight. A player of great finesse, Napier's fancy footwork and subtle flicks appeared ill suited to the more vigorous demands of the lower divisions. However, he proved himself a regular goalscorer at Workington with 25 goals in 58 League appearances and whilst at Brighton he broke the club's post-war scoring record.

He helped Brighton to win promotion to the Second Division in 1971-72 but joined Blackburn after appearing in the opening games of the 1972-73 campaign. Napier left the Goldstone Ground with a record 84 goals in 256 League games (including seven as sub). At Ewood he operated on the right wing for much of his time at the club and for a time his skilful play brightened the gloom of Third Division football. However, his appearances became increasingly spasmodic and he was released by the club at the end of the 1973-74 season.

## NEEDHAM, Paul Andrew
Centre-forward. 1976-1977.
*5ft 11in; 11st 6lb.*
*Born: Oldham, 13 September 1955.*
*Debut: v Bolton Wanderers (h) 21 August 1976 (sub).*
*Career: Harlow & Essex Boys; Birmingham City apprentice June 1971,*

*turning professional in August 1973; Blackburn Rovers July 1976; Aldershot on loan March 1977, signing permanently in April 1977; Chester City June 1979.*

**Appearances:** Football League 4+1; Football League Cup 1+1; Total 5+2.

Andy Needham joined the club after his impressive displays in a tournament in Gibraltar at the end of the 1975-76 season. A tall forward who favoured the centre-forward position, Needham had only appeared in three League games with Birmingham, one of which was as substitute, before joining Blackburn. He began the 1976-77 season on the substitute's bench at Ewood and was discarded after only a handful of appearances. He made more of an impression at Aldershot where he appeared in 95 League games (including three as sub) and scored 29 goals. He made no appearances during a short spell with Chester City at the end of his career.

## NEUTRAL GROUNDS

Ewood Park has been used as a neutral ground for FA Cup matches on a number of occasions. In recent seasons both Chorley and Accrington Stanley have been given permission to play money-spinning ties at Ewood instead of their respective home grounds. On 6 December 1987, Chorley played their second-round tie with Preston North End at Ewood, whilst Accrington Stanley attracted a crowd of 10,801 for their first-round tie with Crewe Alexandra. Both clubs enjoyed mixed fortunes at Ewood for whilst Chorley earned a 1-1 draw from their tie, Accrington crashed to a 6-1 defeat. On 23 February 1959, Ewood Park hosted the second replay of the fifth-round tie between Bolton Wanderers and Preston North End. A goal by Nat Lofthouse was sufficient to give Bolton a victory in front of 51,090 spectators.

Ewood Park has hosted the following FA Cup semi-finals:
1893 Everton 0-0 Preston North End (Replay) (aet)
1895 Aston Villa 2-1 Sunderland
1913 Aston Villa 1-0 Oldham Athletic
1915 Bolton Wanderers 1-2 Sheffield United
1938 Huddersfield Town 3-1 Sunderland
1947 Burnley 0-0 Liverpool (aet)

Blackburn Rovers have themselves been involved in an FA Cup semi-final on 16 occasions, although with replays these have stretched over 20 matches. Details of results and opponents in semi-finals can be found in the section dealing with the FA Cup. However, below is a breakdown on the neutral venues used for the semi-final matches involving Blackburn Rovers:
Anfield, Liverpool 1912 (Replay)
Alexandra Road, Crewe 1889 & Replay
Bramall Lane, Sheffield 1894 & 1911
Derby Cricket Ground 1886
Derby Racecourse 1890
Elland Road, Leeds 1952 (Replay)
Filbert Street, Leicester 1928
Hillsborough, Sheffield 1912 & 1952
Lower Grounds, Aston 1884
Maine Road, Manchester 1958 & 1960
Meadow Lane, Nottingham 1925
Trent Bridge, Nottingham 1885
St Johns, Huddersfield 1882
Town Ground, Nottingham 1893
Whalley Range, Manchester 1882 (Replay)
Victoria Ground, Stoke 1891

## NEW BRIGHTON FC

Formed in 1921, New Brighton Football Club became members of the Third Division North in 1923. The club remained in the Third Division North until losing its Football League status in 1950. Meetings between New Brighton and Blackburn Rovers were restricted to just two wartime games during the 1941-42 season.

**Wartime**

| | | Home | | Away | |
|---|---|---|---|---|---|
| 1941-42 | (FLNS-SC) | W | 5-1 | W | 5-0 |

## NEWCASTLE UNITED FC

The origins of Newcastle United can be traced back to a club called Stanley in 1881. The following year the club changed its name to Newcastle East End. In August 1892, a club called Newcastle West End had been formed and played on a ground which is now St James' Park. When West End went out of existence East End moved to St James' Park and in 1892 they changed their name to Newcastle United. The club was elected to the Second Division of the Football League in 1893 and won promotion following the Test Match series, involving Blackburn Rovers, of 1897-98.

**Football League**

| | | Home | | Away | |
|---|---|---|---|---|---|
| 1898-99 | (Div 1) | W | 4-2 | L | 0-1 |
| 1899-00 | (Div 1) | L | 2-3 | L | 1-4 |
| 1900-01 | (Div 1) | D | 0-0 | L | 0-1 |
| 1901-02 | (Div 1) | D | 0-0 | W | 3-0 |
| 1902-03 | (Div 1) | W | 3-1 | L | 0-1 |
| 1903-04 | (Div 1) | W | 4-0 | L | 1-2 |
| 1904-05 | (Div 1) | W | 2-0 | L | 0-1 |
| 1905-06 | (Div 1) | W | 1-0 | L | 0-3 |
| 1906-07 | (Div 1) | W | 4-0 | L | 1-3 |
| 1907-08 | (Div 1) | D | 1-1 | L | 0-3 |
| 1908-09 | (Div 1) | L | 2-4 | L | 0-2 |
| 1909-10 | (Div 1) | W | 2-0 | L | 1-4 |
| 1910-11 | (Div 1) | W | 3-1 | D | 2-2 |
| 1911-12 | (Div 1) | D | 1-1 | L | 2-4 |
| 1912-13 | (Div 1) | W | 2-0 | W | 1-0 |
| 1913-14 | (Div 1) | W | 3-0 | D | 0-0 |
| 1914-15 | (Div 1) | L | 2-3 | L | 1-2 |
| 1919-20 | (Div 1) | W | 2-0 | D | 0-0 |
| 1920-21 | (Div 1) | D | 3-3 | W | 2-1 |
| 1921-22 | (Div 1) | L | 0-2 | L | 0-2 |
| 1922-23 | (Div 1) | D | 1-1 | L | 1-5 |
| 1923-24 | (Div 1) | W | 2-1 | L | 1-2 |
| 1924-25 | (Div 1) | D | 1-1 | L | 0-4 |
| 1925-26 | (Div 1) | L | 1-2 | W | 7-1 |
| 1926-27 | (Div 1) | L | 1-2 | L | 1-6 |
| 1927-28 | (Div 1) | W | 1-0 | W | 1-0 |
| 1928-29 | (Div 1) | W | 2-0 | W | 2-0 |
| 1929-30 | (Div 1) | W | 4-2 | L | 1-5 |
| 1930-31 | (Div 1) | W | 1-0 | W | 3-2 |
| 1931-32 | (Div 1) | L | 0-3 | L | 3-5 |
| 1932-33 | (Div 1) | W | 2-1 | L | 1-2 |
| 1933-34 | (Div 1) | W | 3-2 | L | 1-3 |
| 1936-37 | (Div 2) | W | 6-1 | L | 0-2 |
| 1937-38 | (Div 2) | W | 2-1 | L | 0-2 |
| 1938-39 | (Div 2) | W | 3-0 | D | 2-2 |
| 1958-59 | (Div 1) | W | 3-0 | W | 5-1 |
| 1959-60 | (Div 1) | D | 1-1 | L | 1-3 |
| 1960-61 | (Div 1) | L | 2-4 | L | 1-3 |
| 1965-66 | (Div 1) | W | 4-2 | L | 1-2 |
| 1978-79 | (Div 2) | L | 1-3 | L | 1-3 |
| 1980-81 | (Div 2) | W | 3-0 | D | 0-0 |
| 1981-82 | (Div 2) | W | 4-1 | D | 0-0 |
| 1982-83 | (Div 2) | L | 1-2 | L | 2-3 |
| 1983-84 | (Div 2) | D | 1-1 | D | 1-1 |
| 1989-90 | (Div 2) | W | 2-0 | L | 1-2 |
| 1990-91 | (Div 2) | L | 0-1 | L | 0-1 |
| 1991-92 | (Div 2) | W | 3-1 | D | 0-0 |

| | P | W | D | L | F | A |
|---|---|---|---|---|---|---|
| Home | 47 | 27 | 9 | 11 | 96 | 54 |
| Away | 47 | 8 | 8 | 31 | 52 | 96 |
| Total | 94 | 35 | 17 | 42 | 148 | 150 |

**Test Matches**

| | Home | | Away | |
|---|---|---|---|---|
| 1897-98 | W | 4-3 | L | 0-4 |

**FA Premiership**

| | Home | | Away | |
|---|---|---|---|---|
| 1993-94 | W | 1-0 | D | 1-1 |

| | P | W | D | L | F | A |
|---|---|---|---|---|---|---|
| Home | 1 | 1 | 0 | 0 | 1 | 0 |
| Away | 1 | 0 | 1 | 0 | 1 | 1 |
| Total | 2 | 1 | 1 | 0 | 2 | 1 |

**FA Cup**

| | | | | |
|---|---|---|---|---|
| 1909-10 | (3) | Away | L | 1-3 |
| 1927-28 | (3) | Home | W | 4-1 |
| 1951-52 | (SF) | Hillsborough | D | 0-0 |
| | (R) | Elland Road | L | 1-2 |

**Wartime**

| | | Home | | Away | |
|---|---|---|---|---|---|
| 1945-46 | (FLN) | L | 1-2 | L | 1-8 |

## NEWELL, Michael Colin

Forward. 1991-
*6ft; 11st.*
*Born: Liverpool, 27 January 1965.*
*Debut: v Barnsley (h) 16 November 1991.*
*Career: Crewe Alexandra on trial September 1983; Wigan Athletic October 1983; Luton Town January 1986 (£100,000); Leicester City September 1987 (£350,000); Everton June 1989 (£1,100,000); Blackburn Rovers November 1991(£1,100,000).*
*Domestic honours with Blackburn Rovers: Second Division Play-off winners: 1992.*
**Appearances:** Premier League 67+1; Football League 18+2; Play-offs 3; FA Cup 7; Football League Cup 10+1; Total 105+4.
**Goals:** Premier League 19; Football League 6; Play-offs 2; FA Cup 6; Football League Cup 7; Total 40.
A strong running forward who is capable of holding the ball until support arrives. Mike Newell got his grounding at Crewe and Wigan Athletic before a £100,000 move took him to Luton Town. He quickly adjusted to life in the First Division and in 1986-87 he finished as joint top scorer

with 12 goals. He moved to Leicester in September 1987 and once again he finished top scorer with 13 League goals in 1988-89. Although not a prolific marksman, Newell's hard working approach was recognised by Everton and in July 1989 he joined the Merseyside club in a million pound plus deal.

Newell struggled to score goals with any regularity on Merseyside and as a result he found himself in and out of the team during his time with the club. Don Mackay made an attempt to bring Newell to Ewood Park during the summer of 1991 but the striker declined the offer. However, in November 1991 he became the first player to cost Blackburn Rovers a million pounds when he accepted an offer from Kenny Dalglish to join the Ewood revolution. Newell scored on his debut and displayed some impressive form as the Rovers ran away from the chasing pack at the top of the Second Division. Tragedy struck in February 1992 when Newell suffered a fractured tibia in the match with Newcastle United at Ewood Park.

Although Dalglish signed Roy Wegerle and Duncan Shearer to compensate for the loss of Newell, neither man was able to provide the leadership which Newell had done before his injury. As the club slipped down the table, Newell returned in time to help ensure that the Rovers claimed the final Play-off place. Newell scored a vital goal in the first leg of the semi-final with Derby County which helped to take the club to Wembley. However, it was in the Play-off Final against Leicester City that Newell carved his own niche in the history of Blackburn Rovers when he converted the penalty which gave the club a 1-0 win and a place in the Premier League. Having formed a good understanding with David Speedie, Newell went on to enjoy an even more successful partnership with Alan Shearer and has been unlucky to be overlooked for international selection. Newell scored 13 goals in 40 League games during 1992-93 despite the fact that he had to adjust to the loss of Shearer mid-way through the season. Newell continued to show outstanding form during the 1993-94 season until he received a serious injury at Old Trafford on Boxing Day 1993. However, although he had only had one reserve-team match in three months, Newell returned to action at Hillsborough in March 1994 and scored the last minute goal which gave the Rovers a 2-1 win. Sadly injuries forced him to miss the final few League games as he had to undergo surgery on a troublesome knee.

## NEWTON, Keith Robert

Right-back. 1958-1969.
*5ft 11in; 11st 2lb.*
*Born: Manchester, 23 June 1941.*
*Debut: v Chelsea (h) 19 September 1960.*
*Career: Didsbury Technical School; Manchester Junior Boys; Spurley Hey Youth Club; Blackburn Rovers non-contract player April 1958, signing professional in October 1958; Everton December 1969; Burnley June 1972; Morecambe 1978-79.*
*International honours with Blackburn Rovers: England: 19 caps (1966-69); England Under-23: 4 caps (1964); Football League: 5 Appearances (1964-68).*
**Appearances:** Football League 306; FA Cup 21; Football League Cup 30; Total 357.
**Goals:** Football League 9; Football League Cup 1; Total 10.
Keith Newton came to Ewood Park as a gangling inside-forward in the late 1950s and left a decade later as England's right-back. Newton was spotted by Blackburn whilst playing junior football in the Manchester area and was a member of the team which lifted the FA Youth Cup in 1959. Newton appeared in the youth team at centre-half but made his debut for the senior team in the left-half position. However, it was at left-back where he first made his mark in the First Division.

Tall and athletic, Newton was a cultured attacking full-back who possessed excellent defensive qualities. His speed and tackling ability made him a formidable opponent on the ground whilst his aerial ability matched that of many central defenders. Newton was eventually switched to right-back and it was in this position that he graduated through the England Under-23 team into the full England squad. Unlucky to miss out on inclusion in the 1966 World Cup squad, Newton established himself as England's first-choice right-back in the late 1960s despite playing in the Second Division. It was during this period that Eddie Quigley tried to persuade Newton that his future lay in midfield. However, although he appeared in this position on a number of occasions, Newton was understandably reluctant to make the switch a permanent one.

In December 1969, after months of speculation, Newton finally left Ewood Park to join Everton for £80,000. He won a League championship medal at Goodison Park in 1969-70 but became unsettled with the way in which he was asked to operate at full-back. In June 1972, he opted to leave Everton for Burnley and helped the Turf Moor club to win promotion to the First Division in the 1972-73 season. He remained at Burnley for the rest of his League career before finally bowing out at the end of the 1977-78 season. On leaving Turf Moor he had a brief spell in non-League football with Morecambe.

## NICOL, Tom

Outside-right/Full-back. 1896-1897.
*Born: Whitburn Scotland, 24 February 1870.*
*Debut: v Nottingham Forest (a) 12 December 1896.*
*Career: Mossend Swifts; Burnley February 1891; Mossend Swifts March 1891; Blackburn Rovers November 1896; Southampton St Mary's cs 1897; Southampton Wanderers 1902.*
**Appearances:** Football League 16; FA Cup 3; Total 19.
**Goals:** Football League 2.
Tom Nicol came to Blackburn Rovers as a forward but made his first-team debut in the left-back position. Although he reverted to his more familiar place in the forward line the following week, Nicol was to appear at full-back on a further three occasions before the end of the 1896-97 season. Totally fearless in the tackle, Nicol was largely used on the right wing at Ewood but went on to become an outstanding full-back with Southampton. After retiring from football he became a publican.

## NIGHTINGALE, Albert

Inside-left. 1951-1952.
*5ft 8in; 10st 3lb.*
*Born: Thrybergh, nr Rotherham, 10 November 1923.*
*Debut: v Notts County (h) 29 September 1951.*
*Career: Sheffield United amateur March 1941, signing professional in June 1941; Chesterfield wartime guest 1942-43 and 1944-45; Huddersfield Town March 1948; Blackburn Rovers September 1951 (£12,000); Leeds United October 1952 (£10,000).*
**Appearances:** Football League 35; FA Cup 7; Total 42.
**Goals:** Football League 5; FA Cup 3; Total 8.
Albert Nightingale made his debut for Blackburn Rovers within two hours of his transfer from Huddersfield Town on 29 September 1951. After a disastrous start to the 1951-52 campaign, Nightingale's fighting qualities were a major factor in the Rovers' League revival and FA Cup

run. When he joined Blackburn he became the club's costliest player but continued to live in Huddersfield as his wife was a schoolteacher in the town. Nightingale never really settled at Ewood and asked for a transfer after being dropped from the first team early in the 1952-53 season. He moved to Leeds United in October 1952 and scored 48 goals in 130 League games for the Elland Road club before a serious knee injury, sustained in the opening game of the 1956-57 season, ended his career.

## NON-LEAGUE OPPONENTS IN THE FA CUP
Blackburn Rovers have enjoyed an excellent record against clubs from outside the Football League in the FA Cup. Only the Corinthians in 1923-24 have made the club suffer the embarrassment of defeat against a team without League status. Below is a full breakdown of the various league competitions which have provided opposition for the club in the FA Cup.

### Alliance Premier League
| | | | | | |
|---|---|---|---|---|---|
| 1979-80 | (2) | Stafford Rangers | (h) | W | 2-0 |

### Amateur
| | | | | | |
|---|---|---|---|---|---|
| 1890-91 | (2) | Chester | (h) | W | 7-0 |
| 1923-24 | (1) | Corinthians | (Crystal Palace) | L | 0-1 |

### Birmingham & District League
| | | | | | |
|---|---|---|---|---|---|
| 1931-32 | (3) | Burton Town | (a) | W | 4-0 |

### Football Alliance
| | | | | | |
|---|---|---|---|---|---|
| 1889-90 | (2) | Grimsby Town | (h) | W | 3-0 |
| | (3) | Bootle | (a) | W | 7-0 |
| | (F) | Sheffield W | (Kennington Oval) | W | 6-1 |

### GM Vauxhall Conference
| | | | | | |
|---|---|---|---|---|---|
| 1988-89 | (3) | Welling United | (a) | W | 1-0 |
| 1991-92 | (3) | Kettering Town | (h) | W | 4-1 |

### Lancashire Combination
| | | | | | |
|---|---|---|---|---|---|
| 1909-10 | (1) | Accrington Stanley | (h) | W | 7-1 |

### Northern League
| | | | | | |
|---|---|---|---|---|---|
| 1890-91 | (1) | Middlesbrough Ironopolis | (a) | W | 3-0 |
| 1973-74 | (1) | Willington Town | (a) | D | 0-0 |
| | (R) | Willington Town | (h) | W | 6-1 |

### Northern Premier League
| | | | | | |
|---|---|---|---|---|---|
| 1973-74 | (2) | Altrincham | (h) | D | 0-0 |
| | (R) | Altrincham | (a) | W | 2-0 |
| 1974-75 | (1) | Matlock Town | (a) | W | 4-1 |

### Southern League
| | | | | | |
|---|---|---|---|---|---|
| 1899-00 | (1) | Portsmouth | (a) | D | 0-0 |
| | (R) | Portsmouth | (h) | D | 1-1 aet |
| | (2R) | Portsmouth | (Villa Park) | W | 5-0 |
| 1906-07 | (2) | Tottenham Hotspur | (h) | D | 1-1 |
| | (R) | Tottenham Hotspur | (a) | D | 1-1 aet |
| | (2R) | Tottenham Hotspur | (Villa Park) | L | 1-2 |
| 1910-11 | (1) | Southend United | (h) | W | 5-1 |
| | (4) | West Ham United | (a) | W | 3-2 |
| 1911-12 | (1) | Norwich City | (h) | W | 4-1 |
| 1912-13 | (1) | Northampton Town | (h) | W | 7-2 |
| | (3) | Reading | (a) | W | 2-1 |
| 1914-15 | (1) | Swansea Town | (a) | L | 0-1 |
| 1979-80 | (1) | Kidderminster Harriers | (a) | W | 2-0 |

## NORTHAMPTON TOWN FC
Founded in 1897 by school teachers connected with the Northampton & District Elementary Schools' Association. The club became founder members of the Third Division of the Football League in 1920. Blackburn Rovers first met Northampton whilst they were a Southern League club in the 1912-13 FA Cup. The clubs have only met on four occasions in the Football League although they have been paired in the Football League Cup as well as the FA Cup. Northampton share the County Ground with Northampton County Cricket Club.

### Football League
| | | Home | | Away | |
|---|---|---|---|---|---|
| 1965-66 | (Div 1) | W | 6-1 | L | 1-2 |
| 1966-67 | (Div 2) | W | 3-0 | L | 1-2 |

| | P | W | D | L | F | A |
|---|---|---|---|---|---|---|
| Home | 2 | 2 | 0 | 0 | 9 | 1 |
| Away | 2 | 0 | 0 | 2 | 2 | 4 |
| Total | 4 | 2 | 0 | 2 | 11 | 5 |

### FA Cup
| | | | | |
|---|---|---|---|---|
| 1912-13 | (1) | Home | W | 7-2 |
| 1929-30 | (3) | Home | W | 4-1 |
| 1955-56 | (3) | Away | W | 2-1 |

### Football League Cup
| | | | | |
|---|---|---|---|---|
| 1965-66 | (2) | Home | L | 0-1 |
| 1974-75 | (2) | Away | D | 2-2 |
| | (R) | Home | W | 1-0 |

## NORTHWICH VICTORIA FC
Formed in 1873, Northwich Victoria have played football on their Drill Field Ground since sometime between 1876 and 1877. It remains the oldest English ground still in current use by any League or former League club. Blackburn Rovers entertained Norwich Victoria at Ewood Park in the second round of the 1892-93 FA Cup. At that time Northwich were themselves members of the Second Division of the Football League. However, goals from Bowdler, Campbell, Sawers and Jack Southworth gave the Rovers a comfortable 4-1 win in front of a crowd in the region of 7,000 spectators.

## NORWICH CITY FC
Founded in 1905, Norwich City joined the Southern League before becoming founder members of the Third Division in 1920. Until the formation of the Premier League in 1992 all League meetings between Blackburn Rovers and Norwich City took place in the Second Division of the Football League. The most memorable meeting between the two clubs took place at Ewood Park on 3 October 1992 when Norwich City came to Blackburn as leaders of the Premier League. However, second placed Rovers turned in an outstanding performance to win 7-1 and so replace Norwich at the top of the table.

### Football League
| | | Home | | Away | |
|---|---|---|---|---|---|
| 1936-37 | (Div 2) | W | 1-0 | D | 0-0 |
| 1937-38 | (Div 2) | W | 5-3 | L | 2-3 |
| 1938-39 | (Div 2) | W | 6-0 | L | 0-4 |
| 1966-67 | (Div 2) | D | 0-0 | W | 1-0 |
| 1967-68 | (Div 2) | D | 0-0 | L | 0-1 |
| 1968-69 | (Div 2) | W | 3-0 | L | 1-3 |
| 1969-70 | (Div 2) | W | 3-1 | W | 1-0 |
| 1970-71 | (Div 2) | W | 2-1 | L | 1-2 |
| 1981-82 | (Div 2) | W | 3-0 | L | 0-2 |
| 1985-86 | (Div 2) | W | 2-1 | L | 0-3 |

| | P | W | D | L | F | A |
|---|---|---|---|---|---|---|
| Home | 10 | 8 | 2 | 0 | 25 | 6 |
| Away | 10 | 2 | 1 | 7 | 6 | 18 |
| Total | 20 | 10 | 3 | 7 | 31 | 24 |

### FA Premiership
| | Home | | Away | |
|---|---|---|---|---|
| 1992-93 | W | 7-1 | D | 0-0 |
| 1993-94 | L | 2-3 | D | 2-2 |

| | P | W | D | L | F | A |
|---|---|---|---|---|---|---|
| Home | 2 | 1 | 0 | 1 | 9 | 4 |
| Away | 2 | 0 | 2 | 0 | 2 | 2 |
| Total | 4 | 1 | 2 | 1 | 11 | 6 |

### FA Cup
| | | | | |
|---|---|---|---|---|
| 1911-12 | (1) | Home | W | 4-1 |
| 1965-66 | (5) | Away | D | 2-2 |
| | (R) | Home | W | 3-2 |

### Football League Cup
| | | | | |
|---|---|---|---|---|
| 1992-93 | (3) | Home | W | 2-0 |

## NOTTINGHAM FOREST FC
Nottingham Forest enjoy the distinction of being one of the oldest football clubs in the world. The club was first formed in 1865 but was not one of the founding members of the Football League in 1888. Elected to the First Division of the Football League in 1892, Nottingham Forest are one of only four English clubs to have won the European Cup. Nottingham Forest first met Blackburn Rovers in competitive football in the third round of the FA Cup in 1879-80. This was the first season that Blackburn had entered the competition but Forest inflicted the club's first FA Cup defeat when they thrashed the Rovers by a margin of 6-0.

## Football League

| | | Home | | Away | |
|---|---|---|---|---|---|
| 1892-93 | (Div 1) | L | 0-1 | W | 1-0 |
| 1893-94 | (Div 1) | W | 6-1 | D | 0-0 |
| 1894-95 | (Div 1) | D | 0-0 | W | 3-2 |
| 1895-96 | (Div 1) | W | 2-0 | L | 2-4 |
| 1896-97 | (Div 1) | D | 0-0 | L | 1-2 |
| 1897-98 | (Div 1) | D | 1-1 | L | 1-3 |
| 1898-99 | (Div 1) | D | 3-3 | W | 1-0 |
| 1899-00 | (Div 1) | W | 2-1 | L | 2-3 |
| 1900-01 | (Div 1) | L | 1-3 | W | 1-0 |
| 1901-02 | (Div 1) | W | 1-0 | L | 0-3 |
| 1902-03 | (Div 1) | D | 2-2 | L | 0-2 |
| 1903-04 | (Div 1) | W | 3-1 | W | 1-0 |
| 1904-05 | (Div 1) | D | 0-0 | L | 2-5 |
| 1905-06 | (Div 1) | D | 1-1 | W | 2-1 |
| 1907-08 | (Div 1) | D | 3-3 | L | 2-3 |
| 1908-09 | (Div 1) | L | 0-3 | L | 1-2 |
| 1909-10 | (Div 1) | D | 2-2 | W | 4-0 |
| 1910-11 | (Div 1) | W | 4-1 | L | 2-5 |
| 1922-23 | (Div 1) | W | 2-0 | L | 0-1 |
| 1923-24 | (Div 1) | D | 1-1 | D | 0-0 |
| 1924-25 | (Div 1) | D | 0-0 | W | 2-0 |
| 1936-37 | (Div 2) | W | 9-1 | L | 0-2 |
| 1937-38 | (Div 2) | W | 5-1 | L | 1-3 |
| 1938-39 | (Div 2) | W | 3-2 | W | 3-1 |
| 1948-49 | (Div 2) | W | 2-1 | L | 0-1 |
| 1951-52 | (Div 2) | W | 3-2 | L | 0-1 |
| 1952-53 | (Div 2) | W | 2-1 | W | 2-1 |
| 1953-54 | (Div 2) | W | 2-0 | W | 1-0 |
| 1954-55 | (Div 2) | L | 0-1 | W | 2-1 |
| 1955-56 | (Div 2) | D | 2-2 | D | 1-1 |
| 1956-57 | (Div 2) | D | 2-2 | L | 1-2 |
| 1958-59 | (Div 1) | W | 3-0 | D | 1-1 |
| 1959-60 | (Div 1) | L | 1-2 | D | 2-2 |
| 1960-61 | (Div 1) | W | 4-1 | D | 1-1 |
| 1961-62 | (Div 1) | W | 2-1 | W | 2-1 |
| 1962-63 | (Div 1) | L | 2-5 | L | 0-2 |
| 1963-64 | (Div 1) | W | 2-0 | D | 1-1 |
| 1964-65 | (Div 1) | D | 1-1 | W | 5-2 |
| 1965-66 | (Div 1) | W | 5-0 | W | 3-0 |
| 1975-76 | (Div 1) | L | 1-4 | L | 0-1 |
| 1976-77 | (Div 1) | L | 1-3 | L | 0-3 |

| | P | W | D | L | F | A |
|---|---|---|---|---|---|---|
| Home | 41 | 19 | 14 | 8 | 86 | 54 |
| Away | 41 | 15 | 7 | 19 | 54 | 63 |
| Total | 82 | 34 | 21 | 27 | 140 | 117 |

## FA Premiership

| | | Home | | Away | |
|---|---|---|---|---|---|
| 1992-93 | | W | 4-1 | W | 3-1 |

| | P | W | D | L | F | A |
|---|---|---|---|---|---|---|
| Home | 1 | 1 | 0 | 0 | 4 | 1 |
| Away | 1 | 1 | 0 | 0 | 3 | 1 |
| Total | 2 | 2 | 0 | 0 | 7 | 2 |

## FA Cup

| | | | | | |
|---|---|---|---|---|---|
| 1879-80 | (3) | Away | L | 0-6 |
| 1903-04 | (2) | Home | W | 3-1 |
| 1951-52 | (3) | Away | D | 2-2 |
| | (R) | Home | W | 2-0 |
| 1985-86 | (3) | Away | D | 1-1 |
| | (R) | Home | W | 3-2 |

## Football League Cup

| | | | | | |
|---|---|---|---|---|---|
| 1961-62 | (3) | Away | W | 2-1 |
| 1979-80 | (2) | Home | D | 1-1 |
| | (R) | Away | L | 1-6 |
| 1981-82 | (3) | Home | L | 0-1 |

## NOTTS COUNTY FC

Originally thought to have been formed in 1862, indeed the club celebrated its centenary in 1962, it is now believed that Notts County became a fully organised football club in December 1864. One of the founder members of the Football League in 1888, Notts County and Blackburn Rovers were frequent opponents in the First Division in the days before World War One. However, since World War Two the club have met only in the Second and Third Divisions.

## Football League

| | | Home | | Away | |
|---|---|---|---|---|---|
| 1888-89 | (FL) | W | 5-2 | D | 3-3 |
| 1889-90 | (FL) | W | 9-1 | D | 1-1 |
| 1890-91 | (FL) | L | 1-7 | W | 2-1 |
| 1891-92 | (FL) | W | 5-4 | D | 2-2 |
| 1892-93 | (Div 1) | W | 1-0 | D | 0-0 |
| 1897-98 | (Div 1) | L | 0-1 | D | 0-0 |
| 1898-99 | (Div 1) | W | 6-0 | L | 3-5 |
| 1899-00 | (Div 1) | W | 2-0 | L | 1-5 |
| 1900-01 | (Div 1) | L | 0-2 | L | 1-2 |
| 1901-02 | (Div 1) | W | 4-2 | L | 0-3 |
| 1902-03 | (Div 1) | L | 1-2 | L | 0-4 |
| 1903-04 | (Div 1) | W | 3-0 | L | 2-4 |
| 1904-05 | (Div 1) | W | 1-0 | L | 1-2 |
| 1905-06 | (Div 1) | L | 1-3 | D | 1-1 |
| 1906-07 | (Div 1) | L | 0-2 | W | 2-1 |
| 1907-08 | (Div 1) | D | 1-1 | W | 2-0 |
| 1908-09 | (Div 1) | L | 0-2 | W | 3-2 |
| 1909-10 | (Div 1) | W | 2-0 | D | 2-2 |
| 1910-11 | (Div 1) | D | 1-1 | L | 0-2 |
| 1911-12 | (Div 1) | D | 0-0 | W | 3-1 |
| 1912-13 | (Div 1) | W | 2-1 | L | 1-3 |
| 1914-15 | (Div 1) | W | 5-1 | D | 1-1 |
| 1919-20 | (Div 1) | D | 1-1 | L | 0-5 |
| 1923-24 | (Div 1) | W | 4-1 | L | 0-3 |
| 1924-25 | (Div 1) | L | 0-2 | D | 0-0 |
| 1925-26 | (Div 1) | W | 4-1 | D | 1-1 |
| 1950-51 | (Div 2) | D | 0-0 | D | 1-1 |
| 1951-52 | (Div 2) | W | 2-0 | W | 1-0 |
| 1952-53 | (Div 2) | W | 3-2 | L | 0-5 |
| 1953-54 | (Div 2) | W | 2-0 | W | 5-0 |
| 1954-55 | (Div 2) | L | 4-5 | L | 1-3 |
| 1955-56 | (Div 2) | W | 2-0 | W | 2-1 |
| 1956-57 | (Div 2) | D | 1-1 | L | 0-2 |
| 1957-58 | (Div 2) | W | 3-0 | D | 1-1 |
| 1971-72 | (Div 3) | L | 0-2 | L | 0-1 |
| 1972-73 | (Div 3) | W | 2-0 | D | 0-0 |
| 1975-76 | (Div 2) | W | 2-1 | L | 0-3 |
| 1976-77 | (Div 2) | W | 6-1 | D | 0-0 |
| 1977-78 | (Div 2) | W | 1-0 | D | 1-1 |
| 1978-79 | (Div 2) | L | 3-4 | L | 1-2 |
| 1980-81 | (Div 2) | D | 0-0 | L | 0-2 |
| 1984-85 | (Div 2) | W | 1-0 | W | 3-0 |
| 1990-91 | (Div 2) | L | 0-1 | L | 1-4 |

| | P | W | D | L | F | A |
|---|---|---|---|---|---|---|
| Home | 43 | 24 | 7 | 12 | 91 | 54 |
| Away | 43 | 9 | 15 | 19 | 49 | 80 |
| Total | 86 | 33 | 22 | 31 | 140 | 134 |

## FA Cup

| | | | | | |
|---|---|---|---|---|---|
| 1883-84 | (SF) | Birmingham | W | 1-0 |
| 1890-91 | (F) | Kennington Oval | W | 3-1 |
| 1893-94 | (SF) | Bramall Lane | L | 0-1 |
| 1908-09 | (1) | Away | W | 1-0 |
| 1980-81 | (3) | Away | L | 1-2 |
| 1991-92 | (4) | Away | L | 1-2 |

## Football League Cup

| | | | | | |
|---|---|---|---|---|---|
| 1963-64 | (2) | Away | L | 1-2 |

## OAKES, John

Outside-right. 1947-1948.
*5ft 10in; 12st.*
*Born: Hamilton, 6 December 1919.*
*Debut: v Derby County (h) 15 February 1947.*
*Career: Wolverhampton Wanderers 1935; Queen of the South January 1937; Heart of Midlothian wartime guest; Hamilton Academical wartime guest; Huddersfield Town wartime guest November 1943; Blackpool wartime guest February 1945; Blackburn Rovers February 1947 (£10,000); Manchester City June 1948; Queen of the South June 1951. Retired 1962. Queen of the South trainer 1964-65 & 1965-66.*
**Appearances:** Football League 35; FA Cup 2; Total 37.
**Goals:** Football League 9.
Within a week of signing Jock Weir from Hibernian, officials of Blackburn Rovers again travelled north of the border to acquire Jackie Oakes from Queen of the South. A sturdily built player with a fine turn of speed and powerful shot, Oakes began his footballing career with Wolverhampton Wanderers before moving to Queen of the South in January 1937. A native of Hamilton, Oakes had played at left-back and

centre-forward as a schoolboy but eventually settled in a wide position. During the war he served in the RAF and toured Belgium with a Scottish Services team. Oakes also represented the Scottish Command in Norway and was a regular guest with Hearts and Hamilton Academical.

Although a regular in the right-wing position during the latter part of the 1946-47 season, Oakes was unable to retain his place during the following campaign. Despite seven goals in his 19 appearances during 1947-48 the club allowed him to move to Manchester City in June 1948. Oakes scored nine goals in 77 League games at Maine Road before returning to Scotland to enjoy a long playing career with Queen of the South. He made his last first-team appearance for Queens on 5 March 1960 but didn't officially retire until 1962. He later spent two seasons with the club as trainer.

### OATES, Graham
Midfield. 1974-1976
*6ft 2½in; 12st 4lb.*
*Born: Bradford, 14 March 1949.*
*Debut: v Grimsby Town (a) 17 August 1974.*
*Career: Tong Street; Mannington Mills; Bradford City February 1970; Blackburn Rovers June 1974 (£15,000 + Don Hutchins); Newcastle United March 1976; Detroit Express (USA) March 1978 (£40,000); Bradford City non-contract 1981; California Surf (USA) 1981; Lidget Green; Dudley Hill Athletic player-manager; Scarborough non-contract 1987; Gainsborough Trinity 1988.*
*Domestic honours with Blackburn Rovers: Third Division championship: 1974-75 (45 apps, 6 gls)*
**Appearances:** Football League 76; FA Cup 4; Football League Cup 6; Total 86.
**Goals:** Football League 10; FA Cup 1; Total 11.
Considering his physique it was not surprising that Graham Oates should have embarked on a career as a centre-half with Bradford City. However, it was as a midfield player that he eventually made his mark at Valley Parade. Gordon Lee snapped Oates up during the 1974 close season and immediately installed him in the Blackburn midfield. His versatility in being able to play in defence, midfield and also attack made him a valuable asset to Lee's promotion chasing team. Oates missed only one League match during the 1974-75 Third Division championship campaign and scored five goals in his first ten League games. Oates remained an ever-present in the Blackburn team until Gordon Lee returned to Ewood to take both Oates and Roger Jones to Newcastle United. However, his time at Newcastle was not particularly successful and in March 1978 he joined the growing exodus to the North American Soccer League.

### O'BRIEN, Joseph
Left-back. 1900-1901.
*5ft 8in; 13st.*
*Born: Glasgow, 1876.*
*Debut: v Sheffield United (a) 13 April 1900.*
*Career: Bailleston (Glasgow); Clitheroe; Sheffield; Reading 1896 to 1900; Blackburn Rovers April 1900; Aberdeen September 1901; Swindon Town cs 1902; Reading cs 1903; Brighton & Hove Albion cs 1904; Swindon Town cs 1905 to cs 1906; Stalybridge Celtic; Haslingden cs 1907.*
**Appearances:** Football League 3.
Joe O'Brien was one of four former Reading players to join Blackburn Rovers around the turn of the century. The somewhat round O'Brien made his debut on Good Friday 1900 when he understudied Allan Hardy. The following season he didn't appear in the first team until April when he appeared twice in the final three League games. O'Brien, who was later described by one commentator as 'exceedingly powerful and full of dash. As strong as a house and never tires', went on to enjoy greater success in the Southern League.

### O'DOWD, James Peter
Half-back. 1926-1930.
*5ft 11in; 12st.*
*Born: Halifax, 26 February 1908; Died: Bournemouth, 8 May 1964.*
*Debut: v Middlesbrough (h) 23 February 1928.*
*Career: St Bees Grammar School; Apperley Bridge (Bradford League);*
*Selby Town; Bradford amateur 1926; Blackburn Rovers December 1926; Burnley March 1930 (£3,000); Chelsea November 1931 (£5,250); Valenciennes (France) September 1935 (£3,000); Torquay United March 1937.*
**Appearances:** Football League 50.
As Blackburn Rovers marched towards Wembley during the latter part of the 1927-28 campaign, Peter O'Dowd appeared in all three of the half-back positions. Although there was no question of this talented youngster appearing at Wembley, there was also no doubting his outstanding promise. At Blackburn O'Dowd challenged Bill Rankin for the centre-half position but it was felt that the enigmatic O'Dowd played a little too much football for such a crucial position. As a result the Rovers opted for the simple but effective style of Rankin and O'Dowd was given the opportunity to carve a niche for himself at left-half.

O'Dowd left Ewood Park in March 1930 to join Burnley but his greatest success came when he moved to Chelsea in November 1931. At Stamford Bridge O'Dowd was to achieve international status whilst playing in the centre-half position he had been unable to command at Ewood. In many ways O'Dowd was a man ahead of his time, a stylist in an age when physique dominated. O'Dowd sampled life on the continent when he fell out with Chelsea and joined Valenciennes in France. He returned to England in March 1937 to link up Torquay United but had to retire when he broke a leg in a trial match with the club.

### OGILVIE, Adam
Goalkeeper. 1893-1897.
*5ft 10in; 13st.*
*Born: Scotland, c.1867.*
*Debut: v Liverpool (h) 1 September 1894.*
*Career: Forfar Athletic; Grimsby Town cs 1888; Blackburn Rovers August 1893; Shrewsbury Town August 1897.*
**Appearances:** Football League 108; FA Cup 12; Total 120.
Adam Ogilvie moved from his native Scotland to Grimsby Town as a utility player in 1888. However, Ogilvie desired to make a career as a goalkeeper and between 1890 and 1892 he was an ever-present in the Grimsby goal during their two seasons in the Football Alliance. Following their election to the newly formed Second Division of the Football League, Grimsby turned to Jimmy Whitehouse as their first-team custodian and Ogilvie reverted to his utility role.

During the 1892-93 season he made seven appearances at left-back, six at centre-half and eight at left-half. It was his desire to play in goal that brought him to Blackburn in August 1893. Although Charlie Watts began the 1893-94 season as the first-choice custodian, he was deposed by Ogilvie after eight games. Until his departure from the club in 1897, Ogilvie totally dominated the goalkeeping position. Tall and well built, Ogilvie was far from the finished article when he arrived at Ewood Park. However, total commitment to the cause and his refusal to be intimated by opposing forwards endeared him to the Blackburn public. He went on to reign supreme in the Blackburn goal, never injured and rarely off form, Ogilvie was unquestionably the finest goalkeeper the club had employed since the formation of the Football League. Although his form began to dip during the 1895-96 season, his former consistency meant that the club had prepared no adequate deputy for Ogilvie. As a result he remained unchallenged for his position as the number-one custodian right up until the time he left for Shrewsbury in August 1897.

### O'KEEFE, James Vincent
Goalkeeper. 1982-1989.
*6ft 2in; 12st 11lb.*
*Born: Birmingham, 2 April 1957.*
*Debut: v Queen's Park Rangers (a) 13 November 1982.*
*Career: Birmingham City July 1975; Peterborough United on loan March 1976; Walsall July 1976; AP Leamington; Exeter City June 1978; Torquay United February 1980; Blackburn Rovers August 1982; Bury on loan October 1983; Blackpool on loan December 1986 to January 1987; Blackpool on loan February to April 1989; Wrexham July 1989; Chorley September 1992; Kidderminster Harriers 1993.*
**Appearances:** Football League 68; FA Cup 1; Football League Cup 7; Full Members' Cup 6; Total 82.
Vince O'Keefe was taken from non-League football to Exeter City by Bobby Saxton in June 1978. Saxton installed him as his first-choice 'keeper and he appeared in 53 League games for the 'Grecians' before moving to Torquay United in February 1980. When Saxton was looking for an understudy to Terry Gennoe at Ewood Park he turned to O'Keefe who had appeared in 108 League games for Torquay. O'Keefe got an early opportunity to experience first-team football following Gennoe's suspension after being sent off at Charlton for a handling offence outside of the area.

However, Gennoe returned after his two match suspension and O'Keefe returned to Central League football. Although O'Keefe appeared on a number of occasions when Gennoe was injured, it was not

Alan Shearer celebrates his 11th goal in 11 matches as he opens the scoring against Oldham Athletic in September 1992.

until the 1986-87 season that he enjoyed a prolonged run in the team. It was in this season that O'Keefe gave his greatest performance for the club when he starred in the Full Members' Cup Final at Wembley. Although Simon Barker carried off the 'Man of the Match' accolade, it was the performance of O'Keefe which enabled the club to return to Blackburn with the trophy.

A broken leg in the fifth match of the 1987-88 season allowed Gennoe to return and the consistency of his performances meant O'Keefe was unable to force his way back into the team. After a loan spell with Blackpool he moved to Wrexham in July 1992. He appeared in 83 League games for the Welsh club and was a member of the team that beat Arsenal in the third round of the FA Cup in January 1992. Today O'Keefe can still be found at Ewood Park on match days as part of the team who look after match sponsors.

### OLD CARTHUSIANS FC
Formed in 1875, the Old Carthusians played their home matches at Charterhouse School. Winners of the FA Cup in 1881 and FA Amateur Cup winners in 1894 and 1897, the Old Carthusians met Blackburn Rovers at Trent Bridge in the semi-final of the FA Cup on 7 March 1885. Goals from Brown (2), Sowerbutts (2) and Lofthouse gave the Rovers a convincing 5-1 win in front of a crowd reported to be in the region of 2,000 people.

### OLD ETONIANS FC
Formed at Eton in 1865, the Old Etonians had dominated the FA Cup competition in the early years of its life. Winners in 1879 and 1882, they had also been Finalists in 1876, 1881 and 1883. Old Etonians and Blackburn Rovers met in the 1882 FA Cup Final at the Kennington Oval on 25 March 1882. It was the first time that Blackburn Rovers had reached the Final but a goal from Anderson, in front of 6,000 spectators, enabled the Old Etonians to lift the Cup by virtue of a 1-0 win.

### OLDHAM ATHLETIC FC
The origins of Oldham Athletic can be traced back to 1895 when a club called Pine Villa was formed to play in the Oldham Junior League. In 1899 Oldham County, the local professional club, folded and Pine Villa were persuaded to take over their ground and change their name to Oldham Athletic. The club was elected to the Second Division in 1907

and have met Blackburn Rovers in three divisions of the Football League as well as the Premiership.

**Football League**

| | | | Home | | Away | |
|---|---|---|---|---|---|---|
| 1910-11 | (Div 1) | W | 1-0 | L | 0-2 | |
| 1911-12 | (Div 1) | W | 1-0 | W | 1-0 | |
| 1912-13 | (Div 1) | W | 7-1 | D | 0-0 | |
| 1913-14 | (Div 1) | W | 2-1 | D | 1-1 | |
| 1914-15 | (Div 1) | W | 4-1 | L | 2-3 | |
| 1919-20 | (Div 1) | L | 0-1 | D | 0-0 | |
| 1920-21 | (Div 1) | W | 5-1 | L | 0-1 | |
| 1921-22 | (Div 1) | W | 3-2 | D | 1-1 | |
| 1922-23 | (Div 1) | W | 1-0 | L | 0-1 | |
| 1953-54 | (Div 2) | W | 4-0 | L | 0-1 | |
| 1971-72 | (Div 3) | L | 0-1 | D | 1-1 | |
| 1972-73 | (Div 3) | D | 1-1 | W | 2-1 | |
| 1973-74 | (Div 3) | L | 0-1 | W | 3-2 | |
| 1975-76 | (Div 2) | W | 4-1 | L | 1-2 | |
| 1976-77 | (Div 2) | W | 2-0 | L | 0-2 | |
| 1977-78 | (Div 2) | W | 4-2 | W | 2-0 | |
| 1978-79 | (Div 2) | L | 0-2 | L | 0-5 | |
| 1980-81 | (Div 2) | W | 1-0 | L | 0-1 | |
| 1981-82 | (Div 2) | D | 0-0 | W | 3-0 | |
| 1982-83 | (Div 2) | D | 2-2 | D | 0-0 | |
| 1983-84 | (Div 2) | W | 3-1 | D | 0-0 | |
| 1984-85 | (Div 2) | D | 1-1 | L | 0-2 | |
| 1985-86 | (Div 2) | D | 0-0 | L | 1-3 | |
| 1986-87 | (Div 2) | W | 1-0 | L | 0-3 | |
| 1987-88 | (Div 2) | W | 1-0 | L | 2-4 | |
| 1988-89 | (Div 2) | W | 3-1 | D | 1-1 | |
| 1989-90 | (Div 2) | W | 1-0 | L | 0-2 | |
| 1990-91 | (Div 2) | W | 2-0 | D | 1-1 | |

| | P | W | D | L | F | A |
|---|---|---|---|---|---|---|
| Home | 28 | 19 | 5 | 4 | 54 | 20 |
| Away | 28 | 5 | 9 | 14 | 22 | 40 |
| Total | 56 | 24 | 14 | 18 | 76 | 60 |

**FA Premiership**

| | | Home | | Away | |
|---|---|---|---|---|---|
| 1992-93 | | W | 2-0 | W | 1-0 |
| 1993-94 | | W | 1-0 | W | 2-1 |

| | P | W | D | L | F | A |
|---|---|---|---|---|---|---|
| Home | 2 | 2 | 0 | 0 | 3 | 0 |
| Away | 2 | 2 | 0 | 0 | 3 | 1 |
| Total | 4 | 4 | 0 | 0 | 6 | 1 |

**FA Cup**

| | | | | | |
|---|---|---|---|---|---|
| 1924-25 | (1) | Home | | W | 1-0 |

**Wartime**

| | | Home | | Away | |
|---|---|---|---|---|---|
| 1916-17 | (LS-PT) | D | 1-1 | L | 0-2 |
| 1917-18 | (LS-PT) | L | 0-2 | L | 0-2 |
| 1918-19 | (LS-PT) | D | 2-2 | L | 0-4 |
| 1939-40 | (NWRL) | L | 1-3 | W | 5-2 |
| 1940-41 | (NRL) | W | 3-2 | L | 0-1 |
| | (LWC) | W | 2-0 | W | 5-1 |
| 1941-42 | (FLNS-FC) | W | 2-1 | D | 2-2 |
| 1942-43 | (FLNS-FC) | W | 8-1 | W | 1-0 |
| | (FLNS-SC) | W | 7-1 | W | 2-1 |
| 1943-44 | (FLNS-FC) | W | 5-2 | W | 4-2 |
| 1944-45 | (FLNS-FC) | D | 1-1 | L | 0-3 |

**OLDHAM, Wilfred**
Centre-forward. 1900-1901.
*Debut: v Liverpool (a) 1 September 1900.*
*Career: Everton February 1898; Blackburn Rovers August 1900; Padiham; Oswaldtwistle Rovers January 1905.*
**Appearances:** Football League 9.
**Goals:** Football League 1.
The centre-forward position had proved something of a headache to the club during the 1899-1900 season and it was in a bid to solve these problems that Wilfred Oldham was signed on the eve of the 1900-01 campaign. Sadly, one goal in the opening eight games, only two of which were won, did little to suggest that he could offer a long-term solution to the club's problems. Oldham made only one further appearance for the club before being released at the end of his only season at Ewood Park.

**O'LEARY, Donal Patrick**
Outside-left. 1954-1956.
*Born: Limehouse, London 24 June 1936.*
*Debut: v Lincoln City (a) 17 December 1955.*
*Career: Blackburn Rovers October 1954 to October 1956.*
**Appearances:** Football League 6; FA Cup 1; Total 7.
**Goals:** Football League 1.
Donal O'Leary was one of a number of young players that Johnny Carey brought to Ewood Park from Ireland in the mid-1950s. Originally a full-back, O'Leary was unexpectedly promoted to the first team at Lincoln in December 1955 at the age of 19. His debut came only one week after his first Central League appearance as a winger. However, he did sufficiently well to earn a brief run with the senior team during the 1955-56 season. In October 1956, O'Leary became homesick and returned to Ireland.

**OLIVER, Alfred**
Outside-left. 1905-1906.
*Born: Bangor, 15 September 1882; Died: Glyn Garth, Menai Bridge, Anglesey, 29 March 1963.*
*Debut: v Notts County (h) 18 March 1905.*
*Career: Beaumaris Grammar School; Beaumaris Town; Bangor 1903-05; Blackburn Rovers March 1905 (£200); Bangor 1906-1914; Llandegfan.*
*International honours with Blackburn Rovers: Wales: 1 cap (1905).*
**Appearances:** Football League 2.
Oliver came to Ewood Park after an impressive performance for Wales in their first-ever win over Scotland in March 1905. Despite his inexperience of League football he was given an early debut by the Rovers but not surprisingly failed to make much impact. The departure of Fred Blackburn to West Ham United ought to have opened the first-team door for Oliver but it was Miles Chadwick who grasped the chance to win the outside-left position. Unhappy with life at Ewood Park, Oliver refused terms for the 1906-07 season and returned to his native North Wales.

**OLIVER, Neil**
Full-back. 1989-1991.
*5ft 11in; 11st 10lb.*
*Born: Berwick-upon-Tweed, 11 April 1947.*
*Debut: v Brighton & Hove Albion (h) 4 November 1989.*

*Career: Coldstream; Berwick Rangers 1986; Blackburn Rovers August 1899; Falkirk cs 1991.*
**Appearances:** Football League 5+1; Football League 0+1; Full Members' Cup 1; Total 6+2.
Oliver was signed by Don Mackay to boost his squad on the eve of the 1989-90 season. A neat and compact player, Oliver acted as understudy to Mark Atkins and Chris Sulley during his stay with the club. However, unable to break into the first team on a regular basis he returned to Scotland to join Falkirk during the 1991 close season.

**O'MARA, John**
Centre-forward. 1972-1974.
*6ft 3in; 11st.*
*Born: Bolton, 19 March 1947.*
*Debut: v Watford (h) 16 September 1972.*
*Career: Margate; Gillingham October 1964; Wimbledon 1968-69; Brentford March 1971; Blackburn Rovers September 1972 (£30,000); Chelmsford City; Bradford City December 1974; Gemiston (South Africa) January 1975.*
**Appearances:** Football League 30+5; FA Cup 5+1; Football League Cup 1; Total 36+6.
**Goals:** Football League 10; FA Cup 2; Total 12.
A record of 28 goals in 53 League matches had made Brentford's John O'Mara a much sought after striker in the early 1970s. However, despite rumours of offers from First Division clubs, it was Ken Furphy who managed to snap up the lanky centre-forward in September 1972. Sadly, O'Mara didn't contribute as much as had been hoped and a return of seven goals in 24 League appearances (including three as sub) was a grave disappointment to Furphy. O'Mara spent much of the 1973-74 season out of the team and in January 1974, in the week that Gordon Lee arrived at Ewood Park, O'Mara rejected a £17,500 move back to Brentford. Lee didn't see O'Mara as part of his future plans and at the end of the season he was released on a free transfer.

**OOZEHEAD GROUND**
Prior to 1876-77 the players and officials of Blackburn Rovers led a rather nomadic existence. However, for the 1876-77 season the club finally found a 'home' of their own at Oozehead. This ground was merely a rented piece of farmland facing Preston New Road on the western side of Blackburn and was not without its problems. Little more than a meadow, a large pool of water in the centre of the field – which was supposedly used for watering the farm stock – was hardly conducive to the needs of a football club. Necessity being the mother of invention, the Rovers experimented with what might be termed a partial artificial surface. Walter Duckworth, one of the founder members of the club, came from a family in the timber business and a few planks of wood covered with turf managed to hide the offending pool. In this unlikely setting the club were able to obtain gate receipts of 6s 6d for the season.

**ORR, John**
Inside-forward. 1908-1920.
*5ft 6½in; 11st.*
*Born: Leith, 1888*
*Debut: v Liverpool (h) 6 April 1908.*
*Career: Blackburn Rovers January 1908 to cs 1920.*
*Domestic honours with Blackburn Rovers: First Division championship:*

*1911-12 (19 apps, 9 gls); 1913-14 (5 apps; 2 gls)*
**Appearances:** Football League 75; FA Cup 10; Total 85.
**Goals:** Football League 30; FA Cup 3; Total 33.
A clever little inside-forward who joined the Rovers from an Edinburgh junior club. Although he suffered from a lack of inches, Orr was a forward who knew his way to goal and proved a valuable addition to the playing staff at Ewood. Orr appeared in 19 League games during the 1911-12 championship season but the arrival of Danny Shea in January 1913 restricted his first-team opportunities. Orr scored 13 goals in 19 wartime appearances and tried to resurrect his career at Ewood after World War One. However, he was only called upon for three League games during the 1919-20 campaign.

**OSWALDTWISTLE ROVERS FC**
Formed in 1877, Oswaldtwistle Rovers met Blackburn Rovers on the

only occasion that they reached the second round of the FA Cup. The match was played on the 21 November 1885 at the Leamington Street Ground in Blackburn. A goal by Hugh McIntyre was sufficient to give Blackburn a 1-0 win in front of an attendance reported to number in the region of 1,000 people.

## OWN-GOALS
The 1938-39 season saw Blackburn Rovers win the Second Division championship with the aid of four own-goals – a record seasonal total for League matches.

The most famous own-goal to be scored by Blackburn Rovers occurred against Wolves at Wembley in the 1960 FA Cup Final. The luckless Mick McGrath tried to cut out a cross from Barry Stobart, only to see the ball fly off his toe into the net.

A number of well-known players have scored own-goals over the years to aid the cause of Blackburn Rovers. In 1949-50 Alf Ramsey, the man who would lead England to a World Cup victory in 1966, scored one of the goals which gave the Rovers a 3-2 victory over Tottenham Hotspur at White Hart Lane.

In the same season, Eddie Quigley, a leading light at Ewood in the 1950s, scored one of Blackburn's two goals in the 3-2 home defeat by Preston North End.

Another man who, like Quigley, went on to manage Blackburn Rovers, was Bobby Saxton and he too came to the aid of the Rovers with an own-goal in a narrow 2-1 win over Plymouth Argyle in November 1972.

In a number of games the opposition has been exceedingly charitable in scoring more than once for the Rovers. In 1908-09, two Manchester United players, Holden and Linkson, scored own-goals to help the Rovers to a convincing 3-0 away win. Two own-goals also helped the Rovers beat Park Road in the first round of the 1881-82 FA Cup competition. In January 1885, goals from Champney and Webster of Romford assisted the Rovers to a rather emphatic 8-0 win in the fourth round of the FA Cup.

## OXFORD UNITED FC
Founded in 1896 as Headington United, the club changed its name to Oxford United in 1960. Elected to the Football League in 1962, following the demise of Accrington Stanley, Oxford pulled off a major shock in the fifth round of the 1963-64 FA Cup competition. Two goals from Jones and one from Calder gave the club a 3-1 win over First Division Blackburn Rovers at the Manor Ground in front of 21,300 spectators.

## Football League

|  |  | Home |  | Away |  |
|---|---|---|---|---|---|
| 1968-69 | (Div 2) | W | 1-0 | L | 1-2 |
| 1969-70 | (Div 2) | W | 2-0 | L | 0-1 |
| 1970-71 | (Div 2) | D | 0-0 | L | 1-2 |
| 1975-76 | (Div 2) | D | 0-0 | D | 0-0 |
| 1979-80 | (Div 3) | W | 2-1 | W | 1-0 |
| 1984-85 | (Div 2) | D | 1-1 | L | 1-2 |
| 1988-89 | (Div 2) | W | 3-1 | D | 1-1 |
| 1989-90 | (Div 2) | D | 2-2 | D | 1-1 |
| 1990-91 | (Div 2) | L | 1-3 | D | 0-0 |
| 1991-92 | (Div 2) | D | 1-1 | W | 3-1 |

|  | P | W | D | L | F | A |
|---|---|---|---|---|---|---|
| Home | 10 | 4 | 5 | 1 | 13 | 9 |
| Away | 10 | 2 | 4 | 4 | 9 | 10 |
| Total | 20 | 6 | 9 | 5 | 22 | 19 |

## FA Cup
| 1963-64 | (5) | Away | L | 1-3 |
|---|---|---|---|---|
| 1984-85 | (4) | Away | W | 1-0 |

## Football League Cup
| 1984-85 | (2) | Home | D | 1-1 |
|---|---|---|---|---|
|  | (R) | Away | L | 1-3 aet |

## Full Members' Cup
| 1986-87 | (3) | Home | W | 4-3 |
|---|---|---|---|---|

## PADIHAM FC
Formed in 1887, Padiham FC met Blackburn Rovers in the third round of the FA Cup in 1883-84. The match was played at the Leamington Street Ground and goals from Brown, Connell (own-goal) and Strachan gave the Rovers a 3-0 win in front of approximately 3,000 spectators.

## PALATINE LEAGUE
The Palatine League was introduced in the mid-1890s as an extra competition for clubs in Lancashire. Games in the Palatine League were played towards the end of the season and, although it was originally intended that clubs should field their strongest teams, it was not unknown for a reserve side to turn out. The Rovers enjoyed their best run in this short-lived competition in 1894-95, when they topped their group having won four and drawn one of their six matches.

## PARKER, Harold
Outside-right. 1951-1953.
*Born: Blackburn, 8 February 1933.*
*Debut: v West Ham United (a) 25 August 1951.*
*Career: Lower Darwen Youth Club; Blackburn Rovers 20 August 1951.*
**Appearances:** Football League 3.
Parker, an 18-year-old local toolmaker, made his first-team debut at Upton Park only a week after becoming a part-time professional with the club. Although he had been on the Blackburn books for some time as an amateur, his experience had been largely limited to the fourth team. He made a quiet debut at West Ham but two days later was retained for the home game with Doncaster Rovers. Parker didn't reappear with the senior team until the final match of the season and this proved to be his last senior appearance.

## PARKER, Stuart John
Centre-forward. 1979-1980.
*6ft 1in; 11st 9lb.*
*Born: Preston , 16 February 1954.*
*Debut: v Millwall (h) 18 August 1979 (sub).*
*Career: Blackpool apprentice July 1970, turning professional in April 1972; Southend United July 1975; Chesterfield February 1977; Sparta Rotterdam (Holland); Blackburn Rovers July 1979; Frecheville CA; Bury September 1982; R.C.Mechelen (Belgium); Preston North End non-contract player September 1983; Chester City non-contract player September 1983; Blackpool non-contract player December 1983; Drogheda; Stockport County February 1984; Witton Albion 1984-85; Irlam Town 1985-86; Runcorn; Barrow; South Liverpool; Northwich Victoria; Hyde United; Lancaster City; Blackpool Mechanics; Irlam Town player-manager; Blackpool Rovers.*
**Appearances:** Football League 5+4; Football League Cup 1; Total 6+4.
**Goals:** Football League 1.
An experienced striker who was brought to Ewood Park by Howard Kendall shortly after his arrival at the club. Parker, who had been playing in Holland before his move to Blackburn, had a record of 33 goals from 114 League games (including 12 as sub) before his move to the continent. His most prolific spell had been at Southend where he had scored 23 goals in 64 League appearances (including two as sub). Unfortunately, the move to Blackburn was not a success and Parker was not retained for a second season. After leaving Blackburn, Parker was unable to resurrect a career in the Football League but was in constant demand in non-League football.

## PARKES, Anthony
Midfield. 1970-1982.
Coach. 1981-
*5ft 10in; 11st.*
*Born: Sheffield, 5 May 1949.*
*Debut: v Swindon Town (h) 5 September 1970.*
*Career: Buxton Town; Blackburn Rovers 21 May 1970 until 27 March 1982; then joined the coaching staff before becoming first team coach under Bob Saxton. Caretaker manager December 1986 until January 1987 when he became assistant manager. Caretaker manager again from August 1991 until October 1991 when he reverted to first team coach.*
*Domestic honours with Blackburn Rovers: Third Division championship: 1974-75 (46 apps 5 gls).*
**Appearances:** Football League 345+5; F.A.Cup 21; Football League Cup 21; Total 387+5.
**Goals:** Football League 38; F.A.Cup 4; Football League Cup 3; Total 45.
A loyal one club man, Tony Parkes has given almost a quarter of a century of service to Blackburn Rovers. Although he came to Ewood from non-League Buxton Town as a promising centre-forward, he operated for virtually all of his playing career as a hard working midfield player. Parkes had struggled to make much impression as a centre-forward and it was Ken Furphy who first asked him to fill a midfield berth. Parkes was grafter and moving to midfield allowed him to utilise his strengths to the full.

Always an underrated player, he rarely caught the eye, but was always there to link up the play between defence and attack. An inspirational character on the field, he worked tirelessly to cover the gaps in the middle of the park and yet still found time and energy to burst forward to score important goals. Twice he helped the club to gain promotion from the Third Division, in 1975 and 1980, before a badly broken leg signalled the end of his playing career in 1981. Under Howard Kendall he had coupled his playing role with that of youth and reserve-team coach and in the summer of 1981 he became first-team coach under Bob Saxton. When Saxton was dismissed at Christmas 1986, Parkes enjoyed a successful period as caretaker manager and was short-listed for the job on a permanent basis. The arrival of Don Mackay saw Parkes given the position of assistant manager as well as continuing as coach. In August 1991 he was again asked to occupy the manager's chair following the dismissal of Mackay and once again he turned around the team's performances on the field. When the club announced the appointment of the Dalglish-Harford managerial team there was universal approval for the fact that Parkes was to be retained as first-team coach.

### PARKIN, Timothy J.
Central defender 1974-1979.
*6ft 1in; 12st 10lb.*
*Born: Penrith, 31 December 1957.*
*Debut: v Bristol Rovers (a) 8 March 1976.*
*Career: Blackburn Rovers apprentice December 1974, turning professional in March 1976; FF Malmö (Sweden) January 1980 (£20,000); Almondsbury Greenway; Bristol Rovers August 1981; Swindon Town July 1986; Port Vale December 1989; Shrewsbury Town on loan September 1991; Darlington August 1992, joining the coaching staff in 1993; Barrow November 1993, becoming assistant manager in March 1994.*
**Appearances:** Football League 13.
Tim Parkin was a raw-boned youngster who got an earlier than expected chance of first team football towards the end of the 1978-79 season. With Keeley injured John Pickering had little alternative than to pitch the enthusiastic but untried Parkin into the relegation fray. Although good in the air, Parkin's ground work was still a little clumsy and he gave the impression of needing further grooming in the Central League. With Howard Kendall placing great store in the pairing of Keeley and Fazackerley, Parkin was allowed to move to FF Malmö in January 1980. Parkin returned to League football in England in August 1981 when he joined Bristol Rovers and he went on to carve out a very successful career in the lower divisions.

### PARKINSON, James
Inside-forward 1895-1896.
*5ft 9in; 11st 10lb.*
*Debut: v Burnley (a) 13 April 1896.*
*Career: Blackpool; Blackburn Rovers August 1895.*
**Appearances:** Football League 1.
James Parkinson made a favourable impression in the practice sessions before the 1895-96 season. The former Blackpool player showed himself to be a speedy player with the ability to dribble through a crowd. Contemporary reporters suggested that a lack of coolness and patience was his undoing. His only taste of senior action came in April 1896 when he appeared in a much changed Blackburn line-up which crashed 6-0 at Turf Moor.

### PATTERSON, John George
Goalkeeper. 1945-1957.
*5ft 8½in 10st 3lb.*
*Born: East Cramlington, 6 July 1922..*
*Debut: v Bolton Wanderers (a) 5 January 1946 (FAC).*
*Career: North Shields; Nottingham Forest amateur; Blackburn Rovers April 1945; Kettering cs 1956; Darwen.*
**Appearances:** Football League 107; FA Cup 5; Total 112.
Jack Patterson was a young goalkeeper who signed professional terms for Blackburn Rovers in April 1945. He first appeared for the club in the Football League North fixture at Blackpool on 8 September 1945 and Patterson finished the season with 15 appearances to his name in that competition. With the restoration of the Football League in 1946, Patterson found himself behind George Marks and Stan Hayhurst in the pecking order at Ewood. It was September 1948 before Patterson received his League debut but the final ten League games of the 1948-49 season found him in possession of the goalkeeping position. Although not the tallest of goalkeepers, the 1949-50 season saw Patterson fight off a challenge from Bill Hughes, a Welsh international, to retain his position in the first team. An ever-present during 1950-51, Patterson's reign as the senior 'keeper came to an end when a fractured arm led to the acquisition of Reg Elvy in November 1951. The consistency of Elvy meant that Patterson made only four more appearances for the club before being released at the end of the 1956-57 season.

### PATTERSON, Mark Andrew
Outside-left. 1979-1988.
*5ft 6in; 10st 10lb.*
*Born: Darwen, 24 May 1965.*
*Debut: v Manchester City (a) 17 September 198 3 (sub).*
*Career: Blackburn Rovers associated schoolboy October 1979,*

*becoming an apprentice in July 1981, and turning professional in May 1983; Preston North End June 1988; Bury February 1990; Bolton Wanderers January 1991.*
*Domestic honours with Blackburn Rovers: Full Members' Cup winners: 1987.*
**Appearances:** Football League 89+12; F.A.Cup 3+1; Football League Cup 4; Full Members' Cup 2+4; Total 98+17.
**Goals:** Football League 20; Football League Cup 1; Full Members' Cup 1; Total 22.
A hard working left-sided midfield player who graduated through the ranks at Ewood Park with Simon Barker. However, whilst Barker went on to greater things with Queen's Park Rangers, Patterson carved out a career in the lower divisions with other local clubs. Patterson forced his way into the side during the 1983-84 season and dislodged Noel Brotherston from his position on the left wing. A speedy left-winger, Patterson also had an eye for goal and scored seven times during his first season of League football.

A player who drifted in and out of the team, Patterson appeared at Wembley as a substitute in the Full Members' Cup Final of 1987. However, the emergence of Scott Sellars on the left side of midfield curtailed Patterson's first-team opportunities and in June 1988 he made the short move to Preston North End. He scored 19 League goals in 55 appearances (including one as sub) for Preston before leaving the plastic pitch of Deepdale for Bury. Ten goals in 42 League games for the Gigg Lane club attracted the attention of Bolton Wanderers and he joined the Burnden Park outfit in January 1991. The 1992-93 season saw him help Bolton gain promotion from the Second Division and in 1993-94 he participated in Bolton's successful run in the FA Cup.

### PAUL, Arthur George
Goalkeeper. 1889-1890.
*Born: Belfast, 24 July 1864; Died: Didsbury, 14 January 1947.*
*Debut: v West Bromwich Albion (a) 11 January 1890.*
*Career: Blackburn Rovers 1889.*
**Appearances:** Football League 1; FA Cup 1; Total 2.
At the time that he joined Blackburn Rovers, Arthur Paul was a noted Rugby Union player having toured Australia and New Zealand and was also on the brink of a highly successful cricketing career with Lancashire. Whilst there was no doubting his temperament his actual goalkeeping technique left much to be desired. His two appearances with the senior team saw him concede five goals and although progress was made in the FA Cup, the Blackburn committee quickly recalled Billy McOwen to replace him.

### PEARCE, Robert G.
Outside-left. 1920.
*Debut: v Liverpool (a) 14 February 1920.*
*Career: Blackburn Rovers amateur February 1920.*
**Appearances:** Football League 1.
Pearce was a young amateur player who was recommended to the club by Jock Simpson, the former Blackburn and England winger. He made his debut at Liverpool in February 1920 but according to one correspondent 'Pearce saw so little of the real play that no accurate estimate of his qualities could be formed.' Pearce was one of 39 different players used during the 1919-20 season and a number of them, Pearce included, were never seen in Rovers' colours again.

### PEARCE, Ian Anthony
Centre-half/Centre-forward. 1993-
*6ft 3in; 14st.*
*Born: Bury St Edmunds, 7 May 1974.*
*Debut: v Shrewsbury Town (a) 9 November 1993 (FLC).*
*Career: Chelsea associate schoolboy November 1988, signing professional in August 1991; Blackburn Rovers October 1993 (£300,000).*
**Appearances:** Premier League 1+4; FA Cup 0+2; Football League Cup 0+2; Total 1+8.
**Goals:** Premier League 1; Football League Cup 1; Total 2.
Kenny Dalglish swooped to sign this 19-year-old England youth international in October 1993. Pearce can play in defence or attack and, although he had made only four substitute appearances for Chelsea up to the start of the 1993-94

season, he had none the less gained a reputation as one of the game's outstanding young prospects. Powerful in the air and skilful on the ground Pearce was a member of the England squad which took part in the under-19 World Cup in Australia during the latter part of the 1992-93 season.

He made an excellent start to his Ewood career by scoring the opening goal in the Reserves' 2-1 defeat of York City only hours after completing his transfer. After having sat on the bench for three senior matches he finally got his chance of first-team action when he came on as substitute against Shrewsbury in the Coca-Cola Cup (formerly League Cup). With the aggregate score at 3-3 and the match in extra-time, Pearce made a dramatic entry to score the winning goal. During the 1993-94 season he has been used as a substitute and usually come on to bolster the forward line. However, many judges believe that he will develop into an outstanding defender, a position he occupies in the Central League team.

## PENALTIES

The penalty-kick was introduced into the game in England during the 1891 close season. A little over 100 years later, Mike Newell took the most important penalty in the history of the club against Leicester City in the Final of the Second Division Play-offs at Wembley. He converted his spot-kick to put the Rovers in the Premier League, although in the closing minutes of the game he also scorned a second opportunity to score from the spot.

The most successful penalty taker in the history of the club remains Billy Bradshaw. He converted his first penalty in a Football League match on the 20 November 1909 against Manchester United at Ewood Park and also scored from a second spot kick in the same game. By the time he converted his last penalty in a League game, on 6 December 1919 at Ewood Park against Derby County, he had scored 20 penalties in League matches and two more in FA Cup-ties.

Ted Harper converted 11 penalties in only two seasons between 1924 and 1926. However, the record for the most penalties to be converted in one season is held by Howard Gayle who was successful on eight occasions during the 1988-89 season. Bobby Langton, who scored seven penalties in 1954-55, might well have reached eight if he hadn't insisted on Tommy Briggs taking a late penalty against Bristol Rovers at Ewood Park on 5 February 1955. Briggs had already scored six goals in the game and his successful conversion of the penalty gave him his seventh.

Surprisingly for such a prolific goalscorer, Briggs was never really a regular penalty taker at Ewood and only scored four of his 140 League goals from the penalty-spot. A number of players, including both Bradshaw and Gayle, have converted two penalties in the same match but only Bill Eckersley has completed this feat in three different games. Surprisingly, the only time that two different players have scored from the penalty-spot in the same match occurred way back in 1923-24 when David Rollo and Jock McKay were both successful against West Bromwich Albion at Ewood Park on 29 October 1923.

Although Blackburn Rovers have twice been involved in penalty shoot-outs in the Final of the Lancashire Manx Cup, winning the trophy on both occasions, the club have only once been involved in a penalty shoot-out in an FA Cup-tie. On 16 March 1993, the sixth-round FA Cup replay with Sheffield United at Bramall Lane was settled by penalties after the teams were tied at 2-2 at the end of extra-time. Unfortunately the Rovers lost the shoot-out 5-3.

## PENNINGTON, Rowland
Goalkeeper. 1890-1893.
*5ft 11in; 11st 9lb.*
*Born: St Helens, 1870.*
*Debut: v Wolverhampton Wanderers (h) 27 September 1890.*
*Career: St Helens Victoria; St Helens Association FC; Whiston; Blackburn Rovers August 1890; Northwich Victoria October 1893.*
*Domestic honours with Blackburn Rovers: FA Cup winners: 1891.*
**Appearances:** Football League 8; FA Cup 2; Total 10.
Rowland Pennington was highly regarded in junior circles before signing for Blackburn Rovers at the start of the 1890-91 season. A joiner by trade, Pennington was athletically built and had a strong muscular arm power that enabled him to deal effectively with the strongest of shots. A staunch teetotaller, by the standards of his time he was the perfect athlete. He caught the eye of Blackburn officials when the Rovers played a friendly match at St Helens against a district team and Pennington gave an outstanding display of goalkeeping for the home side. During his time with Blackburn, Pennington was never more than an understudy, but in March 1891 he received a surprise call to appear in the FA Cup Final at the expense of John Gow. The decision was sufficient to cause Gow to leave the club and in October 1893, Pennington himself left in controversial circumstances. When a decision to experiment with Nat Walton in goal proved successful, Pennington was unceremoniously handed his cards and departed for Northwich Victoria.

## PENTLAND, Frederick Beaconsfield
Forward. 1903-1906.
*5ft 9in; 11st 11lb.*
*Born: Wolverhampton, 18 September 1883; Died: Poole, 16 March 1962.*
*Debut: v Stoke (a) 31 October 1903.*
*Career: Willenhall Swifts; Avondale Juniors; Birmingham August 1900; Blackpool June 1903; Blackburn Rovers October 1903; Brentford May 1906; Queen's Park Rangers May 1907; Middlesbrough July 1908; Halifax Town player-manager February 1913; Stoke City May 1913. Coached in Germany at the outbreak of World War One and was interned for the duration. Coached in France 1920; Athletic Bilbao (Spain) coach 1921-1936; Brentford coach 1936-1937; Barrow manager January 1938 to September 1939.*
**Appearances:** Football League 51; FA Cup 1; Total 52.
**Goals:** Football League 9.
A speedy and manipulative ball player who was brought to Ewood Park from Blackpool in October 1903. Five goals in eight League games with the 'Seasiders' had alerted the Rovers to the potential of Pentland and in October 1903 he made his debut at Stoke in the centre-forward position. He scored seven goals in 18 League games during his first season at Ewood but the start of the 1904-05 season found him out of the senior team. He was recalled in October and although he made occasional appearances in the centre-forward position he was more frequently seen at outside-right. He possessed the ability to send over pinpoint crosses but a tendency towards too much fancy footwork curtailed his effectiveness. He left Ewood in May 1906 to play Southern League football with Brentford. His unusual middle name came about because his father, a former Lord Mayor of Birmingham, was an admirer of Benjamin Disraeli, Earl of Beaconsfield.

## PETERBOROUGH UNITED FC
Founded in 1934 by enthusiasts of the old Peterborough and Fletton Club which had been suspended by the FA during the 1932-33 season and then disbanded. The club was elected to the Football League in 1960 and met Blackburn Rovers in the first round of the 1961-62 Football League Cup competition. The only time the clubs have met in the Football League was in the Third Division in 1974-75.

Football League

|  |  | Home |  | Away |  |
|---|---|---|---|---|---|
| 1974-75 | (Div 3) | L | 0-1 | L | 0-1 |

|  | P | W | D | L | F | A |
|---|---|---|---|---|---|---|
| Home | 1 | 0 | 0 | 1 | 0 | 1 |
| Away | 1 | 0 | 0 | 1 | 0 | 1 |
| Total | 2 | 0 | 0 | 2 | 0 | 2 |

Football League Cup

| 1961-62 | (1) | Away | W | 3-1 |
|---|---|---|---|---|

## PICKERING, Frederick
Centre-forward. 1956-1964 & 1971-1972.
*5ft 11in; 12st 7½lb.*
*Born: Blackburn, 19 January 1941.*
*Debut: v Leicester City (a) 10 October 1959.*
*Career: Blackburn Rovers non-contract player May 1956, signing professional in January 1958; Everton March 1964 (£85,000); Birmingham City August 1967 (£50,000); Blackpool June 1969 (£45,000); Blackburn Rovers March 1971 (£10,000) to February 1972; Brighton & Hove Albion on trial February 1972.*
*International honours with Blackburn Rovers: England Under-23: 3 caps (1963-64).*
**Appearances:** Football League 134; FA Cup 10; Football League Cup 14; Total 158.
**Goals:** Football League 61; FA Cup 5; Football League Cup 8; Total 74.
Fred Pickering was originally groomed in the Rovers' junior and reserve teams as a full-back. He captained the youth team to success in the FA Youth Cup in 1959 before being given his first-team debut at left-back at Leicester City in October 1959. Pickering made little impact and with a number of full-backs on the payroll his prospects appeared bleak.

After several impressive performances at centre-forward in the Central League, Jack Marshall decided to gamble with Pickering in the First Division. Despite his initial clumsiness in approach work, Pickering had the happy knack of being able to put the ball in the back of the net. As the rough edges were gradually removed from his game, Pickering proved to have the pace and power to trouble most defences. With the team chasing the First Division title Pickering became unsettled at Ewood and asked for a transfer. Incredibly, and controversially, the club decided to part company with the unsettled Pickering. A fee of £85,000 took Pickering to Goodison Park and the Rovers spent years, not to mention a small fortune, trying to replace him.

Pickering quickly became a firm favourite on Merseyside and in May 1964 he scored a hat-trick on his England debut against the United States. Curiously he was only capped by England on two further occasions and in 1966 he had the misfortune to miss out on the FA Cup Final because of injury. However the Goodison Park club made sure that the man who scored 56 goals in 97 League appearances whilst on Merseyside was awarded a Cup winners' medal. In August 1967 he moved to Birmingham City and continued his goalscoring with 27 goals in 74 League matches. In June 1969 he returned to Lancashire to join Blackpool and helped the 'Seasiders' to win promotion to the First Division.

After scoring 24 goals in 49 League games (including one as sub) Pickering returned to Blackburn Rovers. Faced with relegation to the Third Division for the first time in their history, Pickering was cast in the role of a Messiah at Ewood Park. Gone, however, was the athletic young centre-forward who had terrorised First Division defences and the ageing striker was unable to prevent the club from slipping out of the Second Division. At the start of the 1971-72 season, the newly appointed Ken Furphy made it clear that he felt that Pickering lacked the required fitness for first-team football and after only one appearance for Furphy he was released by the club. Pickering tried unsuccessfully to revive his career with Brighton but nothing came of it and he left the game.

### PICKERING, John
Manager. 1979.
*Born: Stockton, 7 November 1944.*
*Career: Newcastle United July 1963; Halifax Town September 1965 (£1,250); Barnsley July 1974; Blackburn Rovers reserve-team coach June 1975, appointed assistant manager cs 1978, then caretaker manager October 1978, then manager February 1979 to May 1979;*

*Carlisle United coach 1980-81; Lincoln City assistant manager and coach 1982, then manager July to December 1985; Newcastle United coach 1988; Lincoln City assistant manager 1990; Middlesbrough coach cs 1991.*

John Pickering became a victim of circumstance during his time at Ewood Park and ultimately it was to cost him his position with the club. Within a matter of months he was catapulted from looking after the Central League team at Ewood to managing a team fighting for Second Division survival. When the fight was lost Pickering paid the price with his job. A rough, tough centre-half in his playing days, Pickering had failed to make the grade with Newcastle United but went on to set a new appearance record with Halifax Town. He ended his playing days with Barnsley before accepting Jim Smith's invitation to look after the Central League team at Ewood Park.

Following the departure of Smith and Norman Bodell from Ewood, new manager Jim Iley appointed Pickering as his assistant. Pickering had barely had time to adjust to his new role when Iley was relieved of his duties and Pickering found himself with the unenviable task of trying to pick up the pieces. At first he operated on a caretaker basis but was eventually given a short-term contract until the end of the season. Pickering approach the job with relish and was not afraid to take bold decisions. Early on in his reign he dispensed with the services of assistant coach Bobby Kennedy, who had only arrived in the summer, and appointed Mick Heaton to take charge of the second team.

Although results continued to elude the team Pickering was able to lift the players and supporters alike. Perhaps concerned at his lack of experience, the directors invited Jimmy Armfield, the former Leeds United and Bolton Wanderers manager, to act as an honorary consultant to Pickering. However, to their credit, the directors demonstrated that they were fully prepared to back the man who had almost stumbled into the managers chair by default. The directors sanctioned the signing of Duncan McKenzie from Chelsea for a club record fee of £75,000 and allowed Pickering to sign Mick Rathbone for £40,000 from Birmingham. There was also a sentimental return to Ewood for Dave Wagstaffe when Pickering agreed to pay a token fee for the former Ewood idol. Both McKenzie and Rathbone were to prove excellent acquisitions for the club but, unfortunately, Pickering did not remain at Ewood long enough to reap the benefit of his work.

When the club failed to avoid relegation to the Third Division the directors informed Pickering that his contract would not be renewed when it expired in the summer. However, since leaving Ewood Park, Pickering has rarely been unemployed. He coached at Carlisle United before moving to Lincoln City as coach and later manager. He then had a spell on the coaching staff of Newcastle United and after another brief stint at Lincoln he returned to his native North-East to accept a coaching appointment at Middlesbrough.

### PINKERTON, James R.
Outside-left. 1936.
*5ft 8in; 11st.*
*Born: Rothesay.*
*Debut: v Arsenal (h) 8 February 1936.*
*Career: Bute Athletic; Partick Thistle; Blackburn Rovers February 1936; St Bernards October 1936.*
**Appearances:** Football League 1.
A gardener from Rothesay, Pinkerton was rushed down from Scotland to arrive in Blackburn on the eve of his debut against Arsenal. It was hardly the preparation required to face George Male, England's first-choice right-back, who lined up against him in the Arsenal team. Pinkerton had never experienced this class of football before and a frozen ground, strange surroundings and a struggling Ewood outfit did little to put him at his ease. Blackburn suffered their fourth successive defeat and Pinkerton disappeared into the Central League team never to receive another senior outing.

### PINXTON, Albert Edward
Inside-right. 1933-1936.
*5ft 10in; 11st.*
*Born: Shelton, Hanley 1912 (July quarter).*
*Debut: v West Bromwich Albion (a) 18 January 1936.*
*Career: Stoke City amateur May 1930 to 1932; Stoke St Peter's; Nantwich; Blackburn Rovers May 1933; Cardiff City June 1936; Torquay United May 1937.*
**Appearances:** Football League 3; FA Cup 1; Total 4.
A member of a footballing family, Albert Pinxton's father and two uncles were all professional footballers whilst an uncle was a Football League referee. A goal maker rather than a goalscorer, he none the less netted 23 goals in 51 Central League outings before being given his first-team chance with the Rovers. He was unable to make much impression on a team that was ultimately destined to be relegated and in the summer of 1936 he joined Cardiff City.

Mike Newell scores the winner from the penalty-spot in the 1992 Play-off Final against Leicester City at Wembley

## PLASTIC PITCHES

There have been four Football League clubs who have opted to dig up their natural turf pitches and replace them with artificial surfaces. The first club to do this was Queen's Park Rangers in 1981 and they were followed by Luton Town (1985), Oldham Athletic (1986) and Preston North End (1986). Queen's Park Rangers, Luton Town and Oldham Athletic have all returned to a grass surface and Preston North End were planning to do the same for the 1994-95 season. Blackburn Rovers never played on the plastic pitches at Luton or Preston North End but their record at Loftus Road and Boundary Park is as follows:

| | | | |
|---|---|---|---|
| Queen's Park Rangers: | 1981-82 | L | 0-2 |
| | 1982-83 | L | 2-2 |
| Oldham Athletic: | 1986-87 | L | 0-3 |
| | 1987-88 | L | 2-4 |
| | 1988-89 | D | 1-1 |
| | 1989-90 | L | 0-2 |
| | 1990-91 | D | 1-1 |

## PLATT, Peter

Goalkeeper. 1901-1902.
*Born: Oldham, 1883 (April quarter); Died: Nuneaton, 11 January 1922.*
*Debut: v West Bromwich Albion (a) 2 March 1901.*
*Career: Great Harwood; Oswaldtwistle Rovers; Blackburn Rovers January 1901; Liverpool 1902 to 1904; Luton Town 1905 to 1909; Nuneaton Town.*
**Appearances:** Football League 1.
Peter Platt was still a teenager when he made his debut for Blackburn Rovers at the Hawthorns in March 1901. However, apart from this senior outing the rest of his time at Ewood Park was spent playing in the Lancashire League with the second team. He did rather better at Liverpool where he made 44 League appearances during his two seasons with the club. He enjoyed several seasons as the regular custodian with Luton Town before ending his playing career with Nuneaton Town. He ended his days in the licensed trade in that town before his tragic early death following illness.

## PLAY-OFFS.

1987-88 Second Division Play-offs

| | | | | | |
|---|---|---|---|---|---|
| Semi-Final | 1st Leg | Chelsea | Home | L | 0-2 |
| | 2nd Leg | Chelsea | Away | L | 1-4 |

It was in 1987-88 that Blackburn Rovers first qualified for the end-of-season Play-offs to decide the remaining Second Division promotion place. At that time the Play-offs included a relegation threatened club from the First Division and having finished in fifth position the Rovers were paired with First Division and having finished in fifth position the Rovers were paired with First Division Chelsea over two legs. Don Mackay produced something of a surprise in team selection when he left out Steve Archibald and named Ossie Ardíles as a substitute. Chelsea enjoyed a comfortable 2-0 victory at Ewood in the first leg and although both Archibald and Ardíles were included for the return fixture at Stamford Bridge, the Rovers suffered a crushing 6-1 aggregate defeat.

1988-89 Second Division Play-offs

| | | | | | |
|---|---|---|---|---|---|
| Semi-final | 1st Leg | Watford | Home | D | 0-0 |
| | 2nd Leg | Watford | Away | D | 1-1 aet |
| Final | 1st Leg | Crystal Palace | Home | W | 3-1 |
| | 2nd Leg | Crystal Palace | Away | L | 0-3 |

After narrowly overcoming Watford in a tense two-match affair on the away goals rule, Blackburn Rovers appeared to have taken a major step towards the First Division with a 3-1 win over Crystal Palace at Ewood Park. Sadly, those who felt that the second leg would be a formality were in for a severe disappointment. On a day when the occasion appeared to get to too many of the Blackburn team, Crystal Palace turned the tie around with a stirring 3-0 victory.

1989-90 Second Division Play-offs

| | | | | | |
|---|---|---|---|---|---|
| Semi-final | 1st Leg | Swindon Town | Home | L | 1-2 |
| | 2nd Leg | Swindon Town | Away | L | 1-2 |

The fact that Blackburn Rovers failed to surmount the first hurdle of the Play-offs came as no surprise to most of the Ewood faithful. In truth the team had been somewhat fortunate to actually make the Play-offs and had never really given the impression of looking like promotion candidates. Ossie Ardíles' Swindon Town looked by far the better side over two legs and actually went on the win the Play-off Final at Wembley. However, financial irregularities led the Football League to demoting Swindon back to the Second Division before they had a chance to kick a ball in the top flight.

1991-92 Second Division Play-offs

| Semi-final | 1st Leg | Derby County | Home | W | 4-2 |
|---|---|---|---|---|---|
| | 2nd Leg | Derby County | Away | L | 1-2 |
| Final | | Leicester City | Wembley | W | 1-0 |

At one point in the season Blackburn had held a commanding lead at the top of the Second Division and looked certainties for the championship. However, a run of seven successive defeats saw them slip from first to seventh position so that even a Play-off place was in doubt. The Rovers qualified for the Play-offs only on the final day of the season with a 3-1 win at Plymouth Argyle. Even then they did it the hard way, having gone behind as early as the 12th minute. Fortunately a David Speedie hat-trick ensured that the team lived to fight another day. In view of the club's recent form an air of depression sank over Ewood when Derby raced into a two-goal lead after only 14 minutes of the first leg at Ewood. However, it proved to be the signal for a brave fight back and goals from Scott Sellars and Mike Newell levelled matters by half-time. In a second-half which was totally dominated by the Rovers, two goals from David Speedie enabled the team to travel to Derby with the cushion of a two-goal lead. In front of a highly partisan crowd the Rovers fell behind to an Andy Comyn goal after 23 minutes of the second leg. However, a bravely headed goal by Kevin Moran restored the two goal cushion on 49 minutes and although Ted McMinn put Derby ahead on the night, the Rovers hung on for a 5-4 aggregate victory.

The Final was played at Wembley on 25 May 1992 in front of 68,147 spectators against Leicester City. Leicester had done the double over the Rovers and had finished the season with three points more than the men from Ewood. On a glorious Bank Holiday Monday, the crucial moment of the game occurred on the brink of half-time when David Speedie was felled in the area and George Courtney, in his final match as a senior referee, awarded a penalty. The decision was hotly disputed by Leicester but Mike Newell kept his nerve and swept the ball into the net. As was to be expected the second half was a nerve racking affair. However, despite Newell missing a second penalty, the Rovers hung on to claim their place in the Premier League.

## PLAYING RECORD IN THE FOOTBALL LEAGUE 1888-89 to 1991-92

Below are details of the complete playing record of Blackburn Rovers in the Football League. Blackburn Rovers were one of the founder members of the League and played in three different divisions. Blackburn left the Football League in 1991-92 to participate in the inaugural season of the Premier League.

| | P | W | D | L | F | A |
|---|---|---|---|---|---|---|
| First Division | 2024 | 755 | 467 | 802 | 3379 | 3441 |
| Second Division | 1446 | 583 | 364 | 499 | 2134 | 1981 |
| Third Division | 230 | 104 | 59 | 67 | 299 | 249 |
| Total | 3700 | 1442 | 890 | 1368 | 5812 | 5671 |
| | | | | | | |
| Test Matches/Play-offs | 15 | 4 | 2 | 9 | 18 | 31 |

## PLAYING RECORD IN THE PREMIERSHIP

Blackburn Rovers were one of the founder members of the FA Premier League which became known as the Premiership at the start of the 1993-94 season. Only Aston Villa, Blackburn Rovers and Everton shared the distinction having been founder members of both the Football League and the Premier League. Below are details of their complete playing record in the Premiership.

| P | W | D | L | F | A |
|---|---|---|---|---|---|
| 84 | 45 | 20 | 19 | 131 | 82 |

## PLEASINGTON CRICKET GROUND

The cricket ground at Pleasington was home to Blackburn Rovers following their move from the playing field at Oozebooth. The ground at Pleasington was a little too far from the centre of town to become anything other than a temporary home and within a few months the club had moved to Alexandra Meadows. Today the playing fields at Pleasington are the venue for the club's 'A' and 'B' team matches.

## PLYMOUTH ARGYLE FC

Plymouth Argyle Football Club developed from the Argyle Athletic Club which had been founded in 1886. At first the club played both association football and rugby but when the rugby section was disbanded the membership formed a professional football club in 1903. One of the founder members of the Third Division of the Football League in 1920, Plymouth Argyle have met Blackburn Rovers in both the Second and Third Division but the clubs have never been drawn together in a major cup competition.

**Football League**

| | | | Home | | Away | |
|---|---|---|---|---|---|---|
| 1936-37 | | (Div 2) | L | 2-3 | L | 0-2 |
| 1937-38 | | (Div 2) | W | 2-1 | D | 2-2 |
| 1938-39 | | (Div 2) | W | 4-0 | L | 0-1 |
| 1948-49 | | (Div 2) | W | 2-1 | L | 0-3 |
| 1949-50 | | (Div 2) | W | 1-0 | D | 0-0 |
| 1952-53 | | (Div 2) | L | 1-3 | L | 1-3 |
| 1953-54 | | (Div 2) | L | 2-3 | D | 1-1 |
| 1954-55 | | (Div 2) | D | 2-2 | W | 2-0 |
| 1955-56 | | (Div 2) | W | 2-1 | L | 0-1 |
| 1966-67 | | (Div 2) | W | 3-0 | L | 0-4 |
| 1967-68 | | (Div 2) | D | 1-1 | L | 1-2 |
| 1971-72 | | (Div 3) | W | 3-2 | L | 0-1 |
| 1972-73 | | (Div 3) | W | 3-1 | W | 2-1 |
| 1973-74 | | (Div 3) | W | 2-0 | L | 1-2 |
| 1974-75 | | (Div 3) | W | 5-2 | L | 1-2 |
| 1975-76 | | (Div 2) | W | 3-1 | D | 2-2 |
| 1976-77 | | (Div 2) | W | 2-0 | L | 0-4 |
| 1979-80 | | (Div 3) | W | 1-0 | W | 1-0 |
| 1986-87 | | (Div 2) | L | 1-2 | D | 1-1 |
| 1987-88 | | (Div 2) | D | 1-1 | L | 0-3 |
| 1988-89 | | (Div 2) | L | 1-2 | L | 3-4 |
| 1989-90 | | (Div 2) | W | 2-0 | D | 2-2 |
| 1990-91 | | (Div 2) | D | 0-0 | L | 1-4 |
| 1991-92 | | (Div 2) | W | 5-2 | W | 3-1 |

| | P | W | D | L | F | A |
|---|---|---|---|---|---|---|
| Home | 24 | 15 | 4 | 5 | 51 | 28 |
| Away | 24 | 4 | 6 | 14 | 24 | 46 |
| Total | 48 | 19 | 10 | 19 | 75 | 74 |

## POINTS

The record for the greatest number of points gained in each division is as follows:

| Premier League | 84 points in 1993-94 | |
|---|---|---|
| First Division | 49 points in 1911-12 | |
| Second Division | (2 pts for a win) | 56 points in 1957-58 |
| | (3pts for a win) | 77 points in 1987-88 & |
| 1988-89 | | |
| Third Division | 60 points in 1974-75 | |

The Rovers' record for the lowest number of points gained in each division is as follows:

| Premier League | 71 points in 1992-93 | |
|---|---|---|
| First Division | 20 points in 1965-66 | |
| Second Division | (2pts for a win) | 27 points in 1970-71 |
| | (3pts for a win) | 49 points in 1985-86 |
| Third Division | 46 points in 1973-74 | |

## POOL, Alexander

Half-back. 1919-1925.
*5ft 10in; 11st 10lb.*
*Born: Annan.*
*Debut: v Manchester City (h) 1 October 1921.*
*Career: Solway Star; Blackburn Rovers 1919; Bristol City May 1925; Exeter City August 1926; Stalybridge Celtic June 1929.*
**Appearances:** Football League 17; FA Cup 2; Total 19.

A robust and hard working half-back who came to the club from junior football. Pool was groomed in the Central League team and appeared to offer great promise as either a centre-half or a half-back. After making his first-team debut in October 1921, Pool found himself making only spasmodic appearances until his departure to Bristol City in May 1925. Although he began the 1925-26 season in the first team, Pool made only 12 appearances at Ashton Gate before joining Exeter City in August 1926. During his stay with the Grecians, Pool scored three goals in 74 League appearances before dropping out of the League to join Stalybridge Celtic in June 1929.

## PORT VALE FC

Formed in 1876 as Port Vale, the club adopted the title of Burslem Port Vale in 1884 after moving to that part of the Potteries. The club was one of the original members of the Second Division of the Football League in 1892 but failed to gain re-election in 1896. They returned to the Second Division in 1898 but resigned from the League in 1907. In 1911 the club reverted to the title of Port Vale and in October 1919 they returned to the

Football League when they took over the fixtures of Leeds City. Blackburn Rovers and Port Vale have a history of meetings going back to the days before the Football League was founded. However, the first meeting between the clubs in the League did not take place until the 1954-55 season.

### Football League

| | | | Home | | Away | |
|---|---|---|---|---|---|---|
| 1954-55 | | (Div 2) | W | 2-1 | W | 3-0 |
| 1955-56 | | (Div 2) | W | 7-1 | L | 1-4 |
| 1956-57 | | (Div 2) | L | 2-4 | W | 3-0 |
| 1971-72 | | (Div 3) | W | 3-1 | D | 0-0 |
| 1972-73 | | (Div 3) | L | 0-1 | L | 1-2 |
| 1973-74 | | (Div 3) | D | 1-1 | W | 2-1 |
| 1974-75 | | (Div 3) | D | 2-2 | W | 4-1 |
| 1989-90 | | (Div 2) | W | 1-0 | D | 0-0 |
| 1990-91 | | (Div 2) | D | 1-1 | L | 0-3 |
| 1991-92 | | (Div 2) | W | 1-0 | L | 0-2 |

| | P | W | D | L | F | A |
|---|---|---|---|---|---|---|
| Home | 10 | 5 | 3 | 2 | 20 | 12 |
| Away | 10 | 4 | 2 | 4 | 14 | 13 |
| Total | 20 | 9 | 5 | 6 | 34 | 25 |

### FA Cup

| 1927-28 | (5) | Home | W | 2-1 |
|---|---|---|---|---|
| 1946-47 | (4) | Home | W | 2-0 |
| 1971-72 | (1) | Home | D | 1-1 |
| | (R) | Away | L | 1-3 |

### Full Members' Cup

| 1991-92 | (1) | Away | L | 0-1 |
|---|---|---|---|---|

### Wartime

| | | Home | | Away | |
|---|---|---|---|---|---|
| 1916-17 | (LSPT) | W | 4-0 | L | 1-3 |
| 1917-18 | (LSPT) | L | 1-5 | W | 2-0 |
| 1918-19 | (LSPT) | W | 6-0 | L | 2-3 |

### PORTEOUS, George
Half-back. 1910-1915.
*5ft 8in; 10st 4lb.*
*Debut: v Everton (a) 25 December 1912.*
*Career: Blackburn Rovers April 1910.*
*Domestic honours with Blackburn Rovers: First Division championship 1913-14 (1 app).*
**Appearances:** Football League 6.
George Porteous came to Blackburn Rovers from Scotland as a forward but was developed into a half-back by the club. However, with Albert Walmsley, Percy Smith and Billy Bradshaw firmly in command of the half-back positions, Porteous had to wait until December 1912 before making his senior debut. He went on to deputise for all three regular half-backs during his five outings in the 1912-13 season. He made one appearance, at left-half, during the 1913-14 championship campaign.

### PORTER, Robert
Outside-right. 1887-1889.
*Debut: v Stoke (h) 27 October 1888.*
*Career: Blackburn Rovers 1888.*
**Appearances:** Football League 1.
Although Porter was registered with the Lancashire Association as a Blackburn player for the 1887-88 season he does not appear to have been called upon for the senior team. His sole appearance in the Football League with the Rovers came in the 5-3 home win over Stoke in October 1888. The following week James Beresford resumed his position on the right wing and Porter disappeared from the scene.

### PORTER, Walter S.
Full-back. 1895-1896.
*5ft 9in; 11st 10lb.*
*Born: Mellor.*
*Debut: v Sheffield Wednesday (h) 23 November 1895.*
*Career: Mellor St John's; Blackburn Rovers September 1895; Mellor; Thursday Rangers; St Silas' (Blackburn).*
**Appearances:** Football League 6.
A capable defender who acted as understudy for Brandon and Murray during the 1895-96 season. Although Murray retired at the end of that campaign, Porter was overlooked in favour of Killean and at the end of the season severed his connections with the club after failing to agree terms. His brother Alec, an outside right, appeared occasionally with the second team.

### PORTSMOUTH FC
Formed in 1898, Portsmouth joined the Southern League in 1899 before becoming founder members of the Third Division of the Football League in 1920. Although Blackburn and Portsmouth have a history of League meetings going back to 1927-28 it has been the FA Cup which has produced some of the most titanic struggles between the two teams. Such has been the closeness of these games that two ties have gone to a second replay and had to be settled on a neutral ground.

### Football League

| | | | Home | | Away | |
|---|---|---|---|---|---|---|
| 1927-28 | | (Div 1) | W | 6-0 | D | 2-2 |
| 1928-29 | | (Div 1) | W | 4-0 | D | 2-2 |
| 1929-30 | | (Div 1) | W | 1-0 | L | 0-4 |
| 1930-31 | | (Div 1) | L | 1-2 | L | 0-3 |
| 1931-32 | | (Div 1) | W | 5-3 | L | 0-2 |
| 1932-33 | | (Div 1) | W | 3-2 | L | 0-2 |
| 1933-34 | | (Div 1) | W | 3-2 | L | 0-2 |
| 1934-35 | | (Div 1) | D | 0-0 | L | 1-3 |
| 1935-36 | | (Div 1) | W | 3-1 | L | 1-3 |
| 1946-47 | | (Div 1) | L | 0-1 | L | 1-3 |
| 1947-48 | | (Div 1) | W | 1-0 | D | 1-1 |
| 1958-59 | | (Div 1) | W | 2-1 | L | 1-2 |
| 1966-67 | | (Div 2) | D | 2-2 | D | 1-1 |
| 1967-68 | | (Div 2) | D | 2-2 | L | 1-2 |
| 1968-69 | | (Div 2) | W | 3-1 | W | 1-0 |
| 1969-70 | | (Div 2) | L | 0-3 | L | 0-2 |
| 1970-71 | | (Div 2) | D | 1-1 | L | 1-4 |
| 1975-76 | | (Div 2) | L | 0-3 | W | 1-0 |
| 1983-84 | | (Div 2) | W | 2-1 | W | 4-2 |
| 1984-85 | | (Div 2) | L | 0-1 | D | 2-2 |
| 1985-86 | | (Div 2) | W | 1-0 | L | 0-3 |
| 1986-87 | | (Div 2) | W | 1-0 | L | 0-1 |
| 1988-89 | | (Div 2) | W | 3-1 | W | 2-1 |
| 1989-90 | | (Div 2) | W | 2-0 | D | 1-1 |
| 1990-91 | | (Div 2) | D | 1-1 | L | 2-3 |
| 1991-92 | | (Div 2) | D | 1-1 | D | 2-2 |

| | P | W | D | L | F | A |
|---|---|---|---|---|---|---|
| Home | 26 | 15 | 6 | 5 | 48 | 29 |
| Away | 26 | 4 | 7 | 15 | 27 | 53 |
| Total | 52 | 19 | 13 | 20 | 75 | 82 |

### FA Cup

| 1899-00 | (1) | Away | D | 0-0 |
|---|---|---|---|---|
| | (R) | Home | D | 1-1aet |
| | (2R) | Villa Park | W | 5-0 |
| 1924-25 | (2) | Home | D | 0-0 |
| | (R) | Away | D | 0-0aet |
| | (2R) | Highbury | W | 1-0 |
| 1968-69 | (4) | Home | W | 4-0 |
| 1984-85 | (3) | Away | D | 0-0 |
| | (R) | Home | W | 2-1 |
| 1986-87 | (3) | Home | L | 0-2 |
| 1993-94 | (3) | Home | D | 3-3 |
| | (R) | Away | W | 3-1 |

### PRATT, John T.
Goalkeeper. 1936-1937.
*5ft 9in; 10st 6lb.*
*Born: Workington, 1916 (April quarter).*
*Debut: v Aston Villa (a) 25 April 1936.*
*Career: Cumberland Junior football; Preston North End 1935; Blackburn Rovers amateur April 1936, turning professional in May 1936; Belfast Distillery August 1937; Workington; Carlisle United.*
**Appearances:** Football League 6; FA Cup 2; Total 8.
Pratt was one of five goalkeepers used by the club in the last ten League games of the 1935-36 season. At the time of his debut Pratt was registered as an amateur at Ewood and he didn't sign professional forms until the end of the season. With Jimmy Barron and Jack Hughes ahead of him Pratt had to bide his time before he was given another opportunity with the senior team His chance came at the end of December 1936 when he enjoyed a run of six League and Cup games. However, three of four League games were lost and the club suffered an embarrassing FA Cup exit at the hands of Accrington Stanley. Although there were those who believed that the youngster had a bright future ahead of him, an error strewn display in the defeat by Accrington brought his career at Ewood to an end.

### PREMIERSHIP
Blackburn Rovers became one of the original members of the Premier

Kevin Moran leads Rovers out for their first-ever home game in the Premier League, against Arsenal in August 1992. The Arsenal skipper is Tony Adams.

League when they defeated Leicester City in the Final of the Second Division Play-offs in May 1992. The 1993-94 season saw the competition become known as the 'Carling Premiership'. Blackburn's record in the competition is as follows:

| | | Home | | | | | Away | | | | | |
|---|---|---|---|---|---|---|---|---|---|---|---|---|
| P | W | D | L | F | A | W | D | L | F | A | Pts | Pos |
| 42 | 13 | 4 | 4 | 38 | 18 | 7 | 7 | 7 | 30 | 28 | 71 | 4 |
| 42 | 14 | 5 | 2 | 31 | 11 | 11 | 4 | 6 | 32 | 25 | 84 | 2 |

## PRESTON NORTH END FC

Founded in 1880 by members of the North End Cricket Club, an organisation which had been in existence since 1867, Preston North End became one of the original members of the Football League in 1888. Meetings between Blackburn Rovers and Preston North End were always a special event and often occurred over the Christmas period. On 26 March 1881, Blackburn Rovers visited Preston for a friendly match and inflicted a 16-0 defeat on North End. It was a home fixture against Preston North End on 26 December 1921 which attracted a record League crowd of 52,656 to Ewood Park.

### Football League

| | | Home | | Away | |
|---|---|---|---|---|---|
| 1888-89 | (FL) | D | 2-2 | L | 0-1 |
| 1889-90 | (FL) | L | 3-4 | D | 1-1 |
| 1890-91 | (FL) | W | 1-0 | W | 2-1 |
| 1891-92 | (FL) | L | 2-4 | L | 2-3 |
| 1892-93 | (Div 1) | D | 0-0 | L | 1-2 |
| 1893-94 | (Div 1) | W | 1-0 | W | 1-0 |
| 1894-95 | (Div 1) | D | 1-1 | D | 1-1 |
| 1895-96 | (Div 1) | W | 3-0 | D | 1-1 |
| 1896-97 | (Div 1) | L | 0-4 | L | 1-3 |
| 1897-98 | (Div 1) | W | 1-0 | W | 4-1 |
| 1898-99 | (Div 1) | D | 2-2 | D | 1-1 |
| 1899-00 | (Div 1) | W | 3-0 | L | 0-2 |
| 1900-01 | (Div 1) | W | 3-1 | L | 1-4 |
| 1904-05 | (Div 1) | D | 1-1 | D | 0-0 |
| 1905-06 | (Div 1) | L | 1-2 | L | 1-2 |
| 1906-07 | (Div 1) | D | 1-1 | L | 0-1 |
| 1907-08 | (Div 1) | D | 1-1 | D | 1-1 |
| 1908-09 | (Div 1) | D | 1-1 | L | 0-2 |
| 1909-10 | (Div 1) | D | 2-2 | L | 2-3 |
| 1910-11 | (Div 1) | L | 0-1 | D | 0-0 |
| 1911-12 | (Div 1) | W | 3-0 | D | 2-2 |
| 1913-14 | (Div 1) | W | 5-0 | W | 5-1 |
| 1919-20 | (Div 1) | W | 4-0 | D | 0-0 |
| 1920-21 | (Div 1) | D | 2-2 | L | 2-4 |
| 1921-22 | (Div 1) | W | 3-0 | L | 1-2 |
| 1922-23 | (Div 1) | D | 1-1 | L | 0-1 |
| 1923-24 | (Div 1) | W | 2-0 | W | 1-0 |
| 1924-25 | (Div 1) | L | 0-1 | L | 2-3 |
| 1934-35 | (Div 1) | W | 1-0 | L | 1-3 |
| 1935-36 | (Div 1) | D | 1-1 | L | 0-2 |
| 1946-47 | (Div 1) | L | 1-2 | L | 0-4 |
| 1947-48 | (Div 1) | L | 2-3 | L | 1-2 |
| 1949-50 | (Div 2) | L | 2-3 | L | 1-3 |
| 1950-51 | (Div 2) | W | 2-1 | L | 0-3 |
| 1958-59 | (Div 1) | W | 4-1 | W | 2-1 |
| 1959-60 | (Div 1) | L | 1-4 | L | 3-5 |
| 1960-61 | (Div 1) | W | 1-0 | L | 0-2 |
| 1966-67 | (Div 2) | W | 2-0 | L | 0-3 |
| 1967-68 | (Div 2) | L | 0-1 | W | 5-3 |
| 1968-69 | (Div 2) | W | 1-0 | D | 1-1 |
| 1969-70 | (Div 2) | W | 4-2 | D | 0-0 |
| 1974-75 | (Div 3) | W | 3-0 | D | 0-0 |
| 1978-79 | (Div 2) | L | 0-1 | L | 1-4 |
| 1980-81 | (Div 2) | D | 0-0 | D | 0-0 |

| | P | W | D | L | F | A |
|---|---|---|---|---|---|---|
| Home | 44 | 19 | 13 | 12 | 74 | 50 |
| Away | 44 | 7 | 13 | 24 | 48 | 79 |
| Total | 88 | 26 | 26 | 36 | 122 | 129 |

## FA Cup

| 1899-00 | (2) | Away | L | 0-1 |
|---|---|---|---|---|
| 1925-26 | (3) | Home | D | 1-1 |
| | (R) | Away | W | 4-1 |

## Football League Cup

| 1975-76 | (1) | Away | L | 0-2 |
|---|---|---|---|---|
| | | Home | D | 0-0 |

## Wartime

| | | Home | | Away | |
|---|---|---|---|---|---|
| 1916-17 | (LSPT) | W | 3-2 | W | 2-0 |
| | (LSST) | W | 2-1 | L | 1-3 |
| 1917-18 | (LSPT) | L | 0-2 | L | 0-1 |
| | (LSST) | L | 0-1 | L | 0-2 |
| 1918-19 | (LSPT) | D | 0-0 | D | 2-2 |
| | (LSST) | L | 0-1 | D | 1-1 |
| 1939-40 | (NWRL) | L | 0-3 | L | 0-2 |
| 1940-41 | (NRL) | D | 0-0 | L | 0-1 |
| 1941-42 | (FLNS-FC) | W | 2-1 | W | 2-1 |
| | (FLNS-SC) | D | 3-3 | L | 0-2 |
| 1944-45 | (FLNS-FC) | W | 2-1 | W | 2-0 |
| | (FLNS-SC) | W | 3-2 | L | 2-3 |
| | | | | L | 1-3 |
| | | W | 1-0 | L | 0-5 |
| 1945-46 | (FLN) | L | 0-2 | L | 1-3 |

Note: Blackburn and Preston met on five occasions during the Second Competition of the 1944-45 season.

## PRICE, Christopher John
Right-back/Midfield. 1986-1988 & 1992-1993.
*5ft 7in; 10st 2lb.*
*Born: Hereford, 30 March 1960.*
*Debut: v Leeds United (h) 23 August 1986.*
*Career: Hereford United apprentice June 1976, turning professional in January 1978; Blackburn Rovers July 1986 (£25,000); Aston Villa May 1988 (£125,000); Blackburn Rovers February 1992 (£100,000); Portsmouth February 1993 (£50,000).*
*Domestic honours with Blackburn Rovers: Full Members' Cup winners: 1987; Second Division Play-off winners: 1992.*
**Appearances:** Premier League 2+4; Football League 94+2; Play-offs 3; F.A.Cup 2; Football League Cup 7; Full Members' Cup 6; Total 114+6.
**Goals:** Football League 14.
Chris Price moved to Ewood Park after making 330 League appearances (including three as sub) with Hereford United. During his time at Hereford he scored 17 League goals from the right-back position but in his first season at Ewood he had ten League goals to his name. The prematurely balding Price was a fine attacking full-back who could also operate in midfield. During his first spell at Ewood he appeared in 83 League games before joining Aston Villa after the Rovers failed to gain promotion via the Play-offs in 1987-88. He quickly adjusted to First Division football at Villa Park and made 111 League appearances (including two as sub) before returning to Ewood in February 1992. Following his move from Villa Park, Price scored in both of his first two appearances at right-back but lost his place over the final few matches of the season. He was recalled for the Play-offs and operated on the right-hand side of midfield at Wembley against Leicester City. However, the emergence of David May in the right-back position meant Price had few opportunities to play in the Premier League and in February 1993 he moved to Portsmouth.

## PRICE, John
Outside-right. 1971-1974.
*5ft 4in; 10st 4lb.*
*Born: Easington, 25 October 1943.*
*Debut: v Swansea Town (h) 25 September 1971.*
*Career: Horden Colliery Welfare; Burnley November 1960; Stockport County May 1965; Blackburn Rovers September 1971; Stockport County March 1974.*
**Appearances:** Football League 63+13; FA Cup 4+2; Football League Cup 1+1; Total 68+16.
**Goals:** Football League 12.
A diminutive winger who was brought to Ewood Park by Ken Furphy early in his reign. Although small in stature, Price was a speedy winger whose trickery was always

liable to create openings. His direct style of play was very popular on the terraces and he scored eight goals in 38 League appearances during his first season at the club. However, the remainder of his time at Blackburn found him in and out of the side or occupying a place on the sub's bench. He was eventually allowed to return to Stockport County in March 1974. In two spells with Stockport, Price scored 24 goals in 313 League appearances (including 21 as sub) whilst earlier in is career he had scored two goals in 21 League games with Burnley.

## PRIDAY, Robert Herbert
Outside-left. 1949-1951.
*5ft 9in; 11st 1lb.*
*Born: Cape Town, South Africa, 29 March 1925.*
*Debut: v West Bromwich Albion (a) 19 March 1949.*
*Career: South African football; Liverpool December 1945; Blackburn Rovers March 1949 (£10,000); Clitheroe cs 1951; Northwich Victoria cs 1952; Accrington Stanley December 1952; Rochdale on trial August to October 1953.*
**Appearances:** Football League 44; FA Cup 1; Total 45.
**Goals:** Football League 11.
A South African winger who had joined Liverpool during the last season of wartime football, Bob Priday went on to score six goals in 33 League appearances for the Anfield club. He came to Ewood Park towards the end of the 1948-49 season and became the sixth player during that campaign to occupy the outside-left position. He began the following season as the first-choice outside-left but eventually lost his place to Bob McCraig and then Ernie Edds. Although he was restored to first-team duty during the opening months of the 1950-51 season he eventually lost his place to Billy Fenton. Priday spent some time in non-League football after leaving Ewood before returning to Lancashire to join Accrington Stanley. Unfortunately, he was injured on his debut and made only five League appearances for Stanley before having a trial with Rochdale, which also resulted in only five League games.

## PROCTOR, Benjamin John
Outside-right. 1909-1913.
*5ft 7in; 10st 4lb.*
*Debut: v Tottenham Hotspur (a) 9 February 1911 (FAC).*
*Career: Blackburn Rovers September 1909; Stockport County May 1913.*
*Domestic Honours with Blackburn Rovers: First Division championship: 1911-12 (1 app).*
**Appearances:** Football League 2; FA Cup 1; Total 3.
Proctor had the misfortune to be a promising winger, being described by contemporaries as 'fast and decisive', at a time when the club were well served in that department. When he arrived at Ewood, Garbutt, Anthony and Bracegirdle were competing for the two wide positions and in 1911 Jock Simpson was signed for a record fee. In January 1913 the club brought Joe Hodgkinson to Ewood Park and his arrival signalled the departure of Proctor. During four seasons with the club Proctor had been unable to break into the first team on a regular basis and was not called upon at all during the 1912-13 campaign.

## PROFESSIONALISM
In its earliest days professionalism was very much an 'under the counter' affair and in 1882 the Football Association made a rule which permitted only payment for actual wages lost in addition to expenses. The position of Blackburn Rovers with regard to professionalism was ambiguous from the very outset. Whilst, Dr E.S.Morley, a leading figure at the club and a future chairman, was firmly opposed to professionalism, the fact remains that the Rovers fielded Scottish players who were generally accepted to be professionals.

Whilst the professional status of Hugh McIntyre and Jimmy Douglas was clouded by the fact that both men did have trades outside of football the same could not be said of Fergie Suter. Suter had been paid to appear with Turton in a special competition in 1878 and then joined Darwen. It was believed that he only left Darwen for Blackburn because Rovers' officials had offered him better terms than those he had enjoyed at Darwen.

A stonemason by trade, few if anybody actually witnessed him carrying out his craft in Lancashire. Indeed, it appeared to be common knowledge that Suter had stated that English stone was too difficult to work and hence his decision to play football for a living. The fact that Blackburn Rovers used professionals to help them rise above other clubs in the area did not meet with universal approval. The *Athletic News* in November 1879 stated: 'It looks as if the Blackburn men were afraid to fight out their own battles in a fair and honest manner, and if allowed it would justify other clubs in bringing down the best Scottish players to help them in important encounters.'

The *Blackburn Times* took a similar view when the club arranged for Jock Inglis, the former Glasgow Rangers and Scottish international, to appear in FA Cup-ties during the 1883-84 season. Although neighbouring

Goalkeeper John Butcher, Noel Brotherston and Derek Fazackerley (holding the scarf) join in the celebrations following Blackburn's promotion to the Second Division at the end of the 1979-80 season. On the right (without a shirt) is Duncan McKenzie.

Accrington Football Club found themselves ejected from the 1883-84 and 1884-85 FA Cup competitions no such censures were ever taken against Blackburn Rovers. At a Special General Meeting of the Football Association on 20 July 1885, professionalism was at last recognised. Jimmy Forrest became the first professional to appear for England against Scotland in 1886, whilst Bob Crompton became the first professional to captain the England team.

## PROMOTION

Promotion has been achieved on five occasions during the history of Blackburn Rovers. Details of their playing record in each of these seasons is given below:

1938-39 Second Division to the First Division

| P | W | D | L | F | A | Pts | Pos |
|---|---|---|---|---|---|-----|-----|
| 42 | 25 | 5 | 12 | 94 | 60 | 55 | 1 |

1957-58 Second Division to the First Division

| P | W | D | L | F | A | Pts | Pos |
|---|---|---|---|---|---|-----|-----|
| 42 | 22 | 12 | 8 | 93 | 57 | 56 | 2 |

1974-75 Third Division to the Second Division

| P | W | D | L | F | A | Pts | Pos |
|---|---|---|---|---|---|-----|-----|
| 46 | 22 | 16 | 8 | 68 | 45 | 60 | 1 |

1979-80 Third Division to the Second Division

| P | W | D | L | F | A | Pts | Pos |
|---|---|---|---|---|---|-----|-----|
| 46 | 25 | 9 | 12 | 58 | 36 | 59 | 2 |

1991-92 Second Division to the Premier League

| P | W | D | L | F | A | Pts | Pos |
|---|---|---|---|---|---|-----|-----|
| 46 | 21 | 11 | 14 | 70 | 53 | 74 | 6 |

(Promotion achieved via the Play-offs)

## PROUDFOOT, John

Centre-forward. 1897-1898.
*Born: Scotland.*
*Debut: v Bury (h) 20 February 1897.*
*Career: Patrick Thistle July 1895; Blackburn Rovers February 1897; Everton April 1898; Watford 1902.*
**Appearance:** Football League 36; FA Cup 1; Total 37.
**Goals:** Football League 14.
John Proudfoot arrived in Blackburn in February 1897 and made a goalscoring debut in the 2-1 home defeat by Bury. Proudfoot played at centre-forward in the last seven matches of the season and scored five goals. He missed only one game during the 1897-98 season but could only score a meagre nine goals from 29 League outings. It came as no surprise when the Ewood directors allowed him to move to Everton in April 1898. Proudfoot did much better at Goodison, scoring 30 goals in 84 League games. In 1902 he joined Watford and scored five goals in 12 Southern League appearances for the club.

## PRYDE, Robert Ireland

Centre-half. 1933-1949.
*6ft; 12st.*
*Born: Methil, 25 April 1913.*
*Debut: v Chelsea (h) 21 October 1933.*
*Career: St Johnstone; Brechin City on loan; Blackburn Rovers May 1933; Wigan Athletic player-manager cs 1949.*
*International honours with Blackburn Rovers: Football League: 2 appearances (1941-47).*
*Domestic honours with Blackburn Rovers: Second Division championship: 1938-39 (41 apps, 1 gl); League War Cup runners-up: 1940.*
**Appearances:** Football League 320; FA Cup 25; Total 345.
**Goals:** Football League 11.
Bob Pryde arrived at Ewood Park for a trail with the Central League team at the end of the 1932-33 season. He left 16 years later after making almost 350 League and Cup appearances for the club. Pryde became a

motor-mechanic after leaving school and played part-time football with St Johnstone. He graduated to the first team before joining Brechin City in a loan deal arrangement. After arriving at Ewood, Pryde quickly forced his way into the senior team at left-half. However, it was not until the 1936-37 season that he finally settled in the centre-half position which he would come to dominate at Ewood.

Tall and slim, Pryde was a tough defender whose reading of the game compensated for his suspect pace. His early days at the club were plagued with inconsistency but there was no denying his natural leadership qualities. As the inconsistency evaporated from his game Pryde became a leading figure in the 1938-39 Second Division championship team. Sadly, Pryde was at the peak of his power when war intervened and it fell to him to hold a constantly changing side together during the years of meaningless wartime football.

He scored 11 goals in 180 wartime appearances for the club between 1939 and 1946. Although 33 when League football recommenced it was Pryde who continued to be the dominant force in a struggling team. Determined to bow out whilst still at the top, Pryde delayed his decision to retire from the game in a bid to help the Rovers regain their place in the First Division. He finally called it a day at the end of the 1948-49 season and accepted the position of player-manager with Wigan Athletic.

### PUDDEFOOT, Sydney Charles
Inside-right. 1925-1932.
*5ft 10in; 12st.*
*Born: West Ham, London, 17 October 1894; Died: Southend, 2 October 1972.*
*Debut: v Arsenal (a) 7 February 1925.*
*Career: Park Road School; Conder Athletic; Limehouse Town; West Ham United amateur 1912-13, becoming a professional in 1913-14; Falkirk wartime guest; Falkirk February 1922 (£5,000); Blackburn Rovers February 1925 (£4,000); West Ham United February 1932. Retired cs 1933. Fenerbahçe (Turkey) coach 1933-34; Galatasaray (Turkey) coach 1934-35; Northampton Town manager March 1935 to March 1937. Returned to Turkey in 1937 and coached in Istanbul until 1940.*
*International honours with Blackburn Rovers: England: 2 caps (1925-26); Football League: 2 appearances (1925).*
*Domestic honours with Blackburn Rovers: FA Cup winners: 1928.*
**Appearance:** Football League 250; FA Cup 26; Total 276.
**Goals:** Football League 79; FA Cup 8; Total 87.
Unquestionably one of the finest forwards of his era, Syd Puddefoot began his playing career with junior teams in East London before joining West Ham United. At the time West Ham were members of the Southern League but Puddefoot helped to establish the 'Hammers' in the Second Division of the Football League before moving to Falkirk in February 1922.

Puddefoot, who had been top scorer at Upton Park during each of the three post-war seasons, had been expected to move to a leading club in England and his move to Scotland was something of a sensation. However, the player had guested for Falkirk during the war and was to help the club to a Scottish Cup semi-final appearance. A record of 45 goals in 120 games attracted the attention of Blackburn Rovers and in February 1925 the club paid £4,000 to bring him to Ewood Park. A natural ball player, Puddefoot was seen as the man who could transform the club and lift the gloom which had settled over Ewood in the immediate post-war years. Although, at the age of 30, he was considered to be something of a veteran when he arrived at Blackburn he was still regarded as a major signing. Although a gifted individual, Puddefoot's greatest asset was his seemingly effortless passing ability. As play-maker he had the vision to bring the rest of the team into the game with a succession of pinpoint passes.

It was Puddefoot's vision which enabled him to exploit the changes in the offside law to help Ted Harper to score 43 League goals during the 1925-26 season. As well as play-maker, Puddefoot also had an eye for goal himself and on five occasions his seasonal total in League matches reached double figures. Capped twice by England whilst at Ewood, Puddefoot also picked up an FA Cup winners' medal in 1928. In February

1932, Puddefoot returned to his roots and signed for West Ham United but could not prevent the 'Hammers' from being relegated to the Second Division. When his playing career finally ended in 1932-33 he turned to coaching in Turkey. His only experience of management in England came with a short spell with Northampton Town between 1935-37.

### QUEEN'S PARK FC
Formed in 1867, Queen's Park were one of seven Scottish clubs that participated in the FA Cup during the 1880s. They reached the Final of the competition twice and on both occasions they faced Blackburn Rovers. The meetings, both of which were at the Kennington Oval, were regarded as something of an international affair and on both occasions Blackburn Rovers proved triumphant. In the days before the formation of the Football League, Queen's Park were involved in a number of friendly fixtures with the Rovers.

**FA Cup**

| | | | | |
|---|---|---|---|---|
| 1883-84 | (F) | Kennington Oval | W | 2-1 |
| 1884-85 | (F) | Kennington Oval | W | 2-0 |

### QUEEN'S PARK RANGERS FC
Founded in 1885 as St Jude's Institute FC, the club changed its name to Queen's Park Rangers in 1887. As members of the Southern League they faced Blackburn Rovers in the FA Charity Shield in May1912. The match ought to have been played at the start of the 1912-13 season but was brought forward so that the proceeds of the game could be donated to the Titanic Relief Fund. Queen's Park Rangers became one of the founder members of the Third Division of the Football League in 1920.

**Football League**

| | | Home | | Away | |
|---|---|---|---|---|---|
| 1948-49 | (Div 2) | W | 2-0 | L | 2-4 |
| 1949-50 | (Div 2) | D | 0-0 | W | 3-2 |

| | | | | | |
|---|---|---|---|---|---|
| 1950-51 | (Div 2) | W | 2-1 | L | 1-3 |
| 1951-52 | (Div 2) | W | 4-2 | L | 1-2 |
| 1967-68 | (Div 2) | L | 0-1 | L | 1-3 |
| 1969-70 | (Div 2) | L | 0-1 | W | 3-2 |
| 1970-71 | (Div 2) | L | 0-2 | L | 0-2 |
| 1980-81 | (Div 2) | W | 2-1 | D | 1-1 |
| 1981-82 | (Div 2) | W | 2-1 | L | 0-2 |
| 1982-83 | (Div 2) | L | 1-3 | D | 2-2 |

| | P | W | D | L | F | A |
|---|---|---|---|---|---|---|
| Home | 10 | 5 | 1 | 4 | 13 | 12 |
| Away | 10 | 2 | 2 | 6 | 14 | 23 |
| Total | 20 | 7 | 3 | 10 | 27 | 35 |

**FA Premiership**

| | Home | | Away | |
|---|---|---|---|---|
| 1992-93 | W | 1-0 | W | 3-1 |
| 1993-94 | D | 1-1 | L | 0-1 |

| | P | W | D | L | F | A |
|---|---|---|---|---|---|---|
| Home | 2 | 1 | 1 | 0 | 2 | 1 |
| Away | 2 | 1 | 0 | 1 | 3 | 2 |
| Total | 4 | 2 | 1 | 1 | 5 | 3 |

**Football League Cup**

| | | | | |
|---|---|---|---|---|
| 1986-87 | (2) | Away | L | 1-2 |
| | | Home | D | 2-2 |
| 1990-91 | (3) | Away | L | 1-2 |

**FA Charity Shield**

| | | | |
|---|---|---|---|
| 1911-12 | White Hart Lane | W | 2-1 |

**QUIGLEY, Edward**
Inside-forward. 1951-1956.
Manager. 1967-1970.
*5ft 8½in; 12st 2lb.*
*Born: Bury, 13 July 1921.*
*Debut: v Birmingham City (a) 17 November 1951.*
*Career: Bury September 1941; Sheffield Wednesday November 1947 (£12,000); Preston North End December 1949 (£26,000); Blackburn Rovers November 1951; Bury August 1956; Mossley manager (for six years); Bury coach; Stockport County manager April to October 1966; Blackburn Rovers assistant manager October 1966, becoming caretaker-manager in February 1967 and manager in April 1967 until October 1970, then chief scout and youth coach until June 1971; Stockport County manager May 1976 to April 1977; Blackburn Rovers chief scout 1979 to May 1981; Blackpool chief scout.*
**Appearances:** Football League 159; FA Cup 7; Total 166.
**Goals:** Football League 92; FA Cup 3; Total 95.
Eddie Quigley served the club in several different capacities during an association which stretched over 30 years. He came to Blackburn Rovers as a player in 1951 and later served the club as assistant manager, manager, youth coach and chief scout. As a player Quigley would probably rank amongst the all time greats at Ewood Park with those who watched him in the 1950s.

Big, broad and possibly a little overweight, Quigley was not exactly a picture of athleticism. His build betrayed the fact that he started his footballing career as a full-back before his conversion into the most exquisite of playmakers. Such was his ability that in December 1949 he became the most expensive player in Britain when he moved from Sheffield Wednesday to Preston North End for £26,000. Quigley's languid movements were totally deceptive, for his speed of thought and ability to pass the ball with a surgeon's precision made him a constant threat to even the best of defences. Although he could play either centre-forward or inside-forward, Quigley was at his best when allowed to play in a position which was slightly deeper than normal.

He specialised in long and accurate crossfield passing whilst he possessed a venomous shot which brought 11 goals in his first 12 League games. A regular goalscorer as well as goal maker, Quigley notched 28 goals in 40 League games in 1954-55 and helped the team to register 114 Second Division goals.

Quigley was invited to return to Ewood Park in October 1966 when he was managing Stockport County. The directors wanted to appoint him as coach but Quigley insisted on the title of assistant manager before he would agree to return to Blackburn. The directors agreed and on 31 October 1966, Quigley took up his duties as assistant manager with sole responsibility for coaching at the club. Quigley, the master tactician, soon began to show his influence on Jack Marshall's team selection. Midfield was the area which came under immediate scrutiny with the ageing Bryan Douglas being given a roving commission and rugged defender Walter Joyce being brought in to shadow the opposing team's play-maker.

The changes did not bring an immediate transformation in results and in February 1967 Quigley found himself in sole charge when Jack Marshall parted company with the club. Despite a lack of goals – a problem which was to haunt Quigley throughout his reign – the club became involved in the promotion race. However, the short-comings in front of goal were ultimately to rob the club of the chance of First Division football. In April 1967, Quigley was able to drop the caretaker tag and during the next two seasons he kept the club in the thick of the promotion battle. Unfortunately he was never quite able to find the right blend to mount a serious challenge. His moves in the transfer market were dictated to a certain extent by the financial restraints placed upon him. The likes of Don Martin, Ken Knighton, Allan Hunter and Roger Jones proved tremendously successful investments for Blackburn Rovers.

However others, like Jimmy Fryatt, Brian Hill, Frank Kopel, Bryan Conlon and Alex Russell rarely looked capable of taking the club back to the First Division. As the club entered a new decade it appeared to have lost its way. It was no longer thought of as a First Division club and in October 1970 Blackburn Rovers found themselves languishing at the foot of the Second Division. In a bid to halt the slide the directors decided that Quigley and Johnny Carey, the administrative manager, should switch positions. Obviously unhappy with the move, Quigley declined to comment but was bitterly attacked in the Press for being 'too much of a black board theorist'. Quigley was excluded from working with the first team and was confined to the duties of chief scout and coaching the youth players.

However, when the club lost its Second Division status at the end of the season both Carey and Quigley paid for their failure with their jobs. In the mid-1970s, Quigley brought Stockport County to Ewood Park for a Football League Cup-tie and took great delight in seeing his unfancied team inflict a home defeat on the Rovers. He returned to Ewood again in 1979 to become chief scout under Howard Kendall but lost that position when Bobby Saxton was appointed manager and brought Harold Jarman with him to supervise the scouting activities.

**QUINN, Desmond**
Right-back. 1947-1949.
*Born: Tullyverry, Co Down, Northern Ireland, 21 March 1926.*
*Debut: v Chelsea (h) 1 January 1948.*
*Career: Blackburn Rovers August 1947; Millwall June 1949 to 30 June 1955.*
**Appearances:** Football League 1.
Discovered in Preston junior football, Des Quinn spent two seasons at Ewood Park but was only called upon for first-team action on one occasion. He received the call on New Year's Day 1948 for the home fixture with Chelsea which ended in a 1-1 draw. Two days later Wolverhampton Wanderers visited Ewood Park but Quinn was one of two players who were excluded from the side which had held Chelsea. The 1948-49 season was spent playing Central League football and in June 1949 he moved to London to join Millwall. Quinn went on to make 43 League appearances whilst at the Den.

**QUINN, James Martin**
Centre-forward. 1984-1986.
*6ft 1in; 12st.*
*Born: Belfast, 18 November 1959.*
*Debut: v Crystal Palace (a) (sub) 25 August 1984.*
*Career: Oswestry Town; Swindon Town December 1981 (£10,000); Blackburn Rovers August 1984 (£32,500); Swindon Town December 1986 (£40,000); Leicester City June 1988 (£210,000); Bradford City March 1989; West Ham United on loan December 1989 before signing permanently in January 1990 (£300,000); AFC Bournemouth August 1991 (£40,000); Reading July 1992 (£55,000).*
*International honours with Blackburn Rovers: Northern Ireland: 13 caps.*
**Appearances:** Football League 58+13; FA Cup 4; Football League Cup 6+1; Full Members' Cup 2; Total 70+14.
**Goals:** Football League 17; FA Cup 3; Football League Cup 2; Full Members' Cup 1; Total 23.
A tall, long-legged centre-forward who arrived at Ewood Park from

Swindon Town in August 1984. Quinn was a late-comer to professional football, being plucked from Oswestry Town in December 1981 by Swindon. After a slow start to his professional career at Swindon, Quinn became a regular member of the first team during the 1983-84 season. It was during that campaign that he gave an impressive performance against the Rovers in the FA Cup and in August 1984, Bob Saxton brought him to Ewood Park. Quinn became a permanent substitute during the opening months of the 1984-85 season.

On 8 December 1984 he came on as a late substitute against Sheffield United and scored two goals to give the team a vital 3-1 win. The following week he began a game for the first time and scored another two goals in a 3-0 win at Wolverhampton. With the club chasing promotion, Quinn was finally given an extended run in the senior team but, whilst his goalscoring record was respectable, his form suffered over the final stages of the season. Powerful in the air, Quinn became a regular member of the Northern Ireland squad whilst at Ewood and in 1986 he travelled to Mexico with the Irish squad for the World Cup Finals. On the domestic front things began to go sour for Quinn at Ewood during the 1986-87 campaign.

With the club rooted at the foot of the Second Division he became a target of abuse from the terraces. It appeared to be an act of kindness when the club agreed to Quinn returning to Swindon Town in December 1986. Back in familiar surroundings Quinn regained his old form and became one of the most prolific marksmen outside of the First Division. He helped Swindon gain promotion to the Second Division before joining Leicester City in June 1988. Quinn never really settled at Filbert Street and in March 1989 he moved to Bradford City. Once again he found his goalscoring touch and West Ham United paid a large fee to take him to Upton Park. His career appeared to be coming to an end when he moved to AFC Bournemouth in August 1991 and then Reading just 12 months later. However, the move to Elm Park rejuvenated his career and his goals took Reading to the top of the Second Division in 1993-94 and into the First Division.

## RADFORD, John
Centre-forward. 1978-1979.
*5ft 11in; 12st 12lb.*
*Born: Hemsworth, 22 February 1947.*
*Debut: v Oldham Athletic (h) 25 February 1978.*
*Career: Arsenal apprentice October 1962 , turning professional in February 1964; West Ham United December 1976 (£80,000); Blackburn Rovers February 1978; Bishop's Stortford player-coach and later manager.*
**Appearances:** Football League 36; FA Cup 1; Football League Cup 1; Total 38.
**Goals:** Football League 10; FA Cup 1; Total 11.
A vastly experienced centre-forward who had been a member of Arsenal's double winning team of 1970-71 and who had appeared twice for England whilst at Highbury. Radford scored 111 goals in 379 league games for Arsenal before moving on to West Ham United in December 1976. It was from West Ham that Jim Smith signed Radford in February 1978 in the hope that he would provide the impetus to push the team into a promotion place.

Big and strong, Radford was a hard-working centre-forward who possessed plenty of craft and guile. He made a goal-scoring debut in a 4-2 win over Oldham Athletic and suggested that he might be able to provide the firepower that would take the club back into the top flight. However, a point was carelessly dropped at Charlton in the next game and his second appearance at Ewood resulted in a narrow defeat by Bristol Rovers. Before the next match was played Smith had resigned and gone to Birmingham and the promotion dream just faded away. Radford began the troubled 1978-79 season in possession of the number-nine shirt and he scored four goals in the opening eight matches.

However, only one of those games was won and the club found itself in turmoil at the foot of the Second Division following the dismissal of Jim Iley. Radford remained in the team until March 1979 but was then, rather prematurely, discarded following the arrival of Duncan McKenzie.

Following the club's relegation to the Third Division Radford left Ewood Park to become involved in the licensed trade and non-League football.

## RADIO ROVERS
On 30 October 1993, Blackburn Rovers became the first Premier League club to launch its own match day radio station. Radio Rovers, broadcasting on 1413kHz Medium Wave covers an area in excess of ten square miles around the stadium. The station went on the air three hours before the start of each home match and provided a mixture of music,

The playing strip numbers of Tim Flowers, Lee Makel and Frank Talia make up the new Radio Rovers supporters' line number shown off by producer Gerald Jackson with Jenny North, who would be taking calls, and Susan Smith, manageress of the Blackburn BT shop, who handed over the telephone service.

chat, information, interviews and of course live commentary for those unable to get to the ground. The pioneering team at Radio Rovers were Alan Yardley, Wendy Howard and Gerald Jackson.

## RAITT, David
Full-back. 1928-1929.
*5ft 9in; 11st 6lb.*
*Born: Buckhaven, Fife.*
*Debut: v Everton (h) 13 October 1928.*
*Career: Army football (Warwick Regiment); Buckhaven Victoria; Dundee 1919; Everton May 1922; Blackburn Rovers August 1928 (£350); Forfar Athletic October 1929.*
**Appearances:** Football League 4.
Blackburn Rovers moved to sign the experienced Raitt from Everton following an injury to Jock Hutton. Raitt had appeared in 122 League games for the Goodison Park club during his six seasons on Merseyside. Raitt, who began his career with Dundee after World War One, had arrived at Everton in May 1922 and had immediately helped to steady a suspect defence. However he found he was unable to command a regular place at Goodison and in the 1927-28 championship season he only appeared in six games. When he arrived at Ewood Park he was clearly past his best but for a season he was a valuable understudy to have available to cover the absences of Hutton, Jones and Roxburgh. He was released by the Rovers at the end of the 1928-29 season and returned to Scotland in October 1929 to join Forfar Athletic.

## RALPHS, Bertram Victor H.
Outside-right. 1921-1922.
*5ft 8½in; 11st.*
*Born: Handsworth, 1896 (October quarter).*
*Debut: v Huddersfield Town (a) 5 February 1921.*
*Career: Dennison's FC; Reading cs 1914; Nuneaton; Blackburn Rovers January 1921 (£1,500); Stoke July 1922; Chesterfield July 1926; Crewe Alexandra July 1927 to 1928.*
**Appearances:** Football League 40; FA Cup 1; Total 41.
**Goals:** Football League 6.
Ralphs was signed from Nuneaton in the hope that he could solve the problem outside-right position. The club had already used five men in the right-wing berth before the arrival of Ralphs in January 1921. As well as spaying a fee to Nuneaton, the Rovers also had to pay £50 to Reading before Ralphs could be registered with the Football League. A speedy

type of winger, Ralphs was capable of using either foot and was highly regarded in non-League football. Unfortunately, despite at promising start at Ewood, Ralphs fell away during the 1921-22 season and eventually lost his place to Archie Longmuir. In July 1922 he was allowed to leave Ewood to join Stoke.

## RAMSBOTTOM, Neil
Goalkeeper. 1978-1979.
*6ft; 12st.*
*Born: Blackburn, 25 February 1945.*
*Debut: v Leicester City (a) 20 January 1979.*
*Career: Bury non-contract player August 1963, signing professional in July 1964; Blackpool February 1971; Crewe Alexandra on loan January 1972; Coventry City March 1972; Sheffield Wednesday August 1975; Plymouth Argyle July 1976; Blackburn Rovers January 1978; Miami (USA) summer 1979; Sheffield United October 1979; Bradford City August 1980; AFC Bournemouth August 1983.*
**Appearances:** Football League 10.
Although Neil Ramsbottom had been born and brought up in Blackburn it wasn't until he was into the veteran stage of his career that the opportunity arose to play for his local club. Ramsbottom had appeared in 298 League games with his various clubs before joining Blackburn Rovers on a free transfer to act as understudy to John Butcher. As the team struggled at the foot of the Second Division during the 1978-79 campaign, Ramsbottom finally found himself elevated to first-team goalkeeper after attempts to sign Jim Platt from Middlesbrough broke down. Sadly, Ramsbottom was no longer the 'keeper he had been and a number of errors, including an own-goal at Oldham, did little to help the club's relegation cause. Butcher was recalled for the final stages of the season and Ramsbottom continued his travels. After a spell in America and two League appearances with Sheffield United, Ramsbottom enjoyed a revival in fortunes and made 73 League appearances with Bradford City. He ended his career as a non-contract player with Bournemouth and was called upon for four League games.

## RANDELL, Colin William
Midfield. 1982-1985.
*5ft 9in; 10st 8lb.*
*Born: Skewen, nr Neath, 12 December 1952.*
*Debut: v Wolverhampton Wanderers (a) 28 August 1982.*
*Career: Coventry City apprentice November 1967, turning professional in December 1969; Plymouth Argyle September 1973; Exeter City September 1977 (£10,000); Plymouth Argyle July 1979 (£60,000); Blackburn Rovers August 1982 (£40,000); Newport County on loan March to May 1984; Swansea City July 1985 to May 1987; Barry Town; Briton Ferry manager 1989-90.*
**Appearances:** Football League 72+1; FA Cup 5; Football League Cup 4; Total 81+1.
**Goals:** Football League 7.
An experienced midfield player who was well known to Bobby Saxton, having played for him at both Exeter City and Plymouth Argyle. Although money was tight at Ewood, Saxton invested £40,000 to add Randell to his squad on the eve of the 1982-83 season. A former Welsh international at schoolboy, youth and Under-23 level, Randell had also been on the fringe of a full international cap on several occasions. Although not the quickest of players, Randell read the game well and was capable of opening up defences with his astute passing. Sadly, although Randell had clocked up 327 League appearances (including two as sub) before coming to Ewood, the Blackburn public failed to see the best of the midfield man.

A regular in his first season at Ewood, Randell lost his place early in the 1983-84 season and appeared to be on his way out of the club when he was loaned to Newport County. He began the 1984-85 campaign out of the first team but as the team began to mount a promotion challenge he found himself restored to midfield. It was during this season that he began to show the sort of form which had led Saxton to bring him to Ewood Park. However, when the club failed to achieve promotion Randell was allowed to return to his native Wales.

## RANKIN, William
Centre-half. 1927-1932.
*6ft; 13st 10lb.*
*Born: Dumbarton.*
*Debut: v Arsenal (h) 28 April 1927.*
*Career: Parkhead Juniors; Dundee 1922-23; Blackburn Rovers April 1927 (£4,000); Charlton Athletic March 1932 (£2,650); Burton Town manager June 1933.*
*Domestic honours with Blackburn Rovers: FA Cup winners: 1928.*
**Appearances:** Football League 144; FA Cup 18; Total 162.
**Goals:** Football League 4.
At six feet tall and close to 14 stones in weight, Bill Rankin was a

formidable barrier for opposing forwards to pass. He had an excellent reputation in Scottish football before moving to Ewood towards the end of the 1926-27 season. The following season saw him play a major part in the FA Cup campaign which brought the trophy to the club for a sixth time. Rankin remained a regular in the first team until the 1931-32 season when he lost his place through injury. Although Rankin's defensive qualities were the main strength of his game, he was also capable of intelligent constructive play. He joined Charlton Athletic in March 1932 but after only 26 League appearances for that club he accepted the position of manager with Burton Town. After retiring from the game he was a publican in the Burton area for several years.

## RATCLIFFE, James Barrie
Outside-left. 1958-1964.
*5ft 8in; 10st 13lb.*
*Born: Blackburn, 21 September 1941.*
*Debut: v West Ham United (a) 19 March 1960.*
*Career: Technical High School; Blackburn Rovers amateur May 1958, turning professional in September 1958; Scunthorpe United May 1964 (£4,000); Rochdale July 1965.*
**Appearances:** Football League 36; FA Cup 5; Football League Cup 9; Total 50.
**Goals:** Football League 4; FA Cup 1; Football League Cup 3; Total 8.

Barrie Ratcliffe was the outside-right in the FA Youth Cup winning side of 1959, but became better known as a left-winger. Sadly, Ratcliffe never quite realised the promise he had shown as a youth player. He had been introduced to the first team on a regular basis by Jack Marshall in November 1961, and formed a left-sided partnership with John Byrom. They made a major impact on the team before Ratcliffe's form waned and he was replaced by Joe Haverty. In September 1962, Marshall signed Mike Harrison from Chelsea to fill the outside-left position and after spending two seasons in the Central League Ratcliffe moved to Scunthorpe United. He scored seven goals in 26 League appearances at Scunthorpe before ending his League career with one goal in 12 appearances with Rochdale.

## RATHBONE, Michael John
Left-back. 1979-1987.
*5ft 10in; 11st 13lb.*
*Born: Sheldon, Birmingham, 6 November 1958.*
*Debut: v Wrexham (a) 10 March 1979.*
*Career: Sheldon Heath School, Villa Boys; Birmingham City associated schoolboy February 1974, becoming an apprentice in August 1975, and turning professional in November 1976; Blackburn Rovers on loan*

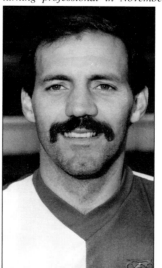

*February 1979, before signing permanently in March 1979 (£40,000); Preston North End August 1987 (£20,000) to May 1991; Darwen August 1991; Halifax Town physiotherapist, becoming manager in December 1992 and then player-assistant manager cs 1993.*
**Appearances:** Football League 270+3; FA Cup 15; Football League Cup 14; Full Members' Cup 4; Total 303+3.
**Goals:** Football League 2.
Popularly known as 'Basil' to the supporters of Blackburn Rovers, Rathbone was initially brought to Ewood Park on a month's loan by John Pickering in February 1979. With the Rovers fighting for their Second Division life Rathbone, a former England Youth international, was sufficiently impressive to be brought to the club on a permanent basis. Although a right-back, Rathbone had to switch over to the

Vince O'Keefe puts off a Reading
striker as he tries a chip shot at
Ewood Park in April 1987.

left to win a regular place in
Howard Kendall's team during
the second half of the 1979-80
season. Despite helping the club
to win promotion, Rathbone
found himself left out of the side
on several occasions during the
1980-81 campaign.

It was not until the arrival of
Bob Saxton that Rathbone finally
established himself as the number
one left-back at the club.
Rathbone suffered a major
setback in October 1983 when he
broke his leg in the away game at
Sheffield Wednesday. However,
his tenacity overcome adversity
and he was restored to the team
for the final three games of the
season. A solid, reliable defender,
Rathbone was also quick to come
forward whenever the opportunity
arose. Indeed, it was his attacking
qualities which enabled the club
to use him in midfield as well as
in defence.

Tragically, an injury sustained
against Chelsea in the opening minutes of the Full Members' Cup semi-
final robbed him of the opportunity of appearing at Wembley in that
competition. Whilst he was out of action the club signed Chris Sulley
from Dundee United and in the summer of 1987 he left Ewood Park to
join Preston North End. Rathbone later combined his playing career at
Preston with that of organising the commercial activities of Darwen
Football Club. He went on to become the physiotherapist at Halifax Town
and as the club slipped towards the GM Vauxhall Conference he was
appointed manager. When Halifax lost League status the club appointed
Peter Wragg as manager because of his experience in non-League
football and Rathbone accepted a position as his assistant.

### READING FC

Founded in 1871, the club first entered the FA Cup in 1877 when they
amalgamated with Reading Hornets. The club was further strengthened
following the amalgamation with Earley FC in 1889. One of the original
members of the Southern League in 1894, the club became one of the
founder members of the Third Division of the Football League in 1920.
Despite their long association with the FA Cup, Reading have only met
Blackburn Rovers once in that competition. The clubs first crossed paths
in the League in the Third Division in 1979-80 and since then they have
only met on four occasions when Reading enjoyed a brief flirtation with
Second Division football in the 1980s.

### Football League

|         |          | Home |     | Away |     |
|---------|----------|------|-----|------|-----|
| 1979-80 | (Div 3)  | W    | 4-2 | D    | 1-1 |
| 1986-87 | (Div 2)  | D    | 0-0 | L    | 0-4 |
| 1987-88 | (Div 2)  | D    | 1-1 | D    | 0-0 |

|       | P | W | D | L | F | A |
|-------|---|---|---|---|---|---|
| Home  | 3 | 1 | 2 | 0 | 5 | 3 |
| Away  | 3 | 0 | 2 | 1 | 1 | 5 |
| Total | 6 | 1 | 4 | 1 | 6 | 8 |

### FA Cup

| 1912-13 | (3) | Away | W | 2-1 |
|---------|-----|------|---|-----|

### REEVES, Thomas Brian

Goalkeeper. 1960-1962.
*5ft 11in; 12st.*
*Born: Skelmersdale, 18 February 1939.*
*Debut: v Manchester United (h) 17 December 1960.*
*Career: Burscough; Blackburn Rovers non-contract player January
1960, signing professional in August 1960; Scunthorpe United May
1962; Southport July 1965; Formby.*
**Appearances:** Football League 12; FA Cup 5; Total 17.
Brian Reeves was one of three goalkeepers who vied for the right to
succeed Harry Leyland in 1960-61. Although Reeves had to wait until

December 1960 before making his debut, he did sufficiently well to be
given an extended run in the first team. Of all the goalkeepers on the
club's books, Reeves was by far the most agile. However, his game
lacked the consistency that was required in the First Division. At times
brilliant, Reeves was also capable of inexplicable errors that cost vital
points. If his dead ball kicking left something to be desired, it was his
inability to deal with crosses which proved to be his Achilles' heel. The
signing of Fred Else in the summer of 1961 limited Reeves to just one
appearance during the 1961-62 season and in May 1962 he moved to
Scunthorpe United. He enjoyed better fortunes in the lower divisions,
making 38 League appearances with Scunthorpe and 143 appearances
with Southport.

### REID, Nicholas Scott

Midfield. 1987-1992.
*5ft 10in; 12st 4lb.*
*Born: Urmston, 30 October 1960.*
*Debut: v Hull City (a) 15 August
1987.*
*Career: Whithall Juniors; Man-
chester City apprentice May 1977,
turning professional in November
1978; Seattle Sounders (USA) on
loan May 1982; Blackburn Rovers
July 1987; Bristol City on loan
September 1992; West Bromwich
Albion November 1992; Wycombe
Wanderers March 1994.*
**Appearances:** Football League
160+14; Play-offs 8; FA Cup 6+2;
Football League Cup 13; Full
Members' Cup 5+1; Total 192+17.
**Goals:** Football League 9; Full
Members' Cup 1; Total 10.
Nicky Reid was picked up on a free
transfer after giving outstanding
service to Manchester City. A
product of the Maine Road South
scheme, Reid made his debut for
City in a UEFA Cup-tie against
Borussia Mönchengladbach and
went on to make 216 League
appearances (including five as sub)
for the club. In 1981 he appeared in the City team which lost the FA Cup
Final replay to Tottenham Hotspur and he also won six England Under-
23 caps whilst at Maine Road.

A player who could play at right-back or in midfield, Reid was
surprisingly granted a free transfer following City's relegation to the
Second Division at the end of the 1986-87 season. Don Mackay brought

him to Ewood Park and installed him as captain in the hope that his experience would prove beneficial to the younger players at the club. A good tackler and strong runner, Reid was asked to hold the midfield together so that players like Simon Barker and Scott Sellars could express themselves creatively.

Reid was to prove vital to the team and, if his value was not immediately appreciated on the terraces, he was to become a popular figure through his surging runs from midfield. Reid lost his place early in the 1991-92 season and his appearances thereafter were, in the main, restricted to the substitute's role. A loan spell with Bristol City was followed by a move to West Bromwich Albion and at the end of the 1992-93 season he was a member of the West Brom side which won promotion to the Second Division via the Play-offs at Wembley. In March 1994 he left West Brom to link up with Simon Garner, a former teammate at Ewood and The Hawthorns, at Wycombe Wanderers. In May 1994, Reid and Garner both helped Wycombe to defeat Preston North End at Wembley in the Third Division Play-off Final.

## REILLY, Frank

Centre-half. 1919-1923.
*5ft 11in; 12st 9lb.*
*Born: Perth 1895.*
*Debut: v Derby County (h) 6 December 1919.*
*Career: Perth Juniors; Falkirk; Blackburn Rovers December 1919 (£5,000); Llanelli August 1923; Weymouth 1924-25.*
**Appearances:** Football League 127; FA Cup 11; Total 138.
**Goals:** Football League 8; FA Cup 1; Total 9.
A physically imposing Scot who arrived at Ewood Park at the same time as David Rollo. The *Lancashire Daily Post Football Annual* of 1920-21 described Reilly as 'a splendid spoiler' and certainly he was a fierce competitor. His rugged tackling saw him dismissed in the local derby with Preston North End at Christmas 1920, but a three-week suspension brought little change to his style of play. He remained a regular in the centre-half position until the closing stages of the 1922-23 season, when injuries began to take their toll. However, Reilly was also facing a strong challenge for his position from Stan Dixon and when the latter took his place for the closing games of the season, Reilly became unsettled and opted to move into non-League football with Llanelli.

## RELEGATION
Blackburn Rovers have had the misfortune to suffer the disappointment of relegation on five occasions. Details of relegation seasons are outlined below:

1935-36 Relegated from the First to the Second Division
| P | W | D | L | F | A | Pts | Pos |
|---|---|---|---|---|---|-----|-----|
| 42 | 12 | 9 | 21 | 55 | 96 | 33 | 22 |

1947-48 Relegated from the First to the Second Division
| P | W | D | L | F | A | Pts | Pos |
|---|---|---|---|---|---|-----|-----|
| 42 | 11 | 10 | 21 | 54 | 72 | 32 | 21 |

1965-66 Relegated from the First to the Second Division
| P | W | D | L | F | A | Pts | Pos |
|---|---|---|---|---|---|-----|-----|
| 42 | 8 | 4 | 30 | 57 | 88 | 20 | 22 |

1970-71 Relegated from the Second to the Third Division
| P | W | D | L | F | A | Pts | Pos |
|---|---|---|---|---|---|-----|-----|
| 42 | 6 | 15 | 21 | 37 | 69 | 27 | 21 |

1978-79 Relegated from the Second to the Third Division
| P | W | D | L | F | A | Pts | Pos |
|---|---|---|---|---|---|-----|-----|
| 42 | 10 | 10 | 22 | 41 | 72 | 30 | 22 |

## RENTON FC
Formed in 1873, Renton were one of seven Scottish clubs to participate in the FA Cup. The 1886-87 season saw them drawn at home to Blackburn Rovers in the second round of the competition. Blackburn managed to hold the Scottish club to a 2-2 draw on 20 November 1886. Renton travelled to Blackburn for the replay and caused a major upset by winning 2-0. Renton's victory brought an end to Blackburn's unbeaten FA Cup run of 24 Cup-ties. Renton won the Scottish Cup in 1885 and 1888 and were runners-up in 1875, 1886 and 1895.

## REPRESENTATIVE HONOURS AT INTERNATIONAL LEVEL
Only international honours which players gained whilst with Blackburn Rovers are included in this section and caps gained with other clubs are not listed. In 1924 the Republic of Ireland began to play separate matches, but prior to this date there was only one Ireland team. The honours are listed in chronological order from 1880, when Fred Hargreaves became the first Blackburn Rovers player to win a full cap, up to the early summer of 1994.

## Full International Appearances
HC = Home International Championship
WCq = World Cup qualifier
WCr1 = World Cup Final Tournament – first round
WCr2 = World Cup Final Tournament – second round
WCqf = World Cup Final Tournament – quarter final
ECq = European Championship qualifier
ECpr = European Championship Preliminary Round
EFr1 = European Championship Final Tournament – first round
USC = United States Challenge Cup
Fr = Friendly
g = goals scored

**Frederick William Hargreaves (England) – 3 appearances**
| 15 Mar 1880 | v | Wales (Wrexham) Fr | W 3-2 |
| 26 Feb 1881 | v | Wales (Blackburn) Fr | L 0-1 |
| 18 Feb 1882 | v | Ireland (Belfast) HC | W 13-0 |

**James Brown (England) – 5 appearances & 3 goals**
| 26 Feb 1881 | v | Wales (Blackburn) Fr | L 0-1 |
| 18 Feb 1882 | v | Ireland (Belfast) HC 2g | W 13-0 |
| 28 Feb 1885 | v | Ireland (Manchester) HC 1g | W 4-0 |
| 14 Mar 1885 | v | Wales (Blackburn) HC | D 1-1 |
| 21 Mar 1885 | v | Scotland (Kennington Oval) HC | D 1-1 |

**John Hargreaves (England) – 2 appearances**
| 26 Feb 1881 | v | Wales (Blackburn) Fr | L 0-1 |
| 12 Mar 1881 | v | Scotland (Kennington Oval) Fr | L 1-6 |

**Doctor Haydock Greenwood (England) – 2 appearances**
| 18 Feb 1882 | v | Ireland (Belfast) HC | W 13-0 |
| 11 Mar 1882 | v | Scotland (Glasgow) HC | L 1-5 |

**Joseph Beverley (England) – 3 appearances**
| 23 Feb 1884 | v | Ireland (Belfast) HC | W 8-1 |
| 15 Mar 1884 | v | Scotland (Glasgow) HC | L 0-1 |
| 17 Mar 1884 | v | Wales (Wrexham) HC | W 4-0 |

**James Henry Forrest (England) – 11 appearances**
| 17 Mar 1884 | v | Wales (Wrexham) HC | W 4-0 |
| 28 Feb 1885 | v | Ireland (Manchester) HC | W 4-0 |
| 14 Mar 1885 | v | Wales (Blackburn) HC | D 1-1 |
| 21 Mar 1885 | v | Scotland (Kennington Oval) HC | D 1-1 |
| 27 Mar 1886 | v | Scotland (Glasgow) HC | D 1-1 |
| 29 Mar 1886 | v | Wales (Wrexham) HC | W 3-1 |
| 5 Feb 1887 | v | Ireland (Sheffield) HC | W 7-0 |
| 26 Feb 1887 | v | Wales (Kennington Oval) HC | W 4-0 |
| 19 Mar 1887 | v | Scotland (Blackburn) HC | L 2-3 |
| 13 Apr 1889 | v | Scotland (Kennington Oval) HC | L 2-3 |
| 15 Mar 1890 | v | Ireland (Belfast) HC | W 9-1 |

**John William Herbert Arthur (England) – 7 appearances**
| 28 Feb 1885 | v | Ireland (Manchester) HC | W 4-0 |
| 14 Mar 1885 | v | Wales (Blackburn) HC | D 1-1 |
| 21 Mar 1885 | v | Scotland (Kennington Oval) HC | D 1-1 |
| 27 Mar 1886 | v | Scotland (Glasgow) HC | D 1-1 |
| 29 Mar 1886 | v | Wales (Wrexham) HC | W 3-1 |
| 5 Feb 1887 | v | Ireland (Sheffield) HC | W 7-0 |
| 26 Feb 1887 | v | Wales (Kennington Oval) HC | W 4-0 |

**John Morris Lofthouse (England) – 6 appearances & 2 goals**
| 28 Feb 1885 | v | Ireland (Manchester) HC 1g | .W 4-0 |
| 14 Mar 1885 | v | Wales (Blackburn) HC | D 1-1 |
| 21 Mar 1885 | v | Scotland (Kennington Oval) HC | D 1-1 |
| 26 Feb 1887 | v | Wales (Kennington Oval) HC | W 4-0 |
| 19 Mar 1887 | v | Scotland (Blackburn) HC | L 2-3 |
| 15 Mar 1890 | v | Ireland (Belfast) HC 1g | W 9-1 |

**John Southworth (England) – 3 appearances & 3 goals**
| 23 Feb 1889 | v | Wales (Stoke) HC 1g | W 4-1 |
| 7 Mar 1891 | v | Wales (Sunderland) HC 1g | W 4-1 |
| 2 Apr 1892 | v | Scotland (Glasgow) HC 1g | W 4-1 |

**William Joseph Townley (England) – 2 appearances & 2 goals**

| 23 Feb 1889 | v | Wales (Stoke) HC | W 4-1 |
| 15 Mar 1890 | v | Ireland (Belfast) HC 2g | W 9-1 |

**John Barton (England) – 1 appearance & 1 goal**
| 15 Mar 1890 | v | Ireland (Belfast) HC 1g | W 9-1 |

**Nathaniel Walton (England) – 1 appearance**
| 15 Mar 1890 | v | Ireland (Belfast) HC | W 9-1 |

(Note: Sources vary as to who actually scored the goals against Ireland. Some suggest Walton scored once, others twice and one claims a hat-trick. Other sources fail to name him amongst the goalscorers).

**Henry Chippendale (England) – 1 appearance**
| 3 Mar 1894 | v | Ireland (Belfast) HC | D 2-2 |

**James Whitehead (England) -1 appearance**
| 3 Mar 1894 | v | Ireland (Belfast) HC | D 2-2 |

**Thomas Brandon (Scotland) – 1 appearance**
| 4 Apr 1896 | v | England (Glasgow) HC | L 1-2 |

**Thomas Edward Booth (England) – 1 appearance**
| 28 Mar 1898 | v | Wales (Wrexham) HC | W 3-0 |

**Frederick Blackburn (England) – 3 appearances & 1 goal**
| 30 Mar 1901 | v | Scotland (Crystal Palace) HC 1g | D 2-2 |
| 22 Mar 1902 | v | Ireland (Belfast) HC | W 1-0 |
| 9 Apr 1904 | v | Scotland (Glasgow) HC | W 1-0 |

**Robert Crompton (England) – 41 appearances**
| 3 Mar 1902 | v | Wales (Wrexham) HC | D 0-0 |
| 22 Mar 1902 | v | Ireland (Belfast) HC | W 1-0 |
| 3 May 1902 | v | Scotland (Birmingham) HC | D 2-2 |
| 2 Mar 1903 | v | Wales (Portsmouth) HC | W 2-1 |
| 4 Apr 1903 | v | Scotland (Sheffield) HC | L 1-2 |
| 29 Feb 1904 | v | Wales (Wrexham) HC | D 2-2 |
| 12 Mar 1904 | v | Ireland (Belfast) HC | W 3-1 |
| 9 Apr 1904 | v | Scotland (Glasgow) HC | W 1-0 |
| 17 Feb 1906 | v | Ireland (Belfast) HC | W 5-0 |
| 19 Mar 1906 | v | Wales (Cardiff) HC | W 1-0 |
| 7 Apr 1906 | v | Scotland (Glasgow) HC | L 1-2 |
| 16 Feb 1907 | v | Ireland (Goodison Park) HC | W 1-0 |
| 18 Mar 1907 | v | Wales (Fulham) HC | D 1-1 |
| 6 Apr 1907 | v | Scotland (Newcastle) HC | D 1-1 |
| 15 Feb 1908 | v | Ireland (Belfast) HC | W 3-1 |
| 16 Mar 1908 | v | Wales (Wrexham) HC | W 7-1 |
| 4 Apr 1908 | v | Scotland (Glasgow) HC | D 1-1 |
| 6 Jun 1908 | v | Austria (Vienna) Fr | W 6-1 |
| 8 Jun 1908 | v | Austria (Vienna) Fr | W11-1 |
| 10 Jun 1908 | v | Hungary (Budapest) Fr | W 7-0 |
| 13 Jun 1908 | v | Bohemia (Prague) Fr | W 4-0 |
| 13 Feb 1909 | v | Ireland (Bradford) HC | W 4-0 |
| 15 Mar 1909 | v | Wales (Nottingham) HC | W 2-0 |
| 3 Apr 1909 | v | Scotland (Crystal Palace) HC | W 2-0 |
| 29 May 1909 | v | Hungary (Budapest) Fr | W 4-2 |
| 31 May 1909 | v | Hungary (Budapest) Fr | W 8-2 |
| 1 Jun 1909 | v | Austria (Vienna) Fr | W 8-1 |
| 14 Mar 1910 | v | Wales (Cardiff) HC | W 1-0 |
| 2 Apr 1910 | v | Scotland (Glasgow) HC | L 0-2 |
| 11 Feb 1911 | v | Ireland (Derby) HC | W 2-1 |
| 13 Mar 1911 | v | Wales (Millwall) HC | W 3-0 |
| 1 Apr 1911 | v | Scotland (Goodison Park) HC | D 1-1 |
| 10 Feb 1912 | v | Ireland (Dublin) HC | W 6-1 |
| 11 Mar 1912 | v | Wales (Wrexham) HC | W 2-0 |
| 23 Mar 1912 | v | Scotland (Glasgow) HC | D 1-1 |
| 15 Feb 1913 | v | Ireland (Belfast) HC | L 1-2 |
| 17 Mar 1913 | v | Wales (Bristol) HC | W 4-3 |
| 5 Apr 1913 | v | Scotland (Chelsea) HC | W 1-0 |
| 14 Feb 1914 | v | Ireland (Middlesbrough) HC | L 0-3 |
| 16 Mar 1914 | v | Wales (Cardiff) HC | W 2-0 |
| 4 Apr 1914 | v | Scotland (Glasgow) HC | L 1-3 |

**Albert Edward Houlker (England) – 1 appearance**
| 3 May 1902 | v | Scotland (Birmingham) HC | D 2-2 |

**Samuel Wolstenholme (England) – 2 appearances**
| 25 Feb 1905 | v | Ireland (Middlesbrough) HC | D 1-1 |
| 27 Mar 1905 | v | Wales (Liverpool) HC | W 3-1 |

**Alfred Oliver (Wales) – 1 appearance**
| 27 Mar 1905 | v | England (Liverpool) HC | L 1-3 |

**William Davies (Wales) – 9 appearances & 5 goals**
| 7 Mar 1908 | v | Scotland (Dundee) HC | L 1-2 |
| 16 Mar 1908 | v | England (Wrexham) HC 1g | L 1-7 |
| 1 Mar 1909 | v | Scotland (Wrexham) HC 2g | W 3-2 |
| 15 Mar 1909 | v | England (Nottingham) HC | L 0-2 |
| 20 Mar 1909 | v | Ireland (Belfast) HC | W 3-2 |
| 28 Jan 1911 | v | Ireland (Belfast) HC 1g | W 2-1 |
| 6 Mar 1911 | v | Scotland (Cardiff) HC | .D 2-2 |
| 13 Mar 1911 | v | England (Millwall) HC | L 0-3 |
| 13 Apr 1912 | v | Ireland (Cardiff) HC 1g | L 2-3 |

**Robert Owen Evans (Wales) – 1 appearance**
| 11 Apr 1908 | v | Ireland (Aberdare) HC | L 0-1 |

**William Bradshaw (England) – 4 appearances**
| 12 Feb 1910 | v | Ireland (Belfast) HC | D 1-1 |
| 14 Mar 1910 | v | Wales (Cardiff) HC | W 1-0 |
| 10 Feb 1912 | v | Ireland (Dublin) HC | W 6-1 |
| 17 Mar 1913 | v | Wales (Bristol) HC | W 4-3 |

**Arthur Cowell (England) – 1 appearance**
| 12 Feb 1910 | v | Ireland (Belfast) HC | D 1-1 |

'Jock' Simpson, capped for England eight times before World War One.

**John Simpson (England) – 8 appearances & 1 goal**
| 11 Feb 1911 | v | Ireland (Derby) HC | W 2-1 |
| 13 Mar 1911 | v | Wales (Millwall) HC | W 3-0 |
| 1 Apr 1911 | v | Scotland (Goodison Park) HC | D 1-1 |

| | | | |
|---|---|---|---|
| 10 Feb 1912 | v | Ireland (Dublin) HC 1g | W 6-1 |
| 11 Mar 1912 | v | Wales (Wrexham) HC | W 2-0 |
| 23 Mar 1912 | v | Scotland (Glasgow) HC | D 1-1 |
| 5 Apr 1913 | v | Scotland (Stamford Bridge) HC | W 1-0 |
| 16 Mar 1914 | v | Wales (Cardiff) HC | W 2-0 |

**Walter Campbell Allison Aitkenhead (Scotland) – 1 appearance & 2 goals**

| | | | |
|---|---|---|---|
| 16 Mar 1912 | v | Ireland (Belfast) HC 2g | W 4-1 |

**Joseph Hodkinson (England) – 3 appearances**

| | | | |
|---|---|---|---|
| 17 Mar 1913 | v | Wales (Bristol) HC | W 4-3 |
| 5 Apr 1913 | v | Scotland (Chelsea) HC | W 1-0 |
| 25 Oct 1919 | v | Ireland (Belfast) HC | D 1-1 |

**Edwin Gladstone Latheron (England) – 2 appearances & 1 goal**

| | | | |
|---|---|---|---|
| 17 Mar 1913 | v | Wales (Bristol) HC 1 gl | W 4-3 |
| 14 Feb 1914 | v | Ireland (Middlesbrough) HC | L 0-3 |

**Daniel Shea (England) – 2 appearances**

| | | | |
|---|---|---|---|
| 14 Feb 1914 | v | Ireland (Middlesbrough) HC | L 0-3 |
| 16 Mar 1914 | v | Wales (Cardiff) HC | W 2-0 |

**David Rollo (Ireland) -7 appearances**

| | | | |
|---|---|---|---|
| 14 Feb 1920 | v | Wales (Belfast) HC | D 2-2 |
| 13 Mar 1920 | v | Scotland (Glasgow) HC | L 0-3 |
| 23 Oct 1920 | v | England (Sunderland) HC | L 0-2 |
| 26 Feb 1921 | v | Scotland (Belfast) HC | L 0-2 |
| 9 Apr 1921 | v | Wales (Swansea) HC | L 1-2 |
| 22 Oct 1921 | v | England (Belfast) HC | D 1-1 |
| 21 Oct 1922 | v | England (West Bromwich) HC | L 0-2 |

**(Northern Ireland) – 5 appearances**

| | | | |
|---|---|---|---|
| 1 Mar 1924 | v | Scotland (Glasgow) HC | L 0-2 |
| 15 Mar 1924 | v | Wales (Belfast) HC | L 0-1 |
| 18 Apr 1925 | v | Wales (Wrexham) HC | D 0-0 |
| 24 Oct 1925 | v | England (Belfast) HC | D 0-0 |
| 20 Oct 1926 | v | England (Liverpool) HC | D 3-3 |

**Patrick Robinson (Ireland) – 1 appearance**

| | | | |
|---|---|---|---|
| 9 Apr 1921 | v | Wales (Swansea) HC | L 1-2 |

**John McKay (Scotland) – 1 appearance**

| | | | |
|---|---|---|---|
| 16 Feb 1924 | v | Wales (Cardiff) HC | L 0-2 |

**William Ronald Sewell (England) – 1 appearance**

| | | | |
|---|---|---|---|
| 3 Mar 1924 | v | Wales (Blackburn) HC | L 1-2 |

**Henry Healless (England) – 2 appearances**

| | | | |
|---|---|---|---|
| 22 Oct 1924 | v | Ireland (Goodison Park) HC | W 3-1 |
| 31 Mar 1928 | v | Scotland (Wembley) HC | L 1-5 |

**Sydney Charles Puddefoot (England) – 2 appearances**

| | | | |
|---|---|---|---|
| 24 Oct 1925 | v | Ireland (Belfast) HC | D 0-0 |
| 17 Apr 1926 | v | Scotland (Manchester) HC | L 0-1 |

**Edward Cashfield Harper (England) 1 appearance**

| | | | |
|---|---|---|---|
| 17 Apr 1926 | v | Scotland (Old Trafford) HC | .L 0-1 |

**John Hutton (Scotland) – 3 appearances**

| | | | |
|---|---|---|---|
| 26 Feb 1927 | v | Ireland (Belfast) HC | W 2-0 |
| 29 Oct 1927 | v | Wales (Wrexham) HC | D 2-2 |
| 25 Feb 1928 | v | Ireland (Glasgow) HC | L 0-1 |

**Herbert Jones (England) – 6 Appearances**

| | | | |
|---|---|---|---|
| 2 Apr 1927 | v | Scotland (Glasgow) HC | W 2-1 |
| 11 May 1927 | v | Belgium (Brussels) Fr | W 9-1 |
| 21 May 1927 | v | Luxembourg (Luxembourg) Fr | W 5-2 |
| 26 May 1927 | v | France (Paris) Fr | W 6-0 |
| 22 Oct 1927 | v | Ireland (Belfast) HC | L 0-2 |
| 31 Mar 1928 | v | Scotland (Wembley) HC | L 1-5 |

**Arthur Rigby (England) – 5 appearances & 3 goals**

| | | | |
|---|---|---|---|
| 2 Apr 1927 | v | Scotland (Glasgow) HC | W 2-1 |
| 11 May 1927 | v | Belgium (Brussels) Fr 2g | W 9-1 |
| 21 May 1927 | v | Luxembourg (Luxembourg) Fr | W 5-2 |
| 26 May 1927 | v | France (Paris) Fr 1g | W 6-0 |
| 28 Nov 1927 | v | Wales (Burnley) HC | L 1-2 |

**Austen Fenwick Campbell (England) – 2 appearances**

| | | | |
|---|---|---|---|
| 22 Oct 1928 | v | Ireland (Goodison Park) HC | W 2-1 |

| | | | |
|---|---|---|---|
| 17 Nov 1928 | v | Wales (Swansea) HC | W 3-2 |

**Arthur Cunliffe (England) – 2 appearances**

| | | | |
|---|---|---|---|
| 17 Oct 1932 | v | Ireland (Blackpool) HC | W 1-0 |
| 16 Nov 1932 | v | Wales (Wrexham) HC | D 0-0 |

**John Iorweth Hughes (Wales) – 1 appearance**

| | | | |
|---|---|---|---|
| 27 Mar 1935 | v | Northern Ireland (Wrexham) HC | W 3-1 |

**Robert Langton (England) – 7 appearances & 1 goal**

| | | | |
|---|---|---|---|
| 28 Sep 1946 | v | Northern Ireland (Belfast) HC 1g | W 7-2 |
| 30 Sep 1946 | v | Republic of Ireland (Dublin) Fr | W 1-0 |
| 13 Nov 1946 | v | Wales (Maine Road) HC | W 3-0 |
| 27 Nov 1946 | v | Holland (Huddersfield) Fr | W 8-2 |
| 3 May 1947 | v | France (Highbury) Fr | W 3-0 |
| 18 May 1947 | v | Switzerland (Zurich) Fr | L 0-1 |
| 19 Nov 1947 | v | Sweden (Highbury) Fr | W 4-2 |

**William Arthur Hughes (Wales) – 5 appearances**

| | | | |
|---|---|---|---|
| 10 Nov 1948 | v | England (Villa Park) HC | L 0-1 |
| 9 Mar 1949 | v | Northern Ireland (Belfast) HC | W 2-0 |
| 15 May 1949 | v | Portugal (Lisbon) Fr | L 2-3 |
| 22 May 1949 | v | Belgium (Liege) Fr | L 1-3 |
| 26 May 1949 | v | Switzerland (Berne) Fr | L 0-4 |

**Edward Crossan (Northern Ireland) – 3 appearances & 1 goal**

| | | | |
|---|---|---|---|
| 1 Oct 1949 | v | Scotland (Belfast) HC/WCq | L 2-8 |
| 7 Oct 1950 | v | England (Belfast) HC | L 1-4 |
| 20 Apr 1955 | v | Wales (Belfast) HC 1g | L 2-3 |

**William Eckersley (England) – 17 appearances**

| | | | |
|---|---|---|---|
| 2 Jul 1950 | v | Spain (Rio de Janeiro) WCr1 | L 0-1 |
| 22 Nov 1950 | v | Yugoslavia (Highbury) Fr | D 2-2 |
| 14 Apr 1951 | v | Scotland (Wembley) HC | L 2-3 |
| 9 May 1951 | v | Argentina (Wembley) Fr | W 2-1 |
| 19 May 1951 | v | Portugal (Goodison Park) Fr | W 5-2 |
| 28 Nov 1951 | v | Austria (Wembley) Fr | D 2-2 |
| 25 May 1952 | v | Austria (Vienna) Fr | W 3-2 |
| 28 May 1952 | v | Switzerland (Zurich) Fr | W 3-0 |
| 4 Oct 1952 | v | Northern Ireland (Belfast) HC | D 2-2 |
| 17 May 1953 | v | Argentina (Buenos Aires) Fr | |
| (abandoned after 21 minutes when the score was 0-0) | | | |
| 24 May 1953 | v | Chile (Santiago) Fr | W 2-1 |
| 31 May 1953 | v | Uruguay (Montevideo) Fr | L 1-2 |
| 8 Jun 1953 | v | United States of America (New York) Fr | W 6-3 |
| 10 Oct 1953 | v | Wales (Cardiff) HC/WCq | W 4-1 |
| 21 Oct 1953 | v | Rest of Europe (Wembley) | D 4-4 |
| 11 Nov 1953 | v | Northern Ireland (Goodison Park) HC/WCq | W 3-1 |
| 25 Nov 1953 | v | Hungary (Wembley) Fr | L 3-6 |

**Ronald Clayton (England) – 35 appearances**

| | | | |
|---|---|---|---|
| 2 Nov 1955 | v | Northern Ireland (Wembley) HC | W 3-0 |
| 30 Nov 1955 | v | Spain (Wembley) Fr | W 4-1 |
| 9 May 1956 | v | Brazil (Wembley) Fr | W 4-2 |
| 16 May 1956 | v | Sweden (Stockholm) Fr | D 0-0 |
| 20 May 1956 | v | Finland (Helsinki) Fr | W 5-1 |
| 25 May 1956 | v | West Germany (Berlin) Fr | W 3-1 |
| 6 Oct 1956 | v | Northern Ireland (Belfast) HC | D 1-1 |
| 14 Nov 1956 | v | Wales (Wembley) HC | W 3-1 |
| 28 Nov 1956 | v | Yugoslavia (Wembley) Fr | W 3-0 |
| 5 Dec 1956 | v | Denmark (Wolverhampton) WCq | W 5-2 |
| 6 Apr 1957 | v | Scotland (Wembley) HC | W 2-1 |
| 8 May 1957 | v | Republic of Ireland (Wembley) WCq | W 5-1 |
| 15 May 1957 | v | Denmark (Copenhagen) WCq | W 4-1 |
| 19 May 1957 | v | Republic of Ireland (Dublin) WCq | W 1-1 |
| 19 Oct 1957 | v | Wales (Cardiff) HC | W 4-0 |
| 6 Nov 1957 | v | Northern Ireland (Wembley) HC | L 2-3 |
| 27 Nov 1957 | v | France (Wembley) Fr | W 4-0 |
| 19 Apr 1958 | v | Scotland (Glasgow) HC | W 4-0 |
| 7 May 1958 | v | Portugal (Wembley) Fr | W 2-1 |
| 11 May 1958 | v | Yugoslavia (Belgrade) Fr | L 0-5 |
| 17 Jun 1958 | v | Soviet Union (Gothenburg) WCr1 | L 0-1 |
| 4 Oct 1958 | v | Northern Ireland (Belfast) HC | D 3-3 |
| 22 Oct 1958 | v | Soviet Union (Wembley) Fr | W 5-0 |
| 26 Nov 1958 | v | Wales (Villa Park) HC | D 2-2 |
| 11 Apr 1959 | v | Scotland (Wembley) HC | W 1-0 |
| 6 May 1959 | v | Italy (Wembley) Fr | D 2-2 |
| 13 May 1959 | v | Brazil (Rio de Janeiro) Fr | L 0-2 |
| 17 May 1959 | v | Peru (Lima) Fr | L 1-4 |
| 24 May 1959 | v | Mexico (Mexico City) Fr | L 1-2 |

| | | | |
|---|---|---|---|
| 28 May 1959 | v | United States of America | |
| | | (Los Angeles) Fr | W 8-1 |
| 17 Oct 1959 | v | Wales (Cardiff) HC | D 1-1 |
| 28 Oct 1959 | v | Sweden (Wembley) Fr | L 2-3 |
| 18 Nov 1959 | v | Northern Ireland (Wembley) HC | W 2-1 |
| 9 Apr 1960 | v | Scotland (Glasgow) HC | D 1-1 |
| 11 May 1960 | v | Yugoslavia (Wembley) Fr | D 3-3 |

**Thomas Royston Vernon (Wales) – 9 appearances & 1 goal**

| | | | |
|---|---|---|---|
| 10 Apr 1957 | v | Northern Ireland (Belfast) HC | D 0-0 |
| 1 May 1957 | v | Czechoslovakia (Cardiff) WCq 1g | W 1-0 |
| 19 May 1957 | v | East Germany (Leipzig) WCq | L 1-2 |
| 26 May 1957 | v | Czechoslovakia (Prague) WCq | L 0-2 |
| 25 Sep 1957 | v | East Germany (Cardiff) WCq | W 4-1 |
| 19 Oct 1957 | v | England (Cardiff) HC | L 0-4 |
| 13 Nov 1957 | v | Scotland (Glasgow) HC | D 1-1 |
| 15 Jun 1958 | v | Sweden (Stockholm) WCr1 | D 0-0 |
| 18 Oct 1958 | v | Scotland (Cardiff) HC | L 0-3 |

**Bryan Douglas (England) – 36 appearances & 11 goals**

| | | | |
|---|---|---|---|
| 19 Oct 1957 | v | Wales (Cardiff) HC | W 4-0 |
| 6 Nov 1957 | v | Northern Ireland (Wembley) HC | L 2-3 |
| 27 Nov 1957 | v | France (Wembley) Fr | W 4-0 |
| 19 Apr 1958 | v | Scotland (Glasgow) HC 1g | W 4-0 |
| 7 May 1958 | v | Portugal (Wembley) Fr | W 2-1 |
| 11 May 1958 | v | Yugoslavia (Belgrade) Fr | L 0-5 |
| 18 May 1958 | v | Soviet Union (Moscow) Fr | D 1-1 |
| 8 Jun 1958 | v | Soviet Union (Gothenburg) WCr1 | D 2-2 |
| 11 June 1958 | v | Brazil (Gothenburg) WCr1 | D 0-0 |
| 15 June 1958 | v | Austria (Boras) WCr1 | D 2-2 |
| 26 Nov 1958 | v | Wales (Villa Park) HC | D 2-2 |
| 11 Apr 1959 | v | Scotland (Wembley) HC | W 1-0 |
| 11 May 1959 | v | Yugoslavia (Wembley) Fr 1g | D 3-3 |
| 22 May 1960 | v | Hungary (Budapest) Fr | L 0-2 |
| 8 Oct 1960 | v | Northern Ireland (Belfast) HC 1g | W 5-2 |
| 19 Oct 1960 | v | Luxembourg (Luxembourg) WCq | W 9-0 |
| 26 Oct 1960 | v | Spain (Wembley) Fr 1g | W 4-2 |
| 23 Nov 1960 | v | Wales (Wembley) HC | W 5-1 |
| 15 Apr 1961 | v | Scotland (Wembley) HC 1g | W 9-3 |
| 10 May 1961 | v | Mexico (Wembley) Fr 2g | W 8-0 |
| 21 May 1961 | v | Portugal (Lisbon) WCq | D 1-1 |
| 24 May 1961 | v | Italy (Rome) Fr | W 3-2 |
| 27 May 1961 | v | Austria (Vienna) Fr | L 1-3 |
| 28 Sep 1961 | v | Luxembourg (Highbury) WCq | W 4-1 |
| 14 Oct 1961 | v | Wales (Cardiff) HC 1g | D 1-1 |
| 25 Oct 1961 | v | Portugal (Wembley) WCq | W 2-0 |
| 22 Nov 1961 | v | Northern Ireland (Wembley) HC | D 1-1 |
| 14 Apr 1962 | v | Scotland (Glasgow) HC | L 0-2 |
| 20 May 1962 | v | Peru (Lima) Fr | W 4-0 |
| 31 May 1962 | v | Hungary (Rancagua) WCr1 | L 1-2 |
| 2 Jun 1962 | v | Argentina (Rancagua) WCr1 | W 3-1 |
| 7 Jun 1962 | v | Bulgaria (Rancagua ) WCr1 | D 0-0 |
| 10 Jun 1962 | v | Brazil (Vina de Mar) WCqf | L 1-3 |
| 6 Apr 1963 | v | Scotland (Wembley) HC 1g | L 1-2 |
| 8 May 1963 | v | Brazil (Wembley) Fr 1g | D 1-1 |
| 5 Jun 1963 | v | Switzerland (Basle) Fr 1g | W 8-1 |

**Michael McGrath (Republic of Ireland) – 18 appearances**

| | | | |
|---|---|---|---|
| 14 May 1958 | v | Austria (Vienna) Fr | L 1-3 |
| 5 Oct 1958 | v | Poland (Dublin) Fr | D 2-2 |
| 5 Apr 1959 | v | Czechoslovakia (Dublin) ECpr | W 2-0 |
| 10 May 1959 | v | Czechoslovakia (Bratislava) ECpr | L 0-4 |
| 1 Nov 1959 | v | Sweden (Dublin) Fr | W 3-2 |
| 11 May 1960 | v | West Germany (Düsseldorf) Fr | W 1-0 |
| 18 May 1960 | v | Sweden (Malmö) Fr | L 1-4 |
| 28 Sep 1960 | v | Wales (Dublin) Fr | L 2-3 |
| 8 Oct 1961 | v | Czechoslovakia (Dublin) WCq | L 1-3 |
| 29 Oct 1961 | v | Czechoslovakia (Prague) WCq | L 1-7 |
| 9 Jun 1963 | v | Scotland (Dublin) Fr | W 1-0 |
| 25 Sep 1963 | v | Austria (Vienna) ECr2 | D 0-0 |
| 13 Oct 1963 | v | Austria (Dublin) ECr2 | W 3-2 |
| 24 May 1964 | v | England (Dublin) Fr | L 1-3 |
| 25 Oct 1964 | v | Poland (Dublin) Fr | W 3-2 |
| 24 Mar 1965 | v | Belgium (Dublin) Fr | L 0-2 |
| 5 May 1965 | v | Spain (Dublin) WCq | W 1-0 |
| 27 Oct 1965 | v | Spain (Seville) WCq | L 1-4 |

**Alexander Derek Dougan (Northern Ireland) – 5 appearances & 2 goals**

| | | | |
|---|---|---|---|
| 3 Oct 1959 | v | Scotland (Belfast) HC | L 0-4 |
| 8 Oct 1960 | v | England (Belfast) HC | L 2-5 |

| | | | |
|---|---|---|---|
| 12 Apr 1961 | v | Wales (Belfast) HC 1g | L 1-5 |
| 25 Apr 1961 | v | Italy (Bologna) Fr 1g | L 2-3 |
| 3 May 1961 | v | Greece (Athens) WCq | L 1-2 |

**Matthew Andrew McEvoy (Republic of Ireland) – 17 appearances & 6 goals**

| | | | |
|---|---|---|---|
| 3 May 1961 | v | Scotland (Glasgow) WCq | L 1-4 |
| 7 May 1961 | v | Scotland (Dublin) WCq | L 0-3 |
| 9 Jun 1963 | v | Scotland (Dublin) Fr | W 1-0 |
| 13 Oct 1963 | v | Austria (Dublin) ECr2 | D 3-2 |
| 11 Mar 1964 | v | Spain (Seville) ECpr 1g | L 1-5 |
| 8 Apr 1964 | v | Spain (Dublin) ECpr | L 0-2 |
| 10 May 1964 | v | Poland (Kracòw) Fr | L 1-3 |
| 13 May 1964 | v | Norway (Oslo) Fr 1g | W 4-1 |
| 24 May 1964 | v | England (Dublin) Fr | L 1-3 |
| 25 Oct 1964 | v | Poland (Dublin) Fr 2g | W 3-2 |
| 24 Mar 1965 | v | Belgium (Dublin) Fr | L 0-2 |
| 5 May 1965 | v | Spain (Dublin) WCq | W 1-0 |
| 27 Oct 1965 | v | Spain (Seville) WCq 1g | L 1-4 |
| 10 Nov 1965 | v | Spain (Paris) WCq | L 0-1 |
| 23 Oct 1966 | v | Spain (Dublin) ECq | D 0-0 |
| 16 Nov 1966 | v | Turkey (Dublin) ECq 1g | W 2-1 |
| 21 May 1967 | v | Czechoslovakia (Dublin) ECq | L 0-2 |

**William Ian Lawther (Northern Ireland) – 2 appearances**

| | | | |
|---|---|---|---|
| 7 Oct 1961 | v | Scotland (Belfast) HC | L 1-6 |
| 9 May 1962 | v | Holland (Rotterdam) Fr | L 0-4 |

**Joseph Haverty (Republic of Ireland) – 2 appearances**

| | | | |
|---|---|---|---|
| 8 Oct 1961 | v | Czechoslovakia (Dublin) WCq | L 1-3 |
| 29 Oct 1961 | v | Czechoslovakia (Prague) WCq | L 1-7 |

**Harold Michael England (Wales) – 20 appearances & 1 goal**

| | | | |
|---|---|---|---|
| 11 Apr 1962 | v | Northern Ireland (Cardiff) HC | W 4-0 |
| 16 May 1962 | v | Brazil (São Paulo) Fr | .L 1-3 |
| 22 May 1962 | v | Mexico (Mexico City) Fr | D 1-1 |
| 20 Mar 1963 | v | Hungary (Cardiff) ECr1 | D 1-1 |
| 3 Apr 1963 | v | Northern Ireland (Belfast) HC | W 4-1 |
| 12 Oct 1963 | v | England (Cardiff) HC | L 0-4 |
| 20 Nov 1963 | v | Scotland (Glasgow) HC | L 1-2 |
| 15 Apr 1964 | v | Northern Ireland (Swansea) HC | L 2-3 |
| 21 Oct 1964 | v | Denmark (Copenhagen) WCq | L 0-1 |
| 18 Nov 1964 | v | England (Wembley) HC | L 1-2 |
| 9 Dec 1964 | v | Greece (Athens) WCq | L 0-2 |
| 17 Mar 1965 | v | Greece (Cardiff) WCq 1g | W 4-1 |
| 31 Mar 1965 | v | Northern Ireland (Belfast) HC | W 5-0 |
| 1 May 1965 | v | Italy (Florence) Fr | L 1-4 |
| 30 May 1965 | v | Soviet Union (Moscow) WCq | L 1-2 |
| 2 Oct 1965 | v | England (Cardiff) HC | D 0-0 |
| 27 Oct 1965 | v | Soviet Union (Moscow) WCq | W 2-1 |
| 24 Nov 1965 | v | Scotland (Glasgow) HC | L 1-4 |
| 1 Dec 1965 | v | Denmark (Wrexham) WCq | W 4-2 |
| 30 Mar 1966 | v | Northern Ireland (Cardiff) HC | L 1-4 |

**Keith Robert Newton (England) – 19 appearances**

| | | | |
|---|---|---|---|
| 23 Feb 1966 | v | West Germany (Wembley) Fr | W 1-0 |
| 2 Apr 1966 | v | Scotland (Glasgow) HC | W 4-3 |
| 24 May 1967 | v | Spain (Wembley) Fr | W 2-0 |
| 27 May 1967 | v | Austria (Vienna) Fr | W 1-0 |
| 21 Oct 1967 | v | Wales (Cardiff) HC/ECq | W 3-0 |
| 24 Feb 1968 | v | Scotland (Glasgow) HC/ECq | D 1-1 |
| 8 May 1968 | v | Spain (Madrid) ECqf | W 2-1 |
| 22 May 1968 | v | Sweden (Wembley) Fr | W 3-1 |
| 1 Jun 1968 | v | West Germany (Hanover) Fr | L 0-1 |
| 5 Jun 1968 | v | Yugoslavia (Florence) ECsf | L 0-1 |
| 6 Nov 1968 | v | Romania (Bucharest) Fr | D 0-0 |
| 11 Dec 1968 | v | Bulgaria (Wembley) Fr | D 1-1 |
| 12 Mar 1969 | v | France (Wembley) Fr | W 5-0 |
| 3 May 1969 | v | Northern Ireland (Belfast) HC | W 3-1 |
| 7 May 1969 | v | Wales (Wembley) HC | W 2-1 |
| 10 May 1969 | v | Scotland (Wembley) HC | W 4-1 |
| 1 Jun 1969 | v | Mexico (Mexico City) Fr | D 0-0 |
| 8 Jun 1969 | v | Uruguay (Montevideo) Fr | W 2-1 |
| 12 Jun 1969 | v | Brazil (Rio de Janeiro) Fr | L 1-2 |

**Barrington Gerard Hole (Wales) – 7 appearances**

| | | | |
|---|---|---|---|
| 22 Oct 1966 | v | Scotland (Cardiff) HC/ECq | D 1-1 |
| 16 Nov 1966 | v | England (Wembley) HC/ECq | L 1-5 |
| 12 Apr 1967 | v | Northern Ireland (Belfast) HC/ECq | D 0-0 |
| 21 Oct 1967 | v | England (Cardiff) HC/ECq | L 0-3 |
| 22 Nov 1967 | v | Scotland (Glasgow) HC/ECq | L 2-3 |

| 28 Feb 1968 | v | Northern Ireland (Wrexham) HC/ECq | W 2-0 |
| 8 May 1968 | v | West Germany (Cardiff) Fr | D 1-1 |

### Eamon Rogers (Republic of Ireland) – 14 appearances & 3 goals

| 22 Nov 1967 | v | Czechoslovakia (Prague) ECq | W 2-1 |
| 15 May 1968 | v | Poland (Dublin) Fr | D 2-2 |
| 30 Oct 1968 | v | Poland (Chorzow) Fr | D 0-1 |
| 10 Nov 1968 | v | Austria (Dublin) Fr 1g | D 2-2 |
| 4 Dec 1968 | v | Denmark (Dublin) WCq | |

(Abandoned after 51 minutes when the score was 1-1)

| 4 May 1969 | v | Czechoslovakia (Dublin) WCq 1g | L 1-2 |
| 27 May 1969 | v | Denmark (Copenhagen) WCq | L 0-2 |
| 8 Jun 1969 | v | Hungary (Dublin) WCq | L 1-2 |
| 21 Sep 1969 | v | Scotland (Dublin) Fr | D 1-1 |
| 15 Oct 1969 | v | Denmark (Dublin) WCq | D 1-1 |
| 5 Nov 1969 | v | Hungary (Budapest) WCq | L 0-4 |
| 8 Dec 1970 | v | Italy (Florence) ECq | L 0-3 |
| 10 May 1971 | v | Italy (Dublin) ECq | L 1-2 |
| 30 May 1971 | v | Austria (Dublin) ECq 1g | L 1-4 |

### Allan Hunter (Northern Ireland) – 6 appearances

| 22 Oct 1969 | v | Soviet Union (Moscow) WCq | L 0-2 |
| 3 Feb 1971 | v | Cyprus (Nicosia) ECq | W 3-0 |
| 21 Mar 1971 | v | Cyprus (Belfast) ECq | W 5-0 |
| 15 May 1971 | v | England (Belfast) HC | L 0-1 |
| 18 May 1971 | v | Scotland (Glasgow) HC | W 1-0 |
| 22 May 1971 | v | Wales (Belfast) HC | W 1-0 |

### Noel Brotherston (Northern Ireland) – 27 appearances & 3 goals

| 16 May 1980 | v | Scotland (Belfast) HC | W 1-0 |
| 20 May 1980 | v | England (Wembley) HC | D 1-1 |
| 23 May 1980 | v | Wales (Cardiff) HC 1g | W 1-0 |
| 11 Jun 1980 | v | Australia (Sydney) Fr | W 2-1 |
| 15 Jun 1980 | v | Australia (Melbourne) Fr | D 1-1 |
| 18 Jun 1980 | v | Australia (Adelaide) Fr 1g | W 2-1 |
| 15 Oct 1980 | v | Sweden (Belfast) WCq 1g | W 3-0 |
| 19 Nov 1980 | v | Portugal (Lisbon) WCq | L 0-1 |
| 14 Oct 1981 | v | Scotland (Belfast) WCq | D 0-0 |
| 18 Nov 1981 | v | Israel (Belfast) WCq | W 1-0 |
| 23 Feb 1982 | v | England (Wembley) HC | L 0-4 |
| 24 Mar 1982 | v | France (Paris) Fr | L 0-4 |
| 28 Apr 1982 | v | Scotland (Belfast) HC | D 1-1 |
| 27 May 1982 | v | Wales (Wrexham) HC | L 0-3 |
| 25 Jun 1982 | v | Spain (Valencia) WCr1 sub | W 1-0 |
| 4 Jul 1982 | v | France (Madrid) WCr2 sub | L 1-4 |
| 13 Oct 1982 | v | Austria (Vienna) ECq sub | L 0-2 |
| 17 Nov 1982 | v | West Germany (Belfast) ECq | W 1-0 |
| 15 Dec 1982 | v | Albania (Tiranë) ECq | D 0-0 |
| 30 Mar 1983 | v | Turkey (Belfast) ECq | W 2-1 |
| 27 Apr 1983 | v | Albania (Belfast) ECq | W 1-0 |
| 24 May 1983 | v | Scotland (Glasgow) HC sub | D 0-0 |
| 28 May 1983 | v | England (Belfast) HC sub | D 0-0 |
| 31 May 1983 | v | Wales (Belfast) HC | L 0-1 |
| 12 Oct 1983 | v | Turkey (Ankara) ECq | L 0-1 |
| 16 Oct 1984 | v | Israel (Belfast) Fr sub | W 3-0 |
| 1 May 1985 | v | Turkey (Belfast) WCq | W 2-0 |

### James Martin Quinn (Northern Ireland) – 13 appearances & 3 goals

| 16 Oct 1984 | v | Israel (Belfast) Fr 1g | W 3-0 |
| 14 Nov 1984 | v | Finland (Belfast) WCq | W 2-1 |
| 27 Feb 1985 | v | England (Belfast) WCq | L 0-1 |
| 27 Mar 1985 | v | Spain (Palma) Fr | D 0-0 |
| 1 May 1985 | v | Turkey (Belfast) WCq | W 2-0 |
| 11 Sep 1985 | v | Turkey (Izmir) WCq | D 0-0 |
| 16 Oct 1985 | v | Romania (Bucharest) WCq 1gl | W 1-0 |
| 13 Nov 1985 | v | England (Wembley) WCq | D 0-0 |
| 26 Feb 1986 | v | France (Paris) Fr | D 0-0 |
| 26 Mar 1986 | v | Denmark (Belfast) Fr sub | D 1-1 |
| 23 Apr 1986 | v | Morocco (Belfast) Fr sub 1g | W 2-1 |
| 15 Oct 1986 | v | England (Wembley) ECq sub | L 0-3 |
| 12 Nov 1986 | v | Turkey (Izmir) ECq | D 0-0 |

### Francis Anthony Stapleton (Republic of Ireland) – 2 appearances & 2 goals

| 6 Sep 1989 | v | West Germany (Dublin) Fr 1g | D 1-1 |
| 2 Jun 1990 | v | Malta (Ta'Qali) Fr sub 1g | W 3-0 |

### Kevin Bernard Moran (Republic of Ireland) – 24 appearances

| 28 Mar 1990 | v | Wales (Dublin) Fr | W 1-0 |
| 25 Apr 1990 | v | Soviet Union (Dublin) Fr sub | W 1-0 |
| 2 Jun 1990 | v | Malta (Ta'Qali) Fr | W 3-0 |

| 11 Jun 1990 | v | England (Cagliari) WCr1 | D 1-1 |
| 17 Jun 1990 | v | Egypt (Palermo) WCr1 | D 0-0 |
| 21 Jun 1990 | v | Holland (Palermo) WCr1 | D 1-1 |
| 25 Jun 1990 | v | Romania (Genoa) WCr2 | D 0-0 |
| | | (won 5-4 on penalties) | |
| 30 Jun 1990 | v | Italy (Rome) WCqf | L 0-1 |
| 17 Oct 1990 | v | Turkey (Dublin) ECq sub | W 5-0 |
| 6 Feb 1991 | v | Wales (Wrexham) Fr | W 3-0 |
| 27 Mar 1991 | v | England (Wembley) ECq | D 1-1 |
| 1 May 1991 | v | Poland (Dublin) ECq | D 0-0 |
| 22 May 1991 | v | Chile (Dublin) Fr | D 1-1 |
| 1 Jun 1991 | v | United States of America (Boston) Fr | D 1-1 |
| 16 Oct 1991 | v | Poland (Poznan) ECq | D 3-3 |
| 30 May 1992 | v | United States of America (Washington) USC | L 1-3 |
| 14 Oct 1992 | v | Denmark (Copenhagen) WCq | D 1-1 |
| 18 Nov 1992 | v | Spain (Seville) WCq | D 0-0 |
| 31 Mar 1993 | v | Northern Ireland (Dublin) WCq | W 3-0 |
| 26 May 1993 | v | Albania (Tiranë) WCq | W 2-1 |
| 8 Sep 1993 | v | Lithuania (Dublin) WCq | W 2-0 |
| 13 Oct 1993 | v | Spain (Dublin) WCq | L 1-3 |
| 20 Apr 1994 | v | Holland (Tilberg) Fr | W 1-0 |
| 24 May 1994 | v | Bolivia (Dublin) (Fr) | W 1-0 |

### Roy Connon Wegerle (United States of America) – 4 appearances & 1 goal

| 30 May 1992 | v | Republic of Ireland (Washington) USC sub | W 3-1 |
| 3 Jun 1992 | v | Portugal (Chicago) USC 1g | W 1-0 |
| 6 Jun 1992 | v | Italy (Chicago) USC | D 1-1 |
| 16 Oct 1992 | v | Saudi Arabia (Riyadh) IC | L 0-3 |

### Alan Shearer (England) – 7 appearances & 2 goals

| 9 Sep 1992 | v | Spain (Santander) Fr | L 0-1 |
| 14 Oct 1992 | v | Norway (Wembley) WCq | D 1-1 |
| 18 Nov 1992 | v | Turkey (Wembley) WCq 1g | W 4-0 |
| 13 Oct 1993 | v | Holland (Rotterdam) WCQ | L 0-2 |
| 9 Mar 1994 | v | Denmark (Wembley) Fr | W 1-0 |
| 17 May 1994 | v | Greece (Wembley) Fr 1gl | W 5-0 |
| 22 May 1994 | v | Norway (Wembley) Fr | D 0-0 |

### Henning Berg (Norway) – 13 appearances & 1 goal

| 30 Mar 1993 | v | Qatar (Doha) Fr | W 6-1 |
| 22 Sep 1993 | v | Poland (Oslo) WCq | W 1-0 |
| 13 Oct 1993 | v | Poland (Poznan) WCq | W 3-0 |
| 10 Nov 1993 | v | Turkey (Istanbul) WCq | L 1-2 |
| 15 Jan 1994 | v | United States of America (Temple, Ariz.) Fr | L 1-2 |
| 9 Mar 1994 | v | Wales (Cardiff) Fr | W 3-1 |
| 20 Apr 1994 | v | Portugal (Oslo) Fr | D 0-0 |
| 19 Jun 1994 | v | Mexico (Washington) WCr1 | W 1-0 |
| 23 Jun 1994 | v | Italy (New York) WCr1 | L 0-1 |
| 28 Jun 1994 | v | Republic of Ireland (New York) WCr1 | D 0-0 |

### Patrik Jonas Andersson (Sweden) – 7 appearances

| 15 Apr 1993 | v | Hungary (Budapest) Fr sub | W 2-1 |
| 28 Apr 1993 | v | France (Paris) WCq | L 1-2 |
| 2 Jun 1993 | v | Israel (Stockholm) WCq | W 5-0 |
| 11 Aug 1993 | v | Switzerland (Boras) Fr | W 2-1 |
| 22 Aug 1993 | v | France (Stockholm) WCq | D 1-1 |
| 8 Sep 1993 | v | Bulgaria (Sofia) WCq | D 1-1 |
| 10 Nov 1993 | v | Austria (Vienna) WCq | D 1-1 |
| 22 May 1994 | v | England (Wembley) Fr | .D 0-0 |
| 1 Jun 1994 | v | Denmark (Oslo) Fr 1gl | W 2-1 |
| 5 Jun 1994 | v | Sweden (Stockholm) Fr | L 0-2 |

### Kevin William Gallacher (Scotland) – 5 appearances & 2 goals

| 28 Apr 1993 | v | Portugal (Lisbon) WCq | L 0-5 |
| 19 May 1993 | v | Estonia (Tallinn) WCq 1g | W 3-0 |
| 2 Jun 1993 | v | Estonia (Aberdeen) WCq | W 3-1 |
| 13 Oct 1993 | v | Italy (Rome) WCq 1g | L 1-3 |
| 17 Nov 1993 | v | Malta (Valletta) WCq | W 2-0 |

### Edward Colin James Hendry (Scotland) – 6 appearances & 1 goal

| 19 May 1993 | v | Estonia (Tallinn) WCq | W 3-0 |
| 2 Jun 1993 | v | Estonia (Tallinn) WCq | W 3-1 |
| 17 Nov 1993 | v | Malta (Valletta) WCq 1g | W 2-0 |
| 23 Mar 1994 | v | Holland (Hampden Park) | L 0-1 |
| 20 Apr 1994 | v | Austria (Vienna) Fr | W 2-1 |
| 27 May 1994 | v | Holland (Utrecht) Fr | L 1-3 |

Stuart Ripley with the England shirt he won against San Marino in November 1993.

**Stuart Edward Ripley (England) – 1 appearance**
17 Nov 1993    v    San Marino (Bologna) WCq         W 7-1

**Graeme Le Saux (England) – 3 appearances**
9 Mar 1994    v    Denmark (Wembley) Fr         W 1-0
17 May 1994    v    Greece (Wembley) Fr         W 5-0
22 May 1994    v    Norway (Wembley) Fr         D 0-0

**David Batty (England) – 1 appearance**
9 Mar 1994    v    Denmark (Wembley) Fr (sub)         W 1-0

**Timothy David Flowers (England) - 1 appearance**
17 May 1994    v    Greece (Wembley) Fr         W 5-0

**Minor International Appearances**
Abbreviated details can be found below of other representative honours gained by players whilst with Blackburn Rovers.

**Victory & Wartime International Appearances**
**Frederick Duckworth (England) – 2 appearances**
1919    v    Scotland (twice)

**Daniel Shea (England) – 2 appearances**
1919    v    Scotland (twice)

**Joseph Hodkinson (England) – 1 appearance**
1920    v    Wales

**Walter Crook (England) – 1 appearance**
1939    v    Wales

**'B' International Appearances**
**William Eckersley (England 'B') – 3 appearances**
1950    v    Holland 'B' (twice), Italy 'B'

**Ronald Clayton (England 'B') – 1 appearance**
1955    v    Yugoslavia 'B'

**Bryan Douglas (England 'B') – 1 appearance**
1956    v    Switzerland 'B'

**Michael McGrath (Republic of Ireland 'B') – 1 appearance**
1957    v    Romania 'B'

**Alexander Derek Dougan (Republic of Ireland 'B') – 1 appearance**
1959    v    France 'B'

**Under-23 International Appearances**
**Ronnie Clayton (England Under-23) – 6 appearances**
1955    v    Denmark Under-23
1956    v    Scotland Under-23, Denmark Under-23
1957    v    Scotland Under-23, Romania Under-23, Czechoslovakia Under-23

**Bryan Douglas (England Under-23) – 5 appearances**
1956    v    Denmark Under-23, France Under-23
1957    v    Bulgaria Under-23, Romania Under-23, Czechoslovakia Under-23

**Thomas Royston Vernon (Wales Under-23) – 1 appearance**
1958    v    Scotland Under-23

**Peter A.Dobing (England Under-23) – 7 appearances & 1 goal**
1959    v    West Germany Under-23, France Under-23
1960    v    East Germany Under-23 1g, Poland Under-23, Israel Under-23, Italy Under-23
1961    v    Scotland Under-23

**Harold Michael England (Wales Under-23) – 11 appearances**
1959    v    Scotland Under-23
1961    v    England Under-23, Scotland Under-23
1962    v    Northern Ireland Under-23
1963    v    Northern Ireland Under-23, England Under-23, Scotland Under-23
1964    v    Northern Ireland Under-23, England Under-23, Scotland Under-23
1965    v    Northern Ireland Under-23

**Christopher Crowe (England under-23) – 2 appearances & 1 goal**
1961    v    Wales Under-23 1g, Scotland Under-23

**Frederick Pickering (England Under-23) – 3 appearances & 4 goals**
1963    v    Wales Under-23 1g, West Germany Under-23
1964    v    Scotland Under-23 3g

**Keith Robert Newton (England Under-23) – 4 appearances**
1964    v    Scotland Under-23, Hungary Under-23, Israel Under-23, Turkey Under-23

**Reginald Blore (Wales Under-23) – 3 appearances & 1 goal**
1964    v    England Under-23 1g, Scotland Under-23
1965    v    Northern Ireland Under-23

**Eamon Rogers (Republic of Ireland Under-23) – 1 appearance**
1966    v    France Under-23

**Anthony John Diamond (Northern Ireland Under-23) 1 appearance**
1989    v    Republic of Ireland Under-23

**Under-21 International Appearances**
**Noel Brotherston (Northern Ireland Under-21) – 1 appearance**
1978    v    Republic of Ireland Under-21

**Simon Barker (England Under-21) – 4 appearances**
1985    v    Israel Under-21 (sub), Republic of Ireland Under-21, Romania Under-21
1986    v    Italy Under-21

**Scott Sellars (England Under-21) – 3 appearances**
1988    v    Scotland Under-21 (sub), France Under-21, Switzerland Under-21

**Alan Wright (England Under-21) – 2 appearances**
1992    v    Spain Under-21, Norway Under-21

**Inter-League Appearances**
**Thomas Brandon (Football League) – 1 appearance**
1891　v　Football Alliance

**George Dewar (Football League) – 1 appearance**
1891　v　Football Alliance

**Jack Southworth (Football League) – 1 appearance**
1893　v　Scottish League

**Thomas Edward Booth (Football League) – 2 appearances**
1897　v　Irish League
1898　v　Irish League

**William Williams (Football League) – 1 appearance**
1898　v　Irish League

**Daniel Hurst (Football League) – 1 appearance**
1899　v　Irish League

**Arnold Whittaker (Football League) – 1 appearance**
1901　v　Scottish League

**Frederick Blackburn (Football League) – 1 appearance**
1901　v　Scottish League

**Robert Crompton (Football League) – 17 appearances**
1902　v　Scottish League
1903　v　Scottish League
1904　v　Scottish league
1907　v　Scottish League, Irish League
1908　v　Scottish league, Irish League
1909　v　Scottish League
1910　v　Scottish League
1911　v　Scottish League
1912　v　Scottish League, Irish League
1913　v　Irish League
1914　v　Southern League (twice), Scottish League, Irish League

**William Bradshaw (Football League) – 4 appearances**
1904　v　Irish League
1905　v　Irish League
1910　v　Southern League
1911　v　Scottish League

**Samuel Wolstenholme (Football League) – 1 appearance**
1905　v　Scottish League

**Albert Edward Houlker (Football League) – 1 appearance**
1902　v　Scottish League

**Edwin Gladstone Latheron (Football League) 5 appearances & 3 goals**
1909　v　Scottish League
1914　v　Southern League (twice), Irish League 2g
1915　v　Scottish League 1g

**Arthur Cowell (Football League) – 1 appearance**
1909　v　Irish League

**William Garbutt (Football League) – 1 appearance**
1910　v　Scottish League

**John Simpson (Football League) – 5 appearances**
1911　v　Scottish League, Southern League, Irish League
1912　v　Irish League
1914　v　Irish League

**Joseph Hodkinson (Football League) – 2 appearances**
1913　v　Scottish League
1914　v　Southern League

**Daniel Shea (Football League) – 2 appearances & 3 goals**
1913　v　Irish League
1914　v　Southern League 3g

**Harry Healless (Football League) – 1 appearance**
1923　v　Irish League

**Sydney Charles Puddefoot (Football League) – 2 app & 1 goal**
1925　v　Scottish League 1g, Irish League

**Herbert Jones (Football League) – 3 appearances**
1927　v　Scottish League
1928　v　Scottish League
1929　v　Irish League

**Austen Fenwick Campbell (Football League) – 2 appearances**
1928　v　Irish League, Scottish League

**Arthur Rigby (Football League) – 1 appearance**
1928　v　Scottish League

**John Bruton (Football League) – 1 appearance**
1934　v　Scottish League

**Robert Ireland Pryde (Football League) – 2 appearances**
1941　v　Scottish League
1947　v　League of Ireland

**Robert Langton (Football League) – 2 appearances**
1947　v　Irish League
1948　v　Scottish League

**John Eric Bell (Football League) – 2 appearances**
1950　v　League of Ireland, Irish League

**William Eckersley (Football League) – 6 appearances**
1950　v　League of Ireland, Irish League
1951　v　League of Ireland
1953　v　League of Ireland, Danish Combination, Irish League

**Ronald Clayton (Football League) – 10 appearances**
1955　v　League of Ireland
1956　v　Irish League, League of Ireland, Irish League
1957　v　Scottish League, Irish League
1959　v　League of Ireland, Irish League, League of Ireland
1960　v　League of Ireland

**Bryan Douglas (Football League) – 4 appearances & 2 goals**
1958　v　Scottish League
1961　v　League of Ireland 2g
1962　v　Irish League, Italian League

**Peter A.Dobing (Football League) – 3 appearances & 3 goals**
1959　v　Irish League, League of Ireland
1960　v　League of Ireland 3g

**Michael McGrath (Football League) – 1 appearance**
1960　v　League of Ireland

**Maurice Woods (Football League) – 1 appearance**
1960　v　League of Ireland

**Keith Robert Newton (Football League) – 5 appearances & 1 goal**
1964　v　Irish League
1965　v　League of Ireland
1966　v　Scottish League
1967　v　Scottish League
1968　v　Scottish League 1g

## REPRESENTATIVE MATCHES AT ALEXANDRA MEADOWS
Alexandra Meadows was selected as the venue for the international match with Wales just a matter of months before Blackburn Rovers moved to the Leamington Street Ground. This was the only international match to be played at the home of the East Lancashire Cricket Club.

**26 Feb 1881 England 0 Wales 1**
**England:** J.P.Hawtrey (Old Etonians); A.Harvey (Wednesday Strollers), A.L.Bambridge (Swifts), J.Hunter (Sheffield Wednesday), F.W.Hargreaves (Blackburn Rovers), T.Marshall (Darwen), T.Rostron (Darwen), J.Brown (Blackburn Rovers), G.Tait (Birmingham Excelsior), J.Hargreaves (Blackburn Rovers), W.Mosforth (Sheffield Wednesday).
**Wales:** R.McMillan (Shrewsbury Engineers); J.R.Morgan (Derby School), S.L.Kenrick (Druids), W.Williams (Druids), W.S.Bell (Shrewsbury Engineers), W.P.Owen (Ruthin), T.Lewis (Wrexham), K.Crosse (Druids), J.Price (Wrexham), U.Goodwin (Ruthin), J.Vaughan (Druids).
*Scorer: Vaughan*
Referee: Mr S.R.Bastard (Upton Park).

## REPRESENTATIVE MATCHES AT EWOOD PARK
Ewood Park was first selected as an international venue in April 1891

when Scotland provided England's opposition. The club had only been operating at Ewood for six months when the Football Association paid them the compliment of selecting the ground for such a prestigious event. However, the FA then caused uproar in the town by failing to select a single member of the Blackburn team in the English line-up. The Blackburn public were not impressed and chose to boycott the event in large numbers. As a result the match produced paltry receipts of £334 and even the *Athletic News* was moved to comment that the exclusion of Jack Southworth and John Barton was 'not only an injustice to the men themselves, but an injustice to England'.

At senior level, Ewood Park has been used for one other full international match, an Under-23 game and a couple of inter-League fixtures.

### 6 Apr 1891 England 2 Scotland 1
**England:** W.R.Moon (Old Westminsters); R.H.Haworth (Preston North End), R.Holmes (Preston North End), A.Smith (Nottingham Forest), J.Holt (Everton), A.Shelton (Notts County), W.I.Bassett (West Bromwich Albion), J.Goodall (Derby County), F.Geary (Everton), E.W.Chadwick (Everton), A.Milward (Everton)
*Scorers: Goodall, Chadwick.*
**Scotland:** J.Wilson (Vale of Leven); W.Arnott (Queen's Park), R.Smellie (Queen's Park), J.Hill (Hearts), J.McPherson (Hearts), I.Begbie (Hearts), F.Watt (Kilbirnie), G.Rankin (Vale of Leven), W.Sellar (Queen's Park), W.H.Berry (Queen's Park), D.Baird (Hearts).
*Scorer: Watt*
Referee: Mr Morrow (Irish Association)
Attendance: 6,000

### 26 Feb 1910 Football League 2 Scottish League 3
**Football League:** J.Dawson (Burnley); R.Crompton (Blackburn Rovers), J.V.Hayes (Manchester United), J.T.Brittleton (Sheffield Wednesday), J.Harrop (Liverpool), W.H.R.Makepeace (Everton), W.Garbutt (Blackburn Rovers), G.H.Holley (Sunderland), J.Parkinson (Liverpool), J.W.Bache (Aston Villa), G.Wall (Manchester United).
*Scorers: Parkinson, Brittleton*
**Scottish League:** J.Brownlie (Third Lanark), A.McNair (Celtic), T.Miller (Falkirk), G.Halley (Kilmarnock), W.Loney (Celtic), J.Hay (Celtic), A.Bennett (Rangers), J.McMenemy (Celtic), J.Quinn (Celtic), A.Devine (Falkirk), R.Templeton (Kilmarnock).
*Scorers: Quinn, Devine, Templeton.*
Referee: T.P.Campbell (Blackburn).
Attendance: 30,000

### 3 Mar 1924 England 1 Wales 2
**England:** W.R.Sewell (Blackburn Rovers); T.Smart (Aston Villa), T.Mort (Aston Villa), F.W.Kean (Sheffield Wednesday), G.Wilson (Sheffield Wednesday), P.Barton (Birmingham), S.Chedgzoy (Everton), D.B.N.Jack (Bolton Wanderers), W.T.Roberts (Preston North End), C.Stephenson (Huddersfield Town), F.Tunstall (Sheffield United).
*Scorer: Roberts*
**Wales:** A.Gray (Oldham Athletic); M.Russell (Plymouth Argyle), J.Jenkins (Brighton & Hove Albion), H.P.Evans (Cardiff City), W.Jennings (Bolton Wanderers), W.Davies (Swansea Town), J.Nicholls (Newport County), L.Davies (Cardiff City), R.Richards (West Ham United), E.T.Vizard (Bolton Wanderers).
*Scorers: W.Davies, Vizard*
Referee: G.N.Watson (Nottingham).
Attendance: 30,000

### 4 Nov 1959 Football League 2 League of Ireland 0
**Football League:** R.Springett (Sheffield Wednesday); J.Armfield (Blackpool), A.Allen (Stoke City), R.Clayton (Blackburn Rovers), P.Swan (Sheffield Wednesday), A.Kay (Sheffield Wednesday), J.Connelly (Burnley), P.Dobing (Blackburn Rovers), D.Viollet (Manchester United), R.Parry (Bolton Wanderers), E.Holliday (Middlesbrough).
*Scorers: Viollet, Connelly.*
**League of Ireland:** K.Blount (Transport); T.Farrell (Shamrock Rovers), E.Blake (Sligo Rovers), R.Nolan (Shamrock Rovers), S.Keogh (Shamrock Rovers), Kelly (Shelbourne), W.Coleman (Drumcondra), J.Hennessey (Shelbourne), D.Leahy (Cork Celtic), T.Hamilton (Shamrock Rovers), L.Tuohy (Shamrock Rovers).
Referee: K.A.Collinge (Altrincham)
Attendance: 20,300

### 20 Apr 1966 England Under-23s 2 Turkey Under-23s 0
**England Under-23s:** A.Stepney (Millwall); L.Badger (Sheffield United), R.Thomson (Wolverhampton Wanderers), B.O'Neil (Burnley), G.Cross (Leicester City), M.Peters (West Ham United), M.Summerbee (Manchester City), E.Hunt (Wolverhampton Wanderers), M.Jones

(Sheffield United), A.Birchenhall (Sheffield United), G.Armstrong (Arsenal).
*Scorer: Armstrong 2*
**Turkey Under-23s:** Artuner; Bugdaypnar, Ozkarsli, Becedek, Y.Sen, Uraz, M.Sen, Dogan, Sari Loglu, Lmastasoglu, Tunaoglu.
Attendance: 9,251

Two schoolboy international matches have also been held at Ewood Park. Below are the details of the result and the England team on both occasions.

### 10 Apr 1976 England Under-18s 2 Scotland Under-18s 2
**England Under-18:** J.I.Shead (Midlands); P.S.Ormerod (Midlands), K.T.Moore (Humberside), C.G.Reeves (Kent), R.J.Hill (Hampshire), K.T.Grimsley (Manchester), C.Nwajiobi (London), P.Whittaker (Burnley), C.P.Green (Hampshire), T.C.Donovan (Humberside), I.Ratcliffe (Staffs). Sub: W.Knox (Northumberland) for P.Whittaker.
*Scorers: Nwajiobi, Hill.*
Attendance 7,212

### 19 Sep 1983 England Under-16s 4 Iceland Under-16s 0
**England Under-16:** F.Digby (Manchester United); S.Ratcliffe (Manchester United), A.Crane (Ipswich Town), K.Keen (West Ham United), T.Adams (Arsenal), D.Anderson (Coventry City), F.Carr (Blackburn Rovers), P.Moulden (Manchester City), D.Beckford (Manchester City), J.Beresford (Manchester City), A.Kilner (Burnley)
*Scorers: Carr 3, Kilner*
Attendance: 2,000

## REPRESENTATIVE MATCHES AT THE LEAMINGTON STREET GROUND
Two international matches were played at the Leamington Street Ground in the mid-1880s. The match with Wales in March 1885 provided J.T.Ward, later to represent Blackburn Rovers, with his only England cap. Ward was the only player in the history of Blackburn Olympic to receive international recognition.

### 14 Mar 1885 England 1 Wales 1
**England:** W.J.H.Arthur (Blackburn Rovers), H.T.Moore (Notts County), J.T.Ward (Blackburn Olympic), N.C.Bailey (Clapham Rovers) J.H.Forrest (Blackburn Rovers), J.M.Lofthouse (Blackburn Rovers), J.K.Davenport (Bolton Wanderers), J.Brown (Blackburn Rovers), C.Mitchell (Upton Park), J.A.Dixon (Notts County), E.C.Bambridge (Swifts).
*Scorer: Mitchell.*
**Wales:** R.H.Mills-Roberts (St Thomas' Hospital); F.R.Jones (Bangor), G.Thomas (Wrexham Olympic), T.Burke (Wrexham Olympic), R.Davies (Druids),. H.Jones (Bangor), J.E.Davies (Oswestry WS), T.Vaughan (Rhyl), J.Wilding (Wrexham Olympic),. G.Farmer (Oswestry WS), W.Lewis (Bangor).
*Scorer: Lewis.*
Referee: Mr Stewart (Glasgow).
Attendance: 5,000

### 19 Mar 1887 England 2 Scotland 3
**England:** R.J.Roberts (West Bromwich Albion); A.M.Walters (Cambridge University), P.M.Walters (Old Carthusians), G.Haworth (Accrington), N.C.Bailey (Clapham Rovers), J.H.Forrest (Blackburn Rovers), J.M.Lofthouse (Blackburn Rovers), F.Dewhurst (Preston North End), T.Lindley (Cambridge University & Nottingham Forest), W.N.Cobbold (Old Carthusians), E.C.Bambridge (Swifts).
*Scorers: Lindley, Dewhurst.*
**Scotland:** J.McAulay (Dumbarton); W.Arnott (Queen's Park), J.Forbes (Vale of Leven), R.Kelso (Renton), J.R.Auld (Third Lanark), L.Keir (Dumbarton), J.Marshall (Third Lanark), W.Robertson (Dumbarton), W.Sellar (Battlefield), J.Allan (Queen's Park), J.McCall (Renton).
*Scorers: Allan, McCall, Keir.*
Referee: Mr Sinclair (Irish Football Association).
Attendance: 10,000.

### RICHARDS, John William
Half-back. 1930-1932.
*5ft 8in; 11st.*
*Born: Rhos-on-Sea, 1909.*
*Debut: v Blackpool (a) 3 January 1931.*
*Career: Wrexham; Blackburn Rovers September 1930; Accrington Stanley August 1934; Darwen September 1934.*
**Appearances:** Football League 2.
Described by the *Lancashire Post Football Annual* of 1930-31 as a 'solid type of wing-half', Richards found first-team opportunities few and far between at Ewood Park. Curiously, his only two senior appearances came

at Bloomfield Road in January 1931 and September 1931. As the club was well served in the half-back department Richards was allowed to leave Ewood at the end of the 1931-32 season.

## RICHARDSON, Lee James
Midfield. 1990-1992.
*5ft 11in; 11st.*
*Born: Halifax, 12 March 1969.*
*Debut: v Bristol City (a) 25 August 1990.*
*Career: Halifax Town trainee August 1986, turning professional in July 1987; Watford February 1989 (£175,000); Blackburn Rovers August 1990 (£250,000); Aberdeen September 1992 (£150,000); Oldham Athletic July 1994.*
*Domestic honours with Blackburn Rovers: Second Division Play-off winners: 1992.*
**Appearances:** Football League 50+12; Play-offs 1+2; Football League Cup 1+1; Full Members' Cup 1; Total 53+15.
**Goals:** Football League 3.
Lee Richardson was brought to Ewood Park on the eve of the 1990-91 season by Don Mackay in a deal which took Andy Kennedy to Watford. A player whose main strength was his ability to pass the ball, Richardson failed to perform with any great consistency during the 1990-91 season. Although he began the following campaign in the first team he lost his place following the arrival of Gordon Cowans in November 1991. Richardson returned to the first team as a substitute during the last few weeks of the season and he appeared at Wembley in that role in the Final of the Play-offs. However, despite his recall, he was allowed to leave Ewood in September 1992 to join Aberdeen. He appeared for the Scottish club in the 1993 Scottish Cup Final but, although he scored a goal against Rangers, he had to be content with a runners-up medal.

## RIGBY, Arthur
Outside-left. 1925-1929.
*5ft 9in; 11st.*
*Born: Chorlton, Manchester, 7 June 1900; Died: Crewe, 25 March 1960.*
*Debut: v Aston Villa (a) 29 April 1925.*
*Career: Manchester district football; Stockport County trial; Crewe Alexandra 1919; Bradford City March 1921 (£1,200); Blackburn Rovers April 1925 (£2,500); Everton November 1929 (£2,000); Middlesbrough May 1932; Clapton Orient August 1933; Crewe Alexandra August 1935 to cs 1937.*
*International honours with Blackburn Rovers: England: 5 caps (1927); Football League: 1 appearance (1928).*
*Domestic honours with Blackburn Rovers: FA Cup winners: 1928.*
**Appearances:** Football League 156; FA Cup 12; FA Charity Shield 1; Total 169.
**Goals:** Football League 41; FA Cup 3; Total 44.
An electrician by trade, Arthur Rigby joined Crewe Alexandra in 1919 following a trial with Stockport County. Although Rigby had begun his footballing career as a goalkeeper he had joined Crewe as a winger and did sufficiently well for Bradford City to pay a sizeable sum to take him into the First Division. Although his bandy legs made him rather ungainly looking on the field, his insatiable appetite for work and exciting brand of wing play brought him enormous success. He joined Blackburn in April 1925 primarily as a left winger but, during the course of his time at the club, he also operated in the inside-left position. Rigby enjoyed a particularly good understanding with Ted Harper and the centre-forward plundered a good many goals from the accurate crosses of Rigby. Rigby won five England caps whilst at Ewood and was a member of the successful 1928 Cup Final team. However, having lost his place at the start of the 1929-30 campaign he asked to be placed on he transfer list and was eventually sold to Everton in November 1929.

## RIGG, Tweedale
Half-back. 1919-1921.
*5ft 9½in; 11st 7lb.*
*Born: Rochdale, 1896 (October quarter).*
*Debut: v Preston North End (h) 30 August 1919.*
*Career: Birkenhead junior; Rochdale cs 1916; Blackburn Rovers April 1919; Rochdale 1923-24; Rochdale assistant trainer 1937-38.*
**Appearances:** Football League 12.
Tweedale Rigg was signed by Blackburn Rovers as the final season of wartime football was drawing to a close. It was a time of great transition at Ewood Park and Rigg found himself installed in the senior team on the return of League football in August 1919. However, Rigg was unable to retain his place after the opening two months of the season and he was released at the end of the 1920-21 season.

## RILEY, Thomas
Full-back. 1902-1905.
*5ft 11in; 11st 6lb.*

*Born: Blackburn, March 1882.*
*Debut: v Sheffield United (h) 13 September 1902.*
*Career: St Mary's College; Chorley; Blackburn Rovers May 1902; Brentford August 1905; Aston Villa April 1906 (£400); Brentwood June 1908; Southampton 1909-10.*
**Appearances:** Football League 22; FA Cup 2; Total 24.
A rather lightweight full-back whose physique prevented him from being anything more than an understudy at Ewood Park. However, he could kick a ball with either foot and was not lacking for pace. His best season at Ewood came in 1903-04 when he featured in 16 First Division matches. In August 1905 he joined Southern League Brentford and did sufficiently well to be included in the England trials. After only 29 Southern League games he joined Aston Villa for a fee of £400, of which £170 came to Blackburn. Unfortunately, his hopes of establishing himself at Villa Park evaporated with a serious knee injury.

## RIPLEY, Stuart Edward
Outside-right.
*5ft 11in; 12st 6lb.*
*Born: Middlesbrough, 20 November 1967.*
*Debut: v Crystal Palace (a) 15 August 1992.*
*Career: Middlesbrough associated schoolboy March 1983, becoming an apprentice in August 1984 before turning professional in December 1985; Bolton Wanderers on loan February to March 1986; Blackburn Rovers July 1992 (£1,200,000).*
*International honours with Blackburn Rovers: England: 1 cap (1993).*
**Appearances:** Premier League 78+2; FA Cup 8; Football League Cup 11; Total 97+2.
**Goals:** Premier League 11; FA Cup 2; Total 13.
Stuart Ripley graduated through the junior ranks of his local club before

making his Football League debut as a substitute in February 1985. He gained further experience of League football during a short loan spell with Bolton Wanderers in March 1986 and became a regular at Middlesbrough during the 1986-87 season. At the end of that campaign Middlesbrough won promotion to the Second Division and the following season Ripley helped them win promotion to the First Division via the Play-offs. Unfortunately, Ripley only enjoyed one season in the top flight before the club was relegated to the Second Division. In 1991-92 he was a member of the Middlesbrough side that won promotion to the Premier League after edging Blackburn from the automatic promotion places.

However, when the Rovers clinched their place in the inaugural Premier League via the Play-offs, Kenny Dalglish paid £1.2 million to bring Ripley to Ewood Park. Although used extensively on the right wing by Kenny Dalglish, Stuart Ripley has the ability to operate on the left with equal effectiveness. He has the pace and ability to go past defenders and can deliver quality crosses for the front men to attack. Ripley is also capable of scoring goals with spectacular strikes. During his time at Ewood, Ripley has developed into one of the game's outstanding wingers. He gained his first England cap in November 1993 when Graham Taylor selected him for the final World Cup qualifying match against San Marino.

## RITCHIE, George Thompson
Centre-forward. 1923-1924.
*5ft 8in; 11st.*
*Born: Maryhill, 16 January 1904; Died: Leicester, 10 September 1978.*
*Debut: v Oldham Athletic (a) 7 April 1923.*
*Career: Maryhill FC; Blackburn Rovers February 1923; Falkirk cs 1924; Leicester City September 1928; Colchester United August 1937.*

**Appearances:** Football League 2.

Described by the *Lancashire Daily Post Football Annual* of 1923-24 as 'a young Scot built on the lines of McKay, and also possesses good footwork'. Unfortunately, his first foray into English football was not a success. Hopes that he would inherit the centre-forward position from Percy Dawson proved unfounded and the emergence of Ted Harper merely ensured that he failed to add to the two appearances he made towards the end of the 1922-23 season. He returned to Scotland to join Falkirk in the summer of 1924 but came back to England in September 1928 to sign for Leicester City. By this time he was no longer a centre-forward but a classy left-half and he went on to appear in 247 League games for the Filbert Street club before ending his career with Colchester United.

## ROBERTS, John Thomas
Goalkeeper. 1966-1967.
*5ft 11in; 12st.*
*Born: Cessnock, N.S.W.Australia, 24 March 1944.*
*Debut: v Blackpool (h) 2 May 1966.*
*Career: Apia Leichardt (Australia); Chelsea on trial January 1966; Blackburn Rovers on trial April 1966, signing professional in August 1966; Chesterfield on loan August 1967, signing permanently in February 1968; Bradford City August 1968; Southend United January 1971; Northampton Town July 1972 to June 1973.*
**Appearances:** Football League 3
An Australian international goalkeeper who came to England for a trial with Chelsea in January 1966. However, when Chelsea declined to sign him he contacted the Rovers and came to Ewood Park on trial. At the time of his arrival the club was struggling at the foot of the First Division and Roberts found himself promoted to the first team for the final few games of the season. Although he was injured in his third match for the club, Jack Marshall had been sufficiently impressed to offer Roberts a contract. However, the signing of John Barton from Preston North End during the 1966 close season meant Roberts had to be content with second-team football during the 1966-67 season. He won a Central League championship medal that season but in August 1967 he opted to join Chesterfield, initially on loan before signing permanently in February 1968. Roberts went on to fulfil the potential he had shown when he first arrived at Blackburn and made 150 League appearances for his subsequent clubs.

## ROBERTS, Thomas
Left-back. 1951-1954.
*Born: Liverpool, 28 July 1927.*
*Debut: v Leicester City (a) 12 April 1952.*
*Career: Skelmersdale United; Blackburn Rovers December 1951; Watford December 1954; Chester February 1956.*
**Appearances:** Football League 6.
Tommy Roberts had the unenviable task of understudying Bill Eckersley during his three years at Ewood Park. A steady, hard-working defender, Roberts was only called upon on six occasions before moving to Watford in December 1954. He made only one appearance for the Vicarage Road club before returning north to make five appearances with Chester during the 1955-56 season.

## ROBERTSON, George
Left-back. 1902-1903.
*Born: Glasgow, 1883.*
*Debut: v Nottingham Forest (a) 4 October 1902.*
*Career: Rutherglen Glencairn; Clyde August 1901; Rangers August 1902; Clyde August 1902; Blackburn Rovers September 1902; Clyde 1903; Birmingham December 1910; Bloxwich Strollers May 1914; Brierley Hill Alliance 1921.*
**Appearances:** Football League 10; FA Cup 3; Total 13.
**Goals:** Football League 1.
Another Scottish import to Ewood Park who got his chance when Neil Logan failed to live up to expectations in the left-half position. Unfortunately, Robertson, who was still relatively inexperienced, fared no better than Logan and after a run of nine games he was axed from the senior team. He made just four more appearances before the end of the 1902-03 campaign before returning to Scotland. He returned to England in December 1910 to join Birmingham and was used far more profitably in a forward position.

## ROBERTSON, James
Inside-right. 1905-1908.
*Debut: v Sunderland (a) 28 October 1905.*
*Career: Vale of Leven; Blackburn Rovers May 1905; Brighton & Hove Albion May 1908 to cs 1909; Falkirk 1911 until 1914; Vale of Leven; Dumbarton May 1921.*
**Appearances:** Football League 78; FA Cup 7; Total 85.

**Goals:** Football League 22.

Jimmy Robertson came to Ewood Park at the end of the 1904-05 season and forced his way into the first team during the following campaign. For a season and a half he was the first-choice inside-right although he did make occasional appearances at inside-left, right-half and even centre-half. He lost his place during the 1907-08 season and left for Brighton in May 1908. Robertson scored five goals in 23 Southern League appearances during his only season at the Goldstone Ground.

## ROBINSON, Alfred
Goalkeeper. 1911-1921.
*5ft 9in; 11st 5lb.*
*Born: Manchester.*
*Debut: v Bury (h) 2 September 1911.*
*Career: Chapel-en-le-Frith; Gainsborough Trinity December 1908; Blackburn Rovers May 1911; Leeds City wartime guest 1916-17; Darwen January 1923.*
*Domestic honours with Blackburn Rovers: First Division championship: 1911-12 (30 apps); 1913-14 (28 apps).*
**Appearances:** Football League 144; FA Cup 12; FA Charity Shield 1; Total 157.

One contemporary critic described Robinson as "A clever, daring and active 'keeper, who is not afraid to dive for the ball at an opponent's feet". Despite his youth, Robinson had held down the goalkeeping position at Gainsborough Trinity on a regular basis prior to joining Blackburn. He left Second Division Gainsborough to become the understudy to Ashcroft at Ewood but did so well on a close season tour of Austria and Hungary that he began the 1911-12 season as the club's first-choice custodian.

Apart from periods of injury, Robinson remained the number-one 'keeper at the club throughout the two championship campaigns. The outbreak of war saw Robinson leave Ewood, when at the peak of his powers, to join the Army. He made only 13 wartime appearances for Blackburn and a further six for Leeds City in 1916-17. After the war Robinson returned to Ewood as the senior goalkeeper but was no longer at the peak of his game. Injuries and the arrival of Ronnie Sewell saw Robinson demoted to the second team and he made only one League appearance during the 1920-21 season. With Sewell firmly entrenched in the goalkeeping position Robinson left the club to join Darwen.

## ROBINSON, Patrick
Outside-right. 1920-1921.
*Born: Belfast, 1892.*
*Debut: v Sunderland (h) 11 September 1920.*
*Career: Distillery; Blackburn Rovers September 1920; Caerphilly cs 1921.*
*International honours with Blackburn Rovers: Ireland: 1 cap (1921).*
**Appearances:** Football League 18.
**Goals:** Football League 2.
Although an Irish international, Pat Robinson proved a major disappointment during his brief spell at Ewood Park. Signed to fill the problem outside-right position, Robinson came with a reputation but failed to sustain it during his time with the club and was placed on the transfer list in May 1920. The Rovers required a fee of £1,500 for Robinson but because the player chose to join Caerphilly, who were in the Second Division of the Southern League and not affiliated to the Football League, Blackburn received no fee for the player.

## ROCHDALE FC
Founded in 1900 as Rochdale Town, the club became a limited company in 1910 and changed its name to Rochdale AFC. One of the founder members of the Third Division North in 1921, Rochdale didn't meet Blackburn Rovers in the Football League until the 1971-72 season. However, apart from wartime football, the clubs had first met in competitive football in the inaugural Football League Cup competition in 1961-62. The following season saw Rochdale pull off a major shock by defeating the Rovers, then a First Division club, in the two-legged League Cup semi-final.

## Football League

| | | | Home | | Away | |
|---|---|---|---|---|---|---|
| 1971-72 | | (Div 3) | W | 3-0 | L | 1-2 |
| 1972-73 | | (Div 3) | D | 1-1 | W | 1-0 |
| 1973-74 | | (Div 3) | W | 3-1 | W | 2-1 |

| | P | W | D | L | F | A |
|---|---|---|---|---|---|---|
| Home | 3 | 2 | 1 | 0 | 7 | 2 |
| Away | 3 | 2 | 0 | 1 | 4 | 3 |
| Total | 6 | 4 | 1 | 1 | 11 | 5 |

## Football League Cup

| | | | | | |
|---|---|---|---|---|---|
| 1960-61 | | (3) | Home | W | 2-1 |
| 1961-62 | | (SF) | Away | L | 1-3 |
| | | | Home | W | 2-1 |
| 1972-73 | | (1) | Home | L | 0-1 |
| 1976-77 | | (1) | Away | W | 1-0 |
| | | | Home | W | 4-1 |

## Wartime

| | | | Home | | Away | |
|---|---|---|---|---|---|---|
| 1916-17 | | (LSPT) | L | 6-1 | L | 0-3 |
| 1917-18 | | (LSPT) | L | 1-3 | L | 0-6 |
| 1918-19 | | (LSPT) | W | 4-2 | L | 1-3 |
| 1939-40 | | (NWRL) | W | 4-2 | W | 5-1 |
| 1940-41 | | (NRL) | W | 2-0 | D | 1-1 |
| 1941-42 | | (FLNS-FC) | W | 8-2 | D | 2-2 |
| 1942-43 | | (FLNS-FC) | W | 6-0 | W | 5-1 |
| | | (FLNS-SC) | D | 2-2 | L | 0-4 |
| | | | W | 3-1 | W | 2-1 |
| 1943-44 | | (FLNS-FC) | W | 6-1 | L | 1-2 |
| | | (FLNS-SC) | W | 3-1 | L | 0-4 |
| 1944-45 | | (FLNS-FC) | W | 3-0 | L | 0-2 |
| | | (FLNS-SC) | W | 3-2 | W | 8-0 |
| | | | W | 4-0 | W | 1-0 |

## RODGERS, Norman

Inside-right. 1920-1924.
*5ft 8in; 12st.*
*Born: Harley Hall, 1891; Died: June 1947.*
*Debut: v Bradford (a) 23 February 1920.*
*Career: Stockport County amateur October 1911, turning professional in April 1912; Blackburn Rovers February 1920.*
**Appearances:** Football League 43; FA Cup 5; Total 48.
**Goals:** Football League 21; FA Cup 3; Total 24.
Norman Rodgers made an immediate impact at Ewood Park with 13 goals in 11 appearances at the back-end of the 1919-20 campaign. A fine marksman, Rodgers achieved the hat-trick twice in succession in the final two matches of the season and his goals helped to keep the club in the First Division. Unfortunately, the following season saw him receive a serious leg injury and although he returned, following an operation, Rodgers was never the same player again. Before his injury, Rodgers had shown himself to be a delightful footballer who possessed a fine shot. Although his work was plain and rarely spectacular, Rodgers did enough to suggest he would be a major asset to the club, until injury tragically affected his career.

## ROGERS, Eamon

Midfield. 1962-1971.
*5ft 9in; 11st 5lb.*
*Born: Dublin, 16 April 1947.*
*Debut: v Stoke City (a) 8 September 1965.*
*Career: Larkview (Dublin junior club); Blackburn Rovers apprentice August 1962, turning professional in May 1965; Charlton Athletic October 1971 (£7,777 plus Barry Endean); Northampton Town on loan November 1972.*
*International honours with Blackburn Rovers: Republic of Ireland: 14 caps (1967-71); Republic of Ireland Under-23: 1 cap (1966).*
**Appearances:** Football League 159+6; FA Cup 4; Football League Cup 14; Total 177+6.
**Goals:** Football League 30; Football League Cup 9; Total 39.
A versatile player, Eamon Rogers originally played at outside-left before finally settling into a midfield role. Rogers fitted the 1960s image to perfection; long hair, sometimes seen with beard or moustache and always with the obligatory shirt outside of his shorts. However, beneath his dishevelled appearance was a rare talent. A small but stocky character, Rogers could use skill or strength to power his way through an opposing defence. Capable of dazzling dribbles, he possessed the most delicate of touches and yet was a hard tackler. He also had an eye for goal and for a time he was used as a striker by Eddie Quigley. Ironically, it was his very versatility that proved to be his undoing at Ewood.

With the sale of Keith Newton to Everton, Quigley selected Rogers to play at right-back and the temperamental Irishman promptly refused. Although he was persuaded to play a couple of matches in that position he made it clear that he did not wish to become a permanent right-back. When he refused to play again he was axed from the team by Quigley. Restored to the midfield for the 1970-71 season, Rogers appeared to become rather disillusioned with life at Ewood following the club's relegation to the Third Division.

As a regular in the Republic of Ireland side he did not want to see his international future jeopardised by Third Division football. When Ken Furphy arranged an exchange deal with Charlton Athletic, Rogers was more than willing to move to London. Sadly, the move was not a success and after a brief spell on loan with Northampton Town Rogers faded from the League scene. Despite his undoubted talents, Rogers remained an enigma throughout his career; a man who was capable of genius, but one who was also fickle and unpredictable.

## ROGERS, William

Outside-right. 1938-1947.
*5ft 7in; 11st 5lb.*
*Born: Ulverston, 3 July 1919.*
*Debut: v West Ham United (a) 29 August 1938.*
*Career: Preston North End August 1937; Blackburn Rovers June 1938; Barrow October 1947 to June 1953.*
*Domestic honours with Blackburn Rovers: Second Division championship 1938-39 (41 apps, 18 gls); League War Cup runners-up: 1940.*
**Appearances:** Football League 73; FA Cup 10; Total 83.
**Goals:** Football League 24; FA Cup 3; Total 27.
Billy Rogers was brought to Ewood Park by Bob Crompton in the summer of 1938 and immediately installed in the outside-right position following the opening game of the 1938-39 season. Crompton had recognised that Jack Bruton's career was at an end and the athletic Rogers proved a more than adequate replacement. He scored 18 goals in 41 League appearances as Blackburn lifted the Second Division title. During the war he scored 26 goals in 72 wartime matches and appeared for the club in the 1940 War Cup Final. After the war he returned to first team action at Ewood but failed to find the consistency he had enjoyed in 1938-39. In October 1947 he moved to Barrow and went on to score 14 goals in 197 League appearances for that club.

## ROLLO, David

Right-back. 1919-1927.
*5ft 7in; 11st 6lb.*
*Born: Belfast, 26 August 1891; Died: Blackpool, 17 February 1963.*
*Debut: v Derby County (h) 6 December 1919.*
*Career: Linfield; Blackburn Rovers December 1919 (£2,000); Port Vale August 1927.*
*International honours with Blackburn Rovers: Ireland: 7 caps (1920-22); Northern Ireland: 5 caps (1924-26).*

**Appearances:** Football League 207; FA Cup 18; Total 225.
**Goals:** Football League 5; FA Cup 1; Total 6.
David Rollo had played for a number of junior clubs in Ireland before linking up with Linfield. Although generally a half-back as a youngster, he proved to be an extremely versatile performer and even appeared for his country on the right-wing. However, it was as a right-back that he came to Ewood Park in order to fill the void left by the retirement of Bob Crompton. Although the task was an unenviable one, the club could not have picked a better man to perform it. A speedy defender who was noted for the length of his clearances, Rollo was a classy player blessed with a perfect temperament.

Never flustered, no matter how great the pressure, Rollo simply got on with the job in a quiet, unfussy manner. Despite being asked to play in various positions during his time at Ewood, the quiet Irishman never complained but simply give of his best in every game. Such was his ability that he was still winning international honours at the age of 35. In August 1927 he finally left Ewood Park to end his playing career with a brief spell at Port Vale.

## ROMFORD FC
Originally formed in 1876, Romford first entered the FA Cup in 1878-79. Romford visited the Leamington Street Ground on 19 January 1884 in the fourth round of the FA Cup. Goals from Rostron, Fecitt (2), Douglas, Sowerbutts (2), and two own-goals gave Blackburn a convincing 8-0 win in front of a crowd in the region of 8,000.

## ROSCAMP, John
Half-back/Forward. 1922-1932.
*5ft 8in; 11st.*
*Born: Blaydon, 8 August 1901; Died: Shrewsbury, 16 August 1939.*
*Debut: v West Bromwich Albion (h) 29 September 193.*
*Career: Wallsend; Blackburn Rovers November 1922; Bradford City April 1932; Shrewsbury Town 1934-35.*
*Domestic honours with Blackburn Rovers: FA Cup winners: 1928.*
**Appearances:** Football League 223; FA Cup 26; FA Charity Shield 1; Total 250.
**Goals:** Football League 38; FA Cup 7; Total 45.
The 1928 FA Cup Final provided Jack Roscamp with the opportunity to carve a niche for himself in the history of Blackburn Rovers. Two goals, the first in the opening minute, in the 3-1 win over Huddersfield Town made Roscamp something of an unlikely hero at Ewood Park. That it should be Roscamp who stole the glory at Wembley was something of a surprise as he had always seemed destined to occupy a 'bit' part on the

Ewood stage rather than a leading role. Much of his early career at the club had been spent as a hard-working, but unspectacular half-back. By no means a regular first-team player, Roscamp used his physical strength to compensate for what he lacked in skill.

The departure of Ted Harper brought an unlikely twist to the career of Roscamp. Having failed to find a suitable replacement for Harper the club experimented with Roscamp in the centre-forward position. He made an immediate impact with seven goals in his first five League games and also claimed the goal which gave the club a 1-0 win over Arsenal in the semi-final of the FA Cup. The 1928-29 season saw Roscamp shunted from centre-forward to the right wing. The transition into a winger was not quite so successful and for the next two seasons he drifted between wing-half, outside-right and centre-forward. In many ways his versatility prevented him from being given the opportunity to settle in one position and he gradually faded from the First Division scene. In April 1932 he finally left Ewood Park to continue his career with Bradford City.

## ROSSENDALE FC
Formed in 1877, the club was reformed as Rossendale United in 1898. Rossendale visited Leamington Street on 11 October 1884 for a first round FA Cup-tie and provided Blackburn with their record victory in that competition. Rossendale were totally overrun by a rampant Blackburn team and lost 11-0 in front of a crowd reported to number 500. The Blackburn team that day was as follows:
Arthur; Hopwood, McIntyre, Forrest, Blenkhorn, Lofthouse, Sowerbutts, A.Barton, A.Birtwistle, Brown, Fecitt.
The goals were scored by Barton (3), Sowerbutts (2), Fecitt (4), Birtwistle and Brown.

## ROSTRON, Thurston
Forward. 1885.
*5ft 5in; 10st 4lb.*
*Born: Darwen, 21 April 1862; Died: 3 July 1891.*
*Debut: v Romford (h) 19 January 1885 (FAC).*
*Career: Helmshore FC., Old Wanderers, Darwen FC; Great Lever during season 1883-84; Darwen 1884 and assisted Blackburn Rovers in January and February 1885.*

**Appearances:** FA Cup 1.
**Goals:** FA Cup 1.
A small but tricky forward who assisted the Rovers during the 1884-85 season. A player with plenty of pace, Rostron had been capped for England whilst still a teenager, making his England debut at Alexandra Meadows in February 1881. He made his debut for Blackburn in the FA Cup-tie with Romford in January 1885 and the following month appeared in a friendly at Derby County. Rostron, who gave good service to Darwen during his career, was employed as a weaver before becoming a bowling green keeper.

## ROTHERHAM UNITED FC
Founded in 1884 with the reformation of Thornhill United (a club which could trace its history back to 1878) and became known at Rotherham County in 1905. In 1925 the club amalgamated with Rotherham Town and changed its name to Rotherham United. Blackburn Rovers and Rotherham United met for the first time in the Football League in the 1951-52 season and most of their League encounters have taken place in the Second Division.

### Football League

|         |         |   | Home |   | Away |
|---------|---------|---|------|---|------|
| 1951-52 | (Div 2) | D | 1-1  | L | 0-3  |
| 1952-53 | (Div 2) | L | 0-1  | D | 0-0  |
| 1953-54 | (Div 2) | W | 3-0  | W | 4-1  |
| 1954-55 | (Div 2) | W | 4-1  | L | 1-5  |
| 1955-56 | (Div 2) | W | 3-1  | L | 2-3  |
| 1956-57 | (Div 2) | W | 3-2  | W | 2-0  |
| 1957-58 | (Div 2) | W | 5-0  | W | 2-1  |
| 1966-67 | (Div 2) | D | 1-1  | L | 1-2  |
| 1967-68 | (Div 2) | W | 3-1  | L | 0-1  |
| 1971-72 | (Div 3) | W | 2-1  | L | 1-2  |
| 1972-73 | (Div 3) | W | 2-1  | D | 1-1  |
| 1979-80 | (Div 3) | L | 0-3  | W | 3-1  |
| 1981-82 | (Div 2) | W | 2-0  | L | 1-4  |
| 1982-83 | (Div 2) | W | 3-0  | L | 1-3  |

|       | P  | W  | D | L  | F  | A  |
|-------|----|----|---|----|----|----|
| Home  | 14 | 10 | 2 | 2  | 32 | 13 |
| Away  | 14 | 4  | 2 | 8  | 19 | 27 |
| Total | 28 | 14 | 4 | 10 | 51 | 40 |

### FA Cup

| 1957-58 | (3) | Away | W | 4-1 |
|---------|-----|------|---|-----|

## ROUND, Paul
Forward/Defender. 1974-1981.
*6ft; 11st.*
*Born: Blackburn, 22 June 1959.*
*Debut: v Millwall (h) 26 March 1977.*
*Career: Blackburn Rovers associated schoolboy November 1974, becoming an apprentice in July 1975, turning professional in August 1977. Released April 1981; Bury; Altrincham; Barrow; Chorley; Rossendale United; Clitheroe.*
**Appearances:** Football League 41+10; FA Cup 4; Football League Cup 5; Total 50+10.
**Goals:** Football League 5.
Paul Round, a powerfully built local youngster, began his Ewood career as a centre-forward before being converted into a centre-half and finally a right-back. A player of great potential, Round was given a number of opportunities to establish himself in each of the three positions. Unfortunately, he failed to make the most of his chances and eventually the club turned to the transfer market to fill the vacancies. After leaving Ewood, Round became active in non-League football.

## ROVERS' COTTAGE
The 'Rovers' Cottage' was in fact the main prize in a club sweep in 1886. Thousands of tickets, which cost 6d, were sold for the draw and each ticket contained a picture of the cottage. The cottage, which was valued at £140 was described as follows: 'The cottage is newly built, palisaded in front, and situate on New Bank Road, near the Rovers' Football Ground, Blackburn. The land is freehold (subject to a yearly ground rent of One Pound Fifteen Shillings), and will entitle the winner to a county vote.' One ticket had six purchasers, although one of the men who shared the ticket was reluctant to participate. However, the six decided to raffle the ticket amongst themselves and the reluctant participant found himself the owner of the ticket. He attended the draw on Wednesday, 17 March 1886 and discovered he had the winning ticket.

**ROXBURGH, Robert**
Full-back. 1924-1931.
*5ft 9in; 11st 10lb.*
*Born; Morpeth, 5 February 1896; Died: Leeds, 1974 (October quarter).*
*Debut: v Burnley (a) 13 September 1924.*
*Career: Morpeth Comrades; Newcastle United November 1920; Blackburn Rovers May 1924 (£375) to 1931. On retirement coached in Holland. Leeds United assistant trainer 1955 until June 1960.*
**Appearances:** Football League 114; FA Cup 13; FA Charity Shield 1; Total 128.
The *Lancashire Daily Post Football Annual* for 1925-26 summed Roxburgh up in the following way: 'Though quick, and a strong neat kicker, he tends to limit his game by over attention to safety first tactics.' Roxburgh had been brought to Ewood Park to provide cover for David Rollo in the right-back position but at the start of the 1925-26 season he found himself as first-choice left-back. However, the arrival of 'Taffy' Jones in December 1925 saw Roxburgh revert to his back-up role until he captured the right-back spot from Rollo at the start of the following season.

Although he made 26 League appearances during the 1926-27 season he was unable to retain the right-back spot following the acquisition of Jock Hutton from Aberdeen. Once again he returned to Central League football and it was not until the 1928-29 season that he finally became a regular member of the first team. The first half of the campaign found him at right-back in place of Hutton whilst in the second half he switched to left-back to replace Jones. It proved to be his most successful season at the club with 38 senior League appearances and six in the FA Cup. Although he began the 1929-30 campaign at right-back, Roxburgh was unable to retain is place and at the end of the 1930-31 season he retired from League football.

**RUSHTON, Walter**
Forward. 1885-1889.
*Debut: v Blackburn Olympic (h) 5 November 1887 (FAC).*
**Appearances:** FA Cup 4.
**Goals:** FA Cup 1.
Little is known about this utility forward who first appeared for the club during the 1885-86 season. His first appearance for the senior team appears to have been in the Potteries in the friendly at Burslem Port Vale on 2 November 1885. However, he didn't become a regular in the first team until the final season of friendly fixtures in 1887-88. It was during this season that he made his first appearance in the FA Cup competition for the club. It should be noted that Rushton has been credited with one League appearance in some sources, but local newspapers do not support this claim.

**RUSSELL, Alexander**
Midfield. 1970-1971.
*5ft 8in; 11st.*
*Born: Seaham, South Shields, 21 February 1944.*
*Debut: v Watford (a) 15 August 1970.*
*Career: Everton December 1961; Southport November 1963; Blackburn Rovers August 1970; Tranmere Rovers July 1971; Crewe Alexandra on loan October 1972; Southport November 1972 to cs 1975; Los Angeles Aztecs 1975; Formby.*
**Appearances:** Football League 22+2; FA Cup 1; Football League Cup 1; Total 24+2.
**Goals:** Football League 4.
When Eddie Quigley surprising moved to bring Alex Russell to Ewood Park in August 1970, he described the former Southport man as 'an Albert Nightingale type of player'. Nightingale had been a teammate of Quigley's at Ewood in the early 1950's and Russell, a grafting type of midfield man, was given a similar role by Quigley during the 1970-71 season. Although he had begun his footballing career at Goodison Park, Russell moved to Southport without making a senior appearance for Everton. At Southport, Russell scored 63 goals in 263 League appearances (including one as sub) before making the move to Ewood Park. Russell made little impression at Ewood in a team which was ultimately relegated to the Third Division for the first time in its history. After only one season at the club he moved to Tranmere Rovers and enjoyed a brief spell on loan with Crewe before returning to Haig Avenue in November 1972.

**RUSSELL, John**
Outside-left. 1901-1902.
*5ft 5in.*
*Born: Carstairs, Lanarkshire, 29 December 1872; Died: Glasgow, August 1905.*
*Debut: v Liverpool (h) 26 April 1902.*
*Career: Glasgow Thistle; Leith Athletic; St Mirren cs 1895; Woolwich Arsenal June 1896; Bristol City cs 1897; Blackburn Rovers March 1902.*

**Appearances:** Football League 1.
Jock Russell was a tricky type of winger who came to Blackburn after scoring 30 goals in 92 Southern and Football League games with Bristol City. Russell had gained an excellent reputation as a direct winger who was capable of scoring goals as well as creating them. However he joined Blackburn at a time when his career was in decline and as a result made just one senior appearance at Ewood Park. His debut came in the final match of the 1901-02 season but he was not retained by the club for the following campaign.

**RUTHERFORD, Septimus**
Outside-left. 1936-1937.
*5ft 10in; 11st 7lb.*
*Born: Percy Main, 29 November 1907.*
*Debut: v Bury (a) 29 August 1936.*
*Career: Blyth Spartans; Portsmouth September 1927; Blackburn Rovers June 1936.*
**Appearances:** Football League 13; FA Cup 1; Total 14.
**Goals:** Football League 1.
The youngest brother of Jock Rutherford, a former Arsenal, Newcastle United and England winger, Sep was a schoolboy international who began his footballing career with Blyth Spartans. He eventually moved to Portsmouth in September 1927 and spent some time as understudy to Freddy Cook, a well established Welsh international. For four seasons Rutherford, a cultured winger with an eye for goal, made the outside-left position his own at Pompey and scored 30 goals in 108 League appearances. His reign at Ewood proved to be a short one as first Frank Baxendale and then Billy Guest took his left-wing spot.

**SALE, Thomas**
Centre-forward. 1936-1938.
*Born: Stoke-on-Trent, 30 April 1910; Died: Stafford, 10 November 1990.*
*Debut: v Everton (a) 14 March 1936.*
*Career: Stoke St Peters; Stoke City amateur August 1929, turning professional in May 1930; Blackburn Rovers March 1936 (£6,000); Stoke City March 1938 (£3,000); Northwich Victoria 1947; Hednesford Town.*
**Appearances:** Football League 65; FA Cup 3; Total 68.
**Goals:** Football League 25; FA Cup 1; Total 26.
An ex-pottery worker who began his professional career with his local club. Sale was originally an inside-left, who had also played as a half-back, until it was realised that his bustling style of play was more suited to the centre-forward position. Sale's move to Ewood Park in March 1936 was the culmination of a protracted search for a proven goalscorer. His eight appearances, seven of which were at inside-left, at the end of the 1935-36 season produced four goals and the following campaign brought 14 goals in 37 League appearances. However, his form during the 1937-38 season began to waver and in March 1938 he was allowed to return to Stoke City.

**SALMON, Michael Bernard**
Goalkeeper. 1978-1983.
*6ft 2in; 13st.*
*Born: Leyland, 14 June 1964.*
*Debut: v Chelsea (h) 15 May 1982.*
*Career: Blackburn Rovers associated schoolboy November 1978, becoming a non-contract player in March 1981, before turning professional in October 1981; Leeds United on loan August to September 1982; Chester City on loan October 1982 to January 1983; Stockport County August 1983; Bolton Wanderers July 1987; Wrexham March 1987 (£18,000); Charlton Athletic July 1989 (£100,000).*
**Appearances:** Football League 1.
Micky Salmon was just 17 at the time of his senior debut for Blackburn Rovers. He was selected by Bob Saxton for the final match of the 1981-82 season when Chelsea visited Ewood Park and left with a 1-1 draw. During his time at Ewood he had loan spells with Leeds United and Chester City but found himself behind Terry Gennoe and Vince O'Keefe in the pecking order at Blackburn. In August 1983 he moved to Stockport County on a free transfer and went on to appear in 118 League matches before joining Bolton Wanderers on a free transfer. Salmon only appeared in 26 League games for the Burden Park club before signing for Wrexham in March 1987. It was at the Racecourse Ground that his career began to blossom and after 100 League games for the Welsh club he was signed by Charlton Athletic in a six-figure deal. Salmon had to fight to become first-choice 'keeper with Charlton but on 8 February 1994 he enjoyed a triumphant return to Ewood Park when he helped Charlton pull off a shock 1-0 win over the Rovers in a fourth-round FA Cup replay.

**SANDERSON, George A.**
Forward. 1891-1893.
*Debut: v Accrington (a) 27 January 1892.*

*Career: Blackburn Rovers November 1891 until cs 1893.*
**Appearances:** Football League 4.
Sanderson spent the majority of his time with Blackburn Rovers playing second-team football. A utility forward, Sanderson appeared in three different forward positions in his four League appearances but was unable to win a regular place in the senior team.

## SANDHAM, William

Forward. 1920-1922.
*5ft 9¾in; 11st.*
*Born: Fleetwood.*
*Debut: v Burnley (a) 15 January 1921.*
*Career: Fleetwood; Blackburn Rovers December 1920; Rochdale June 1922; Fleetwood cs 1923.*
**Appearances:** Football League 4.
**Goals:** Football League 1.
Although Sandham scored a goal on his debut in the local derby with Burnley, he failed to finish on a winning side in each of his four senior outings. Although he possessed a rocket-like shot, he lacked the experience that the club urgently required in the immediate post-war period. He was restricted to Central League football throughout the 1921-22 season before moving to Rochdale in June 1922. Although he was joint top goalscorer at Rochdale in 1922-23 with seven League goals, Sandham was released at the end of that season and resumed his career with Fleetwood.

## SAWERS, William

Forward. 1892-1893.
*Born: Bridgeton, Glasgow, 13 June 1871; Died: Glasgow, 24 October 1927.*
*Debut: v Wolverhampton Wanderers (a) 10 September 1892.*
*Career: Clyde September 1888; Blackburn Rovers August 1892; Stoke cs 1893; Dundee June 1894; Stoke August 1895; Dundee September 1895; Kilmarnock February 1896; Abercorn 1896; Clyde cs 1896.*
**Appearances:** Football League 24; FA Cup 4; Total 28.
**Goals:** Football League 11; FA Cup 3; Total 14.
Bill Sawers was one of several Scottish players who crossed the border to join Blackburn Rovers in the early 1890s. A physical type of player, his strength on the ball made him a difficult man to dispossess whilst his powerful shooting brought 14 League and Cup goals. Although he had the distinction of being the club's leading goalscorer during the 1892-93 season, Sawers was not retained for the following campaign and moved to Stoke.

## SAXTON, Robert

Manager. 1981-1986.
*Born: Bagby, Doncaster, 6 September 1943.*
*Career: Denaby United; Derby County February 1962; Plymouth Argyle February 1968 (£12,000); Exeter City September 1975, then player-manager January 1977 to January 1979; Plymouth Argyle manager January 1979 to May 1981; Blackburn Rovers manager May 1981 to December 1986; Preston North End advisor January 1987; York City manager June 1987 to September 1988; Blackpool assistant manager September 1988; Newcastle United assistant manager 1989, then caretaker manager March to April 1991; Manchester City chief scout October 1991.*
In selecting Bob Saxton to follow Howard Kendall into the manager's office at Ewood Park in May 1981, the directors reverted to their old formula of appointing a man with a proven track record in the lower divisions. In many ways Saxton was a complete opposite of Kendall.

Whilst Kendall had enjoyed a playing career at the highest level, Sexton had amassed over 400 League appearances in the more humble surroundings of Derby, Plymouth and Exeter. He had entered management at Exeter and had led that club into the Third Division before returning to Plymouth to occupy the manager's chair.

Although Saxton arrived at Ewood with his own entourage from Plymouth in the shape of Jim Furnell, Tony Long and Harold Jarman, he none the less appointed long serving Tony Parkes as his coach. He strengthened the playing staff by signing Terry Gennoe from Southampton or £60,000 and paying a similar amount to Swindon Town for Ian Miller. Both men went on to give outstanding service to the club and proved excellent value for money. Having made his initial forays into the transfer market, Saxton found that financial resources became increasing limited. Howard Kendall was always going to be a hard act to follow but without the necessary resources to strengthen the squad, Saxton was faced with a near impossible task. Thus, in the immediate aftermath of Kendall's departure, the best Saxton could hope for was a period of consolidation.

In many ways the excellent job he did in consolidating the club's position in the Second Division worked against him. Always seemingly ill at ease with the media, Saxton never managed to achieve the same rapport with the supporters as Kendall. However, he inspired tremendous loyalty amongst his players and, in turn, he was extremely loyal – some would say too loyal – to them. After three years of steady progress the club found itself heading the Second Division during the 1984-85 season. With the newly signed Jimmy Quinn offering Saxton variety in attack, albeit from the substitute's bench for the first few months, the Rovers headed the table at Christmas.

Having raised the hopes of the supporters the team inexplicably began to fall away. As the slide continued, Saxton antagonised supporters by refusing to move into the transfer market. He insisted that the men who had taken the club to the top should be given the opportunity to complete the job. Sadly, they proved unequal to the task and the failure to win promotion from such a strong position sowed the seeds of unrest on the terraces.

The following campaign was one of complete anticlimax with the club only avoiding relegation in the last match of the season. The 1986-87 season brought a similar story and at Christmas the club was firmly entrenched at the foot of the table. In a bid to change the club's fortunes Saxton sold Jimmy Quinn to Swindon Town and gambled by replacing him with Paul McKinnon, a striker from non-League Sutton United. The gamble proved a disaster and as unrest on the terraces grew, the players tried to deflect criticism from their manager by accepting total responsibility for the club's plight.

The manager had always enjoyed the support of chairman Bill Fox in the boardroom but by Christmas the pressure on Saxton had grown to unbearable proportions. In the middle of the Christmas holiday period the directors finally parted company with the beleaguered manager. Saxton didn't remain out of work for long and accepted an invitation from John McGrath to assist with the coaching at Preston North End. The summer of 1987 saw him appointed manager of York City but on his arrival at the club he found himself without sufficient players to form a team. His hastily assembled side struggled in the Third Division and were relegated at the end of the season.

He declined an offer to join Blackpool as assistant manager in order to help York regain their Third Division status. Having already taken Jim Branagan to York from Preston he appointed Derek Fazackerley as his player-coach. Sadly, he was unable to lift the fortunes of the club and with York anchored at the foot of the table he decided that it would be in everybody's best interests if he left. After leaving York, Saxton returned to Lancashire to take up the position he had earlier declined at Blackpool. However, he remained at Bloomfield Road only a short time before moving to the North-East to become assistant manager to Jim Smith at Newcastle United. He later became caretaker manager at Newcastle following the dismissal of Smith but lost his job at the club when Ossie Ardíles arrived in April 1991. On leaving Newcastle he accepted the position of chief scout at Manchester City.

## SCOTT, William

Manager. 1947.
*Born: Willington Quay, Northumberland, 1893.*
*Career: South Shields amateur 1910s, assistant trainer, masseur and player from 1920 when he turned professional; Crystal Palace wartime guest; Preston North End trainer January 1923, then secretary March 1941 to April 1947; Blackburn Rovers manager April to December 1947; Preston North End manager June 1949 to March 1953; Sunderland assistant manager in 1960.*
Will Scott's was probably the most unfortunate reign of any Ewood manager. He arrived at the club at the end of April 1947 but in December of the same year he had to resign his post on health grounds. Scott's career had begun when he joined South Shields as an amateur but in 1914 thoughts of a future in football were forgotten when he enlisted in the Navy.

He played wartime football with Crystal Palace and was offered professional terms by that club. However, Scott declined the offer and returned to his native Northumberland to link up with South Shields. Whilst still only 26 he took on the duties of assistant trainer at the club and worked closely with manager Jim Lawrence. When Lawrence left the North-East to become manager of Preston North End in 1923, Scott elected to move with him. He remained at Deepdale until his appointment to the manager's position at Ewood Park. During his time at Deepdale, Scott was often given responsibility for team affairs.

The 1947-48 season was only three games old when it was announced that Scott had succumbed to illness. Ordered to take a complete rest, he spent a few weeks away in South Shields whilst Jack Bruton looked after playing affairs at Ewood. Although Scott returned within a matter of weeks it was clear that he was far from well. Like Hapgood, Scott tried to find a winning blend at Ewood by giving some of the younger players a chance to establish themselves in the first team. However, consistency, in terms of both results and performances, continued to elude Scott and the strain began to take its toll on the manager.

On 9 December, 1947, after two heavy defeats at the hands of

Middlesbrough and Sheffield United, Scott tendered his resignation. On accepting his resignation the board invited him to continue to serve the club in a scouting capacity. Having made a complete recovery, Scott returned to the pressure of football management when he accepted the manager's position at Preston North End in June 1949.

In December of that year Scott broke the British transfer record when he signed Eddie Quigley, a future Blackburn player and manager, from Sheffield Wednesday. The 1950-51 season saw Preston win the Second Division title in a campaign that had seen them achieve 14 consecutive victories. He left Deepdale in March 1953 but returned to management in 1960 as assistant to Allan Brown at Sunderland.

## SCOTTISH OPPOSITION

Today, meetings between Blackburn Rovers and Scottish clubs are restricted to pre-season friendlies. However, in the days before the formation of the Football League, Scottish clubs provided attractive opposition for teams like Blackburn Rovers. Furthermore, not only did the Rovers clash with clubs from north of the border in friendlies, but the FA Cup also witnessed a number of meetings between English and Scottish clubs. The first meetings between Blackburn Rovers and a Scottish club to take place at Alexandra Meadows occurred on 2 January 1878 when Partick Thistle were the visitors. The Rovers won 2-1 in front of a gate which was reported to be in the region of 500. However, subsequent visits by Scottish clubs produced some of the club's highest attendances, in pre-League days.

The most memorable clashes between Blackburn Rovers and Scottish clubs took place in the FA Cup competition. Twice, in successive seasons, Queen's Park provided the opposition for the Rovers in the FA Cup Final. Blackburn proved victorious on both occasions and became involved in a sequence of 24 unbeaten FA Cup ties. The sequence came to an end on 27 November 1887, when Scottish club Renton won 2-0 at Blackburn in a second-round replay. In more recent times, the Anglo-Scottish Cup competition of the 1970s saw both Motherwell and Hibernian eliminate the Rovers at the quarter-final stage of the competition.

## SCUNTHORPE UNITED FC

Founded in 1904, Scunthorpe amalgamated with Lindsey United in 1910 to form Scunthorpe and Lindsey United. The club was elected to the Football League in 1950 and dropped the name 'Lindsey' from their title in 1951. Blackburn and Scunthorpe have only crossed swords during the 1972-73 season when both were in the Third Division.

**Football League**

| 1972-73 | | | Home | | Away | |
|---------|---|------|------|---|------|---|
| | | (Div 3) | W | 3-0 | D | 1-1 |

| | P | D | D | L | F | A |
|-------|---|---|---|---|---|---|
| Home | 1 | 1 | 0 | 0 | 3 | 0 |
| Away | 1 | 0 | 1 | 0 | 1 | 1 |
| Total | 2 | 1 | 1 | 0 | 4 | 1 |

## SELLARS, Scott

Midfield. 1986-1992.
*5ft 8in; 10st.*
*Born: Sheffield, 27 November 1965.*
*Debut: v Leeds United (h) 23 August 1986.*
*Career: Leeds United associated schoolboy December 1981, becoming an apprentice in July 1982 and turning professional in July 1983; Blackburn Rovers July 1986 (£25,000); Leeds United July 1992 (£800,000); Newcastle United March 1993 (£700,000).*
*International honours with Blackburn Rovers: England Under-23; 3 caps (1988).*
*Domestic honours with Blackburn Rovers: Full Members' Cup winners: 1987; Second Division Play-off winners: 1992.*
**Appearances:** Football League 194+8; Play-offs 11; FA Cup 11; Football League Cup 12; Full Members' Cup 9; Total 237+8.
**Goals:** Football League 35; Play-offs 2; FA Cup 1; Football League Cup 3; Total 41.
A skilful left-sided midfield player who

proved a bargain buy for Bob Saxton during the summer of 1986. Sellars had graduated through the junior ranks at Elland Road before losing favour during the 1985-86 season. Although he began in a more central midfield position at Ewood Park he ended the 1986-87 campaign on the left wing and helped the club to win the Full Members' Cup at Wembley. During the next three seasons he established himself as one of the most exciting wide midfield players outside of the First Division. Sellars, who liked nothing better than to run at defenders, possessed a powerful shot and was a constant threat at set pieces. Plagued by injuries during the 1990-91 season, Sellars was to play a vital role in the 1991-92 promotion campaign. Having helped the club to climb into the Premier League, Sellars was allowed to return to Elland Road for a large fee. It proved to be an unhappy move and after only seven Premier League games (including one as sub) with Leeds he dropped into the First Division to join Newcastle United. However, he made a quick return to top flight football when Newcastle lifted the First Division championship shortly after his arrival.

## SEWELL, Walter Ronald

Goalkeeper. 1920-1927.
*5ft 10in; 12st 4lb.*
*Born: Middlesbrough, 19 July 1890; Died: Lincoln, 4 February 1945.*
*Debut: v Liverpool (a) 14 February 1920.*
*Career: Wingate Albion; Gainsborough Trinity May 1911; Burnley February 1913; Blackburn Rovers February 1920; Gainsborough Trinity September 1927.*
*International honours with Blackburn Rovers: England: 1 cap (1924).*
**Appearances:** Football League 227; FA Cup 21; Total 248.
Sewell began his career with Wingate Albion and Gainsborough Trinity

before joining Burnley as understudy to Jerry Dawson, the England goalkeeper. With first-team opportunities fairly restricted at Turf Moor, Sewell opted to join Blackburn Rovers in February 1920. Tall and reliable, Sewell helped stabilise an indifferent defence and only missed two matches during the next two seasons. However, the 1922-23 campaign found him dislodged from the first team by Ted Davis and only an injury to the younger man allowed Sewell back into the senior team. Once he had reclaimed first-team place, Sewell was determined not to lose it again and the 1923-24 season found him in commanding form. A true perfectionist, Sewell remained completely unflappable under pressure and his temperament allowed him to ignore errors, no matter how costly. It was this unshakable belief in his own ability that allowed Sewell to fight off the challenge of younger men. A good humoured man, Sewell was a popular figure at the club and a man who could always be relied upon to lift dressing room morale. Sewell's career at Ewood Park came to an end in September 1926 when he broke a leg and retired from the game at the end of the 1926-27 season after an abortive bid to make a comeback.

## SHANAHAN, Terence C.

Outside-left. 1971.
*5ft 10in; 10st 8lb.*
*Born: Paddington, 5 December 1951.*
*Debut: v Swansea City (h) 25 September 1971.*
*Career: Tottenham Hotspur apprentice August 1967 to June 1969; Ipswich Town July 1969; Blackburn Rovers on loan September to October 1971; Halifax Town November 1971; Chesterfield October 1974; Millwall April 1976; Bournemouth July 1977; Aldershot July 1978.*
**Appearances:** Football League 6.
**Goals:** Football League 2.
Although Terry Shanahan was groomed at White Hart Lane and quickly snapped up by Ipswich Town he was, none the less, to spend almost his entire career in the lower divisions. He came to Ewood Park on loan at a time when Ken Furphy was frantically trying to rebuild a side that was in danger of slipping through the Third Division. Shanahan scored two goals in his six League games for the club but was allowed to return to Ipswich on the day that Furphy signed Tony Field from Southport.

## SHARP, Alexander
Inside-left. 1934-1935.
*5ft 7in; 10st 10lb.*
*Born: Dundee.*
*Debut: v Huddersfield Town (h) 1 December 1934.*
*Career: Dundee Violet; East Fife August 1932; Blackburn Rovers November 1934 (£1,000); Hull City October 1935; Raith Rovers cs 1936; Falkirk 1936-37; Raith Rovers cs 1938.*
**Appearances:** Football League 9.
**Goals:** Football League 1.
Although he gained junior fame as an inside-forward, being named as 12th man for a Scottish junior international against Wales, his effective tackling led East Fife to use him as a half-back. He was to spend the best part of two seasons at right-half before returning to the forward line. However, on returning to the front line, his tricky footwork and accurate shooting made him one of the most sought after men in Scottish football. He came to Ewood Park in November 1934 and was immediately given a taste of First Division football. Not surprisingly, Sharp was somewhat overawed at the level of company he found himself in and had to spend a period of grooming in the Central League. He returned for a run of six League games towards the end of the 1934-35 season and made a favourable impression with his typically Scottish style of scheming. Early in the 1935-36 season the club, having a number of young players on the books, agreed to allow Sharp to join Hull City. During his time at Hull he scored five goals in 61 League appearances.

## SHARPLES, George Frank Vincent
Half-back. 1965-1971.
*5ft 11in; 12st 11lb.*
*Born: Ellesmere Port, 20 September 1943.*
*Debut: v West Ham United (h) 20 March 1965.*
*Career: Everton groundstaff June 1959, turning professional in September 1960; Blackburn Rovers March 1965 (£7,000); Southport July 1971 to June 1972.*
**Appearances:** Football League 99+4; FA Cup 5; Football League Cup 4+1; Total 108+5.
**Goals:** Football League 5.

George Sharples was a schoolboy international before joining the Everton groundstaff in June 1959. He was to later win a youth cap whilst with Everton but found his first-team opportunities restricted at Goodison Park. After ten League appearances with Everton he moved to Ewood Park in March 1965 as a possible replacement for Mick McGrath. Sharples began the ill-fated 1965-66 season as first-choice left-half but lost his place as the club continued to struggle at the foot of the First Division. Sharples began the 1966-67 season out of the first team and rather unsettled with life at Ewood Park.

However, he was eventually given the opportunity to form a central defensive partnership with Ronnie Clayton. The chance came about when Dick Mulvaney perforated an ear drum and both Dave Holt and Ben Anderson failed to fulfil his role with any degree of success. The pairing of Clayton and Sharples had been a fairly successful one but Eddie Quigley was of the opinion that they were a little suspect in the air. As a result he bought John Coddington from Huddersfield Town in the summer of 1967 and Sharples again found himself playing Central League football. However, with Clayton coming to the end of his illustrious career Sharples was given another opportunity to establish himself in the first team.

Sadly, a broken leg at the Baseball Ground, Derby on 1 March 1969 finally brought his Ewood career to an end. Sharples remained at Ewood until the summer of 1971 but never again appeared in the first team. In July 1971 he made the short move to Southport and went on to appear in 25 League games (including two as sub) for the Haig Avenue club during the 1971-72 season.

## SHARPLES, Harold
Half-back. 1880-1883.
*Debut: v Bolton Wanderers (h) 19 November 1881 (FAC).*
*Career: Blackburn Rovers 1880.*
*Domestic honours with Blackburn Rovers: FA Cup runners-up: 1882.*
**Appearances:** FA Cup 4.
**Goals:** FA Cup 1.
A player who made little impact at the club apart from his appearances in

the 1881-82 FA Cup run. His first senior outing appears to have been in the home game with Wednesday Strollers in November 1880. The team enjoyed a comfortable 10-1 win in this friendly fixture with Jimmy Douglas, Jack Hargreaves and Jimmy Brown all scoring hat-tricks. Sharples began to appear with increasing regularity during the second half of the 1880-81 season as an understudy to players like Douglas, Fred Hargreaves and Hugh McIntyre. He appeared in the second-round FA Cup-tie with Bolton Wanderers in November 1881 and scored one of the goals which gave the Rovers a 6-2 victory. However, he played no further part in the Cup run until he was selected for the semi-final following an injury to Doc Greenwood. He retained his place in the team and was a member of the first side to represent Blackburn Rovers in an FA Cup Final. However, Sharples lost his place in the team when Greenwood recovered from injury. The only other first-team appearances that Sharples made were in the early part of the 1882-83 season.

## SHAW, Gilbert R.
Inside-left. 1925-1928.
*5ft 8in; 10st 8lb.*
*Debut: v Derby County (a) 20 November 1926.*
*Career: Brierley Hill Alliance; Blackburn Rovers October 1925; Grimsby Town August 1928.*
**Appearances:** Football League 5.
**Goals:** Football League 2.
Although Gilly Shaw celebrated his debut with a goal in a pulsating 5-4 victory over Derby County, the confident young Welshman was unable to claim a regular place in the senior team. Shaw had displayed great promise in the Central League but at the time the club had a wealth of forward talent, including Puddefoot, Harper, McKay, Rigby and Mitchell. Not surprisingly, Shaw was unable to make much progress as regards first-team football at Ewood. He left the club in August 1928 to seek first-team football at Grimsby but failed to make a League appearance with the Mariners.

## SHEA, Daniel
Inside-right. 1913-1920.
*5ft 6in; 11st.*
*Born: Wapping, 6 November 1887; Died: 25 December 1960.*
*Debut: v Notts County (a) 25 January 1913.*
*Career: Pearl United; Manor Park Albion; West Ham United November 1907; Blackburn Rovers January 1913 (£2,000); West Ham United wartime guest; Nottingham Forest wartime guest; West Ham United May 1920 (£1,000); Fulham November 1920; Coventry City cs 1923; Clapton Orient March 1925; Sheppey United October 1926.*

*International honours with Blackburn Rovers: England: 2 caps (1914): England Victory Internationals: 2 appearances (1919): Football League: 2 appearances (1913-14).*
*Domestic honours with Blackburn Rovers: Football League championship: 1913-14 (36 apps, 28 gls).*
**Appearances:** Football League 97; FA Cup 8; Total 105.
**Goals:** Football League 62; FA Cup 3; Total 65.
Despite the intervention of World War One Danny Shea, with 62 goals from 97 League games, proved one of the finest talents to grace Ewood Park. Shea, who came to Ewood from West Ham United, was one of the great

players of his era and one who cost a record fee to bring him to Blackburn Rovers. Regarded as the classic inside-forward, Shea's 28 goals went a long way to bringing the League championship to Ewood Park in 1913-14. An early indication of his goalscoring power had been seen in 1909-10 and 1910-11 seasons when on each occasion he finished as the leading goalscorer in the Southern League.

Unfortunately, the outbreak of war severely disrupted his career and although he returned to Ewood Park in 1919 he was clearly no longer the player he had been. Although he was no longer at the peak of his game he was still a very fine inside-forward and one who was still in demand. The Rovers allowed him to return to London in May 1920 for half the fee that they had paid to bring him to Ewood. At 33, Shea struggled to find a place in the West Ham team and in December 1920 he moved to Fulham. Incredibly, Shea continued to defy those who had written him off and appeared in a further 100 League games with Fulham before joining Coventry City in 1923. Shea ended his career with Clapton Orient before moving into non-League football with Sheppey United. Shea worked in the docks in London's East End before his death at the age of 73 on Christmas Day 1960.

## SHEARER, Alan

Centre-forward. 1992-
*5ft 11in; 11st 3lb.*
*Born: Newcastle, 13 August 1970.*
*Debut: v Crystal Palace (a) 15 August 1992.*
*Career: Southampton associated schoolboy September 1984, becoming a*

*trainee in July 1986 and signing professional in April 1988; Blackburn Rovers July 1992 (£3,300,000).*
*International honours with Blackburn Rovers: England: 7 caps (1992-94).*
**Appearances:** Premier League 55+6; FA Cup 4; Football League Cup 9; Total 68+6.
**Goals:** Premier League 47; FA Cup 2; Football League Cup 7; Total 56.
Although born in Newcastle, Alan Shearer came to prominence on the south coast with Southampton. He joined the club as a schoolboy and graduated through the ranks to make his first-team debut as a substitute against Chelsea on 26 March 1988. He made his first full appearance on 9 April 1988 against Arsenal and rewrote the record books when he netted a hat-trick in a 4-2 win to become the youngest player to score three times in a First Division match. Whilst not the most prolific of goalscorers during his time at the Dell – 23 goals in 118 League matches (including 13 as sub) – Shearer developed into one of the game's outstanding young prospects. If his goalscoring record at The Dell was indifferent his international record was little short of sensational. Eleven England Under-21 appearances whilst with Southampton produced 13 goals and won him promotion to the senior England squad.

He won his first full cap against France in February 1992 and after a disappointing European Championship campaign the following summer, Shearer joined Blackburn Rovers for a British record transfer fee. Shearer made his debut at Crystal Palace on the opening day of the 1992-93 season and scored two sensational long-range goals. Although capable of sniffing out chances at close range, a high proportion of Shearer's goals were of the more spectacular variety. By Boxing Day 1992, Shearer had scored 22 goals in 25 League and Cup games and seemed set to rewrite the goalscoring records at Ewood Park. However, the match with Leeds United at Ewood on Boxing Day resulted in Shearer receiving a serious knee injury. At first it was thought to be a cartilage problem but after an abortive comeback he was diagnosed as having a cruciate ligament injury. Shearer underwent surgery and was out of action for the rest of the season.

Although he appeared, and scored, in a pre-season match in Ireland, Kenny Dalglish insisted on giving Shearer sufficient time to regain his fitness before bringing him back into the team. After sitting out the opening day's fixture at Chelsea, Shearer was given a place on the sub's bench for the next seven League games. He rescued a point at Newcastle when he got off the bench to score an equalising goal and once restored to the centre-forward position he continued his remarkable goalscoring feats. Restored to the England team, Shearer once again looked the complete centre-forward and reached 50 goals for Blackburn Rovers in only 53 full appearances plus another six outings as a substitute. Brave and strong, Shearer has all the attributes required for a striker. Good in the air, he has the ability to shield the ball and is a difficult man to dispossess once bearing down on goal. At Ewood Park Shearer has blossomed into the finest striker in the country and one of the leading marksmen in Europe. The end of the 1993-94 season saw him named as the 'Footballer of the Year'.

## SHEARER, Duncan Nichol

Forward. 1992.
*5ft 10in; 10st 9lb.*

*Born: Fort William, 28 August 1962.*
*Debut: v Barnsley (a) 28 March 1992.*
*Career: Clachnacuddin; Chelsea November 1988; Huddersfield Town March 1986 (free); Swindon Town June 1988 (£250,000); Blackburn Rovers March 1992 (£700,000); Aberdeen July 1992 (£550,000).*
**Appearances:** Football League 5+1; Play-offs 0+1; Total 5+2.
**Goals:** Football League 1.
A prolific goalscorer who inexplicably failed to live up to his reputation during his brief stay at Ewood Park. Shearer was brought to Ewood on the eve of the transfer deadline to ensure that injuries didn't cost the club a place in the Premier League. However, although he scored on his debut he was unable to provide the spark which the team required and was dropped to substitute after only five games to make way for Mike Newell. With Newell restored to fitness, Shearer

Roy Wegerle unleashes a volley in the goalless draw against Sheffield United in the FA Cup quarter-final at Ewood Park in March 1993.

played little part in the Play-offs apart from coming on as a late substitute in the home game with Derby County. Prior to his move to Ewood Park, Shearer had been spearheading Swindon Town's own promotion push with 22 goals from 37 League appearances. This was the sort of goalscoring ratio which was more in keeping with the rest of his career. He left Swindon with a record of 78 goals in 159 League appearances (including three as sub), whilst his record at Huddersfield had been 38 goals from 83 League appearances (including three as sub). The summer of 1992 saw Shearer leave Ewood Park for Aberdeen as Alan Shearer moved in from Southampton. In his first season in Scotland, Shearer continued his goalscoring exploits with 22 goals in 34 League games (including two as sub). Such was his success in Scotland that he was drafted into the Scottish International squad.

### SHEFFIELD PROVIDENCE FC
Formed in 1871, Sheffield Providence played at Hyde Park, Sheffield. Blackburn Rovers played hosts to Sheffield Providence in the first round of the 1880-81 FA Cup competition and enjoyed a comfortable 6-2 victory thanks to goals by Jimmy Brown (3), 'Monkey' Hornby, Dick Birtwistle and Fred Hargreaves,

### SHEFFIELD UNITED FC
Founded in 1889, by members of the Yorkshire County Cricket Club, the club joined the Second Division of the Football League in 1892. Sheffield United have provided the opposition to Blackburn Rovers in more Football League games than any other club. The clubs have met in three different divisions of the Football League as well as in the Premiership.

### Football League

| | | | Home | | Away | |
|---|---|---|---|---|---|---|
| 1893-94 | (Div 1) | W | 4-1 | L | 2-3 |
| 1894-95 | (Div 1) | W | 3-2 | L | 0-3 |
| 1895-96 | (Div 1) | W | 1-0 | D | 1-1 |
| 1896-97 | (Div 1) | L | 1-3 | L | 0-7 |
| 1897-98 | (Div 1) | D | 1-1 | L | 2-5 |
| 1898-99 | (Div 1) | W | 2-1 | D | 1-1 |
| 1899-00 | (Div 1) | D | 3-3 | L | 0-3 |
| 1900-01 | (Div 1) | W | 1-0 | L | 1-2 |
| 1901-02 | (Div 1) | W | 2-1 | L | 1-4 |
| 1902-03 | (Div 1) | W | 2-0 | L | 1-2 |
| 1903-04 | (Div 1) | W | 3-0 | D | 2-2 |
| 1904-05 | (Div 1) | L | 2-4 | L | 1-3 |
| 1905-06 | (Div 1) | W | 2-1 | W | 2-0 |
| 1906-07 | (Div 1) | D | 1-1 | L | 0-3 |
| 1907-08 | (Div 1) | D | 3-3 | L | 2-4 |
| 1908-09 | (Div 1) | L | 0-1 | D | 0-0 |
| 1909-10 | (Div 1) | W | 3-1 | L | 0-3 |
| 1910-11 | (Div 1) | L | 1-2 | D | 1-1 |
| 1911-12 | (Div 1) | W | 1-0 | D | 1-1 |
| 1912-13 | (Div 1) | W | 3-1 | D | 0-0 |
| 1913-14 | (Div 1) | W | 3-2 | D | 1-1 |
| 1914-15 | (Div 1) | L | 1-2 | W | 2-1 |
| 1919-20 | (Div 1) | W | 4-0 | L | 0-2 |
| 1920-21 | (Div 1) | D | 1-1 | D | 1-1 |
| 1921-22 | (Div 1) | L | 2-3 | W | 1-0 |
| 1922-23 | (Div 1) | W | 1-0 | D | 1-1 |
| 1923-24 | (Div 1) | D | 1-1 | L | 0-4 |
| 1924-25 | (Div 1) | D | 2-2 | W | 3-2 |
| 1925-26 | (Div 1) | W | 3-1 | D | 1-1 |
| 1926-27 | (Div 1) | L | 3-4 | L | 3-5 |
| 1927-28 | (Div 1) | W | 1-0 | W | 3-2 |
| 1928-29 | (Div 1) | D | 1-1 | L | 1-2 |
| 1929-30 | (Div 1) | L | 0-1 | W | 7-5 |
| 1930-31 | (Div 1) | W | 2-1 | D | 1-1 |
| 1931-32 | (Div 1) | L | 1-2 | L | 2-3 |
| 1932-33 | (Div 1) | W | 3-0 | L | 1-2 |
| 1933-34 | (Div 1) | W | 3-1 | L | 0-1 |
| 1936-37 | (Div 2) | W | 3-1 | W | 1-0 |
| 1937-38 | (Div 2) | L | 2-3 | D | 1-1 |
| 1938-39 | (Div 2) | L | 1-2 | D | 0-0 |
| 1946-47 | (Div 1) | W | 2-0 | W | 1-0 |
| 1947-48 | (Div 1) | W | 4-0 | L | 1-4 |
| 1949-50 | (Div 2) | L | 0-2 | L | 0-4 |
| 1950-51 | (Div 2) | L | 0-2 | W | 3-0 |
| 1951-52 | (Div 2) | L | 1-5 | D | 1-1 |
| 1952-53 | (Div 2) | L | 1-2 | L | 0-3 |
| 1956-57 | (Div 2) | W | 3-1 | W | 2-0 |
| 1057-58 | (Div 2) | W | 1-0 | L | 2-4 |

| | | Home | | Away | |
|---|---|---|---|---|---|
| 1961-62 | (Div 1) | L | 1-2 | D | 0-0 |
| 1962-63 | (Div 1) | L | 1-2 | D | 1-1 |
| 1963-64 | (Div 1) | D | 2-2 | W | 1-0 |
| 1964-65 | (Div 1) | W | 4-0 | D | 1-1 |
| 1965-66 | (Div 1) | D | 0-0 | L | 0-2 |
| 1968-69 | (Div 2) | W | 1-0 | L | 0-3 |
| 1969-70 | (Div 2) | L | 1-2 | L | 0-4 |
| 1970-71 | (Div 2) | L | 1-3 | L | 0-5 |
| 1976-77 | (Div 2) | W | 1-0 | D | 1-1 |
| 1977-78 | (Div 2) | D | 1-1 | L | 0-2 |
| 1978-79 | (Div 2) | W | 2-0 | W | 1-0 |
| 1979-80 | (Div 3) | W | 1-0 | L | 1-2 |
| 1984-85 | (Div 2) | W | 3-1 | W | 3-1 |
| 1985-86 | (Div 2) | W | 6-1 | D | 3-3 |
| 1986-87 | (Div 2) | L | 0-2 | L | 1-4 |
| 1987-88 | (Div 2) | W | 4-1 | L | 1-3 |
| 1989-90 | (Div 2) | D | 0-0 | W | 2-1 |

| | P | W | D | L | F | A |
|---|---|---|---|---|---|---|
| Home | 65 | 33 | 12 | 20 | 118 | 83 |
| Away | 65 | 14 | 20 | 31 | 74 | 132 |
| Total | 130 | 47 | 32 | 51 | 192 | 215 |

**FA Premiership**

| | Home | | Away | |
|---|---|---|---|---|
| 1992-93 | W | 1-0 | W | 3-1 |
| 1993-94 | D | 0-0 | W | 2-1 |

| | P | W | D | L | F | A |
|---|---|---|---|---|---|---|
| Home | 2 | 1 | 1 | 0 | 1 | 0 |
| Away | 2 | 2 | 0 | 0 | 5 | 2 |
| Total | 4 | 3 | 1 | 0 | 6 | 2 |

**FA Cup**

| 1896-97 | (1) | Home | W | 2-1 |
|---|---|---|---|---|
| 1960-61 | (5) | Away | L | 1-2 |
| 1992-93 | (6) | Home | D | 0-0 |
| | (6R) | Away | D | 2-2aet* |

*Sheffield United won 5-3 on penalties.

**Wartime**

| | Home | | Away | |
|---|---|---|---|---|
| 1945-46 | (FLN) | D | 0-0 | L | 1-2 |

## SHEFFIELD WEDNESDAY FC

Founded in 1867 by the Wednesday Cricket Club, the club was officially known as 'The Wednesday' until June 1929 when the present title was adopted. Members of the Football League since 1892, Sheffield Wednesday have met Blackburn Rovers in three different divisions of the Football League and the Premiership. The clubs first met in competitive action in the 1880-81 FA Cup competition. On 29 March 1890, Blackburn Rovers enjoyed a record 6-1 victory over Sheffield Wednesday in the FA Cup Final. The game also saw Billy Townley produce the first hat-trick in an FA Cup Final.

**Football League**

| | | Home | | Away | |
|---|---|---|---|---|---|
| 1892-93 | (Div 1) | L | 0-2 | W | 3-0 |
| 1893-94 | (Div 1) | W | 5-1 | L | 2-4 |
| 1894-95 | (Div 1) | W | 3-1 | L | 1-4 |
| 1895-96 | (Div 1) | W | 2-1 | L | 0-3 |
| 1896-97 | (Div 1) | W | 4-0 | L | 0-6 |
| 1897-98 | (Div 1) | D | 1-1 | L | 1-4 |
| 1898-99 | (Div 1) | W | 2-0 | W | 2-1 |
| 1900-01 | (Div 1) | D | 2-2 | D | 1-1 |
| 1901-02 | (Div 1) | W | 2-0 | W | 1-0 |
| 1902-03 | (Div 1) | W | 2-1 | D | 0-0 |
| 1903-04 | (Div 1) | D | 0-0 | L | 1-3 |
| 1904-05 | (Div 1) | L | 0-1 | W | 2-1 |
| 1905-06 | (Div 1) | W | 1-0 | W | 1-0 |
| 1906-07 | (Div 1) | L | 0-2 | L | 1-3 |
| 1907-08 | (Div 1) | W | 2-0 | L | 0-2 |
| 1908-09 | (Div 1) | D | 2-2 | W | 2-1 |
| 1909-10 | (Div 1) | D | 0-0 | L | 1-2 |
| 1910-11 | (Div 1) | W | 6-1 | L | 0-1 |
| 1911-12 | (Div 1) | D | 0-0 | D | 1-1 |
| 1912-13 | (Div 1) | L | 0-1 | L | 1-2 |
| 1913-14 | (Div 1) | W | 3-2 | L | 1-3 |
| 1914-15 | (Div 1) | D | 1-1 | D | 1-1 |
| 1919-20 | (Div 1) | W | 1-0 | D | 0-0 |
| 1926-27 | (Div 1) | D | 2-2 | W | 3-0 |

| | | Home | | Away | |
|---|---|---|---|---|---|
| 1927-28 | (Div 1) | W | 3-1 | L | 1-4 |
| 1928-29 | (Div 1) | W | 4-1 | L | 0-1 |
| 1929-30 | (Div 1) | L | 0-1 | L | 0-4 |
| 1930-31 | (Div 1) | W | 5-2 | W | 3-1 |
| 1931-32 | (Div 1) | L | 1-6 | L | 1-5 |
| 1932-33 | (Div 1) | D | 1-1 | D | 1-1 |
| 1933-34 | (Div 1) | W | 3-1 | L | 0-4 |
| 1934-35 | (Div 1) | W | 2-1 | D | 2-2 |
| 1935-36 | (Div 1) | W | 3-2 | D | 0-0 |
| 1937-38 | (Div 2) | W | 1-0 | D | 1-1 |
| 1938-39 | (Div 2) | L | 2-4 | L | 0-3 |
| 1948-49 | (Div 2) | W | 2-1 | L | 0-3 |
| 1949-50 | (Div 2) | D | 0-0 | L | 0-2 |
| 1951-52 | (Div 2) | D | 0-0 | L | 0-2 |
| 1955-56 | (Div 2) | D | 2-2 | L | 1-5 |
| 1959-60 | (Div 2) | W | 3-1 | L | 0-3 |
| 1960-61 | (Div 2) | D | 1-1 | L | 4-5 |
| 1961-62 | (Div 1) | L | 0-2 | L | 0-1 |
| 1962-63 | (Div 1) | W | 3-0 | L | 0-4 |
| 1963-64 | (Div 1) | D | 1-1 | L | 2-5 |
| 1964-65 | (Div 1) | L | 0-1 | L | 0-1 |
| 1965-66 | (Div 1) | L | 1-2 | L | 1-2 |
| 1970-71 | (Div 2) | W | 3-2 | D | 1-1 |
| 1979-80 | (Div 3) | L | 1-2 | W | 3-0 |
| 1980-81 | (Div 2) | W | 3-1 | L | 1-2 |
| 1981-82 | (Div 2) | L | 0-1 | D | 2-2 |
| 1982-83 | (Div 2) | L | 2-3 | D | 0-0 |
| 1983-84 | (Div 2) | D | 0-0 | L | 2-4 |
| 1990-91 | (Div 2) | W | 1-0 | L | 1-3 |

| | P | W | D | L | F | A |
|---|---|---|---|---|---|---|
| Home | 53 | 25 | 15 | 13 | 89 | 61 |
| Away | 53 | 9 | 12 | 32 | 53 | 114 |
| Total | 106 | 34 | 27 | 45 | 142 | 175 |

**FA Premiership**

| | Home | | Away | |
|---|---|---|---|---|
| 1992-93 | W | 1-0 | D | 0-0 |
| 1993-94 | D | 1-1 | W | 2-1 |

| | P | W | D | L | F | A |
|---|---|---|---|---|---|---|
| Home | 2 | 1 | 1 | 0 | 2 | 1 |
| Away | 2 | 1 | 1 | 0 | 2 | 1 |
| Total | 4 | 2 | 2 | 0 | 4 | 2 |

**FA Cup**

| 1880-81 | (2) | Away | L | 0-4 |
|---|---|---|---|---|
| 1882-83 | (SF) | Huddersfield | D | 0-0 |
| | (SFR) | Manchester | W | 5-1 |
| 1889-90 | (F) | Kennington Oval | W | 6-1 |
| 1902-03 | (1) | Home | D | 0-0 |
| | (R) | Away | W | 1-0 |
| 1904-05 | (1) | Home | L | 1-2 |
| 1959-60 | (SF) | Maine Road | W | 2-1 |
| 1965-66 | (6) | Home | L | 1-2 |
| 1988-89 | (4) | Home | W | 2-1 |

**Football League Cup**

| 1981-82 | (2) | Home | D | 2-2 |
|---|---|---|---|---|
| | | Away | W | 2-1 |
| 1992-93 | (SF) | Home | L | 2-4 |
| | | Away | L | 1-2 |

**Wartime**

| | | Home | | Away | |
|---|---|---|---|---|---|
| 1944-45 | (FLNS-SC) | D | 2-2 | L | 0-2 |
| 1945-46 | (FLN) | W | 2-1 | D | 1-1 |

## SHEPSTONE, Paul T.A.

Midfield. 1990-1992.
*5ft 8in; 10st 6lb.*
*Born: Coventry, 8 November 1970.*
*Debut: v Bristol City (a) 25 August 1990.*
*Career: Coventry City associated schoolboy 1985-86, becoming a trainee in July 1987 before turning professional in November 1987; Birmingham City July 1989 to March 1990; Atherstone United; Blackburn Rovers May 1990; York City (on loan) March 1992; Motherwell June 1992 (£60,000); Stafford Rangers 1993; Wycombe Wanderers January 1994 until February 1994; Stafford Rangers March 1994.*
**Appearances:** Football League 16+10; FA Cup 0+1; Football League

Cup 1; Full Members' Cup 1; Total 18+11.
**Goals:** Football League 1.
Don Mackay signed Paul Shepstone from Atherstone United to add a little more depth to the playing staff at Ewood Park. Shepstone had failed to make the grade with Coventry City and Birmingham City but got his chance at Ewood during the disappointing 1990-91 season. His only goal for the club produced three invaluable points against Middlesbrough at Ewood Park and helped to keep the club just above the relegation places. Although he played in a couple of early season games during 1991-92 the influx of expensive new talent saw Shepstone relegated to the Central League team. He left Ewood in the summer of 1992 to try his luck in Scotland with Motherwell but since then has returned to the English non-League scene.

## SHERWOOD, Timothy Alan
Midfield. 1992-
*6ft 1in; 11st 4lb.*
*Born: St Albans, 6 February 1969.*
*Debut: v Middlesbrough (a) 22 February 1992.*
*Career: Watford apprentice February 1986, becoming a professional in February 1987; Norwich City July 1987 (£175,000); Blackburn Rovers on loan February 1992, signing permanently in a £500,000 deal later in the same month.*

**Appearances:** Premier League 76+1; Football League 7+4; FA Cup 7+1; Football League Cup 11; Total 101+6.
**Goals:** Premier League 5; FA Cup 1; Total 6.
Sherwood started his career at Watford but left Vicarage Road after only 32 League appearances (including nine as sub) to join Norwich City. At Carrow Road he was used as something of a utility player, appearing at right-back, in midfield and central defence. However, it was in midfield that he established himself during the 1990-91 season. Whilst with the East Anglian club, Sherwood, a former youth international, gained four England Under-21 caps. The early part of the 1991-92 season was not the happiest of times for Sherwood and a club suspension was followed by a loss of senior status at Carrow Road.

In February 1992, Kenny Dalglish brought Sherwood to Ewood Park on loan before signing him for a £500,000 fee. Unfortunately, Sherwood didn't enjoy the best of form following his move from Norwich and figured in only 11 League games (including four a sub). Although he had played no part in the Play-off matches, Sherwood began the 1992-93 season in midfield and appeared far happier in a higher grade of football than he had in the Second Division. An attacking midfield player whose vision can create openings in opposing defences, Sherwood's constructive use of the ball is matched with a competitive spirit. When injuries began to restrict Kevin Moran's appearances during the 1993-94 season, Sherwood was given the captaincy and many commentators felt him to be on the fringe of full England honours.

## SHERRINGTON, John
Half-back. 1895-1897.
*Debut: v Bury (a) 27 March 1897.*
*Career: Blackburn Rovers November 1895.*
**Appearances:** Football League 1.
Although Sherrington spent the best part of two seasons at Ewood Park he was never anything more than a reserve-team player. His sole appearance with the first team was at left-half in the 3-0 defeat at Bury in March 1897.

## SHORROCK, F.
Full-back. 1883-1886.
*Debut: v Darwen Old Wanderers (h) 5 December 1885 (FAC).*
*Career: Blackburn Rovers 1883.*
**Appearances:** FA Cup 1.
Little is known about this full-back who appeared for the club in the third round of the 1885-86 FA Cup competition against Darwen Wanderers. His first senior appearance came during the 1883-84 season when he played at left-back in the 8-0 win over Darwen and then retained his place for three of the next four matches. However, the 1884-85 season found Turner and Suter as the regular full-back pairing and Shorrock appears to have been used as an understudy for both the regular full-backs. He took the place of Turner in his one FA Cup appearance.

## SHREWSBURY TOWN FC
Founded in 1886, Shrewsbury Town were elected to the Football League in 1950. Blackburn Rovers and Shrewsbury Town first met in the Football League in the Third Division in the early 1970s but it was not until the 1980s that they became regular combatants in the Second Division.

**Football League**

|         |           | Home |     | Away |      |
|---------|-----------|------|-----|------|------|
| 1971-72 | (Div 3)   | W    | 1-0 | L    | 1-7  |
| 1972-73 | (Div 3)   | D    | 0-0 | L    | 0-2  |
| 1973-74 | (Div 3)   | W    | 2-0 | L    | 0-3  |
| 1980-81 | (Div 2)   | W    | 2-0 | D    | 1-1  |
| 1981-82 | (Div 2)   | D    | 0-0 | W    | 2-1  |
| 1982-83 | (Div 2)   | W    | 1-0 | D    | 0-0  |
| 1983-84 | (Div 2)   | D    | 1-1 | L    | 0-1  |
| 1984-85 | (Div 2)   | W    | 3-1 | L    | 0-3  |
| 1985-86 | (Div 2)   | D    | 1-1 | L    | 0-2  |
| 1986-87 | (Div 2)   | W    | 2-1 | W    | 1-0  |
| 1987-88 | (Div 2)   | D    | 2-2 | W    | 2-1  |
| 1988-89 | (Div 2)   | L    | 0-1 | D    | 1-1  |

|       | P  | W | D | L | F  | A  |
|-------|----|---|---|---|----|----|
| Home  | 12 | 6 | 5 | 1 | 15 | 7  |
| Away  | 12 | 3 | 3 | 6 | 8  | 22 |
| Total | 24 | 9 | 8 | 7 | 23 | 29 |

**FA Cup**

|         |     |      |   |     |
|---------|-----|------|---|-----|
| 1977-78 | (3) | Home | W | 2-1 |

**Football League Cup**

|         |     |      |   |        |
|---------|-----|------|---|--------|
| 1993-94 | (3) | Home | D | 0-0    |
|         | (R) | Away | W | 4-3aet |

## SILVESTER, Peter Dennis
Inside-right. 1976.
*5ft 11in; 11st 8lb.*
*Born: Wokingham, 19 February 1948.*
*Debut: v Notts County (h) 9 October 1976.*
*Career: Reading apprentice December 1964, turning professional in February 1966; Norwich City February 1970 (£20,000); Colchester United on loan October to November 1973; Southend United February 1974 to January 1977 (£11,000); Baltimore Comets May to August 1974 & May to August 1975; Vancouver Whitecaps July to August 1976; San*

*Diego Jaws May to July 1976; Blackburn Rovers on loan October to November 1976; Washington Diplomats April to August 1977; Cambridge United August 1977; Maidstone.*
**Appearances:** Football League 5.
**Goals:** Football League 1.
An experienced striker who was brought to Blackburn on loan by Jim Smith during the 1976-77 campaign. With limited financial resources Smith had to be convinced that Silvester would be able to inject some punch into the Blackburn attack before bringing him to Ewood on a permanent basis. Powerful in the air, Silvester was a traditional type of centre-forward who had enjoyed a successful time with Norwich, 37 goals in 113 League appearances (including one as sub), before moving to Southend. He appeared in five League games for Blackburn but was substituted in three and only produced one goal. In deciding not to sign Silvester on a permanent basis Smith said: "He has most of the attributes required by a striker except the very important one of pace."

### SIMPSON, John
Outside-right. 1911-1921.
*5ft 5in; 11st.*
*Born: Pendleton, Manchester, 25 December 1885; Died: 4 January 1959.*
*Debut: v Sheffield United (a) 28 January 1911.*
*Career: Laurieston Juniors 1903; Glasgow Rangers trial 1906-07; Falkirk 1906-07; Blackburn Rovers January 1911 (£1,800); Falkirk wartime guest. Remained on Blackburn's books until 1921 although he didn't play again after receiving injuries during World War One when with Falkirk.*
*International honours with Blackburn Rovers: England: 8 caps (1911-14): Football League: 5 appearances (1911-14).*
*Domestic honours with Blackburn Rovers: First Division championship: 1911-12 (35 apps, 2 gls); 1913-14 (34 apps, 2 gls).*
**Appearances:** Football League 151; FA Cup 17; FA Charity Shield 1; Total 169.
**Goals:** Football League 15; FA Cup 7; Total 22.
Blackburn Rovers paid a record transfer fee of £1,800 to bring 'Jock' Simpson to Ewood Park. Although his parents were Scottish, Simpson had been born in Pendleton, near Manchester but had been taken to Scotland by his family whilst still a young boy. Thus Simpson developed his footballing talents north of the border and whilst still the driver of a horsedrawn omnibus he entered the world of professional football with Falkirk. Simpson quickly rose to prominence with the Scottish club and was likened by many commentators to the legendary Billy Meredith. A number of English clubs, Blackburn included, tried to lure him south of the border but Simpson always rejected their overtures.

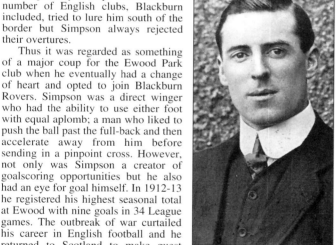

Thus it was regarded as something of a major coup for the Ewood Park club when he eventually had a change of heart and opted to join Blackburn Rovers. Simpson was a direct winger who had the ability to use either foot with equal aplomb; a man who liked to push the ball past the full-back and then accelerate away from him before sending in a pinpoint cross. However, not only was Simpson a creator of goalscoring opportunities but he also had an eye for goal himself. In 1912-13 he registered his highest seasonal total at Ewood with nine goals in 34 League games. The outbreak of war curtailed his career in English football and he returned to Scotland to make guest appearances with Falkirk. He made one wartime appearance for Blackburn in 1916 but when peace was restored a serious ankle injury prevented him from resuming his career.

### SIMPSON, William Stewart
Half-back. 1921-1922.
*5ft 9in; 11st 7lb.*
*Debut: v Manchester City (a) 24 September 1921.*
*Career: Solway Star; Blackburn Rovers January 1921; Aberaman Athletic cs 1922.*
**Appearances:** Football League 4.
Simpson came to Blackburn from the Annan club Solway Star with Alec Pool in January 1921. Whilst Pool made 17 League appearances for the Rovers before going on to enjoy a League career with Bristol City and Exeter, Simpson found his career stagnating at Ewood. He had four

senior outings in 1921-22 but was not retained at the end of the season and left Blackburn to join Aberaman Athletic.

### SIMS, Harry Christopher
Full-back. 1958-1966.
*5ft 11in; 12st 6lb.*
*Born: Liverpool, 6 December 1939.*
*Debut: v Leicester City (a) 26 October 1963.*
*Career: Blackburn Rovers groundstaff October 1958, turning professional in April 1959; Clitheroe cs 1966; Great Harwood.*
**Appearances:** Football League 13.
A sturdily built defender who could operate at either full-back or in the half-back line. Sims, who had made his debut in October 1963, was given the opportunity to stake a claim for the left-back position following the Cup exit at Oxford United in February 1964. Unfortunately, with so little first-team experience behind him he was unable to make the most of his chance. Although he began the 1964-65 season in the number-two shirt he found himself out of the team after only two matches and he did not reappear again during the rest of his time at Ewood. In November 1964 he turned down a move to Rotherham United after the terms between the clubs had been agreed. He later declined a move to Barrow before moving into non-League football with Clitheroe in the summer of 1966.

### SKINNER, Craig Richard
Outside-right. 1985-1992.
*5ft 10in; 11st.*
*Born: Heywood, 21 October 1970.*
*Debut: v Exeter City (h) 3 October 1989 (FLC) (sub).*
*Career: Blackburn Rovers associated schoolboy October 1985, becoming a trainee in July 1987, before turning professional in June 1989; Plymouth Argyle August 1992.*
**Appearances:** Football League 11+5; FA Cup 1; Football League Cup 0+1; Full Members' Cup 3; Total 15+6.
**Goals:** Full Members' Cup 1.
A product of the youth system at Ewood Park, Skinner was a rather lightweight right-winger who made his senior debut as a substitute in October 1990. He enjoyed a brief run in the first team during the early part of the 1991-92 season when Tony Parkes was acting manager. However, he hardly got a look in following the arrival of Kenny Dalglish and a number of expensive signings. In August 1992 he moved to Plymouth Argyle with Keith Hill in the deal which brought Nicky Marker to Ewood Park.

### SMAILES, Matthew
Half-back. 1925-1927.
*5ft 10in; 12st.*
*Born: Lancaster, 25 March 1899.*
*Debut: v Bury (a) 2 January 1926.*
*Career: Annfield Plain; Blackburn Rovers October 1925; West Ham United June 1927; Coventry City May 1930; Ashington August 1931.*
**Appearances:** Football League 4.
A well-built defender who was earmarked as a likely successor to Harry Healless when he arrived at Blackburn. However, Smailes only managed to break into the senior team on four occasions during his stay at Ewood Park. In June 1927 he was allowed to move to West Ham United and appeared in seven League games at Upton Park before moving to Coventry City. In August 1931, Smailes joined Ashington after making 11 appearances for Coventry.

### SMEATON, John R.
Inside-left. 1936-1938.
*5ft 8in; 11st.*
*Born: Perth; Died: February 1984 (aged 69).*
*Debut: v Norwich City (h) 19 September 1936.*
*Career: Stone Thistle; St Johnstone 1934; Blackburn Rovers July 1936; Sunderland June 1938; St Johnstone cs 1947, becoming player-coach cs 1948.*
**Appearances:** Football League 38.
**Goals:** Football League 9.
Jock Smeaton came to Ewood Park on a free transfer in July 1936 and was regarded as a promising young player who might well develop into a first-team prospect. As a part-time professional with St Johnstone, Smeaton had combined his football with an apprenticeship in the carpentry trade but became a full-time professional at Ewood. Smeaton, who had made only a handful appearances with St Johnstone, had the ability but not the consistency to become a long term fixture in the first team. In June 1938, Bob Crompton allowed him to join Sunderland and

after the war he returned to Scotland to link up once more with St Johnstone. He went on to become player-coach at that club and made his final appearance for St Johnstone in April 1950.

**SMETHAMS, John Charles**
Outside-left. 1910-1911.
*Born: Congleton, 1886.*
*Debut: v Sheffield Wednesday (h) 26 November 1910.*
*Career: Blackburn Rovers August 1910.*
**Appearances:** Football League 3.
Smethams had only one season at Ewood Park during which he acted as understudy to Walter Anthony on the left wing. He made just three appearances at a time when Anthony was struggling for consistency and during the latter part of the campaign Smethams found that Walter Cameron was preferred to both men at outside-left.

**SMITH, Albert**
Right-half. 1891-1892.
*Debut: v Preston North End (a) 14 November 1891.*
*Career: Blackburn Rovers November 1891.*
**Appearances:** Football League 7.
Smith appeared briefly for Blackburn Rovers during the 1891-92 season. He made his debut shortly after joining the club and enjoyed a run of seven mid-season appearances before losing his place to Geordie Dewar. Football League records show that he was not retained for the 1892-93 season.

**SMITH, George**
Inside-right/Right-half. 1903-1906.
*5ft 8½in; 11st.*
*Born: Preston, 1879; Died: Southampton, 3 July 1908.*
*Debut: v Everton (a) 1 September 1903.*
*Career: Leyland; Preston North End July 1899; Aston Villa June 1901; New Brompton 1902-03; Blackburn Rovers May 1903; Plymouth Argyle 1906; Southampton 1907.*
**Appearances:** Football League 58; FA Cup 3; Total 61.
**Goals:** Football League 4.
George Smith began his Ewood career as an inside-forward but proved something of a disappointment and quickly lost his first-team place to Fred Pentland. However, the former Preston and Aston Villa man reclaimed his first-team place towards the end of the season playing in the right-half position. The switch appeared tailor-made for Smith as his knowledge of forward play allowed him to put the ball into areas which were beneficial to the front men.

As well as his creative play from the midfield, Smith was also a useful defender. Surprisingly the experiment with Smith in the half-back line was not continued in 1904-05 and once again he found himself in the inside-forward position. Throughout the rest of his time at Ewood he found himself in and out of the side and made only 13 League appearances during 1905-06. After leaving Ewood he played in the Southern League with Plymouth Argyle and Southampton. He had made a favourable impression during his first season at the Dell when he suddenly collapsed and died during the summer of 1908.

**SMITH, James M.**
Manager. 1975-1979.
*Born: Sheffield, 17 October 1940.*
*Career: Sheffield United amateur 1957, turning professional in January 1959; Aldershot July 1961; Halifax Town July 1965; Lincoln City Mach 1968; Boston United player-manager 1968 to 1972; Colchester United player-manager October 1972 until June 1975, retired from playing 1973; Blackburn Rovers manager June 1975 until March 1978; Birmingham City March 1978 until February 1982; Oxford United manager March 1982 until June 1985; Queen's Park Rangers manager June 1985 until December 1988; Newcastle United manager December 1988 until March 1991; Middlesbrough coach March 1991; Middlesbrough coach Mach 1991; Portsmouth manager June 1991.*
The man who would later become widely known as 'Bald Eagle' was, at 34 years of age, the youngest incumbent of the manager's office in the history of Blackburn Rovers. Like Furphy and Lee before him, Smith arrived in Blackburn as a young manager who had proved he could achieve success on the pitch without breaking the bank. A typically tough Yorkshireman, Smith began his playing career with Sheffield United but failed to graduate to the senior team.

However, he went on to clock up 241 League appearances (including one as sub) with Aldershot, Halifax Town and Lincoln City before dropping out of the Football League to become player-manager of Boston United. Success at York Street was rewarded with the player-managership of Colchester United whom he led into the Third Division. Although he came from a similar background to both Furphy and Lee, Smith had the advantage of inheriting a winning team at Ewood.

However, after a bright start, the team found it difficult to adjust to Second Division football. As a result Smith was forced to do some hasty rebuilding despite the club's limited financial resources. He opted to sign two veterans in Dave Wagstaffe and Gordon Taylor and they rewarded his judgement by helping the club to retain its Second Division status.

Having survived a troubled first season, Smith began to build a team which reflected his own approach to the game. Unfortunately, although he managed to create a side capable of the most exciting brand of attacking football, it was also one that was flawed by unpredictability.

Even so, a blend of youth – in the shape of Bradshaw, Hird, Bailey, Keeley and Brotherston – and experience, as epitomised by Wagstaffe Taylor and Radford, was greeted with universal approval on the terraces. Sadly, a team which was well placed for promotion lacked the required consistency to achieve the club's ultimate ambition. As the promotion flame of 1977-78 began to die, Smith accepted the managership of Birmingham City. Within weeks he had returned to Ewood to take his assistant, Norman Bodell, to Birmingham.

Smith enjoyed mixed fortunes at Birmingham, experiencing both relegation and promotion with the club before being axed in February 1982. A few months later he took over at Oxford United and enjoyed his most successful period as a manager. He took unfashionable Oxford from the Third to the First Division before moving to London to join Queen's Park Rangers. Within a year he was losing to Oxford at Wembley in the League Cup Final. In 1987-88 he took Queen's Park Rangers to fifth position in the First Division and then accepted the managerial hot seat at Newcastle United. At Newcastle he appointed another former Blackburn manger, Bob Saxton, as his coach. However, even Smith could not overcome the backstage politics at Newcastle. After almost regaining the First Division place they had lost in 1988-89 he tendered his resignation in March 1991. Smith was quickly approached to take up a coaching position at Middlesbrough but eventually returned to management with Portsmouth in June 1991.

During his first season with Pompey he was unlucky to lose an FA Cup semi-final against Liverpool in a penalty shoot-out. In his second season the club only just missed an automatic promotion place from the Second Division and then lost out in the Play-offs to sixth-placed Leicester City. In January 1994, Smith returned to Ewood with Portsmouth in the third round of the FA Cup and saw his team earn a replay in a pulsating 3-3 draw. However, his former club had the last laugh as the Rovers won by a convincing 3-1 margin in the replay.

**SMITH, John**
Centre-forward. 1946-1947.
*6ft; 11st 9lb.*
*Born: Batley, 17 February 1915.*
*Debut: v Portsmouth (a) 31 August 1946.*
*Career: Whitehall Printers (Leeds); Dewsbury Moor Welfare; Huddersfield Town amateur June 1932, turning professional in October 1932; Newcastle United September 1934 (£2,500); Manchester United February 1938 (£6,500); Blackburn Rovers March 1946 (£3,000); Port Vale May 1947, later assisting Macclesfield.*
**Appearances:** Football League 30; FA Cup 4; Total 34.
**Goals:** Football League 12.
A former English schoolboy player, Jack Smith was approaching the veteran stage of his career when Eddie Hapgood brought him to Ewood Park in March 1946. Smith, who had scored 73 goals in only 112 League games with Newcastle, scored five goals in his nine appearances in the Football League North for the Rovers before the restoration of the Football League in August 1946. Whilst Hapgood introduced a number of young players into the team he continued to keep faith with Smith as leader of his attack. It was only after the departure of Hapgood that Smith lost his place in the first team and in May 1947 he left the club for Port Vale.

**SMITH, Percy James**
Centre-half. 1910-1920.
*5ft 10in; 11st 9lb.*
*Born: Burbage Spring, Leicestershire, 1880 (April quarter); Died: Watford, 18 April 1959.*

*Debut: v Woolwich Arsenal (a) 15 October 1910.*
*Career: Hinckley Town; Preston North End cs 1902; Blackburn Rovers May 1910; Fleetwood player-coach cs 1920; Nelson secretary-manager cs 1925 to May 1927; Bury manager May 1927 to January 1930; Tottenham Hotspur manager January 1930 to April 1935; Notts County manager June 1935 to October 1936; Bristol Rovers manager November 1936 to November 1937.*
*Domestic honours with Blackburn Rovers: First Division championship: 1911-12 (31 apps, 1 gl); 1913-14 (33 apps; 3 gls).*
**Appearances:** Football League 172; FA Cup 20; FA Charity Shield 1; Total 193.
**Goals:** Football League 5; FA Cup 1; Total 6.
Percy Smith, Preston's veteran centre-forward, was signed by Blackburn Rovers during the 1910 close season. Smith, who had scored 90 goals in 239 League appearances for the Deepdale club, was brought to Ewood to provide cover for the forward positions. However, the 1910-11 season

began with Blackburn struggling to find an adequate replacement for George Chapman in the centre-half position. Smith, who had some experience of the position, was given his opportunity to fill the gap and after an indifferent start, a 4-1 reversal at the hands of Woolwich Arsenal, he became the regular centre-half. There was little finesse about Smith's game. He had been a big, bustling type of centre-forward and he brought the same energetic style to his defensive play. Totally dominant in the air, Smith was a solid and reliable defender who performed with great consistency during two championship campaigns. Smith left Ewood in the summer of 1920 to become player-coach at Fleetwood and in 1925 he entered League management with Nelson. Smith possessed a shrewd tactical brain and spent over a decade in Football League management with five different clubs.

## SMITH, William A.
Left-back. 1892-1893.
*Born: Blackburn.*
*Debut: v Stoke (a) 3 April 1893.*
*Career: Kearsley; Blackburn Rovers July 1892.*
**Appearances:** Football League 1.
Smith made his solitary appearance for Blackburn Rovers in the final League match of the 1892-93 campaign. Smith, who had been brought to Blackburn to act as understudy to Johnny Forbes, had previously seen Jimmy Forrest moved to left-back whenever Forbes was unavailable. Many believed that Smith ought to have had more opportunities than he did with the first team. However, the Blackburn committee preferred to put their faith in their Scottish contingent.

## SMITH, William Henry
Utility. 1952-1960.
5ft 10in; 11st 6lb.
*Born: Plymouth, 7 September 1926.*
*Debut: v Bury (a) 29 November 1952.*
*Career: Plymouth United; Plymouth Argyle August 1945; Reading August 1947; Northampton Town July 1948; Birmingham City March 1950; Blackburn Rovers December 1952; Accrington Stanley player-coach July 1960 to March 1962.*
**Appearances:** Football League 119; FA Cup 9; Total 128.
**Goals:** Football League 10; FA Cup 2; Total 12.
Bill Smith was brought to Ewood Park from Birmingham City with Tommy Briggs in December 1952. However, after only four League games, Smith lost his inside-left position and had to wait until the final three League games of the season before being restored to the senior team. By this time Smith had

moved to right-half and it was in this position that he won a regular place during the 1953-54 campaign. Smith, who based his game on solid tackling and astute judgment, lost his place to Ronnie Clayton at the start of the 1954-55 season and it was not until the latter part of the campaign that he found a niche at right-back.

However by the middle of the following season he had lost his place to Ken Taylor and reverted to his role of general understudy. Throughout his time at Ewood Park, Smith was constantly moved to cover gaps at full-back, half-back and inside-forward. He was a genuine utility player and could be relied upon to turn in a solid performance no matter what role he was asked to play. In July 1960, Smith left Ewood Park to become the player-coach at Peel Park. He had the misfortune of being the joint caretaker manager at the time that the Accrington Stanley club lost its League status in March 1962.

## SOMERS, Peter
Inside-right. 1900-1902.
*Born: Avondale, Lanarks, 3 June 1878; Died:27 November 1914.*
*Debut: v Glossop North End (a) 27 February 1900.*
*Career: Motherwell Celtic; Cadzow Oak; Hamilton Athletic 1897; Glasgow Celtic 1897; Blackburn Rovers on loan February 1900 (£200); Glasgow Celtic 1902 (£120); Hamilton Academical 1910.*
**Appearances:** Football League 76; FA Cup 2; Total 78.
**Goals:** Football League 13.
A constructive inside-forward who had the ability to create chances for others, Peter Somers was brought to Ewood Park in a rather curious loan deal. The Rovers had to pay Celtic a fee of £200 to take him to Ewood but the Scottish club retained the right to recall him to Glasgow at the end of the loan period. He stayed at Ewood for two seasons before Celtic paid £120 to take him back to Scotland. The Rovers offered a large fee to keep him but the Celtic manager was adamant that Somers should return to Glasgow. In Scotland he helped Celtic to lift six Scottish championships between 1904-05 and 1909-10 before moving to Hamilton Academical in 1910. He became a director of Hamilton before his tragic early death in November 1914.

## SORLEY, John
Forward. 1893-1895.
*Born: Scotland.*
*Debut: v Sunderland (a) 9 December 1893.*
*Career: New Milns; Newcastle East End early 1891; Newcastle United December 1892; Middlesbrough 1893; Blackburn Rovers September 1893; Burton Swifts May 1895; Hebburn Argyle 1897.*
**Appearances:** Football League 26; FA Cup 1; Total 27.
**Goals:** Football League 9.
Jock Sorley was a something of a legendary figure on Tyneside having captained the East End club and scored in Newcastle United's first League game. At Blackburn, Sorley was tried in the centre-forward position on several occasions following his move from the North-East and scored on his debut against Sunderland. However, his play lacked the required consistency and in May 1895 he opted to join Burton Swifts. The Burton club offered Sorley the same terms as he was getting at Blackburn and also provided a job for him outside of the game.

## SOUTH SHIELDS FC
South Shields FC joined the Second Division of the Football League in 1919. In 1922-23 the club were drawn at home to Blackburn Rovers in the third round of the FA Cup and fought out at 0-0 draw in front of 18,750 spectators. Five days later South Shields travelled to Blackburn and pulled off a major Cup shock when they returned to the North-East with a 1-0 victory under their belts. In 1930 the club moved from its Horsley Hill Road ground in South Shields to Redheugh Park in Gateshead. As a result of the move the club changed its name to Gateshead and retained its Football League membership until 1960.

## SOUTH SHORE FC
Formed in the late 1870s the club merged with Blackpool FC in December 1899. Blackburn Rovers visited the South Shore club in the second round of the 1883-84 FA Cup competition and enjoyed a comfortable 7-0 victory. Goals from Avery (2), Suter, Sowerbutts (2), Douglas and McIntyre in front of a crowd reported to number in the region of 700 gave the Rovers a place in the next round.

## SOUTHAMPTON FC
Founded in 1885, most of the founders were linked with the young's men's association of St Mary's Church. The club played under the title of Southampton St Mary's until the adoption of the present name in 1897. One of the original members of the Third Division of the Football League in 1920, Southampton and Blackburn Rovers first met in the League in 1936-37. All the Football League meetings between the clubs took place in the Second Division.

## Football League

| | | Home | | Away | |
|---|---|---|---|---|---|
| 1936-37 | (Div 2) | W | 1-0 | D | 2-2 |
| 1937-38 | (Div 2) | W | 4-0 | L | 0-1 |
| 1938-39 | (Div 2) | W | 3-0 | W | 3-1 |
| 1948-49 | (Div 2) | L | 1-2 | L | 0-3 |
| 1949-50 | (Div 2) | D | 0-0 | L | 1-3 |
| 1950-51 | (Div 2) | W | 1-0 | D | 1-1 |
| 1951-52 | (Div 2) | L | 0-1 | L | 1-2 |
| 1952-53 | (Div 2) | W | 3-0 | L | 1-6 |
| 1975-76 | (Div 2) | D | 1-1 | L | 1-2 |
| 1976-77 | (Div 2) | W | 3-0 | L | 0-2 |
| 1977-78 | (Div 2) | W | 2-1 | L | 0-5 |

| | P | W | D | L | F | A |
|---|---|---|---|---|---|---|
| Home | 11 | 7 | 2 | 2 | 19 | 5 |
| Away | 11 | 1 | 2 | 8 | 10 | 28 |
| Total | 22 | 8 | 4 | 10 | 29 | 33 |

## FA Premiership

| | Home | | Away | |
|---|---|---|---|---|
| 1992-93 | D | 0-0 | D | 1-1 |
| 1993-94 | W | 2-0 | L | 1-3 |

| | P | W | D | L | F | A |
|---|---|---|---|---|---|---|
| Home | 2 | 1 | 1 | 0 | 2 | 0 |
| Away | 2 | 0 | 1 | 1 | 2 | 4 |
| Total | 4 | 1 | 2 | 1 | 4 | 4 |

## FA Cup

| | | | | |
|---|---|---|---|---|
| 1947-48 | (4) | Away | L | 2-3 |
| 1983-84 | (5) | Home | L | 0-1 |

## SOUTHEND UNITED FC

Founded in 1906 and former members of the Southern League, Southend United became founder members of the Third Division of the Football League in 1920. League meetings between Blackburn Rovers and Southend did not occur until the Rovers lost their Second Division status in the early 1970s. Ewood Park has not proved to be a lucky ground for Southend as they have failed to win on five visits in the League and two in the FA Cup.

### Football League

| | | Home | | Away | |
|---|---|---|---|---|---|
| 1972-73 | (Div 3) | W | 2-1 | W | 1-0 |
| 1973-74 | (Div 3) | W | 1-0 | D | 1-1 |
| 1074-75 | (Div 3) | W | 1-0 | D | 2-2 |
| 1979-80 | (Div 3) | D | 1-1 | W | 1-0 |
| 1991-92 | (Div 2) | D | 2-2 | L | 0-3 |

| | P | W | D | L | F | A |
|---|---|---|---|---|---|---|
| Home | 5 | 3 | 2 | 0 | 7 | 4 |
| Away | 5 | 2 | 2 | 1 | 5 | 6 |
| Total | 10 | 5 | 4 | 1 | 12 | 10 |

### FA Cup

| | | | | |
|---|---|---|---|---|
| 1910-11 | (1) | Home* | W | 5-1 |
| 1938-39 | (4) | Home | W | 4-2 |

*Note: Match originally drawn to be played at Southend.

## SOUTHPORT FC

The Southport Central Football Club which was to join the Football League in 1921 was formed in 1888, although a club bearing the title of Southport FC had been formed in the town in 1881. Southport Central played in the Lancashire League, Lancashire Combination and the Central League prior to becoming one of the founder members of the Third Division North. The club changed its name to Southport Vulcan during the 1918-19 season but the following campaign saw them alter the title to Southport FC. Although Blackburn and Southport had met in the FA Cup and wartime football, the clubs did not meet in the Football League until the 1973-74 season. It was in this season that the clubs met for the only time in the Football League Cup.

### Football League

| | | Home | | Away | |
|---|---|---|---|---|---|
| 1973-74 | (Div 3) | W | 2-1 | D | 2-2 |

| | P | W | D | L | F | A |
|---|---|---|---|---|---|---|
| Home | 1 | 1 | 0 | 0 | 2 | 1 |
| Away | 1 | 0 | 1 | 0 | 2 | 2 |
| Total | 2 | 1 | 1 | 0 | 4 | 3 |

## FA Cup

| | | Home | | Away | |
|---|---|---|---|---|---|
| 1883-84 | (1) | Home | W | 7-0 |
| 1921-22 | (1) | Home | D | 1-1 |
| | (R) | Away | W | 2-0 |
| 1926-27 | (3) | Away | L | 0-2 |

## Football League Cup

| | | | | |
|---|---|---|---|---|
| 1973-74 | (1) | Away | D | 1-1 |
| | | Home | W | 3-1 aet |

## Wartime

| | | Home | | Away | |
|---|---|---|---|---|---|
| 1916-17 | (LSPT) | W | 4-0 | W | 3-2 |
| 1917-18 | (LSPT) | L | 0-1 | L | 1-2 |
| 1918-19 | (LSPT) | L | 2-3 | L | 0-3 |
| 1939-40 | (NWRL) | W | 5-0 | L | 1-4 |
| 1941-42 | (FLNS-FC) | W | 2-0 | L | 2-3 |
| 1942-43 | (FLNS-FC) | D | 2-2 | W | 2-1 |
| 1943-44 | (FLNS-FC) | W | 3-0 | L | 1-3 |
| | (FLNS-SC) | W | 5-0 | W | 2-1 |
| 1944-45 | (FLNS-FC) | W | 4-2 | L | 2-7 |

## SOUTHWORTH, James

Right-back. 1887-1892
*5ft 10½in; 12st.*
*Died: Australia, 1940.*
*Debut: v Accrington (h) 15 September 1888.*
*Career: Blackburn Wednesday; Silver Star; Blackburn Olympic; Chester; Blackburn Olympic; Blackburn Rovers 1887.*
**Appearances:** Football League 21; FA Cup 6; Total 27.
The brother of Jack Southworth, James had played in junior circles before joining Blackburn Olympic. He had a spell in Chester before returning to Blackburn to link up with Olympic and then Blackburn Rovers. He formed an impressive full-back partnership with Joe Beverley during the latter part of the 1887-88 season and the following campaign saw him miss only three of the club's matches in the inaugural season of the Football League. An exceptionally athletic player, his speed, strong kicking and heading ability made him a powerful full-back. During the summer months he was a popular figure on the running tracks and won many prizes for his sprinting ability. The 1889-90 season saw Tom Brandon and Johnny Forbes installed in the full-back positions and Southworth was restricted to only two League appearances.

## SOUTHWORTH, John

Centre-forward. 1887-1893.
*Born: Blackburn, December 1866; Died: Wavertree, Liverpool, 16 October 1956.*
*Debut: v Blackburn Olympic (h) 5 November 1887 (FAC).*
*Career: Inkerman Rangers; Brookhouse Rangers; Brookhouse Perseverance; Blackburn Olympic 1883-84; Higher Walton; Accrington guest; Vale of Lune guest; Chester 1886; Blackburn Olympic; Blackburn Rovers 1887; Everton August 1893. Retired through injury 1895.*
*International honours with Blackburn Rovers: England: 3 caps (1889-92): Football League: 1 appearance (1893).*
*Domestic honours with Blackburn Rovers: FA Cup winners: 1890; 1891.*
**Appearances:** Football League 108; FA Cup 24; Total 132.
**Goals:** Football League 97; FA Cup 24; Total 121.
Jack Southworth was Blackburn Rovers' first truly prolific goalscorer. Popularly known as 'Skimmy' because of his speed, Southworth began his footballing career at the age of 12 when he formed a junior club named Inkerman Rangers. He later played for two clubs, Brookhouse Rangers and Brookhouse Perseverance, which acted as nurseries for Blackburn Olympic and in 1883-84 he was selected for the Olympic's second team. The officials of Blackburn Olympic were quick to recognise the potential of Southworth and he was made captain of the second team and first reserve for the first team. It was at this early stage in his career that Southworth rejected an opportunity to join Blackburn Rovers in favour of staying with Olympic.

His career might well have come to a premature end for he received a serious injury to his right knee whilst making a guest appearance with Accrington. He had to turn to goalkeeping for a while due to a loss of mobility caused by the injury. Having helped Olympic to defeat the Rovers in the 1885 Lancashire Cup Final, Southworth found his career threatened again by a serious injury to his left knee that occurred whilst he was guesting for Vale of Lune. However, despite continued problems with his knees, Southworth signed as a professional with Blackburn Olympic. A keen musician, Southworth was one of seven brothers who were interested in music and in 1886 he took a job in a theatre in Chester. He played with Chester for a time before returning to Blackburn Olympic to resume his career as a centre-forward. Having overcome his injury problems he became a great success as a leader of the attack and in 1887-88 he finally left Olympic to join Blackburn Rovers.

A contemporary wrote that: 'His dodging, his neat passing, his speed and general accuracy in shooting won the hearts of the numerous frequenters of the Leamington ground.' Another commentator wrote that: 'He is built for speed, he plays an unselfish game, he's good at doing tackles and has excellent judgement.' Southworth captained the Blackburn team which entered the Football League and he went on to win three England caps and two FA Cup winners' medals whilst at the club. In August 1893, Everton paid £400 for his services and in his first season on Merseyside he netted 27 goals in 22 games. His second season with Everton saw him score nine goals in nine appearances before a knee injury finally forced him to retire from the game.

On leaving football he turned to music and became a professional violinist. He appeared with the Halle Orchestra, the BBC Northern Orchestra and Liverpool Philharmonic and was versatile enough to play the trombone, euphonium and tuba as well as the violin. For 30 years he was a member of the Pier Pavilion Orchestra in Llandudno. His brother James also played for the Rovers at the same time as Jack and despite having a reputation for speed, Jack always maintained that James was the faster of the two brothers.

### SOWERBUTTS, Joseph Edward
Forward. 1881-1887.
*Born: Blackburn, 1864.*
*Debut: v Southport (h) 20 November 1883 (FAC).*
*Career: Blackburn Rovers 1881.*
*Domestic honours with Blackburn Rovers: FA Cup winners: 1884; 1885; 1886.*
**Appearances:** FA Cup 20.
**Goals:** FA Cup 16.

Joe Sowerbutts was one of the men who figured prominently with Blackburn Rovers during the 1880s. He began to feature in the first team with increasing frequency during the 1881-82 season. However, it was in 1883-84 that he found himself a regular member of the Blackburn forward line. He featured in three FA Cup Finals and proved to be a prolific goalscorer in this competition. He continued to be a regular first-team player up to the end of the 1886-87 season but does not appear to have figured in the team after the match with Blackburn Olympic in December 1887.

### SPEEDIE, David Robert
Forward. 1991-1992.
*5ft 7in; 11st.*
*Born: Glenrothes, 20 February 1960.*
*Debut: v Portsmouth (h) 17 August 1991.*
*Career: Barnsley October 1978; Darlington June 1980; Chelsea June 1982 (£65,000); Coventry City July 1987 (£750,000); Liverpool February 1991 (£675,000); Blackburn Rovers August 1991 (£400,000); Southampton July 1992 (£400,000); Birmingham City on loan October 1992 to January 1993; West Bromwich Albion on loan January 1993 to March 1993; West Ham Untied on loan March 1993 to May 1993; Leicester City July 1993.*
*Domestic honours with Blackburn Rovers: Second Division Play-off winners: 1992.*
**Appearances:** Football League 34+2; Play-offs 3; FA Cup 2; Football League Cup 2; Total 41+2.
**Goals:** Football League 23; Play-offs 2; FA Cup 1; Total 26.

Although he stayed at Ewood Park for only a season, David Speedie acquired 'cult' status amongst the supporters of Blackburn Rovers. Don Mackay signed the experienced Speedie on the eve of the 1991-92 season after attempts to sign Gary

Lineker and Teddy Sherringham failed. A fiery little Scot, whose aggressive nature fell foul of many referees, Speedie had the ability to play as a striker or in midfield. Tigerish in the tackle and brilliant in the air, Speedie had been signed for Liverpool by Kenny Dalglish just before the manager decided to leave the Anfield club. In October 1991, Speedie was reunited with Dalglish when his former Liverpool boss accepted the challenge of trying to restore the fortunes of Blackburn Rovers. Speedie and Mike Newell provided the cutting edge to the Blackburn attack and the combative little Scot created havoc amongst opposing defences. Although he missed ten games through 'suspension' or injury, his 23 League goals, including two hat-tricks, propelled the club towards the Premier League. Speedie played a major part in the club's success in the Play-off victory over Derby with two second half goals which gave the Rovers a 4-2 victory. In the Final at Wembley, it was Speedie who forced a Leicester defender to upend him in the area and so give Newell the chance to score from the spot.

Having played such a crucial role in the success of Blackburn Rovers it came as a something of a surprise when the club agreed to allow Speedie to move to Southampton. Although the club were reluctant to let him go Southampton insisted in him being included in the package which brought Alan Shearer to Ewood Park. Whilst Shearer set the Premier League alight, Speedie failed to settle on the south coast and had loan spells with Birmingham City, West Bromwich Albion and West Ham United before signing for Leicester City in July 1993. The 1993-94 season saw him spearhead Leicester's challenge to win promotion to the Premiership, although he was sent off in the Play-off semi-final and missed the Wembley victory over Derby County.

### SPEIGHT, Michael
Midfield. 1980-1982.
*5ft 10½in; 12st 7lb.*
*Born: South Elmsall, Yorkshire, 1 November 1951.*
*Debut: v Cardiff City (a) 16 August 1980 (sub).*
*Career: Sheffield United apprentice January 1968, turning professional in May 1969; Blackburn Rovers July 1980 (£40,000); Grimsby Town August 1982 (£25,000); Bury on loan March 1983; Chester City player-coach 1984, becoming player-manager.*
**Appearances:** Football League 50+1; Football League 6; Total 56+1.
**Goals:** Football League 4.

Mickey Speight was signed by Howard Kendall following the club's promotion to the Second Division in 1980. Speight was an experienced campaigner who had appeared in 199 League games (including 15 as sub) for Sheffield United and also won international recognition with the England 'B' team. A strong central midfield player with a powerful shot, Speight was also used in defence from time to time during his stay at Ewood Park. Although a regular under Kendall, Speight did not find favour with Bob Saxton and in August 1982 he joined Grimsby Town.

### STAFFORD RANGERS FC
Formed in 1876, Stafford Rangers were members of the Alliance Premier League when they were drawn away to Blackburn Rovers in the second round of the 1979-80 FA Cup competition. Goals from Andy Crawford and Duncan McKenzie gave Blackburn a comfortable 2-0 win in front of a crowd of 5,422 spectators. The Rovers went on to reach the fifth round of the competition before narrowly losing to Aston Villa in a replay.

### STAPLETON, Francis Anthony
Centre-forward. 1989-1991.
*5ft 11in; 13st.*
*Born: Dublin, 10 July 1956.*
*Debut: v Oldham Athletic (h) 19 August 1989.*
*Career: Arsenal St Martins (Dublin); Bolton Athletic (Dublin); Manchester United trial; Wolverhampton Wanderers trial; Arsenal apprentice June 1972, turning professional in September 1973; Manchester United 28 August 1981 (£900,000); Ajax Amsterdam (Holland) August 1987; Derby County on loan March 1988; Le Havre (France); Blackburn Rovers August 1989; Aldershot non-contract September 1991; Huddersfield Town non-contract player-coach October 1991; Bradford City player-manager December 1991 until May 1994.*
*International honours with Blackburn Rovers: Republic of Ireland: 2 caps (1989-90).*
**Appearances:** Football League 80+1; Play-offs 2; FA Cup 4; Football League Cup 5; Full Members' Cup 1; Total 92+1.
**Goals:** Football League 13; FA Cup 1; Football League Cup 1; Total 15.

Although well into the veteran stage of his career, it was still regarded as something of a coup that Don Mackay should be able to persuade Frank Stapleton to join Blackburn Rovers. During his time with Arsenal and Manchester United, Stapleton was regarded as one of the finest centre-forwards in the country. Although not the most prolific of goalscorers – 75 goals in 225 League games (including two as sub) with Arsenal and 60 goals in 223 League games (including 19 as sub) with United – there was no denying that Stapleton was a brave and creative front runner. Stapleton had a difficult first season a Ewood Park and didn't look completely match fit during the opening months of the campaign. None the less he helped to guide the team into a third successive Play-off appearance.

The summer of 1990 saw Stapleton set a new goalscoring record for the Republic of Ireland and he was also included in the Irish squad which did so well in the World Cup Finals. Although the 1990-91 season found the Rovers struggling at the wrong end of the Second Division, a rejuvenated Stapleton performed admirably throughout the season. He finished the season as the club's leading goalscorer with ten League goals but was not retained by Don Mackay. He appeared as a non-contract player with Aldershot and Huddersfield Town, where he was player-coach, before accepting the position of player-manager with Bradford City. In May 1994 he was axed from his job at Bradford after narrowly missing out on reaching the Second Division Play-offs.

### STARBUCK, Philip Michael
Forward. 1990.
5ft 10in; 10st 13lb.
Born: Nottingham, 24 November 1968.
Debut: v Ipswich Town (a) 8 September 1990.
Career: v Nottingham Forest associated schoolboy January 1983, becoming an apprentice in July 1985 and turning professional in August 1986; Birmingham City on loan March 1988; Hereford United on loan February to March 1990; Blackburn Rovers on loan September 1990; Huddersfield Town August 1991.
Appearances: Football League 5+1.
Goals: Football League 1.
Phil Starbuck came to Ewood Park on loan after the club had made a disappointing start to the 1990-91 season. In the third match of his loan spell he scored a last minute goal which gave Blackburn a 4-1 win over Leicester City, a result which to prove the season's biggest winning margin. Starbuck, a utility forward at Forest, was not the fleetest of front men and this may explain why he started only nine League games at Nottingham whilst making a further 27 appearances as a substitute.

### STAVELEY FC
Formed in 1875, the club played at the Recreation Ground, Staveley, Chesterfield. Staveley and Blackburn Rovers met twice in the FA Cup in the days before the Football League and on both occasions Blackburn enjoyed a comfortable margin of victory.

**FA Cup**

| | | | | |
|---|---|---|---|---|
| 1883-84 | (4) | Home | W | 5-1 |
| 1885-86 | (4) | Home | W | 7-1 |

### STEPHAN, Harold W.
Half-back. 1942-1948.
5ft 5in; 10st 12lb.
Born: Farnworth, 24 February 1924.
Debut: v Bolton Wanderers (a) 5 January 1945 (FAC).
Career: Blackburn Rovers amateur September 1942, turning professional in December 1943; Leicester City wartime guest 1944-45; Accrington Stanley September 1948; Mossley May 1949.
Appearances: Football League 13; FA Cup 2; Total 15.
Goals: Football League 1.
Originally an inside-forward, Stephan appeared on the Ewood scene during World War Two. He scored 15 goals in 20 wartime games during the 1943-44 season and finished the wartime programme with 35 goals from 82 appearances. The first season after the war saw Eddie Hapgood give Stephan a run in the first team but he made little impression on a struggling side. The following season saw him make one appearance for the senior team and attempts to revive his League career with Accrington Stanley failed to produce a League appearance.

### STEPHENSON, Roy A.
Inside-forward. 1957-1959.
5ft 6in; 10st 3lb.
Born: Crook, 27 May 1932.
Debut: v Bristol City (a) 9 November 1957.
Career: Sunnyside Juniors; Burnley June 1949; Rotherham United September 1956; Blackburn Rovers November 1957 (£5,000); Leicester City March 1959; Ipswich Town July 1960; Lowestoft Town June 1965.
Appearances: Football League 21; FA Cup 6; Total 27.
Goals: Football League 5.
Roy Stephenson had begun his football career with 27 goals in 78 League games at Burnley before leaving Turf Moor for Rotherham United. A total of 14 goals from 43 League games at Millmoor was sufficient for Johnny Carey to move to sign Stephenson in November 1957. A utility forward, Stephenson was immediately brought into the team at inside-left

but switched to inside-right after only six appearances. As Rovers' promotion campaign went into its final stages Stephenson found himself excluded from the team in favour of Tom Johnston, a new signing from Leyton Orient. The 1958-59 season found Stephenson totally out of favour with only five League appearances and in March 1959 Matt Gillies paid £8,000 to install him in a Leicester City team that was fighting against relegation from the First Division. The following season found him unable to break into the Leicester team and in July 1960 he was signed by Alf Ramsey at Ipswich Town. Stephenson went on to play a leading role in the Ipswich Town team which won the Second and First Division championship in successive seasons. During his time in East Anglia he scored 21 goals in 144 League games.

### STEVENSON, Hugh
Half-back. 1907-1912.
Debut: v Woolwich Arsenal (a) 30 March 1907.
Career: Woolwich; Maryhill; Blackburn Rovers January 1907; St Mirren June 1912; Great Harwood 1919.
Appearances: Football League 58; FA Cup 4; Total 62.
Goals: Football League 3.
The 1909-10 Lancashire Daily Post Football Annual described Stevenson as 'a well built player, with a remarkable turn of speed'. The writer went on to say that he was 'primarily effective in defensive tactics' and that 'he pushes the ball nicely ahead for the forwards'. Although it was expected that Stevenson would develop into an outstanding half-back, the fact remains that by the time the above comments were made, his best days at Ewood Park were behind him. Indeed, the 1909-10 season brought only six League appearances for Stevenson and although he managed 19 games the following season it came as no surprise when he returned to Scotland.

### STOCKPORT COUNTY FC
Founded in 1883 as Heaton Norris Rovers, the club changed its name to Stockport County in 1890. Elected to the Second Division of the Football League in 1900, the club lost its League status in 1904 but returned in 1905 when the Second Division was increased in size. Despite its long association with the Football League, Stockport County only met Blackburn in the League during the 1937-38 season.

**Football League**

| | | Home | | Away | |
|---|---|---|---|---|---|
| 1937-38 | (Div 2) | W | 3-0 | W | 1-0 |

| | P | W | D | L | F | A |
|---|---|---|---|---|---|---|
| Home | 1 | 1 | 0 | 0 | 3 | 0 |
| Away | 1 | 1 | 0 | 0 | 1 | 0 |
| Total | 2 | 2 | 0 | 0 | 4 | 0 |

**FA Cup**

| | | | | |
|---|---|---|---|---|
| 1968-69 | (3) | Home | W | 2-0 |

**Football League Cup**

| | | | | |
|---|---|---|---|---|
| 1969-70 | (1) | Away | W | 2-0 |
| 1974-75 | (1) | Away | W | 2-0 |
| 1976-77 | (2) | Home | L | 1-3 |

**Wartime**

| | | Home | | Away | |
|---|---|---|---|---|---|
| 1916-17 | (LSPT) | L | 2-4 | L | 1-7 |
| 1917-18 | (LSPT) | L | 1-6 | L | 0-6 |
| 1918-19 | (LSPT) | L | 0-4 | L | 0-1 |
| 1942-43 | (FLNS-FC) | W | 4-0 | L | 2-3 |
| 1943-44 | (FLNS-FC) | W | 8-2 | W | 2-1 |

### STOKE CITY FC
Founded sometime in the 1860s by employees of the North Staffordshire Railway Company. The original club went bankrupt in 1908 and a new club was formed. One of the original members of the Football League, the club lost League status in 1890 but returned after an absence of only

12 months. The club resigned from the League in 1908 and did not return until 1919.

## Football League

|         |         | Home |     | Away |     |
|---------|---------|------|-----|------|-----|
| 1888-89 | (FL)    | W    | 5-2 | L    | 1-2 |
| 1889-90 | (FL)    | W    | 8-0 | W    | 3-0 |
| 1891-92 | (FL)    | W    | 5-3 | W    | 1-0 |
| 1892-93 | (Div 1) | D    | 3-3 | D    | 2-2 |
| 1893-94 | (Div 1) | W    | 5-0 | L    | 1-3 |
| 1894-95 | (Div 1) | W    | 6-0 | L    | 1-5 |
| 1895-96 | (Div 1) | W    | 3-1 | L    | 0-3 |
| 1896-97 | (Div 1) | W    | 2-1 | L    | 0-1 |
| 1897-98 | (Div 1) | D    | 1-1 | L    | 1-2 |
| 1898-99 | (Div 1) | W    | 4-1 | W    | 1-0 |
| 1899-00 | (Div 1) | W    | 3-0 | L    | 0-2 |
| 1900-01 | (Div 1) | W    | 3-2 | L    | 0-2 |
| 1901-02 | (Div 1) | W    | 6-1 | D    | 2-2 |
| 1902-03 | (Div 1) | D    | 1-1 | W    | 2-0 |
| 1903-04 | (Div 1) | W    | 2-0 | L    | 2-6 |
| 1904-05 | (Div 1) | W    | 4-0 | L    | 0-4 |
| 1905-06 | (Div 1) | W    | 3-0 | L    | 0-3 |
| 1906-07 | (Div 1) | W    | 3-1 | D    | 1-1 |
| 1922-23 | (Div 1) | L    | 1-5 | D    | 1-1 |
| 1933-34 | (Div 1) | W    | 4-1 | L    | 0-2 |
| 1934-35 | (Div 1) | L    | 0-1 | L    | 1-3 |
| 1935-36 | (Div 1) | L    | 0-1 | L    | 0-2 |
| 1946-47 | (Div 1) | L    | 0-2 | D    | 0-0 |
| 1947-48 | (Div 1) | W    | 2-0 | L    | 1-2 |
| 1953-54 | (Div 2) | W    | 3-0 | L    | 0-3 |
| 1954-55 | (Div 2) | W    | 2-0 | D    | 1-1 |
| 1955-56 | (Div 2) | W    | 3-0 | W    | 2-1 |
| 1956-57 | (Div 2) | W    | 1-0 | L    | 1-4 |
| 1957-58 | (Div 2) | W    | 1-0 | W    | 4-2 |
| 1963-64 | (Div 1) | W    | 1-0 | L    | 1-3 |
| 1964-65 | (Div 1) | D    | 1-1 | D    | 1-1 |
| 1965-66 | (Div 1) | L    | 0-1 | L    | 2-3 |
| 1977-78 | (Div 2) | W    | 2-1 | L    | 2-4 |
| 1978-79 | (Div 2) | D    | 2-2 | W    | 2-1 |
| 1985-86 | (Div 2) | L    | 0-1 | D    | 2-2 |
| 1986-87 | (Div 2) | W    | 2-1 | L    | 0-1 |
| 1987-88 | (Div 2) | W    | 2-0 | L    | 1-2 |
| 1988-89 | (Div 2) | W    | 4-3 | W    | 1-0 |
| 1989-90 | (Div 2) | W    | 3-0 | W    | 1-0 |

|       | P  | W  | D  | L  | F   | A   |
|-------|----|----|----|----|-----|-----|
| Home  | 39 | 28 | 5  | 6  | 101 | 37  |
| Away  | 39 | 9  | 8  | 22 | 42  | 76  |
| Total | 78 | 37 | 13 | 28 | 143 | 113 |

## FA Cup

| 1905-06 | (1) | Away | L | 0-1 |
|---------|-----|------|---|-----|
| 1961-62 | (4) | Away | W | 1-0 |

## Football League

| 1968-69 | (2) | Home | D | 1-1 |
|---------|-----|------|---|-----|
|         | (R) | Away | W | 1-0 |

## Wartime

| 1916-17 | (LSPT) | D | 1-1 | L | 1-4  |
|---------|--------|---|-----|---|------|
| 1917-18 | (LSPT) | L | 1-8 | L | 0-16 |
| 1918-19 | (LSPT) | L | 0-6 | L | 0-7  |
| 1945-46 | (FLN)  | W | 5-1 | L | 0-5  |

## STONEHOUSE, Kevin
Forward. 1979-1983.
*5ft 11in; 11st 10lb.*
*Born: Bishop Auckland, 20 September 1959.*
*Debut: v Rotherham United (h) 29 September 1979.*
*Career: Shildon; Blackburn Rovers July 1979; Huddersfield Town March 1983; Blackpool March 1984; Darlington July 1987; Carlisle United on loan March 1989; Rochdale July 1989.*
**Appearances:** Football League 77+8; FA Cup 2; Football League Cup 3+1; Total 82+9.
**Goals:** Football League 27; Football League Cup 2; Total 29.
Although he enjoyed productive spells with Blackpool and Darlington, it was at Ewood Park that Kevin Stonehouse enjoyed his greatest success in the Football League. He had come to the club as a youngster from the North-East and Howard Kendall quickly blooded him in the senior team early in the 1979-80 season. However, his lack of experience forced

Kendall to recall Joe Craig to the first team and Stonehouse returned to the Central League for further grooming. He returned to senior action in 1980-81 and notched ten goals in 26 Second Division outings (including four as sub). Under Bob Saxton he became a regular member of the first team and his ability to play in midfield as well as attack made him an invaluable asset to a club with a rather threadbare playing staff. Unfortunately he appeared to lose his way during the 1982-83 season and in March 1983 he was transferred to Huddersfield Town.

## STOTHERT, James
Inside-forward. 1888-1889 & 1891-1892.
*Debut: v Bolton Wanderers (h) 8 December 1888.*
*Career: Bohemians; Blackburn Rovers 1888 & 1891; Darwen Dimmocks 1892; Knuzden April 1892; Brierfield; Lincoln City December 1893; Bacup cs 1896.*
**Appearances:** Football League 1.
**Goals:** Football League 1.
Stothert was literally picked from the crowd to make his first-team debut in the local derby with Bolton Wanderers on 8 December 1888. Plans for the match were thrown into disarray when Herbert Fecitt turned up for the game with an injured arm and was unable to play. With no 12th man available the Blackburn officials began to scour the crowd for a likely replacement. The man elected was James Stothert, a player with the local Bohemians junior club. Although it would appear to have been a dream debut in that he scored one of the goals which enabled Blackburn to gain a 4-4 draw, contemporary critics thought otherwise. The correspondent of the *Lancashire Daily Post* wrote: 'Stothert who, from nervousness or some other cause, played a wretchedly bad game. He was a complete hindrance instead of a help to the Rovers and more than once got in the way of Townley, and all through prevented that player from doing anything. Stothert, it is true kicked a goal, but it was more through good luck than good management.'

Whilst the criticism seems rather harsh on a man who turned up to the match as a spectator it becomes increasingly so when it is remembered that Stothert was a full-back and not a forward. In the circumstances it was hardly surprising that Stothert had been reluctant to play and turned out only after a great deal of persuasion. Stothert later appeared on the Blackburn books as a full-back but did not make any more first-team appearances. In February 1892 he was suspended for 14 days for playing for Darwen Dimmock whilst still registered with the Rovers and in April he was again suspended when a similar instance occurred with Knuzden. The second suspension was *sine die* but this was subsequently lifted and Stothert later signed for Lincoln City.

## STRACHAN, Thomas
Forward. 1880-1886.
*Born: Blackburn, 1860.*
*Debut: v Park Road (h) 29 October 1881 (FAC).*
*Career: Blackburn Rovers 1880; Darwen 1886.*
*Domestic honours with Blackburn Rovers: FA Cup winners: 1886; FA Cup runners-up: 1882.*
**Appearances:** FA Cup 21.
**Goals:** FA Cup 5.
'Tot' Strachan was a regular member of the Blackburn team during the early part of the 1880s. Strachan appeared in the friendly match with Bolton Wanderers on 9 October 1880 and scored two goals in a 7-0 win. On 25 October he scored four goals in a 9-0 win over Manchester Wanderers, but had to wait until the following season for his next senior match. A member of the team which lost the 1882 FA Cup Final, Strachan was unfortunate not to appear in the 1884 or 1885 Cup Finals. However, he returned to the team that won the trophy for a third successive season in 1886.

## STRINGFELLOW, John
Left-half. 1891-1893.
*Debut: v Derby County (h) 2 January 1892.*
*Career: Blackburn Rovers November 1891.*
**Appearances:** Football League 4.
One of ten players who made fewer than ten appearances for the club during the 1891-92 season. The numerous team changes went some way to explaining the club's disappointing ninth place in the Football League. Stringfellow was given four games in the left-half position towards the end of the season and did sufficiently well to be retained for the following campaign. However, the 1892-93 campaign brought the arrival of Harry Marshall to the left-half position and Stringfellow was never selected for the first team again.

## STUART, James

Centre-forward. 1894-1895 & 1896-1897.
*Debut: v Stoke (h) 15 September 1894.*
*Career: Albion Rovers; Blackburn Rovers September 1894; Rossendale cs 1895; Blackburn Rovers August 1896.*
**Appearances:** Football League 15.
**Goals:** Football League 5.
Stuart first came on the scene at Ewood Park at a time when the club was desperately searching for a centre-forward. Initially he made a decent showing with a goal on his debut and another on his second senior outing. Had he maintained this early show of speed and trickery he might well have been retained. However, his form fell away and at the end of the season he was allowed to leave the club. He returned in August 1896 to make a further two League appearances for the club and to score the only goal in a 1-0 home win over Liverpool in September 1896.

## SUART, Ronald

Right-back/Centre-half. 1949-1955.
*5ft 11½in; 12st 7lb.*
*Born: Kendal, 18 November 1920.*
*Debut: v Chesterfield (a) 24 September 1949.*
*Career: Netherfield; Blackpool January 1939; Blackburn Rovers September 1949; Wigan Athletic player-manager 1955; Scunthorpe United manager May 1956 to May 1958; Blackpool manager May 1958 to February 1967; Chelsea assistant manager April 1967, caretaker manager October 1967 and manager October 1974 until April 1975; general manager April 1975 until 1978 and finally chief coach until February 1983; Wimbledon chief scout in 1992.*
**Appearances:** Football League 176; FA Cup 11; Total 187.
A product of junior football in the Barrow area, Ron Suart attracted the attention of Blackpool whilst he was playing for Netherfield. He appeared in Central League football with Blackpool during the 1938-39 season but the outbreak of war delayed his League debut for the Seasiders until August 1946. Having established himself during wartime football he became one of the cornerstones of the Blackpool team in the immediate post-war years. Sadly, injury robbed him of a place in the 1948 FA Cup Final and when he could no longer command a regular first-team place at Bloomfield Road he looked to pastures new.

Suart arrived at Blackburn in September 1949 after having appeared in 103 League games for Blackpool. Initially he was seen as cover for the full-back positions but Suart broke into the team in September 1949 at centre-half, a position he had filled at Blackpool in 1946-47. Eventually, Suart won a place in his more familiar full-back position and became something of a fixture in the team. The prematurely balding Suart's main assets were his reading of the game and impeccable timing and it was these qualities that made him a reliable defender who was difficult to beat. In September 1955, keen to enter football management, Suart left Ewood Park to become player-manager of Wigan Athletic. In 1956 he was appointed manager of Scunthorpe United and in May 1958 he returned to Blackpool to take over the manager's position at Bloomfield Road. After nine, often turbulent years, with the Seasiders, Suart left Blackpool for the calmer waters of Chelsea's backroom staff. During 16 years at Stamford Bridge he occupied various positions including manager and general manager.

## SUBSTITUTES

Substitutes were first used in League games during the 1965-66 season. The first player to come onto the field as a substitute for Blackburn Rovers in a League match was John Byrom on 6 November 1965 when he replaced the injured Mick McGrath. It was John Byrom who became the first goalscoring substitute for the club when he netted in the 4-2 win over Newcastle United on 13 November 1965. Simon Garner holds the record for the greatest number of substitute appearances with the club, having appeared in 29 League matches for the club from the bench. The record for the most substitute appearances in one season for Blackburn Rovers is held by Lenny Johnrose who appeared from the bench on no fewer than 20 occasions during the 1990-91 season. Of these, 17 were in League matches, two in the FA Cup and one in the Football League Cup. Under the old rule of only a single substitute the 1972-73 season saw the greatest number of substitutes used in a single season. During the club's ultimately futile chase for promotion from the Third Division they used 30 substitutes in League matches. However, since 1986-87, two substitutes have been allowed and in 1991-92 the club used a staggering 70 substitutes in 46 League matches.

## SULLEY, Christopher Stephen

Left-back. 1987-1992.
*5ft 9in; 11st.*
*Born: Camberwell, 3 December 1959.*
*Debut: v Ipswich Town (h) 11 March 1987 (FMC).*
*Career: Chelsea apprentice July 1976, turning professional in August*

*1978; AFC Bournemouth March 1981; Dundee Untied July 1986 (£15,000); Blackburn Rovers on loan March 1987, signing permanently in April 1987 (£15,000); Port Vale August 1992 (free); Preston North End July 1993.*
*Domestic honours with Blackburn Rovers: Full Members' Cup winners: 1987.*
**Appearances:** Football League 134; Play-offs 5; FA Cup 6; Football League 6; Full Members' Cup 5; Total 156.
**Goals:** Football League 3.
A quiet unassuming full-back who amassed over 150 senior appearances in a little over five seasons with the club. Sulley had made his League debut with AFC Bournemouth and had appeared in 206 League games (including one as sub) for that club before moving to Scotland in the summer of 1986. He was brought to Blackburn by Don Mackay and made his debut against Ipswich Town in the semi-final of the Full Members' Cup. An attacking full-back, Sulley struck up a good understanding with Scott Sellars and together they formed a delightful left-sided partnership. In 1988-89 he lost his place to John Millar and in 1990-91 was again playing Central League football. However, on both occasions he returned to the senior team to make the left-back position his own. Although he began the 1991-92 season as the first-choice left-back, the arrival of Alan Wright from Blackpool ended his first-team career at Ewood. He joined Port Vale on a free transfer in the summer of 1992 and appeared in 40 League games for the Potteries club before returning to Lancashire in July 1993 to join Preston North End.

## SUNDAY FOOTBALL

The club's first experience of Sunday Football came on 27 January 1974 during the industrial upheaval caused by the dispute between the government and the coal-miners. The three-day week necessitated Sunday football and Ewood's biggest crowd of the season, 10,989 spectators, turned up to watch Blackburn defeat Shrewsbury 2-0. Other Sunday matches played during that season were a 2-1 win over Southport and a 0-0 draw with Tranmere Rovers. In recent season's the end of season Play-offs have also involved Sunday football whilst live televised matches on Sky have resulted in a number of fixtures being put back 24 hours for a 4pm Sunday kick-off. However, perhaps the most memorable Sunday fixture remains the 1987 Full Members' Cup Final against Charlton Athletic at Wembley.

## SUNDERLAND FC

Sunderland Football Club began life in 1879 as the Sunderland and District Teachers' Association FC before changing its name to Sunderland AFC in 1880. The club was elected to the Football League in 1890 and enjoyed a long spell of top flight football. Indeed, it wasn't until 1970-71 that Blackburn Rovers and Sunderland actually met in a Football League match outside of the First Division.

**Football League**

|         |         |   | Home |   | Away |
|---------|---------|---|------|---|------|
| 1890-81 | (FL)    | W | 3-2  | L | 1-3  |
| 1891-92 | (FL)    | W | 3-1  | L | 1-6  |
| 1892-93 | (Div 1) | D | 2-2  | L | 0-5  |
| 1893-94 | (Div 1) | W | 4-3  | W | 3-2  |
| 1894-95 | (Div 1) | D | 1-1  | L | 2-3  |
| 1895-96 | (Div 1) | L | 2-4  | L | 1-2  |
| 1896-97 | (Div 1) | L | 1-2  | W | 1-0  |
| 1897-98 | (Div 1) | W | 2-1  | L | 1-2  |
| 1898-99 | (Div 1) | W | 3-2  | W | 1-0  |
| 1899-00 | (Div 1) | L | 1-2  | L | 0-1  |
| 1900-01 | (Div 1) | L | 0-1  | L | 0-2  |
| 1901-02 | (Div 1) | L | 0-1  | L | 2-3  |
| 1902-03 | (Div 1) | L | 0-2  | D | 2-2  |
| 1903-04 | (Div 1) | L | 1-3  | L | 0-2  |
| 1904-05 | (Div 1) | W | 2-1  | L | 1-2  |
| 1905-06 | (Div 1) | L | 0-3  | L | 0-3  |
| 1906-07 | (Div 1) | W | 2-1  | L | 0-1  |
| 1907-08 | (Div 1) | W | 4-2  | L | 0-4  |
| 1908-09 | (Div 1) | W | 8-1  | W | 1-0  |
| 1909-10 | (Div 1) | D | 0-0  | D | 0-0  |
| 1910-11 | (Div 1) | L | 0-1  | D | 2-2  |
| 1911-12 | (Div 1) | D | 2-2  | L | 0-3  |
| 1912-13 | (Div 1) | W | 4-0  | W | 4-2  |
| 1913-14 | (Div 1) | W | 3-1  | L | 1-2  |
| 1914-15 | (Div 1) | W | 3-1  | L | 1-5  |
| 1919-20 | (Div 1) | W | 3-0  | L | 0-2  |
| 1920-21 | (Div 1) | W | 2-0  | L | 0-2  |
| 1921-22 | (Div 1) | L | 1-2  | L | 1-3  |
| 1922-23 | (Div 1) | D | 0-0  | L | 3-4  |
| 1923-24 | (Div 1) | W | 3-2  | L | 1-5  |
| 1924-25 | (Div 1) | D | 1-1  | L | 0-1  |

| | | | | | | |
|---|---|---|---|---|---|---|
| 1925-26 | (Div 1) | W | 3-0 | L | 2-6 | |
| 1926-27 | (Div 1) | L | 0-2 | W | 5-2 | |
| 1927-28 | (Div 1) | D | 0-0 | L | 0-1 | |
| 1928-29 | (Div 1) | W | 2-0 | L | 1-3 | |
| 1929-30 | (Div 1) | W | 5-3 | L | 1-3 | |
| 1930-31 | (Div 1) | W | 3-0 | L | 2-8 | |
| 1931-32 | (Div 1) | W | 5-2 | D | 2-2 | |
| 1932-33 | (Div 1) | L | 1-3 | L | 2-4 | |
| 1933-34 | (Div 1) | D | 0-0 | L | 0-3 | |
| 1934-35 | (Div 1) | D | 0-0 | L | 0-3 | |
| 1935-36 | (Div 1) | D | 1-1 | L | 2-7 | |
| 1946-47 | (Div 1) | L | 1-2 | L | 0-1 | |
| 1947-48 | (Div 1) | W | 4-3 | W | 1-0 | |
| 1964-65 | (Div 1) | W | 3-2 | L | 0-1 | |
| 1965-66 | (Div 1) | W | 2-0 | L | 0-1 | |
| 1970-71 | (Div 2) | L | 0-1 | L | 2-3 | |
| 1975-76 | (Div 2) | L | 0-1 | L | 0-3 | |
| 1977-78 | (Div 2) | D | 1-1 | W | 1-0 | |
| 1978-79 | (Div 2) | D | 1-1 | W | 1-0 | |
| 1985-86 | (Div 2) | W | 2-0 | W | 2-0 | |
| 1986-87 | (Div 2) | W | 6-1 | L | 0-3 | |
| 1988-89 | (Div 2) | D | 2-2 | L | 0-2 | |
| 1989-90 | (Div 2) | D | 1-1 | W | 1-0 | |
| 1991-92 | (Div 2) | D | 2-2 | D | 1-1 | |

| | P | W | D | L | F | A |
|---|---|---|---|---|---|---|
| Home | 55 | 25 | 15 | 15 | 106 | 73 |
| Away | 55 | 11 | 5 | 39 | 56 | 131 |
| Total | 110 | 36 | 20 | 54 | 162 | 204 |

**FA Cup**

| | | | | | |
|---|---|---|---|---|---|
| 1889-90 | | (1) | Home | W | 4-2 aet |
| 1892-93 | | (3) | Home | W | 3-0 |
| 1938-39 | | (5) | Away | D | 1-1 |
| | | (R) | Home | D | 0-0 aet |
| | | (2R) | Hillsb'gh | W | 1-0 aet |
| 1959-60 | | (3) | Away | D | 1-1 |
| | | (R) | Home | W | 4-1 |

**Football League Cup**

| | | | | |
|---|---|---|---|---|
| 1962-63 | (5) | Away | L | 2-3 |

**Full Members' Cup**

| | | | | |
|---|---|---|---|---|
| 1988-89 | (2) | Home | W | 2-1 |

**Wartime
League War Cup**

| | | | | |
|---|---|---|---|---|
| 1939-40 | (3) | Home | W | 3-2 |

**SUTER, Fergus**
Full-back. 1880-1889.
*Born: Glasgow.*
*Debut: v Sheffield Providence (h) 30 October 1880 (FAC).*
*Career: Partick Thistle; Glasgow Rangers; Turton 1878; Darwen 1879; Blackburn Rovers September 1880.*
*Domestic honours with Blackburn Rovers: FA Cup winners: 1884; 1885; 1886; FA Cup runners-up: 1882.*
**Appearances:** Football League 1; FA Cup 38; Total 39.
**Goals:** FA Cup 3.
Fergie Suter belonged to that band of Scotsmen who brought back-door professionalism to England in the days before the Football League. Suter first came to play in Lancashire in 1878 when he appeared for Turton in a local Cup competition that the club had organised. He received payment for his services and 12 months later he was playing with Darwen FC. Suter was a stonemason by trade and Darwen officials claimed that he received no payment for his services. However, shortly after joining Darwen it would appear that Suter gave up his trade because he claimed that English stone was too difficult to work with. Although he

had no other source of income, Suter still appeared to enjoy a fairly comfortable lifestyle.

Certainly a benefit game between Darwen and Turton was played in the spring of 1879 with the proceeds going to Suter and fellow Scot Jimmy Love. In 1880, this tall, strong full-back with the obligatory Victorian moustache decided to leave Darwen for 'personal reasons'. There was uproar when he announced that he would join Blackburn Rovers and Darwen officials immediately accused the Rovers of offering him better terms – even though they had always denied paying Suter. Suter, who would have a good claim to be the first professional player to be employed by Blackburn, made a major contribution to the club's rise to prominence in the 1880s. He appeared in four FA Cup Finals for the club and picked up three winners' medals and only Scotland's policy of not selecting players from England prevented him from winning the caps he so richly deserved.

At Blackburn, Suter partnered Doc Greenwood at full-back. Greenwood, an England international and former public schoolboy was the very epitome of the amateur footballer. The contrast in their background was reflected in their styles of play, but the 'English' gentleman and the 'Glaswegian' professional formed the club's first successful full-back partnership.

**SUTTIE, Thomas**
Left-back. 1907-1915.
*5ft 8in; 11st 4lb.*
*Born: Lochgelly, 1883.*
*Debut: v Sheffield Wednesday (h) 6 April 1907.*
*Career: Leith Athletic; Blackburn Rovers April 1907; Darwen; Great Harwood September 1919.*
*Domestic honours with Blackburn Rovers: First Division championship: 1911-12 (7 apps).*
**Appearances:** Football League 103; FA Cup 7; Total 110.
Contemporaries described Suttie as a strong, dour defender who was full of zeal and energy. He came to Blackburn after helping Leith to win the Second Division championship in Scotland and proved a valuable servant for the club. Suttie looked anything but the finished article on his arrival at Ewood, but with rigorous training he blossomed into a fine left-back. To many other clubs he would have been a regular in the first team but at Ewood he was competing with Arthur Cowell for the left-back spot. Although Suttie enjoyed lengthy spells in the first team in seasons 1907-08 and 1908-09, he found himself playing second fiddle to Cowell for most of his time at the club. However, Suttie was always a loyal clubman and was quite content to play second-team football whilst awaiting his chances with the first team.

**SVARC, Robert Louis**
Inside-forward. 1975-1978.
*5ft 7in; 11st 2lb.*
*Born: Leicester, 8 February 1946.*
*Debut: v Fulham (h) 4 October 1975.*
*Career: Leicester City apprentice October 1961, turning professional in March 1963; Lincoln City December 1968; Barrow on loan September to October 1970; Bolton United cs 1972; Colchester United December 1972; Blackburn Rovers October 1975; Watford on loan September 1977. Retired January 1978 due to injury.*
**Appearances:** Football League 42+8; FA Cup 4; Football League Cup 3+1; Total 49+9.
**Goals:** Football League 16; FA Cup 1; Football League Cup 3; Total 20.
Bobby Svarc was well known to Jim Smith when the Blackburn manager invested £25,000 to bring him to Ewood Park in October 1975. Although money was tight Smith believed that the fee, which was a record for Colchester, would prove a wise investment. Svarc, a proven goalscorer, had been a teammate of Smith at Lincoln City before following him to Boston, Colchester and finally Blackburn. Svarc, who didn't have the build to play as a target man, had proved himself as a tough little foraging type of inside-forward in the lower divisions. He had begun his career in the First Division with Leicester City and arrived at Ewood with a record of 79 goals from 189 League outings (including five as sub). Although he had joined a club that was struggling to find its feet following promotion to the Second Division, Svarc made a creditable start to his Ewood career. After a settling in period, Svarc was just beginning to find his touch in front of goal with four goals in six games when he was hit by cartilage problems. As a result he was kept out of action from the end of February 1976 until the start of the following season. The 1976-77 season found Svarc a regular member of the team and he finished the campaign as the club's leading goalscorer with 14 goals from 37 League and Cup appearances (including nine as sub). The arrival of Jack Lewis from Grimsby Town in August 1977 made Svarc surplus to requirements at Ewood Park. Tragically, a loan spell at Watford ended on his first

appearance when Svarc received a serious injury which ended his footballing career. Following his retirement from the game Svarc settled in Blackburn and became involved in a burglar alarm business.

## SWANSEA CITY FC
Founded in 1912 as Swansea Town, the club changed its name to Swansea City in February 1970. Blackburn Rovers and Swansea Town first crossed swords in competitive football in the 1914-15 FA Cup competition. It was Swansea City who pipped Blackburn Rovers for a place in the First Division in 1980-81 when the men from Wales took the final promotion place on goal difference. However, their time in the top flight was short lived and at the end of the 1983-84 season they slipped into the Third Division.

**Football League**

|         |         |   | Home |   | Away |
|---------|---------|---|------|---|------|
| 1936-37 | (Div 2) | W | 2-1  | L | 0-1  |
| 1937-38 | (Div 2) | W | 3-1  | L | 2-3  |
| 1938-39 | (Div 2) | W | 4-0  | L | 1-2  |
| 1949-50 | (Div 2) | W | 2-0  | L | 0-2  |
| 1950-51 | (Div 2) | W | 3-0  | W | 2-1  |
| 1951-52 | (Div 2) | W | 3-1  | L | 1-5  |
| 1952-53 | (Div 2) | W | 3-0  | D | 1-1  |
| 1953-54 | (Div 2) | W | 1-0  | L | 1-2  |
| 1954-55 | (Div 2) | W | 4-1  | W | 3-2  |
| 1955-56 | (Div 2) | W | 3-0  | L | 1-2  |
| 1956-57 | (Div 2) | W | 5-3  | L | 1-5  |
| 1957-58 | (Div 2) | D | 2-2  | W | 4-0  |
| 1971-72 | (Div 3) | L | 1-2  | W | 1-0  |
| 1972-73 | (Div 3) | W | 3-0  | D | 2-2  |
| 1980-81 | (Div 2) | D | 0-0  | L | 0-2  |
| 1983-84 | (Div 2) | W | 4-1  | W | 1-0  |

|       | P  | W  | D | L  | F  | A  |
|-------|----|----|---|----|----|----|
| Home  | 16 | 13 | 2 | 1  | 43 | 12 |
| Away  | 16 | 5  | 2 | 9  | 21 | 30 |
| Total | 32 | 18 | 4 | 10 | 64 | 42 |

**FA Cup**

| 1914-15 | (1) | Away | L | 0-1 |
|---------|-----|------|---|-----|
| 1938-39 | (3) | Home | W | 2-0 |
| 1954-55 | (3) | Home | L | 0-2 |

**Football League Cup**

| 1960-61 | (2) | Away | W | 2-1 |
|---------|-----|------|---|-----|

## SWARBRICK, James
Outside-left. 1901-1903.
*Born: Lytham St Annes, Lancashire 1881.*
*Debut: v Sheffield Wednesday (a) 22 March 1902.*
*Career: Blackpool Red Star; Marton Combination; Blackpool Etrurians; Blackburn Rovers November 1901; Accrington Stanley on loan April 1903; Brentford cs 1903; Grimsby Town August 1905; Oldham Athletic May 1907; Southport Central November 1909; Stoke May 1910; Burslem Port Vale August 1911; Swansea Town December 1912.*
**Appearances:** Football League 15; FA Cup 1; Total 16.
A dexterous dribbler with plenty of speed, Swarbrick was a formidable man on the wing when on top of his game. Sadly, his promotion to the first team at Ewood Park was followed by a slump in form and in April 1903 he was loaned to Accrington Stanley to help them clinch the Lancashire Combination title. After leaving Blackburn his career followed a rather nomadic path but he enjoyed some success, particularly with Grimsby Town.

## SWIFT, Edward
Right-half. 1899-1900.
*Debut: v Everton (h) 25 November 1899.*
*Career: Black Diamonds; Blackburn Rovers April 1899.*
**Appearances:** Football League 2.
Swift came to Ewood Park with Sam McClure from the Black Diamonds club of Workington. The Rovers had actually travelled to Workington to watch Swift when they had been impressed with McClure and returned to Ewood with the signatures of both men. Swift had developed quite a reputation in Workington for his half-back play but his only two appearances for the Rovers came in consecutive games in November and December 1899. Although the right-half position was proving something of a problem to fill, Swift was continually overlooked until the return of Geordie Anderson closed the door on further first-team opportunities.

## SWINDELLS, John
Centre-forward. 1957-1959.

5ft 9in; 11st 9lb.
*Born: Manchester, 12 April 1937.*
*Debut: v Swansea Town (a) 28 September 1957.*
*Career: Manchester City amateur May 1955; Blackburn Rovers amateur June 1957, turning professional in November 1957; Accrington Stanley December 1959 (£1,200); Barnsley June 1961; Workington February 1962; Torquay United July 1963; Newport County July 1964 to June 1965; Altrincham August 1965 (£500).*
**Appearances:** Football League 9.
**Goals:** Football League 1.
Once an amateur on the books of Manchester City, Jack Swindells joined the Rovers during the reign of Johnny Carey and signed professional forms after completing his National Service. A former England youth international, Swindells began as a left-winger at Ewood before being moved into a more central position. He had an impressive goalscoring record with the Central League team at Ewood with over 50 goals in two and a half seasons. In December 1959 he made the short move to Peel Park in search of first-team football and scored 28 goals in 65 League games for Stanley before joining Barnsley in the summer of 1961. He enjoyed a moderately successful career in the lower divisions before moving into non-League football with Altrincham.

## SWINDON TOWN FC
Founded in 1881, Swindon Town became members of the Southern League in 1894 before joining the Football League as founder members of the Third Division in 1920. Swindon have proved something of a bogey side for Blackburn in knock-out football with the men from Ewood Park failing to register a single win in either FA Cup, Football League Cup, Full Members' Cup or Play-off competitions.

**Football League**

|         |         |   | Home |   | Away |
|---------|---------|---|------|---|------|
| 1969-70 | (Div 2) | W | 2-0  | L | 0-1  |
| 1970-71 | (Div 2) | W | 1-0  | L | 0-3  |
| 1974-75 | (Div 3) | W | 2-0  | L | 0-2  |
| 1979-80 | (Div 3) | W | 2-0  | L | 0-2  |
| 1987-88 | (Div 2) | D | 0-0  | W | 2-1  |
| 1988-89 | (Div 2) | D | 0-0  | D | 1-1  |
| 1989-90 | (Div 2) | W | 2-1  | L | 3-4  |
| 1990-91 | (Div 2) | W | 2-1  | D | 1-1  |
| 1991-92 | (Div 2) | W | 2-1  | L | 1-2  |

|       | P  | W | D | L | F  | A  |
|-------|----|---|---|---|----|----|
| Home  | 9  | 7 | 2 | 0 | 13 | 3  |
| Away  | 9  | 1 | 2 | 6 | 8  | 17 |
| Total | 18 | 8 | 4 | 6 | 21 | 20 |

**Premier League**

|         | Home |     | Away |     |
|---------|------|-----|------|-----|
| 1993-94 | W    | 3-1 | W    | 3-1 |

|       | P | W | D | L | F | A |
|-------|---|---|---|---|---|---|
| Home  | 1 | 1 | 0 | 0 | 3 | 1 |
| Away  | 1 | 1 | 0 | 0 | 3 | 1 |
| Total | 2 | 2 | 0 | 0 | 6 | 2 |

**Play-offs**

|         | Home  | Away  |
|---------|-------|-------|
| 1989-90 | L 1-2 | L 1-2 |

**FA Cup**

| 1967-68 | (3) | Away | L | 0-1 |
|---------|-----|------|---|-----|
| 1969-70 | (3) | Home | L | 0-4 |

**Football League Cup**

| 1968-69 | (3) | Away | L | 0-1 |
|---------|-----|------|---|-----|

**Full Members' Cup**

| 1987-88 | (1) | Home | L | 1-2 |
|---------|-----|------|---|-----|

## TALBOT, Frank Leslie
Inside-forward. 1930-1936.
5ft 11in; 11st 10lb.
*Born: Hednesford, 3 August 1910.*
*Debut: v Manchester United (a) 11 April 1931.*
*Career: Hednesford Town; Blackburn Rovers October 1930; Cardiff City June 1936; Walsall June 1939; Bath City wartime guest; Walsall 1945.*
**Appearances:** Football League 90; FA Cup 6; Total 96.
**Goals:** Football League 20; FA Cup 1; Total 21.
For four of his six seasons at Ewood Park, Les Talbot found it extremely difficult to break into the senior team. During those four seasons he made

37 appearances and had only eight goals to show for his efforts. However, the 1934-35 campaign began with Talbot installed in the inside-right position after trials at inside-left and centre-forward had proved rather disappointing. A return of nine goals from 30 League appearances suggested Talbot was finally finding his niche in the team. A forceful type of inside-forward, who was particularly useful in the air, Talbot enjoyed a formidable right-wing partnership with Jack Bruton which was always liable to break down opposing defences. The 1935-36 season saw him switched to inside-left but without the same degree of success. In June 1936 he joined Cardiff City in a deal which also took Albert Pinxton to Ninian Park. One of four footballing brothers, his brother Alex, played at centre-half for Aston Villa.

### TAYLOR, Gordon
Winger. 1976-1978.
*5ft 6in 11st 2lb.*
*Born: Ashton-under-Lyne, 28 December 1944.*
*Debut: West Bromwich Albion (a) 13 March 1976.*
*Career: Mossley Road County Primary School; Ashton-under-Lyne Grammar School; Ashton Schoolboys; Lancashire Schoolboys; Curzon Ashton FC 1959-60; Bolton Wanderers amateur June 1960, turning professional in January 1962; Birmingham City December 1970 (£18,000); Blackburn Rovers March 1976; Vancouver Whitecaps (Canada) (on loan) June to August 1977; Bury June 1978. Retired 1980 and became secretary of the PFA.*
**Appearances:** Football League 62+2; FA Cup 2+1; Football League Cup 2; Total 66+3.
**Goals:** Football League 3.
A high profile role with the Professional Footballers' Association has tended to obscure a successful playing career that stretched over two decades. Outstanding schoolboy performances brought Taylor to the attention of Manchester United and Arsenal as a youngster but he opted to join Bolton Wanderers, the club he had supported from the terraces. He signed amateur forms in June 1960 and in January 1962 he became a professional with the club. Although he made his debut for Bolton in March 1963, it was not until January 1964 that he won a regular place on the Wanderers' left wing. A diminutive, stocky winger who was equally at home on either flank, Taylor's powerful running and explosive shooting was a threat to any defence. He appeared in 258 League games (including five as sub) for Bolton

and scored 41 goals before moving to Birmingham City in December 1970.

Taylor helped Birmingham to win promotion to the First Division in 1972 and was a member of the 1972 and 1975 FA Cup semi-final teams. Taylor moved to Ewood Park in March 1976 at a time when the club was desperately clinging to its Second Division status. He arrived at Ewood Park with Dave Wagstaffe, a fellow veteran, and their experience and guile helped the club to avoid relegation. Although Taylor was dogged by injuries during his stay at Ewood, he proved himself to be the perfect clubman and one who was very popular with the supporters. The summer of 1977 found him playing in the North American Soccer League with Vancouver but he returned to Blackburn to spend one final season with the club before ending his career with Bury. It was during his two seasons at Gigg Lane that Taylor became deeply involved with the work of the PFA and he joined that organisation on a full-time basis on his retirement from playing.

Taylor was appointed secretary of the PFA in 1981 and has become one of the most eloquent advocates that the game of football has ever had. His thoughtful and diplomatic approach to the game's problems has earned him the admiration of not only his own members but also that of most genuine lovers of the game. In 1989, the late Bill Fox tried to install Taylor as chief executive of the Football League but was unable to overcome the opposition of certain First Division clubs. Taylor remained at the PFA and has continued to provide the sort of vision and leadership which is so sadly lacking in those who try to run the game.

### TAYLOR, Kenneth Gordon
Right-back. 1950-1964.
*5ft 9in; 11st 9lb.*
*Born: South Shields, 15 March 1931.*
*Debut: v Leeds United (h) 4 December 1954.*

*Career: Blackburn Rovers January 1950 to June 1964; Morecambe cs 1964.*
**Appearances:** Football League 200; FA Cup 22; Football League Cup 11; Total 233.
Ken Taylor graduated through the junior ranks at Ewood Park and went on to give over a decade of loyal service to Blackburn Rovers. Taylor spent his first four years at Ewood in the junior ranks before moving up to Central League football. However, within months of his second-team debut he found himself thrust into action in the Second Division. A steady rather than spectacular defender, Taylor's brand of football was always 'safety first' but his solid reliability earned him 35 League appearances during the successful 1957-58 promotion campaign. Although he had to compete with the likes of Eckersley, Whelan, Bray and Newton for a full-back position, Taylor's consistency brought him 200 League appearances for the club. He made his final first-team appearance in March 1964 and during the summer of that year he moved into non-League football with Morecambe.

### TAYLOR, Reginald
Secretary-manager. 1936-1938.
*Born: cs 1873.*
*Career: Preston North End assistant secretary 1922, then secretary 1925; Blackburn Rovers secretary April 1936, then secretary-manager October 1936 until April 1938, then reverting to secretary.*
The resignation of Arthur Barritt as secretary-manager in March 1936 was followed by the appointment of Reg Taylor to the position of secretary in April 1936. Taylor had begun his career in football administration as assistant secretary of Preston North End in 1922. He was later promoted to the position of secretary and retained that post until he came to Ewood Park in April 1936. Whilst at Deepdale he had gained a reputation as one of the game's finest administrators.

The 1936-37 season began with Taylor looking after administrative matters and the directors in charge of team selection. By the end of October the team was struggling at the foot of the Second Division with the directors' record of team management coming under increasing criticism. In response to the growing pressure the directors promptly put Taylor in charge of team affairs as well as administration.

The result was fairly predictable. A man who had no previous experience of team management could do little to lift the fortunes of the club. Although the team managed to finish in 12th position in the League, the FA Cup provided a major shock when the Rovers went out at the hands of Third Division North club Accrington Stanley. The following season saw the team struggling at the foot of the Second Division and, with relegation a distinct possibility, a movement began to bring Bob Crompton back to the club. In April 1938 Crompton, with Taylor's blessing, returned to assist Taylor. With relegation averted the directors appointed Crompton to the position of manager and allowed Taylor to return to administrative matters.

### TAYLOR, Royston
Midfield. 1976-1979.
*5ft 8in; 10st 11lb.*
*Born: Blackpool, 28 September 1956.*
*Debut: v Leicester City (h) 16 September 1978.*
*Career: Preston North End associated schoolboy April 1972, becoming an apprentice in May 1972 before turning professional in October 1974; Sunderland non-contract player; Blackburn Rovers November 1976 to cs 1979. Barrow; Workington; Barrow.*
**Appearances:** Football League 3.
**Goals:** Football League 1.
A promising young midfield player who came to the club after a short period as a non-contract player with Sunderland. Taylor had begun his career as a schoolboy with Preston and made three senior appearances with the Deepdale club before moving to the North-East. Taylor was brought to Ewood Park by Jim Smith but had to bide his time in the Central League before being given his chance by Jim Iley in September 1978. Unfortunately, Taylor was thrown into a team whose confidence was low and as a result failed to make much impression. He made his final appearance in the last match of the season and was then released.

Ronnie Clayton pictured at Ewood Park with the Great Britain XI. Left to right are: Dave Mackay, Bobby Moore, Alan Kelly, Eamonn Rogers, Bobby Moncur, Tommy Gemmell, Geoff Hurst, Keith Newton, Roger Hunt, Fred Pickering and Mike England.

## TAYLOR, William

Outside-right. 1892-1893.

*Born: Edinburgh 1870; Died: 23 July 1949 (aged 79).*

*Debut: Derby County (h) 7 January 1893.*

*Career: Dalry Primrose; Heart of Midlothian; Blackburn Rovers November 1892; Heart of Midlothian 1893; Leith Athletic 1900.*

**Appearances:** Football League 10; FA Cup 3; Total 13.

**Goals:** Football League 1; FA Cup 1; Total 2.

Although news of Taylor's impending transfer reached the columns of the local Press in November 1892, the player didn't actually appear in Blackburn until two months after his signing. It was said that Taylor had received an attractive offer to join Blackburn and that he was to receive more than fellow Scots, Harry Marshall and Geordie Anderson. A prolific goalscorer whilst in Scotland, Taylor was a cultured winger who came to Blackburn with a fine reputation. Strangely, Taylor never quite found his form in Lancashire and after appearing in the final ten League games of the 1892-93 season he returned to continue his career in Scotland .

## TELEVISION

Blackburn Rovers participated in the first match, other than an FA Cup Final, to receive television coverage. The match was the fifth-round FA Cup-tie with Charlton Athletic at The Valley on 8 March 1947. It was not a happy occasion for the Rovers as they lost to a single Charlton goal. Since that time the club have featured in numerous games which have been included in edited highlights form.

On 17 February 1983, the BBC televised the fifth-round FA Cup-tie with Southampton live from Ewood Park. The following season the fifth-round home tie with Manchester United received similar treatment. Unfortunately both games were lost.

Perhaps the most memorable live match was the screening of the Play-off victory over Leicester City at Wembley on 25 May 1992.

Entry into the Premier League saw Blackburn Rovers feature in seven live screenings on Sky Television during the 1992-93 season. Sky also televised the FA Cup replay with Sheffield United live, whilst ITV covered both of the semi-finals of the Coca-Cola Cup live.

The 1993-94 season saw an increased number of League games televised live by Sky, including the two titanic battles with Manchester United over the Christmas and Easter holiday period. As the race for the Premiership title drew to a close, the Rovers found that four of their final seven League matches were selected for live screening. This brought to 11 the total number of the club's League matches which were screened live during the 1993-94 season. The importance of television revenue to

the club can be judged by the fact that £2 million was earned during each of the first two seasons of Premiership football.

## TEST MATCHES

It was at the end of the 1897-98 season that Blackburn Rovers became embroiled in the test match series which would determine the promotion and relegation issues. At that time it was customary for the bottom two clubs in the First Division and the top two clubs in the Second Division to meet to decide promotion and relegation places. Thus Blackburn Rovers lined up with Stoke and Second Division Burnley and Newcastle to battle it out for two First Division places. The games were played at the end of April and although the Rovers brought one or two familiar faces back to Ewood Park to assist them, the matches did not go well. Their results were as follows:

| | | | | | |
|---|---|---|---|---|---|
| 21 Apr v | Burnley | Home | L | 1-3 |
| 23 Apr v | Burnley | Away | L | 0-2 |
| 28 Apr v | Newcastle United | Home | W | 4-3 |
| 30 Apr v | Newcastle United | Away | L | 0-4 |

At the end of the series the table read:

| | P | W | D | L | F | A | Pts |
|---|---|---|---|---|---|---|---|
| Stoke | 4 | 2 | 1 | 1 | 4 | 2 | 5 |
| Burnley | 4 | 2 | 1 | 1 | 5 | 3 | 5 |
| Newcastle United | 4 | 2 | 0 | 2 | 9 | 6 | 4 |
| Blackburn Rovers | 4 | 1 | 0 | 3 | 5 | 12 | 2 |

To all intents and purposes Blackburn Rovers FC was now a Second Division club. However, Burnley drafted a resolution proposing that the First Division be enlarged and that Newcastle United and Blackburn Rovers should take the vacant places. The proposal was passed and Blackburn Rovers survived. At the meeting which determined the club's fate, John Lewis voted against the proposal because he was genuinely opposed to extending the number of clubs in the First Division.

## TESTIMONIAL MATCHES

Throughout the history of Blackburn Rovers the club has rewarded loyal service with at testimonial or benefit match.

Below are details of some of these matches:

| | | | | | |
|---|---|---|---|---|---|
| 23 Feb | 1885 | v | Blackburn Olympic | Home |
| L 1-4 | (John Duckworth) | | | |
| 31 May | 1886 | v | Preston North End | Home |
| D 0-0 | (Hugh McIntyre) | | | |

| | | | | |
|---|---|---|---|---|
| 7 Feb | 1886 | v | Preston North End | Home |
| W 2-0 | (Fergie Suter) | | | |
| 20 May | 1889 | v | Bolton Wanderers | Home |
| D 1-1 | (Joe Beverley) | | | |
| 10 Mar | 1890 | v | Preston North End | Home |
| D 2-2 | (Jim Forrest) | | | |
| 16 Feb | 1892 | v | Everton | Home |
| W 2-1 | (Nat Walton) | | | |
| 31 Oct | 1892 | v | Darwen | Home |
| W 2-0 | (Jack Southworth) | | | |
| 30 Oct | 1893 | v | Everton | Home |
| L 0-1 | (Harry Campbell) | | | |
| 15 Oct | 1894 | v | Preston North End | Home |
| W 2-1 | (Geordie Dewar) | | | |
| 21 Oct | 1895 | v | Preston North End | Home |
| D 1-1 | (Joe Heyes) | | | |
| 11 Sep | 1905 | v | Preston North End | Home |
| D 0-0 | (Arnold Whittaker) | | | |
| 27 Apr | 1920 | v | John Lewis XI | Home |
| D 0-0 | (Jock Simpson) | | | |
| 22 Apr | 1935 | v | Glasgow Rangers | Home |
| W 1-0 | (Jack Bruton) | | | |
| 18 Apr | 1961 | v | Eckersley Select XI | Home |
| L 9-11 | (Bill Eckersley) | | | |
| 15 May | 1976 | v | Manchester City | Home |
| W 2-1 | (Mick Heaton & Andy Burgin) | | | |
| 7 May | 1979 | v | Everton | Home |
| W 4-2 | (Stuart Metcalfe) | | | |
| 5 May | 1980 | v | Preston North End | Home |
| D 0-0 | (Derek Fazackerley) | | | |
| 18 May | 1983 | v | Everton | Home |
| W 2-0 | (Tony Parkes) | | | |
| 16 May | 1984 | v | Burnley | Home |
| W 3-1 | (Norman Bell) | | | |
| 14 May | 1985 | v | Northern Ireland | Home |
| W 3-1 | (Fred O'Donoghue) | | | |
| 12 May | 1987 | v | Preston North End | Home |
| W 2-1 | (Glenn Keeley) | | | |
| 19 Aug | 1988 | v | Newcastle United | Home |
| D 2-2 | (Simon Garner) | | | |
| 11 Sep | 1990 | v | Manchester City | Home |
| L 0-2 | (Noel Brotherston) | | | |
| 10 Oct | 1992 | v | Aberdeen | Home |
| W 3-1 | (Terry Gennoe) | | | |

Two testimonial matches which did not feature a normal Blackburn line-up were those for Bryan Douglas and Ronnie Clayton. The Douglas Testimonial was held on 20 October 1969 and involved a Douglas XI, made up of past and present Blackburn players, against an All Star XI. In front of a crowd of 16,851 the Douglas XI won by 10 goals to 6 thanks to goals from Douglas (3), Pickering (2), Vernon, MacLeod (2) and Dobing (2). On 2 December 1970 a Manchester City/Liverpool XI beat a Great Britain XI by seven goals to five. Both Clayton and Bryan Douglas turned out for the Great Britain XI in the second half and the game attracted a crowd of 11,407.

## THOMAS, Edward
Inside-forward. 1960-1962.
*5ft 9in; 10st 9lb.*
*Born: Newton-le-Willows, 23 October 1933.*
*Debut: v Manchester City (h) 13 February 196.*
*Career: Everton October 1951; Blackburn Rovers February 1960 (as part of the Roy Vernon transfer to Everton); Swansea Town July 1962; Derby County August 1964 (£6,000); Orient September 1967 (£5,000); Nuneaton 1968; Heanor Town cs 1968.*
**Appearances:** Football League 37; FA Cup 2; Football League Cup 5; Total 44.

**Goals:** Football League 9; FA Cup 1; Football League Cup 5; Total 15.
Eddie Thomas came to Ewood Park as part of the club's biggest ever transfer transaction. Everton parted with £25,000 and Thomas to take an unsettled Roy Vernon to

Goodison Park in February 1960. Although Thomas was Everton's leading goalscorer at the time of the transfer he was not seen as a direct replacement for Vernon. That position went on to Chris Crowe who was later acquired from Leeds United and Thomas, who had scored 39 goals in 86 League games at Goodison, did not gain a regular place in the first team until the latter part of the 1960-61 season. During his time at Blackburn he had various spells in the first team without ever really suggesting that he might provide a long-term solution to the inside-forward positions. The highlight of his time at the club was a four goal display in the 4-0 win over Bristol Rovers in a League Cup replay in October 1961. A regular scorer with the reserves, Thomas left Ewood Park in July 1962 to sign for Swansea Town. He scored 21 goals in 68 League games at Swansea before moving to Derby County in August 1964. He left the Baseball Ground with a record for 43 goals in 105 League games (including three as sub) before ending his career with two goals in 11 appearances with Leyton Orient.

## THOMPSON, Christopher David
Centre-forward. 1983-1986.
*5ft 11in; 12st 2lb.*
*Born: Walsall, 24 January 1960.*
*Debut: v Huddersfield Town (h) 27 August 1983 (sub).*
*Career: Bolton Wanderers July 1977; Lincoln City on loan March 1983; Blackburn Rovers August 1983; Wigan Athletic July 1986; Blackpool July 1988; Cardiff City March 1990; Walsall non-contract February 1991.*
**Appearances:** Football League 81+4; FA Cup 10; Football League Cup 5; Total 96+4.
**Goals:** Football League 24; FA Cup 2; Total 26.
Chris Thompson was snapped up by Bob Saxton from neighbouring Bolton on the eve of the 1983-84 season. He got his chance to break into the Blackburn team when Norman Bell was injured in the opening game of the season. The injury ended Bell's career and Thompson took the opportunity to establish himself in the first team. Thompson proved a workmanlike partner for Simon Garner, but a return of eight goals in 33 League games (including two as sub) hardly suggested prolific marksmanship. However, Thompson proved something of a revelation during the early part of the 1984-85 season with nine goals from his first ten League games. His form was so good that Jimmy Quinn, a £40,000 summer arrival from Swindon, was kept on the substitute's bench until the middle of December. Unfortunately Thompson was unable to maintain his strike rate but still ended the season as the club's leading goalscorer with 15 League goals. The following season was a disappointing one for everyone at Ewood and Thompson, like so many others, failed to reproduce his best form. In July 1986 he left the club to make the short move to Wigan Athletic.

## THOMPSON, John Ernest
Centre-forward. 1931-1936.
*5ft 10in; 12st.*
*Born: New Biggin, 1909 (July quarter).*
*Debut: v Sheffield Wednesday (h) 29 August 1931.*
*Career: Benfieldside School; Stakeford U; Ashington amateur 1927-28; Bradford on trial; Carlisle United September 1928; Bristol City June 1929; Bath City February 1930; Blackburn Rovers April 1931; Manchester United November 1936 (£4,500); Gateshead March 1938.*
**Appearances:** Football League 171; FA Cup 8; Total 179.
**Goals:** Football League 82; FA Cup 2; Total 84.
Ernie Thompson was plucked from non-League football and went on to become a prolific goalscorer for the club at a time when its fortunes were beginning to wane. Thompson had begun his career in his native North-East and had the distinction of appearing in three trials with three different clubs, in three different positions, all within the space of a week. An amateur player with Ashington, he was offered professional terms after appearing at right-half in a 1928-29 pre-season trial. He declined the offer and went to Bradford to play at centre-half for Park Avenue in another pre-season game. Finally, he turned out at inside-right for Carlisle United and signed amateur forms for the club.
    Within three weeks he had done sufficient to be awarded a professional contract by the Cumbrian club. He was a regular goalscorer with the reserves at Carlisle and helped the club to win the Cumberland Cup and the Second Division title of the North Eastern League. The end of the 1929-30 season saw him leave Carlisle when the club couldn't afford to pay his summer wages. Thompson joined Bristol City in June 1929 but in February he moved to Bath City and helped them win the Southern League title. His manager at Bath was Ted Davis, a former goalkeeper at Ewood Park, and he arranged a trial with Blackburn which resulted in him joining the club in April 1931. He scored on his debut on the opening day of the 1931-32 season but soon found himself playing Central League football at Ewood. However he returned to the side at the start of October and ended his first season at Blackburn with 21 goals

from 35 League games. During the course of his first campaign at Ewood, Thompson developed into an excellent leader of the line. Tall and strong with pace to match, Thompson became one of the First Division's outstanding centre-forwards with 17 goals in 40 League games during 1932-33. Tragedy struck on 4 November 1933 when the Rovers beat Wolves 7-1 at Ewood Park with Thompson scoring a hat-trick.

Just four minutes from the end of the match he tried to score his fourth goal, collided with the goalkeeper and broke a leg. It was an injury that was to keep him out of action for the remainder of the season. He regained his fitness and was again the club's top scorer when he netted 15 goals in 38 League games during the 1935-36 season. Sadly, his goals were not enough to prevent the club from slipping in the Second Division for the first time in its history. The 1936-37 season was only a few months old when Thompson moved to Old Trafford. However, he didn't enjoy the same amount of success in Manchester with just one goal in three League appearances before returning to his native North-East to join Gateshead.

### THOMPSON, Robert
Goalkeeper. 1898-1900.
*5ft 11in.*
*Born: 11 February 1878.*
*Debut: v Stoke (a) 11 March 1899.*
*Career: Whalley; Blackburn Rovers November 1898.*
**Appearances:** Football League 9.
Shortly after joining the club from local non-League football, Thompson found himself promoted to the number two 'keeper behind James Carter. However, towards the end of the campaign Thompson was given a run of six League games and did sufficiently well to begin the 1899-1900 season as the first-choice 'keeper. In truth, Thompson's promotion came about because Carter was in dispute with club officials. Two of the opening three games were lost and Thompson, who was particularly weak at kicking the ball, was excluded in favour of Albert Knowles. Thompson spent the rest of the campaign vying for place in the Lancashire Combination team and left the club at the end of the season.

### THORLEY, Dennis
Midfield. 1980.
*6ft; 10st 10lb.*
*Born: Stoke, 7 November 1956.*
*Debut: v Exeter City (a) 12 April 1980 (sub).*
*Career: Stoke City July 1976; Blackburn Rovers on loan March to May 1980.*
**Appearances:** Football League 2+2.
A former teammate of Howard Kendall at Stoke City, the Blackburn manager brought Thorley to Ewood Park on loan for the final promotion run-in of 1979-80. Thorley, who made just 13 League appearances with Stoke (including four as sub), deputised for Kendall in two League games and made a further two appearances as a substitute. Whilst he didn't let anybody down he was not signed on a permanent basis at the end of the season.

### THORNEWELL, George
Outside-right. 1927-1929.
*5ft 7in; 10st 7lb.*
*Born: Romiley, 8 July 1898; Died: Derby, 6 March 1986.*
*Debut: v Burnley (a) 31 December 1927.*
*Career: Rolls Royce 1916-17; Nottingham Forest amateur 1917; Derby County amateur 1918, turning professional in September 1919; Blackburn Rovers December 1927; Chesterfield August 1929; Newark Town February 1932.*
*Domestic honours with Blackburn Rovers: FA Cup winners: 1928.*
**Appearances:** Football League 41; FA Cup 6; FA Charity Shield 1; Total 48.
**Goals:** Football League 4; FA Cup 1; FA Charity Shield 1; Total 6.
A nippy little winger who had the misfortune to break a collar-bone in the FA Cup-tie with Exeter City in January 1928. Although the injury kept him out of action for several weeks he returned to play his part in the FA Cup victory over Huddersfield Town at Wembley. Somewhat lightweight in build, Thornewell, a winger who liked to hug the touch-line, relied upon his exceptional pace to beat the opposing full-back. However, as well as sprinting down the touch-line, Thornewell was not averse to cutting inside and having a crack at goal himself. One contemporary commentator said that Thornewell: "Does his work neatly and seldom wastes a ball." Thornewell lost his first-team place during the latter part of the 1928-29 campaign when Jack Roscamp was moved from centre-forward to the right wing. Unable to regain his place he opted to join Chesterfield on the eve of the 1929-30 campaign.

### THORPE, Levi
Right-half. 1920-1922.
*5ft 8in; 10st 7lb.*
*Born: Seaham Harbour, 18 November 1889.*
*Debut: v Bradford (a) 23 February 1920.*
*Career: Seaham Harbour; Blackpool February 1911; Burnley October 1913; Blackburn Rovers February 1920; Lincoln City September 1922; Rochdale June 1924.*
**Appearances:** Football League 85; FA Cup 7; Total 92.
**Goals:** Football League 1.

Levi Thorpe entered League football with Blackpool and enjoyed great success at Bloomfield Road, appearing in 92 consecutive League matches for the club. A move to Burnley in October 1913 was not quite so successful but after a season of being in and out of the side, Thorpe settled down to become a first-team regular during the 1914-15 season. After the war, Thorpe continued his career at Turf Moor until his move to Ewood Park in February 1920. He made his debut for the club on the same day that he was transferred from Burnley and became an automatic choice for the right-half position. The 1921-22 *Lancashire Daily Post Football Annual* said of Thorpe: 'Right-half and captain, an invaluable member of the side. Is a schemer of parts, and a local favourite.' Thorpe remained at the heart of the side until the latter part of the 1922-23 season. The emergence of Harry Healless resulted in Thorpe being allowed to move to Lincoln City in September 1922.

### TIERNEY, Thomas Timothy
Forward. 1895-1897 & 1898.
*5ft 7in; 11st 3lb.*
*Born: Cheshire 1875.*
*Debut: v Nottingham Forest (h) 14 September 1895.*
*Career: Whitton Albion; Chorley; Blackburn Rovers June 1985; New Brighton Tower cs 1897; Blackburn Rovers on loan April 1898; Chorley; New Brighton Tower June 1899; Luton Town 1901; Gainsborough Trinity August 1902.*
**Appearances:** Football League 21; Test Matches 2; Total 23.
**Goals:** Football League 3.
Tierney had the ability to be become an outstanding player but sadly his game lacked consistency. He joined the Rovers in the summer of 1895 from Chorley but was unable to win a regular place during the 1895-96 season. However, he proved himself to be an invaluable understudy by appearing in four different forward positions and made a goalscoring debut in the home match with Nottingham Forest. The 1896-97 season saw him given a run in the team during the early part of the campaign before he lost his place to more consistent performers. The summer of 1897 saw him move to New Brighton Tower but he returned to Ewood in April 1898 to appear in the penultimate League game of the season. He was one of four former players who were brought back to the club over the final weeks of the season in a bid to stave off relegation. He then returned to New Brighton via Chorley before ending his career with spells at Luton Town and Gainsborough Trinity.

### TODD, Paul Raymond
Inside-left. 1950-1951.
*5ft 11½in; 12st 7lb.*
*Born: Middlesbrough, 8 May 1920.*
*Debut: v Sheffield United (a) 19 August 1950.*
*Career: Wolverhampton Wanderers trial; Leicester City trial; RAF football; Doncaster Rovers September 1945; Blackburn Rovers July 1950 (£10,000); Hull City October 1951 (£6,500); King's Lynn player-manager May 1953; Worksop Town manager.*
**Appearances:** Football League 46; FA Cup 1; Total 47.
**Goals:** Football League 13.
A scheming type of inside-forward who also had an eye for goal, Paul Todd failed to impress both Wolves and Leicester City in pre-war trials and began his career in the more sparse surroundings of Doncaster Rovers. He helped Doncaster to two Third Division North titles, in 1947 and 1950, and on 9 March 1947 he was married in the morning and scored two goals against Darlington in the afternoon. He was brought to Ewood Park by Jackie Bestall, his former manager at Doncaster, in the

summer of 1950 after scoring 51 goals in 160 League appearances with Doncaster. Todd showed great consistency during his first season at Ewood and only missed three League games. However, the arrival of Albert Nightingale from Huddersfield Town in September 1951 resulted in Todd being allowed to move to Hull City.

## TOMLINSON, James
Centre-half. 1900-1901.
*5ft 11in.*
*Born: Blackburn.*
*Debut: v Bolton Wanderers (a) 30 March 1901.*
*Career: Blackburn Rovers August 1900; Nelson 1902; Darwen cs 1903-04; Brentford cs 1904; Norwich City cs 1908.*
**Appearances:** Football League 1.
Tomlinson was regarded as an outstanding young prospect when he arrived at Ewood Park on the eve of the 1900-01 season. His long legs enabled him to cover a lot of ground and also allowed him to intercept many a pass that was not intended for him. Good in the air, Tomlinson was a formidable defensive barrier but was also a player who was capable of finding his forwards with accurate passes. Unfortunately, with Bob Haworth, Sam McClure and Kelly Houlker forming an impressive half-back line, Tomlinson found little scope for first-team football. He returned to the non-League game for a time before playing in the Southern League with Brentford and Norwich City.

## TOMLINSON, Robert W.
Right-back. 1945-1951.
*5ft 10¼in; 10st 12lb.*
*Born: Blackburn, 4 June 1924.*
*Debut: v Bolton Wanderers (a) 5 January 1946 (FAC).*
*Career: Feniscowles; Blackburn Rovers January 1943; Accrington Stanley September 1948; Mossley 1949; Halifax Town June 1951.*
**Appearances:** Football League 25; FA Cup 4; Total 29.
Bob Tomlinson joined Blackburn during World War Two but only appeared in seven wartime matches for the club. The 1946-47 season found him playing Central League football and apparently going nowhere. However, the appointment of Will Scott as manager changed Tomlinson's fortunes. The new manager decided to begin the new season with an experimental full-back pairing of Tomlinson and George Higgins. Even when Scott succumbed to ill health, Tomlinson did well enough to retain his place during the caretaker stewardship of Jack Burton. However, after 24 League appearances during the 1947-48 season he lost his place and didn't appear for the senior team again. A move to Accrington Stanley didn't work out and Tomlinson spent some time playing with Mossley before his transfer to Halifax Town in June 1951. Tomlinson appeared in nine League games for Halifax during the 1951-52 season.

## TORQUAY UNITED FC
Although founded in 1898, Torquay United have had very little contact with Blackburn Rovers throughout their long history. Torquay were elected to the Third Division South of the Football League in 1927 but the 1971-72 season was the only time the two clubs met in the League.

### Football League
| | | | Home | | Away | |
|---|---|---|---|---|---|---|
| 1971-72 | | (Div 3) | W | 1-0 | L | 1-3 |

| | P | W | D | L | F | A |
|---|---|---|---|---|---|---|
| Home | 1 | 1 | 0 | 0 | 1 | 0 |
| Away | 1 | 0 | 0 | 1 | 1 | 3 |
| Total | 2 | 1 | 0 | 1 | 2 | 3 |

## TOTTENHAM HOTSPUR FC
Founded in 1882, Tottenham Hotspur were elected to the Second Division of the Football League in 1908. The first competitive meeting between Blackburn Rovers and Tottenham Hotspur came in the 1906-07 FA Cup competition when Tottenham were still members of the Southern League. A number of closely fought FA Cup-ties have been played over the years but perhaps the most memorable League meeting for Blackburn supporters was the 7-2 drubbing of Spurs at Ewood Park in the 1963-64 season.

### Football League
| | | | Home | | Away | |
|---|---|---|---|---|---|---|
| 1909-10 | | (Div 1) | W | 2-0 | L | 0-4 |
| 1910-11 | | (Div 1) | W | 3-0 | D | 2-2 |
| 1911-12 | | (Div 1) | D | 0-0 | W | 2-0 |
| 1912-13 | | (Div 1) | W | 6-1 | W | 1-0 |
| 1913-14 | | (Div 1) | D | 1-1 | D | 3-3 |
| 1914-15 | | (Div 1) | W | 4-1 | W | 4-0 |
| 1920-21 | (Div 1) | D | 1-1 | W | 2-1 |
| 1921-22 | (Div 1) | D | 1-1 | L | 1-2 |
| 1922-23 | (Div 1) | W | 1-0 | L | 0-2 |
| 1923-24 | (Div 1) | L | 0-1 | L | 1-2 |
| 1924-25 | (Div 1) | D | 1-1 | L | 0-5 |
| 1925-26 | (Div 1) | W | 4-2 | L | 2-4 |
| 1926-27 | (Div 1) | W | 1-0 | D | 1-1 |
| 1927-28 | (Div 1) | W | 2-1 | D | 1-1 |
| 1933-34 | (Div 1) | W | 1-0 | L | 1-4 |
| 1934-35 | (Div 1) | W | 2-0 | L | 0-1 |
| 1936-37 | (Div 1) | L | 0-4 | L | 1-5 |
| 1937-38 | (Div 1) | W | 2-1 | L | 1-3 |
| 1938-39 | (Div 2) | W | 3-1 | L | 3-4 |
| 1948-49 | (Div 2) | D | 1-1 | L | 0-4 |
| 1949-50 | (Div 2) | L | 1-2 | W | 3-2 |
| 1958-59 | (Div 1) | W | 5-0 | L | 1-3 |
| 1959-60 | (Div 1) | L | 1-4 | L | 1-2 |
| 1960-61 | (Div 1) | L | 1-4 | L | 2-5 |
| 1961-62 | (Div 1) | L | 0-1 | L | 1-4 |
| 1962-63 | (Div 1) | W | 3-0 | L | 1-4 |
| 1963-64 | (Div 1) | W | 7-2 | L | 1-4 |
| 1964-65 | (Div 1) | W | 3-1 | L | 2-5 |
| 1965-66 | (Div 1) | L | 0-1 | L | 0-4 |
| 1977-78 | (Div 2) | D | 0-0 | L | 0-4 |

| | P | W | D | L | F | A |
|---|---|---|---|---|---|---|
| Home | 30 | 16 | 7 | 7 | 57 | 32 |
| Away | 30 | 5 | 4 | 21 | 38 | 85 |
| Total | 60 | 21 | 11 | 28 | 95 | 117 |

### FA Premiership
| | | Home | | Away | |
|---|---|---|---|---|---|
| 1992-93 | | L | 0-2 | W | 2-1 |
| 1993-94 | | W | 1-0 | W | 2-0 |

| | P | W | D | L | F | A |
|---|---|---|---|---|---|---|
| Home | 2 | 1 | 0 | 1 | 1 | 2 |
| Away | 2 | 2 | 0 | 0 | 4 | 1 |
| Total | 4 | 3 | 0 | 1 | 5 | 3 |

### FA Cup
| 1906-07 | (2) | Home | D | 1-1 |
|---|---|---|---|---|
| | (R) | Away | D | 1-1 aet |
| | (2R) | Villa Park | L | 1-2 |
| 1910-11 | (2) | Home | D | 0-0 |
| | (R) | Away | W | 2-0 |
| 1924-25 | (3) | Away | D | 2-2 |
| | (R) | Home | W | 3-1 |
| 1937-38 | (3) | Away | L | 2-3 |
| 1959-60 | (5) | Away | W | 3-1 |

### Football League Cup
| 1988-89 | (3) | Away | D 0-0 |
|---|---|---|---|
| | (R) | Home | L 1-2 aet |

## TOURS
Blackburn Rovers have embarked on a number of pre and post season tours during their history. In the early days these tours were usually visits to play the odd match or two in Scotland and later Ireland. However at the conclusion of the 1910-11 season, Blackburn Rovers undertook a 12-day tour of Austria and Hungary. The tour was arranged by The First Vienna Football Club who paid the Rovers a guaranteed sum of money to undertake the trip and arranged a schedule of six games for the Ewood club.
Details of the trip are outlined below:
25 May 1911 v Vienna Association W 9-1
28 May 1911 v Oldham Athletic L 0-1
31 May 1911 v Oldham Athletic W 5-2
2 Jun 1911 v Budapest Athletic W 4-1
4 Jun 1911 v Magyar Testgyakoriok W 4-0
5 Jun 1911 v Ferencvárosi Torna W 8-1

The opening match saw Percy Smith score four goals with his head, three from corners by Walter Anthony and a fourth from a free-kick by the same player. Joe Clennell notched a hat-trick, whilst Eddie Latheron and an own-goal completed the scoring. In the third game of the tour, the Rovers and Oldham Athletic met for a second time to compete for a silver cup, valued at £20 0s 0d which had been presented by the Vienna club. The fourth match was a rugged affair with the Hungarian team resorting to physical tactics to try to prevent the Rovers from securing victory. However, two goals from Joe Clennell and one each from Billy Bradshaw and Bob Crompton were sufficient to ensure a comfortable victory. The

Rovers off on a sightseeing trip during their visit to Austria and Hungary in May 1914.

fifth match saw goals from Davies, Latheron, Orr and Clennell giving the touring team a comfortable victory. In light of the previous match, Bob Crompton was prompted to say that the home team had played in a most gentlemanly manner.

The final match was regarded as the most important of the tour as Ferencvárosi had a reputation for defeating touring teams from England. However, within ten minutes the Rovers found themselves with a three goal lead and then Joe Clennell scored what seemed to be a perfectly legitimate fourth goal. To the amazement of the Blackburn team, the referee decided to rule out the goal and minutes later awarded the home side a penalty. When this was missed he immediately ordered it to be retaken and when the Blackburn players argued with the official he promptly left the field. He was followed by Crompton and other Blackburn players and following a long discussion the official agreed to return if he could have his own way over the penalty. Whilst this heated debate was taking place under the grandstand, the Hungarian player who had missed the spot kick was busily engaged in rehearsing his penalty kick technique. The game restarted with a penalty and the ball was promptly dispatched into the back of the Blackburn net. The game was said to have 'proceeded merrily, with the Rovers still scoring'. However, 15 minutes from the end, Davies received a blow in the face from the opposing goalkeeper, just as he was about to put the ball into the net. Davies suffered damage to two teeth and the home custodian hastily fled from the pitch. At this point the crowd turned somewhat ugly and Davies was attacked by a spectator as he left the pitch at the end of the match. A threatening mob were held at bay by police with drawn sabres as the coaches of the Blackburn party were brought into the ground. As they left the arena a stone broke a window but fortunately no one was injured.

Apart from this unfortunate incident, the men from Blackburn enjoyed a wonderful trip and amongst other things enjoyed a day's sail down the Danube, visited the Royal Palace of Schonbraum, the country residence of the Emperor France Joseph and were entertained at a champagne warehouse at Budapest. Following the success of this first continental expedition the Rovers accepted an offer to tour Hungary, Austria and Germany at the end of the 1913-14 season. The results of that tour were as follows:

11 May v Ferencváros L 1-2
12 May v Magyar Testgyakoriok Kore L 1-2
14 May v Sunderland (in Budapest) L 2-3
18 May v Wiener AFC W 4-1
24 May v Hertha BSC W 4-1
25 May v Viktoria Cologne W 4-2

More recent end of season tours have seen Blackburn Rovers visit Germany in 1952, 1960 and 1966, Czechoslovakia in 1972 and Denmark in 1973. In 1965-66 the club undertook a short pre-season tour of Holland but it was Don Mackay in 1989 who introduced touring as a regular part of pre-season preparations. Blackburn Rovers have also acted as host to a number of touring clubs over the years. In 1888-89 the club defeated a Canadian touring team 4-1 and in 1891-92 another Canadian touring team suffered in identical defeat. The Australian club Vienna FC visited Ewood Park in December 1935 and were beaten 2-1 and in January 1955 Linz ASK were defeated 6-2 at Ewood. The erection of the floodlighting system resulted in visits from Werder Bremen in November 1958 (won 3-1), Biel in October 1959 (won 10) and Venlo in April 1960 (won 6-2). However, friendlies against continental opposition have tended to be the exception rather the rule with the most recent example being the visit of Bohemians Prague in August 1972 (won 4-0).

## TOWNLEY, William J.
Outside-left. 1886-1892 & 1893-1894.
*5ft 10in; 10st 6lb.*
*Born: Blackburn, 4 February 1866; Died: 30 May 1950.*
*Debut: v Renton (h) 27 November 1887 (FAC).*
*Career: Blackburn Swifts; Blackburn Olympic; Blackburn Rovers 1886; Stockton July 1892; Blackburn Rovers August 1893; Darwen July 1894; Manchester City September 1896 to cs 1897. Coaching on the continent from 1909 to 1934; Karlsruher SC (Germany) 1909; Fürth (Germany) 1914; Munich (Germany) 1919; Hamburg (Germany) 1921; Kroningen (Holland) 1921; Sweden 1923; Switzerland 1924; Fürth (Germany) 1926; Frankfurt (Germany) 1927; Hamburg (Germany) 1929; Fürth (Germany) 1930; Hanover 1932 to 1934. Returned to England in 1934.*
*International honours with Blackburn Rovers: England: 2 caps (1889-90).*
*Domestic honours with Blackburn Rovers: FA Cup winners: 1890; 1891.*
**Appearances:** Football League 97; FA Cup 26; Total 123.
**Goals:** Football League 37; FA Cup 14; Total 51.
A native of Blackburn, Billy Townley became the first man to prove to be a worthy successor to Jack Hargreaves on the left wing of Blackburn Rovers. Noted for his speed, Townley was an early example of the classic winger. Townley had been a member of the Blackburn Swifts Football Club for 12 months after leaving school and from there he progressed to Blackburn Olympic. At Olympic he was used as a centre-forward and it was in this position that he first joined Blackburn Rovers. However, after

Blackburn Rovers visited Hungary in May 1914, shortly before the outbreak of World War One. Rovers players standing at the back are (from left to right): A.Walmsley, unknown, J.Clennell, A.Cowell, G.R.Chapman, P.J.Smith, E.G.Latheron, J.Hodkinson, A.Robinson, W.Bradshaw, J.Johnston.

a handful of appearances leading the Rovers' attack he was moved to the left wing.

A schoolmaster by profession, Townley formed a dynamic left-wing partnership with Nat Walton for most of his time with the Rovers. Both fast and tricky, Townley could not only send over pinpoint crosses but was also a dangerous marksman in his own right. In 1891 he became the first man to score a hat-trick in an FA Cup Final when his three goals helped to give the Rovers a resounding 6-1 victory over Sheffield Wednesday. On leaving Blackburn he appeared for several clubs whilst still continuing his profession of schoolmaster. Indeed, despite his success in the game he did not turn his back on the classroom until he began his coaching career. As a coach, Townley worked extensively abroad between 1909 and 1934. His son, John Chadwick Townley, was on the books of Tottenham Hotspur, Brighton and Clapton Orient between the wars.

## TRANMERE ROVERS FC
Founded in 1883, Tranmere Rovers joined the Third Division North in 1921 and won the title in 1937-38. The following season saw the first League game between Blackburn and Tranmere but the clubs did not meet again in the League until 1971-72.

**Football League**

|         |          |      | Home |      | Away |
|---------|----------|------|------|------|------|
| 1938-39 | (Div 2)  | W    | 3-2  | D    | 1-1  |
| 1971-72 | (Div 3)  | W    | 4-1  | W    | 3-1  |
| 1972-73 | (Div 3)  | D    | 2-2  | D    | 1-1  |
| 1973-74 | (Div 3)  | D    | 0-0  | D    | 1-1  |
| 1974-75 | (Div 3)  | W    | 2-1  | D    | 1-1  |
| 1991-92 | (Div 2)  | D    | 0-0  | D    | 2-2  |

|       | P  | W | D | L | F  | A  |
|-------|----|---|---|---|----|----|
| Home  | 6  | 3 | 3 | 0 | 11 | 6  |
| Away  | 6  | 1 | 5 | 0 | 9  | 7  |
| Total | 12 | 4 | 8 | 0 | 20 | 13 |

**Wartime**

| 1941-42 | (FLNS-SC) | Away | W | 5-0* |
|---------|-----------|------|---|------|

*Note: Only one game was played.

## TRANSFERS
In July 1992, Blackburn Rovers smashed the British transfer record when Alan Shearer was signed from Southampton for £3,300,000. However, this was not the first time that Blackburn created history in the transfer market. In January 1911, the club set a new British record when they paid Falkirk £1,800 for Jock Simpson and just 12 months later they broke this record when £2,000 was paid to bring Danny Shea from West Ham United.

For many years the most expensive player at the club was Jack Bruton who cost £6,500 from Burnley. The first five figure fee was paid in January 1947 when Jock Weir, Hibernian's centre-forward, was signed for £10,000. However, the move was not a success and a little over 12 months later Weir returned to Scotland to join Celtic for £7,000. The record fee paid for Oakes was overtaken by the £15,000 reported to have been paid for Albert Nightingale from Huddersfield Town in October 1951.

However, within a month a new record had been established when Eddie Quigley joined the club from Preston North End for a fee reputed to be £20,000. The 1960s gradually saw a spiralling of transfer fees and in May1970, Blackburn Rovers paid their highest fee up to that point when Jimmy Kerr was signed from Bury for £65,000. Tragically, Kerr only played 11 League games for the club before a serious injury forced him into premature retirement. The fee paid for Kerr was not beaten until John Pickering paid Chelsea £75,000 for Duncan McKenzie in March 1979. In August 1990, Lee Richardson joined the club from Watford in a deal that was reputedly worth £250,000. However, this involved Andy Kennedy making the opposite journey and it was though that only £50,000 actually changed hands.

In December 1990 the club paid a record £250,000 to sign Bobby Mimms from Tottenham Hotspur. This deal marked the beginning of Jack Walker's active involvement in the activities of Blackburn Rovers and it wasn't long before a new record was established. In January 1991 the Rovers signed Steve Livingstone from Coventry City for £450,000 and also bought Tony Dobson, another Coventry player, for a further £250,000. The first £500,000 transfer occurred in August 1991 when David Speedie joined the club from Liverpool. The arrival of Kenny Dalglish and Ray Harford to Ewood Park in October 1991 signalled the real beginnings of the Ewood transfer revolution. Details of transfers into the club from October 1991 until the end of the 1993-94 season are outlined below.

| Oct | 1991 | Alan Wright (Blackpool) | £500,000 |
|---|---|---|---|
| Nov | 1991 | Colin Hendry (Manchester City) | £700,000 |
| Nov | 1991 | Mike Newell (Everton) | £1,100,000 |
| Nov | 1991 | Garry Tallon (Drogheda United) | £30,000 |
| Nov | 1991 | Gordon Cowans (Aston Villa) | £200,000 |
| Feb | 1992 | Chris Price (Aston Villa) | £100,000 |
| Feb | 1992 | Tim Sherwood (Norwich City) | £500,000 |
| Mar | 1992 | Roy Wegerle (Queen's Park Rangers) | £1,100,000 |
| Mar | 1992 | Duncan Shearer (Swindon Town) | £750,000 |
| Mar | 1992 | Matt Dickins (Lincoln City) | £250,000 |
| Jul | 1992 | Lee Makel (Newcastle United) | £160,000 |
| Jul | 1992 | Stuart Ripley (Middlesbrough) | £1,200,000 |
| Aug | 1992 | Alan Shearer (Southampton) | *£3,300,000 |
| Aug | 1992 | Wayne Burnett (Leyton Orient) | £75,000 |
| Aug | 1992 | Frank Talia (Sunshine George, Australia) | £150,000 |
| Sep | 1992 | Nicky Marker (Plymouth Argyle) | *£500,000 |
| Nov | 1992 | Simon Ireland (Huddersfield Town) | £200,000 |
| Jan | 1993 | Patrik Andersson (Malmö FF) | £800,000 |
| Jan | 1993 | Henning Berg (Lillestrøm) | £400,000 |
| Mar | 1993 | Kevin Gallacher (Coventry City) | *£1,500,000 |
| Mar | 1993 | Graeme Le Saux (Chelsea) | *£650,000 |
| Aug | 1993 | Andy Morrison (Plymouth Argyle) | *£250,000 |
| Sep | 1993 | Paul Warhurst (Sheffield Wednesday) | £2,700,000 |
| Sep | 1993 | Ian Pearce (Chelsea) | £300,000 |
| Oct | 1993 | David Batty (Leeds United) | £2,750,000 |
| Nov | 1993 | Tim Flowers (Southampton) | +£2,000,000 |
| Jul | 1994 | Chris Sutton (Norwich City) | £5,000,000 |

*Total fee includes player/s in part exchange.
+A world record fee for a goalkeeper.

**TURNBULL, Peter**
Centre-forward. 1895-1896 & 1898.
*5ft 7in; 11st 5lb.*
*Born: Lanquhar, 1875.*
*Debut: v Sunderland (a) 7 September 1895.*
*Career: Glasgow Rangers; Burnley March 1893; Bolton Wanderers on loan Mach 1895; Blackburn Rovers April 1895 (£75); Glasgow Rangers May 1896; Blackburn Rovers on loan April 1898; Millwall Athletic cs 1898; Queen's Park Rangers August 1899; Brentford November 1900.*
**Appearances:** Football League 26; FA Cup 1; Total 27.
**Goals:** Football League 7; FA Cup 1; Total 8.
Peter Turnbull could fill any of the inside-forward positions but was used primarily as a centre-forward whilst at Ewood Park. Blessed with natural athleticism, Turnbull knew how to control the ball at speed and was a difficult man to dispossess. A proven goalscorer, Turnbull didn't enjoy the best of fortunes in a Blackburn side that had only just escaped relegation to the Second Division. His subsequent career was far more successful than his stint at Ewood Park.

**TURNER, David J.**
Midfield. 1972-1974.
*5ft 9in; 11st 12lb.*
*Born: Retford, 7 September 1943.*
*Debut: v Bolton Wanderers (h) 2 September 1972 (sub).*
*Career: Newcastle United amateur August 1960, turning professional in October 1960; Brighton & Hove Albion December 1963; Blackburn Rovers August 1972 to cs 1974.*
**Appearances:** Football League 23+2; FA Cup 1; Total 24+2.
A vastly experienced player who came to Ewood Park from Brighton on a free transfer at the same time as Kit Napier made the move from the Goldstone Ground. He was unfortunate to suffer cartilage trouble during the latter part of the 1972-73 season after making 21 appearances (including one as sub) in the Third Division. On returning to fitness he spent most of his time using his experience to guide the youngsters in the Central League team. Turner was freed at the end of the 1973-74 season.

**TURNER, Thomas Stuart**
Outside-left. 1929-1936.
*5ft 4in; 8st 10lb.*
*Born: Glasgow.*
*Debut: v West Ham United (h) 31 August 1929.*
*Career: St Rocks Juniors (Glasgow); Raith Rovers 1923-1924; Blackburn Rovers May 1929; Arbroath cs 1936.*
**Appearances:** Football League 113; FA Cup 2; Total 115.
**Goals:** Football League 24.
Towards the end of his career at Ewood Park *The Lancashire Daily Post Football Annual* said of Turner: 'Can be ranked among the most accomplished outside-lefts in the country. Yet he has generally to stand down for speedier men. A willing servant and intelligent footballer, this little man with a vicious shot, makes even international opponents seem amateurish when they try to counter his cleverness at close quarters.' The man who was popularly known as 'Tucker' Turner came to Ewood Park in May 1929 from Raith Rovers. He began the 1929-30 season on the left-wing but lost his place to Arthur Cunliffe in January 1930. The brilliance of Cunliffe meant that Turner had to spend the next three seasons playing mainly Central League football. However, when Cunliffe left the club in the summer of 1933, Turner was restored to the first team. In January 1934, Turner had to surrender his first-team place to Jackie Milne. Once again Turner had to bide his time in the Central League until Milne's departure once again opened the first-team door to him. Sadly, the 1935-36 season proved to be the swan-song at Ewood Park for a player whose ability had never been fully realised during his time with the club. The summer of 1936 saw him return to his native Scotland to join Arbroath.

**TYNE ASSOCIATION FC**
An amateur club based in the North-East who provided the first opposition to Blackburn Rovers in the FA Cup on 1 November 1879. The Rovers enjoyed a comfortable 5-1 home victory thanks to goals from Jimmy Brown (2), John Lewis and John Duckworth (2).

**TYSON, William George**
Inside-forward. 1937-1938.
*5ft 7in; 10st 12lb.*
*Born: Skerton, Lancaster 1916 (January quarter).*
*Debut: v Newcastle United (a) 26 March 1938.*
*Career: Lancaster Schoolboys; Skerton Athletic; Southport amateur June 1933; Glentoran 1934; Lancaster Town October 1935; Accrington Stanley September 1936; Blackburn Rovers October 1937 (with R.Mortimer for a combined fee of £1,200); Boston Untied August 1938; Accrington Stanley October 1938; Southport June to September 1939; Accrington Stanley wartime guest August 1944.*

**Appearances:** Football League 6.
**Goals:** Football League 2.
Billy Tyson enjoyed his greatest success in the Football League at neighbouring Peel Park. Twelve goals in 26 League games and two sound performances against the Rovers in the FA Cup were sufficient to persuade Ewood officials to bring him to Ewood Park with Bob Mortimer in October 1937. Whilst Mortimer went straight into the first team. Tyson had to bide his time in the Central League. At Accrington he had been something of a bustling type of inside-forward, but one who was also astute in his use of the ball. He broke into the Blackburn team during the latter stages of the 1937-38 season when he appeared in six of the final nine League games. However these proved to be his only senior outings at Ewood and 12 months after joining the club he returned to Peel Park after a short stint with Boston United.

**UPTON PARK FC**
Formed in 1866, Upton Park were one of the original 15 entrants into the first FA Cup competition in 1871-72. Blackburn Rovers visited Upton Park in the fifth round of the 1883-84 FA Cup competition and earned a 3-0 victory thanks to goals by Inglis and Lofthouse (2). A stalwart of the amateur game, Upton Park played as the 'Great Britain' team in the 1900 Olympic Games in Paris and returned with the gold medal.

**VAUSE, Peter G.**
Outside-left. 1934-1938.
*5ft 9¾in; 11st 6lb.*
*Born: Chorley, 1914 (July quarter).*
*Debut: v Huddersfield Town (h) 9 November 1935.*
*Career: Balshaw's Grammar School; Leyland Motors; Blackburn Rovers amateur September 1934; Blackpool on trial 1938-39; Darwen September 1938; Rochdale December 1938 to 1940-41.*
**Appearances:** Football League 7; FA Cup 1; Total 8
**Goals:** Football League 1
A schoolteacher at Poulton-le-Fylde, Peter Vause enjoyed a meteoric rise from non-League to First Division football. He joined Blackburn as an amateur and came into the first team after only six games in the Central League. Vause made five appearances during 1935-36 season and a further two the following campaign. However, the arrival of Billy Guest in January 1937 closed the first-team door on Vause and he returned to non-League football for a spell before trying to relaunch his career with Rochdale.

**VENTERS, Alexander**
Inside-forward. 1947-48.
*5ft 7in; 11st 9lb.*
*Born: Cowdenbeath, 9 June 1913. Died: 30 April 1959.*
*Debut: v Bolton Wanderers (h) 15 March 1947.*
*Career: Southend Rovers (Fife); St Andrews United 1930; Cowdenbeath 1930-31; Glasgow Rangers November 1933; Third Lanark cs 1945; Blackburn Rovers February 1947 (£1,000); Raith Rovers February 1948. Retired May 1948.*
**Appearances:** Football League 25
**Goals:** Football League 7
Alec Venters finally came to Ewood Park some 14 years after the club first tried to entice him south of the border. In 1933 a fee of £3,000 had been agreed with Cowdenbeath for Venters and the Ewood club had even gone as far as arranging work for him as a printer when the player declined the move south. Instead of coming to Blackburn Venters moved to Glasgow Rangers and developed into an outstanding play-maker. Venters was capped three times by Scotland and also made six appearances for the Scottish League side. He also collected four championship medals and was twice a member of the Rangers side which lifted the Scottish Cup. At the end of the war he left Rangers for Third Lanark but in February 1947 he was finally persuaded to try his luck in England with Blackburn Rovers. Even then negotiations were protracted because Venters, a former compositor in the printing industry, had a licensed house in Scotland and preferred to travel south on match days rather than settle in Blackburn. Although into the veteran stage of his career the canny little Scot revitalised the Blackburn attack. It was Venters who provided the guile and craft which enabled the Blackburn team to escape relegation at the end of the 1946-47 season. The following season he was not quite so effective and as a result he was allowed to return to Scotland to join Raith Rovers in February 1948.

**VERNON, Thomas Royston**
Inside-left. 1954-1960.
*5ft 9in; 10st 2lb.*
*Born: Ffynnongroew, nr Holywell, Flintshire, 14 April 1937; Died: Blackburn, 5 December 1993.*
*Debut: v Liverpool (h) 3 September 1955.*
*Career: Rhyl Grammar School XI; Flintshire Schools XI; Mostyn YMCA*

*Juniors; Welsh YMCA; Mostyn YMCA; Blackburn Rovers groundstaff March 1954, turning professional in March 1955; Everton February 1960 (£27,000 + Eddie Thomas); Stoke City March 1965 to April 1970 (£40,000); Halifax Town on loan January 1970; Capetown FC (South Africa); Great Harwood 1970 until January 1972.*
*International honours with Blackburn Rovers. Wales: 9 caps (1957-58). Wales Under-23: 1 cap (1958).*
**Appearances:** Football League 131; FA Cup 13; Total 144.
**Goals:** Football League 49; FA Cup 3; Total 52.

One of Ewood's 'Carey Chicks', Roy Vernon was a superbly gifted player whose exceptional skill and perception had few equals. A creative player who struck a dead ball with tremendous power, Vernon came to Ewood from school and went on to become a Welsh International who appeared in the 1958 World Cup finals in Sweden. At Ewood he had made his debut as an 18-year-old and by 19 he had won his first Welsh cap. Although capable of the most breathtaking wizardry on the pitch, Vernon was also temperamentally unpredictable. Following the departure of Johnny Carey to Everton, Vernon began to grow increasingly disillusioned with life at Ewood Park. He continually clashed with Dally Duncan and in February 1960 he followed his mentor to Goodison Park in the deal which brought Eddie Thomas to Blackburn. Ironically, Vernon had once been offered a trial at Everton but had opted to join the Blackburn groundstaff. A member of the side which brought the First Division championship to Goodison Park in 1962-63, Vernon developed into one of the finest creative players of his era.

Yet as well as creating chances for others Vernon also maintained a highly respectable goalscoring record of his own. He left Everton in March 1965 after scoring 101 goals in just 176 League appearances and at Stoke he scored 22 goals in 87 League games (including three as sub). In January 1970 he had a brief spell on loan with Halifax Town before spending some time in South Africa. He returned to Lancashire in September 1970 to join former Ewood colleagues Ronnie Clayton and Bryan Douglas at Great Harwood. Together the three former internationals took the Northern Premier League club into the first round of the FA Cup for the first time in its history. Vernon retired from the game in January 1972.

**WADDINGTON, John**
Central-defender/Midfield. 1973-1979.
*5ft 11in; 11st 7lb.*
*Born: Darwen, 16 February 1952.*
*Debut: v Brighton & Hove Albion (h) 6 October 1973.*
*Career: St Mary's College, Blackburn; Blackburn Schoolboys; Liverpool May 1970; Darwen; Blackburn Rovers August 1973; Vancouver Whitecaps on loan summer 1977; Bury August 1979.*

*Domestic honours with Blackburn Rovers: Third Division championship: 1974-75 (21 apps, 4 gls).*

**Appearances:** Football League 139+9; FA Cup 12; Football League Cup 7+1; Total 158+10.

**Goals:** Football League 18; FA Cup 2; Total 20.

Although a local youngster, John Waddington entered the world of professional football at Liverpool in May 1970. Unfortunately, a severe bout of glandular fever led to him being released by the Anfield Club before he could make his mark in the game. On recovery from illness, Waddington obtained a trial at Ewood Park. He quickly passed his trial and medical at Blackburn and within a matter of weeks he had also graduated to the first team at centre-half. Although his original position had been centre-forward, it was as a defender that Waddington was to carve a niche for himself at Ewood. Although not the quickest of defenders, his power in the air and the strength of his tackling made him a formidable opponent. Throughout his time at the club he found himself in competition with men like Derek Fazackerley, John McNamee, Graham Hawkins and Glenn Keeley and as a result he could never quite establish himself in the first team. An ability to play in midfield provided him with further first-team opportunities but his lack of pace proved to much of an Achilles' heel in this position. He played in the North American Soccer League with Vancouver Whitecaps in the summer of 1977 and ended his League career with a brief spell at Bury.

**WADE, John James**
Outside-right. 1894-1895.
*Debut: v Sheffield Wednesday (h) 29 September 1894.*
*Career: Darwen August 1891; Blackburn Rovers September 1894.*
**Appearances:** Football League 1.
**Goals:** Football League 2.

Although Wade made a dramatic debut at Ewood Park in September 1894, he was unable to win a regular place on the Rovers' right wing. Wade had enjoyed great success at the nearby Barley Bank ground in Darwen before moving to Blackburn at the start of the 1894-95 season. He had won a regular place in the Darwen team at the end of February 1891 and had only missed one League game during the 1892-93 season. Although he had lost his way a little during the 1893-94 campaign, the Blackburn committee had been sufficiently impressed to offer him terms in September 1894. Wade's final League match at Barley Bank had been on 8 September 1894 when he scored one goal in the 6-0 win over Lincoln City. At the end of that month he made his debut for Blackburn as understudy to Jimmy Haydock and scored two goals in a 3-1 win over Sheffield Wednesday at Ewood. However, the following week saw Haydock return and Wade was not called upon again for the senior team.

**WAGSTAFFE, David**
Outside-left. 1976-1978 & 1979-1980.
*5ft 8in; 10st 8lb.*
*Born: Manchester, 5 April 1943.*
*Debut: v Bristol City (a) 1 January 1976.*
*Career: Manchester City May 1960; Wolverhampton Wanderers December 1964; Blackburn Rovers on loan January to February 1976; Blackburn Rovers March 1976; Blackpool August 1978; Blackburn Rovers March 1979.*
**Appearances:** Football League 74+3; FA Cup 4; Football League Cup 4; Total 82+3.
**Goals:** Football League 7.

Dave Wagstaffe came to Ewood Park in the twilight of his career and became a great favourite on the terraces with his glorious passing ability. Perhaps the finest uncapped winger of his era, Wagstaffe had begun as a youngster with Manchester City but enjoyed his greatest success at Wolverhampton Wanderers. At his peak there was no finer left winger in the country and it was a tragedy that he was overlooked for full representative honours.

Jim Smith first brought him to Blackburn on loan in January 1976 to help lift his struggling team away from the foot of the Second Division. Although his blistering pace had faded, Wagstaffe had added craft and guile to his game and his ability to pass the ball with great accuracy made him ideally suited for a creative role in midfield. Problems over the fee required by Wolves appeared to have ended hopes of a transfer but fortunately an agreement was reached and Wagstaffe returned in March on a permanent basis.

Hugely popular with the supporters, Wagstaffe revelled in his deeper role and struck up a successful partnership with young John Bailey on the left-wing. Whilst Bailey made attacking runs from his left-back position, Wagstaffe peppered long range passes all round the field. There was uproar when Wagstaffe left the club in rather controversial circumstances on the eve of the 1978-79 season. Indeed, the decision to part with Wagstaffe totally alienated manager Jim Iley to supporters and was one of the factors in his downfall in October 1978.

In March 1979, John Pickering brought Wagstaffe back to Ewood Park in an attempt to save the club from slipping into the Third Division. Unfortunately, 'Waggy' was injured in his second match and this effectively ended his senior career. After becoming involved in local football in the Blackpool area he returned to live in the Midlands. Ironically, for a player who relied totally on skill and ability, Dave Wagstaffe was the first player in the Football League to be shown a red card following the introduction of the card system. Wagstaffe received his marching orders at Orient on 2 October 1976 but the Rovers held on to win 1-0.

**WALKER, Jack**
Vice-President.

A life-long supporter of Blackburn Rovers Football Club, Jack Walker became the club's benefactor following the sale of his Walker Steel empire for £330 million. Although still active in business, he found the time to take control at Ewood Park and map out a new and exciting future for a club he had supported as boy. It was in 1945 that Jack's father Charles, had started a tiny sheet metal working and car body repair business with just £80. Following the death of his father, Jack and brother Fred continued to build up the business until they had an £80,000 turnover by 1956. In that year the Walkers entered the steel stockholding business and began their remarkable success story. Although Walker had moved to Jersey he still took an interest in his local football club and in turn the club appointed him Senior Vice-President. He immediately funded the signings of Bobby Mimms, Steve Livingstone and Tony Dobson which enabled the club to escape from the floor of the Second Division in 1990-91.

Following the dismissal of Don Mackay at the start of the 1991-92 season it was Walker who suggested that Kenny Dalglish was the man to revive the club's fortunes. On 12 October 1991, the former Liverpool man was duly installed as manager with Ray Harford, the former Wimbledon manager, appointed as his assistant. Ranked at 24 in the list of the wealthiest individuals in Britain in 1994, Walker has provided the funds which have seen Blackburn Rovers become one of the most powerful clubs in the country. Under the expert management of Dalglish and Harford, Walker has seen his beloved Rovers finish as runners-up in the Premier League and enter Europe after only two seasons in the top flight. At the same time he has provided the finance to redevelop three sides of the stadium and turn it into one of the finest in the country. In seeing Blackburn Rovers become once again a major force in football. 'Uncle Jack', as Walker is popularly known, has not only fulfilled his own dream but also that of thousands of his fellow Blackburnians.

**WALMSLEY, Albert**
Right-half. 1904-1920.
*5ft 9½in; 11st 12lb.*
*Born: Blackburn, 21 October 1885.*
*Debut: v Newcastle United (a) 26 October 1907.*
*Career: St Peter's (Blackburn); Darwen; Blackburn Rovers May 1904; Stockport County July 1920 to 1922-23.*
*Domestic honours with Blackburn Rovers: First Division championship: 1911-12 (37 apps); 1913-14 (37 apps, 1 gl).*
**Appearances:** Football League 272; FA Cup 28; Total 300.

**Goals:** Football League 6.

Charles Francis' early history of Blackburn Rovers describes Albert Walmsley as 'A rare worker, with consistency as an outstanding characteristic, he was keenness personified. As he made little fuss on the field, he did not always catch the eye, but close students of the game appraised him at his true value.' Walmsley had played in local junior circles before enjoying a couple of seasons with Darwen. Walmsley moved to Ewood Park in May 1904 but made very little impact during his early years at the club. However, he bided his time playing reserve-team football before establishing himself in

*Life-long supporter Jack Walker greets new manager Kenny Dalglish, as they embark on an exciting future for Blackburn Rovers*

the senior side during the 1907-08 season. Although not as spectacular in his approach to half-back play as his partner Billy Bradshaw, Walmsley was blessed with an unquenchable thirst for work and boundless enthusiasm. A regular in two championship winning sides, Walmsley was at the peak of his career when World War One brought a halt to the Football League. He appeared in 35 wartime matches before returning to Ewood to make 19 League appearances during the first season after the war. In July 1920 he left Ewood to join Stockport County.

**WALMSLEY, Joseph**
Secretary. 1896-1903.
A native of Blackburn, Joseph Walmsley was the manager of a Blackburn cotton mill before succeeding Tom Mitchell as secretary of Blackburn Rovers towards the end of 1896. A shrewd businessman and an excellent judge of football, Walmsley had been a player with Blackburn Olympic in his younger days. He took over the stewardship of Blackburn Rovers

at a time when the club's fortunes were in decline. The succession of talented Scots that Mitchell had been able to acquire was coming to an end and as a result the club could no longer sustain its position as a dominant force in the game. Indeed, relegation to the Second Division in 1898 was only avoided because of a restructuring of the League. Sadly, although Walmsley was held in high regard in Blackburn as a first class administrator, the manner of his departure proved to be one of the darker episodes in the history of Blackburn Rovers.

Following the club's narrow escape from relegation at the end for the 1902-03 season, accusations were made that Walmsley had tried to arrange an important end of season clash with Everton (*see Bribery*).

Walmsley steadfastly denied the accusation and many believed that he had made a jocular remark which was taken out of context by others. A report of the joint commission of the FA and League took a different view on the matter and suspended Walmsley from having any further connection with the game. As a result of the suspension the club had no alternative but to advertise for a new secretary and Walmsley sought alternative employment. In November 1903, Walmsley had the license of the Florence Hotel in Blackburn transferred to him. The previous occupant of the Florence Hotel had been Bob Crompton's father.

### WALMSLEY, Richard
Right-back. 1912-1923.
*5ft 8in; 11st.*
*Born: Blackburn.*
*Debut: v Preston North End (h) 30 August 1919.*
*Career: Blackburn Trinity; Blackburn Rovers August 1912 to cs 1923; Lancaster Town.*
**Appearances:** Football League 38; FA Cup 1; Total 39.
The football correspondent of the *Blackburn Times* in 1919 described Richard Walmsley as 'A powerfully built youth who has figured at full-back with some success. He is fast, possess plenty of skill and never knows when he is beaten.' Although he had joined the club following the winning of the 1912 First Division title, Walmsley had to wait until the first match for the 1919-20 season to make his League debut. However he had appeared in 21 wartime matches prior to his appearance at Ewood against Preston North End in August 1919. He made 31 League appearances during the first season after the war as either a full-back or wing-half with the majority of these appearances being at right-back. However, the 1920-21 season saw David Rollo in possession of the right-back spot and Walmsley didn't reappear in the senior team until October 1921. By this time he was clearly no more than an understudy to Rollo and he left Ewood at the end of the 1922-23 season to move into non-League football.

### WALSALL FC
Founded in 1888 by the amalgamation of Walsall Swifts and Walsall Town as Walsall Town Swifts. Blackburn had played friendlies against the Walsall clubs prior to the amalgamation but didn't meet Walsall FC, as they became known in 1896, in the League until the 1971-72 season. Walsall had first joined the Football League in 1892, but lost their place in 1895. They returned 12 months later but dropped out again in 1901. Walsall returned to the League in 1921 as one of the founder members of the Third Division North.

**Football League**

|  |  |  | Home |  | Away |  |
|---|---|---|---|---|---|---|
| 1971-72 | (Div 3) | D | 1-1 | D | 0-0 |  |
| 1972-73 | (Div 3) | W | 2-0 | W | 2-0 |  |
| 1973-74 | (Div 3) | L | 0-2 | L | 0-2 |  |
| 1974-75 | (Div 3) | D | 3-3 | W | 3-1 |  |
| 1988-89 | (Div 3) | W | 3-0 | W | 2-1 |  |

|  | P | W | D | L | F | A |
|---|---|---|---|---|---|---|
| Home | 5 | 2 | 2 | 1 | 9 | 6 |
| Away | 5 | 3 | 1 | 1 | 7 | 4 |
| Total | 10 | 5 | 3 | 2 | 16 | 10 |

**FA Cup**

|  |  |  |  |  |
|---|---|---|---|---|
| 1930-31 | (3) | Home | D | 1-1 |
|  | (R) | Away | W | 3-0 |

### WALTER, Joseph D.
Outside-right. 1926-1928.
*5ft 7½in; 11st.*
*Born: Bristol, 16 August 1895.*
*Debut: v Manchester City (a) 17 March 1926.*
*Career: Bristol Rovers 1919; Huddersfield Town May 1922; Bath City; Taunton United May 1925; Blackburn Rovers March 1926; Bristol Rovers 1928; Bristol City groundsman for three years in early 1930s.*
**Appearances:** Football League 27.
**Goals:** Football League 2.
Walter scored 12 goals in 82 League games for Bristol Rovers before leaving his native city to join Huddersfield Town in May 1922. His time at Huddersfield was not quite so successful with five goals in 55 League games and he returned to his native South-West to play non-League football. Blackburn Rovers offered him the opportunity to resurrect his League career in March 1926 when they signed him to understudy Jack Crisp. Although he made only one appearance during 1925-26, the following season saw him begin the campaign as the first-choice outside-right. However, he failed to find any degree of consistency and he spent most of the latter part of the season out of the team. He made only three appearances in 1927-28 before returning to his native city to rejoin Bristol Rovers. He didn't appear for the senior team back at Eastville but later spent three years as groundsman to Bristol City.

### WALTON, Nathaniel
Inside-left/Goalkeeper. 1884-1893.
*5ft 8in; 10st 12lb.*
*Born: Preston, 1867; Died: Blackburn, 3 March 1930.*
*Debut: v Blackburn Olympic (h) 6 December 1884 (FAC).*
*Career: Witton FC; Blackburn Rovers 1884; Nelson cs 1893; Blackburn Rovers trainer 1898 to 1906.*
*International honours with Blackburn Rovers: England: 1 cap (1890).*
*Domestic honours with Blackburn Rovers: FA Cup winners: 1886; 1890; 1891.*
**Appearances:** Football League 110; FA Cup 29; Total 139.
**Goals:** Football League 37; FA Cup 12; Total 49.
*The Blackburn Times* of 5 April 1890 said of Walton: 'Nat is one of the most sterling players going. He is a thoroughly reliable man at every point of the game. He is always good, though perhaps rarely brilliant ...' Without doubt the left-wing combination of Nat Walton and Billy Townley was one of the most effective in the history of the club. Walton first came into the senior team at Blackburn during the 1884-85 season and went on to win a regular place as an industrious inside-forward. He was unfortunate to miss out on the 1885 FA Cup Final when he found himself excluded in favour of George Haworth, the Accrington half-back. His exclusion had little to do with form but came about because the club switched formation to play with three half-backs. However, 12 months later he won an FA Cup winners' medal and he won two more in 1890 and 1891. Walton had to wait until 1890 before receiving England recognition and it was perhaps fitting that he should line-up alongside Townley on his only international appearance. As ageing legs began to slow him down, Walton lost his first-team place and made the decision to try his luck in a different position. After only two second-team appearances as a goalkeeper he became the club's number one custodian during the 1892-93 season. However, at the end of that season he became embroiled in a dispute with the club and moved to Nelson. On leaving football he returned to Blackburn to follow his original trade of coach builder, but soon returned to Blackburn Rovers as their trainer.

### WALTON, William Ewart
Full-back. 1894-1896.
*5ft 6in; 11st.*
*Debut: v Sheffield United (h) 26 December 1894.*
*Career: Clitheroe; Fleetwood Rangers; Blackburn Rovers August 1894; Blackburn Park Road.*
**Appearances:** Football League 5.
**Goals:** Football League 1.
Walton was a typically robust full-back of his era who spent much of his time at the club with the second team. He made his debut at right-half on Boxing Day 1894 and scored one goal in a 3-2 win over Sheffield United His remaining appearances with the club all came in the 1895-96 season when he understudied Tom Brandon and Johnny Murray in the full-back positions.

### WARD, James Thomas
Full-back. 1886-1887.
*Born: Blackburn, 28 March 1865.*
*Debut: v Renton (a) 20 November 1886 (FAC).*
*Career: Furthergate School, Blackburn; Little Harwood 1879; Blackburn Olympic 1881; Blackburn Rovers cs 1886.*
**Appearances:** FA Cup 2.
Jimmy Ward had the distinction of being the only player of the Blackburn Olympic club to win international honours. It was fitting that he should win his only England cap, against Wales in March 1885, in his native Blackburn. A member of the Olympic side which took the FA Cup out of London for the first time in its history in 1883, Ward remained loyal to Olympic almost right up until the club's demise. Ward's strong kicking and muscular approach was very popular with the public of Blackburn. He joined the Rovers for the 1886-87 season but decided to retire from the game at the end of that campaign to concentrate on his hotel business.

### WARHURST, Paul
Utility. 1993-
*6ft 1in; 14st.*
*Born: Stockport, 26 September 1969.*
*Debut: v Liverpool (a) 12 September 1993.*
*Career: Manchester City trainee July 1986, turning professional in July 1988; Oldham Athletic October 1988 (£10,000); Sheffield Wednesday*

*July 1991 (£750,000); Blackburn Rovers September 1993 (£2,700,000).*
**Appearances:** Premier League 4+5; Football League Cup 1; Total 5+5.
An athletic central defender who made a name for himself as a
goalscoring centre-forward with Sheffield Wednesday during the 1992-
93 season. Such was his progress in attack that by the end of the season
he had led the line in both the FA Cup and Football League Cup Finals
for Sheffield Wednesday and had also been brought into the England
standby squad. During his career Warhurst has played in both full-back
positions, centre-back, midfield and centre-forward. His speed, and

control, coupled with his passing and shooting ability, make him a
versatile performer. Warhurst came through the junior ranks at
Manchester City but moved to Oldham Athletic without appearing in the
senior team at Maine Road. At Boundary Park he appeared in 67 League
games (including seven as sub) before being sold to Sheffield Wednesday
for an enormous profit.

He switched from centre-back to centre-forward following an injury
to David Hirst and his goals took Wednesday to two Cup Finals during
the 1992-93 season. Warhurst, who had worked with Ray Harford at
England Under-21 level, was originally set to join Blackburn during the
1993 close season. However, following Wednesday's failure to sign
Brian Deane from Sheffield United they pulled out of the deal and
Warhurst signed a new contract for the Hillsborough club. However, in
September 1993 the deal was resurrected and Warhurst moved to Ewood
for a £2.7 million fee. Both Kenny Dalglish and Harford envisaged
Warhurst's role at Ewood to be in midfield. However, tragedy struck at
Swindon on 2 October when Warhurst suffered a broken leg. The injury
kept him out of first-team contention until March 1994 and he spent the
final few weeks of the season on the bench as he tried to regain match
fitness.

## WARING, Clement
Centre-forward. 1899-1900.
*Debut: v Liverpool (a) 3 February 1900.*
*Career: Blackburn Rovers October 1899.*
**Appearances:** Football League 1.
A reserve centre-forward who made his sole first-team appearance at
Liverpool in February 1900. He got his chance in place of Ben Hulse but
made little impression in a 3-1 defeat. Waring was not retained at the end
of the season.

## WARING, William
Inside-left. 1889-1890.
*Debut: v West Bromwich Albion (h) 30 November 1889.*
*Career: Blackburn Rovers August 1889; Darwen May 1890.*
**Appearances:** Football League 1.
Waring made his sole appearance for Blackburn Rovers on the day that
Jack Southworth scored four in the 5-0 home win over West Bromwich
Albion. Waring got this opportunity for first-team football when Nat
Walton missed his only game of the 1889-90 campaign. However, the
consistency of Walton and Harry Campbell in the inside-forward
positions meant that Waring had to be content with second-team football
during his time at the club. In May 1890 he made the short move to
Barley Bank to join Darwen.

## WARTIME FOOTBALL
During both World Wars, the Football League competition was
abandoned and replaced by regionalised football. In World War One
Football League clubs played in a Lancashire or Midland group, although
five clubs in the South joined with Southern League clubs to play in a
London Combination. The Lancashire and Midland groups were divided
into a Principal Tournament and a Subsidiary Tournament. The latter was
played towards the end of the season when the Principal Tournament had
been completed.

A system of regionalised football was also adopted during World War
Two and the FA Cup competition was abandoned until 1945, when it was
resumed on a home and away basis. Blackburn Rovers found wartime
football to be a fairly meaningless affair. During both World Wars the
club struggled to maintain any consistency in team selection with a whole
host of guest players being used. One season of League football (1914-
15) was played at the start of World War One but Blackburn Rovers
closed down operations during the 1915-16 season because the club
thought it inappropriate to play football at a time of such carnage in
Europe. However, they began to play in 1916-17 as it was felt that it
might provide some respite for the population from the rigours of war.

The war brought an end to the careers of a number of the men who
had won two championships for the club and wartime football saw a
number of former Rovers players come out of retirement to help the club.
The oldest of these was Edgar Chadwick who had first appeared for the
club during the 1887-88 season. The greatest loss during the war was that
of Eddie Latheron who was killed by a German shell in October 1917. As
one might expect, results during World War One were particularly poor.
The 1917-18 season saw the club lose 27 of their 30 fixtures in the
Lancashire Section Principal Tournament.

They recorded only two wins and one draw and on 10 November
1917, lost 16-0 at Stoke. There was little relief in the Subsidiary
Tournament with one win and five defeats.

World War Two brought the deaths of Albert Clarke and Frank
Chivers from the Second Division championship winning side of 1938-
39. It also brought the death of Bob Crompton in March 1941 when the
manager collapsed and died shortly after watching the Rovers play
Burnley. Once again the results of matches during World War Two were
fairly meaningless with numerous guest players turning out for the club.
Outlined below is a brief summary of the club's wartime record:

### World War One

| | | P | W | D | L | F | A |
|---|---|---|---|---|---|---|---|
| 1916-17 | Lancashire Section-Principal Tournament | 30 | 10 | 4 | 16 | 52 | 66 |
| | Lancashire Section-Subsidiary Tournament | 6 | 2 | 0 | 4 | 11 | 15 |
| 1917-18 | Lancashire Section-Principal Tournament | 30 | 2 | 1 | 27 | 22 | 126 |
| | Lancashire Section-Subsidiary Tournament | 6 | 1 | 0 | 5 | 3 | 13 |
| 1918-19 | Lancashire Section-Principal Tournament | 30 | 5 | 4 | 21 | 35 | 83 |
| | Lancashire Section-Subsidiary Tournament | 6 | 0 | 2 | 4 | 6 | 18 |

### World War Two

| | | P | W | D | L | F | A |
|---|---|---|---|---|---|---|---|
| 1939-40 | Abandoned Football League Programme | 3 | 0 | 1 | 2 | 3 | 5 |
| | North West Regional League | 22 | 7 | 4 | 11 | 37 | 40 |
| | League War Cup | 8 | 6 | 0 | 2 | 18 | 9 |
| 1940-41 | North Regional League | 32 | 9 | 10 | 13 | 49 | 60 |
| | League War Cup | 4 | 2 | 0 | 2 | 11 | 10 |
| 1941-42 | Northern Section - 1st Competition | 18 | 10 | 6 | 2 | 40 | 24 |
| | Northern Section - 2nd Competition | 22 | 10 | 6 | 6 | 40 | 31 |

Billy Guest heads high into the West Ham goalmouth during the 1940 Wartime Cup Final at Wembley. The other Blackburn player is Jack Weddle.

| 1942-43 | Northern Section - 1st Competition | 18 | 9 | 3 | 6 | 56 | 43 |
| | Northern Section - 2nd Competition | 18 | 9 | 4 | 5 | 45 | 35 |
| 1943-44 | Northern Section - 1st Competition | 18 | 10 | 2 | 6 | 47 | 32 |
| | Northern Section - 2nd Competition | 16 | 8 | 3 | 5 | 30 | 27 |
| | Lancashire Cup Competition* | 2 | 2 | 0 | 0 | 5 | 1 |
| 1944-45 | Northern Section - 1st Competition | 18 | 7 | 4 | 7 | 30 | 29 |
| | Northern Section - 2nd Competition | 24 | 13 | 2 | 9 | 62 | 51 |
| 1945-46 | Football League North | 42 | 11 | 7 | 24 | 60 | 111 |
| | FA Cup | 2 | 0 | 0 | 2 | 1 | 4 |

*Note: These two Lancashire Cup matches against Blackpool Services were not included in the Northern Section - 2nd Competition.

## WATFORD FC

Founded in 1891 when West Herts and Watford St Mary's amalgamated, the club became founder members of the Third Division of the Football League in 1920. Blackburn and Watford did not meet in the Football League until Watford's promotion to the Second Division at the end of the 1968-69 season. In 1971, Watford manager Ken Furphy left the Vicarage Road club to take charge at Ewood Park following relegation to the Third Division. The records show that meetings between the clubs have generally been tight affairs with honours even after 22 League matches.

### Football League

| | | | Home | | Away | |
|---|---|---|---|---|---|---|
| 1969-70 | | (Div 2) | W | 1-0 | W | 2-0 |
| 1970-71 | | (Div 2) | L | 2-3 | L | 1-2 |
| 1972-73 | | (Div 3) | D | 0-0 | W | 3-1 |
| 1973-74 | | (Div 3) | W | 5-0 | D | 0-0 |
| 1974-75 | | (Div 3) | D | 0-0 | D | 0-0 |
| 1980-81 | | (Div 2) | D | 0-0 | D | 1-1 |
| 1981-82 | | (Div 2) | L | 1-2 | L | 2-3 |
| 1988-89 | | (Div 2) | W | 2-1 | D | 2-2 |
| 1989-90 | | (Div 2) | D | 2-2 | L | 1-3 |
| 1990-91 | | (Div 2) | L | 0-2 | W | 3-0 |
| 1991-92 | | (Div 2) | W | 1-0 | L | 1-2 |

| | P | W | D | L | F | A |
|---|---|---|---|---|---|---|
| Home | 11 | 4 | 4 | 3 | 14 | 10 |
| Away | 11 | 3 | 4 | 4 | 16 | 14 |
| Total | 22 | 7 | 8 | 7 | 30 | 24 |

## WATSON, James William

Left-half. 1920-1923.
*5ft 8½in; 11st.*
*Born: Darwen 1896 (July quarter).*
*Debut: v Bradford (h) 5 March 1921.*
*Career: Darwen Olympic; Blackburn Rovers September 1920; Accrington Stanley May 1923; Clitheroe August 1925; Darwen cs 1926 to cs 1928.*
**Appearances:** Football League 12.

William Watson played in 11 of the final 13 matches of the 1920-21 season and appeared to have a bright future ahead of him. Unfortunately, he received a serious injury in a pre-season trial match and missed the opening two months of the 1921-22 season. Once he'd recovered he found himself unable to break into the senior team. The first-team door was finally closed to Watson with the emergence of Harry Healless and Jimmy McKinnell in the half-back positions during the 1922-23 season. Watson moved to Accrington Stanley in May 1923 and went on to make 72 League appearances for the Peel Park club. His strong tackling proved a benefit to the Accrington defence until he dropped into the Lancashire Combination with Clitheroe in 1925. Watson later went on to captain Darwen for a couple of seasons.

## WATSON, Lionel P.

Inside-forward. 1902-1905.
*Born: Southport.*
*Debut: v Sunderland (a) 25 October 1902.*
*Career: All Saints' School, Southport; Laurel Rovers, Southport; High Park, Southport 1899; Southport Central 1900; Manchester City July 1901; Blackburn Rovers October 1902; West Ham United 1905.*
**Appearances:** Football League 55; FA Cup 6; Total 61.
**Goals:** Football League 19; FA Cup 1; Total 20.

A cultured inside-forward who came to Ewood Park with a reputation for playing good football in October 1902. Watson had learned his trade in the Southport area before making his League debut with Manchester City in October 1901. He made only one League appearance at Maine Road before moving to Blackburn in October 1902. Able to play in either inside-forward position, Watson failed to live up to expectations during the 1902-03 season and was restricted to just nine first-team outings in the League. However, he established himself the following season and missed only three League games whilst his 14 League goals easily made him the club's top goalscorer. Although rather on the slow side, Watson was a difficult man to dispossess and one whose play was full of trickery. However, his lack of pace proved a major handicap and he eventually lost his place during the 1904-05 season before leaving for West Ham United.

### WATTS, Charles
Goalkeeper. 1893-1894.
*5ft 9in.*
*Born: Middlesbrough, 1872; Died: Newcastle, November 1924.*
*Debut: v Darwen (a) 2 September 1893.*
*Career: Middlesbrough Ironopolis 1892; Blackburn Rovers June 1893; Burton Wanderers 1894; Blackburn Brooks on loan; Newcastle United May 1896 becoming assistant trainer in 1906 until April 1908.*
**Appearances:** Football League 9.
Charlie Watts was a rather robust goalkeeper who made good use of his solid physique. Although reluctant to leave his native North-East, the improved wages to be found at Blackburn proved the deciding factor in persuading him to move to Lancashire. Watts had something of a reputation as a gambler and after leaving football became a well-known racing tipster. With Nat Walton in dispute with the club and headed for Nelson, Watts was given the first-team goalkeeping position at at start of the 1893-94 season. A safe and agile custodian, Watts was famed for his ability to punch the ball well clear of the danger area. He lost his place in November 1893 to Adam Ogilvie and his comments on the committee's decision cost him a week's suspension. Although he was unable to regain his place from Ogilvie he later went on to make 98 League appearances for Newcastle before joining their training staff.

### WEBBER, John V.
Forward. 1947-1948.
*5ft 9in; 11st 1lb.*
*Born: Blackpool, 2 June 1920.*
*Debut: v Middlesbrough (a) 22 March 1947.*
*Career: Hyde United; Blackburn Rovers February 1947; Ashton United 1948.*
**Appearances:** Football League 8.
**Goals:** Football League 1.
The arrival of Jack Webber to Ewood Park was rather overshadowed by the fact that he arrived on the same day that a club record fee of £10,000 was paid to Hibernian for Jock Weir. Ironically, Webber got his chance of first-team action when Weir pulled a thigh muscle in training. Although Webber contributed a number of clever moves on his debut at Middlesbrough, a fluffed chance early on seemed to affect his confidence in front of goal. None the less his intelligent use of the ball suggested a bright future. Webber was a product of Blackpool junior football and had played a good deal of football in Madagascar and India while serving in the East Lancashire Regiment. He marked his Central League debut at Ewood with a goal but had to wait until the start of the 1947-48 season before winning a regular first-team place. He kept his place in a much changed attack during the opening games of the season but was axed after appearing in four of the first five games. He later underwent a cartilage operation before leaving Blackburn to return to non-League football.

### WEBSTER, Montague V.
Forward. 1919-1920.
*5ft 7½in; 11st 6lb.*
*Born: Catford.*
*Debut: v Sheffield United (a) 20 October 1919.*
*Career: Blackburn Rovers 1919; Watford August 1920.*
**Appearances:** Football League 2.
Webster was recommended to Blackburn by Billy Garbutt, a former Blackburn winger. He got his first-team opportunity in October 1919 when an injury crisis side-lined a number of senior players. Unfortunately, Webster fluffed an early chance when he shot over the bar from close range and this appeared to affect his confidence. Despite a 2-0 defeat, Webster was retained for the following match but moved from inside-right to the left wing. He enjoyed a much better game but the Rovers crashed 3-0 at Everton and Webster was one of three players who lost their places for the next match. He was not called upon again for the first team and in August 1920 he moved to Watford.

### WEDDLE, John Robson
Centre-forward. 1938-1943.
*5ft 9in; 12st 5lb.*
*Born: Sunderland, 5 November 1905; Died: Blackburn, 21 November 1979.*
*Debut: v Tranmere Rovers (h) 27 August 1938.*
*Career: Fatfield Albion; Portsmouth September 1927; Blackburn Rovers May 1938, then joined the coaching staff becoming head trainer in June 1949 and remaining in that position until May 1961.*
*Domestic honours with Blackburn Rovers: Second Division championship 1938-39 (42 apps, 16 gls).*

**Appearances:** Football League 42; FA Cup 7; Total 49.
**Goals:** Football League 16; FA Cup 2; Total 18.
Jack Weddle spent 11 seasons as the bustling, wholehearted leader of the Portsmouth attack. He scored more than a hundred goals for Pompey and appeared in the 1929 and 1934 FA Cup Finals for the Fratton Park club. Although he came to Blackburn as his playing days were coming to an end, Weddle proved to be an astute signing for Bob Crompton. Weddle fitted perfectly between Len Butt and Albert Clarke and he was regarded as the 'father figure' of the team which clinched the Second Division title in 1938-39. After World War Two he joined the training staff at Ewood and graduated through the third and second teams to become head trainer in July 1949. Weddle was twice honoured by the Football League by being put in charge of representative teams whilst on the coaching staff at Ewood. He left the club in May 1961.

### WEDNESDAY OLD ATHLETIC FC
Formed in 1874, Wednesday Old Athletic provided opposition for Blackburn Rovers in the days before the Football League. Blackburn Rovers travelled to Wednesday Old Athletic for a fifth round FA Cup-tie on 11 February 1882. In front of a crowd reported to be in the region of 8,000 spectators the Rovers enjoyed a 3-0 win thanks to goals from Lofthouse, Avery and Strachan.

### WEGERLE, Roy Connon
Forward. 1992-1993.
*5ft 8in; 10st 2lb.*
*Born: Johannesburg, South Africa, 19 March 1964.*
*Debut: v Bristol Rovers (a) 7 March 1992.*
*Career: Tampa Bay Rowdies (USA); Chelsea July 1986 (£100,000); Swindon Town on loan March 1988; Luton Town July 1988 (£75,000); Queen's Park Rangers December 1989 (£1,000,000); Blackburn Rovers March 1992 (£1,100,000); Coventry City March 1993 (part-exchange for Kevin Gallagher).*
*International honours with Blackburn Rovers: United States of America: 2 caps (1992).*
**Appearances:** Premier League 11+11; Football League 9+3; FA Cup 4+1; Football League Cup 3+3; Total 27+18.
**Goals:** Premier League 4; Football League 2; FA Cup 2; Football League Cup 4; Total 12.

A wonderfully talented striker whose brilliant individualism has been sought after by a number of clubs in recent years. Wegerle was discovered in South Africa by the former Ipswich Town goalkeeper, Roy Bailey, and had a brief trial with Manchester United before moving to the USA. He played football with Tampa Bay Rowdies before moving to England to link up with Chelsea. He appeared in 23 League games (including eight as sub) at Stamford Bridge and also played seven League games with Swindon Town on loan. However, Wegerle failed to make much impact and was allowed to move to Luton Town in July 1988. It was at Luton that he began to show his true potential and ten goals in 45 League appearances (including six as sub) was sufficient to persuade Queen's Park Rangers to pay a million pounds for his services. After a disappointing start to his career at Loftus Road, Wegerle began to live up to his fee.

His ability to twist and turn defenders inside out and to score the most spectacular of goals made him a great favourite with the fans. Following the serious injury to Mike Newell during the 1991-92 season, Kenny Dalglish moved to bring Wegerle to Ewood Park. However the team began to lose its rhythm and as a result fell from the top of the table to a place outside of the Play-off zone. With Wegerle unable to find his form Newell was rushed back into the team and Wegerle had to settle for a place on the bench. The club's second one million pound player played no part in the successful Play-off campaign and the arrival of Alan Shearer found Wegerle a permanent occupant of the substitute's bench. The serious knee injury sustained by Shearer on Boxing Day 1993 finally gave Wegerle an opportunity of regular first-team football.

At last he began to show the Ewood faithful his silky skills and he scored a brilliant last minute goal to beat Newcastle United in the fifth round of the FA Cup. However, despite his individual brilliance, Wegerle was unable to lead the line in the same way as Shearer and at times his unpredictability was as confusing to his own colleagues as it was to the opposition. Although he had graduated to international status with the United States during his time at Ewood, Kenny Dalglish used Wegerle as the makeweight in the deal which brought Kevin Gallagher to Ewood Park.

## WEIR, John Britton
Centre-forward. 1947-1948.
*5ft 8in; 11st 10lb.*
*Born: Fauldhouse, 20 October 1923.*
*Debut: v Sunderland (h) 1 February 1947.*
*Career: Leith Renton; Hibernian; Cardiff City wartime guest; Blackburn Rovers January 1947 (£10,000); Glasgow Celtic February 1948 (£7,000); Falkirk October 1952.*
**Appearances:** Football League 23.
**Goals:** Football League 7.
Blackburn Rovers had to pay a club record fee of £10,000 to bring Jock Weir to Ewood Park in January 1947. He fully lived up to expectations on the ice bound grounds which greeted his arrival in England. However, once the grounds began to thaw, Weir's form began to slump and he was further handicapped by an injury he received at Grimsby over the Easter period. Inexplicably, Weir fared little better in the 1947-48 season and appeared to be totally unable to adapt to his new environment. He lost his place after the first three games of the new season brought no points and had spells playing Central League football.

He even appeared on the right wing on several occasions and although he scored eight goals in nine second-team games, his occasional senior appearances remained disappointing. A deal with Cardiff City was arranged but collapsed at the last minute and reports of a transfer back to Hibernian came to nothing. Clubs were circulated in January 1948 that the Rovers were prepared to part with their first five figure signing and another deal was arranged with Cardiff City. However, the player refused the Welsh club's terms and in February opted to return to Scotland to join Celtic. He enjoyed great success in Glasgow, scoring 42 goals in 114 appearances for Celtic.

## WELLING UNITED FC
Formed in 1963, Welling United were members of the GM Vauxhall Conference when they gained a plumb FA Cup draw at home to Second Division Blackburn Rovers in January 1989. A Ronnie Hildersley goal enabled Blackburn to survive the third-round tie in front of 3,850 spectators.

## WEST BROMWICH ALBION FC
Founded in 1879 and known as West Bromwich Strollers until the name of the club was changed to West Bromwich Albion in 1880. Blackburn and West Bromwich Albion met on a number of occasions prior to the formation of the Football League but the most thrilling match was a 7-6 win for Blackburn on 22 October 1886 at the Leamington Street Ground. One of the founder members of the Football League, Albion have been one of Blackburn's most frequent opponents in the League.

### Football League

| | | Home | | Away | |
|---|---|---|---|---|---|
| 1888-89 | (FL) | W | 6-2 | L | 1-2 |
| 1889-90 | (FL) | W | 5-0 | L | 2-3 |
| 1890-91 | (FL) | W | 2-1 | L | 0-1 |
| 1891-92 | (FL) | W | 3-2 | D | 2-2 |
| 1892-93 | (Div 1) | W | 2-1 | W | 2-1 |
| 1893-94 | (Div 1) | W | 3-0 | L | 1-2 |
| 1894-95 | (Div 1) | W | 3-0 | L | 0-2 |
| 1895-96 | (Div 1) | W | 1-0 | L | 2-3 |
| 1896-97 | (Div 1) | L | 1-2 | L | 0-1 |
| 1897-98 | (Div 1) | L | 1-3 | D | 1-1 |
| 1898-99 | (Div 1) | W | 4-1 | L | 2-6 |
| 1899-00 | (Div 1) | W | 2-0 | L | 0-1 |
| 1900-01 | (Div 1) | D | 1-1 | D | 1-1 |
| 1902-03 | (Div 1) | W | 1-0 | L | 3-5 |
| 1903-04 | (Div 1) | W | 2-0 | L | 1-2 |
| 1911-12 | (Div 1) | W | 4-1 | L | 0-2 |
| 1912-13 | (Div 1) | L | 2-4 | D | 1-1 |
| 1913-14 | (Div 1) | W | 2-0 | L | 0-2 |
| 1914-15 | (Div 1) | W | 2-1 | D | 0-0 |
| 1919-20 | (Div 1) | L | 1-5 | L | 2-5 |
| 1920-21 | (Div 1) | W | 5-1 | D | 1-1 |
| 1921-22 | (Div 1) | L | 2-3 | W | 2-0 |
| 1922-23 | (Div 1) | W | 5-1 | L | 0-3 |
| 1923-24 | (Div 1) | W | 4-0 | D | 3-3 |
| 1924-25 | (Div 1) | W | 1-0 | D | 1-1 |
| 1925-26 | (Div 1) | L | 1-2 | D | 1-1 |
| 1926-27 | (Div 1) | D | 0-0 | L | 0-2 |
| 1931-32 | (Div 1) | W | 2-0 | L | 1-4 |
| 1932-33 | (Div 1) | D | 4-4 | W | 3-1 |
| 1933-34 | (Div 1) | W | 4-0 | W | 1-0 |
| 1934-35 | (Div 1) | W | 3-0 | D | 2-2 |
| 1935-36 | (Div 1) | W | 3-1 | L | 1-8 |
| 1938-39 | (Div 2) | W | 3-0 | L | 0-2 |
| 1948-49 | (Div 2) | D | 0-0 | L | 1-2 |
| 1958-59 | (Div 1) | D | 0-0 | W | 3-2 |
| 1959-60 | (Div 1) | W | 3-2 | L | 0-2 |
| 1960-61 | (Div 1) | W | 2-1 | W | 2-1 |
| 1961-62 | (Div 1) | D | 1-1 | L | 0-4 |
| 1962-63 | (Div 1) | W | 3-1 | W | 5-2 |
| 1963-64 | (Div 1) | L | 0-2 | W | 3-1 |
| 1964-65 | (Div 1) | W | 4-2 | D | 0-0 |
| 1965-66 | (Div 1) | L | 0-1 | L | 1-2 |
| 1975-76 | (Div 2) | D | 0-0 | D | 2-2 |
| 1986-87 | (Div 2) | L | 0-1 | W | 1-0 |
| 1987-88 | (Div 3) | W | 3-1 | W | 1-0 |
| 1988-89 | (Div 2) | L | 1-2 | L | 0-2 |
| 1989-90 | (Div 2) | W | 2-1 | D | 2-2 |
| 1990-91 | (Div 2) | L | 0-3 | L | 0-2 |

| | P | W | D | L | F | A |
|---|---|---|---|---|---|---|
| Home | 48 | 30 | 7 | 11 | 104 | 54 |
| Away | 48 | 10 | 13 | 25 | 58 | 95 |
| Total | 96 | 40 | 20 | 36 | 162 | 149 |

### FA Cup

| | | | | |
|---|---|---|---|---|
| 1884-85 | (6) | Away | W | 2-0 |
| 1885-86 | (F) | Kennington Oval | D | 0-0 |
| | (R) | Derby | W | 2-0 |
| 1890-91 | (SF) | Stoke | W | 3-2 |
| 1891-92 | (2) | Away | L | 1-3 |
| 1893-94 | (1) | Away | W | 3-2 |
| 1895-96 | (1) | Home | L | 1-2 |
| 1911-12 | (SF) | Anfield | D | 0-0 |
| | (R) | Sheffield | L | 0-1 aet |
| 1951-52 | (5) | Home | W | 1-0 |
| 1881-82 | (3) | Away | L | 2-3 |

## WEST HAM UNITED FC
Founded in 1900 following the disbandment of the Thames Ironworks Club. West Ham were elected to the Second Division of the Football League in 1919 and won promotion to the First Division in 1922-23. In 1956-57 both clubs were promoted from the Second Division together with West Ham going up as champions and Blackburn finishing as runners-up. On 26 December 1963, West Ham United suffered their heaviest defeat when Blackburn Rovers recorded an 8-2 victory at Upton Park. Curiously, West Ham travelled to Ewood Park two days later and left with a 3-1 win under their belts.

### Football League

| | | Home | | Away | |
|---|---|---|---|---|---|
| 1923-24 | (Div 1) | D | 0-0 | W | 1-0 |
| 1924-25 | (Div 1) | L | 0-1 | L | 0-2 |
| 1925-26 | (Div 1) | W | 1-0 | L | 1-2 |
| 1926-27 | (Div 1) | W | 4-1 | W | 5-1 |
| 1927-28 | (Div 1) | W | 1-0 | L | 3-4 |
| 1928-29 | (Div 1) | W | 2-0 | D | 3-3 |
| 1929-30 | (Div 1) | D | 3-3 | W | 3-2 |
| 1930-31 | (Div 1) | W | 1-0 | L | 3-4 |
| 1931-32 | (Div 1) | L | 2-4 | W | 3-1 |
| 1936-37 | (Div 2) | L | 1-2 | L | 1-3 |
| 1937-38 | (Div 2) | W | 2-1 | L | 0-2 |
| 1938-39 | (Div 2) | W | 3-1 | W | 2-1 |
| 1948-49 | (Div 2) | D | 0-0 | L | 1-2 |
| 1949-50 | (Div 2) | W | 2-0 | W | 2-0 |
| 1950-51 | (Div 2) | L | 1-3 | W | 3-2 |
| 1951-52 | (Div 2) | W | 3-1 | L | 1-3 |
| 1952-53 | (Div 2) | W | 3-0 | D | 0-0 |
| 1953-54 | (Div 2) | W | 4-1 | L | 1-2 |
| 1954-55 | (Div 2) | W | 5-2 | W | 5-2 |
| 1955-56 | (Div 2) | W | 4-1 | W | 3-2 |
| 1956-57 | (Div 2) | L | 0-2 | W | 3-1 |
| 1957-58 | (Div 2) | W | 2-1 | D | 1-1 |
| 1958-59 | (Div 1) | L | 1-2 | L | 3-6 |
| 1959-60 | (Div 1) | W | 6-2 | L | 1-2 |
| 1960-61 | (Div 1) | W | 4-1 | L | 2-3 |
| 1961-62 | (Div 1) | W | 1-0 | W | 3-2 |
| 1962-63 | (Div 1) | L | 0-4 | W | 1-0 |
| 1963-64 | (Div 1) | L | 1-3 | W | 8-2 |
| 1964-65 | (Div 1) | W | 4-0 | D | 1-1 |

| | | | | | | |
|---|---|---|---|---|---|---|
| 1965-66 | (Div 1) | L | 1-2 | L | 1-4 |
| 1978-79 | (Div 2) | W | 1-0 | L | 0-4 |
| 1980-81 | (Div 2) | D | 0-0 | L | 0-2 |
| 1989-90 | (Div 2) | W | 5-4 | D | 1-1 |
| 1990-91 | (Div 2) | W | 3-1 | L | 0-1 |

| | P | W | D | L | F | A |
|---|---|---|---|---|---|---|
| Home | 34 | 21 | 4 | 9 | 71 | 43 |
| Away | 34 | 13 | 5 | 16 | 66 | 68 |
| Total | 68 | 34 | 9 | 25 | 137 | 111 |

**FA Premiership**

| | | Home | | Away | |
|---|---|---|---|---|---|
| 1993-94 | | L | 0-2 | W | 2-1 |

| | P | W | D | L | F | A |
|---|---|---|---|---|---|---|
| Home | 1 | 0 | 0 | 1 | 0 | 2 |
| Away | 1 | 1 | 0 | 0 | 2 | 1 |
| Total | 2 | 1 | 0 | 1 | 2 | 3 |

**FA Cup**

| | | | | |
|---|---|---|---|---|
| 1910-11 | (4) | Away | W | 3-2 |
| 1947-48 | (3) | Home | D | 0-0 aet |
| | (R) | Away | W | 4-2 aet |
| 1955-56 | (5) | Away | D | 0-0 |
| | (R) | Home | L | 2-3 aet |
| 1965-66 | (4) | Away | D | 3-3 |
| | (R) | Home | W | 4-1 |

## WESTBY, Jack Leslie
Right-back.
*5ft 10¼in; 11st 12lb.*
*Born: Aintree, 20 May 1916.*
*Debut: v Aston Villa (h) 27 January 1938.*
*Career: Orrell; Burscough; Blackburn Rovers January 1937; Liverpool May 1944; Southport August 1947; Runcorn 1948-49; Ellesmere Port Town 1949-50; Bootle 1952-53.*
**Appearances:** Football League 2.
Blessed with a fine physique, Jack Westby was given a professional engagement with the Rovers after appearing as an amateur in the Mid-Week League. He made his debut against Aston Villa in January 1938 and did sufficiently well to be retained for the following match against Bradford. Unfortunately, the trip to Bradford proved a nightmare experience for several Blackburn players. A 7-1 thrashing at the hands of the Yorkshire club saw Westby lose his first-team place. In the face of competition from Billy Hough and Ernest Lanceley, Westby was unable to regain the right-back position. He appeared in 18 wartime matches including nine after his move to Liverpool in May 1944.

## WESTCOTT, Dennis
Centre-forward. 1948-1950.
*5ft 11in; 12st 7lb.*
*Born: Wallasey, 2 July 1917. Died: Stafford, 13 July 1960.*
*Debut: v Southampton (a) 21 August 1948.*
*Career: Wallasey Grocers; Leasowe Road Brickworks (Wallasey); Everton trialist January/February 1935; New Brighton amateur December 1935, turning professional in January 1936; Wolverhampton Wanderers July 1936 (£300); Blackburn Rovers April 1948; Manchester City February 1950 (£12,500); Chesterfield June 1952 to cs 1953; Stafford Rangers.*
**Appearances:** Football League 63; FA Cup 3; Total 66.
**Goals:** Football League 37.
Although Dennis Westcott began his League career with ten goals in 18 League appearances with New Brighton, it was with Wolves that he earned his reputation as a free-scoring centre-forward. He joined Wolves in July 1936 and took only 109 matches to notch 100 goals for the Molineux club. By the time he left Wolves for Blackburn in April 1948, Westcott had scored 124

goals in 144 League and Cup games. Hopes that Westcott would provide the firepower to lift the club back into the First Division at the first attempt were not realised. Whilst Westcott did his part with 21 goals, the only player to reach double figures, the rest of the team seemed ill equipped for promotion. The 1949-50 season brought little change with Westcott again being the only man able to find the net with any regularity. Although he was sold to Manchester City in February 1950, he still remained the leading goalscorer at Ewood for the season and was once again the only player to reach double figures with 16 goals. Westcott continued his goalscoring exploits at Maine Road with 37 goals from 72 League games and in 1952-53 he ended his League career with 21 goals in 40 League appearances for Chesterfield.

## WHALLEY, Jeffrey H.
Outside-left. 1967-1972.
*5ft 8in; 9st 11lb.*
*Born: Rossendale, 8 February 1952.*
*Debut: v Aston Villa (a) 21 March 1970.*
*Career: Blackburn Rovers apprentice August 1967, turning professional in February 1970; Croatia (Australia); Great Harwood February 1977.*
**Appearances:** Football League 2; Football League Cup 1; Total 3.
Jeff Whalley was one of several young players who made their debuts during the 1969-70 season. However, whilst Terry Eccles, Mick Wood and Ray Charter enjoyed varying degrees of success with the first team, Whalley was restricted to just three appearances in three seasons. His most outstanding display with the first team came in a friendly against Manchester United in March 1970 and this earned him a recall to the senior squad. However, following a 3-0 defeat by Swindon Town he was again relegated to the Central League team and his last senior appearance came in a 4-1 defeat at Lincoln City in the Football League Cup in September 1971.

## WHARTON, John Edwin
Winger. 1948-1953.
*5ft 6in; 10st 4lb.*
*Born: Bolton, 18 June 1920.*
*Debut: v Barnsley (h) 28 August 1948.*
*Career: Plymouth Argyle amateur October 1935, turning professional June 1937; Preston North End July 1939 (with James Hunter for £5,500); Carlisle United wartime guest 1939-40; Liverpool wartime guest 1941-42; Blackburn Rovers wartime guest 1942-43 and 1943-44; Bolton Wanderers wartime guest 1942-43; Rochdale wartime guest 1943-44;*

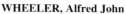

*Manchester City March 1947 (£5,000); Blackburn Rovers June 1948; Newport County February 1953 (with Leslie Graham for £4,000); Wigan Athletic cs 1955.*
**Appearances:** Football League 129; FA Cup 9; Total 138.
**Goals:** Football League 15; FA Cup 2; Total 17.
A much travelled winger who could operate on either flank. Wharton came to Ewood Park as part of the deal which took Jackie Oakes and Verdi Godwin to Manchester City in June 1948. A wholehearted and plucky type of winger. Wharton enjoyed mixed fortunes whilst at Ewood. His most productive season for Blackburn was in 1951-52 when he appeared in 35 League games and 8 FA Cup-ties, including two semi-final matches.
Although he began on the left, Wharton was used just as much on the right flank throughout his time at Blackburn. He left the club in February 1953 when he moved in a double-deal with Les Graham to Newport County. Wharton's son Terry, also a winger, played professional football with Wolves and Bolton Wanderers in the 1960s.

## WHEELER, Alfred John
Outside-right. 1947-49.
*5ft 6¼in; 9st 2lb.*
*Born: Fareham, 6 April 1922.*
*Debut: v Charlton Athletic (h) 27 March 1948.*
*Career: Portsmouth amateur; Blackburn Rovers April 1947; Swindon Town July 1949 to August 1951.*
**Appearances:** Football League 21.
**Goals:** Football League 5.
Alfred Wheeler was a promising right winger who was found playing

Army football on Salisbury Plain by Jack Bruton. Wheeler was not the usual sort of speedy winger but one who preferred craft and guile to outright pace. Described by contemporary critics as 'a two-footed intelligent craftsman' he was given several opportunities to establish himself during the 1948-49 season. However, he failed to do so and in July 1949 he moved to Swindon Town where he scored four goals in 23 League games.

## WHELAN, David
Full-back. 1953-1963.
*5ft 8in; 11st 6lb.*
*Born: Bradford, 24 November 1936.*
*Debut: v West Ham United (h) 27 August 1956.*
*Career: Wigan Boys Club; Blackburn Rovers December 1953; Crewe Alexandra January 1963.*
*Domestic honours with Blackburn Rovers: FA Cup runners-up: 1960.*
**Appearances:** Football League 78; FA Cup 9; Total 87.
**Goals:** Football League 3.
Although the product of a Rugby League environment, being brought up in Wigan, Dave Whelan joined the Ewood staff as a youngster and worked his way up to the senior team. He made his first-team debut at Ewood Park in November 1956 in an unfamiliar right-half position but

was later given three outings at right-back as understudy to Ken Taylor. The 1957-58 season saw him make occasional appearances at left-back until an injury to Taylor allowed Whelan to play in the final seven League games. Six of these games were won and promotion to the First Division was achieved. Whelan began the 1958-59 season at right-back and his naturally aggressive play was a complete contrast to the more cultured style of Eckersley.

He suffered an injury in the match with Preston at Ewood on 11 October 1958, moved on to the wing for the rest of the game and ended up by scoring two goals. Unfortunately the injury, a pull hamstring, side-lined him for several months. Whelan eventually returned to the team at left-back and as injuries began to plague Eckersley, it was in this position that Whelan finally settled. Tragically his Ewood career came to an end when he was carried from Wembley's hallowed turf with a broken leg during the 1960 FA Cup Final. He was released by the Rovers without ever returning to senior duty and dropped into the lower divisions with Crewe Alexandra. He made 115 League appearances for Crewe before leaving the game to return to Wigan as a market trader.

With the same determination that he had shown as a tough tackling defender, Whelan built up his business interests until he owned a whole chain of supermarkets. In the mid-1970s he sold his business and joined the ranks of the millionaires. However, unwilling to retire, Whelan built up a chain of sports shops throughout the North and pursued his own sporting interests following Rugby League at Wigan.

## WHITEHEAD, James
Inside-right. 1893-1897.
*Born: Church, 1870. Died: Accrington, August 1929.*
*Debut: v Darwen (a) 2 September 1893.*
*Career: Bank House Rovers; Peel Bank Rovers; Accrington cs 1890; Blackburn Rovers August 1893; Manchester City September 1897; Accrington Stanley December 1899.*
*International honours with Blackburn Rovers: England: 1 cap (1894).*
**Appearances:** Football League 85; FA Cup 8; Total 93.
**Goals:** Football League 22; FA Cup 2; Total 24.
Born and brought up in Church, James Whitehead was only 12 years of age when he was playing at inside-right for a local club called Bank House Rovers. He was later selected for the second team of Peel Bank Rovers but his abilities were quickly recognised and he was promoted to

the senior team. He moved into League football with Accrington and scored 23 goals in 73 League appearances before joining Blackburn Rovers in August 1893. Short and stocky, Whitehead could hold his own with any opponent who physically tried to intimidate him. He was a master of the dribble and possessed a powerful shot. However, his creative use of the ball enabled him to open up defences at will and he was not afraid of winning the ball in the tackle. He was a regular member of the first team until the 1896-97 season but moved to Manchester City after failing to agree terms with Blackburn for the 1897-98 campaign. Whitehead returned to his roots in December 1899 to play for Accrington Stanley.

## WHITEHEAD, William
Forward. 1889-1893.
*Debut: v Derby County (a) 6 September 1890.*
*Career: Blackburn Rovers August 1889.*
**Appearances:** Football League 3; FA Cup 1; Total 4.
**Goals:** Football League 1.
Whitehead scored on his League debut in opening game of the 1890-91 season. Unfortunately, the Rovers were defeated 8-5 at Derby County and Whitehead made only one further appearance during that season. Although retained, he didn't make any senior appearances during the 1890-91 season and his final appearance came in January 1893. A player named Whitehead appeared for the club during 1886-87 season and it is thought that it may well have been William Whitehead. This player appeared in the second round FA Cup-tie at Renton in November 1886 but did not appear in the replay.

## WHITESIDE, Arnold
Right-half. 1932-1949.
*5ft 7in; 9st 12lb.*
*Born: Calder Vale, 6 November 1911.*
*Debut: v Liverpool (h) 12 November 1932.*
*Career: Woodplumpton Juniors; Blackburn Rovers amateur January 1932 signing professional in March 1932.*
*Domestic honours with Blackburn Rovers: Second Division championship: 1938-39 (33 apps, 1 gl): League War Cup runners-up: 1940.*
**Appearances:** Football League 218; FA Cup 21; Total 239.
**Goals:** Football League 3.
A weaver by trade, Arnold Whiteside had to be brought out of the Calder Vale mill where he worked to sign for Blackburn Rovers. His previous club had been Woodplumpton Juniors and there were many who believed that Whiteside was too lightweight to meet the requirements of the professional game. However, Whiteside's work-rate in the Central League made a favourable impression on most observers and in November 1932 he was given a first-team debut. Whiteside didn't establish himself as a first-team regular until January 1934 when he was given the left-half position. By March he had switched to right-half and remained the regular choice in that position until the end of the 1936-37 season. He lost his way during 1937-38 and, having made only 11 appearances, was put on the transfer list. When no other clubs moved in for Whiteside, Bob Crompton decided to take another look at him and restored him to the first team in September 1938. It proved to be a wise decision as Whiteside was one of the architects of the side which went on to win the Second Division title.

An original midfield dynamo, Whiteside appeared in the 1940 War Cup Final and went on to make 150 appearances for the club in wartime football. After the war he helped to provide experience and stability in a struggling side until age began to limit his effectiveness. His appearances became increasingly restricted and he was freed by the club at the end of the 1948-49 season.

## WHITTAKER, Arnold
Outside-right. 1899-1908.
*5ft 5in; 9st 10lb.*
*Born: Blackburn, 1880.*
*Debut: v Preston North End (h) 14 October 1899.*
*Career: Queen's Park 1898; Accrington Stanley April 1898; Blackburn*

*Rovers May 1899; Accrington Stanley May 1908.*
*International honours with Blackburn Rovers: Football League: 1 appearance (1901).*
**Appearance:** Football League 250; FA Cup 15; Total 265.
**Goals:** Football League 57.
Whittaker was discovered by Accrington Stanley when playing as a full-back in local junior football. However, his speed made him an obvious candidate for a place on the wing and it was in this position that he joined Blackburn Rovers. During his early years at Ewood Park he was by far the speediest man at the club and his skilful dribbling ability, coupled with a powerful shot, made him a dangerous raider. A fact which was amply demonstrated when he scored a hat-trick on his debut against Preston North End. An ankle injury restricted his appearances during the 1904-05 season and although he was later to resume his first team place he was never quite the same player. Even so, Whittaker remained the first choice for the right wing position until midway through the 1907-08 season. Having lost his first-team place at Ewood he returned to Accrington Stanley in May 1908.

**WHITTAKER, (Bernard)**
Inside-left. 1888-1889.
*5ft 5in; 11st.*
*Debut: v Preston North End (h) 12 January 1889.*
*Career: Blackburn Rovers 1888.*
**Appearances:** Football League 4
**Goals:** Football League 1
Football League records give no indication as to the Christian name of the player called Whittaker who appeared in four League games during the 1888-89 season. Some sources refer to an initial 'J', but *The Blackburn Times* in September 1950 carried a photograph of a gentlemen named 'Bernard' Whittaker who was reported to have played at inside-right for Blackburn Rovers during the 1888-89 season. Whittaker actually played at inside-left in four of the final six games of the inaugural season of League football. His only goal was scored in the 3-1 defeat by Everton and records show that he was not retained for the 1889-90 season.

**WHITTAKER, Walter**
Goalkeeper. 1900-1901.
*5ft 11in; 12st 1lb.*
*Born: Manchester, 20 September 1878; Died: 1927.*
*Debut: v Glossop North End (a) 27 February 1900.*
*Career: Molyneaux FC (Manchester League); Buxton; Newton Heath February 1895; Fairfield 1896-97; Grimsby Town May 1897 (£60); Reading 1898; Blackburn Rovers February 1900; Grimsby Town December 1901 (£150); Derby County April 1903; Brentford 1904; Reading 1905; Clapton Orient 1907; Exeter City 1910; Swansea Town player-manager cs 1912; Llanelli manager cs 1914 to November 1914.*
**Appearances:** Football League 52; FA Cup 1; Total 53.
Although not the most consistent custodian in the club's history, Walt Whittaker had shown flashes of the brilliance which illuminated a long and distinguished career. Reputed to be the youngest player in the Second Division when he signed for Newton Heath in February 1895, Whittaker had no shortage of employers throughout his career. Although he missed only two games in a season and a half with the club, Whittaker found the Blackburn climate not to his liking. He suffered frequent bouts of ill health but remained untouched as first team goalkeeper until his surprising departure in December 1901. His fall from grace at Ewood followed a League game at Grimsby in October 1901. Whittaker, a former Grimsby player, asked permission to stay behind after the match to renew old acquaintances. Permission was refused and Whittaker was instructed to return to Blackburn with the team. However, Whittaker 'accidentally' missed the train and had to spend the night in Grimsby. The Blackburn directors were far from amused and promptly dropped him for the next match. Billy McIver stepped into his place and Whittaker found the youngster impossible to shift. Unwilling to play reserve team football, Whittaker returned to Grimsby in December 1901.

**WHITTLE, Maurice**
Left-back. 1963-1966.
*5ft 8in; 10st 11lb.*
*Born: Wigan, 5 July 1948.*
*Debut: v Portsmouth (a) 21 August 1968 (sub).*
*Career: Blackburn Rovers apprentice June 1963, turning professional in October 1966; Oldham Athletic May 1969; Fort Lauderdale Strikers (USA) April 1977; Barrow October 1977; Wigan Athletic March 1980; coaching in Finland 1984-85; Barrow manager cs 1985.*
**Appearances:** Football League 5+2.
Maurice Whittle had been groomed in the Central League team at Ewood Park to provide cover for the half-back positions. He won a Central League championship medal whilst with the club but was unable to make the break through into the senior team on a regular basis. All his first team

appearances came during the 1968-69 season and in May 1969 he moved to Oldham Athletic. Whittle was to enjoy great success at Boundary Park and scored 39 goals in 312 League games (including five as sub). It was whilst at Oldham that Whittle was successfully converted into an attacking full-back. After leaving Oldham he spent a short time in America with Fort Lauderdale Strikers before returning to England to play non-League football with Barrow. He made a brief return to League football with 21 appearances for Wigan Athletic before returning to Barrow as manager.

**WHYTE, Crawford**
Left-back. 1930-1935.
*5ft 10in; 11st 10lb.*
*Born: Ryehope, 4 December 1907; Died: Exmouth, 11 August 1984.*
*Debut: v Derby County (a) 26 December 1930.*
*Career: Wallsend Secondary School; Walker Park; Crawcrook; Blackburn Rovers April 1930; Bradford July 1935; Tranmere Rovers August 1936; Ashington; Hartlepools United August 1937; Clapton Orient August 1938; Floriana (Malta).*
**Appearances:** Football League 87; FA Cup 1; Total 88.
Crawford Whyte had a thorough grounding in junior football before joining Blackburn Rovers in April 1930. He arrived at Blackburn as understudy to 'Taffy' Jones and ultimately succeeded him in the left-back spot at the start of the 1933-34 season. A rugged competitor, Whyte possessed a strong clearance and had the pace to cope with most wingers who tried to pass him on the outside. Was thought to be vulnerable to those who cut inside but, none the less, Whyte remains one of the most underrated full-backs in the club's history. He eventually lost the left-back position early in 1935 to Walter Crook and in July of that year he moved to Bradford.

**WHYTE, John**
Half-back. 1927-1929.
*5ft 8in; 11st.*
*Debut: v Newcastle United (h) 12 March 1927.*
*Career: St Johnstone 1924-25; Blackburn Rovers March 1927; Everton September 1929.*
**Appearances:** Football League 26
**Goals:** Football League 2
Fast and strong, John Whyte was a fierce competitor who made up for a lack of polish with his wonderful reading of the game. A former coal-miner, Whyte was exceptionally unfortunate with injuries during his time at Blackburn and as a result he was rarely able to show the form that had persuaded the club to sign him. He moved to Goodison Park in September 1929 but did not figure in the League team on Merseyside.

**WIGAN ATHLETIC FC**
Wigan Athletic came into being following the demise of Wigan Borough from the Football League in 1931. Founded in May 1932, Athletic had to wait until 1978 before being elected into the Football League. Although Blackburn and Wigan have met in the Lancashire-Manx Cup competition, the only truly competitive meeting between the clubs came in the Football League Cup.

**Football League Cup**

| | | | | |
|---|---|---|---|---|
| 1986-87 | (1) | Away | W | 3-1 |
| | (2) | Home | W | 2-0 |

**WIGHTMAN, John Renton**
Left-half. 1937-1947.
*Born: Duns, 2 November 1912; Died: Blackburn, 20 April 1964.*
*Debut: v Norwich City (a) 23 January 1937.*
*Career: Scarborough; York City; Bradford July 1934; Huddersfield Town January 1935; Blackburn Rovers January 1937; Carlisle United August 1947; Blackburn Rovers back-room staff June 1948.*
**Appearances:** Football League 66; FA Cup 5; Total 71.
**Goals:** Football League 2.
A wholehearted player who became a popular and much respected back-room boy at Ewood Park. Wightman had appeared in five League games for York City before moving to Bradford in September 1934. Wightman made 17 League appearances for Bradford before appearing in 64 League matches with Huddersfield Town. He left Leeds Road in January 1937 and made his debut at Norwich along with Len Butt and Billy Guest. Wightman remained an ever-present until the end of the season. A sturdy wing-half who was one of the most polished players in the years immediately preceding World War Two. Unfortunately an ankle injury kept him out of action for nearly 12 months during the Second Division championship campaign of 1938-39. After six years in the RAF during the war he returned to Ewood Park to play in the first post-war season . He then joined Carlisle United and made 36 League appearances during the 1947-48 season before deciding to retire from the game. In June 1948

he was appointed coach to the 'A' team and was later appointed second team trainer, a position he held at the time of his death. Whilst on the coaching staff at Ewood he helped to groom many local players who went on to become star names.

### WILCOX, Jason Malcolm
Outside-left. 1986-
*5ft 10in; 11st 6lb.*
*Born: Farnworth, 15 March 1971.*
*Debut: v Swindon Town (h) 16 April 1990.*
*Career: Blackburn Rovers associated schoolboy June 1986, becoming a trainee in July 1987 and a professional in June 1989.*
**Appearances:** Premier League 62+4; Football League 49+8; FA Cup 9; Football League Cup 9+1; Full Members' Cup 2; Total 131+13.
**Goals:** Premier League 10; Football League 4; FA Cup 1; Total 15.

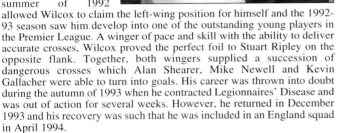

A pacey left-winger who graduated through the youth development scheme at Ewood Park and went on to become a member of the England international squad towards the end of the 1993-94 season. He made his debut in April 1990, but it was not until the 1991-92 season that Wilcox finally established himself in the team. Although a two-footed winger, Wilcox favours the left but because of the form of Scott Sellars had to operate on the right for much of the 1991-92 season. Unfortunately, injury prevented him from participating in the play-off matches.

The departure of Scott Sellars in the summer of 1992 allowed Wilcox to claim the left-wing position for himself and the 1992-93 season saw him develop into one of the outstanding young players in the Premier League. A winger of pace and skill with the ability to deliver accurate crosses, Wilcox proved the perfect foil to Stuart Ripley on the opposite flank. Together, both wingers supplied a succession of dangerous crosses which Alan Shearer, Mike Newell and Kevin Gallacher were able to turn into goals. His career was thrown into doubt during the autumn of 1993 when he contracted Legionnaires' Disease and was out of action for several weeks. However, he returned in December 1993 and his recovery was such that he was included in an England squad in April 1994.

### WILKIE, John
Inside-left. 1895-1898.
*5ft 7in; 12st.*
*Debut: v Sheffield Wednesday (h) 23 November 1895.*
*Career: Partick Thistle cs 1894; Blackburn Rovers November 1895; Glasgow Rangers May 1898; Middlesbrough August 1900; Partick Thistle October 1904 to May 1905; Hibernians cs 1905.*
**Appearances:** Football League 75; FA Cup 5; Test Matches 2; Total 82.
**Goals:** Football League 17; FA Cup 1; Total 18.
Wilkie arrived in Blackburn in November 1895 and made an immediate impact when he scored the opening goal in a 2-1 win over Sheffield Wednesday at Ewood Park. A tricky type of creative player, Wilkie was joined at Blackburn in May 1896 by John Campbell his former left-wing partner at Partick Thistle. The two provided Blackburn with a formidable left-wing pairing in attack for a further two seasons. However, in May 1898 both players opted to return to Scotland to join Rangers. Wilkie didn't enjoy the same degree of success with Rangers that Campbell achieved and only appeared in three games during the championship winning season of 1898-99. He made 11 League appearances the following campaign when the title was retained but didn't appear for

Rangers in the Scottish Cup Final of that season. He returned to England in August 1900 to score eight goals in 28 League appearances with Middlesbrough before returning to Scotland to end his playing career.

### WILKIE, T.
Goalkeeper. 1889.
*Born: Glasgow.*
*Debut: v Preston North End (a) 7 December 1889.*
*Career: United Abstainers (Glasgow); Blackburn Rovers November 1889.*
**Appearances:** Football League 5
One of a number of Scots brought to Blackburn by Tom Mitchell, Wilkie was signed from the Glasgow junior team United Abstainers. He seemed to be settling into the side quite well until an unfortunate incident in his fourth appearance saw him credited with a dubious 'own-goal'. The following week he experienced a personal nightmare in a 4-2 home defeat by Everton. Nerves completely got the better of him and his performance was so poor that the club couldn't risk playing him again. Wilkie was unable to come to terms with his nervous disposition and returned to Scotland.

### WILKINSON, David L.
Outside-left. 1948-1950.
*5ft 8in; 9st 2½lb.*
*Born: Sunderland, 28 May 1928.*
*Debut: v Luton Town (a) 6 September 1948.*
*Career: North Shields; Blackburn Rovers July 1948; Bournemouth & Boscombe Athletic June 1950; Berwick Rangers August 1952.*
**Appearances:** Football League 1.
Wilkinson came to Ewood Park from the RAF after playing as an amateur with North Shields. He received lightning promotion at Ewood as injuries meant he was called into the first team after only five Central League appearances. Unfortunately, perhaps because of his lack of experience, his colleagues appeared reluctant to give him much of the ball and thus he experienced a relatively quiet debut as the team slumped to a 2-0 defeat. The rest of his time at Ewood was spent with the Central League team until a free transfer at the end of the 1949-50 season saw him move to Bournemouth. He scored three goals in eight League appearances with Bournemouth before moving into Scottish football with Berwick Rangers.

### WILKINSON, Neil
Right-back. 1971-1977.
*5ft 7in; 10st.*
*Born: Blackburn, 16 February 1955.*
*Debut: v Lincoln City (a) 18 November 1972 (FAC).*
*Career: Blackburn Rovers apprentice August 1971, turning professional in February 1973. Released February 1977; Cape Town (South Africa); Great Harwood; Port Vale July 1978; Crewe Alexandra October 1978.*
*Domestic honours with Blackburn Rovers: Third Division championship: 1974-75 (2 apps).*
**Appearances:** Football League 27+3; FA Cup 2; Football League Cup 5+1; Total 34+4.
Neil Wilkinson graduated through the ranks at Ewood Park before making his first-team debut in November 1972, whilst still an apprentice. Shortly afterwards he turned professional but was unable to win a regular place in the side until injury ruled Mick Heaton out during the 1975-76 season. Wilkinson, who had been sent off in an FA Cup-tie with Altrincham in December 1973, failed to live up to his promise and Jim Smith chose to use Derek Fazackerley and Kevin Hird at right-back during the 1976-77 season. Wilkinson tried his luck in South Africa after being released in February 1977, but returned to League football with Port Vale in July 1978. He made just seven appearances for the Potteries club before enjoying his most successful spell in the Football League with Crewe Alexandra. Wilkinson went on to make 75 League appearances (including seven as sub) for the Gresty Road club.

### WILLIAMS, William
Outside-right. 1898-1901.
*Debut: v Everton (a) 1 September 1898.*
*Career: Everton January 1894; Blackburn Rovers May 1898; Bristol Rovers; Newton Heath August 1901.*
*International honours with Blackburn Rovers: Football League: 1 appearance (1898).*
**Appearances:** Football League 31.
**Goals:** Football League 1.
The curiously named William Williams came to Ewood Park from Everton with a good reputation for wing play. He played some fine games for Blackburn during the 1898-99 season but failed to reproduce his best form at the start of the following campaign. Williams had the sort of pace that could worry the best of defences and had the ability to turn on a

sixpence. However, as his form began to waver he became the target of some barracking from the terraces and this resulted in a further slump in confidence. Having lost his place in the first team Williams left the Football League to play with Bristol Rovers before joining Newton Heath on the eve of the 1901-02 season.

## WILLIAMSON, John
Forward. 1956-1957.
*6ft; 12st.*
*Born: Manchester, 8 May 1929.*
*Debut: v Hull City (h) 30 Mach 1956.*
*Career: Manchester Corporation Transport Department; Oldham Athletic amateur; Manchester City August 1949; Blackburn Rovers March 1956.*
**Appearances:** Football League 9.
**Goals:** Football League 3.
A thoughtful type of footballer whose lack of bite and shooting power handicapped his progress at Ewood Park. Johnny Carey had first noticed Williamson's potential in 1949 when he was an unknown junior playing for the Manchester Corporation Transport Department team. Carey, who was the Manchester United captain at the time, was coaching the Transport team and tried to persuade Williamson to join United. However, the youngster was a keen Manchester City fan and opted for the Maine Road club.

Williamson scored 18 goals in 59 League games with Manchester City before signing for Blackburn in March 1956. He scored one goal in four appearances during the closing stages of the 1955-56 season and began the following campaign at inside-right in the first team. It had been hoped that Williamson would be able to provide the type of generalship that the departed Eddie Quigley had done before him. Sadly, Williamson never looked like an adequate replacement for Quigley and he lost his place after only four matches. He was to make one further appearance for the club before being released at the end of the 1956-57 season.

## WILLIAMSON, Philip J.
Central-defender. 1979-1982.
*Born: Macclesfield, 19 June 1962.*
*Debut: v Charlton Athletic (a) 5 September 1981 (sub).*
*Career: Blackburn Rovers apprentice July 1979, turning professional in September 1980.*
**Appearances:** Football League 0+1.
Williamson had the misfortune to graduate through the junior ranks at a time when Keeley and Fazackerley reigned supreme at the heart of the Blackburn defence. Williamson vied with David Mail and Julian Marshall for the position of main understudy to the regular first-team pairing. He made his sole appearance for the first team at Charlton in September 1981 when he came on a substitute for Glenn Keeley. However, only Mail emerged as a real challenger to the dominance of Keeley and Fazackerley and both Williamson and Marshall received free transfers.

## WILLIAMSON, Thomas Robertson
Centre-half. 1922-1924.
*5ft 9in; 11st 6lb.*
*Born: Dalmuir, Glasgow, 8 February 1901.*
*Died: Norwich, 1 April 1988 (in a house fire).*
*Debut: v Burnley (a) 21 October 1922.*
*Career: Kilbowie Ross Dhu; Kirkintilloch Rob Roy; Blackburn Rovers March 1922; Third Lanark June 1924; Stoke City December 1926; Norwich City July 1931; Frost's Athletic July 1934.*
**Appearances:** Football League 19.
**Goals:** Football League 1.
Tom Williamson came to Blackburn from Kirkintilloch Rob Roy six months after Frank Crawley had been signed from the same club. A former ship's plater on the Clyde, Williamson made an outstanding debut against Burnley but contracted blood poisoning in his first season at the club and was out of action for several months. The early part of the 1923-24 season found Williamson sharing the centre-half position with Stan Dixon but he later made appearances in both wing-half positions as well as inside-right. Williamson went on to play over 150 League games for Stoke and 85 League games for Norwich City. Tragically he died in a house fire in April 1988 when it was thought that he fell asleep whilst smoking.

## WILLINGTON TOWN FC
Founded in 1906 as Willington Temperance, the club became known as Willington Town in 1911. A member of the Northern League in 1973 when they were drawn at home to Blackburn Rovers in the first round of the 1973-74 FA Cup competition. A crowd of 4,600 watched a 0-0 draw in the North-East and on Monday 3 December 1973, Willington travelled to Ewood Park for the replay. Because of the three-day week which

Garbett (left) scores Rovers' third goal against Willington Town in the first round of the 1973-74 FA Cup competition.

existed at the time due to the industrial dispute in the mining industry, the match was played in the afternoon. Some 4,025 spectators saw the Rovers move into the second round thanks to a 6-1 win which included goals from Field, O'Mara 2, Garbett, Napier and Parkes.

## WILLIS, John Johnson
Forward. 1954-1958.
*Born: Boldon, Durham, 28 May 1934.*
*Debut: v Doncaster Rovers (h) 1 October 1955.*
*Career: Blackburn Rovers August 1954; Accrington Stanley July 1957; Mossley; Aston Villa June 1958.*
**Appearances:** Football League 1.
An aircraftman and former dental technician, John Willis made his debut as a young untried centre-forward in a Second Division meeting with Doncaster Rovers at Ewood Park. He made little impression on the experienced Charlie Williams, who later became a well known stand-up comic. Although he tried to use the ball whenever he could, the pace of Williams prevented him from posing too much of a threat to the visiting team. Willis moved to Accrington Stanley in July 1957 but failed to break into the League team at Peel Park. A short spell with non-League Mossley was followed by one League appearance with Aston Villa.

## WILMINGTON, T.
Outside-right. 1896-97.
*Debut: v Bolton Wanderers (a) 12 September 1896.*
*Career: Burnley; Blackburn Rovers August 1896; Nelson.*
**Appearances:** Football League 9.
Wilmington came to Ewood Park after failing to make the first team at Burnley. He got his chance at Blackburn in the third match of the 1896-97 season and did sufficiently well to retain his place on the right wing. However, two successive four-nil defeats led to him losing his place in the team and he was only recalled for one further outing before being released at the end of the season.

## WILSON, Joseph
Centre-half. 1904-1908.
*Born: Wigan, 1884.*
*Debut: v Woolwich Arsenal (a) 17 February 1906.*
*Career: Wigan County; Darwen; Blackburn Rovers 1904; Brighton & Hove Albion May 1908; Millwall cs 1909; Rochdale September 1920; Fleetwood player-coach cs 1921.*
**Appearances:** Football League 43; FA Cup 3; Total 46.
**Goals:** Football League 4.
Joe Wilson was signed from Darwen to provide the club with more cover for the centre-half position. He won a regular place in the side in September 1906 but was unable to retain it for the following season. Wilson was a tall, commanding figure whose battling qualities were well respected by his more illustrious international colleagues. The 1907-08 season found him out of the side and although he returned briefly during November and December 1907 he was unable to retain his place. After leaving Ewood he spent a season with Brighton before enjoying great success at Millwall. He scored 30 goals in 238 League appearances for Millwall before joining Rochdale in September 1920.

## WILSON, Robert
Goalkeeper. 1937-1938.
*6ft 1in; 12st.*

*Born: Blantyre*
*Debut: v Sheffield United (a) 9 October 1937.*
*Career: Bellshill Athletic; Blackburn Rovers trial 1936, signing professional in January 1937; Falkirk June 1938; Nelson; Blackburn Rovers wartime guest 1940-41.*
**Appearances:** Football League 3.
A successful trial with the Central League team at Ewood Park earned Wilson a first-team debut against Sheffield United at Bramall Lane in October 1937. Although a well-built custodian, Wilson's weak kicking ability proved something of an Achilles' heel and led to United's goal in a 1-1 draw. Never a first choice during his time at the club, Wilson made a further two appearances during the 1937-38 season before returning to Scotland in June 1938. Wilson also appeared in four wartime games for Blackburn during the 1940-41 season.

### WILSON, Thomas Carter
Outside-left. 1898-1899.
*5ft 7in; 11st 7lb.*
*Born: Preston, 20 October 1877.*
*Debut: v Everton (a) 1 September 1898.*
*Career: Fishwick Ramblers; Ashton-in-Makerfield; West Manchester; Ashton Town; Manchester City; Ashton North End; Oldham County 1896; Swindon Town 1897; Blackburn Rovers May 1898; Swindon Town May 1899; Millwall Athletic May 1900; Aston Villa April 1901; Queen's Park Rangers cs 1902; Bolton Wanderers May 1904; Leeds City December 1906; Manchester United February 1908; Chorley manager; Rochdale chairman October 1919, becoming manager during the 1920-21 season until March 1923.*
**Appearances:** Football League 1.
A skilful winger with a good turn of speed, the much travelled Wilson arrived at Blackburn from Swindon in May 1898. He made his debut in the opening game of the 1898-99 season but two days later was replaced by Daniel Hurst. The consistency of Hurst meant Wilson was unable to win a recall to the senior team and in May 1899 he returned to Swindon. Wilson had no shortage of employers during a long career and eventually ended up a chairman of Rochdale in October 1919. It was during Wilson's tenure of office that Billy Bradshaw was appointed as player-manager at Spotland Road. When Rochdale and Bradshaw parted company during the 1920-21 season it was Wilson who stepped into the breach to take over the managerial position.

### WILSON, William
Left-back. 1963-1972.
*5ft 8½in; 11st 1lb.*
*Born: Seaton Delaval, 10 July 1946.*
*Debut: v Chelsea (h) 13 February 1965.*
*Career: Blackburn Rovers September 1963; Portsmouth January 1972.*
**Appearances:** Football League 246+1; FA Cup 14; Football League Cup 16; Total 276+1.
Billy Wilson was a tough tackling, terrier-like defender who proved to be the perfect full-back foil for Keith Newton. Wilson came to Ewood from the North-East and progressed through the junior teams at Blackburn before making his first-team debut in February 1965. Although he could operate on either flank, it was at left-back that he finally settled following the switch of Walter Joyce to a midfield role. Wilson remained a consistent performer until the departure of Newton appeared to unsettle him. As the club began to slide towards the Third Division in 1970-71, Wilson's own form began to suffer and as a result he lost his place in the side for a short time. Although reluctant to sample life in the Third Division, Wilson was persuaded to remain until a suitable move came along.

However, it was clear that he was disenchanted with life at Ewood and Wilson was no longer in the first team when he finally got the move he wanted. At Portsmouth his form and appetite for football returned and he went on to make 194 League appearances (including six as sub) for Pompey before retiring from the game.

### WIMBLEDON FC
The origins of Wimbledon FC can be traced back to 1889 although the club did not become members of the Football League until 1977. As a non-League club Wimbledon caused a major sensation in the FA Cup in January 1975 when they visited Turf Moor, the home of First Division Burnley, and left with a 1-0 victory under their belts. Causing major upsets became something of a speciality for Wimbledon and perhaps the greatest of these was when they beat Liverpool in 1988 FA Cup Final.

**Football League**

| | | | Home | | Away | |
|---|---|---|---|---|---|---|
| 1979-80 | | (Div 3) | W | 3-0 | L | 0-1 |
| 1984-85 | | (Div 2) | W | 2-0 | D | 1-1 |
| 1985-86 | | (Div 2) | W | 2-0 | D | 1-1 |

| | P | W | D | L | F | A |
|---|---|---|---|---|---|---|
| Home | 3 | 3 | 0 | 0 | 7 | 0 |
| Away | 3 | 0 | 2 | 1 | 2 | 3 |
| Total | 6 | 3 | 2 | 1 | 9 | 3 |

**FA Premiership**

| | | Home | | Away | |
|---|---|---|---|---|---|
| 1992-93 | | D | 0-0 | D | 1-1 |
| 1993-94 | | W | 3-0 | L | 1-4 |

| | P | W | D | L | F | A |
|---|---|---|---|---|---|---|
| Home | 2 | 1 | 1 | 0 | 3 | 0 |
| Away | 2 | 0 | 1 | 1 | 2 | 5 |

**Football League Cup**

| | | | | | |
|---|---|---|---|---|---|
| 1985-86 | | (2) | Away | L | 0-5 |
| | | | Home | W | 2-1 |

**Wins**
The record for the most wins in a season in each division is as follows:

| Premiership | 25 | wins | 1993-94 |
|---|---|---|---|
| Division One | 20 | wins | 1911-12 & 1913-14 |
| Division Two | 25 | wins | 1938-39 |
| Division Three | 25 | wins | 1979-80 |

The record for the fewest wins in a season in each division is as follows:

| Premiership | 20 | wins | 1992-93 |
|---|---|---|---|
| Division One | 7 | wins | 1897-98 |
| Division Two | 6 | wins | 1970-71 |
| Division Three | 18 | wins | 1973-74 |

The record for the best home and away win is as follows:
Home 9-0 v Middlesbrough 6 November 1954
Away 7-0 v Bootle 15 February 1890 (FAC)

### WITTON FC
A club which provided opposition to Blackburn Rovers in the days before the formation of the Football League. Witton and Blackburn were drawn together in the third round of the 1884-85 FA Cup competition. On 22 December 1984, Blackburn enjoyed a comfortable 5-1 away win thanks to goals from Forrest, Brown, Sowerbutts, Lofthouse and Fecitt.

### WOLSTENHOLME, Samuel
Right-half. 1904-1908.
*Born: Little Lever, 1878 (July quarter).*
*Debut: v Bury (a) 3 September 1904.*
*Career: Darley Vale; Farnworth; Farnworth Alliance 1896; Horwich 1897; Everton late 1897; Blackburn Rovers May 1904; Norwich City April 1908; Croydon Common cs 1908; Norwich City April 1909; Chester 1913.*
*International honours with Blackburn Rovers: England: 2 caps (1905); Football League: 1 appearance (1905).*
**Appearances:** Football League 98; FA Cup 7; Total 105.
**Goals:** Football League 1; FA Cup 1; Total 2.
The signing of Wolstenholme, a current international, from Everton was something of a major coup for Blackburn Rovers. Although the prematurely balding Wolstenholme looked older than his 25 years, he still had plenty to offer in terms of top-class football. Wolstenholme was immediately installed in the right-half position and his intuitive reading of the game was well received at Ewood Park. Although not the most robust of tacklers, Wolstenholme also figured at right-back and centre-half during his time at Blackburn. He moved to Norwich City in April 1908 and then helped Croydon Common into the Southern League before returning to Norwich in April 1909. Wolstenholme was coaching in Germany when war was declared and as a result was interned along with fellow England internationals Steve Bloomer and Fred Spikesley.

### WOLVERHAMPTON WANDERERS FC
Founded in 1877 and one of the 12 founder members of the Football League in 1888. Blackburn and Wolves met in three FA Cup semi-finals

in five years between 1888 and 1893 and it wasn't until 1966 that the clubs met outside of the First Division in the Football League. In 1960 the clubs met in the FA Cup Final and Wolves enjoyed a resounding 3-0 victory in a game which was marred by the injury which resulted in Dave Whelan sustaining a broken leg.

## Football League

| | | | Home | | Away | |
|---|---|---|---|---|---|---|
| 1888-89 | | (FL) | D | 2-2 | D | 2-2 |
| 1889-90 | | (FL) | W | 4-3 | W | 4-2 |
| 1890-91 | | (FL) | L | 2-3 | L | 0-2 |
| 1891-92 | | (FL) | W | 2-0 | L | 1-6 |
| 1892-93 | | (Div 1) | D | 3-3 | L | 2-4 |
| 1893-94 | | (Div 1) | W | 3-0 | L | 1-5 |
| 1894-95 | | (Div 1) | W | 5-1 | D | 3-3 |
| 1895-96 | | (Div 1) | W | 3-1 | W | 2-1 |
| 1896-97 | | (Div 1) | W | 2-0 | D | 1-1 |
| 1897-98 | | (Div 1) | L | 2-3 | L | 2-3 |
| 1898-99 | | (Div 1) | D | 2-2 | L | 1-2 |
| 1899-00 | | (Div 1) | W | 2-1 | L | 0-4 |
| 1900-01 | | (Div 1) | W | 2-0 | D | 2-2 |
| 1901-02 | | (Div 1) | W | 2-0 | L | 1-3 |
| 1902-03 | | (Div 1) | W | 1-0 | L | 0-2 |
| 1903-04 | | (Div 1) | D | 1-1 | L | 0-1 |
| 1904-05 | | (Div 1) | W | 3-0 | L | 0-2 |
| 1905-06 | | (Div 1) | W | 3-1 | L | 1-2 |
| 1932-33 | | (Div 1) | W | 1-0 | L | 3-5 |
| 1933-34 | | (Div 1) | W | 7-1 | L | 3-5 |
| 1934-35 | | (Div 1) | W | 4-2 | L | 1-2 |
| 1935-36 | | (Div 1) | W | 1-0 | L | 1-8 |
| 1946-47 | | (Div 1) | L | 1-2 | D | 3-3 |
| 1947-48 | | (Div 1) | W | 1-0 | L | 1-5 |
| 1958-59 | | (Div 1) | L | 1-2 | L | 0-5 |
| 1959-60 | | (Div 1) | L | 0-1 | L | 1-3 |
| 1960-61 | | (Div 1) | W | 2-1 | D | 0-0 |
| 1961-62 | | (Div 1) | W | 2-1 | W | 2-0 |
| 1962-63 | | (Div 1) | W | 5-1 | L | 2-4 |
| 1963-64 | | (Div 1) | D | 1-1 | W | 5-1 |
| 1964-65 | | (Div 1) | W | 4-1 | L | 2-4 |
| 1966-67 | | (Div 2) | D | 0-0 | L | 0-4 |
| 1976-77 | | (Div 2) | L | 0-2 | W | 2-1 |
| 1982-83 | | (Div 2) | D | 2-2 | L | 1-2 |
| 1984-85 | | (Div 2) | W | 3-0 | W | 3-0 |
| 1989-90 | | (Div 2) | L | 2-3 | W | 2-1 |
| 1990-91 | | (Div 2) | D | 1-1 | W | 3-2 |
| 1991-92 | | (Div 2) | L | 1-2 | D | 0-0 |

| | P | W | D | L | F | A |
|---|---|---|---|---|---|---|
| Home | 38 | 22 | 8 | 8 | 83 | 44 |
| Away | 38 | 8 | 7 | 23 | 58 | 102 |
| Total | 76 | 30 | 15 | 31 | 141 | 146 |

## FA Cup

| | | | | | |
|---|---|---|---|---|---|
| 1888-89 | | (SF) | Crewe | D | 1-1 |
| | | (R) | Crewe | L | 1-3 |
| 1889-90 | | (SF) | Derby | W | 1-0 |
| 1890-91 | | (3) | Home | W | 2-0 |
| 1892-93 | | (SF) | Nottingham | L | 1-2 |
| 1896-97 | | (2) | Home | W | 2-1 |
| 1911-12 | | (3) | Home | W | 3-2 |
| 1919-20 | | (1) | Home | D | 2-2 |
| | | (R) | Away | L | 0-1 |
| 1959-60 | | (F) | Wembley | L | 0-3 |

## WOMBWELL, Richard
Inside-forward. 1908-1910.
*5ft 6in; 12st.*
*Born: Nottingham, 1879.*
*Debut: v Bolton Wanderers (h) 29 February 1908.*
*Career: Bulwell; Ilkeston Town December 1898; Derby County May 1899; Bristol City August 1902; Manchester United March 1905; Heart of Midlothian January 1907; Brighton & Hove Albion June 1907; Blackburn Rovers February 1908; Ilkeston Town August 1910.*
**Appearances:** Football League 15.
**Goals:** Football League 1.
A gifted playmaker who came to Ewood Park at the end of his playing career. Wombwell, who had appeared in the Hearts side which lost the 1906-07 Scottish Cup Final to Celtic, arrived at Blackburn with two other Brighton players, Walter Anthony and Joseph Lumley. Wombwell featured in ten of the final 12 games of 1907-08, but the following season

saw his experience being used to marshal the younger players in the second team.

## WOOD, Michael J.
Left-back/Utility. 1970-1978
*5ft 11in; 10st 13lb.*
*Born: Bury, 3 July 1952.*
*Debut: v Norwich City (a) 31 January 1970.*
*Career: Blackburn Rovers apprentice July 1968, turning professional in February 1970; Bradford City 8 February 1978 (£15,000); Halifax Town August 1982; Dudley Hill Athletic; Guiseley.*
*Domestic honours with Blackburn Rovers: Third Division championship: 1974-75 (18 apps).*
**Appearances:** Football League 140+8; FA Cup 10+1; Football League 6+1; Total 156+10.
**Goals:** Football League 2.
A solid reliable defender who graduated through the junior ranks at Ewood Park. Wood broke into the team with a crop of other young players – including Terry Eccles, Ray Charter and Jeff Whalley – during the 1969-70 season. The following season saw Wood being given greater opportunities as the club slipped towards the Third Division. Although essentially a left-back, Wood also played at centre-half and in midfield at different times during his time at Ewood Park. A sound defensive player, Wood was strong in the tackle and good in the air. Wood became a valuable member of the first-team squad but was never destined to acquire the same status as his contemporary Derek Fazackerley. Sadly, Wood was plagued by injuries throughout much of his time at the club and this restricted his first-team appearances. In February 1978 he moved to Bradford City and appeared in 146 League games (including three as sub) before ending his career with 81 League appearances (including one as sub) with Halifax Town.

## WOOD, William
Left-half. 1927-1933.
*5ft 8½in; 10st 4lb.*
*Born: Blackburn.*
*Debut: v Chelsea (h) 5 March 1932.*
*Career: Blackburn Rovers amateur June 1927, turning professional in November 1927; Burnley March 1933; Mansfield Town 1934; Chorley cs 1934; Darwen 1935.*
**Appearances:** Football League 7
Wood spent a number of years in the second and third teams at Ewood Park on the left wing before finally settling in the left-half position. He was acclaimed as a second 'Billy Bradshaw' until an ankle injury hindered his progress. Not the speediest of players, Wood was a tricky individual who used the ball constructively. He moved to Turf Moor in March 1933 and made seven League appearances for Burnley before joining Mansfield Town. After making five League appearances for Mansfield he returned to Lancashire to play in non-League football with Chorley and Darwen.

## WOODS, Maurice
Centre-half. 1956-1963.
*6ft; 12st 6lb.*
*Born: Skelmersdale, 1 November 1931.*
*Debut: v Middlesbrough (h) 24 November 1956.*

*Career: Burscough; Everton amateur 1947, becoming a professional in November 1949; Blackburn Rovers November 1956 (£6,000); Hakoah (Australia) cs 1963; Luton Town July 1965; Stockport County July 1966; Drumcondra; Stockport County trainer, then manager April 1970 until December 1971; Southport coach 1974.*
*International honours with Blackburn Rovers: Football League: 1 appearance (1960).*
*Domestic honours with Blackburn Rovers: FA Cup runners-up: 1960.*
**Appearances:** Football League 260; FA Cup 30; Football League Cup 17; Total 307.
**Goals:** Football League 2; FA Cup 1; Total 3.
Although not the biggest of central defenders, Matt Woods strode the pitch like a colossus. He simply dwarfed forwards of bigger

Blackburn's John Radford is foiled by Wrexham goalkeeper Dai Davies at the Racecourse Ground in March 1979.

physique and imposed his presence on all those around him. A man who never shirked a challenge, Woods was probably one of the finest uncapped centre-halves of his era. Christened Maurice but known to everyone as Matt, Woods was a born leader and was able to organise his defensive colleagues. As a youngster he moved from junior football to become an amateur with Everton in 1947 and two years later signed professional forms with the Goodison club. Whilst in the Army he played football with Western Command but at Goodison he struggled to break into the first team.

Woods was the second Evertonian to arrive at Ewood Park during the 1956-57 season, with Harry Leyland having been signed in August 1956. Superb timing and power meant that Woods had total supremacy in the air whilst his ability to tackle with either foot and his sheer strength meant few relished his challenges. With Ronnie Clayton and Mick McGrath on either side of him Woods was a member of one of the finest half-back lines ever to play for the club. Woods appeared in all 42 League games in 1957-58 when the club won promotion to the First Division on the final Saturday of the season.

Two years later he appeared in the 1960 FA Cup Final but, although he was honoured at inter-league level, full international honours escaped him. The early 1960s found him holding off the challenge of the immensely talented Mike England. However, at the end of the 1962-63 season he decided to bow to the inevitable and retired from League football to emigrate to Australia. It was rather ironic that on the other side of the world he won the international honours that had eluded him for so long in England. Having captained the Australian international team Woods returned to England to play with Luton Town in July 1965. He made 34 League appearances for Luton before moving to Stockport County in July 1966. After appearing with Stockport in 85 League games Woods ended his playing career in Ireland with Drumcondra. Woods became trainer and later manager with Stockport County and also had a spell as coach to Southport whilst they were still in the Football League.

### WOOLFALL A.
Goalkeeper. 1879-1883.
*Debut: v Sheffield Providence (h) 30 October 1880 (FAC).*
*Career: Blackburn Rovers 1879; Blackburn Olympic 1883.*
**Appearances:** FA Cup 3.
Popularly known as 'Woody', Woolfall vied with Roger Howarth for the goalkeeping position following the retirement of Tom Greenwood, the club's first goalkeeper. Woolfall received his first opportunities with the senior team during the 1879-80 season but had to wait until the following campaign before edging ahead of Howarth in the pecking order. Towards the end of his time with the Rovers, Woolfall turned out at centre-forward with the second team as the club preferred to groom the young Herbie Arthur in goal. Ultimately, Arthur would replace both Woolfall and Howarth as the number one custodian at Ewood Park.

### WOOLLEY, Horace G.
Outside-right. 1937-1938.
*Debut: v Bradford (a) 29 January 1938.*
*Career: Partick Thistle October 1935; Blackburn Rovers May 1937.*
**Appearances:** Football League 1.
Woolley, who joined the club from Partick Thistle, made his debut as a last minute replacement for Percy Dickie. Woolley was in fact third choice for the right-wing position as Dickie had been deputising for the injured Jack Bruton. Woolley could not have chosen a more inappropriate day to make his debut as the Rovers were routed 7-1 at Bradford. The following week the club signed Charles Luke from Huddersfield Town and Woolley was not retained for the following season.

## WORKINGTON FC

Members of the Football League between 1951 and 1977, Workington and Blackburn Rovers only came together in competitive football in the Football League Cup competition. The first meetings took place in 1964-65 when Blackburn were a leading light in the First Division and Workington were in the Third. However, after holding Blackburn to a 0-0 draw in front of a crowd of 11,763 spectators, Ken Furphy led his Workington team to a major victory at Ewood Park. A crowd of 6,282 watched in disbelief as Workington romped to a 5-1 win.

### Football League Cup

| | | | | | |
|---|---|---|---|---|---|
| 1964-65 | (3) | Away | D | 0-0 | |
| | (R) | Home | L | 1-5 | |
| 1971-72 | (1) | Home | W | 2-0 | |

## WREXHAM FC

Founded in 1873 and the oldest Association Football club in Wales. One of the original members of the Third Division North in 1921, Wrexham and Blackburn Rovers did not meet in competitive football until the fourth round of the inaugural Football League Cup competition in December 1960. Although only 14 League matches have been played these have tended to be tight affairs and have produced no fewer than nine draws.

### Football League

| | | | Home | | Away | |
|---|---|---|---|---|---|---|
| 1971-72 | (Div 3) | W | 2-1 | D | 1-1 | |
| 1972-73 | (Div 3) | D | 1-1 | D | 0-0 | |
| 1973-74 | (Div 3) | L | 1-2 | D | 2-2 | |
| 1974-75 | (Div 3) | D | 0-0 | D | 1-1 | |
| 1978-79 | (Div 2) | D | 1-1 | L | 1-2 | |
| 1980-81 | (Div 2) | D | 1-1 | W | 1-0 | |
| 1981-82 | (Div 2) | D | 0-0 | L | 0-1 | |

| | P | W | D | L | F | A |
|---|---|---|---|---|---|---|
| Home | 7 | 1 | 5 | 1 | 6 | 6 |
| Away | 7 | 1 | 4 | 2 | 6 | 7 |
| Total | 14 | 2 | 9 | 3 | 12 | 13 |

### Football League Cup

| | | | | | |
|---|---|---|---|---|---|
| 1960-61 | (5) | Home | D | 1-1 | |
| | (R) | Away | L | 1-3 aet | |

## WRIGHT, Alan Geoffrey

Left-back. 1991-
*5ft 4in; 9st 4lb.*
*Born: Ashton-under-Lyne, 28 September 1971.*
*Debut: v Grimsby Town (h) 26 October 1991.*
*Career: Blackpool trainee August 1988, turning professional in April 1989; Blackburn Rovers October 1991 (£500,000).*
*International honours with Blackburn Rovers: England Under-21: 1 cap.*
**Appearances:** Premier League 31+6; Football League 32+1; Play-offs 3; FA Cup 5; Football League Cup 8; Total 79+7.
**Goals:** Football League 1.
Alan Wright was Kenny Dalglish's first signing for Blackburn Rovers following his appointment as manager in October 1991. Wright, although one of the smallest players in the game, remains a tremendous prospect being a left-back who has the speed and skill of a winger. Wright quickly adjusted to the pace of Second Division football following his arrival from Blackpool and only missed one game out of 34 before assisting the club into the Premier League via the Play-offs. He began the 1992-93 season playing in midfield before Tony Dobson's suspension saw Wright return to his more familiar left-back position. Unfortunately he was plagued by a hernia problem and the need for an operation brought an early end to his season. Whilst Wright was out of action the club signed Graeme Le Saux from Chelsea and such was his form during the 1993-94 season that Wright was unable to retain his first-team place. Wright eventually returned to the team when Jason Wilcox succumbed to illness in October 1993. Although he played impressively on his return to the

team, Wright found himself out of favour once Wilcox was restored to full fitness. As Le Saux graduated into England's left-back, Wright had to settle for a place on the substitute's bench.

## WRIGHT, Archibald Watson

Inside-forward. 1951-1953.
*5ft 5in; 9st 10lb.*
*Born: Glasgow, 23 November 1924.*
*Debut: v Sheffield United (h) 18 August 1951.*
*Career: Rutherglen; Glencairn Juniors; Hamilton Academical 1946-47; Clyde 1947-48 (£6,000); Falkirk 1949-50; Blackburn Rovers May 1951 (£10,000); Grimsby Town July 1953; Accrington Stanley June 1954 (£1,000); Netherfield cs 1957; Horwich RMI manager 1960; Airdrieonians manager February 1963.*
**Appearances:** Football League 22.
**Goals:** Football League 10.
A former Scottish schoolboy international, Archie Wright had appeared for Falkirk against Blackburn Rovers in a friendly match in May 1951. Wright certainly impressed the Ewood club and signed for Blackburn before the month was out. Wright began the 1951-52 season in the first team but lost his place after the opening three games failed to produce a point. He made occasional appearances before featuring at inside-left in the final six League games. However, although a typically crafty Scotsman, Wright rarely looked like winning a regular first-team place throughout his stay at Ewood. He moved to Grimsby in the summer of 1953 and scored nine goals in 39 League games before returning to Lancashire to join Accrington Stanley in June 1954. Wright was far more prolific in terms of goalscoring at Peel Park and netted 27 goals in 80 League games.

## WRIGHT, Glenn M.

Midfield. 1972-1974.
*Born: Liverpool, 27 May 1956.*
*Debut: v Halifax Town (a) 16 April 1974.*
*Career: Blackburn Rovers apprentice October 1972.*
**Appearances:** Football League 1.
Glenn Wright made his debut as a 17-year-old apprentice at the end of the 1973-74 season. He was not overawed by the occasion and quickly adjusted to the pace of the game. He made a favourable impression on his debut but surprisingly failed to progress to the professional ranks.

## WRIGLEY, Bernard Joseph

Goalkeeper. 1921-1923.
*5ft 9in; 11st 6lb.*
*Born: Clitheroe, 1894; Died: Manchester, 28 April 1965.*
*Debut: v Cardiff City (h) 2 January 1922.*
*Career: Clitheroe Royal Blues; Clitheroe Amateurs; Great Harwood; Blackburn Rovers amateur August 1921 (£25); Lincoln City September to December 1924; Great Harwood.*
**Appearances:** Football League 1.
Bernard Wrigley signed for Blackburn Rovers following a successful pre-season trial in August 1921. Wrigley was seen as the man to understudy Ronnie Sewell and he got his chance of First Division football when injury kept Sewell out of the meeting with Cardiff City in January 1922. Sadly, it was not a happy experience. Wrigley struggled to come to terms with crosses and his inability to judge the flight of the ball resulted in a 3-1 defeat for Blackburn. Wrigley was released at the end of the season and joined Lincoln City before returning to local non-League circles.

## WYLES, Thomas C.

Centre-forward. 1945-1946.
*Born: Bourne, 1 November 1919; Died: October 1990.*
*Debut: v Bolton Wanderers (a) 5 January 1946 (FAC).*
*Career: Peterborough United; Everton February 1938; Blackburn Rovers wartime guest 1943-44; signing permanently in October 1945; Bury May 1946; Southport November 1946 (£200); Bangor City cs 1950; Spalding United; Prescot Cables manager.*
**Appearances:** FA Cup 2.
**Goals:** FA Cup 1.
A former schoolboy international, Cec Wyles joined Blackburn Rovers during World War Two after failing to make the senior team at Goodison Park. He was the top goalscorer at Ewood Park during the 1945-46 season when the club played in the regionalised Football League North. Wyles hit 16 goals in 22 League appearances as well as one in the FA Cup. His most memorable moment came on 27 October 1945 when he scored all four goals in a 4-1 win over Burnley at Turf Moor. In May 1946 he moved to Bury and a few months later, after just two League

appearances, he joined Southport. He scored 49 League goals in 143 outings with Southport and in 1947-48 established a post-war total of 25 goals which was not surpassed until 1962-63. A motor mechanic by trade, Wyles moved into non-League football in the summer of 1950 when he joined Bangor.

### WYLIE, Thomas
Left-back. 1921-1926.
*5ft 7in; 10st 8lb.*
*Born: Darvel, c.1899.*
*Debut: v Sheffield United (h) 19 February 1921.*
*Career: Darvel local football; Queen of the South; Blackburn Rovers February 1921 to cs 1926; Darwen 1926; Swindon Town December 1926.*
**Appearances:** Football League 174; FA Cup 17; Total 191.
A terrier like full-back who came to Blackburn Rovers from Queen of the South and went on to captain the Ewood side. He formed an excellent full-back partnership with David Rollo and for a little over four seasons Wylie was a permanent fixture in the left-back position. He lost his place during the 1925-26 season and the emergence of 'Taffy' Jones during the latter part of the campaign saw Wylie leave the club during the close season. After a short spell with Darwen he returned to League football to join Swindon Town in December 1926.

### YARWOOD, John
Centre-half. 1895-1896.
*5ft 6½in; 10st 4lb.*
*Born: Bacup.*
*Debut: v Burnley (a) 13 April 1896.*
*Career: Accrington; Blackburn Rovers May 1895.*
**Appearances:** Football League 1.
Commenting on the talent available in the second team in September 1895, the football correspondent of the *Lancashire Daily Post* said of Yarwood: 'Of the halves, Yarwood will be worth a place in the first eleven. He is a fearless tackler, and a fine shot at goal.' However, Yarwood's only senior outing came when a much changed Blackburn team visited Turf Moor on 13 April 1896. Perhaps it was not surprising that a team which showed five changes from the previous match should lose by a six goal margin.

### YORK CITY FC
The present York City FC came into being in 1922 and was elected to the Third Division North of the Football League in 1929. York have been rare but welcome visitors to Ewood Park having failed to score on any of their four trips to Blackburn. However, although the Rovers have proved victorious in two Cup meetings at Bootham Crescent the trip to York has brought little reward in terms of points in the Football League. On 10 October 1960 both clubs met at York in the very first Football League Cup match that either club had played.

**Football League**

|  |  | Home |  | Away |  |
|---|---|---|---|---|---|
| 1971-72 | (Div 3) | W | 3-0 | W | 1-0 |
| 1972-73 | (Div 3) | W | 2-0 | L | 0-1 |
| 1973-74 | (Div 3) | W | 4-0 | L | 0-1 |
| 1975-76 | (Div 2) | W | 4-0 | L | 1-2 |

|  | P | W | D | L | F | A |
|---|---|---|---|---|---|---|
| Home | 4 | 4 | 0 | 0 | 13 | 0 |
| Away | 4 | 1 | 0 | 3 | 2 | 4 |
| Total | 8 | 5 | 0 | 3 | 15 | 4 |

**Football League Cup**

|  |  |  |  |  |
|---|---|---|---|---|
| 1960-61 | (1) | Away | W | 3-1 |
| 1966-67 | (3) | Away | W | 2-0 |

### YOUNG, William
Right-half. 1934-1937.
*5ft 7in 10st 4lb.*
*Born: Paisley.*
*Debut: v Aston Villa (a) 21 November 1936.*
*Career: Clydebank Juniors; Blackburn Rovers September 1934 (£200); St Mirren June 1937.*
**Appearances:** Football League 6.
Blackburn Rovers had to beat off the challenge of Sunderland to sign Young in September 1934. He arrived at Ewood Park as a promising youngster who it was thought would develop into a constructive type of half-back. All his League appearances at Blackburn came in the middle part of the 1936-37 season when he understudied Arnold Whiteside in the right-half position. However, by the end of that season Whiteside and Jock Wightman were clearly established as the senior half-backs at the club and Young left Ewood to join St Mirren.

# Subscribers

| | | | |
|---|---|---|---|
| 1 | Mike Jackman | 40 | Barbara Carr |
| 2 | Harry & Emilia Jackman | 41 | Nigel Shaw |
| 3 | Jim Creasy | 42 | Dr L C Cavannagh |
| 4 | Mike Davage | 43 | P A Ormerod |
| 5 | Garth Dykes | 44 | Alan Dyson |
| 6 | Derek Jones | 45 | John Philip Howarth |
| 7 | J Veglio | 46 | Daniel & Joseph Oldrieve |
| 8 | Andy Carruthers | 47 | Daniel Heyworth |
| 9 | The Loftus Family | 48 | Timothy Read |
| 10 | Derek Hyde | 49 | Andrew C Strand |
| 11 | Jonny Stokkeland | 50 | Ian M Collum |
| 12 | Vernisse Sylvain | 51 | Charlie Lucas |
| 13 | Mr T D Culshaw | 52 | Stephen W Bickerton |
| 14 | Michael James Baron | 53 | B R MacKenzie |
| 15 | Philip Dewhurst | 54 | Mr D J Rogerson |
| 16 | Robin, Nicola & Martin Duckworth | 55 | S Forrest |
| 17 | Bruce A S Skeer | 56 | Andy Turner |
| 18 | Mr David Bamber | 57 | T Conroy |
| 19 | Mark Bentley | 58 | Damian Potter |
| 20 | Tony Tomlinson | 59 | Shaun Rudge |
| 21 | Mr J Slater | 60 | Peter S Bolton |
| 22 | R S Briggs | 61 | Peter Schofield |
| 23 | T Owen | 62 | Dave Walton |
| 24 | M B Ainsworth | 63 | P N Heath |
| 25 | Roy Miller | 64 | Stuart Burke |
| 26 | Jonathan D Bibby | 65 | B V Morris |
| 27 | Graham Race | 66 | John Farrer |
| 28 | Pete Longman | 67 | A P Boardman |
| 29 | Brian Bone | 68 | Andrea Stephenson |
| 30 | Pete Garratty, Diego Garcia | 69 | Simon C R Wilkinson |
| 31 | Philip Black | 70 | M J Moore |
| 32 | Brynley James Juliff | 71 | Edward Calvert |
| 33 | Tim Eccles | 72 | John Milton Mitchell |
| 34 | Mark Ramsden | 73 | Phil Spragg |
| 35 | Keith A Barnes | 74 | John Root |
| 36 | Derek L Barnes | 75 | Neil Edwin Pickering |
| 37 | Steve Ball | 76 | Bernard Clarke |
| 38 | Martin Jolly | 77 | R Haworth |
| 39 | M Ormerod | 78 | Roy Grierson |

| | | | | |
|---|---|---|---|---|
| 79 | D W Wike | | 121 | David George |
| 80 | D E Gordon | | 122 | Roger Haydock |
| 81 | Ian Hobro | | 123 | Nigel Graeme Penberthy |
| 82 | R Sourbutts | | 124 | Sappi |
| 83 | Peter Walsh | | 125 | Jonathan Charles Bond |
| 84 | E M Gabbott | | 126 | Philip Aaron John Bond |
| 85 | S J Parker | | 127 | Frank M Kay |
| 86 | L Billington | | 128 | Stephen McNulty |
| 87 | David Hope | | 129 | Tony Catlow |
| 88 | Mr Frank Sutcliffe | | 130 | Craig Clark |
| 89 | Paul S Nolan | | 131 | E Gibbons |
| 90 | J Wilkinson | | 132 | Walter Thompson |
| 91 | K Hocking | | 133 | James Armstrong |
| 92 | Ian Whalley | | 134 | Robert Haworth |
| 93 | C J Clancy | | 135 | A J Carter |
| 94 | K J Merrill | | 136 | A G Parker |
| 95 | Mark Oddie | | 137 | Sharon Winstanley |
| 96 | H Wark | | 138 | S J McCourt |
| 97 | L Sleigh | | 139 | Chris Gorman |
| 98 | Brian D Clarke | | 140 | Simon Banfield |
| 99 | Ian Jordison | | 141 | D A Poland |
| 100 | Gary Stevens | | 142 | I A Aspin |
| 101 | M J Bailey | | 143 | Carl J Barlow |
| 102 | J M Dugdale | | 144 | Andrew J Barlow |
| 103 | John Brindle | | 145 | Gary Lawrenson |
| 104 | Steven Pirie | | 146 | Emma Lawrenson |
| 105 | Michael Whalley | | 147 | Jason Middleton |
| 106 | J M Wilkinson | | 148 | J Hulme |
| 107 | E Caruana | | 149 | Martin Clark |
| 108 | David J Elliott | | 150 | Neil Morris |
| 109 | M Summer | | 151 | Keith Maudsley |
| 110 | Tony Gillett | | 152 | P J Duckworth |
| 111 | K Sunderland | | 153 | A F Hayman |
| 112 | Jim Ollerton | | 154 | D Cowburn |
| 113 | Peter Watson | | 155 | Ross H McGhee |
| 114 | A J Roberts | | 156 | Mr D I Slater |
| 115 | Kevin Hope | | 157 | David Hall |
| 116 | Mrs Houghton | | 158 | David Brown |
| 117 | David Stanley | | 159 | M A McKay |
| 118 | Matthew Taylor | | 160 | A J McKay |
| 119 | Sue Rayton | | 161 | Gregg Schofield |
| 120 | Norman Halliwell | | 162 | H Livesey |

| | | | | |
|---|---|---|---|---|
| 163 | Gordon Matthews | 205 | Andrew Ferguson |
| 164 | Tom Denial | 206 | John B Holden |
| 165 | F B N Cropper | 207 | Derek R Lavin |
| 166 | Geoff C Mather | 208 | Paul Loftus |
| 167 | David Allan Hacking | 209 | G K Scott |
| 168 | David Taylor | 210 | Samuel Flaherty |
| 169 | Jim Jenkinson | 211 | Frank Bland |
| 170 | John Burrow | 212 | Terry Kennedy |
| 171 | Paul W Lang | 213 | J V Classick |
| 172 | Keith Fitzpatrick | 214 | Peter B Jump |
| 173 | Roy Partington | 215 | Andrew Payne |
| 174 | A Haines | 216 | Mark Ian Jarrett |
| 175 | Tom | 217 | Paul Marsden |
| 176 | Fred Gillibrand | 218 | Stephen D Ward |
| 177 | Michael Costello | 219 | David Moore |
| 178 | M Crabtree | 220 | K Burrow |
| 179 | David A Jepson | 221 | Andrew P Holden |
| 180 | Ian Waddington | 222 | Brian Sim |
| 181 | Alan Gosling | 223 | Ian M Parker |
| 182 | Dave Pickup | 224 | Frank Wilkinson |
| 183 | M Haworth | 225 | Philip J Duckworth |
| 184 | John Frederick St John Bottomley | 226 | Jeff Brown |
| 185 | John James (Jim) Fowler | 227 | Mark Hoythornthwaite |
| 186 | Adam J Fowler & Jonathan | 228 | J A Woods |
| 187 | Nicholas Williams | 229 | J M Davison |
| 188 | Roger Hudson | 230 | Gary |
| 189 | Ian Futter | 231 | Michael Teasdale |
| 190 | C G Cheetham | 232 | Peter Teasdale |
| 191 | A C Van-Der-Linden | 233 | Graham Halsall |
| 192 | Gordon Wilkinson | 234 | Ian Smith |
| 193 | Caradog Roberts | 235 | Simon Alexander Smith |
| 194 | Michael Edward Taylor | 236 | Gordon Leigh |
| 195 | Sue Holden | 237 | Paul Brown |
| 196 | Nathan Scott Earrey | 238 | John Morris |
| 197 | Jennifer Taylor | 239 | J Brooks |
| 198 | Maureen Ellis | 240 | Mr H G A Peters |
| 199 | Alan Raymond Birkbeck | 241 | David Lofthouse |
| 200 | Lynne Dorman | 242 | A Lord |
| 201 | Ian Teasdale | 243 | Eric Kinder |
| 202 | Gary Warburton | 244 | Peter Burch |
| 203 | Norman Eccles | 245 | Graham Burch |
| 204 | Alan Ward | 246 | John Cotton |

247 John Robinson
248 Ian Edmundson
249 C A Lowe
250 Peter Horner
251 Kevin Bayman
252 R B Smith
253 A Woodworth
254 Anthony Foley
255 W J Pomfret
256 Martin Brunnschweiler
257 Stuart Kay
258 J D Parker
259 Steven Eddleston
260 Matthew Bridges
261 Paul Yates
262 B J Nutter
263 N K D Cort
264 Peter Atherton
265 Allan Davy
266 Philip Ramsbottom
267 J R Blackshaw
268 Lee Bridges
269 Harry Walmsley
270 Christopher Mullin
271 Oliver Clay
272 Gardner
273 Tony Whipp
274 Pasquale Forte
275 David Jessop
276 J Dunn
277 Ian Partington
278 Simon Shaw
279 John Speak
280 Kenny Turner
281 Simon O'Donnell
282 S Bell
283 John Pittard
284 Simon Pittard
285 Louise Walsh
286 Bill Rain
287 Richard Newmark
288 Stephen Cowell

289 John Cowell
290 Jess Craig
291 D Lavelle
292 Gordon Moulding
293 David Shaw
294 Paul Shaw
295 G P Schofield
296 Bill Gardner
297 Susan Gregson
298 J P Rushton
299 A Wilson
300 L D Harrison
301 J Graham Pawson
302 Mr Jim Standing
303 William Leonard Ferguson
304 Robert Sturgess
305 H & D Dodd
306 John Hacking
307 Andrew Ainsworth